D1879265

COMPANION

TO

JOHNSON'S DICTIONARY,

BENGALI AND ENGLISH

Owing to the antiquity and rarity of this book, certain pages are regrettably absent, and readability is compromised due to the blurring of the original text. If you possess any insights regarding the availability of these missing sections, kindly inform us. Your assistance is crucial in ensuring the completion of this significant work for the benefit of future generations.

COMPANION

TO

JOHNSON'S DICTIONARY,

BENGALI AND ENGLISH.

PECULIARLY CALCULATED

FOR THE USE OF EUROPEAN AND NATIVE STUDENTS.

THE THIRD, IMPROVED EDITION.

TO WHICH IS APPENDED

THE BENGALI ALPHABET, ETC.

BY

JOHN MENDIES,

Late of Serampore.

GYAN

Published by

Gyan Publishing House
5, Ansari Road
Daryaganj, New Delhi-110002
Phone: 011-47034999, 9811692060
E-mail: books@gyanbooks.com

Distribution Network
gyanbooks.com
India, USA, Canada, UK, Australia

© Publisher

All rights reserved. No part of this work may be reproduced, stored, adapted, or transmitted in any form or by any means, electronic, mechanical, photocopying, micro-filming, recording or otherwise, or translated in any language, without the prior written permission of the copyright owner and the publisher.

ISBN: 978-81-212-5568-4 (HB)
First Published, 1851

2nd Impression 2024

Printed at: Gyan Press, Delhi.

The book is sold subject to the condition that it shall not, by way of trade or otherwise, be lent, resold, hired out, or otherwise circulated without the prior publisher's written consent.

COMPANION TO JOHNSON'S DICTIONARY, BENGALI AND ENGLISH

Author: SAMUEL JOHNSON, JOHN MENDIES

COMPANION

TO

JOHNSON'S DICTIONARY,

BENGALI AND ENGLISH.

PECULIARLY CALCULATED

FOR THE USE OF EUROPEAN AND NATIVE STUDENTS.

THE THIRD, IMPROVED EDITION.

TO WHICH IS APPENDED

THE BENGALI ALPHABET, ETC.

BY

JOHN MENDIES,

Late of Serampore.

CONCEAL, IF YOU COME TO AN ERROR, CAST NOT REPROACH,
FOR NO MORTAL CAN BE FREE FROM FAULT. *Hafez.*

CALCUTTA:

PRINTED BY C. B. LEWIS, AT THE BAPTIST MISSION PRESS, 24, LOWER CIRCULAR ROAD:

AND SOLD

AT THE BAPTIST MISSION PRESS; AT THE CALCUTTA SCHOOL-BOOK SOCIETY'S DEPOSITORY, No. 10, GOVERNMENT PLACE, EAST, ALSO BY MESSRS. THACKER, SPINK AND CO., ST. ANDREW'S LIBRARY; AND MESSRS. P. S. D'ROZARIO AND CO., DALHOUSIE SQUARE.

MDCCCLXXVI.

PREFACE.

The utility of the Bengáli language is too evident and too firmly established to require any further demonstration. The Sacred Scriptures, long since translated, printed, and widely circulated over the vast extent of the country—the Establishment of Government, Missionary, and Private Seminaries in various parts of Bengal—the currency of the language in the Presidency and Mufassal Civil and Criminal Courts of Justice—the extensive daily familiar and commercial intercourse of Europeans with the Natives of the country afford, beyond all doubt, ample motives for the study and cultivation of this most useful language. Hence a great many works have already been compiled by eminent European and Native gentlemen towards facilitating its acquisition.

With a view to render his humble services, the compiler was induced, some twenty-nine years back, to undertake the compilation of an Abridgment of Johnson's Dictionary in English and Bengáli, for assisting both European and Native students in acquiring the respective languages. Six years subsequent to that period he designed to give a second edition of the aforesaid work, together with this volume as its companion, but unforeseen obstacles frustrated the execution of his design, and disheartened him from pursuing the object any further.

However, through the unbounded mercy of a gracious Providence, after a long interval, he is enabled to embrace the present opportunity of redeeming the pledge then made, by giving a second edition of both the volumes, corrected, enlarged and, in some instances, abridged and condensed. Many additional terms have been introduced, which are not to be found in any other work of a similar nature.

To prevent disappointment, it is to be observed that a Dictionary, professedly of the Bengáli language, must include not only the pure Bengáli terms used by the learned, but many words of mixed origin which are in common use, derived from Arabic, Persian, Hindi and low Bengáli, which occur daily in the conversation of people of different grades.

In submitting this volume to the candid judgment of a generous public, the compiler is well aware of the difficulty of pleasing every body, therefore he will not pretend to say any thing by way of recommending it, but simply begs leave to quote the opinions of the best judges of the language:—"The compiler of this work, (Companion to Johnson's Dictionary,) as the latest in the field, has been enabled to avail himself of the labours of many predecessors, which he certainly has done with very commendable diligence. On the whole this work is decidedly superior to others of its kind. The opinion is entertained, in which we incline fully to coincide, that this would answer to the student all the ordinary purposes of a complete dictionary. The compiler is a laborious, diligent, and meritorious individual, and we have great pleasure in recommending his work to more general notice."*

Another eminent oriental scholar now in India says:—" Your Bengáli and English Dictionary I have often consulted with advantage, and should be ready to recommend it any day even in its previous form."

In conclusion, the compiler begs leave to say that should his work be deemed deserving of encouragement from a generous public, he humbly trusts that a share of their patronage may be kindly extended to it.

Calcutta, *January*, 1851. J. MENDIES.

ADVERTISEMENT

to the third Edition.

The compiler begs to announce to the public that in the present edition he has introduced, partly in the body of the work, and partly in an Appendix, numerous rare, though useful words, omitted in the former edition, and many others collected from various sources, but chiefly from the late Dr. Carey's Bengáli Dictionary. The work has been condensed and compressed in printing with a view to economy, so as to bring it within a reasonable size and price, without causing the least confusion, by striking out many words of Persian or Arabic origin seldom looked for in a Bengáli Dictionary.

The Compiler further begs to state that, without in the least wishing to be ostentatious, he has availed himself of the present opportunity, for inserting another testimonial to his labours,—the opinion of a well-known oriental scholar regarding the work, entitled, " Abridgment of, and Companion to, Johnson's Dictionary: English and Bengáli and vice versâ."—The learned critic says:—" This is the title of a new edition, just issued, of a work which has been long before the public. We have long been acquainted with the second of these volumes, and found it to be, for all ordinary purposes, the most handy of all Bengáli and English dictionaries. It is much more complete than either Morton's or Marshman's, and not much more bulky than the latter. In this new edition the number of pages has been reduced, principally by condensing the explanations of Bengáli words. The paper also is better than before. We have not had time to examine the new edition carefully, nor to test the English and Bengáli volume. But from our acquaintance with the Compiler, we have no hesitation in recommending the work most cordially."†

The compiler begs to tender his grateful thanks to the generous and discerning public for the prompt disposal of the second edition of his dictionary. To supply the urgent demand for his work, he has been induced to publish the present edition with great labour and at a heavy outlay, trusting solely in their generosity to indemnify him, by patronizing the work.—*Sept.* 1856.

* Vide *Calcutta Christian Observer for* 1838. † Ibid. *March*, 1851.

EXAMPLES OF BENGALI CONTRACTIONS.

এলুয়া -খেলুয়া, -মেলুয়া, *to be read* এলুয়াখেলুয়া *and* এলুয়ামেলুয়া.
গর্ভ -বেদনা, -যন্ত্রণা, „ গর্ভবেদনা *and* গর্ভযন্ত্রণা.
গ্রাহকতা, -ত্ব, „ গ্রাহকতা *and* গ্রাহকত্ব.
তুরী, *s.* a trumpet; -বাদক, „ তুরীবাদক, a trumpeter.

N. B.—These and similar ones are to be observed throughout the Work.

Abbreviations used in this Dictionary.

a. adjective.
acct. account.
ad. adverb.
ana. anatomy.
arith. arithmetic.
astro. astronomy.
bot. botany.
che.*, *chem.*, *chym. chemistry.
comp. composition.
conj. conjunction.
***e. g. (exempli gratia)*,** as for example.
Eng. English.
f.*, *fem. feminine.
fig. figuratively.
gend. gender.
geo. geography.
gram. grammar.
im. sd. imitative sound.
***ibid.*, *idem*,** the same.
imp. imperative.
insepar. inseparable.
interj.*, *intj. interjection.
lit. literally.
masc. masculine.
math. mathematics.
met. metaphorically.
mytho. mythology.
neg. par. negative particle.
part. participle.
ph.*, *phra. phrase.
pl. plural.
Port. Portuguese.
prep. preposition.
pron. pronoun.
s. substantive.
v. a. verb active.
v. n. verb neuter.
v. caus. causal verb.
***vide*,** see.
voc. part. vocative particle.

*** The asterisks prefixed to words denote that they are derived either from the Persian or the Arabic root.

The double daggers denote that the words have both a Persian and a Bengáli meaning.

The superior figures that may be found in the body of the work refer to the NOTES at the end of the Dictionary.

Bengáli Verbal Roots.

আগল্ .. আগলন	জন্মা .. জন্মান	থাক্ .. থাকন	বল্ক .. বল্কন
আটকা .. আটকান	জর্ .. জরণ	থাম্ .. থামন	বহ্ .. বহন
আন্ .. আনন	জান্ .. জানন	থামা .. থামান	বাঁধ্ .. বাঁধন
উঠ্ .. উঠন	জানা .. জানান	থিৎ .. থিতন	বাছ্ .. বাছন
উঠা .. উঠান	জুড়া .. জুড়াম	থিতা .. থিতান	বাজ্ .. বাজন
উল্ট .. উল্টন	জ্বল্ .. জ্বলন	থুক্ .. থুকন	বাজা .. বাজান
কৃ .. করণ	ঝর্ .. ঝরণ	দা .. দেওন	বাড়্ .. বাড়ন
কপ্চা .. কপ্চান	ঝাঁটা .. ঝাঁটান	দংশ .. দংশন	বাড়া .. বাড়ান
কমা .. কমান	ঝঁক্ .. ঝঁকন	দর্শা .. দর্শান	বুঝ্ .. বুঝন
করা .. করাণ	ঝাড়্ .. ঝাড়ন	দল্ .. দলন	ভাঁড়া .. ভাঁড়ান
কষ .. কষণ	ঝিমা .. ঝিমান	দেখ্ .. দেখন	ভাজ্ .. ভাজন
কহ .. কহন	ঝুল্ .. ঝুলন	দেখা .. দেখান	ভিজা .. ভিজান
কাট্ .. কাটন	টন্টনা .. টনটনান	ধড়্ফড়া .. ধড়্ফড়ান	ভুক্ত .. ভুক্তন
কামড়া .. কামড়ান	টল্ .. টলন	ধম্কা .. ধম্কান	ভুল্ .. ভুলন
খণ্ডা .. খণ্ডান	টান্ .. টানন	ধর্ or ধৃ .. ধরণ	ভুলা .. ভুলান
খা .. খাওন	টাল্ .. টালন	ধার্ .. ধারণ	ভূ .. হওন
খাট্ .. খাটান	টিক্ .. টিকন	ধুন্ .. ধুনন	মাখ্ .. মাখন
খাম্চা .. খাম্চান	টিপ্ .. টিপন	ধো .. ধোওন	মাখা .. মাখান
খুল্ .. খুলন	ঠকা .. ঠকান	নম্প্ .. নম্পন	মাগ্ .. মাগন
খেঁচ্ .. খেঁচন	ঠাওরা .. ঠাওরাণ	নাচ্ .. নাচন	মাঙ্গ্ .. মাঙ্গন
গঠ্ .. গঠন	ঠার্ .. ঠারণ	নাটা .. নাটান	মান্ .. মানন
গড় .. গড়ন	ঠিক্রা .. ঠিক্রাণ	নাম্ .. নামন	মার্ .. মারণ
গড়া .. গড়ান	ঠুক্ .. ঠুকন	নামা .. নামান	মিট্ .. মিটন
গাঁজ .. গাঁজন	ঠেক্ .. ঠেকন	নোয়া .. নোয়ান	মিটা .. মিটান
গাদ্ .. গাদন	ডরা .. ডরাণ	পড় .. পড়ন	মিলা .. মিলান
ঘট্ .. ঘটন	ডল্ .. ডলন	পলা .. পলায়ন	মিশা .. মিশান
ঘবরা .. ঘবরাণ	ডাক্ .. ডাকন	পা .. পাওন	যড়া .. যড়ান
ঘর্ষ্ .. ঘর্ষণ	ডিঙ্গা .. ডিঙ্গান	পিট্ .. পিটন	যা .. যাওন
ঘুষা .. ঘুষান	ডুব্ .. ডুবন	পুঁচ্ .. পুঁচন	যাচ্ .. যাচন
ঘের্ .. ঘেরণ	ডুবা .. ডুবান	পুছ্ .. পুছন	রচ্ .. রচন
ঘোলা .. ঘোলান	ঢাল্ .. ঢালন	পোড়া .. পোড়ান	রহ .. রহন
চড় .. চড়ন	ঢুক্ .. ঢুকন	পোহা .. পোহান	রাঁধ্ .. রাঁধন
চম্কা .. চম্কান	ঢুকা .. ঢুকান	ফাঁদ্ .. ফাঁদন	রাখ্ .. রাখন
চল্ .. চলন	ঢুল্ .. ঢুলন	ফাঁপ্ .. ফাঁপন	রাগ্ .. রাগন
চিবা .. চিবান	ঢুলা .. ঢুলান	ফাট্ .. ফাটন	লড় .. লড়ন
চুষ্ .. চুষ	ঢুষা .. ঢুষান	ফির .. ফিরণ	লাগা .. লাগান
চেঁচা .. চেঁচান	তড়পা .. তড়পান	ফিরা .. ফিরাণ	লেপ্ .. লেপন
ছড়া .. ছড়ান	তলা .. তলান	ফুকরা .. ফুকরাণ	শুক্ .. শুকন
ছাড় .. ছাড়ন	তুবড় .. তবড়ন	ফুট্ .. ফুটন	শুধরা .. শুধরাণ
ছান্ .. ছানন	তুল্ .. তুলন	ফুল্ .. ফুলন	সহ্ .. সহন
ছিটা .. ছিটান	তোলা .. তোলান	ফুস্লা .. ফুস্লা	সাজা .. সাজান
ছিল .. ছিলন	ত্যজ্ .. ন্যজন	ফেল্ .. ফেলন	হঠ .. হঠন

N. B.—All the Verbal Roots are to be observed as above.

THE BENGALI ALPHABET.

Vowels, (অচ or স্বর.)

অ	আ	ই	ঈ	উ	ঊ	ঋ	ৠ	ঌ	ৡ	এ	ঐ	ও	ঔ
a	á	i	í	u	ú	ri	rí	li	llí	e	ai	o	au

Consonants, (হল or ব্যঞ্জন.)

ক	খ	গ	ঘ	ঙ
ka	kha	ga	gha	uṉa
চ	ছ	জ	ঝ	ঞ
cha	chha	ja	jha	iṉa
ট	ঠ	ড	ঢ	ণ
ṭa	ṭha	ḍa	ḍha	áṇa
ত	থ	দ	ধ	ন
ta	tha	da	dha	na
প	ফ	ব	ভ	ম
pa	pha	ba	bha	ma
য	য়	র	ল	ব
ja	ya	ra	la	wa
শ	ষ	স	হ	ক্ষ
sha	sha	sa	ha	ksha

জ় za ড় ṛa ঢ় ṛha

Letters and their Symbels.

অ	ই	ঈ	উ	ঊ	এ	ঐ	ও	ঔ	য	র	র	ন	ল	ব	ম	ঋ	ং	ঃ	ঁ
া*	ি	ী	ু	ূ	ে	ৈ	ো	ৌ	্য	্র	র্	্ন	্ল	্ব	্ম	ৃ	ng	ah	n̲

Combinations of Symbols.

কা	কি	কী	কু	কূ	কে	কৈ	কো	কৌ	ক্য	ক্র	র্ক	ক্ন	ক্ল	ক্ব	ক্ম	কৃ	কং	কঃ	কঁ
ká	ki	kí	ku	kú	ke	kai	ko	kau	kya	kra	rka	kna	kla	kwa	kma	kri	kang	kah	kan̲

* The symbols are thus named: ákár; hraswa or short ikár; dírgha or long íkár; short and long ukár; ekár; aikár; okár; aukár; kya, kra, árka, kna, kla, kwa, kma, kri, all these are called phalás; annswar; bisarga; chandra-bindu.

Compound Letters, called

Ánka-phalá.

ঙ্ক	ঙ্খ	ঙ্গ	ঙ্ঘ	ঙ্ঙ
nka	nkha	nga	ngha	nguṉa
ঞ্চ	ঞ্ছ	ঞ্জ	ঞ্ঝ	ঞ্ঞ
ncha	nchha	nja	njha	niṉa
ণ্ট	ণ্ঠ	ণ্ড	ণ্ঢ	ণ্ণ
nṭa	nṭha	nḍa	nḍha	ṉṉa
ন্ত	ন্থ	ন্দ	ন্ধ	ন্ন
nta	ntha	nda	ndha	nna
ম্প	ম্ফ	ম্ব	ম্ভ	ম্ম
mpa	mpha	mba	mbha	mma
ঞ্জ	—	ন্ল	ঙ্ব	—
nja	——	nla	nwa	——
ন্শ	ন্ষ	ন্স	ন্হ	ঙ্ক্ষ
nsha	nsha	nsa	nha	nksha

Áska-phalá.

স্ক	স্খ	দ্গ	দ্ঘ	ঙ্ক্ষ
ska	skha	dga	dgha	uṉástra
শ্চ	শ্ছ	ব্জ	ব্ঝ	জ্ঞ
shcha	shchha	bja	bjha	ggyaṉ
ষ্ট	ষ্ঠ	ব্ড	ব্ঢ	ষ্ণ
shṭa	shṭha	bḍa	bḍha	shna
স্ত	স্থ	ব্দ	ব্ধ	হ্ণ
sta	stha	bda	bdha	ahrna
স্প	স্ফ	দ্ব	দ্ভ	হ্ম
spa	spha	dba	dbha	ahmma
হ্জ	—	হ্ল	হ্ব	—
ahja	——	ahla	ahwa	——
ট্শ	ট্ষ	ট্স	ট্হ	ট্ক্ষ
ṭsha	ṭsha	ṭsa	ṭ'ha	ṭksha

Consonants may be doubled or combined thus :

ক্ক চ্চ হ্ন জ্জ ত্থ দ্দ দ্ধ প্ত গ্ম ব্ব ল্ক ল্ট ব্দ ল্প ল্ল,

These are used for elegance or expedition :

ক্র	ক্ত	ত্ত	গু	শু	হু	ত্র	ত্ত্র	হৃ	দ্রু	দ্রূ
kra	kta	tta	gu	shu	hu	tra	ttra	hri	dru	drú
রু	রূ	হ্ন	হ্য	স্তু	স্ত্র	গ্ধ	ৎ	শ্রী	৭	৺
ru	rú	ahna	ahja	stu	stra	gdha	t	shrí	ganesh	Íshwar

Numerical Figures.

১ ২ ৩ ৪ ৫ ৬ ৭ ৮ ৯ ০

*Fractions.**

৴	৵	৶	।০	।৴	।৵	।৶	।।০	।।৴	।।৵	।।৶	৸০	৸৴	৸৵	৸৶	১
$\frac{1}{16}$	$\frac{1}{8}$	$\frac{3}{16}$	$\frac{1}{4}$	$\frac{5}{16}$	$\frac{6}{16}$	$\frac{7}{16}$	$\frac{1}{2}$	$\frac{9}{16}$	$\frac{10}{16}$	$\frac{11}{16}$	$\frac{3}{4}$	$\frac{13}{16}$	$\frac{14}{16}$	$\frac{15}{16}$	1

* The fractions are of a Rupee, or 16 ánás ; a ser, or 16 chhaṭáks ; also of one káhan, or 16 pans. In land measure ।০ stands for 5 kátás or ¼ of a bighá of 20 kátás. In dry measure, it is 10 sers, or ¼ of a man (maund) of 40 sers ; consequently in accounts it undergoes a slight variation from that of the reckoning by a Rupee or 16 ánás.

COMPANION

TO

JOHNSON'S DICTIONARY.

BENGALI' AND ENGLISH.

অ, THE first vowel in the Bengálí alphabet. It has the sound of *a* in f*a*ther, and sometimes of *o* in G*o*d; but when it is final, that of *a* in Americ*a*. It is inherent in every consonant, and must be sounded with it, unless its place be occupied by another letter or by this mark (্) called hasanta, which shows that the vowel is suppressed. In composition it gives the word it precedes a privative or negative meaning. অন is substituted when it precedes a vowel.

অই, *ad.* yon, yonder, there : *pron.* that.

অঋণী, *a.* free from debt, not in debt.

অংশ্, *v.* to be divided; to share out.

অংশ, *s.* a share, a part, a portion.

অংশনীয়, *a.* divisible, shareable.

অংশা, *v. a.* to divide, to share out.

অংশাংশ, *s.* distinct shares, allotment.

অংশাংশি, *s.* a division into shares.

অংশিত, *a.* shared out, divided, allotted.

অংশী, *s.* a partner, a sharer, co-partner.

অংশু, কিরণ, *s.* a ray, a ray of light.

অংশুমান, *a.* radiant : *s.* the sun.

অকণ্টক, *a.* free from thorns or vexations.

অকথক, *s.* a bad speaker.

অকথন, *a.* silent : *s.* silence.

অকথনীয়, *a.* unspeakable, obscene.

অকথা, *s.* bad word, obscene language.

অকথিত, *a.* not spoken, not divulged.

অকথোপকথন, *s.* silence, taciturnity.

অকথ্য, *a.* unspeakable, obscene.

অকপট, *a.* sincere, frank, ingenuous.

অকবি, *s.* a poetaster, a bad poet.

অকর, *a.* maimed; free from taxes.

অকরুণ, *a.* unmerciful, unfeeling.

অকর্ত্তব্য, *a.* inexpedient, impracticable.

অকর্ম্ম, *s.* improper action : *a.* useless.

অকর্ম্মক, *a.* in *gram.* intransitive.

অকর্ম্মঠ, *a.* not diligent, negligent.

অকর্ম্মণ্য, *a.* useless, worthless, idle.

অকর্ম্মমাত্র, *s.* merely an improper action.

অকর্ম্মান্বিত, *a.* inactive, idle, indolent.

অকল্পিত, *a.* unfeigned, genuine, true.

অকষ্টকল্পনা, *s.* ease of mind, tranquillity.

অকস্মাৎ, *ad.* unexpectedly, suddenly.

অকস্মাদ্বাসনা, *s.* a whim, caprice.

অকাতর, *a.* not distressed : *s.* at ease.

অকাপট্য, *s.* sincerity, honesty, frankness.

অকার, *s.* the letter অ.

অকারণ, *a.* without cause or reason.

অকার্য্য, *a.* useless : *s.* an improper work.

অকার্য্যাক্ষম, *a.* unfit for business.

অকার্য্যচিন্তা, *s.* a building castle in the air.

অকাল, *a.* premature : *s.* a famine.

অকালজ, অকালজাত, *a.* abortive.

অকালে, *ad.* prematurely, untimely.

অকিঞ্চন, *a.* destitute, poor, needy.

অকিঞ্চিৎ, *s.* nothing; insignificant.

অকীর্ত্তি, *a.* infamous : *s.* a want of fame.

অকীর্ত্তিমান্, *a.* infamous, not renowned.

অকুতোভয়, *a.* safe, free from danger.

অকুমারী, *s.* a virgin, a maid.

অকুলন, অকুলান, *a.* not at hand, lacking, wanting, inadequate, insufficient.

*অকুফ, *s.* sense, understanding.

অকূল, *a.* shoreless, boundless.

অকূলপাথার, *s.* a shoreless ocean.

অকৃতজ্ঞ, *a.* ungrateful, unthankful.
অকৃতার্থ, *a.* unsuccessful.
অকৃতী, *a.* unskilful, inexpert, unfit.
অকৃত্রিম, *a.* inartificial, genuine.
অকেযয়া, *a.* useless, unfit for any work.
†অক্ত, *a.* smeared, plastered : *s.* season.
অক্রম, *s.* want of succession, irregularity.
অক্রিয়া, *s.* inaction, improper action.
অক্রীত, *a.* unpurchased, unbought.
অক্লেশ, *s.* absence of distress or fatigue.
অক্লেশে, *ad.* without difficulty, easily.
অক্ষ, *s.* a die, spots on dice ; a myrabolan ; 16 máshás ; a cart, a wheel.
অক্ষক্রীড়া, *s.* play at dice.
অক্ষতযোনি, অক্ষতা, *s.* a virgin.
অক্ষয়, অক্ষয়ণীয়, imperishable, durable.
অক্ষর, *s.* a letter, type : *a.* imperishable.
অক্ষরচুঞ্চু, *a.* writing swiftly and well.
অক্ষরজীবী, living by writing : *s.* a writer.
অক্ষি, লোচন, চক্ষু, নয়ন, নেত্র, *s.* an eye.
অক্ষিকুটক, *s.* the eye-ball.
অক্ষিন্ন, *a.* not pained, not distressed.
অক্ষিপীড়া, *s.* pain or disease of the eye.
অক্ষীণ, *a.* not wasted, not decayed.
অক্ষুণ্ণ, *a.* not pulverized.
অক্ষুব্ধ, অক্ষুভিত, *a.* unexcited, unagitated.
অক্ষেম, *a.* unlucky, inauspicious.
অক্ষোভ, *s.* freedom from agitation.
অক্ষোভিত, *a.* unexcited, not put in motion.
অক্ষোভী, *a.* not exciting or irritating.
অক্ষৌহিণী, *s.* a complete army consisting of 109,350 foot, 65,610 horse, 21,870 chariots, and 21,870 elephants.
অখণ্ডনীয়, *a.* infrangible, incapable of being broken, refuted, or repelled.
অখণ্ডিত, *a.* unconfuted, unbroken, whole.
অখাত, *a.* undug : *s.* a natural pond.
অখাদ্য, *a.* not fit for food, not eatable, forbidden as an article of food.
অখিন্ন, *a.* unregretted, unwearied.
অখ্যাত, *a.* not renowned, inglorious.
অখ্যাতব্য, *a.* unworthy of renown, dishonorable, disgraceful.
অখ্যাতি, *s.* dishonor, disgrace, obloquy.
অগ, *a.* immovable : *s.* a mountain, a tree.
অগড়বগড়, *a.* medley, odds and ends, nicknacks, promiscuous, bad and good mixt.

অগণিত, *a.* not counted, not calculated.
অগণ্য, *a.* innumerable, of no account.
অগতি, অগতিক, *a.* motionless, remediless, unprotected, forlorn.
অগতিক্রিয়া, *s.* promptness : *a.* unprocrastinating.
অগত্যা, *ad.* desperately, without resource.
অগত্যাস্বীকার, *s.* the consenting to any thing when there is no choice left.
অগদ, *s.* medicament, medicine.
অগদ্য, *a.* destitute of prose : *s.* bad prose.
অগন্তব্য, অগমনীয়, *a.* immovable, impassable, inaccessible.
অগম, *a.* unfathomable ; not honorable, not respectable, disregarded.
অগমতা, *s.* dishonor, disrespect, disregard.
অগম্য, *a.* impassable, inaccessible, impracticable, incomprehensible.
অগস্তি, অগস্ত্য, *s.* name of a Hindu sage.
*অগাড়ি, *ad.* before, prior to, sooner : *s.* the place in front ; also, *vide* আগাড়ি.
অগাধ, *a.* profound, very deep.
অগুণ, *s.* bad quality : *a.* useless, worthless.
অগুণী, *a.* worthless : *s.* not a magician.
অগুণ ভূত, *a* become worthless, useless.
অগুরু, *s.* agallochum or lignum aloes, or the tree which produces it ;[1] also the tree from which Bdellium is produced :[2] *a.* not weighty, unimportant, light, trivial.
অগুরুশিংশপা, *s.* a timber tree (dalbergia sissoo.)
অগুহ্য, *a.* unconcealable.
অগো, a vocative particle employed in a respectful address.
অগোচর, *a.* unperceived, not in presence.
অগোচরে, *ad.* unknowingly, clandestinely.
অগোত্র, *a.* of no family : *s.* want of family.
অগোর, *s.* lignum aloes ;[3] another tree.[4]
অগ্নি, *s.* fire, the god of fire, the regent of the south-east quarter, the power of digestion, bile, the name of a plant.[5]
অগ্নিকণা, *s.* a spark of fire.
অগ্নিকল্প, *a.* excessively hot, ignited, red hot.
অগ্নিকার্য্য, অগ্নিক্রিয়া, *s.* the burning of the dead, or any religious act to the performance of which fire is necessary.
অগ্নিকুমার, *s.* a digestive medicine; a plant.
অগ্নিকোণ, *s.* the south-east quarter.
অগ্নিক্রীড়া, *s.* a play of fireworks, bonfire.

অগ্নিগড়, *s.* an expedient to cure the bite of the whipthong snake.

অগ্নিচিৎ, *s.* a funeral pile, a sacrificial pile.

অগ্নিপরীক্ষা, *s.* trial by fire.

অগ্নিপূজক, *s.* a fire-worshipper, a Pársi.

অগ্নিপূজা, *s.* the worship of the god Agni.

অগ্নিপ্রতাপ, the force or heat of fire.

অগ্নিপ্রস্তর, *s.* a flint.

অগ্নিবৎ, *ad.* fiery, passionately, like fire.

অগ্নিবর্দ্ধক, *a.* assisting digestion, provocative, digestive, increasing fire. [row.

অগ্নিবাণ, *s.* fire-arms, a rocket, a fiery ar-

অগ্নিবৃদ্ধি, *s.* the strengthening of appetite.

অগ্নিমন্থ, *s.* a small tree (Premna spinosa).

অগ্নিময়, *a.* abounding with fire, fiery.

অগ্নিমান্, *a.* passionate, fiery.

অগ্নিমান্দ্য, *s.* the want of appetite.

অগ্নিযন্ত্র, *s.* fire-arms, a fire-rocket.

অগ্নিশর্ম্মা, *s.* a sarcastic expression applied to a violently passionate man.

অগ্নিষ্টোম, *s.* a particular sacrifice.

অগ্নিসংস্কার, *s.* consecration by fire.

অগ্নিসংস্কৃত, *a.* consecrated by fire.

অগ্নিসদৃশ, *a.* resembling fire, passionate.

অগ্ন্যস্ত্র, *s.* fire-arms.

অগ্ন্যুৎপাত, *s.* a fiery meteor, a comet.

অগ্ন্যুৎসব, *s.* a bonfire.

অগ্র, *s.* the place in front, a nib, a peak, a point or forepart, a pinnacle, a preliminary : *ad.* before, further, onward.

অগ্রগ, *a.* preceding : *s.* a precursor.

অগ্রগণ্য, *a.* deserving of the first place, entitled to precedence.

অগ্রগত, *a.* gone before, preceded.

অগ্রগামী, *a.* preceding, forerunning : *s.* a forerunner, a precursor, a leader.

অগ্রজ, *a.* first-born : *s.* an elder brother.

অগ্রণী, *a.* leading : *s.* a leader, a duke.

অগ্রদানী, *s.* particular order of bráhmans.

অগ্রদেশ, *s.* the front, the place in front.

অগ্রনিয়ম, *s.* a previous decree, predestination, a preliminary regulation.

অগ্রপশ্চাৎ, *ad.* backwards and forwards, sooner or later. [before.

অগ্রবর্ত্তী, *a.* preceding, standing or going

অগ্রভাগ, *s.* the forepart, foremost part.

অগ্রমাস, *s.* an induration of the liver.

অগ্রসর, *a.* preceding, moving in front.

অগ্রসরণ, *s.* making progress. [point.

অগ্রসূক্ষ্মীকৃত, *a.* sharpened, tapered to a

অগ্রসূচক, *a.* indicating previously.

অগ্রসূচনা, *s.* a foreboding, a presentiment.

অগ্রসূচনীয়, *a.* indicable beforehand.

অগ্রসূচান, *s.* the forewarning a person.

অগ্রসূচিত, *a.* previously indicated.

অগ্রস্থ, অগ্রস্থিত, *a.* situated in front.

অগ্রহণীয়, অগ্রহীতব্য, *vide* অগ্রাহ্য.

অগ্রহায়ণ, *s.* a Hindu month, (Nov.-Dec.)

অগ্রহীতা, *s.* a disinterested person.

অগ্রাহক, *a.* disinterested.

অগ্রাহ্য, *a.* unacceptable, inadmissible.

অগ্রিম, *a.* first, principal, best, chief, eldest.

অগ্লমাণ, *a.* unable to speak or articulate.

অগ্রে, *ad.* in the first place, formerly, forward, previously, afore.

অগ্রেঅগ্রে, *ad.* forwards, onwards, before.

অগ্রেদিধিষু, *s.* a bráhman who is husband to a twice-married woman.

অগ্রেসর, *a.* preceding, forerunning.

অঘ, *s.* sin, guilt, wickedness, crime.

অঘন, *a.* cloudless; not crowded (as trees, &c.)

অঘবান, *a.* sinful, guilty, wicked.

অঘাট, *a.* destitute of a landing place : *s.* that which is not a landing place.

অঘোর, *a.* not terrible, not dreadful : *s.* a name of Shiva.

অঘোরপন্থী, *s.* an order of fanatics who eat every kind of filthy things.

অঙ্ক, *s.* a mark, a badge, a cypher, a numerical figure, the flank, lap, or side ; *fig.* the bosom, the heart : *v. a.* to mark.

অঙ্কক, *s.* one who marks, an accountant.

অঙ্কক্রম, *s.* a series of figures.

অঙ্কন, *s.* a marking, the paging of a book, the act of distinguishing a thing by putting some mark upon it. [ed.

অঙ্কনীয়, requiring a mark, fit to be mark-

অঙ্কপাত, *s.* the entering of numbers in an account.

অঙ্কপূরণ, *s.* multiplication.

অঙ্কবিদ্যা, অঙ্কশাস্ত্র, *s.* arithmetic.

অঙ্কবিদ্যাব্যবসায়ী, *s.* an arithmetician.

অঙ্কবৃদ্ধি, *s.* addition, multiplication, the increasing of a sum, a raising the price, or revenue, extortion, an overcharge.

অঙ্কস্থ, অঙ্কস্থিত, অঙ্কস্থায়ী, *a.* placed on the side (as a child), cherished. [sion.
অঙ্কহরণ, *s.* a decreasing of numbers, divi-
অঙ্কার, *s.* a flat or sharp in music.
অঙ্কিত, *a.* marked, paged. [a germ.
অঙ্কুর, *s.* a plantlet, a seed-bud, a sprout,
অঙ্কুরিত, *a.* germinated, sprouted, budded.
অঙ্কুরিতযৌবনা, *a. f.* in the first bloom of
অঙ্কুশ, *s.* an iron goad or hook. [youth.
অঙ্গ, *s.* a limb, a member; the body.
অঙ্গঅবশ, *s.* the palsy.
অঙ্গগ্রহ, *s.* a spasm, the cramp, pain.
অঙ্গচ্ছেদ, *s.* mutilation, amputation.
অঙ্গজ, *a.* born of one's body: *s.* a son.
অঙ্গজা, *s.* a daughter.
অঙ্গঠা, or আঙ্গঠা, *s.* a chafingdish. [Báli.
অঙ্গদ, *s.* an armlet; son of monkey king
অঙ্গন, *s.* a court-yard, *vulg.* a compound.
অঙ্গনা, *s.* a well-shaped woman.
অঙ্গন্যাস, *s.* a ceremony which consists in touching certain parts of the body.
অঙ্গপ্রত্যঙ্গ, *ad.* in all parts, cap a pie.
অঙ্গবশ, *s.* the use of the limbs.
অঙ্গভঙ্গি, *s.* a distortion of the body whether voluntary or by disease.
অঙ্গভঙ্গিমা, *s.* distortedness of the body.
অঙ্গরক্ষিণী, *a.* guarding body: *s.* a coat.
অঙ্গরাখা, *s.* a coat, a jacket, a gown.
অঙ্গসঙ্গ, *s.* contact with the body, coition, obsequious attendance upon any one.
অঙ্গসঙ্গী, *a.* adhering to the body, sticking closely, obsequiously attending.
অঙ্গাবশ, *a.* paralytic: *s.* the palsy.
অঙ্গার, *s.* charcoal, a coal, cinder.
অঙ্গারক, *s.* the planet Mars, Tuesday.
অঙ্গী, embodied, corporeal: *ad.* acquies-
অঙ্গীকরণ, *s.* act of acquiescing. [cingly.
অঙ্গীকার, *s.* acquiescence, engagement, promise, agreeing to a proposal. [to do.
অঙ্গীকৃত, *a.* agreed to, promised, engaged
অঙ্গীভূত, *a.* become a member or constituent part of any thing.
অঙ্গুরী, *s.* a ring for the finger or toe.
অঙ্গুরীয়, অঙ্গুরীয়ক, আঙ্গুটী, *s. idem.*
অঙ্গুলি, *s.* a finger or toe; -দা, to meddle, intermeddle; -চাল, to slide the fingers forward, to converse by the motions of fingers; -ঠার, to make signs with the finger; -সুড়সুড়া, to feel an inclination or itch, to intermeddle with an affair, have a finger in the pye: also অঙ্গুলী.
অঙ্গুলিগলি, *s.* space between the fingers
অঙ্গুলিগ্রন্থি, *s.* a knuckle. [or toes.
অঙ্গুল্যগ্র, *s.* a finger's end.
অঙ্গুষ্ঠ, *s.* the thumb, the great toe.
অঙ্গুষ্ঠানা, অঙ্গুস্থানা, *s.* a thimble.
*অঙ্গুর, *s.* a grape. In *Sanskrit* দ্রাক্ষা.
অঙ্ঘ্রি, *s.* the foot, leg; root of a tree.
অঙ্ঘ্রিপ, *s.* tree. অঙ্ঘ্রিতল, a foot sole.
অচ্, *s.* in *gram.* a term used to denote that all the vowels are included between these two letters. [steady.
অচকিত, *a.* not startled, not alarmed,
অচক্রী, *a.* not crooked, upright, honest.
অচতুর, *a.* dull, inactive, not clever.
অচরিত্র, *a.* fickle; without incident.
অচল, *a.* immovable, resolute, firm, unable to move, decrepit: *s.* a mountain.
অচলতা, *s.* immovableness. [per conduct.
অচলন, *a.* not current, obsolete: *s.* impro-
অচলনীয়, *a.* immovable, not removable.
অচলিত, *a.* not current or passable.
অচিকিৎসা, *s.* quackery, neglect of medi-
অচিন্তনীয়, *a.* incomprehensible. [cine.
অচিন্তা, *s.* a neglect of care or anxiety.
অচিন্তিত, *a.* unthought on, unexpected.
অচির, *a.* of short duration, transitory.
অচিরস্থায়ী, *a.* fugitive, temporary.
অচেতন, *a.* void of sensation, insensible.
অচেতনা, *s.* the want of sensation.
অচেল, *a.* naked, without a garment.
অচেষ্ট, *a.* without exertion, inactive.
অচেষ্টা, *s.* neglect of exertion.
অচ্ছ, *a.* transparent, good: *ad.* well.
অচ্ছট, *a.* destitute of glory or splendour.
অচ্ছদ, *a.* uncovered, destitute of bark.
অচ্ছিন্নত্বক্, *s.* an uncircumcised person.
অচ্ছেদনীয়, *a.* imperforable, indivisible.
অচ্ছেদিত, *a.* not perforated.
অচ্যুত, *a.* not subject to flux or decay; an epithet applied to Vishnu: *s.* a shrub.[1]
অজ, *a.* unproduced: *s.* a god, a he-goat, Spirit, or the male principle of creation.
অজগর, a large serpent, boa constrictor.

অজগরবৃত্ত, *a.* indolent, lazy, careless.
অজঘন্য, *a.* irreprehensible, unblamable.
অজয়, *a.* invincible, unconquerable.
অজয়ী, *a.* unsuccessful in war.
অজশৃঙ্গী, *s.* the name of a plant.
অজস্র, *a.* incessant, continual. [ture.
অজা, *s.* a she-goat, Matter, or plastic na-
অজাগর, *s.* *vide* অজগর; a small plant.[1]
অজান, *a.* unacquainted with. [sickness.
‡অজার, *a.* without a paramour : *s.* disease,
*অজুরা, *s.* pay for labour.
অজেয়, *a.* invincible, unconquerable.
অজ্ঞ, *a.* ignorant, unwise, uninformed.
অজ্ঞতা, *s.* ignorance, want of knowledge.
অজ্ঞাত, *a.* unknown, unacquainted with.
অজ্ঞাতপিতৃক, *s.* a bastard. [a thing.
অজ্ঞাতসার, *a.* without the knowledge of
অজ্ঞাতে, *ad.* unperceivedly, by stealth.
অজ্ঞান, *a.* ignorant, unlearned, unwise : *s.* ignorance, false knowledge, wrong idea.
অজ্ঞানতঃ, *ad.* unwisely, ignorantly.
অজ্ঞানতম, *a.* most ignorant. [ledge.
অজ্ঞানতা, *s.* ignorance, a want of know-
অজ্ঞানপূর্ব্বক, *ad.* ignorantly, erroneously.
অজ্ঞানী, *a.* unwise, ignorant, unlearned.
অজ্ঞানে, *ad.* foolishly, unwisely.
অজ্ঞেয়, *a.* incomprehensible.
অজ্বর, *a.* free from decrepitude, distress,
অজ্বলনীয়, *a.* incombustible. [or disease.
অঞ্চল, *s.* a border, outskirt, a part or quarter of a town or any place, a district.
অঞ্জন, *s.* collyrium, calcined antimony used as a pigment for the eyes.
অঞ্জনা, *s.* a species of lizard; the mother of the monkey god Hanumán. [joined.
অঞ্জলি, *s.* two handsful, both open hands
*অঞ্জাম, *s.* a supply, the finishing of any
অঞ্জীর, *s.* a guava; a fig, fig-tree. [thing.
অটঙ্কিত, *a.* untwanged.
অটল, *a.* incontrovertible, immovable, unchangeable, irrevocable, irrefragable.
অটলকথা, *s.* an irrefragable argument.
অটট, *a.* unbroken, uninjured.
অটোল, *a.* not dented, smooth, even.
অট্টহাস, *s.* a horselaugh, roar of laughter.
অট্টালিকা, *s.* a house, a palace. [movable.
অটৈল, *a.* unanswerable, irrefragable, im-

অটৈলকথা, *s.* an unanswerable argument.
অড়র, অড়হর, *s.* a species of pulse.[2]
অণু, *s.* an atom, a particle. [eggs.
অণ্ড, *s.* an egg, roe, spawn; -প্রসব, to lay
অণ্ডকটাহ, *s.* the universe.
অণ্ডকোষ, *s.* a testicle.
অণ্ডজ, *a.* produced from an egg, oviparous.
অণ্ডদ্রব, *s.* the loss of firmness thro' fear.
অণ্ডাকার, *a.* oval, elliptical : *s.* an ellipsis,
অণ্ডাকৃতি, *a.* *idem.* [an oval
অতঃপর, *ad.* afterwards, hereafter.
অতএব, *conj.* therefore, wherefore.
অতল, *a.* bottomless : *s.* the first of the infernal spheres or worlds of the Hindus
অতলস্পর্শ, *a.* unfathomable, bottomless
অতসী, *s.* flax (Linum usitatissimum).
অতি, *prep.* prefixed to a word it conveys the idea of excess, usually expressed by the words very, exceedingly.
অতিকায়, *a.* gigantic, huge.
অতিক্রম, *s.* outrage, tyranny, transgression, exceeding of prescribed bounds
অতিক্রমণ, *s.* a transgressing, the surpassing or exceeding of a thing.
অতিক্রমী, *a.* outrageous, transgressing : *s.* a tyrant, a transgressor.
অতিথি, *s.* a guest, a stranger.
অতিথিদ্বেষী, *a.* inhospitable.
অতিথিভক্ত, *a.* devoted to guests.
অতিথিশালা, *s.* a house for guests.
অতিথিসেবক, *a.* hospitable.
অতিথিসেবা, *s.* hospitality.
অতিবাদ, *a.* excessive, exceeding, immoderate : *ad.* excessively, exceedingly.
অতিব্যয়, *s.* prodigality, profusion.
অতিব্যয়ী, *a.* prodigal : *s.* a spendthrift.
অতিরিক্ত, *a.* superabounding, excessive.
অতিরেক, *s.* a surplus, excess.
অতিশয়, *a.* much, exceeding, excessive, great : *ad.* exceedingly, excessively.
অতিশয়োক্তি *s.* garrulity, talkativeness.
অতিশ্রম, *s.* fatigue, weariness.
অতিশ্রমী, *a.* laborious, plodding.
অতিশ্রান্ত, *a.* excessively fatigued, wearied.
অতিসার, অতীসার, *s.* a diarrhœa, dysen-
অতীত, *a.* past, elapsed, gone. [tery.
অতীতকাল, *s.* in *gram.* the preter tense.

অতীন্দ্রিয়, *a.* imperceptible by the senses.
অতীয়ত্তা, *s.* immensity, abundance.
অতুঙ্গ, *a.* dwarf, short, diminutive.
অতুর, *a.* weak, infirm, sickly.
অতৃপ্ত, *a.* unsatisfied.
অতৃপ্তি, *s.* dissatisfaction.
অতোক, *a.* childless, without posterity.
অত্যন্ত, *a.* excessive, great, immoderate, abundant : *ad.* very, excessively.
অত্যর্থ, *a.* excessive, exceeding: *ad.* excessively.
অত্যল্প, *a.* very few, very small.
অত্যাচার, *s.* violence, outrage, oppression.
অত্যাচারী, *a.* outrageous, violent, oppressive.
অত্যাবশ্যক, *a.* urgent, pressing.
অত্যুত্তম, *a.* best, excellent, superlative.
অত্র, *ad.* here, in this, in this place.
অত্রত্য, *a.* belonging to this place.
অথ, *conj.* hence, moreover, and.
অথচ, *conj.* also, and.
অথবা, *conj.* otherwise, or else, or, alias.
অথর্ব্ব, *a.* very old, superannuated : *s.* the name of one of the Vedas.
অথো, *conj.* furthermore, hence, moreover, and.
অদক্ষ, *a.* awkward. অদগ্ধ, *a.* unburnt.
অদত্ত, *a.* not given, ungiven.
অদত্তা, *a.* not given in marriage: *s.* a spinster.
অদন, *s.* food, a meal ; the act of eating.
অদনীয়, *a.* eatable, fit for food.
‡অদল, *a.* not lobated, apetalous : *s.* impression of a seal, a resemblance.
অদল্‌বদল্, *s.* exchange, permutation, barter.
অদাতা, *a.* not liberal, penurious, stingy.
অদান্ত, *a.* unsubdued, uncontrolled.
*অদাবৎ, *s.* enmity, malice, ill-will, spite.
অদায়াদ, *a.* without an heir, unclaimed.
অদার, *a.* unmarried, single.
অদিতি, *s.* the mother of the Hindu gods.
অদিৎসু, *a.* not inclined to bestow.
অদিষ্ট, *a.* unknown : *s.* the reverse of fate.
অদীক্ষিত, *a.* unconsecrated.
অদূরতা, ত্ব, *s.* vicinity, nearness.
অদৃক্, অন্ধ, আন্ধলা, কাণা, *a.* blind, sightless.
অদৃশ্য, *a.* invisible, not to be seen.
অদৃশ্যতা, *s.* invisibility.
অদৃষ্ট, *a.* unseen, unperceived : *s.* fate, destiny, luck, unseen danger.
অদৃষ্টি, *a.* blind : *s.* a malignant look.
অদেখা, *a.* unseen, unperceived.
অদেয়, *a.* not proper to be given, not due.
অদ্ভুত, *a.* preternatural, supernatural, wonderful, strange, marvellous, amazing.
অদ্মর, *a.* ravenous, gluttonous, greedy.
অদ্য, আজি, *ad.* to-day.
অদ্যকার, অদ্যতন, *a.* of this day, belonging to to-day.
অদ্যকাররাত্রি, *ad.* to-night, this night.
অদ্যতনভূতকাল, *s.* preterimperfect tense.
অদ্যতনানদ্যতনভূতকাল, pluperfect tense.
অদ্যাপি, *ad.* still, yet, now, to this day.
অদ্যাবধি, *ad.* from to-day, till this day.
অদ্রব্য, *s.* a non-entity, a vanity.
অদ্রি, শৈল, গিরি, পর্ব্বত, *s.* a mountain.
অদ্বয়, *a.* single, not two.
অদ্বয়বাদী, *a.* sincere, upright.
অদ্বিতীয়, *a.* unique, peerless, only, alone, sole.
অদ্বিধা, *a.* indivisible, single, whole.
অদ্বৈত, *a.* only, single : *s.* unity.
অদ্বৈতজ্ঞান, *s.* the idea of the unity of God.
অধঃ, *ad.* beneath, below, down.
অধঃমুখী, *s.* pudendum muliebre.
অধম, *a.* vile, base, mean, low, vulgar, plebeian.
অধমর্ণ, *s.* a debtor.
অধমাধম, *a.* excessively low or vile.
অধর, *s.* the lower lip.
অধর্ম্ম, অধর্ম্মতা *s.* irreligion, impiety, injustice, unrighteousness, ungodliness.
অধর্ম্মময়, *a.* full of irreligion or injustice.
অধর্ম্মাচরণ, *s.* irreligion, impiety.
অধর্ম্মী, অধার্ম্মিক, *a.* unrighteous, irreligious, ungodly, impious, unjust.
অধর্ম্মেরধন, *s.* unjustly acquired riches.
অধস্তন, *a.* lying beneath, situated under.
অধস্তাৎ, *ad.* beneath, from below.
অধস্থ, অধস্থিত, *a.* situated below.
অধশ্ছেদ, *s.* a denominator or divisor placed beneath.
অধি, *prep.* (used only in composition) ; it usually conveys the idea of possession, right, appropriation, belonging to, &c.
অধিক, *a.* much, more, more than.
অধিকন্তু, *ad.* especially, particularly, principally : *conj.* also, furthermore.
অধিকরণ, *s.* the possessing of a thing ; in *gram.* the seventh or locative case.
অধিকাংশ, *s.* the greatest part, a majority

অধিকাংশতঃ, *ad.* for the most part.
অধিকাধিক, *ad.* more and more.
অধিকার, *s.* an estate, a reign, a government, a kingdom, a right, a privilege, inheritance, possession, title. [right.
অধিকারিতা, *s.* proprietorship, proprietary
অধিকারী, *a.* possessing a right or privilege : *s.* a proprietor, an owner.
অধিকৃত, *a.* possessed, enjoyed as a right.
অধিকৃতি, *s.* possession, right. [ed.
অধিক্ষিপ্ত, *a.* turned away, sent, despatch-
অধিগত, *a.* known, attained, found.
অধিগম, *s.* an acquiring or obtaining.
অধিগম্য, *a.* obtainable, knowable, acquira-
অধিদেবতা, *s.* a guardian deity. [ble.
অধিদৈবত, *s.* theology, a god considered as the regent over any part of nature.
অধিপ, অধিপতি, *s.* a king, a sovereign, a master, a lord, a captain, a chieftain, a governor, an owner, a commander.
অধিবাস, *s.* a ceremony preliminary to the coronation, marriage, &c.
অধিভূত, *s.* nature, material parts of creation, viz. air, earth, water, fire, &c.
অধিমাস, *s.* an intercalary month.
অধিরাজ, *s.* an emperor, a sovereign.
অধিষ্ঠাতা, *s.* a regent, a president, a ruler.
অধিষ্ঠাত্রী, *a.* presiding, ruling, governing.
অধিষ্ঠান, *s.* abiding, a habitation, a possession, practice, the doing of a thing.
অধিষ্ঠিত, *a.* situated, possessed of, settled.
অধীত, *a.* read, instructed, studied.
অধীতি, *s.* study, instruction, a lecture.
অধীন, *a.* subject to, dependent on.
অধীনতা, *s.* servitude, subjection, slavery.
অধীরা, *a.* placid, not impetuous.
অধীশ্বর, *s.* a sovereign, a lord.
অধুনা, *ad.* now, lately, recently.
অধৃতি, *s.* laxity, want of restraint.
অধৃষ্ট, *a.* unassuming, diffident, modest.
অধৃষ্টতা, *s.* modesty, diffidence.
অধেয়, *a.* uncontainable, unassumable.
অধৈর্য্য, *s.* impatience, intemperateness.
অধোগতি, *s.* a descent, a going down.
অধোগমন, *s.* a descending, a going down.
অধোগামী, *a.* descending, sinking. [down.
অধোদৃষ্টি, *s.* a downcast look, a looking
অধোবদন, *a.* downcast, dejected, ashamed.
অধোভুবন, *s.* the infernal region, Pátála.
অধ্যক্ষ, *s.* a chief, ruler, governor, superintendent, a commander, a guardian.
অধ্যক্ষতা, অ, *s.* superintendentship, guardianship, pre-eminence.
অধ্যক্ষর, *s.* the mysterious syllable ওঁ.
অধ্যয়ন, *s.* a reading, study, a lecture.
অধ্যস্ত, *a.* substituted for ; placed over.
অধ্যাত্ম, *a.* spiritual ; inherent in a person's
অধ্যাত্মবিদ্যা, *s.* self-knowledge. [nature.
অধ্যাপক, *s.* a teacher, an instructor.
অধ্যাপকতা, *s.* office of a teacher. [ing.
অধ্যাপন, অধ্যাপনা, *s.* instruction, teach-
অধ্যাপনীয়, অধ্যাপ্য, *a.* fit to be taught.
অধ্যাপয়িতা, *s.* an instructor, a preceptor.
অধ্যাপিত, *a.* taught, instructed in science.
অধ্যায়, *s.* a lesson, a section, a chapter.
অধ্যারোহী, *a.* ascending upon. [ing.
অধ্যাহরণ, *s.* a supplying ellipsis in writ-
অধ্যাহার, *s.* in *gram.* an ellipsis. [reads.
অধ্যেতা, *s.* a student, a reader, one who
অধ্যেয়, *a.* unfit to be meditated on.
অধ্ব, *s.* a road, a highway, a path.
অন, *s.* a particular note in music, a breve.
অনঙ্গ, *a.* unembodied : *s.* a name of Kámdev the Indian Cupid.
অনজ্ঞান, *a.* unknowing : *s.* a stranger.
অনধিকার, *s.* a want of right to a possession or office ; -চর্চ্চা, officiousness.
অনধিকৃত, *a.* unpossessed, uninherited.
অনধিগত, *a.* unknown.
অনন্ত, *a.* endless, eternal : *s.* a name of Vishnu, also of a deified serpent.
অনন্তক, *a.* endless, boundless.
অনন্তগৌর, *s.* a note in Hindu music.
অনন্তচতুর্দ্দশী, *s.* a feast sacred to Vishnu.
অনন্তব্রত, *s.* a vow sacred to Vishnu
অনন্তভাব, *s.* endlessness, eternity.
অনন্তময়, *a.* boundless, endless, eternal.
অনন্তমাত্র, *a.* truly eternal, boundless.
অনন্তমূল, *s.* the name of a plant.[1] [next.
অনন্তর, *ad.* after, afterwards : *a.* near,
অনন্তরাশি, *s.* in *algeb.* infinite quantity.
অনন্তরূপী, *a.* protean, multiform.
অনন্তা, *s.* a name of Durgá ; a plant.[2]
অনন্য, *a.* the same, not different, identical.

অনপত্য, অনপত্যক, *a.* childless.
অনপত্রপ, *a.* shameless, bold, impudent.
অনপরাধেদণ্ডী, *s.* a victim, one suffering for no crime.
অনপহৃত, *a.* not stolen or taken away.
অনপায়, *a.* not subject to loss, uninjurious.
অনপেক্ষ, *a.* independent, satisfied.
অনবরত, *a.* incessant, perpetual, constant.
অনভিজ্ঞ, *a.* ignorant, stupid.
অনভিজ্ঞতা, *s.* ignorance, stupidity.
অনমস্য, *a.* unworthy of honour.
*অনমোল, *a. vide* অমূল্য.
অনর্ঘ্য, *a.* invaluable, high-prized.
অনর্জ্জিত, *a.* unacquired.
অনর্থ, *a.* useless, answering no purpose.
অনর্থক, *a.* unmeaning, useless, vain.
অনর্থকতা, *s.* uselessness, vanity.
অনর্পিত, *a.* not appointed or delegated.
অনল, *s.* fire; a species of reed.[1]
অনশন, *s.* abstinence from food.
অনাচার, *s.* improper conduct, impurity.
অনাচারী, *a.* impure, unclean, wicked.
অনাড়ম্বর, *a.* unostentatious, modest.
অনাথ, *a.* unprotected, forlorn, orphan.
অনাথিনী, *a. fem.* forlorn, unprotected.
অনাদর, *s.* disrespect, want of civility.
অনাদি, *s.* eternal, without beginning.
অনাদিতা, *s.* eternity.
অনাদেয়, *a.* inadmissible, unacceptable.
অনাদেয়তা, *s.* inadmissibility.
অনাদ্য, *a.* not prior, not first.
অনাধৃষ্য, *a.* unconquerable, invincible.
অনান্নাস, *s.* pineapple (Bromelia ananas).
অনাবশ্যক, *a.* unnecessary, needless.
অনাবৃত, *a.* uncovered, unguarded, exposed.
অনাবৃষ্টি, *s.* drought, a scarcity of rain.
*অনামৎ, *a.* whole, entire.
অনাময়, *s.* health.
অনাময়তা, -ত্ব, *s.* healthiness.
অনামিকা, অনামা, *s.* the ring-finger.
অনায়ক, *a.* without owner, unclaimed.
অনায়ত, *a.* not extended, short.
অনায়ত্ত, *a.* independent, untamed.
অনায়াস, *s.* ease, facility: *a.* easy.
অনায়াসকৃত, *a.* easily done, or made.
অনায়াসে, *ad.* easily, without difficulty.
অনারত, *a.* incessant, perpetual.

অনাশ্রিত, *a.* not dependant on.
অনাসিক, *a.* noseless.
অনাস্থা, *s.* incredulity, want of confidence.
অনাস্থিক, *a.* incredulous.
অনাস্থেয়, *a.* incredible, unfit to be confided.
অনাস্বাদু, *a.* tasteless, insipid.
অনাহত, *a.* not smitten: *s.* the breast.
অনাহার, *a.* fasting: *s.* abstinence.
অনাহারী, *a.* fasting, living without food.
অনাহূত, *s.* uncalled, uninvited.
অনিঃশব্দ, অনিঃস্বন, *a.* not silent, noisy.
অনিঃশ্বাস, *a.* breathless: *s.* want of breath.
অনিকট, দূর, *a.* distant.
অনিঙ্গন, *a.* immovable.
অনিচ্ছ, অনিচ্ছু, অনিচ্ছুক, *a.* averse, involuntary, unwilling, reluctant, indifferent.
অনিচ্ছা, *s.* disrelish, aversion, reluctance.
অনিত্য, *a.* temporary, fugitive, transitory.
অনিত্যচিন্তা, *s.* a whim, fancy, caprice.
অনিত্যতা, অনিত্যরূপ, *s.* temporariness.
অনিবারিত, *a.* not hindered, not resisted.
অনিবার্য্য, *a.* irresistible, stubborn.
অনিমিষ, *a.* unwinking, vigilant.
অনিমিষে, *ad.* vigilantly, narrowly, closely.
অনিয়ত, *a.* incessant, perpetual, constant, unresolved, unfixed, undetermined, unregulated, uncontrolled.
অনিয়ন্ত্রিত, *a.* uncurbed, unbridled, unrestrained.
অনিয়ম, *a.* irregular: *s.* absence of a rule.
অনিয়মিত, *a.* not regulated, undetermined.
অনিরুদ্ধ, *s.* the husband of Ushá.
অনির্বচন, *s.* the not asserting of a thing.
অনির্বাচ্য, *a.* indescribable, undefinable.
অনির্বাহ, *s.* want, indigence, need.
অনির্বিণ্ণ, *a.* indifferent, needy, indigent.
অনির্বৃতি, *s.* wretchedness, want, need.
অনিল, বায়ু, *s.* the wind, air.
অনিশ, *a.* nightless, incessant, continual.
অনিষিদ্ধ, *a.* unprohibited, unforbidden.
অনিষ্ট, *a.* undesired, ominous, evil.
অনিষ্টক, *a.* occasioning evil, or ill-luck.
অনিষ্টলাভ, *s.* misfortune.
অনিষ্টশঙ্কা, *a.* foreboding of evil.
অনিষ্টসূচক, *a.* indicating evil, ominous.
অনিষ্ঠা, *s.* unsteadfastness, unsteadiness.
অনিস্বন, *s.* silence: *a.* silent.
অনিহ্নোতা, *s.* one who does not deny a fact.

অনীক, অনীকিনী, *s.* an army, forces.
অনীকাশ, *a.* unlike, unparalleled.
অনীচ, *a.* not low or base. অনীত, *a.* not
অনীতি, *s.* injustice, immorality. [taken.
অনীদৃশ, *a.* not thus, unlike, dissimilar.
অনীশ্বরবাদ, *s.* atheism, a denial of God.
অনীশ্বরবাদী, *a.* denying God: *s.* an atheist.
অনীশ্বরপরায়ণ, *a.* atheistical, impious.
অনীহ, *a.* indifferent, careless.
অনু, *prep.* (used only in composition); it conveys the idea of following, following upon, consequent, according to.
অনুকম্পা, *s.* pity, compassion, tenderness.
অনুকম্পিত, *a.* affected with pity.
অনুকরণ, *s.* an imitation: *a.* imitative.
অনুকরণশব্দ, *s.* an imitative sound.
অনুকর্ষ, *s.* the axle-tree of a carriage.
অনুকর্ষণ, *s.* a drawing, attraction.
অনুকল্প, *s.* an alternative, a secondary
অনুকার, *s.* an imitation. [injunction.
অনুকারী, *a.* imitating, mimicking.
অনুকূল, *a.* coinciding, friendly to, assisting, co-operating, acting in concert.
অনুকূলতা, -ত্ব, *s.* *vide* আনুকূল্য.
অনুকূলবায়ু, *s.* a fair or favorable wind.
অনুক্ত, *a.* not mentioned, not spoken.
অনুক্তি, *s.* not a word, an improper ex-
অনুক্রচক, *a.* serrated, dentated. [pression.
অনুক্রম, *s.* a succession, order, a series.
অনুক্রমণিকা, *s.* an index, table of contents.
অনুক্রোশ, *s.* tenderness, compassion, pity.
অনুক্ষণ, *ad.* at every instant, perpetually.
অনুখাল, *s.* a creek.
অনুগত, *a.* attached to, dependent on.
অনুগম, *s.* a following, a consequence.
অনুগমন, *s.* a following, a woman's burning with the corpse of her husband.
অনুগম্য, *a.* fit or deserving to be followed.
অনুগামী, *a.* following, consequent upon, devoted to, imitating, servile.
অনুগৃহীত, *a.* favored, honored.
অনুগ্রহ, *s.* grace, favor, kindness.
অনুচর, *s.* an attendant, a follower.
অনুচারী, *a.* attending, following.
অনুচিত, *a.* unfit, improper, wrong.
অনুচ্চ, *a.* not high, low, humble, lowly.
অনুজ, *a.* younger, junior.

অনুজীবী, *a.* living upon: *s.* a servant.
অনুজ্ঞা, *s.* a command, injunction; -পালক, obedient; -পালন, obedience.
অনুতাপ, *s.* repentance, regret, remorse.
অনুতাপি, *a.* penitent, regretting.
অনুত্তান, *a.* lying with the face downwards: *s.* a supine posture.
অনুদয়, *s.* the not rising of a luminary.
অনুদাত্ত, *a.* unaccented. [as the day.
অনুদিন, *ad.* daily, every day, as constant
অনুদৈর্ঘ্য, *a.* longitudinal.
অনদ্দিষ্ট, *a.* not regarded, unascertained.
অনুদ্দেশ, *s.* want of attention to an object.
অনুদ্দেশ্য, *a.* not to be regarded.
অনুদ্বেগ, *s.* freedom from perplexity.
অনুদ্যত, *a.* not engaged, not about to do.
অনুদ্যম, *s.* want of effort, not an effort.
অনুধাবন, *s.* a pursuit, consideration, reflection, meditation.
অনুনয়, *s.* submission, intreaty, humility.
অনুনয়ী, *a.* humble, submissive.
অনুন্নতানত, *a.* level, horizontal.
অনুন্নীত, *s.* non-elevation.
অনুপদিষ্ট, *a.* uninstructed, untaught.
অনুপপত্তি, *s.* inconclusive argument for supporting a doctrine or hypothesis.
অনুপম, *a.* incomparable, unequalled,
অনুপমা, *s.* a dissimilitude. [peerless.
অনুপমিত, *a.* uncompared.
অনুপমেয়, *a.* incomparable.
অনুপযুক্ত, *a.* unfit, improper, inconsistent.
অনুপযোগ, *s.* unsuitableness, inutility.
অনুপস্থিতকল্পনা, *s.* absence of mind.
অনুপস্থিতচিন্তা, *s.* absence of thought.
অনুপাত, *s.* proportion, arithmetical pro-
অনুপাতক, *s.* a small crime. [portion.
অনুপান, *s.* a vehicle for a medicine.
অনুপাম, *s.* *idem;* also, *a.* *vide* অনুপম.
অনুপায়, *s.* want of expedient.
অনুপায়ী, *a.* not contriving, not using ex-
অনপার্শ্ব, *a.* lateral. [pedients.
অনুপ্রয়াস, or অনুপ্রাস, *s.* after endeavour or labour, an accumulation of words from the same root, alliteration.
অনুপ্রস্থ, *a.* latitudinal, transverse.
অনুবৎসর, *ad.* yearly, every year.
অনুবন্ধ, *s.* offence, guilt, an element of

language, viz. a root, an affix, an augment, the permutation of a letter.
অনুবর্ত্তনীয়, *a.* probable, possible.
অনুবর্ত্তী, *a.* following, attendant upon.
অনুবাদ, *s.* a response, an abusive reply.
অনুবৃত্তি, *s.* a consequence, a following.
অনুবোধ, *s.* an after-thought.
অনুব্জ, *a.* crooked, awry, not erect.
অনুভব, *s.* experience, experimental knowledge, a guess, an inference, a supposition, a hypothesis, a surmise.
অনুভববিরুদ্ধ, *a.* contrary to experience.
অনুভবসিদ্ধ, *a.* proved by experience.
অনুভবে, *ad.* experimentally. [cation.
অনুভাব, *s.* firm opinion, certainty; indi-
অনুমতি, *s.* acquiescence, consent, permission, a commandment; -দা, to permit.
অনুমন্তা, *s.* one who gives permission.
অনুমরণ, অনুমৃতা, *s.* a woman's burning herself on a separate pile. [thesis.
অনুমান, *s.* a guess, an inference, a hypo-
অনুমানকর্ত্তা, *s.* one who infers. [ference.
অনুমানবিরুদ্ধ, *a.* contrary to legitimate in-
অনুমানসিদ্ধ. *a.* proved or established by
অনুমানে, *ad.* probably. [inference.
অনুমাপক, *a.* leading to an inference.
অনুমাপিত, *a.* forced as an inference.
অনুমিত, *a.* inferred, guessed.
অনুমিতি, *s.* an inference, a guess.
অনুমেয়, *a.* inferrible.
অনুযায়ী, *a.* following, arising as a consequence from some circumstance.
অনুযোগ, *s.* a reproof, a reprehension.
অনুযোগী, *a.* reproving, reprehending.
অনুযোজ্য, *a.* reprehensible. [fond of.
অনুরক্ত, *a.* attached to, enamoured with,
অনুরক্তি, *s.* love, affection, fondness.
অনুরঞ্জক, *a* giving pleasure, causing delight, pleasing, gratifying. [ject.
অনুরঞ্জন, *s.* attachment, delight in an ob-
অনুরাগ, *s.* attachment, fondness, love, af-
অনুরাগী, *a.* affectionate, fond. [fection.
অনুরাধা, *s.* the 17th lunar mansion.
অনুরুদ্ধ, *a.* complied with, conceded to.
অনুরূপ, *a.* corresponding with, like.[ing.
অনুরূপী, *a.* assuming same habit, imitat-
অনুরোদ্ধা, *s.* one who shows partiality.

অনুরোধ, *s.* complaisance, partiality. [ing.
অনুরোধী, *a.* partial, complaisant, conced-
অনুলিপ্ত, *a.* anointed, smeared with.
অনুলেপ, *s.* an unguent, anointing.
অনুলেপক, anointing : *s.* one who anoints.
অনুলেপন, *s.* the anointing with unguents.
অনুলোম, *a.* favorable, helping forward, going with the grain or with the hair.
অনুলোমজ, *a.* produced or born in due gradation or order.
অনুশীলন, *s.* study, attention, devotedness to any science ; -কৃ, to study.
অনুশীলনীয়, *a.* deserving to be studied.
অনুশোক, *s.* repentance, regret, remorse.
অনুশোচক, *s.* one who repents or regrets.
অনুশোচন, *s.* the repenting of an action.
অনুশোচনীয়, *a.* requiring repentance.
অনুশোচিত, *a.* repented of, regretted.
অনুশোচী, *a.* repenting, regretting.
অনুশ্রব, *a.* learned by dictation.
অনুষঙ্গ, *s.* attachment, love ; agreement.
অনুষ্টুপ, *s.* a measure of verse, viz. 32 syllables, or 4 lines of 8 syllables each.
অনুষ্ঠাতব্য, *a.* fit to be practised.
অনুষ্ঠাতা, *s.* one who does or practises.
অনুষ্ঠান, *s.* practice, a practising, application, diligence, a topic of discourse.
অনুসন্ধান, *s.* an aim, search, research, enquiry, investigation, scrutiny.
অনুসন্ধানী, *a.* inquisitive, curious.
অনুসন্ধানীয়, *a.* ascertainable, investigable.
অনুসন্ধায়ী, *a.* searching, seeking, enquiring, investigating, scrutinizing.
অনুসরণ, *s.* the following of a person.
অনুসরণীয়, *a.* fit to be followed, inferrible.
অনুসার, *s.* a consequence, conformity.
অনুসারী, *a.* following, according with.
অনুসারে, *ad.* according to, in virtue of.
অনুসূচক, *a.* reflecting, indicating.
অনুসূচনা, *s.* reflection, indication.
অনুসূচনীয়, অনুসূচয়িতব্য, *a.* indicable.
অনুসূচিত, *a.* known, reflected on.
অনুস্বার, *s.* the nasal character ং.
অনূঢ়, *a.* unmarried : *s.* a bachelor.
অনূঢ়া, *a. fem.* unmarried : *s.* a spinster.
অনেক, *a.* many, much, abundant.
অনেকধা, *ad.* of many sorts : *a.* various.

অনেড়মুক, *a.* entirely deaf and dumb.
অন্‌কী, *s.* a flea, an annoying insect.
অন্ত, *s.* an end, extremity; death: *a.* near.
অন্তঃকরণ, *s.* the heart, will, inward agent.
অন্তঃকরণবর্ত্তী, *a.* innate, in-dwelling.
অন্তঃক্রুদ্ধ, *a.* inwardly vexed, enraged.
অন্তঃপাতী, *a.* included, internal: *s.* vicinity.
অন্তঃপুর, *s.* female apartments, a seraglio.
অন্তঃসলিল, *s.* subterraneous water; a secret, concealed idea. [destructive, fatal.
অন্তক, *s.* death, Yama: *a.* mortal, deadly,
অন্তকর, *a.* mortal, deadly: *s.* a destroyer.
অন্তকাল, *s.* the time of death.
অন্ততঃ, *ad.* at last, finally, in the end.
অন্তর, *ad.* in, within, between.
অন্তর, *s.* interval, distance: *a.* own: *ad.* without, except: *conj.* and, moreover.
অন্তরঙ্গ, *s.* a relative, a near friend. [cy.
অন্তরঙ্গতা, *s.* relationship, kindred, intima-
অন্তরতা, *s.* inwardness, inclusiveness; outwardness, exclusiveness.
অন্তরস্থ, *a.* inner, internal, situated within.
অন্তরা, *ad.* betwixt, between, near, except: *s.* a line in poetry, the verse of a song.
অন্তরাপত্যা, or অন্তর্বত্নী, *a.* pregnant.
অন্তরায়, *s.* an impediment, an obstacle.
অন্তরাল, *s.* the space between two objects.
অন্তরিত, *a.* inward, internal. [a bird.
অন্তরীক্ষ, *s.* sky, atmosphere; -চর aerial:
অন্তরীপ, *s.* a cape, a promontory, a head-
অন্তরীয়, *s.* a lower garment. [land.
অন্তরে, *ad.* between, betwixt, except.
অন্তর্গত, *a.* included, forgotten.
অন্তর্জ্জলী, *s.* the immersing of the body of a dying person into the Ganges.
অন্তর্জ্জাত, *a.* excited within, inborn.
অন্তর্দ্ধান, *s.* a disappearing, a vanishing
অন্তর্দ্ধানী, *a.* becoming invisible. [away.
অন্তর্দ্ধি, *s.* invisibility, a concealed state.
অন্তর্দ্ধ্যান, *s.* inward meditation.
অন্তর্বর্ত্তী, *a.* internal, inward, included, contained, situated within.
অন্তর্বেদি, *s.* Doáb, the country included between the Ganges and Yamuná.
অন্তর্ভূত, *a.* included, contained, internal.
অন্তর্যামী, *a.* pervading, heart-searching.
অন্তর্হিত, *a.* vanished, disappeared.

অন্তিক, *a.* near, proximate, adjacent, conti-
অন্তিকতম, *a.* very near, close to. [guous.
অন্তিম, *a.* extreme, final, last, very near.
অন্তিমকাল, *s.* the time of death.
অন্তে, *ad.* at last, in the end, in fine.
অন্ত্য, *a.* last, ultimate, a hundred billions: *s.* last term in the rule of proportion.
অন্ত্যজ, *a.* junior, youngest; plebeian.
অন্ত্যেষ্টি, *s.* a funeral sacrifice.
অন্ত্যেষ্টিক্রিয়া, *s.* funeral obsequies.
অন্ত্র, *s.* entrails, the bowels, the viscera.
অন্ত্রবিদ্যা, *s.* splanchnology.
অন্ত্রাপপ্লাবক, *s.* the epiploon or caul.
*অন্দর, *a.* within. অন্দরে, *ad.* within.
*অন্দাজ, *s.* a guess, a cast.
*অন্দাজী, guessing, by guess. [fear.
*অন্দেশা, *s.* thought, reflection, doubt,
অন্ধ, অন্ধক, কাণা, *a.* blind, sightless.
অন্ধকার, *s.* darkness: *a.* dark, obscure.
অন্ধকূপ, *s.* a well overgrown by weeds.
অন্ধগোলাঙ্গুলন্যায়, *a.* implicit, led by the
অন্ধতমস, *s.* gross darkness. [nose.
অন্ধযষ্টি, *s.* a blind man's staff.
অন্ধলা, অন্ধ, কাণা, *a.* blind, sightless.
অন্ধস, *s.* food, boiled rice.
অন্ধস্কন্ধারোহণ, *s.* a making shift, the cripple's riding on the shoulders of the blind for the purpose of assisting each other with sight and locomotion.
*অন্ধিয়ারা, *s.* darkness.
অন্ধিসন্ধি, *s.* a chink, a crevice, a flaw.
*অন্ধের, *a.* very dark; mysterious; un-
অন্ন, *s.* food, boiled rice. [just.
অন্নজল, *s.* board, maintenance.
অন্নদাতা, *s.* a supporter, a charitable man.
অন্নপূর্ণা, . a goddess, the Hindu Ceres.
অন্নপ্রাশন, *s.* the ceremony of giving a child rice for the first time.
অন্নরস, or অপক্বরস, *s.* chyle.
অন্য, *pron.* another, other, different.
অন্যতম, *pron.* the best of all others.
অন্যতর, *pron.* rather, either, other, differ-
অন্যত্র, *ad.* elsewhere. [ent.
অন্যথা, *s.* contrary, reverse: *ad.* contrariwise: *a.* contrary, different, void, null.
অন্যদা, *ad.* at another time. [eigner.
অন্যদেশী, অন্যদেশীয়, *a.* foreign: *s.* a for-

অন্যপথ, *s.* a different road. [other.
অন্যপূর্ব্বা, *a.* previously betrothed to an-
অন্যমত, *s.* another manner; another sect: *ad.* otherwise, in another way.
অন্যমতে, *ad.* otherwise, by other means.
অন্যমনস্ক, *a.* absent in mind, averse.
অন্যান্য, *a.* others; mutual.
অন্যায়, *s.* injustice, outrage, impropriety.
অন্যায়ী, *a.* unjust, oppressive.
অন্যোন্য, *a.* reciprocal, mutual.
অন্বিত, *a.* agreeing with, connected with, possessed of, fraught with, inherent in.
অন্বিষ্ট, *a.* sought, required.
অন্বেষণ, *s.* enquire, search, research.
অন্বেষণীয়, *a.* desirable, fit to be searched.
অন্বেষিত, *a.* sought, required.
অন্বেষী, *a.* searching, inquisitive.
অপ্, উদক, জল, নীর, বারি, সলিল, *s.* water.
অপ, *prep.* it usually gives the idea of taking from, or doing a thing badly.
অপকর্ম্ম, *s.* improper conduct, a mean action, an unworthy action.
অপকর্ষ, *s.* an evil tendency, a wrong bias.
অপকর্ষণ, *s.* an unfair seizing, a biasing.
অপকলঙ্ক, *s.* an indelible stain, a disgrace.
অপকার, *s.* a detriment, an injury.
অপকৃত, *a.* hindered, prevented, opposed.
অপকৃতি, *s.* opposition, a bad action.
অপকৃষ্ট, *a.* low, bad, inferior, debased.
অপক্রম, *s.* a retreat, flight, absconding.
অপক্করস, or অন্নরস, *s.* chyle.
অপগত, *a.* gone, departed, deviated from.
অপঘাত, *s.* a tragical or sudden death, [murder.
অপঘাতমৃত্যু, *s. idem.*
অপচয়, *s.* loss, detriment, waste. [office.
অপচয়ভাগী, *s.* the keeper of an insurance
অপচিত, *a.* lost, dispersed, wasted.
অপচিতি, *s.* loss, detriment, waste, dispersion; respect, honour, reverence.
অপচ্ছায়া, *s.* an apparition, a phantom.
অপদেবতা, *s.* spectre, apparition, a goblin.
অপবাদ, *s.* censure, an accusation, a libel.
অপবাদিত, *a.* accused, censured.
অপবাদী, *a.* libelling, defaming, accusing.
অপবিত্র, *a.* unholy, impure, unclean.
অপব্যয়, *s.* prodigality, profusion. [derer.
অপব্যয়ী, *a.* prodigal, profuse: *s.* a squan-

অপভাষা, *s.* low or vulgar language.
অপমান, *s.* dishonor, disgrace, disrespect, an affront, an indignity, an insult.
অপমানী, *a.* dishonorable. disgraceful.
অপমৃত্যু, *s.* unnatural or untimely death.
অপযশঃ, *s.* infamy, disgrace, dishonor.
অপর, *a.* another, other: *ad.* also.
অপরাজিতা, *s.* a plant (Clitorea ternatea).
অপরাধ, *s.* guilt, sin, a fault, crime.
অপরাধবর্দ্ধক, *a.* aggravating crimes.
অপরাধী, *a.* criminal, guilty, sinful.
অপরামর্শ, *a.* unadvisable.
অপরামৃষ্টা, *a.* undefiled: *s.* a virgin.
অপরাহ্ন, *s.* the afternoon. [wife.
অপরিগৃহীতা, *s.* a chaste woman, a lawful
অপরিগ্রহ, *a.* unacceptable: non-accept-
অপরিণয়ন, *s.* celibacy. [ance.
অপরিমিত, *a.* unmeasured, immoderate.
অপরিষ্কার, *a.* impure, unclean, vague.
অপরিহার্য্য, *a.* irrefutable, unanswerable.
অপরীক্ষিত, *a.* untried, unexamined.
অপরূপ, *a.* ugly, distorted, queer, preternatural, singular, strange, surprising.
অপর্য্যায়, *a.* irregular, immethodical.
অপলাপ, *s.* the denial of a thing, scandal, detraction, evasion, low discourse.
অপলাপী, *a.* slandering, belying, denying.
অপস্পষ্ট, *a.* not clear, unintelligible.
অপসরণ, *s.* a withdrawing, a retreating.
অপস্মার, *s.* the epilepsy, falling sickness.
অপস্মারী, *a.* epileptic, having epilepsy.
অপহত, *a.* murdered, killed, ruined.
অপহরণ, *s.* a purloining, a plundering.
অপহার, *s.* plunder, pillage, thievery, larceny, robbery, depredation.
অপহারিত, *a.* plundered, pillaged.
অপহৃত, *a.* stolen, gained by plunder.
অপহ্নব, *s.* denial, concealment.
অপহ্নুত, *a.* denied, concealed.
অপাংনিধি, *s.* the sea, ocean. [cocted.
অপাক, *s.* indigestion: *a.* unripe, uncon-
অপাঙ্গ, *s.* the outer corner of the eye, a lame person: *a.* deformed, ugly.
অপাদান, *s.* in *gram.* the ablative case.
অপার, *a.* shoreless, boundless, impassa-
অপার্য্যমাণ, *a.* impracticable. [ble.
অপি, *conj.* also, and, likewise, moreover.

অপীন, *a.* not thick, plump, or large.
অপূর্ণ, *a.* not full ; -কালজ, abortive.
অপূর্ব্ব, *a.* unprecedented, unexperienced, unparalleled, eminent, excellent, uncommon, remarkable : *s.* fate, destiny.
অপেক্ষ, *a.* expecting, expectant.
অপেক্ষক, *a.* expecting : *s.* an expectant.
অপেক্ষণ, *s.* act of expecting.
অপেক্ষণীয়, *a.* *vide* অপেক্ষ্য, [rather.
অপেক্ষা, *s.* expectation, hope : *ad.* than,
অপেক্ষিত, *a.* expected, waited for.
অপেক্ষী, *a.* expecting, waiting for. [for.
অপেক্ষ্য, *a.* fit to be expected or waited
অপোড়, *a.* unburnt, incombustible.
অপ্রকাশ, *a.* secret, private, sinister.
অপ্রকাশে, *ad.* privately, secretly.
অপ্রকৃত, *a.* spurious, improper.
অপ্রচুর, *a.* insufficient ; তা insufficiency.
অপ্রণালী, *s.* an irreglarity, an anomaly.
অপ্রতিকার্য্য, *a.* irremediable, irretrievable.
অপ্রতিভ, *a.* nonplussed, confounded.
অপ্রতিম, *a.* unparalleled, peerless.
অপ্রতীতি, *s.* incredulity, unbelief.
অপ্রতুল, *s.* need, want, exigency, a strait.
অপ্রত্যক্ষ, *a.* not evident, absent.
অপ্রত্যয়, *s.* incredulity, unbelief, mistrust.
অপ্রত্যয়ী, *a.* unbelieving, incredulous.
অপ্রথ, *a.* not known, not public, irregular.
অপ্রথা, *s.* a want of publicity, irregularity.
অপ্রথিত, *a.* unpublished, not noted.
অপ্রবৃত্ত, *a.* not engaged, not excited. [ness.
অপ্রবৃত্তি, *s.* non-excitation, non-engaged-
অপ্রবেশ, *s.* a not entering : *a.* inaccessible.
অপ্রবেশনীয়, অপ্রবেশ্য, *a.* impenetrable.
অপ্রমাণ, *s.* destitute of proof or evidence.
অপ্রমাদ, *s.* caution, safety, heed.
অপ্রমিধানী, *a.* precipitate, venturesome.
অপ্রমেয়, *a.* incapable of proof, improbable.
অপ্রয়াস, *a.* easy, slight : *s.* ease.
অপ্রয়াসে, *ad.* easily, without labour.
অপ্রয়োগ, *s.* an inferior object.
অপ্রয়োজক, *a.* ineffectual. [cessary.
অপ্রয়োজন, *s.* want of necessity : *a.* unne-
অপ্রলাপ, *s.* coherent speech.
অপ্রশস্ত, *a.* narrow, scanty, strait.
অপ্রস্তুত, *a.* not ready, unprepared, confounded, nonplussed, unable to reply.

অপ্রাচীন, *a* not ancient, not old, modern,
অপ্রাচুর্য্য, *s.* insufficiency. [new.
অপ্রাণী, *a.* inanimate.
অপ্রাপ্ত, *a.* unobtained.
অপ্রাপ্তকল্যাণ, *a.* unfortunate, unsuccess-
অপ্রাপ্তকাল, *a.* inopportune. [ful.
অপ্রাপ্তি, *s.* scarcity : *a.* not gainful, scarce.
অপ্রামাণিক, *a.* improbable, unauthentic.
অপ্রামাণ্য, *s.* improbability, inauthenticity.
অপ্রিয়, *a.* unamiable, not beloved.
অপ্রীতি, *s.* want of love, dislike, disgust.
অপ্সরা, *s.* a species of demi-gods, the fabled courtezans of the Hindu heaven.
অফিম, *s.* opium ; properly অহিফেন.
অফিমী, *a.* addicted to eating opium.
অফুরণ, *s.* non-decay, non-expenditure : *a.* not expended; uncontracted; endless.
অব, *prep.* it usually gives the verb or other word to which it is prefixed, an ablative sense, or sinks its value; sometimes it gives to verbs of motion the sense of motion downwards : *ad.* now.
অবকাশ, *s.* leisure, opportunity.
অবকাশক্রমে, *ad.* at leisure, leisurely.
অবক্তব্য, *a.* not fit or proper to be spoken, unspeakable, unutterable.
অবক্রয়, *s.* an unfair purchase.
অবক্ষেপ, *s.* an irony, a sarcasm, a jeer.
অবগণ্ড, *s.* an infant, a babe.
অবগত, *a.* known, acquainted with.
অবগতি, *s.* knowledge, acquaintedness.
অবগাহন, *s.* immersion, bathing, ablution.
অবগাহিত, *a.* immersed, baptized, plunged,
অবচূর্ণ, *s.* coarse powder. [dipped.
অবচ্ছিন্ন, *a.* limited, bounded.
অবচ্ছেদ, . a limit, a boundary.
অবজ্ঞা, *s.* contempt, despite, disregard.
অবজ্ঞাত, *a.* despised, contemned.
অবজ্ঞাতব্য, *a.* despicable, contemptible.
অবজ্ঞেয়, *a.* *idem.* [cavity.
অবট; *s.* a cavern, a pit, hole, a sinus, a
অবতান, or চন্দ্রাতপ, *s.* an awning.
অবতার, *s.* a descent, incarnation. [tion
অবতারণ, *s.* the descending from a situa-
অবতারণিকা, *s.* a quotation ; a boat.
অবতীর্ণ, *a.* descended, incarnate.
অবথব, *a.* decrepit, embecile.

অবদীর্ণ, *a.* rent, torn, chopt, cracked, cleft.
অবধান, *s.* attention, care, regard.
অবধানতা, *s.* attentiveness, carefulness.
অবধারিত, *a.* emphatic, settled, fixed on.
অবধি, *s.* extremity, limit: *ad.* from.
অবধূত, *a.* devoted to God but not attending on ceremonies: *s.* a class of fanatics.
অবধ্য, *a.* not deserving death, not to be slain.
অবনত, *a.* bowed, bent down.
অবনতকায়, *a.* bent-bodied, bowed.
অবনতি, *s.* a bowing, condescension.
অবনমন, *s.* a depressing, a bending down.
অবনাট, *s.* disagreement, discord.
অবনামক, *a.* deflecting: *s.* a deflector.
অবনি, or অবনী, *s.* the earth, the world; -পতি, or -পাল, *s.* a king, a sovereign.
অবয়ব, *s.* a limb, a number, a feature, aspect, form, a constituent part.
অবরত, *a.* desisted, ceased.
অবরতঃ, *ad.* after, afterwards, beneath.
অবরতি, *s.* cessation.
অবরুদ্ধ, *a.* obstructed, blockaded, besieged.
অবরূঢ়, *a.* descended, dismounted.
অবরোদ্ধা, *s.* a besieger, one who blocks up.
অবরোধ, *s.* a blockading, a shutting up, a besieging; a cover, a lid; a seraglio.
অবরোহ, *s.* a descent, an alighting.
অবরোহণ, *s.* a descending, an alighting.
অবরোহী, *a.* descending, alighting.
অবর্ত্তমান, *a.* non-existent, absent, dead.
অবলজ্জা, *s.* false modesty.
অবলম্ব, *s.* a prop, a support, a perpendicular.
অবলম্বন, *s.* the act of propping or supporting, a fulcrum, a support, a prop.
অবলম্বনীয়, *a.* proper to be depended on.
অবলম্বিত, *a.* depended, dependent.
অবলম্বী, *a.* depending on, hanging on.
অবলা, *a.* dumb, weak: *s.* a woman.
অবলুণ্ঠন, *s.* a rolling, a wallowing.
অবলুণ্ঠিত, *a.* rolled, wallowed.
অবলেপন, *s.* a smearing or plastering.
অবলেহ, *s.* a lapping; a lozenge.
অবলোকন, *s.* the looking at, or surveying of an object; -কৃ, to view.
অবলোকনীয়, *a.* fit to be seen or viewed, visible.
অবলোকিত, *a.* viewed, surveyed, beheld, seen.
অবলোকী, *a.* looking, surveying.

*অবল, *a.* first, chief, best.
অবশ, *a.* not under control, benumbed, unruly, ungoverned, mutinous.
অবশিষ্ট, *a.* left, remaining, surplus.
অবশেষ, *s.* residue, remnant, remainder.
অবশেষে, *ad.* at last, finally.
অবশ্য, *a.* unruly; certain, necessary: *ad.* certainly; -করণীয়, or -কর্ত্তব্য, highly important, indispensably necessary.
অবশ্যায়, *s.* frost, cold; pride.
অবসন্ন, *a.* wearied, fatigued, exhausted, relaxed, decayed, ended, declined.
অবসর, *s.* leisure, opportunity.
অবসরকাল, *s.* a holiday, a vacation, a leisure time.
অবসরক্রমে, *ad.* at leisure, leisurely.
অবসান, *s.* the extinction or exit of a thing, conclusion, decline.
অবসায়, *s.* an end, declination, a decision.
অবস্তু, *a.* vain, unsubstantial.
অবস্তুতা, *s.* vanity, unsubstantialness.
অবস্থা, *s.* condition, a situation, a predicament, a state, affliction, distress.
অবস্থাতা, *s.* one who settles in a place.
অবস্থান, *s.* a residing, lodging, settling, a residence, the settling upon a spot.
অবস্থান্তর, *s.* another state or condition.
অবস্থিত *a.* situated, settled.
অবস্থিতি, *s.* a dwelling, residence, a settlement.
অবস্থেয়, *a.* capable of being dwelt in.
অবহেলা, *s.* disregard, disrespect, contempt, a disregarding of authority.
অবহেলন, *s.* the disregarding of authority.
অবহেলায়, *ad.* carelessly, negligently.
অবাক্, *a.* speechless, mute, unable to reply, dumb: *ad.* beneath, below.
অবাচী, *a.* south: *s.* the south.
অবাচ্য, *a.* unfit to be spoken or mentioned.
অবাধা, *s.* not a hinderance or obstruction.
অবাধিত, *a.* unobstructed, unrestrained.
অবাধ্য, *a.* uncontrollable, obstinate.
অবান্তর, *a.* intervolved, included.
অবার, *s.* the hither side of a river.
অবারণীয়, অবার্য্য, *a.* inevitable, irresistible.
অবারিত, *a.* unguarded, unrestrained, unconfined, free, unobstructed.
অবার্য্যমাণ, *a.* not suffering resistance.
অবিচার, *s.* unjust judgment, injustice.

অবিচার্য্য, অবিচারণীয়, *a.* uninvestigable.
অবিচিন্তনীয়, অবিচিন্ত্য, *a.* inscrutable, incomprehensible, inconceivable.
অবিচ্ছেত্তব্য, *a.* indivisible, inseparable.
অবিচ্ছেদ, *s.* not division, union.
অবিদ্য, *a.* unlearned, uninstructed, ignorant, unsearchable, beyond knowledge.
অবিদ্যমান, *a.* unperceived, absent. [laws.
অবিধান, *s.* the want of laws : *a.* without
অবিধি, অবিধানী, *a.* lawless, illegal, illicit.
অবিনশ্বর, *a.* imperishable, indestructible.
অবিনোদ, *s.* sadness, cheerlessness.
অবিবাহ, *s.* celibacy : *a.* unmarried.
অবিবাহিত, *a.* unmarried : *fem.* অবিবাহিতা.
অবিবেচক, *a.* injudicious, inconsiderate : *s.* one who does not discriminate.
অবিবেচনা, *s.* a want of consideration, discrimination, or investigation.
অবিমত, *a.* not averse to, not disinclined.
অবিরত, অবিরাম, *a.* undesisted, incessant.
অবিরুদ্ধ, *a.* not opposed to a thing.
অবিরোধ, *s.* peace, concord, harmony.
অবিরোধী, *a.* not contentious, peaceable.
অবিলম্ব, *a.* prompt, without delay.
অবিলম্বিত, *a.* not delayed, not postponed.
অবিলম্বে, *ad.* immediately, without delay.
অবিশেষ, *s.* a want of distinction.
অবিশেষ্য, *a.* undistinguishable.
অবিশ্বসিত, *a.* not trusted, not confided in.
অবিশ্বস্ত, *a.* perfidious, treacherous, disho-
অবিশ্বাস, *s.* incredulity, distrust. [nest.
অবিশ্বাসী, *a.* mistrustful, unbelieving.
অবিশ্বাস্য, *a.* unworthy of trust, unfaithful.
অবীরা, *s.* one who has neither husband
অবুঝ, *a.* stupid, senseless. [nor son.
অবুদ্ধি, *a.* senseless, idiot, simple, foolish.
অবুদ্ধিমান্, *a.* unwise, notof clearintellect.
অবৃন্ত, *a.* sessile, void of a peduncle or pe-
অবৃষ্টি, *s.* want of rain, drought. [dicle.
অবেক্ষক, *a.* viewing, examining : *s.* one who views or examines.
অবেক্ষণ, *s.* a survey, an inspection.
অবেক্ষণীয়, *a.* capable of being closely in.
অবেক্ষা, *s.* attention, inspection. [spected.
অবেক্ষিত, *a.* inspected, surveyed.
অবেলা, *s.* the want of time, the conclusion of the day, a deficiency in the tides.

অবৈদ্য, *a.* not a doctor : *s.* a quack doctor.
অবৈদ্যক, *a.* heterodox, not in the veda.
অবৈধ, *a.* unwarranted, irregular.
অবৈধকর্ম্ম, *s.* superstition.
অবৈধকর্ম্মক, অবৈধকারী, *a.* superstitious.
অবৈর, *a.* free from enmity.
অবৈরী, *a.* not hostile, not in enmity.
অবোদ্ধব্য, *a.* incomprehensible.
অবোধ, *a.* senseless, dull, stupid, ignorant : *s.* want of understanding.
অব্জ, *s.* the moon, a conch : Dhanwantari, a lotus,[1] a thousand millions.
অব্দ, *s.* a year, an æra ; a cloud.
অব্ভ্র, *s.* a cloud.
অব্যক্ত, *a.* unperceived, imperceptible, indistinct, latent, vague, unintelligible.
অব্যক্তগণিত, or বীজগণিত, *s.* algebra.
অব্যবস্থা, *s.* want of laws or regulations.
অব্যবস্থিত, *a.* irregular, undisciplined.
অব্যবহার, *s.* not a custom, an improper custom : *a.* obsolete, uncommon. [use.
অব্যবহারিত, *a.* not brought into common
অব্যবহার্য্য, *a.* impracticable, unfit to be brought into common use. [clinable.
অব্যয়, *a.* undiminishable : in *gram.* inde-
অব্যয়ী, *a.* not expending, wasting or decaying : in *gram.* indeclinable. [word.
অব্যয়ীভাব, *s.* an indeclinable compound
অব্যর্থ, *a.* infallible, efficacious.
অব্যাজ, *a.* not delaying, summary.
অব্যাজে, *ad.* immediately, without delay.
অভ্রুবন, অভ্রুবান্, *s.* an infant, a babe.
অভদ্র, *a.* not good, evil, bad, unfavorable.
অভদ্রতা, *s.* not goodness, badness. [exist.
অভব্য, *a.* unseemly, uncomely, unfit to
অভব্যরাজ, *a.* highly clownish : *s.* a stu-
অভয়, *s.* security, safety. [pid clown.
অভয়া, *s.* a tree (Terminalia citrina).
অভরণ, *s.* an ornament, a jewel. [less.
অভরসা, অভরসাত্তি, *a.* desponding, hope-
অভাগা, *a.* destitute, wretched, forlorn.
অভাগিনী, *a.* *fem.* *idem.* [unfortunate.
অভাগ্য, *a.* unfortunate : *s.* misfortune.
অভাজন, *a.* unfit, not trust-worthy.
অভাব, *s.* non-existence, non-entity, a deficiency, a failure, disagreemant. [a thing.
অভাবতঃ, *ad.* through the non-existence of

অভাবে, *ad.* without, except.
অভি, *prep.* it usually indicates that the action expressed by the word to which it is prefixed has a direction towards the object, or in front thereof.
অভিগমন, *s.* the going towards an object.
অভিগামী, *a.* going towards an object.
অভিজাত, *a.* born of a noble race, learned.
অভিজ্ঞ, *a.* wise, learned, skilful.
অভিজ্ঞানপত্র, *s.* a certificate.
অভিধান, *s.* a dictionary, a vocabulary.
অভিনব, *a.* recent, new, modern.
অভিনয়, *s.* a representation, a theatrical entertainment, a comedy, a play.
অভিনিবিষ্ট, *a.* engaged in, devoted to.
অভিনিবেশ, *s.* the devoting of one's self to a pursuit, intentness, application.
অভিনেতা, *s.* an actor, a comedian.
অভিন্ন, *a.* unseparated, unbroken, whole, entire : *s.* an integer or whole number.
অভিপ্রায়, *s.* a design, aim, an object, a scope, intention, the moral of a fable.
অভিপ্রেত, *a.* intended, aimed at, designed.
অভিপ্রেতসিদ্ধ, *a.* successful.
অভিপ্রেতসিদ্ধি, *s.* success : *a.* successful.
অভিবাদ, *s.* a salutation by prostration at the feet of a superior. [ence.
অভিবাদন, *a.* salutation, obeisance, rever-
অভিবাদনীয়, *a.* respectable, venerable.
অভিভব, *s.* humbling, defeat, humiliation.
অভিভূত, *a.* subdued, defeated, humbled.
অভিভূতি, *s.* a defeat, a conquest.
অভিমত, *a.* approved, wished, chosen.
অভিমান, *s.* pride, self-esteem, feeling an affront so keenly as to disregard life.
অভিমানী, *a.* selfish, appropriating, proud, unable to bear an affront, sullen.
অভিমুখ, *a.* facing : *ad.* towards.
অভিযুক্ত, *a.* applied, to, grafted in, accused in a court of law. [aggressor.
অভিযোক্তা, *s.* a plaintiff, an assailant, an
অভিযোগ, *s.* application of one thing to another, the commencement of a lawsuit, a military attack, perseverance.
অভিযোগী, *a.* accusing, leading an attack.
অভিরত, *a.* delighted with, devoted to.
অভিরাম, *a.* beautiful, agreeable, pleasing
অভিরুচি, *s.* a taste or relish for a thing, an inclination, an attachment.
অভিলষণীয়, *a.* desirable, delectable.
অভিলষিত, *a.* desired, wished for, coveted.
অভিলাষ, *s.* a wish, a desire, lust.
অভিলাষী, *a.* desirous, covetous, sensual.
অভিলিখিত, *a.* inserted, written.
অভিশপ্ত, *a.* cursed, imprecated. [accused.
অভিশস্ত, *a.* censured, blamed, reproached,
অভিশস্তি, *s.* censure, blame, calumny.
অভিশাপ, *s.* an imprecation, a curse.
অভিষিক্ত, *a.* anointed, installed to office.
অভিষেক, *s.* installation to office.
অভীপ্সিত, *a.* wished for, desired, loved.
অভীষ্ট, *a.* *idem* ; -লাভ, success. [nate.
অভেদ, *s.* similarity : *a.* alike, indiscrimi-
অভ্যন্তর, *a.* internal, inward, interior.
অভ্যন্তরে, *ad.* internally, inwardly.
অভ্যর্ণ, *a.* near, proximate, approached.
অভ্যসনীয়, অভ্যস্য, *a.* capable of being studied, requiring study.
অভ্যস্ত, *a.* studied, learnt by heart.
অভ্যস্তবিদ্যা, *a.* acquired science by study.
অভ্যাস, *s.* study, practice, a habit.
অভ্যাসী, *a.* studious ; কৃত, studied.
অভ্যুত্থান, *s.* a rising to welcome.
অভ্যুদয়, *s.* welfare, prosperity ; হউক, Good morning to you, Good be to you.
অভ্র, *s.* cloud ; the sky ; talc mineral.
অভ্রম, *s* an affront, disgrace, indignity, not an error : *a.* affronted, dishonored.
অভ্রষ্ট, *a.* not fallen from virtue.
অমঙ্গল, *s.* a disaster, calamity, evil omen.
অমঙ্গলকর, অমঙ্গলকারী, *a.* inauspicious.
অমঙ্গলসূচক, *a.* indicating evil, ominous.
অমঙ্গল্য, *a.* calamitous, disastrous, omin-
অমন, *ad.* thus, so. [ous.
অমনি, *ad.* thus, so, as ; the same ; gratis.
অমনোনীত, *a.* not chosen, not approved.
অমনোযোগ, *s.* inattention. [less.
অমনোযোগী, *a.* inattentive, remiss, care-
অমর, *a.* immortal : *s.* an immortal, a god.
অমরকুল, *s.* the race of immortals.
অমরণ, *s.* a not dying. [immortal.
অমরণীয়, অমর্তব্য, *a.* not liable to death,
অমরাবতী, *s.* the residence of Indra.
‡অমরুত, *a.* airless, calm : *s.* a guava.

অমর্ত্ত্য, *s.* not the earth : *a.* not earthly.
অমর্য্যাদা, *s.* affront, disrespect, dishonor, disgrace, want of civility or politeness.
অমর্ষ, *s.* displeasure, impatience, anger.
অমর্ষণ, *a.* displeased, angry, impatient.
***অমল্**, *s.* jurisdiction, government, office; -দার্, an officer, a corporal. [ment.
***অমলপত্তি**, *s.* hemming, hem of a gar-
***অমলাফিআলা**, *s.* officers, attendants.
অমাত্য, *s.* a courtier, an adviser, a senator,
***অমানৎ**, *s.* a deposit. [a statesman.
অমানব, *a.* not human; uninhabited.
অমানী, *a.* not proud, meek, not self-im-
অমান্য, *a.* not respectable. [portant.
অমাবস্যা, *s.* the day before the new moon.
অমামসী, *s.* the day of the new moon.
অমিত, *a.* unmeasured. [life.
অমিয়া, *s.* nectar, ambrosia, the water of
অমুক, *s.* such a one, a certain person.
অমুক্তি, *s.* want of liberty: *a.* unliberated.
অমুল, *a.* destitute of a root or origin.
অমূলক, unfounded, of suspected origin.
অমূল্য, *a.* invaluable; of no value
অমৃত, *a.* not dead : *s.* nectar, ambrosia, water of life, water, poison, immortality.
অমৃতা, *s.* the name of three drugs.[1]
অমেলক, *a.* discordant, disuniting.
অমেলন, *s.* the want of union, disunion.
অমোক্ষণ, *s.* the not relinquishing of a
অমোঘ, *a.* infallible, effectual. [thing.
অম্বর, *s.* apparel, clothing, ambergris, the sky, a cloud, cotton.
অম্বরীতমাক, *s.* tobacco richly dressed.
অম্বা, **অম্বালিকা**, *s.* a mother. [phant.
***অম্বারি**, **অমারি**, *s.* the haudá of an ele-
অম্বিকা, *s.* a name of Durgá ; a mother.
অম্বু, or **অম্ভস্**, *s.* water.
অম্বুবাচী, *s.* a name given to three days in the month of Ásháṛha, on which the earth is supposed to be menstruous.
অম্ময়, *a.* aqueous, watery.
***অম্মা**, *s.* a mother, an aunt.
অম্র, *s.* a mango; properly আম্র.
অম্রুত, *s.* nectar, ambrosia, water of life.
অম্ল, *a.* acid, sour, tart; -বেতস, sorrel.
অম্লতা, -ত্ব, *s.* acidity, sourness.
অম্লপিত্ত, *s.* an acidity on the stomach.

অম্লাক্ত, *a.* acidulated, mixed with acids.
অম্লিকা, *s.* tamarind and its tree.[2]
অয়, *s.* good luck or fortune.
অযথার্থ, *a.* improper, unrighteous, not
অযথার্থপর্শুকা, *s.* a false rib. [real.
অযথার্থব্যয়, *s.* extravagant expenditure.
অযথার্থব্যয়ী, *a.* profuse, prodigal, squandering, extravagant.
অয়ন, *s.* a going, motion, a road, course of the sun north or south of the equator.
***অয়মা**, *s.* grant of land, freehold; -দার্, a
অযশঃ, *s.* dishonor, infamy. [freeholder.
অয়স্, or **লৌহ**, *s* iron.
অয়স্কান্ত, *s.* a loadstone, magnet.
অযাতন, *a.* free from agony or torment.
অযাতনা, *s.* freedom from torment.
অযাত্রা, *s.* ominous or bad journey. [real.
অযাথার্থিক, *a.* ungodly, unrighteous, not
অযাথার্থ্য, *s.* unrighteousness, want of rea-
অযুক্তি, *s.* not a logical argument [lity.
অযুক্তিসিদ্ধ, *a.* not proved by reason.
অযুত, *a.* ten thousand.
অযোগ্য, *a.* unfit, incapable, unworthy, incompetent, unable, unsuitable.
অয়োগ্র, *s.* pestle, a club shod with iron.
অয়োঘন, *s.* a smith's anvil.
অযোত্র, **অযোত্রী**, *a.* destitute, poor, needy.
অযোধ্যা, *s.* the name of a city, Oude.
অযোনি, *a.* not born in the common way
অর, *a.* quick, speedy. [of generation.
***অরক্**, *s.* juice, moisture, perspiration.
অরক, *s.* moss, several aquatic plants.
অরঘট্ট, **অরঘট্টক**, *s.* a machine for drawing water, a large pit or well.
অরণা, *s.* a buffalo. ***অরজ্জা**, *a.* cheap.
অরণি, *s.* two pieces of dry wood used to procure fire by friction. [gadfly.
অরণ্য, *s.* forest, a wilderness; -মক্ষিকা, a
অরণ্যজ, *a.* produced in a forest.
অরণ্যস্থ, *a.* situated in a forest.
অরন্ধন, *a.* improper for cooking: a feast observed on the last day of Bhádra.
অরব, *a.* silent, mute: *s.* an arabian.
***অরবি**, *a.* arabian, arabic. [ciosum.
অরবিন্দ, *s.* water-lily (Nelumbium spe-
অরমান, *s.* disappointment, dishonor, dis-
অরর, or **অররি**, *s.* a door. [tress.

অরহর, *s.* a plant (Cytisus cajan.)
অরহস্য, *a.* not private, not secret, public.
অরাজক, *a.* destitute of a king, kingless.
অরাজকসময়, *s.* an interregnum.
অরাল, *a.* crooked, bent: *s.* pitch or rosin; a rutting elephant.
অরি, অরাতি, *s.* enemy, a foe. অরিতা, enmity.
অরিষ্ট, *s.* happiness, pleasure, misery, a sign of death, spirituous liquor, garlic, a crow, buttermilk, a seraglio.
অরীতি, *s.* an improper usage or custom.
অরুংষিকা, a disease, tinea or scaldhead.
অরুচি, *s.* disrelish, antipathy, aversion.
অরুচ্য, *a.* not agreeable, not palatable.
অরুণ, *s.* dawn, aurora; charioteer of the sun; the sun: *a.* dark-red or purple.
অরুণোদয়, *s.* first appearance of the dawn.
অরুণোদয়কাল, *s.* peep of day, the dawn.
অরুন্তুদ, *a.* corrosive, sharp, biting.
অরুন্ধতী, *s.* in *mytho.* wife of Vashishṭha.
অরে, অরেরে, *ad.* O, sirrah, soho.
অর্ক, *s.* the sun; -পক্ষ, the sun-flower.
অর্গল, or অর্গলা, *s.* a bar or bolt.
অর্ঘ, *s.* the price of an article; respect shown to superiors and guests.
অর্ঘ্য, *a.* proper as a present to a superior.
অর্চক, *a.* worshipping: *s.* a worshipper.
অর্চন, *s.* the act of worshipping.
অর্চনা, অর্চা, *s.* worship, homage, adoration.
অর্চনীয়, অর্চ্য, *a.* respectable, honorable, worthy of worship, honor or respect.
অর্চিত, *a.* worshipped, honored, respected.
অর্জক, *a.* acquiring: *s.* one who acquires.
অর্জন, *s.* a collecting, acquirement.
অর্জনীয়, *a.* acquirable, procurable.
অর্জান, *s.* a causing to collect or procure.
অর্জিত, accumulated, procured, collected.
অর্জুন, *s.* one of the five suns of Pándu; a colour, a white colour: *a.* white.
অর্ণব, *s.* the sea, ocean; -পোত, or -যান, a ship, a sea-boat.
অর্ণস্ *s.* water.
অর্ণা, *a.* wild, untamed (applied to cattle).
অর্দন, *s.* censure, reproach, hatred, abhorrence.
অর্ত্তি, *s.* pain; the end of a bow.
অর্থ, *s.* a scope, a meaning, sense, signification, an acceptation, purport, reason, a motive; wealth, riches.
অর্থক, *a.* concerning, answering an end.
অর্থকর, *a.* profitable, advantageous.
অর্থনা, *s.* a petition, a request, a scope, a desire, wish, a begging.
অর্থাৎ, *ad.* namely, that is to say, viz., videlicet, in fact, in fine.
অর্থান্তর, *s.* another meaning or explanation.
অর্থান্তরে, *ad.* otherwise.
অর্থাপত্তি, *s.* inference from facts or circumstances.
অর্থিত, *a.* desired, requested, petitioned.
অর্থিতা, *s.* circumstance of being desirous, the office or condition of a plaintiff.
অর্থী, *a.* rich; supplicating, desirous: *s.* a plaintiff, a petitioner, a beggar.
অর্থে, *ad.* about, for the sake of.
অর্থ্য, *a.* desirable, (what is) to be requested: *s.* object of desire, a scope, an end.
অর্দ্ধ, *a.* half, moiety; -শরীর, a wife.
অর্দ্ধগঙ্গা, *s.* the river Káverí.
অর্দ্ধচন্দ্র, *s.* a crescent, a half-moon, semicircle.
অর্দ্ধনিশা, অর্দ্ধরাত্র, *s.* midnight.
অর্দ্ধক্রবাণ, *a.* lisping, speaking like an infant.
অর্দ্ধভোজন, *s.* half a meal, a tiffin.
অর্দ্ধমাত্রাবশিষ্ট, having only half remaining.
অর্দ্ধাঙ্গ, *s.* apoplexy, palsy; a wife, half the body.
অর্দ্ধাঙ্গরোগী, *a.* paralytic.
অর্দ্ধেক, *a.* half, half of a thing.
অর্প, *v. a.* to appoint, delegate, employ, place, or deposit, to make an oblation.
অর্পণ, *s.* a delivering up, a bestowing, appointing or delegating, an offering up.
অর্পণীয়, অর্পয়িতব্য, *a.* fit to be appointed, delegated, deposited or offered.
অর্পা, *s.* the appointing of a person, an offering, a placing, a depositing.
অর্পিত, *a.* appointed, delegated, placed, deposited, put in, offered.
অর্প্য, *a. vide* অর্পণীয়: *s.* a post, an office, a trust.
অর্ব্বাচীন, *a.* contrary, modern, recent; inexperienced: *ad.* contrariwise.
অর্ব্বুদ, *a.* a hundred millions: *s.* a wen.
অর্ব্বুদঅর্ব্বুদ, *a.* hundreds of millions.
অর্য্য, *s.* a master, a lord, an owner, a man of the trading or vaishya tribe.
অর্য্যা, or অর্য্যাণী, *s.* a vaishya woman.
অর্শ, *v.* to pertain, appertain, belong to.
অর্শ, অর্শস, *s.* the piles or hemorrhoids.

অর্শস, *a.* afflicted with the piles. [ing.
অর্শী, *s.* coming into possession, succeed-
অর্হ, *a.* right, fit, worthy, capable, liable
to, deserving of, belonging to.
অর্হণীয়, or অর্হ্য, *a.* capable, right, wor-
thy, fit, possible, probable.
অর্হিত, *a.* suited, fitted, proper, right.
অল, *s.* yellow orpiment, the sting of a
bee, the forceps of a centiped, a tenon.
অলং, *ad.* in vain, uselessly, ornamentally,
enough : *a.* sufficient. [thing.
অলংক্রিয়া, *s.* the adorning of a person or
অলক, *s.* a curl of hair, a ringlet, side curl.
অলকা, *s.* city of Kuvera; mode of paint-
ing the face used by women. [with lac.
অলক্ত, অলক্তক, *s.* lac, paper saturated
অলক্ষণ, *a.* having an ominous sign.
অলক্ষ্ম, *a.* unfortunate, forsaken by for-
অলক্ষ্য, *a.* undistinguishable. [tune.
অলগর্দ্দ, *s.* a black and most deadly va-
riety of the Cobra de capello.
অলঙ্করণ, *s.* the act of adorning a thing.
অলঙ্করণীয়, *a.* capable of being adorned.
অলঙ্কার, *s.* an ornament, an ornament of
অলঙ্কারবান, *a.* ornamental. [speech.
অলঙ্কারশাস্ত্র, *s.* the science of rhetoric.
অলঙ্কৃত, *a.* adorned, ornamented. [Cupid.
অলঙ্গ, *s.* a name of Kámdew, the Indian
অলঞ্জর, *s.* a water-jar, a large pitcher.
অলড়, *a.* immoveable, steady, stable.
*অল্‌বত্তা, *ad.* certainly, assuredly.
*অল্‌বেলা, *s.* a huká with a long snake.
অলভ্য, *a.* unobtainable, unprofitable.
অলস, *a.* idle, inactive, slothful, indolent;
-ছাড়ন, a yawning or gaping. [house.
অলসবাস, *s.* a summer-house, a pleasure
অলি, *s.* a humble bee, scorpion, the In-
dian cuckoo; wine, a crow. [head.
অলিক, *ad.* useless, in vain; *s.* the fore-
অলিকুল, or অলিগণ, *s.* a swarm of bees.
অলিখিত, *a.* unwritten, not recorded.
অলিপ্সু, *a.* not covetous, not greedy.
অলী, *a.* stinging : *s* a bee, a scorpion.
অলীক, *a.* useless, vain, false, not beloved.
অলীকতা, *s.* falsehood, vanity.
*অলুফা, *s.* food obtained at free cost.
অলফাদার, *s.* the holder of a sinecure.

অলুফাদারী, *s.* the holding of a sinecure.
অলুব্ধ, *a.* undesired, uncoveted. [woman.
অলো, *voc. par.* used in addressing a low
অলোকিত, *a.* unseen, unperceived. [tle.
অল্প, *a.* few, small, little : *s.* a few, a lit-
অল্পতা, *s.* fewness, scarcity. [dence.
অল্পপ্রমাণক, *a.* resting on slight evi-
অল্পবিষয়, *s* a trifling concern or affair.
অল্পবুদ্ধি, *a.* having little understanding.
অল্পব্যয়ী, *a.* sparing, economical, thrifty.
অল্পমূল্য, *s.* a small price : *a.* low-priced.
অল্পস্বল্প, *s.* a very few, a few, a little.
অল্পাপেক্ষা, *s.* a very small expectation.
অল্পাপেক্ষায়, *ad.* within a little, very
অল্পায়ু, *a.* short-lived, young. [near.
অল্পাহার, *s.* abstinence, moderation.
অল্পাহারী, *a.* abstemious, moderate.
অল্পীকৃত, diminished, reduced to a few.
অল্পীভূত, *a.* become few, diminished.
অল্পে ২, *ad.* by little and little, by de-
অশক্ত, *a.* unable, weak, infirm. [grees.
অশক্তি, *s.* weakness, infirmity : *a.* weak.
অশক্য, *a.* impossible, impracticable.
অশঙ্ক, *a.* fearless, bold, secure. [security.
অশঙ্কা, *s.* freedom from fear, boldness,
অশঙ্কিত, *a.* not alarmed, undaunted.
অশন, *s.* the act of eating; boiled rice.
অশব্দ, *a.* silent, still, mute, noiseless.
অশাম্য, *a.* unappeasable, unassuageable.
অশাস্ত্র, *a.* unlawful, illegal, unscriptural.
অশাস্ত্রীয়, *a.* inconsistent with the law.
অশাস্য, *a.* ungovernable, uncontrolable.
অশিক্ষিত, *a.* untaught, unlearned.
অশিত, *a.* eaten, satisfied.
অশিশু, *a.* childless : *fem.* অশিশ্বী.
অশিষ্ট, *a.* unpolite, undisciplined, unpo-
lished, ungoverned, neglected, saucy,
insolent, rude, savage, profligate, vulgar.
অশীতি, *a.* eighty, fourscore; -গুণ, eighty-
অশীতিতম, *a.* the eightieth. [fold.
অশীতিপর, *a.* past eighty years of age.
অশীল, *s.* indifference : *a.* indifferent.
অশুচি, *a.* impure, unclean, foul.
অশুদ্ধ, *a.* impure, inaccurate, incorrect.
অশুদ্ধি, *s.* a want of purity : *a.* impure.
অশুভ, *a.* unbecoming, unpropitious, bad,
evil : *s.* misfortune, evil, calamity.

অশুভক্ষণ, *s.* unpropitious moment.
অশুল্ক, *a.* gratis, without pay.
অশেষ, *a.* boundless, endless, infinite.
অশেষজ্ঞ, *a.* all-wise, knowing the whole.
অশেষতঃ, *ad.* infinitely, endlessly. [plete.
অশেষপ্রকার, *a.* perfect, unbounded, com-
অশেষরঙ্গী, *a.* various, parti-colored.
অশেষরূপে, *ad.* wholly, entirely.
অশোক, *s.* a tree :[1] *a.* free from grief, hap-
অশৌচ, *s.* uncleanness, impurity. [py.
অশ্মগর্ভ, *s.* an emerald.
অশ্মজ, *s.* red chalk, red ochre.
অশ্মরী, *s.* stone or gravel in the bladder.
অশ্রদ্ধ, *a.* incredulous, unbelieving.
অশ্রদ্ধা, *s.* distrust, disbelief, incredulity, incredibility, disregard, sneer.
অশ্রবণীয়, or **অশ্রাব্য**, *a.* unfit to be heard.
অশ্রম, *s.* activity : *a.* indefatigable.
অশ্রমী, *a.* not laborious or indefatigable.
অশ্রান্ত, *a.* unwearied, not fatigued.
***অশ্রাফ**, *s.* nobles, grandees, gentlemen.
অশ্রি, *s.* edge or point of sword, a corner,
অশ্রু, or **অশ্র**, *s* a tear. [an angle.
অশ্রুকোষ, *s.* the lachrymal sac.
অশ্রুগর্ত্তচ্ছিদ্র, *s.* the lachrymal duct.
অশ্রুত, *a.* unheard, not heard of. [tears.
অশ্রুপাত, *s.* the falling or trickling of
অশ্রুমুখ, *a.* suffused with tears.
অশ্রেষ্ঠ, *a.* not the best, common.
অশ্লিষ্ট, *a.* not embraced, not surrounded.
অশ্লেষ, *s.* discord, dislike, a misunderstanding, a separation, disjunction.
অশ্লেষা, *s.* the 9th Hindu stellar mansion.
অশ্ব, *s.* a horse; গন্ধা, a plant;[2] -চিকিৎসক, or -বৈদ্য, a farrier; -চিকিৎসা, farriery; -পাল, a groom; -শালা, a stable.
অশ্বতর, *s.* a mule ; a swift elephant.
অশ্বতরী, *s.* a female mule.
অশ্বত্থ, *s.* name of a tree (Ficus religiosa).
অশ্বমেধ, *s.* the sacrificing of a horse.
অশ্বাবরোহণ, a dismounting from a horse.
অশ্বারূঢ়, *a.* mounting a horse : *s.* a horse-
অশ্বারোহ, *s.* horsemanship, riding. [man.
অশ্বারোহক, *a.* the same with অশ্বারূঢ়.
অশ্বারোহণ, *s.* the mounting of a horse.
অশ্বিনী, *s.* the first stellar mansion.
অশ্বিনীকুমার, *s.* the physicians of heaven.

অশ্বী, or **ঘোটকী**, *s.* a mare.
অষুধ, **ঔষধ**, **ভেষজ**, *s.* a medicine.
অষ্ট, *a.* eight; -গুণ, eight-fold.
অষ্টক, *s.* a pod of cotton; in *poe.* a stanza of eight lines; a portion of the veda.
অষ্টকা, *s.* the 8th day of the moon's wane in Pausha and Mágha on which offerings are made to deceased ancestors.
অষ্টকোটিতম, *a.* the eighty millionth.
অষ্টদিক, or **অষ্টদিগ**, *s.* the eight points of the compass, viz. four cardinal and four intermediate ones.
অষ্টদিক্‌পাল, *s.* eight gods who guard the eight quarters of the universe.
অষ্টধা, *ad.* of eight sorts, eight-fold.
অষ্টধাতু, *s.* eight metals, viz. gold, silver, copper, brass, bell-metal, tin, lead, iron.
অষ্টবসু, *s.* a class of gods consisting of
অষ্টম, *a.* the eighth. [eighth.
অষ্টমী, *a.* the eighth, (of a lunar day).
অষ্টসিদ্ধি, s. eight modes of power by which a person's desires or undertakings may be accomplished.
অষ্টাঙ্গ, *s.* eight members of the body on which Hindus make religious marks.
অষ্টাঙ্গপ্রণাম, *s.* a salutation made by prostrating one's self. [forty-eighth.
অষ্টচত্বারিংশ, **অষ্টাচত্বারিংশত্তম**, *a.* the
অষ্টাচত্বারিংশৎ, *a.* forty-eight.
অষ্টাত্রিংশ, **অষ্টাত্রিংশত্তম**, *a.* the thirty-
অষ্টাত্রিংশৎ, *a.* thirty-eight. [eighth.
অষ্টাদশ, **অষ্টাদশম**, *a.* eighteen.
অষ্টাদশগুণ, *a.* multiplied by eighteen.
অষ্টাদশধা, *ad.* of eighteen sorts.
অষ্টাদশাঙ্গ, *s.* a popular medicine composed of eighteen ingredients.
অষ্টানবত, **অষ্টানবতিতম**, *a.* the ninety-
অষ্টানবতি, *a.* ninety-eight. [eight.
অষ্টাপঞ্চাশ, **অষ্টাপঞ্চাশত্তম**, *a.* the fifty-
অষ্টাপঞ্চাশৎ, *a.* fifty-eight. [eighth.
অষ্টাবক্র, *a.* deformed, bent in eight directions : *s.* the name of a famous sage.
অষ্টাবিংশ, **অষ্টাবিংশতিতম**, *a.* the twenty-
অষ্টাবিংশতি, *a.* twenty-eight. [eighth.
অষ্টাশী, **অষ্টাশীতি**, *a.* eighty-eight.
অষ্টাশীত, **অষ্টাশীতিতম**, *a.* eighty-eighth.
অষ্টাষষ্ট, **অষ্টাষষ্টিতম**, *a.* sixty-eighth.

অষ্টাষষ্টি, a. sixty-eight. [eighth.
অষ্টাসপ্তত, অষ্টাসপ্ততিতম, a. the seventy-
অষ্টাসপ্ততি, a. seventy-eight. [tagon.
অষ্টাস্র, or অষ্টাশ্রি, a. octagonal: s. an oc-
অস্থি, s. the stone of a fruit. [all over.
অষ্টেপৃষ্ঠে, ad. on all sides in every part,
অষ্টোত্তরশত, a. an hundred and eight.
অষ্ঠীবদস্থি, s. the knee-pan (rotula).
অষ্ঠীবন, s. the knee.
অসংখ্য, a. innumerable, incalculable.
অসংখ্যক, a. unnumbered, innumerable.
অসংখ্যা, s. non-calculation, not a total.
অসংজ্ঞ, a. insensible, swooned.
অসংযুক্ত, a. unconnected, not in contact.
অসংযোগ, s. disunion, disjunction, non-contact; want of necessaries. [joined.
অসংলগ্ন, a. unconnected, incoherent, dis-
অসংশয়, a. undoubted, certain, sure.
অসংসৃষ্ট, a. not associated or united.
অসংস্কৃত, a. unconsecrated, unacquired.
অসংস্থান, অসংস্থিতি, s. a want of substance, property, or consistence.
অসকৃৎ, ad. often, frequently.
অসখ্য, s. a want of agreement or friendship, hatred, a misunderstanding.
অসঙ্গ, a. solitary, alone. [tent.
অসঙ্গত, a. improper, unlikely, inconsis-
অসঙ্গতাচরণ, s. inconsistent conduct. [ty.
অসঙ্গতি, s. improbability, want of proper-
অসৎ, a. unholy, ungodly, wicked, perverse, incontinent, non-existent.
অসৎকর্ম্ম, s. wickedness, evil conduct, a bad action, lasciviousness, whoredom.
অসৎসংসর্গ, s. evil company or connec-
অসতর্ক, a. inattentive, inadvertent. [tion.
অসতী, a. *fem.* unchaste, impure.
অসতীপতি, s. a cuckold. [gate.
অসত্তম, a. flagrant, most wicked, profli-
অসত্ত্ব, s. non-existence, a non-entity.
অসত্য, a. untrue, false.
অসন্ততি, অসন্তান, s. a want of posterity.
অসন্তুষ্ট, a. displeased, dissatisfied.
অসন্তোষ, s. displeasure, dissatisfaction.
অসন্দিগ্ধ, a. undoubted, unsuspected, sure.
অসন্নিধান, অসন্নিহিত, a. not near, distant.
*অসবাব, s. furniture, accoutrements, goods, tools, apparatus, baggage.

অসভ্য, a. rude, rustic, savage, uncivilized, unpolite, unsocial, unfit for society.
অসভ্যতা, -ত্ব, s. an unfitness for society, unsocialness, unpoliteness, rusticity.
অসম, a. uneven, unlike, not level, un-
অসমক্ষ, s. absence. [common.
অসমঞ্জস, a. unequal, unlike.
অসমবিদ্য, a. not equally learned.
অসময়, s. an improper time, a time of misfortune: a. premature, out of season.
অসময়ে, ad. in an improper time, too late, out of season, prematurely.
অসমর্থ, a. unable, incapable, feeble.
অসমসাহস, a. possessed of extraordinary boldness: s. extraordinary courage.
অসমসাহসী, a. uncommonly bold.
অসমান, a. unequal, not smooth or level.
অসমানত্রিকোণ, s. a scalene triangle.
অসমাপক, a. not finishing. [ple.
অসমাপকক্রিয়াপদ, s. in *gram.* a partici-
অসম্পন্ন, a. unfinished, imperfect, not accumulated, not acquired. [tions.
অসম্পর্ক, a. destitute of adherents or rela-
অসম্পর্কীয়, a. unrelated, not associated
অসম্পূর্ণ, a. incomplete, imperfect. [with.
অসম্পূর্ণকীট, s. the aurelia of an insect.
অসম্পূর্ণতা, -ত্ব, s. incompleteness.
অসম্প্রদায়িক, a. unsocial, unfit for or unconnected with a society, unembodied.
অসম্প্রীতি, s. want of love or communion.
অসম্বন্ধ, s. a want of connection: a. destitute of connection, unconnected.
অসম্বন্ধীয়, a. unrelated, unconnected with.
অসম্ভব, a. uncommon, strange, inconsistent, astonishing, unusual, incompatible, improbable, unreasonable. [bility.
অসম্ভাবনা, s. inconceivableness improba-
অসম্ভাবনীয়, অসম্ভাব্য, a. impossible, improbable, unlikely, unreasonable.
অসম্ভাষণা, s. inaffability, unpoliteness.
অসম্ভুক্ত, a. unenjoyed, unpossessed.
অসম্ভ্রম, s. disgrace, dishonor, an affront, indignity: a. destitute of respect.
অসম্মত, a. averse, reluctant.
অসম্মতি, s. reluctance, aversion. [tress.
অসহিষ্ণু, a. impatient, unable to bear dis-
অসহিষ্ণুতা, -ত্ব, s. impatience.

অসহ্য,*a.* intolerable, unsufferable. [ness.
অসহ্যতা,*s.* intolerableness, unsufferable-
অসাক্ষাৎ, *ad.* in the absence, behind one's back; -কার, not present, absent.
অসাক্ষ্য, *s.* a want of testimony.
অসাড়, *a.* benumbed, insensible.
অসাধনীয়, *a.* impossible, impracticable.
অসাধারণ, *a.* particular, uncommon.
অসাধু, *a.* unrighteous, bad immoral.
অসাধ্য, *a.* impossible, impracticable.
অসাধ্বী, *a.* fem. unchaste, immoral.
অসাবধান, *a.* inadvertent, careless, inattentive, thoughtless, unguarded.
অসামঞ্জস্য, *s.* a want of equality.
অসামর্থ্য, *s.* inability, a want of power.
অসামান্য, *a.* not common, particular.
অসাম্য, *s.* a want of similarity, equality, or likeness, a want of equilibrium.
অসার,*a.* unsubstantial, worthless: *s.* the sappy or white part of timber.
অসি, *s.* a sword, cimeter; -কোষ, a scab-
অসিত, *a.* not white, black. [bard.
অসিদ্ধ, *a.* not proved, accomplished, completed or perfected, unboiled. [proof.
অসিদ্ধি, *a.* unproved: *s.* a not having
অসিপত্র, *s.* blade and sheath of a sword, sugar-cane; one of the Hindu hells.
অসীম, unbounded, unlimited, immense.
অসুখ, *a.* unhappy, uncomfortable.
অসুখী, *a.* unhappy, miserable.
অসুগম, *a.* not easy, difficult. [ster.
অসুর, *s.* a demon, an evil spirit, a mon-
অসুসার, *s.* a want of pecuniary means.
অসুস্থ,*a.* ill, sick, uncomfortable, unquiet.
অসুস্থির,*a.* unstable, unsettled, unsteady.
অসূয়া, *s.* detraction, slander, malice.
অসৃষ্ট, *a.* uncreated, unmade, not formed.
অসৌষ্ঠব, *s.* ugliness, disagreeableness.
অস্ত, অস্তম্ *s.* the setting of the heavenly
অস্তকাল, *s.* the sun-set. [bodies.
অস্তগত, *a.* set, gone below the horizon.
অস্তগিরি, অস্তাচল, *s.* the western mountains behind which the sun sets.
অস্তবল্, *s.* *(English)* a stable.
অস্তাবলম্বন, *s.* the setting of a luminary.
অস্তাবলম্বী, *a.* setting, resting on the western part of the horizon.

অস্তি, *ad.* present, now, at this time: *v.*
অস্তু, *v. imp. md.* be it so, let it be. [it is.
অস্ত্র, *a.* weapon, missile weapon, an edge-tool; -কার, or -নির্ম্মাতা, an armourer; -চিকিৎসক, surgeon; -চিকিৎসা, surgery.
অস্ত্রচিকিৎসাবিদ্যা, *s.* the science of sur-
অস্ত্রজ্ঞ, অস্ত্রবিৎ, *a.* skilled in arms. [gery.
অস্ত্রধারক, *a.* bearing arms; *s.* an armed
অস্ত্রধারণ, *s.* the bearing of arms. [man.
অস্ত্রধারী, *a.* taking arms, bearing arms.
অস্ত্রবৃষ্টি, *s.* a shower of missile weapons.
অস্ত্রবৈদ্য, *s.* a surgeon. [weapons.
অস্ত্রমার্জ্জক, *s.* a furbisher, a polisher of
অস্ত্রযুদ্ধ, *s.* a battle with weapons. [tools.
অস্ত্রশস্ত্র, *s.* arms, armour, implements,
অস্ত্রাগার,*s.*armoury, a magazine, an arse-
অস্ত্রাঘাত, *s.* the stroke of a weapon. [nal.
অস্ত্রাহত, *a.* smitten with a weapon.
অস্থান, *s.* the want of a place, a wrong place, the privy parts of either sex.
অস্থানস্থ, *a.* misplaced, mislaid. [fixed.
অস্থাবর,*s.*not a fixture: *a.* moveable, un-
অস্থায়, অস্থায়ি, unfathomable, very deep.
অস্থায়ী, *a.* unlasting, fleeting, temporary.
অস্থি, *s.* a bone; -কোন, corner of a bone.
অস্থিচর্ম্মাবশিষ্ট, *a.* emaciated, mere skin
অস্থিত, *a.* unsettled, unfixed. [and bone.
অস্থিতি, *s.* the want of place, situation, or property: *a.* not in a situation.
অস্থিতিস্থাপক, *a.* inelastic.
অস্থিত্ব, *s.* ossification.
অস্থিত্বক্, *s.* in *ana.* the periosteum.
অস্থিবৎ, *a.* osseous, resembling bone.
অস্থিবিদ্যা, *s.* osteology.
অস্থির,*a.*unstable, wavering, floating, capricious, fugitive, transitory, volatile.
অস্থিরচিত্ত, *a.* irresolute, unsteady, fickle.
অস্থিরতা, অস্থৈর্য্য, *s.* instability, fickleness, waveringness, unsettledness.
অস্থিরবাদী, *a.* equivocating. [opinion.
অস্থিরবুদ্ধি, *a.* unsettled in judgment or
অস্থিরমতি, *a.* fickle-minded unsteady.
অস্থিরাকার,*a.* chaotic, of unsettled form.
অস্থিসমর্পণ,*s.*the committing of the bones of a dead person to the Ganges.
অস্থূল, *a.* not thick, not gross.
অস্থেয়, or অস্থাতব্য, *a.* unfixable.

অস্থ্যগ্র, *s.* the end of a bone.
অস্পষ্ট, *a.* indistinct, inarticulate, obscure.
অস্পষ্টে, *ad.* obscurely, underhand.
অস্পৃশ্য, *a.* out of reach, intangible.
অস্পৃশ্যতা, -ত্ব, *s.* intangibility.
অস্পৃহ, *a.* indifferent, reluctant.
অস্পৃহা, *s.* indifference, reluctance.
অস্ফুট, *a.* indistinct, inarticulate, obscure, enigmatic, not bent, not broken.
অস্মদ, *pron.* I; in *comp.* our, us.
অস্মদীয়, *a.* our, belonging to us.
অস্মার্ত্ত, *a.* immemorial; -কাল, time immemorial.
অস্মৃতি, *s.* want of recollection.
অস্যপর, *a. phrase,* after this, hereafter.
অস্র, *s.* a tear; corner, an angle.
অস্রু, *s.* a tear; -পাত, shedding of tears.
অস্রোতঃ, *s.* not a stream: *a.* stagnant.
অস্ব, *a.* not a person's own, poor.
অস্বচ্ছ, *a.* obscure, dull, opake.
অস্বাদু, *a.* insipid, disgusting.
অস্বাস্থ্য, *s.* indisposition, illness, uneasiness.
অস্বাস্থ্যগ্রস্ত, *a.* ill, indisposed.
অস্বীকার, *s.* non-acquiescence, refusal, denial.
অস্বীকৃত, unacknowledged, unacquiesced.
অহ, or অহহ, *intj.* astonishing! wonderful! excellent! oh! aha! alas! heyday!
অহং, or অহম্, *pron.* I.
অহঃ, or অহন্, *s.* a day; -পতি, the sun.
অহঙ্কার, *s.* self-importance, pride, egotism.
অহঙ্কারী, *a.* proud, self-important, vain.
অহঙ্কারে, *ad.* proudly, self-importantly.
অহঙ্কৃত, *a.* self-important, selfish, proud.
অহমিকা, *s.* egotism, vanity, pride.
অহম্মতি, *s.* conceit, selfishness, self-love.
অহরহ, *ad.* daily, every day.
অহর্নিশি, *ad.* day and night.
অহল্যা, *s.* a celestial courtezan; wife of Gautama.
অহি, *s.* a snake, a serpent.
অহিংসা, *s.* harmlessness, a not injuring.
অহিংসিত, *a.* uninjured, not mal-treated.
অহিক, *a.* worldly, uugodly, irreligious.
অহিকলোক, *s.* a worldly-minded man.
অহিত, *s.* injury, a disadvantage.
অহিতকারী, *a.* injurious, disadvantageous.
অহিতুণ্ডিক, *s.* a juggler who plays with snakes.
অহিতেচ্ছা, *s.* malevolence.
অহিতেচ্ছু, or অহিতেচ্ছুক, *a.* malevolent.
অহিতৈষী, *a.* not benevolent, malevolent.
অহিনকুলতা, *s.* mortal enmity like that between ichneumon and the serpent.
অহিপূতন, *s.* an ulcer in the anus of children caused by uncleanliness.
অহিফেণ, *s.* saliva and hood of a snake; opium, a poppy (Papaver somniferum).
অহিভয়, *s.* mistrust, a dread of insidious persons, (snakes in the grass).
অহিভুক, *a.* serpentivorous: *s.* a peacock.
অহৃদ্য, *a.* unamiable, not beloved.
অহৃষ্ট, *a.* sad, not glad, not merry.
অহে, a *voc. par. ad.* O, ho! soho!
অহেতুক, *a.* causeless, groundless.
অহো, a vocative particle: *intj.* wonderful! O brave! alas! poor creature.
অহোরাত্র, *ad.* day and night.
*অহ্বাল, *s.* a state, a condition.

আ, the 2nd or long vowel. It has the sound of *a* in asthm*a*. In *comp.* when prefixed to verbal roots or nouns, it usually adds to the word the idea of extension, operation, or possession to a certain extent, and sometimes that of diminution: *intj.* aye! true!
আইআই, *intj.* fie! shame!
আইও, আইওস্ত্রী, *s.* a married woman.
আইওসুআ, *s.* a beloved wife.
আইজ, or অ দ্য, *ad.* to-day.
আইঢাই, *s.* palpitation caused by thirst, fever, or anxiety, a writhing.
*আইন, *s.* a regulation, a rule, a law, a statute.
*আইনা, *s.* a looking-glass, a mirror.
*আইন্দা, *ad.* in future, hereafter.
*আইব, *s.* a fault, a crime, a blot.
আইবড়, আইবুড়, *a.* unmarried: *s.* bachelor.
আইবুড়ত্ব, *s.* celibacy, bachelorship.
*আইয়া *s.* a waiting maid, a nurse maid.
*আইয়াম, *s.* a season, time.
আইল, *s.* a balk, a ridge, embankment.
আইস্, *v.* to come, to approach.
আইসন, *s.* a coming, the act of coming.
আঈ, *s.* a maternal grandmother.
আউ, আউমাউ, *intj.* Oh! ah! alas!
আউশ, *a.* spring (rice), ripening in a short time; -ধান, or -ধান্য, spring-rice.

*আএমা, *s.* charity-land, land given for less than its value: *ad.* gratis, freely.
আএমাদার, *s.* a holder of charity-land.
আওট্, *v.* to inspissate, to thicken with boiling, to weld, to stir round.
আওটন, আওটান, *s.* the welding of metals, the boiling of milk, inspissation.
আওটা, *s. idem: a.* stirred round, thickened, welded, tempered.
আওড়্, *v.* to read, to repeat. [ing.
আওড়, *s.* a whirlpool, a reading, repeat-
আওড়ন, আওড়ান, *s.* the reading or repeating of a passage from a book.
আওড়া, *v. a.* to read, recite, rehearse.
আওতা, *a.* shady, covered, concealed.
আওভাও, *s.* current usage; a welcome.
আওয়া, *s.* a polypus of the nose.
আওর্, *v.* to ooze, to trickle: *a.* more.
*আবরঙ্গ, *s.* a throne, a chair of state.
*আবরৎ, *s.* a woman, a wife.
আওরা, *a.* oozing, running, as the eyes.
আওরাণ, আওরাণি, *s.* a slight shower, the trickling of the eyes with a cold.
*আবলিয়া, *s.* companions: *a.* chief, venerable, respectable.
আং, *s.* the body, a limb, a member.
আংটা, *s.* a chafing dish. আংটী, *s.* a ring.
আংশিক, *a.* having a right to a share.
আঃ, *intj.* aye, aye! Oh aye! ah! alas!
আঁ, *ad.* yes; a particle of assent; lowing
আঁআঁ, *ad.* yes, yes. [of a calf.
আঁইট, *s.* severity, tightness.
আঁইষ, or আইশ, *s.* the scales of a fish.
আঁওট, *s.* the breadth-end of cloth. [ther.
আঁওত্, *v.* to become flaccid, to droop, wi-
আঁওতা, *a.* drooping, flaccid, withered.
আঁওতান, *s.* a drooping, becoming flaccid.
আঁওল, *s.* the secundines. [rabolan.
আঁওলা, *s.* dried fruit of the Emblic my-
আঁক্, *v. n.* to be marked: *v. a.* to mark; -করিয়াউঠ or ডাক্, to cry out as a tiger.
আঁক, *s.* a mark, a numerical figure; an eye; a goal; -কাট, to make a mark.
আঁকড়্, *v. a.* to grasp, to enfold, to catch.
আঁকড়ষী, *s.* a hook with a long handle.
আঁকড়া, *s.* a hook to hang things on.
আঁকড়াআঁকড়ি, *s.* a mutual grasping.
আঁকড়ান, *s.* the grasping with the arms.
আঁকড়ি, *s.* a tendril, cirrhus.
আঁকড়িআ -চলন, to strut; -যাওন, to be contorted with excessive pain or cold.
আঁকড়ী, *s.* a vetch (Vicia sativa).
আঁকড়ীঘুঙ্গনি, *s.* fried vetch.
আঁকন, আঁকনি, *s.* a marking, the paging of a book, a writing down of numbers.
আঁকা, *a.* marked, burnt to the vessel.
আঁকাআঁকী, *s.* a mutual making of marks.
আঁকান, *a.* marked, page, numbered: *s.* a marking, the paging of a book.
আঁকাবাঁকা, *a.* tortuous, crooked, winding.
আঁকুবাঁকু, *s.* eagerness, haste.
আঁখ্, *v. n.* to vibrate, to oscillate.
আঁখা, *v. a.* to vibrate, to fan.
আঁখান, *s.* a fanning, a causing to vibrate: *a.* fanned, made to vibrate.
আঁখি, *s.* an eye.
আঁচ্, *v.* to wash the mouth after eating.
আঁচ, *s.* flame, heat; fault, blame.
আঁচড়্, *v.* to tear, to lacerate, scratch.
আঁচড়, *s.* a bruise, a laceration, a rent.
আঁচড়া, *v.* to tear, scratch, or scrape, to lacerate, to comb the hair, to card flax.
আঁচড়ান, *s.* a tearing, or lacerating, a scratching, combing, or carding: *a.* torn, lacerated, combed, carded. [ing.
আঁচড়ানিয়া, *a.* tearing, lacerating, scratch-
আঁচতাকুড়, *s.* a place where sweepings, &c. are thrown, a sink.
আঁচমন, *s.* a rinsing or washing the mouth after a meal, a sipping of water.
আঁচল, আঁচলা, *s.* the border of a cloth.
আঁচা, *v. n.* to wash the mouth; to guess.
আঁচান, *s.* a rinsing; a guessing.
আঁচার, *s.* a pickle. [guessing.
আঁচাআঁচি, *s.* a mutual examination or
আঁচিল, *s.* a wart, a mole, a pimple.
আঁজলা, *s.* the palms of the hands joined.
আঁজি, *s.* the plastering of a wall merely to stop the holes; the border of cloth.
আঁজিনা, *s.* a species of lizard; a pustule on the eyelid; also, আঞ্জিনেয়.
আঁট্, *v. a.* to bind, to tighten, to pull tight. আঁটিয়া ধরণ, to hold fast.
আঁটকুড়া, *a.* childless; *fem.* আঁটকুড়ি.

আঁটন, *s.* the tightening of a bandage.
আঁটনি, *s.* tightness, severe language.
আঁটরা, *a.* firm, stout, strong. [severe.
আঁটা, আঁটাল, *a.* tight, scanty, too small;
আঁটাআঁটি, *a.* too tight, scanty, severe.
আঁটালি, or **আঁটালু**, *s.* a dog-tick.
আঁটি, *s.* tightness, scantiness, severity, restraint; a sheaf, a bundle; also, অষ্টি.
আঁটু, or **আঁঠু**, *s.* the knee.
আঁটুগাড়ন, *s.* a kneeling down.
আঁটো, *a.* left after eating: *s.* orts.
আঁড়ি, *s.* the decay attending a weaned
আঁড়িয়া, *s.* *idem;* also, a bull. [child.
আঁত, *s.* the bowels, entrails, intestines.
আঁতড়ী, *s.* intestines, entrails, gut, tripe.
আঁতমারণ, আঁতমারা, *s.* a starving, abstinence, the drawing in of the belly.
আঁতমোড়া, *s.* seed-vessel of screw-tree.[1]
আঁতসা, *s.* a kind of sweetmeat. [man.
আঁতুড়,-ঘর, *s.* the room of a lying-in wo-
আঁৎকা, *v. n.* to fear, to dread. [terror.
আঁৎকান, আঁৎকানি, *s.* fear, dread, horror,
আঁদি, *a.* blind-folded: *s.* *vide* আঁধি.
আঁধলা, অন্ধ, কাণা, *a.* blind, sightless.
আঁধার, *s.* darkness, gloom: *a.* dark.
আঁধারি, *s.* darkness; the straw laid on the roof to finish the thatching; the nails used to join boards.
আঁধি, *s.* the thin layer of straw laid on a roof previously to thatching; a storm.
আঁধিসাঁধি, *s.* a crevice, a nook or corner.
আঁধুয়া, *a.* concealed, covered over with weeds (as a pond, a pit, or a well).
আঁব, or **আম্র**, *s.* a mango.
আঁবআদা, *s.* a plant (Curcuma amada).
আঁবুই, *s.* a brother's wife's mother, a sister's husband's mother. [tree.
আঁবুয়া, *a.* belonging to a mango or its
আঁশ্, *v. n.* to become somewhat dry.
আঁশ, *v. a.* to pick hemp, cotton, oakum, &c.: *s.* fibres (of a stringy fruit), bark (of a tree), pubes or nap (of cloth), the roughness of unplaned wood.
আঁশাণ, *s.* the slightly drying of a thing.
আঁশান, *s.* a picking of cotton, hemp, &c.
আঁশাল, আঁশুয়া, *a.* stringy, fibrous.
আঁষি, *s.* the scales of a fish.

আঁষ্টীয়, *a.* fishy; -গন্ধ, a fishy scent.
আক, or **ইক্ষু**, *s.* a sugarcane.
আকট, *a.* severe, hard-hearted.
আকন্দ, আকন্দ, *s.* the swallow wort.[2]
***আকবৎ**, *s.* end, conclusion: *ad.* finally.
আকবতিহামার, *s.* a cable. [Akbar.
***আকবর**, *a.* great, noble: *s.* the emperor
আকর, *s.* a mine, a spring, a source, a quarry, grit, grittiness, a root, origin.
আকরা, *a.* undone, not done.
আকরোট, *s.* a walnut, a walnut tree.[3]
আকর্ষ, *s.* a tendril, cirrhus.
আকর্ষক, *a.* drawing, attracting: *s.* any thing which attracts or draws.
আকর্ষণ, *s.* the drawing, attracting, or seizing of a thing, attraction.
আকর্ষণী, *s.* a tendril; a spasm; science,
আকর্ষিণী, *a.* attractive. [what attracts.
আকর্ষিত, *a.* drawn, attracted. [pected.
আকস্মিক, *a.* coming unexpectedly, unex-
আকা, *s.* a hearth, a furnace, a kiln.
আকাঁড়া, *a.* lusty, jolly, plump; imperfectly cleansed (as rice from its husk).
আকাঁড়ান, *a.* imperfectly cleansed from
আকাঙ্ক্ষণীয়, *a.* desirable. [the husk.
আকাঙ্ক্ষা, *s.* desire, expectation, a wish.
আকাঙ্ক্ষিত, *a.* desired, expected.
আকাঙ্ক্ষিতব্য, or **আকাঙ্ক্ষ্য**, *a.* desirable.
আকাঙ্ক্ষী, *a.* desirous, waiting, expecting.
আকাট, *s.* a want of rain, drought; want
আকাটা, *a.* uncut, unclipt. [of charity.
আকার, *s.* a form, an appearance, a shape, a figure, a statue, a likeness, the letter আ, also the vowel mark (া).
আকাল, *s.* a famine, dearth, scarcity.
আকালিক, *a.* premature, unseasonable.
আকাশ, *s.* the sky, atmosphere, air, space,
আকাশগঙ্গা, *s.* the milkyway. [æther.
আকাশগামী, *a.* moving in the air, aerial.
আকাশচর, আকাশচারী, *a.* *idem.* [con.
আকাশদীপ, *s.* an elevated lantern, a bea-
আকাশবাণী, *s.* a voice from heaven.
আকাশবিদ্যা, *s.* pneumatics.
আকাশবিহারী, *a.* air-traversing.
আকাশমণ্ডল, *s.* the atmosphere.
আকাশী, *a.* aerial, airy, celestial.
আকাশীরঙ্গ, *a.* cærulean, azure.

আক্কি, *intj.* an expression of surprize, Oh!
•আকিক, *s.* a carnelion stone. [what?
আকিঞ্চন, *s.* endeavour, labour, exertion.
আকীর্ণ, *a.* overspread, sprinkled, inter-
আকু, or ইক্ষু, *s.* a sugarcane. [spersed.
আকুঞ্চন, *s.* exertion, labour, endeavour.
আকুঞ্চিত, *a.* curled, tortuous, contorted.
আকুণ্ঠিত, *a.* non-plussed, confounded.
আকুল, *a.* troubled, agitated, distressed,
আকুলতা, *s.* agitation, distress. [confused.
আকুলান, *s.* deficiency, want, exigency.
আকুলিত, *a.* agitated, disturbed, distract-
আকুলিতচিত্ত, *a.* troubled in mind. [ed.
আকুলীকৃত, or আকুলীভূত, *a.* confounded,
confused, non-plussed. [likeness.
আকৃতি, *s.* an image, a shape, a form, a
আকৃষ্ট, *a.* drawn, attracted, plowed.
আকৃষ্টি, *s.* attraction, persuasion.
*আকেকল, *s.* understanding, wisdom.
আক্রম, *s.* invasion, a seizing upon.
আক্রমণ, *s.* a seizing, invasion, seizure
আক্রমণীয়, *a.* seizable, capable of being
আক্রা, *a.* dear (not cheap). [invaded.
আক্রান্ত, *a.* invaded, seized, held.
আক্রামক, *a.* invading, seizing: *s.* one
who seizes, an invader, an usurper.
আক্রুষ্ট, *a.* resented, wept over, lamented.
আক্রোশ, *s.* resentment, hatred, a curse,
abuse, a cry, regret, lamentation.
আক্রোশক, *a.* reproving, cursing, censur-
ing, reproaching, imprecating.
আক্রোশনীয়, *a.* censurable, reproachable.
আক্ষারণা, *s.* aggression, accusation, ca-
আক্ষারিত, *a.* attacked, abused. [lumny.
আক্ষিপ্ত, *a.* reproached, reproved.
আক্ষুটী, *a.* merciless, savage: *s.* a virago,
a vixen, a female savage. [savage.
আক্ষুটীয়, *a.* merciless, implacable, rude,
আক্ষেপ, *s.* reproof, reproach, an irony.
আক্ষেপক, *a.* reproving, reproaching, sar-
castic: *s.* reprover, he who reproaches.
*আক্সর, *a.* single, only, alone.
আখড়া, *s.* an orchestra, a choir of sing-
ers, an assembly, a place of assembly.
আখড়াধারী, holding an assembly: *s.* the
chief of a choir of singers. [choir.
আখড়াবালা, *s.* a singer of poems, one of a

আখণ্ড, whole, entire, perfect, unbroken.
আখর, *s.* a letter, type; *properly* অক্ষর.
আখা, *s.* a hearth, furnace, a kiln. [tion.
*আখির, আখিরী, *s.* the end, a termina-
আখু, *s.* a rat, a mouse; -ভুক, a cat.
আখুট, *s.* a childish whim, caprice.
*আখন্, আখুন্দ, *s.* a tutor, a teacher.
*আখেজ়, *s.* a dispute, contention.
আখেট, *s.* a hunting, a pursuit, terror.
আখেটী, *a.* alarming, horrid, terrific.
*আখের, *s.* an end, a conclusion.
*আখ্তা, *s.* a castrated horse, a gelding.
*আখ্বার, *s.* news, reports.
আখ্রোট, *s.* *vide* আকরোট.
আখ্যা, *s.* a name, a title, a term.
আখ্যাত, *a.* denominated, titled. [city.
আখ্যাতব্য, *a.* declarable, worthy of publi-
আখ্যান, *s.* a word, a saying, a name, a
descriptive character, a denomination.
আখ্যানার্হ, *a.* deserving renown.
আখ্যায়িকা, *s.* a history, narrative, a tale.
আখ্যেয়, worthy of publicity or renown.
আগ্, *s.* fire; the forepart, the place in
front, priority, the end, point, or ex-
tremity, an excess, a fortune-telling;
-বাড়া, to proceed, to make progress.
আগড়া, *s.* chaff, the husk of corn, mildew.
আগড়ী, proceding: *ad.* in the first place.
আগণ্য, *a.* not counted, not reckoned.
আগত, *a.* come, arrived; -কল্য, to-morrow.
আগতপ্রায়, *ad.* nearly come or arrived.
আগতোলন, *s.* a divination by counting a
handful of cowries by pairs, an odd
number indicates good luck. [ticable.
আগন্তব্য, *a.* provable, approachable, prac-
আগন্তু, or আগন্তুক, *a.* arrived at a place,
আগন্তুকলাভ, *s.* a perquisite. [come.
আগবাড়ান, *s.* an advancing; ambition.
আগম, *s.* the veda, science in general; a
legal deed for property; an inserted
letter or syllable; a coming or arrival.
আগমজ্ঞ, *a.* versed in the veda.
আগমন, *s.* an arrival, approach, a coming.
আগমনপত্র, *s.* the notice of any one's
arrival; a summons, a writ.
আগমনীয়, or আগম্য, *a.* capable of being
overcome, approachable, practicable.

আগমবক্তা, *s.* one eloquent in the veda.
আগমিত, *a.* studied, read, acquired.
আগম্নী, *s.* a plant (Bryonia scabrella).
আগল, *v. a.* to restrain, to prevent.
আগল, *a.* not dissolved, not crumbling.
আগলা, or আগলান, *s.* a preventing or restraining, a taking care of.
আগলি, *a.* before, first, former, preceding.
‡আগা, *s.* the tip, point, or peak, a nib; a title of honor among Musalmáns.
আগাও, *s.* anticipation, advance.
আগাছা, *s.* a wild or useless tree.
আগাড়ি, *ad.* before, prior to, sooner; *s.* the place in front; the ropes tied to a horse's forefeet when in the stable.
আগাড়িপিছাড়ি, *s.* ropes by which the fore and hind legs of a horse are tied in the stable: *ad.* before and behind.
আগাম, *a.* giving in advance: *s.* the anticipation of a payment, an advance.
আগামিদর্শী, *a.* fore-seeing, provident.
আগামী, *a.* preceding, coming, about to come; also, *vide* আগাম.
আগার, *s.* a house, a room, a receptacle.
আগালিয়া, *s.* the forepart of a bamboo.
আগাহ, *s.* an advance (of money).
আগু, *a.* preceding, before, first of all.
আগুড়ী, *s.* an advance (of money): *a.* foremost, before, preceding, forward.
আগুতে, *ad.* before, forwards, beforehand.
আগুদল, *s.* the vanguard of an army.
আগুন, অগ্নি, আগ্, *s.* fire.
আগুনখাগী, *s.* the woman who burns with the corpse of her husband is so called.
আগুনবৎ, *a.* like fire, fiery, touchy.
আগুনময়, *a.* fiery, ignited, igneous.
আগুনলাগন, আগুনলাগা *s.* the being set on fire, the setting fire to any thing.
আগুনিয়াবাত, *s.* St. Anthony's fire.
আগুনিয়াবাণ, *s.* a fiery arrow.
আগুয়ান, *a.* preceding: *s.* a precursor, a leader.
আগে, *ad.* first, before, onwards, forwards.
আগোড়, *s.* a door made of mats.
আগ্নেয়, *a.* fiery, igneous, piquant, provocative.
আগ্নেয়াস্ত্র, *s.* fire-arms, a rocket.
আগ্র, *a.* eager, urgent, zealous, persevering.
আঘর্ষণ, *s.* in *music*, an accessory grace.

আঘাট, *s.* not a landing-place, a bad one.
আঘাত, *s.* a blow, a hurt, a stroke, injury, a plague.
আঘাতী, *a.* hurt, wounded.
আঘূর্ণন, *s.* a whirling round, a rolling.
আঘূর্ণিত, *a.* whirled round, rolled.
আঘোষণ, *s.* a crying or proclaiming.
আঘ্রাণ, *s.* a smelling, a scent.
আঘ্রাণীয়, *a.* fit to be smelled, odorous.
আঘ্রাত, *a.* smelled to, scented.
আঙটী, আঙঠী, *s.* a finger or toe ring.
আঙঠা, *s.* a chafingdish.
আঙ্গরা, or আঙ্গার, *s.* charcoal, coals, cinders.
আঙ্গরাখা, *s.* a jacket, a coat, a frock.
আঙ্গরাটীয়া, *a.* like coals, black, burnt.
আঙ্গল্, *v. a.* to finger a thing.
আঙ্গলান, *s.* a meddling or fingering of a thing.
আঙ্গলানিয়া, *a.* fingering, meddling.
আঙ্গিনা, *s.* a court-yard, a square court.
আঙ্গুটী, আঙ্গুঠী, *s.* a finger or toe ring.
আঙ্গুল, *s.* a finger, a toe; -ফুটা, -মট্কা, or -মট্কান, the snapping of the fingers.
আঙ্গুলহাড়া, *s.* a whitlow.
আঙ্গুষ্ঠানা, or আঙ্গুস্তানা, *s.* a thimble.
আঙ্গুলী, *s.* a finger, a toe.
আচ, আচু, *s.* a shrub, the root of which is used in dying (Morinda tinctoria).
আচকা, *ad.* uncounted, unmeasured, by guess.
আচক্ষণ, *s.* a speaking, eloquence.
আচমন, *s.* a rinsing the mouth after a meal, or as a religious ceremony.
আচমনীয়, *a.* proper to be rinsed.
আচম্বিত, আচমকা, *a.* suddenly, unawares.
আচরণ, *s.* a habit, behaviour, an usage.
আচরণীয়, আচরিতব্য, *a.* proper to be observed as a line of conduct.
আচরিত, *a.* acted, accustomed, done as a custom.
আচানক, *a.* sudden, unexpected.
আচান্ত, *a.* rinsed, washed (the mouth).
আচাভুয়া, *a.* surprising, astonishing.
আচার, *s.* conduct, common practice, usage, a rule of conduct; a pickle, sauce.
আচারবিচার, *s.* usage, custom, practice, the manners and customs of a people.
আচারভ্রষ্ট, *a.* apostatized, apostate.
আচারান্বিত, *a.* acting rightly, punctilious.
আচারী, *a.* acting, conducting.
আচার্য্য, *s.* a teacher, preceptor, tutor, a prophet.

আচার্য্যাণী, *s.* a prophetess, a tutoress.
আচালা, *a.* unsifted.
আচোট, *s.* a blow, a stroke: *a.* uncultivated, undug.
আচ্ছন্ন, *a.* covered, concealed, protected.
আচ্ছা, *a.* good, unexceptionable: *ad.* well.
আচ্ছাদক, *a.* covering, protecting: *s.* a lid, a cover, a roof, an awning.
আচ্ছাদন, *s.* the act of covering, a cover, clothes.
আচ্ছাদনীয়, আচ্ছাদয়িতব্য, *vide* আচ্ছাদ্য.
আচ্ছাদিত, *a.* covered, protected.
আচ্ছাদ্য, *a.* requiring to be covered.
আচ্ছিন্ন, *a.* amputated, cut off, confiscated.
আচ্ছেদ, *s.* confiscation, amputation.
আচ্ছেদন, *s.* the act of cutting off, or confiscating, the amputating of a limb.
আচ্ছেদী, *a.* confiscating: *s.* a confiscator.
আছ্, *v. n.* to be, to exist, to live.
আছড়্, *v. a.* to dash, to strike, to smite.
আছড়ন, *s.* the act of dashing a thing.
আছড়া, *v. a. vide* আছড়্: *a.* beat on the washing-board, dashed, threshed: *s.* a dashing, a sprinkling; -দা, to sprinkle.
আছড়ান, *s.* the dashing of a thing, the threshing of corn: *a.* dashed, threshed.
আছড়ানিয়া, *a.* dashing: *s.* a thresher.
আছাড়, *s.* a beating of clothes in washing, a blow, a fall; -মার্, to dash or throw down violently; -খা, to slip so as to fall.
আছোলা, *a.* not lopped or trimmed, not shaved down or stripped off its bark.
আজ, or অদ্য, *ad.* to-day.
*আজগইবী, আজগবী, *ad.* unexpectedly, suddenly.
আজন্ম, *ad.* from one's birth.
আজন্মকাল, *ad.* from the time of birth.
*আজব্, *a.* queer, surprizing, wonderful.
আজবতামাসা, *s.* a wonderful exhibition.
*আজমান্, *s.* a trying or bringing to the test.
আজমায়েশ, *s.* trial, a temptation.
*আঁজা, *s.* a cry to Moslems for prayer.
আজাড়্, *v. a.* to clear, to empty: *s.* sail-cloth, canvass; -কৃ, to empty, vacate.
*আজাদ, *a.* free, liberated: *s.* a poem.
আজাদী, *s.* deliverance, freedom, liberty.
আজান, আঞ্জান, *a.* unknown.
আজানু, *ad.* reaching to the knee, (the hands.)
*আজাব, *s.* punishment, vengeance; fault.
*আজার, *s.* sickness, a disease, affliction.
আজারী, *a.* diseased, afflicted, troubled.
আজি, *ad.* to-day; also, *s.* war, conflict.
আজিকার, *a.* belonging to this day.
*আজিজ, *a.* poor, helpless, needy.
*আজিম, *a.* honorable, respectable, great.
আজীব, *ad.* during life, as long as one lives: *s.* a means of support.
আজীবন, *a.* living upon: *s.* a living, a livelihood.
আজু, or অদ্য, *ad.* to-day.
*আজুরা, *s.* pay, hire; -দার, a jobber.
আজু, *s.* labor without pay, gratis labor.
আজ্ঞপিত, আজ্ঞাপ্ত, *a.* ordered, commanded.
আজ্ঞা, *s.* a command, a decree, an order, an injunction, a precept; -কৃ, or -দা, to order, to command; -মান্, to obey.
আজ্ঞাকরণ, *s.* the giving of orders.
আজ্ঞাকারী, *a.* obedient, obsequious.
আজ্ঞাত, আজ্ঞাপিত, commanded, enjoined.
আজ্ঞাতব্য, *a.* fit to be commanded.
আজ্ঞানুক্রমে, *ad.* according to orders.
আজ্ঞানুবর্ত্তী, *a.* obsequious, obedient.
আজ্ঞানুযায়ী, *a.* obedient to orders.
আজ্ঞানুসারে, *ad.* according to orders.
আজ্ঞাপক, *a.* giving orders: *s.* one who gives orders, a commander.
আজ্ঞাপত্র, *s.* a written law, a warrant, a mandate, a written command.
আজ্ঞাপন, *s.* the act of giving orders.
আজ্ঞাবজ্ঞা, *s.* contempt of orders.
আজ্ঞাবর্ত্তিতা, *s.* obedience, submission.
আজ্ঞাবর্ত্তী, *a.* obedient, submissive.
আজ্ঞাবহ, *idem*: *s.* an obedient servant.
আজ্ঞাভঙ্গ, *s.* disobedience, a transgression.
আজ্ঞালঙ্ঘন, *s.* *idem.*
আজ্য, *s.* ghi or clarified butter.
আঝাল, *a.* not pungent; not soldered.
*আঞ্জাম *s.* the doing of a thing, an end.
আঞ্জিনা, *s.* a stye; a kind of lizard.[1]
আঞ্জিনেয়, *s.* a species of lizard.[2]
আঞ্জীর, *s.* a guava, a fig (Ficus carica).
আট, *a.* eight; -গুণ, eight-fold; -চল্লিশ, forty-eight; -ত্রিশ, thirty-eight.
আটক, *s.* an obstacle, obstruction, a hindrance, a prohibition, a stoppage.
আটকাল, আটকোল, *s.* a guess.
আটচালা, *s.* a bungalow with a veranda all round.
আটপটাঙ্গ, *s.* show, pageantry, pomp.

আটপলিয়া, *a.* octagonal.
আটপাটি, *a.* arranged in eight rows.
আটপিটা, *a.* active, laborious, expert.
আটপৌরিয়া, *a.* wearable both night and day, (applied to clothes). [sant.
আটপ্রহর, *ad.* perpetual, continual, incessant.
আটল, *s.* a bamboo trap to catch fishes.
আটলা, *s.* a pad for a porter's head; also,
আটষট্টি, আটষষ্টি, *a.* sixty-eight, [বিড়া.
আটসত্তা, *s.* accounts, book-keeping; -নবীস, a book keeper, an accountant.
আটা, *s.* bird-lime, gum; wheaten flour.
আটাইশ, or আঠাইশ, *a.* twenty-eight.
আটাইশা, or আঠাইশা, *a.* twenty-eighth.
আটাকাটা, *s.* a bird-twig, a perch.
আটাত্তর, or আটসত্তর, *a.* seventy-eight.
আটানই, or আটানব্বই, *a.* ninety-eight.
আটান্ন, *a.* fifty-eight. [glutinous.
আটাপারা, আটাল, *a.* ropy, viscid, gluey,
আটার, or আঠার, *a.* eighteen.
আটারঞ্জি, আঠারঞ্জি, *a.* the eighteenth.
আটালি, আটালু, আঠালু, *s.* a dog-tick.
আটাশী, *a.* eighty-eight. [pregnancy.
আটাসীয়া, *a.* born in the eighth month of
আটি, *s.* a wisp, a sheaf, a bundle (of hay, straw, &c.); the stone of a fruit.
আটোপ, *s.* pride, self-importance.
আটক, *v. n.* to be obstructed, to be detained or entangled: *s.* restraint.
আটকন, *s.* the restraining of a thing.
আটকা, *v. n.* to obstruct, impede, imprison: *s.* a restraining, a stoppage.
আটকাই, *s.* an obstruction.
আটকান, *s.* a restraining, stopping, or confining: *a.* bound, confined, distrained.
আটকানি, *s.* an obstruction, an arrest.
আঠা, *s.* bird-lime, size, gum, paste, slime, any glutinous or viscid substance.
আঠি, *s.* the stone of a fruit.
আড়, *v. n.* to bend, to lie athwart.
আড়, *a.* athwart, aslant, sideway: *s.* width, a crook or bend; -কৃ, to make athwart; -হ, to recline; -ভাঙ্গ, to straighten.
আড়করণ, *s.* the making of a thing aslant.
আড়কাটা, or আড়কাঠা, *s.* a cross-beam.
আড়কাটি, *s.* a steerer, a pilot, a steersman; a weaver's rod.
আড়কাঠ, *s.* beam laid across, cross-beam; the name of a country, also of a coin.
আড়গড়া, *s.* repository for horses, a stable; a place encircled with wooden railings.
আড়ঙ্গ, *s.* a mart, staple, an emporium, a manufactory; a collection of images at a festival; -ঘাটা, landing-place where the Hindu idols are collected; -ছাটা, cleansed from husk at the mart (rice).
আড়ঙ্গীয়, *a.* brought from a mart.
আড়চক্ষু, *a.* leering, glancing, side-looking.
আড়ড়, *a.* cramped, stiffened, benumbed.
আড়ৎ, *s.* the mart occupied by a forestaller.
আড়দীর্ঘ, *a.* long and wide. [staller.
আড়দ্দার, *s.* a monopolist, a forestaller.
আড়দ্দারী, *s.* a monopoly, forestalling.
আড়ন, *s.* a bending or becoming crooked.
আড়পার, through and through, across.
আড়ভাঙ্গন, *s.* the straightening of a thing.
আড়ভাঙ্গা, *s. idem.* [angles.
আড়মাবলা, *a.* not square, not at right
আড়ম্বর, *s.* a roaring, loud sound, empty noise, a war-drum, excessive preparations, much ado, excitement, apology, the eyelid, arrogance, passion, happiness, a rubbing the body to cure pain.
আড়ম্বরী, *a.* proud, ostentatious, prolix.
আড়রী, *s.* the brink of a bank. [refuse.
আড়সা, *a.* neglected, rejected, lying as
আড়া, bent, laid athwart: *s.* a fish-trap, a perch, a cross-beam, proportion, dimension; -ভাঙ্গ, to straighten. [revenge.
আড়াআড়ি, athwart, diagonally: *s.* mutual
আড়াই, *a.* two and a half; -প্রহর, a time equal to two o'clock (of day or night).
আড়ান, *a.* bent, made crooked, laid across.
আড়ানি, *s.* a screen or large fan.
আড়ামোড়া, *s.* a yawning and stretching.
আড়াল, *s.* a screen, a shelter, ambuscade.
আড়ালে, *ad.* slyly, secretly, behind.
আড়ি, *s.* a wager, stake; a grudge, hatred, malice; a measure of capacity; name of a fish; -পাত, to lie in wait, to peep.
আড়িপাতন, *s.* a lurking, a lying in wait.
আড়রা, *s.* a pretext for delay, an apology.
আড়ুরি, or আড়ুলি, *s.* a precipice, a cliff.
আড়ে, *ad.* crosswise, sidewise, diagonally.

আড়েঅগোচরে, or আড়েআবডালে, *ad.* concealedly, secretly, clandestinely.
আড়েআড়ে, *ad. vide* আড়ে. [a perch.
আড্ডা, *s.* station, a post, a stage, a stand;
আঢ়ি, আঢ়ক, *s.* a measure of capacity esteemed to be equal to two maunds.
আঢ্য, আঢ্যেল, *a.* rich, opulent, wealthy.
আণ্টাল, *s.* a ball of earth or wood.
আণ্ডা, অণ্ড, ডিম্ব, *s.* an egg. [laying eggs.
আণ্ডাল, আণ্ডালি, *a.* having eggs or roes,
আতঙ্ক, *s.* fear, panic, dread, awe; disease.
আতঙ্গ, *s.* fear, a panic, dread, awe.
আতঞ্চন, *s.* a chymical test, a solvent; a pestilence, a calamity; gratification.
আতপ, *s.* sunshine, heat, sun-dried; -চাল্, rice being unhusked without boiling.
আতপত্র, *s.* an umbrella, a parasol.
আতর, *s.* fare for crossing a river.
*আতর্, *s.* essence (of roses, &c).
*আতশ্, *s.* fire; -বাজী, fireworks.
*আতশী, *a.* fiery; -চস্‌মা, a burning glass.
আতস্, *a.* flaxen. [na reticulata).
আতা, আতৃপ্য, *s.* a custard apple (Anno-
আতাই, *a.* officious: *s.* a free songster.
আতান্তরে, *ad.* in these circumstances.
আতায়ী, deceitful, crafty: *s.* a kite; -পনা, -গিরী, craftiness, swindling, knavery.
আতালে, *s.* a long shelf, a scaffold.
আতিথেয়, *a.* hospitable.
আতিথ্য, *a.* hospitable: *s.* hospitality.
আতিদেশিক, *a.* imputing what belongs to one person to another, transferring.
আতিশয্য, *s.* excess, excessiveness.
আতু, a vocative used in calling a dog.
আতুর, *a.* sick, afflicted, distressed.
আত্ত, *a.* received, accepted. [a striving.
আত্তি, *s.* labor, effort, endeavor, exertion,
আত্ম, *a.* self, one's self; -কলহ, domestic broil; -কৃত, self-made; -দোষ, own fault.
আত্মকার্য্য, *s.* a person's private affairs.
আত্মগরিমা, *s.* vaunt, self-conceit. [ens.)
আত্মগুপ্তা, *s.* cowhage (Carpopogon pruri-
আত্মগ্রাহী, *a.* selfish, self-aggrandizing.
আত্মঘাত, *a.* self-murder, suicide.
আত্মঘাতক, *s.* one who commits suicide.
আত্মঘাতী, *a.* committing suicide.
আত্মচ্ছিদ্র, *s.* one's own defect or fault.
আত্মজ, *a.* springing from self: *s.* a son.
আত্মজা, *s.* daughter. [knowledge.
আত্মজ্ঞান, *s.* the knowledge of spirit, self-
আত্মতত্ত্ব, *s.* true nature of spirit. [ship.
আত্মতা, *s.* spirituality, identity, friend-
আত্মদেবতা, *s.* a guardian or family god.
আত্মন্, *a.* self, one's self, own.
আত্মনিন্দা, *s.* self-reproach. [verbs.
আত্মনেপদ, *s.* in *gram.* the middle voice of
আত্মপরীক্ষা, *s.* self-examination.
আত্মপ্রশংসা, *s.* self-applause, egotism.
আত্মবঞ্চক, *a.* self-deceiving.
আত্মবঞ্চনা, *s.* self-deception. [self.
আত্মবৎ, আত্মতুল্য, equal to, or like one's
আত্মবন্ধু, *s.* a near relation. [trol.
আত্মবশ, *a.* under one's own power or con-
আত্মবশতা, -ত্ব, *s.* self-control.
আত্মবশতাপন্ন, আত্মবশীভূত, *vide* আত্মবশ.
আত্মবান্ধব, *s.* a first cousin.
আত্মবিক্রয়, *s.* the selling of one's self.
আত্মবিক্রয়ী, *a.* selling one's self.
আত্মবিস্মৃত, *a.* forgetful of one's own words
আত্মবিস্মৃতি, *s.* self-oblivion. [or actions.
আত্মবোধ, *s.* self-knowledge, a knowledge
আত্মম্ভরি, *a.* selfishly voracious. [of spirit.
আত্মশ্লাঘা, self-applause, vanity, egotism.
আত্মশ্লাঘী, *a.* self-applauding, conceited,
আত্মসদৃশ, *a.* like one's self. [vain.
আত্মসাৎ, *a.* own, proper, one's own.
আত্মহত্যা, *s.* self-murder, suicide.
আত্মহন্তা, *s.* one who commits suicide.
আত্মহা, *a.* self-destroying: *s.* a suicide.
আত্মা, *s.* spirit, self, Brahma, the soul.
আত্মাধীন, আত্মায়ত্ত, *a.* independent. [ed.
আত্মাভিমত, *a.* self-approved, self-applaud-
আত্মাভিমানী, *a.* self-applauding, vain.
আত্মীয়, *a.* belonging to one's own self: *s.* a relation, an intimate friend; -কুল, one's own family; -বৎ, like a relation.
আত্মীয়তা, *s.* relationship, friendship, inti-
আত্মোৎকর্ষ, *s.* self-excellence. [macy.
আত্যন্তিক, *a.* entire, complete, excessive.
আত্রেয়ী, menstruous: *s.* name of a river.
আত্রেয়ীঘ্ন, *a.* defiling a menstruous wo-
আত্‌লস্, *s.* a rich sort of silk cloth. [man.
আদ. *a.* half: *s.* a moiety.
আদকপালিয়া, *s.* half a head-ache.

আদখান, আদখানী, *a.* half: *s.* an half.
আদখেঁচড়া, *a.* half-done, bad, vile.
আদজা, *s.* half of one: *a.* half.
আদড়, *a.* half-aged, half, 20 cubits (cloth).
*আদৎ, *s.* a habit, a custom, an usage.
আদতে, *ad.* naturally, habitually. [lation.
*আদদ; *s.* a number, numeration, a calcu-
*আদব, *s.* instruction, teaching, manners, custom, politeness, civility, urbanity.
*আদম্, or আদম্জাৎ, *a.* human.
আদমী, *s.* a man, a descendant of Adam.
আদর, *s.* respect, honor, veneration, es-
আদরক, or আদা, *s.* ginger. [teem.
আদরণীয়, আদর্য্য, আদৃত, *a.* respectable, honorable, venerable, reverend.
আদরা, *s.* a mark or sign, a landmark.
আদরান্বিত, *a.* venerable, respectable.
আদর্শ, *s.* pattern, original, a specimen,
*আদল, *s.* a judge; a stamp. [a mirror.
আদলা, *s.* half of a paisá, a half brick.
আদলি, *s.* half a rupee. [nalis.)
আদা, আদুক, *s.* ginger (Zinziber offici-
আদাআদি, *a.* half: *ad.* half and half.
আদাংশ, *s.* a half, equal shares.
আদাংশী, আদাভাগী, *s.* partner at equal
আদাড়, *s.* a jakes, a place of filth. [shares.
আদাড়িয়া, *a.* filthy, polluted, of a dung-
আদান, *s.* a receiving, a taking. [hill.
আদানপ্রদান, *s.* an interchange, barter.
*আদাবৎ, *s.* hatred, strife, enmity.
আদায়, *s.* a receiving; the paying of a
*আদালত, *s.* a court of justice. [debt.
আদালতী, *a.* dispensing justice, belonging to, or acting in a court of justice.
আদি, *a.* prior, initial, beginning, first; in *comp.* as an affix it implies et cetera.
আদিকারণ, *s.* a first or primary cause, a moving cause; in *algebra*, analysis.
আদিতেয়, *s.* a god, the son of Aditi.
আদিত্য, *s.* a god; the sun.
আদিত্ব, *s.* priority, precedence
আদিদেব, *s.* in *mytho.* this name is applied both to Náráyana and to Shiva.
আদিভূত, *a.* first-existent: *s.* Brahma.
আদিম, *a.* first, prior, initial.
আদিয়া, *s.* a measure equal to six seers.
আদিরাজ, *s.* the first king, (Prithu).

আদিষ্ট, *a.* commanded, directed, recommended; -সন্ধি, a peace made by surrendering a portion of territory.
আদীপন, *s.* a pigment with which a bridegroom's seat is painted by the bride.
*আদীল, *a.* righteous, just, equitable, like, alike: *s.* one who distributes justice.
আদুড়, *a.* open, uncovered, exposed, bare.
আদুড়িয়া, *a.* half, half-grown, imperfect.
আদৃত, *a.* honored, respected, esteemed.
আদৃষ্টি, *ad.* as far as the sight reaches.
আদেখা, *a.* unseen, unperceived.
আদেশ, *s.* a command, an ordinance, an injunction, a precept.
আদেশক, আদেষ্টা, *s.* one who gives orders, a legislator, a commander.
আদেশন, *s.* the act of giving a command.
আদেশিত, *a.* commanded, ordered.
আদেশ্য, *a.* proper to be commanded.
আদো, *a.* first, prior, preceding, initial.
আদৌ, *ad.* in the first place. [law.
আদ্দাশ, *s.* a complaint, petition, a suit at
আদ্দাশী, *s.* a plaintiff, a petitioner.
আদ্য, *a.* first, preceding, prior, the least or first root of the affected square.
আদ্যন্ত, আদ্যান্ত, *ad.* from the first to the last: *s.* the beginning and the end.
আদ্রক, or আদা, *s.* ginger. [spect.
আদ্রিয়মাণ *a.* showing, or obtaining re-
আধ, *a.* half: *s.* a moiety.
আধখেঁচড়া, *a.* half-done, bad, vile.
আধপেটা, *a.* scanty, half-satisfying.
আধমন, *s.* a pledge, a pawn, deposit.
আধর্ষণ, *s.* the convicting of a crime.
আধর্ষিত, *a.* convicted in a court of law, convinced, overcome in argument.
আধলি, *s.* half a rupee, eight-anna piece.
আধা, *a.* half: *s.* a moiety.
আধাআধি, *a.* half: *ad.* half and half.
আধান, *s.* a pledge, a taking, a holding.
আধার, *s.* a receptacle, a vessel, that which supports or sustains, a substratum.
আধারস্থ, *a.* situated in a receptacle.
আধি, *s.* anxiety, expectation, a pledge.
আধিক্য, *s.* abundance, excess, overplus.
আধিপত্য, lordship, sovereignty, govern-
আধীকরণ, *s.* the making a pledge. [ment.

আধুরীয়, *a.* half-grown, half-old.
আধুনিক, *a.* recent, modern.
আধূত, *a.* shaken, agitated.
আধৃত, *a.* contained, supported.
আধেক, *a.* half, half an one.
আধেয়, *a.* fit to be supported or contained.
আধোয়া, *a.* unwashed, unrinsed. [ous.
আধ্মাত, *s.* flatulence, war, battle: sonor-
আধ্মান, *s.* flatulence, inflation. [tation.
আধ্যান, *s.* thought, contemplation, medi-
আন্, *v. a.* to bring, to fetch: *a.* another,
আনখা, *a.* strange, not seen before. [other.
আনত, *a.* inclined, gently bowed.
আনন, *s.* the act of bringing; the face, the mouth; the first term in progression.
আনন্তর্য্য, *s.* posteriority, succession.
আনন্ত্য, eternity, boundlessness. [mirth.
আনন্দ, *s.* joy, felicity, pleasure, happiness,
আনন্দজনক, *a.* joy-inspiring, pleasure-giv-
আনন্দদায়ক, or আনন্দদায়ী, *a. idem.* [ing.
আনন্দনীয়, *a.* fit to be rejoiced in.
আনন্দভৈরব, *s.* a particular note in music.
আনন্দমনাঃ, *a.* joyful, glad-hearted.
আনন্দময়, *a.* happy, full of joy.
আনন্দযুক্ত, *a.* joyful, glad.
আনন্দলহরী, *s.* a surge of joy or pleasure.
আনন্দলাড়ু, *s.* a bride-cake. [joy.
আনন্দসাগর, *s.* a sea of joy, a fulness of
আনন্দি, *s.* joy, gladness, happiness.
আনন্দিত, আনন্দী, *a.* joyful, happy, glad.
আনন্দে, *ad.* gladly, in the midst of joy.
আনন্দোৎসব, *s.* a joyous feast.
আনয়ন, *s.* the bringing of a thing.
আনয়নীয়, *a.* proper to be brought.
আনল, অনল, অগ্নি, আগ্, *s.* fire.
আনলকুণ্ড, *s.* a fiery pit.
আনা, *s.* the act of bringing; a sixteenth part, the sixteenth part of a rupee.
আনাগোনা, *s.* a coming and going, intercourse, an ado about any thing.
আনাজ, corn, greens, vegetables. [place.
আনাড়, *a.* abstruse, secret: *s.* a secret
আনাড়িপনা, *s.* awkwardness, clumsiness.
আনাড়ী, *a.* clumsy, awkward, ignorant, inexpert, clownish, stupid.
আনান, or আনীত, *a.* brought, fetched.
*আনামৎ, *ad.* the whole, just as it was.

আনায়, *s.* a fishing-net. [ther.
আনায়িত, *a.* brought by the orders of ano-
*আনার, *s.* a pomegranate; *see* দাড়িম্ব.
আনারস, *s.* pineapple (Bromelia ananas).
আনারসী, *a.* pineapple-shaped, of the taste of pineapple, somewhat acid.
আনি, *s.* 16th part, 16th part of a rupee; an edge, a point; -মাজা, a small trowel.
আনীত, or আনান, *a.* brought, fetched.
আনীস, *s.* liquor distilled out of anis-seed.
আনুকূল্য, *s.* assistance, patronage, favor.
আনুগত্য, *s.* affection, attachment to a person, an implicit dependence.
আনুপূর্ব্ব, আনুপূর্ব্বী, *s.* an uninterrupted succession, a rank, a row. [cession.
আনুপূর্ব্বক, *ad.* in order, in regular suc-
আনুভব্য, *a.* specious, hypothetical.
আনুমানিক, *a.* probable, specious, ideal, inferrible, deducible.
আনুরক্তি, *s.* pleasure, attachment.
আনুষঙ্গিক, *a.* agreeing in construction with, analogous, connected.
আনেতব্য, *a.* fit or proper to be brought.
আনেতা, *s.* a person who brings a thing.
*আনোখা, *a.* not seen before, strange.
আনোট, আনোঠা, *s.* a ring for the toe.
আন্তরিক, *a.* inward, internal. [closed.
আন্তরীণ, *a.* inward, internal, included, en-
আন্ত্রিক, *a.* inward, affecting the bowels.
আন্দলা, or আন্ধলা, *a.* blind, sightless.
*আন্দাজ, *s.* a guess, a conjecture, a throw, appraisement; in *mus.* time, a mode.
আন্দাজী, *a.* guessing, by guess.
*আন্দেশা, *s.* thought, anxiety, fear, suspicion, care, concern, meditation.
আন্দোলন, *s.* act of swinging, agitation.
আন্দোলনীয়, *a.* agitable, balancing.
আন্দোলিত, *a.* swung, oscillated, agitated.
আন্ধসিক, *s.* a cook; বৃত্তি, cook's service.
আন্ধিয়ারা, আন্ধের, *a.* dark: *s.* darkness.
আস্রি, *s.* a point, an edge, the upper end.
আন্বীক্ষিকী, *s.* logic, metaphysics. [mind.
আন্যমনা, *a.* otherwise-minded, absent in
আপ, *s.* one of the terrestrial gods called Vasus: *a.* self, one's own self.
আপগা, *s.* a river or stream. [fortune.
আপজ্জনক, occasioning calamity or mis-

আপণ, *s.* a market, a shop.
আপৎকাল, *s.* a time of adversity.
আপত্তি, *s.* objection, a remonstrance, expostulation, excuse; also, *vide* আপদ্.
আপদ, *s.* a misfortune, calamity, an accident, danger, adversity, an evil.
আপদগ্রস্ত, *a.* unfortunate, distressed.
আপন, *pron.* own; your.
আপনকার, *pron.* thy, thine, your.
আপনাআপনি, *ad.* of one's self, spontane-
আপনার, *pron.* own, our, your. [ously.
আপনি, *pron.* self, you, your honor.
আপন্ন, *a.* seized by, affected by, wrought
*আপস্, *pron.* self, ownself. [on.
আপস্মিল, *s.* a compromising, amicable
আপাক, *s.* a potter's kiln. [settlement.
আপাকা, *a.* unripe, imperfect.
আপাঙ্গ, *s.* a plant (Achyranthes aspera.)
আপাত, *s.* a falling, present time, passing instant, appointed time, opportunity.
আপাতক, *ad.* at the present moment: *a.*
আপাতকমরণ, *s.* sudden death. [sudden.
আপাততঃ, *ad.* now, instantly, immediately.
আপাদনীয়, *a.* liable to, obtainable.
আপাদ, -পর্য্যন্ত, -মস্তক, from head to foot.
আপামর, *ad.* even to the most vile.
আপার, *a.* boundless, numerous, innumer-
আপি, *pron.* self, one's self, itself. [able.
আপিল, *s. English*, an appeal.
আপিলণ্ট, *s. English*, an appellant.
আপীন, *s.* the udder of a cow; fat.
আপূপিক, *s.* a baker, a confectioner.
আপ্ত, own; obtained, revealed, authentic
আপ্তগ্রাহী, *a.* avaricious, greedy. [mony.
আপ্তবচন, *s.* a revelation, authentic testi-
আপ্তসার, accounting self the sole object.
আপ্যায়িত, *a.* refreshed, re-animated. [ing.
আপ্লব, আপ্লবন, *s.* the act of overflow-
আপ্লাব, *s.* an overflowing, a flood. [tum.
আপ্লাবক, *a.* overspreading: *s.* the omen-
আপ্লাবন, *s.* an overflowing, a flood.
আপ্লাবিত, *a.* overflowed, suffused.
আপ্লুত, *a.* bathed, overflown, suffused.
*আফজুদ্, *ad.* more, more than, extraordi-
*আফৎ, *s.* the same as আপদ্. [nary.
আফা, *s.* the leaping of fishes over a weir.
আফাকল, *s.* a weir for catching fish.

F

আফানি, *s.* the flouncing of a fish.
আফিঙ্গ, আফিম, অহিফেণ, *s.* opium.
আফিঙ্গখোর, *s.* an opium-eater, a sot.
আফিমী, *a.* addicted to the use of opium.
*আফ্সোস্, *s.* woe, grief: *intj.* alas!
*আব, *s.* water; -কার, a distiller, vintner.
আবকারী, *s* the business of a distiller; duty levied on distilleries.
*আবখোরা, *s.* a small drinking vessel.
আবছায়া, *s.* a fleeting or light shadow.
আবজ্, *v. a.* to shut a door, to close up.
আবজান, *s.* the shutting of a door. [cuse.
আবডাল, *s.* a cover, screen, shelter, ex-
আবদার, *s.* a selfish crying or repining.
*আবদার, *s.* a water-cooler. [cooled.
আবদারখানা, *s.* a room where water is
আবদারী, *s.* the office of a water-cooler.
আবনূস, or আবলুস্, *s.* ebony.
আবন্ধ, *s.* a yoke-rope, a tying tight.
আবর, *s.* a mean and ignorant person.
আবরক, *a.* skreening, concealing, veiling: *s.* a skreen; talc mineral.
আবরণ, *s.* the act of skreening or conceal-
আবরণীয়, *a.* concealable. [ing.
আবরণীয়তা, *s.* concealableness. [ment.
*আবরা, *s.* outerfold or outside of a gar-
*আবরু, *s.* chastity, honor, reputation.
আবরুদার, *a.* honorable, of good repute.
আবর্জ্জনী, *s.* refuse, sweepings, rubbish.
আবর্ত্ত, *s.* a whirlpool, an eddy, circular motion, the spiral turn of a screw.
আবর্ত্তক, *a.* turning round: *s.* in *ana.* the vertebræ of the spine.
আবর্ত্তন, *s.* a returning, a turning round, a circular motion, an eddy.
আবর্ত্তনী, *s.* a crucible. [stirring.
আবর্ত্তিত, *a.* stirred round, thickened by
*আব্বল, *a.* first, chief, principal, best.
*আব্লাৎ, *s.* the appurtenances of an estate, trees and other property, &c.
*আব্লাদ, *s.* descendant, posterity, race.
আবলী, *s.* a row, a range, a rank. [rily.
আবশ্য, *ad.* certainly, assuredly, necessa-
আবশ্যক, *a.* necessary, indispensable, expedient: *s.* necessity, expediency.
আবশ্যকতা, -ত্ব, *s.* necessity, expediency, importance, indispensableness.

আবহমান, *a.* flowing on, flowing in, passing on, customary, usual. [generation.
আবাচ্য, *s.* the male and female parts of
*আবাজ, *s.* voice, a sound, a report.
*আবাদ, *s.* cultivation, the settlement of a town or province.
*আবাদি, *a.* arable, cultivated, settled.
আবার, *ad.* again. [from a child.
আবাল, *a.* childish, belonging to a child,
আবালকাল, *s.* infancy, childhood.
আবালবৃদ্ধ, *ad.* both young and old.
আবালবৃদ্ধবনিতা, *ad.* wholly, including men, women and children.
আবাল্য, *ad.* from infancy. [cle
আবাস, *s.* a residence, a home, a taberna-
আবাহক, *a.* calling, bringing to a place.
আবাহন, *s.* an approach, an invitation.
আবাহিত, *a.* invited, brought near. [near.
আবাহ্য, *a.* fit to be invited or brought
আবিধ, *s.* an awl, a drill, augur, a piercer.
আবির্ভাব, *s.* an unfolding, a developing.
আবির্ভূত, *a.* unfolded, evolved, developed.
আবিষ্ট, *a.* engaged in, devoted to, possessed by, engrossed.
আবীর, *s.* a kind of red powder.
আবু, *s.* a wen. আবুআ, *a.* having a wen.
আবুড়া, আবড়াখাবুড়া, *a.* rough, uneven.
আবৃত, *a.* concealed, covered, skreened.
আবৃত্ত. *a.* circulated, revolved, stirred.
আবৃত্তি, *s.* a returning, a repetition, a revolution, a spiral turn.
আবেদক, *a.* making known his case: *s.* he who enters a suit in a court of law.
আবেদন, *s.* a representation. [tition.
আবেদনলিপি, *s.* an affidavit, a plea, a pe-
আবেদিত, represented, entered as a suit.
আবেদ্যমান, *a* under the circumstance of being made known or represented.
আবেশ, *s.* engagedness of mind, devoted-
আবেশক, *a.* persuasive, engaging. [ness.
আবেশন, *s.* a workshop, a manufactory, an entrance, a halo round the sun.
আবোর, *s.* cloud: *a.* clownish, stupid, low,
আব্দির, *a.* yearly, annual. [awkward.
আভরণ, *s.* an ornament, a jewel.
আভা, or আভাস, *s.* brilliancy, splendour, clearness, an appearance, a semblance.
আভাষ, *s.* a prologue, preface, preamble.
আভাষণ, *s.* an addressing, conversation.
আভিজাত্য, *s.* nobility, greatness of birth.
আভিজাত্যাপন্ন, *a.* noble, of high birth.
আভিমুখ্য, *s.* the front of an object.
আভীর, *s.* a cow-keeper, a herdsman.
আভীরী, *s.* a female cow-keeper.
আভ্যাসিক, *a.* eminent in studying.
আম, *s.* a mango; mucus, slime: *a.* raw, unburnt, (as earthenware, bricks, &c.)
*আমখাস, *s.* common and peculiar, inferior and superior, plebeian and noble.
আমগন্ধি, *a.* smelling like the funeral pile.
আমচুর, আমশী, *s.* dried mangoes.
আমড়া, আম্রাত, আম্রাতক, the hog plum.[1]
*আমদ্, *a.* come, arrived.
*আমদনী, আমদানী, *s.* importation, an income, import: *a.* imported.
*আমদ্‌রফত, *s.* a coming and going.
*আমদা, আমমদা, *a.* overmuch, abundant.
*আমদানীরফতানী, *s.* importation andex-
আমন, *s.* winter rice. [portation.
আমন্ত্রণ, *s.* a calling, an invitation.
আমন্ত্রণীয়, *a.* fit to be called or invited.
আমন্ত্রিত, *a.* called, invited.
আমপানস, *s.* a cold, running of the nose.
আমবাত *s.* a disease, an itchy swelling.
আমবিকার, *s.* a diarrhœa, a dysentery.
আময়, *s.* a disease, sickness.
আময়াবী, *a.* diseased, sick.
আমরক্ত, *s.* the bloody flux or dysentery.
আমরা, *pron.* we, us.
আমরুল, *s.* a plant (Oxalis corniculata.)
*আমল, *s.* a district, period of a ruler's government, reign; addictedness (to eating opium, smoking, &c.)
আমলকী, *s.* a tree (Phyllanthus emblica.)
*আমলতাস্, *s.* the same with সোদালি.
আমলা, *s.* an officer; also, *vide* আমলকী.
আমলাসারগন্ধক, *s.* pure sulphur.
আমলেট, *s.* the name of a fish.[2]
আমশী, আমচুর, *s.* dried mangoes.
আমশূল, *s.* the colic, the griping.
আমসত্ত্ব, *s.* inspissated mango juice.
আমহরিদ্রা, a plant (Curcuma reclinata.)
আমা. *a.* unburnt (bricks). [digestion.
আমাজীর্ণ, a disease said to arise from in-

আমাকে, or আমারে, *v.* to me. [nister.
আমাত্য, *s.* a courtier, a counsellor, mi-
আমাদা, *s.* a plant (Curcuma amada.)
*আমানৎ, *a.* deposited with, delivered to, confided with : *s.* a deposit.
আমানী, *s.* rice gruel, water of boiled rice.
আমান্ন, *s.* raw rice, uncooked rice.
আমার, *pron.* my, mine ; দিগকে, to us.
আমারদের, or আমারদিগের, *pron.* our.
*আমারী, *s.* the haudá of an elephant.
আমাশয়, *s.* a diarrhœa; the stomach.
আমি, *pron.* I, I myself.
*আমিন্, *ad.* amen, so be it.
*আমিল, *s.* a governor, a superintendent.
আমিষ, *s.* flesh, food, enjoyment, a pleasing object, a bribe, lust, desire.
আমিষাশী, *a.* carnivorous, eating flesh.
আমিক্ষা, cheese, curds of two-milk-whey.
*আমীন, *s.* a superintendent, supervisor, an overseer, surveyor, a commissioner.
আমীনী, *s.* the office of an overseer, &c.
*আমীর্, *s.* a nobleman, a grandee.
আমীরওমরা, *s.* nobility, grandeur.
আমীরজাদা, *s.* the son of a nobleman.
আমীরউল্‌ওমরা, *s.* a nobleman, lord of lords, a title of Musalmán ministers.
আমীরাণা, আমীরী, *s.* nobility, grandeur.
আমুক্ত, *a.* clothed, invested, accoutred.
আমুলী, *a.* practical, artificial.
আমূল, *ad.* radically, fundamentally, to the root : *s.* a cause, origin. [pound.
*আমেজ্জ, *a.* mixed : *s.* a mixture, a com-
আমোদ, *s.* enjoyment, pleasure ; a scent, fragrance, festivity, fame. [sure.
আমোদন, *s.* the communicating of plea-
আমোদান্বিত, *a.* joyous, glad, gratified.
আমোদিত, *a.* gratified, gladdened, made
আমোদিনী, *s.* a tune in music. [cheerful.
আমোদী, *a.* gratifying, enlivening. [tified.
আমোদীয়া, *a.* joyful, full of delight, gra-
আম্বরীতামাক, *s.* scented huká tobacco.
আম্বল, *a.* sour, acid ; a dish of acid and
আম্বলতা, *s.* acidity. [other vegetables.
আম্র, আঁব, আম, *s.* a mango. [আমড়া.
আম্রাত, আম্রাতক, *s.* the hog plum ; *vide*
আম্রেড়ন, *s.* a tautology, repetition.
আম্রেড়নীয়, *a.* fit to be often repeated.

আম্রেড়িত, *a.* often repeated : *s.* tautology.
আম্ল, *s.* acidity ; the tamarind.
আম্লিকা, আম্লী, *s.* tamarind and its tree.[1]
আয়, *s.* income, gain, receipts, imports.
আয়ত, *a.* long, wide : *s.* a parallelogram.
আয়তচতুরস্র, *a.* quadrangular : *s.* a quad-
আয়তদীর্ঘচতুরস্র, *s.* a rhomboid. [rangle.
আয়তন, *s.* dimension, extent, a groundplot, an altar, a shed for sacrifices.
আয়তসমচতুরস্র, *s.* a parallelogram.
আয়তসমলম্ব, *a.* rectangular : *s.* a rectan-
আয়তার্দ্ধ, *s.* half an oblong. [gle.
আয়তি, *s.* future state or time, majesty, dignity, a meeting or junction, length.
আয়ত্ত, *a.* subject to, docile.
আয়ত্ততা, -ত্ব, *s.* subjection, dependence.
আয়ত্তি, *s.* love, attachment, subjection, a boundary, a limit, power, strength.
আয়ত্তিকৃত, *a.* brought into subjection.
*আয়না, *s.* a mirror, a looking-glass.
*আয়ন্দা, *a.* future, approaching.
আয়ব্যয়, *s.* an income and expenditure.
আয়ব্যয়স্থিতি, state of a person's affairs.
*আয়া, *s.* a nurse, waiting maid : *a.* come.
আযা, *s.* a paternal grandfather.
আয়াতন, *s.* a ground-plot ; a dimension.
আয়াপাণা, *s.* a medicinal plant.[2]
আয়াবস্থিতি, *s.* stock, a capital, income.
‡আয়াম, *s.* length, extent; a season, time.
আয়াস্, *s.* exertion, labor, effort, fatigue.
আয়ী, *s.* a maternal grandmother.
*আয়ীন, *s.* a law, a regulation, a rule.
আয়ু, আয়ুঃ, *s.* a period of life, age, a life-
আয়ুঃক্ষয়, *s.* the decline of life. [time.
আয়ুঃশেষ, *s.* the end of life.
আয়ুর্দ্দায়, আয়ুস্, *s.* a lifetime, age.
আয়ুধ, *s.* armour, a weapon, arms.
আয়ুর্বৃদ্ধি, *s.* longevity, the length of life.
আয়ুর্ব্বেদ, *s.* the science of medicine.
আয়ুর্ব্বেদী, *s.* a physician, a doctor.
আয়ুষ্কর, *a.* causing longevity.
আয়ুষ্মান, long-lived ; *s.* an yuga [gevity.
আয়ুষ্য, vital, life-preserving, giving lon-
আয়োজক, *a.* collecting, procuring : *s.* one who procures articles for a festival.
আয়োজন, *s.* preparation, the act of collecting articles, a making provision.

আয়োজনীয়, *a.* fit to be collected for any work.
আয়োজিত, *a.* collected, procured.
আয়োজ্য, *a.* the same with আয়োজনীয়.
আয়োধন, *s.* war, a battle, combat.
আর, *conj.* and, also: *ad.* furthermore, more: *pron.* else, other, another.
আরআর, *a.* more, still more: *pron.* other.
*আরক, *s.* juice, moisture, perspiration, spirit.
আরক্ত, *a.* reddish, flesh-coloured.
আরগণ, *s.* *English*, an organ.
*আরজ, আরজী, *s.* a petition, a request.
*আরজু, *a.* cheap, not dear.
আরণা, *s.* a wild buffalo.
আরণ্য, *a.* sylvan, wild, belonging to a forest.
আরতি, *s.* cessation; a wave-offering.
*আরদলী, *s.* a courier, one who runs before the pálki of a rich man.
আরন্ধ, *a.* the same with অরন্ধন.
আরব, *s.* an Arabian, native of Arabia.
আরবার, *ad.* again, another time.
আরবী, *a.* Arabian, Arabic.
আরব্ধ, *a.* begun, commenced.
আরভটী, *s.* a branch of the dramatic art.
আরমান, *s.* a desire, a wish; *vide* অরমান.
আরম্ভ, *s* a beginning, a commencement.
আরম্ভন, *s.* the commencing of a thing.
আরম্ভনীয়, *a.* fit to be commenced.
আরসুলা, *s.* a cockroach, blatta.
আরা, *s.* an awl, a saw; -কষ, a sawyer.
আরাৎ, *ad.* near; distant.
আরাতি, *s.* an enemy, an opponent.
আরাধক, *a.* worshipping: *s.* worshipper.
আরাধন, *s.* the act of worshipping.
আরাধনা, *s.* worship, prayer, attendance.
আরাধনীয়, আরাধ্য, *a.* adorable, worshipful, fit to be worshipped, placable.
আরাধিত, *a.* worshipped, supplicated.
আরাম, *s* a pleasure-garden, ease, health, comfort.
আরামী, comfortable, healthy.
*আরিন্দা, *s.* a tax-gatherer.
আরিশ, *s.* the piles or hemorrhoids.
আরু, *s.* a hog, a crab, a pitcher.
আরূঢ়, *a.* mounted on, riding on.
আরে, *a.* vocative particle used in calling a person angrily or contemptuously.
আরো, *ad.* more, still more.
আরোগ্য, *s.* health: *a.* healthy.
আরোপ, attributing to, placing on, transmutation, a substitution, imputation.
আরোপণ, *s.* the act of transferring a quality from one to another.
আরোপণীয়, আরোপ্য, *a.* capable of being transferred or imputed to another.
আরোপিত, *a.* transformed, transferred, imputed, feigned, forged, counterfeit.
আরোহ, *s.* ascension, a mounting upon.
আরোহক, *a.* mounting upon: *s.* a rider.
আরোহণ, *s.* the act of mounting upon, ascending, or climbing, the getting into a vehicle, a staircase, ladder, a vehicle.
আরোহণীয়, *a.* capable of being mounted upon or ascended: *s.* a vehicle.
আরোহী, *a.* mounting upon, climbing, ascending a height: *s.* a rider.
আর্জন, *s.* the procuring or accumulating of things, the planting of trees.
আর্জনীয়, *a.* planting, procuring: *s.* a planter.
আর্জিত, *a.* planted, procured.
আর্ত, *a.* distressed, vexed, grieved.
আর্তব, *s.* the menses, a flower: menstrual.
আর্তি, *s.* pain, distress; the end of a bow.
আর্ত্বিজ্য, *s.* the office of a family priest.
আর্থিক, *a.* acquainted with any particular subject, versed in any science.
আর্থিকতা, *s.* science, a good knowledge of any subject or of any science.
আর্দ্র, *a.* wet, moist, clammy, cool.
আর্দ্রক, আদ্রক, আদা, *s.* ginger.
আর্দ্রা, *s.* name of a particular star, also the eighth mansion in the zodiac.
আর্দ্রিত, *a.* wetted, moistened, cool.
আর্য্য, *a.* noble, venerable, respectable, excellent, apposite: *s.* a friend, preceptor.
আর্য্যক, *s.* a paternal grandfather.
আর্য্যা, *s.* name of Durgá; kind of metre.
আর্শি, *s.* a mirror, a looking-glass.
আর্ষ, আর্ষ্য, belonging to ancient sages.
আর্ষবিবাহ, *s.* the marriage of a sage.
আর্সভ্য, *s.* a young bull in honor of Shiva.
আল, *v. n.* to moulder, to be spoiled (as boiled rice.) আলিয়া-যা, to moulder.
আল, *s.* a sting, forceps, a tenon, a sharp point; yellow-orpiment: *a.* not boiled in its preparation (applied to rice.)

আলকাতরা, *s. Port.* tar, pitch. [hage.[1]
আলকুশী, *s.* a plant which produces cow-
*আলখাল্লক, *s.* a gown, a frock-coat.
আলগল্লতা, *s.* a parasitical plant.[2]
আলগা, *a.* loose, unconnected, lax, open,
আলগামি, আলগী, *s.* looseness. [slack.
আলগোচ, *a.* upright, balanced, poised : *s.* the lifting of a thing up so as not to touch another thing. [raise itself up.
আলগোচি, *s.* the first efforts of a child to
আলগোচে, *ad* in equipoise, on tiptoe.
আলচালু, *s.* rice which is cleansed from its husk without boiling. [glottis.
আলজি, আলজিহ্বা, *s.* the uvula, or epi-
আলটপ্পা, *ad.* easily, without effort.
আলতা, *s.* lac, leaves impregnated with lac.
*আলবত্তা, *ad.* truly, certainly, surely.
আলবাল, *s. vide* দাঁদা.
*আলবেলা, *s.* a huká with a long snake.
*আলম, *s.* the earth, the world.
আলম্ব, *s.* a prop, a fulcrum, a support.
আলম্বন, *s.* dependence, reliance. [lied on.
আলম্বনীয়, *a.* trustworthy, fit to be re-
আলম্বরুহ, *s.* climbing or parasitical plant.
আলম্বিত, *a.* suspended, depended on.
আলয়, *s.* a house, a habitation, home.
আলসিয়া, *a.* indolent, inactive, idle.
আলস্য, *s.* indolence, inactivity, laziness; -ত্যাগ, -ছাড়ন, a stretching and yawning.
আলস্যামি, *s.* sluggishness, sloth, indo-
আলা, *a.* spoiled, tainted, rancid. [lence.
আলাই, -বালাই, *s.* ruin, a misfortune, a calamity, an affliction. [different.
*আলাদা, আলাহেদা, *a.* separate, distinct,
আলান, *s.* a chain, fetter, a tie, a tether, a rope, string, a post: *a.* spoiled (rice).
আলাপ, *s.* conversation, intercourse, communication, acquaintance. [voice.
*আলাপজ্জারি, *s.* in *music*, a modulation of
আলাপন, *s.* the conversing with a person.
আলাপনীয়, *a.* conversible, affable. [ty.
আলাপামক, *a.* fond of conversation, chat-
আলাপিত, *a.* conversed or conferred with.
আলাপিনী, *s.* a kind of lute. [versing.
আলাপী, আলাপীয়, *a.* affable, chatty, con-
আলাপ্য, *a.* affable, conversible.
আলাবু, *s.* the bottle gourd.[2]

আলেয়া, *s.* an apparition, ignis fatuus.
আলি, or আলী, *s.* a balk, a ridge, a dam, a dike, a row, a race, a rank, a family, a woman's female companion, a tenon.
আলিঙ্গন, *s.* a hugging or embracing.
আলিঙ্গনীয়, *a.* fit to be embraced.
আলিঙ্গিত, *a.* embraced, hugged.
আলিঙ্গ্য, *s.* a small drum; *see* আলিঙ্গনীয়.
আলিঞ্জর, *s.* a large earthen water-jar.
আলিন্দ, *s.* a terrace before a house.
আলিপনা, আলিম্পন, *s.* the plastering or whitewashing of a house at a festival.
আলিশিরা, *s.* a cornice, a battlement.
আলু, *s.* a potato, a yam; -বুখারা, Bukhárá prunes, a sort of plum.*
আলুনি, *a.* fresh, unsalted, insipid.
*আলুফা, *s.* free-food, perquisite, profit.
আলুয়া, *a.* mouldered, loose, open.
আলুয়ামালুয়া, *ad.* confusedly, disorderly.
আলে, *a.* fatigued, wearied, dissolved.
আলেখ্য, *a.* unwritten, blank.
*আলেম, *a.* learned: *s.* a learned man.
আলো, আলোক, *s.* light, brightness.
আলোকন, *s.* the perceiving of a thing.
আলোকনা, *s.* perception, discovery, vision, a sight, a survey, a view. [vable.
আলোকনীয়, *a.* perceptible, visible, obser-
আলোকিত, *a.* seen, perceived, viewed.
আলোচন, *s.* trial, a viewing, a perceiving.
আলোচনা, *s.* trial, examination, investigation, perception, a survey.
আলোচনীয়, *a.* investigable, fit to be examined or surveyed. [tigated.
আলোচিত, *a.* examined, surveyed, inves-
আলোড়ন, *s.* a stirring up of liquid, the agitating of a subject, maceration.
আলোড়িত, *a.* stirred up, agitated.
আলোময়, *a.* full of light, luminous.
আল্পিন, or আল্ফিন, *s. Eng.* a pin.
আল্মারী, *s. Port.* a bureau, a chest of drawers, a book-case, a shelf.
আশংসনীয়, *a.* supposable, doubtful, not ascertainable, desirable.
আশংসা, *s.* a supposition, a doubt, hesitation, uncertainty, desire, wish.
আশংসিত, *a.* supposed, doubted, desired.
*আশক, *s.* a lover, an affectionate person.

আশঙ্কনীয়, *a.* dreadful, horrible, fearful.
আশঙ্কা, *s.* awe, fear, terror, dread, danger, peril.
আশঙ্কান্বিত, *a.* fearful, timorous.
আশঙ্কিত, *a.* alarmed, feared, dreaded.
*আশনা, *a.* familiar : *s.* a friend, a lover.
আশনাই, *s.* familiarity, friendship, love.
আশনাসূত্র, *s.* a very fine kind of thread.
আশপাশ, *ad.* on all sides, all round.
আশয়, *s.* an aim, a scope, an object, tendency, intention, hope, a receptacle.
আশয়সিদ্ধ, successful, prosperous, hopeful.
*আশরফী, *s.* a gold mohur, or coin.
আশা, *s.* hope, expectation, trust, desire, a side, a quarter or region ; a staff.
আশাক্রমে, *ad.* in hope, expectingly.
আশান্বিত, আশাপন্ন, *a.* entertaining hope, full of expectation, desirous.
আশাবন্ধ, *a.* restrained or held fast by hope.
আশাবন্ধ, *s.* an obligation ; a cobweb.
আশাভঙ্গ, *s.* disappointment, defeat of hope.
আশিত, *a.* eaten, satisfied.
আশিস, *s.* a blessing, benediction.
আশী, *s.* the fangs of a serpent : *a.* eighty.
আশীর্ব্বাদ, *s.* a blessing, a benediction.
আশীর্ব্বাদী, *a.* benedictory.
আশু, *ad.* soon, speedily, quickly : *vide* আউশ.
আশুকোপী, *a.* touchy, passionate, fretful.
আশুতুষ্ট, *a.* soon pleased, easily gratified.
আশুতুষ্টি, *s.* speedy gratification.
আশুতৃপ্ত, *a.* quickly satisfied.
আশুতৃপ্তি, *s.* speedy satisfaction.
আশুতোষ, soon pleased, placable ; Shiva.
আশুভাব, *s.* swiftness, a vagary.
*আশকারা, *a.* apparent, clear, public.
আশ্চর্য্যিত, *ad.* suddenly, unexpectedly.
আশ্চর্য্য, *a.* marvellous, astonishing, miraculous, strange, surprizing, supernatural, wonderful, admirable ; -জ্ঞান, -বোধ, astonishment, surprise, wonder.
আশ্রম, *s.* a hermitage, monastery, a residence ; -ভ্রষ্ট, excommunicated.
আশ্রমী, *a.* pertaining to a hermitage, belonging to a religious community.
আশ্রয়, আশ্রা, *s.* an asylum, refuge, shelter, resource, a protection, a defence.
আশ্রয়ণীয়, আশ্রেয়, *a.* proper to take refuge in, fit to be resorted to.
আশ্রিত, *a.* secured, placed in safety, dependent.
আশ্লিষ্ট, *a.* embraced, hugged.
আশ্লেষ, *s.* an embrace, a hug.
আশ্বসিত, আশ্বস্ত, আশ্বাসিত, *a.* encouraged, comforted, animated.
আশ্বাস, *s.* encouragement, hope, comfort, animation.
আশ্বিন, *s.* a Hindu month containing part of September and part of October.
আষাঢ়, *s.* a Hindu month containing part of June and part of July.
আষাঢ়া, *s.* 20th and 21st Hindu stellar mansions, the first is called পূর্ব্বাষাঢ়া, and the other উত্তরাষাঢ়া.
আস, *s.* a bow : *intj.* ah ! oh ! *v. a.* to come.
আসক্ত, *a.* attached to, enamoured.
আসক্তচিত্ত, enamoured, attached with all the heart.
আসক্তি, *s.* love, attachment.
আসঙ্গ, *a.* incessant : *ad.* incessantly, constantly : *s.* society, fellowship.
আসত্তি, *s.* an approach, a meeting, a junction, an intimate union, gain, profit.
আসন, *s.* a seat, a carpet, a stool, chair, act of sitting, a sitting cross-legged.
আসনপীঠ, *s.* Sartorius or taylor's muscle.
আসনস্থ, *a.* seated, placed on a seat.
আসন্দী, *s.* a small stool, a chair, altar.
আসন্ন, *a.* approached, near, approaching.
আসন্নকাল, *s.* the time of death.
আসব, *s.* rum, spirits distilled from sugar.
*আসবাব, *s.* goods, chattels, baggage, furniture, an apparatus.
*আসবার, *s.* a horseman, a rider, one who rides a vehicle.
আসবারী, *s.* horsemanship, ridership.
*আসমান, *s.* heaven, sky, atmosphere.
আসমানী, *a.* heavenly ; azure, sky-blue.
আসমানীরং, *s.* sky colour : *a.* sky-blue.
*আসর, *s.* an assembly, a convention.
*আসল, *s.* an origin, an original : *a.* genuine.
আসলচোব, যষ্টিমধু, *s.* licorice.
আসা, আসাবাড়ি, *s.* a staff, a mace, a club.
আসাদিত, *a.* obtained, gained.
*আসান, *a.* easy : *s.* facility, benefit, advantage, gain.
আসানী, *s.* facility, ease.
আসাপ, *s.* a toad.
আসাবরদার, *s.* a mace-bearer, a lictor.
আসাবরদারী, *s.* office of a mace-bearer.
আসামী, *s.* a client, a defendant, a convict.

আসিদ্ধ, taken into custody, imprisoned.
*আসুদা, *a.* filled, satisfied with food.
আসুর, *s.* a demon; surgery; mustard: *a.* diabolical (as, a mode of marriage.)
আসুরবিবাহ, *s.* a mode of marriage in which the bride is given for a price.
আসুরিক, আসুরী, demoniacal, diabolical, audacious, savage (in the above sense.)
আসুরীচিকিৎসক, *s.* a surgeon.
আসুরীচিকিৎসা, *s.* surgery.
আসেধ, *s.* custody, imprisonment.
আসেধক, *a.* committing to custody: *s.* he who commits another to custody.
আসেধনীয়, আসেধ্য, *a.* liable to an arrest.
আস্কন্দিত, *s.* the gallop of a horse.
আস্কিরাপিটা, আস্কে, *s.* a kind of pancake.
আস্ত, *a.* whole, unbroken, entire.
আস্তবল, *s.* *English*, a stable.
আস্তব্যস্ত, *a.* distracted, hurried, troubled.
আস্তর, *s.* a lining, a plastering, the first coating in painting, a covering.
আস্তরণ, *s.* a carpet, a bed, bed-clothes.
আস্তানা, *s.* the threshold of a door.
আস্তিক, *a.* believing the being of a God.
আস্তিকতা, *s.* faith in the existence of a God.
*আস্তীন, *s.* a sleeve.
আস্তীর্ণ, আস্তৃত, *a.* spread out, laid out.
আস্তে, *ad.* slowly, gently, faintly: *a.* slow.
আস্তেসুস্তে, *ad.* at ease, leisurely, slowly.
আস্থা, *s.* confidence, faith, reliance, assurance, dependence, trust, a prop or stay.
আস্থাই, *s.* the key note in music.
আস্থিক, *a.* believing, trusting, depending, laborious, attentive, firm.
আস্থিকতা, -ত্ব, *s.* believership, faith, exertion, firmness, dependence, attention.
আস্পদ, *s.* business, an affair, a situation, a dignity, authority, a boast, a vaunt.
আস্পর্দ্ধা, *s.* emulation, self-exaltation, rivalry, ambition, a boast, a vaunt.
আস্পর্দ্ধাম্বিন, *a.* self-important, ambitious, challenging, boasting, vaunting.
আস্পর্দ্ধিত, *a.* emulated, aspired to, rivalled, boasted, vaunted.
আস্ফালন, *s.* a flouncing, a floundering, flapping, a clapping, self-importance.
আস্ফালিত, *a.* flounced, flapped, clapped.
আস্ফোট, *s.* a clapping of one hand on the other arm as the combatants do.
আস্ফোটন, *s.* the blowing of a flower.
আস্ফোটনী, *s.* awl, augur, a gimlet, drill.
আস্মাকীন, belonging to us, of our party.
আস্য, *s.* a face, a countenance, a visage.
আস্বাদ, *s.* savour, relish, taste.
আস্বাদন, *s.* a tasting of food, relish, savour.
আস্বাদনীয়, আস্বাদ্য, *a.* fit to be tasted, agreeable to the taste.
আস্বাদু, আস্বাদী, *a.* well-tasted, delicious, nice.
আহ, *intj.* ah! aha!
আহত, *a.* smitten, beaten, hurt, injured.
আহনন, *s.* a smiting, hammering.
আহননীয়, আহন্তব্য, *a.* maleable, vulnerable.
আহব, *s.* a sacrifice; war, a combat.
আহবনীয়, *a.* sacrificial.
আহরণ, *s.* act of collecting, a bringing of things, a seizing; removal.
আহরণীয়, আহর্ত্তব্য, *a.* proper to be collected.
আহর্ত্তা, *s.* one who brings; one who eats.
আহা, *intj.* alas! ah! aha!
আহার, *s.* food, a meal, a repast, diet; a taking.
আহারক, bringing, collecting: *s.* he who brings; in *ana.* the pabulous orifice.
আহারত্যাগ, *s.* relinquishment of food.
আহার-পথ, or -প্রণালী, *s.* the alimentary canal.
আহারান্বেষী, *a.* seeking for food.
আহারার্থী, *a.* hungry, desirous of food.
আহারী, *a.* feeding, gluttonous.
আহারেচ্ছা, *s.* hunger, appetite.
আহারেচ্ছু, or আহারেচ্ছুক, *a.* hungry.
আহারোপযুক্ত, *a.* fit for food, eatable.
আহার্য্য, *a.* fit to be brought, fit to be eaten, incidental, adventitious, necessary.
আহিত, *a.* placed, fixed, deposited.
আহীরী, *s.* a cow-keeper, a milkman.
আহুত, *a.* offered, sacrificed.
আহুতি, *s.* a burnt offering or sacrifice.
আহূত, *a.* called, invited, summoned.
আহৃত, *a.* taken, eaten, brought.
আহো, *intj.* what! yes! alas!
আহোপুরুষিকা, *s.* a boasting, a vaunting, self-pride.
আহ্নিক, *a.* daily, diurnal.
আহ্নিকতত্ত্ব, *s.* a book of daily ceremonies.
আহ্লাদ, joy, mirth, gladness, exultation.
আহ্লাদজনক, *a.* causing joy, gladdening.

আহ্লাদবিশিষ্ট, *a.* joyful, glad, exulting.
আহ্লাদমগ্ন, *a.* immersed in joy. [ing.
আহ্লাদযুক্ত, *a.* joyful, glad, merry, exult-
আহ্লাদিত, *a.* pleased, glad, merry.
আহ্লাদী, or আহ্লাদীয়া, *a.* joyful, joyous, glad, mirthful, festive.
আহ্বান, *s.* a call, an invitation, summons.
আহ্বানপত্র, *s.* a summons, an invitation
*আহ্বাল, *s.* a state, a condition. [note.

ই, the third vowel in the Bengáli alphabet. It has the sound of i in him. In *comp.* it assumes this form (ি) called hraswa ikár : *ad.* even, indeed, very.
ইঃ, an *intj.* expressive of anger, sorrow, distress, compassion, or calling.
ইকার, *s.* the letter ই, or its symbol (ি).
ইকুণ, *s.* a louse.
ইক্ষু. *s.* sugarcane ; যন্ত্র a sugar-mill.
ইক্ষুমেহ, *s.* a kind of gonorrhœa or gleet.
*ইখ্তিয়ার *s.* subjection, control.
*ইখলাস, *s.* esteem, regard.
ইঙ্গিত, *s.* a hint, nod, a wink, a signal.
ইঙ্গিতে, *ad.* indirectly, by nods or signal.
ইচড়, *s.* green or immature jak-fruit.
ইচ্ছা, *s.* will, the will, desire, a wish, a propensity, a bias, choice, inclination.
ইচ্ছাক্রমে, at will, freely, spontaneously.
ইচ্ছাধীন, *a.* subject to one's own will.
ইচ্ছানুসারে, *ad.* as you please, freely.
ইচ্ছান্বিত, *a.* desirous of, wishing for.
ইচ্ছাপূর্ব্বক, *a.* voluntary : *ad.* voluntarily.
ইচ্ছাপ্রযুক্ত, *ad.* with one's own will.
ইচ্ছাবান্, *a.* voluntary, spontaneous.
ইচ্ছামত, *a.* corresponding with the desire.
ইচ্ছামতে, *ad.* according to the will.
ইচ্ছু, ইচ্ছুক, *a.* desirous, solicitous, willing.
ইচ্‌লামাছ, *s.* a prawn, a shrimp. [counts.)
*ইজ্রা, *a.* brought over, carried over (in ac-
*ইজার, *s.* a pair of trowsers ; a farming ; -দার, a farmer ; -দারী farmership.
ইজারবন্দ, *s.* a tape or tassel for trowsers.
ইজারা, *s.* a farm ; revenue of a farm.
*ইজারী, *s.* a strong sort of cloth.
ইজের, *s.* trowsers, breeches, pantaloons.
ইজ্যা, *s.* a sacrifice, an oblation, worship.
ইঞ্চাক, *s.* a shrimp, a prawn.
*ইঞ্জিল, *s.* the gospel, New Testament.
ইট, ইটল, ইটা, ইটাল, ইটু, *s.* a brick.
ইটখোলা, *s.* place where bricks are made.
ইটবালা, *s.* a maker or seller of bricks.
ইটময়, ইটীয়, *a.* brick, made of bricks.
ইটল্ *v. a.* to pelt with bricks.
ইটলান, *s.* pelting of bricks at any one.
ইটাভিটা, *s.* house and its appurtenances.
ইতঃ, *ad.* hence, from this. [mean, low.
ইতর, *a.* other, another ; common, vulgar,
ইতরকথা, *s.* rustic or low language.
ইতরথা, *ad.* otherwise, in another way.
ইতরবিশেষ, *s.* a distinction, a disparity.
ইতরভাষা, *s.* rustic or low language.
ইতরলোক, a plebeian, low people. [day.
ইতরেদ্যুঃ, on another day, on some other
*ইতলা, ইত্তিলা, *s.* information, intelligence.
ইতস্ততঃ, *ad.* hither and thither.
ইতি, *ad.* thus far, thus, hitherto.
*ইত্তিফাক, *s.* friendship, union, chance, an incident, a thinking. [the interim.
ইতিমধ্যে, *ad.* during this, meanwhile, in
ইতিহ, *s.* traditional instruction, advice.
ইতিহাস, *s.* a narrative, history, legend.
ইতোমধ্যে, *ad.* during this, meanwhile.
ইত্থম্ভূত, *ad.* thus, such, like.
ইত্যনুমানে, according to this inference.
ইত্যনুসারে, *ad.* according to this.
ইত্যবসরে, *ad.* in the mean time, at this opportunity, at this time, during this.
ইত্যাদি, *ad.* etcetera, and so forth.
ইদং, *ad.* this, that, the same.
ইদানী, *ad.* now, of late, lately. [sent.
ইদানীন্তন, *a.* new, recent, modern, pre-
ইনাকে, ইনারে, to this person. [a gift.
*ইনাম ইনাম, এক্রাম, *s.* a reward, largess,
ইনার, *ad.* this person's. ইনি, this person.
*ইন্তিজাম, *s.* order, regularity. [holden.
*ইন্তিজার, *a.* expecting, looking for, be-
ইন্তিজারী, *s.* expectation, a looking for.
*ইন্তিহা, *a.* finished : *s.* an end, a summit,
*ইন্তিহাম, *s.* an examination. [a limit.
ইন্দারা, *s.* a well, a large well.
ইন্দীবর, *s.* the blue lotus. [of the moon.
ইন্দু, the moon ; -কলা ; -রেখা, -লেখা, digit
ইন্দুকান্ত, *s.* the name of a gem.
ইন্দুর, *s.* a rat, a mouse, (generic name.)

ইন্দ্র, *s.* the sovereign of the gods; human soul, animal soul, night, an organ of sense, a division of Jambu-dwípa or the continent of Asia. [sect.[1]
ইন্দ্রগোপ, *s.* a fire fly, a lady-bird, an in-
ইন্দ্রজাল, *s.* legerdemain, juggling, conjuring; a net with artificial fish, flowers, etc. suspended over the Rása temple.
ইন্দ্রজালবিদ্যা, *s.* science of magic or leger-
ইন্দ্রজালিক, magical, deceptive. [domain.
ইন্দ্রজালিকা, *a.* deceptive, juggling, illusive.
ইন্দ্রনীল, *s.* a sapphire; a thrill in music.
ইন্দ্রপদ, *s.* Indraship, the office of Indra.
ইন্দ্রযব, *s.* the seed of an Indian shrub.[2]
ইন্দ্রলুপ্ত, *s.* baldness, morbid baldness.
ইন্দ্রাণী, *s.* the consort of Indra; a shrub.[3]
ইন্দ্রায়ুধ, *s.* Indra's weapon, the rainbow.
ইন্দ্রাশন, *s.* the tender tops of hemp dried; also, the seeds of Abrus precatorius.
ইন্দ্রাসন, *s.* the throne of Indra. [tion.
ইন্দ্রিয়, *s.* organs of sensation and percep-
ইন্দ্রিয়গণ, *s.* all the organs. [the senses.
ইন্দ্রিয়গোচর, *a.* perceptible, present to
ইন্দ্রিয়ঘ্ন, *a.* destructive to the senses, debilitating, stupifying.
ইন্দ্রিয়দমন, *s.* self-controul, self-denial.
ইন্দ্রিয়দোষ, *s.* evil propensity, concupis-
ইন্ধন, *s.* fuel, firewood. [cence.
*ইন্‌ফিসাল, *s.* a decision, the adjustment or termination of an affair, a settling.
*ইন্‌সাফ, *s.* decision of a cause, right, jus-
ইপ্সু, *a.* desirous, coveting. [tice, equity.
ইব, *a.* as, like, resembling. [gion.
*ইমান, *s.* faith, belief, conscience, reli-
ইমানদার, *a.* faithful: *s.* a believer.
ইমানদারী, *s.* the condition of a believer.
*ইম্‌তিহান্, *s.* an examination, proof, trial.
ইম্‌তিহানী, belonging to an examination.
*ইম্‌লা, orthography, a writing correctly.
ইম্‌লি, or অম্লিকা, *s.* tamarind and its tree.
ইয়ৎ, *ad.* so much, thus much.
ইয়ত্তা, *s.* fixed quantity, definiteness, limit.
ইয়ত্তাভাব, *s.* unlimitedness.
ইয়ত্তারহিত, *a.* unlimited, indefinite.
ইরম্মদ, *s.* submarine fire. [ardent spirits.
ইরা, *s.* goddess of speech; speech; earth;
*ইরাদা, *s.* desire, inclination, a wish.

G

ইলশা, or ইলিশ, *s.* the name of a fish.[4]
ইলাবৃতবর্ষ, *s.* the most central of the nine geographical divisions of the earth.
ইলেক, *s.* a line, a stroke, a dash, a streak.
*ইলেম, *s.* science, art, learning.
*ইল্লৎ, *s.* filth, dirt, ordure; -খানা a privy.
ইল্লতী, *a.* filthy, fœtid, abominable.
*ইশারা, *s.* a nod or wink, a sign, token.
*ইশ্‌তিহার, *s.* a proclamation, a notice; -নামা, a written proclamation.
ইষ, *s.* the month usually called Áshwin.
ইষু, *s.* an arrow, a versed sine.
ইষুধি, or তরকশ, *s.* a quiver.
ইষুরমূল, *s.* a plant (Aristolochia indica).
ইষ্ট, *a.* desired, wished for, cherished, beloved, reverenced, respected, approved
ইষ্টক, or ইষ্টকা, *s.* a brick.
ইষ্টকর্ম্ম, *s.* a wished-for work; in *arith.* an operation with assumed numbers.
ইষ্টদেব, ইষ্টদেবতা, *s.* a tutelary deity, a particular god a person worships.
ইষ্টি, *s.* volition, will, desire, wish; a sacrifice, a preceptor, a spiritual guide.
ইস্, an interjection expressive of pain, anger, or sorrow: *s.* surprise. [ket.
ইস্কাতর, *s.* a scrutoire, a box, cabinet, cas-
ইস্তক, from, from this place. [clusive.
ইস্তকলাগাদি, from this place to that, in-
ইস্তিআমাল, *s.* a practice, a custom, habit.
ইস্তিমরারী *ad.* always, constantly.
*ইস্তিয়াফা, *s.* pardon, forgiveness; relin-
ইস্ত্রি, *s.* a smoothing-iron. [quishment.
*ইস্পন্দ, *s.* particular drugs the smoke of which is said to keep off evil spirits.
ইস্পাগুল, ইসবগুল, *s.* a plant (Plantago
ইস্পাত, *s. Port.* steel. [isphagula.)
*ইসম, *s.* a name, title; নবীস্, a muster-master; -নবীসী, muster-mastership.
ইহ, *pron.* this, here; -কাল, the present life or time; -লোক, the present world.
ইহা, *pron.* this; -ছাড়া, -ব্যতিরেক, besides,
ইহাতে, *ad.* in this. [beside this.
ইহারঅধিক, *ad.* at most, more than this.
ইহারপর, *ad.* after this, hereafter.
ইহারপূর্ব্বে, *ad.* before this, formerly.
ইহারমধ্যে, *ad.* in the interim, within this.
ইহারা, *pron.* they, these persons.

ঈ, the 4th vowel. In *comp.* it is expressed by this symbol (ী) called dirgha-ikár, and has the sound of i long.
ঈকার, *s.* the letter ঈ, or the symbol (ী).
ঈক্ষণ, *a.* seeing, beholding, looking at.
*ঈজাদ, *s.* invention : *a.* invented.
ঈতি, *s.* calamity befalling the rural peasantry.
*ঈদ, *s.* a festival, a holiday.
ঈদৃক, or ঈদৃশ, *ad.* thus, such, resembling this.
ঈর্ষ্যা, *s.* envy, spite, malice.
ঈর্ষ্যান্বিত, ঈর্ষ্যাবান, ঈর্ষী, *a.* spiteful, malicious, envious, malevolent.
ঈশ, *s.* God, lord, master, name of Shiva, the supreme; beam of a plough.
ঈশলাঙ্গলিয়া, a plant (Gloriosa superba).
ঈশান, *s.* splendour ; name of Shiva : *a.* north-east ; -কোণ, north-east quarter.
ঈশু, *s.* Jesus, the Redeemer of mankind.
ঈশু খ্রীষ্ট, *s.* Jesus Christ, the Saviour.
ঈশ্বর, *s.* God, the Creator, Supreme Lord.
ঈশ্বরত্ব, *s.* Godhead, the attributes of God.
ঈশ্বরনিষেধ, or ঈশ্বরপ্রতিষেধ, *s.* atheism.
ঈশ্বরনিষ্ঠ, *a.* firmly relying on God.
ঈশ্বরপরায়ণ, ঈশ্বরভক্ত, devoted to God.
ঈশ্বরী *s.* a goddess, an empress, a queen.
ঈষ, or ঈষা, *s.* the beam of a plough.
ঈষৎ, *ad.* a little, somewhat, slight.
ঈষদুষ্ণ, *a.* lukewarm; -তা, lukewarmness.
ঈষদ্গভীর, *a.* shallow, not very deep.
ঈষদ্গুণ, *s.* slender abilities, a smattering.
ঈষদ্দর্শন, *s.* a glance, a slight view.
ঈষদ্দোষ, *s.* a peccadillo, a slight fault.
ঈষদ্ধাস্য, *s.* a slight laugh, a smile.
ঈষদ্ধাস্যবদন, *s.* a smiling countenance.
ঈষদ্বক্র, somewhat crooked, bent, curved.
ঈহা, *s.* study, a striving, endeavour.

উ, the fifth vowel; it has the sound of u in full. In *comp.* it is expressed by this symbol (ু) called hraswa-ukár : *intj.* Oh ! expressive of pain.
উআঁচুআঁ, *a.* spoiled in the cooking.
উই, *s.* a termite, a white-ant; -নন্দন, a white-ant hill.
উইপোকা, *s.* a termite, a white-ant.
উঃ, উ, *intjs.* expressing assent, surprize, compassion and anger; aye ! ha !
উচ, উচা, *v. a.* to stir up, to raise up, to peck (as birds), to strip a thatch, straw, or grass, to collect, gather (as grain).
উচ, *a.* exalted, high, lofty, tall.
উঁচকপালিয়া, *a.* having a high forehead.
উঁচন, উঁচান, *a.* torn off (as thatch from a house), collected (as grain).
উঁচনীচা, *a.* high and low, rough, uneven.
উঁচল, উঁচলা, *v.* to toss up, agitate (as corn or a liquid), to bubble, to boil over.
উচলন, উঁচলান, *a.* agitating : *s.* the agitating or falling out of a vessel.
উছল, উছলা, *v. a.* to be agitated, to leap, to skip, to overflow.
উঁছা, *v. a.* to take up, to lift up, to peck the thatch.
উঁছান, a lifting up, pecking, a gathering.
উঁধিপোকা, *s.* the male of the white-ant when it has acquired wings.
উহ, *pron.* that man or woman, he, she.
উঁহুঁ, a particle of refusal or denial, no.
উহ, *v. a.* to rasp, to file.
উক, *s.* a file, a rasp ; a meteor, a torch, a firebrand ; sugarcane : stray, strange.
উকট, *a.* intolerable, hot, mad, furious.
উকটীয়া, *a.* belonging to the hot season.
উকড়ী, *s.* a skimmer, ladle ; a mark tattooed by Hindu women on the forehead.
উকা, *s.* a rasp, a file ; meteor a torch, a firebrand, a flaming wisp of straw.
উকার, *s.* the letter উ, or the symbol (ু).
*উকালৎ, *s.* an embassy, pleadership, attorneyship, agency, a deputation.
উকালৎনামা, *s.* the credentials of an ambassador or agent, a power of attorney.
উকি, *s.* a peep ; a straining to vomit ; -উঠ, to retch in vomiting ; -মার, to peep.
উকিউঠন, *s.* the act of retching to vomit.
উকিঝুকি, *s.* a peep, a peeping or prying ; -মার, to peep, to pry.
উকিমারণ, or উকিঝুকিমারণ, *s.* the act of peeping.
*উকীল, *s.* an attorney, a pleader (in a court) an ambassador, an agent.
উকীলী, *s.* the business or office of an attorney or ambassador ; a negociation.
উকুণ, or উকুন, *s.* a louse ; a bug.
উকুণীয়পোকা, *s.* a weevil.
উকুণে, *a.* lousy : *ad.* lousily.

উকুনবাড়ি, *s.* a bambu hook used to separate short straw, &c. from the corn.
উকলী, উখলী, *s.* a wooden mortar.
উক্ত, *a.* spoken, mentioned, related, said.
উক্তানুক্ত, *a.* spoken and not spoken.
উক্তি, *s.* a word, a speech, an expression, [a sentence.
উখ্, *v. a.* to rasp, to file.
উখ, উখা, *s.* a rasp, a file; a saucepan.
উখড়্, *v. a.* to pass away (as time), to break the string and get loose (a paper kite).
উখড়া, *s.* food made of parched rice and [molasses.
উখড়াখকড়া, *a.* dishevelled.
উখড়ী, *s.* a skimmer, a ladle, a spoon.
উখাড়্, *v. a.* to pluck up, to root up.
উগর্, *v. n.* vomit, to throw up.
উগরণ, or উগরাণ, *s.* the act of vomiting, any substance vomited: *a.* vomited.
উগরিয়াখাওন, *s.* act of chewing the cud.
উগ্র, *a.* hot, peevish, snappish, surly, violent, cross, passionate, pungent.
উগ্রগন্ধ, উগ্রগন্ধা, *a.* strong-scented.
উগ্রতা, -ত্ব, *s.* heat, ardour, violence, pungency, peevishness, passionateness.
উগ্রস্বভাব, *a.* passionate, hot-tempered.
উদ্ঘারণ, *s.* the uncovering of a thing.
উদ্ঘোশ, *s.* the introduction of a topic.
উচ, *a.* high, lofty, tall, elevated.
উচকা, উচক্কা, *a.* unruly, headstrong, mischievous, bold, impudent, insolent.
উচল, উচলা, উচলন, *vide* উঁচল, &c.
উচাটন, *s.* a being sad, gloomy or sullen.
উচাটনমনাঃ, gloomy, sad, heavy-hearted.
উচাটী, *a.* inclined to gloominess.
উচিত, *a.* proper, fit, suitable, convenient.
উচুঙ্গা, *s.* a species of gryllus or cricket.
উচোট, *s.* a trip, a stumble; -খা, to trip, [stumble.
উচ্চ, high, lofty, tall, elevated.
উচ্চটা, pride, arrogance; a custom, usage.
উচ্চণ্ড, *a.* quick, hasty, expeditious.
উচ্চতা, -ত্ব, *s.* height, tallness, elevation
উচ্চপদ, *s.* a high office. [streperous.
উচ্চভাষী, *a.* noisy, brawling, shouting, ob-
উচ্চড, *a.* droll, humorous, jocular.
উচ্চরিত, *a.* pronounced, uttered, expressed, said, spoken. [disquietude.
উচ্চাটন, *a.* gloomy, sullen, sad: *s.* sadness,
উচ্চাবচ, *a.* uneven, various, multiform.

উচ্চার, *s.* pronunciation, utterance; excrement, filth, manure.
উচ্চারণ, *s.* pronunciation, utterance.
উচ্চারণীয়, উচ্চারয়িতব্য, *a. vide* উচ্চার্য্য.
উচ্চারিত, pronounced, uttered. [spoken.
উচ্চার্য্য, fit to be pronounced, uttered, or
উচ্চার্য্যমান, *a.* proceeding from the mouth.
উচ্চিঙ্গড়া, *s.* a gryllus, a cricket.
উচ্ছে, a vegetable (Momordica muricata).
উচ্চৈঃ, *ad.* loud, aloud, on high.
উচ্চৈঃশব্দ, *s.* a loud sound, a loud voice.
উচ্চৈঃশ্রবা, *a.* deaf, high-eared: *s.* Indra's [steed.
উচ্চৈঃস্বর, *s.* loud voice or sound.
উচ্চৈঃস্বরে, *ad.* aloud, with a noise.
উচ্ছন্ন, *a.* ruined, destroyed, subverted, laid waste, stript of, relinquished.
উচ্ছন্নতা, -ত্ব, *s.* perdition, ruin, desolation.
উচ্ছিন্ন, *a.* cut off, ruined, destroyed.
উচ্ছিন্নতা, *s.* excision, ruin, desolation.
উচ্ছিষ্ট, *a.* left, remaining, rejected.
উচ্ছিষ্টতা, *s.* a remnant, orts, refuse.
উচ্ছৃঙ্খল, *a.* loose, unrestrained, irregular, self-willed, perverse, licentious.
উচ্ছৃঙ্খলতা, *s.* irregularity, confusion, disorder, unrestrainedness, licentiousness.
উচ্ছেদ, *s.* excision, ruin, devastation.
উচ্ছেদন, *s.* the devastation of a country.
উচ্ছেদনীয়, or উচ্ছেদ্য, *a.* capable of being cut off, requiring to be eradicated.
উচ্ছ্রয়, উচ্ছ্রায়, *s.* a height, elevation.
উচ্ছ্রিত, *a.* elevated, increased, sprung up, produced, exalted, grown, prosperous.
উছড়্, *v. n.* to vomit, to throw up.
উছড়ন, *s.* the act of vomiting.
উছনিয়া, *a.* squandering away, ruining.
উজ্, *v. n.* to move against the stream, to swim or move up the stream. [right,
উজ, উজা, *a.* straight, direct, sincere, up-
উজাই, *a.* swam up the stream (applied to fishes): *s.* a common report.
উজাড়, *a.* desolate, uninhabited, desert.
উজন, *a.* against the grain, or stream.
উজনিয়া, *a.* going against the stream. wandering out of its place (as fish).
*উজর, *s.* an excuse, an apology.
উজল্, *v. n.* to be tossed, to be agitated.
উজল, *s.* a tossing or agitating.

উজলপাজল, *ad.* topsyturvy, confusedly.
উজলা, *v. a.* to toss, to agitate: *s.* light.
উজলান, *s.* the tossing of a thing; a being tangled.
উজাউজি, *ad.* straight and fair.
উজাড়, *a.* desolate, uninhabited: *s.* a wilderness, a deserted place.
উজান, the upper country: *a.* against the stream or current, against the grain.
উজি, *s.* a common report, a fiction.
*উজির, a minister, a counsellor of state.
উজিরী, *s.* the office of a minister of state.
উজ্জট, *a.* waste, ruined, desolate, desert.
উজ্জড়, উজ্জড়ন, *s.* a stripping off or eradicating, eradication, destruction, ruin.
উজ্জ্বল, *a.* luminous, bright, clear, glossy: *s.* a blazing, brightness, illumination.
উজ্জ্বলতা, -ত্ব, *s.* brightness, luminousness.
উজ্জ্বলন, *s.* the act of blazing up.
উজ্জ্বলা, *s.* a blaze, splendour, brightness.
উজ্জ্বলিত, *s.* kindled, illuminated.
উজ্ঝিত, *a.* left, abandoned, relinquished.
উঞ্ছ, *v. a.* to dry rice by the fire after it has been soaked for being husked.
উঞ্ছ, a gleaning, the collecting of grains.
উঞ্ছন, *s.* the act of gleaning: *a.* dried by the fire (only applied to rice).
উট, *v. n.* to rise up, to heave, to scale off.
উট, or উষ্ট্র, *s.* a camel.
উটকানা, *s.* an unguent for cleaning the body.
উটকরা, *a.* foreign, unknown, vagrant.
উটজ, *s.* a hut of leaves, a thatched house.
উটন, উটনা, *s.* the taking of daily supply of money or goods on credit.
উটনাখরচ, *s.* the expense of supply as above.
উট্‌ক, or উট্‌কা, *v. a.* to search for.
উট্‌কন, or উট্‌কান, *s.* the act of searching.
উট্‌কানীয়া, *a.* seeking, searching, sought.
উটকো, *a.* straying, wandering.
উটুঙ্ক, *s.* a clue, a guide.
উঠ্, *v. a.* to rise, to mount.
উঠ, *s.* rising up, a mounting, elevation: *a.* risen.
উঠন, *s.* the act of rising or mounting, a climbing up, or landing; a court-yard.
উঠা, *v. a.* to cause to rise or ascend, to raise up, set up, to elevate, to exalt, to remove, to eradicate, to awake.
উঠাউঠি, *ad.* repeatedly, importunately.
উঠান, *s.* a raising up, the causing to rise, mount, or ascend, the removing or effacing of a thing; a court-yard.
উঠাপড়া, *s.* a rising and falling.
উঠিত, *a.* erect, risen, mounted, spent.
উঠ্‌তি, *s.* a vent or sale for goods, the breaking up of an assembly.
উড়, *v. n.* to fly, to mount in the air.
উড়কী, *s.* the handle of a culinary vessel; the tattooing on the face or body.
উড়ন, *s.* the act of flying.
উড়নী, *s.* a covering sheet, an upper garment.
উড়নীয়, *a.* flying, taking flight, fledged.
উড়া, *s.* act of flying: *v. a.* to cause to fly.
উড়ান, *s.* the act of wasting profusely, a squandering; a causing dust, etc. to fly.
উড়ানঘাই, *s.* a trick, circumvention.
উড়ানচণ্ডীয়া, *a.* wasting, profuse, extravagant.
উড়ানী, *s.* waste, extravagance.
উড়ানীয়া, *a.* wasting, extravagant, squandering.
উড়াবাও, *s.* the venereal disease.
উড়ী, or উড়ীধান, *s.* wild rice.
উডু, *s.* any constellation in the moon's path.
উডুউডু, *a.* on the wing, on tiptoe, agitated, anxious, ready to take flight.
উডুক্কা, *a.* fledged, able to fly.
উডুপ, *s.* a raft, a float; the moon.
উডুপতি, *s.* the moon.
উডুম্বর, *s.* a wild fig;[1] the threshold of a house; copper; a sort of leprosy.
উড়্‌তী, *a.* flighty, airy, light, vain.
উড্ডয়ন, *s.* a flying, the act of flying.
উড্ডীং, *s.* a leap upwards, a bound.
উড্ডীং ফুড্ডীং, *s.* a jumping and frisking.
উড্ডীয়মান, *a.* flying, in the act of flying.
উৎ, an inseparable preposition, when prefixed to a word, conveys the idea of a degree of elevation or ardour.
উত, *s.* heat, fire: *a.* sewed, woven.
উতর্, *v. n.* to arrive, to come, to descend.
উতর, *s.* an answer; an alighting.
উতরখানা, *s.* a baiting place, an inn.
উতরা, *s.* the arriving at a place.
উতল্, *v. n.* to overflow, to bubble to boil over.
উতলন, *a.* overflowing, boiling over.
উতলপাতল, *ad.* up and down: *s.* the shaking or stirring up of a liquid.

উতলা, *a.* impatient, troubled : *s.* an over-
উতার, উতারা, *s* a copy, duplicate. [flow.
উতালা, impatient, uneasy, hasty, anxious.
উতুল, *v. n.* to boil over, to overflow.
উৎক, *a.* anxious, regretting, sad, vexed.
উৎকট, *a.* bad, painful, troublesome, disagreeable, excessive, mad, furious, drunk.
উৎকটভোক্তা, *s.* one who eats excessively.
উৎকণ্ঠা, *s.* regret, care, anxiety, melancholy, sullenness, vexation, uneasiness.
উৎকণ্ঠিত, *a.* dejected, distressed, anxious, thoughtful, vexed, sullen, melancholy.
উৎকণ্ঠিতা, *a. fem.* anxiously waiting for, or expecting (her husband or lover).
উৎকর্ষ, *s.* excellence, abundance.
উৎকলিকা, *s.* anxiety, thought, care.
উৎকুণ, or উকুণ, *s,* a louse.
উৎকৃষ্ট, *a.* excellent, best, elevated, good.
উৎকৃষ্টতা, -ত্ব, *s.* goodness, excellence.
উৎকোচ, ঘুষ, *s.* a bribe. [transgression.
উৎক্রম, *s.* a leap, a jump, irregularity,
উৎক্রান্ত, *a.* leaped up, transgressed.
উৎক্রোশ, *s.* an osprey, an eagle, (Falco-
উৎক্ষিপ্ত, tossed up, thrown up [utkrosa.
উৎক্ষেপ, *s.* a tossing up, a throwing up.
উৎক্ষেপক, *a.* throwing up : *s.* one who
উৎক্ষেপণ, *s.* a throwing up. [throws up.
উৎক্ষেপণীয়, capable of being thrown up.
উৎখাত, *s,* eradication, destruction, ruin.
উৎখাতী, destructive, subversive, ruinous.
উত্তপ্ত, *a.* hot, heated, burnt up, excited.
উত্তম, *a.* chief, best, excellent, very good.
উত্তমকর্ম্ম, *s.* a good or excellent work.
উত্তমতা, -ত্ব, *s.* excellence, superiority.
উত্তমপদ, *s.* a high office, chief seat.
উত্তমর্ণ, *s.* a creditor, a money-lender.
উত্তমসাহস, *s.* a capital punishment.
উত্তমাঙ্গ, *s.* the head, chief member. [tion.
উত্তমার্হ, *a.* improvable, capable of meliora-
উত্তর, *v. n.* to arrive at a place, to alight, to land from a ship or boat.
উত্তর, *a.* subsequent, posterior, ulterior, succeeding; north : *s.* an answer; the north quarter; a consequence; arrival.
উত্তরউত্তর, *ad.* successively, gradually.
উত্তরকর্ত্তা, *s.* one who replies or answers.
উত্তরকাল, *s.* future time, a future state.
উত্তরক্রিয়া, *s.* funeral obsequies or rites.
উত্তরখণ্ডন, *s.* a refutation, a rejoinder.
উত্তরণ, *s.* the act of arriving, alighting, or
উত্তরণস্থান, *s.* a baiting place. [landing.
উত্তরণীয়, *a.* capable of being got through, crossed over, or arrived at. [entia.)
উত্তরদন্ত, *s.* the furthest tooth (dens sapi-
উত্তরদাতা, *s.* one who gives a reply.
উত্তরদায়ক, উত্তরদায়ী, *a.* answering, re-
উত্তরদিক, *s.* the north quarter. [plying.
উত্তরদেশ, *s.* the north country.
উত্তরপক্ষ, *s.* reply to an argument, minor proposition in a syllogism. [word.
উত্তরপদ, *s.* last member of a compound
উত্তরপ্রত্যুত্তর, *s.* a dialogue, the pleadings in a law suit, a dispute, altercation.
উত্তরপ্রদ, *a.* giving a reply. [du zodiac.
উত্তরফল্গুনী, *s.* 12th mansion in the Hin-
উত্তরভাদ্রপদ, *s.* the twenty-sixth mansion in the Hindu zodiac. [able.
উত্তরযোগ্য, *a.* deserving a reply, answer-
উত্তরসাক্ষী, *s.* a witness testifying upon what he has heard from others.
উত্তরসাধক, *s.* one who directs all the minutiæ of a religious ceremony, an umpire, an auxiliary, a prompter.
উত্তরস্থান, *s.* a baiting place, an inn.
উত্তরাধিকার, *s.* an inheritance.
উত্তরাধিকারপত্র, *s.* a will, a testament.
উত্তরাধিকারিতা, heirship, proprietorship.
উত্তরাধিকারী, *s.* an heir, a successor.
উত্তরান্তর, *s.* a reply which is inapplicable to the charge, another reply.
উত্তরাভাস, *s.* a prevarication, equivocal reply; in *law,* an apparent reply.
উত্তরায়ণ, *s.* the sun's path north of the equator, the tropic of Capricorn.
উত্তরাষাঢ়া, *s.* 21st mansion in the Hindu
উত্তরাসঙ্গ, *s.* an outer garment. [zodiac.
উত্তরী, *s.* outer garment passed over the right shoulder and under the left arm; the sacred thread when thus worn.
উত্তরীয়, *s.* the upper flowing garment.
উত্তরে, *ad.* at last, afterwards. [quently.
উত্তরেণ, *ad.* northerly, northwards, subse-
উত্তরেদ্যুঃ, *ad.* to-morrow, on a future day.
উত্তরোত্তর, *ad.* more and more.

উত্তর্জনা, *s.* a threatening, a dunning.
উত্তলন, *s.* over flowing of ariver or pond; a running or boiling over of a liquid.
উত্তান, supine, lying on the back, shallow.
উত্তানকারী, *a.* lying in a supine posture.
উত্তানশয়, *a. idem;* also, *s.* an infant.
উত্তাপ, *s.* heat, ardour, fervour, zeal.
উত্তাপন, *s.* the making of a thing hot.
উত্তাপনীয়, *a.* capable of being heated.
উত্তাপিত, *a.* heated, made hot.
উত্তারণ, *s.* the causing to arrive or alight.
উত্তীর্ণ, arrived, got over, escaped, rescued.
উত্তেজনা, *s.* a polishing, importunity, dun-
উত্তোলক, *a.* elevating, raising up. [ning.
উত্তোলন, *s.* the raising or elevating of a thing, a boiling over, an overflowing.
উত্তোলনদণ্ড, *s.* a lever. [or elevated.
উত্তোলনীয়, *a.* capable of being raised up
উত্তোলিত, *a.* elevated, raised up, made to boil over, or to overflow. [gusted.
উত্ত্যক্ত, *a.* rejected, abandoned, vexed, dis-
উত্থ, rising, standing erect, arising from.
উত্থল্, *v. n.* to overflow, to boil over.
উত্থলন, *s.* an overflowing, a boiling over.
উত্থলিত, *a.* overflown, boiled over.
উত্থান, *s.* a raising, rising, or getting up.
উত্থানৈকাদশী, *s.* a festival observed in honor of Vishnu's rising from his sleep.
উত্থাপক, *a.* raising up: *s.* one who raises up, a raising machine, an elevator.
উত্থাপন, *s.* the act of raising up; in *arith.* the producing of the answer or result.
উত্থাপনা, *s.* elevation, a raising up.
উত্থাপনীয়, উত্থাপয়িতব্য, *a. vide* উত্থাপ্য.
উত্থাপিত, elevated, raised up. [elevated.
উত্থাপ্য, *a.* capable of being raised up, or
উত্থিত, *a.* erect, risen, exalted.
উত্থিতি, *s.* erection, elevation, a rising up.
উৎপতন, *s.* a leaping up, a mounting.
উৎপত্তি, *s.* production, a production.
উৎপন্ন, *a.* produced, arisen from.
উৎপল, *s.* a waterlily, a lotus. [dication.
উৎপাটন, *s.* a rooting up, eradicating, era-
উৎপাটনীয়, উৎপাটয়িতব্য, *a. vide* উৎপাট্য.
উৎপাটিত, *a.* eradicated, rooted up.
উৎপাট্য, *a.* capable of being rooted up, requiring to be eradicated.
উৎপাত, *s.* ruin, outrage, danger, tumult violence, provocation, a portent.
উৎপাতগ্রস্ত, involved in ruin or calamity, persecuted, suffering violence. [ing.
উৎপাদক, *a.* producing, exciting, occasion-
উৎপাদন, a bringing forth, a producing.
উৎপাদনযোগ্য, *a.* producible, productible.
উৎপাদনীয়, উৎপাদয়িতব্য, উৎপাদ্য, *a.* capable of being produced, producible.
উৎপাদিত, *a.* produced, arisen from.
উৎপাদ্যমান, *a.* coming into existence.
উৎপ্রেক্ষা, *s.* a simile, similitude, a resemblance, a metaphor, an illustration.
উৎপ্লব, *s.* a jump, a leap, a bound.
উৎপ্লবন, *s.* a leaping up, a jumping.
উৎপ্লুত, leaped up, bounded, sprung up.
উৎফুল্ল. *a.* expanded, blown, gladdened.
উৎস, *s.* a spring, a fountain, a cascade.
উৎসঙ্গ, *s.* the bosom, the lap, the hips.
উৎসব, *s.* a festival, holiday, festivity.
উৎসবান্বিত, joined with festivities, convi-
উৎসর্গ, *s.* a gift, offering, oblation. [vial.
উৎসর্জন, *s.* the offering of an oblation.
উৎসর্জনীয়, or উৎসৃজ্য, *a.* proper to be offered, fit for an oblation.
উৎসাহ, *s.* zeal, courage, energy, effort, eagerness, perseverance, enterprize.
উৎসাহশীল, *a.* active, zealous, courageous, ardent, eager, sanguine, enterprizing.
উৎসুক, *a.* zealous, eager, energetic; peni-
উৎসৃষ্ট, offered in sacrifice, given. [tent.
উৎসেচন, *s.* a throwing of water upwards.
উদ, *s.* an otter; water.
উদক, *s.* the north quarter.
উদক, *s.* water. [*nically,* dwarf.
উদগ্র, *a.* pointing upwards, high, tall; *iro-*
উদম, *a.* unrestrained, open, candid, free.
উদমাদা, *a.* sincere, unsuspecting, cheerful, docile, simple, thoughtless.
উদয়, *s.* rise, rising into view. [serpent.
উদয়কাল, *s.* time of sun-rising; name of a
উদয়গিরি, *s.* the eastern mountain.
উদর, *s.* belly, bowels;-রস, gastric fluid.
উদরসর্ব্বস্ব, voluptuous, gluttonous: *s.* an
উদরস্থ, *a.* situated in the belly. [epicure.
উদরস্থবলয়, *s.* in *ana.* the abdominal ring.
উদরাধোদেশ, *s.* the abdomen, the pelvis.

উদরাধোদেশপার্শ্বদ্বয়, *s.* two flanks, the inguina.
উদরাময়, *s.* dysentery, diarrhœa.
উদরী, *a.* abdominous, corpulent, dropsical.
উদরে, *ad.* inclusively, inwardly.
উদরোর্দ্ধদেশ, *s.* the epigastric region.
উদার, *a.* munificent, liberal, generous, noble, grand, gentle, frank.
উদারতা, *s.* grandeur, munificence, liberality
উদারসংজ্ঞক, or উদারাখ্য, *a.* ambiguous.
উদাস, *s.* solitude, misanthropy, sadness, anxiety: *a.* stoical, sad, sorrowful.
উদাসী, উদাসচিত্ত, *a.* lonely, retired, cynical, misanthropic, regretting, anxious.
উদাসীন, wandering, homeless: *s.* a mendicant, a recluse, a cynic, a misanthrope.
উদাসীনতা, *s.* mendicity, misanthropy.
উদাহরণ, an example to illustrate a rule.
উদাহরণীয়, উদাহর্ত্তব্য, উদাহার্য্য, *a.* capable of being illustrated by an example.
উদাহৃত, *a.* exemplified, illustrated by an example, famed, named, spoken.
উদিত, *a.* risen into view, come into fashion; spoken, expressed, bound, tied.
উদিতকাল, *s.* the time of sun-rise.
উদীচী, *s.* the north quarter.
উদীচীন, *a.* northern.
উদীচ্য, *s.* the north-west, northern country.
উদুম্‌ধূমা, *a.* rustic, inactive and corpulent.
উদুম্বর, *s.* a species of fig-tree.
উদুখল, উখলী, *s.* a large wooden mortar.
উদ্‌গত, *a.* ascended, risen, vomited.
উদ্‌গতবাষ্প, *s.* effluvia, ascending steam.
উদ্‌গম, *s.* ascension, a going upwards, a mounting up; knowledge, an idea.
উদ্‌গমন, *s.* act of ascending or mounting.
উদ্‌গমনীয়, *a.* capable of being ascended.
উদ্‌গাতা, *s.* a chanter of the Sáma-veda.
উদ্‌গার, *s.* a vomiting, a belching.
উদ্‌গারণ, *s.* the act of vomiting.
উদ্‌গীথ, *s* a portion of the Sáma-veda, the expression of the triliteral name ওঁম্.
উদ্‌গীর্ণ, *a.* vomited, thrown up.
উদ্‌গূর্ণ, *a.* excited, stimulated, stirred up.
উদ্দংশ, *s.* a gadfly, musquito, gnat.
উদ্দন্তুর, *a.* large-toothed, tusked, terrific, tall.
উদ্দাম, *a.* unrestrained, unconfined, free.
উদ্দিষ্ট, *a.* regarded, designed, agreed upon.
উদ্দীপক, *a.* luminous, glowing, splendid.
উদ্দীপন, *s.* a blazing up, a glowing.
উদ্দীপ্ত, *a.* illuminated, made to shine.
উদ্দেশ, *s.* a motive, scope, vestige, trace.
উদ্দেশক, *s.* one who acts from motive.
উদ্দেশ্য, *a.* recognizable, an aim.
উদ্দেষ্টা, *s.* one who does an action with a certain scope or design.
উদ্ধত, *a.* audacious, bold, rude: *s.* a king's wrestler.
উদ্ধরণ, *s.* the act of extricating or delivering a person or thing, deliverance.
উদ্ধরণীয়, উদ্ধর্ত্তব্য, উদ্ধার্য্য, *a.* extricable.
উদ্ধার, *s.* deliverance, rescue; the extracting of matter from a book.
উদ্ধারকর্ত্তা, *s.* a deliverer, a saviour; one who extracts passages from books.
উদ্ধারিত, *a.* drawn forth, extracted.
উদ্ধুত, or উদ্ধৃত, *a.* tossed up, cast up.
উদ্ধৃত, *a.* rescued, extricated, extracted.
উদ্বন্ধন, *s:* the act of hanging a person or animal.
উদ্বন্ধনমৃত, *a.* dead by hanging.
উদ্বমন, *s.* the act of vomiting, a belching.
উদ্বর্ত্ত, *s.* an overplus: *a.* left, remaining.
উদ্বর্ত্তিত, left as a remainder or overplus.
উদ্বাহ, *s.* marriage, matrimony.
উদ্বিগ্ন, *a.* perplexed, uneasy, anxious, excited.
উদ্বিগ্ন-চিত্ত, -মনাঃ, *a.* troubled in mind, anxious.
উদ্বিড়াল, or উদ্র, *s.* an otter.
উদ্বৃত্ত, *a.* left as a surplus or remainder.
উদ্বেগ, *s.* perplexity, anxiety, uneasiness, dejection; the betel-nut.
উদ্বেগী, *a.* perplexed, anxious, perturbed, agitated.
উদ্বোধ, *s.* the recognizing of a thing, recognition, recollection.
উদ্বোধক, *a.* putting in mind: *s.* a remembrancer.
উদ্বোধন, *s.* the act of recognizing a thing.
উদ্ভট, *a.* well known, unwritten yet current, excellent: *s.* a tortoise; the sun.
উদ্ভব, *s.* a coming into existence, birth, the production of a thing.
উদ্ভাব, *s.* a tending upwards, heat, steam, smoke.
উদ্ভিদ, *a.* sprouting, germinating, vegetating.
উদ্ভিদ্বিদ্যা, *s.* science of botany.
উদ্ভিন্ন, *a.* perforated, split, opened.
উদ্ভূত, *a.* brought into existence, produced.
উদ্যত, *a.* prepared to do (an act), about to do (a thing), engaged, ready.

উদ্যম, *s.* readiness for action, exertion, effort, promptness; -দাতা, he who excites.

উদ্যমি, *a.* active, busy, prompt.

উদ্যান, *s.* a garden, a park, a grove.

উদ্যানপাল, *s.* a gardener, a forester.

উদ্যাপন, *s.* the accomplishing of a thing.

উদ্যুক্ত, *a.* engaged in, prepared for action.

উদ্যোগ, *s.* endeavour, effort, exertion, enterprize, attempt, industry, zeal, fervor.

উদ্যোগভঙ্গ, *s.* frustration of an effort.

উদ্যোগী, **উদ্যোগান্বিত**, *a.* active, industrious, zealous, energetic, fervent, prompt.

উদ্রেক, appearance, a beginning, attempt.

উদ্রেকভঙ্গ, *s.* disappointment. [view.

উদ্রেকী, *a.* gaining ground, coming into

উধার, *s.* a loan, a debt.

উন্, *v. n.* to melt, to dissolve.

উনন, **উনান**, *s.* a melting, a dissolving; a furnace, a hearth: *a.* melted, dissolved.

উনার, *pron.* his, that person's.

উনি, *pron.* he, that person.

উনুই, *s.* a fountain, a spring, a cascade.

উন্দধুন্দ, *s.* a commotion, a riot, a tumult, an uproar, anarchy, confusion, a mob.

উন্দুর, or **উন্দুরু**, *s.* a rat, a mouse. [ed.

উন্নত, *a.* increased, elevated, arisen, exalt-

উন্নতনাভি, *a.* having an elevated navel.

উন্নতস্তন, *a.* having elevated nipples.

উন্নতানত, **উন্নতাবনত**, risen and fallen, elevated and depressed. [advancement.

উন্নতি, *s.* increase, exaltation, prosperity,

উন্নয়ন, *s.* the elevating of a thing, deliberation, discussion, reasoning, logic.

উন্নামন, *s.* the elevating of a thing.

উন্মত্ত, *a.* frantic, mad, crazy, intoxicated.

উন্মত্ততা, *s.* madness, intoxication. [son.

উন্মত্তপ্রলাপ, *s.* ravings of a delirious per-

উন্মনাঃ, *a.* thoughtful, agitated, regretting.

উন্মাদ, *s.* madness, mania, folly, extravagance: *a.* mad, extravagant.

উন্মাদক, occasioning mania, intoxicating.

উন্মাদক্ষেত্র, *s.* a maniac, a mad person.

উন্মাদন, *s.* a being mad or intoxicated.

উন্মাদী, *a.* mad, maniacal, intoxicated.

উন্মান, **উন্মিতি**, *s.* a weighing, weight mea-

উন্মানবিষয়ক, *a.* statical. [sure, value.

উন্মীলন, *s.* the opening of the eyes.

উন্মীলিত, *a.* opened (applied to the eyes).

উন্মুখ, *a.* pointing upwards, engaged in an action: *s.* an effort, an exertion.

উন্মূলক, *a.* eradicating: *s.* one who eradi-

উন্মূলন, eradication, rooting up. [cates.

উন্মূলিত, *a.* eradicated, rooted up. [tion.

উন্মেষ, *s.* a discovery, perception, sensa-

উপ, a preposition which usually conveys the idea of vicinity or resemblance.

উপকথা, *s.* tittle-tattle, a story, a tale.

উপকরণ, *s.* any thing superadded, a supplemental oblation, a sauce.

উপকরণীয়, capable of being superadded.

উপকর্ণিকাগ্রন্থি, *s.* the paroitid gland.

উপকার, *s.* assistance, help, benefit, advan-

উপকারক, *a.* assisting, helping. [tage.

উপকারকর্ত্তা *s.* an assistant, a helper.

উপকারজ্ঞ **উপকারমনাঃ**, *a.* grateful.

উপকারজ্ঞতা, -জ্ঞ, *s.* gratitude.

উপকাররত, *a.* beneficent, benevolent.

উপকারী, *a.* helping, assisting.

উপকৃত, *a.* holpen, assisted.

উপকৃতি, *s.* the same as উপকার

উপকোষ, *s.* in *ana.* capsular membrane.

উপক্রম, *s.* commencement, an attempt.

উপক্রান্ত, *a.* commenced, attempted.

উপগত, *a.* approached, attached to.

উপগম, *s.* approach, the approach of the

উপচ, *v.* to overflow, boil over. [sexes.

উপচন **উপচান**, *a.* overflowed, boiled over. *s.* an overflowing, a boiling over.

উপচয়, *s.* plenty, abundance, an excess.

উপচার, *s.* service, a practice, usage, profession, practice of medicine, a bribe.

উপচিত, *a.* collected, increased, improved.

উপজ, *v. n.* to acquire, to accrue, to come into being, to occur. [occurred.

উপজাত, *a.* produced, acquired, accrued,

উপজিহ্বা, *s.* uvula, the epiglottis. [trade.

উপজীবিকা, *s.* livelihood, maintenance, a

উপজীবী, *a.* living upon, dependent on.

উপজীব্য, *a.* producing a livelihood.

উপজ্ঞা, *s.* intuitive knowledge.

উপড়, *v. a.* to root up, to eradicate.

উপড়ন, **উপড়ান**, *s.* act of uprooting, eradication: *a.* eradicated, extirpated.

উপঢৌকন, *s.* a present, a gift, a largess.

উপতন্তু, *s.* a small fibre, a fibrilla. [flicted.

উপতপ্ত, *a* anxious, heated, distressed, af-

উপতাপ, *s.* heat, pain, mental distress, dis-

উপতাপিত, *a.* put in pain, distressed. [ease.

উপতারা, *s.* the iris of the eye.

উপত্যকা, *s.* a valley at the foot of a hill.

উপদংশ, *s.* the venereal disease.

উপদল, *s.* the calyx of a flower.

উপদিষ্ট, *a.* instructed, taught. [parition.

উপদেবতা, *s.* a demi-god, a phantom, an ap-

উপদেশ, *s.* teaching, instruction, advice.

উপদেশক, *a* giving instruction, instructive : *s.* the same with উপদেশকর্ত্তা.

উপদেশকর্ত্তা, *s.* an instructor, a teacher, a preceptor, a preacher, a school-master.

উপদেশনীয়, উপদেশ্য, *a.* worthy of instruction, teachable, capable of instruction.

উপদেশী, *a.* instructive, edifying.

উপদেষ্টা, *s.* the same as উপদেশকর্ত্তা.

উপদ্রব, *s.* calamity, ravage, ruin, outrage, injury, oppression, tyranny, a portent.

উপদ্রবী, *a.* calamitous, tyrannical, oppressive, disastrous, ruinous, portentous.

উপদ্রাক্ষা, *s.* the uvula or epiglottis.

উপদ্রুত, *a.* oppressed, injured, hurt, tyrannized over, ruined, ravaged.

উপদ্বীপ, *s.* an island, a small island.

উপধান, *s.* a bolster, a pillow, a cushion.

উপধি, fear, dread, circumvention; a wheel.

উপনয়ন, *s.* the investiture of a bráhman with the paitá or sacerdotal thread.

উপনাম, *s.* a surname, a nickname; -দা, to give a nickname. [ed and sealed.

উপনিধি, *s.* a deposit of articles undescrib-

উপনিষদ, *s.* the philosophical part of the veda; the doctrine of matter and spirit.

উপনীত, *a.* invested with the paitá; arrived.

উপন্যাস, *s.* a prologue, a tale, a story.

উপন্যাসবক্তা, *s.* one who delivers a prologue of a discourse, a story-teller.

উপপতি, *s.* a paramour, a gallant.

উপপত্তি, *s.* provision, maintenance, favour, assistance, demonstration, production

উপপত্নী, *s.* a concubine, a kept woman.

উপপদ, *s.* words used adverbially instead of nouns in any given case. [plished.

উপপন্ন, *a.* supplied, provided for, accom-

উপপর্শুকা, *s.* in *ana.* the false ribs.

উপপাতক, উপপাপ, *s.* a venial crime.

উপপাতকী, *a.* guilty of venial crimes.

উপপাদন, *s.* the proving or establishing of a proposition by reason or argument.

উপপাদনীয়, উপপাদ্য, *a.* capable of being proved by reason or argument.

উপপাদিত, *a.* proved or established by reason or argument, accomplished.

উপপ্লব, *s.* a portent, portentous phenomenon; Ráhu; an eclipse; an affray.

উপপ্লুত, *a* eclipsed, seen as a portent.

উপবন, *s.* a garden, park, artificial forest.

উপবনরক্ষক, *s.* a forester, a gardener.

উপবাস, *s.* a religious or voluntary fast.

উপবাসী, *a.* fasting : *s.* one who fasts.

উপবিদ্য, *a.* knowing inferior sciences.

উপবিদ্যা, *s.* an inferior science, such as painting, legerdemain, dancing, &c.

উপবিষ্ট, *a.* seated, entered.

উপবীত, *s.* the paitá or sacred thread.

উপবীতী, *a.* wearing a sacred thread.

উপবেশক, *a.* sitting : *s.* one who sits.

উপবেশন, *s.* act of sitting; -কর্ত্তা, one who [sits.

উপভুক্ত, *a.* enjoyed, possessed.

উপভোক্তা, *s* one who enjoys. [cation.

উপভোগ, *s.* luxurious enjoyment, gratifi-

উপভোগফল, *s.* usufruct, enjoying profits.

উপভোগ্য, *a.* proper to be enjoyed.

উপমা, or উপমিতি, *s.* a comparison, simile, a likeness, a resemblance, a metaphor.

উপমাকর্ত্তা. *s.* one who uses similitudes.

উপমাতা, *s.* a wetnurse, a nurse; one who compares one thing with another.

উপমাবিশিষ্ট, *a.* metaphorical, figurative.

উপমিত, or উপমেত, *a.* compared.

উপমেয়, or উপমাতব্য, *a.* comparable.

উপমেয়তা, -ত্ব *s.* comparableness.

উপযম, *s.* marriage, matrimony.

উপযাচক, *a.* requesting, petitioning : *s.* one who requests a thing, a petitioner.

উপযাচিত, *a.* requested, prayed to, or for.

উপযুক্ত, *a.* suitable, fit, proper, becoming.

উপযুক্ততা, *s.* fitness, suitableness.

উপযোগ, *s.* suitableness to a want. food.

উপযোগিতা, *s.* utility, suitability, fitness.

উপযোগী *a.* useful, suitable, fit, proper.

উপর, *s.* the top, height: *ad.* upon, over.
উপরক্ত, *a.* pained, afflicted, seized by a calamity; eclipsed: *s.* in *mytho.* Ráhu.
উপরগস্তি, *s.* a superintendent over watch- [men.
উপরত, *a.* ceased, stopped, desisted.
উপরতস্পৃহ, *a.* indifferent, stoical.
উপরতি, *s.* cessation, a stopping; pleasure.
উপরভাগ, *s.* the upper part. [another.
উপরাউপরি, *ad.* in succession, one upon
উপরাগ, *s.* a full eclipse; a calamity.
উপরাম, *s.* cessation, a stop, breaking off.
উপরি, *ad.* above, upon, upper: *a.* other.
উপরিখরচ, *s.* extra expenses. [person.
উপরিদৃষ্টি, *s.* looking of evil spirits upon a
উপরিদেবতা, *s.* aerial or malignant spirit.
উপরিফাঁপরি, *a.* other, another.
উপরি-বায়, -বাতাস, *s.* a malignant spirit.
উপরিভাগ, *s.* the upper part.
উপরিষ্টাৎ, *ad.* from above, above, up.
উপরিস্থ, উপরিস্থিত, *a.* situated above.
উপরুদ্ধ, *a.* skreened, protected, defended.
উপরে, *ad.* up, upon, upwards.
উপরের, *ad.* upper, the topmost one.
উপরোধ, *s.* partiality, protection, support, defence, favour, kindness. [tection.
উপরোধ্য, *a.* defensible, deserving of pro-
উপর্য্যুপরি, *ad.* one above another, higher [and higher.
উপল, *s.* a stone, a rock.
উপলক্ষ, উপলক্ষণ, *s.* a synecdoche, an inference, an indication, illustration.
উপলক্ষিত, *a.* inferred from, deduced.
উপলক্ষ্য, *a.* inferrible, deducible.
উপলব্ধ, *a.* guessed, understood, received.
উপলব্ধি, perception, conception, surmise, the understanding, gain, acquisition.
উপশম, *s.* an alleviation, relief, abating.
উপশমক, *a.* alleviating, relieving.
উপশম-কারক, -কারী, *a.* alleviating, appeasing: *s.* one who alleviates. [peasing.
উপশান্তি, *s.* alleviation, tranquillity, an ap-
উপশ্রুত, *s.* a commencement, a beginning.
উপসংব্যান, *s.* the upper garment.
উপসংহার, destruction, finishing, an end.
উপসর্গ, *s.* an inseparable preposition; a symptom of a disease; a portent.
উপসর্জ্জন, *a.* secondary, subordinate: *s.* something secondary or subordinate.
উপসর্পক, *a.* approximating: *s.* a favorite.
উপসর্পণ, *s.* an approaching, access.
উপস্ত্রী, *s.* a concubine, a kept woman.
উপস্থ, *s.* generative organs of both sexes, the hip, the arms: *a.* near, proximate.
উপস্থিত, *a.* near, standing near, present, arrived, ready at hand. [speaker.
উপস্থিতবক্তা *s.* eloquent person, a ready
উপস্বত্ব, *s.* profit, gain, income, perquisite, proceeds, the produce of the soil.
উপহত, *a.* smitten, struck, hurt.
উপহসিত, *a.* laughed at, smiled at.
উপহার, *s.* an offering, a present, a gift.
উপহাস, *s.* a smile, ridicule, a jest, joke.
উপহাসক, *s.* a jester, one who ridicules.
উপহাসযোগ্য, *a.* ridiculous, laughable.
উপাখ্যান, *s.* a tale, a story, a narrative.
উপাঙ্গ, *s* subordinate part, a subdivision.
উপাত্ত, *a.* admitted, taken for granted
উপাদান, *s.* abstraction, a cause, a formal
উপাদানকারণ, *s.* proximate cause. [cause.
উপাদেয়, *a.* excellent, admissible.
উপাদেয়তা, *s.* admissibility, excellency.
উপাধান, *s* a cushion, a pillow, a bolster.
উপাধি, *s.* surname, a title, an attribute.
উপাধ্যায়, *s.* an instructor, teacher, tutor.
উপাধ্যায়তা, tutorship, office of a teacher.
উপানৎ, *s.* a shoe, a slipper.
উপান্ত, *a.* near, proximate.
উপায়, *s.* an expedient, a remedy, a stratagem, a method, means, way, resource.
উপায়ক্ষম, *a.* able to contrive means.
উপায়চিন্তক, *a.* meditating expedients.
উপায়চিন্তা, *s.* a contrivance.
উপায়ন, *s.* a present, a gift. [means.
উপায়ী, *a.* making use of expedients, using
উপার্জ্জক, *a.* acquiring, accumulating.
উপার্জ্জন, *s.* an accumulation, an acquisition, gain, earnings, savings. [cures.
উপার্জ্জনকর্ত্তা, *s.* one who acquires or pro-
উপার্জ্জনীয়, *a.* acquirable, fit to be earned
উপার্জ্জিত, acquired, accumulated, laid up.
উপাস, *s.* a religious or voluntary fast.
উপাসক, *a.* attending upon, propitiatory, supplicatory: *s.* a servant, worshipper.
উপাসন, *s.* the act of serving a person, supplication, prayer, intercession.

উপাসনা, *s.* service, worship, attendance, assiduity, supplication, intercession.
উপাসনাকর্ত্তা, *s.* one who sedulously attends on a superior, a petitioner.
উপাসনীয়,উপাস্য, deserving assiduous attention, placable, adorable, worshipful.
উপাসিত, assiduously served or attended.
উপাস্যমান, *a.* receiving sedulous attention.
উপাস্থি, *s.* a cartilage, gristle.
উপাস্থিবৎ, *a.* cartilaginous, gristly.
উপুড়, or উবুড়, *a.* prostrate, reversed.
উপেক্ষক, *a.* disregarding, neglecting.
উপেক্ষণ, *s.* the act of disregarding a thing.
উপেক্ষণীয়, *a.* deserving of disregard.
উপেক্ষা, *s.* neglect, disregard.
উপেক্ষিত, *a.* neglected, contemned, disregarded.
উপেত, *a.* approached, connected with.
উপেন্দ্র, *s.* a name of the god Krishna.
উপোষণ, *s.* a religious fast, a fast.
উপোষিত, *a.* fasted, observed as a fast.
উব, *v. n.* to depart, disappear, vanish, or evaporate, to dissolve away : *a.* erect.
উবর্‌, *v. n.* to be plentiful, to abound, to superabound; to go to stool.
উবরণ, উবরাণ, *s.* a superabounding, a being plentiful : *a.* abundant, plenteful.
উবরা, *v.* to make abundant or plenteous: *s.* abundance : *a.* abundant, plentiful.
উবল, *s.* the swell of a liquid in boiling; search, enquiry, a vestige.
উবলন, উবলান, *s.* a boiling over or swelling up in boiling : *a.* made to boil over.
উবী, উবু, *a.* erect, high, exalted, elevated.
উবুড়, or উপুড়, *a.* prostrate, reversed.
উচ্চ, *a.* erect, high, elevated : *s.* height.
উভয়, *pron.* both, two together.
উভয়তঃ, *ad.* in both respects, mutually, between themselves, on both sides.
উভয়ত্র, *ad.* in both places.
উভয়পার্শ্বস্থ, *a.* situated on both sides.
উভয়পার্শ্বীয়, *a.* belonging to both sides.
উভয়ে, *ad.* mutually, jointly, conjointly.
উভরণ, *s.* the unlading of a ship or boat.
উভরায়, *ad.* with a loud voice.
উম, an *interj.* indicating anger, interrogation, assent, or cordiality; also, *a.* hot.
*উমদ্‌, *s.* a grandee : *a.* rich, opulent.

*উমরা, *s.* a nobleman, an opulent man.
উমরাই, *s.* grandeur, nobility, opulence.
উমা, *s.* a name of Durgá; linseed; alas!
উমান, *s.* the sounding of a depth.
উমাপতি, *s.* Shiva, the husband of Umá.
উমী, *a.* stupid, ignorant, clownish.
*উম্মেদ, *s.* hope, expectation.
উম্মেদবার, *a.* hoping, expecting : *s.* an expectant.
উম্মেদবারী, *s.* condition of an expectant.
উরঃ, *s.* the breast, the bosom, the chest.
উরগ, *a.* crawling, creeping : *s.* a reptile.
উরশ্ছদ, *s.* a breastplate, a coat of mail.
উরানুঘাই, *s.* trick, an evasion, an excuse.
উরু, *a.* great, ample, large : *s.* the thigh.
উরোগামী, *a.* creeping, crawling, going on the belly.
উর্ণনাভ, মাকড়সা, *s.* a spider.
উর্ণা, *s.* wool, fur, felt.
উর্ব্বরা, *a.* arable, fertile, prolific : *s.* a rich soil.
উর্ব্বশী, *s.* name of a celestial courtezan.
উর্ব্বী, *s.* the earth.
উর্ষ, *v. n.* to leak, to admit the rain (as a leaky roof.)
উর্ষণ, *s.* a leaking. উর্ষণিয়া, *a.* leaky.
উল, *v. a.* to set a thing down, to descend.
উলঙ্গ, *a.* naked, unclothed, bare.
উলঙ্গতা, -ত্ব, *s.* nakedness, nudity.
উলঙ্গিনী, *s.* a naked woman.
উলট্‌, *v. n.* to be reversed or turned upside down.
উলট্‌কম্বল, *s.* a plant (Abroma angusta.)
উলট্‌পালট, *s.* a turning, disorder.
উল, উলুখড়, *s.* a kind of thatching grass.
উলুউলু, *s.* a shout uttered by women on joyous occasions : *a.* nearly descended.
উলূক, পেচক, পেঁচা, *s.* an owl (Strix ulula ?)
উলুটুলু, *s.* the motion of the eyes when intoxicated or sleepy.
উল্কা, *s.* a meteor, a torch, a firebrand.
উল্কাধারী, *s.* a link-boy, a torch-bearer.
উল্কাপাত, *s.* the falling of a meteor.
উল্কামুখী, কেখেঁশিয়ালো, খেঁখী, *s.* a fox.
উল্কি, *s.* a sort of tattooing practised by Hindu women on the chin and nose.
উল্টা, *v.* to turn upside down, to reverse.
উল্টা, *a.* upside downwards, wrong, contrary, reversed; -কৃ, to reverse.
উল্টান, উল্টন, *s.* a turning upside down. *a.* turned, topsyturvy, reversed.
উল্টাপাল্টা, *ad.* topsyturvy, confusedly.

উল্টাবুঝ, *s.* a perverted mind, a misinterpreting, a misunderstanding. [fusedly.
উলটপল, *s.* hurly burly, confusion : *ad.* con-
উল্মুখ, *s.* a meteor, a torch, a firebrand.
উল্লঙ্ঘক, transgressing : *s.* a transgressor.
উল্লঙ্ঘন, *s.* a transgressing, a violating.
উল্লঙ্ঘনীয়, উল্লঙ্ঘ্য, *a.* transgressible.
উল্লঙ্ঘা, *s.* a transgression, violation.
উল্লঙ্ঘিত, *a.* transgressed, exceeded, passed
উল্লম্ফ, *s.* a jump, a leap, spring. [over.
উল্লম্ফপ্রোল্লম্ফ, *s.* a leaping and jumping.
উল্লসিত, *a.* elated with joy, glad. [joy.
উল্লসিতব্য, *a.* capable of being elated with
উল্লাস, *s.* joy, delight, exultation, vivacity.
উল্লাসক, *a.* exciting joy, elating the mind.
উল্লাসিত, *a.* elated with joy, glad.
উল্লিখিত, *a.* uttered, enunciated, tossed, dared, painted, delineated, described.
উল্লূক, *s.* an owl; a name of Indra.
উল্লেখ, উল্লেখন, *s.* a specifying, mentioning, enunciating; a digging. [fever.
উল্বণ, *a.* apparent : *s.* a symptom; bilious
উল্বণক্ষেত্র, *s.* the body when considered as the seat of disease.
উল্লস, *v.* to be elated, to be full of joy.
উশনা, *s.* Shukra the regent of Venus.
উশীর, উবীর, *s.* root of a grass, khaskhas.
উষঃকাল, উষস্, *s.* the morning, the dawn.
উষণ, *s.* pepper, black pepper.
উষা, *s.* the dawn of day; the daughter of king Vána and wife of Aniruddha.
উষাকাল, *s.* the dawn of day, the morning.
উষিপিষি, *s.* an uneasy sensation, the fidgets, a restless uneasiness.
উস্ক, উস্কা, *v. a.* to repair a fire, to trim the wick of a lamp, to instigate.
উস্কন, উস্কাণ, *s.* a stirring up, instigating, a repairing (fire), trimming of a wick.
উস্কণি, *s.* instigation, a stirring up.
উষ্ট্র, উট, *s.* a camel, dromedary. [gry.
উষ্ণ, *a.* warm, hot, sultry; passionate, an-
উষ্ণকাল, *s.* summer, hot weather.
উষ্ণতা, -ত্ব, *s.* heat, sultriness, fervour, ardour, passion, warmth.
উষ্ণস্বভাব, উষ্ণত, angry, passionate, hasty.
উষ্ণা, *a.* cleansed by scalding or boiling.
উষ্ণানুষ্ণ, *a.* hot or cold, temperate.
উষ্ণানুষ্ণতা, *s.* temperament, heat or cold.
উষ্ণান্বিত, passionate, furious, angry, fiery.
উষ্ণিক, *s.* a kind of verse consisting of four lines of seven syllables each.
উষ্ণীষ, উষ্ণীক, *s.* a turban; a diadem.
উষ্মা, *s.* heat, ardour, warmth, rage, anger,
উষ্মান্বিত, *a.* hot, angry, fervent. [choler.
উস্, *v.* to serve the pedal with rice, &c.; *interj.* expressive of pain or surprise.
*উস্তাদ, *s.* a teacher, a tutor, a preceptor.
উস্তাদী, *s.* tutorship, preceptorship.
*উস্বাস, *s.* a doubt, hesitation.
উস্বাসী, *a.* hesitating.
উহাড়, *s.* a case, a cover, sheath. [alas!
উহু, উহুউহু, *intj.* expressive of pain; oh!

ঊ, the sixth vowel; having the sound of ú long; in *comp.* it assumes this form (ূ) called dírga-úkár. [oh!
ঊঃ, an *interj.* expressive of sudden pain;
ঊর্ধ, ঊঁধার, *a.* high, elevated : *ad.* on high.
ঊকার, *s.* the letter ঊ, or the symbol (ূ).
ঊখলি, উদূখল, *s.* a large wooden mortar.
ঊঢ়া, *a.* married : *s.* a married woman.
ঊত, *a.* woven : *s.* cloth, stuff.
ঊর্ধা, *a.* high, lofty : *s.* a soaring up. [fewer.
ঊন, *a.* in *comp.* (one) less, short, minus,
ঊনচত্বারিংশ, *a.* the thirty-ninth.
ঊনচত্বারিংশৎ, ঊনচল্লিশ, *a.* thirty-nine.
ঊনত্রিংশ, ঊনত্রিংশত্তম, *a.* twenty-ninth.
ঊনত্রিংশৎ, ঊনত্রিশ, *a.* twenty-nine.
ঊনত্রিশা, *a.* the twenty-ninth.
ঊননই, ঊননব্বই, ঊননবতি, *a.* eighty-nine.
ঊননবতিতম, *a.* the eighty-ninth.
ঊনপঞ্চাশ, ঊনপঞ্চাশৎ, *s.* forty-nine.
ঊনপঞ্চাশত্তম, *a.* the forty-ninth.
ঊনবিংশ, ঊনবিংশতিতম, *a.* nineteenth.
ঊনবিংশতি, ঊনিশ, *a.* nineteen.
ঊনবুকা, *a.* spiritless, destitute of energy.
ঊনষষ্ঠ, ঊনষষ্টিতম, *a.* the fifty-ninth.
ঊনষষ্টি, ঊনবাইট, *a.* fifty-nine.
ঊনসত্তর, ঊনসপ্ততি, *a.* sixty-nine.
ঊনসপ্তত, ঊনসপ্ততিতম, *a.* the sixty-ninth.
ঊনাশী, ঊনাশীতি, *a.* seventy-nine.
ঊনাশীত, ঊনাশীতিতম, *a.* seventy-ninth.
ঊনিশ, ঊনবিংশতি, *a.* nineteen.
ঊনিশা, *a.* the nineteenth.

উই়ী, উই়পোকা, *s.* a white-ant, termite.
উরু, or উরুৎ, *s.* the thigh.
উরুগামী, *a. fem.* crural. [caste.
উরুজ, *a.* born from the thigh: *s.* Vaishya
উরুস্তম্ভ, *s.* a tumour in the thigh.
উর্ণনাভ, মাকড়সা, *s.* a spider.
উর্ণা, *s.* wool, fur, felt.
উর্ণায়ু, *a.* made of wool: *s.* a blanket.
*উর্দ্দু, *a.* belonging to the royal army.
উর্দ্দুজবান, *s.* the court language, or the dialect of the Persian-Hindí.
উর্দ্দুবাজার, *s.* the market of the army.
উর্দ্ধ, উর্দ্ধ, *a.* high, lofty, elevated, up.
উর্দ্ধক, *s.* heartburn, flatulency.
উর্দ্ধগত, *a.* elevated, gone up, ascended.
উর্দ্ধগতি, *s.* an ascent, elevation.
উর্দ্ধগমন, *s.* ascension, upward motion.
উর্দ্ধগামী, উর্দ্ধগ, *a.* ascending, going up.
উর্দ্ধজানু, *a.* long-thighed, thick-kneed.
উর্দ্ধতা, *s.* height, elevation.
উর্দ্ধদৃষ্টি, *s.* the act of looking upward.
উর্দ্ধবাহু, *s.* a devotee with up-lifted arm.
উর্দ্ধরেতাঃ, expelling sperm upwards,: *s.* a devotee who observes strict chastity.
উর্দ্ধশ্বাস, *s.* expiration, difficult breathing.
উর্দ্ধস্থ, *a.* superior, above, upper.
উর্দ্ধস্থিত, situated above, superior, upper.
উর্দ্ধাংশ, *s.* in *ana.* the fundus uteri.
উর্ম্মি, *s.* a wave, a billow, a whim.
উর্ম্মিমৎ, *a.* undulated, wavy, plicated.
উর্ম্মিমত্তা, *s.* undulation, waviness.
উষর, *a.* saline, salt: *s.* saline earth.
উষা, *s.* the morning twilight, the dawn.
উহা, উহাপোহা, *s.* investigation, reasoning, the supplying of an ellipsis.
উহ্য, requiring to be supplied, elliptical.

ঋ, the seventh vowel; it has the sound of ri in rill. In *comp.* it assumes this form (ৃ) called kri-phalá.
ঋক্, *s.* the name of a veda; a bear.
ঋকার, *s.* the letter ঋ or its symbol (ৃ).
ঋক্ষ, *s.* a bear; the constellation Ursa
ঋগ্বেদ, *s.* one of the four vedas. [minor.
ঋগ্বেদী *a.* professing the Rig-veda.
ঋচ, *s.* a hymn to any god, a form of praise, any sentence in the Rig-veda.
ঋজু, *a.* straight, sincere, honest. [honesty.
ঋজুতা, *s.* straightness, rectitude, sincerity,
ঋজুস্বভাব, *a.* honest, sincere, upright.
ঋণ, *s.* a loan, a debt; in *alge.* minus.
ঋণগ্রস্ত, *a.* involved in debt, indebted.
ঋণগ্রহণ, *s.* the borrowing of money.
ঋণী, *a.* indebted: *s.* a debtor. [flux.
ঋতু, *s.* a season; the menses, menstrual
ঋতুমতী, menstruous, having the menses.
ঋতুরক্ষা, *s.* the commerce of the sexes on the 4th day after the menses appear.
ঋতুরাজ, *s.* the spring, season of spring.
ঋতে, *ad.* except, besides.
ঋত্বিক্, ঋত্বিজ, *s.* a sacrificial or family priest. These are three, viz. the আচার্য্য, the পুরোহিত, the ঋত্বিজ্ or ঋত্বিক্.
ঋদ্ধি, *s.* increase, riches, store, wealth, opulence, prosperity. [of Jaina saints.
ঋষভ, *a.* excellent, great: *s.* a bull; a chief
ঋষি, *s.* a sage; -গণ a body of sages.
ঋষিকুল, *s.* the race or family of a sage.
ঋষ্টি, *s.* a calamity, evil omen; a sword.
ঋষ্যমুখ, *s.* in *myth,* a mountain famed for having been the residence of the monkey king Sugríva, the ally of Ráma.
ঋষ্যশৃঙ্গ, *s.* name of a famous sage who had the horns of a deer on his head.

ৠ, eighth vowel: rarely used; in *comp.* it is expressed by this mark (ৄ).
ৠকার, *s.* the letter ৠ, or that character which expresses the sound of rí.

ঌ, the ninth vowel. It is seldom used.
ঌকার, *s.* the letter ঌ, or the character which expresses the sound of li.

ৡ, tenth vowel; it is scarcely ever used.
ৡকার, *s.* the letter ৡ, or the character which expresses the sound of lí.

এ, the eleventh vowel; it has the sound of e in there. In *comp.* it is expressed by this symbol (ে) called ekár: *pron.* this.
এঅবধি, or এই অবধি, *ad.* henceforth.
এই, *pron.* this, very, even this.
এইক্ষণে, *ad* now, immediately, instantly.

এইকারণ, *con.* hence, for this reason, where-
এই-জন্যে-নিমিত্তে, *con.* for this cause. [fore.
এইধারা, এইডাঁড়া, *s.* this method, custom,
এইপ্রকার, *ad.* thus, such. [or habit.
এইবার, *ad.* this time, now.
এইমত, or এইরূপ, *ad.* thus, this way.
এইমাত্র, *ad.* just now, just this moment.
এইহেতুক, for this, wherefore, insomuch.
এঁষে, or এঁবেষা, *s.* an ulcer in the mouth or between the hoofs of cattle.
এঁবেবলি, *s.* the name of a plant.
এক, *a.* one; also, *article*, a, an.
একআড়া, *a.* being of the same size.
একআদ, *a.* half, the half of one.
একই, *pron.* the same, sole, identical, the
একইশ, *a.* twenty-one. [self-same.
একএক, *ad.* severally, each, one by one,
একক, *a.* one, single alone. [every one.
এককড়া, *s.* a single cauri. [word.
এককথা, *a.* consistent; coherent: *s.* one
এক-কর্ণিকা, *a.* monogynous; -কেশর, monandrous; -গর্ভ, unilocular.
এককর্ম্মা, doing the same work, engaged in the same profession: *s.* a competitor.
এককালীন, *a.* coeval, simultaneous.
এককালে, *ad.* at the same time, at once.
এককুড়ি, *a.* twenty, a corge.
একখান, একখানি, *a.* one, one piece.
একগাঁইয়া, belonging to the same village.
একগাছ, *a.* single (as cord, hair, &c.)
একগাড়, *ad.* in the same condition.
একগুঁয়া, *a.* self-willed, obstinate, headstrong, perverse.
একঘরিয়া, *a.* unsocial, recluse, secluded.
একঘাইয়া, unremitting, continual (fever).
একচক্ষুয়া, *a.* one-eyed, having one eye.
একচত্বারিংশ, *a.* the forty-first.
একচত্বারিংশৎ, একচল্লিশ, *a.* forty-one.
একচর, *a.* solitary: *s.* a rhinoceros.
একচালা, *a.* of one thatched roof: *s.* a shed,
একচিত্ত, *a.* unanimous, attentive. [a hovel.
একচেটিয়া, monopolized: *s.* a monopolist.
একচেটিয়াব্যবসায়, *s.* a monopoly.
একচেটিয়াব্যবসায়ী, *s.* a monopolist.
একচেষ্ট, *a.* having the same object.
একচ্ছায়াশ্রিত, *a.* placed under equal obligation: *s.* a joint bondsman.

একছুটিয়া, *a.* having a single garment on.
একজন, *s.* a person, an individual.
একজাই, *ad.* repeatedly, frequently, incessantly: *s.* a list, inventory.
একটা, *a.* one, an entire one.
একটানা, *s.* a single line: *a.* extended: *ad.* in a right line; running in one stream.
একটী, *a.* one, merely one, only one.
একটু, একটুক, or একটুকি, *a.* a little, small, some, very small: *s.* a morsel.
একটুখানি, *s.* a morsel, a small piece, a bit.
একডালিয়া, *a.* having a single branch: *s.* (*fig.*) the male organ of generation.
একডৌল, *a.* uniform, of one make.
একঢল, *ad.* together, in one body.
একঢাল, having a regular slant, slanting.
একতন্ত্বী, *a.* having the same object, rival: *s.* a rival, a competitor.
একতন্ত্রী, *a.* having one string; subject to
একতম, *a.* one of the many. [one lord.
একতর, *a.* either, one of the two: *ad.* alike.
একতরফ, *a.* on the same side. [paper.)
একতা, *s.* oneness, sameness; a sheet (of
একতালা, *a.* having only one floor or story: *s.* a single lock. [samum.
একতিল, *a.* very little, or as a grain of se-
একতীর, *ad.* as far as an arrow shot. [ther.
একত্র, *ad.* in one place, collectedly, toge-
একত্রিংশ, একত্রিশা, *a.* the thirty-first.
একত্রিংশৎ, একত্রিশ, *a.* thirty-one.
একত্ব, *s.* oneness, sameness, identity.
একদন্ত, *s.* an appellation of Ganesha.
একদা, *ad.* once, at once, at one time.
একদিক্, *a.* apart, aside, on one side.
একদেশ, *s.* a particular part of any thing, a province, the same country.
একদেশস্থ, একদেশ, একদেশীয়, *a.* belonging to the same country or place.
একধর্ম্ম, *s.* the same religion, office, or rule of duty; also, *a. vide* একধর্ম্মী.
একধর্ম্মী, *a.* professing the same religion, observing the same duties, analogous.
একধা, *a.* single, simple, one kind only.
একধান, *a.* very little, as a grain of rice.
একনলী, *a.* running in the same channel, having a single barrel. [namesake.
একনামা, *a.* having the same name: *s.* a

একপ, একপো, *s.* quarter sera, a 4th part.
একপঞ্চাশ, একপঞ্চাশত্তম, *a.* the fifty-first.
একপঞ্চাশৎ, একান্ন, *a.* fifty-one. [leaves.
একপত্র, *s.* a single leaf : *a.* having simple
একপদী, *a.* having one foot or line, holding the same office or employment.
একপরাগক, *a.* monandrous. [mous.
একপরামর্শ, *s.* the same opinion : *a.* unani-
একপরামর্শক, একপরামর্শী, *a.* agreeing in the same opinion, unanimous.
একপাটা, *s.* a covering sheet made with a single breadth of the cloth.
একপান, *s.* a dose or draught.
একপাশ, একপাশীয়া, *a.* having one side ; aslant : *ad.* on one side. [a lock.)
একপেঁচিয়া, *a.* opening at one turning (as
একপেট, *a.* united in the same plan of collusion or deception.
একপ্রকার, *a.* uniform, of one sort. [lord.
একপ্রভুক, *a.* monarchical, subject to one
একপ্রভুত্ব, *s.* a monarchy. [time.
*একবক্ত, *a.* simultaneous, coeval, at one
একবগল, *ad.* on one side.
একবচন, *s.* in *gram.* the singular number.
একবয়সীয়া, *a.* of the same age. [timent.
একবাক্য, *a.* unanimous : *s.* the same sen-
একবাক্যতা, *s.* agreement, unanimity.
একবাগিয়া, *a.* tenacious, dogmatical, pertinacious, obstinate : *ad.* on one side.
একবাগে, *ad.* on one side, in one part.
একবার, একবারগী, *ad.* once, one time,
*একবাল, *s.* a total sum. [suddenly.
একবিংশ, একবিংশতিতম, *a.* the twenty-
একবিংশতি, একুশ, *a.* twenty-one. [first.
একবিন্দু, *s.* a single drop, a little, a drop.
একবিশ, *a.* twenty, a corge. [rival.
একবিষয়ী, *a.* having the same object : *s.* a
একব্যবসায়ী, *a.* following the same trade.
একভক্ত, *a.* eating once in 24 hours.
একভক্তব্রত, *s.* a vow of eating once in 24
একভাব, *a.* intimate, equal. [hours.
একমনাঃ, *a.* unanimous, of one accord.
একমন্ত্রণা, *s.* the same opinion or design.
একমাটিয়া, *a.* once plastered over with earth (applied to Hindu idols.)
একযুক্তি, *s.* the same judgment or opinion : *a.* of the same design or opinion.

একযুটি, *a.* of the same age or size, equal.
একযোট, *a.* of the same clan : *s.* one connected by the same common tie. [ther.
একযোনি, *a.* uterine, born of the same mo-
একরত্তি, *s* a grain, a very small quantity.
একরূপ, *a.* alike, similar, same, resembling.
একরোখা, *a.* obstinate ; one-edged.
একলা, একল, *a.* alone, solitary, single.
একলাই, *a. idem* : *s. vide* একপাটা.
একলাদুকলা, *ad.* one or two together.
একশাড়িয়া, *a.* lonely, recluse, unsocial.
একশিরা, *s.* swelled testicles, a disease.
একশেষ, *a.* having same issue or termina-
একষট্টি, একষষ্টি, *a.* sixty-one. [tion.
একষষ্ট, একষষ্টিতম, *a.* the sixty-first.
একসঙ্গী, *a.* united, collected, keeping company together, compact ; accomplice.
একসত্তর, একাত্তর, *a.* seventy-one.
একসমান, *a.* uniform, level, even, smooth.
একস্বামিক, *a.* having the same master or
একহায়নী, *s.* a heifer one year old. [lord.
একহারা, *a.* single, not double.
একা, *a.* alone, solitary. [same form.
একাকার, *a.* alike, uniform, having the
একাকিনী, *a. fem.* alone, solitary, single.
একাকী, *a.* alone, solitary, single.
একাকৃতি, *a.* having same shape or form, si-
একাগ্র, *a.* devoted to one pursuit. [milar.
একাগ্রতা, *s.* a pursuit of one sole object.
একাতপত্রা, *a.* governing the whole world.
একাত্মতা, *s.* the being of one only spirit.
একাত্মবাদ, *s.* the sentiment or doctrine that there is one only spirit.
একাত্মবাদী, *a.* asserting or maintaining the doctrine of one only spirit.
একাদশ, এগার, *a.* eleven.
একাদশকর্ণিকা, *a.* enneagynous.
একাদশকেশর, *a.* enneandrous.
একাদশধা, *ad.* of eleven sorts or kinds.
একাদশবিধ, *a.* consisting of eleven sorts, or, of eleven kinds. [eleven terms.
একাদশরাশিকা, *s.* the rule of proportion of
একাদশাস্র, *s.* a polygon with eleven angles.
একাদশী, *a.* the eleventh (lunar day.)
একাদিক্রম, *a.* successive, uninterrupted.
একাদিক্রমে, *ad.* successively, regularly.
একাদোকা, *ad.* merely one or two.

একাধার, *a.* having the same receptacle.
একাধিকরণ, *a.* having the same relation, being in same place, or predicament: *s.* the same place or predicament.
একাধিপতি, *s.* a sovereign, a monarch.
একাধিপত্য, *s.* a monarchy.
একানই, একানব্বই, *a.* ninety-one.
একানিয়া, *a.* only, single, solitary.
একান্ত, or একান্তি, *a.* effectual, leading to one result, excessive, private. [day.
একান্তরা, *a.* eating one meal every other
একান্ন, *s.* the same food: *a.* messing together; fifty-one. [mate.
একান্নভুক্‌, *a.* messing together: *s.* a mess-
একাবয়ব, *a.* made of the same members, similar, like, resembling, uniform.
একাভিলাষী, *a.* pursuing the same object,
একায়ত্ত, *a.* subject to one only. [rival.
একার, *s.* the vowel এ, or the symbol (ে).
একার্ণব, *s.* a mixed mob or multitude; a general inundation, a deluge.
একার্থ, *a.* having same meaning, intent,
একাশী, *a.* eighty-one. [or scope.
একাশীয়া, *a.* inclining to one side, aslant.
একাহ, a single day: *a.* ephemeral, lasting
একাহার, *s.* a single meal. [one day.
একাহারী, *a.* eating once in twenty-four hours; living on the same food. [cal.
একি, *a.* alike, similar, same, equal, identi-
*একিদা, *s.* faith, belief, trust, confidence.
*একীন, *a.* true, certain, exact, sure.
একুড়্যা, *a.* solitary, unsocial; odd, single.
একুড়্যাসওদা, *s.* a monopoly.
একুন, *s.* a sum, a total.
একুনে, *ad.* in the whole, altogether.
একুশ, *a.* twenty-one. একুশীয়া, *a.* twenty-
একেএকে, *ad.* one by one. [first.
একেলা, *a.* alone, single, solitary. [alone.
একেশ্বর, *a.* alone, depending on one's self
একোদ্দিষ্ট, *a.* performed with the same
একোপম, *a.* similar, resembling. [view.
*একরার, *s.* a promise, an agreement, an assurance, an attestation.
একরারনামা, *s.* a written agreement, a promissory note, an indenture, a bond.
এক্ষণে, *ad.* now, instantly, at this moment.
এখন, এখনি, *ad.* now, immediately.
এখনতক, এখনপর্য্যন্ত, *ad.* still, till now.
এখনহইতে, *ad.* hence, henceforward.
এখনাবধি, *ad.* hence, from this time.
এখান, *s.* this place; this, this piece.
এখানকার, *a.* belonging to this place.
এখানহইতে, *ad.* from this place.
এখানে, *ad.* here, in this place.
এখ্‌তিয়ার, এখ্‌তিয়ারী, *s.* authority, power will, choice, election, control: *a.* subject to one's will or control.
*এগানা, *a.* single, sole, singular, agreed, unanimous: *s.* kindred, relation.
এগার, একাদশ, *a.* eleven.
এগারক্রি, *a.* the eleventh.
এজন্যে, *ad.* hence, wherefore, therefore.
এটে, *s.* thick root of the plantain tree.
এড়্‌ or এড়িয়া-দা, *v.* to cast (a net), to release, relinquish, loosen, unloose.
এড়, *a.* deaf. এড়মূক, *a.* deaf and dumb.
এড়ক, *s.* a ram, a wild goat. [releasing.
এড়ন, *s.* casting a net, escaping, flying off,
এড়া, *a.* left, rejected, liberated.
এড়াণ্ডন, *s.* act of escaping or fleeing.
এড়াকানি, *s.* the turning a deaf ear.
এড়াটিয়া, *a.* filthy, loathsome, abominable.
এড়ান, *s.* act of relinquishing, a setting at liberty: *a.* liberated, relinquished.
এড়ানি, *s.* relinquishment, rejection.
এণ, *s.* a deer, an antelope.
এণ্টা, এণ্টাল, *s.* a play-ball of lac, metal,
এণ্ডা, অণ্ড, ডিম্ব, *s.* an egg. [bone, &c.
এত, *pron.* so much, so long, so many, so.
এতকাল, *ad.* so long time.
এতক্ষণ, *ad.* all this while.
এতগুলি, এতগুলিন, *ad.* so much. [parts.
এতচ্চতুষ্টয়াত্মক, *a.* consisting of these four
এতজ্জন্য, *ad.* for this reason, from this
এতৎ, এতদ্‌, *pron.* in *comp.* this. [cause.
এতৎকাল, *s.* this time.
এতৎকালীন, *a.* modern, belonging to this
এতৎকালে, *ad.* now, at this time. [time.
এতত্তুল্য, *a.* equal to this, like this, similar.
এতদনন্তর, *ad.* afterwards, after this.
এতদন্তর, *ad.* besides this, after this.
এতদবধি, *ad.* so far, from this, to this.
এতদর্থ, *s.* this meaning or scope.
এতদর্থে, *ad.* for this, for this motive.

এতদা, এতদানীং, *ad.* now, at this time.
এতদুপরি, *ad.* hereupon, upon this, upon [this person.
এতদ্দূর, *ad.* so far, very far.
এতদ্দেশ, *s.* this place, country or province.
এতদ্দেশস্থ, *a.* situated in this country.
এতদ্দেশী, *a.* belonging to this country.
এতদ্দেশীয়, *a.* *idem.* [this.
এতদ্ভিন্ন, *a.* distinct from this: *ad.* beside
এতন্মধ্য, *s.* the midst or the inside of this.
এতন্মধ্যে, *ad.* during this, in the meantime, in the interim, in the midst of this.
এতন্মাত্র, *ad.* merely this, only this.
এতবার, *ad.* often, so many times.
এতর্হি, *ad.* now, at present, thus.
এতাদৃক, এতাদৃশ, similar, like, resembling this, such, like this: *ad.* thus.
এতাবৎ, *ad.* thus much, thus far, so much.
এতাবতা, *ad.* thus, by this means, by this.
এতাবন্মাত্র, *a.* merely this, simply this.
এতাবান্, *a.* thus, similar.
এতেক, *ad.* so many, so much, so long.
*এত্তেলা, *s.* news; also, *vide* ইতলা.
এত্তেলানামা, *s.* a news-paper, a notice.
*এৎনা, *ad.* so much, thus much. [day.
*এৎবার, *s.* trust, confidence, faith; Sun-
এৎবারী trusty, faithful; born on Etwár.
*এৎমাম, *s.* a farm of lands or a district.
এৎমামদার, *s.* the farmer of a district.
এথা, *ad.* here, in this place.
এদিক, *ad.* this way, in this direction.
এদিকওদিক, *ad.* this way and that way.
এদিকস্থ, *a.* situated in this direction.
এদিগ্, *s.* this side, this point or direction.
এদিগে, *ad.* this way, in this direction.
এদিগেওদিগে, *ad.* on this side and on that.
এধার, *s.* this border or edge, this side.
এধারওধার, *ad.* this way and that, here [and there.
এধারে, *ad.* on this side.
এনিমিত্তক, *a.* arising from this cause: *ad.* from this cause, hence, wherefore.
এনিমিত্তে, *ad.* for this cause, wherefore.
এপর্য্যন্ত, *ad.* thus far, hitherto. [side.
এপাশ, এপার্শ্ব, *s.* this side: *ad.* on this
এপাশওপাশ, *ad.* on this and that side,
এপাশে, *ad.* on this side. [here and there.
এপ্রকার *s.* this sort: *a.* thus, such.
এপ্রকারে, *ad.* thus, in this manner.

এপ্রযুক্ত, *ad.* therefore, wherefore, on this account, inasmuch, hence, hereupon.
এফোড়ওফোড়, *ad.* through and through.
এব, an emphatic particle: even, indeed.
এবং, *conj.* and, also, likewise, moreover.
*এবজ, *s.* a substitute, change, exchange.
এবজী, *ad.* instead of, in lieu of.
এবম্প্রকার, *a.* such, such like, of this sort.
এবম্বিধ, *ad.* this sort, such.
এবম্ভূত, *a.* such, the like kind.
এবার, *ad.* this time, this once.
*এবারৎ, *s.* a reading, the text of a work.
এবে, *a.* now, at this time.
*এবন, *s.* a son, a male offspring.
এমত, *a.* thus, in this manner.
এমতে, *ad.* thus, in this manner.
এমন, এমনি, *a.* thus, so, like this.
এমনে, *ad.* thus, this way, this side.
*এমান, এমানদার, *vide* ইমান, &c. [room.
*এমারৎ, *s.* a building, a house, an upper-
এমারতী, *a.* belonging to a building.
এমুড়া, *s.* this end, this extremity.
এমুড়াওমুড়া, *ad.* from this end to that.
এরণ্ড, *s.* the castor-oil tree.
*এরাক, *s.* the province of Irák.
এরাকী, *a.* belonging to Irák, of Irák.
এরূপ, *a.* thus: *s.* this form.
এরূপে, *ad.* thus, in this manner.
*এলবাস, *s.* clothes, garments.
এলা, *s.* large cardamom; also the plant.
এলাইচ, *s.* cardamoms.
*এলাকা, *s.* union, connection. [ther.
এলাকাদার, *s.* one connected with ano-
এলাচী, *s.* cardamoms.
এলাচীকড়ি, *s.* a species of spotted cauri.
এলাচীদানা, *s.* a kind of comfit.
*এলাজ, *s.* a medicine, a remedy.
*এলাহি, *a.* relating to God, providential.
এলাহিয়ত, *s.* divinity, godhead. [fused.
এলুয়া, *a.* unconnected, loose, random, con-
এলুয়াকথা, or এলোকথা, *s.* random talk.
এলুয়া -থেলুয়া, -মেলুয়া, *a.* confused, scattered, loose: *ad.* confusedly, pellmell.
এষ, *pron.* this, not that.
এস্থানে, *ad.* here, in this place.
এহেতুক, *a.* caused by or arising from this: *ad.* on this account, from this, hence.

ঐ, the twelfth vowel; in *comp.* it is expressed by this mark (ৈ) called ai-kár: *pron.* that: *ad.* yon, yonder. [larity.
ঐকমত্য, *s.* an agreement, sameness, simi-
ঐকাগ্র্য, *s.* consistency, perseverance.
ঐকান্তিক, *a.* complete, entire, exclusive.
ঐকান্তিভাব, *s.* completeness, entireness.
ঐকার, *s.* the letter ঐ, or the symbol (ৈ).
ঐকাহিক, *a.* tertian: *s.* a tertian. [gate.
ঐক্য, *s.* unity, amity, oneness, an aggre-
ঐচ্ছিক, *a.* voluntary, wilful.
ঐতরেয়োপনিষদ্, *s.* one of the Upanishads or philosophical part of the veda.
ঐতিহ্য, *s.* traditional knowledge.
ঐন্দ্রজালিক, *a.* magical, juggling.
ঐন্দ্রিয়ক, *a.* relating to the organs of perception, or action, evident to the senses.
ঐমত, *a.* so such: *ad.* in that manner, thus.
*ঐরান, *s.* a forest, a wilderness.
ঐরাবৎ, *s.* name of Indra's elephant; a fabled hydra: *a.* large, very large, huge.
ঐরি, *s.* enemy, adversary. ঐরিতা, enmity.
ঐশ্বর, ঐশ্বরী, *a.* divine, relating to God.
ঐশ্বর্য্য, *s.* grandeur, glory, pomp, wealth, greatness, majesty, state.
ঐশ্বর্য্যবান, ঐশ্বর্য্যযুক্ত, *a.* grand, glorious, majestic, stately, pompous, wealthy.
ঐশ্বর্য্যশালী, *a.* ambitious, aspiring, stately.
ঐশ্বর্য্যান্বিত, *a.* grand, glorious, majestic.
ঐস্থানে, *ad.* there, yon, yonder, thither.
ঐহিক, *a.* pertaining to this world.
ঐহিকদর্শী, *a.* worldly-minded.
ঐহিকলোক, *s.* a worldly-minded person.

ও, the 13th vowel; in *comp.* its substitute is (ো) called o-kár: a *voc. par.* *pron.* he, that: *conj.* and, too, also.
ওআক, *s.* the night raven; effort for vo-
ওআকবক, *s.* the night raven. [miting.
ওআড়, *s.* a case, a pillow-case, a sheath.
ওআদা, *s.* a promise, a promised time.
*ওএরান, *s.* wilderness, forest. [trinity.
ওঁ, the sacred syllable denoting the Hindu
ওঁক, *s.* the bellowing of a bull.
ওঁচলা, *s.* sweepings, dirt, refuse, trash.
ওঁচান, *s.* shuffling and tying up straw for thatching; a raising the hand to strike.
ওঁচা, *a.* refuse, rejected; low, mean, vile.
ওক, *s.* a house, a place, a haunt.
ওকড়া, *s.* the name of three plants.
*ওকর, *s.* excellence, superiority, honor.
ওকার, *s.* the letter ও, or the mark (ো).
*ওকালৎ, or ওকালতী, *s.* attorneyship.
ওকালৎনামা, *s.* a power of attorney.
ওখান, *s.* that place, that piece.
ওখানে, *ad.* there. in that place. [vomited.
ওগরা, *s.* rice-conjee; act of vomiting: *a.*
*ওগৈরহ, *s.* and the like, etcetera. [dress.
ওগো, a *voc. par.* used in respectful ad-
ওঘ, *s.* a multitude; velocity of a stream.
ওঙ্কার, ওম্, *s.* mystic syllable ওঁ which see.
*ওজ্র, *s.* excuse, a pretence. [three, etc.
ওজঃসংজ্ঞক, *a.* odd number; as, one, five,
*ওজন, *s.* weight, measure; দার a weigh-
*ওজুর, *s.* an excuse, a pretence. [man.
ওজস্, *s.* life, the vitality, light, manifestation, strength: *a.* uneven, unequal.
ওজোগুণ, *s.* the quality of vitality or dis-
ওঝা, *s.* snake-catcher, an exorcist. [play.
ওঝালি, *s.* the profession of an exorcist.
ওটবন্দী, *s.* a regulation of the rent to be paid for cultivating waste land.
ওটার, *s.* a seam, a sewing, a girth.
ওঠন, ওঠা, *s.* a rising up, an ascending.
ওঠান, *s.* the act of raising up.
ওড়যোড়, *s.* a wrapping one's self up.
ওড়ন, *s.* a flying, the act of flying.
ওড়ফুল, *s.* a shrub and its flower.
ওড়ষা, *a.* foreign, ignorant of the lan-
ওড়া, *s.* flight, the act of flying. [guage.
ওড়ান, *s.* a causing to fly, a squandering.
ওৎ, *s.* an ambush, ambuscade, a screen.
*ওতন, *s.* house, a dwelling, residence.
ওতু, *s.* a cat; প্লুত, *ad.* by fits and starts.
ওতে, ওতেঘাতে, *ad.* concealedly, privately.
ওথা, *ad.* there, in that place.
ওদন, *s.* boiled rice, food.
ওদিক, *s.* that way, that point, that side.
ওদিগে, *ad.* on that side, that way, yonder.
ওদেষ্ট, *a.* harsh, cacophonic, unmusical as
ওদো, *s.* damp, moist, wet. [avoice.
ওপার, *s.* the opposite shore, across.
ওম্, *s.* the sacred syllable of the Hindu
*ওমর, *s.* age, the life-time. [trinity.

ওর়, *s.* a boundary, end, limit : *pron.* his.
*ওরক, *s.* the leaf of a book, a sheet of [paper.
*ওরমা, *s.* a stitch, a sewing.
*ওরম্বা, *a.* bold, daring, dauntless, vicious; [foreign.
*ওরেব, *s.* a diagonal.
ওল, *s.* the root of Arum campanulatum.
ওলন্দামটর, *s.* a rouncival pea.
ওলন, *s.* a dismounting, alighting, descending from, a lowering; a plumb line.
ওলা, *v.* to lower, cause to descend : *s.* descent; a sugar-ball; a purging by stool.
ওলাউঠা, *s.* the spasmodic cholera morbus.
ওলান, *s.* a causing to descend, the landing of goods, the launching of a vessel.
ওলো, *inf. voc. par.* used by women when addressing those of their own sex.
ওষ, *s.* dew, frost, cold, snow. [plants.
ওষধি, or ঔষধি, *s.* annual or herbaceous
ওষধীশ, *s.* the moon. [at work.
ওষা, *v.* to serve the pedal with rice when
ওষাণ, *s.* a serving of the pedal with rice.
ওষকা, ওস্কাণ, *vide* উষ্ক, &c.
ওষ্ঠ, *s.* the lip, *properly* the upper lip.
ওষ্ঠাগত, *a.* situated on the lips (as life).
ওষ্ঠাগতপ্রাণ, *s.* the life on the lips (dying).
ওষ্ঠাধর, *s.* the upper and lower lips.
ওষ্ঠ্য, *a.* labial; -বর্ণ, the class of labial letters, viz. উ ঊ প ফ ব ভ ম ব ও ঔ.
ওসার, *a.* wide : *s.* width, breadth.
ওসারকরণ, *s.* a dilating, a making wide.
ওসারল, *a.* broad, wide, of good width.
*ওস্তখদুস্, *s.* a medicinal drug (Stoechas).
ওস্তা, *s.* a hoarding up, amassing.
*ওস্তাদ, *s.* a teacher, a preceptor, a tutor.
ওস্তাদী, *s.* tutorship, teachership; trickery.
ওহানে, *ad.* there, thither, in that place.
ওহে, a *voc. par.* used in prayer, O, oh; also, in addressing one's equals.
ওহো, *intj.* O ho! take care! mind!

ঔ, the 14th vowel; pronounced as ou in out; in *comp.* thus (ৌ) called au-kar.
ঔকার, *s.* the letter ঔ, or the mark (ৌ).
ঔচিত্য, *s.* fitness, suitableness, propriety.
ঔচ্চ, *s.* height, elevation, altitude.
ঔডুম্বর, made of fig-tree wood; coppery : *s.* Yama; copper; a kind of leprosy.

ঔৎকট্য, *s.* importunity, excessiveness, fury, madness, ebriety, rashness. [tion.
ঔৎকর্ষ্য, *s.* excellency, superiority, perfec-
ঔহর, *a.* gross, palpable. [digious.
ঔৎপাতিক, *a.* portentous, outrageous, pro-
ঔৎসর্গিক, *a.* relating to a gift, natural.
ঔৎসুক্য, *s.* zeal, ardour, exertion, anxiety.
ঔদরিক, *a.* gluttonous, voracious, greedy.
ঔদশ্বিত, *s.* diluted buttermilk. [lity.
ঔদার্য্য, *s.* munificence, candour, libera-
ঔদাস্য, *s.* sadness, solitude, misanthropy.
ঔদ্ধত্য, *s.* violence, tyranny, a tumult.
ঔদ্বাহিক, *s.* marriage gift to a woman.
ঔপচারিক, *s.* what is imputed to another.
ঔপনায়িক, *a.* relating to the sacred thread.
ঔপসর্গিক, *a.* symptomatic, portentous.
ঔপম্য, *s.* a comparison, a resemblance.
ঔপাধিক, *a.* belonging to a modification of matter, or to predominating property.
ঔপায়িক, *a.* expedient, right, fit, proper.
*ঔবল, *a.* first, best, chief, superior.
*ঔরৎ, *s.* a woman, a wife. [ful descent.
ঔরস, *a.* lawfully begotten, natural : *s.* law-
ঔরসজাত, *a.* legitimate, lawfully born.
ঔরসসন্তান, *s.* a legitimate child.
ঔরসাভাবে, *ad.* in case of there not being lawful or legitimate offspring. [son.
ঔর্দ্ধদেহিক, funeral, due to a deceased per-
ঔর্ব্ব, *s.* submarine fire. [excessiveness.
ঔল্বণ্য, *a.* excessive : *s.* superabundance,
ঔষধ, ভেষজ, *s.* medicine, drug, a remedy.
ঔষধকর্ত্তা, *s.* medicine-maker, apothecary.
ঔষধবিক্রেতা, *s.* a druggist, an apothecary.
ঔষধসেবন, *s.* the using of medicines.
ঔষধীয়, *a.* medicinal, medical.
ঔষধোপদেশ, *s.* medical advice.
ঔষ্ম, *s.* heat, ardour, fervency.
ঔষ্মানুষ্ম, *s.* temperament, climate.
ঔষ্ট্রক, *s.* a herd of camels.

ক, The first consonant of the Bengáli alphabet. It has the sound of k.
কই, কোথায়, *ad.* where? in what place?
কঈ, *s.* the name of a kind of fish.
কউতর, কবুতর, পায়রা, *s.* a pigeon.
কএক, *pron.* some, a few, several.
*কএদ, *s.* imprisonment, confinement.

কএদখানা, *s.* a prison, a gaol. [soner.
কএদী, *a.* imprisoned, confined: *s.* a pri-
কএরাখানী, *a. fem.* brawling, querulous.
কংস, *s.* white-brass, bell-metal; a famous king; -মাক্ষিক, a particular pyrite.
কংসবণিক, *s.* a brazier, a coppersmith.
কঃ *pron.* who? what? [of age.
কঁটালাবাছুর, *s.* a calf under three months
ককা, *v. a.* to cackle, to groan, to moan.
ককান, ককানি, *s.* a cackling, a groaning, a
ককার, *s.* the letter ক. [moaning.
ককুৎ, *s.* the hump of a bull.
ককুদ্, *s. idem;* a mark or sign of royalty, a mountain-peak, excellency. [region.
ককুভ, *s.* a point of the compass, space, a
কককক, *s.* a giggling, a tittering.
কক্ষ, *s.* the arm-pit, the side, the flank, the end of the lower garment.
কক্ষ, কক্ষ্যা, *s.* a hawser, a rope to fasten an elephant, a woman's girdle, an inclosure of a courtyard, part of a chariot.
কখ, or কখাদি, *s.* the Indian alphabet.
কখন, *ad.* when? at any time, ever.
কখনও, *ad.* never; sometimes.
কখনকখন, *ad.* sometimes, now and then.
কঙ্ক, *s.* a heron; a name of Yudishthira.
কঙ্কট, *s.* a coat of mail, an insignia.
কঙ্কণ, *s.* a bracelet, a small bell.
কঙ্কত, কঙ্কতিকা, চিরণী, *s.* a hair-comb.
কঙ্কত্রোটি, কাঁকিলা, *s.* the name of a fish.
কঙ্কর, *s.* coarse sand, gravel.
কঙ্করোল, *s.* name of a tree, and a plant.
কঙ্কাল, *s.* the skeleton, the loins, waist.
কঙ্গাল, কঙ্গালী, *a.* poor, indigent, needy.
কঙ্গালপনা, *s.* poverty, want, penury, beg-
কচ, *v. n.* to be dislocated. [gary.
কচ, *s.* hair; son of Vrihaspati; a scar, cicatrix, a dried sore; *a.* unsquare.
কচড়া, *s.* a cable, a halter, a tether, rope.
কচনার, *s.* name of a tree and its flower.
কচা, *v. n.* to shoot forth, to bud.
কচা, *s.* a stake or staff, grit; a dislocation.
কচান, *s.* shooting forth, a budding.
কচাল, *s.* a dispute, a wrangling. [babe.
কচি, tender, soft, young; -ছেলিয়া, a brat,
কচিত, *ad.* sometimes; *vide* কদাচিৎ.
কচু, কচাঁ, *s.* the generic name of Arum.

কচুরী, *s.* a kind of fried cake. [rustling.
কচ্‌কচ, *s.* a murmuring, a grumbling, a
কচকচি, কচ্‌ঘচি, *s.* a murmur, contention.
কচ্‌কচিয়া, *s.* the name of a bird.
কচ্চাবচ্চা, *s.* children, little ones.
কচ্ছ, *s.* a shore, low watery place; end of the garment worn round the waist.
কচ্ছপ, *s.* a tortoise, a turtle.
কচ্ছু, *s.* the itch, a scab.
কচট্, *v. a.* to knead, to temper, crush.
কচটান, *s.* act of kneading, a tempering.
কচ্যান, *s.* a budding, a sprouting.
কচ্‌ল, or কচ্‌লা, *v. a.* to rub clothes or anything between the hands in washing it.
কচলন, কচ্‌লান, কচ্‌লানি, *s.* the rubbing of cloth in washing, a scrubbing, rinsing.
*কজ্জিয়া, *s.* a quarrel, a dispute.
কজ্জল, কজ্বল, *s.* lampblack, eye-paint.
কজ্জলী, *s.* Ethiops mineral.
কঞ্চি, *s.* a branch or twig of bambu.
কঞ্চু, *s.* the slough or skin of a snake.
কঞ্চুক, *s. idem;* armour, mail; a bodice.
কঞ্চুকাল, *s.* a variety of cobra de capello.
কঞ্চুলিক, *s.* a woman's bodice. [maker.
কঞ্জর, *s.* Brahma, the sun, belly, a rope-
কট, *v. n.* to fade, wither: *s.* the hip, the hip and loins, an elephant's temples, a mat, a fixed period, a treaty, a bond.
কট, *ad.* suddenly, unexpectedly, hastily.
কটক, *s.* a camp, a circle, bracelet, a ring, ring for drawers, or for an elephant's tusk; a city, a royal metropolis, tableland, brow of a hill; a city in Orissá.
কটকলেজা, *s.* a climbing plant.
কটকী, *s.* the name of a medicinal plant.
কটকীপাড়িয়া, *a.* having coloured border (as cloth); *lit.* Cuttack-bordered.
কটবেল, *s.* the elephant apple.
কটরা, *s.* a copper or brass cup. [cifera.)
কটলবট, *s.* a kind of fig-tree (Ficus lac-
কটলবর্ণ, *s.* the name of a kind of salt.
কটা, *v.* to fade, wither: *a.* faded, flaccid, tawny, sallow, wan: *pron.* how many?
কটাক্ষ, *s.* a glance, an indirect glance, an
কটাক্ষদর্শন, *s. idem.* [ogling look.
কটাচক্ষুয়া, *a.* cat-eyed, yellow-eyed.
কটাৎ, কটাস, *ad.* suddenly, hastily.

কটার়, *s.* a dagger, a poniard, a dirk.
কটাল, *s.* the spring tide : *a.* faded, flaccid.
কটাহ, *s.* a caldron, a boiler, a young buffalo, tortoise shell, the infernal region.
কটি, কটী, *s.* the loins, the waist, the hips.
কটিতট, কটিদেশ, *s.* loins, hips, the waist.
কটিপ্রোথ, *s.* the posteriors, the buttocks.
কটিবন্ধনী, *s.* a girdle, a zone. [quality.
কটিয়া, *a.* hard, disagreeable, of an inferior
কটু, *a.* pungent, acrimonious, hot, harsh, disagreeable, costive : *s.* costiveness.
কটুকথা, কটুবাক্য, *s.* obscenity, scurrility.
কটুকাটব্য, *s.* scurrility, abusive language.
কটুতা, -ত্ব *s.* costiveness; pungency, acri-
কটুতুম্বী, *s.* a kind of bitter gourd. [mony.
কটুবাদী, *a.* abusive, scurrilous, provoking.
কটুরোহিণী, *s.* name of a medicinal plant.
কটূক্তি, *s.* harsh word, obscenity, scurrility.
কটূত্তর, *s.* a severe reply, abusive language.
কটোর, *s.* a cup, a cup of metal.
কটকটানি, *s.* a twinging, throbbing. [frog.
কট্‌কটিয়া, *a.* clattering ; -বেঙ, a species of
কট্‌কিনা, *s.* difficulty, severity, harshness, roughness: *a.* farming at a rack-rent.
কটকিনাদার, *s.* one who acts severely ; one who lets land at a rack-rent.
কট্‌কিনাদারী, *s.* severity, rigidness ; the letting land at a rack-rent.
কটকোবালা, *s.* a conditional bargain or sale which is subject to penalties in case of failure, a deed of sale.
কট্টার, *s.* a dagger, a poniard, a dirk.
কট্‌ফল, *s.* a nut used in medicine.
কঠিন, *a.* hard, solid, rigid, harsh, severe, cruel, morose, inflexible, austere, unfeeling, inhuman, difficult, abstruse.
কঠিন -চিত্ত, -স্বভাব, *a. vide* কঠিনহৃদয়.
কঠিনতা. *s.* hardness, solidity, severity, inflexibility, austerity, rigidity, harshness, relentlessness, difficulty, abstruseness.
কঠিনহৃদয়, কঠিনান্তঃকরণ, *a.* hard-hearted, severe, cruel, inhuman, unfeeling.
কঠোর, কঠোরতা, *vide* কঠিন, &c.
কড়, *s.* a particular kind of bracelet.
কড়ক্‌, *v. n.* to heal, to cicatrize ; কড়কিয়া উঠ, to heal up, to cicatrize.
কড়কচ, *s.* a superior kind of salt.
কড়কা, *v. n. vide* কড়ক্‌ ; also, to bud : *s.* a stalk, a scion, sucker, a cause or original, a descendant, a supporter, an heir.
কড়কান, *s.* the closing or healing of a sore or wound ; the scolding of a person.
কড়ম, *a.* the stalk of a potherb ; cause, original of any thing ; a preserver.
কড়রা, *a.* hard, strong, firm, harsh.
কড়া, *s.* a ring, a ring or handle for drawers, pictures, etc., the link of a chain, an iron or copper boiler, a corn or callosity, a medicinal preparation, a cauṛi, the stirnum or breast-bone when somewhat prominent : *a.* strong, hard, severe.
কড়াই, *s.* pulse, legumes; a fry-pan.
কড়াকড়া, *a.* dried into balls (as boiled rice).
কড়াৎ, *ad.* gratingly, done with effort.
কড়ানিয়া, *s.* the reckoning by cauris.
কড়ার, *s.* any composition or cement which becomes hard or strong ; a promise.
কড়ারকাঠি, *s.* a shell-cutter's instrument.
কড়ি, *s.* a cowry, cauṛi; an earring; a beam.
কড়িক্‌, *v. n.* to begin to heal, to cicatrize
কড়িকাঠ, *s.* a beam, a balk. [as a sore.)
কড়িকুষ্টা, *a.* avaricious, niggardly, venal.
কড়িয়া, *a.* small : *s.* a beam : -আঙ্গুল, little
কড়িয়াল, rich, opulent, wealthy. [finger.
কড়িয়ালী, *s.* the bit of a bridle.
কড়ুবা, *a.* acrid, bitter, pungent, rancid.
কড়্‌কড়ি, *s.* grittiness, roughness, crashing.
কণ, *s.* a particle, atom, hilum or eye of a seed, spark of a gem, a twang.
কণা, *s.* an atom, a spark, a drop ; long-
ক'ণ, the corner of the nails. [pepper.
কণিকা, *s.* a particle, a grain, a drop, an
কণুই, কফোণি, *s.* the elbow. [atom.
কণ্‌কণ্‌, *s.* a throbbing pain. [sounds.
কণকনিয়া, *a.* tinkling, giving out musical
কণ্টক, *s.* a thorn, prickle, horripilation, a foe, enemy, danger, a fish-bone.
কণ্টকভুক্‌, উষ্ট্র, উট, *s.* a camel.
কণ্টকিকীট, *s.* a hairy caterpillar.
কণ্টকিফল, কণ্টাফল, *s.* the jack fruit.
কণ্টকী, *s.* the egg-plant and its fruit.
কণ্টিকারী, *s.* a plant (Solanum jacquini).
কণ্ঠ, *s.* the throat ; ভূষা, -মালা, a necklace.
কণ্ঠস্থ, *a.* placed or sticking in the throat.

কণ্ঠা, *s.* the neck just above the collar-bone.
কণ্ঠাগত, *a.* coming to the throat (as life).
কণ্ঠাস্থি, *s.* the collar-bone, the clavicle.
কণ্ঠিধারী, *a.* wearing a necklace : *s.* the neck.
কণ্ঠিবদল, *s.* marriage of the Vaishnavas.
কণ্ঠী, *a.* guttural : *s.* a necklace.
কণ্ঠ্য, *a.* guttural ; বর্ণ, the class of guttural letters, viz. অ আ এ হ ক খ গ ঘ ঙ
কণ্ড, *a.* guttural, of the throat. [its husk.
কণ্ডন, *s.* the process of cleaning rice from
কণ্ডু, কণ্ডুয়া, *s.* an itching, eruption, the itch.
কণ্ডুয়ন, *s.* the itching of a pimple.
কণ্ডুয়মান, *a.* scratching, itching, itchy.
কণ্ডুয়িত, *a.* scratched, rubbed.
কণ্ডোল, *s.* a basket, a meat-safe ; -বীণা, a mean or vulgar lute.
কৎ, *s.* a nib ; catechu or Japan earth.
কত, কতি, *ad.* how much ? how many ?
কতক, *a.* some, a few, several : nux-vomica.
কতকটা, *a.* some, an uncertain number.
কত -কাল, -ক্ষণ, *ad.* how long ? some time.
কতগুলা, কতগুলি, *ad.* how many ?
কতটা, কতটী, কতটিন, *ad.* how many ?
কতটুক, কতটুকি, *ad.* how much ? so little.
কতদিন, *ad.* how long ? how many days ?
কতবার, *ad.* how often ? many times.
কতরণ, কতরাণ, *s.* the shearing of sheep, a cutting or clipping of cloth, etc.
*কতল, *s.* murder, slaughter, destruction.
*কতা, *s.* a piece of land, a share, a portion.
কতার, *s.* a series, a row, range, file, rank
কতিপয়, *a.* some, a few, several : *ad.* how
কতেক, *a.* few, somewhat. [many ?
কৎকৎ, *s.* a palpitation of the heart.
কৎবেল, *s.* the same with কটবেল.
কথং, *ad.* why ? how ? what ?
কথক, *s.* a speaker ; -তা, office of a speaker.
কথন, *s.* a speaking or uttering ; a word.
কথনীয়, কথয়িতব্য, *vide* কথা.
কথা, *s.* a word, a sentence, a speech, a
কথাচোর, *s.* a plagiary. [story.
কথাপ্রবন্ধ, *s.* a set form of words, a studied speech, a literary composition.
কথাপ্রসঙ্গ, *s.* the introduction of a topic, discourse, a topic of conversation.
কথাবার্তা, *s.* conversation, chitchat; news.
কথায়, *ad.* verbally, orally, in words.
কথায় কথায়, *ad.* in conversation. [rister.
কথাসচিব, *s.* a pleader, a solicitor, a bar-
কথাসঞ্চার, *s.* a fame, a report.
কথিত, *a.* spoken, mentioned, expressed.
কথোপকথন, *s.* conversation, free intercourse, dialogue, conference. [tioned.
কথ্য, *a.* fit to be spoken, proper to be men-
কথ্যমান, *a.* under mention, mentioning.
কথ্যাকথ্য, *a.* fit and unfit to be mentioned.
কদক্ষর, *s.* bad writing, scrawl, bad letters.
কদন্ন, *s.* bad or disagreeable food.
কদম, *s.* a pace, a footstep, foot; *vide* কদম্ব.
কদভ্যাস, *s.* a bad habit, evil practice.
কদমা, *s.* the name of a sweetmeat.
কদম্ব, *s.* a tree (Nauclea cadumba). [tion.
কদম্বক, *s.* a crowd, a multitude, a collec-
কদম্বকুসুম, *s.* the flowers of the Nauclea.
কদম্বকুসুমাকার, *a.* globular. [or thing.
*কদর, *s.* the value or worth of a person
কদরদান *s.* one who knows the value or worth of a person or thing.
কদর্য্য, *a.* base, bad, disagreeable, unpleasant to the touch, depraved, abominable.
কদর্য্যতা, *s.* badness, disagreeableness, de-
কদলী, *s.* plantain and its tree. [pravity.
কদা, *ad.* when ? at what time ?
কদাকার, *a.* ugly, ill-shaped, uncouth.
কদাচ, *ad.* seldom, scarcely ever, at any
কদাচন, *ad.* sometimes, seldom. [time.
কদাচার, *a.* wicked, profligate, abandoned.
কদাচিৎ, *ad.* rarely, scarcely ever, some times, seldom, occasionally. [and then.
কদাপি, *ad.* at some time, sometimes, now
*কদিম, *a.* old, ancient, former, prior : *s.*
কদু, কদুয়া, *s.* a pumpkin. [the East.
কদুক্তি, *s.* abuse, scurrility, bad words.
কদুষ, *a.* lukewarm, hot and cold.
কধী, কধু, *ad.* when ? when, at any time.
কনক, *s.* gold ; the name of several plants.
কনকচম্পক, কনকচাঁপা, *s.* a flower tree.
কনকতেল, *s.* the name of a drug.
কনকধুতুরা, *s.* a species of thorn-apple.
কনকাই -ঘোড়া, -টাট্টু, Kankái horse or po-
কনাৎ, *s.* a tent-fence, an outer tent. [ny.
কনিষ্ঠ, *a.* youngest, least, inferior, junior.
কনিষ্ঠতা, *s.* minority, inferiority.
কনিষ্ঠা, *s.* the little finger.

কনী, *s.* a small pond or pit (for fishing).
কনীয়ান, *a.* younger, inferior, junior.
কনোজ, *s.* the name of a country.
কন্থা, *s.* a devotee's coat of shreds; a well.
কন্দ, *s.* bulbous root, raw or coarse sugar, a kind of sweetmeat. [chasm, a cave.
কন্দর, *s.* a glen, a defile, a deep valley, a
কন্দর্প, *s.* a name of the Indian Cupid.
কন্দল, *s.* reproach, censure, a quarrel, a dispute, contention, war.
কন্দু, *s.* a sauce-pan, a frying-pan.
কন্দুক, *s.* a ball made of flowers.
কন্ধর, *s.* the neck; a cloud.
কন্যা, *s.* the sign Virgo; a daughter, a virgin, a young woman, a bride.
কন্যাকর্ত্তা, *s.* the guardian of a bride, the guardian of an unmarried woman.
কন্যাকাল, *s.* the time of youth or virginity.
কন্যাদান, *s.* the giving of a daughter in
কন্যাভাব, *s.* virginity. [marriage.
কন্যাভাবে, *ad.* as a daughter. [ter.
কন্যাভার, *s.* burden or charge of a daugh-
কন্যাযাত্রী, *s.* guest who attends the bride
কন্যারাশি, *s.* the sign Virgo. [nate.
কন্যারাশীয়, *a.* shame-faced, timid, effemi-
কন্যাসম্প্রদান, *s.* the same as কন্যাদান.
কন্যাসহচরী, *s.* a bride's-maid. [critical.
কপট, *s.* deceit, a trick: *a.* deceitful, hypo-
কপটতপস্বী, *s.* a religious impostor.
কপটতা, *s. vide* কাপট্য. [part.
কপটবেশ, *s.* a feigned character, assumed
কপটবেশধারী, *a.* acting an assumed part.
কপটবেশী, *a. idem*: *s.* a player.
কপটী, deceitful, acting an assumed part.
*কপড়ধুল, *s.* curtain gauze.
কপর্দ্দ, কপর্দ্দক, *s.* the matted hair of Shiva; a small shell called cowry or cauṛi.
কপাট, *s.* a door or window shutter.
কপাটী, *s.* operculum of a univalve shell; দাঁতকপাটী, locked-jaws. [fate.
কপাল, *s.* the forehead; *fig.* destiny, luck,
কপালসন্ধি, *s.* a peace made by two hostile parties on equal terms. [dus.
কপালী, *s.* a lintel; Shiva; a class of Hin-
কপালীয়, *a.* fortunate, lucky. [cabbage.
কপি, *s.* an ape, a monkey; a pulley; a
কপিকল, *s.* a pulley, a block.

কপিত্থ, *s.* the same with কটবেল.
কপিল, *s.* a sage, the founder of Sánkhya philosophy; fire: *a.* tawny, brown.
কপিশাবক, *s.* a cabbage, brocoli.
কপীন, *s.* cloth worn by the poor or devotees to cover their privities, a clout.
কপুচ্ছল, *s.* the right lock, কপুচ্ছিক, the left lock, of hair tied on the crown at the investiture with the sacred thread
কপোত, or কপোতিকা, *s.* a pigeon.
কপোল, *s.* the cheek, the temple.
কপ্‌চা, *v.* to clip, trim a hedge with shears; to begin to talk (as the parrots).
কপ্‌চান, *s.* a clipping, a trimming; first attempt of a bird to imitate human voice.
কপ্‌টা, *v.* to clip, to cut with scissors or
কপ্‌টান, *s.* the act of clipping. [shears.
কপ্নী, *s.* the same as কপীন or কৌপীন.
কফ, *s.* phlegm, a cold or catarrh.
কফঘ্ন, *a.* efficacious to remove a cold.
কফজ, *a.* arising from phlegm or a cold.
*কফন্, *s.* a shroud, a winding-sheet.
*কফিলা, *s.* a caravan, travelling company.
কফী, *a.* ill with a cold, subject to colds.
*কফনি, *s.* a piece of cloth worn on the neck by Musalmán mendicants.
*কব, *ad.* when? what time? [amulet.
কবচ, *s.* defensive armour; an armlet; an
কবচপাঠ, *s.* the text used as a charm.
কবচী, *a.* armed, wearing defensive armour.
*কবজ, *s.* receipt, the hand, the gripe, pos-
কবজী, কবয়ী, *s. vide* কই. [session.
কবন্ধ, *s.* a headless trunk; a demon.
*কবর, *s.* a grave, a tomb; -কন, a grave-digger; -গাহ, -স্থান, a burial ground.
কবরী, *s.* a braid of hair; acidity.
কবল, *s.* a mouthful, a morsel.
*কবলতি, *s.* a receipt, acknowledgment.
কবলিত, *a.* swallowed, eaten, glutted.
*কবা, *s.* a pretence, a deception, a trick.
*কবাইদ, *s.* military exercise.
কবাট, *s.* a door or window shutter.
*কবাব, *a.* roasted: *s.* a roast.
কবাবচিনি, *s.* cubeb, allspice.
কবার, *ad.* how often? how many times?
কবালা, *s.* a bill of sale, a deed of transfer.
কবি, *s.* a poet, a writer of taste; a cabbage.

কবিতা, *s.* a poem, a verse, poetry, versifi-
কবিত্ব, *s.* poetry, poetship. [cation.
কবিরাজ, *s.* a physician, a doctor.
কবীরপন্থী, *s.* a follower of Kabíra.
কবীলা, *s.* a family, a wife. [*fem.* কবুতরী
কবুতর, *s.* a pigeon ; -খানা, a pigeon-house :
*কবূল, *s.* an acknowledgment, dèclaration.
কবূলতি, *s.* a written acknowledgment.
কবে, *ad.* when; when? on what day?
কব্জা, কব্জী, *s.* the wrist ; a hinge.
কব্য, *s.* an oblation to deceased ancestors.
কভী, *ad.* at any time, some time.
কভু, *ad.* any time, even at any time.
কম্, *v.* to be deficient, to decrease, fail.
কম, কমতি, *a.* defective, less, inadequate,
কমক, *s.* a helper, an associate. [deficient.
কমঠ, *s.* a tortoise, a turtle.
কমণ্ডলু, *s.* a devotee's earthen water-pot.
কমন, *a.* lewd, libidinous, desirous; beau-
tiful, desirable : *v.* to be less, to be short.
কমনীয়, *a.* desirable, beautiful, agreeable.
কমনে, *ad.* where? whither? somewhere.
কমর, *s.* the loins, the waist ; -বন্দ, a girdle
for the loins, ; -বন্দী, a girding the loins.
কমল, *s.* waterlily, lotus, an aquatic plant.
কমলা, *s.* a name of Lakshmí ; an orange.
কমলানেবু, কমলানিম্বু, *s.* an orange.
কমলিনী, *s.* an assemblage of waterlilies.
কমা, *v. a.* to lessen, to abate, to diminish.
কমান, *s.* a diminishing, an abatement (in
value or price) ; a cross-bow. [less.
কমী, *s.* abatement, paucity : *a.* wanting,
কমীজ, *s. Port.* a shirt, a shift, chemise.
*কমীনা, *a.* mean, low, base, vile, wicked.
কমীনী, *a. fem. idem : s.* lowness, baseness.
*কম্‌কীমত *a.* cheap, low-priced, of small
কম্‌কুঅৎ, *a.* weak, infirm, feeble. [value.
কম্‌জাত, *a.* base, low, mean, low-bred.
কমজোর, *a.* weak, infirm, debilitated.
কম্‌জোরী, *s.* debility, weakness, infirmity.
কম্‌তী, *s.* a diminution, a defect : *a.* less.
কম্প, কম্পন, *s.* a trembling, a quaking,
agitation, a vibration, tremour. [ing.
কম্পজ্বর, *s.* an ague, a fever with shiver-
কম্পনীয়, *a.* capable of trembling, agitable.
কম্পবান, *a.* trembling, quivering. [ing.
কম্পবায়ু, *s.* flatulency attended by shiver-
কম্পবায়ুগ্রস্ত, *a.* paralytic, palsied.
কম্প্রমান, trembling, quaking, quivering,
palpitating, vibrating, being agitated.
কম্পান্বিত, *a.* quivering, tremulous.
কম্পাস্, *s.* a pair of compasses. [turbed.
কম্পিত, *a.* made to tremble, agitated, dis-
কম্পোক্ত, *a.* unripe, imperfect, immature.
কম্‌বখ্‌ৎ, *a.* wretched, unfortunate.
কম্‌বখ্‌তি, *s.* wretchedness, misfortune.
কম্বল, *s.* the dewlap ; a blanket, woollen rug.
কম্বু, *s.* a shell, conch ; bracelet ; the neck.
কম্বুগ্রীবা, a neck marked like a spiral shell.
কম্বি, *s.* a blanket, a woollen rug.
কম্‌বেশ, *ad.* more or less, nearly, there-
কয়লা, *s.* charcoal, a coal. [abouts.
কয়াল, *s.* a weighman ; his hire, কয়ালী.
কর, *s.* the hand ; revenue, tax ; proboscis ;
করই, *s.* a storehouse, a granary. [a ray.
করকচ, *s.* a kind of black sea-salt.
করকচি *s.* unripe shell of the cocoanut.
করকটিয়া, *a.* stunted (as vegetables).
করকনা, বঙ্ক্ষণ, *s.* the hip. [hailstorm.
করকা, *s.* hail; ascetic's water-pot ; -পাত, a
করকোষ্ঠী, *s.* lines in the palm of the hand.
করগ্রহণ, *s.* the receiving of tribute ; the
receiving a person in marriage.
করগ্রাহক, করগ্রাহী, collecting revenue : *s.*
a collector of revenue or taxes. [cup.
করঙ্ক, *s.* the head, a vessel, cocoanut-shell
করচা, *s.* a written assessment, a levy.
করঞ্জ, করঞ্জা, *s.* the same as করঙা.
করণ, *s.* a doing or making, the agent or
means by which a work is performed.
করণক, *ad.* (used only in *comp.*) by means
of, by the instrumentality of.
করণীয়, *a.* proper to be done, practicable.
করণ্ড, *s.* a wicker-basket ; a bee-hive.
করঙা, *s.* an acid fruit, and its tree.
করতল, *s.* palm of the hand ; subjection.
করতলে, *ad.* in subjection, under controul.
করতাল, ঝাঁঝ, *s.* a cymbal. [hands.
করতালী, *s.* a cymbal, a clapping of the
করদাতা, *s.* one who pays tribute.
করদায়ক, or করদায়ী, *a.* paying tribute.
করপল্লব, *s.* conversation by the fingers.
করপুট, *s.* the joining of the hands to-
gether as a token of respect.

করপুটে, *ad.* with the hands respectfully
করবাল, *s.* a sword, a cimeter. [joined.
করবী, করবীর, *s.* the oleander flower tree.[1]
করভ, *s.* young of an animal; the meta-
করম, *s.* an action, fate, luck. [carpus.
করমচা, করমর্দ্দ, করমর্দ্দক, *s. vide* করঞ্চা.
করমালা, *s.* a rosary, bead-roll.
করল, *s.* the name of a bird.[2]
করলা, *s.* a vegetable and its plant.[3]
করশাখা, *s.* a finger, the fingers. [hands.
করশোথ, *s.* an œdematous swelling of the
করা, *s.* a doing or making: *a.* done.
করাঘাত, *s.* a slap, a blow with the hand.
করাটিয়া, *a.* stunted in growth.
করাণ, *s.* a causing to be done or made.
করাণী, *s.* a collector of tribute; a clerk.
করাত, করপত্র, *s.* a saw. করাতী, a sawyer.
করার, করারনামা, *s. vide* একরার, &c.
করাল, *s.* coral, pitch, a mixture of oil and pitch: *a.* great, high, lofty, formidable.
করিকুম্ভ, *s.* frontal globes of an elephant.
করিবক, *s.* a variety of the white heron.[4]
করিশুণ্ড, *s.* the trunk of an elephant.
করী, *s.* an elephant.
করীন্দ্র, *s.* the leader of a herd of elephants, a very excellent elephant.
*করীম, *a.* beneficent, generous, liberal.
করুই, *s.* a storehouse, a granary. [cy.
করুণা, *s.* pity, compassion, clemency, mer-
করুণানিধান, *s.* a sea of compassion: *a.* very compassionate. [hearted.
করুণাময়, *a.* full of compassion, tender-
করুল, *s.* the osprey or fishing eagle.[5]
করেলা, *s.* the same as করলা.
করোট, *s.* the skull, the cranium.
কর্কট, *s.* crab; Cancer; a kind of serpent; -রাশি, sign Cancer; -শৃঙ্গী, a plant.[6]
কর্কটী, *s.* a female crab; also, *vide* কাঁকুড়.
কর্কন্ধু *s.* a name of the jujube fruit.
কর্কর, *s.* gravel, grating noise or sensation, the sensation felt from dust in the eye.
কর্করিয়া, *a.* gritty, full of nodules.
কর্কশ, *a.* rigid, harsh, rough, hard, violent, unfeeling, cruel, unkind, miserly.
কর্জ, *s.* a loan, debt; -আদায়, -শোধ, the paying of a debt; -দাদন, giving a loan.
কর্জদার, কর্জী, *s.* a debtor, one who owes.

কর্জপত্র, *s.* a bond, a promissory note.
কর্ণ, *s.* the ear; rudder of a ship or boat; in *mytho.* one of the sons of Kunti.
কর্ণ, -কুহর, -ছিদ্র, -রন্ধ্র, *s.* the ear-hole.
কর্ণগুথ, কর্ণমল, *s.* the ear-wax.
কর্ণগোচর, *s.* the cognizance of the ear: *ad.* within hearing. [insect.
কর্ণজলৌকা, *s.* a species of centipes; also an
কর্ণদর্পণ, *s.* an earring, ear-ornament.
কর্ণধার, *s.* a helmsman, a steersman.
কর্ণপাক, *s.* a tumour in the ear.
কর্ণ, -ফুল, -কড়ি, -পালী, *s.* an ear-ornament.
কর্ণবেধ, *s.* the boring of the ear.
কর্ণমূল, *s.* the root of the ear.
কর্ণরোগ, *s.* a disease of the ear.
কর্ণশষ্কুলী, *s.* the hollow of the ear.
কর্ণাকর্ণি, *s.* a whispering together.
কর্ণাট, *s.* the name of a country; -বচ, orris
কর্ণিক, *s.* a mason's trowel. [root.
কর্ণিকা, *s.* earring; middle finger; pericarp
কর্ণিকার, *s.* pericarp of a lotus. [of lotus.
কর্ণেজপ, *s.* a talebearer, a whisperer.
কর্ত্তন, *s.* a cutting, clipping, a trimming.
কর্ত্তনী, *s.* a pair of scissors; parings.
কর্ত্তব্য, *a.* fit to be done, necessary, incumbent, practicable, proper, fit. [ness.
কর্ত্তব্যতা, *s.* practicability, propriety, fit-
কর্ত্তব্যাকর্ত্তব্য, *a.* practicable or impracticable, proper or improper. [shears.
কর্ত্তরিকা, কর্ত্তরী, *s.* a pair of scissors or
কর্ত্তা, *s.* an agent, a master, the doer of any thing, a governor; the agent of a verb.
কর্ত্তৃক, *s.* (in *comp.*) done by agency of that which is expressed by the first member.
কর্ত্তৃত্ব, *s.* agency, mastership, authority, management, rule, government.
কর্ত্তৃত্বপদ, *s.* the office of governing, the state or condition of a governor.
কর্ত্তৃত্বভার, *s.* the care or responsibility of government or of agencyship.
কর্ত্তৃপদ, *s.* the office of an agent or director; in *gram.* the agent of a verb.
কর্ত্তৃবাচ্য, *s.* in *gram.* the active voice.
কর্ত্রী, *s.* a female agent, the mistress of a family, a governess, a matron.
কর্দ্দ, কর্দ্দম, *s.* dirt, mud, mire, clay.
কর্দ্দমময়, *a.* dirty, abounding with mud.

কর্দ্দমাক্ত, *a.* smeared with mud or dirt.
কর্পট, *s.* old and patched garments.
কর্পাস, *s.* the cotton, the cotton plant.
কর্পূর, *s.* camphor; -যুক্ত, camphorated.
কর্ব্বুর, *a.* variegated, speckled, spotted.
কর্ম্ম, *s.* an action, work, a deed, an office, an employment, an affair, a matter; in *gram.* the object of a verb.
কর্ম্মকর, *s.* a workman, a labourer.
কর্ম্মকর্ত্তা, *s.* a workman, the superintendent of any business, a labourer.
কর্ম্মকাণ্ড, *s.* the body of religious ceremonies established by custom or law.
কর্ম্মকার, *s.* a blacksmith, an armourer.
কর্ম্ম, -কারক, -কারী, *a.* doing effecting any purpose : *s.* one who does any work.
কর্ম্মকীলক, *s.* a washer, a washerman.
কর্ম্মকুশল, *a.* skilled in any business.
কর্ম্মক্ষম, *a.* capable of work, able to work.
কর্ম্মচারী, *a.* engaged in a work : *s.* a collector of revenues, a steward, a factor.
কর্ম্মচ্যুত, *a.* cashiered, dismissed, discharged.
কর্ম্মচ্যুতি, *s.* a dismission, a cashiering.
কর্ম্মজ্ঞ, *a.* acquainted with religious duties, [or labour.
কর্ম্মঠ, *a.* diligent, laborious.
কর্ম্মণিবাচ্য, *s.* in *gram.* the passive voice.
কর্ম্মণ্য, *a.* fit for work, serviceable. [rites.
কর্ম্মন্, *s.* work, labour, action, religious
কর্ম্ম -পটু, -নিপুণ, *a.* eminent at any work.
কর্ম্মনৈপুণ্য, *s.* cleverness in business.
কর্ম্মপারক, *a.* capable of any work.
কর্ম্মফল, *s.* the fruit of human actions.
কর্ম্মবিপাক, *s.* the consequence of human actions; a book treating on the subject.
কর্ম্মভূমি, *s.* in *geo.* the middle part of India reckoned as a place of sanctity.
কর্ম্মভোগ, *s.* suffering or enjoyment of the consequences of evil or good actions.
কর্ম্মশীল, *a.* industrious, laborious, diligent.
কর্ম্মসচিব, *s.* a minister, a counsellor.
কর্ম্মসাধন, *s.* the means of accomplishing a
কর্ম্মস্থান, *s.* place of employment. [work.
কর্ম্মাদি, *s.* work and its consequences.
কর্ম্মানুযায়ী, *a.* according to one's actions.
কর্ম্মানুসারে, *ad.* according to actions.
কর্ম্মানুষ্ঠান, *s.* commencement of a work.
কর্ম্মান্ত, *s.* end of an action or undertaking.
কর্ম্মান্তে, *ad.* at the end of an action.
কর্ম্মান্বিত, *a.* industrious, diligent.
কর্ম্মাবৃত, *a.* officially protected; busy.
কর্ম্মার, *s.* a blacksmith; a brazier.
কর্ম্মারম্ভ, *s.* commencement of an action.
কর্ম্মার্হ, *a.* useful, fit for any work.
কর্ম্মাসক্ত, *a.* laborious, industrious.
কর্ম্মিষ্ঠ, *a.* industrious, skilful, fit for work.
কর্ম্মী, *a.* fit for any work, ingenious.
কর্ম্মোদ্যোগ, *s.* industry, diligence.
কর্ম্মোদ্যোগী, *a.* laborious, active, diligent.
কর্ম্মোপযুক্ত, *a.* useful, fit for any work.
কর্ষ, *s.* a sicca weight of gold or silver; tillage; a beleric myrabolan. [man.
কর্ষক, *a.* drawing, ploughing : *s.* a ploughman.
কর্ষণ, *s.* the act of drawing or ploughing.
কর্ষণীয়, *a.* capable of being drawn, or attracted; fit to be ploughed. [bridle.
কর্ষিণী, *s.* a plough-woman; the bit of a
কর্ষিত, *a.* drawn, ploughed, tilled.
কর্হি, *ad.* when? at what time?
কর্হিচিৎ, *ad.* sometimes, occasionally.
কল, *s.* semen virile; any piece of machinery, an engine, a machine, the lock of a gun, a trap, an elastic spring; a shoot, a scion, a sprout; a mouthful.
কলই, *s.* tin, tinning; -কর, to tin a vessel.
কলইকর, or কলইগর, *s.* a tinman.
কলকল, *s.* a hum, buz, a hubbub.
কলঙ্ক, *s.* rust, a stain, a blemish, a stigma, an imputation of crime, a crime, guilt.
কলঙ্কভঞ্জন, *s.* the freeing of a person from guilt, the removal of crime or blame.
কলঙ্কী, *a.* stained, blemished, charged with crime; *fem.* কলঙ্কিনী. [কালমেঘ.
কলপ, *s.* paste, starch, varnish; নাথ, *vide*
কলম, *s.* a pen; a scion, ingraftment, a cutting of any plant: *a.* ingrafted.
কলমকর্ত্তনী, *s.* a penknife, a pen-cutter.
কলমকাঠি, *s.* writing reed, wooden pen.
*কলমজারী, *a.* engaged in work, busy.
*কলমতরাশ, *s.* a penknife, a pen-cutter.
*কলমদান, *s.* a standish, a writing box.
*কলমা, *s.* a word, a prayer, oraison.
কলমী, *a.* crystallized : *s.* nitre, crystallized salt; an aquatic plant. [stalk.
কলম্ব, *s.* Columbo root; an arrow; a plant-

কলরব, *s.* a dove, pigeon, the black cuckoo; a murmur, clamour, a buz, a din.
কলশ, *s.* a water-pot, a pitcher, a jar.
কলশী, or কলসী, *s.* *idem.*
কলশীপিঁড়ি, *s.* a bench for water-pots.
কলস, *s.* a pinnacle; a pitcher.
কলহ, *s.* quarrel, brawl, squabble, contention.
কলহকর্ত্তা, *s.* a brawler, a wrangler.
কলহী, *a.* quarrelsome, contentious.
কলা, *v.* to sprout; to act in the manner of a machine: *s.* the mechanic art; a digit of the moon; fraud, deceit; a plantain; the menses, menstrual discharge.
কলাই, or কলায়, *s.* vetches, peas, pulse.
কলান, *s.* a sprouting; the rehearsing of a theme before exhibition; the working of a machine: *a.* sprouted, germinated.
কলাপ, *s.* an ornament, a zone, a peacock's tail, a multitude, a quiver, the moon; the name of a Sanskrit grammar.
কলাপাতী, *s.* a calking; a calker.
কলাপী, *s.* a peacock; one versed in Kaláp.
কলাবউ, *s.* a plantain tree representing the wife of Ganesha, and is worshipped.
কলি, *s.* 4th or present age of the world; joining strip; a flower-bud; wet-lime.
কলিকা, *s.* an unblown flower; pipe-bowl, the tobacco vessel of the huká; a cup.
কলি -কাল, -যুগ, *s.* the fourth or present age of the world (or, the age of vice).
কলিঙ্গ, *s.* in *geo.* a country between Cuttack and Madras; the name of a bird.
কলিচূণ, *s.* wet-lime, lime for whitewashing.
কলিত, *a.* numbered, reckoned, known, understood, acquired, separated, divided.
কলু, *s.* an oilman, oilman caste.
কলুষ, *s.* sin, a crime, guilt, defilement, filth.
কলুষান্বিত, কলুষী, *a.* guilty, sinful, vile, filthy, foul.
কলেজা, যকৃৎ, *s.* the liver.
কলেবর, দেহ, *s.* the body.
কল্ক, *s.* sediment, ordure, the ear-wax, sin, orts, filth.
কল্কল, *s.* a rippling, or brawling sound.
কল্কলা, *v. n.* to brawl, to ripple, to make a rippling noise (as of water or stream.)
কল্কলান, *s.* a rippling sound, a brawling.
কল্কলানি, *s.* a rippling, a surf, a brawling.
কল্কলীয়, *a.* brawling, contentious.

কল্কী, *s.* the tobacco-bowl of a huká; the tenth and last incarnation of Vishnu.
কল্‌শা *s.* a diadem, a tiara or cross.
কল্‌তানি, *s.* serum, the sanies, matter.
কল্প, *s.* a contrivance, a scheme, a purpose, an opinion, a report, a period of 432,000,000 years; a sacred writing, one of the six vedángas; an option.
কল্পতরু, *s.* a fabled tree in Indra's paradise which yields fruit to every one's desires; *fig.* a very generous person.
কল্পন, *s.* the forming of a plan or scheme.
কল্পনা, *s.* a scheme, a contrivance, a plan, a forgery, a counterfeit, an imitation.
কল্পনীয়, *a.* capable of being contrived or devised, fit to be designed or purposed.
কল্পিত, *a.* contrived, counterfeit, feigned, fictitious, made by art, designed, invented, purposed, devised, artificial.
কল্‌বল, কল্‌বলানি, *s.* tumultuous noise.
কল্‌বলি, *a.* brawling: *s.* a tumult.
কল্মষ, *s.* sin, filth, moral impurity; one of the hells of the Hindus.
কল্য, *s.* to-morrow, yesterday; health: *a.* recovered; deaf, deaf and dumb.
কল্যকা, *ad.* to-morrow, yesterday.
কল্যাণ, *s.* welfare, prosperity, happiness.
কল্যাণকর্ত্তা, *s.* a beneficent person.
কল্যাণপ্রার্থক, *s.* a well-wisher.
কল্যাণী, *a.* successful, prosperous, happy, fortunate.
কল্যাণীয়, *a.* worthy of good fortune.
কল্যাবধি, *ad.* from yesterday, till to-morrow.
কল্ল, *a.* deaf, deaf and dumb.
কল্লা, কল্লী, *a.* wicked, froward, abominable.
কল্লোল, *s.* the roaring of the sea, the noise of a tumult, noise produced in gargling.
কল্‌সা, *s.* the gills of a fish; the cheek.
*কশম্‌কশ, *s.* strait, distress, affliction.
কশা, *s.* a whip, scourge, cat-o'-nine-tails.
কশাকশি, *s.* a struggle; a tightening to the utmost; scantiness, insufficiency.
কশাড়, *s.* a kind of grass (Scirpus kysoor).
কশেরু, *s.* backbone, spine; *see* কশেরুখণ্ড.
কশেরুখণ্ড, *s.* a division of Jambu-dwípa.
কশ্চন, or কশ্চিৎ, *pron.* some one, any one, whosoever, a certain person.
কশ্যপ, *s.* in *mytho.* a famous sage.

কষ, *v.* to rub any thing hard, to tighten, to tan, to try with the touch-stone.
কষ, *s.* a touch-stone, tanning, the tanning principle, or substance : *a.* tight.
কষণ, *s.* a testing, trying by touch-stone, a tightening, the tanning of leather.
কষণী, *s.* tightness, astringency, severity.
কষা, close-fisted; *s.* harsh, astringent taste.
কষাণি, *s.* purulent matter, sanies, serum.
কষায়, *s.* a harsh taste : *a.* tawny, astrin-
কষী, *s.* a line drawn with a pen. [gent.
কষীদা, *s.* a kind of needle-work : *a.* tight.
কষুরা, *a.* astringent, harsh to the taste.
কষ্ট, *s.* trouble, difficulty, suffering, distress, pain : *a.* suffering, impervious.
কষ্টকর, *a.* distressing, vexatious, painful.
কষ্টকল্পনা, *s.* a cavil, false objections, an attempt to distress an opponent.
কষ্টকল্পিত, *a.* contrived with difficulty.
কষ্টশ্রেষ্ঠ, *s.* great trouble or distress.
কষ্টসাধ্য, *a.* difficultly accomplishable.
কষ্টি; *s.* a test, a trial, a touch-stone.
কষ্টিপাথর, *s.* a touch-stone. [juice.
কস্, *s.* the jaw, lower part of the cheek;
কস্কষাণি, *s.* a grinning, snarl; friskiness.
কসৎ, **কস্লত**, *s.* labour, fatigue, practice.
কসব, *s.* trade, a profession; whoredom.
কসবা, *s.* a small town or village, hamlet.
কসবী, *s.* a whore, a common prostitute; -বাজ, whoremonger; -বাজী, whoring.
*__কসম__, *s.* an oath, an asseveration.
*__কসায়ী__, *s.* a butcher; -খানা, a butchery.
কসালা, *s.* distress, pain, anguish, trouble.
কসুর, *s.* an abatement, a failure, a coming short, deficiency, fault, a defect.
*__কস্ত__, **কস্দ্**, *s.* study, practice, a wish, a desire, a purpose, a project, a scope.
কস্তুরা, *s.* an oyster, a bivalve shell-fish.
কস্তুরিকা, **কস্তুরী**, *s.* musk, a lily, a plant.[1]
কস্মিন্কালে, *ad.* when? at what time?
কহ, *v. a.* to speak, to say, to mention, to tell, to announce, to rehearse.
কহন, *s.* the act of speaking or saying.
কহর, *s.* rage, indignation, vengeance, severity, chastisement, judgment.
কহা, *s.* the recital or mention of any thing, the speaking of any thing.
কহা-কহি, **-বলা**, conversation, disputation.
কহুয়া, *a.* eloquent, talkative, garrulous.
কাই, *s.* starch, paste; rice-flour paste.
কাইট, *s.* the dirt of a huká or tobacco pipe, lees, dregs, sediment, dross.
কাইত, *a.* on one side, aslant. [phyrio.)
কাইম, *s.* an aquatic bird (Gallinula por-
কাইল, *ad.* to-morrow, yesterday.
কাএত, *s.* a person of the writer caste.
*__কাএদা__ *s.* a rule, a law, a constitution.
*__কাএম__, *a.* erect, firm, steadfast, fixed.
কাএমী, *s.* steadfastness, firmness.
কাওয়া, *v. a.* the same as কাবা. [Hindus.
কাওরা, *s.* a hog-keeper, a low caste of
কাংস্য, *s.* bell-metal, a gong, musical plate; -কার, -বণিক, a brazier, brass-founder.
কাঁক, *s.* a heron; the side, the flank.
কাঁকই, *s.* a comb, instrument to card cot-
কাঁকড়া, *s.* a crab; a timber tree.[2] [ton.
কাঁকড়াবিছা, *s.* a scorpion. [nata.)
কাঁকড়াশৃঙ্গী, *s.* a plant (Asclepias gemi-
কাঁকণ, *s.* a bracelet or ring for the wrist.
কাঁকতল্পী, *s.* a bundle carried on the hip.
কাঁকবিরালি, *s.* a tumour in the armpit.
কাঁকর, *s.* gravel, nodules, pebbles, grit.
কাঁকরীয়া, *a.* stony, gravelly, nodular.
কাঁকরোল, *s.* a plant (Momordica mixta).
কাঁকলা, *s.* an aromatic drug.
কাঁকলাস, *s.* a species of lizard.[3]
কাঁকালি, *s.* the waist, the loins, hips, side.
কাঁকিনী, *s.* a female full grown; a female buffalo : *a.* very high (applied to trees).
কাঁকিলা, *s.* the same as কঙ্কত্রোটি.
কাঁকুড়, **কাঁকুড়ী**, *s.* a species of cucumber.[4]
কাঁখ, **কাঁখতালী**, *s.* the flank, armpit, side.
কাঁচ, *s.* crystals of quartz, glass, crystal; -কলা, green plantain; -লবণ, rock salt.
কাঁচকলস, *s.* a glass bottle or pitcher.
কাঁচড়া, *s.* a plant growing in marshes.
কাঁচপাত্র, *s.* a glass, glass vessel, a bottle.
কাচমণি, *s.* glass, crystals of quartz.
কাঁচলি, *s.* a woman's bodice, a stays.
কাঁচা, *a.* imperfect, unripe, uncooked, raw, green, ignorant, not versed in business.
কাঁচাহলদী, *s.* turmeric, zedoary.[5]
কাঁচী, *s.* a pair of scissors, shears, a sickle : *a.* below the standard (as weight, etc.)

কাঁজি, *s.* rice-water, rice-gruel, sour gruel.
কাঁজিয়াল, *s.* the spathe of a plantain tree.
কাঁট, *s.* the clitoris.
কাঁটা, *s.* a thorn, thistle, a fish-bone, a fork, skewer, a sharp point, an enemy.
কাঁটাকুড়, *s.* a place full of thorns, a place of extreme distress or difficulty.
কাঁটানটিয়া, *s.* a species of amaranthus.[1]
কাঁটাপালখ্যা, *a.* pin-feathered, unfledged.
কাঁটাবাঁশ, *s.* a thorny species of bambu.
কাঁটাবাবলা, *s.* a tree (Mimosa arabica).
কাঁটাবিশিষ্ট, কাঁটাময়, *a.* thorny, thistly.
কাঁটাল, *a.* thorny : *s.* the jak-fruit. [fruit.
কাঁটালকোষ, *s.* the edible part of the jak-
কাঁটালিকলা, *s.* a variety of plantain.
কাঁটাশিঙ্গুর, *s.* a species of oak.[2]
কাঁটি, *s.* female scurrility ; the bullet of a fishing net ; beads ; the natural ring of colours round the neck of a parrot.
কাঁঠাল, *s.* the jak-fruit.[3]
কাঁঠালি, *s.* a particular manner of sewing or stitching ; a variety of plantain.
কাঁঠী, *s.* the bullet of a fishing net.
কাঁড়, *v. n.* to separate grain from its husk.
কাঁড়ন, *s.* the act of cleaning rice from its husk ; the using a person with scurrility.
কাঁড়নি, *s.* the wages paid for cleaning grain ; the making use of scurrilities.
কাঁড়রা, *a.* thick, clumsy ; -বুলবুল, a bird.[4]
কাঁড়া, *v.* to husk grain : *a.* cleansed from the husk or bran : *s.* a bambu oil vessel.
কাঁড়ান, *s.* a causing to cleanse grain from its husk : *a.* cleansed from its husk.
কাঁড়ি, *s.* a heap or collection, stack, pile.
কাঁড়িকরণ, *s.* making of heaps, a piling up.
কাঁড়িয়া, *s.* a small earthen jar or pitcher.
কাঁত, or কাঁথ, *s.* wall, mud wall, a ruin.
কাঁতড়া, or কাথড়া, *s.* the ruins of a town.
কাঁথা, *s.* a coat of shreds, a ragged quilt.
কাঁথী, *s.* a high shore or bank of a river.
কাঁদ, *v.* to weep, to cry, to howl. [ing.
কাঁদন, *s.* a crying, weeping, wailing, howl-
কাঁদনি, *s.* a weeping or howling ; a ditty sung by snake-catchers. [ing.
কাঁদনিকলা, *s.* lamentation, weeping, wail-
কাঁদা, *v. a.* to cause a person to weep : *s.* a weeping ; a verge, a shore, a margin.
কাঁদাকাদ্দি, *s.* a mutual weeping or howling.
কাঁদাকাটী, *s.* cry, lamentation. [eaves.
কাঁদাড়ি, *s.* a spout, drain, trench ; under-
কাঁদালিবাড়ি, *s.* a rod to tread out corn.
কাঁদি, *s.* a cluster, a bunch (of fruits).
কাঁদিকাঁদি, *ad.* by clusters or bunches.
কাঁধ, or কাঁধা, *s.* the shoulder.
কাঁধা, *s.* border, a rim, edge of a cup, a margin, a verge, a shore, a bank, a mound.
কাঁধাড়ি, *s.* brow of a hill ; place under the
কাঁপ, *v.* to quake, tremble, shake. [eaves.
কাঁপন, *s.* a quaking, a shaking, a trembling.
কাঁপনি, *s.* quaking, shaking, trembling.
কাঁপা, *s.* fishing trap, a trap to catch birds, a band of cords for tying up straw.
কাঁসর, *s.* plate of bell-metal used as a musical instrument ; a disease of the liver.
কাঁসরিয়া, *s.* one whose liver is morbidly en-
কাঁসা, *s.* bell-metal, white-brass. [larged.
কাঁসারি, *s.* a brazier, a coppersmith.
কাক, *s.* a crow ; *fem.* কাকী, or কাকিনী.
কাকচরিত্র, *s.* art of divination, astrology.
কাকচরিত্রী, *a.* divining : *s.* an astrologer.
কাকচা, *s.* mustard-straw, mustard-stalks.
কাকচিঞ্চী, *s.* the seed of Abrus precatorius which has a black spot on it. [ber.
কাক-তন্দ্রা, -নিদ্রা, *s.* a light sleep or slum-
কাকতালীয়ন্যায়, *a.* sudden, unexpected.
কাকতুল্য, *a.* crow-like, crafty.
কাকপক্ষ, *s.* the temporal locks of hair.
কাকবন্ধ্যা, *a.* having only a single child : *s.* a woman who bears only one child.
কাকলা, *s.* a kind of perfume.
কাকলাস, *s.* a kind of lizard, chameleon.
কাকলী, *s.* a low and agreeable note.
কাকা, *s.* uncle, father's younger brother ; note of a crow ; -তুআ, a kind of parrot.
কাকাক্ষিগোলকন্যায়, *a.* ambidextrous.
কাকাবলী, *s.* a flock of crows.
কাকিণী, *s.* a cubit ; five gandás or twenty cauri, a cauri. [female crow.
কাকী, *s.* younger paternal uncle's wife ; a
কাকু, *s.* (used in vulgar sense) a plantain, the thumb, membrum virile. [scream.
কাকুক্তি, কাকুতি, *s.* a moan, cry of distress, a
কাকুতিমিনতি, *s.* supplication, intreaty.
কাগ, কাগা, কাক, *s.* a crow.

কাগচা, *s.* a paper-maker. [cument.
কাগজ, *s.* paper ; -পত্র, record, written do-
কাগজী, *s.* a paper-maker : *a.* thin-skin-
ned ; -নেবু, or -লিম্বু, a variety of lime.
কাগারি, কাকারি, পেচা, *s.* an owl.
কাঙ্কর, *s.* calcareous nodule, gravel, pebble.
কাঙ্কালী, *s.* the waist, the loins. [licum.)
কাঙ্গনী, *s.* a species of grass (Panicum ita-
কাঙ্গাল, কাঙ্গালী, *a.* poor, needy, wretched.
কাঙ্গালীপনা, *s.* poverty, wretchedness.
কাঙ্গুর, *s.* a basket in which the water of
the Ganges is carried to sacred places.
কাচ, *v.* to wash linen ; to act an assumed
part, to feign : *s.* glass, crystal, quartz ;
a feigned character, a disguise.
কাচতিয়া, কাচি, *s.* a sickle, a reaping hook.
কাচন, *s.* a washing of clothes ; a feigning.
কাচা, *v. a.* to cause to wash (clothes).
কাচা, *a.* washed : *s.* a shroud; coarse cloth.
কাচান, *a.* washed, cleansed, finished.
কাচুবা, *s.* a comedian, a feigned character.
কাছ, *s.* nearness to, vicinity ; a shore.
কাছা, *v.* to overtake, to approach, near.
কাছা, *s.* the tuck of the lower garment.
কাছা-আলগা, -ঢীলা, *a.* slovenly, careless,
loose, lewd, lascivious, unprincipled.
কাছাকাছি, *ad.* very near, near each other.
কাছাড়, *s.* the high banks of a river.
কাছাধরা, *s.* a sycophant, a satellite.
কাছান, *s.* the overtaking of any one.
কাছারী, *s.* a court-house, court of justice.
কাছিম, *s.* a tortoise, an aquatic turtle.
কাছী, *s.* a hawser, a cable, a thick rope.
কাছে, *ad.* near, in the vicinity.
কাজ, *s.* work, labour, duty, business.
কাজল, *s.* stibium, lampblack for eyelids.
কাজলনতা, *s.* a vessel to make lampblack.
কাজলা, *s.* a species of parrot ;[1] a wedge, a
কাজলি, *s.* a variety of sugarcane. [peg.
কাজিয়া, *s.* dispute, a squabble, a fray.
*কাজী, *s.* a judge, a Musalmán judge.
কাজীউলকুজ্জাৎ, *s.* a Musalmán chief judge.
কাজুবাদাম, *s.* cashoo nuts.
কাঞ্চড়া, *s.* the name of a plant.[2] [apple.[4]
কাঞ্চন, *s.* gold; mountain ebony ;[3] thorn-
কাঞ্চনময়, *a.* golden, made of gold, aurifer-
কাঞ্চনসন্ধি, *s.* a perpetual alliance. [ous.

কাঞ্চী, *s.* a zone, a girdle ; name of a city.
কাঞ্জী, কাঞ্জিক, *s.* rice-gruel, sour gruel.
কাট, *v. a.* to cut, clip, to gnaw, to deduct
(wages, etc.), to pass (as time). কাটিয়া
ফেল, to cut down, to cut off. [vessel.
কাট, *s.* wood, timber ; -কুআ, large wooden
কাটকুট, *s.* a cutting and chopping.
কাটছাতা, *s.* a fungus growing on wood.
কাটন, *s.* the act of cutting or clipping.
কাটনকুটন, *s.* act of cutting and chopping.
কাটনা, *s.* a spinning, work of spinning.
কাটনি, *s.* a spinster ; wages of spinning.
কাটনিয়া, *s.* one who spins thread.
কাটা, *s.* a cutting : *a.* cut, cut off.
কাটাই, কাটানী, *s.* wages for spinning or cut-
কাটাও, *s.* a kind of needle work. [ting.
কাটাকাটী, *s.* mutual slaughter or cutting.
কাটান, *s.* a causing to be cut, the channel
of a river, the passing away of time.
কাটার, *s.* a dagger, a poniard, a dirk.
কাটারী, *s.* a bill-hook, a cleaver.
কাটী, *s.* a bit of stick, a chip, a splinter.
কাটুরা, or কাঠুরিয়া, *s.* a wood-cutter.
কাঠ, *s.* wood, timber ; -কুআ, a trough bail-
ing vessel ; -ছাতা, a wood-fungus.
কাঠখড়া, *s.* a hard kind of chalk. [closure.
কাঠগড়া, *s.* a railing, a stockade, stake-en-
কাঠগোলাব, *s.* China rose (Rosa chinen-
কাঠঠোকরা, *s.* a wood-pecker.[5] [sis.)
কাঠনেকার, *s.* a straining to vomit.
কাঠপিপীড়া, *s.* a species of large ant.
কাঠবিষ, *s.* vegetable poison.
কাঠবিড়াল, *s.* a squirrel. [num zambac.)
কাঠমল্লিকা, *s.* a species of jasmine (Jasmi-
কাঠরা, *s.* a prison ; a house made of wood,
a place enclosed by stakes : *a.* wooden.
কাঠসোলা, *s.* a species of light-wood.[6]
কাঠা, *s.* a measure of land (about 20 cu-
bits square), a measure of capacity.
কাঠকালি, *s.* the working of a sum in sur-
veying or land-measuring.
কাঠাম, *a.* wooden, framed with wood.
কাঠাল, *a.* woody, firm, full-grown, adult.
কাঠিন্য, *s.* severity, harshness, roughness,
hardness, unfeelingness.
কাঠী, *s.* a wand, splinter, a piece of stick ;
a writing reed, a key, a scabbard.

কাঠুয়া, *a.* wooden, hard : *s.* a wood-cutter.
কাঠুরিয়া, *s.* one who cuts and sells wood.
কাড়্, *v. a.* to cleanse, to take out of, to take out from, to snatch, to seize.
কাড়ন, *s.* a taking out of or from, a snatching or seizing, the act of cleaning.
কাড়া, *v.* to await an omen by the fall of flowers placed on the head of an image.
কাড়া, *a.* cleansed out : *s.* a sort of drum ; -কাঠি, hooked stick to clean an oil-mill.
কাড়াকাড়ি, *s.* a reciprocal snatching.
কাড়ান, *s.* the expecting of the fall of flowers which is laid on the head of an idol.
কাণ, *s.* the ear ; -দা, to listen, to hearken; -মল, to pull or twist one's ears.
কাণকুআ, *s.* the gills of a fish.
কাণকোটারী, *s.* a kind of insect, julus.
কাণখড়কিয়া, *a.* quick of hearing, retentive.
কাণ -খড়িকা, -খুটনী, -খুকসী, *s.* an ear-pick.
কাণখাড়া, *a.* listening, attentive.
কাণচটা, *s.* a fungus growing on trees.
কাণজুল্পি, *s.* a lock of hair on the temples.
কাণতড়পা, *s.* an ornament for the ear.
কাণপাকা, *s.* a painful tumour in the ear.
কাণপাটা, *s.* the flap of the ear.
কাণপাতল, *a.* quick of hearing, babbling.
কাণভাঙ্গচি, *s.* the prejudicing of a person.
কাণভাঙ্গান, *s.* a whispered slander.
কাণমলা, কাণমুচড়া, *s.* the same as কাণুটি.
কাণমাগুর, কানিমাগুর, *s.* name of a fish.[1]
কাণা, *a.* blind, one-eyed, perforated, broken : *s.* brim or edge of a cup or pot.
কাণাকাণি, *ad.* ear to ear, by whispers ; to the brim : *s.* a whispering, tête-à-tête.
কাণাচি, *s.* place under the hinder eaves.
কাণাচিয়া, *a.* situated under the hinder eaves : *s.* an eaves-dropper.
কাণাড়ি, *s.* act of listening, eaves-dropping ; -পাতা, a listener, an eaves-dropper.
কাণাৎ, *s.* the curtains or walls of a tent.
কাণাভাঙ্গা, *a.* broken at the brim or edge.
কাণি, *s.* a rag, tatter, a piece of cloth ; a moulding; the jagg on the top of a post ; the end or corner of a sail : *a.* eared.
কাণিপোঁদা, tattered, ragged, poor, penny-less : *s.* a tatterdemalion.
কাণুটি, *s.* pulling or twisting of the ears, a warning.
কাণেকাণে, *ad.* to the brim ; in the ear.
কাণোড়া, *a.* obsequious, attentive, servilely obedient, under subjection or controul.
কাণ্চা, or কাণ্চী, *s.* a quarrelsome and scurrilous woman, a scold, a virago.
কাণ্ড, *s.* a stalk or stem, the trunk of a tree ; an arrow ; a section or chapter.
কাণ্ডার, কাণ্ডারী, *s.* fence or screen of cloth ; a pilot, a helmsman, a steersman.
কাণ্ডারোপণ, *s.* the ceremony of planting four arrows on four sides of an idol.
কাণ্ডী, *s.* a heap or collection, stack, pile.
কাৎ, *s.* side, division, value, rate, price.
কাতর, *a.* troubled, distressed, anxious.
কাতরতা, *s.* trouble, distress, anxiety.
কাতরাণ, কাতরাণি, *s.* a moan, a complaint, distress, anguish, agony.
কাতরোক্তি, *s.* a complaint, expression of distress.
কাতলা, *s.* the name of a fish ;[2] a cant word used by robbers to signify a man.
কাতা, *s.* coir, coir cable.
কাতান, কাতানী, *s.* a butcher's cleaver, a bill-hook, a parang, a binder's knife.
কাতার, *s.* a row, a rank, a line, a file.
কাতারকাতার, *ad.* in files, in rows, in a line.
কাতারি, *s.* a sort of pots for curds.
কাতারী, *s.* a pair of shears ; shell-cutter's saw.
কাতি, *s.* a shell-cutter's saw ; a canister.
*কাতীব, *s.* a scribe, a writer, a teacher.
কাতুর, *s.* a seat on the Indian oil-mill.
কাতুরকুতুর, *s.* the sensation of tickling.
কাতে, *ad.* on the side of, on account of.
কাতেকাতে, *ad.* invidiously, pryingly.
*কাতেল, *s.* one who kills, an executioner.
কাত্যায়নী, *s.* a name of the goddess Durgá.
কাদম্বরী, *s.* spirituous liquor extracted from the flowers of Nauclea orientalis.
কাদম্বিনী, *s.* assemblage of clouds.
কাদা, কাদাকিচা, *s.* mud, mire, dirt, soft clay.
কাদাখোঁচা, *s.* a snipe, a fen-fowl.[3]
কাদা -টিয়া, -ড়িয়া, *a.* muddy, dirty, sloppy, turbid.
কাদান, *s.* the making a place muddy.
কাদাময়, কাদাল, *a.* muddy, dirty, sloppy.
*কাদের, *a.* able, powerful, mighty.
কান্দা, *s.* a bill-hook, a cleaver.
কানন, *s.* a thicket, forest, wood, wilderness.
কানীন, born of a virgin : *s.* child of a virgin.

কানুড়, *s.* a plant (Crinum toxicarium).
*কানুন, *s.* a law, a statute, a regulation.
কানুনগো, *s.* an officer who keeps the public records, the master of the rolls.
কান্ত, *s.* a husband, iron : *a.* desirable, beloved, dear, beautiful, highly esteemed ; -কড়া, an iron caldron ; -লোহ, steel.
কান্তা, *s.* a wife, a beautiful woman.
কান্তার, *s.* bad, difficult or dangerous road, a forest ; a red variety of sugarcane.
কান্তি, *s.* beauty, splendour, light, brilliance ; a beautiful woman; wish, desire.
কান্তিকর, *a.* causing light or splendour, illuminating, exciting desire. [beauty.
কান্তিপুষ্টি, *s.* preservation of splendour or
কান্তি -বিশিষ্ট, -মান্, -যুক্ত, *a.* beautiful, splendid, brilliant, luminous, bright.
কান্তিলোহ, *s.* steel, bright or excellent iron.
কান্দ, *v. n.* to weep, to cry, to bewail, to lament, to howl (as an animal).
কান্দনীয়, *a.* cross, crying, crying aloud.
কান্দুয়া, *a.* weeping, howling, crying.
কান্দুয়াবাঘ, *s.* the hunting leopard.
কাপ, *s.* a false appearance, a pantomime, a show, a pretence ; the nib of a pen.
কাপট্য, *s.* deceitfulness, craftiness, trickery, dissimulation. [rel, attire.
কাপড়, *s.* cloth, linen cloth, wearing appa-
কাপড়্যা, *s.* linen-draper, cloth-merchant.
কাপালি, *s.* pálki-maker, a class of Hindus.
কাপাস, *s.* cotton-wool, the cotton plant.[1]
কাপাসীয়, *a.* cotton, made of cotton, dry.
কাপুরি, *a.* impregnated with camphor.
কাপুরুষ, *s.* a coward, mean-spirited man.
কাপুরুষত্ব, *s.* cowardice, want of energy.
কাপট্যা, কাপ্ট্যামি, the same as কৃপণ, &c.
কাপ্তেনী, *a.* lending money at 500 per cent. to minor heirs of large estates.
*কাফর, কাফের, *s.* an infidel, a Jew, an
কাফরি, *s.* an African, a negro. [idolator.
কাফী, *a.* useful, advantageous : *s.* coffee.
কাবলী -বুট, -মটর, *s.* a variety of pea.
কাবা, *v.* to inspissate, thicken any preparation by boiling: *s.* caudle. [cloak.
*কাবা, *s.* a pretence, excuse ; coffee ; a
কাবাইদ, *s.* military exercise. [allspice.
কাবাব, *a.* roasted : *s.* a roast; -চিনি, cubebs,
কাবার, *s. Port.* the last day of the month.
কাবারী, *a.* due at the month's end : *s.* a
*কাবিল, *a.* able, learned. [bambu lath.
কাবু, *a.* within power : *s.* power, controul.
কাব্য, *s.* poetry, a poem ; -কর্ত্তা, a poet, writer of poetry ; -গ্রন্থ, -শাস্ত্র, a book of poems.
কাব্যত্ব, *s.* the characteristic of a poem.
কাব্‌ল্যা, *s.* a wedge, a peg, a stake.
কাম, *s.* desire, lust ; god of love ; object,
কামগ, *a.* unrestrained, licentious. [work.
কামগোজার, *a.* active, eminent in business.
কামজ, *a.* spontaneous, arising from desire
কামঠা, *s.* a bow, a cross-bow. [or lust.
কামড়, *s.* the biting of any thing, a bite.
কামড়ন, *s.* the act of biting, a biting.
কামড়া, *v.* to bite, to snap, gnaw ; to produce a griping pain, to throb. [fling.
কামড়াকামড়ি, *ad.* mutually biting or scuf
কামড়ান, *s.* a biting, griping, throbbing.
কামড়ানি, *s.* colic, a griping pain. [pain.
কামড়াহ্যা, কামড়ান্যা, *a.* biting : *s.* a colic
কামদ, *a.* gratifying, yielding the desire.
কামধেনু, *s.* the name of a fabulous cow.
কামনা, *s.* prayer, supplication, a request, a desire, a wish, appetite, lust.
কামপীড়া, *s.* the pains of love or lust.
কামরা, *s.* a closet, a room, a bed-room.
কামরাঙ্গা, *s.* the crab-apple and its tree.[2]
কামরূপ, *a.* assuming any form at will : *s.* a district in the North of Bengal.
কামরূপী, *a.* assuming any shape at will.
কামল, *a.* libidinous, lustful : *s.* jaundice.
কামলা, নেবা, *s.* the jaundice. [shave.
কামা, *v.* to earn, to acquire by labour ; to
কামাই, *s.* gains, earnings, savings ; also, neglect, absence, deficiency.
কামাতুর, *a.* sick with love, lustful.
কামান্, *s.* a cross-bow, a cannon, artillery.
কামান, *s.* the act of shaving ; an earning.
কামানল, *s.* the fire of lust, lechery.
কামানী, *s.* the hire of a barber ; a fiddle-bow ; the sticks in a paper kite.
কামান্ধ, *a.* blinded by lust or love.
কামার, *s.* a blacksmith, a whitesmith.
কামারশালা, *s.* a smith's shop, a forge.
কামার্ত্ত, কামার্থী, *a.* lewd, lascivious, libidinous, wanton, lecherous, amorous.

কামিজ, s. *Port.* a shirt; a shift, chemise.
কামিনী, s. a lascivious or beautiful woman;
a flowering shrub (Murraya exotica).
কামী, কামুক, a. lascivious, lustful, lewd.
কাম্য, a. desirable, delectable, voluntary.
কাম্যমরণ, s. voluntary death, suicide.
কায়, s. the body; -পুত্র, a low class of Hin-
কায়কৃত, a. done by the body. [du.
*কায়দা, s. a rule, a custom, a manner, an
institute, the rules of grammar, a basis.
কায়ফল, s. a medicinal nut. [some.
কায়বারী, a. resolute, insulting, quarrel-
কায়মনোবাক্য, *ad.* with the body, mind
and speech, heartily, in every respect.
কায়স্থ, a. corporal: s. the writer caste.
কায়স্থিত, a. situated in the body, corporal.
কায়া, দেহ, শরীর, অঙ্গ, s. the body.
কায়িক, শারীরিক, দেহী, a. bodily, corporeal.
কারক, a. doing, effecting, causing, accom-
plishing: s. an agent, a doer.
কারকিত, a. complete, perfect, finished.
*কারকুন, s. an agent, a superintendent.
কারখানা, s. a manufactory, a workhouse.
কারণ, s. a cause, a reason, motive, an oc-
casion, a principle: *prep.* for.
কারণকর্ণ্য, s. a deficiency, want, strait.
কারণতা, -ত্ব, s. causality. [sonable.
কারণযুক্ত, a. having a proper cause, rea-
কারণীভূত, a. become a cause or motive.
*কারবান্, s. a caravan, body of travellers.
কারবার, s. business, a negociation, trade.
কারবারী, a. fit for business, active, indus-
*কারবালা, s. a burial ground. [trious.
কারসাজি, s. artifice, tricks; a doing.
কারা, কারাগার, s. a jail, a prison, a gaol.
*কারাবা, s. a large phial for rose water.
কারি, s. an effect, an action, issue, action,
act, agency, an artificer. [man.
কারিকর, or কারিগর, s. a mechanic, work-
কারিকরী, or কারিগরী, s. mechanic labour,
mechanics, workmanship.
কারিকা, s. an actress, a dancing girl; act,
action, profession, agency; sharp pain;
usury: *a. fem.* acting, doing, causing.
কারিতা, -ত্ব, s. agency, causality. [agent.
কারিন্দা, s. a workman, a mechanic; an
কারী, a. acting, causing, occasioning.

কারু, s. a mechanic, artificer, an agent, a
maker, a trade; a painful ulcer. [ful.
কারুন্দিয়া, a. expert, active, diligent, use-
কার্কশ্য, s. hard-heartedness, cruelty, un-
feelingness, roughness, niggardliness.
কার্ণিস, s. *Eng.* a cornice.
কার্ত্তিক, s. a Hindu month containing part
of Oct. and part of Nov.; name of a god.
কার্দা, কাটারী, s. a bill-hook, a cleaver.
কার্পণ্য, s. niggardliness, parsimony, stingi-
কার্পা, s. gum Sandarach. [ness.
কার্পাস, s. cotton; also *vide* কাপাস.
কার্ম্মণ, s. magic, sorcery, witchcraft.
কার্ম্মুক, s. a bow; a bambu.
কার্য্য, s. business, duty, work, undertak-
ing, an affair, office, a deed, an effect.
কার্য্য-কর্ত্তা, -কারক, s. an agent, a workman.
কার্য্যকারিতা, s. workmanship, agency.
কার্য্যক্রমে, *ad.* in the course of business.
কার্য্যান্ত, *ad.* at the end of the business.
কার্য্যান্বেষী, a. seeking for employment.
কার্য্যার্থী, a. desirous of employment.
কার্য্যোদ্যোগ, s. industry, activity, zeal.
কার্য্যোদ্যোগী, a. active, industrious.
কাল, s. time, a season, weather, a space of
time, the time of death; Yama, death
personified; in *gram.* a tense; a. black,
dark-blue, swarthy, sable; -কাট, -ক্ষেপ,
to spend time; -কাসুন্দা, a plant.[1]
কাল -কাটন, -কাটান, s. a spending of time.
কালকিষ্ট, a. filthy, black, squalid, dirty.
কালকূট, s. venom, mortal or deadly poison.
কালক্রমে, *ad.* in process of time.
কালক্ষেপ, কালক্ষেপণ, s. the spending of
কালখণ্ড, or যকৃৎ, s. the liver. [time.
কালছুঁচা, s. a variety of the musk rat.[2]
কালজাম, s. a tree and its fruit.[3] [indica).
কালজীরা, s. a plant and its seed (Nigella
কালতিল, s. a variety of the sesamum.[4]
কালতুলসী, s. a species of basil.[5]
কালতুল্য, a. death-like, deadly, destructive.
কালধর্ম্ম, s. the line of conduct suited to
any particular time or season.
কালধুতুরা, s. a species of the thorn-apple.[6]
কালনাগিনী, s. a species of serpent.
কালপেচা, s. a kind of owl (Stryx infausta).
কালফুটকী, s. a small species of bird.[7]

কালবটের, *s.* a species of quail.[1]
কালবসুমাছ, *s.* the name of a fish.[2]
কালবাত, *s.* the name of a particular tune or method of singing by response.
কালবাতী, *s.* one well versed in the kálwát.
কালবৈশাখী, *a.* tempestuous, stormy.
কালমরিচ, *s.* black pepper.
কালমুগ, *s.* a variety of pulse.[6]
কালমেঘ, *s.* a febrifuge plant (Justicia paniculata).
কালযবন, *s. fig.* a tyrant, a monster.
কালযাপন, *s.* spending of time.
কালশিরা, *s.* a bruise, the livid colour of a bruise.
কালসর্প, কালসাপ, *s.* the black and most mortal variety of the Cobra de capello.
কালসূত্র, *s.* the Hindu hell.
কালস্বরূপ, *a.* death-like, fatal, solemn, awful.
কালা, *a.* deaf, cold, black : *s.* a fish-spear; -কর, a dyer of black; -মুখ, black-faced.
কালাগ্নি, *s.* the universal conflagration at the end of the world.
কালান্তক, *s.* epithet of Yama, who puts an end to time.
কালান্তর, *s.* another time, a different time.
কালাপাতী, *s. Port.* a calking; a calker.
কালাবতু, *s.* twisted silver and silk thread.
কালাশুদ্ধি, কালাশৌচ, *s.* an impure time, the time of impurity.
কালি, *s.* in *arith.* product of a sum, result or working a sum; goddess Kálí; ink; the flowers of onions : *ad.* to-morrow.
কালিকা, *s* goddess Kálí : *ad.* to-morrow.
কালিচা, কালীচা, *s.* a scar, mark of a bruise
কালিনী, *a.* destructive, deadly, ruinous.
কালিন্দী *s.* a name of the river Yamuná.
কালিমা, *s.* blackness, darkness.
কালিষ্ঠ, *a.* weatherbeaten, sunburnt, tawny.
কালিষ্ঠবর্ণ, *s.* a tan colour : *a.* tawny.
কালী, *s.* ink; the goddess Kálí; a stain, a stigma : *a.* black, filthy, squalid.
কালীন, or কালীয়, *a.* relating to time.
কাল্পনিক, *a.* feigned, false, hypocritical, artificial, fictitious : *s.* a hypocrite.
কাল্পনিকতা, *s.* hypocrisy, dissimulation.
কাল্য, *a.* squalid, dingy; pleasant talk.
কাশ, *s.* a cough; a kind of grass.[4]
কাশন্দি, *s. vide* কাসন্দি, কাস, &c.
কাশিয়া, *s* a tall species of grass.[4]
কাশী, *s.* the name of the city of Benares.
কাশ্মীর, *s.* the name of a country.
কাশ্মীরী, *a.* belonging to Káshmír.
কাষ্ঠ, *s.* wood, timber, fuel.
কাষ্ঠপাদুকা, *s.* a clog, a sandal.
কাষ্ঠময়, *a.* woody, wooden, well wooded.
কাষ্ঠমল্ল, *s.* a raft of timber.
কাষ্ঠা, *s.* a point of the compass, space, a tract, a region, a place, a site, a limit, a boundary, excellence, superiority.
কাষ্ঠাসন, *s.* a stool, a bench.
কাষ্টিক, *s. Eng.* caustic, a cautery.
কাস্নি, *s.* endive (Cichorium endivia).
কাস, *v. n.* to cough : *s.* a cough, rheum.
কাসকর, *a.* occasioning cough.
কাসঘ্ন, *a.* good to remove a cough.
কাসন, *s.* the act of coughing.
কাসন্দি, *s.* sauce, pickle, a pickle made of mango, tamarind, and mustard seed.
কাসপীড়িত, *a.* afflicted with a cough.
কাসরোগ, *s.* a cough, the consumption.
কাসী, *s.* a cough; the consumption.
*কাসীদ, *s.* a courier, a messenger.
কাসীস, *s.* copperas, green vitriol.
কাসুয়া, *a.* afflicted with a cough.
কাস্তিয়া, *s.* a sickle; চোরা, a name of a bird.
কাহকে, *ad.* to any one, to some one.
কাহণ, কার্ষাপণ, *s.* 16 panas of 1280 cauris.
কাহাকে, কাহারে to whom? what person?
কাহার, *s.* pálki-bearer : *ad.* whose? -দিগকে, to whom? -দের, -দিগের, whose?
কাহারবা, *s.* a kind of dance.
কাহিনী, *s.* a tale, a story, a narration, a history.
কাহিল, *a.* weak, faint, weary, ill.
কাহিলী, *s.* weakness, faintness, illness.
কি, or কিং, *pron.* what?
*কিংখাব, *s.* a kind of silk or brocade.
কিংশুক, *s.* a flower tree (Butea frondosa).
কিঙ্কর, দাস, *s.* a servant, a slave.
কিঙ্করতা, -ত্ব, *s.* servitude, slavery.
কিঙ্কিণী, *s.* a girdle set with small bells, small bell, any tinkling ornament.
কিচড়, or কিচা, *s.* mud, mire, dirt, slime.
কিচির-কিচির, -মিচির, কিচ্মিচ্, *s.* a chirping or chattering noise.
কিচ্কিচ্, *s.* the grating of sand between the teeth.
কিছু, *pron.* some, a little, any (thing).
কিছুকিছু, *pron.* some, a little, somewhat.

কিন্তাত, *ad.* what sort ! how altered for the worse ! (in a ludicrous sense.)

কিজানি, *ad.* perhaps, lest, for fear of.

কিঞ্চন, *pron.* some ; any, a little.

কিঞ্চিৎ, *pron.* some, any, a few, a little, somewhat, very little.

কিঞ্চিদপেক্ষা, *ad.* within a little, almost.

কিঞ্চুলুক, কেঁচুয়া, *s.* a worm, the earthworm.

কিট্‌কিট্, কিট্‌কিটা, *a.* dirty, filthy, squalid.

কিট্‌মিট্, কিড়্‌মিড়, *s.* the same as কিড়িমিড়ি.

কিড়া, or কীড়া, *s.* a worm, a maggot.

কিড়িমিড়ি, কিড়্‌মিড়নি, *s.* the grinding or gnashing of the teeth through rage.

কিণ্, *v. a.* to buy, to acquire by purchase.

কিণ, *s.* a wart, a mole, a corn or callosity, a cicatrix, a scar, a wood-insect.

কিণন, *a.* buying, a purchasing. [trade.

কিণাবেচা, *s.* a buying, and selling, traffic,

কিতা, *s.* a share, a parcel or spot of ground.

কিতাকিতা, *s.* shares : *ad.* in parcels.

*কিতাব, *s.* a book ; -খানা, a library.

*কিতাবৎ, *s.* the learning to write, writing.

কিনা, *phra.* that is to say, videlicet : *s.* a purchase; hatred, malice: *a.* purchased.

কিনার, কিনারা, or কিনারী, *s.* a shore, an edge, a margin, a brim, a hem.

কিনারায়, *ad.* ashore, on the brink.

কিন্তু, *conj.* but, moreover, further.

কিন্নর, *s.* fabled beings with horses' heads.

কিন্নরবর্ষ, *s.* a division of the earth.

কিপর্য্যন্ত, *a.* how far ? how long ? *ad.* till

কিপ্রকার, *ad.* how ? what kind ? [when ?

*কিফাইৎ, *s.* gain, profit, gain on trade.

কিফাইতী, *a.* saving, profitable. [lent !

কিবা, *pron.* what ? what ! *ad.* how excel-

কিমত, *a.* how ? in what way ? [intention ?

কিমর্থে, *ad.* why ? wherefore ? with what

*কিমা, *a.* minced : *s.* prepared molasses for the tobacco ; -কৃ, to mince flesh.

কিমাকার, *ad.* what sort ? how formed ? *a.* of an uncertain or uncommon form.

*কিমিআ, গরী, chemistry ; -গির, chemist.

কিমিআবিদ্যা, *s.* the science of chemistry.

*কিম্‌খাব, *s.* a. sort of brocade.

কিম্পচান, *s.* a miser : *a.* miserly, niggardly.

কিম্বদন্তী, *s.* a rumour, common report.

কিম্বা, *conj.* or, else, otherwise, either.

কিম্ভূত, what ? how ? what kind ? [what !

কিম্ভূতকিমাকার, *a.* what sort ! how ? like

কিয়ৎ, *pron.* some, a few, a little. [ago.

কিয়ৎকাল, *ad.* how long ? some little time

কিয়ৎকালে, *ad.* in a short time.

কিয়দ্দিন, *ad.* how long ? some days ago.

কিয়ান, *pron.* what ? some.

কির, *v. a.* to expunge, erase, cross out.

কিরণ, *s.* a ray, sun-beam ; an erasure.

কিরণমাত্র, *s.* a mere ray. [splendid.

কিরণময়, কিরণান্বিত, *a.* radiant, refulgent,

কিরা, *s.* an oath; কৃ, or খা, to take an oath.

কিরাট, *s.* a miser ; a dealer. [চিরতা.

কিরাত, *s.* a mountaineer, a savage ; *vide*

কিরীচ *s.* a sword, a dagger, poniard, dirk.

কিরীট, *s.* a crest, tiara, diadem, a crown.

কিরূপ, *a.* what sort ? what kind ? *ad.* how ?

কির্‌কির, *s.* a grating sensation.

কির্‌কিরা, *s.* cut work upon a ring.

*কিমিচী, *a.* crimson, scarlet.

কিল, *ad.* certainly, indeed : *s.* the fist, box ; -দাগড়া, callous, hardened by beating.

কিলা, *v.* to beat with the fist ; -কিলি,

কিলান, *s.* beating with the fist. [fisticuffs.

কিলানি *s.* a beating or blow with the fist.

কিলাস, *s.* a blotch, a whitish mark.

কিল্‌কিল, *s.* a jumbling or rippling sound.

কিল্লা, *s.* a fort ; -দার, the governor of a fort ; -দারী, the office of a killádár.

কিশোর, *s.* a colt, young of any animal, a child under fifteen years of age.

*কিশ্‌তী, *s.* a ship, a boat, a tray, emulation, a particular movement in chess.

কিশ্‌মিশ, *s.* raisin, dried grapes.

কিস্তি, *s.* an instalment ; a boat. [ments.

কিস্তিবন্দী, *s.* agreement to pay by instal-

*কিস্‌মৎ *s.* a part, division ; fortune, fate.

*কিস্সা, *s.* a story, tale ; -গো, a story-teller.

কীকস, *s.* a bone ; a worm : *a.* hard.

কীট, কীড়া, *s.* an insect, a worm, a maggot.

কীটময়, *a.* full of insects, maggoty.

কীটমাত্র, *s.* a mere insect. [contempt).

কীটস্থকীট, *s.* an insect living on insect, (in

কীদৃক্, কীদৃশ, *ad.* of what sort ? how ?

*কীমুক্ত, কিমখ্ত, *s.* a kind of leather.

*কীমৎ, *s.* the price or value of a thing.

কীর, *s.* a parrot ; a native of Káshmír.

কীরাট, কীকট, *a.* niggardly, penurious, miserly, avaricious, poor : *s.* a miser.
কীর্ত্তন, *s.* a shouting, a singing praise, celebrating, a singing in concert.
কীর্ত্তনিয়া, কীর্ত্তন্যা, he who shouts or sings.
কীর্ত্তি, reputation, celebrity, fame, renown.
কীর্ত্তিকর, *a.* making famous, praising.
কীর্ত্তিগায়ক, *s.* a flatterer, a panegyrist.
কীর্ত্তিপতাকা, *s.* a badge of fame or honour.
কীর্ত্তিবর্ণনা, *s.* a panegyric, an eulogy.
কীর্ত্তিমান্, *a.* renowned, famed, celebrated.
কীল, *s.* a pin, a wedge, a peg, a nail, a bolt, the fist, a box, a blow : *v. a.* to box, blow.
কীলক, *s.* a pin, a wedge, a peg, a spike.
কীলা, *v. a.* to box, to beat with the fist.
কীলাকীলি, *s.* pugilism, a boxing, fisticuffs.
কীলান, কীলন, *s.* a striking with the fist.
কীলাল, *s.* water, blood, honey ; -ধি, the sea.
কীলিত, *a.* wedged up, pinned, beaten.
কু, a prefix used in *comp.* meaning evil, bad, contemptible, base, diminutive.
*__কুঅৎ__, *s.* power, force, strength, ability.
কুআ, *s.* a well ; -ড়া, or -শা, a mist, a fog.
কুঁকড়, *v. n.* to shrivel up, to contract.
কুঁকড়ি-মুকড়ি, -সুকড়ি, *a.* nipped or chilled with cold, shrivelled, contracted.
কুচ, *s.* a small heron ; the seed of Abrus precatorius, used as a weight.
কুঁচবক, *s.* a species of crouching heron.
কুঁচি, *s.* a brush, a bristle brush, a tooth-brush.
কুঁচিয়া, *s.* the Indian eel fish.[1]
কুঁচিয়াচক্ষুয়া, *a.* having small eyes.
কুঁচিলা, *s.* the nux vomica and its tree.[2]
কুঁজ, *a.* deformed, hump-backed : *s.* a gugglet.
কুঁজড়, *a.* scurrilous, mean, abusive.
কুঁজি, *a.* (*fem.*) hump-backed : *s.* a key.
কুঁড়, *s.* a small fen or morass.
কুঁড়, কুঁড়া, *s.* the inner husk of rice.
কুঁড়ি, কুঁড়ী, *s.* the bud, or calyx of a flower ; a cup, a bowl, a basin, a betel-basin.
কুঁড়িয়া, *s.* a cottage, small hut ; a stone mortar, a student's water-pot ; -পাথর, a stone-bowl ; -হাঁড়ি, salt-maker's pot.
কুঁড়কাড়, *s.* a pit, a low land for rice.
কুঁড়মুড়, *s.* the sound of gnawing bone.
কুঁথ, *v. n.* to groan, to strain at stool.
কুঁদ, *v.* to skip, jump ; to turn in a lathe.
কুঁদ, *s.* a turner's lathe ; -কাঠ, a piece of turnery ; the posts of a lathe.
কুঁদন, *s.* a skipping, a jumping ; the turning of any thing in a lathe.
কুঁদনফাঁদন, *s.* a frisking or jumping for joy.
কুঁদনি, *s.* the act of skipping or jumping.
কুঁদবাটালি, *s.* a turner's chisel.
কুঁদরকী, *s.* the frankincense tree.[3]
কুঁদলা, কুন্দল, *s.* a quarrel, a dispute.
কুঁদলীয়া, কুন্দলীয়া, quarrelsome, litigious.
কুঁদা, *s.* a gun-stock : *a.* turned in a lathe.
কুঁদার, কুন্দার, *s.* a turner.
কুঁদি, *s.* a washerman's mallet to beat cloth.
কুঁদো, *a.* thick ; -কাঠ, a block, log of wood.
কুঁপ, *a.* having crooked or distorted arms.
কুক, *s.* a loud voice, the barking of a dog.
কুকর, *a.* having a crooked hand.
কুকর্ম্ম, *s.* an evil action, wickedness, sin.
কুকর্ম্মমাত্র, *s.* a mere crime ; merely crime.
কুকর্ম্মা, কুকর্ম্মী, *a.* wicked, vicious, sinful.
কুকাপ, *a.* evil, difficult, dark : *s.* a difficulty, a dilemma, darkness.
কুকার্য্য, *s.* an evil action, wickedness, sin.
কুকিল, *s.* Indian cuckoo (Cuculus indicus).
কুকুড়া, *s.* a fowl, gallinaceous fowl.
কুকুন্দর, *s.* the cavities of the loins.
কুকুর, *s.* a dog ; -ছা, a puppy ; -মাছী, a dog tick ; -রব, barking of a dog ; *fem.* কুকুরী.
কুকুরজিহ্বা, *s.* the name of a fish.[4]
কুকুরশুঙ্গা, *s.* the name of a plant.[5]
কুকো, *s.* a large species of cuckoo.[6]
কুক্কুট, *s* a cock, a fowl ; *fem.* কুক্কুটী.
কুক্কুটধ্বনি, *s.* the crowing of a cock.
কুক্কুভ, *s.* a wild cock ; an oily gloss.
কুক্কুর, *s.* a cur, a dog ; *fem.* কুক্কুরী.
কুকুচি, কটি, বঙ্ক্ষণ, *s.* the hip joint.
কুক্রিয়, *a.* wicked, sinful, profligate.
কুক্রিয়া, *s.* a bad action, a crime, a sin.
কুক্রিয়াকর্ত্তা, *s.* the doer of a bad action.
কুক্রিয়াকারী, *a.* wicked, profligate.
কুক্রিয়াম্বিত, *a.* guilty, sinful.
কুক্ষি, *s.* the belly, the cavity of the abdomen.
কুগঠন, কুগড়ন, *s.* bad workmanship.
কুগতিক, *s.* misconduct, misfortune, calamity.
কুগ্রহ, *s.* an inauspicious planet.
কুঘটন, *s.* an evil occurrence, a mishap.
কুচ্ছী, কুৎসী, *s.* an offensive speech, abuse.

কুঙ্কুম, *s.* saffron; red powder play-balls.
কুচ্, *v. a.* to cut, to cut into small chips, to chip: *s.* the sound of cutting.
কুচ, a chip; woman's breast, pap; a march.
কুচকলিকা, কুচকোরক, *s.* a woman's breast.
কুচকাচা, *s.* chips and shaving. [conspiracy.
কুচক্র, *s.* evil society, a circle of bad men;
কুচক্রী, *s.* an evil adviser, evil companions.
কুচন, কুচান, *s.* cutting into bits; shrinking.
কুচমর্দ্দন, *s.* playing with a woman's breasts.
কুচরিত্র, *s.* an evil inclination or bias.
কুচর্য্যা, *s.* evil conduct, bad habit.
কুচল, *a.* small, little, minute; *vide* খেঁচল.
কুচা, *v. a.* to chip, to gnaw: *s.* a chip, a shaving, a splinter, a fragment.
কুচাগ্র, *s.* the nipple of the breast.
কুচি, *s.* a brush, confectioner's brush; chip,
কুচিকিৎসক, *s.* a quack doctor. [bit, strip.
কুচিকিৎসা, *s.* quackery, bad acts in physic.
কুচিন্তক, *a.* thinking evil, contriving evil: *s.* one who plots mischief. [evil.
কুচিন্তা, *s.* an evil thought, the plotting of
কুচিন্তাকারী, *a.* plotting or contriving evil.
কুচিলা, *s.* nux vomica: *vide* কুঁচিলা.
কুচেল, *a.* ill-clothed, shabbily attired.
কুচেষ্টক, *a.* doing evil, mischievous. [chief.
কুচেষ্টা, *s.* an exertion to do evil of mis-
কুচ্কি, *s.* the groins, hollow of the hips.
কুছন্দ, *s.* doggerel poetry, mean poems.
কুচ্ছা, *s.* slander, obloquy, accusation, stain a blot, a disgrace, libel, censure, blame.
কুচ্ছাবাদী, *s.* a slanderer, an accuser.
কুচ্ছিত, *a.* ugly, bad, evil, uncomely.
কুচরামুচরা *s.* fragments and small chips.
কুছ্, *pron.* some, a little, any (thing).
কুজ, *s.* an earthen water-bottle; Tuesday, the planet Mars: *a.* hump-backed.
কুজড়, কুজড়া, *a.* low, base, mean, vulgar.
কুজড়বৃত্তি, কুজড়ামি, *s.* meanness, vulgarity.
কুজন, *s.* a low, mean, or vulgar person.
কুজা, *a.* deformed, crooked, hump-backed: *s.* an earthen water-bottle, a gugglet.
কুজ্ঝটিকা, কুজ্ঝটি, *s.* a mist, a fog.
কুজ্ঞান, *s.* an evil idea or design, craft.
কুজ্ঞানী, crafty, having evil idea or design.
কুঞ্চিকা, *s.* the seeds of কুঁচ; *vide* কুঁচিয়া.
কুঞ্চিত, *a.* warped, shriveled, curled.

কুঞ্জ, *s.* ivory; a grove, a bower, arbour.
কুঞ্জর, elephant; in *comp.* chief, eminent, noble.
কুঞ্চিকা, কুঞ্চী, কুঁজিকাঠি, *s.* a key. [noble.
কুট্, *v. a.* to pound, to beat, to pulverize: *s.* a pinch or sudden gripe. কুট্ করিয়া, with a sudden pinch or gripe. [shaving.
কুট, *s.* a piece of straw or stick, a chip, a
কুটন, *s.* a beating or pounding to powder: pounded to pulp. [between, a pimp.
কুটনা, *a.* fit to be beat to a pulp: *s.* a go-
কুটনী, she who peels vegetables; a procuress, a bawd; -পনা, business of a bawd.
কুটরী, *s.* an apartment, a room, a cabin.
কুটরীয়া, belonging to the hollow of a tree.
কুটরিয়াপেচা, *s.* a species of owl. [pulp.
কুটা, *v. a.* to cause to pound or beat to a
কুটা, কুটাকাটা, *a.* cut and chopped: *s.* a bit of straw or stick, a chip, a shaving.
কুটান, *s.* a causing to pound.
কুটার্থ, *s.* a quibble, a covered design.
কুটি, *s.* a morsel, a bit of stick or straw, a splinter, a small chip; the leprosy.
কুটিকরা, *a.* pounded, pulverized.
কুটিকুটি, *ad.* by small particles, by bits.
কুটিচর, *s.* a porpoise, the sea-hog.
কুটিয়া, *a.* leprous: *s.* a leper. [insidious,
কুটিল, *a.* crooked, insincere, disingenuous.
কুটিলতা, -ত্ব, *s.* crookedness, insincerity.
কুটিলান্তঃকরণ, *a.* insincere, fraudulent.
কুটী, *s.* an assembly; also, *vide* কুঠী.
কুটীর, *s.* a shed, hovel, booth, hut, a stall.
কুটুম্ব, *s.* a kinsman, a relative by marriage.
কুটুম্বতা, *s.* relationship, kindred. [ship.
কুটুম্বিতা, *a.* related to any one: *s.* relation-
কুটুম্বী, *s.* householder, master of a house.
কুটকুট্, কুটকুটনি, *s.* a throb, a twinging or itching sensation, querulousness.
কুটকুটিয়া, *a.* peevish, querulous. [ress.
কুটনী, *s.* a go-between, a bawd, a procu-
কুটপাট্, *a.* excessive (laughter). [bud.
কুট্মল, *s.* an unopened bud, an opening,
কুষ্ঠ, *s.* the leprosy; a tree.
কুঠরী, *s.* an apartment, a cottage, a cabin, a room, the body of a carriage.
কুঠার, *s.* an axe, a hatchet.
কুঠী, *s.* a house, a palace, the house of an employer, a factory, a banking-house.

কুঠীৱালা, *s.* a banker, an agent, a merchant, the owner of house, a landlord.
কুঠীয়া, কুঠ্যা, *a.* leprous; indolent, (in contempt.)
কুঠীয়াবেঙ্গ, *s.* a toad, landfrog.
কুড়্, *v.* to collect, to pick up, to glean.
কুড়, *s.* the leprosy; a medicinal drug; in *comp.* a heap, a pile; a bighá; *vide* বিঘা.
কুড়কালি, *s.* the working a sum in land measure, and giving the result in bighás.
কুড়ন, কুড়ান, *s.* the act of picking up or collecting: *a.* picked up, gathered.
কুড়নীয়া, কুড়ানীয়া, *a.* found, picked up.
কুড়ল, *s.* fishing eagle or osprey;[1] an axe.
কুড়া, *v. a.* to collect, to pick up, to glean.
কুড়া, *s.* a bighá of land; *vide* বিঘা.
কুড়ালি, কুড়ুল, *s.* an axe, a hatchet.
কুড়ি, *s.* leprosy; a score, twenty; -কুষ্ঠ, leprosy.
কুড়িয়া, *s.* a hut, a shed, a stall: *a.* leprous; inactive, lazy, indolent (in contempt).
কুড়ুক, *a.* about to hatch (as a hen).
কুডৌল, *a.* deformed, shapeless, clumsy.
কুড্য, *s.* a wall, plastering of a wall.
কুড়্যা, *a.* leprous; indolent, torpid, slow, lazy.
কুড়্যামি, *s.* indolence, torpitude, slowness, laziness.
কুণ্, *s.* vibration of a string.
কুণ্‌কুণ্, *s.* a griping pain in the bowels.
কুণপ, *s.* a corpse, a dead body.
কুণী, *s.* a whitlow; the elbow; withered arm.
কুণুয়া, কুণো, *a.* slinking into a corner, shy, bashful, timid.
কুণোবিড়াল, *s.* a tom-cat.
কুণোবেঙ্গ, *s.* a species of frog or toad.
কুণোমি, *s.* shyness, a shrinking from sight.
কুণ্ঠ, কুণ্ঠিত, *a.* indolent, stupid, silly.
কুণ্ড, *s.* a pit, sacrificial pit, a bowl; a bastard.
কুণ্ডল, *s.* earring; a coil of rope.
কুণ্ডলধারী, *a.* wearing earrings.
কুণ্ডলাকার, কুণ্ডলাকৃতি, *a.* circular, annulous.
কুণ্ডলী, *a.* coiling, winding, assuming a spiral form; -পাকা, to coil, to twine.
কুণ্ডলীপাকানা, *a.* serpentine.
কুণ্ডিকা, কুণ্ডী, *s.* a basin, a hemispherical vessel.
কুৎ, *s.* the ascertaining the quantity of an article by guess: *a.* ascertained by guess; -কৃ, to ascertain by guess.
কুতঃ, *ad.* whence? from which?
কুতপ, *s.* great or disagreeable heat, the eighth hour, or the middle of the day.
কুতপকাল, *s.* hottest part of the day, or the midday.
কুতর, *a.* bad, evil, bad in kind.
কুতুপ, *s.* a small leathern bottle for oil, etc.
*কুতুব, or কুতুবখানা, *s.* a library.
কুতুরকাতুর, *s.* a tickling, a tickling sensation.
কুতু, *s.* a large leathern bottle for oil, etc.
কুতুহল, *s.* eagerness, vehemence, briskness, sport, pleasure, merriment, gratification.
কুতুহলী, *a.* sportive, playful, gratifying, vehement, impetuous, brisk, active.
কুৎকরণ, *s.* the ascertaining of the quantity of an article by guess.
কুত্তা, *s.* a cur, a dog. কুত্তী, *s.* a bitch.
কুত্র, *ad.* where? in what place?
কুত্রচিৎ, *ad.* wherever, wheresoever.
কুত্রাপি, *ad.* wherever, wheresoever, any where, somewhere.
কুৎসা, *s.* censure, blame, calumny, blot, reproach, slander, accusation, ugliness.
কুৎসাকারক, কুৎসাবাদী, *a.* reproaching, calumniating, censorious, slanderous.
কুৎসাময়, *a.* vile, full of evil, disgraceful, reproaching, scandalous, ugly, deformed.
কুৎসিত, *a.* ugly, low, mean, vile, deformed, disagreeable, disgusting, hateful.
কুথলী, *s.* a checkered cloth, a horse-cloth.
কুদাঁড়া, *s,* evil conduct, an evil course of actions.
কুদাল, কুদালি, *s.* a digging hoe.
কুদালিয়া, *s.* the name of a plant.[2]
কুদিন, *s.* an unlucky day, a cloudy day.
কুদেশ, *s.* a bad or unhealthy country, a country subject to injustice.
*কুদরৎ, *s.* power, might, force, ability.
কুদরতী, *a.* powerful, able, forcible.
কুধারা, *s.* an evil custom, evil conduct.
কুনাম, *s.* infamy, a bad reputation.
কুনীতি, *s.* low or perverted morals.
কুন্‌কুন্, *s.* a throbbing, a griping pain.
কুন্‌কুনানি, *s.* a throbbing pain.
কুন্তল, *s.* hair of the head, a lock of hair; barley.
কুন্থন, *s.* a groaning, a straining at stool.
কুন্দ, *s.* frankincense; a lathe; -কর, a turner; -বাটালি, a turner's chisel.
কুন্দন, *s.* a leaping, jumping, skipping.
কুন্দল, *s.* a quarrel, a dispute, wrangling.
কুন্দলীয়া, *a.* quarrelsome, disputacious, litigious.
কুন্দুরু, *s.* incense, frankincense.

কুন্দুরুকী, *s.* the frankincense tree.[1] [etc.
কুপ, কুপা, *s.* a large leathern bottle for oil,
কুপথ, কুপন্থা, *s.* a bad road, evil con duct.
কুপথগমন, *s.* the going in an evil way.
কুপথগামী, *a.* going in an evil way.
কুপথ্য, *a.* unwholesome, hurtful (as diet): *s.* unwholesome diet. [advice.
কুপরামর্শ, *s.* evil counsel, intrigue, bad
কুপরামর্শী, *a.* giving bad counsel, caballing: *s.* one who gives evil counsel.
কুপিত, *a.* angry, vexed, provoked; -বায়ু, an aggravated state of flatulency.
কুপ্রিয়, *a.* despicable, base, low, mean.
কুবক্তা, *s.* an incorrect or bad speaker.
কুবচ, *a.* calumnious, slanderous.
কুবচন, *s.* abuse, obscenity, scurrility.
কুবলয়, *s.* a waterlily (in general).
কুবাক্য, *s.* an evil speech, obscene word.
কুবাক্যবাদী, *a.* speaking evil or obscenely.
কুবাস, *s.* disagreeable scent. কুবাসী, fœtid.
কুবিক্রম, tyrannical, oppressive. [cision.
কুবিচার, *s.* unfair judgment, a wrong de-
কুবিচারকর্ত্তা, *s.* an unfair or unjust judge.
কুবিবেচনা, *s.* an unfair investigation.
কুবুদ্ধি, *s.* a perverted understanding, craft.
কুবের, *s.* Indian Plutus, god of wealth.
কুব্জ, *a.* crook-backed, hump-backed.
কুব্জীকৃত, *a.* made to be deformed. [cond.
*কুমক, *s.* help, a sidesman, a helper, a se-
কুমড়া, *s.* a kind of gourd; -ঘণ্ট, a dish made of kumṛá;[2] -বড়ি, kumṛá balls.
কুমন্ত্র, *s.* evil counsel; a charm to do evil.
কুমন্ত্রণা, *s.* evil counsel or advice, intrigue.
কুমন্ত্রী, *s.* an evil counsellor.
কুমরিকাপোকা, *s.* the Spanish fly.
কুমার, *s.* a lad, a son, a boy, a prince, the heir apparent; Kárttika; a potter.
কুমারিকা, *s.* a virgin, a girl, a young girl; a wooden catch; the Spanish fly.
কুমারিকাখণ্ড, *s.* in *geo.* a division of the earth; it contains India, etc.
কুমারী, *s.* a young girl, a daughter, a virgin, a girl; Durgá; a portion of Jambu dwipa, cape Comorin; a plant.[3]
কুমারীপূজা, *s.* a ceremony at the festival of Durgá, in which a girl is worshipped as a representative of the goddess.
কুমারীভোজন, *s.* a religious repast at the festival of Durgá, in which a girl is fed as the representative of the goddess.
কুমীর, কুমুর, *s.* same as কুম্ভীর. [lotus.
কুমুদ, *s.* the white and red variety of the
কুমুদিনী, কুমুদ্বতী, *s.* assemblage of lotuses.
কুমকুম, *s.* saffron; redstuff play-balls.
কুম্প, *a.* having a crooked arm.
কুম্ভ, *s.* a jar, a pitcher; the frontal globes of an elephant; the sign Aquarius.
কুম্ভক, *s.* a religious ceremony which consists in closing the nostrils and mouth.
কুম্ভকর্ণ, *s.* one of the brothers of Rávana.
কুম্ভকামলা, *s.* the dropsy, watery disease.
কুম্ভকার, *s.* a potter, maker of earthenware.
কুম্ভরাশি, *s.* the sign Aquarius.
কুম্ভলগ্ন, *s.* the time of the day in which the sign Aquarius rises above the horizon.
কুম্ভিল, *s.* a thief, a pickpocket, a plagiarist, a paraphrast, a wife's brother.
কুম্ভীপাক, *s.* one of the Hindu hells.
কুম্ভীর, *s.* a crocodile, an alligator.
কুযশঃ, *s.* a bad name, a blasted reputation.
কুযশোবিশিষ্ট, *a.* dishonorable, infamous.
কুযাত্রা, *s.* a bad or inauspicious journey.
কুযুক্তি, *s.* evil counsel, unjust decision.
কুর, *v. a.* to scrape thin, to gnaw through.
কুরঙ্গ, *s.* a deer, an antelope.
কুরঙ্গনয়না, *a.* fawn-eyed, deer-eyed.
কুরচিপোনা, *s.* the name of a fish.[4]
কুরণ, *s.* a scraping, scratching: *a.* scraped
কুরণী, *s.* a cocoanut-scraper. [thin.
কুরণ্ড, *s.* the sarcocele, the hydrocele.
কুরল, *s.* the osprey (Falco halietas).
কুরীতি, *s.* a bad custom, an evil habit.
কুরু, *s.* in *mytho.* name of a famous king.
কুরুই, *s.* gravel, nodules of limestone.
কুরুক্ষেত্র, *s.* a country near Delhi, where the famous battle was fought between Kuru and Pandu, in which the whole race of the former was destroyed.
কুরুচি, *s.* disgust, distaste, dislike, loss of
কুরুজ, *s.* the wards of a lock. [appetite.
কুরুবর্ষ, *s.* the most northerly division of the earth called Uttara-kuru.
কুরূপ, *s.* an ugly or uncourth form, a bad conformation: *a.* ugly, deformed.

কুরূপতা, -ত্ব, *s.* ugliness, deformity.
কুরূপী, *a.* ill-formed, uncouth, ugly.
কুরুট, *s.* sweepings, filth, dirt, rubbish.
কুর্‌কুর্‌, *s.* the barking of a little dog.
কুরকুরণি, *s.* a scratching, a tickling, lust.
কুর্ণিস, *s.* a bow, obeisance.
কুর্ত্তা, *s.* a coat, a jacket. [to gambol.
কুর্দ, *v. a.* to play, to skip, to leap, to frisk,
কূর্পর, *s.* the elbow, knee : *a.* subject to.
কুল্‌, *v. a.* to abound, to be sufficient.
কুল, *s.* lineage, a race, a family, a tribe, pedigree, extraction, a flock or herd; a fan for winnowing corn;[1] the jujube.
কুলকণ্টক, *s.* one who is a plague to his family, (*lit.*) a thorn of the family.
কুলকলঙ্ক, *s.* one who is a disgrace to the family, a family stain or dishonour.
কুলকুচ, *s.* the gargling of the mouth.
কুলক্রিয়া, কুলকর্ম্ম, *s.* the duties of a family.
কুলক্ষণ, *s.* an evil or inauspicious mark.
কুলক্ষণাক্রান্ত, *a.* marked by inauspicious.
কুলক্ষয়, *s.* the decay of a family.[marks.
কুলগরিমা, কুলগৌরব, *s.* family pride.
কুলগ্ন, *s.* an inauspicious ascension of one of the signs of the zodiac.
কুলচ্যুত, *a.* fallen from family privileges.
কুলজ, কুলজাত, *a.* born of a good family.
কুলজী, *s.* a genealogy, a family register.
কুলটা, *s.* a whore, prostitute, a courtezan.
কুলটাপতি, *s.* whore's husband, a cuckold.
কুলদর্প, *s.* family pride or importance.
কুলধর্ম্ম, *s.* family duty, duties of a family.
কুলন, *s.* a being sufficient : *a.* sufficient.
কুলবতী, *f.* reputable, of respectable family.
কুলবধূ, *s.* a virtuous wife, a good wife.
কুলবধূতা, *s.* virtue or chastity in a wife.
কুলভঙ্গ, *s.* a fall from family honour.
কুলভ্রষ্ট, *a.* expelled from family honour.
কুলমর্য্যাদা, *s.* family respectability.
কুলমান, or কুলশীল, *s.* family honour.
কুলসী, *s.* articles tied in a sheaf of straw for the convenience of carriage.
কুলস্ত্রী, *s.* a virtuous woman, a house wife.
কুলা, *v.* to possess, abound, to be sufficient : a fan to winnow corn. [family.
কুলাঙ্গার, *s.* one who is a disgrace to his
কুলাচার, *s.* a family usage or custom.
কুলাচার্য্য, *s.* a family registrar, a family priest who selects marriage matches.
কুলান, *s.* a being sufficient: *a.* sufficient.
কুলানীয়, *a.* supervisng, superintending.
কুলায়, *s.* a nest, a place of residence.
কুলাল, *s.* a potter; -চক্র, a potter's wheel.
কুলি, *s.* *Telianga*, a potter, a labourer.
কুলিচা, *s.* a kind of sweetmeat or biscuit.
কুলিয়াকাড়া, *s.* a thorny shrub.[2]
কুলিশ, *s.* the thunderbolt of Indra.
কুলীন, *a.* of noble descent: *s.* a nobleman.
কুলীনতা, -ত্ব, nobility, grandeur. [crab.
কুলীর, *s.* a crab; -শৃঙ্গী, the antennæ of a.
কুলুপ, *s.* a lock, a padlock; -কাঠি, a key.
কুলোদ্ভব, *s.* the origin of a family.
কুল্‌কুচ, *s.* the gargling of the mouth.
কুল্‌কুল্‌, কুল্‌কুলা, *s.* a gargling or rinsing.
কুল্‌চুর, *s.* smashed dry jujube pickle.
কুল্য, *s.* a wicker fan to winnow corn; a
কুল্ল, *ad.* only, wholly, in all. [bone.
কুল্লই, *s.* a nodule, gravel, gravel-stones.
কুল্লা, *s.* the gargling of the mouth.
কুশ, *v. a.* to hew timber, to hack.
কুশ, *s.* one of the seven continents of the Hindus; a son of Rama; sacred grass.[3]
কুশন, *s.* the hewing of timber, a hacking.
কুশল, *s.* welfare, peace, happiness, talent, ability, virtue: *a.* eminent in, clever.
কুশলী, *a.* prosperous, happy, lucky.
*কুশাদা, *a.* extensive, wide, spacious.
কুশাসন, *s.* mat of kusha grass, a hassock.
কুশী, *s.* a plough-share; a pod of cotton; a spoon-like vessel used for libations.
কুশীল, *a.* evil-disposed, wicked, spiteful.
কুশীলতা, *s.* wickedness, evil bias of mind.
কুশূল, *s.* a cup-board, a barn, a granary.
কুষী, *s.* the kernel of a mango-stone.
কুষীদ, কুসীদ, *s.* usury; -গ্রাহী, an usurer.
কুষ্ঠ, or কুষ্ঠরোগ, *s.* the leprosy.
কুষ্ঠঘ্ন, *a.* good to cure the leprosy.
কুষ্ঠময় *a.* leprous, full of leprosy.
কুষ্ঠরোগী, or কুষ্ঠী, *a.* leprous : *s.* a leper.
কুষ্মাণ্ড, *s.* the same as কুমড়া. [sumption.
কুষ্মাণ্ডখণ্ড, *s.* medicine for the cure of con-
কুসুম, flower; safflower; the menses.
কুসুম্ভ, *s.* the safflower plant.[4]
কুস্তাকুস্তি, *s.* mutual wrestling or scuffling.

কুস্তি, *s.* a wrestling; -গীর্, a wrestler.
কুস্বপ্ন, *s.* ominous dream, the nightmare.
কুহক, *s.* delusion, fascination, sorcery; a
কুহকী, *s.* a sorcerer, a juggler. [sorcerer.
কুহর, *s.* a cavity, a hole; the ear-hole.
কুহু, *s.* the new moon; note of the cuckoo.
কুহেড়িকা, কুহেড়ী, *s.* a mist, fog, haze.
কূচিকা, *s.* a painting brush.
কূট, *s.* a mountain-peak, a ream of paper, a heap, a water-jar, hammer, a mallet, ploughshare, plough, a deer-trap; illusion, deceit, falsehood: *a.* low, mean.
কূটক, *s.* a ploughshare; the eyeball.
কূটযন্ত্র, *s.* a snare, deer-trap, a net. [able.
কূটস্থ, *a.* unchangeable, uniform, unalter-
কূটাগার, *s.* an attic, an upper room.
কূটার্থ, *s.* obscurity, ambiguity, a fiction.
কূড়, *s.* a ream of paper; an end, a clue.
কূড্য, *s.* a wall. কূতনী, a sort of cloth or
কূথলী, *s.* a satchel, a wallet, a bag. [stuff.
কূপ, কুআ, *s.* a wall. কূপোদক, well-water.
কূপক, *s.* a mast, a stake in the ground.
কূপমণ্ডুক, *s.* a frog in the well, a man who has not seen the world.
কূর্চ্চ, *s.* space between the eyebrows.
কূর্চ্চিকা, *s.* inspissated milk. [boiling.
কূর্দ্দন, *s.* amusement, play, jumping, gam-
কূর্ম্ম, *s.* a tortoise, a turtle.
কূর্ম্মপিঠিয়া, *a.* tortoise-backed, gibbous.
কূর্ম্মপুরাণ, *s.* a book on Hindu religion.
কূর্ম্মাবতার, *s.* Vishnu's 2nd incarnation.
কূল, *s.* shore, bank, a heap, mound, a pond, the rear of an army; the jujube.'
কূলি, *s.* a porter, a labourer. [the bank.
কূলিকূলি, *ad* to the brim: *a.* reaching to
কৃ, *v. a.* to do, to make, to perform.
কৃকলাস, *s.* a lizard, a chameleon.
কৃচ্ছ্র, *s.* torment, pain, distress, difficulty, penance: *a.* distreseed, tormented.
কৃচ্ছ্রগত, *a.* tormented, suffering anguish or distress, engaged in a severe penance.
কৃচ্ছ্রলব্ধ, *a.* hard-earned, hard-acquired.
কৃৎ, *a.* doing, performing: *s.* affixes converting the roots into verbal nouns.
কৃত, *a.* done, performed, made.
কৃতকর্ম্মা, কৃতকার্য্য, *a.* skilful, fortunate,
কৃতকৃতার্থ, কৃতকৃত্য, *a. idem.* [successful.

কৃতঘ্ন, *a.* ungrateful, unthankful.
কৃতঘ্নতা, *s.* ingratitude, unthankfulness.
কৃতজ্ঞ, *a.* grateful, thankful.
কৃতজ্ঞতা, *s.* gratitude, thankfulness.
কৃতদার, *a.* married, wedded.
কৃতনিত্যক্রিয়, *a.* having performed the usual daily ceremonies of religion.
কৃতবিক্রয়, *a.* disposed of by sale, sold.
কৃতাঞ্জলি, -পুট, *a.* with the hands joined in a humble manner. [er; conclusion.
কৃতান্ত, *s.* death, Yama, universal destroy-
কৃতাপরাধ, *a.* guilty, criminal.
কৃতার্থ, *a.* successful, prosperous.
কৃতার্থী, *a.* desirous of success, thankful.
কৃতি, *s.* an act, action, deed.
কৃতিতা, -ত্ব, *s.* learning, talent, ability, an accomplishment, wisdom, piety, virtue.
কৃতী, *a.* learned, accomplished, expert, active, good, wise, virtuous, pious.
কৃত্তি, *s.* the skin, the hide of an antelope.
কৃত্তিকা, *s.* the Pleiades; Karttika's nurse.
কৃত্য, *s.* duty, a work, a motive, a cause.
কৃত্রিম, *a.* artificial, fictitious, counterfeit.
কৃৎস্ন, *a.* all, entire, the whole.
কৃদন্ত, *a.* terminated with one of the affixes used in the formation of verbals.
কৃপণ, *s.* a miser, a niggard: *a.* miserly, penurious, avaricious, mean, stingy.
কৃপণতা, *s.* niggardliness, parsimony. [ous.
কৃপণস্বভাব, *a.* miserly, niggardly, penuri-
কৃপণাশয়, *a.* mean, penurious, abject.
কৃপয়া, *ad.* graciously, compassionately.
কৃপা, *s.* compassion, pity, mercy, tenderness, kindness, clemency, grace, favour.
কৃপাকর, কৃপান্বিত, *a.* compassionate, pitiful, gracious, merciful, kind, tender.
কৃপাকর্ত্তা, *s.* a kind or merciful man.
কৃপানিধি, কৃপাসিন্ধু, *s.* an ocean of grace or mercy, a sea of compassion.
কৃপাপাত্র, *s.* an object of pity.
কৃপাবত্তা, *s.* mercifulness, favourableness.
কৃপাবলোকন, *s.* a look of pity, compassion, or kindness, a gracious look.
কৃপাবান্, কৃপালু, *a.* gracious, merciful, compassionate, pitiful, kind, tender.
কৃপাময়, *a.* full of compassion or mercy.
কৃপার্থী, *a.* desirous of compassion or pity.

কৃফলা, *s.* the class of compounds of which ৠ is the last member, the symbol (ৄ)
কৃমি, *s.* a worm, a maggot, an insect, the [lac insect.
কৃমিকর, *a.* breeding worms.
কৃমিঘ্ন, *a.* anthelmintic, worm-destroying.
কৃমিময়, *a.* abounding with worms. [ated.
কৃশ, *a.* meagre, wasted, lean, thin, emaci-
কৃশতা, -ত্ব, *s.* meagreness, thinness.
কৃশাঙ্গী, *a.* slender, delicate, slender-waist- [ed.
কৃশানু, *s.* fire; name of a plant.[1]
কৃষক, *a.* cultivating: *s.* a husbandman.
কৃষাণ, *s.* a husbandman, peasant, farmer.
কৃষাণী, *s.* husbandry, agriculture. [ing.
কৃষি, *s.* cultivation, agriculture, plough-
কৃষিকর্ম্ম, *s.* business of cultivating land.
কৃষিজীবী, *a.* living by agriculture. [man.
কৃষিলোক, *s.* an agriculturist, a husband-
কৃষিবল, *s.* a husbandman, a farmer.
কৃষ্ণ, *a.* black, dark-blue: *s.* the ninth incarnation of Vishnu; a black colour.
কৃষ্ণকেলি, কৃষ্ণচূড়া, *s.* two flower plants.[2]
কৃষ্ণজীরক, কৃষ্ণজীরা, *s.* same as কালজীরা.
কৃষ্ণতা, -ত্ব, *s.* blackness, blueness.
কৃষ্ণতুলসী, *s.* *vide* কালতুলসী. [privities.
কৃষ্ণদূর্ব্বা, *s.* a cant name for the hair of the
কৃষ্ণপক্ষ, *s.* the wane of the moon.
কৃষ্ণপক্ষীয়, *a.* bastard, illegitimate; obs-
কৃষ্ণপরায়ণ, *a.* devoted to Krishna. [cure.
কৃষ্ণবর্ণ, *a.* black, dark-blue.
কৃষ্ণবাবুই, *s.* a variety of the basil.[3]
কৃষ্ণমুগ, কৃষ্ণমুদগ, *s.* the same as কালমুগ.
কৃষ্ণসার, *s.* the black antelope.[4]
কৃষ্ণাভ্র, *s.* black talc, a black cloud.
ক্লৃ, *s.* the compound letter kli. [ed.
ক্লৃপ্ত, *a.* denominated, yclept, fixed, appoint-
ক্লৃফলা, *s.* that class of compound letters of which the last member is ঌ.
কে, or কেটা, *pron.* who? what person?
কেআ, কেআফুল, কেওড়া, *s* *vide* কেতক.
কেআরি, *s.* a garden bed; an anthelmintic medicine for cattle.
কেউ, *pron*, any one, some one. [pello.
কেউটিয়াসাপ, *s.* a variety of Cobra de ca-
কেউবা, কাক, বায়স, *s.* a crow,
কেও, *pron.* who is that?
কেই, কেঁইবীচি, *s.* seed of tamarind and [বকল.
কেঁউকেঁউ. *s.* the yelling of a dog.
কেঁএ, *s.* native of Keyán; *a.* quarrelsome, disputatious, captious, dogmatical.
কেঁকর, *s.* the creaking sound of a cart.
কেঁকোঁ, *s.* the croaking sound of a frog.
কেঁচ, *v. n.* to become raw, or inexpert.
কেঁচা, *s.* a kind of hog spear or pike.
কেঁচো, কেঁচুয়া, *s.* a worm, earthworm.
কেঁচকোল, *s.* a marble, ball of dried earth.
কেঁতুর, *s.* the sordes of the eye.
কেঁদ্, *v.* to weep (as *advl. pa.*): *s.* a tree.
কেঁদুআবাঘ, or কেঁদোবাঘ, *s.* a wolf.
কেঁদো, *a.* thick, clumsy: *s.* a wolf.
কেকর, *a.* crooked, squint-eyed.
কেকা, *s.* the call or note of a peacock.
কেচিৎ, *pron. pl.* some: *s.* some persons.
কেচুআ, কেচো, *a.* hypocritical, dissembling.
কেজুয়া, *a* useful, serviceable.
কেঠুআ, *a.* wooden, woody: *s.* a vessel to bale a boat, a large wooden bowl.
কেঠুআখটী, *s.* a wood-market.
কেঠুআনেড়, *s.* dry or hard ordure.
কেণ, *v. a.* to cause to purchase: *a.* bought: *s.* the act of purchasing.
কেণন, *s.* a buying, a purchasing.
কেণা, *a.* bought, purchased: *s.* a purchase.
কেণাবেচা, *s.* bargain and sale, traffic.
কেন্নো, *s.* a particular species of insect.
কেতক, কেতকী, *s.* a fragrant flower tree.[5]
কেতন, *s.* a flag, banner; a house, abode.
কেতাব, *s.* a book; -খানা, a library.
কেতু, *s.* the 9th planet in the Hindu system; in *astro.* the dragon's tail or descending node, a comet, ensign, a flag.
কেতুমালবর্ষ, *s.* a division of Jambu-dwipa.
কেদরাণী, *s.* liquid filth, the sordes.
কেদার, *s.* a field, a mountain; -নাথ, name [of Shiva.
কেদেরা, *s.* *Port.* a chair.
কেন, *ad.* why? wherefore?
কেননা, *ad.* for, because.
কেন্দুয়া, or কেন্দুয়াবাঘ, *s.* a wolf. [circle.
কেন্দ্র, *s.* in *astro.* the poles; centre of a
কেবল, *s.* simple, mere: *ad.* alone, only, ab- [solutely, certainly.
কেবা, *pron.* who?
কেমন, *ad.* how? what sort?
কেয়াল, *a.* winnowed, clean, marketable.
কেয়ূর, *s.* an ornament for the arm.
কেরবাল, *s.* a paddle, a small oar.

কেরাণী, *s.* a scribe, a writer, a clerk, accountant.

কেরাম, *s.* a cramp, a staple.

*কেরায়া, *s.* rent, hire, tenancy; -দার, a renter, a tenant; -দারী, tenantship.

কেলা, *v. a.* to peel, to skin: *s.* a plantain.

কেলান, *a.* peeled, skinned: *s.* the act of peeling, stripping or skinning.

কেলি, *s.* play, diversion, sport, fun.

কেলিকুতুহল, *s.* sport, pleasure, enjoyment.

কেলিগৃহ, *s.* a play-house, a theatre.

কেল্যানী, *s.* rice-gruel, sour gruel.

কেশ, *s.* the hair of the head, a mane.

কেশজ, *a.* produced from hair.

কেশব, *a.* hairy, shaggy: *s.* a name of Vishnu.

কেশবিন্যাস, *s.* the dressing of the hair.

কেশবেশ, *s.* the adorning of the hair.

কেশমার্জনী, *s.* a comb, a hair-brush.

কেশর, *s.* the filament of a flower; saffron.

কেশরাজ, কেশরিয়া, *s.* name of a plant.[1]

কেশরী, *s.* a hair: *a.* maned, having hair.

কেশহীন, *a.* bald, destitute of hair.

কেশাকর্ষণ, *s.* a pulling of the hair.

কেশী, কেশযুক্ত, *a.* hairy, having hair.

কেষী, *s.* the kernel of a mango stone.

কেহ, কেহু, *pron.* any body, any one, some one.

কৈ, *ad.* where? in what place?

কৈঁলা, কৈলা, *a.* tender, young: *s.* a sucking calf.

কৈঁলাবাছুর, *s.* a sucking calf.

কৈঙ্কর্য্য, *s.* servitude, slavery.

কৈতব, *s.* craftiness, deceit, fraud, a swindling.

*কৈদ, *s.* imprisonment; -খানা, a gaol.

কৈদী, *s.* a prisoner, a captive, a convict.

*কৈফ, *s.* intoxicating things, intoxication.

*কৈফিঅৎ, *s.* a doubt, a circumstance.

*কৈফী, *a.* addicted to intoxicating things: *s.* a tippler, a drunkard.

কৈবর্ত্ত, *s.* a fisherman; a class of Hindus.

কৈবল্য, *s.* identity with or absorption into the divine essence, emancipation.

কৈভোল, *s.* the name of a fish.[2]

কৈরব, *s.* the lotus, the waterlily.

কৈলাস, *s.* in *mytho.* the paradise of the Hindus, the residence of Shiva.

কৈশোর, *s.* boyhood, the time of boyish youth.

কো, *s.* a well, a fog or mist.

কোআড়া, কোআশা, *s.* a mist or fog, haze.

কোঁ, *s.* a groaning or croaking sound.

কোঁইট, *s.* a condition, a stipulation, a bet, a clause.

কোঁক, *s.* the flank, side, hip.

কোঁকড়, কোঁকড়া, *v.* to shrivel up, to curl, to crimp, to curl up, to shrink, to shrivel: *s.* a crumple, a curl, a contraction, a crisped place in a leaf, a fold.

কোঁকড়, কোঁকড়ান, *a.* shrivelled, crisped crimped, puckered: *s. vide* কোঁকড়ানি.

কোঁকড়ানি, *s.* a shrivelling up, a curling of hair, a crumpling of paper or cloth.

কোঁকা, *v. a.* to groan, to moan, to grunt.

কোঁকান, *s.* the act of groaning, a moaning.

কোঁকানি, *s.* a groan, a moan, a moaning.

কোঁকুড়, *v. n.* to shrink up, to shrivel, to contract, to become curled or crisped.

কোঁকোঁ, *s.* a groaning or croaking sound.

কোঁচ, *s.* a sheaf of fish spears, a harpoon.

কোঁচকা, কোঁকচা, *s.* a snarl in a rope occasioned by its being overtwisted.

কোঁচড়, *s.* the lap end of a garment tucked up in front just about the waist.

কোঁচড়াতমাক, *s.* a kind of tobacco.

কোঁচড়ায়াদাদু, *s.* a ringworm of the waist.

কোঁচনীপাড়া, *s.* a woman of Kuch Behar.

কোঁচবক, *s.* a species of heron.

কোঁচবেহার, *s.* the name of a country.

কোঁচা, *s.* the tuck of the lower garment: *v. a.* to plait, to pucker.

কোঁচান, *s.* a plat, the plaiting of cloth: *a.* puckered.

কোঁচাবহ, *s.* a train-bearer.

কোঁচাল, *a.* wearing the tuck of the garment long.

কোঁট, *s.* the clitoris.

কোঁড়, *s.* the tender stem of a bambu.

কোঁড়ক, or কোঁড়কছাতা, *s.* a mushroom.

কোঁড়ল, *s.* the hydrocele, the sarcocele.

কোঁড়া, *s. vide* কোঁড়; also, the loop-hole of an ornament, or of a gilt button.

কোঁৎ, *s.* a groan, a straining effort.

কোঁতা, কোঁতান, *vide* কোঁথ, &c.

কোঁৎকা, *s.* a club, a bludgeon: *v.* to beat, to bang; কোঁতকিয়া-দা, to beat, bang.

কোঁথ, কোঁথা, *v. n.* to groan, to grunt, to strain, to moan: *s.* a groan, a grunt.

কোঁথন, কোঁথান, *s.* the act of groaning or moaning, a grunting or straining.

কোঁথপাড়ন, *s.* the uttering of groans or plaintive sounds, a straining at stool.

কোঁথানি, *s.* a groaning, straining at stool.
কোঁথানীয়া, *a.* groaning, moaning.
কোঁদন, *s.* the same as কুঁদন.
কোঁদল, *s.* a dispute, a quarrel.
কোঁদলীয়া, *a.* disputatious, quarrelsome, captious.
কোঁদা, *v.* to cause to turn in a lathe : *a.* turned in a lathe : *s.* turning in a lathe.
কোঁদান, *s.* the causing to turn any article in a lathe : *a.* turned in a lathe.
কোঁপা, *a.* crooked-armed : a wooden instrument used by bricklayers to beat the mortar of a terrace roof and floor.
কোঁস্তা, *s.* a besom, a scrubbing brush.
কোক, *s.* a wolf, ruddy goose; a chameleon; a date-tree, a Sanskrit amatory work.
কোকনদ, *s.* the red lotus or waterlily.
কোকরন্দা, কোকশিমা, *s. vide* কুকুরশুঙ্গা.
কোকিল, *s.* the cuckoo; -ধ্বনি, his note.
কোঙ্কণ, *s.* the name of a country.
কোজাগর, *s.* a festival in honour of Lakshmí observed at full moon in Ashwina.
কোট, কোট্ট, *s.* a tower, a fort, citadel.
কোটন, *s.* the act of pounding or beating to a powder, the mincing of meat.
কোটনা, *s.* a pimp, a pander, a cuckold.
কোটনা, -পনা, -মি, *s.* the office of a pimp.
কোটর, *s.* the hollow part in a tree, a den.
কোটরিয়াপেচা, *s.* a species of owl.
কোটা, *v.* to beat to powder, to stamp, to pound, to mince, to reduce to a pulp.
কোটানি, *s.* a part of a fish or fruit given as a reward for cutting or peeling them.
কোটাল, *s.* a constable, a watchman.
কোটালী, *s.* the office of a constable or watchman, the police of a city.
কোটি, কোটী, *a.* a crore or ten millions : *s.* a sword-point; a wager, engagement.
কোটিকল্প, *ad.* for ever : *lit.* enduring through a crore of kalpas.
কোটীর, *s.* a cottage, hut, hovel, shed.
কোটীশ্বর, *s.* the lord of a crore of rupees.
কোট্যর্দ্ধ, *a.* five millions or half a crore.
কোট্যুদ্ধার, *s.* the fulfilling of an engagement, a solution.
কোঠ, *s.* a fort, squares on a chess board; the marks of leprosy; the ringworm.
কোঠরী, *s.* an apartment, a room, a cabin.

কোঠা, *s.* a mansion, house, brick-house.
কোঠি, *s.* a mansion, brick-house; *vide* কুঠী.
কোড়, *v. a.* to dig, to bore through.
কোড়ন, *s.* a boring, piercing or digging.
কোড়া, *s.* a whip, a cart, a scourge.
কোড়াবরদার, *s.* one whose office is to beat.
কোণ, *s.* an angle, a corner; the elbow.
কোণটানা, *a.* diagonal : *s.* a diagonal line.
কোণা, *s.* an angle, a corner.
কোণাকোণি, *ad.* cornerwise, diagonally.
কোণাচি, *s.* corner lath of a thatched roof.
কোণী, *a.* crooked-armed, angular : *s.* the elbow.
কোণুআ, *a.* angular, crooked.
কোতখানা, *s.* a guard-house, room for arms.
*কোতবা, *s.* a Muhammadan prayer.
কোতবাল, কোতবালী, *s. vide* কোটাল, &c.
কোতরা, *s.* a sort of treacle or molasses.
কোতল, *s.* a spare horse or palki following the train of an Indian grandee.
*কোতাহী, *s.* neglect, a deficiency, poverty.
কোথ, *s.* sore eyes, gangrene.
কোথা, *ad.* anywhere, where?
কোথাও, *ad.* any where, even in any place.
কোথাতা, *ad.* whence? from what place?
কোদ, কোদ্রব, *s.* sort of grain.[a]
কোদাল, কোদালী, *s.* a spade, a digging hoe.
কোদালিয়া, *s.* a digger, a pioneer; a plant.
কোন্, *pron.* who? what? which?
কোন, *a.* any, some; -কালে, at any time; -ক্রমে, in what order? how in any way; -খানে, where? somewhere; -প্রকারে, -মতে, in any way, in some way.
কোন্দল, *s.* quarrel, a dispute, wrangling.
কোন্দলীয়া, *a.* quarrelsome, disputatious.
কোপ, *s.* anger, rage, fury, wrath; stroke of a weapon, a blow; a spit of earth.
কোপকাপ, *s.* strokes and cuts, blows.
কোপখেকুয়া, *s.* he who has received blows.
কোপত, *ad.* through anger or rage, angrily.
কোপদ, *a.* occasioning anger, provoking.
কোপন, *a.* the being angry : *a.* furious.
কোপবান্, *a.* angry, wrathful, passionate.
কোপসা, *a.* dug down so as to retain the water for the cultivation of rice; -ভুমি, land which has been thus dug.
কোপা, *v.* to provoke any one to anger to incense, to irritate : *s. vide* কোঁপা.

কোপাকোপি, mutual or reciprocal anger.
কোপান, *s.* a provoking to anger; a cutting: *a.* provoked to anger. [tion.
কোপানি, *s.* anger, rage, wrath, provoca-
কোপান্বিত, কোপাবিষ্ট, *a.* wrathful, furious, angry, rancorous, passionate, ferocious.
কোপাল, কোপালক, *a. idem.* [corous.
কোপী, *a.* angry, passionate, wrathful, ran-
কোবিদ, *a.* learned, wise: *s.* a learned man.
*কোবিলা, *s.* a wife, a housewife.
কোমর, *s.* the loins, the waist.
কোমরকষাই, *s.* the pay or hire of a messenger, or *lit.* for girding his loins.
কোমরবন্দ, *s.* a girdle for the waist, a belt.
কোমরবন্দী, *s.* the girding of the loins.
কোমরভাঙ্গা, *a.* broken-backed.
কোমরী, *a.* lumbar; having the lumbago.
কোমরীবাত, *s.* the sciatica. [tle, bland.
কোমল, *a.* tender, soft, delicate, mild, gen-
কোমলতা, -ত্ব, *s.* tenderness, softness, gentleness, mildness, blandness.
কোমল -প্রকৃতি, -স্বভাব, or -হৃদয়, *a.* tender, mild, gentle, tender-hearted, good-natured: *s.* good nature, gentleness.
কোমলান্তঃকরণ, *a. idem.* [formed.
কোমলাকৃতি, *a.* tender, delicate, delicately
কোর, *a.* curved, winding; concave.
কোরক, *s.* a plant bud, unblown flower; the stopping or distraining of goods.
কোরকদার, *s.* a bound bailiff, a distraining officer, a sheriff's officer.
কোরকদারী, *s.* the office of a distrainer.
কোরকার, *s.* crookedness, a curvature.
কোরকী, *a.* ordering a distraint.
কোরণ, *s.* a scraping, a grating to powder.
কোরণ্ড *s.* the hydrocele, the sarcocele.
কোরবী, করবী, *s.* the oleander flower tree.
কোরা, *v. a.* to grate, to rasp, to scrape: *a.* unadulterated, unbleached (as cloth).
‡কোরাণ, *a.* grated, rasped: *s.* the act of grating; also, the Moslem Qurán.
‡কোরাণী, *s.* a grating or rasping: *a.* well versed in, or swearing by, the Qurán.
কোল, *s.* a raft, a haven, harbour, a port, a jujube, a hog, the bosom, the embrace, a class of Hindus, the Kols. [a codicil.
কোলপাতী, *s.* a supplement, a postscript,
কোলপোঁছা, *a.* clearing the bosom (a mother's last child is so called.) [cow.
কোলা, *s.* a swelling on the dewlap of a
কোলাকোলি, *s.* a mutually embracing.
কোলাৎ, *s.* the bark of the petiole of a palmyra leaf used to make ropes with.
কোলানি, encouragement, welcome, hope.
কোলাবেঙ্গ, *s.* a large species of frog.
কোলাহল, *s.* sound of a tumult, shouting.
কোলে, *ad.* in the bosom, in the arms.
কোষ, *s.* treasure, a treasury, a cocoon of silk, a bud, a sheath, scabbard, scrotum, testicle, the eyeball, the womb, an egg, a ball or globe, the edible part of the Jak fruit, a seed-vessel, nutmeg, a dictionary or vocabulary, a receptacle.
কোষখসা, *s.* castration, emasculation.
কোষফল, *s* a berry with a fragrant pulp.
কোষবৃদ্ধি, *s.* the sarcocele, the hydrocele.
কোষা, *s.* a canoe, a boat-shaped sacrificial vessel: *v. a.* to shave wood or metal.
কোষাগার, *s.* a place for money, a treasury.
কোষাণ, *a.* shaved so as to taper to a point at each end: *s.* the act of thus shaving.
কোষাধিপতি, *s.* a treasurer, a paymaster.
কোষাধীশ, কোষাধ্যক্ষ, *s. idem.*
কোষী, *s.* a small sacrificial vessel in the shape of a boat, a sauce-boat.
কোষ্টা, *s.* hemp, jute.
কোষ্ঠ, *s.* a granary, an apartment; the stomach; ordure, evacuation by stool.
কোষ্ঠবদ্ধ, *s.* costiveness: *a.* costive.
কোষ্ঠশুদ্ধি, *s.* evacuation by stool.
কোষ্ঠা, *s.* the same as কোষ্ঠ.
কোষ্ঠাশ্রিতবায়ু, *s.* flatulency, inward wind.
কোষ্ঠী, *s.* a horoscope, destiny, fate ascertained by casting one's nativity.
কোহাড়া, কোহাশা, *s.* a fog, mist, haze.
কোহো, *pron.* any one, any body. [tees.
কৌক্কুটিক, *s.* a hypocrite, a class of devo-
কৌটা, *s.* a canister, a small box, a casket.
কৌটিল্য, *s.* crookedness, insincerity, craft, concealed conduct, deceit, dishonesty.
কৌড়ি, *s.* a cauri or shell current as money.
কৌতর, কপোত, *s.* a pigeon. [diversion.
কৌতুক, *s.* a show, a spectacle, sport, fun,
কৌতুকী, *a.* sportive, jocular, funny: jester

কৌতুকীয়, *a.* jocose, funny : *s.* a jester, a zany.
কৌতুকেয়, *a.* showy, laughable.
কৌপীন, *s.* a piece of cloth worn by the poor merely to cover the privities.
কৌবেরী, *s.* seat of Kuvera ; north quarter.
কৌম, *s.* a nation, a tribe.
কৌমার, *s.* youth, childhood, the time of youth.
কৌমারী, *s.* the divine mothers or energies of the gods, divine energy of Kárttika.
কৌমুদী, *s.* the moon ; rays of the moon ; a title given to several books.
কৌরব, *s.* family or race of king Kuru.
*কৌল, *s.* a promise, engagement, a vow.
কৌলটেয়, *a.* descended from a harlot.
কৌলিক, *a.* belonging to a family.
কৌলীন্য, *s.* nobility of birth, nobility.
কৌশল, *s.* welfare, happiness ; policy, a contrivance, art, device, a stratagem.
কৌশলক্রমে, *ad.* by a contrivance or stratagem.
কৌশলবাক্য, *s.* artful discourse.
কৌষেয়, *a.* silken, made of silk.
কৌস্তুভ, *s.* the breast-jewel of Vishnu.
ক্ন, *s.* kna, the compound of ক and ন.
ক্নফলা *s.* kna class of compound letters.
ক্য, *s.* kya, the combination of ক and য.
ক্যফলা, *s.* the class of compound letters ক্য kya, or the symbol (্য).
ক্যাঁক্, *s.* the sound of some birds.
ক্যাঁচ্, *im. sound* of cutting soft bodies.
ক্যাঁৎ, *im. sd.* expressive of a sudden kick : ক্যাঁৎ করিয়া, suddenly, unexpectedly
ক্র, *s.* kra, or the combination of ক and র.
ক্রকর, *s.* a saw ; a poor man ; a partridge.
ক্রকচ, করাত, *s.* a saw.
ক্রতু, *s.* a sacrifice, an offering, worship.
ক্রন্দন, *s.* wailing, weeping, crying, lamentation ; the howling of an animal.
ক্রন্দনকারী, *a.* weeping, lamenting.
ক্রন্দনশীল, *a.* inclined to weeping, sorrowful.
ক্রন্দনীয়, *a.* lamentable, fit to be wept.
ক্রন্দিত, *a.* wept, lamented.
ক্রফলা, *s.* those compound letters of which র is the last member, the symbol (্র).
ক্রব্য, *s.* flesh, raw flesh, meat.
ক্রব্যাদ, *s.* a rákshas, a giant, a cannibal.
ক্রম, *s.* a step, a degree, series, order, succession.
ক্রমনিম্ন, *s.* a slope, a declivity.
ক্রমভঙ্গ *s.* an interruption in a series.
ক্রমশঃ, *ad.* gradually, regularly, in regular order, successively, in rotation.
ক্রমাগত, *a.* regular, uninterrupted, successive, regularly succeeding each other.
ক্রমানুযায়ী, *a.* following the direct order of a series : *ad.* successively.
ক্রমানুসার, *s.* the direct order of a series.
ক্রমানুসারে, *ad.* successively, in rotation. in direct succession, in a regular series.
ক্রমিক, *a.* successive, gradual, regular.
ক্রমে, *ad.* gradually, successively.
ক্রমেক্রমে *ad.* gradually, by degrees.
ক্রমোৎক্রম, *s.* fits and starts, irregularity.
ক্রয়, *s.* a purchase, the act of buying.
ক্রয়কর্ত্তা, *s.* a purchaser, one who buys.
ক্রয়ণ, *s.* the act of purchasing any thing.
ক্রয়ণীয়, *a.* purchasable, marketable.
ক্রয়বিক্রয়, *s.* buying and selling, trade, traffic.
ক্রয়ার্থী, *a.* desirous of purchasing.
ক্রয়ী, *a.* purchasing, dealing.
ক্রয্য, *a.* exhibited for sale, purchasable.
ক্রান্ত, *a.* stepped, gone, passed over.
ক্রান্তি, *s.* ascension, a surmounting, surpassing ; in *acct.* third part of a cauṛi.
ক্রায়ক, *a.* purchasing : *s.* a purchaser.
ক্রান, *s.* a complete reply, a rejoinder, the confutation of a plea.
ক্রিমি, *s.* an insect, a worm, a maggot.
ক্রিমিঘ্ন, *a.* anthelmintic : *s.* a plant.[1]
ক্রিমিদানা, *s.* cochineal.
ক্রিমিময়, *a.* abounding with worms.
ক্রিয়া, *s.* act, a deed, work, affair, action, religious act ; -কুট, a body of works.
ক্রিয়াকর্ত্তা, *s.* the doer of a work, an agent.
ক্রিয়াপদ, *s.* in *gram.* a verb.
ক্রিয়াবান্, *a.* abounding in works, meritorious.
ক্রিয়াবিশেষণ, *s.* in *gram.* an adverb.
ক্রীড়া, *s.* play, sport, a game, wantonness, sensual gratification.
ক্রীড়াকৌতুক, *s.* sport, pastime, enjoyment. pleasure ; the connection of the sexes.
ক্রীড়াবান্, *a.* gamesome, playful.
ক্রীত, *a.* bought, purchased.
ক্রুদ্ধ, *a.* enraged, angry, vexed.
ক্রূর, *a.* cruel, unfeeling, hard-hearted, severe, harsh, pitiless, terrible, hard, solid.

ক্রূরতা, ক্রূরত্ব, s. cruelty, unfeelingness, hard-heartedness, severity, harshness.
ক্রূরস্বভাব, a. naturally unfeeling, pitiless.
ক্রেতব্য, a. purchasable, fit for market.
ক্রেতা, s. a purchaser, a customer.
ক্রেয়, a. purchasable, marketable. [lap.
ক্রোড়, s. the bosom, breast or embrace,
ক্রোড়পত্র, s. a supplement, an appendix, a postscript, a codicil to a will.
ক্রোধ, s. anger, wrath, fury, rage, passion.
ক্রোধযুক্ত, a. angry, wrathful, vengeful,
ক্রোধান্বিত, ক্রোধী, a. *idem.* [furious.
ক্রোর, a. ten millions: s. the osprey.
ক্রোল, s. the fishing eagle or osprey.[1]
ক্রোশ, s. about two English miles.
ক্রৌঞ্চ, s. a species of heron, the name of a mountain, and of a demon. [tinents.
ক্রৌঞ্চদ্বীপ, s. in *geo.* one of the seven con-
ক্ল, s. a compound character of ক and ল.
ক্লফলা, s. that class of compound letters the last member of which is ল.
ক্লান্ত, s. wearied, fatigued, tired, languid.
ক্লান্তি, a. weariness, fatigue, languor.
ক্লান্তিকর, a. fatiguing, wearisome. [ed.
ক্লিন্ন, a. moist, wet, damp, musty, corrupt-
ক্লিশিত, a. vexed, perplexed, afflicted, distressed, plagued, tormented. [ed, lean.
ক্লিষ্ট, distressed, fatigued, wearied, pinch-
ক্লিষ্টতা, s. affliction, distress, weariness.
ক্লিষ্টশরীর, afflicted, distressed, suffering.
ক্লীব, a. neuter, impotent, hermaphrodite.
ক্লীবত্ব, s. neutrality, impotence, the condition of a hermaphrodite.
ক্লীবলিঙ্গ, s. in *gram.* the neuter gender.
ক্লেদ, s. moisture, pus, ichor, filth in a liquid state, the sordes of the body.
ক্লেশ, s. distress, difficulty, perplexity, a strait, suffering, trouble, molestation, pain or anguish, labour, worldly care.
ক্লেশক, ক্লেশকর, a. distressing, vexatious, troublesome, afflictive, molesting.
ক্লেশজনক, ক্লেশদায়ক, a. *idem.*
ক্লেশন, s. the act of giving trouble.
ক্লেশযুক্ত, ক্লেশান্বিত, a. distressing, afflictive, persecuting, distressed, afflicted.
ক্লেশিত, a. brought into trouble or distress.
ক্লোম, s. the bladder, urinary vessel.

ক্ব, *ad.* where? in what? s. a compound letter which expresses the sound kwa.
ক্বচিৎ, *ad.* somewhere, seldom, rarely.
ক্বণ, or ক্বণক্বণ, s. the sound of a stringed instrument, or of a metallic vessel.
ক্বণিত, a. twanged, made to sound.
ক্বণক্বণিয়া, a. giving out a ringing sound.
ক্বথিত, a. decocted, boiled, stewed.
ক্বফলা, s. the name of all those compound letters of which ব is the last member.
ক্বাথ, s. a decoction, extract, resin.
ক্ষ, s. kshya, a compound of ক and ষ; but being the last letter of the alphabet, it may well stand in its proper place.

খ, the 2nd consonant; it has the sound of kh: s. the sky, the air, the atmosphere.
খই, s. parched or fried grain; ;চুর, a kind
খইন, a. deep, navigable. [of sweetmeat.
খইয়াখোলা, s. a vessel for parching corn.
খইয়াগোখুরা, s. a variety of the Cobra de
খইল s. oil-cake; the ear-wax. [capello.
খএণ, s. kind of rice which is fried freely.
খএর, খদির, s. catechu, and its tree.[2]
খএরীবক, s. a species of heron.
খক্, s. a sound expressive of hawking.
খকার, s. the letter খ.
খগ, a. moving in the air, aerial: s. an aerial inhabitant, a bird. [of birds.
খগপতি, s. a name of Garura the king
খগাবগা, a. mean, inferior, bad of its kind.
খগেন্দ্র, খগেশ, খগেশ্বর, s. *vide* খগপতি.
খগোল, s. the planisphere, the starry hea-
খগোলবিদ্যা, s. astronomy. [vens.
খচ, s. a ball of things tied together.
খচর, s. a mule, a mongrel: a. aerial, moving in the air. [beset, inlaid.
খচিত, a. set as precious stones in a socket,
খচিল, s. a ball, a bullet.
খজাকা, খজ, s. a ladle, a spoon,
*খজানা, s. wealth, treasure, revenue.
খজাঞ্চী, s. a treasurer, a paymaster.
খঞ্জ, a. lame, limping: s. a metre of two
খঞ্জন, s. the wagtail; a tonjohn. [lines.
খঞ্জনী, খঞ্জরী, s. a tabor, a small drum.
খঞ্জর, s. a dagger, a poniard, a dirk.
খট, s. a kind of grass; phlegm.

খটাডম্বুর, *s.* a tabor, insignia of Shiva.
খটি, *s.* a multitude, a heap, pile, a quantity; consultation, advice, machination.
খটিকা, *s.* chalk, reeds used as firewood.
খট্খট্, *s.* a clattering sound. [a road.)
খট্খটিয়া, *ad.* rough and disagreeable (as
খট্মল, *s.* a bug. খটী, *s.* chalk. [mock.
খট্টা, *s.* a bedstead, couch, a bier, a ham-
খট্টাঙ্গ, *s.* a trident, Shiva's weapon.
খট্টাচ্ছাদন, *s.* a coverlet, a counterpane.
খট্টাশ, খটাশ, *s.* the pole-cat, a civet-cat.[1]
খড়, *s.* straw, stubble; thatching grass.
খড়কী, *s.* a private door, back door.
খড়জালী, *s.* a sort of salt.
খড়ম, *s.* a sandal, a clog, a patten; -পায়া,
খড়রা, *s.* a currycomb. [sandal-footed.
খড়র্খড়র্, খড়র্মড়র্, *s.* a rattling sound.
খড়হাঁস, *s.* a species of wild duck.
খড়া, *s.* the mark of a graduated vessel; a report, news, information.
খড়াকাটা, *a.* marked, graduated: *s.* the graduating of a glass or other measure.
খড়ি, *s.* a consultation, advice, a machination; chalk; a kind of coarse grass.
খড়িকা, *s.* a grass tooth-pick; coarse grass.
খড়িকাখাওন, *s.* the picking of the teeth.
খড়িকামুটি, *a.* striped (applied to cloth).
খড়িঞ্চি, খড়িটী, *s.* a sort of mortar used to plaster the mud walls of a house.
খড়িটীকরণ, *s.* the plastering of a house.
খড়িয়া, *a.* white, chalky, pale, hoary: *s.* the name of a river in Nadiyá. [white.
খড়িয়ামারণ, *s.* the leaves of a tree turning
খড়ী, *s.* chalk, fuel, coarse grass used as
খড়ীমাটী, চাক্‌খড়ী, *s.* chalk. [fuel.
খড়ুআ, *a.* made of straw or coarse grass.
খড়ুআঘর, *s.* a hut made of straw or grass.
খড়্খড়্, *s.* a clattering or rattling sound.
খড়্খড়ান, *s.* producing a clattering sound by striking of hard bodies. [a pálki.
খড়্খড়ি, খড়্খড়িয়া, *s.* a venetian window;
খড়্গ, *s.* a cimeter; horn of a rhinoceros.
খড়্গকোষ, *s.* the sheath of a cimeter.
খড়্গী, *a.* armed: *s.* a rhinoceros. [tual.
খণ্ড্, *v.* to remove, depart, become ineffec-
খণ্ড, *s.* a piece, fragment, a section, part, chapter, raw sugar, a cluster of houses.

খণ্ডক, *a.* breaking to pieces, removing: *s.* one who breaks, or expiates offences.
খণ্ডকপালিনী, *a. fem.* unfortunate, unlucky.
খণ্ডকপালীয়া, *a. masc. idem.*
খণ্ডখণ্ড, *ad.* in pieces, piece by piece: -কৃ, to cut up, to quarter, to cut to pieces.
খণ্ডচতুষ্টয়, *s.* four pieces or quarters.
খণ্ডত্রয়, *s.* three pieces or parcels,
খণ্ডদ্বয়, *s.* two pieces or halves.
খণ্ডন, *s.* the act of cutting to pieces, the rescinding of an order, the refuting of an argument, the removing of a calamity, the thwarting of a scheme.
খণ্ডনকর্ত্তা, *s.* one who breaks, removes danger or misfortune, or expiates crimes.
খণ্ডনা, *s.* a fracture, a remonstrance, refu-
খণ্ডনীয়, খণ্ডিতব্য, *a. vide* খণ্ড্য. [tation.
খণ্ডপ্রলয়, *s.* a partial destruction of the universe; a quarrel, disunion.
খণ্ডবিখণ্ড, *a.* reduced to fragments.
খণ্ডা, *v. a.* to divide, to break, to refute, to rescind or revoke, to remove, to thwart, to avert: *s.* a refutation, a revocation.
খণ্ডাখণ্ডি, *s.* mutual refutation, reciprocal thwarting, or breaking to pieces.
খণ্ডান, *s.* a breaking to pieces, a removing of danger or misfortune, a rescinding, a refuting, the expiation of crimes.
খণ্ডিত, broken to pieces, averted, removed, repealed, refuted, revoked. [refutable.
খণ্ড্য, *a.* removable, repealable, revokable,
*খত, *s.* a bond, a note of hand, a letter, a writing, a hand writing.
*খতনা, *s.* circumcision. [end.
*খতম, খতমা, *s.* a conclusion, a sealing, an
*খতমি, *s.* the seed of the common holyhock (Alcea rosea) used in medicine.
*খতর, *s.* recollection, thought, remembrance; danger, fear, risk.
খতরা, *s.* danger, fear, risk, a venture.
খতা, *v.* to calculate, to cast up a sum, to settle an account: *s.* a fault, a crime.
খতান, *a.* reckoned up: *s.* a reckoning up, casting up of accounts. [count book.
খতিয়ান, *a.* containing accounts: *s.* an ac-
খতুয়া, decayed, rotten, rent, torn. [loss.
*খতুর, *s.* a coming, a passing, an entering;

খতো, *s.* a disease of the eyelids; decay, the rot in wood, etc.: *a.* rent, rotten.
খতকী, *s.* a purchase; a bill of sale.
খদরণ, *s.* the chasing of a person or animal
খদি, or খদিকা, *s.* parched corn. [away.
খদির, খএর, *s.* catechu or Japan earth.
খদের, *s.* a purchaser, a customer.
খদ্যোত, *s.* a fire-fly, the sun.
খধূপ, *s.* a sky-rocket, firework.
খনক, *s.* a rat; a miner, a digger, a burglar.
খনন, *s.* a digging, a mining; -কর্ত্তা, a dig-
খননীয়, *a.* fit to be dug. [ger, miner.
খনা, *s.* a hog-spear, a snuffling: *a.* nasal.
খনাখনা, nasal, uttered through the nose.
খনি, *s.* a mine, a quarry, a hole, a cave.
খনিত, *a.* dug, excavated. [vessel.
খন্‌খন, *s.* a jarring sound of a cracked
খন্‌খনা, *v. n.* to emit a jarring sound.
খন্‌খনান, খন্‌খনানি, *s.* the jarring sound emitted by a cracked vessel. [ring.
খন্‌খনিয়া, *a.* having a jarring sound, jar-
খন্তা, খন্তী, খনিত্র, *s.* a digging hoe, a spud,
খন্দ, *s.* the harvest, a crop. [a spade.
খন্দক, *s.* a ditch, trench, a moat, a gutter.
খপ্‌করিয়া, *ad.* quickly, hastily, suddenly.
খপরা, খপরৈল, *s.* a tile, a roofing tile.
খপুর, *s.* betel-nut tree (Areca catechu); garlic, a water-jar; city of Harischandra, fabled to be situated in the air.
খপুষ্প, *s.* a flower in the air (sarcastically, the impossibility of an undertaking).
খপ্পর, *s.* crown of the head; a knave.
*খফা, *a.* wrathful, angry, enraged, vexed.
খফগী, *s.* anger, wrath, rage, vexation.
*খবর, *s.* news, information, intelligence.
খবরগীর, *s.* a spy, a scout; a protector.
খবরদার, *a.* careful, active, attentive.
খবরদারী, *s.* care, attention. [impure.
*খবীশ, *a.* malicious, malignant, wicked,
*খম্, *a.* twisted, crooked, coiled: *s.* a fold, a coil, a noose; a curl, a ringlet.
*খমীর, *a.* leavened, fermented. [pinch.
খমচা, *s.* a pinch, a handful: *v. a.* to gripe,
খমচান, *s.* the act of pinching, a griping.
খমচানি, *s.* a pinch, a grasp, a griping.
খমদার, *a.* crooked, twisted, coiled, curled.
*খম্বা, *s.* a post, a pillar, a stake.

*খয়র, *a.* beneficial, well, good: *s.* goodness, welfare, health, happiness.
খয়রা, *a.* light brown: *s.* a species of fish.[1]
*খয়রাৎ, *s.* a charity, a gift, alms-giving.
খয়রাতী, *s.* a gift, alms: *a.* intended for a gift, given or received in charity.
খয়া, *a.* decayed, worn out, injured.
খর, *s.* an ass, a demon, a rákshas slain by Ráma, heat, catechu: *a.* hot, rigid, sharp, pungent, cruel, harsh, brittle.
*খরগোশ, *s.* a hare, a rabbit. [bass.
খরচ, *s.* expenditure, money, expense: *a.*
খরচপত্র, *s.* money for expenses.
খরচবরদার, *s.* a servant whose office is to supply the household expenses.
খরচা, *s.* expense, the costs of a law suit.
খরচী, *a.* expensive, extravagant: *s.* a stick used in knitting nets; fee of a prostitute.
খরণস, sharp-nosed; acute organ of smell.
খরতর, *a.* excessively sharp, very keen.
খরপত্র, *s.* a red variety of basil; the Teak or Indian oak (Tectona grandis).
খরপোড়, *a.* well-baked, well-burnt, (applied to pottery, bricks, bread, etc.)
খরবুজ, খরবুজা, *s.* the musk-melon.[2]
খরশাণ, *a.* sharp, pungent: *s.* dried to-
খরশূলা, *s.* the name of a fish.[3] [bacco.
খরসা, *s.* a receptacle for a spindle.
খরা, *v. a.* to overbake, calcine: *a.* overbaked, calcined; hot, dry: *s.* a hare.
খরাণ, or খরাণিয়া, *a.* overbaked, calcined, burnt in parching or baking.
খরাব, *a.* bad, evil, spoiled, rotten, wicked.
খরাবী, *a.* evil, badness, wickedness, ruin.
খরীদ্, *s.* a purchase. খরীদা, *a.* purchased.
খরীদার, *s.* a purchaser, one who buys.
*খরীদগী, *s.* the same as খতকী.
খর্‌খর্, *a.* rough, sharp; -করিয়া, quickly.
খর্জু, *s.* the itch, a cutaneous eruption.
খর্জ্জূর, খর্জ্জূরী, *s.* date-fruit, and its tree.[4]
খর্পর, *s.* a beggar's dish; the skull, crown of the head; a collyrium for the eyes.
খর্ব্ব, *a.* dwarf, pigmy; ten thousand mil-
খর্ব্বতা, -ত্ব, *s.* dwarfness, shortness. [lions.
খল, *a.* deceitful, guileful, artful, crafty, dishonest, knavish: *s.* a stone-mortar.
খলকাহিনী, *s.* a novel, a legend, a story.

খলৎ, *a.* deceitful, unsteady, slippery.
খলতত্ত্ব, *s.* the searching for a knave.
খলতা, deceitfulness, swindling, knavery.
খলন, *s.* a slipping, a blundering, a slip of the tongue, a slip of moral conduct.
খলবাক্য, *s.* a deceitful speech. [knave.
খলবিবরণ, *s.* a feigned story, history of a
খলবিবেচনা, *s.* a swindling opinion.
খলবুদ্ধি, *s.* a deceitful idea or sense.
খলমন্ত্রণা, *s.* the advice of deceitful men.
খলমূষল, *s.* a mortar and pestle.
খলল, *s.* a tumult, a disturbance; a failure.
খলা, *v. n.* to consent inconsiderately.
খলাস, *s.* deliverance, emancipation.
খলাসী, *s.* a sailor, an artillery-man.
খলি, *s.* the ear-wax; mustard-oil cake.
*খলিফা, *s.* a sovereign, a master wrestler or cock-fighter, a cook, a taylor.
খলিশা, *s.* the name of a fish.[1]
খলু, *ad.* truly, certainly, indeed.
খল্‌খলা, *v. n.* to make a noise like water when agitated, to laugh immoderately.
খল্‌খলান, খল্‌খলানি, *s.* the sound uttered in laughter, sound of agitated water.
খল্‌বল্, খল্‌বলি, *s.* a tumult, a hubbub.
খল্ল, *s.* a creek, canal, trench, a deep hole.
খল্লী, *s.* a shooting pain; mustard-oil cake.
খস্, *v. n.* to fall, to fall off as leaves, etc., to be loose. পেট-খস, to miscarry.
খসণ, খসণী, *s.* a falling of leaves or fruits from a tree, the falling of a meteor. পেট-খসণ, miscarriage, abortion.
খসা, *v. a.* to open, to loosen, to take out.
খসাণ, *a.* opened, made loose, taken out: *s.* the act of loosening, or taking out.
খস, *s.* the itch, scabrosity: *a.* rough, scab- [rous.
*খসম, *s.* a husband, spouse.
খসুয়া, *a.* diseased with the itch, scabby.
খস্‌খস্, *s.* the roots of a species of grass[2] used to make door-screens for the hot season: *ad.* quickly: *a.* scabrous, rough.
খস্‌ড়া, *s.* a rough copy; a waste-book.
খা, *v. a.* to eat, corrode, abrade, wear off.
খাই, খাইন, *s.* a ditch, a trench, a pit.
খাইদ, *s.* alloy, slag or dross of metals.
খাউকী, *s.* a pretence, imposition. [cious.
খাউড়াল, খাউন্তিয়া, *a.* ravenous, greedy, vora-

খাওন, *s.* the act of eating, or corroding.
খাওনদাওন, *s.* an eating and feeding.
খাওনিয়া, *a.* entertaining, feeding others.
খাওয়া, *s.* *vide* খাওন,: *a.* eaten, corroded. *v. caus.* to entertain, to feed; to abrade.
খাওয়াখায়ি, *s.* an eating and giving food.
খাওয়ান, *s.* the act of feeding or entertaining, the corroding of a thing.
খাওয়ামলম, *s.* a caustic plaster. [lems.
*খাঁ, *s.* a title of Paṭhán tribe of the Mos-
খাঁই, *s.* a desire, greediness, want.
খাঁকতি, *s.* abatement, a deficiency.
খাঁকরি, *s.* grit, sand, sediment. [phlegm.
খাঁকার, *s.* a disgrace, a blot; a hawking,
খাঁচা, *s.* a coop, a bird-cage, an aviary.
খাঁজ, *s.* a mortise, dovetail, groove.
খাঁজকাটা, *a.* grooved, dovetailed.
খাঁড়, *s.* raw sugar, molasses, treacle.
খাঁড়া, *s.* a cimeter, a sword.
খাঁড়াধারী, *a.* checkered, striped.
খাঁড়ি, *s.* an inlet, a frith, a strait.
খাঁড়ুয়া, *s.* a clout worn by female children.
খাঁদা, খাঁদুয়া, *a.* noseless, snub-nosed, flat-
খাঁদী, *a. fem. idem.* [nosed.
*খাক, *s.* earth, dust, ashes.
খাকী, খাগী, *a.* eating, devouring.
খাকুই, *s.* a cotton-mill.
খাগ, *s.* horn of a rhinoceros; a cimeter.
খাগড়া, *s.* a species of reed or grass.[3]
খাণ্ডন, খাঞ্জন, *s.* a sword with long blade.
খাঙরা, *s.* a broom, a besom.
খাজা, *s.* a kind of sweetmeat: *a.* hard.
খাজাকাঁটাল, *s.* a jak fruit, the substance of which is firm and hard. [cashier.
*খাজাঞ্চী, *s.* a treasurer, a cash-keeper, a
খাজানা, *s.* treasure, revenue, ground-rent
খাজূর, খর্জ্জূর, *s.* a date, date-tree. [juice.
খাজূরগুড়, *s.* molasses made from date-tree
খাজূরছড়ি, *s.* the midrib of the branch of date-tree, a kind of striped cloth.
খাজূররস, *s.* the juice of the date-tree.
খাঞ্চা, *s.* a tray, a salver, a large dish.
খাট্, *v. a.* to labour, serve, work, effect: *v. a.* to operate, to answer an end.
খাট, *s.* bed, bedstead: *a.* dwarf, short, small; কৃ to shorten, humble, subdue.
খাটদৃষ্টি, *a.* short-sighted, penurious.

খাটন, *s.* labouring at any work, the answering a designed end. [nial service.
খাটনি, *s.* effecting, labouring, doing me-
খাটনা, *s.* pay of labour, wages, task, toil.
খাটনীয়া, *s.* a labourer, a workman.
খাটমল, *s.* a bug (Cimex lictularia).
খাটলা, *s.* a screen, a fence; a bedstead.
খাটলী, *s.* a small or common bedstead.
খাটা, *v. a.* to superintend, or set persons to work, to apply, to suspend, to put to the test: *s.* an effect: *a.* acid, sour.
খাটাখাটি, *s.* a labouring in society.
খাটান, *s.* superintending of workmen, a setting men to work, effecting, trying.
খাটাল, *s.* space between beams or posts.
খাটাশি, *s.* perfume found in the zibet-cat.
খাটি, *a.* refined (as metal), clear, unmixed, unadulterated, explicit, plain. [talk.
খাট্টা, *a.* acid, sour; -পাকান, nonsensical
খাড়ল, *s.* a crack, a crack in the earth.
খাড়া, *a.* erect, upright, steep, straight, standing, perpendicular; at sight: *s.* the stalk of a plant, the long and torulose legume of some trees, a loment. [ly.
খাড়াখাড়া, *ad.* forthwith, instantly, quick-
খাড়াহুণ্ডী, *s.* a bill payable at sight.
খাড়ু, *s.* an ornament for a woman's wrists.
খাণ, *s.* a piece, individual thing.
খাণখাণ, *ad.* in pieces, piece by piece.
খাণি, *s.* a piece; a mine, a pit, a quarry.
খাণিক, *s.* a little, an instant, a short time.
খাত, *s.* a ditch, a moat, a pond, a pit.
খাতক, *s.* a debtor, a borrower of money.
খাতকী, *a.* promissory (as a note or bond).
খাতা, *s.* an assembly, a party, a plot of ground, a row, a stratum, a place of trade, an account book, a ledger.
খাতাখাতা, *ad.* in parties, in rows, in files.
খাতাবাড়ী, *s.* export or import warehouse.
*খাতির, *s.* the heart, soul, mind, esteem, respect, care, choice, a sake, the will.
খাতিরজমা, *a.* comforted, tranquil, contented: *s.* satisfaction, assurance.
খাতিরজমায়ী, *s.* tranquillity, stedfastness.
খাতিরদার, *s.* one who kindly treats.
খাতিরদারী, *s.* esteem, kind treatment.
খাতিরনদারৎ, *s.* inattention, disregard.

খাতিরপসন্দ, *a.* desired, chosen approved.
খাতের, *s.* thought: *ad.* on account of, for.
*খাতা, *a.* convicted: *s.* a fault, a failure.
খাদ, *s.* alloy, dross or scoriæ of metals.
খাদক, *a.* eating, devouring, corroding: *s.*
খাদন, *s.* an eating, corroding. [an eater.
খাদি, *s.* a short piece; a truncheon, club.
খাদিখাদি, *ad.* in short pieces. [stroyed.
খাদিত, *a.* eaten, devoured, corroded, de-
*খাদিম, *s.* a servant, an attendant. [lent.
খাদ্য, *a.* eatable, fit for food, edible, escu-
খাদ্যমান, *a.* under the process of being
খাদ্যাখাদ্য, *a.* fit or unfit for food. [eaten.
খান, *s.* a place, a situation; a piece.
খানকী, *s.* a prostitute, a harlot, a whore; -খোর, -বাজ, a whoremonger; -বাজী, whoremongery; বাড়ী, a bawdy-house; -টোলা, -পল্লী, -পাড়া, the part of the town inhabited by prostitutes. [ry.
খানকীপনা, খানকীমি, *s.* whoredom, harlot-
খানখান, *ad.* in pieces, piece by piece.
*খানপোশ, *s.* a cover of wicker works for
খানসামা, *s.* a steward, a butler. [a tray.
খানসামাগিরী, *s.* the business of a butler.
‡খানা, *s.* a ravine, a pool, a pit, a ditch; a meal, dinner, diet; a house. [ges.
*খানাখরচ, *s.* table expenses, board wa-
*খানাখারাব, *a.* ruined, spoiled, destroyed.
খানাখারাবী, *s.* ruin, destruction. [sons.
*খানাজঙ্গী, *s.* a duel, a contest of two per-
*খানাজাদ, *s.* a son by a slave girl; a lad.
খানাবাড়ি, *s.* a dwelling-house, habitation.
খানিক, *s.* a little; breach in a wall.
খানিল, *s.* a house-breaker, a burglar.
খাপ, *s.* a scabbard, a sheath: *a.* thick, waterproof (applied to cloth).
খাপবুনন, *a.* thickly woven, close-woven.
খাপরা, খাবরা, *s.* a roof tile, a potsherd.
খাপরেল, *a.* tiled, covered with tile: a tile.
খাপরেলী, *a.* tiled; -ঘর, a tiled-house.
*খাপা, *a.* angry, wrathful, enraged.
খাবরি, *s.* hemispherical vessel; the skull.
খাবল, খাবলা, *s.* a mouthful, a handful.
খাবার, *a.* fit or ready for eating, eatable.
খাবি, খাবিখাওন, *s.* a struggling for life when drowning, the panting of fishes when dying by the stench of the water.

*খাম, *a.* raw, imperfect, bad, inferior : *s.* the sealing of a letter; a pillar. [air.
*খামখেয়াল, *s.* a building of castles in the
খামখেয়ালী, *a.* building castles in the air.
*খামখা, *ad.* certainly, undoubtedly, suddenly, unexpectedly, nolens volens.
খামার, *s.* a threshing floor. [már.
খামারিয়া, *a.* spoiled; pertaining to a khá-
খামচা, *v. a.* to pinch, to gripe, to take up a handful : *s.* a pinch, a handful.
খামচান, *s.* the act of pinching : *a.* pinched.
খামচানি, *s.* a pinch, a sudden gripe, colic.
*খামিন্দ, *s.* a master, a lord, a husband.
*খাম্বা, *s.* a post, a pillar, a stake.
খারা, *s.* a pod of cotton : *a.* upright, just, honest; payable without deduction.
খারাই, *s.* rectitude, honesty, uprightness.
খারী, *s.* a particular measure of capacity.
খারীজ, *a.* excluded, dismissed, banished.
খারীজদাখিল, *s.* the delivering in of a dismissal or resignation.
খারুআ, *s.* a kind of coarse red cloth.
খারেজা, *s.* a catchword.
খাল, *s.* a creek, an inlet, a bay.
*খালা, *s.* a mother's sister. [tured.
খালাড়ী, *s.* a place where salt is manufac-
খালাস, *s.* a deliverance, release, the deliverance of a woman in travail.
খালাসপত্র, *s.* a deed of release; a charm for the delivery of a woman in travail.
খালাসী, *s.* a sailor, a matross; rescue.
*খালিসা, *s.* a revenue collector's office; land held immediately of government.
খালী, *a.* empty, void, blank, simple, vacant, unengaged : *s.* a mother's sister.
খালীহাত, *a.* empty-handed, pennyless.
*খালু, *s.* a mother's sister's husband.
খালুই, or খারুই, *s.* a vessel of bambu rods used by fishermen to preserve fish.
খাস, *a.* select, good, excellent, fine, elegant, mature, pure, peculiar, own.
খাসা, *a. idem* : *s.* a kind of cloth. [habit.
*খাসিঅৎ, *s.* natural disposition, conduct,
খাসী, *s.* a castrated sheep, goat, or other animal; the inhabitant of Khásiá.
খাস্ত, *a.* bad, evil, inferior, ugly.
খাস্তা, *s.* choice; badness, worthlessness.

খিঁচ্, *v. a.* to draw, to pull, to attract, to writhe, to contract by convulsions.
খিঁচ, *s.* a dispute; a difference in opinion, or in account; -মিটা, to settle a dispute.
খিঁচন, *s.* a pulling, a drawing of the body by convulsions or the like, a writhing.
খিক্, খিক্খিক্, *s.* a giggling sound, gig-
খিখি, খেঁকর, খেঁকশিয়াল, *s.* a fox. [gling.
খিচ, *v. a.* to grin, to set the teeth, to dispute, to be angry, waspish or pettish.
খিচড়, *s.* dirt : *a.* vulgar, scurrilous, low.
খিচড়ি, *s.* a medley; a dish made of rice, pulse, ghi, and spices; mixed, blended.
খিড়ৗয়া, *a.* vulgar, scurrilous, obscene.
খিচা, *v. a.* to cause one to grin, to scold.
খিচান, *s.* the causing a person to grin.
খিচানিয়া, *a.* scolding, grinning, angry.
খিচিমিচি, *s.* a grinning, fretfulness, a petty quarrel, a dispute about a trifle.
খিচ্খিচা, *a.* fretting at trifles, impatient.
খিচ্ড়া, *a.* low, vulgar : *s. vide.* খিচড়ি.
খিট, *s.* rust, a crack; উঠা, to scale off.
খিটা, খিটিয়া, *a.* rusty, cracked, broken.
খিটিমিটি, খিট্খিট্, খিট্মিট্, *s.* a perpetual scolding, peevishness, murmuring.
খিট্খিটা, *v. n.* to scold, to fret, to complain, to be querulous, to be peevish.
খিট্খিটান, খিট্খিটানি, *s.* a fretting or being peevish, a jarring or contending.
খিট্খিটিয়া, খিট্মিটিয়া, *a.* fretful, peevish, querulous, murmuring, dissatisfied.
খিড়কী, *s.* a window; a back-door, private
খিড়কীদার, খিড়কীপথ, *s. idem.* [door.
খিতাব, *s.* a title, an honorary name.
খিদা, ক্ষুধা, *s.* hunger, appetite.
*খিদ্মৎ, *s.* service, attendance. [table.
খিদ্মৎগার, *s.* a servant, one who waits at
খিদ্মৎগারী, *s.* service, the office of a man who waits at table. [regretting.
খিদ্যমান, distressed, sorrowful, grieving,
খিন্ন, *a.* distressed, melancholy.
খিন্খিন্, *s.* a discontented moan.
খিন্খিনিয়া, *a.* discontentedly moaning.
খিরকিচ্, *s.* intricacy, perplexity.
খিল, *s.* land not in tillage, sward, a tingling or numbedness, a peg, a wedge, a bolt, a pin : *v. a.* to turn an arch.

খিলকা, *s.* a coat worn by Moslem mendi-
খিলঘরা, *s.* a staple for a bolt. [cants.
খিলন, *s.* the driving of a wedge ; an arch.
খিলা, *v. a.* to turn an arch, to drive in a wedge or pin, to pin up; to nail up.
খিলান, *s.* an arch, an arched turret, a vault, a dome : *a.* arched, pinned.
খিলানীয়, *a.* arched, vaulted, domed.
খিলী, *s.* an arch, a tunnel, a funnel, a packet of betel or of any other thing.
খিলখিল্, *im. sd.* used to express a gig-
*খিলাৎ, *s.* an honorary dress. [gling.
খুঁআঁড়, *s.* a cowpen, sheepfold, a hog-sty.
খুঁইয়া, *a.* small, little, diminutive, mean.
খুঁচ্, *v. n.* to prick or punch, to thrust the bill (as birds do), to thrust ; to gripe.
খুঁচ্, *s.* an easy cutting sound of a knife.
খুঁচড়, খুঁচড়া, *v. a.* to stir up a fire.
খুঁচড়ন, খুঁচড়ান, *s.* a stirring up of fire.
খুঁচি *s.* the straw introduced in repairing a thatched roof; a small rice-basket.
খুঁজ, *v. a.* to seek for, to search out.
খুঁজন, *s.* the act of seeking or searching.
খুঁজি, *s.* a seeking, a search.
খুঁট্, *v.* to pick, glean, to pick up (as birds do), to scratch a pimple ; to compare.
খুঁট, *s.* corner, end (of cloth), comparison, trial; খুঁটিয়ালওন, to compare and take.
খুঁটআঁখরিয়া, *a.* writing an illegible hand.
খুঁটঝাড়া, *s.* all, the whole : *ad.* wholly.
খুঁটনি, *s.* a dot, a point, a flaw.
খুঁটর্, or খুঁটরা, *v. a.* to scratch up anything, to scratch a pimple, to pick.
খুঁটরণ, or খুঁটরাণ, *s.* the act of scratching up or picking : *a.* scratched up.
খুঁটরণি, or খুঁটরাণি, *s.* a scratching up.
খুঁটর্মুটর্, খুঁরটামুটর, *s.* a slight quarrel, a bickering, dispute, contention.
খুঁটা, *v. a. vide* খুঁট্ ; also, to match, to compare with : *s.* a wedge, a peg, a pin.
খুঁটাখুঁটি, *s.* a mutual comparison.
খুঁটান, *s.* a comparing with, a matching : *a.* compared with, matched with.
খুঁটী, *s.* a post, a stake, a wooden pillar.
খুঁট্খাঁট, *s.* the end or corner of a garment.
খুঁড়্, *v. a.* to dig, to throw up earth (as a hog), to express surprise at an excess.
খুঁড়ন, *s.* a digging, an expression of surprise at an excess in eating, etc. [sign.
খুঁত, *s.* a stain, blemish, a flaw, fault, a bad
খুঁতুর্খুঁতুর্, *s.* a sobbing (as children do).
খুঁৎখুঁৎ, খুঁৎমুৎ, *s.* a doubt, the expression of unwillingness to do a thing.
খুঁৎখুঁতিয়া, খুঁৎমুতিয়া, *a.* doubtful, doing a thing unwillingly, or with ill-will.
খুক্, *s.* hawking or coughing sound : *v. a.* to hawk, to cough. [dandruff.
খুকী, *s.* a fœtus, a babe, a little girl; scurf,
খুক্খুক্, *s.* the noise made in coughing.
খুক্খুকা, *v. n.* to cough, to wheeze.
খুক্খুকান, *s.* the act of coughing. [ket.
খুক্খুকানি, *s.* fit of coughing ; a small bas-
খুক্নী, *s.* a female infant, a little girl.
খুঙ্গী, *s.* an oblong ratan box for pens, etc.
খুঙ্গীপুঁথি, *s.* books and oblong ratan box.
খুচ, *ad.* suddenly, unexpectedly, hastily.
খুচুর্খুচুর্, *ad.* quickly : *a.* little at a time.
খুজ, *v. a.* to seek, to search.
খুজন, *s.* the act of seeking or searching.
খুজর, *a.* small, little, insignificant, mean.
খুজরা, *a.* by retail, little at a time.
খুজী, খুজীতল্লাসী, *s.* search, enquiry.
খুজ্লা, *v. n.* to itch, to scratch.
খুজলান, *s.* act of itching, a scratching.
খুজ্লানি, *s.* an itching, the itch.
খুজ্লী, *s.* itches, scab.
খুঞ্চিয়া, *s.* a tray, a salver, a charger.
খুট্খুট্, *s.* the sound of striking on wood.
খুড়্, *v. a.* to pick up, to compare, to dig.
খুড়তত, খুড়াত, *s.* a junior paternal uncle; -ভগিনী, or -ভাই, a cousin, a junior paternal uncle's daughter or son.
খুড়ন, *s.* a digging, picking up, comparing.
খুড়া, or খুড়াত, *s.* a junior paternal uncle.
খুড়ী, *s.* the wife of a junior paternal uncle.
খুদ্, *v. a.* to dig, to excavate, to carve.
খুদ, *s.* refuse, broken rice or other grain.
খুদা, *v. a.* to dig, to cause to cut or dig.
খুদী, *s.* broken rice : *a.* little, small.
খুদীখুদী, *a.* very small, diminutive. [old.
খুন্খুন্, *s.* a discontented moan : *a.* very
খুন্তি, খনিত্র, খন্তা, *s.* a spud or spade.
খুপ্করিয়া, *ad.* quickly, hastily, suddenly.
খুব, *a.* good, excellent, elegant, beautiful.

খুররি, *s.* a hovel, shed, hut, a pigeon-hole.
খুবরিখাবরি, *a.* rough, full of holes.
খুবরিখুবরি, *a.* little, small, make-shift.
*খুবসুরৎ, *s.* beautiful, handsome, graceful.
*খুবানি, *s.* an apricot, a wall-fruit.
*খুবি, *s.* beauty, elegance, grace.
খুর, *s.* a hoof; foot of a bedstead; a razor.
খুরণস, *a.* sharp-nosed.
খুরশী, *s.* a chair, a stool; a noose, a rope to tie a calf.
খুরা, *s.* the foot of a bedstead, etc., the bottom of a glass or brass cup.
খুরাক, *s.* food, provisions, daily food, diet.
খুরাকী, *s.* the money advanced for food.
খুরী, *s.* a small earthen cup or basin.
খুর্খুর্, *s.* a quick pace with short steps.
খুরখুরিয়া, *a.* moving with quick and short steps.
খুর্পা, *s.* a grass-cutter's spud.
খুর্মা, *s.* a sweetmeat, dried date-fruit.
খুল্, *v. n.* to open, to expand, to unloose.
খুলন, *s.* opening, a loosening, untying.
খুলাসা, *ad.* plainly, openly, sincerely : *a.* clear, plain, open, sincere : *s.* a digest.
খুলী, *s.* cranium, skull, a hemispherical earthen vessel used by confectioners.
খুল্লতাত, *s.* a father's younger brother.
*খুশ্. *s.* joy, pleasure: *a.* joyful, pleasant; -খুরাক্ a dainty food; -খুরাকী, feeding daintily; -জুবান, eloquent, speaking fluently; -তবা, a jester: blithe, gay, boxom; তবাজী, a jest, pleasing expression; -রেজ্জা, good-natured, kind.
*খুশামদ, *s.* flattery, praise, curry favour.
খুশামদী, খুশামদিয়া, *s.* a flatterer, a sycophant.
খুশী, *s.* pleasure, happiness, joy.
*খুশ্কী, *a.* on foot, by land.
*খুশ্খৎ, *s.* penmanship, good writing, fine letters.
খুশখবর, *s.* good news, the gospel.
খুশ্খবরী, *a.* pertaining to good news.
খুশ্গপ্প, *s.* pleasant chat, a pleasant story.
খুশ্ডৌল, *a.* handsome, comely, graceful.
খুশ্নবীস, *s.* good writer, a writing-master.
খুশ্নবীসী, *s.* business of a writing-master.
খুশ্নমা *a.* neat, pretty.
খুশ্নাম, খুশ্নামী, *s.* a good name or reputation.
খুশ্পোশাক, *s.* a good clothing, fine dress.
খুশ্পোশাকী, *a.* well-dressed, gay showy.
খুশ্বক্ত, *a.* joyful, airy; *s.* a good season.
খুশ্বক্তি, *s.* pleasure, joy, gladness.
খুশ্বো, *s.* an agreeable scent, fragrance.
খুশ্মিজাজ, *a.* happy, pleased, in humour.
খুষ্, *a.* quick, swift : *ad.* quickly, swiftly.
খুষ্, *v.* to cough, to tickle in the throat.
খুষণ, *s.* the act of coughing, a wheezing.
খুষ্খুষাণি, খুষ্খুষি, *s.* a fit of coughing.
খুষ্কণ, *s.* a coughing, an exciting.
‡খুস্কা, *v. n.* to cough : *s.* boiled rice.
খুস্কাণ, *s.* the act of hawking, a coughing.
খুস্কী, *s.* cough; excitement; dandruff.
খুস্, *v. a.* to separate corn from its husk : *ad.* quickly, instantly.
খুসড়্, *v. a.* to tuck or wrap up, to put a thing by.
খুসড়ন, *s.* a tucking or wrapping up.
খুসনি, *s.* a witch; the separating of barley or other grain from the husk.
খুসরাণ, *a.* tucked in a bundle or bale.
খুসরাণি, *s.* a tucking into a bundle.
খুসিমুসি, *s.* a stretching and yawning.
খুসুর্, *v. a.* to tuck or thrust in a thing.
খুস্খুস্, খুসখুসনি, *s.* a coughing, wheezing sound in the throat.
খুন, *s.* blood, slaughter, murder; -জারী, the shedding of blood.
খুনখরাবী, *s.* murder, bloody deeds.
খুনাখুনি, *s.* mutual bloodshed, slaughter.
খুনী, খুনীয়া, *a.* bloody, murderous, cruel : *s.* a murderer, a cut-throat.
খেই, খেই, *s.* fibres of thread, a thread-end.
*খেআনৎ, *s.* perfidy; detriment, loss.
‡খেআল, *s.* a thought, an imagination : *a.* composed of good cotton or flax.
খেংরা, খেঙ্গরা, *s.* a besom, a broom.
খেঁউড়, *s.* a vulgar or scurrilous song.
খেঁক্, *s.* the yelp of a dog, shakal, or fox.
খেঁক্চান, *s.* a teazing, importunity.
খেঁকশিআল, or খেঁকর, *s.* a fox.
খেঁকশিআলী, or খেঁখী, *s.* a female fox.
খেঁকা, *v. a.* to scold, to snarl, to threaten : *v. n.* to be impatient or fretful.
খেঁকান, *a.* repulsed, driven away : *s.* a driving away, a being fretful or impatient.
খেঁকানি, *s.* fretfulness, impatience.
খেঁকানিয়া, *a.* passionate, peevish, fretful.
খেঁকারি, *s.* a hem or half cough.
খেঁকী, *a. fem.* snarling, ill-natured.
খেঁখানিয়া, *a.* peevish, importunate, teasing.

খেঁচ্, *v. a.* to pull tight, to gird close, to twitch, to snatch, to tug, to draw.
খেঁচন, *s.* the act of pulling or drawing, a contraction of the body by spasms.
খেঁচা, *s.* a spasm, a stitch, the cramp, a pulling : *v. a.* to draw, to pull forcibly.
খেঁচ্কা, *v. a.* to dun, to importune, to solicit, to tease, to urge : *s.* importunity, an emergency, an exigency, a difficulty.
খেঁচ্কান, *a.* importuned, solicited : *s.* the reiteration of a request, importunity.
খেঁচ্কানি, *s.* importunity, solicitation.
খেঁচ্ড়া, *a.* obscene, vulgar, coarse, scurrilous, base.
খেকুআ, *s.* devourer, an eater.
খেঘাট, *s.* a ferry, a place where a ferry-boat plies.
খেঙ্গরা, *s.* a besom, a broom.
খেচর, *a.* aerial, moving in the air.
খেট, *s.* a village, a suburb.
খেটক, *s. idem ;* Balarám's club, a club, bludgeon.
খেটা, *s.* a club, a bludgeon, a mace.
খেড়ি, *a.* dwarfish, thin, spare.
খেত, *s.* a field, a wife; -পাপড়া, a medicinal plant.
খেতখোলা, *s.* a field, husbandry, tillage.
*খেতাব, *s.* a denomination, a title.
খেদ, *s.* distress, pain, regret, grief, remorse, vexation, affliction, repentance.
খেদকর্ত্তা, *s.* one who regrets or repents.
খেদজনক, *a.* producing regret or repentance, afflictive, distressing.
খেদড়্, খেদড়া, *v.* to drive away, to spring game : *s.* the chasing of an animal.
খেদড়ন, or খেদড়াম, *s.* the act of driving away, the springing of game.
খেদন, *s.* distress, regret, vexation, affliction.
খেদযুক্ত, খেদিত, *a.* the same as খেদান্বিত.
খেদা, *v.* to drive, expel, to drive away, to drive cattle, to chase away.
খেদান, *s.* the driving away of a person or animal.
খেদানিয়া, *s.* one who repulses another.
খেদান্বিত, *a.* distressed, repentant, afflicted in mind, grieved, regretting.
খেদিতব্য, খেদ্য, *a.* distressful, worthy of regret.
খেপ্, *v. a.* to storm, to rage, to rave, to be angry : *a.* as much as is borne or carried at one time : *s.* a batch.
খেপন, *s.* the act of raging or raving with fury.
খেপলাজাল, *s.* a kind of fishing net.

খেপা, *v. a.* to plague, to aggravate, to provoke, to tease : *a.* mad, raving, foolish.
খেপান, *s.* the act of exciting any one to anger : *a.* excited to rage, provoked.
খেপানি, *s.* excitement, provocation.
খেমী, *s.* a casket, a basket, a work-basket.
খেয়, *s.* a ditch, a moat, a trench.
খেয়া, *s.* a ferry, the motion or plying of a ferry-boat, the rowing of a boat.
খেয়াঘাট, *s.* a ferry, place where a ferry-boat plies.
খেয়ানৌকা, *s.* a ferry-boat.
*খেয়াল, *s.* understanding, imagination, a whim; a kind of air or song.
খেল্, *v. n.* to play, move freely (as a machine).
খেলন, *s.* the act of playing or sporting.
খেলনা, খেলানি, *s.* plaything, toy, gewgaw.
খেলা, *s.* play, sport, fun, gambol : *v.* to excite to play, to make a machine play.
খেলাখেলি, *s.* a mutual play, a playing.
খেলাড়, খেলাড়িয়া, খেলাড়ু, *a.* playful, gamesome, sportive : *s.* a playful person.
*খেলাৎ, *s.* an honorary dress.
খেলান, *s.* the causing of machinery to move freely, a stimulating to play.
খেলানিয়া, *a.* fit to play with.
খেলান্বিত, *a.* playful, gamesome, sportive.
*খেলাফ্, *a.* opposed to, passed : *s.* failure.
খেলি, *s.* play, sport, a gambol, a frolic.
*খেশ, *s.* a desire, a wish ; a rug, a stuff.
*খেশারৎ, খেশারতী, *s.* deficiency, loss.
খেশারী, *a.* a species of pulse.[1]
খেস্, *s.* kin, a kindred, relatives.
খৈ, *s.* parched-rice flower ; -চুর, a sweet-meat.
খৈমণ্ড, *s.* rice-flower gruel or conjee.
খৈরী, খৈরীবক, *s.* a species of heron.[2]
‡খো, *s.* brickbats ; disposition, nature.
খোআ, *s.* brickbats, bricks broken small ; cream of milk : *a.* lost : *v.* to loose.
খোআন, *s.* the being lost, a losing : *a.* lost.
খোআনিয়া, *s.* a wasteful person, a spendthrift.
*খোআব, *s.* a dream, idle fancy.
*খোআর, *s.* loss, injury : *a.* bad, corrupt.
খোঁআড়ি, *s.* a hog-sty, a sheepfold.
খোঁচ, *s.* a pointed piece of bambu lath ; a measure, a measuring bambu lath.
খোঁচা, s. any thing pointed used to punch.
খোঁচান, *s.* act of thrusting or punching.

খোঁচাখোঁচি, *s.* a mutual thrusting.
খোঁটন, *s.* a picking up, a scratching off the top of a pimple or scab, a comparing.
খোঁটা, *s.* a pin, peg, stake : *v. a.* to cause to pick up ; to match, to compare with.
খোঁটান, *s.* a causing to pick up little articles, comparing or matching of things: *a.* picked up, matched, compared.
খোঁড়, খোঁরাড়, the same as খুঁড়, খুঁআড়.
খোঁড়া, *v. a.* to cause to dig, or excavate ; to limp, be lame : *a.* dug, excavated ; lame, halt, crippled, limping.
খোঁড়ান, *s.* the causing a spot to be dug ; a limping : *a.* dug ; lame. [lameness.
খোঁড়ানি, *s.* the wages of digging ; a limping,
খোকা, *s.* an infant, a babe ; *fem.* খুকী.
খোজ, *s.* search, enquiry, a trace, a vestige.
খোজন, *s.* the act of searching or seeking.
খোজা, *s.* a eunuch ; a searching. [dustán.
খোট্টা, *a.* Hindustáni, belonging to Hin-
*খোদ, *a.* own, ownself : *v.* to dig, carve.
খোদকস্তা, *a.* (land) let to resident tenants.
খোদকারিকর, *s.* a carver, an engraver.
খোদকারিকর্ম্ম, *s.* a carving, an engraving.
খোদকারী, *s. idem ;* a carver, an engraver.
খোদন, *s.* a digging, a picking of the teeth.
‡খোদা, *s.* God : *v.* to cause to dig, carve, or engrave ; -তালা, God the Creator.
খোদাই, *s* godhead, attributes of God.
খোদাবন্দ, *s.* a master, a husband, a man of God, a term of respect to superiors.
খোন, *s.* a spear, a hog-spear ; a tray ;-কার, one whose business is to circumcise.
খোনা, *a.* speaking through the nose.
খোন্চা, *s.* a salver, a tray, a charger.
খোপ, *s.* a coop or box for pigeons.
খোপচাল, *s.* side roof of a thatched house.
খোপরী, *s.* skull, cranium ; cottage, hut.
খোপা, *s.* a knot of hair tied on the head.
খোপাল, *a.* wearing the hair tied in a knot.
খোয়, *s.* a disposition, nature, manners.
খোয়বেগড়া, *a.* ill-disposed, unmannerly.
‡খোর, *s.* the name of a disease ; an eater.
খোরা, *s.* a particular drinking vessel.
খোরাক, খোরাকী, same as খুরাক, খুরাকী.
*খোর্মা, *s.* dish prepared by salting flesh and frying it in butter ; dry date-fruit.

খোল, *a.* hollow : *s.* the shell of a cocoa-nut, a sheath, socket, case, a kind of drum, the frame of a drum or tom-tom.
খোলকর্ত্তাল, *s.* a drum and cymbal.
খোলন, *s.* a loosening, opening, untying.
খোলস, *s.* the slough of a serpent.
খোলসছাড়া, *a.* (snake) having cast its skin.
খোলা, *a.* open, loose, free, unobstructed, conspicuous : *s.* a field, a toy, a tile, a potsherd, a pot used to bake or parch articles, rind : *v. a.* to cause to open.
খোলাসা, *a.* open, plain, frank, downright.
খোলুতা, *a.* open, free, clear, bright.
খোস, *s.* the itch, an itching eruption.
খোসড়া, *a.* rough, waste : *s.* a waste-book.
খোসা, *s.* husk, shell of corn, a pod, the peel or rind ; chaff, bran, a ligament.
খোসান, *s.* a cleansing from the husk.
খ্যাংখ্যাতান, *s.* the act of fretting.
খ্যাংখ্যাতানি, *s.* fretfulness, discontent.
খ্যাত, *a.* denominated, named, renowned.
খ্যাতি, *s.* character, fame, renown, a denomination, a name, a title, a nickname.
খ্যাত্যাপন্ন, *a.* renowned, famous, celebrated.
*খাঞ্চা, *s.* a salver, a plate, a try.
*খ্বাব, খোআব, *s.* a dream, idle fancy.
*খ্বার, *s.* corruption, evil conduct : *a.* bad.
*খ্বাহিশ, *s.* wish, desire, will, inclination.

গ, the third consonant : when affixed to words, it signifies moving or going.
গইড়, *s.* a large wave, a billow ; tumour of the small-pox ; a layer of thatch.
গইড়পড়া, গইড়পাড়ন, *s.* the beating of a billow ; laying on of layers of a thatch.
গইড়পাতন, *s.* the laying on of layers.
গইরা, *a.* deep, profound : *s.* deep water.
গএর, *s.* phlegm, saliva, hawked phlegm.
গঁগঁ, *s.* a roaring or bellowing sound.
গঁবরা, *s.* the mock temple and horse exhibited at the Muharram festival.
গঁবার, *a.* stupidly ignorant, rustic, rude.
গঁবারী, *s.* stupid ignorance, rusticity.
গকার, *s.* the letter গ.
গগণ, *s.* the sky, the atmosphere, the firmament.
গগণকুসুম, *s.* a flower in the air ; *fig.* any thing absurd or impossible.

গগণচর, গগণচারী, *a.* aerial, moving in the air.

গগণভেলা, *s.* a species of pelican.[1]

গগণমণ্ডল, *s.* the whole body of the atmosphere.

গগণস্থ, *a.* situated in the sky.

গগণোপরি, *ad.* above the sky.

গগরী, *s.* a pitcher, a water-pot.

গগা, *v. n.* to groan, to moan.

গগান, *s.* a groaning or moaning.

গগানি, *s.* a groan, a moan.

গঙ্গা, *s.* the river Ganges; -জল, Ganges water; a sweetmeat; -পুত্র, the doma caste.

গঙ্গাজলী, *a.* white, cream-coloured (as a shawl); swearing by the Ganges water.

গঙ্গাজলীয়া, *s.* one who thus administers an oath.

গঙ্গাটেঙ্গ, *s.* a prawn, a shrimp.

গঙ্গাধর, *s.* a name of Shiva.

গঙ্গাপ্রাপ্তি, গঙ্গালাভ, *s.* the arrival on the shore of the Ganges to die there, the casting of a corpse into the Ganges.

গঙ্গাবাসী, *a.* residing near the Ganges.

গঙ্গাযমুনারঙ্গী, *s.* parti-coloured.

গঙ্গাযাত্রা, *s.* the carrying of a sick person to the Ganges that he may die there.

গঙ্গাযাত্রী, *a.* going to the river Ganges.

গঙ্গাসাগর, *s.* the place where the Ganges disembogues itself into the ocean.

গঙ্গাস্নান, *s.* ablution in the river Ganges.

গচ, *a.* coarse and closely woven, thick.

গচ্ছ, *s.* a deposit, a pledge; a tree.

গচ্ছিত, *a.* pledged, deposited: *s.* a pledge.

গচ্ছ, *v. a.* to receive a thing deposited.

গচ্ছা, *v. a.* to deliver in trust or charge, to deposit, deliver: *s.* promise, pledge.

গচ্ছান, *a.* deposited, placed in a person's charge: *s.* the act of depositing with.

গচ্ছানি, *s.* the making of a deposit.

গজ, *s.* an elephant; a bishop (at chess); a yard, a carpenter's rule; *vide* ছিঁচকা; -কাঠি, a yardwand; -চক্ষুয়া, squint-eyed.

*গজগীর, *s.* a plasterer, one who makes a pavement, a terrace or pavement.

গজগীরী, *s.* the making of a terrace or pavement, a terrace, pavement.

গজঘণ্টা, *s.* a bell hung on an elephant's neck.

গজ-দন্ত, -দাঁত, *s.* an elephant's tusk, ivory.

গজপতি, *s.* the master of an elephant (a title applied to all the Hindu kings).

গজপিপ্পলী, *s.* a climbing plant.*

*গজব, *s.* anger, wrath, fury, curse.

গজমুক্তা, গজমোতা, *s.* a very large pearl.

গজর, *v. a.* to grumble, to murmur; *s.* a grumbling, a murmuring.

গজরা, *s.* an ornament for the wrist of women.

গজস্কন্ধ, *a.* elephant-shouldered.

গজা, *v. n.* to sprout, shoot out: *s.* a bud, sprout, a sweetmeat: *a.* elephant-eyed, squint-eyed, cock-eyed; -চক্ষুয়া, squint-eyed; -রূঢ়, riding on an elephant.

গজান, *s.* a sprouting or shooting out.

গজানন, *a.* elephant-faced; *s.* god Ganesha.

গজাল, *s.* a pin, a large nail, a peg, plug; a fish.

গজী, *s.* a kind of coarse cloth.

গজ্‌গজ্‌, গজ্‌গজানি, *s.* an inward murmuring.

গজ্‌গজা, *v. n.* to murmur inwardly.

গজ্‌গজান, *s.* a muttering, murmuring.

গঞ্জ, *v. a.* to treat a person with opprobrious or disrespectful language.

গঞ্জ, *s.* a mart, a place for merchandize; a mine of jewels; a tavern; contempt.

গঞ্জন, গঞ্জনা, *s.* treating of a person with contempt or reproachful language.

গঞ্জা, *v. a.* to vilify, to abuse: *s.* a tavern, a distillery, a liquor shop.

গঞ্জিফা, or গাঞ্জিবা, *s.* a pack of cards.

গঠ্‌, *v. a.* to fabricate, to make, to mould, to construct, to build, to erect.

গঠন, *s.* a framing or moulding, a making, shaping or building, a make, structure.

গঠিত, *a.* made, framed, moulded, erected.

গড়্‌, *v. a.* to make, fabricate, form, mould, to erect, to build, to roll; -কু, to bow.

গড়, *s.* obstacle, fence, screen, ditch, moat, fort, fortification, a breastwork, a fastness, medium, average; wood on which the pedal works; a bow, a salutation.

গড়ই, or গড়ুক, *s.* the name of a fish.

গড়কাঠ, *s.* wood on which the pedal works.

গড়কাঠি, *s.* a shell-cutter's instrument.

গড়খাই, *s.* a moat, a ditch, a trench.

গড়গড়, *s.* a thundering or rattling sound.

গড়গড়িয়া, *s.* an ornament worn by women.

গড়ন, *s.* act of making or fabricating, a make, shape, form, figure, fabrication.

গড়নকাঠ, *s.* a timber for building.

গড়নদার, গড়নিয়া, *s.* an artist, a maker.
গড়নী, *s.* the hire or pay of an artificer.
গড়সুন্দর, *s.* a tree (Mimosa arabica).
গড়া, *v. a.* to cast, to fabricate, to make, to lie, to recline, to run out, to roll: *a.* wrought, forged, made: *s.* coarse cloth.
গড়াগড়ি, *s.* the act of wallowing or rolling about; -দা, to wallow, to roll about.
গড়ান, *s.* a casting (of metal), a rolling, a causing to fabricate or make, a reposing: fabricated, cast, sloping, inclined.
গড়ানিয়া, *a.* sloping, aslant, slippery.
গড়াপেটা, *a.* made, formed, fabricated.
গড়াল, a mouthful; gayála or Bos gavæus.
গড়ি, *s.* a large wave, a billow; a tumour after the small-pox; a layer of thatch.
গড়িমসী, idleness, delay, procrastination.
গড়িয়া, *a.* indolent, shrinking from labour.
গড়িয়াকাঠ, *s.* beams laid under a granary.
গড়িয়াগোরু, *s.* a bullock that lies down at [work.
গড়িয়ান, aslant, inclined, sloping.
গড়িয়ামি, *s.* indolence, sloth, torpor.
গড়ু, *s.* a hump, goitre, wen, bronchocele.
গড়ুর, *a.* hump-backed; having a wen, afflicted with a goitre; *s.* the regent of birds.
গড়ে, *ad.* in the gross, on an average.
গড়গড়া, *v. n.* to thunder, to rattle, rumble.
গড়্গড়ি, *s.* thunder, rattling sound.
গড্ডালিকা, *s.* disorder, confusion; a sheep.
গড়্বড়ি, গড়বিড়ি, *s.* confusion, disorder, a confused mixture, a tumult, a hubbub.
গণ্, *v. a.* to reckon, to count, to enumerate, to calculate, to account.
গণ, *s.* a kind, a genus, a party, a flock, a tribe, a class, a troop, a body of troops, or attendants, a number in arithmetic; the list of dhátus or Sanskrit roots.
গণক, *s.* an astrologer, fortune-teller, calculator of nativities, an arithmetician.
গণকতা, -ত্ব, *s.* the calculating of a nativity, divination, astrologership, astro- [logy.
গণতা, ত্ব, *s.* partiality, collusion.
গণতাকার, *s.* a partizan, a partial person.
গণতাকারী, partial, prejudiced in favour of.
গণৎকার, *s.* an astrologer, an astronomer.
গণন, *s.* a counting, a casting up, a reckoning, the making of a calculation.

গণনকর্ত্তা, *s.* a calculator, an accountant.
গণনা, *s.* arithmetic, a calculation, a sum, an account, a number, numeration.
গণনীয়, গণয়িতব্য, *a.* calculable, numerable.
গণপতি, *s.* name of Ganesha; a ringleader.
গণবদ্ধ, *a.* bound or confined to a party.
গণা, *v. a.* to cause to count or calculate: *a.* counted, calculated: *s.* a counting.
গণাক্রান্ত, *a.* drawn by a sect or party.
গণাগণি, mutual counting: *ad.* by parties.
গণাগাথা, *s.* a calculation: *a.* counted.
গণাগোষ্ঠী, *s.* a generation, race, lineage.
গণান, *s.* a causing to calculate or count: *a.* [counted.
গণিয়ারী, *s* a small tree.[1]
গণিকা, *s.* a harlot, a prostitute. [house.
গণিকাগৃহ, গণিকালয়, *s.* a brothel, a bawdy-
গণিত, *a.* enumerated, counted, accounted: *s.* arithmetic, an arithmetical treatise.
গণিতশাস্ত্র, science, or book of arithmetic.
গণীভূত, *a.* entered into or joined to a party, hereditary (applied to a disease).
গণেশ, *s.* Ganesha, or the god of wisdom.
গণেশচতুর্থী, *s.* in the month of Bhádra the day on which Ganesha is worshipped.
গণেশজননী, *s.* a name of Durgá.
গণ্গণ্, *s.* the blazing or glowing of fire.
গণ্গণিয়া, *a.* glowing, ready to blaze.
গণ্তি, *s.* a calculation, an enumeration.
গণ্ড, *s.* the cheek, the side of the face, elephant's temples; a boil, pimple, a mark.
গণ্ডক, *s.* a rhinoceros; also, *vide* গণ্ডাকিয়া.
গণ্ডগোল, *s.* a tumult, an uproar, hubbub, a mob, a mutiny, an insurrection.
গণ্ডগোলিয়া, *a.* tumultuous, noisy, mobbing.
গণ্ডগ্রাম, *s.* a principal village. [the face.
গণ্ড -দেশ, -প্রদেশ, -স্থল, *s.* the cheek, side of
গণ্ডদেশস্থ, *a.* situated on the cheek.
গণ্ডমালা, *s.* an inflammation of the glands of the throat attended with pustules.
গণ্ডমূর্খ, *a.* pre-eminently ignorant.
গণ্ডশৈল, *s.* a part of mountain or rock cast down by some convulsion of nature.
গণ্ডা, *a.* four (a reckoning by the tale).
গণ্ডাকিয়া, *s.* a method of counting by gan- [dás or fours.
গণ্ডার, *s.* a rhinoceros.
গণ্ডি, *s.* a goitre, a wen, bronchocele, trunk of a tree; a bow, circle, halo, rainbow.

গণ্ডী, *s.* a bow, a rainbow; a circle.
গণ্ডূষ, *s.* a handful of water for washing the mouth; the tip of an elephant's trunk.
গণ্য, *a.* calculable, numerable, notable.
গৎ, *v. a.* to deliver to a person's custody.
গত, *a.* gone, past, last; *ad.* by-gone; -কাল, past time; -কীর্ত্তি, sunk in reputation.
গত -কল্য, -দিন, -দিবস, *s.* yesterday.
গতপ্রমায়ু, *a.* dying, past recovery.
গতপ্রভ, *a.* dim, of decayed splendour.
গতমর্য্যাদ, *a.* bereft of former respect.
গতর, গাত্র, গা, অঙ্গ, শরীর, *s.* the body.
গতরাত্রি, *s.* the past night, yesternight.
গতরাল, *a.* fat, plump, fleshy, large-bodied.
গতর্জ্জমা, *s.* indolence; collectedness, arrears.
গতা, *v. a.* to deposit, deliver up.
গতাগত, *s.* a going and coming.
গতাব্দ, *a.* antedated, out of date, or use, obsolete.
গতান, *s.* a depositing with, a pledging.
গতানুগতিক, following or imitating others.
গতানুসূচনা, the inutility of after-thought.
গতায়াত, *s.* intercourse, coming and going.
গতায়ু, *a.* dying, expiring, past recovery.
গতার্থক, retrospective, looking past events.
গতি, *s.* motion, going, progress, a procession, a course, a condition of life, a refuge, an expedient, fate, fortune.
গতিক, *s.* a condition, circumstance, a position, a resource, an expedient, a scope.
গতিক্রিয়া, *s.* delay, procrastination, trifling.
গতিবিধি, *s.* intercourse.
গতিবিহীন, *a.* motionless, helpless, without resource.
গতিয়া, or গত্যা, *a.* lazy, indolent, inactive, dilatory, procrastinating.
গতিযোগ্য, *a.* passable, fit for motion.
গতিরহিত, গতিহীন, *a.* same as গতিবিহীন
গতিশক্তি, *s.* the power of motion.
গদ্, *s.* the heaviness of a former meal.
গদ, *s.* a disease, sickness, speech, a word.
গদা, গদায়ুধ, *s.* a club, a mace, a bludgeon.
গদাঘাত, *s.* a stroke with a club.
গদাধর, *s.* a name of Balarám.
গদাযুদ্ধ, *s.* a battle with clubs or bludgeons.
গদি, গদিয়া, *s.* a cushion, mattress, pillow, a seat, a bench.
গদিত, *s.* spoken, said.
গদিয়ান্, *a.* possessed of a seat or bench.
গদী, *a.* bearing a mace, armed with a club.
গদ্গদ, *a.* interrupted by sighs: *ad.* sobbingly; -বাক্য, speech interrupted by sobs; -ভাষী, speaking with sobs.
গদ্দি, *s.* a jest, a joke, a repartee, a taunt.
গদ্দিযোগ্য, *a.* proper to be made a jest of.
গদ্য, *s.* prose; pleasantry, humour.
গদ্যচ্ছন্দ, *s.* prose, a measured prose.
গদ্যযোগ্য, গদ্যার্হ, *a* fit for prose, prosaic.
গন্তব্য, *a.* passable, accessible, practicable.
গন্তা, *s.* a traveller, one who goes, a goer.
গন্ত্রী, *s.* a cart or car drawn by oxen.
গন্ধ, *s.* a scent, a smell, odour, a perfume, fragrance, a relationship, a connection; -প্রিয়, fond of scents; -মাদন, the name of a mountain; -যুক্ত, scented, fragrant.
গন্ধক, *s.* sulphur, brimstone; sandal-wood.
গন্ধকাষ্ঠ, *s.* lignum aloes, sandal-wood.
গন্ধগোকুল, *s.* a species of polecat.[1]
গন্ধপাষাণ, *s.* sulphur, brimstone.
গন্ধবণিক্, *s.* a perfumer, druggist, apothecary.
গন্ধবিরজা, *s.* a kind of medicinal resin.
গন্ধবেণা, *s.* the lemon grass.[2]
গন্ধমার, *s.* the Indian wormwood.[3]
গন্ধমালতী, *s.* a variety of rice; a flowering climber.[4]
গন্ধমূষিক্, *s.* the musk-rat.
গন্ধরস, *s.* myrrh.
গন্ধরাজ, *s.* the king of flowers.[5]
গন্ধর্ব্ব, *s.* the choristers of heaven.
গন্ধর্ব্ববিদ্যা, *s.* the polite arts, viz. music, etc.
গন্ধর্ব্ববিবাহ, *s.* a marriage in which the parties make the contract.
গন্ধা, *v.* to perfume, emit scent: *a.* stinking, fetid.
গন্ধাদিদান, *s.* an offering of perfumes, etc. to the deceased ancestors.
গন্ধাধিবাস, *s.* a preliminary offering of perfumes.
গন্ধান, *s.* the emitting of a scent: *a.* fetid.
গন্ধী, *s.* a bug, a flying-bug; a druggist.
গপ্, গপ্‌গপ্, *s.* a gulping sound.
গপ্প, *s.* chitchat, tattle, a story, tale, report.
গপ্পসপ্প, *s.* tittletattle, chitchat.
গপ্পিয়া, গপ্পী, *a.* talkative, garrulous, addicted to telling stories.
গবড়ী *v. n.* to cast the young, to miscarry, to fail.
গবড়া, *v. a.* to write unintelligibly, to do a work clumsily, or so as to spoil it.
গবড়ান, *s.* the doing a thing clumsily, a writing badly: *a.* badly written, or done.

গবা, *s.* a cow; a simpleton, an idiot.
গবাক্ষ, *s.* a window-blind like ox's eye.
গবাক্ষদ্বার, *s.* passage through a window.
গবাসন, *s.* a skinner, a currier, a tanner.
*গবাহ, *s.* a testimony. গবাহী, *s.* a witness.
গব, *a.* pregnant, big with young.
গব্য, *a.* produced from a cow, fit for a cow: *s.* produce of a cow, viz. milk, butter, ghi, cowdung, etc.; a bow-string.
গব্যূতি, *s.* a measure of two krosha.
গভস্তি, *s.* a ray of light, a sun-beam.
গভস্তিমৎখণ্ড, *s.* one of the divisions of the earth.
গভীর, *a.* deep, profound, grave.
গভীরতা, -ত্ব, *s.* depth, profundity, gravity.
গভীরধ্বনি, *s.* a deep or grave sound.
*গম্, *a.* withdrawn, concealed: *s.* grief.
গম, গোম, গোধুম, *s.* wheat.
গমক, *s.* plant and its fruit;[1] a bag to conceal the rosary or beads when praying.
গমন, *s.* a going, motion, a march, progress; coition. গমনার্হ, গমনীয়. *vide* গম্য.
গমনরহিত, motionless, still, immovable.
গমনশীল, *a.* inclined to motion, mobile.
গমনাগমন, *s.* intercourse, free communication.
গমনাসক্ত, fond of walking, mobile.
গমাগম, *s.* intercourse, going and coming.
*গম্‌খোর, *a.* anxious, thoughtful.
গম্‌খোরী, *s.* anxiety, thoughtfulness.
গম্ভারী, *s.* a tree (Gmelina arborea).
গম্ভীর, *s.* deep, profound, grave.
গম্ভীরতা, -ত্ব, *s.* depth, profundity, gravity.
গম্য, *a.* accessible, movable, practicable, fit to be travelled or gone over.
গম্যাগম্য, *a.* practicable or impracticable.
গয়া, *s.* the name of a city in Behár.
গয়াকরণ, *s.* making a pilgrimage to Gayá.
গয়ার, গয়ের, *s.* phlegm, saliva, spittle.
গয়াল, *s.* a species of ox; a variety of rice.
গয়ালী, গয়ালীয়া, *a* residing at Gayá.
গয়াশ্বত্থ, *s.* a species of fig tree.[2]
গয়াসুর, *s.* the name of a giant.
*গর্, *ad.* without, besides, except.
*গরক, *a.* sinking, drowning, going down.
গরগণ্ড, *s.* a goitre, a wen, bronchocele.
গরণ:খাঁদা, *s.* a hare lip: *a.* hare-lipped.
*গরজ, *s.* desire, necessity, exigency.
গরজী, *a.* necessitous, desirous, inclined.
গরদ, *s.* a kind of silk cloth.
*গরদা, or গ [illegible], *s.* dust.
গরম্, *a.* passionate, hot, warm.
গরমী, *s.* warmth, passion, heat; venereal disease.
গরম্‌পোশ, *a.* wearing warm clothing.
গরম্‌মেজাজ, *a.* passionate, hot-headed.
গরল, *s.* venom, poison, virus; a kind of disease.
গরলী, *a.* venomous, poisonous.
গরাণ, *s.* the name of a tree,[3] its bark is used in tanning: *a.* deep-rooted.
গরাদি, or গরাদিয়া, *s.* a rail, a palisade, a pale, a range of paling, a balustrade.
গরিমা, *s.* self-importance, vanity, a boast, pride.
গরিমান্বিত, *a.* self-important, vain.
গরিষ্ঠ, *a.* most important, honourable, reverend, superior; difficult of digestion.
*গরীব, *a.* poor, needy, indigent, humble.
গরীবানা, *a.* fit for or according to the poor.
গরীবী, *s.* poverty, humility, indigence.
গরীয়ান, *a.* the same as গরিষ্ঠ.
গরু, *s.* a cow (generic name); *fig.* a simpleton.
গরুড়, *s.* regent of birds, Vishnu's steed; a large vulture, or a gigantic crane.
গরুৎ, *s.* a wing, a feather.
গরুত্মান, *a.* winged, feathered.
গরুবৎ, *ad.* cow-like, stupidly, sillily.
গরুরহাঁছী, *s.* a dilemma.
গর্,-আদালত, -ইনসাফ, injustice, a wrong.
গর্‌আশল, *a.* destitute of an origin.
গরকবুল, *s.* a denial, a not confessing.
গর্গর, *s.* redness with rage, anger, rage, fury.
গর্গরী, *s.* a jar, a pitcher, a jug.
গর্গরীয়া, *a.* red with rage or fury, furious.
গর্গা, *s.* a spear; a species of fish.[4]
*গর্‌জানবিৎ, *a.* unknown, unacquainted.
গরজানির, *a.* absent, not of the party.
গর্জ্জ, *s.* a roar, a bellow, a growl.
গর্জ্জন, *s.* a growling, a roaring, bellowing, a threatening, thunder, passion, rage, fury, tumult of war; name of a tree.[5]
গর্জ্জনতৈল, *s.* wood-oil.
গর্জ্জনী, *s.* a bellowing, roaring, thunder, a threatening.
গর্জ্জিত, *a.* threatened, scolded: *s.* an elephant in rut, the rumbling of thunder.
*গর্‌তকসীর, *a.* faultless, innocent, without a fault; *s.* innocence, faultlessness.
*গর্‌তজবীজ, *s.* injustice, a wrong.

*গর্‌তদবীর, s. carelessness, inattention.
গর্ত্ত, s. a hole in the ground, a cave, an excavation, a burrow, a cavity.
গর্ত্তময়, গর্ত্তযুক্ত, a. full of holes or pits.
গর্দন, or গর্দান, s. the neck. [neck.
গর্দানী, s. the turning out a person by the
*গর্‌দিশ, s. circulation, a circuit. [cloth.
গর্দ্দখোর্‌, a. concealing dust : s a kind of
গর্দ্দভ, s. an ass, a donkey; a beetle; scent.
গর্দ্দভবৎ, a. ass-like, foolish, stupid.
গর্দ্দভী, s. a she-ass, a genny ass.
*গর্‌পসন্দ, s. disapprobation, dislike.
গর্‌বক্ত, s. a being out of time: a. untimely.
গর্‌বাজিবী, a. wrong, improper, unjust.
গর্ব্ব, s. pride, arrogance, haughtiness, scorn, self-sufficiency. [scornful, proud.
গর্ব্বযুক্ত, গর্ব্বান্বিত, a. arrogant, haughty,
গর্ব্বামুকী, a. *fem. idem.*
গর্ব্ভিণী, গর্ব্ভিনী, a. pregnant. [glorious.
গর্ব্বিত, a. arrogant, proud, haughty, vain-
গর্ব্ভ, s. an embryo, a fœtus, the gravid uterus, a child, the womb ; the spatha of a plant, the bed of the Ganges.
গর্ব্ভক, s. a chaplet of flowers worn in the
গর্ব্ভঘাতিনী, a. causing abortion. [hair.
গর্ব্ভ- চ্যুত,-পতিত,|abortive, untimely birth.
গর্ব্ভজ, গর্ব্ভজাত, a. arising from pregnancy, born of a man's wife by another person.
গর্ব্ভদাস, s. the son of a female slave.
গর্ব্ভধারণ, s. conception in the womb.
গর্ব্ভপাত, গর্ব্ভস্রাব, s. miscarriage, abortion.
গর্ব্ভবতী, or গর্ব্ভিণী, a. pregnant.
গর্ব্ভ- বেদনা, -যন্ত্রণা, -যাতনা, s. the throes of labour, the pains of child-birth.
গর্ব্ভস্থ, a. in the womb, seated internally.
গর্ব্ভাগার, s. a lying-in chamber. [tion.
গর্ব্ভাধান, s. a ceremony to ensure concep-
গর্ব্ভ শঙ্কা, s. apprehension of pregnancy.
গর্ব্ভাষ্টম, s. eighth month of pregnancy: a eight years old (as a proper season for investing a lad with the sacred thread).
গর্ব্ভোৎপাদন, s. impregnation.
গর্হ, গর্হা, s. scurrility, reviling, a censure, a reproach, a blame, a disgrace.
*গর্‌হক, a. wrong, improper, unjust.
গর্হণীয়, or গর্হ্য, a. censurable, reproachable, contemptible, abominable.

গর্‌- হাজির্‌, a. absent, হাজিরী, absence.
গর্হিত, a. reviled, despised, disgraced, reproached, treated with scurrility.
গল্‌, v. v. to dissolve, melt, ooze, burst, suppurate, wear out, to escape through the bars of a cage, or walls of a prison.
গল, or গলদেশ, s. the neck.
গলই, গলুই, s. the prow of a ship or boat.
গলইয়া, s. one who manages the prow of
গলকম্বল, s. the dewlap of an ox. [a boat.
গলগণ্ড, s. a goitre, a wen, bronchocele.
গলগ্রহ, গলগ্রহণ, s. the same as গলহস্ত.
গলত্তি, s. a melting or dissolving (as salt, sugar, etc.) ; an error, a mistake.
গলন, গলনি, s. a melting, a dissolving, the bursting of a tumour, escape thro' a bar.
গলনীয়, a. malleable, soluble, dissolvable.
*গলবা, s. superiority, pre-eminence.
গলভঙ্গ, s. hoarseness, roughness of voice.
গলরোগ, s. a disease of the neck or gullet.
গলহস্ত, s. the throttling of a person : a. holding by the neck, collaring a person.
গলা, v. a. to melt, dissolve, burst, force out: s. the neck, gullet, throat; a loud voice: a. melted, dissolved, putrefied, burst.
গলাখুষ্‌কী, or গলাখুষ্‌খুষ্‌ণী, s. a cough, a tickling or wheezing in the throat.
গলা -খেঁকরাণ, -খেঁকরাণি, *vide* গলাখেঁকারি.
গলাখেঁকার্‌, v. to clear the throat by coughing up phlegm : s. a coughing.
গলাখেঁকারি, s. a coughing, the clearing of the throat by coughing up phlegm.
গলাগলা, ad. huggingly, neck to neck, reaching to the neck, dissolved.
গলাগলি, s. mutual holding of the neck.
গলাচাপন, গলাচাপা, s. same as গলাটিপী.
গলাট, a. worn out, dissolved, putrid, rotten.
গলাটেলা, s. a scolding loud voice. [ten.
গলাটিপন, গলাটিপা, s. same as গলাটিপী.
গলাটিপী, s. a throttling, a strangling or choking of a person or animal. [posed.
গলাটিয়া, a. dissolved, putrid, burst, decom-
গলাধঃকরণ, s. the swallowing of a thing, the power of swallowing. [cing.
গলাধরণ, s. the act of hugging or embra-
গলাধরা, s. the hugging of a person : a. seizing the throat (as acrid substances).

গলান, *a.* dissolved, melted, made to pass through an opening : *s.* act of melting.
গলানিয়া, *a.* solvent, dissolvent.
গলানী, *s.* the wages given for melting, etc.
গলায়দড়িয়া, *a.* died by hanging (a ghost).
গলাবন্ধ, *s.* a neckcloth, a cravat, a stock.
গলাভাঙ্গা, *a.* hoarse, broken-necked.
গলাস, গলাসী, *s.* a noose, slip-knot, neck-rope, halter.
গলাসীগিরা, *s.* a slip-knot.
গলি, *s.* a lane, an alley, a narrow passage.
গলিঘুঁজি, *a.* crooked, tortuous and narrow.
গলিত, *a.* dissolved, melted, decomposed, burst, passed through a small opening.
গলিতকুষ্ঠ, *s.* that stage of leprosy when the body is ulcerous and fingers drop off.
গলিতকুষ্ঠী, *a.* afflicted with above leprosy.
গলিয়া, *s.* one who manages the prow.
*গলীজ, *s.* filth, mud, dirt: *a.* filthy, dirty.
গলুই, *s.* the prow of a ship or boat.
গল্‌গল, *s.* garrulity; a kind of mortar or cement made with resin and tar.
গল্‌গলা, *v. n.* to talk excessively, or very fast.
গল্‌গলিয়া, *a.* garrulous, talkative.
*গল্‌ৎ, গল্‌তি, *s.* a mistake, an error.
গল্প, *s.* a story, chitchat, idle talk, palaver.
গল্পীয়া, *a.* talkative, chatty, gossiping.
গল্লা, *v.* to tie up sheaves, bind straw, etc. in bundles : *s.* a sheaf, a wisp, a bundle.
গল্লাচিঙ্গড়ি, *s.* a large species of prawn.
গল্বা, *s.* grain; ascendency over others
গস্‌গসা, *v.* to be hot with fever, to glow.
গস্‌গসীয়া, *a.* hot, feverish, glowing.
*গস্ত, *s.* a walking about, a sauntering.
গস্তান, *s.* a strumpet, a whore, a harlot.
গস্তানী, *a.* whorish, sensual, licentious.
গহগহ, *s.* a crowd, the din of a crowd.
গহন, *s.* a forest, a thicket : *a.* impervious.
গহনা, *s.* an ornament, a trinket, a jewel.
গহরা, গহেরা, *a.* deep, profound : *s.* depth.
গহরী, *s.* delay, procrastination, a demurrage.
গহীন, গহীর, *a.* deep, profound.
গহ্বর, *s.* a deep valley, a ravine, a defile, cave, hole, a den; an arbour, a bower.
গা, *v. a.* to sing, to chant; to calk.
গা, *s.* the body, surface of any thing; -তুল, to rise, get up; কাঁপ্‌, to tremble.
গাইন, *s* a singer, a songster, a chorister.
*গাইব, *s.* a disappearing, vanishing away.
গাইল, *s.* scurrility, abusive language.
গাই, গাভী, *s.* a cow. গাইগোরু, *s.* cattle.
গাওন, *s.* a singing; a calking; -দার, a calker.
গাওয়া, *s.* vocal music, singing of a tune.
গাওনী, *s.* the calking of a boat or ship.
গাং, *s.* the Ganges, river in general; -চিল, a kind of gull; -ফড়িঙ্গ, a kind of grasshopper; -সালিক, a species of marten.
গাঁ, *s.* a village, a hamlet.
গাঁই, *a.* belonging to a village.
গাঁইট, *s.* a knot, a knob, a knuckle, a joint, a bale.
গাঁইটকাটা, *s.* a cutpurse, a pickpocket.
গাঁইটশূলা, *s.* pain in the knuckles, a whitlow.
গাঁইঠ, গাঁঠি, the same as গাঁইট, &c.
গাঁইয়া, *a.* residing in the village, rustic : *s.* a villager, a clown, a rustic.
গাঁগাঁ, *s.* a roaring or bellowing sound : *ad.* from village to village, at every village.
গাঁজ, *v. n.* to beat, foam, froth up : *s.* froth.
গাঁজন, *s.* beating to foam or froth.
গাঁজলা, *a.* frothy, covered with foam : first milk.
গাঁজা, *s.* the tops of hemp used as a narcotic : *v. a.* to beat into foam, to froth.
গাঁজাখোর, গাঁজিয়াল, *a.* smoking hemp as a narcotic : *s.* a smoker of hemp.
গাঁজাখোরী, *s.* the habit of smoking gánjá.
গাঁজাবালা, *s.* a seller of hemp.
গাজিয়া, *s.* a wallet, a grass-cutter's bag, a purse.
গাঁটরি, গাঁঠরি, *s.* a bundle, bale, a package.
গাঁটা, *v. a.* to tie knots, to lie in wait : *s.* a listening in private, a lying in wait.
গাঁটাগাঁটি, *a.* wrestling : *ad.* at every joint.
গাঁটিছাড়া, *s.* a marriage ceremony of tying the bride and the bridegroom together.
গাঁটিবন্দী, *a.* packed up in a bale : *s.* a packing of bales; -কৃ, to pack up in bales.
গাঁঠলী, *s.* a stopping the progress of the venom of a serpent by incantations.
গাঁঠলীপাড়ন, *s.* the act of stopping the progress of the venom of a serpent.
গাঠা, *v. a.* to tie knots, knit stocking, etc.
গাঁড়, *s.* a prominent navel; the anus.
গাঁড়পোল, *s.* a pelican.[1]
গাঁড়ার, *s.* a rhinoceros; a low class of the Hindus.
গাঁড়ি, or গাঁইড়, *s.* the anus, the vent.
গাঁড়িয়া, গাঁড়ু, গাণ্ডু, *s.* a catamite.

গাঁড়িয়াগুবলি, *s.* abuse, excessive scurrility.
গাঁতান, *a.* threaded, strung, arranged.
গাঁতি, *s.* a kind of iron cross-crowbar.
গাঁতী, *s.* the insertion or introduction of an article among a number of others.
গাঁতীজমা, *s.* the including of a small lot of land in a more general rent.
গাঁথ্, *v. a.* to knit, thread beads; to plait, unite, construct, build, arrange, poke.
গাঁথন, *s.* a knitting, a knotting, a stringing of beads, etc., the arranging of bricks.
গাঁথনি, *s.* the hire or quality of arranging bricks, the workmanship of a building, a threading of beads or flowers.
গাঁথা, *v. a.* to join, make up; to cause to be threaded, to cause bricks to be arranged in a building: *a.* spitted, knitted, threaded, strung, orderly arranged.
গাঁথান, *a.* caused to be strung or arranged: *s.* a causing to join, arrange, or string.
গাথানি, *s.* fee to join (a coin), the hire of arranging bricks, or threading beads, etc.
গাধি, *s.* ill-scent; -লাগ, to be affected by stench (as fishes); -পোকা, a flying-bug.
গাঁহাক, *s.* a purchaser, a buyer, a customer.
গাকাঁটা, লোমাঞ্চ, *s.* horripilation.
গাখসা, *s.* abortion, miscarriage.
গাগরা, *s.* a kind of fish.[1] গাগী, a kind of parrot.
গাগরী, *s.* a pitcher, a water-pot.
গাঘামান, *s.* a causing of perspiration, a being interested in an affair.
গাছ, *v. n. vide* গাছা; -মরিচ, chilly, red-pepper.[2]
গাছ, গাছা, *s.* a tree, a plan, a single one: *e. g.* এক গাছা রসী, a single line or string; এক গাছ চল, a single hair.
গাছড়া, *s.* vegetables, plants and trees.
গাছবাটা, *s.* a kind of betel-box or stand of brass made in the form of a lustre.
গাছবেড়া, *s.* enclosure with trees or hedges.
গাছা, *v. n.* to grow, to sprout, spring up.
গাছান, *s.* vegetation, a training up plants.
গাছী, *s.* single one (hair, etc.)
গাছুআ, climbing or living on trees; -ইন্দুর, tree-rat.
গাছুড়িয়া, *a.* expert at climbing trees.
গাজন, *s.* a stall in honour of Shiva at the charak-pujá, penance by self-torture.
গাজর, *s.* a carrot (Daucus carota).

গাজুরগুজুর, *s.* a rumbling of the bowels.
গাড়্, *v. a.* to plant, to fix a stake in the ground, to bury: *s.* a mine, a pit, hole.
গাড়ন, *s.* act of fixing a stake or post in the ground, or of burying any thing.
গাড়বান, গাড়ীবান, *s.* a carter, coachman.
গাড়বানী, *s.* office of a carter or coachman.
গাড়র, or গাড়ল, *s.* a sheep in general.
গাড়রিয়া, or গাড়লিয়া, *s.* a shepherd.
গাড়া, *s.* a hole, a pit: *a.* planted, buried; thick (applied to cloth, or any liquid).
গাড়ী, *s.* a carriage, cart, waggon, hackery, a coach; a hole, pit: *a.* deep.
গাড়ীবালা, *s.* a driver or maker of a carriage.
গাড়ু, *s.* a curvature of the spine, a wen in the neck, a water-vessel with a spout.
গাঢ়, *a.* dense, crowded, excessive, deep (as sleep), close (embrace), thick, inspissated (liquids); -দধি, thick curds; -প্রবাস, inhabiting a long time; -প্রণয়, -প্রীতি, -প্রেম, excessive love; -মুষ্টি, close-fisted.
গাঢ়া, *s.* a cave, a ditch, an abyss, a thick forest: *a.* thick (applied to liquids).
গাঢ়ান্ধকার, *s.* thick or excessive darkness.
গাঢ়ালিঙ্গন, *s.* a hug, a close embrace.
গাণপত্য, *a.* belonging to Ganesha.
গাণ্ডার, খড়্গী, *s.* a rhinoceros.
গাণ্ডিব, or গাণ্ডীব, *s.* a bow, Arjuna's bow.
গাণ্ডু, গাঁড়ু, গাঁড়িয়া, *s.* a catamite.
গাণ্ডেপিণ্ডে, *a.* full to the throat.
গাতাগামড়ি, *s.* the Japan earth (Terra Japonica).
গাতুয়া, *a.* indolent, idle, lazy, torpid.
গাতোলন, গাতোলা, গাত্রোত্থান, *s.* a getting up, act of rising when lying or seated.
গাত্র, *s.* the body, the surface of any thing.
গাত্রকণ্ডু, গাত্রকণ্ডুয়া, *s.* an itching, the itch.
গাত্রপাক, *s.* giddiness, vertigo, staggers.
গাত্রমর্দ্দন, *s.* the rubbing of the body.
গাত্রমার্জ্জনী, *s.* a towel, a napkin.
গাথক, *a.* skilful in singing: *s.* a chanter, a singer.
গাথা, *s.* a verse or stanza, a poem to be sung, vulgar or barbarous language.
গাদ্, *v. a.* to cram, to ram, to force down, to press, to fix a stake.
গাদ, *s.* lees, dregs, scum, a sediment.
গাদন, গাদনি, *s.* cramming of any thing, charging of a gun, a ramming down.

গাদপুনর্নবা, গাদপুন্যা, *s.* name of a plant.[1]
গাদা, *v. a.* to cause to cram, or ram down : *s.* an ass; a heap, a stack, a rick, a ream.
গাদাগাদি, *s.* a mutual cramming.
গাদী, *s.* ten quires of paper; a heap ; a cushion, state seat, a raised place, altar.
গাদীগাদী, *ad.* by heaps, in piles. [cants.
গাদীপতি, *s.* the chief of a body of mendi-
গাদুলমযামী, *s.* indolence, slothfulness.
গাধা, *s.* an ass, donkey ; a stupid person ;
গাধাবৎ, *ad.* ass-like, stupidly. [*fem.* গাধী.
গান, *s.* song, vocal music, act of singing ; -কর্তা, a singer, a songster : -বাদ্য, song and music : -শক্তি, an ability to sing ; -শ্রবণ, the hearing of song or vocal music ; -শ্রোতা, one who hears singing.
গানাসক্ত, *a.* fond of singing or vocal music.
গাপ্, *v. a.* to deny a thing, to conceal.
গাপন, *s.* the concealing of a fact, denial.
গাপা, *v. a.* to cause to deny or conceal.
গাপান, *s.* a causing to deny or conceal.
গাপোসা, *a.* idle, lazy, indolent.
*গাফিল্, *a.* negligent, idle, inattentive.
গাফিলী, *s.* inattention, negligence.
গাফুলা, *v.* to strut, swagger, swell with pride, to appear consequential. [tial.
গাফুলানিয়া, *a.* strutting, vain, consequen-
গাফুলানী, *s.* self-consequence, stateliness.
গাব, *v.* to become turbid, rusty, or filthy : *s.* a semen virile ; a tree and its fruit.[2]
গাবড়া, *s.* idle talk, chitchat, tittletattle.
গাবা, *v. a.* to stir up a liquid to make it turbid, to stir a thing, divulge a secret, to blab out ; -নিল, a kind of reed.[3]
গাবান, *a.* stirred up so as to become turbid, divulged, blabbed out.
গাবানি, *s.* the stirring up of water so as to make it turbid, the divulging of secrets.
গাবানিয়া, *s.* a tell-tale, tale-bearer, a tattler, a divulger of secrets.
গাভা, গাবা, *s.* a fœtus, the gravid uterus, pregnancy ; the spatha of a plant.
গাভারী, *a.* heavy with young, pregnant ; heavy with a cold or fever.
গাভিণ, or গাবিন, *a.* pregnant.
গাভী, or গাবী, *s.* a cow. [one, a surfeit.
গামধুরাণ, *s.* the cloying or satiating of any
গামোচা, or গাম্‌চা, *s.* a towel, a handkerchief, a napkin. মলাট, *s.* an apron.
গামোড়া, *v.* to yawn, stretch : *s.* a yawning or stretching ; -দা, to yawn, stretch.
গাম্‌ড়া, *s.* the midrib of the palm leaf.
গাম্ভারী, *s.* the same as গম্ভারী. [ousness.
গাম্ভীর্য, *s.* depth, gravity, profundity, seri-
গাম্‌লা, *s.* a hemispherical earthen vessel.
গায়, *ad.* on or along the surface. [ster.
গায়ক, *a.* singing : *s.* a singer, chanter, song-
গায়কঘটা, *s.* a choir, a body of singers.
গায়ত্রী, *s.* sacred stanza of the Rig-veda, which none but bráhmans repeat mentally ; a measure of verse in the veda.
গায়ত্রীচ্ছন্দ, *s.* the Gáyatri metre.
গায়পায়, *s.* the body, the person of a man.
গায়ভাঙ্গন, *s.* a drooping, a debility.
*গারৎ, *s.* plunder, rapine, devastation, destruction, ruin, consumption.
গার্হপত্য, *s.* householdership.
গার্হস্থ্য, *s.* the condition of a householder : *a.* pertaining to a house dweller.
গাল্, *v. a.* to dissolve, to melt, to break a boil, to strain out the liquor, to milk.
গাল, *s.* the cheek ; a story, talk ; abuse.
গালগুল, *s.* a common report, town-talk.
গালন, *s.* a melting of metals, a dissolving of salt, etc., a straining off, a milking.
গালা, *v. a.* to melt metals, to dissolve any thing : *s.* sealing-wax, lac.
গালাকাঠি, *s.* a stick of sealing-wax.
গালাগালি, *s.* abusive language, scurrility.
গালাঘুষা, *s.* a common report, rumour.
গালান, গালানি, *s.* melting of metals, dissolving of salt, etc. ; price for melting.
গালি, গালী, *s.* abusive language, scurrility.
*গালিচা, *s.* a particular sort of carpet.
*গালিব, *a.* overcoming, excelling. [my.
*গালিম, tyrannizing : *s.* a tyrant, an ene-
গালুআ, *s.* a boaster, a talkative person.
গালুনিয়া, *a.* abusive, brawling, scurrilous.
গাহক, গাথক, *s.* singer, songster. [fishes.
গিজ্‌গিজ্, *s.* a crowd, multitude, a shoal of
গিঞ্জি, *a.* impervious, thick set, crowded.
গিন্নী, *s.* the mistress of a house, a wife.
*গিদড়, গিধড়, *s.* a jackal, a shakal.
গিধ, *s.* a species of vulture ;[4] *fem.* গিধিনী.

গিনা, *s.* a small metallic or earthen cup.
গিমা, a potherb (Chironia centauroides).
গির, *s.* a word, a speech, saying.
গিরগিটী, *s.* a species of lizard.[1]
গিরদা, *s.* a side pillow, a pillow, a bolster.
গিরা, *s.* a knot, a joint, a knuckle.
গিরি, *s.* a mountain, hill, rock; a mouse.
গিরিজা, *s.* a name of the goddess Durgá.
গিরিন্দ্র, *s.* the Himálaya mountains.
*গিরেফ্তার, *a.* seized, apprehended.
গিরেফ্তারী, *s.* a seizure, apprehension.
গির্জা, *s.* a church, a place of worship.
গিল, *v. a.* to swallow, to strip, to plunder.
গিলন, *s.* act of swallowing or gulping.
গিলনি, *s.* a swallowing, a gulping.
গিলা, *v. a.* to cause to swallow, to feed: *s.* a kidney, the seeds of Mimosa scandens; a backbiting, censure.
*গিলাফ্, *s.* a case, a cover; winter sheet.
গিলিত, *a.* swallowed, glutted, enclosed.
*গিলিম, *s.* a carpet of a peculiar make.
গিল্লা, গিল্লাগুজারী, *s.* a backbiting, talebearing, discontent, censure, reproach.
গিল্লাগুজার, *a.* censorious, abusive, backbiting.
গীঃ, *s.* a word, a sentence.
গীত, *s.* a song, an ode, a hymn.
গীতকর্ত্তা, *s.* a singer, one who composes songs.
গীতশ্রবণ, *s.* the hearing of songs.
গীতা, *s.* the name of a famous poem.
গীর্ব্বাণ, *a.* immortal: *s.* a deity.
গু, *s.* dung, excrement, ordure, filth, rust.
গুআ, *s.* the betel-nut; the anus.
গুআমউরী, *s.* anis-seed, also the plant.[2]
গুঁজ্, গুঁজড়্, *v. a.* to tuck in, to thrust in.
গুঁজড়ন, গুঁজড়ান, *a.* tucked in: *s.* the act of tucking or thrusting in.
গুজড়নি, গুজড়ানি, *s.* a thrusting or tucking in.
গুঁজড়া, *v. a.* to tuck in, to thrust in.
গুঁজন, গুঁজনি, *s.* the act of tucking in.
গুঁজী, *s.* an awl, a plug, a cork, a stopple.
গুঁড়, *v. a.* to crumble, pulverize, reduce to powder: *s.* crumbs, fragments, powder; the cross beams of a ship or boat: *a.* pulverized, crumbled, powdered.
গুঁড়গাড়া, *s.* fragments, crumbs, powder.
গুঁড়ন, গুঁড়ান, *s.* the act of crumbling or pulverizing: *a.* pulverized, powdered.

গুঁড়া, *v. a.* to cause to reduce a substance to powder: *s.* fragments, crumbs, powder: *a.* crumbled, pulverized.
গুঁড়াটুঁড়া, গুঁড়ামুঁড়া, *s.* fragments, crumbs, powder.
গুঁড়ি, *s.* flour, powder; the trunk of a tree, a tuberous root, a piece of timber.
গুঁড়িকাঠ, *s.* the trunk of a tree, a timber.
গুঁড়িপিপিড়া, *s.* a species of black ant.
গুগলী, *s.* a species of snail.
গুগ্গুল, *s.* bdellium; the lignum aloes.[3]
গুচি, গুচ্ছি, *s.* a tuft of hair, grass, etc., a bunch, a nosegay, a sheaf, a collection, a floating stake or wager in gambling.
গুচ্ছার,গুচ্ছির, *s.* some, a little, a few; *e. g.* গুচ্ছির ঘাস, a little grass, etc.
গুচ্ছ, *s.* a cluster, a bunch, a nosegay, a tuft of hair or grass, a bundle, a sheaf, a collection, a necklace of 32 strings.
গুছ, গুছা, *a.* to collect in clusters, collect and lay in proper order, to arrange.
*গুজব্, *s.* a flying report, a town-talk.
*গুজর্, *v. a.* to pass away, to go by: *s.* admission; a cow-keeper, a dairyman.
গুজরহ, *ad.* by means of, by the hand of.
গুজ্‌রাতীএলাচি, *s.* the true cardamoms.[4]
*গুজ্‌রান, *s.* a living, support: *a.* spent, passed by, gone, passing away, going.
*গুজরী, *s.* ornament for the ankles worn by women; a female personification of music; a dairymaid, a gujar's wife.
*গুজ্‌শ্তা, *a.* past, gone, passed away.
*গুজ্‌রা, *s.* a ferry; also, *vide* গুজ্‌রান.
গুজগুজ, গুজগুজনি, *s.* tale-bearing, whispering, tattle, garrulity, gossipping.
গুজগুজিয়া, *a.* talkative, blabbing.
গুঞ্জ, গুঞ্জা, *s.* a plant, its seed, called রতি; a humming, a buzzing noise; a tavern.
গুঞ্জন, গুঞ্জরণ, *s.* hum of a bee, echoing of any voice, a low murmuring sound.
গুঞ্জর্, *v. n.* to hum a tune, to utter a low murmuring sound, to hum as bees do.
গুঞ্জিত, *a.* filled with the humming of bees, or with any low murmuring noise.
গুট্, *v. a.* to roll up, to collect together.
গুটন, *a.* rolled up, furled, gathered: *s.* the furling or rolling up of any thing.
গুটনি, *s.* the rolling up of any thing.

গুটলী, *s.* ball or pellet of dung, etc.; fruit-
গুটা, গুটান, the same as গুট্, &c. [stone.
গুটি, *s.* in *comp.* one, a single or merely one
individual of the kind; also, *vide* গুটী.
গুটিক, *s.* a collection, a quantity, a heap.
গুটিকা, *s.* a pill, a pellet, a ball, a cocoon.
গুটিকাপাত, গুটিপোকা, *vide* গুটীপাত, &c.
গুটিগুটি, *ad.* one by one, by slow steps.
গুটিলা, *s.* a hard ball of dung. [the hips.
গুটিলি, *s.* the stone of a fruit, a swelling in
গুটী, *s.* a ball, a pill, bolus, a fruit when
first formed, stone of a fruit, the small-
pox, a cocoon or silk ball, men in dice.
গুটীপাত, *s.* the casting of lots, a lottery.
গুটীপোকা, *s.* a silk-worm, aurelia.
গুঠলী, *s.* the stone of a fruit.
গুড়্, *v. a.* to roll up, to furl, to pack up.
গুড়,*s.* raw-sugar, molasses, treacle: -পিঠা,
gingerbread; -কামারী, a thorny shrub.[1]
গুড়ক, *s.* a medicated lozenge; tobacco.
গুড়ত্বক, *s.* cinnamon, or rather cassia bark.
গুড়ন, গুড়নি, গুড়ান, the same as গুটন, &c.
গুড়মুড়া, গুল্‌, এড়ী, *s.* the heel.
গুড়া, *v. a.* to roll up, to furl, to pack up.
গুড়াকু, *s.* tobacco mixed with molasses.
গুড়ি, *s.* a stooping posture, a crouching.
গুড়িগুড়ি, *ad.* by little and little, crouching-
ly, in a stooping posture. [tioner.
গুড়িয়া, *a.* made of raw-sugar: *s.* a confec-
গুড়কতমাক, *s.* tobacco mixed with treacle.
গুড়ুম্, গুড়ুম্‌গুড়ুম্, *ad.* with repeated reports
of artillery, or sudden claps of thunder.
গুড়্‌গুড়্, *s.* a running quickly, sound arising
from thundering or beating of a drum.
গুড়্‌গুড়িয়া, *a.* rattling, running with quick
and short steps: *s.* a species of quail.[2]
গুড়্‌গুড়ী, *s.* a small huká; a kind of quail.[2]
গুণ, *s.* a quality, property, attribute, ten-
dency, virtue, power, effect, stretch,
accomplishment, an advantage; three
properties of matter, viz. *Satwa*, the
principle of existence or truth; *Raja*,
that of passion; and *Tama*, that of dark-
ness or ignorance; sackcloth, gunny;
track-rope, tow-line; bow-string; gold
or silver thread, wire. In *comp.* preceded
by a numeral, it signifies as many times;
e. g. চতুর্গুণ, four times as much, or four-
fold, etc.; a charm, magic, witchcraft.
গুণক, *s.* in *arith.* a multiplier. [eulogy.
গুণ্ -কথন, -প্রশংসা, -বর্ণনা, *s.* a panegyric,
গুণকরণ, *s.* amelioration, improvement, the
effecting of medicine, or of a charm.
গুণ-কার, -কৃৎ, -কারক, -কারী, *a.* improving,
advantageous, effectual, beneficial.
গুণকীর্ত্তি, *s.* a eulogy, panegyric. [gyrist.
গুণগাথক, *a.* praising, eulogizing: *s.* a pane-
গুণগান, *s.* a chanting of praise, panegyric.
গুণচট, *s.* sackcloth, unny.
গুণচরিত্র, *s.* a panegyric, an eulogy.
গুণচ্ছেদ, *s.* cutting of any of the threads of
the paitá: *a.* having its threads cut.
গুণজনক, *a.* productive of good: *s.* a tutor.
গুণজ্ঞান, *s.* a sense of the virtues of others.
গুণটানা, *s.* the drawing of the track-rope
of a boat: *a.* drawing the track-rope.
গুণটুন, *s.* qualities, ropes and cords, sacks.
গুণদর্শন, *s.* being successful, taking effect.
গুণন, *s.* in *arith.* multiplication.
গুণপনা, *s.* virtue, talent, ability, skill.
গুণপরীক্ষা, *s.* the trial or proof of virtue.
গুণবত্তা, *s.* an accomplishment. [qualities.
গুণবর্ণন, *s.* the relating of virtues or good
গুণবাদী, *a.* praising, eulogizing, grateful.
গুণবান্, গুণশালী, গুণী, *a.* possessed of tal-
ents or virtues, ingenious, accomplish-
ed, talented, distinguished, virtuous.
গুণযোগ, *s.* the study of science.
গুণসাগর, গুণসিন্ধু, গুণার্ণব, *a.* an ocean of
virtues or good qualities. [of virtues.
গুণা, *s.* wire, gold or silver wire; -কর, mine
গুণাখ্যান, *s.* a panegyric, an eulogy.
গুণাগুণ, *s.* virtues and defects of any one.
গুণান্বিত, *a.* virtuous, accomplished.
গুণার্হ, *a.* suited to virtues or good quali-
গুণিন্, *s.* a magician, a sorcerer. [ties.
গুণীভূত, *a.* become accomplished or useful.
গুণ্‌গুণ্, *s.* a humming, humming sound.
গুণ্‌গুণা, *v. a.* to hum, snuffle. [fling noise.
গুণ -গুণান, -গুণানি, -গুণি, *s.* humming, snuf-
গুণ্ড, lascivious, lewd, profligate; *fem.* গুণ্ডী.
গুণ্ডমি, গুণ্ডপনা, *s.* lasciviousness, lewdness,
letchery, profligacy, libertinism.
গুণ্ডিকা, *s.* powder, dust, saw-dust.

গুঁত, *v. a.* to thrust, to stab, to gore, to ram, to punch : *s.* a thrust, a stab.
গুঁতন, *s.* a punching, goring, stabbing : *a.* gored, punched, thrust at, stabbed.
গুঁতখুরিয়া, গুঁতনিয়া, *a.* goading, accustomed to gore (applied to horned animals).
গুঁতা, *v. a.* to punch, thrust, to ram, gore, to stab, to knock : *s.* a stab, a thrust.
গুঁতাগুঁতি, *s.* a mutual stabbing or goring.
গুঁতান, *s.* the act of thrusting or goring, a stabbing, a ramming, a beating down.
গুৎস, গুচ্ছ, a tuft, bunch, cluster, nosegay.
গুদ, *s.* the anus, pudendum muliebre.
গুদড়, *s.* rags and the like stuff, a quilt.
গুদড়ী, গুধড়ী, *s.* a bed quilt, a quilt, a rug.
গুদকম্প, *s.* a very great degree of fear.
গুদা, *s.* marrow ; a kind of bird. [house.
গুদাম, *s.* a warehouse, magazine, a store-
গুদারা, *s.* a ferry, the plying of a ferry.
গুদারাঘাট, *s.* landing-place of a ferry boat.
গুদারানৌকা, *s.* a ferry, a ferry-boat.
গুদী, *s.* a dock-yard, a dock for shipping.
গুন, *s.* a sack, bag, wallet, pack, gunny.
*গুনজাইশ, *s.* capacity, gain, advantage.
গুনজাইশী, *a.* gainful, advantageous.
*গুনাহ্‌, *s.* a crime, sin, guilt, a fault.
গুনাহ্‌গার, *a.* guilty, sinful, criminal.
গুনাহ্‌গারী, *s.* faultiness, sinfulness ; a fine.
গুপো, *a.* secret, not manifest (as blows).
গুপোঘা, *s.* a secret blow, assassination.
গুপ্‌চুপ্‌, *a.* silent: *s.* a kind of sugar plum.
গুপ্ত, *a.* concealed, hidden, secret, guarded.
গুপ্তকথা, গুপ্তবাক্য, *s.* a secret, secret word.
গুপ্তবেশ, *s.* disguise, a concealed habit.
গুপ্তঃবেশে, *ad.* in disguise, *incog.*
গুপ্তভাব, *s.* a concealed state. [tinely.
গুপ্ত -ভাবে, -রূপে, *ad.* concealedly, clandes-
গুপ্তা, *s.* a woman who conceals her amours.
গুফ্‌, *s.* a mountain-pass, a ravine.
গুবর্‌, *v. a.* to write badly or blottedly.
গুবরিয়া, *a.* pertaining to cow-dung.
গুবরিয়াডাঁটা, *s.* a kind of potherb.
গুবরিয়াপোকা, *s.* a species of beetle.
গুবাক, *s.* the betelnut and its tree.[1]
গুম্‌, *v. n.* to be mouldy or musty (as hay or corn when stacked up) : *s.* a discontinuing at intervals to lay eggs.

গুমট, *s.* heat, sultriness, closeness.
গুমটকাল, *s.* hot season, sultry weather.
গুমটিয়া, *a.* mouldy, tainted, musty.
গুমর্‌, *v. a.* to buzz, murmur : *s.* buzzing sound : pride, haughtiness ; advantage.
গুমরণ, গুমরাণ, *s.* a buzzing, a re-echoing, the act of rebellowing, a rumbling.
গুমরা, *v. a.* to buzz, to rebellow, to rumble, to echo : *s.* the nightmare.
গুম্‌শো, গুম্‌সা, *a.* mouldy, musty, stale.
*গুমান, *s.* a suspicion, a fancy, pride.
গুমানী, *a.* suspicious, fanciful, capricious, [proud.
*গুমাশ্‌তা, *s.* an agent, a factor.
*গুম্বজ, *s.* a tower, a turret, a dome, vault.
গুম্‌সন, *s.* the growing musty or stale.
গুয়া, *s.* the betel-nut ; the anus.
গুরী, *a.* white, fair : *s.* a fair woman.
গুরু, great, heavy, important, honorable, accented : *s.* spiritual guide, a preceptor, a teacher, a parent, a superior.
গুরুজন, *s.* a superior, a guru. [weighty.
গুরুতর, *a.* *compar. deg.* more important,
গুরুতল্পগ, *s.* a violater of his guru's bed.
গুরুতা, -ত্ব, *s.* importance, weight, greatness, honorableness, glory, majesty.
গুরুদক্ষিণা, *s.* a fee given to a guru.
গুরুদত্ত, given by a preceptor or superior.
গুরুদশা, *s.* death of a parent or superior.
গুরুদীক্ষিত, *a.* put in possession of his mantra by his guru or spiritual guide.
গুরুদেব, *s.* a preceptor, a spiritual guide, a parent, a superior.
গুরুনিন্দক, *a.* censuring or reproaching superiors : *s.* one who does so.
গুরুনিন্দা, *s.* the reproaching or censuring, of a preceptor or superior.
গুরুপত্নী, *s.* the wife of a spiritual guide.
গুরুপাক, *a.* difficult of digestion.
গুরুপাপ, *s.* a great crime, heinous offence.
গুরুবরণ, *s.* making an oblation to a guru.
গুরুবর্ণ, *s.* a long or accented vowel.
গুরুবার, or বৃহস্পতিবার, *s.* Thursday.
গুরুবোধ, *s.* a firm conviction, a clear idea.
গুরুভক্ত, *a.* devoted to a spiritual guide.
গুরুভক্তি, *s.* devotedness to a preceptor.
গুরুভাব, *s.* preceptorship, weightiness.
গুরুভার, *s.* a heavy load, a great weight.

গুরুসুখ, *s.* great happiness.

গুরুহত্যা, *s.* the murder of a guru, a parricide.

গুরূক্তি, *s.* the sayings of a preceptor.

গুরূচ্চারণ, *s.* pronunciation of a long or accented vowel; words uttered by a guru.

গুরূত্তর, *s.* the answer of a preceptor.

গুরূপাসনা, *s.* attendance on the lectures or instructions of a preceptor.

গুরুরা, *v. a.* to cause a palpitation.

গুরুরাণ, *s.* occasioning of a palpitation.

গুর্বঙ্গনা, *s.* a preceptor's wife; a mother or other superior female relation.

গুর্বারাধনা, *s.* the respect due to a preceptor, to a parent, or a superior.

গুর্বিণী, *a.* pregnant, with child.

গুর্বী, *a.* pregnant, weighty, great, heavy, important: *s.* wife of a spiritual guide.

গুল্, *v. a.* to melt, dissolve (in a liquid): *s.* a ferrule with which a pedal, etc. is shod; a ball of charcoal, a fire-ball; the snuff of a candle or lamp; the burnt tobacco of a huká; a globe, a ball.

*গুল্, *s.* a nose, a flower; -দাউদী, a flower plant;[1] -নর্গিশ্, a kind of narcissus;[2] -মস্ত, a drug; -মেন্দি, a flower plant.[3]

গুল, গুলক, *s.* a collection, a multitude, a number.

*গুলকন্দ, *s.* conserve of roses.

গুলকাটা, *s.* the shaving of a piece of wood to make it round; a pair of snuffers.

গুলঞ্চ, *s.* a medicinal climbing plant.[4]

গুলতরাশ, *s.* a pair of snuffers.

গুলতি, *s.* rice-pap; pellet-bow, cross-bow.

গুলন, *s.* the dissolving of a substance in a liquid.

গুলবাঘা, *s.* a hyena.

*গুলর, *s.* a species of wild fig-tree.[5]

*গুল্শকর, গুল্শকরী, *s.* conserve of roses.

গুলা, গুলাক, *s.* a multitude, a collection.

*গুলাচীন, *s.* a small fragrant flower-tree.[6]

গুলানার, *s.* a species of pomegranate tree with double flowers but no fruit.

গুলাপাশ, *s.* a receptacle for rose-water.

গুলাব, *s.* a rose, rose-water.

গুলাবাস, *s.* the same as কৃষ্ণকেলি.

গুলাবী, *a.* pink, rosy, rose-scented, rose.

গুলালতুলসী, *s.* a kind of fragrant plant.[7]

গুলি, *s.* a pill, bolus, a ball, bullet: a number, some few; *e. g.* কতগুলি, some few.

গুলিক, গুলিন, *s.* a few, a number, some.

গুলিবাঁট, *s.* a casting of lots, a lottery, a sharing out by lot, or by casting dice.

গুলিয়া, *a.* globular: *s.* a kind of fish.

গুলিস্তান, garden of roses; name of a book.

গুলী, *s.* a pill, bolus, a ball, bullet, a pellet, a bullet of earth, a cannon ball.

গুল্গাল, *s.* a hubbub, a noise, a clamour, common or town talk, a general report.

*গুল্গুলা, *s.* a kind of fritters.

গুল্তাই, গুল্লল, *s.* a pellet-bow, a cross-bow.

গুল্ফ, *s.* the ankle. গুল্ফাস্থি, ankle-bone.

গুল্ম, *s.* a shrub, bush; induration of the mesenteric glands; division of an army.

গুল্মী, *a.* abounding with bushes or shrubs, afflicted with the disease called gulma.

গুল্ল, গোড়মুড়া, এড়ী, *s.* the heel.

গুহা, *s.* a ravine, cavern, a dell, a valley, a cave.

গুহ্য, *a.* concealable: *s.* the anus.

গুহ্যতা, *s.* concealableness, secresy.

গুহ্যদেশ, *s.* the anus, the private parts.

গুহ্যস্থান, *s.* a recess, a private place.

গূ, *s.* ordure, excrement, dung, filth, rust.

গূঢ়, *a.* concealed, abstruse, mysterious.

গূঢ়জ, *a.* illegitimate, bastard.

গূঢ়তা, *s.* secresy, concealedness, abstruseness.

গূঢ়পাদ, *s.* a serpent, a snake.

গূঢ়পুরুষ, *s.* a scout, a spy.

গূঢ়াভিমানী, *a.* proud of obscurity, affecting abstruseness or mystery.

গূয়া, *a.* smeared with ordure, having the scent of ordure; -বাবলা, a small tree;[8] -লেকড়া, or -শালিক, a species of bird.[9]

গৃঞ্জন, *s.* a carrot; poisoned flesh.

গৃধ্, *a.* greedy: *s.* a vulture; *vide* গিধ.

গৃধ্রসী, *s.* pains about the loins, lumbago.

গৃহ, *s.* a house, a habitation; -কর্ত্তা, master or builder of a house; -কর্ম্ম-কার্য্য, domestic duties, household work, building of a house; -জাত, homeborn; -দাহ, burning of a house; -দাহক, an incendiary; -বাসী, a house-dweller; -মধ্য,-মাঝ, inside of a house; -রক্ষা, guarding of a house; -রক্ষাকর্ত্তা, guardian of a house.

গৃহগোধিকা, *s.* the small house lizard.

গৃহচ্ছিদ্র, *s.* a family quarrel, family fault.

গৃহবাজ, *s.* a tumbler pigeon.

গৃহবিচ্ছেদ,*s.* family dispute, domestic feud.
গৃহভঙ্গ, *s.* the breaking down of a house.
গৃহভেদী, *a.* sowing dissension in a family, officious, betraying family secrets.
গৃহশূন্য, *a.* destitute of a house.
গৃহস্থ, *a.* residing or situated in a house: *s.* a house-dweller, a householder.
গৃহস্থধর্ম্ম,*s.* duties incumbent on a house-
গৃহস্থায়ী, *a.* residing in a house. [holder.
গৃহস্থাশ্রম,*s.*the conditionof a householder.
গৃহস্থিত, situated or dwelling in a house.
গৃহিণী, *s.* a wife, mistress of a house.
গৃহী, *a.* domestic, worldly, not ascetic.
গৃহীত, *a.* received, taken, accepted.
গৃহীতবিদ্য, গৃহীতশাস্ত্র, *a.* versed in science.
গৃহে, *ad.* at home, in the house.
গৃহ্য, *s.* a ritual of domestic duties.
গেঁউড়, *s.* a tuberous root. [foam or froth.
গেঁজ, *v. n.* to ferment, to be covered with
গেঁজ, *s.* the plumula or sprout of a seed, a pustule when first beginning to form.
গেঁজলা, *a.* in a state of fermentation, covered with froth or foam: *s.* biestings.
গেঁজা, *v. a.* to beat into a foam, to cause to ferment: *s.* tops of hemp; biestings.
গেঁজান, *s.* act of beating to foam or froth.
গেঁজ্যা, *s.* a purse, bag; grass-cutter's bag.
গেঁজ্যাল, *a.* addicted to gánjá: *s.* a sot.
গেঁটা, গেঁটিয়া, *a.* knotty, knobby, genicu-
গেঁটাগোঁটা, *a.* the same as গেড়া. [lated.
গেঁঠান, *s.* the tying of a knot.
গেঁড়া, *a.* stout, plump, short and thick.
গেঁড়ি, *s.* a species of snail; *vide* বদনা.
গেঁড়িভাঙ্গাকেউটিয়া,*s.* a variety of Cobra de
গেঁড়িশামুক, *s.* a species of snail. [capello.
গেঁডু, *s.* a ball for play, a granulated root.
গেঁড়ুআ, *s.* a ball of flowers. [to faulter.
গেঁড়্গেঁড়্, *v. n.* to make a faultering noise,
গেঁদড়া, *s.* a kind of sweetmeat.
গেঁদা, or গেন্দা, *s.* a marygold.[1]
গেঙ্গাড়ি, *s.* the cry of a watchman.
গেঙ্গান, *s.* a whining cry or lamentation.
গেণ্ডু, গেণ্ডুক, *s.* a ball for play. [box.
গেব্যা, *s.* a drawer, a till, a division in a
গেয়, *a.* fit or proper to be sung.
গের, *v. n.* to fall, to drop down: *s.* a knot.
গেরণ, *s.* a falling down; an eclipse.

গেরা, *v. a.* to cast or throw down. [down.
গেরান,*s.* a throwing down, thrown or cast
গেরী,-মাটী,*s.* red-ochre, ruddle, red earth.
গেরেস্তার, *a.* clever, prudent, respectable.
*গের্দ, *a.* circular: *s.* a circle, a boundary.
গের্দবার, *a.* surrounding on all sides.
গের্দবারী, *s.* a being on all sides; a police-
গেলা, *v. a.* to cause to swallow. [officer.
গেলান, গেলানি, *s.* a causing to swallow.
গেলুয়া, *a.* loquacious, talkative, boasting.
গেহ, *s.* a habitation, a house. [village.
গৈগাঁ, *s.* the country, opposed to a city, a
গৈরা, *a.* deep: *s.* a deep place, an abyss.
গৈরিক, *s.* red-ochre, ruddle, red earth.
গৈষী, *a.* desirous of talents or virtues.
গো, *s.* a cow, ox; betel-nut; *voc. part.* used in respectfully addressing a person.
গোআলনী, *s.* a milkmaid, a dairymaid.
গোআলা, *s.* a cow-keeper, a dairyman.
গোআলাপাড়া, *s.* the part of a town or village inhabited by cow-keepers. [spy.
গোএন্দা, *s.* spy, a scout; -গিরী, office of a
গোঁ, *s.* advantage, opportunity; a projection in masonry; a bellowing sound.
গোঁগোঁ, *s.* a bellowing sound.
গোঁজ, *s.* a peg, a wooden pin, a stake.
গোঁজা, *v. a.* to thrust straw into old thatch for repairing it: *s.* a peg, pile, stake.
গোঁড়, *s.* a lump, ball, clod; a prominence, a swelling; *a.* prominent, gibbous.
গোঁড়নাভি, *s.* a prominent navel.
গোঁড়া, *s.* prominence, a ball; a bigot, blind partizan, a flatterer, leader of a band.
গোঁড়াচূণ, *s.* quicklime, lime of cockle shells.
গোঁড়াঝিনুক, *s.* species of shell-fish.
গোঁড়ানেবু, *s.* a variety of lime.
গোঁড়াম, গোঁড়ামি, *s.* bigotry, partizanship, bloated praise, bombast, flattery.
গোঁদ, *s.* gum, gum arabic, gum of Mimosa
গোঁফ, *s.* mustaches, whiskers. [arabica.
গোঁফাল, *a.* having large mustaches. [oxen.
গোঁয়ারা, *s.* panniers, baskets borne by
গোকর্ণ, *s.* a short span; a snake; antelope.
গোকল, *s.* oblation of straw made to a cow.
গোকিল, *s.* a pestle; a plough.
গোকুল, *s.* a herd of cows, a cow-pen.
গোক্ষুর, গোখুরী, *s.* the name of a plant.

গোখাদক, *a.* eating beef: *s.* a beef-eater.
গোখুরসাপ, *s.* a variety of the Cobra de capello.
গোগা, *a.* dumb, speechless.
গোগৃহ, *s.* cow-house.
গোগোল, *s.* a hemorrhoidal tumour.
গোগ্রাস, *s.* the taking up of a mouthful.
গোঘৃত, *s.* clarified butter (of cow's milk).
গোঙর, গোঙরা, *v. n.* to make a noise like a person oppressed by the nightmare.
গোঙরাণ, গোঙরাণি, *s.* the effort to speak while having the nightmare.
গোঙ্গা, *a.* dumb, speechless: *s.* a large cauri.
গোঙ্গান, গোঙ্গানি, *s.* the nightmare.
গোচ, *s.* a bunch, a wisp, a sheaf, a tuft, a nosegay, a custom, a habit; the instep.
গোচর, *a.* perceptible: *s.* in presence, cognizance: *ad.* before, in the presence of.
গোচরাণ, *s.* the grazing or feeding of cattle.
গোচরাণি, *s.* a cow pasture.
গোচা, *v. a.* to collect into bundles: *s.* a handful, a tuft, a bunch, a wisp, a sheaf.
গোচাগোচা, *ad.* by handfuls, by tufts.
গোচান, *s.* collecting of things into sheafs or bundles: *a.* collected into bundles.
গোচানি, *s.* collection into bunches or bundles.
গোচারক, *s.* a cowkeeper, cowherd.
গোচারণ, *s.* the pasturing of cattle.
গোচিকিৎসক, *s.* a quack doctor, a cow-doctor.
গোচিকিৎসা, *s.* quackery.
গোচোর, *s.* a cow-stealer.
গোছ, গোছা, the same as গোচ, &c.
গোছাল, গোচাল, *a.* tied in bunches, bundles, or sheafs; neat and clever, tidy.
গোট, *s.* a silver chain for the waist.
গোটা, *a.* whole, entire, unbroken, uncut, undivided: *s.* gold or silver lace; a thing that is whole, an integer; betel-nut.
গোটাকত, *s.* a number, a quantity, a few.
গোটানাল, *s.* a foaming at the mouth from the bite of a serpent; slaver, saliva.
গোটাল, *a.* whole, entire, unbroken, uncut.
গোটেটোমোটো, *a.* rolled up, gathered.
গোঠ, *s.* a herd, a flock, a drove, a company; a cow-pen, station for cowherds.
গোঠছাড়া, *a.* straggled from the herd.
গোঠবাঁধন, *s.* the assembling or collecting into a herd, a gathering in company.
গোঠবিহারী, *s.* the name of an annual fair.
গোড়, *s.* the foot; sore of small-pox; the base, bottom, a foundation, a pedestal.
গোড়-গাঁইট, -গাঁঠি, গুল্ফ, *s.* the ankle.
গোড়মুড়া, গুল, এড়ী, *s.* the heel.
গোড়শূল, *s.* a corn or callosity under the foot.
গোড়া, *v. n.* to overtake, approach, to draw near: *s.* the base of a pillar, etc., the foundation of a building, origin, source.
গোড়াগোড়ি, *ad.* wholly, from the foundation, origin, or source.
গোড়াঘেঁষা, *a.* in contact with the base of a thing.
গোড়ান, *s.* overtaking, approaching, drawing near: *a.* approached, come to pass.
গোড়াবধি, *ad.* from the origin or source.
গোড়াবাঁধন, *s.* the earthing up of plants, etc.; the confirming of a proposition.
গোড়ারি, গুড়মুড়া, গুল, এড়ি, *s.* the heel.
গোডিম, গোডিব, *a.* unfledged, callow.
গোডুম্বা, *s.* the water-melon.
গোণী, *s.* a sack, a bag, sackcloth, gunny.
*গোতা, *s.* immersion, a diving, a dipping.
গোত্র, *s.* a race, lineage, pedigree, family extraction, an ancestor, a patriarch.
গোত্রজ, *a.* lineal, lineally descended.
গোত্ব, *s.* cowship. গোপতি, *s.* a bull.
গোথুবৈ, *a.* curled, curly, knotty, snarly.
গোদ, *s.* the elephantiasis, or swelled leg.
গোদন্ত, *s.* a cow's tooth; the sulphate of arsenic; -হরিতাল, yellow-orpiment.
গোদন্তমণি, *s.* a chrysoprasus.
গোদা, *a.* afflicted with the elephantiasis.
গোদাচিল, *s.* the common Indian kite.
গোদান, *s.* a gift of cows.
গোদানী, *s.* a tattooing of the body, branding.
গোদাবরী, *s.* the name of a river.
গোধা, *s.* a fence of leather worn on the left arm by archers; an alligator.
গোধিকা, *s.* the guana, an alligator.
গোধূম, *s.* wheat; -চূর্ণ, wheaten meal, flour.
গোধূলি, গোধূলিকাল, *s.* evening twilight.
গোধেনু, *s.* a cow, a milch-cow.
গোনাগোষ্ঠী, *s.* a family or lineage reckoned to the original progenitor.
গোপ, *s.* a cow-keeper, a milk-man, a butterman, a dairyman.
গোপগণ, *s.* a body or fraternity of cow-keepers.

গোপগৃহ, *s.* the house of a cow-keeper.
গোপন, *s.* the act of concealing any thing, privacy, secresy, concealment.
গোপনস্থল, গোপনস্থান, *s.* a place of concealment, a retreat, a recess.
গাপনীয়, গোপ্য, *a.* concealable. [tinely.
গোপনে, *ad.* privately, secretly, clandes-
গোপাঙ্গনা,*s.* a dairymaid, dairyman's wife, a female cow-keeper, a milkmaid.
গোপায়িত, *a.* concealed, hidden, guarded.
গোপার্ব্বণ, *s.* a festival of cows and calves.
গোপাল, *s.* a name of Krishna; *vide* গোপ.
গো-পালক,-রক্ষক, *s.* a cow-keeper.
গোপালন, *s.* the nourishing of cows.
গোপালয়, *s.* the residence of a dairyman.
গোপিকা, *s.* a dairywoman, a milkmaid.
গোপিনী, গোপী, *s. idem.*
গোপী -কুল, -গণ, *s.* a body of milkmaids.
গোপীমাটী, *s.* yellow-ochre. [maids.
গোপীবল্লভ, *s.* Krishna, the lover of milk-
গোপুচ্ছ, *s.* a cow's tail; a kind of monkey.
গোপো, *s. fig.* all a person's household.
গোপ্তা, *s.* he who conceals; *fem.* গোপ্ত্রী.
গোবদা, *a.* thick, clumsy, unwieldy.
গোবধ, *s.* the killing of a cow.
গোবর, গোময়, *s.* cow-dung, manure.
গোবরা, *v. a.* to write badly; *s.* a shrub.
গোবরাট, *s.* the sill, threshold of a door.
গোবরাণ, *s.* the writing in a blotted and illegible manner: *a.* illegibly written.
গোবরাণি, *s.* blotted or illegible writing.
গোবরাণিয়া, *a.* writing in a blotted illegible manner: *s.* one who thus writes.
গোবরিয়াচাঁপা, *s.* the same as গুলাচীন,
গোবরিয়াডাঁটা, *s.* a species of potherb.
গোবরিয়াপোকা, *s.* a large species of beetle.
গোবাঘা, *s.* a hyena.
গোবিন্দ, *s.* a name of Krishna.
গোবৈদ্য, *s.* a cow-doctor, a quack doctor.
গোময়, গোবর, *s.* cow-dung, manure.
গোমাংস, *s.* beef, cow's flesh.
গোমায়ু, *s.* a jackal; the bile of the cow.
গোমুখ, *s.* a cow's mouth; a musical instrument; a bag to cover the hand while counting the beads; a noted chasm in the Himálaya, the source of the Ganges.
গোমুড়, *s.* cow's head, skull of a dead cow.
গোমূঢ়, *a.* stupidly ignorant, cow-like.
গোমূত্র, *s.* the urine of a cow.
গোমেদক, *s.* a topaz; a kind of poison.
গোমেধ, *s.* the sacrifice of a cow. [man.
গোয়ালা, গোবালা, *s.* a cow-keeper, a butter-
†গোর, *a.* fair, white: *s.* a grave, a tomb.
গোরক্ষণ, *s.* the act of tending cows.
গোরক্ষা, *s.* the preservation of cows.
গোরক্ষী, *s.* a plant (Solanum rubrum).
গোরস, *s.* the fluid productions of a cow, viz. milk, whey, curds, butter-milk.
*গোরস্থান, *s.* a burial ground.
গোরা, *a.* white, fair; *fem.* গোরী, গুরী.
গোরু, *s.* a cow, an ox; a man (in irony).
গোরোচনা, *s.* a bright yellow pigment, or that vomited by a cow as a scibulæ. It is used in medicine, and painting.
গোর্দ্দ, *s.* the brain, dregs, refuse.
গোল, *s.* a globe, a ball, noise, clamour, turmoil, tumult, hubbub, a mob: *a.* round, globular, circular; -কাঠ, timber.
গোলক, *s.* a widow's bastard; a ball, globe.
গোলদার, *s.* a monopolist, wholesale dealer.
গোলদারী, *s.* a monopoly, the profession of
*গোলন্দাজ, *s.* artillery troops. [a goldár.
গোলন্দাজী, *s.* the business of golandáz.
গোলমরিচ, *s.* black pepper.
গোলমাল, *s.* tumult, confusion, disorder.
গোলা, *v. a.* to spread a report, to divulge, to blab, reveal: *a.* dissolved: *s.* a storehouse, granary, a barn; a ball, cannon ball; liquid earth and cow-dung used for coating or smearing the floors.
গোলাগুলি, *s.* balls and their ammunition.
গোলাঙ্গুল, *s.* the tail of a cow; a species of monkey, or the baboon. [earth, etc.
গোলান, *a.* dissolved: *s.* the dissolving of
গোলানি, *s.* the dissolution of earth, etc.
*গোলাব, *s.* a rose, rose-water.
গোলাবারুদ, *s.* powder and ball. [loured.
গোলাবী, *a.* rosy, made of roses, rose-co-
গোলাস, *s.* a fungus, a toadstool. [earth.
গেলাহাঁড়ি, *s.* a pot for liquid cowdung and
গোলী, *s.* a bullet, a ball, a pill, a bolus.
গোলোক, *s.* the paradise of Krishna.
*গোশল, *s.* bathing; -খানা, a bath.
গোশালা, গোশাহী, *s.* a cow-house.

গোশৎ, *s.* flesh, meat. [a drove of cows.
গোষ্ঠ, *s.* a flock, herd, cowpen, cowpasture,
গোষ্ঠী, *s.* lineage, descent, kindred, family, race, clan; genealogy, pedigree; assembly, a meeting; conversation, discourse
গোষ্পদ, *s.* the print of a cow's foot.
গোস্‌বারা, *s.* an ornament for the ear; an index of a zamindári account.
গোসর্গ, *s.* the dawn, the break of day.
গোসর্প, গোসাপ, *s.* the guana.
গোসা, *s.* anger, wrath, fury, rage.
গোস্তনী, *s.* a grape. [-হাড়, cow-bone.
গো-হত্যা, -হিংসা, killing or injuring a cow;
গোহালী, গোশালা, *s.* a cow-house.
গৌড়, *s.* a province lying north of the Ganges, the central part of Bengal.
গৌড়ী, *s.* spirit distilled from molasses.
গৌড়ীয়, *a.* belonging to Gaur province.
গৌণ, *a.* inferior, subordinate: *s.* inferiority, subordination; delay. [dinate.
গৌণতা, -ত্ব, *s.* inferiority, the being subor-
গৌতম, *s.* a name of Buddha; also that of a sage, the author of Nyáya philosophy.
গৌর, *a.* fair, white, pale, red, clean, pure.
গৌরব, *s.* importance, weight, glory, greatness, majesty, grandeur, honour.
গৌরবান্বিত, গৌরববান্, *a.* important, great, respectable, honourable, glorious.
গৌরবাসন, *s.* the seat of honour.
গৌরাঙ্গ, *a.* white-bodied, white, fair.
গৌরাঙ্গী, *a. fem. idem: s.* a fair woman.
গৌরী, *s.* a name of Durga, a young girl of eight years old, a maid, a virgin.
গৌরীপাট, *s.* lower stone of the Linga.
গ্যান্‌গ্যানানি, *s.* a whining cry, a whimper.
গ্যান্‌গ্যানিয়া, *a.* whimpering, whining.
গ্রথিত, *a.* built, arranged orderly (as stones or bricks); written; sewed, strung.
গ্রন্থ, *s.* a book, volume, writing, Scripture.
গ্রন্থক, *s.* a builder, a writer, a wickerman.
গ্রন্থকর্ত্তা, গ্রন্থকার, *s.* an author, a compiler, a writer, a writer of a literary work.
গ্রন্থগৌরব, *s.* the authority of a book.
গ্রন্থন, *s.* stringing of beads, etc., compiling of a work, the arranging of bricks.
গ্রন্থনীয়, *a.* capable of being written, composed, or orderly arranged.

গ্রন্থি, *s.* a knot, a knob, a knuckle, a joint.
গ্রন্থিত, *a.* orderly arranged, platted, knotted, sewed, strung, written, compiled.
গ্রন্থিবন্ধন, *s.* the same as গাঁটছাড়া,
গ্রস্ত, *s.* swallowed, involved in, eclipsed.
গ্রস্তাস্ত, *s.* the setting of the eclipsed sun or
গ্রস্তোদয়, *s.* the rising of the same. [moon.
গ্রহ, *s.* a planet; a holding, acceptance, tenacity, reception; -পতি, the sun.
গ্রহণ, *s.* an eclipse; a taking, receiving, accepting, seizing; কৃ, to accept, seize.
গ্রহণকাটা, *s.* a hare lip.
গ্রহণার্হ, *a.* worthy of acceptance, acceptable, plausible, satisfactory.
গ্রহণী, *s.* a dysentery, flux, a diarrhœa.
গ্রহণীয়, *a.* the same as গ্রাহ্য.
গ্রহপীড়া, *s.* the evil influence of a planet.
গ্রহীতা, *s.* a recipient, a receiver, a person who takes or accepts any thing.
গ্রাম, গাঁ, *s.* a village, a hamlet.
গ্রামণী, *s.* a village barber, the chief man of a village: *a.* best, excellent, chief.
গ্রামস্থ, *a.* situated in village, rustic.
গ্রামী, *a.* pertaining to a village, rustic.
গ্রাম্য, *a.* tame, domestic, rustic, rural, village; -দেবতা, rural-god; -ধর্ম্ম, copulation.
গ্রাস, *s.* a mouthful; eating of a mouthful.
গ্রাসাচ্ছাদন, *s.* food and raiment. [a shark.
গ্রাহ, *s.* a taking, acceptance, a reception;
গ্রাহক, *a.* taking, receiving, acquiring. *s.* a purchaser, one who accepts or receives.
গ্রাহকতা, *s.* receivership, purchasership.
গ্রাহী, *a.* taking, receiving, obtaining, procuring, acquiring: *s.* a receiver.
গ্রাহ্য, *a.* acceptable, worthy of being accepted, received, or regarded.
গ্রীবা, *s.* the nape of the neck, the neck.
গ্রীবাবন্ধনী, *s.* a neckcloth, a cravat.
গ্রীষ্ম, *a.* hot, warm, sultry: *s.* the hot season, sultry weather, heat, warmth.
গ্রীষ্মকর, *a.* causing heat, hot.
গ্রীষ্মকাল, *s.* the hot season, sultry weather.
গ্রীষ্মকালীন, *a.* of the hot season, summer.
গ্রীষ্মযুক্ত, গ্রীষ্মান্বিত, *a.* hot, sultry.
গ্লানি, *s.* languor, lassitude, fatigue; a slander, a censure, reproach, backbiting.
গ্লানিকর্ত্তা, *s.* a slanderer, a censurer.

ঘ, the 4th consonant; it has the sound of *h-g* in *log*-house; -কার, the letter ঘ.
ঘট্, *v. n.* to occur, to happen, to befall.
ঘট, *s.* an earthen water-pot, a jug, pitcher.
ঘটক, *s.* a negotiator of marriages.
ঘটকতা, *s.* office of a marriage negotiator.
ঘটকালি, *s. idem;* also, the fee given him.
ঘটন, *s.* a happening, an occurring.
ঘটনা, *s.* an occurrence, event, accident.
ঘটনীয়, *a.* liable to happen, probable.
ঘটপটাদি, *s.* a term signifying objects in general; *lit.* pitchers, clothes, etc.
ঘটা, *v. a.* to cause, to occasion an event.
ঘটা, *s.* a concourse, a crowd, ado, parade, pomp, a public procession. [sion.
ঘটাটঙ্কার, *s.* the sound of a great proces-
ঘটাটোপ, *s.* a tilt, covering (of pálki, etc.)
ঘটান, *s.* a causing to take place.
ঘটিকা, *s.* the ankle; period of 24 minutes.
ঘটিত, *a.* happened, occurred, relating to.
ঘটিতব্য, *a.* probable, liable to happen.
ঘটী, *s.* a clock, watch; a brass water-pot.
ঘটীযন্ত্র, *s.* well-machine for raising water.
ঘট্ট, *s.* a quay or wharf, a landing-place.
ঘট্টী, *s.* a private wharf or landing-place.
ঘট্টীঘোষণা, *s.* the communicating of news, the making a thing public.
ঘড়া, *s.* a pitcher, a water-pot.
ঘড়িয়াল, *s.* a crocodile; a bellman.
ঘড়ী, *s.* an hour; a clock, a watch.
ঘড়ীবালা, *s.* a watch-maker; a bellman.
ঘড়্ঘড়্, *s.* rattling in the throat, a purring.
ঘড়্ঘড়া, *v. a.* to pur, to rattle in the throat.
ঘড়্ঘড়ান, *s.* the purring of a cat, the making a rattling sound in the throat.
ঘড়্ঘড়িয়া, *s.* a hyena.
ঘড়্ঘড়ী, *s.* the rattling in the throat at the approach of death; a top, a whirligig.
ঘণ্ট, *s.* a kind of vegetable curry.
ঘণ্টা, *s.* a bell, a clock-bell; an hour; -ধ্বনি, -রব, bell-ringing; -বাদক, a bell-ringer.
ঘণ্টাপথ, *s.* a highway through a village.
ঘণ্টিকা, *s.* uvula, the epiglottis.
ঘণ্টী, *s.* a small bell. ঘণ্টু, a string of bells.
ঘন্, *v. a.* to dig up the earth (as hogs do): *a.* struck (as old rupees; but not কল.)
ঘন, *s.* a metallic plate to ring; a number, an assemblage, a cloud, solidity, extension: *a.* dense, thick, as trees, etc., impervious, crowded, incessant, incrassated, inspissated, thickset, close, near.
ঘনকাল, *s.* rainy season, cloudy weather.
ঘনগিরা, *a.* full of knots, close knots.
ঘনঘন, *ad.* incessantly, repeatedly, often.
ঘনতা, *s.* thickness, solidity, density, cras-
ঘনমূল, *s.* a cube root. [situde, closeness.
ঘনা, *v. a.* to overtake, to come near.
ঘনাঘন, *a.* solid, thick, close, near, impervious: *s.* a cloud, collision, Indra.
ঘনান, *s.* a coming near, an overtaking.
ঘনাবৃত, *a.* inspissated, thickened by boil-
ঘনিষ্ঠ, *a.* close at hand, very near. [ing.
ঘনিষ্ঠতা, *s.* proximity, a being very near.
ঘনী, *s.* a bambu cage-trap to catch fish.
ঘনীভূত, *a.* inspissated, become thick or in-
ঘনুগা, *s.* a paramour, a pimp. [cessant.
ঘবর্, *v. n.* to be confused or nonplussed.
ঘবরণ, *s.* a being confused or nonplussed.
ঘবরা, *v. a.* to confound, to nonplus, to perplex, to confuse, to discompose.
ঘবরাণ, *s.* the exciting of confusion or perplexity, the disturbing of one's mind.
ঘবরাণী, ঘবরায়ী, *s.* perturbation, confusion, discomposure, perplexity, non-
ঘমোরী, *s.* the prickly heat. [plus.
ঘর্, *s.* a house, a dwelling, a building, a loop, a buckle hole, a groove, a family.
ঘরকন্না, *s.* a household, a house-keeping.
ঘরকোটালী, *a.* taking justice in one's own
ঘরঘর, *ad.* from house to house. [hand.
ঘরট্ট, *s.* a mill, a machine.
ঘরণী, *s.* a wife, a female house-keeper.
ঘরবসত, *s.* a home, a residence, the ceremony of bringing a newly married woman to reside at her husband's house.
ঘর-ভাঙ্গন, -ভাঙ্গা, *s.* breaking up a family; the breaking of a house. [in a family.
ঘরভাঙ্গানী, *a.* causing dissension or breach
ঘরসন্ধান, *s.* officiousness, a prying into another's household concerns. [affairs.
ঘরসন্ধানী, *a.* officious, prying into family
ঘরা, *s.* a receptacle, a drawer, a passage,
ঘরাও, *a.* domestic, intestine. [a hole.
ঘরাঘরি, *ad.* between family or neighbours.

ঘরামী, *s.* a hut-builder, a thatcher.
ঘরামীগিরী, *s.* the business of a thatcher.
ঘরুআ, *a.* domestic, home-made, of a house.
ঘরে, *ad.* at home; -বাহিরে, at home and abroad.
ঘরেঘরে, *ad.* in or at every house.
ঘঘর, ঘর্ঘরাণি, *s.* the rattling of wheels, a rattling sound, a purring.
ঘর্ম্ম, ঘাম, *s.* perspiration, sweat.
ঘর্ম্মজনক, *a.* sudorific, causing perspiration.
ঘর্ম্মাক্ত, *a.* covered with perspiration.
ঘর্ম্মার্ত্ত, *a.* perspiring, in a perspiration.
ঘর্ষ্, *v. a.* to rub, to file, to polish, to grind, to abrade, to wipe, to varnish.
ঘর্ষক, *a.* rubbing, filing: *s.* one who rubs or files; an instrument for rubbing, etc.
ঘর্ষণ, *s.* a rubbing, grinding, filing, friction.
ঘর্ষিত, *a.* rubbed, cleaned, filed, polished.
ঘষ্, ঘষণ, the same as ঘর্ষ, ঘর্ষণ.
ঘষণি, *s.* a rubbing, grinding, friction.
ঘষা, *v.* to produce friction, to cause to rub or polish: *a.* rubbed, filed, polished.
ঘষাণ, *s.* a producing friction, a causing to file or rub: *a.* rubbed, filed, polished.
ঘষাণী, *s.* the production of friction, the filing or polishing of a thing.
ঘষি, *s.* the powder of dried cow-dung.
ঘা, *s.* a knock, blow, cut, gash, wound, sore, an ulcer; -দা, -মার, to strike, to knock; -খেকুয়া, callous, weather-beaten.
ঘাই, *s.* the wheel in which silk is rolled in manufacturing it; flouncing of a fish in water; -লাড়া, a moving about in anger.
ঘাইট, *s.* a fault, crime, misdemeanor, guilt, sin; abatement, defect, flaw: *a.* less.
ঘাইটবাড়ি, *a.* less or more.
ঘাঁইট, ঘাঁট্, *v. a.* to stir up, to stir or mix.
ঘাঁটন, ঘাঁটনি, *s.* a mixing or stirring up.
ঘাঁটা, *v. a.* to rouse up, to stimulate: *a.* stirred up, mixed: *s.* the blade-bone or scapula of an animal; a corn, callosity.
ঘাঁটান, *a.* roused up, stirred up: *s.* the rousing up of a person or animal.
ঘাঁটি, *s.* track of animals, a watch-post, an ambush, road for thieves to retreat by.
ঘাঁটু, ঘণ্টাকর্ণ, ঘণ্টেশ্বর, *s.* names of a god who presides over itches.
ঘাঁটুভাঙ্গাসংক্রান্তি, *s.* a ceremony in honour of ঘাঁটু.

ঘাঁটো, *s.* a kind of theatrical dance.
ঘাঁৎ, *v. a.* to affect the heart, to speak so as to strike the heart.
ঘাঁতন, ঘাঁতনি, *s.* speaking or acting so as to strike or affect the hearts of others.
ঘাখেকুয়া, *a.* callous, wounded, weather-beaten, hardened by beating; *fem.* ঘাগী.
ঘাঘরা, *s.* a petticoat, an apron, a gown.
ঘাঘরি, *s.* a rabbet, a groove.
ঘাট্, *v. a.* to be deficient, to fall short.
ঘাট, *s.* a quay, wharf, landing-place, a ferry, mountain pass; -মার্, to smuggle; -মারণ, a smuggling; -মারণিয়া, a smuggler; -মারা, a smuggling; a smuggler.
ঘাটা, *v. a.* to abate, to diminish, reduce, to lessen: *s.* a corn, callosity, a sore.
ঘাটান, *s.* reducing or abating the value of a thing, the diminishing of a thing.
ঘাটী, *s.* a fault, a crime; a watch-post.
ঘাড়, ঘাড়ি, *s.* the hinder part of the neck.
ঘাড়গর্দান, the neck. ঘাড়ান, assent by nod.
ঘাত, *s.* a knock, a blow, wound.
ঘাতক, *a.* smiting, striking: *s.* a murderer, striker.
ঘাতন, *s.* a smiting, hurting, killing.
ঘাতুক, *a.* destructive, murderous, cruel.
ঘানি, ঘানিগাছ, *s.* an oil-mill.
ঘাম্, *v. n.* to sweat, perspire: *s.* sweat, perspiration.
ঘামন, *s.* a sweating, a perspiring.
ঘাময়, *a.* full of ulcers or wounds.
ঘামা, *v. a.* to cause to sweat or perspire.
ঘামাক্ত, *a.* covered with perspiration.
ঘামাচি, *s.* the prickly heat.
ঘামান, *s.* a causing to perspire: *a.* made to perspire.
ঘামুখ, *s.* the opening of a sore or ulcer.
ঘারেঘোরে, *ad.* by signs, by inuendoes, privately, secretly, figuratively.
ঘালি, *a.* wounded: *s.* a sore, cut, an ulcer.
ঘাশূন্য, *a.* free from wounds or ulcers.
ঘাস, *s.* grass, meadow grass, hay.
ঘাসকাটা, ঘাসিয়াড়া, *s.* a grass-cutter.
ঘাসময়, *a.* full of grass, grassy.
ঘাসাহারী, *a.* graminivorous, feeding on grass.
ঘাসুড়ীয়া, *a.* *idem*: *s.* a grass-cutter.
ঘাসুয়া, *a.* of grass, grassy.
ঘি, clarified butter; -কুমারী, *see* ঘৃতকুমারী.
ঘিচ্পিচ্, ঘিঞ্জি, *a.* dense, crowded, impervious.
ঘিন্, *s.* the same as ঘৃণা.

ঘিন্‌ঘিন্, *s.* the whining cry of a child.
ঘিয়া, *a.* oily, butyraceous, shining.
ঘির্, *v. a.* to surround, to hedge round.
ঘিরণ, *s.* a hedging round, a fencing in.
ঘুঁজি *a.* crooked, tortuous, concealed.
ঘুঁজিশিঙ্গা, *a.* having very crooked horns.
ঘুঁট্, *v. a.* to grind by rubbing, to rub so as to polish, to look well into affairs.
ঘুঁটন, *s.* the act of rubbing or grinding, the looking well into any affair.
ঘুঁটনি, *s.* a rubbing or grinding in a mortar, the looking well into business; the instrument used in rubbing or polishing.
ঘুঁটি, *s.* gravel, nodule, ball, a die, men in chess or in other games, hairs left uncut in shaving, a decoction for infants.
ঘুঁটিফেলা, *s.* casting of lots; throw of a die.
ঘুঁটিয়া, *s.* dried cakes of cow-dung used for fuel.
ঘুঁড়ী, *s.* a paper kite; a mare.
ঘুঁৎঘুঁৎ, *s.* the grunting of a pig.
ঘুঁৎঘুঁতিয়া, *a.* grunting, restive: *s.* a pig.
ঘুঘু, *s.* a dove, a wood-pigeon.
ঘুঘুরফাঁদ, *s.* a dove's snare, the reward attendant on an imprudent action.
ঘুঘুরা, ঘুঘুরিয়া, *s.* mole-cricket; *vide* ঘুঘুঁরা.
ঘুঙ্গুর, *s.* small bells, a string of small bells.
ঘুচ্, *v. n.* to remove, to open, to yield, to pass away, to disappear.
ঘুচন, *a.* removed, yielded to, opened, passed away: *s.* a removing, a yielding, the taking off clothes, a passing away.
ঘুচা, *v. a.* to open, to loosen, to rescind, to cancel, to rub out, to dispel, to remove.
ঘুচান, *s.* the repealing of a law, the rubbing out of an old score, the dispelling of danger, the removing of misfortune.
ঘুট, ঘুটি, *s.* the ankle; a kind of jujube.
ঘুটমণ্ডল, *s.* confusion, disorder.
ঘটী, *s.* the ankle; a chessman, or rather small nodules used in play.
ঘুট্‌ঘুট্, *s.* great darkness, gloom.
ঘুট্‌ঘুটিয়া, *a.* gloomy, blinding, very dark.
ঘুট্‌না, *s.* the knee; a muller.
ঘুড়ি, ঘুড়ী, *s.* a paper kite; a mare.
ঘুণ্, *v. a.* to dig up the earth (as swine).
ঘুণ, *s.* the name of a wood insect.
ঘুণাক্ষর, *a.* without pains: *s.* a hint.
ঘুণী, *s.* a kind of bambu fish-trap.
ঘুণ্‌ঘুণ্, *s.* the buzz of humble bees or large beetles.
ঘুণ্‌ঘুণা, *v. n.* to buz, to growl.
ঘুণ্‌ঘুণান, ঘুণ্‌ঘুনানি, *s.* a buzzing sound.
ঘুণ্‌ঘুণানিয়া, *a.* buzzing about, growling.
ঘুণ্টী, ঘুণ্ডী *s.* a button; -ঘরা, a button-hole.
ঘুপ্‌ঘাপ, *s.* the flouncing of large fishes.
ঘুম্ *v. n.* to sleep, to slumber: *s.* sleep.
ঘুম, *s.* sleep, slumber; -পাড়া, to lull one to sleep.
ঘুমগড়িয়া, *a.* slothful, sleepy.
ঘুমটুম, *s.* sleep and slumber.
ঘুমন, *s.* the act of sleeping, repose.
ঘুমন্ত, *a.* asleep, sleeping, dozing.
ঘুমপাড়ান, *s.* the lulling of a child to sleep.
ঘুমপাড়ানী, *a.* lulling children to sleep.
ঘুমভাঙ্গন, *s.* the awaking out of sleep.
ঘুমভাঙ্গা, *a.* awake, roused from sleep.
ঘুমভাঙ্গান, *s.* the rousing one from sleep.
ঘুমা, *v.* to sleep, to lull, to excite sleep.
ঘুমান, *s.* a sleeping; *a.* asleep, sleeping.
ঘুমে, *ad.* while asleep, in a slumber.
ঘুর, *v.* to whirl, turn round, roll, revolve.
ঘুঘুঁরা, *s.* the mole-cricket; a sort of ulcer.
ঘুল্, *v.* to stir liquids, to dissolve in water.
ঘুলন, *s.* a dissolving, stirring, agitating.
ঘুষ্, *v. a.* to repeat, proclaim, talk about, to enter, run into; to box: *s.* a bribe.
ঘুষ, *a.* small (fishes): *s.* a fist, box, fist-blow.
ঘুষখেকুআ, *a.* venal, corrupt.
ঘুষড়্, *v.* to enter, to creep or retreat into, to expunge.
ঘুষড়ন, *s.* the creeping, retreating, or entering into a place, expunging.
ঘুষড়া, *v.* to force in, thrust in: decoction of herbs.
ঘুষড়ান, *s.* a forcing in, a thrusting in.
ঘুষণ, ঘুষণি, *s.* declaring of a thing; a boxing; entering or running into a place.
ঘুষা, *v.* to box, give fist-blows; to cause to enter: *a.* small (fishes): *s.* a fist, a box.
ঘুষাঘুষি, *s.* a reciprocal boxing, pugilism.
ঘুষামাছ, *s.* small fishes.
ঘুস্কা, *v. a.* to creep in, to enter, to penetrate.
ঘুস্কান, *s.* a causing to creep in or enter.
ঘুস্কী, *s.* a loose female, a private prostitute.
ঘুষ্ট, *a.* uttered, sounded, made. [vocal.
ঘুষ্‌টুষ, *s.* bribes, peculation.
ঘূর, *v. n.* to turn, revolve, swing. [whirl.
ঘূরণ, *s.* a turning, a revolving, swinging, a

ঘূরণি, *s.* a revolution, a whirl, a turning.
ঘূরপাক, *s.* a distortion, a twist, a whirl.
ঘূরা, *v. a.* to turn, to whirl, to subvert.
ঘূরাণ, *s.* the whirling, turning or swinging of a thing round, the spinning of a top.
ঘূরাণিয়া, *a.* wandering, revolving, whirling round.
ঘূরাণিয়াবাতাস, *s.* a whirlwind.
ঘূর্ণ, *s.* a revolution, a turn, a whirl, a rolling : *a.* whirling, turning, revolving.
ঘূর্ণজল, *s.* a whirlpool, an eddy.
ঘূর্ণবায়ু, ঘূর্ণবাতাস, *s.* a whirlwind, a cyclone.
ঘূর্ণমান, ঘূর্ণায়মান, *a.* turning, revolving, whirling, swinging round, rolling.
ঘূর্ণা, *s.* a giddiness, a vertigo ; a turning, a whirling motion ; a whirlpool, eddy.
ঘূর্ণি, *s.* a circular motion, a revolution ; a swinging, turning, vertigo ; a whirligig.
ঘূর্ণিত, *a.* turned round, revolved, whirled.
ঘৃণা, *s.* disgust, hatred, antipathy, abhorrence, a nausea, a dislike.
ঘৃণাকর, *a.* causing disgust, exciting nausea.
ঘৃণাযুক্ত, *a.* malevolent, full of disgust.
ঘৃণার্হ, *a.* disgusting, detestable, hateful.
ঘৃণিত, *a.* abhorred, hated, abominated.
ঘৃণ্য, *a.* abominable, hateful, disgusting.
ঘৃত, ঘি, *s.* clarified butter, ghi.
ঘৃতকুমারী, *s.* an ornamental plant.[1]
ঘৃতকুম্ভ, *s.* a jar of clarified butter.
ঘৃতকুল্যা, *s.* a pond of clarified butter.
ঘৃতময়, *a.* abounding with clarified butter.
ঘৃষ্ট, *a.* rubbed, polished, abraded.
ঘেউআ, *a.* full of wounds or ulcers.
ঘেঁচ, ঘেঁচা, *v. a.* to supplant, to frustrate, to shuffle cards or other articles.
ঘেঁচড়া, *a.* scurrilous, obscene, vulgar.
ঘেঁচান, *s.* a supplanting, the shuffling of cards : *a.* supplanted, shuffled.
ঘেঁচু, *s.* a species of plant (Arum orixense).
ঘেঁট্, *v. a.* to meddle with, to intermeddle.
ঘেঁটা, *v. a. idem.*
ঘেঁটান, *s.* the meddling with a person or animal.
ঘেঁটু, *s.* the same as **ঘাঁটু**, which see.
ঘেঁষ্, *v. a.* to rub against, to come in contact : *s.* pitch : *a.* thickly crowded.
ঘেঁষণ, *s.* a rubbing : *a.* rubbed.
ঘেঁষড়, or **ঘেঁষড়া**, *v. n.* to draw along the ground, to trail, to run, to drag.
ঘেঁষড়ন, ঘেঁষড়ান, ঘেঁষড়ানি, *s.* the trailing or drawing of things along the ground.
ঘেঁষা, *v. a.* to cause to rub, to rub, polish : *a.* rubbed, filed, polished.
ঘেঁষাঘেঁষি, *a.* close, thick, crowded.
ঘেঁষাণ, *s.* a causing to rub, the filing or rubbing of a thing so as to polish it.
ঘেঙ্গা, *v. a.* to entreat, to importune, pray : *s.* intreaty, importunate.
ঘেঙ্গান, *s.* the act of intreating or importuning.
ঘেঙ্গানি, *s.* importunity, incessant intreaty.
ঘেঙ্গানিয়া, *a.* importunate, troublesomo.
ঘেট্, *v. n.* to fail, to decrease, to diminish.
ঘের্, *v. a.* to surround, to encompass, to enclose, to invest, to impound.
ঘেরঘার, *s.* a boundary, a hedge.
ঘেরণ, *s.* a surrounding, a fencing, an encircling, the inclosing of a field or garden, the investing of a city.
ঘেরা, *v. a.* to cause to surround ; to invest, to besiege : *s.* a circle, a bound hedge, a fence : *a.* surrounded, fenced in.
ঘেরাণ, *s.* the surrounding or fencing of a thing : *a.* fenced in, surrounded.
ঘৈরা, *s.* depth : *a.* deep.
ঘোঁজ, *s.* a corner, crook or bend in a road, a crooked outlet from a person's yard.
ঘোঁট, *s.* the agitating of a topic of conversation, the rubbing of a substance in a mortar, a mouthful (of liquid).
ঘোঁটন, *s.* the canvassing of an affair, the rubbing of any thing in a mortar.
ঘোঁটনা, *s.* a pestle, a muller.
ঘোঁটা, *v. a.* to cause the canvassing of an affair, to cause to be rubbed in a mortar : *a.* agitated, stirred up, rubbed.
ঘোঁটান, *s.* causing an affair to be canvassed, causing to be rubbed in a mortar : *a.* agitated, canvassed, rubbed.
ঘোঁটামারণ, *s.* a pawing with the forefoot.
ঘোঁৎ, ঘোঁৎঘোঁৎ, *s.* the grunting of a hog.
ঘোঁৎঘোঁতিয়া, *a.* grunting : *s.* a pig, a hog.
ঘোঙা, *s.* a snail ; a musical instrument.
ঘোঙাকড়ি, *s.* a genus of shell or Cyprea.
ঘোঙ্গরা, *a.* deep-sounded, hoarse, guttural : *v. n.* to utter a deep note.
ঘোঙ্গরাণী, *s.* a deep or hoarse sound.

ঘোঙ্গা, *s.* a metal plate, a gong.
ঘোটক, *s.* a horse; *fem.* ঘোটকী. [race.
ঘোড়্, *s.* hinder part of a shoe; -দৌড়, horse-
ঘোড়গাড়ি, *s.* a carriage drawn by horses.
ঘোড়তোলা, *a.* pulled up behind (as shoes).
ঘোড়বেড়, *s.* spread around, wrapped round.
ঘোড়শালা, ঘোড়াশালা, *s.* a stable.
ঘোড়া, *s.* a horse; *fem.* ঘোড়ী, or ঘুড়ী.
ঘোড়াচড়া *s.* a riding, a horseman, cavalry.
ঘোড়ানিম, *s.* a variety of the Melia azadi-
ঘোড়ামুগ, *s.* a kind of pulse.[1] [rachta.
ঘোড়ারু, *s.* an elk: *a.* fond of riding.
ঘোণা, *s.* a sort of musquito curtain.
ঘোণ্টা, *s.* the betel-nut tree.
ঘোপ, *s.* a large bush: *a.* dark, bushy.
ঘোপঘাপ, *s.* large bushes, windings.
ঘোপনগর, *s.* a port, an harbour.
ঘোপাল, *a.* bushy, abounding with bushes.
ঘোমটা, *s.* a veil for the face; -দা, to veil.
ঘোর, *a.* terrific, gloomy, dark, dreadful, awful, formidable, tremendous; intricate, abstruse, occult, recondite: *s.* darkness, gloom, horror, dread.
ঘোরতর, *a.* very dreadful, gloomy, awful.
ঘোরতা, -ত্ব, *s.* awfulness, dreadfulness, obscurity, gloominess, gloom, darkness.
ঘোরভাঞ্জন, *s.* the dispelling of gloom.
ঘোরা, *v. a.* to revolve, to whirl, to turn. *s.* a whirling: *a.* revolving, whirling.
ঘোরাণ, *s.* causing of a thing to revolve.
ঘোরার্থ, ঘোরাল, *a.* recondite, mysterious, ambiguous, vague, dark, obscure.
ঘোরেঘারে, *ad.* darkly, obscurely, by signs
ঘোল, *s.* buttermilk; an eddy. [or tokens.
ঘোলমহন, *s.* the churning of butter.
ঘোলমহনী, *s.* a churning stick; a plant.[2]
ঘোলা, *v. a.* to make muddy, to dissolve: *a.* turbid, muddy, semifluid, dissolved.
ঘোলাটিয়া, *a.* muddy, turbid, semifluid.
ঘোলান, *s.* a stirring of water to make it turbid: *a.* dissolved, turbid, semifluid.
ঘোলানিয়া, *a.* dissolving, making muddy.
ঘোলানী, *a.* thick, turbid, muddy.
ঘোষ, *s.* a sound, a cry, an appellation, an appellation applied to herdsmen.
ঘোষণা, *s.* a proclamation, a sermon, public preaching; -দা, or -কৃ, to proclaim.
ঘোষণাপত্র, *s.* a written proclamation.
ঘোষণাবিক্রয়, *s.* a public or auction sale.
ঘোষা, *v. a.* to proclaim, to publish, make known, to preach, to inculcate.
ঘোষাণ, *s.* a proclaiming, a publishing, a preaching: *a.* proclaimed, published.
ঘোষিত, *a.* proclaimed, published, preached, declared, inculcated.
ঘোর, *s.* meditation, deep reflection.
ঘ্ন, *a.* destructive, ruinous; only used as the last member of a compound word.
ঘ্যানঘ্যানানি, *s.* a whining cry of a child.
ঘ্রাণ, *s.* a scent, a smell, act of smelling.
ঘ্রাণেন্দ্রিয়, *s.* the sense of smelling.
ঘ্রাত, *a.* smelled to, scented.

ঙ, the fifth consonant. It is scarcely ever used except when compounded with another letter; -কার, the letter ঙ.

চ, the sixth consonant; it has the sound of ch in child: *conj.* and, also.
চআল, *s.* the jaw-bone; -ধরু, to have the locked jaw, to be seized with Tetanus.
চই, *s.* a kind of pepper (Piper chuvya).
চক, *s.* a market-place, a square.
চকবন্দী, চকমিলন, *s.* a square of buildings.
চকরচকর, *s.* a lapping, a lapping sound.
চকা, চক্রবাক, *s.* the ruddy goose;[3] *fem.* চকি,
চকাচকি, *s.* *idem.* (the generic name).
চকার, *a.* the letter চ. [ful, affrighted.
চকিত, *a.* timorous, alarmed, startled, fear-
চকোর, *s.* a species of partridge;[4] timber.
চকোরকাঠ, *s.* a timber (the best). [ping.
চক্চক্, *a.* shining, vivid, clear, glaring; lap-
চক্চকানি, চক্চকি, চকমকানি, *s.* brightness, brilliancy, lustre, clearness, glare.
চক্চকিয়া, *a.* glaring, bright, glittering.
চকনামা, *s.* a tally of land; *vide* চকবন্দি.
চক্মক্, *s.* a glaring, a glittering, a flash.
চক্মকা, *v. n.* to shine, flash, glare, glitter.
চকমকি, *s.* a flash, a glare, glitter; a flint.
চকমকিপাথর, *s.* a flint.
চক্মকিয়া, *a.* glaring, radiant, flashing.
চক্লা, *s.* a district, province, estate, manor, a number of villages. [the manor.
চক্লাদার, *s.* owner of a district, a lord of
চক্লাদারী, *s.* the office of a chakládár.

চক্র, *s.* a wheel, a potter's wheel, a discus, a circle, a period of time, a revolution, an army, combination, plot, conspiracy, a realm, a province, region, a multitude, a heap, a whirlpool, a system, a form of military array, the ruddy goose.
চক্রটক্র, চক্রমক্র, *s.* combinations, conspiracies, plots, wheels and the like.
চক্রপাণি, *a.* wielding the discus: *s.* Vishnu.
চক্রবর্ত্তী, *a.* seated in a province or estate: *s.* lord of a manor, master of an estate, ruler of a province, an emperor, a king.
চক্রবাক, *s.* the ruddy goose (Anas casarca).
চক্রবাত, *s.* a hurricane, a whirlwind, a cy-
চক্রবৃদ্ধি, *s.* compound interest. [clone.
চক্রাকার, চক্রাকৃতি, *a.* circular, round.
চক্রী, *s.* Vishnu, an emperor, governor of a province; a potter, oilman, a juggler, an informer, a serpent, a ruddy goose.
চক্ষাচক্ষি, *ad.* face to face, eye to eye.
চক্ষু, *s.* the eye; -টিপ, to wink; -ফুটা, to undeceive, blindfold; -মটকা, to beckon.
তোর চক্ষুর মাথা খা, may you be blind.
চক্ষুপীড়া, চক্ষুরোগ, *s.* disease of the eyes.
চক্ষুঃশ্রবা, *s.* a snake. চক্ষুঃস্থ, situated in the
চক্ষুক্ষেলান, *s.* scaling of the eyes. [eye.
চক্ষুর্গোচর, *a.* visible, present to the eye.
চক্ষুর্দান, *s.* the giving of sight to an idol.
চঙ্গ, *a.* handsome, good, eminent, sound,
*চঙ্গা, *a.* recovered from disease. [healthy.
চঙ্গাই, *s.* recovery, a cure, health, good-
চঙ্গারী, *s.* a kind of basket. [ness, beauty.
চঞ্চনিয়া, *a.* throbbing, shifting, uneasy.
চঞ্চল, *a.* fickle, changeable, capricious, unsteady, inconstant, fluctuating, fluid.
চঞ্চলতা, *s.* fickleness, instability, capriciousness, inconstancy, changeableness.
চঞ্চলা, *s.* lightning; a name of Lakshmí.
চঞ্চু, *s.* the bill of a bird, a beak.
চঞ্চুপুট, *s.* the bill of a bird when shut.
চঞ্চুসূচি, *s.* the taylor bird (Sylvia sutoria).
চট্, *v. n.* to split, break off, shiver off: *s.* sackcloth, canvas: *ad.* hastily.
চটক, *s.* show, gaudiness; a sparrow; *fem.*
চটন, *s.* a splitting, a cracking. [চটকি.
চটা, *a. a.* to cause to crack or break into shivers: *s.* a splinter, a small chip.

চটাচট, চটাং, *s.* cracking sound of a whip.
চটাচটি, *s.* alienation, breach, quarrel.
চটান, *s.* a plain, a strand; a breaking off in splinters; *a.* splintered, shivered.
চটাল, *a.* broad, wide, spacious.
চটী, *s.* a sackcloth, canvas, a mat, a flat thin rod of split bambu. (-মার, to slap.
চট্কনা, চট্কানা, *s.* a slap with the flat hand;
চট্কা, *v.* to knead, temper clay: *s.* a shrub.[1]
চট্কান, *s.* a kneading: *a.* kneaded.
চট্কানি, *s.* the kneading of dough, etc.
চট্কানিয়া, *s.* one who kneads.
চট্চট্, *ad.* speedily, quickly; -করণ, a being viscid, sticky or gummy.
চট্চটানি, *s.* viscidity, clamminess. [cid.
চট্চটিয়া, *a.* gummy, glutinous, viscous, vis-
চট্পট্, *a.* quick: *ad.* quickly, speedily.
চট্পটিয়া, restless, active, fluent, talkative,
চট্পটী, *s.* activity, restlessness. [voluble.
চড়্, *v. n.* to mount, to ascend, to go on board a boat or ship, to climb: to slap.
চড়, *s.* a slap, a slap on the face. [of rice.
চড়ুই, চটই, *s.* a sparrow; -নখো, a variety
চড়ক্, *v.* to grow worse, to throb, twinge.
চড়ক, চরক, *s.* the swinging festival.
চড়কন, *s.* a twinging, a smarting.
চড়কল, *a.* excessive, very painful.
চড়ন, *s.* the act of mounting, ascending, or climbing up, the going on board a boat.
চড়নদার, *s.* a supercargo.
চড়া, *v. a.* to place or set on a thing, to bend a bow, to raise, to slap: *s.* a shallow, a shoal: *a.* bent, high, exalted.
চড়াও, *s.* an invasion, an attack, an onset, an inroad, an assault, an aggression.
চড়াওকারক, *s.* an invader, an aggressor.
চড়াকথা, *s.* loud language, bullying language, an emphatical expression.
চড়াচড়ি, *s.* a mutual slapping on the face, the sport vulgarly called leap-frog.
চড়াং, *s.* a cracking or snapping sound.
চড়াদর, *s.* a high price: *a.* high-priced.
চড়ান, *s.* causing to mount or ride, act of placing a thing upon a shelf, fire, etc.; bending of a bow, a raising the price.
চড়ানিয়া, *a.* elevating, increasing. [wide.
চড়াপড়া, *a.* neutralized, balanced, high and

চড়াশব্দ, *s.* an accent, loud noise.
চড়্চড়্, *s.* a cracking or crackling noise; the rending of the heart with distress.
চড়্চড়ী, *a.* making a crackling or sputtering noise: *s.* curry of only small fishes.
চড়্তি, *s.* an increase, advance in price.
চণক, *s.* gram, a sort of pea (Cicer arietinum).
চণ্ড, *a.* very passionate, furious, great, very strong, violent, angry, enraged. [lence.
চণ্ডতা, *s.* rage, fury, excessive passion, vio-
চণ্ডাল, *s.* an outcast, a scamp: *a.* cruel.
চণ্ডালতা, *s.* the condition of an outcast.
চণ্ডালীয়া, *a.* low, vulgar, unprincipled.
চণ্ডিকা, *s.* a name of Durgá. [exploits.
চণ্ডী, *s. idem;* a poem which celebrates her
চণ্ডু, *s.* the common monkey; a rat.
চণ্ডুল, *s.* a species of lark. [fourth.
চতুঃপঞ্চাশৎ, fifty-four. **চতুঃপঞ্চাশত্তম**, fifty-
চতুঃপার্শ্ব, *s.* the four sides, all the sides.
চতুঃপার্শ্বস্থ, *a.* situated on all sides.
চতুঃশত, *a.* four hundred.
চতুঃশালা, *s.* a cluster of four houses.
চতুঃষষ্ট, **চতুঃষষ্টিতম**, *a.* the sixty-fourth.
চতুঃষষ্টি, *a.* sixty-four. [fourth.
চতুঃসপ্ততি, seventy-four; **-তম**, the seventy-
চতুঃসীমা, *s.* a border or boundary on all sides; **-বচ্ছিন্ন**, bordered on all sides.
চতুর, *a.* four; clever, acute, active, ingenious, dexterous, artful, crafty, cunning.
চতুরংশ, *s.* four quarters or shares; **-কৃ**, to
চতুরক্ষর, *s.* four letters. [quarter.
চতুরক্ষরীয়, *a.* compound of four letters.
চতুরঙ্গ, *a.* (an army) composed of four parts, or full complete, viz. elephantry, chariotry, cavalry, and infantry.
চতুরঙ্গবল, *s.* an army composing as above.
চতুরঙ্গিনী, *a. fem gen.* the same as **চতুরঙ্গ**.
চতুরতা, **-ত্ব**, *s.* dexterity, acuteness, activity, cleverness, ingenuity, artfulness.
চতুরশীতি, *a.* eight-four; **-তম**, eighty-4th.
চতুরস্র, *a.* quadrangular, square. [ma.
চতুরানন, *a.* four-faced; epithet of Brah-
চতুরালী, *s.* craftiness, dexterity, acuteness.
চতুর্গুণ, *ad.* fourfold: *a.* quadruple.
চতুর্থ, or **চতুর্থী**, *a.* the fourth.
চতুর্থাংশ, *s.* a quarter, the fourth part.
চতুর্দশ, *a.* fourteen. **চতুর্দশী**, *a.* fourteenth.
চতুর্দিক্, **চতুর্দিক্ষু**, *ad.* on all sides. [ing.
চতুর্দিকস্থ, situated on all sides, surround-
চতুর্দিগে, *ad.* on all sides, all around.
চতুর্দিগ্ব্যাপক, *a.* occupying all sides.
চতুর্দোল, **চতুর্দোলা**, *s.* a litter, a sedan.
চতুর্দ্ধা, *a.* fourfold, of four sorts.
চতুর্দ্ধাশান্তি, *s.* a religious ceremony.
চতুর্নবতি, *a.* ninety-four; **-তম**, ninety-4th.
চতুর্বর্গ *s.* four objects of human pursuit, viz. love, riches, religion and beatitude.
চতুর্বর্ণ, *s.* the four classes of Hindus, viz. bráhman, kshetri, vaishya, and sudra; the four principal colours, viz. white, black, blue and red; four letters.
চতুর্বিংশতি, twenty-four; **-তম**, twenty-4th
চতুর্বিধ, *a.* of four sorts, of four kinds.
চতুর্বেদ, *s.* the four vedas, viz. the Sáma, Rik, Yajur, and the Atharva. [vedas.
চতুর্বেদজ্ঞ, *a.* acquainted with the four
চতুর্ভুজ, *a.* four-armed; epithet of Vishnu.
চতুর্মুখ, *a.* four-faced; an epithet of Brahma: *s.* the name of a medicine.
চতুর্যুগ, *s.* the four yugas, or ages, viz. Satya, Tretá, Dwápara and Kali.
চতুশ্চত্বারিংশ, **চতুশ্চত্বারিংশত্তম**, the forty-
চতুশ্চত্বারিংশৎ, *a.* forty-four. [fourth.
চতুষ্কোণ *a.* quadrangular: *s.* a quadrangle.
চতুষ্টয়, *a.* four; *e. g.* **জনচতুষ্টয়**, four men
চতুষ্পত্রী, *a.* quadrifoliate.
চতুষ্পদ, *a.* four-footed: *s.* a quadruped.
চতুষ্পাঠী, *s.* a college, an academy.
চতুষ্পাদ, *a.* four-footed: *s.* a quadruped.
চতুষ্পার্শ্ব, *s.* the four sides.
চতুষ্পার্শ্বে, *ad.* on all sides, all around.
চতুস্ত্রিংশ, **চতুস্ত্রিংশত্তম**, the thirty-fourth.
চতুস্ত্রিংশৎ, *a.* thirty-four.
চত্বর, *s.* a courtyard, a sacrificial ground.
চত্বারিংশ, **চত্বারিংশত্তম**, *a.* the fortieth.
চত্বারিংশৎ, *a.* forty.
চনা, *s.* the same as **চণক**. [album).
চন্দন, **চন্দনকাঠ**, *s.* sandal-wood (Santalum
চন্দন-পীড়া-পাটা, *s.* a sandal-wood grind-
চন্দনা, *s.* a species of parrot. [ing stone.
চন্দনাদিতৈল, *s.* a medicinal oil extracted from sandal-wood and other ingredients.
চন্দা, *s.* a subscription, a collection.
চন্দ্র, **চাঁদ**, *s.* the moon; **-মুখী**, *f.* moon-faced.

চন্দ্রকলা, *s.* the digit of the moon.
চন্দ্রকান্ত, *s.* a precious stone, jasper.
চন্দ্রকোণা, *s.* name of a town near Burdwan.
চন্দ্রগ্রহণ, *s.* an eclipse of the moon.
চন্দ্রচূড়, crescent-crested; epithet of Shiva.
চন্দ্রব্রত, *s.* a vow or duty peculiar to kings; the coronation oath. [jáb river.
চন্দ্রভাগা, *s.* one of the streams of the Pan-
চন্দ্রমণ্ডল, *s.* the lunar orb.
চন্দ্রমল্লিকা, *s.* a beautiful flowering plant.[1]
চন্দ্রমা, চন্দ্রিমা, *s.* the moon.
চন্দ্রহার, *s.* a kind of ornamental neck-
চন্দ্রহাস, *s.* a kind of sword. [chain.
চন্দ্রাতপ, চাঁদআ, *s.* an awning, a canopy.
চন্দ্রানন, *a.* moon-faced.
চন্দ্রাভাস, *s.* a paraselene, a mock-moon.
চন্দ্রিকা, *s.* moon-light, the lunar rays.
চন্দ্রোদয়, *s.* the rising of the moon.
চপ্, *ad.* quickly, speedily, hastily. [risk.
চপট, *s.* the open or flat palm; jeopardy,
চপরাস, *s.* a buckle, breastplate, badge.
চপরাসী, *s.* a police officer, a person distinguished by a badge of office.
চপল, *a.* unsteady, wavering, tremulous, fickle, swift, expeditious, instantaneous.
চপলতা, -ত্ব *s.* unsteadiness, tremulousness, fickleness, swiftness, expedition.
চপলা, *fem. vide* চপল. *s* name of Lakshmí; lightning; a coquette, a harlot, whore.
চপেট, *s.* a slap, the flat palm. [palm
চপেটাঘাত, *s.* a slap, a blow with the flat
চপ্‌কন্, *s.* a sort of man's frock or gown.
চপ্‌চপ্, *ad.* quickly, speedily, hastily,
চবিলা, *a.* blithe, buxom, merry, gay, active.
চব্বিশ, twenty-four, চব্বিশা, twenty-fourth.
চমক, *s.* a twinkling brightness, a flash, a glance, a panic: *v. a.* to heat slightly.
চমকিত, *a.* aghast, affrighted, alarmed.
চমড়া, *s.* leather, skin, hide. [ment.
চমৎকার, *s.* surprize, astonishment, amaze-
চমৎকারী, *a.* surprizing, astonishing.
চমৎকৃত, *a.* surprized, astonished, amazed.
চমন্, *s.* a flower-garden, a bed of flowers.
চমরী, *s.* the Yak or Tartarian ox, a fly-brush; a compound pedicel. [sel.
চমস, *s.* a ladle, a spoon, a spoon-like ves-
*চমিনাফরোশ, *s.* a dealer in leather.

চমূ, *s.* an army, a squadron. [tering.
চম্‌কন, *s.* a starting, a shuddering, a glit-
চম্‌কা, *v. a.* to start, to shudder, to shrug, to flash, glitter, coruscate; to parch.
চম্‌কান, *s.* a startling, a starting, a flashing, coruscation: *a.* slightly parched, startled, flashing, coruscant. [cation.
চম্‌কানি, *s.* a start, shudder, a flash, corus-
চম্‌কী, *s.* a kind of small tinsel ornaments.
চম্‌চম্, *ad.* with shrinking and startling.
চম্‌চা, *s.* a spoon, a ladle.
চম্পক, *s.* a fragrant yellow flower tree.[2]
চম্পট, *s.* a withdrawing, absconding, van-
চমেলি, *s.* a species of jasmine.[3] [ishing.
চয়, *s.* a multitude, an assemblage, a collection, a heap, mound, a ridge of earth.
চয়ন, *s.* a collecting, a culling (of flowers).
চয়নীয়, *a.* fit to be gathered or collected.
চর্, *v. n.* to graze, to pasture: *s.* a scout, a spy, an emissary: *a.* movable, mobile.
চরক, *s.* the name of a writer on medicine; the book written by Charaka; the swinging festival, the machine for swinging.
চরকগাছ, *s.* the machine for swinging.
চরকপূজা, *s.* the worship or religious ceremony of swinging in honour of Shiva.
চরকসংক্রান্তি, *s.* day of charak-pujá. [lass.
চরকা, *s.* spinning-wheel, a capstan, wind-
চরকি *s.* a kind of firework, a small wheel, a wheel, a reel, a jenny, a cotton machine, a pillory; a winch, a crank.
চরণ, *s.* the foot; a poetical foot; a grazing, a pasturing, a feeding in a pasture.
চরণদাসী, *s.* a wife; a sandal, clog, patten.
চরণপ্রসাদাৎ, a complimentary expression meaning thro' the kindness of (—) foot.
চরণযুগল, চরণযুগ্ম, *s.* the two feet.
চরণসেবক, *a.* serving the foot, a phrase equal to "humble servant" in English.
চরণসেবা, serving the foot, humble service.
চরণামৃত, *s.* the water in which a bráhman dips his the; *lit.* the nectar of the foot.
চরণায়ুধ, *s.* a cock, a chanticleer.
চরণোদক, *s.* the same as চরণামৃত.
চরণোপান্ত, *ad.* near the foot, at the foot.
চরতা, *s.* a species of nettle.
*চরফ্, *a.* active, vigilant, attentive.

চর্ব, *a.* active, spirited: *s.* fat, suet. [fat.
চর্বী, *s.* fat, suet, tallow; -দার, greasy,
চরভট্টী, *s.* pride, self-complacency, self-applause, the voice of merriment.
চরম, *a.* last, ultimate, final; western, west.
চরমকাল, *s.* the time of death.
চরস, *s.* a kind of intoxicating drug.
চরসী, *a.* addicted to the smoking of চরস.
চরা, *v.* to feed and attend cattle. [world.
চরাচর, movable and immovable: *s.* the
চরাণ, *s.* the tending or feeding of cattle.
চরাণি, *s.* the grazing or feeding of cattle.
চরাণী, *s.* a pasture, meadow. [customary.
চরিত, *a.* moved, acted, done, instituted;
চরিতার্থ, prosperous, successful in an un-
চরিতার্থী, desirous of success. [dertaking.
চরিত্র, *s.* a history; conduct, disposition,
চরিষ্ণু, *a.* active, mobile, movable. [usage.
চরু, *s.* a meat-offering, oblation of milk.
চরুস্থালী, *s.* a plate for the meat-offering.
চরুহোম, *s.* the oblation of a meat-offering.
চর্চ্চা, *s.* reflection, consideration, deliberation, action, mention; an anointing.
চর্চ্চাপিপীড়া, *s.* a species of small ant.
চর্ব্বণ, *s.* a chewing, a masticating.
চর্ব্বণীয়, চর্ব্ব্য, *a.* masticable, that may be
চর্ব্বিত, *a.* chewed, masticated. [chewed.
চর্ব্বিতচর্ব্বণ, *s.* a tautology, a repetition.
চর্ভট, or চর্ভটি, *s.* the same as চরভট্টী.
চর্ম্ম, *s.* a skin, a hide, leather; a shield.
চর্ম্মকার, *s.* a tanner, currier, shoe-maker.
চর্ম্মচটিকা, *s.* a smaller species of bat.
চর্ম্মপাদুকা, *s.* a leathern shoe. [shield.
চর্ম্মী, *a.* bearing a shield: *s.* one who bears a
চর্য্য, *a.* practicable, incumbent, customary.
চর্য্যা, movable: *s.* perseverance in religious austerities; custom, practice, habit.
চল্, *v. n.* to go, to set off on a journey, to act, to pass on, to flow, to pass current.
চল, চলৎ, *s.* motion, action, conduct.
চলচ্ছক্তি, চলৎশক্তি, *s.* the power of motion.
চলন, *s.* motion, walk, a habit, conduct, a custom: *a.* current, customary, habitual.
চলনার্হ, *a.* passable, fit to pass.
চলনী, *s.* a petticoat, a skirt.
চলা, *v. a.* to cause to move or act, to urge on, to drive: *s.* motion, action, currency.
চলাচল, steadfast and wavering, unfixed.
চলাচলি, *s.* reciprocal motion, currency.
চলান, *s.* a driving, despatching, impelling, urging on; an invoice, a pass, a permit.
চলাবুলা, *s.* much ado about anything, a
চলি, *s.* a journey, a race, course. [fuss.
চলিত, moved, sent, gone, current, custom-
চলিতব্য, *a.* movable, fit to be moved. [ary.
চলিষ্ণু, *a.* movable, unsteady, fluid.
চলুক, *s.* a handful of water; undulation.
চল্ক, *v. n.* to move, to flow, to flap over.
চল্কন, *s.* spilling, flowing or flapping over.
চল্কা, *v. a.* to spill, to agitate (as liquid).
চল্কান, *s.* the agitating of a fluid. [fluid.
চলচলিয়া, *a.* movable, unstable, unsteady,
চল্তি, *s.* an action, course, conduct, cus-
চল্লিশ, *a.* forty; -গুণ, forty-fold. [tom.
চল্লিশা, *a.* fortieth; of forty (cubits): *s.* defect in sight at about forty years of age.
*চশম্, *s.* the eye, a fountain; -খোর, ungrateful; -খোরী, ingratitude.
চশমা, *s.* a pair of spectacles, an eyeglass.
চষ্, *v. a.* to plough; to till, to cultivate.
চষক, *s.* a drinking vessel, a kind of cup.
চষণ, *s.* a ploughing up of land, a tilling.
চষা, *v. a.* to cause to plough: *s.* the tilling or ploughing of land: *a.* ploughed.
চষাচষি, *s.* a ploughing about, a tilling.
চষাণ, *s.* a causing to plough, the ploughing of a field: *a.* ploughed. [ing.
চষাণি, *s.* a ploughing; wages for plough-
চষিত, *a.* ploughed, tilled, prepared to sow.
চষী, *a.* ploughing; worming in. [fingers.
চষীপোকা, *s.* an insect which infects the
চহলা, *s.* clay, soft mud, dirt, mire.
চা, *v. a.* to ask, wish, look upon, look, see: *s.* a wish, desire, volition, will; tea.
চাইট, *s.* a kick backwards, -মার, to kick.
চাউনি, *s.* a wish, a request, a look, a view.
চাউল, *s.* unhusked rice, uncooked rice.
চাউলমুগরা, *s.* name of a medicinal drug.
চাওন, *s.* a desiring, a wishing, a seeing.
চাওয়া, *s. a.* wish, a requisition, a request.
চাওয়াচাওয়ি, *s.* mutual desire, emulation.
চাঁই, *s.* a clod, a large turf or piece of earth; a chief, a leader, a protector.
চাঁচ্, *v. a.* to scrape, to shave, to pare off.

চাঁচ, *s.* a coarse mat made of split reeds.
চাঁচন, *s.* the act of scraping or shaving.
চাঁচনি, *s.* a scraping, the shavings of wood.
চাঁচর, curled, crisped, crimpled: *s.* a curl. a bonfire made at the Dola festival.
চাঁচরকেশ, *s.* a curl, curled or crisped hair.
চাঁচা, *v. a.* to cause to scrape or shave off: *a.* scraped, shaved, pared off.
চাঁচি, *s.* scrapings, shavings, parings.
চাঁড়াল, *s.* an outcast, a class of Hindus.
চাঁড়ালীয়া, *a.* vile, base, vulgar, low.
চাঁদ, চন্দ্র, *s.* the moon; -মুখী, moon-faced
চাঁদআ, চন্দ্রাতপ, *s.* an awning, a canopy.
চাঁদনী, *s.* an awning; a porch, portico, open building on pillars; the moon-light.
চাঁদা, *s.* a subscription; the name of a fish.[1]
চাঁদাড়, *s.* side-ridge of a thatched house.
চাঁদী, *a.* white, clear: *s.* silver; the crown of the head, space above the forehead.
চাঁদোয়া, *s.* an awning, a canopy, a portico.
চাঁপকলী, *s.* an ornament for the neck.
চাঁপা, *s.* an earring: -কলা, the best plantain;[2] -নটিয়া, a potherb;[3] also *vide* চম্পক
চাঁপী, *s.* edible parenchyma of the jak fruit.
চাক্, *v. a.* to taste: *s.* a ripping open.
চাক, *s.* a wheel, a circle, a discus, a honey-comb, the comb of a wasp or hornet.
চাক, -খড়ী, *s.* chalk; -দয়াল, a small bird.[4]
চাকন, *s.* tasting, trying the taste or relish.
চাকনি, *s.* a tasting, a trying the taste.
চাকনিয়া *a.* tasting, skilled in tasting.
চাকনী, *a.* tasting, trying the relish.
চাকভ্রমী *a.* revolving, turning like a wheel.
চাকর, *s.* a servant, domestic; *fem.* চাকরানী
*চাকরা, *s.* land given as reward of service.
চাকরানা, *s.* land allowed for the expenses of collecting the revenue. [business.
চাকরী, *s.* a post, service, an employment,
চাকলা, *a.* circular: *s.* the same as চক্লা, &c.
চাকশূল, *s.* a medicinal plant or drug.
চাকা, *v.a.* to cause to taste food: *s.* a circle, a wheel, a disc: *a.* tasted, relished.
চাকী *s.* a mill, a grinding stone, a circular body, a spindle used to spin twine.
চাকু, চাকুছুরী, *s.* a claspknife, a penknife.
চাকুন্দা, *s.* name of a plant (Cassia Tora).
চাকুলিয়া, চাকুল্যা, *s.* a species of fern.[5]

চাকচকা, *s.* brilliance, splendour, lustre.
চাকচিকিনি, *a.* declining in brilliance.
চাকতী, *s.* a wafer, a flat round slice.
চাকতীগুড়, *s.* flattened molasses. [eyes.
চাক্ষুষ, *a.* evident, visible, before one's
চাখন, *s.* a tasting, a trying the flavour.
চাখড়া, *s.* a name given to the orange.
চাগ্, *v. n.* to commence (as a disease,) to begin to exert one's self in any action.
চাগন, *s.* the access of the paroxysm of a disease, a stirring up to motion.
চাগনি, *s.* the access of a paroxysm, a rousing of one's self to motion.
চাগা, *v. a.* to exert to raise up a heavy body, to stimulate, to rouse up, to cause to rise, to bring on a paroxysm.
চাগান, *s.* exertion to raise up a heavy body, the rousing of an animal: *a.* roused.
চাগানি, *s.* a stimulating or rousing up.
চাচা, চাচ্চা, *s.* a father's brother, an uncle.
চাচাত, *a.* derived from an uncle; -বহিনী, an uncle's daughter; -ভাই, an uncle's son.
চাচী, *s.* a father's brother's wife, an aunt.
চাচ্কী, *a.* easily coaxed or wrought upon, unstable: *s.* the coaxing of a person.,
চাঞ্চল্য, *s.* fickleness, instability, unsteadiness, activity, agility, fluidity.
চাট্, *v v.* to lick, to lap.
চাটন, *s.* a licking, a lapping of any thing.
চাটনি, *s.* act of licking; a kind of sauce.
চাটা, *v. a.* to cause to lick: *a.* licked.
চাটাচাটি, *s.* a mutual licking or lapping.
চাটান, *s.* a causing to lick: *a.* licked.
চাটানি, *s.* the licking of a thing.
চাটি, চাটী, *s.* backward kick (of a horse); -মার to kick; -মারণ kicking backwards.
চাটিম, *a.* fit to be sucked; -কলা, a plantain.
চাটু, *s.* pleasing or soft words, flattery.
চাটুবাদী, *a.* flattering: *s.* a flatterer, a parasite, a sycophant, a jester, a cheat.
চাটুয়া, *s.* the flat palm of the hand.
চাটুক্তি, *s.* a flattering, flattery, adulation.
চাটে, *ad.* wholly, entirely, altogether.
চাড়, *s.* hurry, necessity; a wrench, lever.
চাড়া, *a.* high, steep: *s.* a wrench, lever, a prop, fulcrum; fixing of a bowstring.
চাড়াশব্দ, *s.* an emphatic word, loud voice.

চাড়ী, *s.* pole to force a boat, a lever, prop.
চান, *s.* the track or trace of a fish in the water; bathing, ablution (incorrectly).
চাণক্য, *s.* name of a sage, and of his poems.
চাণ্ডাল, *s.* an outcast, a low caste Hindu.
চাণ্ডালী, চাণ্ডালীন, *s.* a female outcast.
চাতক, *s.* the name of a species of swallow.
চাতকিনী, চাতকী, *s.* female swallow. [plot.
চাতর, *s.* a gang of robbers; a conspiracy,
চাতাল, *s.* a plain space, a sheet of water, a terrace, the roof of a house.
চাতুরী, *s.* activity, cleverness, craftiness, deceit, fraud, roguery, female infidelity.
চাতুর্বর্ণ্য, *a.* relating to the four castes.
চাতুর্মাস্য, *a.* continuing four months.
চাতুর্য্য, *s.* activity, cleverness, craftiness, unsteadiness, deceit, fraud, roguery.
চাদর, *s.* a sheet, a covering or bed sheet.
চান্দনী, *s.* the moon-light; an awning.
চান্দা, *s.* the same as চাঁদা, which see.
চান্দ্র, *a.* lunar; -মান, lunar time; -মাস, do. month; -মাসিক, reckoned by lunar time.
চান্দ্রায়ণ, *s.* the name of a religious vow.
চাপ্ *v. a.* to press by a weight, to press down, to compress, to cover, to conceal, to quash, to smother, to place upon.
চাপ, *s.* a turf, clod, lump, pressure, burden, a block used in printing calicoes, the platen of a printing press, a bow.
চাপড়, *s.* a slap; a butcher's axe, cleaver.
চাপড়া, *v. a.* to slap, beat: *s.* turf, a clod.
চাপড়ান, *s.* the act of slapping or beating.
চাপড়ানি, *s.* a slap, the slapping a person.
চাপন, *s.* a pressing down, squeezing, compressing, concealing, quashing, stifling.
চাপল্য, *s.* the same as চপলতা, which see.
চাপা, *v. a.* to put any thing into a press, to lay a weight on a thing, to print: *s.* a cover, a press, the lever of a press.
চাপাচাপি, *s.* a mutual pressing, pressure.
চাপান, *s.* the covering of a thing, the laying of a weight, a printing: *a.* pressed down, pressed, compressed, printed.
চাপানি, *s.* pressure, pressure of a crowd.
চাপুয়া, *a.* curdled, sticking together in clods.
চাপুয়াদই, *s.* coagulated milk.
চাপে২চাপে, চাপ্‌চাপ, *ad.* in clods or lumps.

চাপ্‌টা, *a.* pressed, flat; -লি, a squatting posture.
চাপ্‌টী, *s.* a fish; female organ.
চাব্, *v. a.* to chew, to masticate.
চাবড়া, *s.* a turf, a clod, a square clod.
চাবনি, *s.* a view, a sight, desire, a wish.
চাবা, *v. a.* to persuade, to excite a desire, to show: *a.* desired, asked for, wished.
চাবা, *v. a.* to chew, to cause to masticate.
চাবাচাবি, *s.* a looking at one another.
চাবান, চাবন, *s.* a chewing, a masticating.
চাবানি, *s.* mastication, chewing.
চাবী, *s. Port.* a key; -কুলুপ, lock and key.
চাবুক, *s.* a whip, scourge; -সবার, a horse-breaker, a horse-jockey, a good horseman; -সবারী, riding, horsemanship.
চাম, *s.* skin, leather, hide; -ছাড়া, -খোল, to skin, flay; -আটুলু, a kind of tick.
চামচা, খজাকা, *s.* a spoon, a ladle.
চামচিকা, চামগুদড়ী, the same as চর্ম্মচটিকা.
চামড়, *a.* sticking, adhesive, elastic, sticky, viscous.
চামড়মাংস, *s.* gristle, cartilage.
চামড়া, *s.* a skin, hide, leather, parchment.
চামড়ী, *s.* scurf, dandruff; touchwood; skin, hide, leather: *a.* very dry and light.
চামদল, *s.* a cutaneous disease; small-pox.
চামনিকী, চামনী, *s.* a nit, egg of a louse.
চামর, চামরী, *s.* a fly-brush, a fly-flapper made of the tail of the cow of Tartary.
চামসা, *a.* stinking like dried skin. [scurf.
চামাটি, চামাতী, *s.* a razor-strop; dandruff,
চামার, চর্ম্মকার, *s.* a tanner, a currier, a skinner, a shoe-maker, a cobbler.
চামারালু, *s.* a species of yam. [gold.
চামীকর, *s.* gold; -ময়, golden, made of
চার্, *v. a.* to procure the germination of seed, to level the surface of any thing.
চার, *a.* four: *s.* a spy, a scout; a bait.
চারখান, *s.* a sort of check cloth.
চারটা, *ad.* only four; few, little: *s.* little.
চারণ, *s.* a dancer, actor of note, a reciter of shástras; planting out of seedlings.
চারপায়া, *a.* four-footed: *s.* a quadruped.
চারপায়ী *s.* a bedstead, a couch, a stool.
চারবায়ু, *s.* a zephyr, a gentle breeze.
চারা, *v.* to plant out seedlings: *s.* a plant, a seedling; means, remedy, aid, help.
চারাটারা, *s.* plants and seedlings.

চারাগিয়া, *a.* dealing in plants, raising plants from seed : *s.* a nursery-man.

চারি, *a.* four ; -আনা, four ánás, a 4th part ; -কোণা, quadrangular ; four corners.

চারিদিগে, *ad.* on all sides, all around.

চারিপাইয়া, চারিপায়ী, *vide* চারপায়া, &c.

চারিপাশ, *ad.* on all sides : *s.* four sides.

চারি-পুআ, *a.* full, complete, entire, whole ; four quarters or a sera ;-গুণ, fourfold.

চারিভাগ, *s.* four shares ;-কৃ, to quarter.

চারু, *a.* handsome, beautiful, agreeable, elegant.

চারুতা, *s.* beauty, elegance.

চার্বঙ্গী, *a.* beautiful, handsome, elegant, symmetrical : *s.* a handsome woman.

চার্বাক, *s.* a sophist, a materialist, atheist.

চাল্, *v. a.* to remove, to dispel, to drive, to sift any thing, to over-run.

চাল, *s.* conduct, behaviour, walk, gait; the pitched roof ; unhusked rice.

চালক, *a.* clever, active, lively, brisk.

চালকী, *a.* dealing in rice : *s.* a rice-dealer.

চালতা, *s.* the name of a tree and its fruit.[1]

চালন, *s.* the causing to move, the removing or sifting of any thing.

চালনা, *s.* the sifting of corn, etc. motion onwards.

চালনী, *s.* a sieve, a colander.

চালা, *v. a.* to remove, to drive cattle, to transport, to manage, to urge forwards : *s.* conduct, management ; a hut, a stall.

চালাক, *a.* active, brisk, lively, clever.

চালাকী, *s.* activity, liveliness, cleverness.

চালাচালি, *s.* reciprocal motion or sifting.

চালান, *s.* management ; a driving, urging forwards; the letting of an arrow or gun ; dispatching of goods, an invoice, a pass.

চালানিয়া, *a.* urging forward ; superintending : *s.* a superintendent, a manager.

চালানী, *s.* the dispatching of goods, an invoice, a pass for goods.

চালি, *s.* a custom, a habit, practice, a fashion, gait, a walk, motion ; unhusked rice ; stage of a boat ; a hanging-shelf.

চালিত, *a.* moved, in motion.

চালু, *s.* unhusked or sifted rice : *a.* swift.

চালুনী, *s.* a sieve, a colander ; *vide* চেলুনী,

চাল্লি, *s.* quick motion, a running.

চাল্লিশ, চাল্লিশা, the same as চল্লিশ, &c.

চাষ্, *v. a.* to plough : *s.* cultivation, agriculture, tillage, a ploughing.

চাষবাষ, *s.* agriculture, tillage, husbandry.

চাষা, *a.* clownish, awkward, clumsy : *s.* a clown, a ploughman, a husbandman.

চাষাড়িয়া, *a.* rustic, clownish, clumsy, awkward.

চাষাধোবা, *s.* a class of Hindus.

চাষামী, *s.* clownishness, rusticity.

চাষী, *a.* ploughing : *s.* a ploughman, a tiller.

চাষীকৈবর্ত্ত, *s.* a class of Hindus.

চাহন, *s.* a looking, wishing, want, desire.

চাহা, *s.* a kind of snipe ; a wish.

চাহারম, *a.* fourth : *s.* Moslem funeral rite.

চিঅ, চিআ, *v. a.* to awaken, to stimulate.

চিঅন, চিআন, *s.* awakening of a person : *a.* awake, wakened ; -কটাল, spring-tide.

চিঅন্ত, *a.* awakened, stimulated.

চিঁ, চিঁচিঁ, *s.* the chirping noise of birds.

চিক্, *v. a.* to smooth, to polish ; to scream ; *s.* a scream ; a sort of lattice or screen.

চিকন, *a.* oily, unctuous ; *s.* embroidery.

চিকনকর, or চিকনগর, *s.* an embroiderer.

চিকনদোজ, *s.* *idem.*

চিকা, *v.* to smooth, polish ; to solder : *s.* a musk-rat.

চিকান, *s.* the smoothing of the hair, etc.

চিকাশ, *a.* clear, fair (applied to weather)

চিকিৎসক, *s.* a physician, a doctor.

চিকিৎসনীয়, *a.* curable, remediable.

চিকিৎসা, *s.* science of medicine, medical treatment, administration of medicine.

চিকিৎসিত, *a.* attended by a doctor, physicked.

চিকিৎস্য, *a.* curable, remediable.

চিকিন, *a.* flat-nosed, snub-nosed.

চিকিমিকি, *a.* sudden or successive flashing.

চিকিল, *s.* mud, mire, clay, sludge.

চিকী, *a.* bad, rotten (as betel-nut).

চিকীগো, *s.* bad or rotten betel-nut.

চিকীর্ষা, *s.* a desire to perform any thing.

চিকীর্ষিত, *a.* required to be done.

চিকীর্ষু, *a.* desirous of doing a thing.

চিকুর, *s.* the hair, the hair of the head.

চিকুরারি, *s.* an epithet given to a barber.

চিকোর, *s.* the red partridge.[2]

চিক্কণ, *a.* unctuous, oily, greasy, glossy, slippery, smooth, sleek.

চিক্কণতা, or চিক্কণাই, *s.* unctuosity, slipperiness, oiliness, smoothness, polish.

চিক্কা, ছুঁচা, s. a musk-rat.
চিক্কড়, s. a thunder-bolt.
চিক্‌চিক্‌, s. glossiness; a vivid light.
চিকচিকিনী, s. a glow, a vivid light.
চিক্‌না, a. oily, smooth, greasy; polished.
চিক্‌মিক্‌, s. a flash, a glance of light.
চিঙ্গড়া, চিঙ্গড়ি, s. a shrimp, a prawn.
চিঙ্গড়িপোড়া, shrunk up (as fried prawn).
চিঙ্গড়িমাছ, s. a shrimp, a prawn fish.
চিচিঙ্গা, s. the snake-gourd.[1]
চিচ্‌কার, s. the same as চিৎকার.
চিচ্ছক্তি, s. the power of intellect.
চিঞ্চা, s. the tamarind tree and its fruit.
চিট, s. rust, mouldiness, mildew.
চিটা, s. mouldiness, the smut of corn, mildew; a chit, a note: a. viscous, clammy.
চিটাগুড়, s. liquid molasses for tobacco.
চিটী, s. a letter, a note, a chit, a note of hand, a bank note, a draft, an order.
চিট্‌কল, a. spread out, patent.
চিট্‌চিটিয়া, a. viscid, ropy, sticky, tenacious
চিট্যা, a. mouldy, rusty, viscous, clammy.
চিট্যাগুড়, s. liquid molasses for tobacco.
চিট্যামি, চিট্যারোগ, s. mouldiness, rust.
চিঠী, s. a letter, a note an assignment.
চিড়্‌, v. n. to cut, to be exasperated, to fret.
চিড়, s. a slit, a crack; vexation, passion.
চিড়ন, s. cracking, fretting, being vexed.
চিড়মারণ, s. the splitting any thing.
চিড়া, s. rice soaked and flattened: v. a. to teaze, to vex, to exasperate. [son.
চিড়ান, s. a teazing, exasperating of a per-
চিড়িক্‌, s. a twinging, a throbbing pain.
চিড়িকমারণ, s. the shooting of a pain.
চিড়িমার, s. a fowler, a bird-catcher.
চিড়িয়া, s. a bird; -খানা, an aviary, a cage.
চিড়কন, চিড়্‌কানি, s. the twinging of a sore.
চিড়্‌কা, v. n. to twing, to twitch. [sion.
চিড়্‌চিড়, s. exasperation, petulance, pas-
চিড়্‌চিড়্‌, চিড়্‌চিড়িয়া, a. captious, peevish, cross, splenetic, testy: s. a plant.[2]
চিড়্‌বিড়্‌, s. the sensation of itching. [ing.
চিড়্‌মিড়িয়া, a. throbbing, twinging, smart-
চিৎ, s. the soul, intellect, the heart: a. lying on the back, turned upside down, supine: v. a. to recline, to lie on the back.
চিতই, চিতইপিটা, s. a sort of riceflour cake.
চিতলমাছ, s. a species of fish.[3] [wort.[4]
চিতা, a. spotted: s. a funeral pile; lead-
চিতাকড়ি, s. a spotted kind of Cyprea.
চিতাচ্ছাদন, s. a shroud for the dead.
চিতাপড়ন, s. a becoming mouldy.
চিতাবস্ত্র, s. a shroud for the dead.
চিতাবাঘ, চিত্রব্যাঘ্র, s. a leopard.
চিতাভস্ম, s. the ashes of the funeral pile.
চিতাভূমি, s. the place of a funeral pile.
চিতারোহণ, s. ascending of a funeral pile.
চিতারোহিণী, a. ascending the funeral pile.
চিতাহরিণ, s. the Axis or spotted deer.
চিতিসাপ s. a species of snake. [outcry.
চিৎকার, s. a scream, a squalling noise, an
চিৎকারশব্দ, s. a loud noise, a scream.
চিত্ত, s. the mind, the reasoning faculty, the heart, the affections. [tions.
চিত্তচোর, s. one who steals away the affec-
চিত্তনিবেশী, devoted to an object, zealous.
চিত্তবাদ, s. the sentiment of the heart.
চিত্তবাধ, s. a disgust, displeasure, ill will.
চিত্তভাব, s. the state or bias of the heart.
চিত্তভ্রম, s. a mistake, vagrancy of mind, a
চিত্তরম্য, agreeable to the heart. [vagary.
চিত্তান্তর, a. averse, disgusted, dissatisfied.
চিত্তোচ্চাটন, s. pensiveness, melancholy.
চিত্তোদ্বেগ, s. perplexity, anxiety of mind.
চিৎপট্টাং, চিৎপাত, s. the falling into a reclining posture with the face upwards.
চিত্র, s. a picture, a painting, printed linen, a miracle, astonishment, a circlet or mark, a variegated colour: a. variegated, speckled, surprising, astonishing.
চিত্রকর, চিত্রকার, s. a painter, artist, drafts-
চিত্রকাব্য, s. alliteration, an acrostic. [man.
চিত্রকারী, a. painting, variegating.
চিত্রগুপ্ত, s. the registrar of Yama. [dy.
চিত্রবিচিত্র, a. variegated, checquered, gau-
চিত্রভানু, s. the sun; fire; a name of Shiva.
চিত্রলেখা, s. in *mytho.* a female famous for describing every thing at her will.
চিত্রহস্ত, a. having the hand reversed.
চিত্রা, s. a star in the spike of Virgo.
চিত্রিণী, a. surprising, ravishing (applied to a particular description of women).
চিত্রিত, or চিত্রীকৃত, a. painted, variegated, speckled, spotted, checquered.

চিদাত্মা, *s.* the intellectual soul, spirit, God.
চিদাভাস, *s.* a semblance of intellect or spirit.
চিদ্রূপ, *a.* intelligent, amiable.
চিন্, *v. a.* to recognise, to know.
চিনকী, *a.* small, dwarf, diminutive.
চিনন, *s.* a recognising, a knowing.
চিনা, *v.* to point out : *a.* known, acquainted with: *s.* a Chinese; -জোঁক, small leech.
চিনান, *s.* a causing to know, pointing out.
চিনাপরিচয়, *s.* familiar acquaintance, intimacy.
চিনী, or চীনী, *s.* sugar ; a Chinese.
চিন্‌চিন্, *im. ad.* of a twinging sensation.
চিন্‌চিনীয়া, *a.* acute, sharp (as pain).
চিন্ত, *v. a.* to be anxious, to be thoughtful.
চিন্তক, *a.* thoughtful, anxious.
চিন্তন, *s.* a thinking, reflecting, pondering, cogitation.
চিন্তনীয়, *a.* deserving care or reflection.
‡চিন্তা, *s.* thoughtfulness, care, anxiety, a cogitation, a thought, meditation.
চিন্তাকারক, চিন্তাকারী, *a.* careful, anxious.
চিন্তাজ্বর, *s.* a fever arising from anxiety.
চিন্তান্বিত, *s.* thoughtful, pensive, anxious.
চিন্তামণি, *s.* a fabulous gem ; a medicine.
চিন্তিত, *a.* thought on, anxious, perplexed.
চিপ্, চিপড়্, *v. a.* to squeeze, express (the juice), to press out, to wring (water).
চিপড়ন, চিপড়ানি, *s.* a squeezing with the hand.
চিপড়া, *v. a.* the same as চিপ্.
চিপড়ান, *s.* the act of squeezing or pressing out : *a.* squeezed, pressed out.
চিপন, *s.* a squeezing, a pressing out.
চিপিটক, *s.* rice soaked and parched.
চিব্, *v. a.* to masticate, to chew.
চিবন, *s.* a chewing, masticating : *a.* chewed.
চিবনি, *s.* mastication, the chewing of food.
চিবনিয়া, *a.* eminent at masticating food.
চিবান, *s.* the act of chewing : *a.* masticated.
চিবা, *v. a.* to chew, to masticate : *s.* masticated betel-leaf.
চিবুক, *s.* the chin.
চিমট্, *v. a.* to grasp, to pinch, to nip.
চিমটন, *s.* a grasping, pinching, nipping.
চিম্‌টা, *v. a.* to grasp, pinch, nip : *s.* a pair of forceps or pincers, a pair of tongs.
চিম্‌টী, *s.* a pair of pincers or nippers, a pinching ; -কাট্, to pinch, nip, grasp.
চিম্‌টীকাটন, *s.* the pinching of any one.
চিমড়্, *v. a.* to adhere, to shrivel, stick to.
চিম্‌ড়ন, *s.* an adhering, a sticking close.
চিম্‌ড়া, *v.* to make a thing stick : *s.* a pod, shell of a pea, a skin, a shell, a husk : *a.* elastic, flexible, lean, dried, tough.
চিমড়ান, *s.* a causing to shrink or to stick close : *a.* flexible, tough. dried.
চিয়ন, *a.* roused, awake, active, alert.
চিয়ান, *s.* a rousing, awakening, stimulating.
চির্, *v.* to rend, tear, split ; to be rent.
চির, *ad.* of old, of long standing : *s.* a rent : *a.* long (time); -কাল, long time; -ক্ষত, old wound, ulcer ; -জীবী, long-lived ; -দুঃখী, long afflicted or distressed ; -সঞ্চিত, long hoarded ; -সুখী, long or lastingly happy.
চিরকারী, *a.* dilatory, slow, loitering.
চিরকালাবধি, *ad.* from, or for a long time.
চিরকালিক, চিরকালীন, *a.* old, ancient, lasting, perennial, chronic, inveterate.
চিরঞ্জী, *s.* a kind of dried fruit.[1]
চিরণ, *s.* a tearing, rending, lacerating.
চিরতা, *s.* a kind of medicinal plant.[2]
চিরন্তন, *a.* old, of long standing, ancient.
চিরন্তন, *a.* old, ancient, antique.
চিররোগ, *s.* a chronic disease.
চিররোগী, *a.* valitudinary, long-diseased.
চিরস্থায়ী, *a.* durable, of long continuance.
‡চিরা, *v. a.* to cause to cleave or tear : *a.* torn, rent : *s.* a parti-coloured turban ; maidenhood ; -উতার, to deflour.
*চিরাগ, *s.* a lamp ; -দান, a lamp-stand.
চিরাগী, *s.* fee given to a Moslem priest.
চিরাণ, *s.* the causing to cleave wood.
চিরাণী, *s.* the wages of cleaving wood.
চিরাৎ, *ad.* of old : *s.* a long time.
চিরুণ, চিরুণী, চিরুণী, কঙ্কতিকা, *s.* a comb.
চিরুণদাঁতী, *a.* comb-toothed, pectinated.
চিল, *s.* the common Indian kite.[3]
চিলম, *s.* the tobacco bowl of the huká.
চিলমচি, *s.* a brass washing bason.
চিলা, *a.* spotted : *s.* the same as চিলাঘর.
চিলাঘর, *s.* a small room on the top of a house to cover the stair-case.
চিল্ল, *s.* sore-eye, a kite : *a.* sore-eyed, bleareyed.
*চিহারা, *s.* the face, the aspect, a form.
চিহ্ন, *s.* a sign, mark, a badge, a scar, a spot, vestige, token, signal, a trace.
চিহ্নিত, *a.* marked, signed, denoted by a mark.

চিহিঁ, চীঁহী, *im. sd.* of a horse's neighing.
*চীজ্, *s.* a thing, an article, furniture.
চীজবস্ত,*s.* furniture, baggage, equipage.
চীৎকার, *s.* a screaming, an outcry.
চীন, *s.* a deer; millet; China; -দেশ, Chinacountry; -দেশীয় China, Chinese.
চীনা,*s.* millet, a species of grass (Panicum miliacium); a Chinese : *a.* China.
চীনানারাঙ্গি,, *s.* a shrub and its fruit.[1]
চীনাসিন্দূর, *s.* China minium or redlead.
চীনী, *s.*sugar; a Chinese; -কাঁটালী,-চাম্পা, very sweet varieties of the plantain.
চীর, *s.* cloth, clothes, a rag, old and torn cloth, bark; also, the same as চীরবস্ত্র.
চীরবস্ত্র, *s.*cloth made of vegetable fibres; the dress of a devotee, a coat of shreds.
চীরবস্ত্রী,*a.* wearing the dress of a devotee.
চীর্ণ, *a.*split, divided, rent, torn.
চু, *v. n.* to ooze out, to leak, to distil.
চুআ, *v. n. idem : v. a.* to cause to leak : *s.* a rat, a medicine, a sort of perfume.
চুআন,*s.* the leaking of liquors, an oozing out : *a.* leaked, oozed out. [ing.
চুওন, চুয়ন,*s.* a leaking, oozing out, a flow-
চুঁ, চুঁয়, *v. n.* to burn away, to be burnt.
চুঁআ, চুয়া, *v.a.* to burn, to calcine, to tan.
চুঁক, *v. a.* to whet a knife, set a razor, etc.
চুঁক্, *v. a.* to strip corn from the ear, to strip flowers or seeds from the stalks.
চুঁচড়া,*a.* small, minute : *s.* name of a town.
চুঁচি,চুচী, *s.* the nipple, breast, the paps.
চুঁচিমলন,*s.* a rubbing of a woman's breast.
চুক্, *v. n.* to miss, to mistake, to err, to transgress, to settle, to decide.
চুক, *s.* a mistake, an error, a blunder, a fault, an oversight; the Indian sorrel.
চুকন,*s.* an erring, making a mistake, settling an affair; a whetting, sharpening.
চুকনি,*s.* accommodation, settling an affair.
চুকপালঙ্গ, চুকশাক, *s.* the Indian sorrel.[2]
চুকা, *v. a.* to decide, to adjust, to settle : *a.* acid, sour : *s.* the Indian sorrel.
চুকান, *s.* the deciding or adjusting of an affair, the settling of a dispute.
চুকানিয়া, *s.* one who settles or adjusts.
চুকে, *ad.* by mistake, inadvertently.
চুক্চাক্, *s.* failure, errors and mistakes.
চুকচুক, *a.* glossy, shining, oily. [ment.
চুক্তি, *s.* a bargain, a contract, an agree-
চুক্র, *s.* acid seasoning, acidity; sorrel, tamarind.
*চুগল, -খোর, *s.* a backbiter.
চুগলখোরী, *s.* a backbiting, a slandering.
চুগলী,*s.* backbiting, slander, talebearing.
চুঙ্গী,*s.* a socket, a tube, a pipe, oil-vessel, a mortise hole, barrel of a gun, a cup.
চুট, *v. a.* to strike, to smite, to hit.
চুট্‌কি,চুট্‌কী,*s.* a pinch; ring for the toes; a mouse : *ad.* some, a little. [ble.
চুটকিয়া, *a.* small, little, trifling, despica-
চুড়া, *s.* rice soaked and flattened.
চুড়ী,*s.* a kind of bracelet usually made of gold, silver, ivory, horn, glass, lac, etc.
চুণী,*s.* a ruby : *a.* small, little; -মুক্তা small pearl.
চুত, *s.* female organ, the anus.
চুতড়, *s.* the buttocks, the back side.
চুন্, *v. a.* to select, to choose, to pick out : to pucker or crisp cloth.
চুনন, *s.* a picking, selecting of a person or thing, the puckering of a thing.
চুনা, *a.* small : *s* a small species of fish.
চুনাট, *a.* puckered, crisped, plaited.
চুনিন্দা, *a.* select, choice, chosen.
চুপ, *s.* silence, quietness : *a.* quiet, hush, still, silent : *ad.* be quiet; *intj.* hold! be still! -কৃ, to be silent; -করা, to silence, to quiet; -কর,-মার, be quiet.
চুপ্চাপ, *s.* silence, caution, secresy.
চুপড়িয়া, *a.* like a basket, large : -আলু, a yam.[3]
চুপড়ী,*s.* a basket; -আলু a yam.
চুপন *s.* a hacking, smiting with a weapon.
চুপিচুপি, চুপেচাপে,*ad.* slily, secretly, cautiously, silently, slinkingly.
চুপ্‌ষ্, চুপস্, *v.* to imbibe, suck in, sink (as ink.
চুপ্‌ষান,চুপ্‌সন,*s.* a sinking, imbibing paper).
চুব, *v.* to dip, immerse, plunge; to prick.
চুবন, *s.* a pricking, ducking, immersing.
চুবনি, চুবানি, *s.* a ducking, immersion.
চুবা, *v.* to dip, plunge, immerse; to prick: *a.* immersed : *s.* a ducking, immersion.
চুবাচুবি, *s.* mutual ducking or immersion.
চুবান, *s.* act of pricking, ducking, dipping or immersing : *a.* pricked, immersed.
চুম্, *v. a.* to kiss, to come in contact.
চুমা, *s.* a kiss; -খাওন, or -লওন, to kiss.

চুমাচাটা, *s.* a kissing; *lit.* kissing and licking.
চুমাচুমি, *ad.* mutually kissing.
চুমুক, *s.* a sip, a mouthful (of liquid).
চুমুরী, *s.* the spatha of the cocoanut.
চুমকী, *s.* a kind of small tinsel ornaments.
চুমকুড়ী, *s.* a chirping with the lips to entice or coax a bird or other animal.
চুম্বক, *a.* kissing, touching upon a topic, laconic: *s.* a summary, an abstract, an index, short-hand; a loadstone, magnet; -পাথর, -প্রস্তর, -মণি, loadstone, magnet.
চুম্বন, *s.* a kiss, a kissing; -কর্ত্তা one who kisses.
চুম্বনীয়, *a.* deserving to be kissed.
চুম্বা, *s.* a kiss. চুম্বিত, *a.* kissed.
চুয়াড়, *s.* a mountaineer, a savage.
চুরট, *s.* a roll of tobacco, a cigar.
চুরি, চুরী, *s.* theft, robbery, a pilfering.
চুল, *s.* hair of the head, a lock of hair.
চুলটুল, *s.* hair, locks of hair.
চুলা, চুল্লী, *s.* a portable hearth, a furnace, a fireplace.
চুলুক, *s.* a handful of water; mire, mud.
চুলকনা, চুলকনি, চুলকানা, *s.* itches, an itching, the sensation of itching; lust.
চুলকা, *v. n.* to itch, to tickle, to scratch.
চুলকান, *s.* itching, a tickling, scratching.
চুলকানী, *s.* an itching, a pimple, the itch; lust.
চুল্কী, *s.* a lock of hair, a curl.
চুলচুল, চুলবুল, *s.* fickleness, unsteadiness.
চুলবুলিয়া, *a.* fickle, unsteady, inconstant, active.
চুঁচুঁ, *s.* the chirping of birds.
চুচুক, *s.* the nipple, the breast, the paps.
চূড়া, *s.* a lock of hair, a crest, a top-knot, a pinnacle, a turret, a mountain peak, a plume, a diadem; flattened rice.
চূড়ান্ত, *s.* a conclusion, a decision, result, issue.
চূড়ামণি, *s.* a gem to be worn in the crest, jewel of a crown; in *comp.* it signifies chief, eminent; *e. g.* পণ্ডিতচূড়ামণি, chief of the learned; মূর্খচূড়ামণি, chief of the ignorant, or supremely ignorant.
চূড়িয়া, *s.* mantle or wrapper for the body.
চূড়ো, *s.* the same as চূড়া, which see.
চূণ, *s.* quicklime, powdered lime; -কাম, a whitewashing; -বালী plaster or mortar.
চূণটি, or চূণতি, *s.* lime-vessel of a betel-box.
চূণা, *s.* quicklime, dry or powdered lime.
চূণারী, *s.* a burner or maker of lime.

চূত, *s.* the mango, also, the mango tree.[1]
চূর, *a.* pulverized: *s.* fragment, powder; a fulness.
চূরচার, *s.* pieces and fragments.
চুরচুর, *a.* overflowing, completely, quite (drunk or full.)
চূর্ণ, *v. a.* to pulverize, crumble, break into fragments.
চূর্ণ, *s.* lime; powder, a crumble.
চূর্ণক, *s.* a discourse to maintain a sentiment or thesis laid down as a topic, the expounding of such a sentence.
চূর্ণন, *s.* the pounding or pulverizing of any thing.
চূর্ণাঙ্গ, *a.* broken-limbed.
চূর্ণিত, *a.* powdered, pulverized, crumbled.
চূর্ণীকৃত, *a.* reduced to powder or crumbs.
চূষ., *v. a.* to suck, to imbibe.
চূষণ, *s.* imbibing or sucking of a thing.
চূষিত, *a.* sucked, imbibed.
চূষণী, চূষী, *s.* a coral or other plaything for little children to suck.
চেঁউড়, *s.* a leg of mutton, a haunch of venison.
চেঁচ, চেঁচা, *v. n.* to bawl, to scream.
চেঁচাচেঁচি, *s.* a loud noise, a squabble.
চেঁচাড়ি, *s.* the scrapings of a bambu rod.
চেঁচান, *s.* a bawling, a crying out, a vociferating: *a.* bawled, spoken aloud.
চেঁচানি, *s.* a bawling, a cry, a scream.
চেঁচানিয়া, *s.* one who speaks loud.
চেঁট, the human penis; -কাটানি circumcision.
চেঁটিয়া, *s.* the male organ of generation.
চেঙ্গ, *s.* name of a kind of fish;[2] -ড়াম, -ড়ামি, puerility, childishness, boyishness.
চেঙ্গড়া, *a.* young, youthful; wide, expanded: *s.* a lad, a boy, a youngster.
চেঙ্গড়ী, *fem.* youthful: *s.* a girl; a prawn.
চেঙ্গারী, *s.* a flat kind of basket.
চেঙ্গয়ামাছ, *s.* a species of fish.[3]
চেট, চেটক, *s.* a servant, a slave.
চেটা, চেটাই, *s.* a mat, a mat to sit or sleep on.
চেটাল, চেটকা, *a.* broad, wide, flat, shallow.
চেটী, চেড়ী, *s.* a female servant or slave.
চেটুয়া, *s.* the flat palm of the hand.
চেটো, *s.* *idem;* also, *a.* young, full grown.
চেটা, *s.* manhood, adult age.
চেড়া, *v. a.* to provoke, to exasperate.
চেড়ান, *s.* the provoking of a person.
চেৎ, *v. a.* to convince, to make a person take notice: *ad.* if, though, perhaps.

চেতঃ, *s.* the mind, intellect, the reasoning faculty, understanding, the sensorium.
চেতন, *s.* the soul, understanding, consciousness, intelligence, wisdom, a sensation, reflection, an idea, a sentient being.
চেতনরূপী, *a.* intelligent, sentient.
চেতনা, *s.* sensation, life, feeling, stimulus.
চেতনা -করা, -করাণ, *s.* the act of stimulating, exciting, or admonishing. [alive.
চেতনান্বিত, *a.* intelligent, sensible, sentient,
চেতনেশ্বর, God as the fountain of wisdom.
চেতা, *v. a.* to stimulate, to awaken, to convince, to make a person feel.
চেতান, *s.* the convincing or stimulating of a person : *a.* stimulated, excited.
চেতানি, *s.* stimulation, excitation.
চেতানিয়া, *s.* one who stimulates or excites.
চেৎ, *conj.* if, though : *ad.* although.
চেপ্টা, *a.* compressed, flattened, flat.
চেপ্টানাকা, *a.* flat-nosed, snub-nosed.
চেরা, *v. a.* to cleave, split, tear, to cause to cleave or tear : *a.* torn, split, cleft.
চেরাণ, *s.* the causing to cleave, split, or tear any thing : *a.* split, cleft, torn.
চেরাণি, *s.* a cleaving, splitting, tearing.
চেরাণী, চেরাই, *s.* wages for cleaving or
চেল, *s.* cloth, clothes, garment. [tearing.
চেলনা, *s.* a particular sort of cloth.
চেলা, *v. a.* to hew, to chip : *s.* a chip; a disciple, a scholar, a mate ; a fish.[1]
চেলাকাট, *s.* a chip, a large and long chip.
চেলি, *s.* silken cloth, satin. [washed.
চেলুনী, *s.* water in which rice has been
চেষ্টক, *a.* acting, endeavouring, persevering : *s.* one engaged in an undertaking.
চেষ্টন, *s.* the acting, engaging or endeavouring to do or accomplish a thing.
চেষ্টা, *s.* action, application, exertion, endeavour, labour, pursuit, search, effort; কৃ,- or -পা, to make an effort, to exert.
চেষ্টা -কারক, কারী, *a.* active, exerting, seeking : *s.* one who exerts or seeks.
চেষ্টাচরিত্র, activity, attention to business.
চেষ্টান্বিত, engaged, eager, active, zealous.
চেষ্টিত, *a.* sought, engaged in, laboured for, endeavoured. [sought after
চেষ্টিতব্য, *a.* proper to be laboured for or

চৈ, *s.* a kind of pepper (Piper chuvia.)
চৈচৈ, a *voc. par.* used in calling ducks.
চৈতন্য, *s.* sensation, consciousness, feeling, knowledge, the soul, spirit, a name of God ; the leader of a sect of Hindus.
চৈতন্যকারক, *a.* stimulating, exciting : *s.* he who stimulates or excites to action.
চৈত্য, *s.* a large tree under which a stone or the image of an idol is placed.
চৈত্র, *s.* a Hindu month, part of March and part of April; -রথ, paradise of Kuvera.
চো, *v. n.* to ooze out, to leak, to drop, to drip, to distil, to shed out : *s.* a well.
চোআ, *v. a.* to cause to leak or ooze out: *v. n.* to ooze out : *a.* leaked, oozed.
চোআন, or চোওন, *s.* the oozing, leaking, dripping, or distilling of a liquid.
চোআলি, *s.* the jaws, the jawbone. [cined,
চোঁআ, *v. a.* to burn, calcine : *a.* burnt, cal-
চোঁআন, চোঁয়ান, *s.* burning or calcining of any sort of grain : *a.* calcined, burnt.
চোঁআনি, *s.* calcining of grain to powder.
চোঁকা, *v. a.* to sharpen, whet, to strop or set a razor : *a.* whetted, keen, sharp.
চোঁকান, *s.* the whetting of a knife or other edge tool : *a.* whetted, sharpened.
চোঁকানি, *s.* the whetting of a knife, etc.
চোঁকাল, *a.* whetted, sharp, acute, keen.
চোঁচ, *s.* a splinter, the internal woody fibres of a palm or other tree.
চোঁচা, *v. a.* to strip off seeds, to run (with all the might). *a.* rough (as a writing): *e. g.* a rough copy, a rough draught.
চোঁচাল, *a.* abounding with woody fibres.
চোঁতা, *a.* rough, applied to writings : *e. g.* a rough copy : *s.* a pocket-book.
চোক, *s.* desire, liking, pleasure, *vide* চৌক.
চোকা, *v. a.* to adjust, to settle, whet : *s.* an adjustment : *a.* sharp, strong (as liquor, acid, bitter, etc.) ; adjusted, settled.
চোকাল, চোখাল, *a.* sharp, whetted, keen.
চোখা, *v.* to whet, sharpen ; -রাম, a pimp.
চোখান, *s.* the sharpening of an edge tool.
চোঙ্গা, *s.* a tube, pipe ; a girl (in irony.)
চোট, *s.* a hurt, blow, contusion, stroke, wound; -মার, to wound; -লাগ, to hurt.
চোটখেকুয়া, *a.* wounded, hurt, bruised.

চোটা, *v. a.* to cut, chop, to smite, strike: *s.* usury, an exorbitant rate of interest.
চোটান, *s.* wounding, striking repeatedly.
চোণা, *v.* to expel urine (as a cow): *s.* urine.
চোনন, *s.* a choosing, a selecting, picking.
চোনা, *v. a.* to cause to select: *a.* selected.
চোপ, *s.* a stroke, the stroke of a weapon.
চোপ্‌ষ, *v. n.* to imbibe, to sink (as paper.)
চোপ্‌ষা, *v. a.* to imbibe moisture, to sink (as paper): *a.* imbibed, moist.
চোপ্‌ষান, *s.* sinking (as paper): *a.* imbibed, admitting the ink to sink into it.
চোপ্‌ষানি, *s.* the imbibing of ink by paper.
চোপা, *v. a.* to strike with a weapon, to cause to strike; *s.* the face; the rind.
চোব, *s.* a mace, a staff; -দার, a mace-bearer; -দারী, the office of a mace-bearer.
চোবচিনী, *s.* China root, an aromatic drug,
চোবল, *s.* the attempt of a snake to bite.
চোবা, *s.* rind of a fruit, a tegument, peel.
*চোবুতরা, *s.* a terrace or summer-house; a custom-house; a police-office.
চোয়ালি, চোহালি, *s.* the lower jawbone.
চোর, *s.* a thief, a robber, a pilferer.
চোরকাঁটা,, চোরপুষ্পী, *s.* a kind of grass the seeds of which stick in the clothes.
চোরছিদ্র, *s.* a peep-hole, a crevice.
চোরা, *a.* stolen, clandestine, hidden, secret.
চোরাও, *a.* stolen: *s.* theft, robbery, pilfering.
চোরাগর্ত, *s.* a pitfall, covered pit.
চোরাঘা, চোরাঘাত, *s.* a blow in secret, assassination.
চোরাপথ, *s.* a bye-road.
চোরাবালি, *s.* a quicksand.
চোরী, *s.* theft, robbery, thievery.
চোলক, *s.* a cuirass, armour; rind. [fleece.
চোষ্, *v. a.* to suck, to imbibe, to wring, to fleece.
চোষক, *a.* sucking: *s.* an extortioner, a blood-sucker, one who sucks. [in.
চোষণ, *s.* a sucking, imbibing, drinking in.
চোষা, *v.* to cause to suck: *s.* suction: *a.* sucked.
চোষাণ, *s.* a sucking: *a.* sucked.
চোষাণি, *s.* suction, imbibing.
চোহাড়, *s.* a tribe of mountaineers, savages.
চৌআ, *s.* a square plat of ground dug in order to raise up embankments.
চৌআত্তর, *a.* seventy-four.
চৌআন্ন, *a.* fifty-four.
চৌআল্লিশ, *a.* forty-four.
চৌআল্লিশা, *a.* the forty-fourth.
চৌক, *a.* four: *s.* the eye; in *acct.* four pans marked thus (।•); a square, a market.
চৌকষ, *a.* circumspect, attentive, vigilant.
চৌকষাই, চৌকষী, *s.* circumspection, attention, vigilance, caution, watchfulness.
চৌকা, *s.* a square plat of ground marked out, on which a Hindu dresses his food.
চৌকাঠ, *s.* a door frame.
চৌকালা, *s.* a harpoon with four prongs.
চৌকি, a chair, a bench, a stool; guard, watch; -দা, to mount guard, to watch; -ঘর, -থানা, a watch-house, guardhouse.
চৌকিদার, *s.* a watchman, a sentinel.
চৌকিদারী, *s.* the office of a watchman.
চৌকিপহারা, *s.* a guarding, a watching.
চৌকিয়া, *a.* by fours: *s.* a watchman.
চৌকোণ, *a.* quadrangular, square.
চৌকোণা, *a.* square: *s.* a square.
চৌকোশী, *a.* four kros distance, or in extent.
চৌখোপী, *a.* square, having four roofs.
*চৌগান্, *s.* a kind of play, crickets or cats.
চৌগুণ, চতুর্গুণ, *a.* four-fold.
চৌঘড়ি, *s.* the space of four hours.
চৌঘরা, *a.* having four receptacles.
চৌচাপটে, *ad.* on all sides, all along, flat.
চৌচালা, *s.* a hipped roof, a bungalow.
চৌট, or চৌঠ, *a.* a fourth, one-fourth.
চৌটা, or চৌঠা, *a.* the fourth.
চৌটী, or চৌঠী, *s.* a fourth, a quarter.
চৌড়া, *a.* wide, broad.
চৌড়াই, *s.* width, breadth.
চৌতারা, *a.* four-stringed: *s.* a summer-house.
চৌত্রিশ, thirty-four. চৌত্রিশা, thirty-4th.
চৌথ, চৌথাই, *s.* a fourth part, a quarter.
চৌদিগ, *s.* four quarters of the heavens.
চৌদিগে, *ad.* on all sides, all around.
চৌদোল, *s.* a palankeen, a litter, a pálki.
চৌদ্দ, or চৌদ্দা, *a.* fourteen.
চৌদ্দক্কি, *a.* the fourteenth.
চৌধুরী, *s.* a title of honour indicating chief of four.
চৌপল, চৌপহল, *a.* square: *s.* a square bottle.
চৌপলীয়া, *a.* quadrangular.
চৌপাঠী, *s.* a college, a school, academy.
চৌপাড়, or চৌপাড়ি, *s.* a die, dice.
চৌপাড়িখেলা, *s.* play at dice.

চৌপায়া, *a.* four-footed, quadruped.
চৌপালা, *s.* a pálki, a litter, marriage pálki.
চৌপিঠা, *a.* handy, active, clever, vigilant.
চৌবাচ্চা, *s.* a reservoir, a vat, pit, cistern.
চৌবাড়ী, *s.* a college, a school, academy.
চৌমাথা, *s.* the same as চৌরাহ.
চৌর, *s.* a thief, a robber, a burglar.
চৌরস, *a.* smooth, even, level, flat, plain.
চৌরসী, *s.* smoothness, evenness, level.
চৌরানই, চৌরানব্বই, *a.* ninety-four.
চৌরাশী, *a.* eighty-four. [cross-road.
চৌরাহা, *s.* place where four roads meet, a
চৌরী, or চঁৌরী, *s.* a flyflap: *vide* চামর.
চৌর্য্য, চৌরী, *s.* theft, robbery, burglary.
চৌর্য্যবৃত্তি, *s.* the practice of theft, theft,
চৌসর, *s.* dice, play at dice. [robbery.
চৌহারা, *a.* quadruple, having four folds.
চ্যাঁট, *s.* the male organ of generation.
চ্যাঁটকাটানি, *s.* circumcision. [freed.
চ্যুত, *s.* a mango: *a.* fallen from, dismissed,
চ্যুতি, *s.* dismissal, leave, release, freedom.

ছ, 7th consonant; sounds as *chh* in *much-haste*: *a.* six: *intj.* pugh; -কার, letter ছ.
ছই, *s.* a roof or covering over boats.
ছউক্তি, *a.* the sixth. [board.
ছক, *s.* a square or checker in a chess-
ছক্কাপঞ্জা, *s.* imposition, a trick, deceit, imposture, fraud; *lit.* sice-cinque.
ছককাঠি, *s.* a shell-cutter's tool. [cauris.
ছকড়া, *s.* a bullock-cart, a hackery; six
ছটা, *s.* light, lustre, splendour: *a.* six.
ছটাক, *s.* the sixteenth part of a sera.
ছটাকফটাক, *s.* a chhaták or little more.
ছটক্, ছটকা, *v. n.* to desert, withdraw, fly out (as gun-lock) to spring: *a.* shed out.
ছট্কান, *s.* flying out of a spring or gun-lock; withdrawing from an assembly: *a.* squeezed or forced out, expelled.
ছট্কানি, *s.* a flying out, a withdrawing.
ছট্কানিয়া, *a.* flying out: *s.* a withdrawer.
ছট্কাফট্কা, *a.* speckled, spotted, freckled.
ছট্ফট, *s.* the tossing, turning or struggling of a person in pain, fever, etc., struggling of an animal for its liberty.
ছট্ফটা, *v. a.* to struggle for liberty, to flutter, to toss about in pain.

ছট্ফটান, ছট্ফটানি, *s.* the struggling of an animal for its liberty, the tossing of a person with violent disease or pain.
ছট্ফটিয়া, restless, unsteady, struggling fluttering, tossing and turning.
ছট্ফট্যামি, *s.* a struggling, a fluttering.
ছড়্, *v. n.* to skin, to flay, to fall in a scattered manner, to scatter, to sprinkle.
ছড়, *s.* a spear; flagstaff; a scratch, bruise.
ছড়া, *v. a.* to scatter, strew, to sow seed, to sprinkle, disperse, dissipate, to cause to skin: *s.* a sparkling; a string (of beads,) a cluster, bunch (of plantains).
ছড়াছড়ি, *s.* profusely scattering of things about, waste, a skinning (an animal).
ছড়াঝাঁটি, *s.* a sprinkling and weeping.
ছড়ান, ছড়ন, *s.* a skinning, a flaying, scattering, a throwing about, sprinkling, a dispersing: *a.* scattered, dispersed.
ছড়ানি, *s.* a skinning, flaying, a scattering about, the dispersion of a multitude.
ছড়ানিয়া, *a.* wasteful, lavish, scattering about: *s.* one who flays, a scatterer.
ছড়ী, *s.* a switch, a twig, a thin stick; a distemper which drys up a person. [urine.
ছড়্‌ছড়্, *im. sd.* of the falling of water or
ছত্র, *s.* an umbrella, a fungus, mouldiness.
ছত্রধারী, *a.* holding an umbrella: *s.* a king.
ছত্রভঙ্গ, *s.* a forlorn state, widowhood; anarchy, a loss of empire or dominion.
ছত্রাকার, ছত্রাকৃতি, *a.* like an umbrella, umbrella-formed, umbellate. [umbrella.
ছত্রী, canopied: *s.* tester of a bed, awning,
ছত্রিশ, thirty-six. ছত্রিশা, thirty sixth.
ছদ, *s.* habit, custom; a leaf, blade of grass.
ছদি, *s.* the roof of a house. [disguise.
ছদ্ম, *a.* feigned, disguised: *s.* a covering,
ছদ্মবেশ, *s.* disguise: *a.* disguised, incog.
ছদ্মবেশন, *s.* the putting on of a disguise.
ছদ্মবেশী, *a.* appearing in disguise, assuming a fictitious character: *s.* a player.
ছদ্মরূপী, *a.* acting a concealed part.
ছদ্মরূপে, *ad.* in disguise, incognito.
ছন্দ, *s.* the veda, a verse, metre, poetry, the measure of a verse, cadence.
ছন্দস্, *s.* poetical metre, the measure of the veda, the veda.

ছন্দোগ, *s.* one who sings the Sáma veda; also, the name of a grammar.
ছন্ন, *a.* covered, concealed, secret, solitary, private; foolish; -বেশী, *vide* ছদ্মবেশী.
ছপ্পর, *s.* a thatched roof, tester of a bed.
ছবি, *s.* a drawing, picture, a portrait; beauty, splendour, brilliance, lustre.
ছবিকর, *s.* a picture-painter, a limner.
ছমছম্, *s.* perturbation of the mind.
ছয়, *a.* six; -রিপু, the six vital enemies of mankind, viz. কাম, lust; ক্রোধ, anger; লোভ, covetousness; মোহ, fascination; মদ, pride and মাৎসর্য্য, envy, malice.
ছর্কট্, *v. n.* to splash, to scatter, to break: *v. a.* to throw about, to splash about.
ছর্দ্দি, *s.* a vomiting, a belching.
ছল্, *v. a.* to impose upon, to deceive.
ছল, *s.* contrivance, stratagem, pretence, artifice, pretext, deceit, a trick, a plot.
ছলগ্রাহক, ছলগ্রাহী, *a.* suspecting a person to be an impostor: *s.* one so suspects; an impostor, a cheat, swindler, sharper.
ছলন, *s.* the using of pretences, the imposing upon or cheating of a person.
ছলনা, *s.* a pretence, a trick, a deception, circumvention, fraud. [sharper.
ছলনিয়া, *a.* swindling: *s.* a cheat, swindler,
ছলী, *a. idem*; also a blotch, a scab.
ছলছল্, *a.* watery, flowing, gushing out;
ছষট্টি, *a.* sixty-six. -কৃ, to gush out.
ছা, *v. a.* to thatch, to bottom a chair or bedstead: *s.* the young of an animal.
ছাই, *s.* ashes. [water (when raining).
ছাইট, *s.* a whip, scourge; a beating in of
ছাউনি, *s.* a camp, an encampment, barracks, an awning, a tent, covering of a drum with skin, the bottoming of a chair or bedstead, thatching of house.
ছাউনীতলা, *s.* the space under an awning.
ছাওয়াল, ছ'ওয়াল, *s.* a child, a boy. [hood.
ছাওলামি, *s.* childishness, childhood, boy-
ছাঁ, *s.* a shade, shadow, shelter. [sift.
ছাঁক, *v. a.* to strain, to filtrate, percolate,
ছাঁকন, *s.* straining, filtering, draining off.
ছাঁকনা, *s.* lees; a strainer, a sieve.
ছাঁকনিয়া, *s.* one who strains or sifts.
ছাঁকনী, *s.* a strainer, a sieve, a colander.
ছাঁকা, *v. a.* to cause to strain: *a.* strained.
ছাঁচ, *s.* forming of the fœtus, or of eggs in the womb; a mould; a model, likeness.
ছাঁচনী, *s.* a churning stick.
ছাঁচি, *s.* the eaves of a house.
ছাঁচিখড়, *s.* the thatching grass called উলু.
ছাঁচিতলা, *s.* the space under the eaves.
ছাঁচিপান, *s.* a fine variety of betel-leaf.
ছাঁচুয়া, *a.* cast in a mould, mould-made.
ছাঁট্, *v. a.* to lop off, trim; to clean husked rice: *s.* the cuttings of paper or cloth.
ছাঁটন, *s.* a lopping, a trimming, a clipping of paper, etc., a cleaning of husked rice.
ছাঁদ্, *v. a.* to tie the legs of a cow to prevent its kicking when milked. [ters.
ছাঁদ, *s.* poetical metre, the strokes of let-
ছাঁদন, or ছাঁদনি, *s.* the tying the legs of a cow to prevent kicking when milked.
ছাঁদনদড়ী, *s.* a cord used to tie the legs of
ছাক, *v. a.* to strain, to sift. [a cow.
ছাকন, *s.* the act of sifting or straining.
ছাকনি, *s.* a strainer, a sieve, a colander.
ছাকনী, *s.* one who strains liquor. [clear.
ছাকা, *v. a.* to cause to strain: *a.* strained,
ছাগ, *s.* a goat, he-goat; -বলি, sacrifice of a goat; -মাংস, goat's flesh; *fem.* ছাগী.
ছাগল, *s.* a goat; -নাদি, dunga of goats.
ছাগলগোজিয়া, *a.* goatish, letcherous.
ছাগলাদ, *s.* a medicine made of a hermaphrodite goat and other ingredients.
ছাট, ছাটন, the same as ছাঁট, ছাঁটন.
ছাট, *s.* a switch to strike grasshoppers.
ছাটন, *s.* a clipping, a trimming, cleaning.
ছাটনি, *s.* the clippings of paper or cloth.
ছাটা, *v. a.* to cause to clip or trim a thing, or to lop a tree, to cause to husk rice: *a.* clipped, lopped, cleaned from the husk.
ছাটান, *s.* a causing to clip, trim or lop a tree, a causing to cleanse rice: *a.* clipped, shorn, trimmed, lopped, cleansed.
ছাটানী, *s.* a causing to clip, trim, etc.
ছাড়্, *v.* to relinquish, to abandon, desert, evacuate, to leave off, depart from, to abate, to unloose, discharge, withdraw, liberate, emancipate, divorce (a wife).
ছাড়চিঠী, ছাড়লিপি, *s.* a release, a passport, a clearance for goods.

ছাড়ন, *s.* the relinquishing or abandoning of an undertaking, or of a habit, the loosing of a person or animal.
ছাড়া, *v. n.* to procure the release of any one, to object, discharge, rescue, extricate, to separate, disperse, to cashier.
ছাড়া, *s.* a releasing, relinquishing: *a.* left, excepted, deserted: *e. g.* লক্ষ্মীছাড়া, deserted by fortune, unfortunate. [tion.
ছাড়াছাড়ি, mutual relinquishing, separa-
ছাড়ান, *s.* the setting of a prisoner or an animal at liberty, act of extricating, redeeming, discharging, or separating.
ছাড়ানি, *s.* relinquishment, liberation, a release, extrication ; a key. [leasing.
ছাড়ানিয়া, *a.* relinquishing, liberating, re-
ছাত, *s.* the flat roof of a house, a terrace.
ছাতা, *s.* an umbrella, a parasol; a fungus, a mushroom, mouldiness.
ছাতাটিয়া, ছাতাপড়া, *a.* mouldy, fungous.
ছাতাবরদার, *s.* an umbrella-bearer.
ছাতার, ছাতারিয়া, *s.* the name of a bird.
ছাতি, *s.* an umbrella ; the breast, bosom.
ছাতিবালা, *s.* one who carries an umbrella.
ছাতী, *s.* the bosom, the breast, courage, boldness ; an umbrella. [of pulse.
ছাতু, *s.* barley meal, meal of several sorts
ছাত্র, *s.* a scholar, a pupil, a disciple, stu-
ছান্, *v. n.* to knead, to mould. [dent.
ছানন, *s.* the kneading of dough or earth.
ছানা, *v. a.* to knead, strain water (for fishing): *s.* the young of an animal; cream or curds of milk : *a.* moulded, kneaded.
ছানাছানি, *s.* mutual kneading of dough.
ছানাপোরা, *s.* a sort of sweetmeat.
ছানী, *s.* a cataract in the eye, a film or speck on the eye. [of the veda.
ছান্দস, pertaining to the veda : *s.* a teacher
ছাপ, *v. a.* to print, to impress a figure, to skulk, to quash, to overflow.
ছাপ, *s.* a die, a stamp, a seal, a press, an engraved block for printing calico.
ছাপন, *s.* imprinting of a mark, the act of printing, a printing of calicoes; hiding.
ছাপর, *s.* tester of a bed, a thatched roof, a roof over a boat ; -খাট, a bedstead.
ছাপরী, *s.* a paper mould, a strainer.

ছাপা, *v. a.* to cause to be printed, to conceal or suppress anything, to overflow.
ছাপা, *s.* a printing, concealment, suppression : *a.* printed, suppressed, concealed; -কর, a printer, calico-printer; -কল, lithograph or printing press; -খানা, printing-office; -বালা, a printer, a pressman.
ছাপান, *s.* the causing to be printed, the concealing or suppressing of a thing.
ছাপানিয়া, *a.* suppressing, clandestine.
ছাপাযন্ত্র, *s.* lithographic press, a printing
ছাপী, *a.* concealed, suppressed. [press.
ছাপ্পান্ন, *a.* fifty-six. [hood.
ছাবলামি, *s.* childishness, childhood, boy-
ছাবা, *v. a.* to cause to thatch a house, or bottom a chair : *a.* thatched, bottomed.
ছাবান, *s.* a causing to be covered, thatched, or bottomed : *a.* thatched, bottomed.
ছাবানি, *s.* a thatching, a bottoming.
ছাবানী, *s.* due for thatching or bottoming.
ছাবাল, *s.* a child, a boy ; -কাল, childhood,
ছাব্বিশ, *a.* twenty-six. [infancy.
ছাব্বিশা, *a.* the twenty-sixth.
ছায়া, *s.* shade, shadow, covert, refuge, an apparition, reflection ; a petticoat. [dy.
ছায়াটিয়া, ছায়াম্বিত, *a.* umbrageous, sha-
ছায়াপদ, *s.* noting time by shadow. [lite.
ছায়াবৎ, *a.* shadow-like : *s.* attendant, satel-
ছায়ামণ্ডপ, *s.* a house or place built for shade, the space covered by an awning.
ছায়াযুক্ত, ছায়াবায়ু, *a.* shady, umbrageous.
ছার, *a.* vile as asses, abominable, hateful.
ছারকপাল, *s.* bad luck, misfortune.
ছারকপালিয়া, ill-fated, unlucky. [ashes.
ছারখার, *s.* ruin : *a.* ruined, reduced to
ছারপোকা, *s.* a bug (Cimex lictularia).
ছাল, *s.* bark, peel, rind, skin, leather, an integument ; -উঠা, or -তোল, to peel.
ছালন, *s.* sauce, stew, curry. [ring.
ছালনা, *s.* an awning for a wedding ; toe-
ছালনাতলা, *s.* the space under the awning.
ছালা, *s.* a pair of sacks borne by oxen, a pair of panniers, a sack, a bag, a wallet.
ছালিয়া, *s.* a child ; -পিলিয়া, children.
ছাল্টি, *s.* grasscloth ; a canoe of Sál tree.
ছি, or ছিছি, *intj.* fie ! for shame !
ছিঁক, *s.* a sneezing : *v. a.* to sneeze.

ছিঁচ্কা, *s.* a skewer, a thin rod of iron or bambu used to clean the huká tube.
ছিঁচড়্, *v. a.* to drag along the ground.
ছিঁড়্, *v. n.* to tear or rend of itself: *v. a.* to tear, to rend, to pluck. [custom.
ছিঁড়, ছিঁড়নি, *s.* a water-course, a habit, a
ছিঁড়ন, *s.* the act of tearing, a plucking, a
ছিঁড়া, *a.* torn, rent, divided, cut. [tearing.
ছিড়াছিঁড়ি, *s.* mutual plucking or tearing.
ছিকল, *v. a.* to link together, to furbish: *s.*
ছিকলি, *s.* a chain, a link. [a chain, link.
ছিক্কা, *s.* a sneeze, a sneezing.
ছিচকাচোর, *s.* a petty thief, a pilferer.
ছিচকাঁদনিয়া, *a.* peevish, crying for trifles.
ছিট্, *v. a.* to sprinkle, sow seed, to work lattice-work, or the like. [remainder.
ছিট, *s.* chintz; a remnant, a balance, a
ছিটন, *s.* sprinkling, scattering about (of seed): the working of lattice-work.
ছিটনি, *s. idem;* also, a slender rod.
ছিটনিয়া, *s.* one who does lattice-work.
ছিটা, *v. a.* to sprinkle, to strew, to scatter about: *s.* shot, a particle, a drop, atom.
ছিটাগুলি, *s.* shot, gun shot. [ing.
ছিটান, *s.* act of sprinkling or scatter-
ছিটানি, *s.* a sprinkling, aspersion.
ছিটক্, *v. a.* to fly up with a jerk, to throw by a jerk, to jet, to spatter, to sputter, rebound. ছিট্‌কিয়া উঠন, to rebound.
ছিট্‌কন, *s.* the act of spattering, the flying of a thing with a sudden jerk.
ছিটকা, *v. a.* to sprinkle, to fly with a sudden jerk, to jet: *s.* a sling, a slip-knot.
ছিট্‌কান, *s.* the besprinkling of any thing, the flying up with a sudden jerk.
ছিট্‌কী, *s.* a very slender rod, a switch.
ছিট্‌কীনী, *s.* a bolt for a door or window.
ছিদ্র, *s.* a hole, a perforation, a fissure, a fault, a blemish, a flaw, a defect.
ছিদ্রান্বেষী, *a.* seeking for the faults of
ছিন্, *v. a.* to snatch, to seize. [others.
ছিনকুটিয়া, *a.* full of knots. [detaining.
ছিনন, *s.* the seizing of a person or thing,
ছিনা, *v. a.* to shoulder, to strike violently: *s.* the corner of a building or masonry.
ছিনাল, *s.* a strumpet, a whore, a harlot.
ছিনালপনা, ছিনালী, *s.* whoredom, harlotry.

ছিন্ন, *a.* cut, severed, torn, cut down, cut
ছিন্নকর্ণ, *a.* having the ears cut off. [off.
ছিন্নকেশ, *a.* shorn, having the hair cut.
ছিন্নকেশর, *a.* having the mane cropped.
ছিন্ননাসিক, *a.* having the nose cut off.
ছিন্নপাদ, *a.* having the legs cut off.
ছিন্নভিন্ন, *a.* severed, scattered, dispersed.
ছিন্নমস্তক, *a.* decapitated, headless.
ছিন্নমস্তা, *s.* a name of the goddess Kálí.
ছিন্নমূল, *a.* cut down by the root. [off.
ছিন্নহস্ত, *a.* maimed, having the hands cut
ছিপ, *v.* to conceal, hide: *s.* a fishing rod.
ছিপন, *s.* a hiding, a concealing one's self.
ছিপান, *s.* a concealing, hiding, a suppressing: *a.* hidden, concealed, suppressed.
ছিপিকর, *s.* a calico-printer.
ছিপিখানা, *s.* a calico printing factory.
ছিপী, *s.* a cork, a stopple, a stopper.
ছিপ্‌লিয়া, ছিবলা, *s.* a lad, a youngster.
ছিবড়া, *s.* refuse of an article which has been chewed, or the juice extracted.
ছিম, or শিম, *s.* a kidney-bean.
ছিমড়া, ছিমড়ী, *s.* a legume, shell of a pea;
ছিয়াত্তর, *s.* seventy-six. [an orphan.
ছিয়াত্তরীয়া, *a.* pertaining to seventy-six (or to the dreadful famine of Bengal and Behar in the Higira year 1176).
ছিয়ানই, ছিয়ানব্বই, *a.* ninety-six.
ছিয়াশী, *a.* eighty-six.
ছিল্, *v. a.* to strip off the bark, to peel.
ছিলকা, *s.* a peel, a rind, a bark, a husk.
ছিলন, *s.* a peeling, a stripping off bark.
ছিলা, *s.* a bow-string. [pipe; a huká.
ছিলিম, *s.* the bowl of a huká or tobacco
ছিলিমিলি, *s.* a necklace worn by fakirs.
ছিল্ল, *s.* peevishness, great irritability.
ছুঁ, *v. a.* to touch, to come in contact.
ছুঁচ, *s.* a needle, a thin bambu rod used in thatching: *v. a.* to wash the posteriors.
ছুঁচা, ছুঁছা, চিক্কা, *s.* the musk-rat.
ছুঁচাল, *a.* pointed, having a sharp point.
ছুঁচি, *s.* a lying as if inattentive or dead; -পাত, to watch, to lie in wait.
ছুঁচিপাতন, *s.* a watching, a lying in wait.
ছুঁচিয়াবুক্কাল, *s.* the whipthong snake.
ছুঁড়ী, ছুকরী, *s.* a girl. [of any thing.
ছুঁবন, *s.* a coming in contact, the touching

ছুট্, *v. n.* to be discharged, to fly as a ball, to escape, to run away, to break loose.
ছুটকী, *a. fem.* younger.
ছুটন, *s.* a running away, escaping, a flying off.
ছুটনি, *s.* the flying of a bullet, an escape.
ছুটা, *v. a.* to loosen, dispel, fire a gun or crackers: *a.* unconfined, loose.
ছুটাছুটি, *s.* a running speedily, a running about.
ছুটান, *s.* the loosening of a thing, liberating of a person : *a.* let loose, escaped.
ছুটানী, *s.* liberation, exemption, escape.
ছুটালিয়া, *a.* peddling; -ব্যবসায়ী, a pedlar.
ছুটী, *s.* a discharge, a release, a dismission, a furlough, vacation, leave of absence.
ছুড়্, *v. a.* to liberate, to throw, to pelt, to cast away, to discharge or fire a gun.
ছুড়ন, *s.* the discharging of an arrow or ball, a pelting, a throwing.
ছুৎ, *s.* contagion, a touch, a contact.
ছুত, **ছুতা**, *s.* a pretence, an artifice, an excuse.
ছুতল, *s.* a sharper, a swindler.
ছুতার, *s.* a carpenter; -মেস্ত্রী, master-joiner.
ছুনী, *a.* small, very small.
ছুপ্, *v. a.* to press down, to prevail over, to exceed.
ছুপন, *s.* a pressing down, a subduing.
ছুরিকা, **ছুরী**, *s.* a knife; also, a penknife.
ছুল্, *v. a.* to skin, flay, to pare off, prune.
ছুলি, *s.* a kind of blotches on the body.
ছুহারা, *s.* the Arab dried date-fruit.
ছে, *s.* a cut, piece cut off, striking of the pedal when cleansing corn.
ছেআ, *v. a.* to cut into pieces : *s.* a piece cut off.
ছেআনি, *s.* an interval, an intermission, a stop; -দা, to desist, to intermit, stop.
ছেআশী, *a.* eighty-six.
ছেই, *intj.* fie! avaunt! out! go out! away!
ছেঁওড়, *s.* an orphan. [*vide* ছেআনি.
ছেঁক, *v. a.* to foment; to obstuct, stop : *s.*
ছেঁকন, *s.* a stop, a stopping; a fomenting.
ছেঁকা, *s.* a searing, a cauterizing; -দা, to sear, to cauterize, to burn.
ছেঁকচা, *a.* burning hot, burnt with a hot iron.
ছেঁকচাপোড়া, *a.* half burnt, seared.
ছেঁকচি, **ছেঁচকী**, *s.* a dish made of vegetables.
ছেঁচ্, *v. a.* to throw water from a pond, to bale the water from a boat; to bruise.
ছেঁচকা, *s.* an iron skewer, a thin iron rod.
ছেঁচড়্, *s.* a pilferer, a petty thief, a knave.
ছেঁচড়া, *v. a.* to drag: *a.* shameless, low, vile, base : *s.* a bad debtor, a knave, cheat.
ছেঁচড়াছেঁচড়ি, *s.* a mutual dragging.
ছেঁচড়ান, *s.* the dragging of any thing.
ছেঁচড়ামি, *s.* pilfering, vileness, baseness.
ছেঁচড়ী, *a. fem.* vile, base: *s.* a bad debtor.
ছেঁচন, *s.* a bruising; a baling of water.
ছেঁচা, *v. a.* to cause to throw the water out of a pond, to cause to bale a boat, to cause to bruise : *a.* baled out, bruised.
ছেঁচাছেঁচি, *s.* a mutual baling or bruising.
ছেঁচান, *s.* causing to throw out the water of a pond or boat, a causing to bruise.
ছেঁচানি, *s.* the act of baling, a bruising.
ছেঁচোড়্, *s.* a pilferer, petty thief, a knave.
ছেঁড়া, *v. a.* to tear, to rend : *a.* rent, torn.
ছেঁড়াছেঁড়ি, *s.* a reciprocal tearing.
ছেঁদা, *s.* a hole, perforation: *a.* perforated, torn; -কৃ, to perforate, to bore a hole.
ছেক্, *v. a.* to foment, to sear; to arrest, to stop, cease, desist, intermit; *s.* an interval of time, a cessation.
ছেকতড়কে, *ad.* at intervals, by fits and starts.
ছেকন, *s.* a desisting, an intermitting.
ছেটন, **ছেটা**, the same as ছিটন, ছিটা.
ছেদ, *s.* a cut, a hole, the space between words in writing, a pause, an interval.
ছেদন, *s.* the act of cutting, a perforating.
ছেদনীয়, *a.* capable of being cut or perforated, separable, divisible.
ছেনা, *s.* cream, curds; -ভাজা, fried cream.
ছেনাপোরা, **ছেনাবড়া**, a kind of sweetmeat.
ছেপ, *s.* spittle, saliva; -দা, -ফেল, to spit.
ছেমুয়া, *a.* snappish, snarling: *s.* an idiot.
ছেয়াত্তর, **ছেয়াত্তরীয়া**, *vide* ছিয়াত্তর, &c.
ছেয়ানই, **ছেয়ানব্বই**, *a.* ninety-six.
ছেলিয়া, *s.* a child, infant; -খেলা, childish play; -কাল, -বেলা, childhood, infancy.
ছেলিয়াপিলিয়া, *s.* children, young family.
ছেলিয়াম, **ছেলিয়ামি**, *s.* childishness.
ছেলী, *s.* a goat; the spots on the skin of a deer or other animal; a blotch.
ছেলীপড়া, *a.* speckled, spotted, freckled.
ছেষট্টি, *a.* sixty-six.
ছোঁ, *s.* a pouncing, a darting at; -মার্, to pounce, to dart at (as a kite does).

ছোঁআ, *v.a.* to cause to touch, to bring into contact: *a.* touched: *s.* a scare-crow.
ছোঁআচ, unclean, menstruous, contagious.
ছোঁআন, *s.* a causing to touch, the bringing of things into contact: *a.* touched.
ছোঁচ, *v.* to wash the posteriors after evacuation: *a.* greedy: *s.* a musk-rat. [riors.
ছোঁচান, ছোঁচানি, *s.* a washing of the poste-
ছোঁচানী, *s.* the water in which the posteriors has been washed after evacuation.
ছোঁচামি, *s.* greediness, ravenousness.
ছোঁছোঁ, smelling about (for food or gain).
ছোঁড়া, *s.* a boy, a chap, a brat; *fem.* ছুঁড়ী
ছোঁয়া, ছোঁয়ান, *vide* ছুঁ, ছোঁআ, ছোঁআন.
ছোকরা, *s.* a boy; -বাজ, a sodomite; -বাজী,
ছোকরী, *s.* a girl; a slave girl. [sodomy.
ছোট্, *s.* any thing with which to tie.
ছোট, *a.* small, little, trivial, petty, mean, low, younger, humble; -লোক, a plebeian.
ছোটক্ষীরই, *s.* the name of a plant.[1]
ছোটদৃষ্টি, *a.* short-sighted: *s.* meanness.
ছোটন, *s.* the emitting of any thing.
ছোটনোণিয়া, *s.* species of purslain.[2]
ছোটবউ, *s.* a youngest brother's wife, the youngest of a man's wives.
ছোটমা, *s.* a father's youngest wife; riches, the goddess of prosperity. [indicum).
ছোটমেথী, *s.* a plant, its seed (Trifolium
ছোটমোট, *a.* small, little, diminutive.
ছোটলঙ্কা, *s.* capsicum minimum.
ছোটশিকার, *s.* a hare, wild hare.
ছোটা, *v. a.* to set free, to unloose, to send forth, to emit: *a.* let loose, discharged, emitted: *s.* any thing with which to tie.
ছোটান, *s.* the setting any one at liberty, a sending away, the discharging of a gun: *a.* liberated, turned loose.
ছোটিকা, *s.* a snap of the finger.
ছোড়্, *v. a.* to fire a gun: *a.* shooting: *e. g.* গোলা ছোড়্, shooting a bullet.
ছোড়ন, *s.* firing off, discharging of a gun.
ছোড়া, *v. a.* to discharge an arrow, to fire a gun: *a.* discharged from a bow or gun.
ছোড়ান, ছোড়ানী, *s.* a key. [juice, a colour.
ছোপ, *s.* a stain or mark with vegetable
ছোপা, *v. a.* to impress a mark, to dye, to print calicoes: *a.* stained, coloured.
ছোপান, *s.* the dyeing or staining of cloth: *a.* stained, marked, coloured. [cloth.
ছোপানী, *s.* the staining or colouring of
ছোবড়া, *s.* the external coat of cocoanut and other palms, the peel of a plantain.
ছোবল, *s.* the attempt of a snake to bite.
ছোরা, *s.* a large knife, a stiletto, a dagger.
ছোল্, *v. n.* to pare, scrape, peel, to skin.
ছোলন, *s.* a peeling, a paring, a flaying.
ছোলা, *v. a.* to cause to pare off, to scrape: *s.* a kind of pulse:[3] *a.* pared, scraped.
ছ্যা, *intj.* fie! for shame! avaunt!

জ, the 8th consonant; in *comp.* it signifies born, produced; -কার, the letter জ.
জক্মকিয়া, vexed, enraged, provoked, non-
জখম, *s.* an ulcer, wound, hurt. [plused.
*জখমী, *a.* full of ulcers, wounded.
জগচ্ছাসন, *s.* the government of the world.
জগচ্ছাস্তা, *s.* the governor of the world.
জগজ্জনক, *s.* the creator of the world.
জগজ্জননী, *s.* Durgá, mother of the world.
জগঝম্প, *s.* a sort of musical instrument.
জগৎ, *s.* the world, the universe.
জগৎকর্ত্তা, *s.* the governor of the world.
জগত্তারক, জগত্রাতা, *s.* the saviour of the
জগদন্ত, *s.* the end of the world. [world.
জগদন্তক, *a.* world-destroying.
জগদম্বা, *s.* the same as জগজ্জননী. [world.
জগদাত্মক, *a.* identically the same with the
জগদাদি, *s.* the beginning of the world.
জগদাধার, *s.* the air, wind, the supporter or stay of the universe.
জগদাধারকর্ত্তা, *s.* the God of providence.
জগদীশ, জগদীশ্বর, *s.* the Lord of the world, an appellation of Vishnu and Shiva.
জগদীশ্বরী, *s.* a name of Durgá, meaning the queen of the world. [form.
জগদ্ধাত্রী, *s.* a name of Durgá in peculiar
জগদ্যোনি, *s.* a name of Shiva, the earth.
জগন্নাথ, *s.* the Lord of the world, one of the names of Vishnu.
জগন্নাথক্ষেত্র, *s.* the place of the famous temple of Jagannáth in Uṛissá. [good.
জগন্মঙ্গল, *s.* good of the world, the public
জগন্মোহন, *a.* fascinating the world: *s.* the proper name of a man.

জগন্মোহিনী, *a.* fascinating the world : *s.* enchantress or fascinatrix of the world.

*জগহ্, *s.* a place, ground, land.

*জগাৎ, *s.* custom, duty on goods, tribute.

জগাতী, *s.* a collector of the customs.

জগ্‌জগা, *s.* a glittering, shining; leaf-brass.

জঘন, *s.* the hip and loins.

জঘন্য, *a.* last, ultimate, low, vile, base.

জঘন্যজ, *s.* a sudra : *a.* low-born, base.

জঘন্যতা, *s.* baseness, lowness, meanness.

জঙ্গিজাম, *s.* the name of a tree.[1]

জঙ্গম, *a.* movable, removable.

জঙ্গল, *a.* wild, desert : *s.* a forest, wilderness, a thicket, bush, weeds in a field.

জঙ্গলময়, *a.* abounding with wilderness, covered with weeds and bushes.

জঙ্গলাট, *a.* wild, desert, bushy, waste, un-

জঙ্গলী, *a.* wild, sylvan. [cultivated.

জঙ্গাল, *s.* a limit, a boundary, a ridge or balk in rice fields, an embankment.

জঙ্গুল, *s.* poison, venom.

জঙ্ঘা, *s.* the thigh, the leg. [fleet.

জঙ্ঘাল, *a.* marching quick, walking well,

জঙ্ঘোয়া, *s.* short-drawers, breeches.

জজ্‌বজ্, *a.* superabundant, enough, sufficient, plenty, as much as desired.

জঞ্জাল, *s.* trouble, disorder, confusion, misfortune; rubbish, sweepings, refuse.

জঞ্জালিয়া, *a.* troublesome, mischievous.

*জিঞ্জীর, *s.* a chain, shackles, fetters.

জট, *s.* the matted hair of a devotee.

জটলা, *s.* a crowd of people, an assembly.

জটা, *s.* clotted hair of an ascetic, the root of a plant, roots which descend from the branches of the Ficus indica.

জটাকর, *a.* clotting or matting the hair.

জটাজুট, *s.* the clotted hair of Shiva.

জটাধর, জটাধারী, wearing a head of clotted hair: *s.* a devotee; a name of Shiva.

জটামাংসী, *s.* the Indian spikenard.[2]

জটিয়া, জটিল, জটিলা, *a.* wearing matted hair.

জটিয়াবুড়ি, *s.* an old woman with dishevelled matted hair (a bugbear for children).

জটিলাকুটিলা, *s.* the mother and sister of Ayán Ghosa, husband of Rádhá.

জটু, জটুক, *s.* a freckle, spots on the body.

জঠর, *s.* the belly, the womb.

জঠরজ্বালা, জঠরপীড়া, *s* hunger; a pain in the bowels, the colic. [childbirth.

জঠরযন্ত্রণা, জঠরযাতনা, *s.* the throe, pain of

জঠরস্থ, *a.* being or existing in the womb.

জড়্, *v. a.* to wind into a ball, to entangle, to intertwine, to wrap round.

জড়, *a.* stupid, decrepit, inactive, cold, benumbed, collected, crowded, heaped together : *s.* a root, an origin ; -কৃ, to collect, to amass, to heap together.

জড়ক্রিয়, *a.* indolent, procrastinating.

জড়তা, -ত্ব, *s.* stupidity, idiocy, decrepitude, inactivity, benumbedness, frigidity.

জড়ভরত, *s.* a stupid person, an idiot.

জড়মড়, *a.* gathered, collected, contracted.

জড়া, *v. a.* to wrap round, to wind into a ball, to interlace, to cling to, to overlay, to plate, to set precious stones.

জড়াউ, or জড়াও *a.* ornamented, overlayed with gold, set with precious stones.

জড়াজড়ি, *s.* a clinging round each other.

জড়ান, *s.* a winding round, a clinging to: *a.* wound, clasped round, clung to.

জড়ানমড়ান, *a.* rolled, wrapped round.

জড়ানি, *s.* the winding or wrapping of a thing, a clinging to, an interlacing.

জড়ানিয়া, *a.* winding, interlacing : *s.* one who winds or interlaces things.

জড়ানিয়াকল, *s.* a winch, winding machine.

জড়িত, *a.* set with gems, studded, crowded.

জড়িতবাক্য, *s.* crowded talk, sputtered lan-

জড়িবটী, *s.* medicines, drugs. [guage.

জড়িমা, *s.* stupefaction decrepitude, stiffness, congelation, numbness, idiocy.

জড়ীকৃত, *a.* stupified, made insensible or decrepit, reduced to idiocy, congealed, frozen, benumbed, made rigid.

জড়ীভূত, *a.* become stupid, inactive or decrepit, frozen, congealed, benumbed.

জড়ুর, *s.* a freckle, a spot, an eruption.

জড়েমাড়েট, *ad.* wholly, root and branch, completely, entirely, in the gross.

জড়্‌জড়ানী, *s.* viscidity, stickiness.

জড়্‌জড়িয়া, *a.* viscid, tenacious, sticky.

জতু, *s.* lac ; -গৃহ, a house made of lac.

জতুক, *s.* lac, asafœtida, a freckle, a spot.

জতুমণি, *s.* a freckle, a mark on the body.

জন, *s.* a person, a man, individual.

জনক, *a.* producing, causing, begetting: *s.* a father; in *mytho.* the father of Sitá.

জনকতা, -ত্ব, *s.* causality, fatherhood.

জনতা, জনসমূহ, *s.* a multitude, a crowd.

জনন, *s.* birth, production, the producing

জননী, জনয়িত্রী, *s.* a mother. [of a thing.

জনপদ, *s.* any inhabited country, a region.

জনপদাধ্যক্ষ, *s.* the governor of a country.

জনপ্রিয়, *a.* popular, esteemed by all.

জনমানব, *s.* people, men, mankind.

জনম, *s.* birth, production. [king.

জনমেজয়, *s.* the son of Parikshita, a Hindu

জনরব, *s.* a rumour, a report, fame.

জনলোক, *s.* one of the Hindu paradises.

জনশ্রুতি, *s.* a report, a rumour, town-talk.

জনসমূহ, জনতা, *s.* a multitude, a crowd.

*জনাজ়া, *s.* a corpse, a funeral.

জনাজাত, *a.* specifying each person.

*জ়নানা, *s.* a seraglio: *a.* female, relating

জনার, *s.* a species of grain.[1] [to woman.

জনার্দ্দন, *s.* one of the names of Krishna.

জনিত, *a.* born, begot, produced, caused.

জনেজনে, *ad.* individually, one by one.

জন্তু, *s.* an animal; -বিদ্যা, zoology.

জন্তুব্যবচ্ছেদবিদ্যা, *s.* in *ana.* zootomy.

*জ়িন্দার, *a.* alive, living, existing.

জন্ম্, *v. a.* to be born, to be produced.

জন্ম, *s.* birth, production; -দা, to cause to produce, to beget; -লও, to be born.

জন্মকালীন, জন্মগত, *a.* inherent, hereditary.

জন্মতিথি, *s.* a birth-day by the lunar time.

জন্মদাতা, *s.* a father, a parent, one who be-

জন্মদিন, *s.* a birth-day, day of birth. [gets.

জন্মদোষ, *s.* a fault or blemish of birth.

জন্মন, *s.* a being born, a resulting from.

জন্মফের, *s.* transformation, regeneration.

জন্মবৈলক্ষণ্য, *s.* a change or defect in birth.

জন্মভূমি, *s.* a birth-place, a natal soil.

জন্মশোধ, *s.* the great end of life, the paying of the debt of nature, death.

জন্মস্থ, জন্মস্থিত, *a.* connected with birth.

জন্মস্থান, *s.* a native place, a birth-place.

জন্মা, *v. a.* to produce, beget, bring forth, to propagate, to invent, create, cause.

জন্মান, *s.* a producing, a propagating, begetting, the inventing of a thing.

জন্মান্তর, *s.* another birth, a future birth.

জন্মান্তরার্জ্জিত, acquired in a former birth.

জন্মান্তরে, *ad.* in another birth.

জন্মান্ধ, *a.* born blind, born without sight.

জন্মাবধি, *a.* from a person's birth.

জন্মাবা, *s.* the producing of a thing.

জন্মাবামাত্র, *ad.* as soon as it was produced.

জন্মার্জ্জিত, *a.* acquired by a person's birth.

জন্মাষ্টমী, *s.* the birth-day of Krishna.

জন্মিবা, *s.* being born, a being produced.

জন্য, *a.* producible, caused by, arising from: *s.* a cause, a motive, reason.

জন্যে, *ad.* on account of, because, for.

জপ্, *v. a.* to repeat the name of a god, to mutter over prayers. [a prayer.

জপ, *s.* the repetition of prayers, a praying,

জপনিষ্ঠ, *a.* engaged in repeating prayers.

জপনিষ্ঠতা, *s.* engagedness in the prayers.

জপনীয়, *a.* worthy of being repeated. [ry.

জপমালা, জপবটী, *s.* a prayer beads, a rosa-

জপা, *v. a.* to cause to repeat the name of any god, to instigate: *s.* the repetition of prayers; a flowering shrub.[2]

জপান, *s.* the inducing of a person to repeat the name of a god, instigation.

জপ্য, *a.* worthy of being repeated.

জব, *s.* barley. *Properly* যব.

*জ়বর, *a* above, powerful, strong, proud; -দস্ত, supreme, forcible, powerful,; -দস্তি জ়বরী, force, coercion, compulsion.

জবাঁমর্দ, *a.* young, active, alert, agile: *s.* a young man, a hero. [ness, heroism.

জবাঁমর্দী, *s.* youth, agility, activity, alert-

জবান্, *a.* young, active, alert, agile.

*জ়বান্, *s.* the tongue, a language, speech.

জ়বানবন্দি, *s.* a written deposition.

জ়বানী, *a.* verbal, expressed by the tongue.

জবানী, *s.* youth, activity, agility, alert-

জবাব, *s.* an answer, a reply. [ness.

জবাবী, *s.* one who answers: *a.* answering,

জব্জব্, *s.* wetness, dampness. [replying.

জবজবীয়া, *a.* wet, damp, clammy, poachy.

জব্দ, *a.* subdued, reduced, seized, confined.

জম, *v. n.* to congeal, to candy, to coagulate, to freeze; -জানা, to be congealed.

জমক, *s.* show, pomp, parade: *a.* twin.

জমন, *s.* freezing, congelation, coagulation.

জমলা, *s.* total, all, the whole, a collection.
জমা, *v. a.* to collect, to cause to coagulate or congeal : *s.* a collection, an increase, an accumulation, an amount, a total, in *acct.* the creditor side : *a.* collected.
জমাখরচ, *s.* income and expenditure, debtor and creditor sides of an account.
জমাট, *s.* a crowd, an assembly, a congregation, cement, ice, an icicle, a crystal.
জমাদ্দার, *s.* a muster-master, a chief, a captain.
জমাদ্দারী, *s.* the office of a jamáddár.
জমান, *s.* a collecting, a coagulating : *a.* collected, frozen, coagulated.
জমানি, *s.* a collection, coagulation, congelation.
জমানিয়া, *s.* one who collects or coagulates.
জমাবন্দি, *s.* a settlement or account of the revenues of a province, a farm rent.
জমী, জমীন্, *s.* land; -দার, a land-holder.
জমীদারি, জমীন্দারি, *s.* a landed estate.
জমক্, *v. n.* to assemble, to collect.
জমকা, *v. a.* to assemble, to come together.
জমকান, *a.* assembled, collected ; blazing, glowing: *s.* the assembling of a crowd.
জমকানি, *s.* the assembling of a crowd.
জমকাল, *a.* pompous, showy, parading.
জম্বাল, *s.* mud, sludge, clay, mire.
জম্বীর, *s.* a lime, lemon (Citrus acida).
জম্ব, জম্বু, *s.* the rose-apple and its tree ;[1]
জম্বুক, *s.* a shakal, a jackal.
জম্বুদ্বীপ, *s.* the central division of the earth including the whole of Hindustán.
জম্বুদ্বীপস্থ, *a.* situated in Hindustán.
জম্বুবান, *s.* a monkey, a baboon.
জম্ভন, *s.* sexual intercourse, coition.
জয়, *s.* conquest, victory, triumph ; hail ! -কৃ, to conquer, to vanquish, overcome.
জয়করণ, *s.* the obtaining of a victory.
জয়কর্ত্তা, *s.* a conqueror, a vanquisher.
জয়কাতিয়া, *a.* attending on victory, or on a victory and publishing his praise.
জয়কারক, *a.* victorious : *s.* a conqueror.
জয়কারী, *a.* victorious, vanquishing.
জয়জয়কার, *a.* triumphant, victorious.
জয়জয়কারী, *a.* announcing victory.
জয়ঢক্কা, জয়ঢাক, *s.* a war drum, a drum of victory.
জয়ঢাকী, *s.* an army drummer.
জয়ধান, *s.* a species of grain.[2]
জয়ধ্বনি, *s.* a shout or cry of victory.
জয়ন্তী, *s.* the name of a tree.[3]
জয় -পতাকা, -নিশান, *s.* a flag or ensign of victory.
জয়পত্র, *s.* a written declaration of victory.
জয়বাদন, *s.* music on account of a victory.
জয়বান, *a.* victorious, triumphant.
জয়যুক্ত, *a.* belonging to a victory, victorious.
জয়যোগ্য, *a.* worthy of victory.
জয়শৃঙ্গ, জয়শিঙ্গা, *s.* the horn of victory.
জয়িত্রী, *s.* the spice called mace.
জয়ী, *a.* triumphant, victorious: *s.* a victor.
জর্, *v. n.* to digest, to waste away.
*জর, *s.* gold and silver, money, riches.
জর, *s.* decay, decrepitude, old age.
জরণ, *s.* a growing old, the digesting of food.
জরদ্, *a.* yellow ; -গব, an old ox.
জরা, *v. a.* to digest or prepare by chymical process of digestion, to cause to digest: *s.* decrepitude, decay, old age, infirmity: *a.* digested, tabid, decrepit, infirm.
জরাতুর, *a.* decrepit, debilitated, old, infirm.
জরাবস্থা, *s.* decrepitude, old age.
জরায়ু, *s.* the womb, the uterus.
জরায়ুজ, *a.* viviparous, born from the womb.
*জরী, *s.* gold or silver thread.
*জরীব, *s.* the measuring of land, land-surveying, a rod to measure land, a staff.
*জরীমানা, *s.* a fine, damage.
*জরু, *s.* a wife; -লেড়কা, wife and children, a family.
*জরুর, জরুরী, a necessary, important.
জরুরী অৎ *s.* force, violence, compulsion, restraint; want, indigence, necessity.
জর্জ্জর, *a.* perforated, shattered, cracked, jarring, decrepit : *s.* an aquatic plant.
জর্জ্জরিত, *a.* shattered, rent, torn, tattered.
*জর্দ, জর্দা, *a.* yellow, of the colour of gold.
জর্দার, *a.* wealthy, rich, opulent.
জর্দা, *a.* yellow, gold-colour : *s.* turmeric.
জল, *s.* liquor, water ; -দা, to water, to give water; -কৃ, to spring a leak ; -উঠ, to bubble up; -খা, to drink; -ছিটা, to sprinkle; -তোল, to draw water ; -পড়, to leak, to rain ; -সেচ, to water, to bale water.
জলই, *s.* iron pin, peg, nail, joining nail; a fountain.
জলকপি, *s.* a porpoise, riverhog.
জলকর, *s.* the revenue or rent of fisheries.
জলকষ্ট, *s.* a scarcity of water, aridity.

জলকুল্য, *s.* a small pond. [with water.
জলক্রীড়া, *s.* diversion in water, the playing
জলগণ্ড, *s.* a swamp, a marsh, a fen, a bog.
জলগমন, জলযাত্রা, *s.* a voyage by water.
জলঘোটক, *s.* a hippopotamus. [mal.)
জলচর, *a.* moving in water, aquatic (ani-
জলচারী, *a.* moving in water, aquatic.
জলচোর, *s.* a pirate, a water-thief.
জলছত্র, জলসত্র, *s.* a temporary shed in which water, etc. is given to travellers.
জলজ, জলজাত, *a.* produced in water.
জলজন্তু, *s.* an aquatic animal. [tion.
জলটঙ্গী, *s.* a house for pleasure and refec-
জলঢোঁড়া, *s.* a species of harmless snake.
জলতরঙ্গ, *s.* a wave, a musical water-glass.
জলতৃষা, *s.* a thirst for water, thirst.
জলতোলা, *s.* the drawing of water.
জলদ, *a.* giving water : *s.* a cloud.
জলদোষ, *s.* a diseased state of the fluids.
জলধর, *s.* a cloud : the sea.
জলধি, জলনিধি, *s.* the sea, the ocean.
জলনিকাশ, *s.* an outlet for water.
জলপথ, *s.* a way by water ; an outlet for
জলপাই, *s.* a tree and its fruit.[1] [water.
জলপাত্র, *s.* a vessel for water, a water-glass.
জলপান, *s.* refreshment, a breakfast, a tiffin, a repast, the drinking of water.
জলপিপাসা, *s.* thirst, a desire for water.
জলপ্রক্ষালন, *s.* a washing with water.
জলপ্রক্ষালিত, *a.* washed in water.
জলপ্রায়, *a.* watery, like water, marshy,
জলপ্রিয়, *a.* fond of water. [swampy.
জলপ্রেক্ষণ, *s.* a sprinkling with water.
জলপ্রোক্ষিত, *a.* sprinkled with water.
জলপ্লাবন, *s.* an inundation, a deluge.
জলপ্লাবিত, *a.* deluged, inundated.
জলবৎ, *a.* resembling water, liquid, limpid.
জলবর্ষণ, *s.* the falling of a shower.
জলবহন, *s.* a flowing or running of water.
জলবাহন, *s.* a water-vehicle, a ship, a boat.
জলবিকার, *s.* a change of water or fluid.
জলবিম্ব, জলবুজ্‌কুড়ি, জলবুদ্বুদ, *s.* a bubble.
জলবিষুব, *s.* the autumnal equinox.
জলবীচি, *a.* rough, billowing : *s.* a wave
জলভরণিয়া, *s.* a water-bearer.
জলভস্কা, *a.* diluted, watery, insipid.
জলভাটুই, গুগলী, *s.* a species of snail.

জলভীতি, *s.* hydrophobia.
জলমগ্ন, *a.* immersed in water.
জলময়, *a.* watery, deluged, full of water.
জলমাত্র, *s.* mere water, nothing but water.
জলমানুষ, *s.* a mermaid, a seal. [mal.
জলমার্জার, *s.* an otter, an amphibious ani-
জলমিশ্রিত, *a.* mixed with water, diluted.
জলমুহরী, *s.* a drain for water, a canal.
জলমুহান, *s.* a trench, watercourse, canal.
জলযুক্ত, *a.* wet, watery, marshy.
জলযোগ, *s.* a slight repast, a breakfast, luncheon, tiffin, a refection, refreshment.
জললহর, *s.* an aqueduct, a canal for water.
জললহরী, *s.* a surge, a billow, wave.
জলশরাব, *s.* a particular part of the veda.
জলশায়ী, *a.* reposing on water : *s.* Vishnu.
জলসিক্ত, *a.* sprinkled with water, watered.
জলসিঞ্চন, *s.* the sprinkling of water.
জলস্থ, জলস্থিত, *a.* situated in the water.
জলস্পর্শ, *s.* the touching of water.
জলহস্তী, *s.* a crocodile, alligator. [water.
জলহিল্লোল, *s.* the roaring of the sea or of
জলা, *a.* watery, marshy, swampy : *s.* a fen,
জলাকর, *s.* a spring, a fountain. [marsh.
জলাকৃতি, *a.* liquid, aqueous, like water.
জলাকীর্ণ, *a.* inundated, overflowed.
জলাধার, *s.* a receptable for water. [ters.
জলাধিপতি, *s.* Varuna, the god of the wa-
জলাভাব, *s.* drought, a want of water.
জলাভিষিক্ত, *a.* watered, sprinkled with wa-
জলাম, *s.* the secundines, afterbirth. [ter.
জলার্থী, *a.* desirous of water, thirsty.
জলাশঙ্কা, *s.* hydrophobia.
জলাশয়, *s.* a pond, a tank, a reservoir of
জলৌবী, *s.* a kind of sweetmeat. [water.
জলুয়া, *a.* diluted, waterish, thin, tasteless, insipid, watery, wet, serous.
*জলুস, *s.* a king's accession to a throne.
জলসী, *a.* belonging to the government.
জলোদরী, *s.* the dropsy : *a.* dropsical.
জলৌকা, জলিকা, *s.* a leech.
জল্‌জল্‌, জল্‌জলাট, *s.* a glare, a glow, vivid light, refulgence, brightness, lustre.
জল্‌জলা, *v. a.* to glow, to be refulgent.
জল্‌জলান, *s.* the glowing of any thing.
জল্‌জলিয়া, *a.* glowing, lucid, refulgent.
*জলদ্‌, *a.* quick, expeditious, brisk, hasty.

জল্দ্‌বাজ, *a.* quick, hasty, alert, brisk.
জল্দ্‌বাজি, *s* quickness, haste, briskness.
জল্দী, *a.* quick, swift; *ad.* quickly. [ling.
জল্প, *s.* chat, gossip, talk, garrulity, wrang-
জল্পন, *s.* a talking, chatting, gossiping.
জল্পাক, *a.* loquacious : *s.* a chatterer.
জল্পিত, *a.* spoken, uttered, talked about.
*জল্লাদ, *s.* a hangman : *a.* cruel.
জল্লাদি, *s.* the office of a hangman.
*জশন্, *s.* joy, a rejoicing, conviviality.
জশনী, *a.* joyful, rejoicing, convival.
*জহর, *s.* poison, venom, bane; -মোহরা, a
জহরী, *s.* a dealer in poisons. [bezoar.
*জহুরা, *s.* manifestation, a display.
*জহুরী, *s.* a dealer in precious stones.
জহ্নুতনয়া, *s.* a name of the river Ganges.
জা, *s.* a husband's brother's wife.
*জাইগীর, *s.* pension in landed property.
জাইগীরদার, *s.* holder of a grant of land.
জাইগীরদারী, *s.* the office of a jáigirdár.
জাইট, *s.* the cylinder of an oil-mill.
*জাইদাদ, *s.* goods, chattels, property.
জাওয়ালি, *s.* the young of serpents, young and verdant rice plants.
জাওর, *s.* breed, caste; the cud; -কাট, to ruminate, to chew the cud. [cud.
জাওর -কাটান, -কাটা, *s.* the chewing of the
জাঁক, *s.* a multitude, a crowd, pomp, parade, pride, a vaunting, a boasting.
জাঁকজমক, *s.* pomp, parade, a boasting.
জাঁকজমকী, *a.* crowding, pompous, parading.
জাঁকড়, *s.* a condition in buying an article, which if not approved may be returned.
জাঁকাল, *a.* pompous, parading, showy.
জাঁৎ, *v. a.* to press, pull tight, force down.
জাঁত, *s.* a press, a vice; -দা, to press down; -কষ্, to screw up a vice or press.
জাঁতন, জাঁতনি, *s.* the pressing of an article.
জাঁতা, *v. a.* to cause to press down : *s.* a millstone, a pair of bellows: *a.* pressed.
জাঁতাজাতি, *s.* mutually pressing.
জাঁতান, *s.* the causing a person to press a substance: *a.* pressed, compressed.
জাঁতানি, *s.* the causing to press a substance.
জাঁতী, *s.* an instrument to cut betel-nut.
জাগ্, *v. n.* to awake; to force to ripen.
জাগন, জাগনি, *s.* an awaking from sleep.
জাগানিয়া, *a.* watchful : *s.* watchman.
জাগরণ, *s.* a wake, wakefulness, a waking.
জাগরিত, *a.* awaken, awake, vigilant.
জাগরূক, *a.* keeping awake, wakeful.
জাগা, *v, a.* to awaken, to rouse, to stir up, to spring game, to force to ripen fruit.
জাগান, *s.* the rousing or awakening of a person : *a.* awakened, forcibly ripened.
জাগানি, *s.* the awakening of a person.
জাগানিয়া, *a.* forcibly ripe : *s.* a watchman.
জাগ্রৎ, *a.* rising from sleep, awake, alert.
জাগ্রদবস্থা, *s.* a state of wakefulness.
জাঙ্গাল, *s.* a balk, a dam, a dike, a mound, an embankment; verdigris.
জাঙ্গালবাঁধা, *s.* an embankment.
জাঙ্গী, *s.* the leg; the backstays, long ropes of a boat-mast; -কাঠ, a pair of stilts.
জাঙ্গীহরীতকী, *s* the Beleric myrobalan.
জাচ্, *v. a.* to appraise, to inspect, survey; to ask or to force to accept any thing.
জাচন্দার, *s.* an appraiser, an inspector.
জাচন্দারি, *s.* the office of an appraiser.
জাচা, *v. a.* to order goods to be appraised: *a.* appraised : *s.* an appraisal.
জাচাই, *s.* appraisement; -কৃ, to appraise.
*জাজরুর, *s.* privy, a jakes.
*জাজিম, *s.* a fine kind of carpet.
জাজ্বল্যমান, *a.* refulgent, shining, bright.
জাটতত ভগিনী ও ভাই, *s.* a father's elder brother's daughter and son.
জাটি, *s.* the cylinder of an oil-mill. [son.
জাড়, জাড়া, *s.* cold, frost, winter, cold sea-
জাড়কাঁটা, *s.* the pustules on the tongue.
জাড়ি, *a.* cold, wintery : *s.* a kind of decoc-
জাড়িবেঙ্গ, *s.* a toad, a frog. [tion.
জাড্য, *s.* numbness, apathy, rigidity, stupidity, folly, idiocy, coldness, congelation.
জাৎ, *s.* a kind, species; a festival.
জাত, *a.* born, produced, begotten, arising.
জাতক, কোষ্ঠী, *s.* a horoscope. [child.
জাতকর্ম্ম, *s.* a ceremony at the birth of a
জাতকোপ, *a.* become angry, enraged.
জাতকৌতুক, *a.* become gratified, sportive.
জাতক্লেশ, *a.* fallen into distress, afflicted.
জাতপ্রতীতি, *a.* become confident, believing.
জাতপ্রীতি, *a.* producing love, affectionate.
জাতবিদ্য, *a.* become wise, learned.

জাতবিশ্বাস, *a.* believing, confiding, trusting.
জাতমর্য্যাদ, *a.* become respectable.
জাতমাৎসর্য্য, *a.* become envious, envious,
জাতানন্দ, *a.* become glad, joyful, glad.
জাতান্ধ, *a.* born blind. জাতাপত্যা, a mother.
জাতাপবাদ, *a.* accused, spoken evil of.
জাতাপমান, *a.* dishonourable, disgraced.
জাতাভিমান, *a.* become proud, proud.
জাতাভিলাষ, *a.* become desirous, desirous.
জাতাহঙ্কার, *a.* become proud, proud.
জাতাহ্লাদ, *a.* become glad, joyful, glad.
জাতি, *s.* a caste, a tribe, a nation, a genus, a kind, a sort, birth, a nativity; a shrub;[1] -খাবা, a rape; -খা, to ravish; -যা, to lose caste; -মার্, to destroy one's caste.
জাতিখাওয়া, *s.* a violating, deflouring, rape.
জাতি-চ্যুত, -ভ্রষ্ট, *a.* fallen from a caste, outcast.
জাতিটাতি, *s.* nations, tribes.
জাতিধর্ম্ম, *s.* the peculiar duties of a tribe.
জাতিভ্রংশ, *s.* the loss of caste.
জাতিমারা, *s.* a rape, destroying a person's caste.
জাতিস্মর, *s.* the memory of a former birth.
জাতিহারা, *s.* the losing of caste.
জাতী, *s.* mace; -কোষ, -ফল, a nutmeg; *vide* জাতি.
জাতীয়, *a.* belonging to a particular kind.
জাতেষ্টি, *s.* a sacrifice at the birth of a son.
*জাদা, *s.* a son; *e. g.* শাহজাদা, a prince; সাহেব—, son of a gentleman; মাল—, son of a harlot; হারাম—, a bastard.
জাদু, *s.* sorcery, magic, divination, fascination: *a.* beloved, dear. [*fem.* জাদুগরনী.
জাদুগর, জাদুগীর, *s.* a magician, a sorcerer;
জাদুগরি, *s.* the arts of sorcery, magic.
জাদুমণি, *s.* a dearly beloved object, a lovely jewel, a fascinating gem.
জান্, *v.* to know, perceive, discern, discover, to apprehend: *s.* life, knowledge, a wizard, an astrologer, a fortune-teller.
জানন, *s.* a knowing, thinking, supposing.
জানপহচান, *s.* acquaintance, intimacy.
জানবর, *s.* an animal.
জানবাজ, *a.* lively, active, spirited, mettlesome.
জানবিৎ, *a.* known, acquainted.
জানা, *v. a.* to make known, to acquaint, to warn, to admonish, to inform, to demonstrate, to represent; *s.* knowledge of a fact: *a.* known, acquainted.

জানাজানি, *a.* made public: *s.* acquaintance.
জানান, *s.* informing, making known: made known, proclaimed, informed.
জানানি, *s.* certainty, conviction, information.
জানামী, *s.* divination, astrology, sorcery, magic.
জানালা, *s.* *Port.* a window.
জানাশুনা, *s.* sensible evidence of a fact.
*জানিব, *s.* a side, a quarter, surety.
জানিবদার, *s.* a surety, a supporter, a second.
জানিবদারি, *s.* partiality, suretyship.
*জানী, *s.* a recruit, web of the eye; whoremonger.
জানু, *s.* the knee.
জাপ, *s.* a repeating the name of a god.
জাপট্, *v. a.* to clasp a person in the arms, to embrace; জাপটিয়া -লাগ্, to stick, to adhere; জাপটিয়া-ধর্, to clasp, embrace.
জাপটাজাপটী, *s.* a mutual embracing.
*জাফরান, *s.* saffron.
জাব, জাবনা, *s.* a mixture of straw, oil-cake, etc. for cattle.
জাবড়া, *a.* confused, blotted: *s.* the jaw.
জাবা, *v.* to preserve fishes alive; -বাঁশ, a sort of bambu.
জাবানিয়া, *a.* preserved alive.
জাবালি, *s.* young of vermin, or plants of rice.
জাব্দা, *s.* a waste-book, a cash-book.
জাম, *s.* a bason; a tree and its fruit.[2]
জামদান, *s.* a fine sort of figured cloth.
জামদানী, *s.* *idem;* also, a clothes-bag.
জামরুল, *s.* the star-apple and its tree.[3]
জামা, *s.* a frock, a coat, a gown.
জামাই, *s.* a son-in-law; -পুলি, a kind of cake.
জামাইপুলিশিম, *s.* a kind of kidney bean.[4]
জামাতা, জামাই, *s.* a son-in-law.
জামি, *s.* a sister, a good woman.
জামিন্, *s.* a bail, security; -দার্, a surety.
জামিনদারি, *s.* a suretyship, securityship.
জামিনি, *s.* security for debt or for appearance to answer a charge, responsibility.
‡জামির, *s.* a lime, lemon; the heart.
জামুড়া, *s.* a cicatrix, a scar, a corn, a callosity.
জায়, *s.* a list, an inventory, an account.
জায়গা, *s.* a place, ground, land.
জায়গীর, জায়গীরদার, *vide* জাইগীর, &c.
জায়ফল, জাতীকোষ, জাতীফল, *s.* a nutmeg.
জায়বাকী, *s.* the balance of an account.
জায়া, দারা, পত্নী, ভার্য্যা, মাগ, *s.* a wife.
জার্, *v. a.* to waste, to digest, to dissolve, to calcine by chymical process.

জার, *s.* an adulterer, a paramour, a gallant.
জারক, *a.* dissolving, digestive : *s.* a digestive medicine, a dissolvent.
জারজ, *a.* bastard, illegitimate, base-born.
জারণ, *s.* a calcining, calcination, a dissolving, the promoting of digestion.
জারা, *v. a.* to cause to dissolve, waste, or decay : *a.* dissolved, digested.
জারাশঙ্কা, *s.* jealousy (of a wife's fidelity).
জারাশঙ্কিত, *a.* jealous (of a wife's fidelity).
জারী, *s.* manifestation, a making known, a boast; songs sung at the Moharram.
জারুল, *s.* the name of a timber tree.[1]
জাল, *v. a.* to kindle a fire, to light a lamp.
জাল, *s.* a net, a web, snare ; a lattice, an eyelet; magic, illusion, supernatural deception ; flame of fire: *a.* false, forged ; -দা, to kindle fire, to heat over a fire.
জালকাগজ, জালখত, *s.* a forged note.
জালগোটিকা, *s.* bullets of a fishing net.
জালন, *s.* a kindling, lighting a lamp, etc.; [fuel.
জালমাছ, *s.* a shrimp, a prawn.
জালা, *v. a.* to light a fire, candle, or lamp, to heat or burn : *s.* a large jar ; a burning pain, inflammation, distress, anxiety of mind, the burning of wood.
জালান, *s.* the kindling of fire; the teazing of a person : *a.* kindled, heated.
জালানি, *a.* proper for fuel : *s.* a burning.
জালিক, *s.* a spider, a fisher, a fowler, a hunter who uses net, a conjurer, a juggler.
*জালিম, *s.* a tyrant, an oppressor.
জালিয়া, *s.* a fisher, a fisherman.
জালী, *s.* a fringe, a lattice, a net-purse, a network, a web, a film on the eye, the young fruit of a gourd or cucumber.
জালীপড়া, *a.* reticulated; covered by a film.
জাল্‌জাল্‌, *a.* net-like, porous, reticulated.
জাল্‌তি, *s.* a muzzle ; -বাঁধ্‌, to muzzle.
জাল্ম, *s.* a low man, a person of a low tribe.
*জাসু, জাসুস, *s.* a spy, a scout.
* জাহাজ, *s.* a ship, a schooner, bark, yacht.
জাহাজী, *a.* belonging to a ship : *s.* a sailor.
*জাহির, *s.* a display, a manifestation, a discovery : *a.* manifest, public.
জাহিরা, *ad.* openly, evidently, manifestly.
জাহ্নবী *s.* the river Ganges personified.

‡জি, *v. n.* to live, to be alive : *s.* the tongue: *voc. part.* Sir, your honour. [mate.
জিআ, *v. a.* to revive, to give life, to animate.
জিআদা, *a.* more : *s.* an excess.
জিআন, *s.* the animating of a person or animal, the preserving of fish in water.
জিউলি, *s.* a fisherman, a fishmonger.
জিউলী, *s.* a timber tree (Odina woodier).
জিওল, জিবল, *s.* *idem ;* also, a tortoise.
জিওলমাছ, *s.* a tortoise, a turtle.
জিকর, *s.* discourse, conversation, chitchat.
*জিগর, *s.* the heart. জিগির, aloud, manifest.
জিগা, *s.* a tiara, diadem ; the anus. [fest.
জিগির্‌জিগর্‌, *ad.* aloud, manifestly.
জিগীষা, *s.* emulation, rivalry; envy. [ous.
জিঘাংসক, জিঘাংসু, *a.* revengeful, malicious.
জিঘাংসা, *s.* malice, revenge, rancour.
জিজ্ঞাস্‌, *v. a.* to inquire, to ask, to require.
জিজ্ঞাসক, জিজ্ঞাসু, *a.* inquiring, inquisitive, desirous of knowing a thing.
জিজ্ঞাসনীয়, জিজ্ঞাসিতব্য, *a.* *vide* জিজ্ঞাস্য.
জিজ্ঞাসা, *s.* a query, a question, inquiry.
জিজ্ঞাসিত, *a.* asked, inquired after.
জিজ্ঞাস্য, *a.* worthy of research, fit to be inquired into, proper to be required of.
জিঞ্জীর, *s.* a chain, fetters. [bility.
জিঞ্জীরবন্দী, *a.* chained : *s.* joint-responsibility.
জিঞ্জীরা, *s.* place where convicts are transported, chiefly applied to Botany Bay.
জিত্‌, *v. a* to conquer, overcome, subdue, vanquish, win: *a.* won, conquered, etc.
জিতকোপ, *a.* of subdued anger.
জিতন, জিনন, *s.* a conquering, the subduing of an enemy, a winning at play.
জিতনিয়া, *a.* triumphant, conquering.
জিতা, *v. a.* to cause to conquer or win.
জিতাহার, *a.* of subdued appetite for food.
জিতিহরিণ, *s.* the musk-deer. [sions.
জিতেন্দ্রিয়, *a.* continent, of subdued passions.
জিতেন্দ্রিয়ত্ব, *s.* continence, forbearance.
*জিদ্‌, *s.* vexation, opposition, obstinacy.
জিদ্দী, *a.* vexatious, obstinate, opposing.
জিন্‌, *v. a.* to win, conquer, transcend, surpass, eclipse: *s.* a Jaina saga; *vide* জৈন.
জিনীস, *s.* a thing, goods. [ornament.
*জিন্দগানী, জিন্দগী, *s.* life. জিবাইন, *s.* an ornament.
জিব, জিভ, *s.* the tongue, organ of speech.

জিবল, জিওল, s. same as জিউলী. [scraper.
জিবি, জিবচাঁচনী, or জিবছোলা, s. a tongue-
জিম্মা, জিম্বা, s. custody, in trust, in care.
জিয়ল, জিয়লমাছ, s. a tortoise, a turtle.
জির্, v. a. to rest from labour or fatigue.
জিরণ, জিরণি, s. a resting from fatigue.
জিরা, v. n. to cause to rest from fatigue.
জিরাণিয়া, a. resting, tranquillizing.
জিরাপোশ, s. a girdle for the loins.
জির্জির্, a. emaciated, skin and bone.
জিল, s. the treble string of a violin, a high or shrill tone; -টান, to quaver.
*জিলা, s. a province, district, a country; -দার্, ruler of a district; -দারী, his office.
জিলাবন্দী, s. the settlement of a province.
জিলিপী, জিলেবী, s. a kind of sweetmeat.
*জিলেপ, s. a herald, a precursor. [binder.
*জিলদ, s. binding of a book; -গর্, a book-
*জিলা, s. brightness, polish. [showy.
জিলাদার্, a. bright, glaring, tawdry, fine,
জিহ্বা, s. the tongue; -আঁচড়া, same as জিবি.
জিহ্বাকণ্টক, s. an excoriation of the tongue.
জীঅঁচ্পআতী, s. she whose children are all
জীঅক, a. reviving: s. a reviver. [living.
জীঅন, s. a living, existing, being alive.
জীআ, জীআন, the same as জিআ, জিআন.
জীউ, s. life; the tongue. জীগর্, the heart.
*জীন্, s. a saddle; -চড়া, or -বাঁধ্, to saddle; -কস্, a martingal; -পোশ, a saddle-cloth.
জীব, s. life, an animal, the soul, existence, a livelihood, the sentient soul, motion and sensation; a name of Vrihaspati.
জীবজন্তু, জীববর্গ, জীবসমূহ, s. animals.
জীবজ্ঞ, s. self-manifestation.
জীবৎ, a. living, alive, extant.
জীবৎপতিকা ও পুত্রিকা, s. one whose husband and children are living. [of life.
জীবৎমান, alive, living: s. lifetime, season
জীবদ্দশা, s. life, lifetime, state of existence.
জীবন, s. life, existence, lifetime; water; an animal; the name of a tree.[1] [life.
জীবনাবশিষ্ট, a. nearly dead: last spark of
জীবনোপায়, s. state of living, livelihood.
জীবন্ত, জীববান্, জীবযুক্ত, a. alive, living.
জীবন্মুক্ত, a. free from material things.
জীবন্মুক্তি, s. freedom from material things.
জীবন্মৃত, a. dead while living.

জীবন্যাস, s. a giving life to an idol.
জীবলোক, s. a man, men. [der.
জীবহত্যা, s. the killing of an animal, mur-
জীবহিংসা, s. injury to an animal.
জীবাত্মা, s. the vital principle, vitality, soul.
জীবাধান, s. the preserving of life.
জীবিকা, s. a livelihood, maintenance.
জীবিকায়ী, a. tributary, under tribute.
জীবিকাস্ত্র, s. a tool for gaining a livelihood.
জীবিত, a. living, alive, revived: s. life.
জীয়ন্ত, জীবিতবান্, a. living, alive, extant.
জীয়া, v. a. to revive, animate, preserve.
জীয়ান, s. a giving life to, vivification.
জীরক, জীরা, s. cummin seed.[2]
জীর্ণ, a. grown old, decayed, worn out, old, infirm, obstinate, digested; -কৃ, to digest.
জীর্ণঘরা, জীর্ণিঘরা, s. the stomach.
জীর্ণি, s. infirmity, decay, digestion.
জীল, s. a high or shrill tone; -দা, to quaver.
জুআ, s. gaming, playing at dice; -খেলা, a gambling, play; -চোর্, a cheat, a sharper, a knave; -চোরি, a cheating, knavery.
জুআর্, s. flood tide; -ভাটা, flood and ebb
জুআরিয়া, a. brought in by the tide. [tide.
জুআরী, s. a gambler; crookedness.
জুঁই, s. jasmine;[3] louse; -পাপা, a shrub.[4]
জুঁইয়া, s. the plantain tree insect.
জুক্, v. a. to measure, to weigh. [hand.
জুগৎ, s. counsel, contrivance, sleight of.
জুগুপ্সা, s. a reproach, vituperation.
জুঙ্গ, a. confident, bold, impudent, stout.
*জুজ্র, s. a sheet of paper folded in octavo.
জুজু, s. a bugbear, false terror. [size.
জুড়্, v. n. to grow cool, to be cold; to join.
জুড়ন, s. becoming cool or calm; a joining.
জুড়নিয়া, a. cool, calm: s. one who joins.
জুড়া, v. a. to cool, to refresh, to quell.
জুড়ান, s. a cooling or refreshing, a resting from fatigue: a. cooled, refreshed.
জুৎ, s. beauty, symmetry, a good appearance, elegance, fitness; a being in proper order (applied to machinery). [shoe.
জুত্, s. a shoe, a slipper: v. to beat with a
জুতন, জুতনি, s. a flogging with slippers.
জুতল, a. beautiful, elegant, in good order.
জুতা, s. a shoe, a slipper: v. a. to order a person to flog with slippers.

জুতাজুতি, *s.* reciprocal striking with shoes.
জুতান, জুতানি, *s.* a flogging with slippers.
জুতী, *s.* a shoe, a slipper ;-মার্, to beat with shoes ;-খা, to be struck with shoes.
জুবড়্, or জুবড়া, *v. a.* to dip cloth into the dye, to smear any thing by dipping.
জুবড়ন, জুবড়ান, *s.* the dipping of cloth, etc. in a fluid: *a.* dipped, dyed, immersed.
জুবড়ানি, *s.* a dipping, immersion.
জুমল, জুমলা, *s.* the amount of a sum, a total.
জুয়া, জুয়ার, জুয়ারী, *vide* জুআ, &c.
জুল, *s.* a peep, a glance, a side-look.
জুলপি, or জুলফ্, *s.* the hair left full on the temples by way of ornament.
জুলম, *s.* fierceness, tyranny, unfeelingness, cruelty.
*জুলমানা, *s.* a fine, damage.
*জুলাফ, or জুলাব, *s.* a purge, a cathartic.
জুলাফা, জুফা, *s.* a kind of medicinal drug.
জুলী, *s.* a trench, a watercourse, a canal.
জুলজুল, *s.* repeated peeps or glances.
জুহূ, *s.* a sacrificial vessel of wood.
*জুদা, *a.* separate, distinct;-ই, separation.
জুভূ, *s.* a pretence, swindling, imposture.
জুষ, *s.* sauce, broth, soup, porridge.
জৃম্ভণ, জৃম্ভা, *s.* a gaping, yawning, a yawn.
জেটী. *s* the house-lizard ; also, *vide* জেঠাঈ.
জেঠতত, জেঠাত, *s.* an uncle, a father's eldest brother ;-ভগিনী, an uncle's daughter ;-ভাই, an uncle's son, a cousin.
জেঠা, *s.* a father's eldest brother.
জেঠাঈ, জেঠী, *s.* a father's eldest brother's wife.
জেঠামি, *s.* self-importance, vanity.
জেতা, *s.* a conqueror: *v. a.* to cause to conquer.
জেতান, *s.* the making a person victorious : *a.* made to conquer, made victorious.
জেতানি, *s.* a making victorious.
জেতৃনিরা, *a.* giving victory, victorious.
*জেব, *s.* a pocket ;-কাতা, a pickpocket.
জেয়, জেতব্য, *a.* conquerable, vincible.
জের, *a.* brought over in account, beneath.
জেরদস্ত, *a.* subject to, obnoxious to.
জেরবন্দ, *s.* a martingal, a belly-band.
জেরবার, *a.* burdening, heavy.
জেরম্বাদ, *s.* a drug (Zingiber zerumbet).
জেহেল, *s.* *Eng.* a jail, a gaol, a fetter.
জৈন, *s.* a Jaina, one of the Jaina sect.
জৈপাল, *s.* a tree and fruit (Croton tiglia).

*জোআহর, *s.* a gem. জোআহরী, a jeweller.
জোঁক, *s.* a leech, a blood-sucker.
জোঁকন, *s.* the act of measuring a thing.
জোঁকা, *v. a.* to cause to measure: *a.* measured : *s.* the name of a plant.
জোঁকান, *a.* ordered to be measured : *s.* the causing a person to measure a thing.
জোঁকানি, *s.* the measuring of a thing.
*জোখম, *s.* calamity, trouble, loss, danger.
জোঙ্গট, *s.* a desire, a longing desire.
জোঙ্গড়া, *s.* a particular kind of snail.[1]
জোন, *s.* a man, a person ; a hired labourer.
জোনাক, *a.* moon-shining : *s.* a fire-fly.
জোনাকী, জোনাকিপোকা, *s.* a fire-fly.
*জোনাব, *s.* a side, vicinity ; the feet.
*জোবান্, *s.* the tongue, language ;-দরাজ, abusive, scurrilous ; -দরাজি, scurrility, abusiveness ; -বন্দি, a deposition.
*জোর, *s.* force, pressure, strength, compulsion ;, -জোলম্, violence, tyranny.
জোরবার, জোরাবর, *a.* strong, powerful, vigorous.
জোরাবরি, *s.* strength, power.
জোরু, জোরুলেড়কা, the same as জরু, &c.
জোল, *s.* a fen, a marsh, swamp, a ravine.
*জোলা, *s.* a weaver : *a.* ignorant, foolish.
*জোলাব, *s.* a purge, physic, a cathartic.
জোলী, *s.* a ravine, a gutter, a sink, a sewer.
*জোশ, *s.* passion, rage ; gravy, soup, broth.
জৌ, *s.* lac, gum lac ; -বাতা, stick-lac.
জ্ঞ, *s.* perception ; in *comp.* knowing, perceiving ; *e. g.* বেদজ্ঞ, versed in the veda.
জ্ঞা, *v. a.* to know, to perceive. জান্, is constantly substituted for this root.
জ্ঞাত, *a.* aware, known, acquainted with, informed.
জ্ঞাতব্য, capable of being known.
জ্ঞাতসার, *s.* an object of knowledge : *ad.* knowingly.
জ্ঞাতা, *s.* one who knows.
জ্ঞাতি, *s.* a collateral relation, a kinsman.
জ্ঞাতিকুটুম্ব, *s.* relations of every description.
জ্ঞাতিকুল, জ্ঞাতিগণ, *s.* all the collateral relations.
জ্ঞাতিত্ব, -ত্ব, *s.* relationship, kin.
জ্ঞাতৃতা, *s.* experience, genius, knowledge.
জ্ঞান, *s.* knowledge, an idea, wisdom, the perception of an idea, sense, an opinion, persuasion ; -কৃ, to form an opinion.
জ্ঞানকাণ্ড, *s.* the portion of the veda treating of knowledge, distinct from কর্ম্মকাণ্ড.

জ্ঞানকৃত, *a.* done knowingly or intention-
জ্ঞানজ, *a.* arising from knowledge. [ally.
জ্ঞানতঃ, *ad.* knowingly, intentionally.
জ্ঞানদ, *a.* giving knowledge or ideas.
জ্ঞানদাতা, *s.* a preceptor, a spiritual guide.
জ্ঞানদায়ক, *s.* one who communicates ideas.
জ্ঞানদায়ী, *a.* communicating ideas.
জ্ঞানপূর্ব্বক, *ad.* knowingly, intentionally.
জ্ঞানবান্, *a.* wise, sagacious, intelligent.
জ্ঞানান্বিত, জ্ঞানাপন্ন, *a.* wise, knowing.
জ্ঞানিতা, -ত্ব, *s.* wisdom, erudition, sagacity.
জ্ঞানী, *a.* wise, intelligent, sage, knowing.
জ্ঞানেন্দ্রিয়, *s.* organs of sensation or those of hearing, seeing, smelling, tasting and feeling, to which is added the mind.
জ্ঞানোৎপত্তি, *s.* production of knowledge.
জ্ঞানোদয়, *s.* the rise of knowledge.
জ্ঞাপক, *a.* making known, proclaiming: *s.* one who proclaims or makes known.
জ্ঞাপন, *s.* a communicating, an informing, the making of a thing known.
জ্ঞাপনীয়, *a.* capable of being made known, fit to be revealed or made known.
জ্ঞাপয়িতব্য, জ্ঞাপ্য, *a. idem.*
জ্ঞাপিত, *a.* made known, revealed, notified.
জ্ঞেয়, *a.* knowable, cognizable: *s.* an object
জ্যা, *s.* a bow-strong. [of knowledge.
জ্যেঠশ্বশুর, *s.* a husband's or wife's father's eldest brother. [brother's wife.
জ্যেঠশাশ, জ্যেঠশাশুড়ি, *s.* the aforesaid eldest
জ্যেঠা, জ্যেঠতাত, a father's eldest brother.
জ্যেষ্ঠ, *a.* eldest, elder, first born, chief, best, senior, pre-eminent, most excellent.
জ্যেষ্ঠতা, -ত্ব, *s*, primogeniture, seniority.
জ্যেষ্ঠা, *s.* the 18th stellar mansion; the best beloved of one's wives; middle-finger.
জ্যেষ্ঠাধিকার, *s.* the right of primogeniture.
জ্যৈষ্ঠ, *s.* the name of an Indian month containing part of May and part of June.
জ্যৈষ্ঠী, *s.* the common house-lizard.
জ্যোতিঃ, *s.* a heavenly luminary, a star, the sun, light, fire, the pupil of the eye.
জ্যোতিঃশাস্ত্র, *s.* the science of astronomy, a book on the science of astronomy.
জ্যোতির্জ্ঞ, *s.* versed in astronomy. [nomy.
জ্যোতির্বিদ্যা, *s.* astronomy, science of astro-
জ্যোতিরিঙ্গণ, *s.* a fire-fly, a glow-worm.
জ্যোতির্বেত্তা, *s.* an astronomer. [region.
জ্যোতির্মণ্ডল, *s.* the stellar orbs, the stellar
জ্যোতির্ময়, *a.* abounding with stars.
জ্যোতিশ্চক্র, *s.* the zodiac.
জ্যোতিষ, *s.* the science of astronomy including astrology, a star, a luminary.
জ্যোতিষিক, *s.* an astronomer, an astrolo-
জ্যোতিস্, *s.* the same as জ্যোতিঃ. [ger.
জ্যোৎস্না, *s.* moonlight; -রাত্রি, a moonlight
জ্বর, *s.* a fever, an ague. [night.
জ্বরঘ্ন, জ্বরান্তক, *a.* febrifuge, curing fever.
জ্বরাতিসার, *s.* a fever attended by dysen-
জ্বরী, *a.* feverish, diseased, weak. [tery.
জ্বল্, *v.* to burn, to blaze, to enkindle, to smart, to be ardent, eager, distressed.
জ্বলদগ্নি, *s.* a blazing or burning fire.
জ্বলন, *s.* a kindling up, a lighting, blazing of fire, a being zealous, eager or fervent, a being distressed in mind, a smarting.
জ্বলনার্হ, জ্বলনীয়, *a.* fit for fuel, inflammable, combustible. [burning.
জ্বলনী, *a.* virulent, burning: *s.* virulence, a
জ্বলন্ত, *a.* burning, glowing, ardent, pain-
জ্বলা, *s.* inflammation, a burning. [ful.
জ্বলাতন, *a.* wearied, teazed, vexed.
জ্বলান, *s.* a kindling, lighting, burning.
জ্বলানি, *a.* fit for burning, fit for fuel.
জ্বলানিয়া, জ্বালানিয়া, *a.* inflaming, enkindling, exasperating: *s.* an incendiary.
জ্বলানী, *a.* for the purpose of fuel.
জ্বলিত, *a.* lighted, burnt, inflamed, vexed.
জ্বালা, *v. a.* to kindle a fire, to light a lamp or candle, to burn, scald, vex, torment: *s.* a burning, inflammation, smart, virulence, torment, distress, vexation.
জ্বালামুখী, *s.* a volcano, an inflammable pit.
জ্বালাযন্ত্রণা, *s.* distress, vexation, torment, pain or anguish of body or mind.
জ্বালাযুক্ত, *a.* distressed, vexed, pained.
জ্বালিত, *a.* inflamed, burnt, vexed, grieved.

ঝ, the 9th consonant in the alphabet: it has the sound of jh; -কার, the letter ঝ.
ঝক্, *ad.* suddenly, quickly, speedily: *s.* nonsense, rant, idiocy; -মার্, to repent.
ঝকড়া, *s.* a quarrel, a squabble, a dispute, a wrangling, strife, war; -কৃ, to quarrel.

ঝকড়াউ, ঝকড়াটিয়া, *a.* quarrelsome, contentious, wrangling, disputatious, perverse.
ঝকিক্, *s.* a rebuff, huff, reproof, violence.
ঝক্ঝক্, *s.* a vivid luminous appearance.
ঝক্ঝকিয়া, *a.* luminous, shining, radiant.
ঝক্মক্, ঝক্মকানি, *s.* lustre, glare, brightness, a glittering, a shining.
ঝক্মকিয়া, *a.* glaring, luminous, shining
ঝক্মারণ, *s.* a talking nonsense or rant.
ঝক্মারী, ranting, nonsensical : *s.* repentance, regret ;-কৃ, to regret, to repent.
ঝঙ্কার, *s.* the buzzing of bees or wasps.
ঝঞ্ঝন, *s.* a jingling, a rattling, a clanking or rattling noise ;-কৃ, to jingle, rattle.
ঝঞ্ঝনা, *s.* lightning, a thunder-bolt.
ঝঞ্ঝনিয়া, *a.* clanking, jingling, rattling.
ঝঞ্ঝা, *s.* a storm, a tempest, a hurricane.
ঝঞ্ঝাট, *s.* perplexity, trouble, vexation.
ঝঞ্ঝাটিয়া, *a.* troublesome, vexatious.
ঝট্, *s.* quickness, speed. [apace
ঝট্ করিয়া, *ad.* quickly, speedily, hastily,
ঝটাপটি, *s.* a sparring, the sparring of birds.
ঝটিতি, *ad.* quickly, apace, speedily, hastily, summarily, expeditiously.
ঝটক্, *v. a.* to chop off, to lop off. [ing.
ঝটকন, *s.* a lopping off, a docking, behead-
ঝট্কা, *s.* hurricane, storm, squall : *a.* chopped off : *v. a.* to chop off ; to be lean.
ঝট্কান, ঝট্কানি, *s.* a chopping or lopping off, decapitation ; a being emaciated.
ঝট্ঝট্, *ad.* quickly, hastily, suddenly.
ঝড়, *s.* a hurricane, a storm, a tempest.
ঝড়কন, *s.* the repelling a reproof, a scolding, a chiding, a blustering.
ঝড়ঝাঁটা, ঝড়টড়, *s.* a hurricane, a tempest.
ঝড়তুফান, ঝড়বাতাস, *s.* a storm, a tempest.
ঝড়বৃষ্টি, *s.* a storm attended with rain.
ঝড়ি, *s.* a storm, a tempest, rain. [storm.
ঝড়ুয়া, *a.* tempestuous, stormy, fallen in a
ঝণ্ডা, *s.* flagstaff ; a flag, banner, standard.
ঝন্, ঝনৎ, ঝনাৎ, *im. sd.* used to express the clanking of metallic bodies.
ঝনৎকার, ঝনাৎকার, *s.* the clank of metal-
ঝন্কাট, *s.* a door-lintel. [lic bodies.
ঝপ্, *s.* haste, quickness, suddenness.
ঝপ্করিয়া, ঝপ্ঝপকরিয়া, *ad.* quickly, speedily, hastily, immediately, suddenly.

ঝম্প, *s.* a jump, leap, spring ;-দা, to jump,
ঝম্পমোর, *s.* a species of Falcon. [leap.
ঝর্, *v. n.* to leak, ooze out, drip, exude, to fall, shed : *s.* a cascade, a waterfall,
ঝরকা, *s.* a window, venetian blinds.
ঝরণ, *s.* a dripping, oozing, the falling of leaves from a tree, a shedding of corn.
ঝরণা, *s.* a cascade, a cataract, waterfall. a sieve, colander ; a dripping, a falling.
ঝরণী, *s.* strainer : a dripping, flowing.
ঝরা, *v. a.* to pour out, to strain.
ঝরাণ, *s.* the pouring out of the last drop, a straining : *a.* poured out, strained.
ঝরাণি, *s.* the last remains of a vessel.
ঝর্ঝর, *s.* a gugglet, a water-bottle, a dropping sound : *a.* cracked, full of holes.
ঝর্ঝরিয়া, *a.* out of repair, full of holes.
ঝর্ঝরী, *s.* a lattice, a fence, a cymbal.
ঝলক, ঝলকন, *s.* a shining ; a flake of fire.
ঝল্ক, *s.* a dash of waves ; a flake of fire.
ঝলাবর, *a.* fine, gay, elegant, gaudy.
ঝলঝল, ঝল্মল্, *s.* a flapping, a dangling.
ঝলমলিয়া, *a.* flapping, dangling.
ঝল্সা, *v.* to scorch, singe, roast : *a.* scorched, singed, roasted. -কাণা, purblind.
ঝল্সান, ঝল্সানি, *s.* a roasting, scorching,
ঝষ, *s.* fish, a fish. [singeing, burning.
ঝাইল, *s.* solder ; the flame of fire ; a hole dug to drain up the waters of a pond.
ঝাউ, *s.* name of a tree (Tamarix indicus).
ঝাঁই, *s.* a calx, a calcined state ; a sweetmeat made by frying scraped cocoanut and sugar ; freckles on the cheeks.
ঝাঁক্, *v. a.* to shake articles in a sack that they may occupy less space, to be angry, to collect into a swarm, to peep.
ঝাঁক, *s.* a swarm, herd, flock, drove, collection, a brood ;-বাঁধ, to swarm, to flock.
ঝাঁকন, *s.* a shaking or feeling the weight, the being in a passion, a peeping.
ঝাঁকনি, *s.* a shaking, lifting up to ascertain weight, passionate reproof, a peeping.
ঝাঁকবাঁধা, *a.* collected into a swarm or flock.
ঝাঁকর, ঝাঁকরা, *v. a.* to shake articles in a bag so that they may be close together.
ঝাঁকরাণ, *s.* the shaking down of articles in a bag : *a.* shaken, shaken down.

ঝাঁকা, *v. a.* to cause to ascertain the weight, or shake the articles in a bag for space: *a.* shaken together: *s.* a large basket.

ঝাঁঝ, *s.* flame, pungency, heat; a cymbal.

ঝাঁঝরা, *s.* a colander, water-pot. [foration,

ঝাঁঝরী, *s.* a lattice, colander, strainer, per-

ঝাঁঝলি, *a.* ardent, fierce, parched, testy.

ঝাঁঝাঁ, *im. sd.* of cymbal, or barking of dogs.

ঝাঁঝাঁলিয়া, *a.* ardent, glowing, fierce, testy, [passionate.

ঝাঁট্, *v. a.* to sweep a place.

ঝাঁট, *s.* the hair on the privities.

ঝাঁটন, ঝাঁটনি, *s.* the sweeping of a place.

ঝাঁটনিয়া, *a.* sweeping, employed to sweep.

ঝাঁটা, *v. a.* to sweep, to cause to sweep: *s.* a broom, a besom. [fuse, rubbish.

ঝাঁটনি, ঝাটি, *s.* a sweeping; sweepings, re-

ঝাঁটো, *ad.* speedily, quickly, forthwith.

ঝাঁপ্, *v. n.* to leap, to jump, to leap on, to copulate (as animals): *v. a* to shut up, to cover, to overspread, to overrun.

ঝাঁপ, *s.* a mat-door, mat-screen; a leap.

ঝাঁপা, *v. a.* to cause to jump, to leap up for copulation (as animals): *s.* name of two ornaments, a tassel, an epaulet.

ঝাঁপান, *s.* stage erected by snake-catchers to play with snakes, a jump, a leap.

ঝাঁপানিয়া, *a.* playing with snakes.

ঝাঁপাল, *a.* bushy and thick (as trees).

ঝাঁপী, *s.* a covered basket, a work-basket.

ঝাড়, *v. a.* to beat out the dust, to thrash, winnow, to shake off leaves, etc., to expel evil spirit or venom by exorcism.

ঝাড়, *s.* a tuft, bush, shrub; breed of animals, a stock, a pedigree; a chandelier.

ঝাড়ন, *s.* a thrashing, winnowing, a beating out of dust, a shaking off the leaves, etc., the expulsion of evil spirit or venom by exorcism; a towel, napkin, a duster.

ঝাড়া, *v. a.* to cause to shake off dust, to cause to winnow, thrash or shake off the leaves or fruits, to cause to expel evil spirit or venom by exorcism: *a.* beaten, thrashed out, winnowed, full, complete: *s.* search, ordure, a privy, the dusting of clothes, a shaking off leaves, etc.

ঝাড়ান *s.* a causing to beat out dust, a causing to shake off leaves, etc., or to thrash or winnow corn, a causing to expel poison or evil spirit by exorcism.

ঝাড়াল, *a.* bushy, growing in large tufts.

ঝাড়ি, *s.* a bush, shrub; -পথ, a forest-road.

ঝাড়িবন, *s.* a bush, a thicket of brushwood.

ঝাড়ু, *s.* a broom, besom; -বর্দার, a sweeper, a mehtar; -বর্দারী, office of a sweeper.

ঝান, *s.* the fading of a flower or plant.

ঝাপনা, *s.* a film on the eye, dimness.

ঝাবুক, *s.* name of a tree (Tamarix indica).

ঝাব্বা, *s.* an epaulet, a tassel, frills, a tuft.

ঝামর্, *v.* to run or flow as the nose and eyes do with a cold: *s.* a kind of whetstone for sharpening spindles, etc.

ঝামরাণ, ঝামরাণি, *s.* a running of the nose and eyes when a person has a cold.

ঝামা, ঝামক, *s.* a vitrified brick.

ঝাম্প্যান্, *s.* a litter used in ascending hills.

ঝারা, *s.* a stream from a water-pot hung over a plant; a shower-bath, a leaking.

ঝারী, *s.* a water-vessel with a spout, a jug.

ঝাল্ *v. a.* to heat red-hot, to ignite, to [solder.

ঝাল, *a.* pungent, hot, acid.

ঝালঝম্, *s.* hot spicery, hot seasonings.

ঝালন, *s.* a soldering, heating of metals.

ঝালর, *s.* fringes, frills, tassel, edging.

ঝালরদার, *a.* adorned with fringes.

ঝালা, *v. a.* to cause to ignite, or solder.

ঝালান, *s.* a causing to be soldered: *a.* soldered, ignited, heated to redness.

ঝালানি, *s.* soldering, an igniting.

ঝালানী, *s.* pay for soldering or heating.

ঝালাপালা, *s.* faggots and brushwood.

ঝালি, *s.* a hole dug at the bottom of a pond to drain up the waters; solder. [acrid.

ঝালুয়া, *a.* highly seasoned, pungent, hot,

ঝি, *s* a daughter, a girl; -পুত, children.

ঝিক, *s.* the cones of a hearth, small props of earth placed under a boiling pot.

ঝিঁকর, ঝিকুর, *a.* hard, crusty, morose.

ঝিঁকা, *s.* a jerk, the propelling a boat by working at the rudder; -মার্, to propel a boat by the help of the rudder.

ঝিঁঝাঁ, *s.* a species of insect, a tingling sensation felt in a limb by long sitting.

ঝিকিমিকি, ঝিক্‌ঝিক্, ঝিক্‌মিক্, *s.* a glare, a glittering; -কর্, to glitter, to glare.

ঝিঙা, *s.* a cucurbitaceous plant and fruit.[1]
ঝিনুক, *s.* a muscle, a cockle.
ঝিনুকগিলা, ঝিনুকিল, *s.* a species of bird.[2]
ঝিম্, *v. n.* to be drowsy, to nod with sleep.
ঝিমন, *s.* a nodding, a being drowsy.
ঝিমনি, *s.* nodding with sleep, drowsiness.
ঝিমা, *v. a.* to be drowsy, to nod with sleep.
ঝিমান, *s.* the act of nodding : *a.* nodding.
ঝিমানি, *s.* drowsiness, a nodding.
ঝিম্ঝিম্, ।ঝন্ঝিন্, *s.* a tingling sensation.
ঝির্ঝির্, *s.* a leaking in a gentle stream.
ঝিল, *s.* a lake, a shallow lake, a swamp.
ঝিলিমিলি, *s.* a thin kind of curtain gauze.
ঝিল্লি, *s.* a cricket, dragon fly; thin leather.
ঝী, *s.* a daughter, a girl ; -পুত, children.
ঝুঁক, *v. n.* to hitch forward, to bend down, to incline, to stagger, to totter.
ঝুঁকন, *s.* the act of bending or inclining.
ঝুঁকনি, *s.* a hitching of the body forward.
ঝুঁকি, *s.* a hitching forwards, responsibility, a risk : *a.* drunk, intoxicated, tipsy.
ঝুঁকিঝাঁকি, *a.* drunk, sottish, tipsy, fuddled.
ঝুঁকিভাগী, *a.* insuring : *s.* an insurer.
ঝুঁজ্, *v. n.* to ooze out, to flow, to drip.
ঝুঁজকাবেলা, *s.* the early dawn, the dawn.
ঝুঁজর, *s.* heaped measure (of dry goods).
ঝুঁজরখুঁচি, *s.* the last handful to a heap.
ঝুঁট, *s.* the hump (of a bull), a camel's bunch, a crest; a lie, a falsehood, a fib.
ঝুঁট্মুট্, *ad.* falsely, lyingly, stupidly.
ঝুঁটা, *s.* orts, refuse ; a liar, a fibber.
ঝুঁটাঝুঁটি, ঝুঁটামুটি, *s.* a mutual pulling of hair.
ঝুঁটী, *s.* a tuft, the tuft of hair left after tonsure ; a hump, a bunch, a crest.
ঝুড়্, *v. a.* to cut off, to lop, crop, cut, trim.
ঝুড়ন, ঝুড়নি, *s.* a cutting, trimming of a tree, lopping.
ঝুড়ী, *s.* a basket, a scuttle.
ঝুণ্ট, *s.* a shrub, a bush, underwood.
ঝুণ্ড, *s.* a multitude, a flock, a swarm.
ঝুন্, *v. a.* to reprove, to abuse, to scold
ঝুন, ঝুনা, *a.* ripe, dry (as a cocoanut).
ঝুনুর্ঝুনুর্, *s.* tinkling sound of chain, etc.
ঝুপ্, ঝুপুং, *s.* sound of a plunge in water.
ঝুপড়ী, *s.* a cabin, a hut, a shed, a cottage.
ঝুমুর, *s.* a kind of Hindu love songs.
ঝুমকা, ঝুমকি, *s.* an ornament for the ears of women; citron-leaved passion flowers.[3]

ঝুমঝুম, *im. sd.* arising from a child's rattle.
ঝুম্ঝুমী, *s.* a child's rattle.
ঝুম্রা, *a.* shaggy, curly, hairy.
ঝুর, *v. n.* to trickle, to ooze ; to lament.
ঝুরণ, *s.* a trickling ; a lamenting.
ঝুরা, *s.* a crumble, a morsel : *a.* crumbled.
ঝুরাঝারা, *s.* fragments, crumbles, pieces.
ঝুরী, *s.* a kind of sweetmeat ; the roots of the branches of Ficus religiosa.
ঝুর্ঝুর্, *ad.* by morsels or crumbles.
ঝুল, *v. a.* to swing, to hang : *s.* soot.
ঝুলন, *s.* a swinging, a hanging pendent.
ঝুলনযাত্রা, *s.* a festival in honor of Krishna.
ঝুলনী, *s.* a swinging, a cradle, a swing.
ঝুলা, *v. a.* to hang or suspend any thing, to cause a thing to swing : *a.* pendent, pendulous, swinging, oscillatory.
ঝুলাঝুলি, *s.* a mutual swinging.
ঝুলান, *s.* the act of suspending a thing, the causing of a thing to swing.
ঝুলী, *s.* a wallet, bag, a knapsack, a satchel.
ঝুল্ঝাল, ঝুল্টুল্, *s.* soot and filth.
ঝুঠ, *a.* false, feigned, counterfeit.
ঝুঠা, *a. idem : s.* a liar, a fibber.
ঝেঁট্, *v. a.* to sweep, to shake dust out.
ঝেঁটন, *s.* the sweeping of a place.
ঝেঁটা, *s.* a broom, a besom ; -দা, to sweep.
ঝেঁটানিয়া, *s.* a sweeper, one who sweeps.
ঝেঁটানী, *s.* sweepings, brushings, rubbish.
ঝেঁতলা, *s.* a kind of coarse mat ; slippers.
ঝোঁক, *v. a.* to bend down, to incline, to reel, to stagger, to stoop, to totter.
ঝোঁক, *s.* a jerk, a jerking motion, a tottering, staggering, swinging, inebriety.
ঝোঁকন, *s.* a jerking motion, a tottering, a staggering, a bending forward.
ঝোঁকা, *v. a.* to cause to hitch forwards: *a.* tottering, reeling, bent, inclined.
ঝোঁকান, *s.* the act of bending or inclining: *a.* bent, inclined, depressed.
ঝোঁকী, *s.* responsibility, a venture, a risk : *a.* drunk, intoxicated, inebriated, tipsy.
ঝোড়, *s.* a bushy tree, a bush, underwood.
ঝোড়ঝাড়, *s.* bushes and shrubs.
ঝোড়ন, *s.* the lopping of trees or bushes.
ঝোড়া, *v. a.* to cause a tree or a bush to be trimmed : *s.* a large basket, a scuttle.

ঝোড়ান, *s.* the causing a tree or bush to be lopped or trimmed: *a.* lopped, trimmed.
ঝোড়ানী, *s.* the lopping or trimming of a [tree.
ঝোপ, *s.* a bush, a bushy tree.
ঝোপঝাপ, *s.* bushes and shrubs. [hut.
ঝোপড়া, or ঝোপড়ী, *s.* a cottage, a shed, a
ঝোরণ, *s.* a trickling, an oozing, a leaking.
ঝোরণা, *s.* a watercourse, a water-fall, a cataract, a cascade, a drain, a gutter.
ঝোরা, ঝোর্, *s. idem: v. a.* to make to ooze or leak, to cause to trickle. [leak.
ঝোরাণ, *s.* the causing of water to ooze or
ঝোরাণি, *s.* an oozing or leaking. [swing.
ঝোল্, *v. n.* to be pendent, to hang down,
ঝোল, *s.* broth, soup, gravy; a brood.
ঝোলন, *s.* a swinging, a hanging pendent.
ঝোলা, *s.* a swing, a knapsack, a wallet, a wrinkle; -লাগ to be overcome by heat or fatigue; also, *v. a. vide* ঝুলা.
ঝোলাগুড়, *s.* liquid treacle or molasses.
ঝোলান, *s.* a suspending, a causing to oscillate: *a.* made to swing, pendent.
ঝোলানি, *s.* a swinging or suspending.
ঝোলি, *s.* a knapsack, a wallet, a bag.

ঞ, the tenth consonant of the Bengáli alphabet. It is seldom used alone.

ট, the eleventh consonant of the Bengáli alphabet. It has the sound of t hard.
টং, *s.* an elevated shed, a pigeon-house.
টইয়া, টয়, *s.* feather ornament for a drum.
টক্, *v. n.* to be acid: *im. sd.* of a rap, a tap.
টক, *a.* acid, sour, tart: *s.* acidity.
টকুআ, টকো, *a.* acid, sour, tart. [ping.
টকটক, *s.* redness, glowing redness, a rap-
টকটকিয়া, *a.* red, ruddy, blood-coloured.
টক্কর, *s.* emulation, a rap, knock; -লাগ, to [rap, knock.
টগর, *s.* a flowering shrub.[1]
টগরিয়া, *a.* prating, talkative, garrulous.
টঙ্ক, *s.* borax, a spade or hoe, a stone-cutter's chisel, a hatchet, sacrificial knife, a cimeter, a scabbard, anger, the leg.
টঙ্কন, *s.* borax; a spade; the leg.
টঙ্কপতি, *s.* the master of the mint. [ing.)
টঙ্কশালা, টেকশাল, *s.* the mint (for coin-
টঙ্কা, তঙ্কা, *s.* a silver coin, a rupee, money.
টঙ্কার, *s.* the twang of a bow-string, the sound of a stringed instrument, spasm, cramp, astonishment, fame, notoriety.
টঙ্কারিয়া, *s.* a spasm, the cramp.
টঙ্কিত, *a.* estimated, appraised.
টণ্টা, টণ্টাই, *s.* a dispute, quarrel, squabble.
টনক, টনকনাড়া, *s.* the sudden recollection of a thing as if by the ringing of a bell.
টনাৎ, *s.* the sound of a metallic plate.
টন্‌ক, টন্‌কা, *v. n.* to be hard, to be solid; *v. a.* to make hard: *a.* hard, firm, solid.
টন্‌টন্, *s.* throbbing sensation of tumour.
টন্‌টনা, *v. n.* to throb, smart; to be tense.
টন্‌টনানি, *s.* a throbbing; tenseness.
টন্‌টনিয়া, throbbing, painful, tense, tight.
টপ্‌ক, টপ্‌কা, *v. a.* to leap over a fence.
টপ্‌কান, *s.* the act of leaping over a wall.
টপ্‌কানি, *s.* a leaping over a wall.
টপ্‌টপানি, *s.* a continual dripping of rain.
টপ্পা, *s.* a song sung in short solo parts.
টল, *v. n.* to vacillate, stagger, slip, slide.
টলন, *s.* a vacillating, staggering, reeling.
টলনিয়া, *a.* staggering, vacillating, reeling.
টলা, *v. n.* to cause to stagger, slip, slide, to cause to vacillate or shrink from.
টলান, *s.* the making a thing unsteady, the making a person stagger.
টল্‌টল্, টল্‌মল্, *s.* a staggering or tottering motion, a tossing about (as a boat).
টলটলা, *v. n.* to stagger, reel, vacillate.
টল্‌টলিয়া, টল্‌মলিয়া, *a.* tossing about like a boat, staggering, tremulous. [a boat.
টল্‌মলা, *v. n.* to be tossed up and down like
টস্কা, *v. a.* to be brittle or fragile: *a.* brittle.
টহল, *s.* the collecting of materials for a feast; the begging from house to house.
টহলটুকরা, *s.* trifling work, job work.
টহলন, *s.* act of walking, or going about with singing as some beggars do.
টহলা, *v. a.* to put off, to temporize: *s.* a walk for pleasure, or for begging.
টহলানিয়া *a.* temporizing. [val.
টহলিয়া, *a.* collecting articles for a festi-
টা an enclitic particle frequently used in composition; *e. g.* ঘোড়াটা, a horse; একটা, only one, etc. [numbed.
টাউরা, *v. n.* to shrink with cold, to be be

টাউরাণ, টাউরাণি, *s.* a shrinking with cold, a being shrunk up or benumbed.

টাঁক, *v. a.* to appraise, to ascertain, to foretell; to sew, to stitch, to tack together.

টাঁকন, *s.* the appraising of goods, the ascertaining of price; a stitching, a tacking.

টাঁকনি, *s.* appraisement of goods, a stitching, a tacking of things, a patching.

টাকা, *s.* the appraising of goods; a stitch, a tack: *a.* stitched, tacked: *v. a.* to cause to stitch or tack; -**না,** to stitch, to tack.

টাক, *s.* baldness, morbid baldness.

টাকপড়া, *a.* bald, morbidly bald. [ness.

টাকপোকা, *s.* the (insect or) cause of bald-

টাকরা, *s.* the palate or roof of the mouth.

টাকশাল, *s.* the mint (for coining).

টাকা, *s.* a silver coin, a rupee, money.

টাকুয়া, *s.* a spindle, a skewer. [thread.

টাকুর, *s.* a reel, a machine used to twist

টাকুরাই, *s.* a cramp, a spasm.

টাঙ্, *v. n.* to be suspended, to hang. [leg.

টাঙ্গ, *s.* a spade, a hoe, an axe, borax, the

টাঙ্গন, *s.* act of suspending; a hill poney.

টাঙ্গা, *v. a.* to hang up, to suspend: *a.* suspended, hanging. [pended.

টাঙ্গান, *s.* a hanging up: *a.* hung up, sus-

টাঙ্গানি, *s.* the hanging up of a thing.

টাঙ্গ প্রদীপ, *s.* a hanging lamp, a lantern.

টাঙ্গী, *s.* an axe, a battle-axe, a halberd; the male organ of generation. [burnt up.

টাট, টাটা, *v. n.* to smart, to throb, to be

টাট, *s.* a copper dish used in worship; interest by the day; canvass, sackcloth.

টাটান, *s.* a smarting, throbbing, a being burnt up: *a.* painful, withered.

টাটানী, *s.* virulence of pain, a smarting.

টাটি, *s.* a fence, a mat-screen; a privy.

টাটী, *s.* a cup, a mug, a small basin.

টাটু, টাটুয়া, *s.* a poney, country horse.

টাটকা, *a.* fresh, new, not stale.

টান্, *v. a.* to pull, to row, to pull an oar, to draw, attract, drag, tow: *a.* dear, scarce, much in request, hard, harsh, severe: *s.* a pull, the strength of a stream, attraction, force, a spasm, a violent tension.

টানন, *s.* a pulling, drawing, attracting.

টানা, *v. a.* to cause to pull or draw: *s.* a pulling, stretching, the warp of cloth, a spasm, tension; -**না,** to strain, stretch: *a.* drawn, pulled, far, long (a journey).

টানাটানি, *s.* a reciprocal pulling, a rivalry in trade, a struggle, hardship.

টানানি, *s.* a pull, strain, draught, tension,

টানাপ্রদীপ, *s.* a hanging lamp. [a spasm.

টান্‌টোন, *a.* severe, harsh, inflexible; pulling and hauling: *s.* exigency, want.

টাণ্টা, *s.* a dispute, a quarrel, a wrangling.

টাপর, *s.* a tap, a rap, a slight stroke.

টাপা, *s.* a cage for fowls made of wicker work, a musquito screen for babes.

টাপু, *s.* an island, an isle.

টামটুম, *s.* jobs, employment at light work.

টায়টায়, *ad.* equally, neither more nor less.

টাল্, *v. a.* to procrastinate, to dillidally, to trifle, to pretend, to temporize.

টাল, *s.* a pretext, an excuse, procrastination, shuffle, a pretence, a fit of fainting.

টালন, *s.* a procrastinating, a putting off, a shuffling, the using of pretences.

টালনিয়া, *a.* temporizing, procrastinating.

টালাটালি, *s.* a temporizing, procrastina-

টালি, *s.* *Eng.* a tile for flooring. [tion.

টালমটা , *s.* an excuse, an evasion, an equivocation; -**কৃ,** to put off, to shuffle.

টি, an enclitic particle indicative of diminution or affection; *e. g.* মেইয়াটি, the girl; দুটি ভাত, a little rice, etc.

টিআ, টিয়া, *s.* a species of parrot. [stop.

টিক্, *v. n.* to last, continue, endure, stand,

টিকন, *s.* the lasting of any work, a stop-

টিকর, টিকল, *a.* elevated, ridged. [ping.

টিকা, *s.* charcoal dust dough made like a dollar, dried in sun, and used as fire; an ornament for a woman's forehead, a mark on the forehead; inoculation.

টিকাদার, *s.* one who inoculates.

টিকারা, *s.* a kind of kettle-drum.

টিকী, *s.* a small tuft of hair left on the crown of a Hindu, a crest.

টিকাওপড়া, *s.* a plant having sticky seeds.[1]

টিক্‌টিক্, *s.* a ticking noise; a prohibition: *v. n.* to tick.

টিক্‌টিকান, *s.* act of ticking.

টিক্‌টিকানি, *s.* a ticking sound. [noise.

টিক্‌টিকা, *v. n.* to tick, to make a ticking

টিক্‌টিকী, *s.* the common house-lizard.
টিক্‌লী, *s.* a thin slice, a wafer, a lozenge, an ornament for a woman's forehead.
টিটারি, টিটির্, টি টিভ, *s.* the lapwing.
টিট্‌কার, টিট্‌কারি, *s.* a reviling, contempt, reproach; -দা, to revile, reproach, contemn.
টিন্‌টিন্, *s.* the ticking of a watch or bell.
টিপ্, *v. a.* to press, squeeze: *s.* a pressure; eggs of large ants or wasps; *vide* টীপ.
টিপন, *s.* a pinching, squeezing, pressing.
টিপনী, *s.* a commentary, note; a pressing.
টিপা, *s.* a notch, a nick, a mark, indenture.
টিপটিপ, *s.* a fidgeting sensation.
টিপ্‌টিপা, *v. n.* to be on the fidgets.
টিপ্পনী, *s.* a commentary, an annotation, [a note.
টিমক, *s.* a swagger, a boast.
টিম্‌কা, *a.* boasting, bragging, swaggering.
টিম্‌টিম্, *s.* a twinkling and blinking like a lamp when going out, sound of a drum.
টিম্‌টিমা, টিমটিমি, *s.* a small drum.
টী, an enclitic syllable; the same as টি.
টীকা, *s.* a commentary, an inuendo, a [speck.
টীকাকার, *s.* a commentator.
টীপ, *s.* an assignment, a note of hand, a bank-note, a bill of exchange, a draft, a bond, a letter, a voucher.
টু, *im. sd.* used by children in their play.
টুঁক, *v. a.* to tap the sieve or winnowing van while agitating the corn in it.
টুঁকনি, *s.* the tapping of a sieve as above.
টুঁটী, *s.* throat, windpipe; -দাব, to throttle.
টুক্, *v. a.* to prohibit, contradict, thwart, to eat (as insects gnaw paper, etc.)
টুক, *s.* a bit, a slice, a piece, a morsel, a [scrap.
টুকনী, *s.* a small brass water-pot.
টুকরা, *s.* a piece, a fragment, a bit, a parcel, a scrap, a morsel, the spark of gem.
টুকর টুকর, *ad.* piecemeal, in pieces; -কৃ, to cut to pieces, to shatter.
টুকরী, *s.* a basket, a scuttle.
টুকি, টুকী, *s.* a morsel, a small bit, a little.
টুকিটুকি *ad.* by morsels, by little and little.
টুক্‌টুক্ *s.* ruddiness, glow. টুক্‌টুকিয়া, glowing red, ruddy.
টুঙ্কার, *s.* a sound, noise.
টুঙ্গি, *s.* a pigeon-house; a hut, a shed.
টুট্, *v. n.* to be defective, to break, burst: *s.* a deficiency, a defect, loss, a breach.
টুটন, *s.* a breaking, being defective.
টুটী, *s.* the throat; deficiency, defect, loss.
টুন্‌টুন্, *s.* the sound of bells.
টুন্টুক, or টুন্টুনী, *s.* the tailor-bird.
টুপ্, *v. n.* to drop, to fall in drops, distil.
টুপী, *s.* a hat, a cap, a lid or cover.
টুপোকুল, *s.* ripe jujube.
টুম্, টুমটাম্, *s.* a job, light work, job work.
টুমুক, *a.* brittle, weak, fragile.
টুস্কি, *s.* a rap, a tap with the finger.
টেঁ, *im. sd.* of the cry of infants.
টেক, *v. n.* to adhere, to continue, to last, subsist: *s.* a side, a bend, a turning.
টেকন, টেকা, *s.* a continuing, a lasting, a subsisting, a dwelling, a residing.
টেকেটেকে, *ad.* from point to point.
টেটা, *s.* a harpoon, a fish-spear.
টেঁটারী, টেটারী, *s.* a brazier, coppersmith.
টেঁপ, টেঁপাল, *a.* puffed up, bloated.
টেঁপামাছ, *s.* the name of a fish.[1]
টেকাও, *s.* continuance: *a.* strong, durable.
টেকুয়া, টেকো, *s.* a spindle, a skewer.
টেঙ্গরা, *s.* a species of fish.[2] [side.
টেড়্, *v. n.* to be crooked, to lean to one
টেড়া, *a.* askew, awry, crooked, distorted, [oblique.
টেড়াদৃষ্টি, *a.* squint-eyed.
টেনা, *a.* ragged, tattered: *s.* a rag.
টেনাপোঁদা, *a.* ragged: *s.* a tatterdemalion.
টেনী, *a.* small, short; ragged, tattered.
টেপ, টেপন, *s.* a pressing any thing with the finger, a squeeze, a compression.
টেপা, *v. a.* to cause to press or squeeze: *a.* indented, pressed, squeezed.
টের, *s.* certainty, evidence, indication; a border, a verge; -পাওন, to know.
টেরচা, *a.* awry, crooked, distorted, cross,
টেরা, *a.* squint-eyed, cockeyed. [diagonal.
টেরে, *ad* tortuously; on one side or end.
টোঁকন, *s.* a shaking of corn in a sieve.
টোঁকা, *v. a.* to cause corn to be agitated in a sieve, etc.: *a.* sifted, agitated.
টোঁকান, *a.* agitated in a sieve.
টোকর, *s.* a rap; -মার, to rap, to peck.
টোকা, *s.* a kind of umbrella: *a.* worm-eaten: *v. a.* to contradict, eat (as insects).
টোক্‌রা, টোক্‌রী, *s.* a basket, a scuttle.
টোঙ্গর, *s.* a Musalmán (in contempt).

টোটা, *v. a.* to make defective, to break : *s.* a frustrum, a stump, cartridge : *a.* loss.

টোটো, *s.* a lounging about, a rambling.

টোণ, *s.* a quiver for arrows, arrow-case.

টোনা, *s.* a sort of makeshift curtains used by the poor; magic, sorcery, witchcraft.

টোনাটামন, *s.* magic, sorcery, witchcraft.

টোপ, *s.* a fish-bait; a cap, hat, a helmet; a drop; a dent in a metallic vessel.

টোপতোলা, *s.* the mending of a dented vessel; the heads of brass nails.

টোপবৎ, *a.* convex, gibbous, button-like.

টোপর, *s.* a crown, a hat, a helmet.

টোপা, *v. a.* to drop, to distil; *s.* a small cake or lozenge : *a.* mitre-shaped.

টোপান, *a.* fallen in drops : *s.* a dropping, a distilling, a slow falling by drops.

টোপী, *s.* a hat, a cap, a bonnet, a cover.

টোল, *s.* a college, academy, school; a hut, a dent or bruise in a metallic vessel.

টোলখেকুয়া, *a.* bruised, dented, depressed.

টোলটাল, *s.* indentation, bruises, and dents.

টোলপড়া, *a.* bruised, dented, depressed.

টোলা, টোলী, *s.* a part of a town inhabited by particular traders, a ward.

ট্যাঁ, ট্যাঁট্যাঁ, *im. sd.* of the cries of babes.

ট্যাঁস্‌ট্যাঁস্, *s.* insipidity, tastelessness.

ট্যাঁস্‌ট্যাঁসিয়া, *a.* insipid, tasteless, waterish.

ট্যামট্যাম্, *im. sd.* of a small tabour.

ট্যামট্যামী, *s.* a small tabour, a tamborine.

ঠ, the twelfth consonant. It agrees in sound with the *t-h* in pen*t-h*ouse.

ঠং, *s.* the sound of a metallic vessel.

ঠক, *s.* a backbiter, a tale-bearer, a rogue, a swindler, a sharper, an extortioner,

ঠকা, *v. a.* to swindle, over-reach, defraud, cheat, deceive, to outwit, to backbite.

ঠকাঠকি, *s.* a reciprocal defrauding.

ঠকান, *s.* a swindling, defrauding, backbiting : *a.* outwitted, swindled, aspersed.

ঠকানিয়া, *a.* swindling, backbiting, cheating.

ঠকামি, *s.* a backbiting, extortion, fraud.

ঠক্‌ঠক্, *im. sd.* that arising from striking two pieces of wood : *a.* hard, difficult.

ঠক্‌ঠকা, *v. a.* to tap, to rap, to knock at.

ঠক্‌ঠকান, ঠকঠকানি, *s.* a tapping, a rapping.

ঠক্‌ঠকিয়া, *a.* carping, difficult, difficult to deal with, shrewd, sharp. [dy.

ঠক্‌ঠকী, *s.* a dilemma, a difficulty, jeopar-

ঠগ, *a.* swindling, cheating, backbiting : *s.* a swindler, a cheat, a backbiter.

ঠগাই, ঠগামি, *s.* swindling, a cheating, a backbiting, extortion, fraud.

ঠটিয়া, *a.* hard, austere, harsh, disagreeable.

ঠটিয়াকলা, *s.* green kántáli plantain.

ঠঙ্কন, ঠঙ্কনানি, *s.* ringing or jingling sound.

ঠঙ্কনা, *v. n.* to ring, utter a ringing sound.

ঠঙ্কনান, *s.* the making a ringing sound.

ঠঙ্কনিয়া, *a.* sonorous, ringing, gingling.

ঠণ্ডা, ঠণ্ডাই, the same as ঠাণ্ডা, &c. [tarrh.

ঠণ্ডী, *a.* cool, cold : *s.* a cold coolness, a ca-

ঠন্, *s.* sound of a sonorous body. [ness.

ঠন্‌মন্, *s.* a tottering walk through weak-

ঠন্‌মনিয়া, *a.* tottering, unsteady in walk-

ঠমক্‌ঠমক, *s.* show, pomp, coquetry. [ing.

ঠমকী, *a.* showy, pompous : *s.* a coquette.

ঠম্‌ঠমিয়া, *a.* loose, tottering, shaking.

ঠাওর্, ঠাওরা, *v. a.* to consider, to plan, to contrive, to intend, to design, to guess.

ঠাওরণ, ঠাওরাণ, *s.* a considering or determining, a designing, a guessing.

ঠাঁই, *s.* a place, a situation, a space, a station; also, *a.* near, in one's possession.

ঠাকুর, *s.* a god, a lord, a father, a grandfather, Sir, Master, Your worship.

ঠাকুরখুড়া, *s.* a paternal uncle.

ঠাকুরঝী, *s.* a wife's or husband's sister.

ঠাকুরঠুকুর, *s.* a repeated rapping.

ঠাকুরণ, *s.* the same as ঠাকুরাণী. [uncle

ঠাকুরদাদা, *s.* paternal grandfather, great

ঠাকুরদাদী, or ঠাকুরাণীদিদী, *s.* a paternal grandmother, a great uncle's wife.

ঠাকুরপো, *s.* a wife's or husband's brother.

ঠাকুর-বাটী,-বাড়ী,-ঘর, *s.* an idol temple.

ঠাকুর-বাপ,-মা, father's father and mother,

ঠাকুরাণী, *s.* a goddess, the wife of a spiritual guide, a mother, a wife's mother, a lady; also, Madam, Your ladyship.

ঠাকুরালী, *s.* authority, respectability.

ঠাট, *v. n.* to become erect (as the penis).

ঠাট, *s.* a company, a thing, a sketch, a frame, deceit, a show, pomp, affectation.

ঠাটর, *s.* a sketch, a frame.

ঠাটা, *v. n.* to become erect (as the penis).
ঠাটান, *s.* a becoming erect (as the penis).
ঠাটানো, *s.* erection, erection of the penis.
ঠাটারি, *s.* a brazier, a coppersmith.
ঠাট্টা, *s.* mockery, a jibe, a sneer, a jest, a joke, a pun, play, a sarcasm, a squib, a taunt, the ridiculing of a person; -কৃ, to ridicule, to make sport at any one.
ঠাট্টাবাজ, *a.* playful : *s.* a jester, a mocker, a joker, a funny fellow, a merry andrew.
ঠাট্টাবাজি, *s.* mockery, sarcasm, jesting.
ঠাটঠমক, *s.* pomp, show, parade, coquetry.
ঠাটঠমকী, *a.* pompous, showy : *s.* a coquette
ঠাড়, *a.* erect, steep, standing. [tranquil.
ঠাণ্ডা, *a.* cold, cooling, refreshing, agreeable,
ঠাণ্ডাই, *s.* coolness, coldness, agreeableness, comfort, refreshing or cooling things.
ঠাণ্ডী, *s.* a catarrh, a cold (disease).
ঠাপ, ঠাপা, *v. a.* to slap two naked bodies (as in coition) : *s.* the motion of coition.
ঠাপাঠাপি, *s.* mutual slapping (as above).
ঠাপান, ঠাপানি, *s.* the act of slapping two naked bodies (as in coition). [neat.
ঠাম, *a.* elegant, beautiful, well-formed,
ঠায়, *ad.* in that very instant, in that very place, certainly, truly, effectually.
ঠার, *v. a.* to point at, to wink, to make a signal : *s.* an inuendo, a hint, a signal.
ঠারণ, *s.* a winking, a hinting by signals.
ঠারাঠারি, *s.* a mutual winking or nodding.
ঠাস্, *v. a.* to ram down the charge of a gun, to press, to compress, to knead.
ঠাসন, *s.* the ramming down the charge of a gun, a forcing or stuffing in.
ঠাসা, *v. a.* to cause to ram down the charge of a gun : *a.* forced in, rammed down.
ঠাহর্, *v. a.* to reflect, consider, ponder, determine, to think, suppose, to intend, to guess : *s.* idea, reflection, determination, thought, consideration, a guess.
ঠাহরণ, *s.* the considering or meditating upon a thing, a guessing, ascertaining.
ঠাহরা, *v. a.* to consider, to resolve, to determine : *a.* understood, resolved on.
ঠিক, *a.* exact, correct, accurate, true, stable, fixed, proper, precise, just, punctual, direct; -কৃ, to fit, to adjust, to suit; -দা, to add, to cast up a sum, to reckon; -রাখ, to persist : *s.* witchcraft, a charm.
ঠিকর্, *v. a.* to rebound, to bound, spread.
ঠিকরণ, ঠিকরাণ, *s.* a rebounding, a bouncing, a spreading : *a.* rebounded, bounced.
ঠিকরা, *v. a.* to rebound, to bound, spread : *a.* rebounded, bounced : *s.* a potsherd.
ঠিকরী, *s.* a potsherd; -চুনন, to pick shreds.
ঠিকা, *a.* working at job work, working for daily hire, mercenary, hired; -খাট, to work at job work; ঠিকা কর্ম্ম, job work.
ঠিকানা, *s.* certainty, a situation, a residence, a station, the address of a letter.
ঠিক্ঠাক, *a.* correct, accurate, exact, just.
ঠিস্মিন্, ঠিস্মিনা, *s.* a shaking, tottering walk.
ঠিলিয়া, *s.* a water-pot, a pitcher. [tree.
ঠুঁটা, *a.* lame-handed, maimed : *s.* a lopped
ঠুক *s.* a rapping noise : *v. a.* to rap, smite,
ঠুকনি, *s.* a rap, a stroke, a blow. [beat.
ঠুকর্, ঠুকরা, *v.* to peck, to nibble.
ঠুকরণ, ঠুকরাণ, *s.* a pecking, a nibbling.
ঠুকি, *a.* rapping, tapping : *s.* a tap, a rap.
ঠুক্ঠুক্, ঠুক্ঠুকা, *v. a.* to tap, to rap.
ঠুক্ঠুকনি, *s.* a rapping, a tapping. [jar.
ঠুন্ঠুন, *s.* a jarring sound, a jingle; -কৃ, to
ঠুন্ঠুননি, *s.* the ringing of a small bell.
ঠুন্কা, *a.* brittle, fragile : *s.* a sore in the breast or pap of a woman.
ঠুলী, *a.* a ticket in lottery; a hoodwink.
ঠেঁটা, *a.* self-willed, obstinate, contentious.
ঠেঁটামি, *s.* obstinacy, self-will, perversity.
ঠেঁটী, *s.* a widow's garment or petticoat.
ঠেক্, *v. a.* to stop, to obstruct, touch : *s.* a hindrance, an obstruction, a difficulty.
ঠেকনা, *s.* a prop, a stake, a stanchion.
ঠেকা, *v. n.* to touch or strike, to clog, obstruct : *s.* a stake, a prop, a stanchion.
ঠেকাঠেকি, *s.* a mutual touching or striking.
ঠেকান, *s.* a striking or touching, a clogging, or obstructing : *a.* stopped, obstructed.
ঠেকানি, *s.* an obstruction, an insuperable obstacle, a bar or hindrance. [ance.
ঠেকার, *s.* pride, haughtiness, self-import-
ঠেকারিয়া, *a.* proud, supercilious, vain.
ঠেকাল, *a.* difficult, full of obstacles.
ঠেকুয়া, *s.* a prop, a stake, a stanchion.
ঠেকে, *a.* near, proximate; unexpected.

ঠেকেমুড়ে, *ad.* by chance, unexpectedly.
ঠেঙ, *s.* the leg; -তোলা, a paramour.
ঠেঙ্গা, *v. a.* to strike with a staff or bludgeon: *s.* a club, a staff; the thumb.
ঠেঙ্গাঠেঙ্গি, *s.* a reciprocal striking with staffs or clubs, a fighting with staves.
ঠেঙ্গাড়িয়া, or ঠেঙ্গানিয়া, *a.* smiting with club: *s.* one who strikes with a staff.
ঠেঙ্গান, *s.* the act of striking with a staff.
ঠেঙ্গানি, *s.* a striking with a club.
ঠেঙ্গুয়া, *a.* having legs (as prawns, insects).
ঠেল, *v. a.* to push, shove, repel, confute.
ঠেলন, *s.* the act of pushing or shoving, a repelling, the refuting of an argument.
ঠেলা, *v. a.* to cause to push or shove: *s.* a push, a thrust, a shove, a repulsion.
ঠেলাঠেলি, *s.* a press of people, the pushing and shoving of a crowd. [pushed.
ঠেলান, *s.* the causing to push or resist: *a.*
ঠেলানি, *s.* a pushing, a shoving, repulsion.
ঠেলামারণ, *s.* the giving a push or shove.
ঠেস্, *v. n.* to lean against, to lean, to push, to press: *s.* reliance, support, a prop.
ঠেসা, *v. a.* to prop, to support, to implicate; -মার, to jog; -লাগ, to justle.
ঠেসাঠেসি, *s.* a pressing or crowding.
ঠেস্‌ঠাস্, *s.* contract, props and supports.
ঠোঁট, *s.* the lips, the beak, bill of a bird.
ঠোঁটকাটা, *a.* hare-lipped; bold, daring.
ঠোঁটেঠোঁটে, *ad.* in every one's mouth so as to be town-talk: *lit.* bill to bill.
ঠোক, *v. a.* to beat, to strike, to drive a nail, to ram, to rap, to tap. [striking.
ঠোকন, ঠোকনি, *s.* a rapping, a tapping, a
ঠোকনা, *s.* a rap, a tap on the face; a mallet.
ঠোকর, *s.* a pek, a rap, acap, a knock; -লাগন, -খাওন, to trip, stumble; -দেওন, -মারণ. to rap, to tap, to peck, to nibble.
ঠোকরা, *v. a.* to peck, to nibble, to tap.
ঠোকরাণ, *s.* a tapping, pecking, nibbling.
ঠোকরাণি, *s.* nibbling, a peck, a rap, a tap.
ঠোকা, *v. a.* to cause a person to strike, tap, or rap: *s.* a rap, a tap, a knock.
ঠোস, *a.* solid, not hollow. [bead.
ঠোসা, *s.* a blister, vesicle; drop, button,
ঠোসেঠাসে, *ad.* in short, briefly. [tion.
ঠৌর, *s.* stedfastness, certainty, recollec-

ড, the thirteenth consonant in the Bengáli alphabet. It has the sound of d.
ডগর্, *s.* a particular kind of drum.
ডগা, *s.* a point, forepart, a peak, tip, nib. tender stalk of a climber, potherb, etc.
ডগাকড়ি, *s.* a large kind of cauṛi. [peaked.
ডগাল, *a.* pointed, ending in a point or tip,
ডগি, *s.* the forepart or small end of a pole or a bambu: *a.* young and tender.
ডগিরা, *a.* large, high, prominent, rank.
ডগ্‌ডগ্, *s* the glow of a bright red colour.
ডগডগিয়া, *a.* glowing, vividly red.
ডঙ্কা, *s.* a kind of large drum.
ডণ্ড, *s.* a staff, a mace; a fine, punishment.
ডণ্ডা, *s.* the stalk of a plant, a perch for birds, a lamp-stand, a post, a rod.
ডণ্ডী, *s.* a particular tribe of devotees; one who is fined or punished.
ডন্, *s.* a bodily exercise made by wrestlers.
ডব্‌ডবিয়া, *a.* watery, wet, flaccid, limber.
ডমরু, *s.* a kind of small drum like a tabour.
ডমরুমধ্য, *s.* a peninsula, a neck of land.
ডম্ফ, *s.* a kind of drum beat on one side.
ডর্, *v. n.* to be terrified, alarmed, or in fear: *s.* fear, terror, panic, dread, alarm.
ডরফক্কা, *a.* timid, fearful, pusillanimous.
ডরা, *v. a.* to affright, to alarm a person.
ডরাণ, *s.* the putting of a person in fear, a being afraid: *a.* alarmed, frightened.
ডরালু, *a.* afraid, timid, fearful, cowardly.
ডরুক, *a.* timorous, fearful, pusillanimous.
ডল, *v. a.* to grind on a stone, to rub in unguents, to squeeze, to tread, to trample.
ডল্‌করমচা, *s.* white or China caranda.
ডলন, *s.* the rubbing of a thing, a grinding, squeezing, a treading under foot.
ডলনা, *s.* a muller, roller of wood or stone.
ডলা, *v. a.* to cause to rub or grind: *a.* rubbed in, squeezed, ground: *s.* a lump.
ডলাডলি, *s.* a mutual rubbing, or treading.
ডলান, *a.* ground, rubbed in, trod: *s.* a causing to grind or rub, a treading.
ডলানি, *s.* a treading or grinding. [work.
ডল্লক, *s.* a fruit-basket, a tray of wicker
ডহর, ডহরা, *s.* a lake, deep water, the centre cavity or hold of a boat.
ডা, the same with টা, which see.

ডাহিণ, *a.* right (in opposition to left).
ডাইন, or ডাইনী, *s.* a witch, a hag.
ডাইনকোণা, *s.* the name of a fish.[1]
ডাইনপনা, *s.* witchcraft.
ডাইনপিটা, *a.* obstinate, hardened, self-willed.
ডাইনমন্ত্র, *s.* witchcraft, also the incantations used to expel the charm of a witch.
ডাং, *s.* a staff, pole, perch, hanging-shelf.
ডাঁট্, *v.a.* to threaten, to daunt, to punish, to rebuke, to scold : *s.* scolding.
ডাঁট, *a.* unripe, green, hard ; unfeeling.
ডাঁটন, ডাঁটনি, *s.* a scolding, a threatening, the rebuking of a person, a threat.
ডাঁটা, *s.* a stalk, a stem, a handle, a shaft, or upright rod : *a.* threatened, scolded.
ডাঁটাল, *a.* abounding with or full of stalks.
ডাঁটী, *s.* a stem, a stalk, a handle, a shaft.
ডাঁড্, *v. n.* to stand : *s.* a tooth.
ডাঁড়, *s.* a paddle, oar, roost, perch ; a fine, forfeit.
ডাঁড়কাক, *s.* the common carrion crow.
ডাঁড়শ, *s.* the name of a harmless serpent.
ডাঁড়া, *v.* to stand, stand still, or erect : *s.* a custom, habit, a tooth, the back-bone, a standing erect : *a.* erect, perpendicular.
ডাঁড়ান, *s.* a standing, a standing erect.
ডাঁড়াসাঁতার, *s.* a swimming with the body in an erect posture.
ডাঁড়ী, *s.* a waterman, a rower, the beam of a pair of scales.
ডাঁড়ীপাল্লা, *s.* a pair of scales.
ডাঁড়ুকা, *s.* stocks, manacles, shackles, fetters.
ডাঁপ, *s.* a rail, poles used in scaffolding.
ডাঁশ্, *v. n.* to half-ripen (as fruits).
ডাঁশ, *s.* a gad-fly, a large musquito.
ডাঁশা, *v. n.* to half-ripen (as fruits) : *s.* a cross or horizontal bar of wood.
ডাঁশাল, *a.* half-ripe, appearing ripe.
ডাক্, *v. a.* to call, to name. ডাকিয়া পাঠান, to send word, to call, to summon.
ডাক, *s.* a call, a summon, a letter-carrier, a post ; -ছাড়, -পাড়, to shout, to scold.
ডাকঘর, *s.* a post-office, a post house.
ডাকচৌকী, *s.* a post-station, post-stand.
ডাকডোক, *s.* a calling and shouting.
ডাকন, *s* the act of calling or naming.
ডাকপত্র, *s.* post letter, a summon.
ডাকপত্রী, ডাকপাতী, *s.* a letter or billet by post.
ডাকপাখী, *s.* a species of bird.[2]

ডাকপেয়াদা, *s.* a postman, a letter-carrier.
ডাকবালা, *s.* the bearer of a post-bag.
ডাকবাঙ্গী, *s.* a post conveyance of parcel.
ডাকবেহারা, *s.* post bearers of a pálki.
ডাকমারণ, *s.* a robbing of the post.
ডাকমাসুল, *s.* the postage of a letter or parcel.
ডাকহাঁক, *s.* a shout, an outcry.
ডাকা, *v. a.* to cause to call : *s.* a call ; a robber, a highwayman : *a.* called.
ডাকাইত, *s.* a robber, a highwayman, a bandit.
ডাকাইতি, *s.* a robbery, a burglary.
ডাকাডাকি, *s.* a repeated calling, an outcry.
ডাকাতি, *s.* a robbery, an attack to rob.
ডাকাবুকা, *a.* bold, impudent, undaunted, fearless, valiant, daring.
ডাকাবুকামি, *s.* boldness, insolence, fearlessness.
ডাকিনী, *s.* a witch, a virago, a bold woman.
ডাকিনীবং, *a.* crafty, mischievous.
ডাকু, *s.* a robber, a plunderer, a highwayman.
ডাকুয়া, *s.* a postman, a guide.
ডাকে, *ad.* by post : *prep.* calling.
ডাগর, *a.* large, prominent, high, thriving.
ডাঙ্গ, *s.* a stake stuck in the wall to hang clothes on, a hanging-shelf, a roost.
ডাঙ্গস, *s.* a goad, iron hook to drive an elephant.
ডাঙ্গা, *s.* dry land, upland.
ডাঙ্গাপথ, *s.* a road or journey by land.
ডাঙ্গাপথে, *ad.* by land, overland.
ডাড়, *s.* a tooth, fang ; claws of a crab or lobster, a serrature ; wards of a key.
ডাড়কাক, *s.* the common carrion crow.
ডাড়া, *s.* the serrated legs of a crab or lobster.
ডাড়াল, *a.* serrated, like a saw.
ডাণ্ডা, *s.* a staff, a spot, a cricket-bat.
ডাণ্ডী, *s.* a post, stake, yard of a ship, handle.
ডাব, -নারিকেল, *s.* green cocoanut.
ডাবর, ডাবরী, *s.* a pitcher, a water-pot.
ডাবা, *s.* a washing basin ; a mean huká.
ডাবু, *s.* a washhand basin ; a water-pot.
ডামাডোল, *s.* an uproar, an unsettled state.
ডাল্, *a.* to lop a tree, to throw.
ডাল, *s.* a branch, a bough ; split peas.
ডালচীনী, দারচীনী, *s.* cinnamon.
ডালন, *s.* the lopping of a tree ; a throwing.
ডালনা, *s.* a dish made of vegetables.
ডালা, *s.* a fruit-basket, a wicker tray, a cover, a lid : *v. a.* to cause to lop a tree.

ডালি, *s.* a basket full of any articles, or of fruits, etc. for a present; split peas.
ডালিম, *s.* a pomegranate; diseased pork-
ডাহুক, *s.* name of a water-bird.[1] [flesh.
ডি, *s.* a district; also the same with টি.
ডিগবাজী, *s.* a tumbling, a vaulting;-কর, a
ডিগরী, *s. Eng.* a judicial decree. [tumbler.
ডিঙ্গ, *v. a.* to jump over any thing.
ডিঙ্গরা, *a.* roguish, swindling, mean, depraved: *s.* a rogue, cheat, a mean person.
ডিঙ্গরামি, *s.* roguishness, etc. [a boat.
ডিঙ্গা, *v. a.* to jump over a fence: *s.* a ship,
ডিঙ্গান, *s.* the jumping over a fence.
ডিঙ্গী, *s.* small boat, wherry, skiff;-বালা, a
ডিণ্ডিম, *s.* a tabour, small drum. [boatman.
ডিণ্ডির, *s.* the foam of the sea. [district.
ডিবন্দী, *s.* the settling of the revenues of a
ডিবা, *s.* a small box, a pill-box, a canister.
ডিম, ডিম্ব, ডিম্ভ *s.* an egg, a spawn, chrysalis;-ছাড়, to spawn;-পাড়, to lay eggs.
ডিম্বজ, or ডিম্ভজ, *a.* oviparous. [state.
ডিম্বসাঁচ, *s.* the sperm, eggs in an imperfect
ডিম্বিকা, *s.* a bubble, vesicle; a water-fly.
ডিহী, *s.* a small district;-বন্দী, *vide* ডিবন্দী.
ডুকর, ডুকরা, *v. n.* to weep, to cry, lament: ডুকরিয়া কাঁদন, to weep or cry aloud.
ডুকরণ, ডুকরাণ, *s.* a weeping, crying aloud.
ডুকার, *s.* a bawling or crying aloud.
ডুগডুগ, *a.* glowing, vividly red.
ডুগডুগী, *s.* a small drum, a toy drum.
ডুঙ্গী, *s.* a canoe, a skiff, a small boat.
ডুব, *v.n.* to sink, plunge: *s.* diving, immersion;-দেবা, to immerse, to baptize;-দা, -পাড়, or -মার, to plunge, to dive: ডুবিয়া মরণ, to drown: ডুবিয়া যাওন, to sink.
ডুবক, ডুবনিয়া, *s.* one who immerses, or administers baptism, a baptizer, a baptist.
ডুবন, *s.* a diving, a sinking, a being im-
ডুবরী, or ডুবরিয়া, *s.* a diver. [mersed.
ডুবা, *a.* to plunge, to immerse, to baptize, to cause to sink: *a.* immersed, inundated, sunk, drowned, overflown, swampy.
ডুবান, *a.* immersed, plunged: *s.* the immersing of a person or thing. [culty.
ডুবানিয়া, *a.* plunging one in water or diffi-
ডুবারা, *s.* the dobchick or diver.[2]
ডুবারু, *s.* a diver; the dobchick or diver.[2]

ডুবিত, *a.* immersed, dipped, plunged, bap-
ডুবুডুবু, *a.* on the point of drowning. [tized.
ডুমা, *s.* a small bit, a chip, a crumb.
ডুমুর, *s.* a fig, a fig-tree (Ficus glomerata).
ডুমুরিয়া, *a.* large (a sort of small-pox).
ডুম্বর, *s.* a young tiger; a fig, a fig-tree.
ডুরিয়া, *a.* striped, corded: *s.* a dog-keeper.
ডুরী, *s.* line, string, packthread, fine rope.
ডুরীপড়া, *a.* striped, streaked, corded.
ডুলী, *s.* a covered litter, a pálki; a mast.
ডুলাডুলী, *s.* fear and trembling.
ডেউআ, ডেঁফল, *s.* a tree and its fruit.[3]
ডেউআপিপীড়া, *s.* a species of black ant.
ডেঁড়ুআ, *s.* a kind of spade or digging hoe.
ডেঁড়ে, *a.* seamed; punished, fined.
ডেঁপ, *s.* the sucker of a tree, a stage prop.
ডেকরা, ডেঙ্গর, ডেঙ্গরা, vile, rascally, impudent, depraved, letcherous, libertine: *s.* a letcher, a libertine; *fem.* ডেকরী.
ডেকরামি, ডেঙ্গরামি, *s.* depravity, vileness, villany, impudence, rascality, letchery.
ডেগ, *s.* a caldron, a pot, a copper-boiler.
ডেঙ্গুয়া, *s.* a widower;-খাড়া, a kind of pot.
ডেঙ্গুর, *s.* a louse, a large louse. [herb.
ডেড়, ডেড়া, *a.* one and a half. [order.
ডেড়ী, *s.* want, need, poverty, sickness, dis-
ডেনা, *s.* a wing, pinion, a fin, an arm.
ডেবরা, *a.* left-handed, prominent, gibbous.
ডেরা, *s.* a house, tent, the screen of a tent.
ডেলা, *s.* a lump, a clod;-মার, to pelt.
ডোকরা, *v. n.* to lament, to weep, bewail: *s.* an old man (in a ludicrous sense).
ডোকরাণ, *s.* a lamenting, a bewailing,
ডোকরাণি, *s.* lamentation, a bewailing.
ডোঙ্গা, ডোঙ্গী, *s.* a canoe, a skiff; a trough.
ডোবা, *s.* a hole, a pond: *v. a. vide* ডুবা.
ডোম, *s.* a low class of Hindu, a wickerman, basket-maker, scavenger, a dog-killer.
ডোমচিল, *s.* a species of kite. [of song.
ডোমনী, *s.* a female basket-maker; a sort
ডোর, ডোরক, *s.* a fishing line, a line, a string, twine, a rope, a cord.
ডোরা, *s.* a stripe, a streak, the rib of a stocking, a cord, a rope, a line.
ডোরিয়া, ডোরী, the same as ডুরিয়া, ডুরী.
ডোল, *s.* a granary, a store-house; a mast.
ডোলা, ডোলী, *s.* a covered litter, a pálki.

ডৌল, s. a fashion, a form, a shape, a manner, method, an attitude, a mien, gait.
ডৌলডাল, s. shape and fashion, a gait.
ডৌলমাফিক, or ডৌলসার, a. fashionable, according to fashion, well formed.

ঢ, the fourteenth consonant. It has the power of *d h* in holy roo*d-h*ouse.
ঢং, the sound of a bell: s. manners, habit.
ঢক্, v. a. to shove, to push: s. a shove, a push.
ঢক, s. weight (for scales) a thing.
ঢক্কা, s. a drum, a large Indian drum.
ঢঙ্গ, s. an imposter, a swindler; manners.
ঢনা, a. blasted, faded, withered, dried up.
ঢম্মন্, s. a shaking or tottering motion.
ঢম্মনিয়া, a. tottering, exceedingly weak.
ঢপ্, s. the same as ডৌল.
ঢপ্‌ঢপ্, ঢব্‌ঢব্, s. the sound of wet drum.
ঢপ্‌ঢপিয়া, a. sounding like a wet drum.
ঢল্, v. n. to decline, slope, fall, to be aslant, inclined: s. slanting stream, fall of hilly waters in a river: a. loose, slack.
ঢলনাবা, s. mountain streams, descending of muddy hill waters into the rivers.
ঢলা, v. to make known an evil conduct, to be lewd, to proclaim one's own disgrace.
ঢলান, ঢলানি, s. the proclaiming of one's own disgrace by a course of lewdness.
ঢলানী, a. publishing her disgrace by her lewdness: s. a coquette, a lewd woman.
ঢল্ক, v. to demolish, decline, revolve, pass away: a. loose, slack, lax: s. slackness.
ঢল্কন, s. a being demolished; the declining of a luminary: a. loose, not tight.
ঢল্কা, v. a. to demolish, to pass, to decline.
ঢল্কান, s. a passing, declining of a luminary when it has passed the meridian.
ঢল্কানি, s. the declension of a luminary.
ঢল্‌ঢল্, s. a sparkling appearance of a gem or water: a. loose, slack; -কৃ, to sparkle.
ঢলঢলিয়া, a. sparkling, fluid, loose, slack.
ঢস্, v. a. to moulder, to crumble, fall in.
ঢসা, v. a. to cause to crumble or break off in large pieces: a. crumbled down.
ঢসান, s. a causing the banks of a river to break: a. broken, mouldered, fallen in.
ঢাক, v. a. to cover, conceal: s. a big drum.
ঢাককাঠী, s. a drum-stick.
ঢাকন, s. the act of covering or concealing.
ঢাকনা, ঢাকনি, s. a cover, a lid, a covering.
ঢাকনী, s. a cover, a lid: a. *fem.* covering.
ঢাকা, v. a. to cause to cover or conceal: s. name of a city: a. covered, concealed.
ঢাকাঘেরা, s. a screen, a fence, a shade: a. covered, fenced, screened.
ঢাকাঢোকা, a. covered, concealed, fenced.
ঢাকী, s. a drummer.
ঢাকুনী, s. a screen, fence, cover, lid.
ঢাঙ্গা, s. a concourse of people, a mob.
ঢাপ্, v. a. to cover, to conceal. [to cover.
ঢাপা, ঢাপ্‌, s. a covering: a. covered; -দা,
ঢামরা, s. a goose.
ঢাল, v. to pour, to spill, cast in a mould: s a shield; a slope, declivity, obliquity: a. aslant, aslope, inclined, oblique.
ঢালন, s. the act of pouring or casting.
ঢালা, v. a. to cause to pour out, or cast metal in a mould: a. poured out, cast.
ঢালাউবরা, s. the loading and unloading of a boat or other vessels, a pouring over.
ঢালান, a. poured out, cast: s. a causing to pour out liquor, or to cast metals.
ঢালী, a. wearing or using a shield.
ঢিম্মিন্, s. a tottering motion. [flaccid.
ঢিম্মিনা, or ঢিম্মিনিয়া, a. tottering, flabby,
ঢিপ্, s. sound of a blow on the back, or the fall of a clod, a cocoanut, etc.
ঢিপন, ঢিপান, s. a smiting, giving blows.
ঢিপনি, ঢিপানি, s. a smiting with the fist,
ঢিপা, v. to smite with the fist. [pugilism.
ঢিপী, ঢিবি, s. a heap, a pile, accumulation.
ঢিপীঢিপী, ঢিবিঢিবি, ad. in heaps or piles.
ঢিপ্‌ল্যা, s. a piece of wadding, a plug.
ঢিপসা, a. bulky, fat, stout, unwieldy.
ঢিমা, a. mild, gentle, cool, dispassionate.
ঢিল, a. slake: s. a clod, a brickbat; slackness, procrastination; -মার, to pelt at.
ঢিল্‌মিলিয়া, a. flabby, flaccid. [lazy, lax.
ঢিলা, a. loose, slack, flaccid, dilatory, slow,
ঢিলাম, or ঢিলামি, s. slackness, looseness, flaccidity, laxity, negligence, laziness.
ঢু, s. a butting with the head as a ram, etc.
ঢুঁড়্, v. a. to seek, to search: s. search.
ঢুঁড়ন, ঢুণ্ডন, s. a seeking, a searching for.

ঢুঁড়নি, *s.* a seeking, searching, search.
ঢুক্, *v. n.* to enter, to pervade, to intrude.
ঢুঁকন, ঢুকনি, *s.* the entering into a place.
ঢুকা, *v. a.* to thrust, to tuck in, to force in.
ঢুকান, *s.* the act of thrusting or forcing in.
ঢুটনী, *s.* a bawd, a procuress, go-between.
ঢুঁড়ুভ, *s.* a kind of harmless snake. [etc.
ঢুপ্‌ঢাপ্, *im. sd.* of the falling of cocoanut,
ঢুল্, *v. n.* to nod with sleep, to nod, doze,
ঢুল্‌কি, a drum struck by the fingers. [nap.
ঢুলকিবালা, *s.* one who plays on the ḍhulki.
ঢুলঢুল্, ঢুলন, *s.* a nodding with drowsiness.
ঢুলা, *v. n.* to shake, jog, agitate. [(eyes.)
ঢুলুঢুলু, ঢুলঢুলু, *a.* dull, drowsy, half-closed
ঢুষ্, ঢুষা, *v. a.* to butt (as a ram, etc.,) to
enter, to thrust in the head: *s.* a push.
ঢুষণ, ঢুষাণ, *s.* a butting with the head.
ঢুষাঢুষি, *s.* mutual butting with the head.
ঢুষাণিয়া, *a.* butting, pushing with the head.
ঢেউ, *s.* a billow, a wave, a surge; a whim;
-ভাঙ্গ, to scollop, to avoid the billows.
ঢেঁকী, *s.* the pedal; -শালা, the pedal house.
ঢেঁকীকল, *s.* a battering ram. [born.
ঢেঁটা, *a.* insolent, saucy, impudent, stub-
ঢেঁটাম, ঢেঁটামি, *s.* insolence, sauciness, stub-
ঢেঁড়স, *s.* the same as ধেঁড়স. [bornness.
ঢেঁড়রা, or ঢেঁড়ি, *s.* the beat of a drum, a
proclamation by beat of drum.
ঢেঁড়রিয়া, *s.* a drummer, a crier.
ঢেঁড়ী, *s.* a large kind of earring. [lenta.
ঢেঁপ, *s.* the seed-vessel of Nymphæa escu-
ঢেঁশা, *s.* an invidious comparison, a blame.
ঢেকান, ঢেকানি, *s.* a shoving or pushing.
ঢেকান্, *v. a.* to shove, to push. [belch.
ঢেকুর, *s.* a belching, eructation; -তোল, to
ঢেঙ্গা, *a.* tall, high, long. [wicked.
ঢেমন, *s.* an illegitimate child, a bastard: *a.*
ঢেমনঢোষর্ *s.* a bastard, an unlawful child.
ঢেমনা, *s.* a gallant, a paramour.
ঢেমনাসাপ, *s.* a large harmless snake.
ঢেমনী, *s.* a concubine, a kept woman.
ঢের, *a.* many, abundant, much, plenty.
ঢেরা, *s.* a cross mark made as signature,
a sort of reel used to spin packthread.
ঢেরি, ঢেরী, *s.* a heap, a pile, a collection.
ঢেলা, *s.* a lump, a clod; the eye (in con-
ঢো, *v. a.* to carry a burden. [tempt.)
ঢোওন, *s.* the carrying of a burden.
ঢোঁ, ঢোঁস, *s.* loud sound of breaking wind.
ঢোঁড়ন, *s.* the searching for a thing. [seek.
ঢোঁড়া, *s.* a water-snake: *v. a.* to cause to
ঢোক, *s.* a draught, a gulp; -গিল, to gulp.
ঢোকন, *s.* the entering into a place.
ঢোকা, *v. a.* to force or thrust in, to cause
to enter: *a.* entered, forced in. [enter.
ঢোকান, *s.* a causing to enter: *a.* made to
ঢোল, *s.* a drum, a tomtom; a nodding, a
ঢোলকলমী, *s.* a climbing plant. [shaking.
ঢোলন, *s.* a nodding, a swinging freely.
ঢোলনিয়া, *a.* drowsy, lethargic, nodding.
ঢোলা, *v. a.* to cause to swing, to cause to
carry burdens: *a.* hollow: *s.* a nodding.
ঢোলাই, *s.* the hire for cárrying burdens.
ঢোলান, *s.* the transporting of goods or
merchandize from one place to another.
ঢোষা, *v. a.* to cause to butt: *a.* hollow.
ঢোষাণ, *s.* a causing to butt, or to force in.

ণ, the fifteenth consonant. It is scarcely ever used as the initial of a word.
ণত্ব, *s.* the condition or circumstance of the letter ণ. A grammatical term indicating the letter ণ and not ন.

ত, the sixteenth consonant. It has the soft sound of *t* as in Ba*t*-hurst.
*তঅজ্জব, *s.* astonishment, surprize, won-
*তইনাৎ, *s.* attendance. [der.
তইনাতী, *s.* an attendant.
তউ, *s.* a brazen or copper pot. [see.
তৎ, a *contract.* of তরফ, and তলব, which
তক্, *ad.* till, until, to, unto: *a.* sour, acid.
*তকল্লব, *s.* trouble, distress, affliction.
*তকাবী, *s.* money given in advance.
তকিআ, *s.* a pillow, a bolster, a support.
তকিত, *s.* the ascertaining of a thing.
তকু, *a.* the fourth (a term used in some
*তক্ত, *s.* a throne, a state chair. [games.)
তক্তপোস, *s.* a kind of bedstead, a table.
তক্তরয়া, *s.* a state pálki, a portable stage
used in public processions.
তক্তা, *s.* a board, a plank.
তক্তাপোস, *s.* a plank-bottomed bedstead.
*তক্তি, *s.* a slate, a small writing board.

তক্র, *s.* diluted buttermilk. [altercation.
তকরার, *s.* repetition, tautology, dispute,
তকরারী, *a.* disputatious, contentious.
*তক্লীফ, *s.* affliction, distress, hardship.
তক্ষক, *s.* a carpenter, a carver; a fabled
তক্ষণ, *s.* a carving, engraving. [serpent.
তক্ষণি, *ad.* then, at that instant.
তক্ষিত, *a.* carved, engraved, scraped. [sin.
*তক্সীর, *s.* a fault, crime, offence, error,
তক্সীরবার, *a.* faulty, guilty, sinful. [then.
তখন, তখনি, *ad.* then, at that time, even
*তগলব, *s.* an adulteration, a cheating, embezzlement, imposition. [on others.
তগলবী, *a.* adulterated cheating, imposing
*তগীর, *s.* an exchange, dismission from of-
তঙ্কা, টাকা, *s.* a silver coin, a rupee. [fice.
তঙ্কী, *s.* investigation, inquiry, search.
তচ্ছম, *s.* a mollifying, a tranquillizing; -কৃ, to tranquillize that, to mollify that.
তজ্জ, *a.* springing from him, her, or that.
*তজ্বীজ, *s.* examination, search, investigation, scrutiny, judgment, justice.
তঞ্চ *s.* collusion, imposition, fraud.
তঞ্চক, *a.* deceiving, swindling, imposing upon: *s.* a deceiver, swindler, impostor.
তঞ্চকতা, *s.* deceitfulness, swindling, etc.
তট, *s.* a shore, the bank of a river, strand.
তটবর্ত্ম, *s.* a road on the shore or strand.
তটস্থ, *a.* situated on the shore; impartial.
তটাক, তড়াক, or তড়াগ, *s.* a lake, a pond, a pond or pool deep enough for the lotus.
তড়, *s.* a strand, shore; -পথ, a road by land.
তড়প্, *v. a.* to bound, to flounce, to ramp.
তড়পন, *s.* a flouncing, jumping, ramping.
তড়পা, *v. a.* to bounce, jump: *s.* a bundle.
তড়া, *s.* a shore, strand, a coast, the sea
তড়িৎ, *s.* lightning, flash of light. [coast.
তড়্তড়িয়া, *a.* impatient, fickle, smart.
তণ্ডুল, চাউল, *s.* husked rice. unboiled rice
তণ্ডুলকণা, *s.* grains of rice, broken rice.
ততঃ, *ad.* than that, from that, after that.
তত, *pron.* so much, so many.
ততদিন, *ad.* so long, so many days. [that.
ততোধিক, *ad.* twice as much, more than
তৎ, *pron.* he, she, it, that (used in *comp.*)
তৎকথন, *s.* saying that; his or her speech.
তৎকথা, *s.* that word, the same story.
তৎকরণক, তৎকর্তৃক, *a.* done by that, done by his, her or its instrumentality.
তৎকর্ম্ম, *s.* that work, action, or business,
তৎকারণ, *s.* that cause, the cause of that.
তৎকার্য্য, *s.* that work, business, action or
তৎকাল, *s.* that time, that instant. [deed.
তৎকালধী, *s.* the presence of mind.
তৎকালীন, *a.* belonging to that time.
তৎকালে, *ad.* then, at that time.
তৎকৃত, *a.* done by him, her, or that.
তৎক্ষণাৎ, *ad.* thenceforth, immediately.
তৎক্ষণে, *ad.* then, at that instant.
তত্তুল্য, *a.* equal to that, like that, similar.
তত্ত্ব, *s.* a first principle, essence, primitive truth, axiom, accurate idea, genuine nature of a thing, a truth, reality, identity, a mystery, a thing to be sought, search, enquiry, scrutiny; -কৃ, -লও, to scrutinize, search, trace out. [gates.
তত্ত্বকারক, *s.* one who searches or investi-
তত্ত্বজ্ঞান, *s.* the knowledge of first principles, the knowledge of realities.
তত্ত্বজ্ঞানী, *a.* acquainted with the realities: *s.* one who is thus acquainted.
তত্ত্ববাদী, *a.* speaking correctly on any subject, speaking philosophically.
তত্ত্ববার্ত্তা, *s.* an enquiry, search, scrutiny.
তত্ত্ববোধনী, *a.* convincing of the first principle, or primitive truth. [tor.
তত্ত্বাবধারক, *s.* a superintendent, inspec-
তত্ত্বাবধারণ, *s.* superintendence, care, attention, inspection.
তৎপক্ষ, *s.* that side, his or her side, that wing, that wax or wane of the moon.
তৎপক্ষে, *ad.* on that side, on his or her side.
তৎপদস্থ, *a.* occupying that situation.
তৎপর, *a.* eminent, clever, accomplished, able, skilful, dexterous, shrewd.
তৎপরতা, -ত্ব, *s.* skilfulness, dexterity.
তৎপশ্চাৎ, *ad.* after that, after him or her.
তৎপ্রযুক্ত, *ad.* therefore, for that.
তৎপ্রয়োগ, *s.* that impelling cause. [ject.
তৎপ্রসক্তি, তৎপ্রসঙ্গ, *s.* that topic, that ob-
তত্র, *ad.* there, therein, in that place.
তত্রস্থ, *a.* situated there, of that place.
তত্রাপি, *ad.* even, even then, yet, still.
তথা, *ad.* thus, so, there, the same, ditto.

তথাচ, তথাপি, *conj.* notwithstanding, nevertheless, yet, still, even, even thus.
তথায়, *ad.* in that place, there.
তথাস্তু, *phrase.* so be it, amen.
তথৈব, *ad.* so, even so, thus.
তথ্য, *s.* a reality, certainty, accuracy, truth.
তথ্যজ্ঞান, তথ্যবোধ, *s.* an accurate knowledge, a correct idea, a conviction.
তদংশ, *s.* that share, his or her share.
তদংশী, *a.* sharing that, dividing that.
তদধিকার, *s.* that right or proprietorship, a right over him or her.
তদধিকারী, *s.* owner or proprietor of that.
তদনন্তর, *ad.* afterwards, after that, then.
তদনুগ, *a.* following him, her, or that.
তদনুগত, *a.* devoted to him, her, or that.
তদনুগামী, *a.* following him, her, or that.
তদনুযায়ী, *a.* according with that, following upon that, consistent with that.
তদনুরূপ, *a.* resembling him, her, or that, corresponding with that, thus, so.
তদনুসার, *a.* according to that, so.
তদনুসারী, *a.* according with that, agreeing thereto.
তদনুসারে, *ad.* according to that.
তদন্ত, *s.* that scope or end, the object or scope of that, a scope, object, aim, end.
তদন্তর, *ad.* besides, besides that.
তদবধি, *ad.* thenceforth, till then, so far.
তদবস্থ, *a.* thus conditioned, thus situated.
তদবস্থা, *s.* his or that state or condition.
তদভ্যন্তর, *s.* the midst of that : *ad.* in the midst of that.
তদা, *ad.* then, at that time.
তদাদি, *a.* beginning with that.
তদাদিতদন্ত, *s.* all the circumstances which relate to a thing from beginning to end.
তদানীং, *ad.* then, at that time.
তদিতর, *a.* different from that.
তদুক্ত, *a.* spoken by him or her, mentioned in that (book or writing.)
তদুক্তি, *s.* that sentence, his, her or that expression.
তদুচিত, *a.* proper or fitting for that.
তদুত্তর, *s.* that answer, his or her reply: *a.* after him, her, or that ; north of that.
তদুত্তরদিগে, *ad.* to the north of that.
তদুত্তরদেশ, *s.* the country north of that.
তদুপকার, *s.* that assistance, his or her help.
তদুপযুক্ত, *a.* fit for him, her or that.
তদুপযোগিতা, -ত্ব, *s.* that utility or fitness, fitness or usefulness for that purpose.
তদুপযোগী, *a.* useful or fit for that, useful or advantageous to him or her.
তদুপরি, *ad.* thereupon, upon that, upon him or her.
তদেকচিত্ত, *a.* like-minded with him or her.
তদেব, *ad.* the very same thing, identically the same thing, the same.
তদ্গত, *a.* found or being in that, attached to or existing in him, her or that.
তদ্গতিক, *s.* his, her, or that state or condition, his, her or that state of happiness.
তদ্দণ্ড, *s.* that hour, staff, or punishment.
তদ্দেশ, *s.* his, her or that country.
তদ্দ্বারা, *ad.* by or through him, her or that.
তদ্ধিত, *s.* his, her or that benefit or advantage; in *gram.* derivatives formed from complete words, as distinguished from such as are formed from verbal roots.
তদ্বৎ, *a.* like that, resembling.
তদ্বৎপ্রায়, *ad.* almost so, nearly in that manner.
তদ্বাচক, *a.* expressing that, saying that.
তদ্বিপর্যয়, *s.* his, her, or that opposition.
তদ্বিবরণ, *s.* that detail, those circumstances.
তদ্বিবেচনা, *s.* that investigation.
তদ্বিষয়, *s.* that object, wealth, or affair.
তদ্বিষয়ক, *a.* relating to that.
তদ্বৃত্তান্ত, *s.* that detail or recital of particulars.
তদ্ব্যতিরেক, *ad.* without or beside that.
তদ্ব্যবস্থা, *s.* that law, or statute.
তদ্ব্যবস্থানুসারে, *ad.* according to that law.
তদ্ভিন্ন, *a.* apart from that: *ad.* beside that.
তদ্রূপ, *s.* that form ; so, in like manner, such.
তধী, *ad.* then, at that very time.
*তন্, *s.* the body. তনা, *a.* alone, lonely.
তনয়, *s.* a son. তনয়া, *s.* a daughter.
তনিষ্ঠ, *a.* very thin, narrow, or small.
তনু, তনূ, *s.* the body: *a.* minute, delicate, thin, slender ; -কূপ, pores of the skin.
তনুজ *a.* produced from the body: *s.* a son.
তনূজা, *fem. idem : s.* a daughter.
তনূকৃত, *a.* pared, made thin or delicate.
তনূর, *s.* an oven, a furnace.
তনূরুহ, *s.* the hair of the body, feathers of a bird.
*তন্খা, তন্খাই, *s.* search, inquiry, guess, an appraisement; -কৃ, to search.
তন্খা, *s.* wages, assignment on the revenues.

তন্‌খাদার, *s.* one who receives a salary.
তন্‌খাদারী, *s.* the living on a salary.
তন্তু, *s.* a thread, threads of a warp, a cord.
তন্তুবা , তন্তুবায়, *s.* a weaver, a spider.
তন্তুশালা, *s.* a weaver's shop. [tree.
তন্তুসার, *s.* an emaciated person; betel-nut
তন্ত্র, *s.* a thread, the threads of a warp, the strings of a musical instrument, a class of sacred books, a charm; a weaver's loom, a leathern thong: *a.* subservient.
তন্ত্রকাষ্ঠ, *s.* a weaver's loom.
তন্ত্রতা, *s.* contrivance, collusion, intrigue.
তন্ত্রমন্ত্র, *s.* delusion, sorcery, witchcraft.
তন্ত্রসার, *s.* quintessence of the Tantras.
তন্ত্রী, *s.* a musician, a stringed instrument, a professor of the Tantras. [situde.
তন্দ্রা, তন্দ্রী, *s.* drowsiness, sleepiness, las-
তন্দ্রাকর্ষিত, *a.* overcome by sleepiness.
তন্দ্রাবৃত, তন্দ্রাযুক্ত, *a.* sleepy, drowsy.
তন্দ্রালু, *a.* weary, drowsy, sleepy, slothful.
তন্ন, *ad.* not that, not so; an expression of
তন্নগর, *s.* that city or town. [denial.
তন্নতন্ন, *ad.* not so; a repeated denial.
তন্নিকট, *a.* near that, near him or her.
তন্নিকটবর্ত্তী, *a.* being near him, her or that.
তন্নিকটস্থ, *a.* situated near him, her or that.
তন্নিমিত্তক, on that account, for that cause, therefore: *ad.* from or through that.
তন্নিমিত্তে, *ad.* for that, for that reason, on account of that, because of that.
তন্মধ্য, *s.* the midst or inside of that.
তন্মধ্যবর্ত্তী, *a.* including or situated in that.
তন্মধ্যস্থ, *a.* situated in that, situated between them: *s.* that mediator.
তন্মধ্যে, *ad.* during that, in the mean time, in the interim, in that, between that.
তন্মনস্ক, তন্মনাঃ, *a.* so-minded, having that
তন্মাত্র, *ad.* merely that. [mind.
তন্বী, *s.* a thin or slender woman.
তপ, *s.* hot season, summer, heat, warmth.
তপঃশীল, *a.* inclined to devout austerities.
তপঃসাধ্য, *a.* accomplishable by penance.
তপঃসিদ্ধ, *a.* successful by penance.
তপন, *s.* the sun, one of the Hindu hells, heat, inflammation, the hot season.
তপনীয়, *a.* requiring to be heated.
তপস্, *s.* religious austerities, penance, mortification, self-denial, the heaven of devotees, virtue, religious merit; the hot season, the cold or dewy season.
তপস্য, *s.* Phálgun month; devout austerities, penance, religious mortification.
তপস্যামাছ, *s.* the mango-fish.[1]
তপস্বিনী, *a.* religious: *s.* a female devotee.
তপস্বী, *s.* an ascetic, a devotee; mango-fish.
তপূ, in *accts.* specially in land-surveying, signifies before, before that, already.
তপোবন, *s.* the forest in which religious austerities are practised. [austerities.
তপোবল, *s.* power or virtue of religious
তপোভঙ্গ, *s.* the interruption of religious
তপ্ত, *a.* heated, hot. [austerities.
তপ্তকাঞ্চন, *s.* ignited or burnished gold.
তপ্তান্ন, *s.* hot food, hot rice.
তপ্তাম্বুকুণ্ড, *s.* a hot bath.
***তফাৎ**, *s.* distance, difference, distinction, disparity: *a.* distant, separate, absent.
***তফ্‌রীক**, *s.* separation, division, partition.
***তফ্‌সীল**, *s.* an explanation, an analysis, separation, division, a detail.
তব, *ad.* thine, thy.
***তবক্**, *s.* a shelf, a stage, a story, a degree, order, class, a rank, a layer, a stratum.
তবল, তবলক্, *s.* a drum, a tabour.
তবলা, *s.* a caldron, a pot, a kettle, a drum.
***তবাক্**, *s.* a dish or plate made of copper.
***তাবাক্কা**, *s.* hope, expectation.
***তবাজ্জা**, *s.* humility, attention, pretended kindness, compliment. [depravity.
***তবাহী**, *s.* wreck, ruin, distress, perdition,
***তবিয়ৎ**, *s.* state of body or mind, desire.
তবু, তভু, *conj.* even then, yet, still, never-
তবে, *ad.* then, at that time. [theless.
তবুক, *s.* a little drum, a bundle of papers, a list, a catalogue. [lative degree.
তম, *s.* in *gram.* termination of the super-
তমঃ, *s.* the quality of darkness, darkness.
তমস্, *s.* the third quality of matter, or that of darkness; darkness, gloom, sorrow, grief, Ráhu or ascending node.
***তমসুক**, *s.* a receipt, a bond, a writing.
তমস্বিনী, *s.* melancholy temperament.
তমা, *s.* a darkness, gloom, obscurity.
তমাক, তমাকু, *s.* tobacco; -খাও, to smoke.

*তমাচা, *s.* a slap, a blow, a slap on the face.
*তমাম, *a.* all, whole, complete, finis.
তমামী, *s.* integrity, completeness.
তমাল, *s.* the sectarial mark on the forehead; the name of a tree.[1]
তমাশা, *s.* a show, a sight; *vide* তামাশা.
তমোগুণ, *s.* one of the three primeval qualities of matter, viz. inertness (applied to matter), or ignorance, fascination (as regards animated beings).
তমোগুণী, *a.* stupid, ignorant, inert, dull, relating to the quality of inertness, etc.
*তম্বী, *s.* an admonition, reproof, reproach, castigation, punishment.
তম্বু, তম্বুর, *s.* the same as তাম্বু, তাম্বুর.
তর, *s.* a sort, a kind; in *gram.* the termination of the comparative degree.
তরই, or তরুই, *s.* a plant and its fruit.[2]
তরকশ, *s.* a quiver, arrow-case. [quiver.
তরকশী, *a.* quivered: *s.* one who bears a
তরকারী, *s.* garden-stuff, vegetables.
তরক্ষু, *s.* the hyena.
তরখা, *a.* very rough (as the river).
তরঙ্গ, *s.* a wave, billow. তরঙ্গিণী, *s.* a river.
তরজমা, *s.* a translation; -কার, a transla-
তরজা, *s.* a sort of responsive songs. [tor.
তরণ, *s.* the crossing of a river, the getting through a difficulty. [passable.
তরণার্হ, তরণীয়, *a.* capable of being crossed,
তরণি, or তরণী, *s.* a boat, the sun, a float or raft; the succotrine aloe.[3]
তরণিতনয়া, *s.* a name of the river Yamuná.
*তরদ্দুদ, *s.* exertion, labour, engagedness.
তরপণা, *s.* ferriage, passage-money.
তরফ, *s.* a side, a party; -দার, a partizan: partial; -দারী, partiality, attachment.
তরবার, *s.* a cimeter, a sword, a hanger.
তরবুজ, or তরমুজ, *s.* water-melon.[4]
*তরমদান, *s.* a kind of fine cloth.
তরমোটি, *s.* a species of hawk.[5] [quid.
তরল, *a.* tremulous, diluted, thin, fluid, li-
তরলতা, *s.* tremour, fluidity, liquidity.
তরলবুদ্ধি, *a.* inconstant, fickle, light, silly.
তরললোচন, *a.* having tremulous eyes.
তরলিত, তরলীকৃত, *a.* inconstant, liquified.
তরশু, তরশ্ব, *ad.* three days ago, three days
তরস্, *s.* speed, velocity, strength. [hence.
তরস্ত, *a.* expeditious, quick, hasty, fickle.
তরস্বী, *a.* quick, swift, fleet, strong: *s.* a courier or express, a runner, the wind.
*তরহ্, *s.* a sort, a kind, a manner.
তরা, *v. a.* to save, to convey a person over a river, to get a person over a difficulty.
তরাজু, *s.* a pair of scales.
তরাণ, *a.* saved, rescued: *s.* the saving of a person, the getting one over a river.
তরাস, *s.* a kind of umbrella; *impft.* fear.
তরি, তরী, *s.* a skiff, a boat, raft. [tenance.
*তরিবৎ, *s.* education, support, care, main-
*তরীক, *s.* a canon, rule, manner, custom.
তরু, *s.* a tree, shrub, plant; -লতা, a creeper.[6]
তরুণ, *a.* juvenile, young, new, fresh, novel: *s.* a young man, a person of virile age.
তরুণী, *a. fem. idem;* the succotrine aloe.[8]
তরে, *ad.* for, on account of, because of.
*তরোতাজা, *a.* verdant, plump and fresh.
তর্ক, *s.* decision, investigation, examination, reasoning, logic. [a logician.
তর্কক, *a.* investigating: *s.* an investigator,
তর্কপঞ্চানন, *a.* eminent in the তর্কশাস্ত্র.*
তর্কবাগীশ, *a.* eloquent in the তর্কশাস্ত্র.*
তর্কশাস্ত্র, *s.* the science of logic or reasoning, a book treating of logic. [logic.
তর্কশাস্ত্রবেত্তা, *s.* a person acquainted with
তর্কশাস্ত্রানুশীলন, *s.* the study of logic.
তর্কসিদ্ধান্ত, *a.* most eminent in তর্কশাস্ত্র.*
তর্কালঙ্কার, *s.* the jewel of the তর্কশাস্ত্র.*
[* The degrees of the Hindu colleges.]
তর্কিত, *a.* investigated, sought, examined.
তর্কিতব্য, *a.* capable of being examined, reserved for investigation. [logic.
তর্কী, *a.* acquainnted with the science of
তর্কু, *s.* a spindle, a distaff.
তর্জ্জগর্জ্জ, তর্জ্জনগর্জ্জন, *s.* a threat, a loud reprehension, a scolding, threatening.
তর্জ্জন, *s.* scolding, threatening of a person.
তর্জ্জনী, *s.* the forefinger, finger of scorn or
তর্হারিয়া, *a.* fickle, impatient. [threat.
তর্পণ, *s.* the satisfying of a person; the offerings of water made to the ancestors.
তর্পণীয়, *a.* capable of being satisfied or
তর্ম্বরা, *a.* in *music*, shrill, loud. [gratified.
তর্ষা *s.* a chasm, a void space: *ad.* at a distance: *v. a.* to be distressed.

তল্, *v. n.* to sink to the bottom.
তল, *s.* under-part of any thing, the bottom depth, a pit, a hole, a chasm, lowness, inferiority, a stand or support, a base.
তলক্, *ad.* till, until: *a.* strong (as tobacco).
তলদাবাঁশ, *s.* a species of bambu (Bambusa tulda).
তলপেট, *s.* the abdomen, pelvis.
তলপেট্যাল, *s.* a cobler, a bungler.
তলপ্রহার, *s.* a slap, a flat-handed blow.
তলফোড়, তলফোড়া, *s.* a fountain, spring.
*তলব, *s.* a summons; wages; -চিঠী, a written summons.
তলবার, *s.* a sword, a cimeter; -ধারী, a swordsman.
তলভূমি, *s.* a valley, the lowland.
তলস্পর্শ, *a.* fathomable, shallow.
তলা, *v. n.* to sink to the bottom: *s.* the bottom, under part, lower part, base.
তলাগুচি, *a.* aiding secretly, backbiting: *s.* the collecting of things, aid, assistance.
তলাচি, *s.* the bottom part; a cane-mat.
তলাতল, *s.* a division of infernal regions.
তলান, *s.* a sinking to the bottom: *a.* sunk.
তলানি, *s.* the bottom, what settles at the bottom.
*তলাব, *s.* a pond, a pit, a tank.
তলাবাঁধা, *s.* the earthing up of plants, a pavement.
তলায়, *ad.* at the bottom.
তলাস, *s.* search; -কৃ, to search, to seek.
তলাসী, *a.* searching: *s.* a searcher, search.
তলী, *a.* beneath, under, lying at the bottom: *s.* the sole of a shoe, or of the foot.
তলু, *s.* the last player (in a game).
তলুনা, *s.* a large earthen pot.
তলে, *ad.* beneath, under, at the bottom, subject to, under the power of.
তলেতলে, *ad.* beneath, under, secretly.
তল্তল্, *s.* softness, softness of a bog.
তল্তলিয়া, *a.* soft, shaking, quavering as a bog.
তল্প, *s.* a bed, a tower, a turret.
তল্পী, *s.* a bundle, a package, a parcel.
তল্লক্ষণ, *s.* that mark or sign.
তল্লিখিত, *a.* written by him or her: *s.* that writing.
তল্লিপি, *s.* that writing, that treatise.
তল্শোষ, তল্শুষি, *s.* a fountain, spring.
তল্শোষিয়া, *a.* bubbling up, flowing.
তশলা, *s.* a brass vessel; the bar of a door.
তষ্টি, *s.* obstinacy, stiffness, pertinacity.
তষ্টা, তষ্টাশ্বিত, *a.* stiff, obstinate, stubborn.

*তসমা, *s.* a thong, leather, a strap.
তসর, *s.* a coarse sort of silk stuff.
*তসল্লী, *s.* comfort, consolation.
তসিল, *s.* a level bar upon which a pedal works, a pivot, the fulcrum of a lever.
তস্কর, *s.* a thief, a robber.
তস্করী, *s.* thievishness, theft.
*তস্দি, *s.* affliction, trouble, distress.
*তস্বী, *s.* a rosary, a string of beads.
তস্বীর, *s.* a picture, a print, portrait, drawing.
*তস্রি, *s.* the ordinances of a prophet.
তস্য, *pron.* his, hers, its.
*তহ, *s.* a layer, a stratum, a fold.
*তহকীক, or তহকীত, *s.* certainty, examination.
*তহখানা, *s.* a room underground, a cellar.
তহবীল, *s.* treasury, cash, trust; -দার, a cashier, a treasurer; -দারী, treasurership.
তহমৎ, *s.* an accusation, censure, an aspersion.
তহমতী, *s.* an accuser, a censurer.
তহসীল, *s.* a collection of the revenue; -দার, a revenue collector; -দারী, his office.
তা, *s.* a sheet (of paper); a heating: *pron.* that: *v. a.* to heat, bake, blow a fire; -দা, to sit on eggs (as a fowl).
তাই, *pron.* even that: *s.* the clapping of the hands.
*তাইদাদ, *s.* enumeration, a summing up.
তাও, *s.* anger, wrath, heat, a fold of cloth or paper, a sheet of paper; -কৃ, to fold.
তাওন, *s.* a heating, the heating of iron, etc.
তাওয়া, *v. a.* the same as তাবা.
তাওয়ান, *s.* the causing a thing to be heated, a provoking to anger: *a.* heated.
তাং, a *contr.* of তারিখ, তাগাদা, which see.
তাঁইত, *s.* a loom; a cord, catgut, a thong.
তাঁইশ, *s.* care or strictness on business.
তাঁত, *s.* a weaver's sley or geer, a loom, catgut, the string of a musical instrument.
তাঁতকাটা, *a.* fresh cut from the loom.
তাঁতগাড়া, *s.* a hole in the ground in which the treddles of a weaver's loom play.
তাঁতশালা, *s.* a weaver's workshop.
তাঁতী, *s.* a weaver, a cotton-weaver.
তাঁবা, *s.* copper: *a.* copper-coloured, red.
তাক্, তাগ্, *v. a.* to view, look at, aim: *s.* a stage, a shelf, a looking at, aiming.
*তাকৎ, তাকাবী, *s.* force, strength.
তাকন, *s.* looking at or surveying a thing.

তাকা, *v. a.* to look, to view, to aim at.
তাকান, *s.* the looking at : *a.* viewed.
*তাকিদ, *s.* a hastening or urging forward.
তাকিদে, *ad.* quickly, with exertion.
তাকেতাকে, *ad.* in rows, one over another.
তাগা, *s.* thread, silk or thread tied round the arm as a charm : *v. a. vide* তাকা.
তাগাড়, *s.* mortar used for building, the hole or trough in which it is prepared.
তাগাড়ী, *s.* a large wooden vessel, a mason's hod, one who prepares mortar. [nity.
তাগাদগী, *s.* a dunning, urgency, importu-
তাগাদা, *s. idem ;* also, the hastening of a person ; -কৃ, to dun, to be quick.
তাগাবী, *s.* an advance of money. [neglect.
তাচ্ছল্য, তাচ্ছীল্য, *s.* disregard, contempt,
*তাজ, *s.* a tiara, a crown, a mitre, a cap.
*তাজখাজা, *s.* a sort of sweetmeat.
*তাজগী, *s.* freshness, juiciness, greenness.
তাজা, *a.* fresh, green, new, alive, active.
তাজারুজু, *s.* a confronting; -কৃ, to confront.
তাজী, *s.* a particular breed of horses.
তাজীকুকুর, *s.* a greyhound, a bloodhound.
তাড়্, *v.a.* to beat, threaten, to drive away.
তাড়, *s.* a beating, a whipping, chastisement, an ornament worn on the arm by women, a small sheaf; a sort of palm.[1]
তাড়ঙ্ক, *s.* an ornament for the ear.
তাড়তোড়, *s.* a kind of needle-work.
তাড়ন, *s.* the beating, threatening or repelling of any one, a driving away.
তাড়না, *s.* battery, a threat, a reproof.
তাড়নী, *s.* a horsewhip, a riding-whip.
তাড়নীয়, *a.* deserving to be beaten or driven away, worthy of threatening.
তাড়স, *s.* virulence, the pain of a tumour.
তাড়সা, *a.* virulent, painful, sore.
তাড়া, *v. a.* to drive away : *s.* expulsion, a driving away; a threat, a reprimand ; a bundle, sheaf; a balcony; a bar, a bolt.
তাড়াতাড়ি, *ad.* scufflingly, by driving from all quarters, hastily, speedily, quickly.
তাড়ান, *s.* an expelling, a driving away.
তাড়ী, তাড়িকা, *s.* the juice of the fan-palm,
তাডু, *s.* a wooden spoon or ladle. [toddy.
তাণ্ডব, *s.* a dancing ; a sort of grass.
তাৎ, *v.* to heat, to warm : to become hot.

তাৎকালিক, *ad.* of that time. [an intent.
তাৎপর্য্য, *s.* a scope, an object, a design,
তাৎপর্য্যার্থ, *s.* object of one's aim, a scope.
তাত, *s.* a father; heat : *a.* venerable, reverend, respectable ; hot, warm.
তাতরস, তাতরসী, *s.* a saccharine juice.
তাতা, *v. a.* to warm, to heat : *a.* hot, heated.
তাতান, *s.* the heating or warming of a thing : *a.* heated, hot, warm.
তাতালিয়া, *a.* choleric, peevish, cross.
তাতি, *s.* a son, an offspring.
তাদবস্থ, *ad.* in that same way.
তাদর্থ, or তাদর্থ্য, *s.* identity of object, the acquisition of a habit, a habit.
তাদাত্ম্য, *s.* identity, sameness.
তাদৃক্, তাদৃশ, *a.* like, so, such, similar.
তাদৃশাচরণ, *s.* such or similar conduct.
তান, *s.* a tune, the key note in music.
তানপূরা, *s. commonly* তাম্বুরা, which see.
তানা, *s.* the thread of the warp.
তান্ত্রিক, *s.* a scholar, one well versed in the Tantras : *a.* mentioned in the Tantras.
তাপ্, *v. n.* to grow hot, to grieve, to fret.
তাপ, *s.* heat, warmth, distress, smart, a fever, woe ;-দা, to apply heat, foment, to sit on the eggs (as a fowl,) to hatch.
তাপক, *a.* occasioning distress, afflicting.
তাপন, *s.* the act of heating any thing, the being in affliction, a basking ; the sun.
তাপনীয়, তাপার্হ, *a.* capable of being heated, inflammable, capable of suffering.
তাপমাপযন্ত্র, *s.* a thermometer. [ascetic.
তাপস, *a.* doing religious austerities : *s.* an
তাপা, *v. a.* to heat, to occasion distress, to afflict, to give pain, to cause to heat.
তাপান, *s.* a warming, a basking. [flicted.
তাপিত, *a.* heated, excited, distressed, af-
তাবকীন, *a.* belonging to thee, thine.
তাবৎ, *a.* so many, all : *ad.* so long, until.
তাবা, *v. a.* to heat, communicate warmth, to provoke to anger : *s.* a copper or brass vessel, a plate of iron used to bake bread on, thin plate of iron used in the smoking apparatus over which fire is put.
*তাবীজ, *s.* a charm, an amulet.
তাবে, *s.* subjection : *a.* also, -দার, subject to, under control ; -দারী, subjection.

তামকুড়িঘুঘু, *s.* a species of dove. [Hindus.
তামলী, *s.* a retail shopkeeper, an order of
তামস, *a.* inert, stupid, ignorant, partaking of or influenced by the principle of inertness, ignorance or mental darkness.
তামসিক, *a.* stupid, inert, mentally blind.
তামসী, *s.* night, dulness, stupidity : *a. see*
তামা, *s.* copper ; expectation. [তামস.
তামাক, or তামাকু, *s.* tobacco.
*তামাচা, *s.* a slap, a flat-handed blow.
*তামাম, *a.* complete, perfect, the whole.
তামামী, *s.* completion, perfection.
*তামাশগীর, *s.* a spectator, a bye-stander.
তামাশা, *s.* a show, a sight, an exhibition.
তাম্বু, *s.* a tent, a pavilion, a marquee.
তাম্বুর, *s.* a drum, a war-drum.
তাম্বুরচী, তাম্বুরবালা, *s.* a drummer.
তাম্বুরা, *s.* a three-stringed Indian guitar.
তাম্বুল, *s.* the betel-leaf (Piper betel).
তাম্র, তাম্বা, *s.* copper ; -কুণ্ড, copper basin.
তাম্রকার, *s.* a coppersmith, a brazier.
তাম্রকুট, *s.* the tobacco plant.
তাম্রচূড়, copper-crested : *s.* a cock. [girls.
তায়ফা, *s.* a band of musicians or dancing
তার্, *v. a.* to convey over a river, to save, to deliver from difficulty or distress.
তার, *s.* a tone in music, wire, gold thread, musical string, savour, taste.
তারক, *a.* effecting salvation or deliverance : *s.* a saviour, deliverer, or star, the pupil of the eye, a pilot, a helmsman.
তারকষ, *s.* a wire-drawer.
তারকষী, *s.* wire-drawing.
তারকহিল্লোল, *s.* a peculiar note in music.
তারণ, *s.* the crossing over a river, act of saving a person, a float, a raft, a boat.
তারতম্য, *s.* gradually increasing series, the state or condition of more or less.
তারল্য, *s.* fluidity, unsteadiness, fickleness.
তারা, *s.* a star, the pupil of the eye, a planet, an asterism; in *music*, an octave or alto ; also, a name of Durgá.
তারাণা, *s.* a tune or mode of singing.
তারাপতন, *s.* falling of a meteor or star.
তারাপতি, *s.* the moon, a name of Shiva.
তারামণ্ডল, *s.* pupil of the eye, a stellar orb,
তারিখ, *s.* date of the month. [starry region.
*তারিফ, *s.* praise, applause. [thread.
তারীনি, তারমিহ, *a.* made of wire or gold
তারুণ্য, *s.* youth, youthfulness.
তার্কিক, *a.* studying the civil law : *s.* a lawyer, a logician, a sophist, a philosopher.
তার্ক্ষ্য, *s.* a name of Garura, the regent of birds, and of Aruna ; a snake.
তাল, *s.* the fan-palm,[1] a musical time or measure, a clod, a clue, a ball, a span, a slapping on the left arm as wrestlers do, the clapping of hands. [senic.
তালক, *s.* a lock, a bolt, a lath, yellow ar-
তালকাণা, *a.* having no ear for music.
তালগাছ, *s.* the fan-palm or palmyra tree.
তালচঞ্চু, *s.* the common swallow. [palm.
তালচোঁচ, *s.* a swallow, the pith of the fan-
তালতাল, *a.* wound in balls : *ad.* in lumps.
তাল-পত্র-পাত, *s.* the leaf of the fan-palm.
তালবৃন্ত, *s.* a palm-leaf fan.
তালব্য, *a.* palatal -বর্ণ, the class of palatal letters, viz. ই ঈ চ ছ জ ঝ ঞ এ ঐ য.
তালমাখনা, *s.* a tree with edible fruit.[2]
তালমারণ, *s.* a slapping on the left arm.
তালশাঁস, *s.* the tender kernel of tála fruit.
তালা, *s.* a lock, a padlock, the story of a building, sensation of stunning; -মার্, or -লাগ্, to be silent, to be stunned.
*তালাক, *s.* a divorce, a relinquishing, an abandoning, an oath. [written oath.
তালাকনামা, *s.* a bill of divorcement, a
তালাস্ত, *s.* a rest (in music).
*তালিক, তালিকা, *s.* a catalogue, an inventory, an invoice, a manifesto. [teaching.
*তালিম, *a.* learned, clever : *s.* instruction,
তালী, *s.* the clapping of the hands, a stunning, patch ; -দা, to patch, to clap the hands ; -লাগ্, to be stunned.
তালীলাগন, *s.* act of stunning. [mouth.
তালু, তালুকা, *s.* the palate, the roof of the
তালুক, *s.* a manor, a lordship, an estate.
তালুকদার, *s.* the lord of a manor, the owner of an estate, a land-holder. [tálukdár.
তালুকদারী, *s.* the condition or office of a
তালুয়া, *s.* palm of the hand, sole of the foot, roof of the mouth, crown of the head.
তালেবর, *a.* rich, respectable, illustrious.
তাস্, *v. a.* to brush the dust from a thing.

তাস, *s.* a card, gold thread, a frying pan.
তাসন, *s.* a brushing away of dust. [brush.
‡তাসা, *s.* a kind of drum : *v. a.* to cause to
তাসান, *s.* causing to brush : *a.* brushed.
তাহা, *pr.* it, that ; -তে, in that, in it. [pital.
তাহুত, *s.* agreement ; rent ; -খানা, a hos-
তিউড়ী, *s.* a furnace, a portable hearth ; a
তিঁহ, *pron.* he (honorific). [plant.[1]
তিক্ত, *s.* a bitter taste : *a.* bitter, aromatic.
তিক্ততা, -ত্ব, *s.* bitterness. [fragrant.
তিগ্ম, *s.* heat, pungency, the heat of spices: *a.* hot, pungent, acrid, sharp.
তিগ্ম, *a.* sharp, keen, pointed. [cantile.
*তিজারৎ, *s.* merchandize. তিজারতী, mer-
তিড়িংবিড়িং, or তিড়িংমিড়িং, *s.* a quick jumping up ; -কৃ, to jump, to gallop.
তিৎ, *v. a.* to wet, to make damp.
তিত, *a.* bitter ; -পাট, a bitter herb.[2]
তিতর, *s.* the Francoline partridge.
তিতা, *v. a.* to cause to wet, to wet, to moisten : *a.* moist, wet, damp, bitter.
তিতান, *s.* a wetting : *a.* wetted, moistened.
তিতাল্লিশ, *a.* forty-three.
তিতি, a sound used to call hens and cocks.
তিতিক্ষা, *s.* distress, disgust, vexation, anguish, a suffering or enduring. [vexed.
তিতিক্ষিত, তিতিক্ষু, *a.* distressed, disgusted,
তিতিভ, *s.* the cochineal insect.
তিত্তিরি, *s.* the Francoline partridge, the name of a sage, the Yajur-veda.
তিৎপান্ন, or তিপ্পান্ন, *a.* fifty-three.
তিথি, *s.* a lunar day, day of a lunar change,
তিন, *a.* three ; -খান, 3 pieces ; -গুণ, three-
তিনা,ক *s.* a small stick, a bit. [fold.
তিনটা, তিনটি, *a.* three (complete articles).
তিনি, *pron.* he, she (honorific).
তিন্তিড়ী, তিন্তড়ী, *s.* tamarind, tamarind tree.[3]
তিন্দুক, *s.* a kind of ebony.
তিমি, *s.* a large fish, a whale.
তিমিত, *a.* wetted, moist, annoyed. [rena.
তিমির, *s.* darkness, obscurity, the gutta se-
তিমিরনাশক, *a.* dissipating darkness.
তিয়র, *s.* a class of fishermen.
তিয়াত্তর, তিআত্তর, *a.* seventy-three.
*তিয়াদাদ, *s.* a number, a calculation.
তিরস্কার, তিরস্ক্রিয়া, *s.* abuse, insult, reprehension, censure, reproach.

তিরস্কৃত, *a.* abused, censured, insulted, re-
তিরানই, তিরানব্বই, ninety-three. [viled.
তিরাশী, *a.* eighty-three.
তিরোধান, *s.* disappearance, concealment, a cover, a sheath, a veil, a cloak.
তিরোহিত, *a.* covered, hidden, concealed.
তির্য্যক্, *a.* moving tortuously or awry.
তির্য্যগ্যোনি, *s.* a brute animal.
তিল, *s.* sesamum and its plant ;[4] a mole, a freckle, a very small portion, a moment; in accounts the 80th part of a cauri.
তিলক, *s.* a mark on the forehead made of earth or sandal, freckle, mole ; in *comp.* it signifies nobility or pre-eminence : *a.* spotted, freckled, chief, pre-eminent.
তিলকাল, *s.* a moment, a short space of
তিলতিল, *a.* minced, cut into shreds. [time.
তিলতৈল, *s.* oil of sesamum. [ted.
তিলা, *s.* a hill : *a.* dotted, speckled, spot-
তিলাখাজা, *s.* a sort of sweetmeat.
তিলি, *s.* a caste among the Hindus.
তিলিয়া, *a.* dotted, speckled, spotted.
তিলিয়াঘুঘু, *s.* a species of dove.
তিলিয়ালাউ, *s.* a variety of bottle-gourd.[5]
তিলেতাল, *a.* making a great ado about a little thing, mountains of mole-hills : *s.* a great ado about nothing. [heaven.
তিলোত্তমা, *s.* a courtezan of the Hindu
তিলোদন, *s.* a kind of frumenty or ricemilk.
তিষ্ঠ, *a.* stop, stay : *v. a.* to stay, to conti-
তিষ্ঠা, *s.* permanence, stability. [nue.
তিসি, *s.* linseed ; *vide* মসীনা. [folds.
তিহারা, *a.* three-fold, doubled into three
তীক্ষ্ণ, *s.* heat, sharpness, pungency, passion, haste : *a.* hot, pungent, sharp, keen, acute, zealous, active, intelligent.
তীক্ষ্ণকর্ম্মা, *a.* active, zealous ; -ধার, sharp-
তীক্ষ্ণগন্ধক, *s.* Indian horseradish. [edged.
তীক্ষ্ণতা, -ত্ব, *s.* sharpness, pungency.
তীক্ষ্ণবুদ্ধি, *s.* wit, acuteness : *a.* witty, saga-
তীক্ষ্ণবুদ্ধিতা, -ত্ব, *s.* sagacity, wit. [cious.
তীক্ষ্ণাগ্নি, *s.* a strong power of digestion.
তীক্ষ্ণাগ্র, *a.* sharp-pointed. [ing or fishing.
তীবর, *s.* a class of Hindus living by hunt-
তীব্র, *a.* sharp, poignant, pungent, severe, excessive, energetic, urgent ; -গতি, rapidity, swiftness ; -জ্ঞানী, sharp-witted.

তীব্রতর, *a.* very sharp or pungent. [gency.
তীব্রতা, -ত্ব, *s.* sharpness, keenness, pun-
তীব্রধ্বনি, *s.* a sharp or shrill sound.
তীব্রবুদ্ধি, *s.* wit, penetration: *a.* witty, keen.
তীব্রবেদনা, *s.* an agony, excessive pain.
তীয়র, *s.* a sharp note in music, a shrill tone: *a.* shrill, loud [arrow.
তীর, *s.* tin; a shore, a bank, a margin; an
তীরন্দাজ, *s.* an archer. তীরন্দাজি, archery.
তীরবর্ত্তী, তীরস্থ, *a.* situated on a shore.
তীরিত, *a.* finished, completed, ended.
তীর্থ, *s.* a sacred place, a place of pilgrimage, a landing-place at a river side.
তীর্থদর্শন, *s.* the visiting of a sacred place.
তীর্থযাত্রা, *s.* the going to a sacred place.
তীর্থযাত্রী, *a.* going to a sacred place, going on pilgrimage: *s.* a pilgrim.
তু, *conj.* but, or, against, also, and, moreover, indeed; *also,* thou (in contempt).
তুই, *pron.* thou (to an inferior).
তুঁদ, তুন্, *s.* a timber tree (Cedrela toona).
তুঁষ, *s.* chaff, the outer husk of grain.
তুক্, তুকতাক্, *s.* an incantation, a charm.
তুক্ক, *s.* an arrow without a barb, a lire in poetry or the fourth part of a stanza.
তুখড়, তুখার, *a.* strong, able, active, brisk, clever, keen, shrewd. [keenness.
তুখারী, *s.* activity, shrewdness, briskness,
তুঙ্গ, *a.* high, tall, lofty, elevated, chief, principal, passionate, hot: *s.* highest point, top, vortex, altitude of an object.
তুঙ্গতা, -ত্ব, *s.* tallness, height, altitude.
তুচ্ছ, *a.* despised, despicable, mean, contemptible, worthless, insignificant; -কৃ, to despise, undervalue, disregard.
তুচ্ছজ্ঞান, তুচ্ছবোধ, *s.* a mean opinion of any thing, contempt, disregard.
তুচ্ছতা, -ত্ব, *s.* hollowness, emptiness, insignificance, contemptibleness.
তুচ্ছতাচ্ছল্য, *s.* contempt, derision. [ed.
তুচ্ছীকৃত, *a.* degraded, despised, contemn-
তুচ্ছে, *a.* contemptuously, slightingly.
*তুজ্জর, *s.* a trader, a merchant.
তুজ্জরী, *s.* the business of a merchant.
তুড়্, *v. a.* to break, to cut, to cut up a person's character, to criminate, to insult.
তুড়কী, *s.* a leap, a skip, jump; clever.
তুড়ী, *s.* a fillip, snapping of fingers; a leap, skip; -দা, to fillip, to snap the fingers.
তুণ্ড, *s.* the mouth, the face. [*vide* তুত,
তুত, *v. a.* to praise, to applaud, to flatter: *s.*
তুতিয়া, তুত্থ, or তুত্থক, *s.* blue vitriol.
তুতী, *s.* a parrot; other species of birds.[1]
তুন্দ, *s.* the belly, the abdomen, the navel.
তুন্দিক, *a.* having a prominent navel.
তুন্দিভ, তুন্দিল, *a.* corpulent, abdominous.
*তুফান্, *s.* a hurricane, a storm, tempest.
তুফানী, *a.* boisterous, tempestuous.
তুবড়্, *v. n.* to shrivel, to contract, to wrinkle. তুবড়িয়া পড়ন, to become flaccid.
তুবড়ন, *s.* a shrivelling or contracting.
তুবড়ী, *s.* a kind of firework for playing.
তুম্, *pr.* thou: *s.* a tree (Garuga pinnata).
তুমড়ী, *s.* a snake-catcher's pipe.
তুমার, *s.* a heap, a roll, a list, a volume, an account book: *pron.* your, thy, thine.
তুমি, *pron.* thou (to an equal).
তুমুল, *s.* mixed conflict, uproar, tumult, sound of conflict in war, clangor of arms.
তুমুলযুদ্ধ, *s.* close combat, sharp conflict.
*তুমতড়াক্, *s.* magnificence, ostentation.
তুমতড়াকী, *a.* pompous, ostentatious.
তুম্ব, তুম্বী, *s.* the bottle-gourd,[2] the hollow shell of a gourd, a buoy.
তুম্বকী, *s.* a particular kind of drum.
তুরগ, তুরঙ্গ, *s.* a horse; the mind, the heart.
তুরঙ্গম, *s.* a horse; -সৈন্য a trooper.
*তুরঞ্জবীন্, *s.* manna, a medicinal drug.
তুরপণ, *s.* a drill, a fiddle-drill, a gimlet.
তুরপা, *v. a.* to drill a hole; to cut cloth.
তুরপাণ, *s.* drilling of a hole; a cutting of
তুরবণ, *s.* a fiddle-drill, a gimlet. [cloth.
তুরী, *s.* a pencil, brush, shuttle; *vide* তুরী.
তুরুক, *s.* a Turk, a native of Turkey. [lier.
তুরুকসবার, *s.* a trooper, a horseman, a cava-
তুরুকসবারী, *s.* horsemanship. [of horses.
তুরুকী, *s.* native of Turkey; a peculiar breed
তুরুম, *s.* the stocks, shackles; a trumpet.
তুরীয়, তুর্য্য, *a.* the fourth.
তুল্, *v. a.* to weigh, to take or raise up, elevate: *a.* increased: *s.* a pair of scales.
তুলৎ, তুলাৎ, *s.* paper dressed with the sulphate of arsenic (used by Hindus).
তুলধারক, *s.* a weigher, a weighman.

তুলনা, *s.* similarity, equality, comparison.
তুলসী, *s.* sacred basil (Ocymum sanctum).
তুলসীদানা, *s.* a kind of gold necklace.
তুলা, *s.* a weighing, a pair of scales; sign Libra; equality, a resemblance; cotton.
তুলি, or তুলী, *s.* a painter's brush, a hair pencil.
তুলিত, *a.* weighed, raised up.
তুল্‌তুল্, *s.* elasticity, softness, puffiness.
তুল্‌তুলিয়া, *a.* elastic, puffy, pliable, soft.
তুল্য, *a.* comparable, like, resembling, equal to similar; -তন্ত্র, a set of chimes.
তুল্যজ্ঞান, *s.* the esteeming of all alike.
তুল্যতা, -ত্ব, *s.* equality, comparableness, similarity, a resemblance.
তুল্যমূল্য, *a.* alike, equal, of equal value, like-priced.
তুল্যানুতুল্য, *a.* exceedingly like.
তুল্যানুমান, *s.* a parallel case.
*তুশক, *s.* a mattress, a quilted bed.
তুষ্, *v. n.* to be gratified, to be pleased, to please.
তুষ, *s.* chaff, the husk of grains.
তুষার, *s.* frost, hoar frost, rime, cold, snow, ice, thin rain, mist; *a.* cold, frigid, frosty.
তুষানল, *s.* fire made of chaff, a capital punishment.
তুষ্ট, *a.* pleased, glad, gratified.
তুষ্টি, *s.* pleasure, gratification, enjoyment, satisfaction, contentment, happiness.
তুষ্টিকর, তুষ্টিজনক, *a.* pleasing, gratifying.
তুষ্ণীক, or তূষ্ণীক, *a.* silent, taciturn, grave.
তুহিন, *s.* frost, hoar frost, rime; moon-light.
তূ, or তূতূ, *pron.* thou (used to call dogs).
তূণ, or তূণীর, *s.* a quiver, case for arrows.
তূত, *s.* a mulberry, its tree;[1] -পোকা, silk-worm.
তূতিয়া, *s.* vitriol, blue vitriol.
তূরী, *s.* a trumpet; -বাদক, a trumpeter.
তূরীধ্বনি, *s.* the sound of a trumpet.
তূরীবাদ্য, *s.* a trumpet, sound of a trumpet.
তূর্ণ, *a.* swift, expeditious: *ad.* swiftly.
তূর্য্য, *s.* a trumpet: *a.* a fourth.
তূর্য্যাংশ, *s.* a quarter, a fourth part.
তূল, *s.* cotton; a pair of scales; a mulberry.
তূলা, *s.* cotton; -রাশি, the sign Libra.
তূলি, তূলিকা, তূলী, a hair pencil, painting brush.
তূষ্ণীং, *ad.* taciturnly, silently.
তূষ্ণীংশীল, or তূষ্ণীশীল, *a.* taciturn, silent.
তৃণ, *s.* grass, straw, gramineous vegetable.
তৃণগ্রাহী, *s.* amber, electric gem.
তৃণদ্রুম, *s.* the class of palms.
তৃণধান্য, *s.* wild rice, wild grain.
তৃণবৎ, *ad.* like a straw, worthless, insignificant.
তৃণময়, *a.* abounding with grass, grassy.
তৃণরাজ, *s.* the fan-palm or palmyra tree.
তৃতীয়, *a.* the third; -বার, the third time.
তৃতীয়া, *a.* the third (lunar day).
তৃপ্ত, *a.* pleased, satisfied, gratified.
তৃপ্তি, *s.* satisfaction, gratification.
তৃপ্তিকর, *a.* satisfying, gratifying.
তৃষা, or তৃষ্ণা, *s.* thirst, desire, appetite.
তৃষার্ত্ত তৃষিত, *a.* thirsty, athirst.
তৃষ্ণক্, *a.* thirsting, desirous, eager, sensual.
তৃষ্ণাতুর, *a.* thirsty, afflicted with thirst.
তৃষ্ণান্বিত, তৃষ্ণার্ত্ত, তৃষ্ণিত, *a.* thirsty, eager.
তৄ, *v. a.* to cross a river, to get over a difficulty, to pass over. The final ৠ of this root becomes অর্, when it is conjugated: *e. g.* তরি, I cross over.
তেইশ, *a.* twenty-three. তেইশা, *a.* twenty-third.
তেউড়্, *s.* young plants of a plantain tree.
তেউড়ী, *s.* a plant, Convolvulus turpethus.
তেওড়্, *v. a.* to become crooked or warped.
তেওড়া, *a.* crooked, warped, awry: *s.* kind of pulse:[2] *v. a.* to warp, to bend a thing.
তেঁই, *conj.* therefore, for that reason.
তেঁতুল, *s.* the tamarind tree and its fruit.[3]
তেঁতুলিয়া, like tamarind; -বিছা, a centipede.
তেকাটা, তেকোণা, *a.* triangular, three-cornered.
তেকাটামিজ, *s.* the name of a tree.[4]
তেকালা, *s.* a harpoon, a trident.
তেকোঁচা, tucked in at three corners: *s.* an apron.
তেখণ্ডী, *s.* a kind of striped cloth.
তেখেঁচড়া, *a.* vile, base, blackguard.
তেখোঁচা, *a.* three stabs or thrusts.
তেঘেইয়াজ্বর, *s.* a tertian ague.
তেচক্ষুয়া, *a.* three-eyed: *s.* epithet of Shiva.
তেজ, *v. a.* to relinquish, abandon, leave; -জম্মা, to invigorate: *s.* same as তেজস্.
তেজঃপুঞ্জ, *s.* a heap of splendour.
তেজকলম, *s.* a swift pen; a swift writer.
তেজপত্র, or তেজপাত, *s.* the Cassia leaf.[5]
তেজস্, *s.* the most active principle in any thing, splendour, glory, brightness, light, lustre, vitality, ardour, vigour, vividness, rapidity, dignity, consequence, strength, energy, vivacity, power, fame, inability to bear an insult, impatience, spirit, pun-

gency, sharpness, freshness, liveliness, luxuriance in vegetation, brilliance or intenseness of colour, semen virile, fresh butter, bile, the bilious humour.
তেজস্কর, *a.* invigorating, brightening, irradiating, illuminating, exciting. [tive.
তেজস্বী, *a.* ardent, energetic, luminous, active.
তেজারৎ, *s.* trade, commerce. [merce.
তেজারতী, *a.* belonging to trade or commerce.
তেজাল, *a.* energetic, active, powerful, vigorous, bright, brilliant, hot, pungent.
তেজিত, *a.* whetted, polished, burnished.
তেজোময়, *a.* full of energy, full of ardour, splendid, brilliant, bright, active.
তেড়া, *a.* crooked, warped, awry; cock-eyed.
তেড়ামগজু, *a.* obstinate, headstrong.
তেতা, *v. a.* to wet: *a.* wetted, wet or damp.
তেতান, *a.* wetted: *s.* the wetting of a thing.
তেতারা, *a.* three-stringed, three-corded.
তেতালা, *a.* three-storied, having three stories.
তেতাল্লিশ, তিতাল্লিশ, *a.* forty-three. [ries.
তেতুল, তেতুলিয়া, same as তেঁতুল, তেঁতুলিয়া.
তেত্রিশ, *a.* thirty-three. তেত্রিশা, *a.* thirty-third.
তেথর, *a.* three places or ranges. [third.
তেথরী, *a.* consisting of three ranges.
তেপান্তর, *s.* a broad plain, a prairee.
তেপায়া, *s.* a tripod, a teapoy.
তেপেঁচি, *a.* having three turnings (a lock).
তেফড়কা, or তেফড়েঙ্গা, *a.* three-forked.
*তেব, *s.* the science of medicine, medicine.
তেবন, *s.* a garden, a play-ground.
তেমত, তেমন, *a.* resembling that, like that, such: *ad.* in that manner, so. [ner.
তেমনি, *ad.* so, even so, such, in like manner.
তেমনে, *ad.* in that manner. [place.
তেমাত্রা পথ, *s.* three roads meeting in one place.
তেমাথা, *a.* three-headed, pointing 3 ways.
তেমুখা, *a.* three-bladed, having 3 openings.
তেমুহানা, *s.* a place where 3 rivers meet.
তের, তেরো, *a.* thirteen. তেরক্ষি, *a.* the 13th.
তেরেণা, তেল্লানা, *s.* a mode or air of singing.
তের্চা, তের্ছা, তির্ছা, *a.* aslant, awry, crooked.
তেল, or তৈল, *s.* oil, fat; -মাখ, to anoint.
তেলচাটা, or তেলাপোকা, *s.* a cockroach.
তেলচিটা, *a.* musty, oily, gummy, viscid.
তেলচকুচুকিয়া, *a.* glossy, glossy, with oil.
তেলসার, *s.* ebony (Diospyros ebenum).
তেলা, or তৈলবৎ, *a.* oily, glossy, greasy.
তেলাকুচা, *s.* a creeping plant.[1] [Telanga.
তেলাঙ্গা, *s.* a soldier; a red ant; a native of Telanga.
তেলাটিয়া, *a.* smelling of oil, greasy, oily.
তেলানী, *a.* holding oil, oiled, greased.
তেলী, তৈলিক, *s.* an oilman, a dealer in oil.
তেশিরা, *a.* three-nerved, three-striped.
তেষট্টি, *a.* sixty-three. তেহাত্তর, *a.* 73.
তেসরা, *a.* the third. তেহাই, *s.* a third part.
তেসূতী, *s.* cloth wove with tripple thread.
তেহাতা, *a.* three cubits wide or long.
তেহারা, *a.* thrice-doubled, threefold.
তৈজস, *a.* metallic; -পাত্র, a metallic vessel
তৈজসাবর্ত্তিনী, *s.* a crucible, a coppel.
তৈত্তিরীয়, *a.* relating to the Yajur-veda.
তৈয়ার, *a.* ready, prepared, ready-made.
তৈয়ারি, *a.* ready, prepared: *s.* readiness.
তৈল, তেল, *s.* oil, fate; -যন্ত্র, an oil-mill.
তৈলঙ্গ, *s.* a soldier, the Telinga country.
তৈলপা, or তৈলপায়িকা, *s.* a cockroach.
তৈলমর্দ্দন, তৈলাভ্যঙ্গ, *s.* anointing with oil, rubbing on of oil.
তৈলস্ফটিক, *s.* amber. [rubbing on of oil.
তৈলাকর, *s.* seeds that yield oil.
তৈলাক্ত, *a.* oiled, smeared with oil.
তৈলিক, তেলী, *s.* a dealer in oil, an oilman
তো, *s.* a fold, a layer; -কৃ, to fold up.
তোক, *s.* a child, (male or female).
*তোখম, *s.* the seed of vegetables.
*তোখমে -কতান, *s.* linseed; -বালম, a cooing seed; -রেহান, a kind of basil seed.
তোটক, *s.* a kind of metre.
তোড়, *s.* the violence of a stream.
তোড়তাড়, *s.* the rapidity of a stream.
তোড়ন, *s.* the breaking of any thing, dishonour, abusive or insulting language.
তোড়নী, *s.* a broken precipice.
তোড়ল, *s.* an ornament for the wrist.
তোড়া, *v. a.* to change money, to break: *a.* broken: *s.* a purse, a bag of money; a sort of brick used in the cornice.
তোড়াতোড়া, *ad.* by bags full (of rupees).
তোড়াতোড়ি, *s.* mutual recrimination.
তোড়ানি, *s.* ricegruel; the changing of money.
তোড়াদারবন্দুক, *s.* a match-lock. [ney.
তোড়াবন্দী, *s.* a bag of money tied up.
তোত, *s.* a kind of sweetmeat.
তোতলা, *a.* stammering: *s.* a stammerer.

তোতা, *s.* a parrot, a paroquet, the cock of a gun, the pommel of a saddle.
তোতী, *s.* a female parrot or paroquet
তোতো, a word used to express stammer-
তোত্র, *s.* an iron-headed goad. [ing.
তোপ, *s.* a gun, cannon, artillery. [battery.
তোপখানা, *s.* artillery, a park of artillery, a
তোপচী, *s.* an artillery-man, a gunner.
তোপড়া, *s.* a bundle, a portmanteau, a bag.
তোপদাগ, *s.* gunfire, the firing of a cannon.
তোফা, *a.* rare, uncommon, good, excellent, admirable, beautiful, wonderful.
তোবড়া, *v. a.* to cause a thing to shrivel or contract: *s.* a portmanteau, a bag.
তোবড়ান, *s.* the causing a thing to shrivel or contract: *a.* shrivelled, contracted.
*তোবা, *s.* regret, repentance, sorrow.
তোমর, *s.* an iron crowbar.
তোয়, *s.* water; -নিধি, the sea, ocean.
তোয়দ, *a.* giving water: *s.* a cloud.
তোমা, *pron.* you; used only in composition; *e. g.* তোমাকর্ত্তৃক, by your agency.
তোমার, *pron.* your (honorific). [grass.
তোর, *pron.* your (to inferiors): *s.* a kind of
তোরঙ্গ, *s.* a kind of musical instrument.
তোরণ, *s.* a portal, a porch, a gateway.
তোরা, *pron. pl.* you (infer). [mitre-gems.
তোর্‌রা, *s.* a bouquet, a nosegay, a cluster of
তোলক, *s.* a rupee's weight; a weighman.
তোলন, *s.* a raising or lifting up, a throwing up (from the stomach). [tation.
তোলপাড়, *s.* a stormy dispute, violent agi-
তোলা, *v. a.* to raise, to lift up, to cause to erase, eradicate, or take up, to excite vomiting: *s.* a weight of 80 rattis or 105 grains, a rupee weight. [ingdish.
তোলাউনান, *s.* a portable hearth, a chaf-
তোলান, *s.* a throwing up from the stomach: *a.* vomited, lifted up, raised up.
তোলাপাড়া, *s.* the agitating of a subject in the mind, the introducing of a subject.
তোশক, *s.* a cotton-bed, a mattress. [tion.
তোষ, *s.* pleasure, happiness, joy, satisfac-
তোষ্‌, *v. a.* to please, to gratify, to gladden.
তোষক, *a.* gratifying, giving pleasure.
তোষণ, *s.* the act of pleasing or gratifying.
তোষণীয়, *a.* fit or proper to be pleased.

তোষদান, *s.* a cartridge pouch.
তোষাখানা, *s.* a magazine, a storehouse.
তৌল, *v. a.* to weigh: *s.* weight, weighing.
তৌলকর, *a.* weighing: *s.* a weighman.
তৌলন, *s.* the act of weighing a thing.
তৌলা, *v. a.* to cause any one to weigh.
তৌলান, *s.* the causing to be weighed.
ত্যক্ত, *a.* relinquished, deserted, abandoned, left, forsaken, teazed, importuned.
ত্যক্তব্য, *a.* deserving to be left or abandon-
ত্যক্তলজ্জ, *a.* shameless, impudent. [ed.
ত্যজ, *v. a.* to relinquish, abandon, leave.
ত্যজন, *s.* a forsaking, abandoning.
ত্যাগ, *s.* the relinquishing of a thing, abandonment, desertion; -কৃ, to relinquish, abandon, desert, leave, surrender, evacuate, resign, to abstain from, to avoid.
ত্যাগপত্র, *s.* a bill of divorcement.
ত্যাগী, *a.* relinquishing, abandoning.
ত্যাজ্য, *a.* abandoned, relinquished; relinquishable, worthy of being forsaken.
ত্যাজ্যতা, -ত্ব, *s.* relinquishableness.
ত্রপা, *s.* shame, ignominy, modesty. [ful.
ত্রপান্বিত, ত্রপিত, *a.* ashamed, modest, bash-
ত্রয়, *s.* three: *e. g.* মনুষ্যত্রয়, three men.
ত্রয়ঃপঞ্চাশ, ত্রয়ঃপঞ্চাশত্তম, *a.* fifty-third.
ত্রয়ঃপঞ্চাশৎ, *a.* fifty-three.
ত্রয়ঃষষ্টি, *a.* sixty-three; -তম, sixty-third.
ত্রয়ঃসপ্ততি, *a.* seventy-three; -তম, 73rd.
ত্রয়শ্চত্বারিংশ, ত্রয়শ্চত্বারিংশত্তম, *a.* forty-
ত্রয়শ্চত্বারিংশৎ, *a.* forty-three. [third.
ত্রয়স্ত্রিংশ, ত্রয়স্ত্রিংশত্তম, *a.* the thirty-third.
ত্রয়স্ত্রিংশৎ, *a.* thirty-three.
ত্রয়ী, *s.* the three vedas.
ত্রয়োদশ, *a.* thirteen.
ত্রয়োদশাংশ, *s.* the thirteenth part.
ত্রয়োদশী, *a.* the thirteenth (lunar day).
ত্রয়োনবতি, *a.* ninety-three; -তম, 93rd.
ত্রয়োবিংশতি, *a.* twenty-three; -তম, 23rd.
ত্রসরেণু, *s.* an atom, a small particle.
ত্রস্ত, *a.* alarmed, fearing, dreading.
ত্রস্নু, *a.* fearful, timorous, afraid [verance.
ত্রাণ, *s.* salvation, safety, preservation, deli-
ত্রাণকর্ত্তা, *s.* a saviour, a preserver, a guar-
ত্রাত, *a.* saved, delivered, redeemed. [dian.
ত্রাতা, *s.* a saviour, a deliverer, redeemer.
ত্রাস, *s.* fear, awe, terror, dread, alarm.

ত্রাসিত, *a.* put in fear, affrighted, terrified.
ত্রাসী, ত্রাসযুক্ত, *a.* fearful, timid, alarmed.
ত্রাহি, *intj.* save! deliver! ত্রাহিত্রাহি, O save!
ত্রি, *a.* three. ত্রিংশৎ, *a.* thirty.
ত্রিআক্, *s.* treacle, a kind of medicine.
ত্রিংশত্তম, *a.* the thirtieth. [apron).
ত্রিকচ্ছ, *a.* tucked in three places (as an
ত্রিকটু, *s.* three pungent drugs, viz. dried ginger, long-pepper, and black-pepper.
ত্রিকণ্টক, *a.* three-spined, trifurcated.
ত্রিকর্ণিকা, *a.* trigonous. ত্রিকোনা, *a.* trigonal.
ত্রিকাল, *s.* the three tenses of a verb, viz tho present, past, and future.
ত্রিকুল, *s.* three families, viz. that of a person's father, mother, and wife's father.
ত্রিকুট, *a.* three-peaked, three-crested.
ত্রিকেশর, *a.* triandrous. [gonal.
ত্রিকোণ, *s.* a triangle : *a.* triangular, tri-
ত্রিগুণ, *s.* the three primeval qualities of matter, viz. সত্ত্ব, রজস্, and তমস্, which see : *a.* threefold, thrice.
ত্রিচক্র, *a.* three-wheeled.
ত্রিচত্বারিংশ, ত্রিচত্বারিংশত্তম, *a.* the forty-
ত্রিচত্বারিংশৎ, *a.* forty-three. [third.
ত্রিজগজ্জয়ী, *a.* subduing the universe.
ত্রিজগৎ, *s.* the universe, including heaven, earth, and the subterranean regions.
ত্রিজগৎকর্তা, *s.* the creator of the universe.
ত্রিদশ, *s.* a demigod : *a.* the thirteenth.
ত্রিদশাবাস, ত্রিদশালয়, *s.* abode of the gods.
ত্রিদশারি, *s.* infernal spirit, enemy of the
ত্রিদিব, *s.* heaven, sky, atmosphere. [gods.
ত্রিদিবেশ, *s.* a god, a celestial being.
ত্রিদোষ, *s.* a vitiated state of the three humours, viz. bile, blood, and phlegm.
ত্রিধা, *ad.* of three sorts, threefold.
ত্রিধার, *a.* three-edged, trilateral. [toms.
ত্রিধারা, *s.* three streams, habits, or cus-
ত্রিনবত, ত্রিনবতিতম, *a.* the ninety-third.
ত্রিনবতি, *a.* ninety-three. [of Shiva.
ত্রিনেত্র, ত্রিনয়ন, *a.* three-eyed : *s.* epithets
ত্রিপঞ্চাশ, ত্রিপঞ্চাশত্তম, *a.* the fifty-third.
ত্রিপঞ্চাশৎ, *a.* fifty-three. [three-forked.
ত্রিপত্র, ত্রিপত্রক, *a.* trifoliate, three-leaved,
ত্রিপথগা, *s.* Gangá, river Ganges. [tre.
ত্রিপদী, *s.* a tripod, a teapoy; a kind of me-
ত্রিপুণ্ড্র, *s.* three lines on the forehead.
ত্রিপুষ্পক, ত্রিফুলা, *a.* three-flowered.
ত্রিফলা, *s.* the three medicinal fruits of the Hindu physicians.
ত্রিবর্গ, *s.* three objects of human pursuit, viz. love, duty, wealth; three conditions of life, viz. prosperity, equality, decline.
ত্রিবলী, *a.* having three wrinkles or folds.
ত্রিবিক্রম, *s.* the god Vishnu as a dwarf.
ত্রিবিধ, *a.* of three sorts, of three kinds.
ত্রিবেণী, *a.* having the hair tied in three tails : *s.* a confluence of three streams.
ত্রিবেদ, *s.* the three vedas of the Hindus.
ত্রিভঙ্গ, *a.* having the body bent with three convolutions : *s.* an epithet of Krishna.
ত্রিভুবন, *s.* the three worlds ; *vide* ত্রিজগৎ.
ত্রিমুখ, *a.* having three faces or mouths.
ত্রিমূর্তি, *s.* the Hindu Trinity of Brahma,
ত্রিযামা, *s.* the night. [Vishnu and Shiva.
ত্রিযোনি, *s.* a lawsuit from covetousness.
ত্রিরাশিপ, *a.* governing the signs of the
ত্রিরেখ, three-striped, trisulcate. [zodiac.
ত্রিলোক, *s.* the universe ; *vide* ত্রিজগৎ.
ত্রিলোচন, *a.* three-eyed ; epithet of Shiva.
ত্রিশিরা, *a.* three-headed, three-nerved.
ত্রিশূল, *s.* a trident ; Shiva's crest. [dent.
ত্রিশূলধারী, *a.* holding or bearing a tri-
ত্রিষষ্টি, *a.* sixty-three ; -তম, sixty-third.
ত্রিসন্ধ্য, ত্রিসন্ধ্যা, the three periods, viz. the dawn, mid-day, and evening twilight.
ত্রিসপ্ততি, *a.* seventy-three ; -তম, the 73rd.
ত্রিস্কন্ধ, *s.* an astronomer who is versed in three divisions of astrological science.
ত্রিহায়নী, *s.* a heifer three years' old.
ত্রুটি, *s.* a fault, failure, loss, defect, crime, the breaking of a promise, or command.
ত্রেতা, ত্রেতাযুগ, *s.* in Hindu chronology the second age of the world ; three fires.
ত্রৈমাসিক, *a.* quarterly, in three months.
ত্রৈরাশিক, belonging to three signs of the zodiac : *s.* in *arith.* the Rule of Three.
ত্রৈলোক্য, *s.* the universe ; *vide* ত্রিজগৎ.
ত্রোটি, *s.* the beak, the bill of a bird.
ত্র্যক্ষর, *a.* triliteral : *s.* the Hindu Trinity composed of the letters অ, উ, and ম.
ত্র্যবান্তর, *s.* a broad plain, a prairee.
ত্র্যশীতি, *a.* eighty-three; -তম, eighty-third.
ত্র্যম্বক, *s.* a name of Shiva.

ত্র্যহস্পর্শ, *s.* a solar day, a day in which part of three lunar days meet. [days.
ত্র্যাহিক, *a.* tertian, occurring once in three
ত্বক, *s.* skin, an integument, bark, rind of a
ত্বকছিন্ন, *a.* circumcised, cut off. [fruit.
ত্বকছেদ, *s.* circumcision, sign of moslemism
ত্বকছেদন, *s.* the act of circumcising.
ত্বকছেদী, *a.* circumcising, circumcised.
ত্বচ্, *s.* the skin, the integument.
ত্বগ্জ্ঞান, *s.* the sense of feeling. [touch.
ত্বগ্জ্ঞেয়, *a.* palpable, perceptible by the
ত্বঙ্ক, *s.* an imposition, a trick : *vide* তঙ্ক.
ত্বদীয়, *a.* thy, thine, your. [tion.
ত্বরা, *s.* haste, speed, quickness, expedi-
ত্বরান্বিত, *a.* quick, hasty, expeditious.
ত্বরায়, *ad.* speedily, quickly, soon.
ত্বরিত, *a.* hurried, hastened, done expedi-
ত্বর্ত্বরিয়া, *a.* hasty, impatient. [tiously.

থ, the seventeenth consonant in the alphabet : *a.* still, quiet, unable to reply.
থই, থইকর, *s.* a mason, bricklayer. [ter).
থইথই, full and standing (as a crowd, wa-
থইগরী, থইপণা, *s.* the trade of a mason.
থকা, *s.* a bunch of fruit or flowers, a clot.
থকাথকা, *ad.* in bunches, in clusters. [slap.
থককড়, *s.* a blow, a slap ; -মার্, to smite,
থক্থক্, *s.* the quivering motion of raw
থক্থকিয়া, *a.* soft, quivering. [flesh, etc.
থতা, *v. a.* to silence, to nonplus; to pacify.
থপ্ড়া, থপ্পড়্, *s.* an open-hand blow, a slap.
থপ্থপ্যা, *a.* decrepit, shrivelled with age.
থম্কা, *v. n.* to be startled, to stand like a post with fear or surprise. [ing still.
থম্কান, *s.* a being startled, sudden stand-
থম্থমিয়া, *a.* subsiding, moving slowly, tending to rest, slack (as the tide).
থর্, *s.* a row, rank, layer, stratum, brink of a river or stream, fishing net.
থরেথরে, *ad.* in rows, in ranks, in layers.
থর্থর্, *s.* a shivering motion, trembling.
থর্থরা, *v. n.* to palpitate, to be agitated, to tremble, to vibrate, to shiver. [ing.
থর্থরাণ, *s.* trembling, palpitation, shiver-
থর্থরাণি, *s.* a palpitation, trembling.
থর্থরী, থর্মরী, *s.* a trembling, agitation, palpitation, vibration, vertigo.

থর্মা, *a.* half-roasted so as to be juicy.
থল, *s.* a place, station, table-land, flat surface, bottom; swelling (of boil).
থলকুড়ী, *s.* a weed (Hydrocotyle asiatica).
থলপদ্ম, *s.* a beautiful flowering shrub.
থলিয়া, *s.* a bag, a sack ; pelican's pouch.
থলী, *s.* a valley ; also, *idem*.
থলুয়া, *s.* a bunch, a cluster, a tuft.
থল্থল, *s.* dangling motion of an udder.
থল্থলিয়া, *a.* swinging, dangling, pendent.
থলাৎ, *s.* a receiver of stolen goods.
থস্থসিয়া, *a.* soft, puffy, elastic, spungy.
থা, *s.* a place, certainty, a settled state, regularity, a right or proper state.
থাই, *s.* the bottom of a river, etc. ; a row, shelf, a sect or party ; -দা, to fathom.
থাউকা, *a.* altogether, all thrown into a mass: *ad.* by wholesale, in a mass, in a lump.
থাক্, *v. n.* to stay, stop, to pause, desist, to remain, abide, dwell, to continue, to subsist, to endure, exist, to be. [layer.
থাক, *s.* a pause, an interval, stratum,
থাকথাক, *ad.* in rows, on separate shelves.
থাকা, *s.* staying, continuing in any situation, the existing or being of a thing.
থাকে, থাকেথাকে, *ad.* by layers, in strata.
থাড়্, *v. n.* to be erect ; -কৃ, to erect, stand,
থাড়, *a.* erect, standing, perpendicular.
থাড়কাঁতা, *s.* a steep bank or shore.
থাড়া, *v. a.* to erect, to cause to be erect.
থাড়ান, *s.* the causing a thing to stand erect : *a.* erect, erected, made upright.
থাৎ, or থাতা, *v. a.* to appease, to nonplus.
থাতান, *s.* the appeasing, or nonplussing of a person : *a.* calmed, nonplussed.
থান, *a.* whole: *s.* a piece of cloth, coin, etc., a morsel, a place, a sheet (of metal).
থানকষা, *s.* reckoning of price by pieces.
থানছাড়া, *a.* dispersed, broken up, decayed.
থানকুনী, *s.* the same as থলকুড়ী. [to back.
থানথান, *a.* unbroken : *ad.* in pieces ; -কৃ,
থানা, *s.* a military post, a police-station, a watch-house, resort of thieves, a horde.
থানাথানা, *ad.* by pieces, by fragments.
থানাদার, *s.* keeper of a guard-house, constable, bailiff. থানাদারী, his office.
থানে, *ad.* is the same place, in one place.

থামেহম্বীর, *phrase*. I alone, or, I the hero [present.
থাপড়, *s.* flat palm, a slap, pat.
থাপড়া, থাবড়া, *v. a.* to slap, to pat : *s.* a slap, [pat.
থাবড়ান, *s.* a slapping, a patting.
থাবা, *s.* the paw of an animal, the extended palm, a claw, a talon, a fang, a slap.
থাবাথুবা, *ad.* with the palm, by handfuls.
থাম্, *v. n.* to become calm or tranquil, to forbear, desist, to be assuaged, to cool in ardour or zeal, to stop, hold.
থাম, *s.* a pillar, post, stake, block.
থামন, *s.* a becoming tranquil or quiet, a forbearing, being assuaged, a stopping.
থামল, *s.* the levelling a piece of masonry.
থামা, *v. a.* to make tranquil, to assuage, to pacify, to calm, to stop.
থামান, *s.* tranquillizing, causing to subside, assuage, or stop : *a.* tranquillized, made to stop, subside, or slacken pace.
থাল, থালা, *s.* a dish, tray, charger.
থালী, *s.* a dish, pot, vessel. [subside.
থিৎ, *v. n.* to become tranquil, to settle, to
থিতন, *s.* settling or subsiding of liquor.
থিতা, *v. a.* to cause liquor to settle.
থিতান, *s.* the settling of sediments.
থু, *s.* spittle : *intj.* fye : *v. a.* to place, lay.
থুক্, *v. n.* to spit : *s.* spittle ; -দা, -ফেল, to [spit.
থুক্থুক্, *a.* full : *s.* sputtering of saliva.
থুকথুকান, *s.* the sputtering out of saliva.
থুগবুগ, থকথুক, *a.* full (as lice or worms).
থুতনি, থুতী, *s.* the chin, lowest part of face.
থুথ, থুৎকুড়ী, *s.* spittle, saliva ; -দা, to spit.
থুবড়্, *v. n.* to fall flat, to fall on the face.
থুবড়া, *a.* old, dull, decrepit, unmarried (in *irony*) : *s.* an old bachelor ; *fem.* থুবড়ী.
থুবা, *s.* a tuft, cluster, bunch, tassel.
থুবাথুবা *ad.* in tufts, by clusters, in bunches.
থুর্, *v. a.* to hack, chop, mince, cut in pieces.
থুরণ, *s.* the hacking or cutting to pieces.
থুর্থুর্, *s.* shivering or tremulous motion.
থুর্থুরাণ, থুরথুরাণি, *s.* a shaking by weakness, tottering with age or infirmity.
থুর্থুরা, *a.* old, decrepit, crazy, ricketty.
থেঁতল, *v. n.* to be bruised, to be beaten.
থেঁতলন, *s.* the being bruised or beaten.
থেঁতলা, *v. a.* to bruise, to hammer out, to beat, to flatten, to beat black and blue.
থেঁতলান, *s.* the bruising or beating of a person or thing : *a.* bruised, beaten.
থেঁতুয়া, *a.* bruised, flattened, depressed.
থেঁত্যান, *s.* the placing of things in order.
থেবড়া, *v. a.* to press down, flatten : *a.* flat.
থেবড়ান, *s.* a pressing down : *a.* flattened.
থেবড়ানাকা, *a.* flat-nosed, snub-nosed.
থেলুয়া, *a.* flat, wide at the top, patent : *s.* a
থৈকর, *s.* a mason, bricklayer. [cluster.
থৈলা, or থৈলী, *s.* a bag, sack, purse.
থৈলাথৈলা, *ad.* by bagsful, by sacksful.
থোওন, *s.* placing of a thing, a keeping.
থোঁতা, *s.* a chin, bird's beak. [gate.
থোক, *s.* a whole, heap, collection, aggre-
থোকথাক, *ad.* at once, by heaps, in lumps.
থোকে, থোকেথাকে, *ad.* at once, in the whole.
থোকেবিক্রয়, *ad.* by wholesale. [corn.
থোড়, *s.* the spathe of a plantain tree, ear of
থোড়া, *a.* few, very little : *s.* a few, a little.
থোড়াল, *a.* plump, swollen with the ear.
থোতান, *s.* a nonplussing, a flustering.
থোপ, *s.* a cluster, bunch, tassel.
থোপথোপ, *ad.* by bunches, by clusters.
থোপনা, *s.* the chin, the face or mouth.
থোপা, থোবা, *s.* a cluster, bunch, tassel.
থোপাথোপা, *ad.* in clusters, in bunches.
থোবড়া, *v. n.* to cause to fall on the face : *a.* fallen on the face, depressed.
থোবনা, *s.* the chin, the face, the mouth.
থোবাথোবা, *ad.* by clusters, by bunches.

দ, the eighteenth consonant in the alphabet, In *comp.* it signifies giving ; *e. g.* মুক্তিদ, giving salvation, saving.
দই, দধি, *s.* curdled milk, curds.
দইয়াখইয়া, *s.* a disease ; also a plant.
দইয়াল, *s.* the name of a fine song bird.
দং, a *contraction* of দরুণ, and দফে.
দংশ, *v. a.* to bite (as a snake) : *s.* a gadfly, a snake, a tooth, fang, sting, bite.
দংশক, *a.* biting, stinging : *s.* a gadfly.
দংশন, *s.* stinging, biting, bite of a snake.
দংশা, *v. a.* to cause to bite.
দংশান, *s.* the causing an animal to bite.
দংশিত, *a.* bitten, wounded with the teeth.
দংষ্ট্র, দংষ্ট্রা, *s.* a tusk, a fang, a tooth.
দংষ্ট্রী, *a.* stinging, biting : *s.* a hog, snake.

দঁক, *s.* soft dirt, mud, mire, a bog, a marsh.
দক্তি, *s.* a weaver's sley. [tion.
দকদক, *s.* a glowing, redness, an inflamma-
দকদকিয়া, *a.* glowing, fervid, red.
দক্ষ, *a.* clever, active, dexterous, expert, skilful, acute, able : *s.* Brahmá's son.
দক্ষকন্যা, or দক্ষজা, *s.* names of Durgá.
দক্ষযজ্ঞভঙ্গ, *s.* the destruction of Dakshya's sacrifice ; *fig.* an entire failure or disappointment in an undertaking.
দক্ষিণ, *s.* the south, right hand side ; -গম্, or -যা, to go to the abodes of death.
দক্ষিণদিক্, দক্ষিণদিশ্, *s.* the south quarter.
দক্ষিণদিগে, *ad.* southerly, to the south.
দক্ষিণদেশ, *s.* the south country.
দক্ষিণনায়ক, *s.* one who keeps concubines yet has unabated affection for his wife.
দক্ষিণভাগ, *s.* the southern part. [zone.
দক্ষিণসমকোটিবন্ধ, *s.* southern temperate
দক্ষিণহস্ত, *s.* the right hand. [ceptor.
দক্ষিণা, *s.* a fee given to a bráhman or pre-
দক্ষিণাভিমুখ, *a.* facing the south. [south.
দক্ষিণায়ন, *s.* sun's course from north to
*দখল, *s.* possession, a holding subjection.
দখলকার, *s.* a possessor, a holder.
দখলী, *a.* possessed, held, subject to.
*দগা, *s.* deceit, imposture, treachery: -দার, traitor, impostor; -দারী, deceit, perfidy.
দগাবাজ, *s.* a cheat, traitor, impostor.
দগাবাজি, *s.* cheating, deceit, treachery,
দগদগ, *s.* a glowing, redness. [fraud.
দগ্ধ, *a.* burnt, consumed, scorched, singed.
দগ্ধা, *a.* unpropitious (day).
দগ্ধিকা, *s.* half-burnt rice, parched rice.
দঙ্গ, দঙ্গা, *s.* sedition, mutiny, affray, disturbance, uproar, hubbub, tumult.
দঙ্গাবাজ, *a.* seditious, mutinous, factious.
দজ্জাল, *a.* wicked, oppressive, overbearing.
দজ্জালপনা, *s.* wickedness, oppressiveness.
দড়, *a.* hard, firm, tough, stiff, brittle.
দড়া, *s.* a cord, a hawser, a thick rope.
দড়ী, *s.* a cord, a rope, a string. [ysm.
দড়কা, *v. a.* to inflame, irritate : *s.* a parox-
দড়কান, *s.* the bringing on of a paroxysm.
দড়্যা, *s.* a rope-maker, maker of cordage.
দড়্দড়্, *ad.* swiftly, hastily, on a sudden.
দঢ়, *a.* strong, hard, firm, stiff, tough.

দঢ়দঢ়, *ad.* firmly, strongly. [five seras.
দণ, *s.* a measure of capacity containing
দণ্ড, *s.* punishment, chastisement, fine, mulct, staff, stick handle of a tool, stem, an oar, churning staff, an Indian hour, a pole, a pilgrim's staff, a sceptre.
দণ্ড-কর্তা, -দাতা, *s.* one who punishes others.
দণ্ডধর, *a.* holding or bearing the pilgrim's staff, wielding a sceptre : *s.* a king.
দণ্ডধারী, *a.* bearing a staff: *s.* a mendicant.
দণ্ডনায়ক, *s.* a constable, bailiff. [justice.
দণ্ডনীতি, *s.* duties of a king, viz. impartial
দণ্ডনীয়, *a.* punishable, liable to a fine.
দণ্ডবৎ, *s.* prostration, obeisance, a bow : *a.* like a staff ; -কৃ, to bow, to prostrate.
দণ্ডযোগ্য, দণ্ডার্হ, *a.* punishable, finable.
দণ্ডা, *v. n.* to stand erect, to stand still.
দণ্ডাঘাত, *s.* a blow with a staff. [nation.
দণ্ডাজ্ঞা, *s.* a judicial sentence of condem-
দণ্ডায়মান, *a.* standing, standing erect.
দণ্ডাশ্রম, *s.* the condition of a pilgrim.
দণ্ডাশ্রমী, *a.* assuming the pilgrim's staff.
দণ্ডী, *a.* bearing a pilgrim's staff : *s.* a pilgrim, religious mendicant.
দণ্ড্য, *a.* punishable, liable to fine.
দত্ত, *a.* given, bestowed, given away : *s.* a title of the Hindus of the writer caste.
দত্তকপুত্র, *s.* an adopted son.
দত্তপ্রাণ, *a.* yielding to martyrdom.
দত্তা, *a.* given in marriage : *s.* a betrothed
দত্তাত্মা, *a.* self-given (adopted son). [maid.
দদ্রু, *s.* the ringworm, tetter. [curds.
দধি, দই, *s.* curds ; -মন্থন, the churning of
দনু, *s.* one of the daughters of Dakshya.
দনুজ, *a.* born of Danu : *s.* a demon.
দন্ত, *s.* a tooth, the fang of a snake, a tusk.
দন্তকিড়িমিড়ি, *s.* the gnashing of the teeth.
দন্তচ্ছদ, *s.* the lips, covering for the teeth.
দন্তধাবন, *s.* the washing of the teeth.
দন্তবেদনা, or দন্তশূল, *s.* the tooth-ache.
দন্তমূল, *s.* the root or spur of a tooth, the
দন্তযুক্ত, *a.* toothed, tusked, fanged. [gums.
দন্তরহিত, দন্তশূন্য, দন্তহীন, *a.* toothless.
দন্তশোধনী, *s.* a tooth-pick.
দন্তাঘাত, *s.* a blow on the teeth ; a biting.
দন্তী, *a.* tusked : *s.* a medicinal plant ; an
দন্তুর, *a.* having large teeth. [elephant.

দন্ত্য, *a.* dental; -বর্ণ, the class of dental letters, viz. ঌ ৡ ত থ দ ধ ন ল স র.
দন্দান্‌মিস্‌রী, *s.* barleysugar, sweetmeat.
দপট, *s.* pride, self-importance, arrogant behaviour, assuming conduct, severity.
*দফলহ্বি, *s.* delay, the putting off an opportunity.
দফা, *s.* time, a moment, one time.
দফাদফা, *ad.* repeatedly, from time to time.
দফাদার, *s.* a supervisor, superintendent.
দফাদারী, *s.* the business of a superintendent.
দফে, *ad.* again, also, ditto; item.
দফ্‌তর, *s.* a book, journal, record.
দফ্‌তরখানা, *s.* a counting-house, office, record-room, writing-room.
দফ্‌তরপোশ, *s.* a wrapper for account books.
দফ্‌তরী, *s.* a librarian, record-keeper.
দফ্‌রা, *s.* a wave; shove or push.
দব, *v. a.* to tread under foot, to trample.
দবক্, *v. a.* to startle, to withdraw.
দবকন, *s.* a startling at, withdrawing.
দবকা, *v. a.* to startle, withdraw, conceal.
দবকান, *s.* the concealing of any thing.
দবদবা, *s.* state, pomp, dignity.
‡দবা, *v. a.* to trample, suppress: *s.* medicine.
দবাৎ, *s.* an inkstand, standish.
দবান, *s.* a suppressing, treading under foot.
দবিষ্ঠ, দবীয়ান, *a.* remote, farther, afar off.
*দম্, *s.* breath, life, breathing space, moment; deceit, trick, fibs; a boiling or setting on slow fire (in cookery); a spring: *a.* the second (sort).
দম, *s.* punishment, penalty; boast, the spring of the mind, pride, ambition.
দমক, *s.* a single effort, a spirt.
দমন, *s.* keeping in order, bringing in subjection, subduing passions, or an enemy.
দমনকর্ত্তা, *s.* one who subdues or suppresses.
দমনীয়, *a.* capable of being subdued.
দম্‌কল, *s.* a screw-jack, crane; fire engine.
দম্‌কলী, *s.* a squirt, a syringe.
*দম্‌কশ, *a.* drawing breath, breathing.
দম্‌কশী, *s.* a drawing of breath, respite.
দম্‌কা, *v. n.* to sink, to become lower than before: *a.* much, all, the whole.
দম্‌কান, দম্‌কানি, *s.* a sinking or becoming lower.
দম্‌কাটান, *s.* a pulling in a sudden effort, a pulling at an effort by united force.
দম্‌কাবাতাস, *s.* a sudden gust of wind, a squall.
দম্‌খাওন, *s.* a being deceived.
দমড়ী, *s.* one-eighth part of a paisá.
দম্‌দম্‌মিস্‌রী, *s.* barleysugar, a sort of sweetmeat.
দম্‌বাজ, *s.* a deceiver, deceitful person.
দম্‌বাজী, *s.* deceit, trick, imposture.
দম্পতী, *s.* a pair, pair of animals (he and she).
দম্ভ, *s.* self-importance, pride, arrogance, deceit, cheating, hypocrisy, wickedness.
দম্ভোক্তি, *s.* a domineering speech.
দম্য, *a.* capable of being subdued.
দয়া, *s.* pity, compassion, mercy, grace, sympathy.
দয়ানিধি, *s.* ocean of compassion or pity.
দয়াপাত্র, *s.* an object of pity or mercy.
দয়াবান্, or দয়াময়, *a.* full of pity, compassionate, gracious, merciful.
দয়ালু, *a.* compassionate, gracious, merciful.
দয়ালুতা, *s.* compassion, pity, mercy.
দয়াশীল, *a.* merciful, compassionate.
দয়িত, *a.* beloved, accepted, favoured.
দর্, *v. n.* to moulder: *s.* price, value.
দরকার, *s.* want, necessity, importance.
দরকারী, *a.* necessary, important, urgent.
*দরখৎ *s.* a tree, a plant.
দরখাস্ত, *s.* a petition, a request, an application.
*দরগুজর, *s.* forgiveness, a desisting from.
দরজবাব, *s.* a reply, a rejoinder.
*দরজা, *s.* a step, an office, rank, gradation.
দরজী, *s.* a tailor, a seamster.
দর-ঠাহরণ, -ধরণ, *s.* the valuing of goods.
দরণ, *s.* decay, the mouldering away of any thing.
*দরদ্, *s.* pain, anguish, feeling.
দরদ্‌মন্দ, *a.* pained, distressed, feeling.
দরদ্‌মন্দী, *s.* a feeling, pain, anguish.
দরদর, *a.* flowing, trickling, running freely.
দরদী, *a.* pained, suffering, feeling.
*দরপেশ, *s.* before, in the presence.
*দরবাজা, *s.* a door, a gate, a portal.
দরবান, *s.* a porter, a door-keeper.
দরবানী, *s.* the office of a door-keeper.
*দরবার, *s.* a court, a hall of audience.
দরবারিয়া, *a.* frequenting courts of justice.
দরবারী, *a.* of a court, attending court.
*দরবেশ, *s.* a Muhammadan devotee.
দরমা, *s.* a kind of coarse mat of reeds.
দরমাবালা, *s.* a mat-maker, one who sells mats.
দরমাহা, *s.* salary, monthly wages.

দরমাহী, *a.* employed by monthly wages.
*দরমিয়ান, *s.* the midst, an interval : *ad.* in the midst, before, in view.
*দররোজ, *ad.* daily, every day.
দরা, *a.* mouldering, putrid, musty.
দরাজ, *a.* long, wide, ample, capacious.
*দরাম, *s.* the value or price of any thing.
দরিদ্র, *a.* poor, indigent, needy. [ness.
দরিদ্রতা, *s.* poverty, indigence, wretched-
*দরিয়া, *s.* a river, the sea.
*দরিয়াফত, *s.* a conceiving, a thinking, consideration, discrimination. [a valley.
দরী, *a.* modern, new: *s.* a carpet; a glen,
*দরীয়াই, *s.* a sea-faring man : *a.* sea-born.
দরীয়াইঘোড়া, *s.* the morse, the hippopo-
দরুন, *ad.* within, in, of, relating. [tamus.
*দরোবস্ত, *a.* all, the whole, entire.
দর্প, *s.* a boasting, pride, arrogance, self-importance, vanity, courage, energy.
দর্পণ, *s.* a looking-glass, mirror ; the eye.
দর্পপূর্ব্বক, *ad.* arrogantly, proudly.
দর্পিত, *a.* boasted, arrogated. [insulting.
দর্পী, *a.* proud, arrogant, self-important,
দর্ব্বী, *s.* a spoon, a ladle.
দর্ভ, *s.* a species of sacred grass. [view.
দর্শ, *v.* to appear, to be seen, to come into
দর্শক, *a.* seeing, beholding, showing, surveying : *s.* one who sees, or shows.
দর্শন, *s.* a seeing, an interview, a prospect, a scene, a view, a survey, a visit, dream, vision, the eye, a mirror, the doctrines or particular views of the vedas.
দর্শনকর্ত্তা, *s.* one who sees, one who shows.
দর্শনমাত্র, *s.* the mere view of a thing.
দর্শনী, *s.* a present, a gift on a visit. [ful.
দর্শনীয়, *a.* visible, fit to be seen, beauti-
দর্শনীয়তা, *s.* visibility, a visible state.
দর্শা, *v. a.* to show, to exhibit, to display.
দর্শান, *s.* a showing, exhibiting, displaying.
দর্শিত, *a.* seen, viewed, beheld, showed, exhibited, displayed, exposed to view.
দর্শী, *a.* seeing, beholding, viewing. It is used in *comp.* as, দূরদর্শী, বহুদর্শী, &c.
দল, *v. a.* to tread down, trample, knead : *s.* a sheath, leaf, a heap ; thickness.
দল, *s.* a portion, fragment, a gang, party, a body of troops, a blade of grass, or of a knife, a leaf, the petal of a flower, thickness, a sail, an aquatic grass.[1]
দলক, *a.* soaking, unintermitted, incessant
দলদার, *a.* thick ; petalled. [(as a shower).
দলন, *s.* a treading under the feet.
দলপতি, *s.* the leader of a party, the commander of a body of troops.
দলপীপী, *s.* a species of bird.[2]
দলা, *v. a.* to cause to trample on or tread down : *s.* clod, a ball, a lump. [party.
দলাক্রান্ত, *a.* joined to a party, seized by a
দলাদল, *s.* opposite parties, factions. [ing.
দলাদলি, *s.* a mutual trampling or squeez-
দলান, *s.* the trampling of a thing ; a hall.
দলিত, *a.* full blown, expanded, split, broken, divided, trodden on, trodden down.
*দলীজ, *s.* a vestibule, a portico, porch.
*দলীয়া, *s.* a kind of frumenty. [argument.
দলীল, *s.* demonstration, testimony, proof,
দলুয়া, *s.* a particular sort of sugar, a ball of rice : *a.* boggy, quivering like a bog.
দল্‌দল্‌, *s.* the quivering motion of a bog.
দলদলিয়া, or দল্‌দলী, *a.* boggy, marshy.
দল্‌বল, *s.* the suite of a great personage.
দল্লাল, *s.* a broker. দল্লালী, *s.* brokerage.
দশ, *a.* ten ; -খান, ten pieces ; -গুণ, tenfold.
দশক, *s.* in *arith.* ten gandás.
দশকর্ম্ম, *s.* the ten actions necessary to the bráhmans, kshetriyas, and vaishyas.
দশকিয়া, *s.* a small book for teaching nu-
দশত্রি, দশম, *a.* the tenth. [meration.
দশটা, দশটী, *a.* ten (applied to things).
দশদিগ্‌, ten points, viz. four cardinal, four intermediate, the nadir and the zenith.
দশধা, *ad.* of ten sorts, in ten manners.
দশন, *s.* a tooth, a tusk, fang. [shráddha.
দশপিণ্ড, *s.* ten funeral cakes offered before
দশবার্ষিক, *a.* decennial. [the Hindus.
দশবিধসংস্কার, *s.* the ten sacraments of
দশমাংশ, *s.* the tenth part, a tithe.
দশমী, *a.* the tenth (lunar day). [roots.
দশমূল, *s.* a medicament composed of ten
দশমূলপাঁচন, *s.* a decoction of dashmúl.
দশরথ, *s.* a king of Oude, father of Ráma.
দশা, *s.* the frizzled end of cloth, a period or time of life, a state, condition, circumstance, a predicament, a lamp-wick.

দশানন, দশকণ্ঠ, *s.* the names of Rávana.
দশাপন্ন, *a.* placed in a state or condition.
দশাবতার, *s.* the ten incarnations of Vishnu.
দশাহীন, *a.* unlucky, destitute.
দস্ত, *s.* the hand; stool; -**খত**, a signature.
দস্তক, *s.* a voucher, a receipt, a pass for goods, a permit, a passport, a writ.
দস্তা, *s.* pewter, zinc, lapis calaminaris.
দস্তানা, *s.* a pair of gloves.
দস্তুর, *s.* a custom, fashion, a mode, a rule, regulation.
দস্তুরী, *s.* custom, allowance for prompt payment.
দস্যু, *s.* a plunderer, a robber.
দস্যুভয়, *s.* fear of robbers, or thieves.
দস্যুরূপে, *ad.* like a robber.
দহ, *s.* a deep place in a river, an abyss, a whirlpool.
দহন, *s.* the burning of a thing.
দহনীয়, *a.* combustible, intended to be burnt.
দহরম্, দহরম্মহরম্, *s.* love, friendship.
দা, *v. a.* to give, bestow, permit, grant, accord, to dispense with, to pay, to offer.
দা, *s.* a bill-hook, a sickle : *v. a.* to reap.
দাই, *s.* a midwife, a nurse, a cookwoman.
দাউদ, *s.* a ringworm, tetter : king David.
দাউলিয়া, *s.* a reaper, mower.
দাও, দাওঘাৎ, *s.* the convenience of holding, or of giving a blow, an opportunity.
দাওয়া, *s.* a claim, a pretension, an allegation, a charge, a plaint.
দাঁড়, *s.* an oar, a paddle, a perch; penalty, a fine; -**কাক**, a raven; -**টান্**, to row.
দাঁড়ঘরা, *s* an open square near a temple.
দাঁড়ন, *s.* an inflicting of fines or penalties.
দাঁড়া, *v. n.* to stand, to be erect : *s.* a custom, habit, conduct, rule, common practice, a fashion, a method, a mode, a staff, a bat to play with, a perch, a clue, a guide, the backbone : *a.* fined, standing.
দাঁড়াগুলি, *s.* the game of crickets or cats.
দাঁড়াদাঁড়ি, *s.* manners and customs.
দাঁড়াধরণ, *s.* the adhering to a custom.
দাঁড়ান, *s.* a standing erect : *a.* standing.
দাঁড়াশ, *s.* a species of harmless snake.
দাঁড়ী, *s.* a rower, a waterman, an ignorant person, beam of a pair of scales, a narrow causey, the mark (।) or a full stop.
দাঁড়ীপাল্লা, *s.* a pair of scales.
দাঁড়ুকা, *s.* a pair of stocks, a wooden fetter.

দাঁত, *s.* a tooth, a tusk, fang, a serrature.
দাঁতকড়া, *s.* painful tumour of the molaris.
দাঁতকপাটী, *s.* lockjaw, the locked-jaw.
দাঁতখামাটী, *s. idem;* a biting of the lips.
দাঁতন, *s* a small stick used to cleanse the teeth, the cleaning of the teeth.
দাঁতলসা, *s.* a gum-boil, sore in the gum.
দাঁতশূল, দাঁতশূলা, *s.* the tooth-ache.
দাঁতাল, *a.* tusked, having large teeth : *s.* a boar.
দাঁতি, *s.* a snaffle, the having large teeth; locked-jaw; -**লাগ্**, to have locked-jaw.
দাঁতুয়া, *a.* dentate, large-toothed.
দাক্ষ্য, *s.* skill, address, talent, ability, capacity.
দাখিল, *s.* insertion, arrival at, a delivering of.
দাখিলা, *s.* a receipt, acquittance.
দাগ্, *v. a.* to mark, stain, brand : *s.* a mark, a blot, a stain, a blemish, a badge, a cicatrice, a scar; -**দা**, or -**কৃ**, to stain, mark, blot; -**লাগ**, to imbibe a stain or mark.
দাগবালা, *a.* marked, stained, spotted.
দাগরাজি, *s.* repairing of cracks in a roof.
দাগা, *a.* branded, marked; *vide* **দগা**, &c.
দাগী, *a.* spotted, stained, marked, blotted.
দাগড়া, *a.* scabrous, callous, rough.
দাগড়াদাগড়া, *ad.* scabrous, with callosities.
দাঙ্গা, দাঙ্গাবাজ, *vide* **দঙ্গ, দঙ্গা, দঙ্গাবাজ.**
দাড়, দাড়া, *s.* a tooth, a fang, a serrature, serratures on the legs or antennæ of an insect, the forceps of an insect, claws of a crab or lobster, the ward of a key.
দাড়কাক, *s.* a raven, a carrion crow.
দাড়াযুক্ত, দাড়যুক্ত, *a.* serrated, dentated.
দাড়ি, দাঁড়ি, দাড়ী, *s.* the chin, the beard.
দাড়িম্ব, *s.* pomegranate (Punica granata).
দাণ্ডা, *s.* a club, a play bat, the bed-posts.
দাতব্য, *a.* proper to be given.
দাতা, *s.* a giver, a liberal or bountiful person.
দাতৃতা, -ত্ব, *s.* liberality, bountifulness, munificence, generosity, charitableness.
দাতৃত্বশক্তি, *s.* an ability to give, a liberal disposition.
দাত্র, *s.* a sickle, a bill-hook.
দাদ, *s.* equity, law, revenge, the retaliation of an evil; the ringworm; -**মর্দ্দন**, a plant used to cure the ringworm.[1]
দাদখানি, *s.* a fine variety of rice.
দাদন, *s.* an advance of money for work.
দাদনী, *s.* money advanced for work.

দাদনদার, s. one who takes advances.
দাদ্‌রা, s. a kind of responsive song.
দাদা, s. elder brother, a paternal grandfa-
দাদী, s. a plaintiff; a grandmother. [ther.
দাদু, s. ringworm, tetter; a Hindu found-
er of a sect; -পন্থী, a follower of Dádu.
দান, s. the giving of a thing, a donation,
a gift, a largess, a present, alms.
দানকর্ত্তা, s. a giver, one who gives. [son.
দানড়া, s. an overbearing impudent per-
দানপত্র, s. a deed of gift, a grant, a will.
দানব, s. infernal beings, a demon, a titan.
দানবাড়ী, s. a house where gifts are made.
দানবারি, s. a god, an enemy of demons.
দানবীর, s. a man eminent for liberality.
দানশক্তি, s. liberal or generous disposition.
দানশীল, a. generous, charitable, liberal.
দানশীলতা, -ত্ব, s. generosity, liberality.
দানশৌণ্ড, s. exceedingly liberal, generous.
‡দানা, a. prudent, wise: s. a titan, a fiend,
a spectre, demon; beads, seed, grain.
দানাগণ, s. the demons or troops of the
দানাদার, a. granulated, grained. [gods.
দানাধিকারী, s. having a right to gifts.
‡দানী, a. receiving alms or gifts, liberal,
bountiful: s. a vessel, a receptacle.
দানীয়, a. fit to be given, bestowable, due.
দানুয়া, a. offered, given as an oblation.
দানো, s. a titan, a ghost, a demon, a fiend.
দান্ত, a. subdued, tamed, devoted, docile.
দান্তি, self-denial, subjection, submission,
দাপ্‌, দাপা, v. a. to stamp. [humiliation.
দাপ, s. pride, arrogance; a stamping.
দাপনীয়, দাপ্য, a. responsible, amenable,
দাপান, দাপানি, s. a stamping. [finable.
দাপিত, a. condemned, adjudged to pay a
দাপে, ad. with a violent stamping. [fine.
দাব্‌, v. a. to compress, suppress, squeeze,
to press, to subdue, to conceal, to stifle.
দাবন, s. act of compressing, pressing, or
shampooing, the suppressing or con-
cealing of a fact, restraint. [a sash.
দাবন, s. a cord, a skirt, a girdle, a ribbon,
দাবা, v. a. to compress, to suppress, to con-
ceal, to quash: s. a portico or porch;
the queen (in chess); suppression, com-
pression, peculation; also, *vide* দাবী.

2 A 2

দাবা, s. the same as দাওয়া. [forest.
দাবাগ্নি, দাবানল, s. the conflagration of a
দাবান, s. the suppressing or concealing of
a fact, the compressing of a thing.
দাবী, s. a prayer, a request, a supplica-
tion, a demand, a complaint. [dant.
দাবীদার, s. a plaintiff, accuser, a deman-
দাম, s. price, value, cost; a rope, a string,
a ribbon; conferva, weed; a collection.
দামড়া, s. castrated bull, an ox, bullock.
দামড়ী, s. the eighth part of a paisá.
দামন্‌, s. a rope, a girdle, a ribband, the
flap or skirt of a garment. [girdle.
দামনী, s. a tethering rope, a rope, cord, a
দামন্‌জোড়া, a. tied with a rope, tethered.
দামা, s. a clown; a rope, a cord: a. bold.
দামাদ, s. daughter's husband, son-in-law.
দামান, s. the lee side, the lee sheet tackle
দামামা, s. a kind of drum. [in a ship.
দামাল, s. a child when just able to crawl.
দামাসাহী, s. the composition of a debt, an
assessment, a cess. [of a river.
দামোদর, s. a name of Krishna; the name
দাম্বাল, a. peevish, capricious: s. a brat.
দাম্ভিক, a. bullying, blustering, imperious,
proud, boasting, hypocritical. [ness.
দাম্ভিকতা, -ত্ব, s. blusteringness, imperious-
দায়, s. a donation, gift, a nuptial present,
a portion, an inheritance, patrimony,
peril, danger, difficulty, jeopardy, loss,
trouble, an allegation, a lawsuit, a
charge, a pretension, tenure, a debt.
দায়ক, a. giving, bountiful, liberal, muni-
ficent: s. a giver, an accuser. [sible.
দায়গ্রস্ত, a. involved in difficulty, respon-
দায়ঠেকা, s. a being exposed to trouble.
দায়পত্র, s. a protest, a written plaint.
দায়বিভাগ, s. a division of patrimony.
দায়ভাগ, s. a division of patrimony; a book
which treats of the law of inheritance.
দায়মালহাবিশ, s. imprisonment for life.
দায়াদ, s. an heir, a son, a kinsman.
দায়ার্হ, a. claimable, cognizable.
দায়ী, a. munificent, liberal: s. a giver, a de-
fendant, a debtor, a person in trouble.
দার, দারা, s. a wife; -কর্ম্ম, marriage.
দারণ, s. a tearing, a rending, a splitting.

দারদ, *s.* a poison, quicksilver, vermillion.
দারমুচ, *s.* poisonous wood. [cerated.
দারিত, *a.* rent, torn, divided, cracked, la-
দারিদ্র্য, *s.* poverty, indigence. [terer.
দারী, *a.* having many wives : *s.* an adul-
দারু, *s.* wood, timber, spirituous liquors, wine, gunpowder, medicine. [puppet.
দারুক, *s.* Krishna's charioteer ; a doll, a
দারুচিনী, or দালচিনী, *s.* cinnamon.
দারুজ, দারুময়, *a.* wooden, made of wood.
দারুণ, *a.* awful, cruel, unfeeling, difficult, frightful, horrible, terrific, intolerable.
দারোগা, *s.* a peace-officer, a police-officer.
দার্ঢ্য, *s.* force, firmness, stability, validity.
দার্ষ্টান্ত, *s.* the thing elucidated by simile or metaphor, an archetype, prototype.
দাল, দালি, দালী, *s.* split peas, split pulse.
দালান, *s.* a hall, a hall of audience.
দালাল, *s.* a broker. দালালী, *s.* brokerage.
দালিম, দাড়িম, *s.* pomegranate. [sudra.
দাস, *s.* a servant, a slave, a serf, a fisher, a
দাসত্ব, *s.* servitude, slavery, bondage.
দাসস্বরূপ, *a.* like a servant or slave. [maid.
দাসী, *s.* a female sudra, or servant, a bond-
দাস্য, *a.* servile : *s.* slavery, servitude.
দাহ, *s.* a burning, conflagration, combustion, burning of the dead, inflammation, fever-heat, a cautery; -কর্ত্তা, incendiary.
দাহক, *a.* burning, causing to burn, caute-
দাহন, *s.* the burning of a thing. [rizing.
দাহস্থল, *s.* a place to burn the corpse.
দাহিকাশক্তি, *s.* a power of burning.
দাহ্য, *a.* proper to be burnt, combustible.
দাহ্যতা, -ত্ব, *s.* combustibility.
দিং, a *contraction* of দিগর, another.
দিক্, দিগ, *s.* a point of the compass, a quarter of the world ; a side, a part.
*দিক্, *s.* fretfulness, vexation, trouble, perplexity ; -কৃ, to give trouble, to teaze.
দিক্দার, *a.* troublesome, vexatious.
দিক্দারী, *s.* troublesomeness, vexation.
দিক্পতি, or দিক্পাল, *s.* a god who superintends the quarters of the universe.
দিগন্তর, *s.* another quarter of the universe.
দিগম্বর, *a.* naked : *s.* a name of Shiva.
দিগর, *s.* other, another. [the universe.
দিগ্গজ, দিগ্হস্তী, *s.* the guardian-elephant of
দিগ্দর্শন, *s.* look on all sides, a general survey, a general view. [general survey.
দিগ্দর্শী, *a.* looking on all sides, taking a
দিগ্দাহ, *s.* universal conflagration. [ed.
দিগ্ধ, poisoned arrow : *a.* smeared, anoint-
দিগ্বাসাঃ, *s.* a name of Kálí, and of Shiva.
দিগ্বিজয়, *s.* universal conquest.
দিগ্বিজয়ী, *a.* conquering the universe.
দিগ্বিদিগ্, *s.* every part of the atmosphere, every direction. [crimination.
দিগ্বিদিগ্জ্ঞান, *s.* a general knowledge, dis-
দিগ্ভুল, দিগ্ভ্রম, *s.* a being bewildered, mistaking the way to a place. [rection.
দিগ্ভ্রমণ, *s.* a wandering about in every di-
দিগ্ভ্রমণী, *a.* wandering in every direction.
দিৎসা, *s.* generosity, a desire to give.
দিৎসু, *a.* generous, liberal, munificent.
দিদী, *s.* an elder sister, a grandmother.
দিধিষূ, *s.* the second husband of a woman twice married, a twice-married woman.
দিন, *s.* a day ; -কাট্, -টাল্, to spend time.
দিনকাটা, *s.* the spending of time.
দিনকানা, *a.* unable to see in the daytime.
দিন-ক্ষেপ, -ক্ষেপণ, *s.* the spending of time.
দিনচতুষ্টয়, or দিবসচতুষ্টয়, *s.* four days.
দিনটালা, *s.* support, a spending of time.
দিনত্রয়, or দিবসত্রয়, *s.* three days.
দিনদিন, *ad.* daily. দিনড়ী, *a.* daily.
দিনদ্বয়, or দিবসদ্বয়, *s.* two days. [day.
দিননাথ, দিনপতি, *s.* the sun, the lord of
দিনপাত, *s.* support, occupation, spending
দিনমান, *s.* day, daytime. [of time.
দিনরাত, *ad.* day and night, incessantly.
দিনান্ত, or দিনাবসান, *s.* the evening.
দিনিকা, *s.* wages for a day, and day's hire.
দিব, or দিবি, *s.* the sky, the atmosphere.
দিবস, *s.* a day. দিবসে, *ad.* in the day.
দিবসিক, *a.* proper to the day, diurnal,
দিবসীয়, *a.* belonged to the day. [daily.
দিবা, *s.* a day, daytime : *ad.* in the daytime.
দিবাকর, or দিনমণি, *s.* the sun.
*দিৱান্, *s.* a steward, a bannian. [night.
দিবানিশি, *s.* a day and night : *ad.* day and
দিৱানী, *s.* the office of a steward : *a.* civil
দিৱানীঅদালৎ, *s.* a civil court. [(lawsuit).
দিৱান্খানা, *s.* a tribunal, hall of audience.
দিবান্ধ, *s.* an owl : *a.* the same as দিনকাণা.

দিবাপ্রদীপ, *s.* a lamp in the day time (denoting a person of unknown abilities): *a.* useless, eclipsed by superior merit.
দিবাবসান, *s.* the close of the day, evening.
দিবাভাগ, *s.* the day time: *a.* during day.
দিবারাত্রি, *ad.* day and night, incessantly.
দিব্বি, *s.* an oath, an appeal to God.
দিব্য, *a.* divine, excellent: *s.* an oath.
দিব্যচক্ষু, *s.* supernatural vision.
দিব্যজ্ঞান, *s.* supernatural knowledge.
দিব্যাঙ্গনা, *s.* a comely or beautiful woman.
*দিমাগ, *s.* pride, egotism, self-importance.
দিমাগী, *a.* proud, self-important, arrogant.
*দিরিং, *a.* late, tardy, delayed. [energy.
*দিল, *s.* the heart, the mind, prowess,
দিলাসা, *s.* encouragement, comfort, consolation.
দিলগীর, *a.* distressed, sorrowful.
দিলগীরী, *s.* distress of mind, sorrow.
দিলদার, *a.* holding the heart: *s.* a lover.
দিলদিহী, *s.* attention, close application.
দিশা, *s.* a point of the compass, a region.
দিশাহারা, *a.* lost, bewildered, puzzled.
দিশপাশ, *s.* a boundary, a limit, a border.
দিষ্ট, *a.* ordered, allowed: *s.* destiny.
দিস্তা, *s.* a quire of paper; a thin place in cloth caused by a defect in weaving.
দিস্তাপড়া, thin (defect in cloth). [bearer.
দীউটী, *s.* a lamp, a torch; -য়া, a torch-
দীক্ষক, *s.* a priest, a guru, a spiritual guide.
দীক্ষা, *s.* the performance of a sacrifice or oblation, a worshipping, the receiving of instruction or initiatory formula.
দীক্ষিত, *a.* engaged in worship, or in making sacrifices or oblations, engaged in giving instruction or initiatory rites.
দীগী, or দীঘী, *s.* an oblong pond or lake.
দীঘ, দীঘল, *a.* long, extended.
দীঘে, *ad.* lengthwise. [father's mother.
দীদী, *s.* elder sister, elder brother's wife,
দীন, *a.* fallen into decay, poor, needy, miserable, wretched, indigent. [poverty.
দীনতা, *s.* indigence, wretchedness, want,
দীনদয়াময়, দীনদয়ালু, *a.* full of compassion for the indigent, full of pity to the poor.
দীনদৈন্য, *s.* the indigence of the indigent.
দীননাথ, *s.* a protector of the indigent.
দীনভাব, *s.* indigence, wretchedness, want.
দীনমনস্ক, *a.* distressed, low-spirited. [able.
দীনহীন, *a.* poor, wretched, indigent, miser-
দীনহীনতা, *s.* poverty, misery, indigence.
দীনহীনাবস্থা, *s.* poverty, wretchedness.
দীনার, *s.* a coin, a dínár, a gold coin.
দীপ, *s.* a light, a lamp, a lighted candle.
দীপক, illuminating, irradiating, elucidating, perspicuous, beautifying, kindling, inflaming; cordial: *s.* a lamp, a musical mode, rhetorical elegance or perspicuity of expression; an aromatic seed.[1]
দীপকালঙ্কার, *s.* a figure of rhetoric which throws light upon the subject, an elegance of construction.
দীপ -গাছ, -বৃক্ষ, -ঝাড়, *s.* a branched candlestick, a chandelier, a lustre. [shade.
দীপঘেরা, *s.* a shade for a candle, a table-
দীপদান, *s.* a candlestick, a lamp-stand.
দীপন, *s.* a shining, blazing: *a.* inflaming; cordial.
দীপমালা, *s.* a row of lamps.
দীপশিখা, *s.* the flame of a lamp or candle.
দীপাচ্ছাদন, *s.* a shade for a candle.
দীপাধার, *s.* a lamp-stand, a candlestick.
দীপান্তর, *s* another lamp or light.
দীপান্বিতা, *a.* luminous, clear, perspicuous.
দীপ্ত, or দীপিত, *a.* lighted up, illuminated, elucidated, made clear or conspicuous.
দীপ্তি, *s.* light, splendour, illumination, brilliancy, refulgence, effulgence. [light.
দীপ্তিকর, *a.* irradiating, shining, giving
দীপ্তিমান্, দীপ্র, *a.* luminous, shining, illustrious, glorious, refulgent, effulgent, fulgid, radiant, brilliant, bright, clear.
দীপ্যমান, *a.* shining, conspicuous, clear.
দীয়মান, *a.* under bestowment, being bestowed.
দীয়া, *s.* a light, a lamp, candle.
দীয়াকাঠি, দীয়াশলা, *s.* a match (to light).
দীর্ঘ, *a.* long, tall, prolonged; -কায়, tall.
দীর্ঘঈকার, *s.* the letter ঈ or the symbol ী.
দীর্ঘউকার, *s.* the letter ঊ or the symbol ূ.
দীর্ঘকাল, *s.* a long time; -জীবী, long-lived.
দীর্ঘকালস্থায়ী, *a.* continuing a long time.
দীর্ঘচ্ছন্দ, *s.* a long verse, an alexandrine.
দীর্ঘজঙ্ঘ, *a.* long-thighed, spindle-shanked.
দীর্ঘজীবিতা, -ত্ব, *s.* longevity, long life.
দীর্ঘজীবী, *a.* long-lived, living long.
দীর্ঘতা, *s.* length, tallness, protractedness.

দীর্ঘদর্শী, *a.* fore-sighted, far-seeing, prudent, learned : *s.* a vulture. [sigh.
দীর্ঘনিদ্রা, *s.* death. দীর্ঘনিশ্বাস, *s.* a deep
দীর্ঘশব্দ, *s.* protracted sound, a long accent.
দীর্ঘসূত্র, দীর্ঘসূত্রী, *a.* dilatory, slow, tardy, tedious, procrastinating.
দীর্ঘসূত্রতা, *s.* procrastination, delay.
দীর্ঘাকার, *a.* oblong. দীঘে, *ad.* lengthwise.
দীর্ঘায়ু, *a.* long-lived : *s.* longevity.
দীর্ঘিকা, *s.* an oblong pond or lake.
দীর্ঘোচ্চারণ, *s.* a long syllable, emphasis.
দু, *a.* two : *v. a.* to milk an animal.
দুআ, *a.* two ; hated, disliked (as a wife).
দুআর, *s.* a doorway, a gateway, an open-
দুই, *a.* two. দুইটা, *a.* two (entire). [ing.
দুইখান, *a.* two : *s.* two pieces.
দুইগুণ, *a.* two-fold, double, twice.
দুইপ্রহর, *s.* 12 o'clock; -দিন, noon; -রাত্রি,
দুইবার, or দুবার, *a.* twice. [midnight.
দুইমনা, *a.* hesitating, double-minded.
দুঃখ, *s.* affliction, distress, trouble, suffering, wretchedness, labour; -দা, to afflict.
দুঃখদশা, *s.* a state of affliction or trouble.
দুঃখদায়ক, *a.* afflicting, distressing, painful
দুঃখধন্দা, *s.* labour, employment. [misery.
দুঃখভোগ, *s.* the suffering of affliction or
দুঃখভোগী, *a.* suffering affliction or misery.
দুঃখময়, *a.* full of affliction, misery or evil.
দুঃখমাত্র, *s.* wholly affliction, mere trouble.
দুঃখিত, *a.* afflicted, distressed, wretched,
দুঃখী, *a.* *idem ; fem.* দুঃখিনী. [miserable.
দুঃশীল, *a.* malicious, ill-natured, evil-dis-
দুঃশীলতা, *s.* malevolence, malice. [posed.
দুঃসময়, *s.* a time of affliction or distress.
দুঃসহ, দুঃসহ্য, *a.* unbearable, intolerable.
দুঃসাধ্য, *a.* impracticable, difficult.
দুঃসাহস, *s.* rashness, temerity, audacity.
দুঃসাহসী, *a.* daring, rash, presumptuous.
দুঃস্থ, *a.* sunk in distress or trouble.
দুঃস্থতা, *s.* the being in distress. [mare.
দুঃস্বপ্ন, *s.* an ominous dream, the night-
দুঃস্বভাব, *s.* an evil inclination or propensity, an ill-nature, a low disposition.
দুঁড়িয়া, *s.* a kind of basket to catch fish.
দুঁদিয়া, *a.* stubborn, unruly, turbulent.
দুঁদামি, *s.* refractoriness, seditiousness,
দুকাট, *a.* twice-cut (plant). [turbulence.

দুকান, *s.* a shop ; -দার, a shop-keeper.
দুকানদারী, *s.* business of a shop-keeper.
দুকানী, *a.* of a shop : *s.* a shop-keeper.
দুকুল, *s.* the family of father and mother; the family of father and husband.
দুকুলখাকী, *a.* destroying the family of her father and husband (a scurrilous term).
দুকুল, *s.* the two shores of a river.
দুক্কর, *Malay.* *s.* a pig, a hog. [ed.
দুখচেটিয়া, *a.* miserable, afflicted, wretch-
দুখান, *s.* two pieces ; -কৃ, to break in two.
দুগাড়িয়া, *s.* an impostor, a turncoat.
দুগুণ, *a.* twofold, double, twice as much.
দুগ্ধ, *a.* milked : *s.* milk ; -পায়ী, drinking
দুগ্ধপান, *s.* the drinking of milk. [milk.
দুগ্ধপোষ্য, *a.* living on milk : *s.* a babe.
দুগ্ধবতী, *a.* milch, giving milk, having milk.
দুঘেয়া, occurring twice every day (fever).
দুজাতীয়া, *a.* mongrel, hybrid, half-caste.
দুটপ্পা, *a.* laconic, short, brief, concise.
দুটা, or দুটী, *a.* two ; a few, some.
দুটীখানী, *a.* two, some, a very few.
দুঢোক, *s.* two gulps. দুণী, *s.* *vide* দুনী.
দুণ, দুণা, *a.* twofold, double, twice as much.
দুতত্ত্ব, *s.* two objects, a dilemma.
দুথাপড়, *s.* two slaps, two pats.
দুদাঁত, *a.* two-toothed ; *s.* two teeth.
দুদ, *s.* milk ; -খাওয়া, to give suck.
দুদলিয়া, *a.* belonging to two parties, unprincipled : *s.* a turncoat.
দুদিক্, *s.* two directions, two ways, two sides or parties ; -খা, to break or encroach on both sides (as a river).
দুদিক্চতুর, *a.* ambidextrous, clever in both
দুদিগ্দর্শী, *a.* looking two ways. [ways.
দুদীয়া, দুধিয়া, *a.* sucking, giving milk :
দুদু, *s.* milk ; -খা, to suck. [*s.* a plant.
দুধ, *s.* milk ; -দা, or -খাওয়া, to give suck, to suckle ; -ছাড়া, to wean.
দুধখেকুয়া, *a.* sucking, feeding on milk.
দুধচাসি, *s.* small cakes boiled in milk.
দুধতোলা, *s.* a throwing up the milk (as a
দুধিয়াদাঁত, *s.* the milk teeth. [baby).
দুধিয়াবালাক, *s.* a sucking child.
দুন, or দুনা, *a.* double, twice as much.
দুনলী, or দুচুঙ্গী, *a.* double-barrelled.
*দুনিয়া, *s.* the world, the universe.

দুনিয়াদার, *s.* a person engaged in worldly pursuits : *a.* worldly.

দুনিয়াদারী, *a.* worldly, pertaining to the [world.

দুনী, *s.* a coast ship or boat ; a windmill.

দুনুগী, *a.* twice, double.

দুন্দুভি, *s.* a trumpet, a kettle-drum ; name [of a giant.

দুপট্টা, *s.* a sheet made of two breadths of [cloth.

দুপট্টী, *s.* two rows or ranges.

দুপর, *a.* (দিন) midday ; (রাত্রি) midnight.

দুপাক, *a.* twice-boiled : *s.* two turnings.

দুপাটী, *s.* the name of a flowering plant.[1]

দুপেঁচা, দুপেঁচুয়া, *a.* requiring two turns.

দুফাক, *ad.* in two pieces : *s.* two pieces.

দুবলা, *a.* lean, meagre, weak : *s. vide* দুর্ব্বা.

দুবাজু, *a.* having two-coloured wings.

দুভাঁতি, *a.* belonging to both parties.

দুভাতারী, *s.* a twice-married woman : *a.* having two husbands (abusive term).

দুভাষিয়া, or দুভাষী, *s.* an interpreter.

দুম্, *s.* a tail. দুমচী, *s.* a crupper.

দুমড়, *v. a.* to bend, to fold (as paper, etc.)

দুমণি, *s.* the erect hooks fixed in the walls of door pillars for hanging a gate.

দুমুখ, *a.* two-faced, two-bladed, facing two ways, having two heads or openings.

দুমুখসাপ, *s.* an amphisbina, also, a kind of serpent resembling an earthworm.

দুমুড়ি, *s.* two ends, both sides, two heads.

দুমেটিয়া, দুমেটে, দুমেটেম, *a.* twice-coated with clay (applied to Hindu idols).

দুমড়, *v. n.* to bend, to be crooked.

দুমড়া, *v. a.* to bend, to double, to fold.

দুমড়ান, *a.* turned or bent, folded.

দুম্বা, *a.* large-tailed, thick.

দুম্বাভেড়া, *s.* the Cape sheep, large-tailed [sheep.

দুর্, *prep.* in *comp.* it signifies bad, evil, difficult ; *e g.* দুর্নাম, a bad name, etc.

দুরঙ্কিত, *a.* badly marked or described.

দুরঙ্গ, *s.* two colours : *a.* party-coloured.

দুরঙ্গী, *a.* party-coloured, of two colours.

দুরদৃষ্ট, *s.* an ill fate, bad fortune.

দুরদৃষ্টক্ষয়, *s.* the removal of bad destiny.

দুরধীত, *a.* scarcely read, carelessly read.

দুরধ্যয়ন, *s.* a studying with difficulty.

দুরনুজ্ঞা, *s.* a severe or harsh order.

দুরন্ত, *a.* wicked, unmanageable, restive, unruly, cruel, impudent, troublesome.

দুরন্বয়, *s.* a false concord in grammar.

দুরবগত, *a.* difficultly known or acquired.

দুরবস্থা, *s.* adversity, distress, misfortune.

দুরবস্থান, *s.* difficultly residing in a place.

দুরাক্রমণ, *s.* a seizing or invading with difficulty ; an unjust invasion or seizure.

দুরাক্রান্ত, *a.* seized or invaded with difficulty ; seized or invaded unjustly.

দুরাগত, *a.* arrived with difficulty.

দুরাচরণ, *s.* evil conduct, bad actions.

দুরাচরিত, *a.* difficultly practised.

দুরাচার, দুরাত্মা, *a.* profligate, wicked, un- [just.

দুরারূঢ়, *a.* mounted with difficulty.

দুরারোহণ, *s.* a difficult or dangerous as- [cent.

দুরালাপ, *s.* scurrilous language.

দুরাশয়, *a.* evil-minded, wicked, malici- [ous.

দুরাশ্রয়, *s.* an insufficient or insecure re- [fuge.

দুরাশ্রিত, *a.* secured with difficulty.

দুরাসদ, *a.* scarce, hard to procure.

দুরাহ্বান, *s.* a disrespectful invitation.

দুরিত, *a.* sinful ; putrid, rotten : *s.* sin.

দুরিততা, -ত্ব, *s.* putridity, vice, depravity.

দুরী, *a.* two, deuce (used in gambling).

দুরুক্ত, *a.* badly uttered, difficultly spoken.

দুরুক্তি, *s.* a harsh or cruel expression.

দুরুচ্চরিত, *a.* badly pronounced.

দুরুৎসাহ, *s.* rashness, audacity, precipita- [tion.

দুরুপায়, *s.* a bad or unlawful expedient.

দুরূ, *a.* twice, two ways.

দুরূপ, *s.* two forms, two manners.

দুরূহ, *a.* abstruse, difficult, obscure.

দুরূহতা, *s.* abstruseness, difficultness.

দুর্গ, *a.* difficult of access : *s.* a castle, a fortress, a fort, a tower.

দুর্গতি, *s.* distress, poverty, wretchedness, [misery.

দুর্গতিপ্রাপ্ত, *a.* distressed, afflicted, poor.

দুর্গন্ধ, *s.* ill scent, a stench, fœtor : *a.* fœtid, [ill-scented.

দুর্গন্ধী, *a.* fœtid, stinking.

দুর্গবেষ্টন, *s.* the investing of a fort.

দুর্গম, *a.* difficult, impassable, inaccessible.

দুর্গম্য, *a.* difficultly passable, impassable.

দুর্গা, *s.* goddess Durgá ; -পূজা, worship of [Durgá.

দুর্গাক্রমণ, *s.* the taking of a fort.

দুর্গাটুন্টুনী, *s.* the name of a small bird.[2]

দুর্গাধ্যক্ষ, *s.* the governor of a fort.

দুর্গেয়, *a.* difficult to be sung or chanted.

দুর্গোৎসব, *s.* the festival of goddess Durgá.

দুর্গ্রহ, *s.* the taking or holding of a thing
with difficulty, a spasm, the cramp.
দুর্ঘট, *s.* a disagreeable occurrence, a cala-
mity,bad luck:*a.* difficult. [bad fortune.
দুর্ঘটন, দুর্ঘটনা, *s.* a misfortune,calamity,a
দুর্ঘটনীয়, *a.* improbable, unlikely to occur.
দুর্ঘটিত, *a.* calamitous, unlucky, wretched.
দুর্জন, *a.* wicked, ill-natured, surly, male-
volent, tyrannical, unruly, cruel.
দুর্জনতা, -ত্ব, *s.* tyranny, wickedness, ill-
naturedness, surliness, malevolence.
দুর্জয়, *s.* a hard-earned victory: *a.* scarcely
vincible, difficult to be subdued.
দুর্জেয় *a.* hard to be conquered. [able.
দুর্জ্ঞেয়, *a.* difficultly knowable or recogniz-
দুর্দম্য, *a.* difficult to be brought under sub-
দুর্দর্শ, *a.* scarcely visible. [jection.
দুর্দশা, *s.* evil condition,a state of calamity,
misery, or adversity. [sity or calamity.
দুর্দশাগ্রস্ত, দুর্দশাপন্ন, *a.* involved in adver-
দুর্দান্ত, *a.* stubborn, unruly, perverse.
দুর্দিন, *s.* bad weather, a cloudy day.
দুর্দ্ধর্ষ, *a.* confident, bold, impudent. [tate.
দুর্দ্দুরা, *v. a.* to tremble, to shake, to palpi-
দুর্নাম, *s.* a bad name, obloquy, a slander.
দুর্নামক, *s.* the piles, hemorrhoids.
দুর্নামী, *a.* infamous, of bad reputation.
দুর্নিবার, *a.* difficultly resistible.
দুর্নীত, *a.* immoral; got with difficulty.
দুর্নীতি, *s.* bad morals; impolicy, injustice.
দুর্ব্বচন, দুর্ব্বাক্য, *s.* abusive, low, harsh,pro-
fane, or obscene language, scurrility.
দুর্ব্বর্ত্ম, *s.* bad conduct,or road: *a.* profligate.
দুর্ব্বল, *a.* impotent, feeble, weak, infirm.
দুর্ব্বাচ্য, *a.* scarcely utterable,scurrilous,dif-
ficult or unfit to be spoken. [chimæra.
দুর্ব্বাসনা, *s.* an evil desire or propensity, a
দুর্ব্বাসা, *s.* the name of a famous sage.
দুর্ব্বিক্রয়, *s.* a bad sale, a difficult sale.
দুর্ব্বিক্রীত, *a.* badly or unfairly sold.
দুর্ব্বিক্রেয়, *a.* scarcely or difficultly saleable.
দুর্ব্বিধ, *a.* wicked, of a bad sort.
দুর্বুদ্ধি, *s.* stupidity, obstinacy: *a.* wicked,
obstinate, stupid, crafty. [able, restiff.
দুর্বৃত্ত, *a.* unmanageable,unruly, ungovern-
দুর্বৃষ্টি, *s.* an untimely rain, a portentous
দুর্বৈদ্য, *s.* a quack physician. [shower.

দুর্বোধ, *a.* wicked, obstinate,stupid, crafty.
দুর্ভক্ষ্য, দুর্ভক্ষণীয়, *a.* scarcely eatable.
দুর্ভগা, *a.* hated (only applied to a wife).
দুর্ভাগ্য, *s.* a misfortune: *a.* unfortunate.
দুর্ভাবনা, *s.* an evil thought, an evil or ma-
levolent intention, malevolence.
দুর্ভিক্ষ, *s.* a famine, a dearth, scarcity.
দুর্ম্মতি, *a.* obstinate, ill-natured,caballing.
দুর্ম্মদ, *a.* infatuated, blinded with pride,
intoxicated with praise or success.
দুর্ম্মনাঃ, *a.* heavy-hearted, sorrowful, de-
দুর্ম্মন্ত্রণা, *s.* evil counsel,bad advice. [jected.
দুর্ম্মন্ত্রী, *s.* an evil counsellor: *a.* giving evil
দুর্ম্মা, *s.* a half-ripe cocoanut. [counsel.
দুর্ম্মুখ, *a.* scurrilous, abusive. [rubbish.
দুর্ম্মুষ, *s.* a rammer to beat down earth or
দুর্ম্মূল্য, *s.* dearness, a high price: *a.* dear,
of an exorbitant price, high-priced.
দুর্ম্মেধা, *a.* dull, deficient in abilities.
দুর্যোগ, *s.* a bad joining, evil conjuncture:
a. badly joined; cloudy, inclement.
দুর্যোধন, *s.* the name of one of the heroes
of the Mahábhárat. [an evil omen.
দুর্লক্ষণ, *s.* an evil mark, an unlucky sign,
দুর্লঙ্ঘন, *s.* the transgressing of a law, or
overstepping of a limit with difficulty.
দুর্লভ, *a.* difficultly obtainable,scarce,rare.
দুর্লভতা, -ত্ব, *s.* scarceness, rarity.
দুর্লভ্য, *a.* scarcely or difficultly obtainable.
দুর্লালা, *a.* dear, beloved, fond. [tion.
দুর্লোভ, *s.* an evil desire, an evil inclina-
দুল্, *v. n.* to oscillate, to swing, to vibrate.
দুলা, *v. a.* to cause to swing or oscillate.
*দুলা, দুলাহ্, *s.* a bridegroom. [per name.
দুলাল, *s.* a pet, a fondling, fondness; a pro-
দুলালচাঁপা, *s.* a flowering plant.[1]
দুলিচা, *s.* a carpet, a woollen rug.
দুলিয়া, *s.* a particular class of Hindus.
*দুলান, দুলাহীন, *s.* a bride.
*দুল্‌দুল্‌ঘোড়া, *s.* Imám Husain's horse.
*দুশমন, *s.* an enemy. দুশমনী, *s.* enmity.
দুশ্চরিত্র, *s.* an evil disposition: *a.* ill-dis-
posed, vicious, ill-natured. [skin.
দুশ্চর্ম্মা, *s.* a bad skin: *a.* having a rough
দুশ্চিন্তা, *s.* evil thought, malevolence: *a.*
দুষ্কর, *a.* difficult, arduous. [malevolent
দুষ্কর্ম্ম, *s.* an evil act, a crime, fornication.

দুষ্কর্ম্মা, দুষ্কৃতী, *a.* wicked, sinful, profligate.
দুষ্কর্ম্মান্বিত, *a.* wicked, sinful, profligate.
দুষ্কৃত, *a.* evil, wicked : *s.* sin, wickedness.
দুষ্ক্রিয়া, *s.* a wicked action, a crime, forni-
দুষ্ক্রিয়ান্বিত, *a.* guilty, criminal. [cation.
দুঃখ, *s.* affliction, distress, pain, suffering ; -দা, to punish, to afflict ; -পা to suffer.
দুঃখিত, দুঃখী, *a.* the same as দুঃখিত.
দুষ্ট, *a.* wicked, depraved, vile, vicious.
দুষ্টতা, *s.* wickedness, depravity, villany.
দুষ্টভাব, *s.* a depraved condition.
দুষ্টভার্য্য, *a.* having an unfaithful wife.
দুষ্টমতি, *a.* bad-hearted : *s.* an evil mind.
দুষ্টরীতি, *s.* a wicked course, a bad method.
দুষ্টস্বভাব, *a.* wicked, malicious, vicious.
দুষ্টামি, *s.* wickedness, villany. turpitude.
দুষ্পাচ, *a.* indigestible, hard of digestion.
দুষ্পূর, *a.* difficult to please, nice, delicate.
দুষ্প্রকৃতি, *s.* an evil nature or disposition.
দুষ্প্রাপ্ত, *a.* scarcely or difficultly obtained.
দুষ্প্রাপ্তি, *s.* a difficult acquisition.
দুষ্প্রাপ্য, *a.* difficultly obtainable, scarce.
দুসূতী, *a.* made of double threads : *s.* coarse cloth made of double threads. [over.
দুস্তর, দুষ্পার, *a.* difficult, difficult to pass
দুস্তরণীয়, *a.* impassable, difficult to pass
দুস্তোষ্য, *a.* difficult to be pleased. [over.
দুস্থ, *a.* poor, afflicted, miserable. [poverty.
দুস্থতা, *s.* wretchedness, affliction, misery,
দুহাতা, *a.* two cubits long or wide.
দুহাতিয়া, *a.* ambidextrous, double-dealing.
দুহিতা, *s.* a daughter, a female offspring.
দুহ্যমান, *a.* under the operation of milking.
দূত, *s.* a messenger, an ambassador, an angel, a spy, scout, a procurer. [spy
দূতপ্রেরণ, *s.* the sending of ambassador or
দূতী, *s.* a female messenger, a procuress.
দূর, *a.* distant, remote : *s.* a distance : *ad.* far, afar ; -হ, or -যা, to withdraw, shun ; -কৃ, to remove, to dismiss, drive away,
দূরতর, *a.* more distant, very distant. [ous.
দূরদর্শক, *a.* far-seeing, provident, sagaci-
দূরদর্শন, *s.* foresight, penetration, sagacity.
দূরদর্শী, *a.* provident, forecasting, sagacious, prudent : *s.* a learned man, vulture.
দূরবর্ত্তী, *a.* far, distant, remote. [cope.
দূরবীন, দূরবীক্ষণ, *s.* a spying glass, a teles-

দূরস্থ, দূরস্থিত, *a.* situated at a distance.
দূরাদূর, *ad.* everywhere, far and near.
দূরীকরণ, *s.* a removing, a dismissing.
দূরীকৃত, *a.* removed, dismissed.
দূর্ব্বা, *s.* bent-grass, a species of grass.
দূষ্, *v. a.* to condemn, to point out faults, to confute, to convict of an error.
দূষণ, *s.* a fault, guilt, offence. [ing guilt.
দূষণাবহ, *a.* worthy of reproach, occasion-
দূষিকা, *s.* the rheum of the eyes. [tent.
দূষ্য, *a.* blame-worthy, condemnable : *s.* a
দৃক্, *s.* an eye-sight ; in *comp.* it means seeing the thing to which it is affixed.
দৃক্পাত, *s.* a glance, a look, notice.
দৃগ্গোল, *s.* the visible horizon.
দৃঢ়, *a.* firm, hard, tough, strong, stable, tight, fast, strict, sure, irrevocable, inviolable ; -কৃ, to confirm, corroborate.
দৃঢ়জ্ঞান, দৃঢ়বোধ, *s.* a firm persuasion, conviction, confidence, assurance, certainty.
দৃঢ়তম, *a.* very firm, most firm, hardest, tightest, most sure or stable.
দৃঢ়তর, *a.* more or very firm, harder, tighter, stronger, more sure or stable.
দৃঢ়তা, -ত্ব, *s.* firmness, hardness, strength, tightness, stability, sureness. [a rule.
দৃঢ়নিয়মী, *a.* punctual, strictly keeping to
দৃঢ়প্রতিজ্ঞ, *a.* punctual, firm to a promise.
দৃঢ়প্রত্যয়, *s.* confidence, firm belief.
দৃঢ়প্রত্যয়ী, *a.* confident, firmly believing.
দৃঢ়প্রীতি, *s.* constancy, firm love.
দৃঢ়বন্ধ, *s.* a firm bond, a strong obligation.
দৃঢ়বাক্য, *s.* sure word, an affirmation, a confirmation, an asseveration. [promise.
দৃঢ়বাদী, *a.* affirming, asserting, faithful to a
দৃঢ়মাংস, *s.* hard or tough meat, gristle.
দৃঢ়মুষ্টি, *a.* close-fisted, parsimonious.
দৃঢ়ীকরণ, *s.* the making of a thing firm.
দৃঢ়ীকৃত, *a.* made strong or firm, made sure or stedfast, fortified, strengthened.
দৃঢ়ীভাব, *s.* a becoming firm or hard.
দৃঢ়ীভূত, *a.* become strong, firm, or stedfast.
দৃশ্য, *a.* visible, perceptible, fit to be seen.
দৃশ্যত্ব, *s.* visibility, perceptibleness.
দৃশ্যমান, *a.* under the view, under survey.
দৃশ্যাদৃশ্য, *a.* visible and invisible. [evident.
দৃষ্ট, *a.* seen, viewed, observed, apparent,

দৃষ্টকৌরূপ্য, *s.* evident ugliness or deformity.
দৃষ্টতঃ, *ad.* seemingly, ostensibly.
দৃষ্টফলক, *a.* producing evident advantages or consequences. [similitude.
দৃষ্টান্ত, *s.* a simile, a parable, a metaphor,
দৃষ্টি, *s.* vision, sight, look, view, a vision, a scene, a prospect. [sight, in view.
দৃষ্টিগোচর, *a.* perceptible to sight: *ad.* in
দৃষ্টিঘরা, *s.* the pupil of the eye.
দৃষ্টিদোষ, *s.* fault or error in vision. [ing.
দৃষ্টিপাত, *s.* casting a look, looking, regard-
দৃষ্ট্যাবরোধক, *a.* opaque, obstructing vision.
দে, *s.* a god, a demon; a title: *a.* give.
*দেআনৎ, দেআনদ্দারী, *s.* integrity, conscience, honesty, justice, piety. [ous.
দেআনদ্দার, *a.* just, faithful, honest, consci-
দেআলতা, *s.* a kind of red powder.
দেইজ্জী, *s.* a collateral relation. [door
দেউড়ী, *s.* a vestibule, porch, entrance of a
দেউড়ীবান, *s.* a porter, a turnkey. [pujá.
দেউল, *s.* a temple; a patron of the charaka
দেউলিয়া, *s.* a bankrupt; -ন্নি, bankruptcy.
দেউলী, *s.* a religious illumination in honour of the goddess Káli; a bankrupt.
দেওড়, *s.* a volley. [of a thing.
দেওন, or দেওয়া, *s.* the giving or granting
দেওনপাওন, *s.* a giving and receiving.
দেখ, *v.* to see, look, view, observe, visit.
দেখন, *s.* a seeing, a viewing, observing.
দেখা, *v. a.* to show, display, point out: *s.* a seeing, sight, interview, a visit: *a.* seen.
দেখাদৃষ্টে, *ad.* evidently, clearly, openly.
দেখাদেখি, *ad.* face to face: *s.* the imitating of another person, imitation.
দেখান, *s.* the showing or exhibiting of a thing: *a.* shown, exhibited. [thing.
দেখানি, *s.* the showing or exhibiting of a
দেখারু, *a.* perceivable: *s.* one who shows.
দেখাশুনা, *s.* the evidence of both sight and hearing: *a.* seen and heard.
দেড়, or দেড়া, *a.* one and a half.
দেড়ী, *s.* sickness: *a.* half-boiled (rice).
দেদীপ্যমান, *a.* refulgent, conspicuous, resplendent.
দেধান, *s.* a species of grain.[1] [splendent.
দেনদার, *s.* a debtor: *a.* having debts.
দেনদারী, *s.* the condition of a debtor.
দেনা, payable: *s.* a debt, that is to be given.
দেনাপাওনা, *s.* debt and demand or income.
দেনুয়া, *a.* offered as an oblation.
দেব, *s.* a god, a demon, a heathen god, a king, a person of high rank: *voc. c.* Sir.
দেবকী, *s.* the name of Krishna's mother.
দেব-কুসুম, *s.* a clove; -খাত, a natural pond, a river, the ocean; -গণ, the class of god; -গর্জ্জন, thunder; -তুল্য, like the gods.
দেবতা, *s.* deity, the deity, a god; the clouds.
দেবত্র, *s.* the same as দেবোত্তর,
দেবত্ব, *s.* deity, divinity, godhead.
দেবদত্ত, *a.* given by a god: *s.* a term designating one whose name is not known.
দেবদারু, *s.* name of a species of pine tree.*
দেবদূত, *s.* an angel, a divine messenger.
দেবধান, দেবধান্য, *s.* the same as দেধান.
দেবনিন্দক, *s.* a blasphemer of the gods.
দেবনিন্দা, *s.* censure of the gods, blasphemy.
দেবনিষ্ঠ, *s.* a believer in God, a theist.
দেবনিষ্ঠা, *s.* a belief in God, theism.
দেবপূজক, *a.* worshipping heathen gods; *s.* an idolater, a worshipper of demons.
দেবপূজা, *s.* idolatry, the worship of gods.
দেববাণী, *s.* an oracle, a divine word.
দেবমাতৃক, *a.* (land) watered by rain.
দেবযোনি, *a.* descended from the gods; *s.* a demi-god, an infernal being.
দেবর, *s.* a husband's younger brother.
দেবরাজ, *s.* the king of the gods, Indra.
দেবর্ষি, *s.* a divine sage. [gods.
দেবল, দেবস্থল, দেবস্থান, *s.* a temple, a pa-
দেবলোক, *s.* the abode of the gods, heaven.
দেবসভা, *s.* court or assembly of the gods.
দেবসেবা, *s.* idolatry, attendance on gods.
দেবস্ব, *s.* sacred property, a sacred thing.
দেবহিংসক, *s.* one who injures the gods.
দেবহিংসা, *s.* an injury done to the gods.
দেবারাধক, or দেবার্চ্চক, *a.* worshipping the gods: *s.* an idolater. [gods, idolatry.
দেবারাধনা, দেবার্চ্চনা, *s.* the worship of the
দেবালয়, দেবায়তন, *s.* a temple, a pagoda.
দেবালয়কর্ত্তা, *s.* the owner of a temple.
দেবী, *s.* a goddess, a queen.
দেবোত্তর, *s.* endowment of a temple with land or other property, an estate given for the support of the worship of a god.
দেবোপাসক, দেবোপাসনা, *see* দেবারাধক, &c

দেয়, *a.* due, fit to be given, payable.
দেয়াল, *s.* a wall; -গীর, a wallshade. [wall.
দেয়ালী, *a.* building a wall: *s.* builder of a
*দের, *a.* late. দেরী, *s.* lateness, delay.
দেরা, or ডেরা, *s.* a tent, a tent rope.
দেরকা, দেলুকা, *s.* a lampstand, candlestick.
দেশ, *s.* a country, province, place, region.
দেশচ্যুত, *a.* banished from a country.
দেশচলান, *s.* being a disgrace to a coun-
দেশদেশান্তর, *s.* various countries. [try.
দেশধারা, *s.* the custom of a country.
দেশবর্ণনা, *s.* the description of a country.
দেশবিদেশ, *s.* one's own and foreign coun-
দেশবিশেষ, *s.* a particular country. [tries.
দেশব্যবস্থা, *s.* the laws of a country.
দেশব্যবহার, *s.* the custom of a country.
দেশভাষা, *s.* a vernacular language. [try.
দেশভ্রমণ, *s.* wandering through a coun-
দেশভ্রমণী, *a.* strolling, wandering. [try.
দেশময়, *a.* full, abundant all over the coun-
দেশমাসুর, *a.* known all over the country.
দেশরীতি, *s.* the custom of a country.
দেশরূপ, *s.* propriety, correctness.
দেশলা, *s.* a match for lighting. [bly.
দেশসভা, *s.* a parliament, a popular assem-
দেশসভ্য, *a.* eligible to a national assem-
bly: *s.* a member of parliament. [try.
দেশাচার, *s.* a custom prevalent in a coun-
দেশাধিপ, or দেশাধিপতি, *s.* a sovereign, a king, ruler, the governor of a country.
দেশান্ত, *s.* a frontier, the boundary of a
দেশান্তর, *s.* a foreign country. [country.
দেশান্তরগত, *a.* gone to another country.
দেশান্তরপ্রেরিত, *a.* sent to another country.
দেশী, or দেশীয়, *a.* country, belonging, or natural to a country, home-made.
দেহ, the body, matter; -ত্যাগ, -পাত, death.
দেহধারণ, *s.* the assuming of a body.
দেহপুষ্টি, *s.* a pampering of the body.
দেহযুক্ত *a.* embodied, material, corporeal.
দেহরহিত, or দেহহীন, *a.* unembodied, im-
দেহাত্মবাদী, *s.* a materialist. [material.
দেহান্তর, *s.* another embodied state.
দেহী, *a.* corporeal, embodied, material, connected with body: *s.* embodied soul.
দেহুড়ী, *s.* a door, gate, vestibule. [body.
দেহোদ্ভূত, *a.* inborn, natural, born of the

দৈত্য, *s.* a demon, fiend, titan, evil genius.
দৈত্যকুল, *s.* the race or family of titans.
দৈত্যগণ, *s.* the genus of titans. [Venus.
দৈত্যগুরু, *s.* Shukra, regent of the planet
দৈত্যারি, *s.* a god, enemy of the demons.
দৈনন্দিন, or দৈনিক, *a.* diurnal, daily.
দৈন্য, *s.* indigence, poverty, want, need.
দৈন্যদশা, দৈন্যাবস্থা, *s.* a state of poverty.
দৈন্যী, *a.* indigent, needy, wretched, poor.
দৈব, *s.* providence, fate, chance, an incident, a misfortune: *a.* divine, religious, providential, accidental. [remonies.
দৈবকর্ম্ম, *s.* a religious action, religious ce-
দৈবকী, *s.* the name of Krishna's mother.
দৈবকী-নন্দন, -সুত, *s.* names of Krishna.
দৈবঘটনা, *s.* a providential occurrence.
দৈবজ্ঞ, *s.* an astrologer, a fortune-teller.
দৈববাণী, *s.* a divine revelation, an oracle.
দৈবযোগ, *s.* an impulse, a divine interposition, a communion with the deity.
দৈবযোগে, দৈবাৎ, *ad.* accidentally, casually, providentially, unexpectedly.
দৈবাধীন, *a.* under the dominion of provi-
দৈবাপমৃত্যু, *s.* sudden death. [dence.
দৈবারাধনা, *s.* supplication to heaven.
দৈবী, *s.* a providential dispensation.
দৈবোৎপাত, *s.* a providential calamity.
দৈর্ঘ, or দৈর্ঘ্য, *s.* length, longitude.
দো, *a.* two; hated (applied only to a wife).
দোআ, *v. a.* to cause to milk, to milk cattle: *s.* prayer, supplication, blessing.
দোআৎ, *s.* an inkstand. [hire of milking.
দোআনী, *s.* an eighth; a branding iron;
দোআল, *a.* milch; -গাই, a milch-cow.
দো-আসলা, mongrel, hybrid: -আস্তা, coun-
*দোএম, the second (sort). [try-liquor.
দোআঁচলা, two-fringed, double-bordered.
দোআঁশ, *a.* consisting of two ingredients.
দোঁহা, *s.* a kind of verse; the second singer
দোঁহে, *a.* two, both. [in a choir.
দোকতা, *s.* dried tobacco leaves.
দোকর, double, repeated, twice; -কথা, repetition, tautology; -লিখন, a transcript.
দোকলমা, দোকলমিয়া, holding pen with two
দোকা, দোখা, *s.* rope to yoke oxen. [fingers.
দোকাট, *a.* produced by two cuttings or incisions (as the palm-juice); twice cut.

দোকাঠিয়া, *a.* consisting, or made of two pieces of wood, or two sticks. [prices.
দোকাণ্ডিয়া, *a.* of both sides, making two
দোকান, দোকানদার, *s.* same as দুকান, &c.
দোখতী, *s.* a sort of striped cloth.
দোখুঁট, *s.* two corners or protuberances.
*দোখ্তের, *s.* a daughter, female offspring.
দোগজা, *s.* a sort of covering cloth. [fever.)
দোঘেইয়া, *a.* occurring twice a day (as a
দোচুঙ্গী, দোনলী, *a.* double-barrelled.
দোচুটকী *s.* two pinches of any substance.
দোচেরা, *a.* split into two but not separat-
*দোজখ, *s.* hell, infernal region. [ed.
দোজবরিয়া, *a.* twice-married (used in con-
দোজাত্যা, *a.* mongrel, hybrid. [tempt.)
দোটানা, *s.* a dilemma, a pulling two ways.
দোঠকা, *a.* cheating both sides: *s.* a cheat, double-dealer, mischief-maker. [ties.
দোঠকামি, *s.* doing knavery on both par-
দোতন্ত্র, *s.* an option, an alternative.
দোতার, *a.* twisted double (as thread).
দোতারা, *a.* two-stringed (instrument).
দোতালা, *a.* two-storied, locking double.
দোতো, *a.* doubled, folded twice.
দোথর, দোথরী, *a.* occupying two places.
দোদাঁড়িয়া, *a.* having two teeth.
দোদামী, *s.* a kind of needle-worked cloth.
দোদুল্যমান, *a.* swinging, oscillating.
দোধড়ভেপড়, *a.* torn into tatters.
দোধারী, *a.* striped with two stripes.
দোপট্টে, *ad.* in two rows or ranks.
দোপড়া, *s.* a twice-married woman.
দোপাইয়া, *a.* biped, having two feet.
দোপাক, *a.* twice-cooked: *s.* ordure.
দোপাকা, *a.* boiling two pots at once.
দোপাটা, or দোপাট্টা, *s.* a covering sheet.
দোপেঁচা, *a.* turning twice (as a lock).
দোফড়কা, or দোফড়েঙ্গা, *a.* bifurcated.
দোফলা, *a.* producing fruit twice a year.
দোবজা, *s.* a kind of covering cloth.
দোভাঁজ, *a.* mixed, doubled, twice-folded.
দোভাষিয়া, *s.* an interpreter. [two folds.
দোমড়, *v. n.* to be folded double, or into
দোমড়া, *v. a.* to double into two folds, to double: *a.* folded, double, doubled.
দোমড়ান, *s.* the doubling of any thing, the folding a leaf in a book: *a.* doubled.

দোমড়ানি, *s.* the folding of a thing.
দোমনা, *a.* double-minded. [nuts.)
দোমালা, *a.* half ripe (applied to cocoa-
দোর, *s.* a door-way, an opening.
দোরঙ্গা, *a.* partycoloured, piebald. [brid.
দোরঙ্গী, *a.* partycoloured; mongrel, hy-
দোরসা, *a.* altered in taste, half-putrid.
দোল, *s.* a swinging, an oscillatory motion,
দোলট্‌খট্‌, *s.* a dilemma. [oscillation.
দোলন, *s.* a swinging, oscillating. [dle.
দোলনা, *s.* oscillation, a swinging; a cra-
দোলনী, *s.* a swing, a child's cradle.
দোলনীয়, *a.* oscillatory, vibratory.
দোলমাল, *s.* a swinging at random.
দোলযাত্রা, *s.* a festival in honour of Krishna and Rádhá; also that of Ráma.
দোলা, *v. a.* to cause to swing, to impel a swing: *s.* a swing, a litter, a pálkí.
দোলাই, *s.* a kind of mantle, or covering
দোলাদোলী, *s.* a mutual swinging. [cloth.
দোলান, *s.* the causing of a thing to swing.
দোলানি, *s.* the act of swinging. litter.
দোলাবাহক, *s.* a pálkí-bearer, bearer of a
দোলায়মান, *a.* swinging, oscillating.
দোশাখা, *a.* having two branches or pro-
দোষ্‌, *v. a.* to refute, invalidate. [cesses.
দোষ, *s.* a fault, crime, guilt, sin, a vice, a defect, an imperfection, blemish, a flaw, calumny, a vitiated state of any part of the body;-দা, to blame, accuse, calumniate, defame;-কৃ, to offend, to do evil.
দোষকর, *a.* hurtful to health, injurious.
দোষক্ষমা, *s.* the forgiveness of a crime.
দোষক্ষেত্র, *s.* the scene of crime, a criminal, a diseased body. [ator.
দোষগায়ক, *a.* calumniating: *s.* a calumni-
দোষগ্রস্ত, *a.* involved in guilt, guilty.
দোষগ্রাহক, *a.* accusing: *s.* a fault-finder.
দোষণ, *s.* imputation of crimes, the invalidating of a testimony, or argument.
দোষতত্ত্ব, *s.* the ascertaining of crimes.
দোষময়, *a.* full of crimes or faults.
দোষমাত্র, nothing but crime, mere crime.
দোষসূচক, *a.* indicating guilt or crime.
দোষস্বীকার, *s.* the confession of sins.
দোষা, *v. a.* to criminate, to condemn.
দোষাকর, *s.* a source of faults or crimes.

দোষাক্রান্ত, *a.* seized or loaded with crimes.
দোষাঘ্রাত, *a.* guilty, criminal, faulty.
দোষাণ, *s.* a criminating, a finding fault.
দোষাদোষ, *s.* merits and defects, good and
দোষাদোষি, *s.* mutual recrimination. [evil.
দোষান্বিত, *a.* guilty, criminal.
দোষাবহ, *a.* bringing faults or crimes.
দোষাবিষ্ট, *a.* engaged in faults or crimes.
দোষার্হ, *a.* befitting the fault or crime.
দোষী, *a.* culpable, guilty, faulty, criminal, sinful; incorrect, inaccurate: *s.* a criminal; -কৃ, to criminate, to convict.
দোসতিনী, *s.* two wives of the same hus-
দোসর, *s.* a second, a companion. [band.
দোসরা, *a.* the second, another.
*দোস্ত, দোস্দার, *s.* a friend, a companion.
দোস্তানী, দোস্তী, দোসদারী, friendship, kind-
দোহ্, *v. a.* to milk; to draw away. [ness.
দোহক, *a.* milking: *s.* one who milks.
দোহদ, *s.* the longing of a pregnant woman; the fœtus, the embryo; a stain.
দোহন, *s.* the milking of animals. [ed.
দোহনীয়, *a.* milch, capable of being milk-
দোহা, *s.* a couplet, a kind of verse.
দোহাই, *s.* an exclamation or call for justice, an oath, an appeal.
দোহাতা, দোহাতিয়া, the same as দুহাতা, &c.
দোহার, *s.* a second, a prompter.
দোহারা, *a.* double, two-fold; -পীড়া, a re-
দোহারাপীড়িত, *a.* relapsed. [lapse.
দোহারালেখা, *s.* a transcript, a copy.
দৌড়, *v. a.* to run; দৌড়িয়া যাওন, to run, to run swiftly; দৌড়িয়া ধরণ, to overtake.
দৌড়, *s.* a race, a career, a running. [ning.
দৌড়ধাপ, *s.* endeavour, exertion in run-
দৌড়ন, *s.* the act of running, scampering.
দৌড়নি, *s.* a running, a race. [to impel.
দৌড়া, *v. a.* to make any one run, to drive,
দৌড়াদৌড়ি, *s.* a running about: *ad.* hastily, speedily, in great haste, at a run.
দৌড়ান, *s.* a causing to run, a running.
দৌত্য, or দৌত্যকর্ম্ম, *s.* the office of a messenger, ambassadorship, an embassy.
দৌবারিক, *s.* a porter, a door-keeper.
দৌরাত্ম্য, *s.* violence, outrage, oppression.
দৌর্জন্য, *s.* wickedness, violence. [fatigue.
দৌর্ব্বল্য, *s.* weakness, infirmity, weariness,
দৌর্ভাগ্য, *s.* misfortune, ill luck.
*দৌলৎ, *s.* riches, wealth, treasure.
দৌলৎখানা, *s.* a mansion, a house.
দৌলতী, or দৌলৎমন্দ, *a.* rich, wealthy.
দৌহিত্র, *s.* a daughter's son; *fem.* দৌহিত্রী.
দ্যুতি, *s.* light, splendour, lustre.
দ্যুনিশ, *s.* a day and night.
দ্যূত, *s.* dice; -ক্রীড়া, play at dice, gambling.
দ্যোত, *s.* light, lustre, sunshine.
দ্যোতক, *s.* nonsense, unmeaning word.
দ্যোতন, *s.* a revealing, an enlightening.
দ্রব, *a.* liquid, fluid: *s.* fusion, melting; -কৃ, to fuse, to melt; -হ, to be dissolved.
দ্রবভাব, *s.* fluidity, a liquid state.
দ্রবরস, *s.* a fluid or liquid substance.
দ্রবার্হ, *a.* dissolvable, fusible, soluble.
দ্রবিণ, *s.* wealth, substance, gold.
দ্রবীকৃত, *a.* liquefied, made fluid.
দ্রবীভূত, *a.* become fluid or liquid.
দ্রব্য, *s.* a thing, substance, article, materi-
দ্রব্যমূল্য, *s.* price of an article. [al, stuff.
দ্রব্যান্তর, *s.* another thing. [of things.
দ্রব্যায়োজন, *s.* the collecting or preparing
দ্রাক্ষা, *s.* a grape, a raisin; -লতা, a vine.
দ্রাক্ষারস, *s.* wine, the juice of the grapes.
দ্রাঘিমা, *s.* length, longitude.
দ্রাঢ্য, *s.* firmness, solidity, strength. [acid.
দ্রাপক, *s.* elixir of vitriol, diluted sulphuric
দ্রাবক, solvent: *s.* a solvent, a flax assisting
দ্রাবণ, dissolving, melting, fusion. [fusion.
দ্রাবী, *a.* soluble, dissolvable, fusible.
দ্রাম্, *s.* *Eng.* a drachm.
দ্রু, or দ্রুম, *s.* a tree. দ্রুণ, *s.* a scorpion.
দ্রুত, *a.* speedy, hasty, accelerated, quick;
দ্রুতগামী, *a.* swift, fleet. [liquid, fluid.
দ্রুমাঙ্গ, *s.* the branch of a tree. [sers.
দ্রোণ, *s.* a measure of capacity, about 32
দ্রোণকাক, *s.* a raven, a carrion crow.
দ্রোণী, *s.* a kind of boat, a canoe, a raft.
দ্রোহ, *s.* injury, spite, malice, malevolence, envy, murder. রাজদ্রোহ, a treason.
দ্রোহক, দ্রোহী, envious, injurious, malevolent, spiteful, murderous, treasonous.
দ্বন্দ্ব, *s.* a pair, a pair of opposites; as, a man and wife, good and evil, pleasure and pain, etc.; strife, dispute, quarrel.
দ্বন্দ্বজ, *a.* arising from a quarrel or dispute.

দ্বন্দ্বী, quarrelsome, disputatious, litigious.
দ্বয়, s. two, a pair, a brace, a couple; used only as the last member of a compound.
দ্বাঃস্থ, a. standing at the door or gate.
দ্বাচত্বারিংশৎ, a. 42. দ্বাচত্বারিংশত্তম, a. 42nd.
দ্বাত্রিংশৎ, a. 32. দ্বাত্রিংশত্তম, a. 32nd. [row.
দ্বাদশ, a. twelve; -মন্দির, 12 temples in a
দ্বাদশাস্র, s. a dodecahedron, parallelopipedon.
দ্বাদশী, a. the twelth (lunar day.)
দ্বানবতি, a. ninety-two; -তম, ninety-second.
দ্বাপঞ্চাশৎ, a. fifty-two. দ্বাপঞ্চাশত্তম, a. 52nd
দ্বাপর, s. 3rd yuga or chronological period of the Hindus; doubt, uncertainty.
দ্বাবিংশতি, a. twenty-two; -তম, 22nd.
দ্বার, s. a door, passage, entrance, opening, a medium of communication or action.
দ্বারকা, s. a famous city of pilgrimage.
দ্বার -পাল, -রক্ষক, s. a porter, door-keeper.
দ্বারস্থ, or দ্বাস্থ, a. being at a gate or door.
দ্বারা, ad. by, through, by means of.
দ্বারী, or দ্বারিক, s. a door-keeper, a porter.
দ্বাষষ্টি, a. sixty-two; -তম, sixty-second.
দ্বাসপ্ততি, seventy-two; -তম, 72nd. [heard.
দ্বিরুক্তিধর, a. retaining what has been twice
দ্বিকর, s. two hands: a. having two hands.
দ্বিকোণ, two angles: a. having two angles.
দ্বিকর্ণিকা, a. having two pedicels or fruit-stalks.
দ্বিকেশর, a. diandrous, diandrian.
দ্বিকোষ, a. having two seed-vessels.
দ্বিখণ্ড, s. two pieces: a. bisected.
দ্বিগর্ভ, a. bilocular, divided into two cells.
দ্বিগুণ, a. double, twofold, twice.
দ্বিগুণাঙ্ক, s. a peculiar Hindu method of working a sum in multiplication.
দ্বিচত্বারিংশৎ, a. 42. দ্বিচত্বারিংশত্তম, 42nd.
দ্বিচ্ছিন্ন, a. bisected, cut into two.
দ্বিজ, a. twice-born, regenerated: s. a bráhman, a bird, oviparous animal. [birds.
দ্বিজরাজ, s. the moon; Garura, regent of
দ্বিজাত, দ্বিজাতি, a. twice-born: s. a bráhman.
দ্বিজাতীয়, a. of a bráhman; hybrid.
দ্বিজালয়, s. the habitation of bráhmans.
দ্বিজিহ্ব, s. a serpent, a snake.
দ্বিতন্ত্রী, a. two-stringed, having two fibres.
দ্বিতয়, a. twofold, of two sorts, two.
দ্বিতীয়, a. the second.
দ্বিতীয়তঃ, ad. secondly.
দ্বিতীয়া, a. the second (lunar day.) [day.
দ্বিত্র্যহ, ad. in two or three days, the other
দ্বিত্ব, s. a reduplication, repetition. [ties.
দ্বিদল, a. two-leafed, bilobated: s. two parties.
দ্বিদলাক্রান্ত, a. drawn by both parties.
দ্বিদলিয়া, a. siding with both; unprincipled.
দ্বিধা, ad. of two sorts: s. a dilemma, a word having two meanings, a doubtful circumstance, a doubt, hesitancy.
দ্বিধাকম্প, a. doubtful, precarious. [cond.
দ্বিনবতি, a. ninety-two; -তম, the ninety-second.
দ্বিপঞ্চাশ, দ্বিপঞ্চাশত্তম, a. the fifty-second.
দ্বিপঞ্চাশৎ, a. fifty-two.
দ্বিপদ, or দ্বিপাদ, a. two-footed, biped.
দ্বিপুটক, a having two rows of petals.
দ্বিবক্র, a. having two curves, bending two ways: s. in *ana.* the sismoid cavity.
দ্বিবচন, s. the dual number in grammar.
দ্বিবচনান্ত, a. ending with a plural termination.
দ্বিবর্তুল, a. biglobose, bispherical.
দ্বিবিধ, a. twofold, of two kinds: s. two sorts.
দ্বিভাগ, s. two parts or shares; -কৃ, to divide.
দ্বিভুজ, a. two-armed: s. a figure with two sides.
দ্বিমস্তক, দ্বিমুণ্ড, a. two-headed.
দ্বিমুখ, a. having two mouths, two-faced: s. an amphisbina, a deceitful person.
দ্বিমূর্দ্ধা, or দ্বিশিরাঃ, a. two-headed.
দ্বিমূলক, a. springing from two origins.
দ্বিযোনি, a. digynous, having two pistils.
দ্বিরদ, or দ্বিপ, s. an elephant.
দ্বিরাগমন, s. a second coming of a newly married girl to her husband's house.
দ্বিরাবৃত্তি, s. a second return, or revolution.
দ্বিরুক্ত, a. twice spoken, repeated.
দ্বিরুক্তি, s. a repetition, a tautology.
দ্বিরূঢ়, a. twice-married: s. twice-married man.
দ্বিরূঢ়া, s twice-married woman.
দ্বিরূপ, a two-fold, of two sorts, of a double form.
দ্বিরূপী, a. having two forms.
দ্বিরেফ, s. a humble-bee, so called from having two র in its name, viz. ভ্রমর.
দ্বিভোজন, a. eating twice. [teeth.
দ্বিশল্য, a. bicuspidate: s. the grinding
দ্বিষষ্টি, a. sixty-two; -তম, sixty-second.
দ্বিসপ্ততি, a. seventy-two; -তম, 72nd.
দ্বিসমচতুরস্র, s. quadrangle with two equal sides.
দ্বিসমত্রিভুজ, s. an isosceles triagnle.

দ্বিহস্ত, *s.* two hands: *a.* two-handed.
দ্বিহায়নী, *a.* two years' old.
দ্বীপ, *s.* an island, a continent.
দ্বীপান্তর, *s.* another island or continent.
দ্বেষ, *s.* envy, malice, hatred, injuriousness.
দ্বেষক, *a.* injurious, malicious, malevolent.
দ্বেষবাক্য, *s.* a malicious speech.
দ্বেষভাব, *s.* maliciousness, malevolence.
দ্বেষসূচক, *a.* indicating malice or hatred.
দ্বেষাদ্বেষ, *s.* hatred and good will. [volent.
দ্বেষী, *a.* envious, injurious, malicious, male-
দ্বেষ্টা, *a.* malevolent, hostile: *s.* an enemy.
দ্বেষ্য, *a.* deserving to be hated. [kind.
দ্বৈত, *s.* a second of the same nature or
দ্বৈতজ্ঞ, *a.* believing in a plurality of gods.
দ্বৈতজ্ঞান, *s.* belief in a plurality of gods.
দ্বৈতজ্ঞাননিষ্ঠ, *s.* faith in a plurality of gods.
দ্বৈতজ্ঞানী, *a.* the same as দ্বৈতজ্ঞ. [theist.
দ্বৈতবাদ, *s.* polytheism. দ্বৈতবাদী, *s.* a poly-
দ্বৈতাদ্বৈত, *s.* a 2d of the same nature or not.
দ্বৈধ, *s.* ambiguity, dilemma, doubt, double speech, or resource, stratagem, a two-fold form or state, a contest, a duel.
দ্বৈধবাক্য, *s.* a doubtful speech, a dilemma.
দ্বৈধীকৃত, *a.* brought into a dilemma.
দ্বৈমাতুর, *a.* having two mothers: *s.* an epithet of Ganesha and Jarasandha.
দ্ব্যগ্র, *a.* ending in two points, bifid, biceps.
দ্ব্যগ্রমাংসপেশী, *s.* the biceps muscle.
দ্ব্যঙ্গুল, *a.* two fingers wide or long.
দ্ব্যণুক, *s.* a particle, an atom.
দ্ব্যর্থ, *a.* admitting of two meanings.
দ্ব্যর্থকথা, *s.* a quibble, a pun, a bon-mot.
দ্ব্যাহিক, *a.* occurring every other day.
দ্ব্যুদর, *a.* digastric (muscle).

ধ, is nineteenth consonant in the Bengáli alphabet. It is the aspirated dental d.
ধকেল, *s.* a thrust, a push, a shoving in.
ধক্কা, *s.* a push, a shove, a thrust. [tion.
ধক্‌ধক্‌, *s.* a blazing up, glitter, a palpita-
ধক্‌ধকা, *v. n.* to blaze, glow, palpitate.
ধক্‌ধকান, *s.* the blazing up, the palpitating
ধড়, *s.* the body, trunk. [of the heart.
ধড়া, ধড়াই, *s.* old garment, a rag, a piece of cloth worn to cover the privities.
ধড়ীবাজ, *a.* deceitful, crafty, roguish.
ধড়ীবাজী, *s.* roguishness, craftiness.
ধড়্‌ধড়্‌, *s.* sudden palpitation.
ধড়্‌ধড়িয়া, *a.* ragged, hanging in tatters; squirting, soft (as ordure). [tering.
ধড়্‌ফড়্‌, *s.* a struggling, a flouncing, a flut-
ধড়্‌ফড়া, *v. a.* to struggle, flounce, flutter.
ধড়্‌ফড়ান, *s.* a struggling or fluttering.
ধড়্‌ফড়ানি, *s.* a violent struggling.
ধন, *s.* wealth, property, riches, goods, a treasure, property consisting of cattle.
ধনক্ষয়, *s.* the loss or decay of property.
ধনগরিমা, or ধনগর্ব্ব, *s.* the pride of wealth.
ধনগর্ব্বিত, or ধনাভিমানী, *a.* purse-proud.
ধনঞ্জয়, *s.* the god Agni, a name of Arjuna.
ধনপতি, *s.* Kuvera, the god of riches.
ধনবান্‌, *a.* wealthy, rich, opulent, affluent.
ধনবাহুল্য, *s.* abundance of wealth. [riches.
ধন-বৃদ্ধি, *s.* increase of riches; -মাত্র, mere
ধনব্যয়, *s.* the expenditure of wealth.
ধনমত্ত, *a.* intoxicated with wealth, purse-
ধনমূলক, originating from riches. [proud.
ধনরক্ষা, *s.* the preservation of wealth.
ধনরাশি, *s.* a heap or stack of treasure.
ধনলাভ, ধনার্জ্জন, *s.* acquisition of wealth.
ধনলোভ, *s.* desire for wealth or property.
ধনলোভী, *a.* desirous of wealth, covetous.
ধনসঞ্চয়, *s.* the accumulation of wealth.
ধনাকাঙ্ক্ষা, desire for riches, covetousness.
ধনাকাঙ্ক্ষী, ধনার্থী, *a.* desirous of riches, cov-
ধনাঢ্য, *a.* wealthy, affluent, rich. [etous.
ধনাধার, ধনভাণ্ডার, *s.* a storehouse, a trea-
ধনাধিকার, *s.* a right to property. [sury.
ধনাধিকারিতা, *s.* proprietorship of wealth.
ধনাধিকারী, *a.* having a right to property.
ধনাধিপতি, *s.* Kuvera, the god of riches,
ধনাধ্যক্ষ, *s.* *idem.* [a treasurer.
ধনাশা, *s.* a hope for riches, a thirst for
ধনিচা, *s.* the Indian flax-plant.[1] [wealth.
ধনিতা, -ত্ব, *s.* affluence, opulence.
ধনিয়া, *s.* coriander seed; *vide* ধন্যা.
ধনিষ্ঠা, *s.* the 23d stellar mansion. [happy.
ধনী, *a.* rich, affluent, opulent, fortunate,
ধনু, *s.* a bow; the name of a measure.
ধনুঃ, ধনুরাশি, *s.* the sign Sagittarius.
ধনুক, *s.* a bow, the bow of a violin.
ধনুখরা, *s.* a bow for cleaning cotton.
ধনুবৎ, *a.* arcuated, bent, curved, arched.

ধনুরাকর্ষণ, s. the drawing of a bow.
ধনুরাকার, or ধনুরাকৃতি, a. arcuated, bent, curved : s. the segment of a circle.
ধনুর্গুণ, s. a bowstring, the chord of an arc.
ধনুর্দ্ধর, s. an archer, a bowman.
ধনুর্বিদ্যা, s. archery, the science of archery.
ধনুর্ভঙ্গ, s. the breaking of a bow. [wager.
ধনুর্ভঙ্গপণ, s. a firm threat, promise, or
ধনুষ্টঙ্কার, s. the twang of a bowstring;
ধনুস্তম্ভ, s. rigidity from spasms. [spasms.
ধনুস্, s. a bow, a curve, an arc.
ধনেশ, s. appellation of Kuvera. [proud.
ধনোন্মত্ত, intoxicated with wealth, purse-
ধনোপার্জ্জন, s. the acquisition of wealth.
ধন্দা, s. the defective sight, a mistake.
ধন্য, a. praiseworthy. happy, blessed.
ধন্যধন্য, intj. O brave! praiseworthy!
ধন্যবাদ, s. ascription of praise, blessing, a thanksgiving, thanks; -কৃ, to thank.
ধন্যবাদী, a. ascribing praise, thankful.
ধন্যা, ধন্যাক, s. coriander seed, its plant.[1]
ধন্বন্তরি, s. the physician of the gods.
ধন্বী, s. an archer : a. armed with a bow.
ধপ্‌ধপ্, s. the sensation of clearness.
ধপধপা, v. a. to appear clear or bright.
ধপ্‌ধপান, s. an appearing white, a shining.
ধপ্‌ধপিয়া, a. clear, bright, open, white.
ধব, s. a husband; linen, clothes : a. white.
ধবল, a. white : s. white leprosy.
ধবলকুষ্ঠ, s a species of white leprosy.
ধবলকুষ্ঠী, a. leprous, having white leprosy.
ধবলা, a. white. ধবলী, s. a white cow.
ধমন, s. the kindling up of fire.
ধমনী, s. a vein, artery, a nerve.
ধমুক্, s. a threat, a censure, a reproof, a scolding, a chiding, a shock, a report.
ধমক্‌ধামক্, s. threats and reproofs.
ধম্‌কা, v. to threaten, reprove, reprimand, to chide, to scold: s. a pair of bellows.
ধমকাধমকি, s. mutual scolding, a brawling.
ধম্‌কান, s. a scolding, threatening, reprov-
ধম্‌কাবাত, ধম্‌কা, s. a squall of wind. [ing.
ধম্মিল্ল, s. embroidered hair.
ধর্, v. a. to seize, to catch, to hold.
ধরণ, s. the having or holding of a thing, a seizing or apprehending, a ceasing (of a shower,) a stopping (the lax bowels).
ধরণা, s. a scaffold; a dunning; -দা, to dun.
ধরণাদায়ক, a. dunning : s. a dunner.
ধরণিয়া, a. catching, holding, seizing.
ধরণী, s. earth; -পতি, -পাল, a king, sove-
ধরণীতল, s. earth, bottom of earth. [reign.
ধরণীধর, s. a king; a mountain.
ধরণীয়, worthy of regard, or of being controverted, assumable, apprehensible.
ধরা, v. a. to cause to seize or hold; to plaster : s. the earth, seizure, capture, apprehension; -পড়্, to be apprehended.
ধরাই, s. a catching, a holding.
ধরাট, s. an allowance or interest upon money lent for trade, usury, interest.
ধরাণ, s. a causing to seize or apprehend.
ধরাধর, s. a mountain; a name of Vishnu.
ধরাধরি, s. a mutual holding or seizing.
ধরামণ্ডল, s. a terrestrial globe.
ধরায়, a. apprehensible, accountable.
ধরিত্রী, s. the earth. ধর্ণা, s. *vide.* ধরণা,
ধর্ত্তব্য, a. apprehensible, worthy of notice or criticism, accountable, significant.
ধর্ম্ম, s. inherent virtue, nature, temper, character, religious merit, duty, righteousness, justice, religion, piety; name of a god; -পুত্র, a name of Yudhisṭhir.
ধর্ম্মকর্ম্ম, s. piety, godliness, a religious ac-
ধর্ম্মতঃ, ad. piously, rightly, justly [tion.
ধর্ম্মতা, -ত্ব, s. religion, virtue, rectitude.
ধর্ম্মতোভার, s. a duty or obligation to be
ধর্ম্মত্যাগ, s. apostacy. [sacredly fulfilled.
ধর্ম্মত্যাগী, s. an apostate.
ধর্ম্মনিষ্ঠ, establishment in virtue, firmness
ধর্ম্মপত্তন, s. black-pepper. [in religion.
ধর্ম্মপথ, s. the road of religion or virtue.
ধর্ম্মপরায়ণ, devoted to religion or virtue.
ধর্ম্মপরাঙ্মুখ, averse to religion or virtue.
ধর্ম্মপরিবর্ত্তক, s. a proselyte, a convert.
ধর্ম্মপরিবর্ত্তন, s. a conversion, a change of religious profession. [gion or virtue.
ধর্ম্মপালক, a. observing the duties of reli-
ধর্ম্মপালন, s. an observing or practising the duties of religion. [vent, hospital.
ধর্ম্মশালা, s. an almshouse, monastery, con-
ধর্ম্মশাস্ত্র, s. the body of Hindu law, juris-
ধর্ম্মশাস্ত্রকারক, s. a legislator. [prudence.
ধর্ম্মশীল, a. pious, virtuous, religious.

ধর্ম্মসংহিতা, *s.* a digest of laws, a ritual.
ধর্ম্মাত্মা, *s.* the Holy Spirit : *a.* holy, pious.
ধর্ম্মাধর্ম্ম, *s.* religion and the want of it, religion and irreligion, virtue and vice.
ধর্ম্মাধিকরণ, *s.* a court of law, a tribunal.
ধর্ম্মাধিকার, *s.* the right to administer justice, the duties of a sheriff. [do justice.
ধর্ম্মাধিকারী, *s.* a sheriff: *a.* having a right to
ধর্ম্মাধ্যক্ষ, *s.* a spiritual teacher, a bishop.
ধর্ম্মাবতার, *s.* an incarnation of justice or virtue (a term of Hindu flattery).
ধর্ম্মিষ্ঠ, ধর্ম্মী, *a.* virtuous, religious, pious, godly, just, righteous, honest.
ধর্ম্মোপদেশ, *s.* religious instruction.
ধর্ম্মোপদেশক, *s.* a preacher of religion.
ধর্ম্ম্য, *a.* lawful, proper, just, right. [ing.
ধর্ষক, *a.* daring, bold, imposing, over-aw-
ধর্ষণ, ধর্ষণকরা, *s.* the daring of a person to combat, a brow-beating, boldness.
ধল, white, fair:-বস্ত্র, white or washed cloth.
ধাই, *s.* a nurse, a wetnurse, a midwife.
ধাইতেলা, overanointing (a babe) with oil.
ধাউড়িয়া, *s.* a runner, an express, a mes-
ধাউড়্য়া, *s.* expedition, speed, haste. [senger.
ধাউস, or ঢাউস, *s.* a large paper kite.
ধাওন, ধাওয়া, *s.* a going fast, a running.
ধাঁদা, *s.* mistiness or dimness of sight, blindness, a stratagem, trick, a sleight; -লাগ, to overlook, mistake, to wink at.
ধাঁদালাগান, *s.* a confounding, causing mistakes by introducing confusion. [ed.
ধাঁদালী, ধাঁদলানি, dim-sighted, short-sight-
ধাঁধাঁ, *im.sd.* of a brisk motion, or of a drum.
ধাকা, *s.* the sum deposited in gambling.
ধাক্কা, *s.* a push, shove, a thrust, shock.
ধাড়া, *s.* a balance; a row of coarse stitches or patches in cloth ; mat screen or door.
ধাড়ালেপা, *s.* a patching, a patch work, a
ধাড়িয়া, or ধেড়িয়া, *s.* an otter. [patcher.
ধাড়ী, *a.* strong, robust, full grown : *s.* a dam.
ধাতা, *s.* one who nourishes, Providence.
ধাতু, *s.* a principle or humour of the body, as phlegm, wind, and bile ; an organ of sense ; metal, metallic ore, the element or root of a word, semen virile, the matter which oozes in a gleet, the pulse.
ধাতুকাশীশ, *s.* the red sulphate of iron.

ধাতুক্ষয়, *s.* a decay of the vital functions.
ধাতুক্ষরণ, *s.* the oozing of matter in a gleet.
ধাতুঘটিত, *a.* metalline, mixed with metal.
ধাতু-চলা, -বিকার, *s.* a gleet, a gonorrhea.
ধাতুনরম, *s.* a cold, a catarrh. [tric fluid
ধাতুপ, *s.* alimentary juice, chyle, the gas-
ধাতুপাত্র, *s.* a metal dish or cup.
ধাতুপুষ্টি, *s.* nutrition, nourishment, the strengthening of the body by aliment.
ধাতুপুষ্টিকর, *a.* nutritive, nourishing, alimentary, strengthening. [tening.
ধাতুপোষক, *a.* nutritive, nutritious, fat-
ধাতুবাদী, *s.* an assayer, mineralogist, a mi-
ধাতুভেদ, *s.* change in the humours. [ner.
ধাতুময়, *a.* made of metal, metallic.
ধাতুমাক্ষিক, *s.* a sort of mineral substance.
ধাতুমারিণী, borax, copple-dust (a solvent).
ধাতুসাম্য, *s.* a state of perfect health. [ry.
ধাত্রী, *s.* wetnurse, midwife;-কর্ম্ম, midwife-
ধাত্রীবিদ্যা, *s.* obstetric science, midwifery.
ধান্, *s.* grain, rice ; -কাট, to reap; -কাটন, a reaping ; -মাড়ন, a threshing (rice).
ধানমরিচ *s.* a variety of capsicum.[1]
ধানী, *a.* (rice) mixed with unhusked rice.
ধানুষ্ক, ধানুষ্কী, *s.* an archer, a bowman.
ধান্য, *s.* unhusked rice, corn, grain.
ধান্যক্ষেত্র, *s.* a rice-field. ধান্যাদি, *s.* grain.
ধান্যময়, *a.* abounding with rice, or grain.
ধান্যশালী, *a.* (soil) fit for growing rice.
ধাপ, *s.* the step of a stair-case.
ধাব্, *v. a.* to run, to go fast, to scamper.
ধাবক, *s.* a runner, one who goes express.
ধাবড়িয়া, *a.* quick, swift, running express.
ধাবন, ধাবনি, ধাবনা, a running, going fast.
ধাবমান, *a.* running, in the act of running.
ধাবাধাবি, *s.* a promiscuous running.
ধাম, *s.* the body; a house, a dwelling, a place, a spot, a country, dignity, light.
ধামসা, *s.* a kind of kettle-drum.
ধামা, ধামী, *s.* a scuttle or basket of ratan.
ধার্, *v. a.* to borrow, owe, hold as a loan or debt : *s.* a loan, debt, an end, border, boundary, a line, limit, edge of a precipice, or of a weapon, sharpness, distillation, dripping or oozing by drops, a leak, flaw, a stream ; -কৃ, to borrow ; to whet, sharpen ; -মার্, to make blunt.

ধারক, *s.* a holder, one who examines the accuracy of the text in reading the shástras, an umpire : *a.* having, holding.
ধারকতা, -ত্ব, *s.* the office of an umpire.
ধারকরণ, *s.* a borrowing; a harpening.
ধারণ, *s.* a having, holding, maintaining, assuming a habit or shape, supporting, sustaining, upholding; -কৃ, to sustain.
ধারণা, *s.* continuance in aright way, perseverance, fortitude, firmness, resolution, restraint, mental retention, memory, a debt, a sustentaculum. [restrained.
ধারণাবান্, *a.* persevering, firm, resolute,
ধারণাশক্তি, *s.* an ability to be firm, resolution, power of restraint. [straight line.
ধারণী, *s.* any tubular vessel of the body, a
ধারা, *s.* a method, a custom, a habit, a usage, a fashion, a course, a stream, a general practice, a section, conduct.
ধারাক্রমে, *ad.* according to custom or ha-
ধারানুসার, *a.* customary, habitual. [bit.
ধারানুসারে, *ad.* customarily, habitually.
ধারাবাহিক, or ধারাবাহী, *a.* flowing down the stream of custom. [cloud ; a sword.
ধারায়, *a.* apprehensible. ধারাধর, *a*
ধারাল, or ধারযুক্ত, *a.* edged, sharp, keen.
ধারাসম্পাত, *s.* a heavy shower.
ধারী, *s.* an edge, margin : *a.* having, holding ; *e. g.* অস্ত্রধারী, bearing arms, etc.
ধারে, *ad.* ashore ; on credit. [ous, just.
ধার্ম্মিক, *a.* pious, religious, virtuous, righte-
ধার্ম্মিকতা, -ত্ব, *s.* righteousness, justice.
ধার্য্য, *a.* apprehensible, restrainable, retentive; -কৃ, to nominate, determine, assign.
ধার্ষ্ট্য, *s.* impudence, shamelessness. [ment.
ধিং, ধিং ধাং, ধিংপণা, *s.* a tumult, outrage, a confusion, anarchy, sedition.
ধিক্, *intj.* fye or curse on it! woe be to it!
ধিক্কার, *s.* contempt, reproach, censure.
ধিক্কৃত, *a.* cursed, contemned, reviled, cen-
ধিক্ধিক্, *a.* a burning slowly. [sured.
ধিক্ধিকি, *a.* quivering or burning slowly.
ধিমা, *a.* slow, abated, deliberate, cautious.
ধিমায়, *ad.* faintly, softly, deliberately.
ধিষণ, *s.* a name of Vrihaspati. [*a.* wise.
ধী, *s.* understanding, knowledge, an idea :
ধীন্দ্রিয়, *s.* an organ of perception.

ধীবর, *s.* a fisherman. [ous; Vrihaspati.
ধীমান্, *a.* wise, learned, intelligent, sagaci-
ধীর, *a.* wise, learned, sedate, sagacious, grave, deliberate, tranquil, serene, temperate, docile, slow, lazy, steady, firm.
ধীরতা, -ত্ব, *s.* deliberateness, temperateness, sedateness, gravity, steadiness.
ধীরা, *a.* jealous of a lover, yet suppressing resentment;-ধীরা, a jealous woman.
ধীরে, or ধীরেধীরে, *ad.* deliberately, slowly, coolly, sedately. [report.
ধীশব্দ, or ধীধীশব্দ, *s.* a report, a common
ধীসচিব, *s.* a barrister, counsellor, pleader.
ধু, or ধুওন, *v. a.* to wash any thing.
ধুঁদুল, *s.* a climbing plant and its fruit.[1]
ধুকড়ী, *a.* coarse: *s.* a coarse bag, or cloth.
ধুক্ধুক্, *s.* a feeble palpitation, a panting.
ধুক্ধুকা, or ধুক্, *v. n.* to pant, to palpitate.
ধুক্ধুকান, *s.* act of panting, a palpitating.
ধুক্ধুকানি, *s.* an anxiety about any affair.
ধুক্ধুকী, *s.* anxiety, remorse; a neck orna-
ধুক্নি, *s.* a panting ; a blow-pipe. [ment.
ধুচনী, *s.* a kind of basket for washing rice.
ধুত, *a.* agitated, relinquished. [crimes.
ধুতকল্মষ, or ধুতপাপ, *a.* freed from sin or
ধুতী, *s.* the lower garment worn by the natives instead of breeches ; a bribe.
ধুতুরা, *s.* the thorn-apple (Datura metal).
ধুধু, *s.* the blazing up of fire : *a.* wide open.
ধুন্, *v. a.* to clean cotton with a bow.
ধুনখরা, ধুনচি, *s.* a bow for cleaning cotton.
ধুনন, *s.* the cleaning of cotton ; a beating.
ধুননি, *s.* the cleaning of cotton with a bow.
ধুননী, *s.* the price for cleaning cotton.
ধুনারি, or ধুনিয়া, *s.* a cotton-cleaner.
ধুন্দ, *s.* ardour, zeal, fervour, diligence : *a.* great, prodigious, ardent. [uproar.
ধুন্দমারী, *s.* rebellion, sedition, tumult, an
ধুপ, *s.* incense, resin ; a sabre ; the sun.
ধুপী, or ধুবী, *s.* a washerman. [will.
ধুপপনেচ্ছা, *s.* a strong desire, a determined
ধুম, *s.* zeal, ardour, fervour, ado, tumult, pomp : *a.* thick, gross, large, spacious.
ধুমড়ী, *s.* a concubine, a fat vagabond woman, a female Vaishnava. [cherous.
ধুমড়ীমারা, *a.* vagabond, vagrant, lewd, le-
ধুমধাম, *s.* hubbub, tumult, pomp, parade.

ধুম্‌ধুম্, *a.* bulky, heavy, thick, gross.
ধুমুল, *s.* the monotonous beating of a drum to call persons to a festivity or show.
ধুয়া, *s.* the burden or chorus of a song.
ধুর্, *s.* the axletree, a carriage pole; reflection, thought; a load, burden. [burden.
ধুরন্ধর, *a.* bearing a burden : *s.* a beast of
ধুরন্ধরধুরীণ, *a.* chief of those who sustain the burden of office, viz. a king.
ধুল, *s.* a measure of land equal to a káṭhá.
ধু, or ধুধু, *im. sd.* expressive of a blazing up.
ধুঁআ, *s.* smoke, steam, vapour; -দা, to fumigate.
ধুঁআঘরা, *s.* chimney, smoke-tunnel. [gate.
ধুঁআটা, *a.* smoky, like smoke. [place.
ধুঁআদেওন, *s.* the fumigating of a thing or
ধুঁআপথ, ধুঁআফুকার, *s.* a chimney.
ধুনচি, or ধুনী, *s.* a censer, an incense-pot.
ধুনা, ধুনক, *s.* incense, resin of Shála tree.
ধুপ, *s.* incense, resin ; the sun, solar rays ; -ছায়া, solar-shaded (a sort of cloth).
ধুপীত, perfumed with incense, fumigated.
ধুম, *s.* smoke, steam, fume, vapour-; -জাল, -পুঞ্জ, a volume of smoke ; -যোনি, cloud.
ধুমকেতু, *s.* a comet, meteor, a falling star,
ধুমপান, *s.* the smoking of tobacco. [fire.
ধুমময়, *a.* covered with, or full of, smoke.
ধুম্র, *a.* purple, smoke-coloured : *s.* purple.
ধুর্ত, *a.* cunning, subtle, crafty, sly, knavish, roguish : *s.* a gamester, a rogue, a knave, a cheat ; the thorn-apple.
ধূর্ত্ততা, *s.* craftiness, knavery, slyness.
ধুর্ত্তপুষ্প, *s.* the flower of the thorn-apple.
ধুর্ত্তপুষ্পাকার, or ধুর্ত্তপুষ্পাকৃতি, *a.* funnel-shaped, infundibuliform, arytænoid.
ধুর্পত *s.* a particular tune in music.
ধুলা, ধুলি, *s.* dust, pollen ; -মাখন, a smearing with dust; -মাখা, smeared with dust.
ধুলিধূসর, *a.* cinereous, dust or ash coloured.
ধুলিময়, *a.* dusty, covered with dust.
ধুলিমুষ্টি, *a.* dusty : *s.* a handful of dust.
ধূল্যবগুণ্ঠন, *s.* a veil to keep off the dust.
ধূসর, gray ; *s.* gray colour, an ass, oilman,
ধূসা, *s.* flannel. ধূসরী, *a.* gray. [a vulture.
ধুস্তূর, *s.* the thorn-apple (Datura metal).
ধুস্তূরপুষ্প, ধুস্তূরপুষ্পাকার, *see* ধুর্ত্তপুষ্প, &c.
ধৃ, *v. a.* to hold, to seize, to apprehend a criminal, to have, to continue, remain.

2 C 2

ধৃত, *a.* caught, seized, held, taken.
ধৃতরাষ্ট্র, *s.* a king celebrated in the Mahábhárata ; a kind of wild goose, a swan.
ধৃতি, *s.* sacrifice, a religious rite or ceremony, restraint, retention, tenacity, firmness, constancy, a holding, a having, pleasure, satisfaction, happiness, an astronomical yoga, a particular kind of verse or metre.
ধৃতিমান্, *a.* firm, steady, constant, restrained, satisfied, happy. [insolent.
ধৃষ্ট, or ধৃষ্ণু, *a.* impudent, shameless, bold,
ধেঁড়স্, *s.* a vegetable commonly called the
ধেড়ি, *s.* a sort of earring. [ram's horn.
ধেড়, *v. n.* to purge or have a looseness.
ধেঁড়িয়া, or ধাড়িয়া, *s.* an otter. [cow.
ধেনু *s.* kine, a cow, recently calved milch-
ধেয়, *a.* fit or proper to be held in.
ধেয়া, *v. a.* to think upon, to meditate.
ধেয়ান, *s.* meditating, reflection, attention.
ধৈর্য্য *s.* deliberation, temperance, forbearance, steadiness, patience, coolness.
ধৈর্য্যকরণ, *s.* the exercising of forbearance.
ধৈর্য্যধরা, *s.* a maintaining patience.
ধৈর্য্যবান, ধৈর্য্যশালী, *a.* patient, forbearing, temperate, deliberate, cool, steady.
ধৈর্য্যান্বিত, *a. idem.*
ধৈর্য্যাবলম্বন, *s.* restraint, abstinence.
ধৈর্য্যাবলম্বী, *a.* patient, restrained, abstinent.
ধো, *v. a.* to wash, to clean. [nent.
ধোঁকন, *s.* a panting ; a blowing the fire.
ধোঁকা, *v. a.* to cause to pant : *s.* a panting.
ধোঁকানি, *s.* a panting with hard running.
ধোঁড়া, *s.* a species of water-snake.
ধোআট, *s.* alluvial soil, washings.
ধোওন, *s.* the washing of a thing.
ধোকড়, or ধোকড়ী, *s.* a coarse bag, a sack ; the testicles : *a.* coarse. [a doubt.
ধোকা, *s.* an illusion, deception, suspicion,
ধোপ, *s.* washing of clothes : *a.* washed.
ধাপদাস্ত, ধোপাল, *a.* washed, clean.
ধোপা, ধোবা, *s.* a washerman; *fem.* ধোবানী.
ধোমলা, *v.* to seek after a person's health, to inquire, to ask how a person does.
ধোয়া, *s.* a cleansing, washing : *a.* washed,
ধোয়ানি, *s.* washings, dregs. [clean.
ধোমা, *s.* a kind of silk and cotton cloth.

ধৌত, *a.* washed, clean; -কৃ, to wash.
ধৌতকলেবর, ধৌতকায়, *a.* washed, bathed.
ধৌতবস্ত্র, *s.* washed or clean clothes.
ধ্যাতব্য, *a.* fit or proper to be meditated on.
ধ্যাতা, *a.* contemplative : *s. vide* ধ্যানকর্ত্তা.
ধ্যান, *s.* meditation, thought, contemplation, cogitation, reflection. [plates.
ধ্যানকর্ত্তা, *s.* one who meditates or contem-
ধ্যানগম্য, *a.* accessible to meditation.
ধ্যানভঙ্গ, *s.* an interruption of meditation.
ধ্যানযুক্ত, *a.* contemplative, sedate, reflect-
ধ্যানযোগ, *s.* religious abstraction. [ing.
ধ্যানী, *a.* contemplative, thoughtful.
ধ্যেয়, *s.* the object of meditation.
ধ্রুপদ, *s.* a particular tune in music.
ধ্রুব, *ad.* permanently, certainly : *a.* permanent, eternal, continual, fixed, stable, firm, certain, ascertained : *s.* the polar star, the north pole; logic, reasoning.
ধ্রুবকা, *s.* the longitude of a star; a chorus.
ধ্রুব-লোক, *s.* heaven ;-তারা, the polar star.
ধ্বংস, *s.* destruction, ruin, loss, detriment.
ধ্বংসক, or ধ্বংসী, *a.* destructive, ruinous: *s.* a person who ruins, a destroyer.
ধ্বংসন, *s.* destruction, ruin. [ruined.
ধ্বংসনীয়, *a.* destructible, capable of being
ধ্বজ, *s.* a flagstaff, an ensign, a monument, sign, symbol, the penis;-বান, a flagman.
ধ্বজভঙ্গ, *s.* a disease which consists in an inability to erect the penis.
ধ্বজা, ধ্বজী, *s.* a banner, a standard, an ensign, flag, a monument, a sign, symbol.
ধ্বজিনী, *s.* an army; a high landmark.
ধ্বনি, *s.* a noise, sound. ধ্বনিত, *a.* sounded.
ধ্বন্যাত্মক, *a.* sounding, expressing sound.
ধ্বস্ত, fallen, ruined, degraded, destroyed.
ধ্বান, *s.* inarticulate sound.
ধ্বান্ত, *s.* darkness, gloom.

ন, the twentieth consonant; a negative particle, no, not : *a.* nine : *s.* the fourth son or daughter in a large family.
নই, *a.* no, not; new; ninety. [tube.
নইচা, *a.* young (applied to fish) : *s.* a huka
নউক্তি *a.* the ninth. [bagpipe, etc.
*নওবৎ, *s.* a music consisting of drum,
নওবৎখানা, *s.* a music-room, an orchestra.
*নকল, *s.* a copy, a transcript, imitation; a show, mimickry; -নবীস, a copyist.
নকলনবীসী, *s.* the profession of a copyist.
নকলবয়ান, *s.* the reading of a copy.
নকলিয়া, *a.* mimicking, imitating, copying.
*নকশ্‌বন্দ, *s.* a class of Moslem beggars.
নকার, *s.* the letter ন; a denial, refusal,
নকী, *s.* a brass vessel. [negation.
*নকীব, *s.* a forerunner whose office is to proclaim his master's approach. [davas.
নকুল, *s.* ichneumon; one of the five Pán-
*নক্কাশ, *s.* a map-maker, a painter, a lim-
নক্ত, *s.* the night : *ad.* by night. [ner.
নক্তব্রত, *s.* a vow to eat only in the night.
নক্তান্ধ, *a.* unable to see by night. [shark.
নক্র, *s.* a crocodile, an alligator; -রাজ, a
*নক্‌শা, *s.* a feature, countenance, visage; a map, a chart, a picture, a plan.
নক্ষত্র, *s.* lunar mansion, a star, constellation; -পতি, or -রাজ, the moon.
নক্ষত্রমালা, *s.* a row of stars; a kind of neck-
নক্ষত্রলোক, the starry region, sky. [lace.
নক্ষত্রশ্রেণী, *s.* a row of stars.
নক্‌সান, *s.* injury, loss, detriment. [talon.
নখ, নখর, *s.* finger or toe nail, a claw, a
নখচিহ্ন, *s.* a scratch, a mark of the nails.
নখনা, *s.* the spur of a cock, a point.
নখরঞ্জনী, *s.* the same as নরুণ, which see.
*নখরা, *s.* a trick, an artifice, a joke, waggery, coquetry, a sham, a pretence.
নখশূল, a whitlow. নখাস্থি, the os unguis.
নখাগ্র, *s.* the point of a nail or talon.
নখাঘাত, *s.* a stroke with the nails or ta-
নখায়ুধ, *a.* having nails or talons. [lons.
নখী, *a. idem: s.* a bivalve shell; a kind of
নগ, *s.* a mountain, rock, a tree. [perfume.
নগজ, *s.* an elephant; a mountaineer.
নগণ্য, *a.* of no estimation, mean, worthless.
নগদ, *a.* prompt, ready, in hand (applied to money); -টাকা, cash, ready money.
নগদজিনিশ, *s.* articles produced.
নগদবিক্রী, *s.* a sale for ready money.
নগদানগদি, or নগদী, *s.* ready money.
নগর, নগরী, *s.* a city, a town. [a city.
নগরসমীপ, *s.* the vicinity of a city: *a.* near
নগরপ্রান্ত, *s.* the outskirts of a city.
নগরবাসী, or নাগর, *s.* a citizen.

নগরস্থ, *a.* standing or situated in a city.
নগরাক্রান্ত, *a.* held or confined in a city.
নগাম, *s.* a bridle; *vide* লাগাম. [bowels.
নগি, *s.* urine;-গ্রহবন্ধ, constipation of the
নগী, *s.* a standing (as a little child), a pole,
নগ্ন, *a.* naked, uncovered. [a boat-hook.
নগ্নিকা, *s.* a young girl.
নঙ্গর, *s.* an anchor; -কৃ, or -ফেল্, to cast anchor; -তোল্, to weigh anchor.
নঙ্গর -করণ, -ফেলন, *s.* a casting anchor.
নঙ্গরবাড়ী, *s.* anchorage, harbour. [else.
নচেৎ, *ad.* perhaps not, if not; otherwise,
*__নজ্‌দীক্, নজীক__, *a.* near, in the vicinity.
নজ্‌নজ্যা, *a.* poachy, soft, plashy.
*__নজর__. *s.* a view, a sight; a present, a gift.
নজ্জরবন্দ, *a.* fascinated, guarded, watched,
নজ্জরবন্দী, *s.* imprisonment. [imprisoned.
নজ্জরবাজ্, *a.* sharp-sighted: *s.* one who sees or views, one who ogles, a juggler.
নজ্জরবাজী, *s.* sharp-sightedness.
নজ্জরা, *s.* a view, a sight, a present.
নজ্জরানা, *s.* a present, present at meeting.
নঞি, *a.* the ninth. নঞ্, a *neg. part.* no, not.
নট, *s.* a dancer, an actor: *a.* curdled.
নটখট, *s.* an intricate affair, perplexity: *a.* wicked, troublesome, vexatious. [cy.
নটখটী, *s.* perplexity, wickedness, intrica-
নটন, *s.* a ball, dancing. [limbs.
নট্‌পট্, *s.* a struggling, feeble state of the
নটবর, *s.* a fop, a rake, a lewd fellow.
নটিয়া, নট্যা, *s.* several species of amaran-
নটী, *s.* a female dancer; a harlot. [thus.[1]
নট্যালয়, *s.* a brothel, a bawdy-house.
নট্যাশাক, *s.* spinach, amaranthus.
নড়্, *v. n.* to stir, to move; *properly* লড়্.
নড়্, *s.* a kind of reed. নড়ন, *vide* লড়ন.
নড়ী, *s.* a cane, a stick, a staff, a wand.
নড়্বল, or **নড়্বান্**, *a.* abounding in reed.
নত, *a.* bowed down, bent, prostrate, descended, reclined, crooked: *s. vide* নথ.
নতকন্ধর, *a.* bowed, holding down the head.
নতনাসিক, *a.* having a depressed nose.
নতা, *s.* an excuse, a pretence. [papers.
নতি, *s.* humility, a bow, prostration; file of
নতিগাঁথা, *s.* the sewing of loose papers.
*__নতিজা__, *s.* a retribution, a reward.
নতু, *conj.* otherwise, or, but.

নতুবা, *conj.* if not, otherwise, else. [very.
নত্রা, *s.* the ninth day after a woman's deli-
নথ, নতিনী, *s.* a ring for the nose worn by
নদ, *s.* a river, a male river. [women.
নদ্‌নদ্, *s.* softness, plashiness.
নদনদিয়া, *a.* plashy, poachy, soft. [ing.
নদাকার, নদাকৃতি, *a.* like a river, meander-
নদী, *s.* a river, a female river; -কূল, -তট, or -তীর, the bank of a river.
নদীমাতৃক, *a.* fed or watered by rivers.
নদীসিকস্ত, *a.* broken, worn away by a river.
নন, a *negative particle*, no, not. [sister.
ননদ, ননদিনী, ননদী, ননন্দা, *s.* a husband's
ননী *s.* butter, fresh butter. [objection.
ননু, a *part.* used to draw attention to an
নন্দ, *s.* joy, happiness, festivity, pleasure, felicity, prosperity, increase; Indra's paradise; the foster father of Krishna.
নন্দথু, *s.* happiness, pleasure, joy, festivity.
নন্দন, *s.* a son; gladdening. [Krishna.
নন্দনন্দন, *s.* the son of Nanda, a name of
নন্দা, prosperity, increase; a water-jar; a husband's sister; a goddess. [*see* নন্দী.
নন্দি, *s.* gaming, gambling; happiness, joy;
নন্দিক, *s.* a timber tree (Cedrela Toona).
নন্দিনী, *s.* a daughter; a husband's sister.
নন্দী, rejoicing: *s.* one of Shiva's attendants, speaker of a prelude to a drama; one who pronounces a benediction.
নন্দীবৃক্ষ, a timber tree;[2] Indra's paradise.
নন্দোৎসব, *s.* Krishna's birth-day festival.
নম্বড়িয়া, *a.* swinging, pendent.
নপ্‌নপ্, *s.* haste, speed. [eunuch.
নপুংসক, *a.* neuter: *s.* a hermaphrodite, a
নপূর, *s.* a jingling ornament for the feet.
নপ্তা, *s.* a grandson; *fem.* নপ্ত্রী.
নফট্‌কী, *s.* a plant called heart-pea.[3]
নফর, *s.* a servant. নফরালী, servitude, ser-
*__নফা__, *s.* gain, profit, perquisite. [vice.
নব, *a.* new, fresh, young; nine: *s.* panegyric, praise; -কুমার, an infant son; -গ্রহ, the nine planets; -রঙ্গকুল, noble.
নবতা, -ত্ব, *s.* newness, recentness.
নবতি, *a.* ninety; -তম, the ninetieth.
নবদ্বার, *a.* having nine doors: *s.* the body.
নবনত্রা, *s.* the ninth day after childbirth.
নবনারিকা, *s.* a newly married woman.

নবনী, or নবনীত, *s.* butter, fresh butter.
নববধূ, *s.* a bride, a newly married woman.
নবম, *a.* the ninth. নবমী, 9th (lunar day).
নবযৌবন, *a.* young, opening into youth.
নবরত্ন, *s.* the nine gems, viz. diamond, emerald, ruby, garnet, sapphire, topaz, lapis lazuli, pearl, or more probably the cat's eye, and crystal. [nine terms.
নবরাশিকা, *s.* the rule of proportion with
নবসূতিকা, *s.* one newly become a mother.
নবহেমকর, *s.* a newly blown water-lily.
নবাঙ্কুর, *s.* a young sprout.
নবাৎ, *s.* a kind of sweetmeat.
নবান্ন, *s.* new rice, new corn, a festival observed on cutting the first ripe corn.
*নবাব, *s.* a vicegerent, a nawáb, a viceroy.
নবাবী, *a.* of a nawáb: *s.* viceroyship.
নবীন, নবীনতা, the same as নব্য, নব্যতা.
নবোঢ়া, *s.* a newly married person, a bride.
নব্য, *s.* new, fresh, young, modern, novel.
নব্যতা, *s.* newness, novelty, recentness.
নব্যতাপ্রকাশ, *s.* a display of novelty.
নব্যপদ্যচালক, *s.* a schemer, a projector.
নব্বই, or নবতি, *a.* ninety. [sphere.
নভঃ, নভঃস্থল, নভোমণ্ডল, *s.* the sky, atmo-
নমঃ, *s.* a bow, a salutation, obeisance.
নমন, *s.* a descending, stooping, becoming
নমনীয়, *a.* flexible, depressible. [humble.
নমশূদ্র, *s.* a Chandála, an outcaste.
নমস্কার, *s.* a bow, a salutation, obeisance, a prostration; -কৃ, to bow. [tration.
নমস্কৃত, *a.* bowed to, saluted, bowed by pros-
নমস্য, *a.* honourable, venerable, worthy of respect or salutation, reverend. [tion.
নমস্যানমস্য, *a.* worthy or not of saluta-
*নমুদ, *s.* an index, a guide, an appearance, a beginning: *a.* apparent, famous.
*নমুনা, *s.* a pattern, muster, an example.
নম্য, *a.* flexible, depressible; -তা, flexibility.
নম্র, *a.* humble, lowly, condescending, soft, gentle, meek; -প্রকৃতি, -স্বভাব, naturally humble, gentle, meek, lowly.
নম্রতা, *s.* humility, meekness, lowliness, condescension, gentleness.
নম্রান্তঃকরণ, *a.* humble-minded, lowly.
নয়, *ad.* no, is not: *a.* nine: *s.* morality, justice, righteousness, right.

নয়ন, or নয়ান, *s.* an eye; -ঠার, a wink, eye-
নয়নগোচর, *a.* obvious, visible. [sign.
নয়নতারা, *s.* the pupil of the eye.
নয়নপ্রিয়, *a.* agreeable to the sight.
নয়া, *a.* new, fresh, novel, modern.
নয়ানবাণ, *s.* the eye resembling a dart.
নয়ানসুখ, *s.* a sort of fine cloth.
নর, *s.* a man, a male; -ভুক, a cannibal.
নরক, *s.* the infernal region, hell, torment, misery, punishment; ordure; -গামী, going to hell; -ভোগ, the suffering of hell; -যন্ত্রণা, the torments of hell.
নরকী, *a.* hellish, infernal, tormenting.
নরদেব, *s.* a sovereign, a king, a bráhman.
নরপতি, *s.* a king, sovereign, governor.
নরপ্রিয়, *a.* philanthropic, loving mankind.
নরবলি, or নরমেধ, *s.* a human sacrifice.
নরম, *a.* gentle, soft, mild, tender, supple,
নরমা, *v. a.* to mollify, to soften. [pliant.
নরমাণ, *s.* a mollifying, a softening.
নরমী, *s.* softness, mildness, tenderness.
নরলোক, *s.* the earth, the world inhabited
নরসংসর্গ, *s.* human society. [by man.
নরসিংহ, *s.* in *mytho.* the 4th incarnation of Vishnu; an eminent man, a nobleman.
নরসুন্দর, *s.* an epithet given to a barber.
নরাকৃতি, *s.* human form: *a.* human-formed.
নরাঙ্কিত, *a.* ascertained as certain, corrobo-
নরাজ, *s.* beam of a weaver's loom. [rated.
নরাধম, *s.* a vile man: *a.* vilest among men.
নরাধিপতি, *s.* a king, a sovereign, a gover-
নরাধিবাস, *s.* a human residence. [nor.
নরুণ, *s.* an instrument to pare the nails.
নরেন্দ্র, or নরেশ্বর, *s.* a sovereign, a king.
নরোত্তম, *s.* an excellent man, a nobleman.
নর্ত্তক, *s.* a dancer, an actor, a dancing boy.
নর্ত্তকশালা, *s.* a ball-room, a theatre.
নর্ত্তকী, *s.* an actress, a dancing girl.
নর্ত্তন, *s.* act of dancing, acting. [trench.
নর্দ্দমা, *s.* a channel, gutter, drain, canal, a
নর্ম্ম, *s.* sport, fun, amusement, jocularity.
নর্ম্মঠ, *a.* devoted to sport or pleasure: *s.* a nipple; a rake, a lecher, a libertine; sport, amusement, coition. [river.
নর্ম্মদা, *a.* giving pleasure: *s.* name of a
নল, *s.* a tube, a pipe, an earthen spout or pipe, the trachea or windpipe, a reed,

the huká tube, a measuring rod; the name of a famous king; a water-lily.[1]
নলক, s. the drop of a nose-ring; the tibia, the radius, a cylindrical bone, a tube.
নলকযন্ত্র, s. a telescope, a spying-glass.
নলকিনী, or নলকীল, s. the knee-pan or patella.
নলখাগড়া, s. a species of reed.[2]
নলচালা, s. *lit.* the moving of a reed; or, an artifice or incantation for the discovery of stolen goods.
নলদ, s. the nectar of a flower; the Indian spikenard.[8]
নলস্থ, a. of the windpipe, bronchial.
নলা, s. the arm, a cylindrical bone.
নলি, s. a cylindrical bone, a reed on which weavers wind thread for the shuttle.
নলিচা, s. a huká-snake, the tube of a huká.
নলিন, s. a waterlily, lotus; -নয়ন, lotus-eyed.
নলিনী, s. assemblage of waterlilies.
নলিয়া, s. a fowler; -ধনু, a cross-bow.
নলী, s. a tube, the barrel of a gun, the trachea or windpipe, realgar, red arsenic; also, *vide* নলি. [faux or pharynx.
নলীদ্বার, s. the opening to the throat, the
নলীফাঁদাল, v. the caliber of a gun.
নল্প, নল্পা, s. a. to flash, to emit flashes.
নল্পন, নল্পান, s. the flashing of lightning.
নল্যগু, s. the glottis, larynx hole. [cubits.
নল্ল, or নল্, s. a measure of four hundred
নশ্বর, a. liable to destruction, perishable, transitory.
নশ্বরতা, s. perishableness.
নষ্ট, a. dead, perished, spoiled, ruined, lost, debauched; -কৃ, to spoil, ruin, destroy, debauch, deflour, taint, undo, squander.
নষ্টকারক, a. injurious, ruinous, destructive: s. a destroyer, a seducer. [ergy.
নষ্টচেতাঃ, a. foolish, want of heart or en-
নষ্টতা, নষ্টামি, s. roguery, knavery, debauchery, profligacy, pollution, turpitude.
নষ্টা, s. a debauched woman, a strumpet.
নষ্টোদ্ধার, s. the retrieving of an affair.
*নসীব, s. fate, destiny, fortune; a share, a lot.
*নসীহৎ, s. exhortation, instruction.
নস্য, s. snuff; -দান, or -দানী, a snuff-box.
*নস্তালিক, s. a sort of Persian writing.
নহ (তুমি-), নহিস (তুই-), thou art not.
নহি, *neg. par.* no, not; (আমি-), I am not.
নহে, *ad.* no, not (সে), নহেন (তিনি), he is not.

না, *ad.* no, not; or: s. a boat: v. to bathe.
নাই, *ad.* no, not, is not: s. a barber, the navel.
নাইকুণ্ডল, s. the navel.
নাইদ, s. a bathing tub, a jar.
নাইয়া, s. a waterman, a boatman.
*নাউম্মেদ, a. hopeless, helpless, forlorn.
নাউয়াপেটা, a. abdominous, pot-bellied.
*নাএক, s. a corporal in the army.
নাএবী, s. a deputy, a vicegerent. [puty.
নাএবী, s. deputyship: a. belonging to a de-
নাএবীকর্ম্ম, s. the business of a deputy.
নাওন, s. the act of bathing, ablution.
নাং, s. a gallant, a paramour, sweetheart.
নাংচূর্ণী, s. a lewd woman, a strumpet.
নাংনী, a. having a gallant or paramour.
নাক, s. the nose; -ঘড়ঘড়া, -ডাক, to snore, to snort; -তোল, -সেঁটকা, to sneer; -খাঁদা, -থেবড়া, snub-nosed; -ডাকা, a snoring; -তোলন, -তোলা, a sneering at any one; -ফোঁড়া, having the septum of the nose bored; -বেঁকা, crook-nosed, wry-nosed.
নাকড়া, s. a polypus of the nose.
নাকানাকি, *ad.* nose to nose, to the brim.
*নাকারা, useless, fit for nothing: s. a drum.
নাকাল, s. a pair of pincers; *vide* নাকুরা.
নাকি, *ad.* a particle expressing an option or alternative, or not, or no, or what.
*নাকিস্, s. bad, vile, refuse, worthless.
নাকী, a. nasal: s. the ward of a lock.
নাকীকথা, s. a speaking through the nose.
নাকীসুর, or নাকীস্বর, s. a nasal sound.
নাকুয়া, a. having a prominent or fine nose.
নাকেখত, s. the punishment of rubbing a person's nose hard on the ground.
নাকেদম, a. having all the breath or life in the nose as though ready to depart.
নাকেশ্বরীবাঘ, s. a species of tiger, a leopard.
*নাকোঅৎ, a. feeble, weak, infirm.
নাক্ষত্র, নাক্ষত্রিক, a. relating to the stellar mansions.
নাক্ষত্রমাস, s. a stellar month.
*নাখান্দা, a. unable to read. [joyful.
*নাখুশ, a. displeased, not pleased, not
*নাখোদা, s. the captain of a ship.
নাখ্রা, s. a trick, an artifice, deceit, waggery, coquetry, a sham, a pretence.
নাখরাজ, a. rent-free: s. a freehold.
নাখরাবাজ, a. gay, waggish, shamming.

নাগরাবাজী, *s.* gaiety, waggishness.
নাগ, *s.* in *mytho.* a race of fabulous beings[*] in the form of serpents; the spectacle snake, a hydra, a serpent; an elephant.
নাগকূপ, *s.* a burning well, a volcano.
নাগকেশর, or নাগেশ্বর, *s.* a flowering tree.[1]
নাগজ, *s.* vermillion, redlead.
নাগদনা, *s.* a plant (Artimisia vulgaris).
নাগদন্ত, *s.* a pin or peg stuck in a wall; the battlements of a house; ivory.
নাগপাশ, *s.* a Hindu fabulous weapon.
নাগবেল, *s.* a strong climbing plant.[2]
নাগযষ্টি, *s.* a centre-post in a pond.
নাগর, *a.* of a city, town-born, clever, sharp, knowing, nameless, bad, vile: *s.* a denial of knowledge; a citizen; a wag.
নাগরঙ্গ, *s.* an orange.
নাগরদোলা, *s.* a kind of swing.
নাগরমুথা, *s.* a species of grass.[3]
নাগরা, or নাগারা, *s.* a sort of drum.
নাগরাজ, *s.* Vásuki the king of serpents.
নাগরালি, *s.* citizenship.
নাগরী, *a.* of a city: *s.* a citizen; the Nágarí character; an intriguing woman.
নাগরীগুড়, *s.* a fine kind of molasses.
নাগলোক, *s.* Pátála, the infernal regions.
নাগা, *a.* near, armed: *s.* an order of ascetics.
নাগাল, *s.* a vestige, a situation.
নাগিনী, নাগী, *s.* a female serpent or hydra.
নাঙ্গল, *s.* a plough; -চষন, a ploughing.
নাঙ্গলা, *a.* ploughing: *s.* a plough-bullock.
নাচ, *v. a.* to dance, jump, vibrate, shake.
নাচ, *s.* a dance, dancing, gesticulation.
নাচঘর, নাচশালা, *s.* a theatre, a ball-room.
নাচন, নাচনি, *s.* a dancing, skipping.
নাচা, *v. a.* to cause to dance: *s.* act of dancing.
নাচাড়ী, *s.* a particular measure of verse.
নাচান, *s.* the causing a person to dance.
নাচানিয়া, *a.* dancing: *s.* a dancer.
নাচার, *a.* poor, helpless, hopeless, forlorn.
নাচারী, *s.* helplessness, hopelessness.
নাছদুয়ার, *s.* a back-door, a private door.
*নাজীর, *s.* a jailor, an inspector, a superintendent, the chief of the peons.
নাজীরী, *s.* the business of a Názir.
*নাজুক, *a.* delicate, tender, elegant, facetious, genteel: *s.* the sensitive plant.[4]

নাজেহাল, a state of unparalleled wretchedness or misery, excessive fatigue.
নাট, *v. a.* to dance: *s.* a dance, a scene.
নাটক, *s.* a drama, a dramatic writing, a dancer, actor: a. theatrical dancing.
নাটকী, *s.* dancing girl, dramatic writing.
নাটন, *s.* a dancing, acting, performing.
নাটমন্দির, *s.* a ball-room, a theatre.
নাটরাঘাটরা, *a.* topsyturvy: *s.* nicknacks.
নাটা, *v. a.* to reel silk or thread: *a.* dwarf: *s.* a reel for silk, etc.; a climbing shrub.[5]
নাটাই, *s.* a reel for silk or thread.
নাটাঘাঁটা, *a.* towzled, entangled, topsyturvy.
নাটান, *s.* the reeling of silk or thread.
নাটানি, *s.* distress, misery, exigency.
নাটানিয়া, *a.* miserable: *s.* one who reels.
নাটিকা, *s.* a light comedy, a comic play.
নাটিম, *s.* a top, a child's teetotum, toy.
নাটিমাকার, *a.* toy-shaped, pyriform.
নাটিয়াঘাঁটিয়াবাঁচা, *s.* the outliving of the greatest distress or dangerous illness.
নাটুআ, *s.* a dancing boy, a dancer, buffoon.
নাট্য, *s.* a dance, a dancing.
নাট্যবিদ্যা, *s.* the science of dancing.
নাট্য -মন্দির, -শালা, *s.* a theatre, ball-room.
নাঠৌর, *a.* unascertained, uncertain.
নাড়্, *v. a.* to move, to stir, to wag, shake.
নাড়ন, *s.* the act of stirring or shaking.
নাড়া, *v.* to move, stir, wag: *s.* a stirring; straw, stubble: *a.* stirred, shaken.
নাড়াচাড়া, *s.* a stirring and moving about.
নাড়ান, *s.* the stirring of a thing: *a.* moved.
নাড়ানাড়ি, *s.* a moving or stirring about.
নাড়াশীজ, *s.* a species of Euphorbia.[6]
নাড়ী, *s.* a tubular stalk, culm of grass or corn, a blowpipe, the intestines, guts, a blood-vessel, vein, the navel-string, the pulse; -দেখ্, to feel the pulse.
নাড়ীকাটা *s.* cutting the navel-string of a babe.
নাড়ীগতি, *s.* pulsation, motion of the pulse.
নাড়ীগালন, *s.* the extracting of the guts.
নাড়ীছাড়ন, *s.* the cessation of pulsation.
নাড়ীজ্বলন, *s.* a pain in the bowels, hunger.
নাড়ীজ্ঞ, *a.* versed in the doctrine of pulse, skilful in tracing disease by the pulse.
নাড়ীজ্ঞান, *s.* a knowledge of the pulse.
নাড়ীটেপা, *s.* a physician (in contempt).

নাড়ীদেখা, *s.* a feeling of the pulse to ascertain disease.
নাড়ীন্ধম, *s.* a goldsmith. [certain disease.
নাড়ীবিদ্যা, *s.* angiology, or science of veins.
নাড়ীবৈশন, *s.* the cessation of pulsation.
নাড়ীব্রণ, *s.* a fistulous ulcer, a running sore.
নাড়ী-ভুঁড়ী, *s.* intestines, -ময়, veiny, veined.
নাড়ীমরা, *s.* inappetency, loss of appetite.
নাড়ীস্তম্ভ, stoppage of pulsation. [Krishna.
নাড়ু, *s.* a ball-sweetmeat; -গোপাল, image of
*না-তদ্‌বির, *a.* unthinking, unreflecting; -তমাম, unfinished; -তরিবৎ, uneducated; -তালীম, want of instruction or doctrine.
নাতি, *s.* a grandson; *fem.* নাতিনী.
নাতিপুতি, *s.* grandsons, grandchildren.
নাথ, *s.* a lord, master, protector, a ruler, husband; a bullock's nose-rope. [lord.
নাথবান্, *a.* dependent upon a master or
নাদ্, *v. a.* to expel the fæces (as cows, etc.)
নাদ, *s.* a sound, a call, a noise, a roar, the dung of animals, a large earthen pan.
নাদন, *s.* expelling of the fæces by cattle.
নাদনা, *s.* a rammer, a bludgeon; a jar.
নাদপচা, *a.* rotten or tainted while standing in the vessel (applied to rice).
নাদবিন্দু, or চন্দ্রবিন্দু, *s.* the nasal mark.
নাদা, *s.* a large pan; -পেটা, pot-bellied, abdominous.
নাদিত, *a.* made to sound. [dominous.
নাদী, *s.* a pellet or little ball of dung.
নাদুনী, *s.* a kind of boat; skiffs and boats.
নাদোষমাছ, *s.* the name of a fish.[1] [bread.
*নান্, *s.* a flat-bread; -খাতাঈ, a ginger-
নান্‌বাঈ, *s.* a baker of nán, a public cook.
নানক, *s.* the founder of the Shikh religion; -পন্থী, a follower of Nának.
নানা, *a.* various, diverse: *s.* a mother's father.
নানাজাতীয়, *a.* of various sorts. [ther.
নানাত্মবাদ, *s.* the doctrine of every person's possessing a distinct spirit.
নানাত্মা, *s.* distinction of spirit in each person (a tenet of Sánkhya philosophy).
নানাদিক্, *s.* various points of the compass.
নানাদিগ্‌দেশ, *s.* various quarters and countries.
নানাদেশ, *s.* various countries. [tries.
নানাদেশীয়, *a.* belonging to various countries.
নানান, *a.* various, diverse, divers. [tries.
নানাপথ, *s.* various roads or ways.
নানাপ্রকার, নানাবিধ, *a.* of various kinds.
নানাবর্ণ, *a.* of various colours, partycoloured, chequered, of various sorts.
নানাবেশ, *s.* various habits or dresses.
নানাভাব, *s.* various circumstances.
নানামত, *a.* various, of various sects.
নানামতে, *ad.* by every means, variously.
নানারঙ্গ, নানারঙ্গী, *a.* of various colours.
নানারস, *s.* a variety of sentiment.
নানারূপ, various forms: *a.* polymorphous.
নানার্থ, *s.* various meanings, or objects: *a.* having various meanings. [ings.
নানার্থবাচক, *a.* expressing various mean-
নানাশব্দসংগ্রহ, *s.* a dictionary, vocabulary.
নানাশস্ত্র, or নানাস্ত্র, *s.* various weapons.
নানাশাস্ত্র, *s.* various writings, various sciences.
নানাস্থান, *s.* various places. [ences.
নানাস্থানী, *a.* strolling, unsettled, vagrant.
নানী, *s.* a maternal grandmother.
নানোপায়, *s.* various expedients. [prelude.
নান্দী, *s.* praise, a benediction; a prologue,
নান্দীমুখ, *s.* an ancestor. [of ancestors.
নান্দীমুখশ্রাদ্ধ, *s.* an oblation to the manes
না-পসন্দ, unchosen, unapproved; -পাক, unclean, impure, unholy; -পায়দা, unborn.
নাপিত, *s.* a barber; *fem.* নাপ্তিনী.
নাব্, *v. n.* to descend, to purge off by stool.
নাবন, *s.* a descending, a purging by stool.
নাবা, *v. a.* to bathe another person.
নাবাকার, *a.* boat-shaped, cymbiform.
*নাবাকিফ, *a.* unacquainted with, ignorant.
*নাবাজিবী, *a.* not right or just, improper.
নাবান, *s.* the bathing of a person or thing.
নাবাল, *a.* low, not high; -ভূমি, lowland.
নাবালক, *a.* under lawful age: *s.* one under
নাবি, *a.* late in the season. [age, a minor.
নাবিক, *s.* a navigator, a pilot, a helmsman, a sailor, a mariner, a boatman.
নাবুঝ, *a.* dull of understanding, stupid.
নাব্য, navigable, boatable; marine, naval.
নাভি, *s.* the navel, the centre of a circle, the nave of a wheel; -কুণ্ডল, the navel.
নাভিকূপ, *s.* a depression in the navel.
নাভিগোণ্ড, *s.* a prominent navel. [navel.
নাভিদেশ, or নাভিস্থল, *s.* the region of the
নাভিনাড়ীরজ্জু *s.* the umbilical cord.
নাভিসরোবর, *s.* a depressed navel.
নাভ্যধোদেশ, *s.* the pelvis, the abdomen.

নাম্, *v.* to descend, to purge off by stool.
নাম, *s.* a name, reputation, an appellation, a noun ;-কৃ, to repeat a name, to extol; -রাখ্, or -দা, to name, to give a name ; -বাড়া, to promote a person's fame.
নামক, *a.* in *comp.* named, denominated ; bending downward : *s.* the flexor muscle.
নামকরণ, *s.* a naming, repeating of a name.
নামকীর্ত্তন, *s.* the proclaiming of a name.
নামজাদ, *a.* named, renowned, famous.
নামজারী, *s.* the celebration of a name.
নামডাকা, *s.* the calling one by his name.
নামডুবান, *s.* the ruining of one's reputation : *a.* of lost or ruined reputation.
নামতা, *s.* the multiplication table.
নামদার, *a.* named, renowned, famous.
নামধর, নামধারী, *a.* named, called. [noun.
নামধাতু, *s.* a verbal root formed from a
নামধেয়, *s.* a name, an appellation.
নামন, *s.* a descending, a condescending, an alighting, a purging. [accepted.
নামনজুর, *a.* unapproved, null, void, not
নামনা, *s.* the branch roots of Ficus indica.
নামবাচক, নামবাচ্য, *a.* expressing a name : *s.* in *gram.* a proper name. [putation.
নামবাড়ান, *s.* the promotion of fame or re-
নাম-মাত্র, *s.* a mere name;-যশঃ, renown,
নামর্দ্দ, *a.* effeminate, unmanly. [fame.
নামলুব্ধ, *a.* famous, illustrious. [named.
নামা, *v. a.* to cause to descend, to lower : *a.*
নামাউঠা, *s.* the spasmodic cholera morbus.
*না-মাকুল, ignorant ; -মুনাসিব, improper.
নামাঙ্কিত, *a.* marked with a name.
নামান, *s.* a causing to lower, a descending.
নামানন, নামানা, *s.* the not regarding of a saying, a not admitting, or obeying.
নামাবলি, *s.* a sort of cloth printed like chintz with the names of Hindu gods.
নামামৃত, *s.* the nectar of a name.
নামাশ্রয়, *s.* shelter in a name.
নামো, *s.* the bottom, the lower part.
নামোতে, *ad.* beneath, below, under.
নায়, *s.* guidance, instruction.
নায়ক, *s.* a leader, a guide, a conductor, a constable, a chief, a head, a general. In amatory poems, the husband or lover ; *a.* leading guiding, chief, principal.
নায়কাধিপ, *s.* a king, a sovereign.
নায়কীয়, *a.* belonging to a lover, or guide.
নায়িকা, *s.* in amatory poems, the wife or mistress ; a name of Durgá.
নারক, *a.* infernal, hellish : *s.* hell.
নারকী, *a.* impious, hellish, infernal.
নারদ, *s.* the name of a Hindu sage.
নারদীয়, *a.* belonging to the sage Nárada.
নারাঙ্গী, *s.* orange ; -রঙ্গ, orange-coloured.
নারাচ, *s.* an iron arrow ; a shuttle.
নারাজ, *a.* not pleased or satisfied.
নারাজী, *s.* displeasure, dissatisfaction.
নারায়ণ, *s.* God, a name of Vishnu.
নারায়ণক্ষেত্র, *s.* the space of four cubits on each side of the water of the Ganges.
নারায়ণী, *s.* Lakshmí, wife of Vishnu.
নারিকেল, *s.* the cocoanut; -খণ্ড, the medicine prepared with cocoanuts ; a piece of cocoanut ; -তৈল, cocoanut oil ; -দড়ি, coir-rope; -মালা, cocoanut-shell. [kind.
নারী, woman, a female ; -বর্গ, -গণ, woman-
নারীধর্ম্ম, *s.* custom of women, the menses.
নারীপরায়ণ, *a.* attentive or devoted to wo-
নারীপ্রিয়, *a.* fond of women. [men.
নাল, *s.* a tube, tubular stalk or vessel, th culm or stalk of a plant, saliva, slaver ; a horse-shoe ; a fee given at gambling ; -পড়্, to drivel ; -বাঁধ্, to shoe a horse.
নালকী, *s.* a sort of pálki or sedan.
নালপড়া, *a.* drivelling : *s.* a drivelling.
নালবন্দ, *s.* a farrier, a shoeing smith.
নালবন্দী, *s.* farriery, shoeing horses ; a sub-
নালবাঁধন, *s.* shoeing of a horse. [sidy.
নালা, *s.* a rivulet, a trench, a drain, a gut-
নালানিয়া, *a.* drivelling ; gluttonous. [ter.
*নালায়েক, *a.* unworthy, unfit ; not of age.
নালিতা, *s.* a kind of bitter potherb.
নালিফোঁড়, *s.* a defect in weaving of cloth.
*নালিশ, *s.* a complaint, a plaint, suing.
নালিশবন্দ, or নালিশী, *s.* a plaintiff.
নালী, *s.* a tube ; a fistula ; a drain, sluice.
নালুক, *s.* a driveller : *a.* thin, worn.
নাশ, *s.* destruction, ruin, perdition.
নাশক, destroying, ruinous : *s.* a destroyer.
নাশন, *s.* the destroying of a thing. [ble.
নাশনীয়, or নাশ্য, *a.* perishable, destructi-
নাশিত, *a.* destroyed, ruined, spoiled.

নাস্তিক, *a.* bereft of owner, or of property.
নাস, *s.* snuff; -দান, or -দানী, a snuff-box.
নাসা, *s.* the nose; the polypus; a lintel.
নাসাচ্ছিদ্র, or নাসারন্ধ্র, *s.* the nostrils.
নাসাজ্বর, *s.* a fever caused by the polypus.
নাসামল, *s.* the mucus of the nose. [nose.
নাসারোগ, *s.* the polypus, a cancer in the
নাসারোগী, *a.* afflicted with the polypus.
নাসিকা, *s.* the nose; a door-lintel.
নাসিকাগ্র, *s.* the point of the nose.
*নাস্তা, *s.* breakfast, morning meal.
*নাস্তানাবুদ, *a.* ruined, entirely destroyed.
নাস্তি, *phrase.* it is not, empty, wanting.
নাস্তিক, *s.* an atheist, infidel, unbeliever; -পথ, or -মত, atheism, tenets of atheism.
নাস্তিকতা, *s.* atheism, infidelity, unbelief.
নাস্তিক্য, *s.* atheism, infidelity, unbelief.
নাস্তিত্ব, *s.* non-existence, nonentity.
*নাহক, *a.* unrighteous, improper, unjust.
নাহি, *ad.* none, no, not, certainly not.
নি, a *prefix*, meaning under or down; also, completeness, excellence. [diagonal.
নিআড়, *a.* straight, at right angles, not
নিউনি, *s.* a wooden trowel for fine work.
নিংড়, *v. n.* to drip, to fall in drops.
নিংড়ন, dripping of water from wet cloth.
নিংড়া, *v. a.* to wring out, to press, strain, or squeeze out, to force the juice out.
নিংড়ান, *s.* the wringing of wet cloth, the pressing of fruits to express its juice.
নিঃ, a *prefix*, implying separation.
নিঃক্ষিপ্ত, *a.* deposited, pledged, abandoned, rejected, given up, cast away.
নিঃক্ষুব্ধ, *a.* undisturbed, placid, quiet.
নিঃক্ষেপ, *s.* a deposit, a pledge, a throw.
নিঃক্ষেপক, *a.* pledging, depositing with another: *s.* one who deposits.
নিঃক্ষোভ, *a.* tranquil, easy, placid: *s.* quietness, tranquillity, placidity, repose.
নিঃক্ষোভী, *a.* quiet, tranquil, unagitating.
নিঃশঙ্ক, *a.* safe, fearless, secure.
নিঃশঙ্কা, *s.* fearlessness, safety, security.
নিঃশত্রু, *a.* free from enemies, foeless.
নিঃশব্দ, *a.* silent, still, mute, noiseless.
নিঃশস্ত্র, *a.* not armed, unarmed.
নিঃশেষ, entire, complete, uttermost, without remainder; -রূপে, *vide* নিঃশেষতঃ.

নিঃশেষতঃ, *ad.* entirely, wholly, completely.
নিঃশেষিত, *a.* completed, finished. [steps.
নিঃশ্রেণী, *s.* a ladder, staircase, a flight of
নিঃশ্রেয়স, *s.* final beatitude, emancipation.
নিঃশ্বাস, -প্রশ্বাস, *s.* breathing, respiration; -ছাড়, or -ফেল, to respire, to breathe.
নিঃসঙ্গ, *a.* solitary, alone, without society.
নিঃসন্তান, *a.* childless, without posterity.
নিঃসন্দিগ্ধ, *a.* unsuspected, undoubted.
নিঃসন্দেহ, or নিঃসংশয়, *a.* indubitable, unquestionable, doubtless, clear, certain.
নিঃসন্ধি, *a.* whole, seamless, jointless.
নিঃসমর্থ, *a.* unable, incapable, powerless.
নিঃসম্পর্ক, নিঃসম্বন্ধ, *a.* destitute of relatives.
নিঃসম্পাত, *s.* midnight, 12 o'clock night.
নিঃসরণ, *s.* issuing, exuding, oozing, a going forth, a going out, death, a dying.
নিঃসরণকর্ত্তা, *s.* one who goes out.
নিঃসহায়, *a.* destitute of helpers or allies.
নিঃসাধ্বস, *a.* fearless, familiar, tame, bold.
নিঃসান, *s.* tingling of any part, throbbing.
নিঃসার, *a.* pithless, sapless, unsubstantial.
নিঃসারক, going forth: *s.* he who goes out.
নিঃসারণ, *s.* expelling, pushing, driving out.
নিঃসারিত, *a.* expelled, driven out, cast out.
নিঃসাহস, নিঃসাহসিক, নিঃসাহসী, *a.* cowardly, timid, pusillanimous, irresolute.
নিঃসৃত, *a.* extracted, exuded, issued, gone out, or forth.
নিঃস্পন্দ, *a.* not tremulous.
নিঃস্পৃহ, *a.* free from desire, apathetic.
নিঃস্ব, *a.* poor, indigent; destitute, bereft.
নিঃস্বতা, -ত্ব, *s.* poverty, indigence. [rent.
নিঃস্বত্ব, forfeiture, deprivation; -জমা, rack-
নিঃস্বত্বক, *a.* rapacious, confiscating.
নিক, *v. a.* to plaster, smear with cowdung.
নিকট, *s.* vicinity, proximity: *a.* near, adjacent; -বর্ত্তন, a being near, vicinity.
নিকটবর্ত্তী, নিকটস্থ, *a.* near, neighbouring.
নিকটাগত, *a.* come to, approached. [near.
নিকটানিকটি, *ad.* at hand, nearly, almost,
নিকটে, *ad.* in the vicinity, at hand, near.
নিকড়িয়া, *a.* poor, indigent, penniless.
নিকন, *s.* a cowdung plastering: *a.* plastered.
নিকনচুকন, *s.* plastering of a house. [ed.
নিকন্ধিয়া, *a.* headless, shoulderless.
নিকর, *a.* clear, free from taxes and duties.
নিকষা, *s.* the mother of giants: *a.* near.

নিকষাত্মজ, *s.* an imp, a goblin, a giant.
নিকা, *s.* a marriage : *v. a.* the same as নিক্.
নিকাকরণ, *s.* a being married, a marrying.
নিকান, *s.* a plastering with cowdung.
নিকার, *s.* an injury, offence, obstruction.
নিকারী, *a.* injury, hindering, obstructing.
নিকার্য্য, *s.* a habitation, a dwelling.
নিকাশ, *s.* a paying off, clearing up, a dispatching ; an issue or outlet for water.
নিকিরী, *s.* a class of Moslem fishmongers.
নিকুঞ্জ, *a.* penurious, stingy : *s.* a forest of climbers, a bower, arbour, a thicket.
নিকুঞ্জকানন, *s.* a forest of climbing plants.
নিকুঞ্জবিহারী, *a.* roaming or walking for pleasure among thickets or bowers.
নিকৃত, *a.* insincere, cunning, devious, dishonest, perverse, low, mean, base, vile, removed, set aside, dismissed, cheated.
নিকৃতি, *s.* low cunning, dishonesty, abuse, reproach, poverty, rejection, removal.
নিকৃত্রিম, *a.* not counterfeit, unadulterated, inartificial, genuine.
নিকৃষ্ট, *a.* niggardly, bad, low, vile, despised, outcast.
নিকৃষ্টতা, -ত্ব, *s.* badness, vileness, lowness.
নিকেতন, *s.* a house, an abode, habitation.
নিক্তী, *s.* a small pair of scales.
নিক্কণ, *s.* the sound of a lute or harp.
নিক্ষা, নিখী, নিকী, *s.* a nit, a louse.
নিক্ষিপ্ত, *a.* thrown about, dispersed, scattered.
নিক্ষেপ, *s.* a throwing about, casting, dispersion ; pledge, deposit ; an injection.
নিক্ষেপক, *s.* one who throws about, or deposits.
নিক্ষেপণ, *s.* the act of throwing.
নিক্ষেপণীয়, নিক্ষেপ্তব্য, নিক্ষেপ্য, *a.* fit to be thrown about, proper to be deposited.
নিখনন, *s.* interment, burial of a corpse.
নিখরচা, *a.* cost-free, without any charges.
নিখর্ব্ব, *a.* dwarfish ; a billion : *s.* a dwarf.
নিখাটু, without work, idle.
নিখাত, *s.* a pit, moat, cavity, a ditch (as a landmark).
নিখিল, *a.* all, whole, entire, complete.
নিখী, নিকী, নিক্ষা, *s.* a nit, a louse.
নিখুঁত, *a.* free from flaw or blemish, immaculate.
নিগড়, *s.* an iron chain, fetters, shackles, a pair of stocks, elephant's foot-chain.
নিগম, *s.* a town, a city, a market, a fair, a high road, trade, traffic ; the veda.
নিগমজ্ঞ, *a.* acquainted with the veda.
নিগরণ, *s.* a swallowing ; the throat.
*নিগহ-দার, -বান, *s.* a watchman, an overseer, a superintendent.
নিগহ -দারী, -বানী, *s.* overseership, superintendence.
নিগাল, *s.* a horse's throat or neck.
নিগূঢ়, *a.* fast, tight, strict, close, profound, abstruse, hidden, mysterious.
নিগূঢ়কথা, *s.* a mysterious or obscure sentence.
নিগূঢ়ার্থ, mysterious, profound, abstruse ; *s.* a mysterious object.
নিগৃহীত, punished, treated with severity, persecuted.
নিগ্রহ, punishment, harsh treatment, persecution, aversion, disfavour, disdain, dislike, confinement, a binding, a tie.
নিগ্রহকারক, persecuting : *s.* a persecutor.
নিগ্রহণীয়, or নিগ্রাহ্য, *a.* punishable.
নিগ্রহান্বিত, *a.* ill treated, mortified.
নিগ্রাহক, নিগ্রাহী, *a.* persecuting, punishing.
নিঘণ্টু, *s* a list, a table of contents, a vocabulary.
নিঘুষ্ট, *s.* sound, noise.
নিঘ্ন, *a.* docile, yielding, subservient.
নিঙড়্, *v. n.* to wring, to express juice.
নিঙড়ন, *s.* the wringing of wet clothes.
নিঙ্ড়া, *v. a.* to wring out, to wring wet clothes, to exact, to squeeze the poor.
নিঙড়ান, *s.* act of wringing or pressing.
নিঙ্গল, or গিল, *v. a.* to swallow, devour.
নিঙ্গলন, *s.* the swallowing of a thing.
নিচয়, *s.* a collection, a heap, a batch.
নিচু, or নিছু, *a.*, only, alone ; low, below.
নিচোল, *s.* a mantle, a wrapper, a surtout.
নিচ্চোড়, *a.* illiberal, niggardly, parsimonious, base, mean, contemptible.
নিচ্চোড়তা, নিচ্চোড়ামি, *s.* meanness, parsimony.
নিছক, *ad.* undoubtedly, without difficulty.
নিছুড়িয়া, *a.* friendless, orphan, forlorn.
নিজ, *a.* own, one's own ; pure, unmixed.
নিজমতাবলম্বী, *a.* self-opinionated.
নিজঞ্জাল, *a.* free from disorder, confusion, trouble, or care, at ease, tranquil.
নিজতন্ত্রী, *a.* autocratical, independent.
নিজা, *s.* one who is a helpmate to her husband in this world and by burning with his corpse secures him the next.
নিজী, নিজে, *a.* ownself ; -কৃত, made one's own.
নিঝড়, *a.* not tempestuous or stormy, calm.

নিঝাড়ি, *a.* clean, completely emptied.
নিঝুম, *a.* still, close, calm, silent, quiet.
নিট্, *a.* certain, sure, true, exact, neat.
নিট্‌পিটা, *a.* slothful, dilatory, negligent, slow.
নিঠুর, *a.* cruel, harsh, unfeeling.
নিড়্, *v. a.* to weed. নিড়ন, *s.* a weeding.
নিড়বিড়া, *a.* lazy, slow, tardy, loitering.
নিড়া, *v. a.* to weed, to cause to weed.
নিড়ান, *s.* the weeding of a garden.
নিড়ানী, *s.* a weeding-knife.
নিতম্ব, *s.* the posteriors of a woman, buttocks, rump of an animal, a gibbosity.
নিতম্বদেশ, *s.* the posteriors.
নিতরাং, *ad.* always, continually, eternally, perpetually.
নিতল, *s.* a division of the infernal regions.
নিতান্ত, *ad.* entirely, certainly, excessively, quite, downright; -কর্ত্তব্য indispensable.
নিতান্তেচ্ছু, *a.* solicitous, very desirous.
নিতিনিতি, *ad.* constantly, perpetually.
নিত্য, *a.* constant, perpetual, incessant, eternal, continual, daily, regular, fixed: *ad.* always, eternally, continually.
নিত্য-কর্ম্ম, -ক্রিয়া, -কার্য্য, *s.* the daily ceremonies of religion, the daily duties.
নিত্যতা, *s.* perpetuity, constancy, eternity.
নিত্যনিত্য, *ad.* constantly, perpetually.
নিত্যনৈমিত্তিক, *a.* constantly performed to secure some object or advantage.
নিত্যযৌবন, *s.* perpetual youth.
নিত্যশঃ, *ad.* perpetually, constantly, eternally.
নিত্যশঙ্কা, *s.* constant suspicion or fear.
নিত্যস্নান, *s.* the regular duty of ablution.
নিত্যানন্দ, *s.* continual happiness; a chief of Vaishnavas : *a.* continually happy.
নিত্যানিত্য, *a.* eternal and temporary.
নিথর, *a.* still, calm, tranquil, quiet.
নি-দাঁত, *a.* toothless; -দম, breathless, lifeless.
নিদয়, *a.* pitiless, merciless, cruel, severe.
নিদর্শন, *s.* a simile, a type, a pattern, an elucidation, an example, proof, sign.
নিদর্শনপত্র, *s.* a specimen, example.
নিদর্শনী, *a.* showing, elucidating, proving.
নিদাগ, *a.* stainless, spotless, immaculate.
নিদাঘ, *s.* the hot season, heat, sweat.
নিদান, *s.* a first cause, primary or remote cause, purification, correctness, purity, accuracy, an end, a treatise upon the science of medicine: *ad.* at last, at least, at the lowest; -কাল, the time of death.
নিদারুণ, *a.* fearless, bold, cruel, severe.
নিদালী, *s.* an incantation used by burglars to cause a profound sleep.
নিদিধ্যাসন, *s.* a desire to fix the mind intensely on an object, or on God.
নিদিষ্ট, *a.* commanded, spoken, said.
নিদেশ, *s.* a direction, a command, injunction, order, speech, utterance, the word of command; vicinity, proximity.
নিদেশ্য, *a.* fit to be commanded or spoken.
নিদ্রা, *s.* sleep, drowsiness; -কর, narcotic, somnific; -যা, to sleep; -ভাঙ্গ, to awake.
নিদ্রাকর্ষণ, *s.* sleepiness, seized with sleep.
নিদ্রাকুল, নিদ্রাতুর, *a.* distressed with sleep.
নিদ্রাকৃষ্ট, *a.* seized by sleep, sleepy, drowsy.
নিদ্রাগত, *a.* asleep, gone to sleep.
নিদ্রাগার, নিদ্রালয়, *s.* a dormitory, sleeping room.
নিদ্রাজনক, *a.* soporific, narcotic.
নিদ্রান্বিত, নিদ্রাবিষ্ট, drowsy, sleepy, asleep.
নিদ্রাবেশ, *s.* an inclination to sleep.
নিদ্রাভঙ্গ, *s.* the interruption of sleep.
নিদ্রালু, *a.* sleepy, drowsy, lethargic.
নিদ্রিত, or নিদ্রাণ, *a.* asleep, slumbering.
নিধন, poor, needy : *s.* death, destruction, annihilation, disappearance, want, loss.
নিধান, *s.* a gem, jewel, valuable thing, a receptacle.
নিধার, *a.* blunt, dull; debtless.
নিধি, *s.* a valuable thing, a gem, property, a thing found, treasury, granary; an asylum, a nest, a receptacle; the ocean.
নিধু, *a.* pernicious, destructive, ruinous.
নিধুড়া, -ড়্ব, *s.* perdition, destruction, ruin.
নিধুবন, *s.* coition, pleasure, pastime, sport, play, enjoyment; agitation, trembling.
নিধূম, *a.* smokeless, clear.
নিন, or বাটালি, *s.* a carpenter's chisel.
নিনাদ, *s.* a sound, noise, roar, bellow.
নিনাদী, *a.* roaring, making a noise, noisy.
নিন্দক, *a.* reviling, reproaching, abusive.
নিন্দন, *s.* a reproaching, reviling, censure.
নিন্দনীয়, *a.* contemptible, reproachable.
নিন্দা, *s.* reproach, contempt, censure, rebuke.
নিন্দাকর, *a.* reviling, censuring.
নিন্দান্বিত, *a.* reproached, censured, reviled.
নিন্দাবান্দা, *s.* censure and praise.

নিন্দাযোগ্য, নিন্দার্হ, *a.* worthy of censure.
নিন্দিত, *a.* reproached, reviled. [able.
নিন্দিতব্য, *a.* reproachful, blamable, censur-
নিন্দুক, *a.* reproaching, reviling, censuring: *s.* one who reviles or censures.
নিন্দ্য, *a.* deserving reproach, contemptible.
নিপট, *a.* indeed, truly, really, completely.
নিপত, *a.* death, destruction, ruin, an over-
নিপতন, *s.* a falling, going to ruin. [throw.
নিপতনীয়, *a.* liable to falling, fallible.
নিপতিত, *a.* fallen, gone to ruin.
নিপাত, *s.* death, destruction, an overthrow, ruin; in *gram.* an anomaly, irregularity.
নিপাতকারক, *a.* mortal, deadly, murderous.
নিপাতন, *s.* a causing to fall, a destroying, ruining, causing death or destruction; in *gram.* an irregularity or anomaly.
নিপাতনীয়, or নিপাত্য, *a.* capable of being cast down, killed, or destroyed.
নিপাতিত, *a.* cast down, killed, destroyed.
নিপান, *s.* a watering-trough, a milk-pail.
নিপুণ, *a.* eminent, able, expert, clever, skil-
নিপুণতা, -ত্ব, *s.* the same as নৈপুণ্য. [ful.
নিব্, *v. n.* to be extinguished, to expire.
নিবড়্, *v. n.* to be finished, to come to a
নিবড়ন, a being empty or finished. [close.
নিবড়া, *v. a.* to accomplish or finish a work.
নিবড়ান, *s.* a completing: *a.* completed.
নিবদ্ধ, *a.* composed, treated of, discussed.
নিবন্ধ, *s.* an obligation, a voluntary obligation or vow, a subject, topic, treatise.
নিবন্ধন, *s.* a cause, motive, origin; a binding, a confining; compiling of a work.
নিবন্ধা, *s.* an author, a compiler, a lexico-
নিবর্ত্ত, *s.* cessation, restraint. [grapher.
নিবর্ত্তক, causing to cease, putting a stop to.
নিবর্ত্তন, *s.* the putting a stop to, a making to cease, the rescinding of a law.
নিবর্ত্তনীয়, নিবর্ত্তয়িতব্য, নিবর্ত্ত্য, *a.* proper, or requiring to be stopped. [fied.
নিবর্ত্তিত, *a.* made to cease, stopped, paci-
নিবসতি, *s.* a dwelling, a residence, abode.
নিবস্ত্র, নিবস্ত্রী, *a.* unclothed, naked, unclad.
নিবহ, *s.* a multitude, a quantity; all.
নিবা, *v. a.* to extinguish, to put out.
নিবাড়, *s.* completion, a finish, conclusion.
নিবাড়ন, *s.* the completing of a thing.
নিবাত, or নিবাতাস, *a.* sheltered, calm: *s.* a
নিবান, *s.* extinguishing of fire. [calm.
নিবাপ, *a.* fatherless: *s.* funeral cake. [ing.
নিবারক, *a* preventing, prohibiting, hinder-
নিবারণ, *s.* resisting, stopping, preventing, prevention, restraint. [preventible.
নিবারণীয়, নিবার্য্য, *a.* resistible, restrainable,
নিবারা, নিবার্য্যতা, *s.* prevention, restraint.
নিবারিত, *a.* resisted, prevented, hindered.
নিবার্য্যমাণ, *a.* suffering resistance.
নিবাস, *s.* a place of residence, a dwelling, a habitation, a house, a residence.
নিবাসী, *a.* residing, dwelling: *s.* a dweller. a resident, an inhabitant.
নিবিড়, *a.* thick, close (as trees, etc.,) umbrageous, dense, impenetrable, impervious.
নিবিষ্ট, *a.* engaged in, devoted to.
নিবিষ্টতা, *s.* engagedness, devotedness.
নিবীত, *s.* the Bráhmanical thread.
নিবৃত্ত, *a.* made to cease, stopped, hindered.
নিবৃত্তি, *s*, cessation, stoppage, appeased.
নিবেদন, *s.* information, a representation, a request, an offering, a present.
নিবেদনপত্র, *s.* a written request, petition.
নিবেদিত, *a.* offered, mentioned, communicated, made known, represented.
নিবেদ্য, নিবেদনীয়, *a.* fit to be represented or mentioned, fit to be presented.
নিবেদ্যমান, *a.* in the act of being offered.
নিবেশ, *s.* engagedness, devotedness, earnestness, a being interested in.
নিবেশক, *a.* engaging with the mind, entering things into a writing.
নিবেশন, *s.* a house, an entrance, an entry.
নিবেশনীয়, নিবেশ্য, *a.* fit to be engaged in.
নিবেশিত *a.* engaged in with the heart, devoted to, entered in a writing.
নিভাঁজ, *a.* unadulterated, pure, genuine, real, unalloyed, smooth, free from folds.
নিভৃত, secret, private, concealed, seclud-
নিম, or নিম্ব, *s.* the name of a tree.[1] [ed.
নিমক, *s.* salt; -দান, -দানী, a salt-cellar; -হারাম, unfaithful, ungrateful; -হারামী, ingratitude; -হালাল, faithful, grateful, loyal; -হালালী, faithfulness, gratitude.
নিম্‌কবাবী, *a.* young, half fit for roast.
নিম্‌কাজ্জী, *s.* a Moslem petty judge.

নিম্খাসা, *a.* middling, rather good.
নিমগ্ন, dipped, immersed, sunk, drowned.
*নিম্চা, *s.* a small sword, a scimetar.
নিম্জোস, *a.* parboiled, half-boiled.
নিম্দাবা, *s.* the elephant (in chess).
নিমন্ত্র, *s.* invitation, a call; -কৃ, to invite.
নিমন্ত্রক, *a.* inviting: *s.* one who invites.
নিমন্ত্রণ, *s.* an inviting, invitation, call.
নিমন্ত্রণপত্র, *s.* letter or card of invitation.
নিমন্ত্রণীয়, নিমন্ত্র্য, *a.* fit or proper to be invited.
নিমন্ত্রিত, *a.* invited, called.
নিময়, *s.* a change, a succession, an alteration, a barter, an exchange.
নিম্রাজী, somewhat satisfied, half-pleased.
*নিমা, নিমাস্তিন, *s.* a sort of jacket, cloak.
*নিমাজ, *s.* Moslem prayer, a prayer.
নিমিত্ত, *s.* a cause, reason, a motive, an instrumental cause, a source, mark, sign.
নিমিত্তক, *ad.* by, through, caused by, arising from.
নিমিত্ততা, -ত্ব, *s.* causality.
নিমিত্তে, *ad.* for the sake of, on account of.
নিমিষ, *s.* a twinkling of the eye, a moment.
নিমীলক, *a.* shutting the eyes: *s.* a sphincter.
নিমীলন, *s.* winking, closing the eyes.
নিমীলিত, *a.* closed, shut.
নিমুড়িয়া, or নিমুড়্যা, *a.* friendless, orphan, forlorn.
নিমেষ, *s.* a wink, a twinkling of the eye.
নিম্ন, *a.* low, depressed, deep, sunk.
নিম্নগ, descending, going down; deep-flowing.
নিম্নতা, *s.* lowness, a depression, a cavity.
নিম্ব, *s.* lime, lemon, orange, citron.
নিয়ত, *a.* regular, directed, uniform, perpetual.
নিয়তি, *s.* a law, regulation, appointment, destiny, luck, good or bad fortune.
নিয়ন্তা, *s.* a ruler, a director, a regulator.
নিয়ন্তৃতা, *s.* directorship, regulatorship.
নিয়ন্ত্রিত, *a.* not obstructed, free.
নিয়ন্ত্রিতা, *s.* a freedom from obstruction.
নিয়ম, *s.* a regulation, a rule, a law, a law of nature, an agreement, a covenant, a stipulation, a treaty, a contract, assent.
নিয়মকর্ত্তা, *s.* one who makes rules or laws, one who stipulates or covenants.
নিয়মপত্র, *s.* a writing, regulation, a written agreement, a treaty.
নিয়মভঙ্গ, *s.* the making of a rule void, the infraction of a treaty or contract.
নিয়মলঙ্ঘন, *s.* the transgressing of a rule or precept, or the terms of a treaty.
নিয়মিত, নিয়মান্বিত, *a.* orderly, stipulated, agreed on, regulated, covenanted.
নিয়াম, *s.* the same as নিয়ম.
নিয়ামক, *a.* regulating, acting as a prime mover, regulating the motions of machinery: *s.* a regulator, regulating cause.
নিয়ামকতা, -ত্ব, *s.* the condition or office of a regulator, or of regulating cause.
নিযুক্ত, *a.* appointed to an office, appointed, constituted, commanded.
নিযুক্ততা, *s.* a being constituted or appointed to office.
নিযুত, a million, ten lakhs.
নিযুদ্ধ, *s.* a wrestling, a boxing, pugilism.
নিয়োক্তব্য, *a.* eligible to office.
নিয়োক্তা, *s.* commander, one who enjoins, or appoints to office.
নিয়োক্তৃতা, *s.* the office of appointing or commanding.
নিয়োগ, *s.* an appointment to office, an order, a command, a precept, a constitution; in *gram.* the imperative mode.
নিয়োগকর্ত্তা, *s.* one who appoints to office, one who issues precepts or commands.
নিয়োগধর্ম্ম, *s.* in the Hindu law, the appointing of a widow to raise offspring by her husband's brother.
নিয়োগী, *a.* appointed, ordered, commanded.
নিযোজক, appointing to office, commanding, enjoining: *s.* same as নিয়োগকর্ত্তা.
নিযোজন, *s.* the appointing of a person, the laying an injunction upon any one.
নিযোজনীয়, নিযোজ্য, *a.* fit to be appointed, requiring a precept or command.
নিযোজিত, *a.* appointed to office, constituted, ordered, commanded.
নির্, *prep.* in *comp.* it gives the idea of privation, absence, or negation.
নিরংশ, *a.* destitute of a share or lot.
নিরংশী, *a.* destitute of a partner, single.
নিরঙ্কুশ, *a.* unrestrained, free, self-willed.
নিরঙ্কুশতা, *s.* freedom, liberty, free-will.
নিরঞ্জন, *a.* pure, free from stain, holy; free from antimony: *s.* the casting of an idol into the water after its worship is over.
নিরত, *a.* excessively delighted with, very fond of.
নিরনুনাসিক, *a.* not nasal.

নিরন্তর, *a.* having no space between, incessant, unintermitted, solid, impervious.
নিরন্তরাল, *a.* close, solid, having no space between.
নিরন্ন, *a.* destitute of food.
নিরন্বয়, not agreeing with another word in a sentence; destitute of posterity.
নিরপচয়, *a.* free from loss or detriment.
নিরপত্য, *a.* childless, without issue.
নিরপত্রপ, *a.* shameless, immodest, impudent.
নিরপবাদ, *a.* free from accusations.
নিরপরাধ, নিরপরাধী, *a.* innocent, guiltless.
নিরপায়, *s.* security, safety.
নিরপায়ী, *a.* secure, safe.
নিরপেক্ষ, *a.* independent; -তা, independence.
নিরপেক্ষা, *s.* independence, indifference.
নিরব, *a.* silent, mute, quiet.
নিরবকাশ, without leisure, busy: *s.* a want of leisure.
নিরবকাশী, *a.* not at leisure, busy.
নিরবগ্রহ, independent, uncontrolled, self-willed.
নিরবচ্ছিন্ন, *a.* unaffected by, unpossessed of, alone, unadulterated.
নিরবদ্য, *a.* superior, complete, established, high, not mean.
নিরবদ্যবিদ্য, *a.* clever, well-versed.
নিরবধি, *a.* unlimited, endless, boundless.
নিরবয়ব, *a.* destitute of members or component parts, simple, unorganic.
নিরবয়বতা, -ত্ব, *s.* a want of organic structure.
নিরবলম্বন, *s.* a want of dependence.
নিরবলম্বী, *a.* not depending on.
নিরবসর, *a.* without leisure, busy.
নিরয়, *s.* hell, a place of punishment.
নিরর্গল, unobstructed, uncontrolled, easy.
নিরর্থ, নিরর্থক, *a.* useless, vain, fruitless.
নিরর্থকতা, *s.* vanity, inutility, uselessness.
নিরলস, *a.* not idle, not indolent, diligent.
নিরশন, *s.* a not eating: *a.* fasting.
নিরস, *a.* juiceless, dry, sapless.
নিরস্ত, *a.* defeated, desisted, restrained, appeased, assuaged, calmed, allayed.
নিরস্তক, *a.* subduing, calming, allaying.
নিরস্ত্র, *a.* weaponless, unarmed.
নিরহ, *a.* peaceable, pacific, tranquil.
নিরহঙ্কার, humility: *a.* not proud, humble.
নিরহঙ্কারী, *a.* not proud, humble.
নিরহঙ্কৃত, *a.* not grown proud.
নিরাকরণ, *s.* the driving away or expelling of a person, extermination.
নিরাকরণীয়, নিরাকার্য্য, *a.* exterminable.
নিরাকাঙ্ক্ষ, নিরাকাঙ্ক্ষী, *a.* free from desire, contented, satisfied.
নিরাকার, *a.* incorporeal, shapeless, without form.
নিরাকৃত, *a.* expelled, driven away, banished, exterminated.
নিরাকৃতি, *a.* *vide* নিরাকার: *s.* expulsion, extermination.
নিরাক্রোশ, *s.* the absence of displeasure.
নিরাগম, *s.* a not approaching.
নিরাচ্ছন্ন, নিরাচ্ছাদিত, *a.* uncovered, unconcealed.
নিরাচ্ছাদন, *a.* destitute of a covering.
নিরাট, *a.* close, concealed, solid, not hollow.
নিরাতঙ্ক, *a.* safe, secure, fearless.
নিরাধার, *a.* destitute of a receptacle, fulcrum, or support; incessant, continual.
নিরাধারা, *a.* incessant, continual.
নিরানই, or নিরানব্বই, *a.* ninety-nine.
নিরানন্দ, *a.* sad, dejected, joyless, cheerless: *s.* sadness, dejection, displeasure.
নিরানন্দিত, *a.* not gladdened, gloomy, sad.
নিরাপত্তি, নিরাপদ্, *a.* secure, safe: *s.* freedom from misfortune, security, safety.
নিরাপদি, *ad.* in safety, in security.
নিরাবৃত, *a.* uncovered, bare, exposed.
নিরাময়, *a.* free from disease, healthy.
নিরাময়ী, *a.* not diseased, healthy.
নিরামিষ, *a.* destitute of flesh, excluding flesh.
নিরামোদ, নিরামোদী, *a.* joyless, gloomy.
নিরায়ুধ, *a.* destitute of weapons.
নিরালয়, *a.* desert, destitute of habitations.
নিরালস্য, *s.* freedom from indolence: *a.* diligent.
নিরালা, *ad.* privately, in secret.
নিরাশ, *a.* hopeless, despairing.
নিরাশয়, *a.* destitute of a scope or object: *s.* the want of a scope or object.
নিরাশা, *s.* despair, despondency.
নিরাশ্বাস, *s.* discouragement, hopelessness.
নিরাশ্বাসী, *a.* not hoping, discouraging.
নিরাস, *s.* a repelling, a driving away.
নিরাসক, *a.* repelling, repulsive.
নিরাসকতা, *s.* repulsion, repulsiveness.
নিরাসকস্বরূপে, *ad.* repulsively.
নিরাহার, *a.* fasting: *s.* an abstaining from food.
নিরাহারী, abstaining from food, fasting.
নিরীক্ষক, *a.* looking at, gazing at, viewing, observing, seeing: *s.* one who looks.
নিরীক্ষণ, *s.* a looking, seeing, viewing.

নিরীক্ষণীয়, *a.* visible, observable.
নিরীক্ষিত, *a.* viewed, observed with care.
নিরীখ, *s.* a fixed price, a price-current.
নিরীশ্বর, *s* the denial of a God, atheism.
নিরীশ্বরবাদ, *s.* the sentiments of atheism
নিরীশ্বরবাদী, *a.* professing atheism.
নিরুক্ত, *a.* not spoken or mentioned.
নিরুত্তর, *a.* without an answer or reply.
নিরুত্তরণীয়, *a.* unanswerable, indefensible.
নিরুত্তরী, or নিরুত্তরীয়, *a.* not answering.
নিরুত্তাপ, *a.* free from heat, anger, or jealousy, cool: *s.* freedom from heat.
নিরুৎপাত, *s.* safety, security, fearlessness.
নিরুৎসাহ, *s.* a want of effort or courage.
নিরুদ্ধ, *a.* blocked up, besieged, obstructed.
নিরুদ্বিগ্ন, *a.* not perplexed, easy in mind.
নিরুদ্বেগ, *a. idem: s.* freedom from perplexity.
নিরুদ্বেগী, *a.* unanxious, easy.
নিরুদ্বেগে, *ad.* without perplexity, safely.
নিরুদ্যত, *a.* not ready for, not engaged in.
নিরুদ্যুক্ত, *a.* not engaged in exertions.
নিরুদ্যোগ, *s.* a want of zeal or exertion.
নিরুপদ্রব, absence of outrage, tranquillity, peace.
নিরুপদ্রবী, *a.* free from oppression.
নিরুপক্রুত, *a.* not ravaged, not oppressed.
নিরুপম, *a.* peerless, incomparable, unequalled.
নিরুপায়, *a.* remediless, helpless.
নিরুপায়ী, *a.* not contriving, not scheming.
নিরুপেক্ষা, *s.* attention, regard, respect, honour.
নিরূপ, *a.* without form, shapeless.
নিরূপক, *a.* directing, ordering, regulating, ascertaining: *s.* a director, a regulator.
নিরূপকতা, -ত্ব, *s.* directorship.
নিরূপণ, *s.* planning, establishing, settling, fixing, prescribing of a course of life.
নিরূপণীয়, or নিরূপ্য, *a.* assignable, nominable, ascertainable, determinable.
নিরূপিত, *a.* appointed, fixed, assigned, prescribed, nominated, regulated.
নিরোধ, *s.* a blocking up, an obstruction.
নিরোধক, *a.* blocking up, obstructing.
নির্গত, *a.* gone forth, expelled, extracted, past.
নির্গন্ধ, *a.* scentless, stenchless.
নির্গম, *s.* an outlet, an issue, a going forth.
নির্গমণ, *s.* a going out, proceeding, departing.
নির্গুণ, নির্গুণী, *a.* worthless, useless.
নির্গুণতা, -ত্ব, *s.* worthlessness, uselessness.

নির্ঘণ্ট, *s.* survey, table of contents, index.
নির্ঘাত, *s.* a thunderstroke, a severe blow.
নির্ঘোষ, *s.* a sound, sound of a trumpet.
নির্জন, *a.* secluded, solitary, uninhabited, desert, private.
নির্জনে, *ad.* privately, aside.
নির্জয়, *s.* complete conquest.
নির্জর, *a.* free from decrepitude or infirmities of age.
নির্জল, *a.* destitute of water.
নির্জিত, *a.* completely overcome.
নির্জীব, *a.* lifeless, inanimate, weak, languid.
নির্ঝর, *s.* a fountain, a spring, a cascade.
নির্ঝরণ, *s.* a shedding out, an oozing.
নির্ঝরী, *s.* a place abounding in springs.
নির্ণয়, *s.* certainty, the ascertaining of a thing, an agreement, an engagement.
নির্ণয়কর্ত্তা, *s.* one who ascertains or settles.
নির্ণয়নীয়, *a.* ascertainable, determinable.
নির্ণায়ক, *a.* deciding, ascertaining.
নির্ণিক্ত, *a.* cleansed, purified, corrected.
নির্ণীত, *a.* ascertained, settled, determined on, fixed upon, established, confirmed.
নির্ণেতা, *s.* one who decides or ascertains.
নির্দ্দয়, *a.* pitiless, merciless, hard-hearted, unfeeling, inhuman, cruel, relentless.
নির্দ্দয়তা, *s.* unmercifulness, cruelty, severity, unfeelingness, relentlessness.
নির্দ্দয়া, *s.* brutality, cruelty, unfeelingness.
নির্দ্দায়পত্র, *s.* an acquittance, a release.
নির্দ্দিষ্ট, fixed upon, pointed out, identified, nominated, appointed, commanded.
নির্দ্দিষ্টতা, *s.* a being fixed on or appointed, a being nominated or commanded.
নির্দ্দেশ, *s.* appointment, mandate, appropriation, a designation, a testimony.
নির্দ্দেশক, *a.* appointing, appropriating, designating, bearing a testimony: *s.* one who appoints or designates, a witness.
নির্দ্দেশন, *s.* the ascertaining of a circumstance, act of appointing to an office.
নির্দ্দেশনীয়, নির্দ্দেশ্য, *a.* ascertainable, appropriable, capable of proof.
নির্দ্দেশ্যতা, *s.* ascertainableness, appropriability.
নির্দ্দোষ, or নির্দ্দোষী, *a.* free from fault, innocent, blameless, sinless, accurate.
নির্দ্দোষীকৃত, *a.* justified, cleared from guilt.
নির্ধন, wretched, poor, indigent, penniless, needy.
নির্ধনতা, *s.* poverty, penury, want.

নির্ধার, অঋণী, *a.* free from debt.

নির্ধারক, *a.* ascertaining : *s.* one who ascertains.

নির্ধারণ, *s.* the confirming or ascertaining of a thing, an agreement, a covenant.

নির্ধারণীয়, or **নির্ধার্য্য**, *a.* inviolable, not to be relinquished, ascertainable, capable of being settled, fixed, or decided.

নির্ধারিত, *a.* confirmed, ratified, determined, ascertained, settled, decided, covenanted, agreed upon, bargained.

নির্ধার্য্যতা, -**ত্ব**, *s.* a capability of being settled or fixed.

নির্ধূম, *a.* smokeless, clear.

নির্নাম, nameless, stripped of name or honour.

নির্নিষ্ঠ, uncertain, not established.

নির্ব্বংশ, **নির্ব্বংশিয়া**, *a.* without progeny, destitute of race or family.

নির্ব্বচন, *s.* speaking, defining, describing, relating.

নির্ব্বচনীয়, *a.* capable of being spoken or uttered, capable of being narrated.

নির্ব্বচা, *s.* speaking, a description, a narration.

নির্ব্বন্ধ, **নির্ব্বন্ধন**, *s.* bondage, slavery, an obligation, a decree, a detention, seizure.

নির্ব্বল, **নির্ব্বলী**, *a.* weak, powerless, helpless.

নির্ব্বহ, *a.* not flowing, stagnant.

নির্ব্বাণ, *s.* the extinction of any thing, extinguishing of a lamp or fire, final emancipation, annihilation, a disappearance, a departure, cessation, union, repose, vacuity, space, vacuum : *a.* extinguished, extinct, gone out, departed, defunct.

নির্ব্বাণতা, -**ত্ব**, *s.* extinction, extinguishing.

নির্ব্বাত, *a.* airless, calm, close, sultry.

নির্ব্বাদ, censure, blame, reproach, rumour, report, an asseveration, an affirmation.

নির্ব্বার্য্য, *a.* acting fearlessly, undaunted.

নির্ব্বাস, *s.* expulsion, expatriation.

নির্ব্বাসন, *s.* the expulsion of a person from his house, the exiling of a person.

নির্ব্বাহ, *s.* a sufficiency, adequacy, abundance, a livelihood, a competency, provision ; -**কৃ**, to supply or suffice a person.

নির্ব্বাহক, *s.* a manager, one who provides for others, a providing for, supplying.

নির্ব্বাহকতা, -**ত্ব**, *s.* the office or condition of a manager or caterer.

নির্ব্বাহকরা, *s.* the act of providing for.

নির্ব্বিকল্প, *a.* not optional, subject to.

নির্ব্বিকার, *a.* unaltered, uniform, unchanged.

নির্ব্বিঘ্ন, *a.* free from obstacles, safe.

নির্ব্বিঘ্নে, *ad.* without obstacle, safely.

নির্ব্বিণ্ণ, *a.* senseless, distressed, paralyzed.

নির্ব্বিরোধ, *a.* peaceable, free from strife.

নির্ব্বিরোধিতা, -**ত্ব**, *s.* peaceableness.

নির্ব্বিরোধী, *a.* not quarrelsome, peaceable.

নির্ব্বিরোধে, *ad.* peaceably, quietly.

নির্ব্বিষ, *a.* free from venom or poison.

নির্ব্বিষী, *s.* a kind of grass and its root.[1]

নির্ব্বুদ্ধি, *a.* void of understanding, silly, foolish, dull : *s.* want of intellect, folly.

নির্ব্বুদ্ধিতা, -**ত্ব**, *s.* want of intellect, silliness, foolishness, dulness.

নির্ব্বৃতি, *s.* ease, safety, security, final emancipation, happiness, repose, rest, tranquillity, cessation, completion.

নির্ব্বৃত্ত, finished, completed, accomplished, done.

নির্ব্বৃত্তি, accomplishment of an undertaking, satisfaction, final emancipation.

নির্ব্বৃষ্টি, *s.* a want of rain, drought.

নির্ব্বেদন, or **নির্ব্ব্যথ**, *a.* insensible, free from pain.

নির্ব্বোধ, *a.* void of intellect, ignorant, foolish, stupid, senseless, simple, silly, dull.

নির্ব্ব্যথা, *s.* freedom from pain, ease.

নির্ব্ব্যাধি, *a.* free from disease, healthy.

নির্ভয়, *a.* bold, fearless, undaunted, secure, safe.

নির্ভয়বচন, *s.* a promise of security.

নির্ভর, *a.* permanent, confident; excessive, brimful : *s.* centre of gravity ; a fulcrum, prop, dependence : *ad.* excessively.

নির্ভরসা, *s.* despair, despondency.

নির্ভাবনা, *s.* thoughtlessness, inattention, a freedom from care or anxiety.

নির্ম্মদ, *a.* sober, quiet, unexcited, out of rut.

নির্ম্মম, *a.* not considered as one's own.

নির্ম্মমতা, -**ত্ব**, *s.* a want of attachment.

নির্ম্মল, *a.* pure, clear, clean, transparent, limpid, honest, fair (as weather).

নির্ম্মলতা, -**ত্ব**, *s.* cleanness, clearness, purity, transparency, limpidness, honesty.

নির্ম্মলী, a seed used in depurating water.[2]

নির্ম্মলীকরণ, *s.* a purifying, a depurating.

নির্ম্মলীকৃত, *a.* purified, cleaned, depurated.

নির্ম্মাণ, *s.* the forming or making of a thing, a fabricating or building ; -**কৃ**, to fabricate, to build, to make, to form, frame.

নির্মাণকর্তা,নির্মাতা, *s.* a maker, fabricator. a builder, a constructer, an architect.
নির্মায়ক, making,fabricating : *s.* a maker. constructer,fabricator,builder, author.
নির্মাল্য, *a.* destitute of a necklace : *s.* a garland of flowers offered to a god.
নির্মিত, *a.* made, moulded, framed, fabricated, built, wrought, constructed.
নির্মুক্ত, *a.* liberated, set free, released.
নির্মূল, *a.* destitute of a root or origin ;-কৃ, to extirpate, to eradicate, to root out.
নির্মেধ, *a.* dull, stupid, without intellect.
নির্যাস,*s.* extract, a decoction, an infusion, gum, resin, mucus : *a.* firm, positive.
নির্যাসউত্তর, *s.* a positive answer.
নির্যাসরূপে, *ad.* firmly, positively.
নির্লজ্জ, নির্লাজ, *a.* shameless, impudent, immodest, indecent. [impudence.
নির্লজ্জা *s.* a want of shame, immodesty,
নির্লোভ, free from desire : *s.* contentment.
নির্লোভী, *a.* not covetous, contented.
নিলাজ,*a.*shameless, impudent, immodest.
নিলাম,*s.* an auction sale; ballast of a ship.
নিলামঘর, *s.* an auction-room.
নিশা, *s.* night; restitution; -কর, -পতি, the moon ;-পাল,a watchman, night guard.
নিশাচর, *s.* a night-prowler,rákshas,giant; an owl, nocturnal animal,a watchman.
নিশাচরী, *s.* a female rákshas, a giantess, a lewd woman, a nightstrolling woman.
নিশান, *s.* a flag, a sign, a badge, a mark.
নিশানধারী, carrying or holding the flag.
নিশানবর্দার, *s.* one who holds the colours.
নিশানমারণ,*s.* the striking a mark or butt.
নিশানী, *s.* a good marksman; *vide* নিশান.
নিশান্ত,নিশাবসান, *s.* the close of the night.
নিশাভাগ, or নিশীথিনী, *s.* the night.
নিশামধ্য, or নিশীথ, *s.* midnight. [night.
নিশি, *s.* the night ; *ad.* at night, in the
নিশিত,*a.*sharpened,set, whetted, ground.
নিষুতি, *a.* fast asleep, profound sleep.
নিশ্চঞ্চল, *a.* steady, immovable.
নিশ্চয়, *a.* certain, sure, true : *s.* certainty, clear knowledge of a thing ; -কৃ, to ascertain ; -কহ, to affirm, to confirm.
নিশ্চয়কথা, *s.* an affirmation, an assevera-
নিশ্চয়জ্ঞান, *s.* certainty, confidence. [tion.

নিশ্চল, *a.* immovable, fixed, firm, stedfast, stationary, still.
নিশ্চলন, *a.* not current, obsolete.
নিশ্চায়ক, *a.* ascertaining, deciding : *s.* one who ascertains or decides, an umpire.
নিশ্চিত, *a.* ascertained, sure, certain.
নিশ্চিতকর্মা, *a.* acting on sure grounds.
নিশ্চিন্ত, *a.* careless, thoughtless, uncon-
নিশ্চিন্তরূপে, *ad.* carelessly. [cerned.
নিশ্চেষ্ট, *a.* void of motion or exertion, list-
নিশ্চেষ্টা, inaction, want of exertion. [less.
নিশ্বাস, respiration, breath, breathing out, a sigh ; -ছাড়, -ফেল্, to respire, breathe.
নিশ্বাসপ্রশ্বাস, *s.* respiration, breathing.
নিষণ্ণ, *a.* sad, dejected, melancholy.
নিষাদ, *s.* dejection, sadness ; an outcast.
নিষিদ্ধ, *a.* prohibited, forbidden, inter-
নিষিদ্ধতা, *s.* prohibitedness. [dicted.
নিষেক, *s.* the injection of the sperm, the impregnation of the uterus. [ventive.
নিষেদ্ধা, *s.* a prohibiter, a preventer, a pre-
নিষেধ, *s.* prohibition, prevention, hinderance, an interdict, a restriction.
নিষেধক,নিষেধকারক, preventing, prohibitive, preventive : *s.* one who prohibits.
নিষেধকর্তা, *s.* a preventer, a prohibiter.
নিষেধনীয়, or নিষেধ্য, *a.* prohibitable.
নিষ্কণ্টক, *a.* free from thorns or obstacles, free from pain or trouble, at ease.
নিষ্কর, *a.* free from tribute or taxes.
নিষ্কর্মা,নিষ্কর্মান্বিত, unemployed, idle, un-
নিষ্কর্মী, not diligent, useless. [occupied.
নিষ্কর্ষ, *s.* proof, evidence, certainty, decision, an appointment to any office.
নিষ্কর্ষণ, *s.* the coming to a decision.
নিষ্কল, *a.* waned, diminished, impotent.
নিষ্কলঙ্ক,নিষ্কলঙ্কী, *a.* spotless, unstained, not blamable, immaculate. [bearing.
নিষ্কলা, *a.* past menstruation, past child-
নিষ্কাম,নিষ্কামী, *a.* free from lust. [som.
নিষ্কৃতি, *s.* acquittal, clearance, pardon, ran-
নিষ্কৃষ্ট, *a.* ascertained, plain, clear. [ing.
নিষ্কৃষ্টার্থ, ascertained and decided mean-
নিষ্ক্রমণ, *s.* an expelling or bringing out.
নিষ্ক্রান্ত, *a.* expelled, brought out, gone.
নিষ্ক্রামক, *a.* expelling, bringing forth.
নিষ্ক্রিয়, *a.* useless, ineffectual, vain.

নিষ্ঠ, *a.* fixed, established, devoted to, upright, faithful, just.
নিষ্ঠা, *s.* firmness in religion, uprightness, confidence, affiance, certainty : *a.* firm, upright ; -জান্, to be sure, or confident.
নিষ্ঠীব, *s.* spittle, phlegm, saliva, slaver.
নিষ্ঠুর, cruel, unfeeling, unmerciful, hard-hearted, barbarous, inhuman, morose.
নিষ্ঠুরতা, *s.* cruelty, unfeelingness, hard-heartedness, barbarity, inhumanity.
নিষ্ঠেবন, *s.* a spitting, expectoration.
নিষ্ণাত, *a.* learned, of finished education.
নিষ্পাক, *a.* unripe, raw, unconcocted.
নিষ্পত্তি, *s.* a finishing, a decision, a determination, a final settlement, an award.
নিষ্পত্তিকর, *s.* a judge, an umpire, one who decides : *a.* settling, deciding, judging.
নিষ্পত্র, নিষ্পাত, *a.* leafless, without leaves.
নিষ্পন্ন, *a.* accomplished, settled, decided, ordered, finished, concluded, awarded.
নিষ্পাদক, *a.* deciding, accomplishing : *s.* one who decides, or accomplishes.
নিষ্পাদন, *s.* the accomplishing of an undertaking, the deciding of a cause.
নিষ্পাদনীয়, নিষ্পাদ্য, *a.* capable of being brought to a completion or conclusion.
নিষ্পাদিত, *a.* brought to a completion.
নিষ্পাপ, or নিষ্পাপী, *a.* sinless, innocent.
নিষ্পীড়ন, *s.* a wringing out, a squeezing.
নিষ্পীড়িত, *a.* wrung, wrung out, squeezed
নিষ্প্রয়োজন, *a.* needless, unnecessary. [out.
নিষ্ফল, *a.* fruitless, abortive, useless, ineffectual, unprofitable, worthless.
নিষ্ফলতা, -ত্ব, *s.* uselessness, fruitlessness.
নিসর্গ, *s.* natural state; rejection, abandon-
নিসাড়, *a.* benumbed, torpid, rigid. [ment.
নিসিন্দা, *s.* name of a tree. [tion, rescue.
নিস্তার, *s.* salvation, deliverance, preserva-
নিস্তারক, *a.* saving, preserving : *s.* a saviour, a preserver, a deliverer. [liverer.
নিস্তারকর্ত্তা, *s.* a saviour, a preserver, a de-
নিস্তারণ, *s.* act of saving or preserving.
নিস্তার্য্য, *a.* salvable, deliverable.
নিস্তীর্ণ, *a.* delivered, saved, rescued. [led.
নিস্তুল, *a.* unequal, unlike, uneven, unrival-
নিস্তেজ, dull, obscure, blunt, flaccid, weak.
নিস্পন্দ, *a.* still, motionless, inanimate.

নিস্পৃহা, disinterestedness, contentedness.
নিস্পৃহী, *a.* contented, disinterested.
নিস্ব, destitute, poor, penniless, indigent.
নিস্বন, *s.* a bellow, a sound, a loud noise.
নিহত, *a.* killed, smitten, slain.
*নিহায়াৎ, *s.* an extremity, excess : *a.* very, much, excessive : *ad.* at the utmost.
নিহার, নীহার, *s.* frost, cold : *v. a.* to see.
নিহারণ, *s.* a seeing, a viewing, beholding.
নিহালী, or নিহানী, *s.* an anvil. [lation.
নিহ্নব, নিহ্নুতি, *s.* a denial, mistrust, dissimu-
নিহ্নুত, *a.* denied, concealed, mistrusted.
*নীচ, *a.* low, base, plebeian, vile, inferior.
নীচগামী, *a.* descending, going downwards.
নীচজাতি, *s.* a low tribe : *a.* of a low tribe.
নীচতা, -ত্ব, *s.* lowness, baseness, inferiori-
নীচপদ, *s.* a low office or station. [ty.
নীচভাষা, *s.* low or rustic language.
নীচলোক, *s.* a low or mean person.
নীচস্থ, *a.* situated beneath, placed low.
নীচা, *a.* low : *s.* the lower part of a thing, the base, the bottom, a skirt. [turvy.
নীচাউপরে, *ad.* bottom uppermost, topsy-
নীচাচার, *s.* low or mean conduct.
নীচাশয়, *a.* servile, low-minded.
নীচু, *a.* below, low ; -ঘর, a cellar.
নীচে, *ad.* down, below, beneath.
নীচৈঃ, *ad.* slowly, softly, with a low voice.
নীচোক্তি, *s.* a low or mean expression.
নীড়, *s.* a bird's nest. [ed.
নীত, *a.* taken, accepted, received, obtain-
নীতি, *s.* justice, right, morality, ethics.
নীতিকথা, *s.* a moral sentence or discourse.
নীতিজ্ঞ, *a.* acquainted with the rules of morality, civilized. [moral philosophy.
নীতিজ্ঞতা, *s.* an acquaintance with morals,
নীতিজ্ঞাতা, *s.* a moral philosopher.
নীতিতত্ত্ব, *s.* morality, ethics.
নীতিবিৎ, *a.* skilled in ethics or morality.
নীতিবিদ্যা, *s.* ethics, morality, politics.
নীতিবিরুদ্ধ, *a.* opposed to justice or right.
নীতিবেত্তা, *s.* one acquainted with ethics.
নীতিশাস্ত্র, *s.* the science of ethics, a book treating of morals or politics. [tice.
নীতিশিক্ষা, *s.* instruction in morals or jus-
নীয়মান, *a.* that which can be taken.
নীয়া, *s.* the taking of a thing.

নীর, *s.* water, juice, liquor ;-নিধি, the sea, the ocean ; -ময়, watery.
নীরক্ত, *a.* bloodless, without blood, sallow.
নীরতরঙ্গ, *s.* a wave on the water. [less.
নীরদ, *s.* a cloud : *a.* giving water ; tooth-
নীরব, *a.* silent, quiet, mute, speechless.
নীরস, *a.* juiceless, sapless, tasteless.
নীরাগ, *a.* free from anger or passion.
নীরোগ, *a.* free from disease : *s.* health.
নীরোগী, *a.* not diseased, hale, healthy.
নীল, *a.* blue : *s.* indigo, the indigo plant.[1]
নীলকণ্ঠ, *a.* blue-throated : *s.* an appellation of Shiva ; name of a bird ; [2] a peacock.
নীলকর, *s.* an indigo-planter, an indigo-maker, one who dyes things blue.
নীলকান্ত, or নীলকান্তমণি, *s.* a sapphire.
নীলপদ্ম, *s.* the blue waterlily.[3]
নীলবড়ি, *s.* a ball or square of indigo.
নীলবর্ণ, *a.* blue-coloured, blue.
নীলবানর, *s.* a species of monkey.[4]
নীলমণি, *s.* a sapphire, a precious stone.
নীললোহিত, *a.* purple, red and blue.
নীলী, নীলিকা, *s.* the indigo-plant, indigo.
নু, *v. n.* to bend, to incline. [ciency.
*নুকসান, *s.* loss, injury, a defect, a defi-
নুটী, নুটীসুটী, *s.* a ball of any thing wrapped together ; -কৃ, to wrap together.
নুড়, *s.* a wisp of straw or grass ; a wager.
নুড়নুড়, *s.* a hanging pendent, a swinging.
নুড়িসুড়ি, *s.* balls and clods : *a.* rolled up.
নুড়ী, *s.* a pebble, fragment of brick, a mul-
নুণ, লবণ, নিমক, *s.* salt. [ler, a stake.
নুণিয়া, *a.* salt, selling salt : *s.* purslain ; a dealer in salt ; -শাক, purslain. [tion.
নুতি, *s.* praise, adulation, flattery, solicita-
নুন্ন, *a.* sent, ordered, commanded.
নুন্দি, *s.* a fat belly, fatness, corpulency.
নুন্দিপেটা, *a.* fat, corpulent, abdominous.
নুম্বুড়ী, *s.* trachea, wind-pipe, the clapper of a bell, a woman's ear-drops. [ble.
নুয়া, *v. a.* to bend down, to bend, to hum-
নুয়ান, *s.* a bending, the humbling of a person : *a.* bent, inclined, humbled.
*নুর, *s.* splendour, light, the dawn of day.
নুরী, *s.* a particular species of parrot.[5]
নুলা, *a.* lame of the hand, maimed.
নূতন, *a.* new, recent, novel.

নূন, *ad.* certainly, assuredly, probably.
নূপুর, *s.* an ornament for the ankles.
নূহা, *s.* an ornament worn on the wrist.
নৃ, a *prefix*, meaning man ; -কপাল, human
নৃঘ্ন, *s.* a manslayer, a murderer. [skull.
নৃত্য, *s.* a dance, dancing, a ball, a jumping.
নৃত্যকারক, *a.* dancing : *s.* a dancer.
নৃত্যবিদ্যা, *s.* the science of dancing.
নৃত্যশালা, *s.* a ball-room, a theatre.
নৃপ, or নৃপাল, *s.* a king, a sovereign.
নৃপকুল, *s.* a royal race, a royal family.
নৃপতা, -ত্ব, *s.* kingship, sovereignty.
নৃপতি, *s.* a king, a sovereign, a governor.
নৃপবর, *s.* an excellent king.
নৃপাগার, *s.* a king's palace.
নৃপাত্মজ, *s.* a king's son, a prince. [nant.
নৃশংস, *a.* injurious, malevolent, malig-
নৃসিংহ, *s.* the fourth incarnation of Vishnu in the form of a lion, a noble man, a lion of a man, an excellent man.
নেআর, *s.* a broad sort of tape.
নেউট, নেউটা, *v. n.* to turn back, to return.
নেউট, *s.* a tame animal ; -পাড়া, intimacy,
নেউটন, *s.* a returning. [intercourse.
নেউল, *s.* an ichneumon, a weasel.
নেও, *s.* a foundation ; a law. [of a gun.
নেওলা, *s.* a morsel, a mouthful, wadding
নেং, *s.* the leg ; -মার, to push with the
নেংচ, *v. n.* to halt, to be lame. [leg.
নেংচন, *s.* a limping, halting, hobbling.
নংট, or নেংটা, *a.* naked, stripped.
নেংটি, or নেঙ্গুটি, *s.* a piece of cloth worn merely to cover the privities. [mouse.
নেংটিয়া, *a.* naked : *s.* a mouse ; -ইন্দুর, a
*নেক, *a.* pure, holy, good ; -নজর, the eye of mercy ; -নাম, a good name ; -নামী, reputation, fame ; -বক্ত, fortunate.
নেকড়া, -কানি, *s.* a rag, a shred of cloth.
নেকড়িয়া, or নেকড়্যা, *s.* a hyena, a wolf.
নেকা, *a.* playing the buffoon, pretending.
নেকামী, *s.* buffoonery, pretension.
নেকার, *s.* a vomiting, puking, a nausea.
*নেকী, *s.* goodness, holiness, purity.
নেখরা, *s.* a trick, a sham, a pretence, an artifice, a joke, waggery, coquetry.
নেঙা, *a.* left-handed. নেঙ্গ, *s.* a step, a foot-
নেঙ্গড়া, *a.* limping, lame, hobbling. [step.

নেঙ্গি, *s.* a striking with the leg to throw down an opponent in wrestling.
নেঙ্গুচা, *s.* a sausage, a hog's pudding.
*নেঙ্গোড়া, *a.* destitute of race or family (abusive term); *lit.* destitute of feet.
নেজ, *s.* a tail. নেজাড়, *s.* a crupper.
নেজা, *s.* a tail; a spear, a lance, a pike.
নেজামত, *s.* arrangement, government, the administration of criminal justice.
নেজামুড়া, *s.* the tail and the head.
নেজনেজিয়া, *a.* plashy, wet, ropy, slimy.
নেটা, *a.* left-handed, sinister-handed.
নেটাঘেঁটা, *s.* a being tarnished, a tarnish.
নেটুয়া, *s.* a professional dancing boy.
নেড়, or ন্যাড়, *s.* hard excrement, ordure.
নেড়া, *a.* pollard, lopped, shorn, bald, bare: *s.* balladsinger, a Vaishnava (in irony).
নেড়ানেড়া, *a.* shorn, bald, unadorned.
নেড়াশীজ, *s.* the same with নাড়াশীজ.
নেড়ী, *s.* a female Vaishnava, a balladsinger.
নেড়োল, *s.* a species of wild duck.
নেড়্যা, *s.* a Musalmán (in contempt).
নেতব্য, *a.* proper to be received or taken.
নেতা, *s.* one who takes, a receiver, a leader; a rag used in cookery; a rogue.
নেতাড়ি, *s.* a hemistich: *a.* half; -মারা, half-done.
নেতুড়, *a.* slow, inactive, lazy.
নেত্র, চক্ষু, নয়ন, *s.* the eye.
নেত্রগোচর, *s.* an object of sight; *a.* before the eyes
নেত্র-পীড়া, -রোগ, *s.* disease of the eyes.
নেত্ররোগী, *a.* diseased in the eyes.
নেদি, *s.* clods of cowdung dried for fuel.
নেদিষ্ঠ, or নেদীয়ান্, *a.* nearest, very near.
নেদ্‌নেদ্, *s.* softness, plashiness, pulpiness.
নেদ্‌নেদিয়া, *a.* soft, plashy, boggy, pulpy.
নেপা, *s.* a membrane, web of fibres.
নেপাপা, *a.* web-footed, palmipede.
নেপুর, *s.* an ornament for the feet.
নেবা, *s.* the jaundice, a disease of the bile.
নেবু, *s.* a lime, lemon, orange.
নেমি, *s.* the circumference of a wheel or circle.
নেয়ার, or নেয়াল, *s.* a kind of broad tape.
নেয়ে, *s.* a boatman, a waterman.
নেল্, *v. a.* to excite, to stimulate, to set a dog on.
*নেশা, *s.* intoxication, intoxicating drug.
নেশাখোর, *s.* a drunkard.
নেশাখোরী, *s.* drunkenness, inebriety, intoxication.

নেহার্, *v. a.* to look, to view, to behold.
নেহারণ, *s.* a looking, a surveying.
নৈ, *s.* a lump of earth or dough: *a.* new, recent; female (applied to a calf).
নৈকট্য, *s.* vicinity, nearness, proximity.
নৈগম, *s.* a shop-keeper; a portion of the veda.
নৈত্য, *s.* eternity, continuance.
নৈপুণ্য, *s.* cleverness, skilfulness, address, expertness, ability, superiority.
নৈবেদ্য, *s.* an offering, present.
নৈমিত্তক, *a.* causal, producing, procuring, causing.
নৈয়ায়িক, *a.* professing the doctrine of the Nyáya school; a logician.
নৈযুক্ত, *s.* an appointment to office.
নৈরন্তর্য, *s.* incessantness, imperviousness.
নৈরাকার, *s.* incorporiety, formlessness.
নৈরাশ, নৈরাশ্য, *s.* despair, despondency.
নৈর্ঋত, *s.* the south-west quarter; a giant.
নৈর্গুণ্য, *s.* inutility, a want of good qualities.
নৈর্ধন্য, *s.* poverty, wretchedness.
নৈর্মল্য, *s.* purity, transparency, clearness.
নৈষ্কর্ম্ম, *s.* uselessness, inutility.
নৈষ্কিক, *s.* the master of the mint.
নৈষ্ঠ্য, *s.* establishment in any sentiment.
নৈসর্গিক, *a.* natural, arising from nature, humble.
নৈস্ত্রিংশিক, *s.* a swordsman.
নোআ, নোআন, *vide* নুয়া, নুয়ান.
*নোক্তা, *s.* a point, a bird's bill, a spur.
নোক্সান, or নোকসানী, *s. vide* নুক্সান.
নোক্তা, *s.* a point, dot in writing, a blame, stigma.
নোঙ্গর, *s.* a boat or ship anchor.
নোঙ্গরা, or নোঙ্গরাটিয়া, *a.* filthy, beastly.
নোড়, *s.* alloy, base mixture; an acid fruit.
নোড়া, *s.* a muller, a stone muller.
নোণা, *a.* salt, brackish; -টেঙ্গরা, a fish.[1]
নোদী, *s.* a paunch, a large belly; -পেটা, pot-bellied.
নোনা, a tree and its fruit.[2]
নৌ, *s.* a ship, a boat, a skiff.
নৌকা, *s.* a boat; -পথ, a passage by water.
নৌকাগম্য, নৌগম্য, নৌতার্য্য, *a.* navigable.
নৌকাপথে, *ad.* by boat, by ship.
নৌসাদর, *s.* sal-ammoniac.
ন্যক্কার, *s.* a loathing, disgust, a nausea.
ন্যক্কারিত, ন্যক্কৃত, *a.* abhorred, loathed.
ন্যক্কার্য্য, *a.* abominable, disgusting.
ন্যক্ষ, *a.* dwarf, short, base, mean, evil.
ন্যাঙ্চা, *a.* lame, halt, club-footed.

ন্যস্ত, *a.* deposited, pledged, placed.
ন্যস্তক, *a.* saving, hoarding: *s.* a hoarder.
ন্যাকার, *s.* a vomiting, puking, nausea.
ন্যাটা, *a.* left-handed, sinister-handed.
ন্যায়, *s.* one of the six schools in which vedic philosophy is professed; right, justice, truth, equity, law, righteousness, logic: *a.* resembling, like. [er.
ন্যায়ক, *s.* a judge, logician, just reason-
ন্যায়কর্ত্তা, *s.* one who acts rightly, or with equity, one who does justice. [justly.
ন্যায়কারক, doing justice: *s.* one who acts
ন্যায়তঃ, *ad.* according to right or justice.
ন্যায়পূর্ব্বক, *ad.* by a law suit, with justice.
ন্যায়শাস্ত্র, *s.* logic, or the science of philosophy usually called the Nyáya.
ন্যায়ী, *a.* rational, right, just, proper, doing right, doing justice. [at law.
ন্যায্য, *a.* right, just, litigable, recoverable
ন্যাল, *a.* satisfied, sufficient, successful.
ন্যাস, *s.* a deposit, a pledge.
ন্যাসাপহ্নব, *s.* the denial of a deposit.
ন্যুব্জ, *s.* a ladle: *a.* crooked, curved, crook-backed, stooping, looking downwards.
ন্যুব্জীকৃত, *a.* made crooked, bent.
ন্যূন, *a.* less, deficient, defective, wanting.
ন্যূনতা, *s.* defectiveness, deficit, deficiency.
ন্যূনাতিরেক, or **ন্যূনাধিক**, *a.* less or more.
ন্যূনাধিক্য, *s.* a deficiency or excess.

প, the twenty-first consonant in the alphabet. It has the sound of English p.
পইঠা, *s.* steps, stairs, a stair-case.
পইতা, *s.* the Hindu sacerdotal thread.
পংক্তি, *s.* a row, a range, a line, rank; a metre: *a.* ten; -ধারক, a catch-word.
পঁইছা, *s.* a bracelet; the wrist.
পঁইত্রিশ, or **পঁয়ত্রিশ**, *a.* thirty-five.
পঁচাত্তর, seventy-five. **পঁচাশী**, eighty-five.
পঁচানই, **পঁচানব্বই**, *a.* ninety-five.
পঁচিশ, twenty-five. **পঁচিশা**, twenty-fifth.
পঁয়তাল্লিশ, forty-five. **পঁয়ষট্টি**, sixty-five.
পঁহুছ, *v. n.* to arrive, to come, to reach.
পঁহুছন, *s.* the arriving at a place.
পকুর, *s.* a pond, a pool, tank, a reservoir.
পক্তান, *s.* a place where salt is made.
পক্তানি, *a.* belonging to salt manufactory.

পক্ব, *a.* ripe, cooked, mature, concocted,
পক্বতা, *s.* maturity, ripeness. [digested.
পক্বতৈল, *s.* a chymical preparation of oil used as a medicine, boiled oil.
পক্বান্ন, baked meats, a short of sweetcake.
পক্ষ, *s.* an army, a feather, a wing, the feather of an arrow, a side, a flock, a party, a friend, a fortnight; a proposition or side of an argument in logic, a plaint in law, a position advanced, an alternative, contradiction, opposition, rejoinder, reply; in *arith.* primary division.
পক্ষপাত, *s.* collusion, partiality. [zan.
পক্ষপাতী, partial, attached to: *s.* a parti-
পক্ষবান্, *a.* winged, feathered. [tions.
পক্ষভেদ, *s.* a distinction between proposi-
পক্ষরহিত, or **পক্ষহীন**, *a.* destitute of feathers, unfledged, wingless. [true bill.
পক্ষলক্ষণ, *s.* the sign of a valid plaint, a
পক্ষাকার, **পক্ষাকৃতি**, *a.* feather-shaped, like
পক্ষাঘাত, *s.* the palsy, paralysis. [a wing.
পক্ষান্ত, *s.* end of a proposition or plaint, last day of waxing or waning of moon.
পক্ষান্তর, *s.* another side, another view.
পক্ষান্তরে, *ad.* otherwise, on the other side.
পক্ষিগণ, *s.* birds, a class of birds.
পক্ষিণী, *s.* night reckoned with its preceding and succeeding day, a female bird.
পক্ষিনিনাদ, *s.* the singing of birds.
পক্ষিমারা, *s.* a bird-catcher, a fowler.
পক্ষিরাজ, *s.* Gaṛura, the regent of birds; a swift horse; a peacock.
পক্ষী, *a.* winged: *s.* a bird, a fowl.
পক্ষ্ম, *s.* the eyelash, the harl or fibre of a thread, a fibre, the filament of a flower.
*__পগডণ্ডী__, *s.* a footpath in a mountain.
পগার, *s.* a mound, a bank.
পঙ্ক, *s.* mud, mire, clay; sin, guilt.
পঙ্কজ, or **পঙ্কেরুহ**, *s.* a lotus, a waterlily.
পঙ্কজনয়নী, *a. fem.* lotus-eyed.
পঙ্কজবৎ, *a.* resembling the lotus.
পঙ্কজিনী, *s.* an assemblage of waterlilies.
পঙ্কবৎ, *a.* resembling mud, pulpy.
পঙ্কবদম্লরস, *s.* chyle, the gastric juice.
পঙ্কময়, **পঙ্কিল**, *a.* muddy, miry, clayey.
পঙ্কোদ্ধার, *s.* the cleansing a pond or other receptacle of water from the mud.

পঞ্জৎ, *s.* confraternity, a religious society.
পঙ্গপাল, *s.* a locust,[1] a flight of locusts.
পঙ্গু, *a.* lame, crippled, halt: *s.* a cripple.
পচ্, *v. n.* to putrefy, to mortify, to rot.
পচন *s.* a putrefying, a rotting, decaying.
পচা, *v. a.* to promote putrefaction, to macerate: *a.* rotten, putrefied, digested.
পচান, *s.* the causing of a thing to putrefy.
পচানী, *s.* putridity, rottenness, a stiving.
পচাপাচকুয়া, *a.* worn out, rotten, putrid.
পচাভুর, *s.* foppery, glare, outside show.
পচাল, *s.* scurrility: *a.* scurrilous, obscene; -পাড়, to use scurrility, talk obscenely.
পচালপাড়ন, *s.* a talking obscenely.
পচালিয়া, *a.* scurrilous, talking obscenely.
পচ্পচ, *s.* sloppiness, splashiness.
পচ্পচিয়া, *a.* sloppy, poachy, miry, dirty.
পচ্য, *a.* digestible, that may be digested.
পচ্যমান, *a.* under digestion, ripening.
পঞ্চ, *a.* five: *s.* an arbitrator, an assembly.
পঞ্চক, *s.* a tax of a fifth: *a.* relating to five.
পঞ্চকশত, *s.* five per cent.
পঞ্চকোণ, *s.* a pentagon: *a.* pentagonal.
পঞ্চকোল, *s.* five pungent plants,[2] much used in the Hindu পাঁচন, or decoction.
পঞ্চগব্য, *s.* five productions of the cow, viz. dung, urine, curds, milk, and butter.
পঞ্চচত্বারিংশৎ, *a.* forty-five.
পঞ্চচত্বারিংশত্তম, *a.* the forty-fifth.
পঞ্চতপাঃ, *s.* a kind of religious austerity.
পঞ্চতরা, an inland duty on merchandise.
পঞ্চত্রিংশৎ, thirty-five. পঞ্চত্রিংশত্তম, 35th.
পঞ্চত্ব, *s.* death, viz. a resolution into the five primary elements; -পা, to die.
পঞ্চদশ, *a.* fifteen; -ধা, of fifteen sorts.
পঞ্চধা, *ad.* of five sorts. পঞ্চন্, *a.* five.
পঞ্চপঞ্চাশ, পঞ্চপঞ্চাশত্তম, *a.* the fifty-fifth.
পঞ্চপঞ্চাশৎ, *a.* fifty-five.
পঞ্চপল্লব, *s.* the twigs of five trees[3] used as a medicinal preparation.
পঞ্চপাণ্ডব, *s.* five heroes of the Mahábhárata, viz. যুধিষ্ঠির, ভীম, অর্জুন, নকুল, and সহদেব, these are the sons of Pándu, an ancient king of Hastinápur or Delhi.
পঞ্চপ্রকার, or পঞ্চবিধ, *a.* of five sorts.
পঞ্চপ্রদীপ, *s.* five lamps (as an offering).
পঞ্চপ্রাণ, *s.* the five vital airs.
পঞ্চবিংশতি, twenty-five; -তম, the 25th.
পঞ্চভুজ, *a.* pentagonal: *s.* a pentagon.
পঞ্চভূত, *s.* the five elements, viz. earth, water, air, æther, and light or energy.
পঞ্চভূতাত্মা, *s.* the individual as consisting of the five primary elements of matter.
পঞ্চভৌতিক, *a.* material, not spiritual.
পঞ্চম, *a.* the fifth; -বর্ষীয়, quinquennial.
পঞ্চমহাপাতক, *s.* five mortal sins, viz. the murder of bráhman, drinking of spirits, stealing above 80 grains of gold, defiling the bed of a spiritual guide, and the society of a person guilty of mortal sin.
পঞ্চমী, *a.* the fifth (lunar day).
পঞ্চমূল, *a.* composed of five roots.
পঞ্চরত্ন, *s.* the five precious things, viz. gold, silver, pearls, crystal, and copper.
পঞ্চশর, *s.* a name of the Indian Cupid.
পঞ্চাৎ, *s.* an assembly, a company, a jury of a court, a committee for arbitration.
পঞ্চাতী, *s. idem: a.* pertaining to a panchát, (duty) done by a panchát.
পঞ্চানন, *a.* having five faces: *s.* Shiva, a lion, sign Leo.
পঞ্চান্ন, *a.* fifty-five.
পঞ্চাশ, পঞ্চাশৎ, *a.* fifty. পঞ্চাশত্তম, 50th.
পঞ্চাশীতি, *a.* eighty-five; -তম, the 85th.
পঞ্চাস্র, *s.* a pentagon: *a.* pentagonal.
পঞ্জর, *s.* a rib, a side of the body; a cage.
পঞ্জিকা, *s.* an almanac, calendar.
পঞ্জিকাকার, *s.* almanac-maker, an astronomer.
পট্, *v.* to be in the way of succeeding.
পট, *s.* the canvas or ground of a picture, a picture, fine cloth, canvas.
পটকা, *s.* a squib, a cracker; the bladder.
পটকার, *s.* a draughtsman, a limner.
পটল, *s.* mark on the forehead with sandal wood, a basket, a film on the eyes.
পটপটী, *s.* the name of a particular medicine, a pop-gun, a snapping sound.
পটা, *v. a.* to make an undertaking successful, to accomplish a work or design.
পটাকা, *s.* a squib, a cracker.
পটান, *s.* the accomplishment of a work.
পটী, *s.* a cloth, a slip of cloth, a bandage, a roller, a garter, a small strip of land, a quarter or part of a market.
পটীবাঁধা, *s.* the tying of a bandage.

পটু, *a.* eminent, clever, able, expert, skilful, dexterous, diligent, smart, sharp, crafty: *s.* baize, woollen cloth.
পটুআ, *s.* a painter, a limner, an image-maker.
পটুকা, *s.* a girdle, a belt, a sash.
পটুতা,-ত্ব, *s.* expertness, eminence, cleverness.
পটোল, *s.* a cucurbitaceous fruit.[1]
পটোলতোলা, *s.* the gathering of Patola; (*met.*) a dying, death, flight for debts.
পট্‌ক, *v. n.* to fall in wrestling.
পট্‌কন, *s.* a stumble, a slip of the foot; -মার্, to knock down;-খা, to get a fall.
পট্‌কা, *v. a.* to throw down in wrestling.
পট্‌কান, *s.* a dashing, a throwing down.
পট্ট, *s.* a kind of silk; a mark on the forehead.
পট্টবস্ত্র, *s.* silk cloth, satin.
পট্টমহিষী, or পট্টরাণী, *s.* the chief queen.
পট্টী, *s.* the same as পটী.
পট্‌পটিয়া, *a.* snapping, crackling.
পঠন, *s.* a reading, a reciting.
পঠনীয়, পঠিতব্য, পঠ্য, *a.* legible, fit to be read.
পঠিত, *a.* read, repeated, recited.
পঠ্যমান, *a.* in the condition of being read.
পড়্, *v. n.* to fall, drop, to fall into disuse, to occur, happen: *v. a.* to read, repeat.
পড়সী, or পাড়াপড়সী, *s.* a neighbour.
পড়া, *v. a.* to cause to fall, happen, or read, to teach: *a.* fallen, fallow, uncultivated; reading: *s.* a lesson, a throw at dice.
পড়ান, *s.* causing to fall; a teaching, causing to read, casting of dice: *a.* reading.
পড়িয়ান, *s.* the woof of a piece of cloth.
পড়ুয়া, পড়ো, *a.* fallow, waste; reading: *s.* a student, a pupil, scholar, a school boy.
পণ, *s.* a wager, a pledge, a bargain, a stipulation, a condition, a compact; 20 gaṇḍás, or 80 cauṛis;-কৃ, to bet, stake.
পণনীয়, *a.* subject to a wager, negociable.
পণপূরণন্যায়, *s.* the reckoning of a sum or counting of articles over and over.
পণপ্রতিজ্ঞা, *s.* the laying a wager.
পণাপণ, *s.* matter of indifference.
পণিত, *a.* made a matter of trade, laid as wager.
পণিতব্য, *a.* merchantable, saleable.
পণ্ড, *a.* futile, fruitless: *s.* a eunuch, a blank (in a lottery).
পণ্ডশ্রম, *s.* a fruitless labour, a plodding.
পণ্ডশ্রমী, *a.* laborious to no purpose.
পণ্ডা, *s.* learning, philosophy; bráhmans of Jagannáth's temple in Uṛissá.
পণ্ডিত, *a.* learned: *s.* learned man, philosopher.
পণ্ডিতগণ, or পণ্ডিতবর্গ, *s.* a class or society of learned men, or of philosophers.
পণ্ডিততা, -ত্ব, *s.* learning, philosophy.
পণ্ডিতসমাজ, *s.* a society of philosophers.
পণ্ডিতাভিমানী, *a.* esteeming or accounting one's self to be a learned man.
পণ্য, *a.* marketable, saleable: *s.* merchandise.
পতঙ্গ, *s.* a grasshopper, a bird; paper-kite.
পতন, *a.* falling: *s.* a falling, subtraction.
পতনীয়, *a.* fallible, liable to fall.
পতর, *s.* a plate of metal, an iron hoop.
পতাকা, *s.* a flag, an ensign, a pendant, a standard, a weathercock, a signal.
পতাকী, *s.* a standard-bearer.
পতি, *s.* a lord, a master, husband, owner, possessor.
পতিঙ্গা, *s.* a grasshopper, butterfly; a kite.
পতিত, *a.* degraded, fallen, laid down with grass, neglected, uncultivated, fallow; -পাবন, purifying the fallen, or sinful.
পতিপ্রাণা, *a.* loving her husband as her own life, burning with her husband.
পতিবত্নী, *a.* having a husband, married.
পতিব্রতা, *a.* chaste: *s.* a chaste wife.
পতিম্বরা, *a.* choosing her own husband.
পত্তন, *a.* building, founding: *s.* a city, a town, the settling of a colony or town, laying a foundation; advance of money for manufacturing any article.
পত্তনীয়া, *a.* (article) for which money has been advanced beforehand.
পত্নী, *s.* a wife, the female owner of any thing.
পত্র, *s.* a leaf, a blade of grass, the leaf of a book, a letter, a writing; metal plate.
পত্রক, *s.* a leaf, a letter, a writing.
পত্রকুটীর, *s.* a hut of leaves.
পত্রচালাচালি, *s.* correspondence by letters.
পত্রদ্বারা, *ad.* by means of a letter or writing.
পত্রাঙ্ক, *s.* number of the page in a book.
পত্রাবলী, *s.* a list of tickets in a lottery.
পত্রী, *s.* a letter, writing, a bird, an arrow.
পথ, *s.* a road, path, way, route;-হারা, to lose the way, to go astray.
পথখরচ, *s.* road expenses, provision for a journey.

পথঝেঁটানিয়া, *s.* a scavenger, a sweeper.

পথদর্শক, *s.* a guide, one who shows the way.

পথভুল, *s.* a being bewildered.

পথভ্রম, *s.* a mistaking the road.

পথান্তর, *s*, a different road, another way.

পথিক, *s.* a traveller, a passenger.

পথিকাবাস, পথিকাশ্রম, পথিকাশ্রয়, *s.* an inn, a baiting place on the road.

পথিন্, *s.* a road, a way.

পথিমধ্যে, *ad.* on the road, by the way.

পথ্য, *a.* salutary, wholesome : *s.* diet, regimen.

পথ্যদায়ক, *a.* giving wholesome food.

পথ্যাপথ্য, *a.* wholesome or unwholesome.

পথ্যাশী, *a.* feeding on wholesome food.

পদ, *s.* a foot, the foot of a piece of furniture, an employment, a station, office, a rank, a step, an inflected word, a connected sentiment, a place, a site, a mark, a stage, a foot in poetry, a verse.

পদগ, পদ্গ, *a.* going on foot : *s.* a footman.

পদচিহ্ন, *s.* a footstep, a foot mark.

পদচ্যুত, পদভ্রষ্ট, *a.* fallen from a station, discharged from an office.

পদতল, *s.* the sole of the foot.

পদবী, *s.* a title, patronymic name; a way, a road.

পদব্রজে, *ad.* on foot; -যা, to walk, to go on foot.

পদরথী, *s.* stockings, a boot.

পদসংক্রমণ, *s.* the departing from the subject matter of a plaint and complaining of something else in a court of law.

পদসঙ্কীর্ণ, *a.* mixed or compounded (applied to mixed plaints).

পদস্থ, *a.* in possession of an office, fixed in a station.

পদস্থিত, *a.* situated in an office or station.

পদহর, *a.* plagiary : *s.* plagiary, plagiarism.

পদহর্তা, *s.* a plagiarist, a literary thief.

পদা, *v. a.* to applaud, to praise, celebrate.

পদাঘাত, *s.* a kick; -কৃ, to kick.

পদাঙ্ক, *s.* a footstep, the print of the foot.

পদাঙ্কিত, *a.* marked with the foot.

পদাঙ্গুলি, *s.* a toe. পদাঙ্গুষ্ঠ, *s.* the great toe.

পদাতি, or পদাতিক, *s.* a foot soldier, infantry, a foot messenger, a footman.

পদান, *s.* applauding or praising of a person, the marking of the cases of nouns with figures for recognition, the spacing of words in writing, punctuation.

পদানত, পদাবনত, *a.* bowed at the feet.

পদান্তর, another part of a law proceeding.

পদাবলী, *s.* a list of titles; metre, verse.

পদাভিষিক্ত, *a.* installed into an office.

পদার্থ, *s.* material object, substance, property, essence, quality, a thing, thing expressed by a word, a category.

পদার্পণ, *s.* the induction of a person into an office, the installation of a person.

পদাসন, *s.* a footstool, a stool.

পদী, *s.* the tonnage of ships or boats.

পদীপ, or প্রদীপ, *s.* a lamp, light, candle.

পদুয়া, *a.* belonging to an office, official.

পদুয়াবিক্রয়, *s.* wholesale, not retail.

পদেপদে, *ad.* at every step, step by step.

পদ্দি, or পদ্বী, *s.* a title, a surname.

পদ্ধতি, *s.* a road, way, a line, a row, range; a ritual, a manual, a battle array.

পদ্ম, *s.* a lotus, a waterlily;[1] ten billions;

পদ্মকলিকা, *s.* an unexpanded waterlily.

পদ্মবন্ধু, *s.* the sun, a bee, a humble bee.

পদ্মমধু, *s.* the honey of waterlilies.

পদ্মযোনি, পদ্মনাভ, পদ্মাসন, *s.* Brahmá's names.

পদ্মরাগ, পদ্মরাগমণি, *s.* a ruby.

পদ্মলোচন, *a.* having eyes like the lotus.

পদ্মিনী, *s.* assemblage of waterlilies, particular description of delicate women in the amatory writings of the Hindus.

পদ্য, *s.* verse, metre; rule, usage, customary behaviour; idiom of a language.

পদ্যক্রম, *s.* common or customary practice.

পদ্যহীন, *a.* unprecedented, unusual.

পনস, *s.* the same as কাঁঠাল, which see.

পনীর, *s.* cheese; -বালা, a cheese-seller.

পনের, *a.* fifteen. পনেরুয়িঃ, the fifteenth.

পন্থা, *s.* a road, way, path, route; a clue.

পন্থী, *a.* travelling, following the tenets of a sect.

পন্নগ, *s.* a serpent, snake, reptile.

পয়জ্জা, *s.* a shoe, a boot, stockings.

পবন, *s.* the wind, the god of wind.

পবননন্দন, *s.* Bhíma and Hanumán, who are fabled to be the sons of Pavana.

পবিত্র, *a.* pure, clean, holy, sacred.

পবিত্রতা, -ত্ব, *s.* purity, holiness.

পবিত্রীকৃত, *a.* sanctified, purified.

পয়, *s.* a clue, a guide.

পয়ঃ, *s.* milk, water; prosperity, good luck.

*পয়গাম, *s.* a message, a letter.
পয়গাম্বর, *s.* a messenger, a prophet.
*পয়জার, *s.* a slipper, a shoe.
*পয়দা, *a.* produced, born, created.
পয়নালা,পয়োনালা, *s.* drain, gutter, aqueduct, watercourse, a spout, a tube.
পয়মন্ত, *a.* prosperous, fortunate, lucky.
*পয়মাল, *a.* trampled on, ruined, overrun.
পয়স্, *s.* milk, water.
পয়সা, *s.* a copper coin; money.
পয়স্য, *a.* made of milk, produced by milk.
পয়স্বিনী, *a.* milch, giving milk.
পয়ান, *s.* a marching, travelling, going.
পয়ার, *s.* a metre, a measure of verse.
পয়োধর, *s.* the teat or udder of an animal, a woman's breast; a cloud.
পয়োধি, পয়োনিধি, *s.* the sea, the ocean.
পর্, *v. a.* to dress, to put on clothes.
পর, *a.* other, another, different, remote, next, subsequent, following after, inimical, adverse: *s.* a stranger; a feather.
পরকন্ধ, *a.* at another's expense.
পরকলা, *a.* transparent: *s.* glass, crystal.
পরকাল, *s.* another world, a future state.
পরকীয়, *a.* belonging to another.
পরকীয়া, *a. fem.* belonging to another (an epithet of a loose woman). [probation.
পরখ, *s.* an ordeal, experiment, a trial, a
পরখদার, *s.* one who tests or tries.
পরখদারী, *s.* the making of experiments.
পরখাই, *s.* an experiment, a trial, a test.
পরগণা, *s.* a district, a division of a coun-
পরগৃহ, *s.* another person's house. [try.
পরচুল, *s.* false hair, a wig, a periwig.
পরচ্ছায়া, *s.* the shadow of another person.
পরচ্ছিদ্র, *s.* another's faults.
পরছতী, *s.* the eaves of a house.
পরজ, *a.* born of, or produced by, another.
পরণ, *s.* a wearing, dressing, putting on of
পরতঃ, *ad.* by or from another. [clothes.
পরতন্ত্র, *a.* dependent on others, subject.
পরতন্ত্রতা, -ত্ব, *s.* dependence, subjection.
পরতল, *s.* a patch, -লাগা, to patch.
পরত্র, *ad.* about another world; in another, among others, among enemies.
পরদার, *s.* another man's wife; adultery.
পরদারগমন, পরদারাভিগমন, *s.* adultery.

পরদারগামী, *a.* committing adultery: *s.* an
পরদারী, *a.* adulterous. [adulterer.
পরদেশ, *s.* a foreign country. [eigner.
পরদেশী, পরদেশীয়, *a.* foreign: *s.* a for-
পরন্তু, *conj.* but, moreover.
পরপত্র, *s.* a catch-word.
পরপত্রগ, *a.* using a catch-word. [further.
পরপর, *ad.* more and more, further and
পরপাঁউ, *s.* a kind of pigeon. [jilt.
পরপুরুষগামিনী, *s.* an unfaithful wife, a
পরপূর্ব্বা, *a. f.* twice-married; -স্ত্রী, she who
পরব, *s.* a festival, a feast. [is re-married.
পরবশ, *a.* subject to another, dependent.
*পরবা, *s.* fear, care, anxiety, concern.
পরবানগী, *s.* command, order, permission.
পরবানা, *s.* an order, a command, a warrant, a licence, a pass, a passport.
পরবৃত্তি, *s.* another person's livelihood.
পরম, *a.* excellent, chief, sublime, great,
পরমকল্যাণ, *s.* chief blessing. [principal.
পরমকল্যাণবরেষু, *phra.* thou art the object, or worthy of the highest blessing.
পরমকল্যাণীয়, *a.* attending chief blessing.
পরমকারুণিক, *a.* highly compassionate.
পরমগতি, *s.* heavenly bliss. [Spirit.
পরমপুরুষ, *s.* God, the most excellent
পরমপূজনীয়, *a.* highly revered.
পরমলাভ, *s.* happiness, consolation. [tee.
পরমহংস, *s.* an ascetic, self-denying devo-
পরমাণু, *s.* an atom, a particle of matter.
পরমাত্মা, *s.* the supreme Spirit, God.
পরমানন্দ, *s.* excess of joy, sublime plea-
পরমান্ন, *s.* rice-milk, frumenty. [sure.
পরমায়ুঃ, *s.* the period of a person's life, the age of a person. [Being.
পরমার্থ, *s.* an excellent object, a supreme
পরমাহ্লাদ, *s.* great joy, exalted pleasure.
পরমাহ্লাদিত, *a.* highly rejoiced.
পরমেশ্বর, পরব্রহ্ম, *s.* the Supreme God.
পরম্পরা, *a.* communicated from one to another in succession, successive.
পরম্পরাগত, *a.* descended by tradition.
পরম্পরাসম্বন্ধ, *s.* mediate connection.
পরলোক, *s.* another world, a future state.
পরলোকগত, or পরলোকপ্রাপ্ত, *a.* gone to the other world, dead. [death.
পরলোকপ্রাপ্তি, *s.* going to a future state,

পরশ, *v. a.* to touch ; -পিপুল, *s.* a tree.[1]
পরশপাথর, *s.* the philosopher's stone.
পরশাড়া, *s.* a parasitical plant, a parasite.
পরশু, *s.* a battle-axe, hatchet ; *vide* পরশ্ব.
পরশ্রীকাতর, *s.* envious, malicious.
পরশ্ব, *ad.* day after to-morrow, day before yesterday.
পরস্ত্রীগমন, *s.* adultery.
পরস্ত্রীগামী, *a.* adulterous: *s.* an adulterer.
পরস্ত্রীহরণ, *s.* seduction, adultery.
প্ররস্ত্রীহারী, *s.* an adulterer, a seducer.
পরস্পর, *a.* each other, mutual ; mutually.
পরস্মৈপদ, *s.* the active voice of a verb.
পরহস্তগত, *a.* delivered over to another.
পরা, *v. a.* to dress another, to harness an animal ; to put a thing into a socket, to case any thing : *a.* put on, dressed.
পরাক, *s.* a religious vow ; a cimeter.
পরাক্রম, *s.* power, energy, strength, force.
পরাক্রমী, পরাক্রমবিশিষ্ট, powerful, brave, strong, puissant, energetic, forcible.
পরাক্রান্ত, *a. idem ;* drawn by another.
পরাগ, *s.* the pollen of a flower, dust, articles for bathing, an eclipse.
পরাঙ্মুখ, *a.* having the face turned away, averse.
পরাজয়, *s.* defeat, discomfiture, a repulse, loss of a lawsuit, being cast on a trial.
পরাজয়কর্ত্তা, পরাজয়কারক, *s.* a conqueror.
পরাজয়পত্র, *s.* a decree of a legal decision.
পরাজয়ী, *a.* defeated, conquered, subdued.
পরাজিত, *a.* overcome, defeated, subdued, vanquished, repulsed, discomfited.
পরাজেতব্য, or পরাজেয়, *a.* vincible.
পরাজ্ঞাবহ, *a.* under the orders of another.
পরাণ, *s.* the dressing of a person, a harnessing ; also, a *corruption* of প্রাণ life.
পরাৎপর, *s.* God, the most high.
পরাধীন, *a.* dependent on another.
পরাধীনতা, *s.* dependence, subjection.
পরাপবাদ, *s.* the accusing of another person.
পরাবজ্ঞ, *a.* contemptuous, scornful.
পরাবর্ত্তন, *s.* a returning, reverting back.
পরাবর্ত্তনীয়, *a.* returnable, revertible.
পরাবর্ত্তনীয়তা, -ত্ব, *s.* revertibleness.
পরাবর্ত্ত্য, *a.* revertible, returnable.
পরাবৃত্ত, *a.* reverted to, returned.
পরাবৃত্তি, *s.* a reversion, a returning.
পরাভব, *s.* defeat, discomfiture.
পরাভবনীয়, *a.* vincible, vanquishable.
পরাভূত, *a.* defeated, subdued, vanquished, conquered, overcome, discomfited.
পরামনন, *s.* conversion, repentance.
পরামর্শ, *s.* advice, counsel, consultation.
পরামর্শক, *s.* an adviser, a counsellor.
পরামর্শদাতা, পরামর্শদায়ক, *s.* an adviser.
পরামর্শপূর্ব্বক, *ad.* by advice or counsel.
পরামর্শী, *a.* advising, counselling.
পরামাণিক, *s.* the chief man of a tribe, the chairman of an assembly, a barber.
পরামৃষ্ট, *a.* defiled, defloured ; counselled, advised.
পরায়ণ, *s.* devotedness, a votary.
পরার্থ, *ad.* for the sake of others.
পরাস্ত, *a.* the same as পরাভূত.
পরি, an *insepar. prep.* in *comp.* it gives the idea of an increased or accumulated degree of the action or passion.
পরিকপাল, *s.* in *ana.* the pericranium.
পরিকর্ম্ম, *s.* the decoration of the body.
পরিক্ষয়, *s.* complete decay, ruin.
পরিখা, *s.* a ditch, moat ; an encircling.
পরিগৃহীত, *a.* owned, received, accepted.
পরিগ্রহ, *s.* the reserve of an army, the sun near the moon's node, a wife, dependents, servants, a retinue, assent, acceptance, a taking, a root, an origin.
পরিঘ, *s.* bludgeon, a pike ; a glass vessel.
পরিচয়, *s.* the making known, or introducing of one's self, acquaintance.
পরিচর্য্যা, *s.* service, attendance.
পরিচায়ক, *a.* making a person acquainted, causing to know : *s.* he who introduces.
পরিচারক, *a.* attending on : *s.* a servant, attendant.
পরিচারিকা, *s.* female servant.
পরিচিত, *a.* acquainted with, known, intimate.
পরিচ্ছদ, *s.* clothing, a garment.
পরিচ্ছন্ন, *a.* clothed, covered, arrayed.
পরিচ্ছিত্তি, পরিচ্ছেদ, *s.* a partition, a space, a separation, a boundary, a limit.
পরিচ্ছিন্ন, *a.* bounded, limited, separated with a boundary, defined.
পরিজন, *s.* family, member of a family, an attendant.
পরিজ্ঞান, *s.* a complete idea, comprehension, knowledge, detection, conviction.
পরিজ্ঞাপন, *s.* information, conviction.
পরিজ্ঞাপিত, *a.* informed of, convicted.

পরিণত, *a.* curved, deflected, changed.

পরিণতি, *s.* a change of substance, trans-

পরিণয়, *s.* marriage, nuptials. [mutation.

পরিণয়ন, *s.* a giving of marriage.

পরিণাম, *s.* transmutation of a substance, any change, a chymical production.

পরিণামদর্শক, *a.* provident, prudent.

পরিণামদর্শন, *s.* a view of changes likely to take place: *a.* looking into the changes of human affairs. [dence, forecast.

পরিণামদর্শিতা, providence, foresight, pru-

পরিণামদর্শী, *a.* provident, prudent.

পরিণীতা, *a. fem.* married. [flamed.

পরিতপ্ত, *a.* heated, thoroughly heated, in-

পরিতাপ, *s.* heat, agony, torment, distress.

পরিতুষ্ট, *a.* satisfied, contented, pleased.

পরিতোষ, *s.* contentment, satisfaction, gratification, joy, pleasure. [pleasure.

পরিতোষক, *a.* gratifying: *s.* one who gives

পরিত্যক্ত, *a.* relinquished, deserted, left.

পরিত্যাগ, *s.* abandonment, relinquishment.

পরিত্যাগী, *a.* relinquishing, abandoning.

পরিত্যাজ্য, relinquishable, may be forsaken.

পরিত্রাণ, *s.* complete deliverance, salvation.

পরিত্রাণকর্ত্তা, পরিত্রাতা, *s.* a saviour, a deli-

পরিদান, *s.* exchange, barter. [verer.

পরিদেবনা, *s.* wit, prudence. [clothes.

পরিধান, *s.* the wearing or putting on of

পরিধাবন, *s.* consideration, thought, reflection, a running after pursuit.

পরিধি, *s.* the circumference of a circle or ellipsis, a periphery, a disk. [worn.

পরিধেয়, পরিধানীয়, *a.* wearable, fit to be

পরিপক্ব, *a.* ripe, completely ripe, mature, perfect, complete, digested. [ness.

পরিপক্বতা, *s.* ripeness, maturity, complete-

পরিপন্থী, *a.* circumventing: *s.* a circumventor, a foe, an enemy. [a ripening.

পরিপাক, *s.* maturity, ripeness, digestion,

পরিপাটী, *s.* order, regularity, method.

পরিপালিত, *a.* preserved, kept, nourished.

পরিপাল্য, *a.* worthy of being preserved

পরিপূর্ণ, *a.* filled, replete, complete, full.

পরিপূর্ণতা, -ত্ব, *s.* fulness, completeness.

পরিবর্জন, *s* the relinquishing of a thing.

পরিবর্জনীয়, *a.* relinquishable.

পরিবর্জ্জিত, *a.* relinquished, abandoned.

পরিবর্ত্ত, *s.* a requital, a recompense, a retribution, reward, an exchange, a vicissitude, an equivalent substitution, permutation, a barter, reciprocity. [tion.

পরিবর্ত্তন, *s.* exchange, requiting of an ac-

পরিবর্ত্তনীয়, *a.* requitable, exchangeable, may be exchanged or bartered.

পরিবর্ত্তনীয়তা, -ত্ব, *s.* a capacity of being requited or exchanged. [pensing.

পরিবর্ত্তী, *a.* changing, requiting, recom-

পরিবর্ত্তে, *ad.* instead of, in lieu of.

পরিবাদ, *s.* an accusation, a charge, an evil report, a slander, blame. [accuser.

পরিবাদক, *a.* slandering: *s.* a slanderer, an

পরিবাদন, *s.* the accusing of a person.

পরিবাদী, *a.* accusing, slandering: *s.* an ac-

পরিবাদ্য, liable to an accusation. [cuser.

পরিবার, *s.* household, family, relatives.

পরিবিত্তি, *s.* an unmarried elder brother.

পরিবৃত, *a.* surrounded, attended by.

পরিবেত্তা, *s.* a younger brother who marries before his elder brother.

পরিবেদনা, *s.* prudence, caution, pain, repentance, regret ;-রহিত, unregretting.

পরিবেশ, *s.* the sun's disk, circumference.

পরিবেশক, *a.* serving out at table: *s.* one who serves at table.

পরিবেশন, *s.* the serving out at table ;-কর্ত্তা, or পরিবেষ্টা, one who serves at table.

পরিবেশনীয়, *a.* proper to be attended on.

পরিবেষ্টক, surrounding, wrapping round.

পরিবেষ্টন, *s.* a surrounding, a wrapping.

পরিবেষ্টনীয়, *a.* that may be surrounded.

পরিবেষ্টিত, *a.* surrounded, wrapped round.

পরিব্রাজক, *a.* wandering about: *s.* a religious mendicant, a pilgrim, a vagabond.

পরিভব, *s.* disrespect, disregard; defeat.

পরিভাষা, *s.* a glossary of technical terms, conversation, discourse, a speech.

পরিভাষিত, agreed on, conversed, spoken.

পরিভুক্ত, *a.* enjoyed, possessed, [ed.

পরিভূত, *a.* disrespected, despised; defeat-

পরিভোগ, *s.* the enjoyment of any thing.

পরিভ্রম, *s.* a wandering, a mistake, error.

পরিভ্রষ্ট, *a.* fallen, corrupted, degraded.

পরিভ্রামক, *a.* wandering about, mistaking, erring: *s.* a wanderer, a pilgrim.

পরিমাণ, *s.* measure, weighing, size.
পরিমাতা, *s.* one who weighs or measures.
পরিমাপক, *a.* measuring, weighing.
পরিমাপণ, *s.* the causing to be measured.
পরিমায়ক, *a.* measuring, weighing.
পরিমিত, *a.* measured, defined, limited.
পরিমিততা, *s.* measuredness, limitedness.
পরিমিতব্যয়, *s.* frugality, economy.
পরিমিতব্যয়ী, *a.* economical, frugal.
পরিমিতভুক্, temperate, eating moderately.
পরিমিতভোক্তা, *s.* a moderate eater.
পরিমিতাহার, *s.* temperate or limited diet.
পরিমেয়, *a.* measurable, finite, calculable.
পরিমেয়তা, -ত্ব, *s.* measurableness.
পরিরক্ষণ, *s.* the preserving of a thing.
পরিরক্ষিত, *a.* well guarded, kept, preserved.
পরিশুদ্ধ, *a.* cleansed, purified, cleared off, paid.
পরিশুষ্ক, *a.* dried, completely dry.
পরিশেষ, *s.* a complete end, an end, a limit, a boundary, a border.
পরিশোধ, *s.* a paying or clearing off (a debt,) payment, recompense, requital.
পরিশোধক, *a.* clearing off, paying off a debt: *s.* a person who pays a debt.
পরিশোধন, *s.* paying or clearing of a debt.
পরিশোধনীয়, পরিশোধ্য, *a.* payable, due.
পরিশোধিত, cleared off, paid, made pure.
পরিশোষ, *s.* dryness, complete dryness.
পরিশ্রম, toil, exertion, labour, endeavour, fatigue; -বিশিষ্ট, -যুক্ত, *vide* পরিশ্রমী.
পরিশ্রমী, fatiguing, toilsome, wearisome, laborious.
পরিশ্রান্ত, *a.* wearied, fatigued.
পরিশ্রান্তি, toil, fatigue, weariness, labour.
পরিষৎ, *s.* a court, an assembly, audience.
পরিষ্করণীয়, *a.* requiring to be cleaned or purified, requiring to be repaired.
পরিষ্কার, *a.* clean, correct, plain: *s.* cleanness, clearness, transparency, accuracy, the repairing of a building; -কৃ, to clear, to acquit, to polish, to cleanse, refine.
পরিষ্কারক, পরিষ্কারী, *a.* cleansing, purifying, clearing up, polishing, repairing.
পরিষ্কার্য্য, capable of being cleared, polished or refined, requiring reparation.
পরিষ্কৃত, *a.* cleansed, refined, cleared, purified, depurated, cleared up, acquitted.
পরিসমাপনীয়, finishable, may be finished.
পরিসমাপ্ত, *a.* finished, ended, concluded.
পরিসমাপ্তি, a finish, a conclusion, an end.
পরিসর, *s.* the width of any thing, breadth, dimension, space, room: *a.* horizontal.
পরিসীমা, *s.* a limit, a boundary, a border.
পরিস্পন্দন, *s.* vibration, agitation, fluttering.
পরিস্পন্দিত, *a.* vibrating, agitated.
পরিহরণ, *s.* the confuting of an argument, the repelling of a charge.
পরিহরণীয়, *a.* confutable, capable of being repelled.
পরিহসনীয়, *a.* laughable, ridiculous.
পরিহসিত, *a.* laughed at, ridiculed, mocked.
পরিহার, *s.* a confutation, a repulse, disregard, disrespect, disesteem.
পরিহারক, *a.* confuting, repelling, treating with disrespect: *s.* one who confutes.
পরিহার্য্য, *a.* confutable, that may be repelled, deserving disrespect: *s.* a bracelet.
পরিহাস, or পরীহাস, *s.* laughter, ridicule, raillery, mockery, jesting, pleasantry.
পরিহাসক, *s.* a jester, a buffoon: *a.* jesting, ridiculing, railing, mocking.
পরিহাসকর্ত্তা, পরিহাসকারক, *s.* one who ridicules, a mocker, a mimic, a buffoon.
পরিহাসযোগ্য, *a.* worthy of being ridiculed, deserving to be laughed at.
পরিহাসী, *a.* jesting, mocking, ridiculing.
পরিহাস্য, *a.* laughable, ridiculous.
পরিহিত, *a.* clothed, clad, put on as a garment.
পরিহৃত, confuted, repelled, disrespected.
*পরী, *s.* a fairy, an elf.
পরীক্ষক, *a.* trying, bringing to the ordeal, tempting.
পরীক্ষণ, *s.* the trying of a thing, the putting of a thing to the proof.
পরীক্ষণীয়, *a.* capable of proof, requiring to be brought to a trial or proof.
পরীক্ষা, *s.* an ordeal, a test, trial, examination, an experiment, temptation.
পরীক্ষিত, tried, put to the proof, brought to the test, tempted: *s.* name of a king.
পরীক্ষ্য, *a.* subject to a trial or ordeal.
পরীবর্ত্ত, *s.* *vide* পরিবর্ত্ত, &c.
পরীবাদ, *s.* an accusation, censure, blame, reproof.
পরীবার, *s.* a relation, an attendant, a retinue, the sheath of a sword.
পরীবৃত্ত, *a.* exchanged, requited, recompensed.
পরু, *s.* *Port.* a leek, a common potherb.

পরুয়া, *s.* a bladder, packet, a bag, purse.
পরুষ, *a.* unkind, harsh, insulting, severe, scurrilous, rough, rugged.
পরে, *ad.* afterwards, after, hereafter.
পরেত, *a.* dead, gone to another state.
পরেদ্যবি, পরেদ্যুঃ, *ad.* on the next day.
পরোক্ষ, absent, not under one's own eye.
পরোক্ষার্থ, *s.* an invisible object. [others.
পরোপকার, *s.* beneficence, the helping of
পরোপকারক, পরোপকারী, *a.* beneficent, hospitable : *s.* one who assists others.
পরোপকৃত, *a.* assisted by others. [others.
পরোপকৃতি, *s.* beneficence, the helping of
পর্কলা, *a.* transparent : *s.* glass, crystal.
পর্ণ, *s.* a leaf, the betel-leaf. [patch.
পর্ত্তল, *s.* a false bottom, a patch ; -লাগা, to
পর্দা, *s.* a curtain, a skreen, a partition.
*পর্দাপোশ, পর্দাপোশী, *a.* skreening : *s.* a covering, a veil over faults, protection.
পর্পটী, *s.* a kind of red aluminous earth.
পর্ব্ব, *s.* the joint of a bambu or other plant, a knuckle, a gibbosity, a section, a division, a chapter, a festival, a feast.
পর্ব্বত, *s.* a mountain, a rock, a hill.
পর্ব্বতপাশাড়ি, *s.* a valley, the side of a hill.
পর্ব্বতপ্রমাণ, *a.* mountain-sized. [a crag.
পর্ব্বতশৃঙ্গ, পর্ব্বতচূড়া, *s.* a mountain peak,
পর্ব্বতশ্রেণী, *s.* a range of mountains.
পর্ব্বতাকার, *a.* mountain-formed, gibbous.
পর্ব্বতীয়, mountain, alpine, mountainous.
পর্ব্বন্, *s.* a joint, the joint of a bambu or stalk of grass ; the equinox, the solstice, a festival, a holding, an opportunity, an occasion, a chapter, a section.
পর্ব্ববৎ, *a.* geniculated, resembling a joint.
পর্ব্বসন্ধি, *s.* a joint, the moment of the full and change of the moon.
পর্ব্বাহ, *s.* the day of a festival. [terpane.
পর্য্যঙ্ক, *s.* a bed, a bedstead ; -পোশ, a coun-
পর্য্যটন, *s.* a peregrination, a perambulation, a tour, progress. [until, unto.
পর্য্যন্ত, *s.* a limit, a boundary : *ad.* as far as,
পর্য্যবসান, *s.* end, conclusion. [finished.
পর্য্যবসিত, *a.* declined, brought to a close,
পর্য্যাটক, *a.* travelling : *s.* a traveller.
পর্য্যাপ্ত, *a.* obtained, gained ; finished, concluded, voluntary ; enough, sufficient.

পর্য্যাপ্তি acquisition ; warding off a blow.
পর্য্যায়, *s.* regular order, rotation, succes-
পর্য্যায়ক্রমে, in regular succession. [sion.
পর্য্যায়ানুসার, *s.* a turn in rotation.
পর্য্যায়ানুসারে, *ad.* in rotation, in turn.
পর্য্যুষিত, *a.* corrupted, stale, not fresh.
পর্শুকা, *s.* a rib.
পল, *s.* a minute ; straw, flesh, a bevelled edge ; -তোলা, rim of a bevelled edge.
পলক, *s.* eye-lid ; a wink, twinkling of an
পলল, *s.* meat, flesh. [eye ; -মার্, to wink.
পলা, *v. n.* to flee, to escape, to run away : *s.* oil-ladle, a coral, a bead of red lac.
পলাকড়া, পলাকড়ি, *s.* the same as পটোল.
পলাণ্ডু, *s.* an onion (Allium cepa).
পলাতক, *s.* a fugitive, deserter, a runaway.
পলান, or পলাওন, *s.* a running away.
পলানিয়া, *a.* runaway, fugitive, deserting.
পলায়ন, *s.* a running away, escape, flight. an elopement, an absconding. [flight.
পলায়মান, *a.* running away, in the act of
পলায়িত, *a.* fled, run away, absconded.
পলাল, *s.* straw for fodder. [pitiless, cruel.
পলাশ, *s.* a leaf, a beautiful tree :[1] green ;
পলিত, *a.* hoary, gray-haired, old. [lock.
পলিতা, *s.* the wick of a candle or match-
পলুপোকা, *s.* a feathered white-ant.
পল্কা, *v. n.* to be impaired, to decay.
পল্কান, *s.* a being impaired, a decaying.
পল্টন, *s.* a regiment, a corps, an army.
পল্টনীয়া, *a.* belonging to an army or regi-
পলতা, *s.* the leaves of Patola. [ment.
পল্লব, *s.* a twig, a sprout, a young shoot.
পল্লবগ্রাহিতা, *s.* catching at a twig, or at trifling objections, a carping at trifles.
পল্লবগ্রাহিপাণ্ডিত্য, *s.* twig-catching learning, a smattering of learning.
পল্লবগ্রাহী, *a.* twig-catching, catching at every trifling objection, carping.
পল্লবিত, *a.* covered with twigs.
পল্লি, or পল্লী, *s.* a district, canton, hamlet.
পল্লিগ্রাম, *s.* a country, village, hamlet.
পল্লিগ্রামী, *a.* rustic, country. [canal.
পল্বল, *s.* a small pond, a pool, a tank, a
পলবল্, *s.* the same as পটোল.
পশ্, *v. a.* to enter. [ties (ironically).
*পশম, *s.* wool, fur, the hair on the privi-

পশমী, পশমীনা, *a.* woollen, made of wool.
পশমীবস্ত্র, *s.* flannel, broad cloth.
পশু, *s.* a beast, animal; an order of gods.
পশুগণ, or পশুবর্গ, *s.* beasts, the genus or order of beasts, the mammalia.
পশুজাতি, *s.* the genus of beasts, mamma-
পশুজাতীয়, *a.* pertaining to beasts. [lia.
পশুপতি, *s.* the lion, the lord of beasts; an appellation of Shiva. [tle.
পশুপালক, *s.* one who keeps or feeds cat-
পশুবৎ, পশুতুল্য, *a.* beast-like, irrational,
পশুবদাচার, *s.* beastly conduct. [beastly.
পশুবিদ্যা, *s.* the knowledge of beasts.
পশুরক্ষক, *s.* a person who keeps cattle.
পশুরাজ, *s.* the king of beasts, the lion.
পশুসদৃশ, *a.* like a beast. [sequently.
পশ্চাৎ, *ad.* behind, after, afterwards, sub-
পশ্চাত্তাপ, *s.* regret, repentance, remorse.
পশ্চাত্তাপী, *a.* repentant, penitent, regret-
পশ্চাদাগত, *a.* came after, followed. [ting.
পশ্চাদাগমন, *s.* a following after. [follower.
পশ্চাদ্গামী, *a.* following, succeeding: *s.* a
পশ্চাদ্দর্শক, *a.* seeing afterwards, reflecting.
পশ্চাদ্দর্শন, *s.* an afterview, reflection.
পশ্চাদ্দর্শী, reflective, viewing afterwards.
পশ্চাদ্দৃষ্টি, *s.* aftersight, reflection.
পশ্চাদ্ধাবন, *s.* a following or running after.
পশ্চাদ্বর্ত্তী, *a.* following, situated behind.
পশ্চাদ্ভাবনা, *s.* afterthought, reflection.
পশ্চিম, *s.* the west: *a.* western, after, be-
পশ্চিমদিগ্, *s.* the west quarter. [hind.
পশ্চিম, *a.* western, hinder: *s.* the disease of tetanus or locked jaw.
পশ্চিমাস্য, *a.* facing the west.
পষ্ট, *a.* clear, plain, evident. [lect.
পসন্দ, *s.* choice, approbation; -কৃ, to se-
পসরা, *s.* a vessel, a basket for vegetables.
পসলা, *s.* a slight shower, a drizzling.
পসার্, *v.* to extend, expand: *s.* extension.
পসারণ, *s.* a spreading out, extending.
পসারী, *s.* five seras; a druggist, a grocer.
পসুরী, *s.* a weight of five seras.
পস্তা, *v. n.* to repent, to regret: *s.* a piece.
পস্তান, *s.* repentance, regret, remorse.
পস্তানিয়া, *a.* penitent, regretting.
পহর, *s.* a fourth part of the day or night, the space of three English hours.
পহরী, or প্রহরী, *s.* a watchman, a sentry.
পহিলা, *a.* first, the first, before.
পা, *v. a.* to obtain, gain, find, get, receive, suffer, possess, acquire: *s.* the leg, foot.
পাই, *a.* a quarter, a fourth part; in *acct.* 4 pái or 12 pái, are reckoned one áná.
পাইক, *s.* an armed footman, a watchman.
পাইকস্তা, *a.* (land) let to non-resident ten-
পাইকার, *s.* a pedlar, a hawker. [ants.
পাইড়, *s.* a selvage, hem, edge, a breast-summer or beam laid on pillars to support other beams, an architrave, a bambu or beam to support a pitched roof.
পাইন, *s.* solder; -ঝাল, a soldering.
পাওআ, *v. a.* to cause to obtain or suffer, to induce, to procure, to obtain: *s.* acquisition, gain, the obtaining of a thing.
পাওন, *s.* the getting, obtaining, or finding of a thing, the suffering of a thing.
পাওনা, *a.* due, demand, pecuniary claim.
পাংশু, *s.* dust, ashes, manure.
পাঁইজ, *s.* a distaff; the name of a fish.
পাঁইত, *s.* a row, range, continuous line.
পাঁউরুটী, *s.* leavened bread, a loaf.
পাঁউলাগা, *ad.* good-morrow, or more properly, I touch your foot, a salutation.
পাঁক, *s.* clay, mud, mire. [the foot).
পাঁকই, *a.* occasioned by mud (as a sore in
পাঁকাল, clayey, miry: *s.* a species of fish.
পাঁকুটীয়া, *a,* living in mud, muddy.
পাঁচ্, *v. a.* to lance with a lancet.
পাঁচ, *a.* five; -ভৌতিক, material. [livery.
পাঁচট্, *s.* the fifth day after a woman's de-
পাঁচটা, or পাঁচটী, *a.* five, only five.
পাঁচন, *s.* the act of lacning; a decoction; -অস্ত্র, a lancet; -বাড়ী, a rod, a staff.
পাঁচনী, *s.* a twig, a rod, a wand, a cane.
পাঁচবার্ষিক, or পাঁচসনী, *a.* quinquennial.
পাঁচমিশালি, *s.* a promiscuous mixture.
পাঁচা, *v. a.* to cause to lance, to lance, cut slightly: *s.* brine used in making salt.
পাঁচালি, *s.* a particular sort of metre used in poems, a particular mode of singing.
পাঁচীল, *s.* a wall, a brick wall, fence wall.
পাঁচুঞি, *a.* the fifth. পাঁজ, pedigree; foot-
পাঁজর, পাঁজরা, *s.* a rid, the ribs. [print.
পাঁজা, *s.* a wisp, bunch, bundle; brick-kiln.

পাঁজী, *s.* an almanac, a calendar, a directo-
পাঁজীকর, *s.* an almanac-maker. [ry.
পাঁঠা, *s.* a he-goat; a blockhead; *fem.* পাঁঠী.
পাঁঠীবেচা, *a.* disposing of his daughter in marriage for a stipulated sum.
পাঁড়ু, *a.* blanched, reserved for seed.
পাঁড়ুকুমড়া, *s.* a gourd reserved for seed.
পাঁতার, or পাঁথার, *s.* the width of a river;
পাঁতি, *s.* a row, a range, a line. [a flood.
পাঁদাড়, *s.* the back part of a house.
পাঁদাড়িয়া, *a.* of the back part of a house.
পাঁপড়, পাঁপর, *s.* a thin kind of biscuit.
পাঁশ, *s.* the ashes of cow-dung, ashes.
পাক্, *v. n.* to ripen, concoct, suppurate.
পাক, *a.* ripe, cooked: *s.* ripeness, cooking, boiling, twisting, digestion; a circular motion; a screw; -দা, -লাগা, to twist, turn round, writhe; -কৃ, to cook food; -খা, to be twisted; -পা, to digest.
পাককর্ত্তা, *s.* a cook, one who cooks.
পাকখাওন, *s.* a being twisted.
পাকখোলা, *s.* a turnscrew.
পাকচক্র, *s.* deceit, collusion; an eddy, a circular motion, a wheel.
পাকড়্, *v. n.* to seize, to hold.
পাকড়ন, *s.* a seizing or holding. [thing.
পাকড়া, *v. a.* to take or seize a person or
পাকড়ী, *s.* the corolla or petal of a flower, a
পাকতৈল, *s.* prepared or boiled oil. [branch.
পাকনা, *s.* a whirlpool, an eddy in water.
পাকপড়া, *a.* intricate, contorted. [signing.
পাকপাড়া, *a.* insidious, artful, crafty, de-
পাকপাড়ান, *s.* insidiousness, craftiness, artfulness, craft, finesse. [digested.
পাকল, *a.* concocted, ripe, mature, perfect,
পাকলা, *v. a.* to clean, to wash: *a.* washed,
পাকলান, *s.* a washing, a cleaning. [clean.
পাকশালা, *s.* a cook-room, a kitchen.
পাকসাঁড়াশি, *s.* a smith's vice, a turnscrew.
পাকস্থালী, *s.* seething pot, culinary vessel.
পাকা, *v. a.* to cook, to twist, to screw: *a.* cooked, ripe, mature, twisted: *s.* a fan.
পাকাচুল, *s.* gray hair, hoary hair.
পাকাটী, পাটকাটী, *s.* the stalks of hemp.
পাকান, *s.* the cooking of food, a causing to ripen, a twisting; a sort of sweet cake.
পাকাপাকি, *a.* mutually agreed on, settled.

2 G

পাকি, *s.* a bird, the leaves of a venition.
পাকুড়, *s.* a fig tree (Ficus infectoria).
পাকুড়িয়া, *a.* pertinacious.
পাখ, *s.* a wing, a feather; -কাট্, to moult.
পাখরাজ, *s.* a small drum or tabour.
পাখলা, *v. a.* to rinse, to wash, to clean.
পাখলান, *s.* a washing, rinsing, cleaning.
পাখসাট, *s.* a blow with the wings.
পাখা, *s.* a wing, a fan, the fin of a fish, a feather; -কৃ, -ঘুরা, or -ঢুলা, to fan.
পাখী, *s.* a bird; the leaves of a venition.
পাখীমারা, *s.* a fowler, a bird-catcher.
পাখুরা, *s.* a chisel, a fin, the upper arm;
পাখো, *s.* a feather; a whirlpool. [a bird.
পাগ, or পাগড়ী, *s.* a turban.
পাগল, *a.* insane, mad, maniacal, foolish: *s.* a maniac, a madman; *fem.* পাগলী.
পাগলখানা, *s.* an insane hospital.
পাগলা, *s.* a maniac, a madman, an idiot.
পাগলাগারদ, *s.* a mad-house. [foolish.
পাগলাটিয়া, *a.* weak, silly, mad, insane,
পাগলামী, *s.* foolishness, insanity, madness.
পাঙ্, *v. a.* to perceive, to form an idea.
পাঙ্গা, *v. a.* *idem*: *s.* a kind of rock-salt.
পাঙ্গাশ, *s.* name of a fish: *a.* whitish, pale,
পাঙ্গাশীয়া, *a.* tawny, pale, wan. [tawny.
পাচক, *a.* concocting, digestive: *s.* a cook.
পাচকতা, -ত্ব *s.* a digestive quality.
পাচড়া, *s.* the itch. [a decoction.
পাচন, *s.* act of cooking, digesting of food;
পাচিকা, *s.* a cookwoman. [posteriors.
পাছ, *s.* the hinder part, the back side,
পাছকানাচ, *s.* the back part of a house.
পাছড়্, *v. a.* to winnow grain.
পাছড়ন, *s.* the winnowing of grain. [now.
পাছড়া, *v.* to throw in wrestling; to win-
পাছড়ান, *s.* the winnowing of corn; the throwing an antagonist in wrestling.
পাছড়াপাছড়ি, *s.* a grappling in wrestling.
পাছড়ী, *s.* a kind of prepared rice.
পাছদ্বার, *s.* a back-door. [the stern.
পাছা, *s.* the hinder part, buttocks, rump,
পাছাড়, *v. a.* to throw in wrestling: *s.* a fall in wrestling; -মার, to throw down.
পাছাপাছি, *s.* rump to rump. [part.
পাছু, *s.* the rear of an army, the hinder
পাছুড়ী, *s.* a wrapper, an upper garment.

পাছে, *ad.* behind, after, afterwards, subsequently, lest.
পাজা, *s.* a brick-kiln.
পাজামা, *s.* a pair of breeches, trowsers.
পাজী, *a.* low, base, mean, vile, slavish.
পাজীআনা, *s.* meanness, baseness, vileness.
পাজীপুজরা, *a.* very mean, base, low, vile.
পাজীমিজাজ, *a.* mean, obstinate, of bad conduct.
পাজেম, *s.* meanness, baseness.
পাঞ্চজন্য, *s.* Krishna's couch.
পাঞ্চভৌতিক, *a.* material, composed of the five original elements of matter.
পাঞ্জা, *s.* the hand, the claw of a bird or beast; five torches burning on a pole.
পাট, *s.* a folding of clothes in order, an altar, a board, a stool, a throne, a terrace, breadth, extension, sack of corn; a plant,[1] its fibres are used for cordage; silk; the earthen hoops of a well.
পাটন, *s.* a city, a town, a mart, a seaport.
পাটনা, *s.* the name of a city in Behar.
পাটনাই, *a.* produced at, or coming from, Patna.
পাটনী, *s.* a ferryman.
পাটব, *s.* eminence, cleverness, expertness.
পাটবারী, *s.* a tax-gatherer, a bailiff.
পাটভাঙ্গা, *s.* the ceremony of falling on knives at the Charaka festival.
পাটরাণী *s.* the chief wife of a king.
পাটল, *a.* pale-red, rose colour, pale-pink; a kind of rice.
পাটলি, *s.* trumpet flower.
পাটশাক, *s.* jew's mallow used as potherb.
পাটা, *s.* a board, a plank; a lease for land.
পাটালিগুড়, *s.* thin cakes of molasses.
পাটাসেলামী, *s.* a present given to obtain a lease.
পাটিকেল, *s.* a brick.
পাটী, *s.* a flat plate or bar of metal, a bar or rafter, a valve, the four side bars of a bedstead, a mat; one of a pair, a row, *e. g.* জুতার পাটী, a single shoe; দাঁতের পাটী, a single row of teeth.
পাটলী, *s* a large flat boat of burden.
পাটেপাটে, *ad.* in every sack, sack by sack.
পাটোআর, *s.* a silk-mercer; one who strings native bracelets, beads, etc.[1]
পাটোআরী, *s. idem;* also, a tax-gatherer.
পাট্টা, *s.* a lease for land, a patent, a rake.
পাট্‌ঠা, *s.* a wrestler: *a.* young.
পাঠ, *s.* a text, a lesson, a reading, study, perusal.
পাঠক, *a.* reading: *s.* a reader, a student.
পাঠকর্ত্তা, *s.* one who reads, a lecturer.
পাঠক্রম, *s.* order of study, order in reading, style.
পাঠগুরু, *s.* a schoolmaster, a tutor.
পাঠপ্রণালী, *s.* the style of an author.
পাঠশালা, *s.* a school, a seminary.
পাঠশিষ্য, *s.* a pupil, a scholar.
পাঠা, *v. a.* to send, to delegate, to despatch; পাঠাইয়া দা, to send.
পাঠান, *s.* a sending, a delegating; a class of Moslems.
পাঠাপাঠ, *s.* right or wrong reading of a text.
পাঠার্থী, *a.* desirous of reading.
পাঠার্থে, *ad.* for the purpose of reading.
পাঠার্হ, *a.* deserving to be read.
পাঠিত, *a.* caused to be read.
পাঠ্য, *a.* legible, worthy of being read.
পাড়্, *v. a.* to lay, to cast down, to spread, throw down, to gather fruits or flowers.
পাড়, *s.* a breastsummer or crossbeam supporting other beams, a coast, steep bank.
পাড়ন, *s.* act of laying or spreading, a causing to fall, a collecting of fruits, etc.
পাড়া, *v. a.* to cast down, to cause a mat to be spread out, to cause to collect fruit: *s.* a quarter of a town, a canton, hamlet.
পাড়াগাঁ, *s.* a hamlet, small village.
পাড়াগাঁইয়া, *a.* rustic, belonging to a village.
পাড়ান, *s.* the causing to spread a carpet or mat, the causing to collect fruits.
পাড়পড়শী, or **পড়শী**, *s.* a neighbour.
পাড়ি, *s.* a selvage, hem; a passing to the opposite side; -দা, to pass over a river.
পাণ, *s.* betel-leaf, the leaf of Piper betel.
পাণপত্র, *s.* a writing of betrothal, betel-leaf given in conclusion of a marriage.
পাণবাটা, *s.* a betel-box.
পাণমরিচ, *s.* a plant;[2] pepper fried in betel-leaf.
পাণা, *s.* an aquatic weed (Salvinia cucullata).
পাণি, *s.* the hand.
পাণিগৃহীতা, *a.* taken by the hand: *s.* a bride
পাণিগ্রহ, **পাণিগ্রহণ**, *s.* marriage.
পাণ্ডব, *s.* race of Pándu; *vide* পঞ্চপাণ্ডব.
পাণ্ডর, *a.* pale, yellowish white: *s.* a pale colour, red chalk.
পাণ্ডা, *s.* a priest of Jagannáth's temple in Urissá, idol's priest.
পাণ্ডিত্য, scholarship, learning, erudition.
পাণ্ডিত্যপ্রকাশ, *s.* a display of learning.

পাণ্ডু, *a.* yellowish white : *s.* the jaundice; the name of an ancient king of Delhi.
পাণ্ডুবর্ণ, পাণ্ডুর, *a.* white-coloured, white, pale, whitish, wan, yellowish white.
পাণ্ডুরোগ, *s.* the jaundice; dropsy, a dis-
পাণ্ডুলিপি, *s.* a rough draft, a sketch. [ease.
পাণ্ডুলেখ্য, *a.* fit to be drafted or sketched.
পাৎ, *v. a.* to lay down, spread out. [thin.
পাত, *s.* a fall; a leaf; a note, writing: *a.*
পাতক, *s.* sin, guilt, crime; cause of fall.
পাতকী, *a.* sinful, guilty, criminal.
পাতখোলা, *s.* a thin little earthen vessel.
পাতশিয়া, *s.* a mattress laid over a mat.
পাতঞ্জল, *s.* one of the six schools of philosophy, it was founded by Pátanjala.
পাতড়া, *s.* orts, refuse of a meal; ration; a wastebook, rough sketch; -চাটা, -মারা, eating a ration; living upon orts.
পাতনা, *s.* a muster, a specimen. [diluted.
পাতল, পাতলা, *a.* thin, light, lean, slender,
পাতা, *s.* a leaf, blade of grass; -কৃ, to reel
পাতাপা, *a.* web-footed. [silk; to pray.
পাতাল, *s.* the infernal region, hell, a hole, a chasm; -ভেদী, a fountain, a spring.
পাতালপুরী, *s.* the infernal region.
পাতালমুখী, *s.* (*met.*) pudendum muliebre.
পাতি, *a.* small, little, diminutive, petty.
পাতিচোর, *s.* a pilferer, a petty thief. [sin.
পাতিত্য, *s.* a fallen or depraved condition;
পাতিনেড়্যা, *s.* a nickname for a Moslem.
পাতিনেবু, *s.* the best variety of lime.
পাতিপাতি, *s.* a searching minutely.
পাতিব্রত্য, *s.* chastity, devotedness to a hus-
পাতিমৌড়, *s.* a bridal crown. [band.
পাতিশেয়াল, *s.* a fox, a jackal.
পাতিহাঁস, *s.* the common duck, a drake.
পাতী, *s.* a letter, a writing, a note.
পাতুক, *a.* disposed to fall: *s.* a precipice.
*পাতোআন, *s.* exchange, discount, an ex-
পাতোআল, *s.* a helm, a rudder. [change.
পাৎকুঁড়ি, *s.* the bud of a plant, a leaf-bud,
পাৎকুয়া, *s.* a well, a deep well. [muster.
পাত্না, *s.* a jar; a rough sketch, specimen,
পাত্র, *s.* a vessel, a recipient, a bridegroom, a plate, a cup, a jar, the body, a king's minister, counsellor, a person entrusted with an office, propriety, fitness.

পাত্রতা, -ত্ব, *s.* confidence, patronage.
পাথর, *s.* a stone, rock; -কাটা, a stone-
পাথরচূর, *s.* an aromatic plant.[1] [mason.
পাথরী, *s.* the stone or gravel, the tartar
পাথরীয়া, *s.* a stone-cutter. [of the teeth.
পাথস্, *s.* water. [ling expenses.
পাথেয়, *a.* belonging to a road: *s.* travel-
পাদ্, *v. a.* to expel wind backwards.
পাদ, *s.* a foot, leg, step, foot in poetry; a quarter; wind let out; -নিক্ষেপ, a step.
পাদতল, *s.* the sole of the foot.
পাদধূলি, পাদরজ, *s.* the dust of the foot.
পাদন, *s.* the breaking of wind backwards.
পাদপ, *s.* a tree. পাদপদ্ম, *s.* the lotus foot
পাদপীঠ, *s.* a footstool. [(term of flattery).
পাদপ্রক্ষালন, *s.* the washing of the feet.
পাদবিরজাঃ, পাদরথী, *s.* a boot, shoe, slipper, a stocking. পাদাঘাত, *s.* a kick.
পাদবিহীন, *a.* destitute of foot, apodal.
পাদরি, *s.* a priest, minister, clergyman.
পাদস্ফোট, *s.* a kibe, a chilblain.
পাদাঙ্ক, *s.* a footstep, a footprint, track.
পাদাতিক, *s.* a footman, a foot soldier.
পাদার্পণ, *s.* a placing the foot, a stepping.
পাদুআপোকা, *s.* a kind of cimex or bug.
পাদুকা, or পাদু, *s.* a shoe, a slipper.
পাদোদক, *s.* the water in which a bráhman has dipped his feet. [his feet.
পাদ্য, *s.* water offered to a guest to wash
পান, *s.* the act of drinking; -কৃ, to drink.
পানকর্ত্তা, *s.* one who drinks, a drinker.
পানপাত্র, *s.* a drinking vessel. [sottish.
পানমগ্ন, or পানশৌণ্ড, *a.* drunk, intoxicated,
পানসী, *s.* a sort of small covered boat.
পানা, *s.* breadth; lemonade, sherbet; moss: *v.* to induce a cow to give milk freely.
পানার্থী, *a.* thirsty. পানাশক্ত, *a.* sottish.
পানার্থে, *ad.* for the purpose of drinking.
পানী, *s.* water, drinking liquid.
পানীআলা, *s.* a tree and its fruit.[2]
পানীকৌড়ি, *s.* a species of water-bird.[3]
পানীঘড়ী, *s.* a clepsydra.
পানীচরকী, *s.* a water-mill.
পানীভাঁত, *s.* a hydraulic press.
পানীতরাস, *s.* the keel of a ship or boat.
পানীতারা, *s.* a kind of sweetmeat. [ter.
পানীনালা, *s.* an aqueduct, a trench, a gut-

পানপন্থী, *a.* travelling by water, voyaging.
পানীফল, *s.* an aquatic plant and its fruit.[1]
পানীবসন্ত, *s.* the chicken-pox. [water.
পানীভরা, *s.* a water-bearer : *a.* full of
পানীভাঙ্গা, breaking of water : *s.* a female
পানীমুচি, *s.* liquor amnii cyst. [disease.
পানীযন্ত্র, *s.* a hydraulic machine.
পানীয়, *a.* fit for drink, potable : *s.* water.
পানীসা, পান্সা, *a.* watery, diluted, insipid, serous ; -দাঁত, a bleeding tooth.
পানুই, *s.* a pair of slippers, shoes, boots.
পানে, *ad.* towards, near. [ture meal).
পান্তা, *s.* stale rice kept in water (for a fu-
পান্থ, *s.* a traveller, passer by, a passenger.
পান্না, *s.* eating of first meal after a fast.
পাপ, *s.* sin, crime, guilt, wickedness ; -কৃ, to commit sin ; -মিটা, to atone for sin.
পাপকর্ম্ম, *s.* a sinful action, a crime.
পাপকর্ম্মা, *a.* guilty of sin, criminal.
পাপক্ষয়, *s.* mortification of sin. [luck.
পাপগ্রহ, *s.* an evil planet ; calamity, ill-
পাপঘ্ন, sin-destroying, expiating for sin.
পাপড়িখএর, *s.* a kind of catechu. [of sin.
পাপভোগ, *s.* a suffering the consequences
পাপময়, *a.* made up of sin, wholly sin.
পাপা, *s.* *Port.* the Pope, a father.
পাপাচরণ, পাপাচার, *s.* a wicked or sinful
পাপাত্মা, *a.* sinful, wicked. [practice.
পাপাশয়, *a.* wicked, intending evil.
পাপিষ্ঠ, *a.* wicked, guilty, sinful, criminal, highly wicked : *s.* a sinner, a rascal.
পাপী, *a.* sinful, wicked, guilty, criminal ;
পাপোঁচ, *s.* a wipeshoes. [*fem.* পাপীয়সী.
পাপোশ, *s.* a pair of slippers or shoes.
পাব, *s.* space between two joints, a knuc-
পাবদা, *s.* a kind of fish.[2] [kle, a joint.
পাবন, পাবক, *a.* purifying, cleansing.
পাবনতা, -ত্ব, *s.* purification, cleanness.
পামর, *a.* base, vile, despicable, low, wicked, stupid, silly. [stupidity, idiotcy.
পামরতা, *s.* baseness, vileness, meanness
পামরী, *s.* a mean woman ; a sort of cloth
পায়চারী, *a.* going on foot, walking. [ers.
পায়জামা, *s.* a pair of trowsers, long draw-
পায়দল, *a.* pedestrial, on foot. [the feet.
পায়পড়া, *a.* sycophant, servile, falling on
পায়পায়, *ad.* step by step, at every step.

পায়রা, *s.* a pigeon ; *fem.* পায়রী.
পায়স, *s.* frumenty, sweetened rice-milk.
পায়া, *s.* the foot, the leg or foot of a piece of furniture, a situation, office, rank.
পায়ু, *s.* the anus. পার্, *v. a.* to be able.
পার, *s.* across, opposite shore of a river, a working of pedal by the foot. [ver.
পারক, *a.* able, expert, capable, active, cle-
পারকতা, *s.* ability, capability, activity.
পারগ, *a.* well-versed, efficient, skilful, clever, studious, going to the other side.
পারগতা, -ত্ব, *s.* skilfulness, studiousness.
পারঘাটা, *s.* the landing-place where a ferry-boat plies.
পারণ, *s.* the being able to do a thing ; the first meal after a religious fast. [power.
পারতপক্ষ, *a.* the object within a person's
পারতন্ত্র্য, *s.* subjection, subserviency.
পারত্রিক, *a.* same as পারলৌকিক. [ing.
পারদ, *s.* quicksilver, mercury ; extricat-
পারদর্শক, পারদর্শী, seeing the other side, far-seeing, skilful in an art or science.
পারদর্শিতা, *s.* skilfulness in an art or science, a view of the opposite shore.
পারদারিক, *a.* adulterous : *s.* an adulterer.
পারদারিকতা, পারদার্য্য, *s.* adultery.
পারমার্থিক, *a.* spiritual, excellent.
পারম্পর্য্য, *a.* traditional : *s.* tradition, traditional doctrine, continual succession.
পারলৌকিক, *a.* relating to the next world.
পারশব, *s.* a bráhman's son by a shudráni, a son by another's wife, a living corpse.
পারস্ত্রৈণেয়, *s.* an adulterine, son by ano-
পারা, quicksilver, mercury. [ther's wife.
পারাণী, *a.* paid for crossing a river : *s.* hire
পারাণীনৌকা, *s.* a ferry-boat. [for a ferry.
পারাবত, *s.* a pigeon, a dove.
পারাবার, *s.* the ocean, sea, both shores of a river : *ad.* through and through.
পারায়ণ, study ; totality, entireness, completion ; a crossing to the other side.
পারিচ্ছিদ্র্য, *s.* the adjustment of any affair.
পারিজাত, *s.* the coral tree of paradise.[3]
পারিতোষিক, *a.* gratifying, satisfying : *s.* a present, a reward, a gift, a gratuity.
পারিপাট্য, *a.* regular, orderly, neatly.
পারিভাষিক, *a.* technical, not common.

পারিশা, *s.* the name of a species of fish.[1]
পারিষদ, পার্ষদ, *s.* a spectator, attendants, retinue : *a.* belonging to an assembly.
পারুষ্য, *s.* abuse, reproach, scurrility, severity, harshness, violence, defamation, a misdemeanor, an assault.
পার্থক্য, *s.* a separation, a division.
পার্থিব, *a.* earthly, terrestrial.
পার্ব্বণ, *s.* a festival, a feast. [at festivals.
পার্ব্বণী, *s.* presents at festivals : *a.* given
পার্ব্বতী, *s.* a name of Durgá.
পার্য্য, পার্য্যমাণ, *a.* possible, practicable.
পার্শ্ব, *s.* a side, the side of the body.
পার্শ্বগত, *a.* situated on the side, collateral.
পার্শ্বদন্ত, *s.* an eye-tooth.
পার্শ্ববর্ত্তী, পার্শ্বস্থ, *a.* adjacent, situated at the side : *s.* an associate, a companion.
পার্শ্বাস্থি, পর্শুকা, পঞ্জর, পাঁজর, *s.* a rib.
পার্শ্বে, *ad.* aside, privately.
পার্ষ্ণি, *s.* the heel, the rear of an army, the back, a violent woman.
পাল্, *v. a.* to preserve, nourish, support, maintain, educate, to keep a promise.
পাল, *s.* a nourisher, a protector, a flock, a herd, a drove, the copulation of beasts, a sail, a sail cloth ; -তুল্, to hoist a sail.
পালই, *s.* a stack or rick of corn, a granary, a storehouse, a magazine.
পালক, *a.* preserving, nourishing : *s.* a preserver, keeper, protector, a cowherd.
পালকপুত্র, পালকবেটা, *s.* an adopted son.
পালকবেটী *s.* an adopted daughter.
পালকী, *s.* a sort of sedan chair, a pálkí.
পালকুঁড়ি, *s.* a switch, a twig ; pinfeather.
পালখ, *s.* a plume, feather, wing, pinion, the eye-lashes ; -বদলা, to moult.
পালঙ্ক, *s.* beet-root, beet ;[2] a bedstead.
পালঙ্গদানা, *s.* an ornament for the neck.
পালঙ্গপোষ, *s.* a counterpane, a bed-cover.
পালট, *v. n.* to turn, to turn back.
পালটি, *a.* reciprocal, mutual, alternate.
পালন, *s.* the act of nourishing or maintaining, act of keeping or observing.
পালনকর্ত্তা, *s.* a nourisher, a supporter, an observer, one who keeps a thing.
পালনা, *s.* a cradle, rocking bed. [supported.
পালনীয়, পাল্য, *a.* fit to be nourished or

পালা, *s.* the maintenance of a person ; a twig, hoar frost, a time or turn in rotation : *a.* supported, domestic : *v. a.* to nourish, maintain, to flee, run away.
পালাঝালা, *s.* twigs and branches. [wall.
পালাঙ্গা, *s.* a shelf ; small shed on a mud
পালাতক, *a.* running away : *s.* a runaway.
পালান্, *s.* a packsaddle, the udder of an
পালান, *s.* flight, escape, flying. [animal.
পালানিয়া, *s.* a runaway, a deserter.
পালি, *s.* a sail, edge of a weapon, a corner, the tip of the ear, a line, a row, a spot, stain, a causey, a woman with a beard, measure of five sera ; a cockpit.
পালিত, *a.* nourished, protected, educated,
পালিতামাদার, *s.* a tree.[3] [preserved.
পালো, *s.* an infusion, vegetable farina.
পালোবান, *v.* a hero, a wrestler.
পাল্লা, *s.* a pair of scales, space, distance.
পাশ, *s.* a rope, noose, snare, fetters, dice ;
পাশক, *s.* a die, dice. [a side : *ad.* near.
পাশক্রীড়ক, *s.* a gambler : *a.* playing at dice.
পাশক্রীড়া, *s.* play at dice. [the other.
পাশমোড়া, *s.* the turning from one side to
পাশলী, *s.* a toe-ring ; the collar-bone.
পাশা, *s.* dice, a rope for the feet used in climbing palm trees ; an ear-ornament.
পাশাখেলা, *s.* a play at dice, a gambling.
পাশাপাশি, *ad.* abreast, side by side, near.
পাশী, *s.* a frame, one who extracts palm-
পাশুলী, *s.* a ring for the toes. [juice.
পাশ্চাত্য, *a.* western, hinder : *s.* hinder part.
পাষণ্ড, *a.* impious, blasphemous, heretical : *s.* a blasphemer, a heretic. [phemy.
পাষণ্ডতা, *s.* hypocrisy, impiety, heresy, blas-
পাষাণ, *s.* a rock, stone, inequality in a pair of scales, any thing used to equalize it.
পাষাণময়, *a.* full of stones, stony, rocky.
পাষাণহৃদয়, *a.* hard-hearted, unfeeling.
পাষাণী, *s.* pickaxe, a mason's hammer, a stone-cutter's chisel ; -য়া, stony, rocky.
পাস্তি, *s.* dice for playing. [getfulness.
পাসর, পাসরা, *v. n.* to forget, err : *s.* for-
পাসরণ, *s.* forgetting of a thing, erring.
পাহাড়, *s.* a mountain, a hill, a rock.
পাহাড়তলী, *s.* bottom of a hill, a valley.
পাহাড়ী, *s.* brink of a precipice ; a hillman.

পাহাড়ীয়া, *a.* hilly, mountainous, belonging to a mountain : *s.* a mountaineer.
পি, *v. a.* to drink, to smoke tobacco.
পিউড়ি, *s.* yellow ochre. পিওন, a drinking.
পিঁজরা, *s.* a cage, a bird-cage, a fowl-cage.
পিঁড়া, *s.* a stool, raised floor of a house.
পিঁপাড়া, *s.* an ant, emmet, pismire.
পিঁপুল, *s.* long-pepper (Piper longum).
পিক, *s.* the black cuckoo (Cuculus indicus); the spittle when chewing betel.
পিকদান, or পিকাদানী, *s.* a spitting-pot.
পিকবর, *a.* chief of cuckoos : *s.* an appellation applied to an excellent singer.
পিঙ্গ, পিঙ্গড়া, *a.* tawny, brownish-yellow.
পিঙ্গল, *s.* brownish-yellow colour : tawny.
পিঙ্গলা, *s.* a particular vessel of the body.
পিচকারী, *s.* a syringe, a squirt, clyster-pipe ; -দা, to inject, administer enema.
পিচটী, *s.* the concrete rheum of the eyes.
পিচিণ্ড, *s.* the belly, the abdomen, pelvis.
পিচ্ছ, *s.* a peacock's tail, a crest, a tail.
পিচ্ছিল, *s.* sauce mixed with rice-gruel.
পিছ, *v. n.* to fall back, recede, go behind.
পিছপা, *s.* a receding, a falling back.
পিছল, *v. n.* to slip, to slide : *a.* slippery, wet.
পিছলন, *s.* the slipping of the feet.
পিছা, *v. a.* to repel, to cause to go back, to cause to desist ; to fall back.
পিছাড়ী, *s.* the hinder part, the stern, the rear, the hinder feet ropes of a horse.
পিছান, *s.* hinder part; receding, desisting.
পিছাপিছি, *ad.* behind, following behind.
পিছু, পিছে, *ad.* behind, after, afterwards.
পিছুলা, *v. a.* to slip : *a.* last : *s.* slippery.
পিঞ্জ, *v. a.* to card cotton or wool.
পিঞ্জর, *s.* a cage, a bird-cage, the ribs, the thorax.
পিট, *v. a.* to strike, beat, hammer, punish.
পিটন, *s.* a beating, a striking, a hammering.
পিটনা, *s.* a mason's floor-rammer.
পিটা, *s.* a sort of cake : *v. a.* to cause to beat or hammer, to beat, hammer out.
পিটান, *s.* a beating, the causing to beat or hammer : *a.* beaten, hammered out.
পিটাপিটি, *s.* reciprocal beating.
পিটালী, *s.* pulp of rice made into a paste ; a fish.
পিট্‌পিট্, *s.* peevishness ; a tingling, an itching.
পিট্‌পিটা, *v. a.* to itch, tingle.
পিঠ, *s.* the back ; the same with পিড়ী.
পিঠবোকচা, *s.* a knapsack, bundle.
পিঠাপিঠি, *ad.* one after the other, back to back.
পিড়া, *s.* a raised floor, a stool, a portico.
পিড়িঙ্গ, *s.* the name of an edible plant.[1]
পিড়ী, *s.* a stool, a terrace, the pedestal of an idol.
পিণাক, *s.* name of Shiva's bow.
পিণ্ড, *s.* a mass, lump, ball, funeral cake.
পিণ্ডখর্জ্জুর, *s.* Arabian preserved dates.
পিণ্ডদান, *s.* the offering of a funeral cake.
পিণ্ডী, *s.* a mass, lump, ball, funeral cake.
পিণ্ডীকৃত, *a.* become a mass or ball.
পিণ্ডীভূত, *a.* made up into a mass or ball.
পিত্তল, brass ; -ময়, brazen, made of brass.
পিতা, *s.* a father ; -মাতা, parents. [má.
পিতামহ, *s.* a paternal grandfather ; Brah-
পিতামহী, *s.* a paternal grandmother.
পিতৃ, *a.* paternal : *s.* a father.
পিতৃ -কর্ম্ম, -ক্রিয়া, -কৃত্য, *s.* the ceremonies due to ancestors, funeral obsequies.
পিতৃকুল, *s.* paternal race or family.
পিতৃ -ঘাতক, -দ্রোহী, *a.* parricide : *s.* a parricide.
পিতৃধন, *s.* paternal or hereditary property.
পিতৃপক্ষ, *a.* paternal: *s.* paternal relations.
পিতৃপতি, *s.* Yama, the regent of death.
পিতৃপদ, *s.* the office held by a father.
পিতৃপিতামহাদি, paternal ancestry, progenitors.
পিতৃপুরুষ, *s.* paternal ancestors.
পিতৃবান্ধব, *s.* the son of a grandfather's sister, the son of the sister of a father's mother, the son of a father's uncle.
পিতৃব্য, *s.* a paternal uncle.
পিতৃভক্ত, *a.* devoted to a father.
পিতৃভক্তি, *s.* devotedness to a father.
পিতৃমাতৃহীন, *a.* bereft of parents, orphan.
পিতৃলোক, *s.* an ancestor, ancestors, forefathers.
পিতৃস্বসা, *s.* a paternal aunt.
পিতৃহত্যা, *s.* the murder of a father.
পিত্ত, *s.* bile, gall ; -কোষ, the gall-bladder.
পিত্তঘ্ন, *a.* antibilious, destroying bile.
পিত্তজ্বর, *s.* a bilious fever.
পিত্তল, *s.* brass;-ময়, brazen, made of brass.
পিত্তোল্বন, *s.* an excess of bile ; bilious fever.
পিত্র্য, *a.* paternal, hereditary.
পিধান, *s.* a cover, a covering, wrapper, cloak.
পিনিস, *s.* a pinnace, a pleasure boat.
পিন্ধ্, *v. a.* to put on clothes, to dress.

পিন্ধন, *s.* a dressing, putting on of clothes.
পিপা, পিপে, *s.* a barrel, a pipe, a cask.
পিপাসা, *s.* desire, thirst, drought.
পিপাসিত, *a.* athirst, thirsty.
পিপাসী, পিপাসু, পিপাসান্বিত, *a.* thirsty.
পিপীড়া, পিপীলি, পিপীলিকা, *s.* an ant.
পিপুল, or পিপ্পলী, *s.* long-pepper.
পিপুলপাতা, *s.* an ornament for the ear.
পিপ্পলীমূল, *s.* the root of long-pepper.
পিয়া, *v. a.* to cause to drink; a corruption [of প্রিয়.
পিয়াজ, পেয়াজ, *s.* an onion.
পিয়াদা, *s.* a footman, a messenger.
পিয়ারা, *a.* beloved: *s.* a lover; a guava.
পিয়াল, *s.* the name of a fruit tree.[1]
পিয়ালা, *s.* a cup, a tea cup, a water glass.
পিয়ালাবাজ, *s.* a drunkard, a tippler.
পিয়ালাবাজী, *s.* drunkenness, tippling.
পিয়াশাল, *s.* the name of a timber tree.[2]
পিয়াস, *s.* thirst. পিয়াসা, *a.* thirsty.
পিরিচ, or পিরিজ, *s.* *Port.* a saucer.
পিরিতি, প্রীতি, *s.* love, affection, kindness.
পিল, *s.* unfledged bird, a young animal.
পিলা, পিলুই, *s.* the spleen, the spleen dis- [ease.
পিল্‌পিল্, *s.* a crowd, a multitude.
পিলসুজ, *s.* lampstand, candlestick.
পিশাচ, *s.* fiends, demigods with horses' [heads.
পিশু, *s.* a flea. পিশিত, *s.* flesh, meat.
পিশুন, *s.* saffron, a crow; sage Nárada, cotton, a spy; *a.* cruel, wicked, mean, low, base, contemptible, stupid, foolish.
পিশুনতা, *s.* cruelty, wickedness, meanness, [stupidity.
পিষ্, *v. a.* to grind, to bruise.
পিষ্টক, *s.* baked meats, bread, a cake.
পিসা, *s.* a father's sister's husband.
পিসাস, *s.* a wife's or husband's paternal [aunt.
পিসী, *s.* a paternal aunt. [or daughter.
পিস্তুত-ভাই, -বহিন, *s.* a paternal aunt's son
পীআ, *a.* beloved: *s.* a husband, a lover.
পীড়ি, *s.* a stool, a bench, a terrace.
পীট্, *v. a.* to strike, to beat.
পীটন, *s.* a striking, a beating, a hammer- [ing.
পীঠ, *s.* the back, a page or side of a leaf, a stool, a bench, a pedestal, a terrace.
পীঠমর্দ্দ, *s.* a lover who labours to appease an offended or angry mistress.
পীড়্, *v. a.* to cause pain, to bruise, to express the juice of the sugarcane, etc.
পীড়ক, *a.* hurtful, distressing, sore, vexatious: *s.* a persecutor, an oppressor.
পীড়ন, *s.* act of giving pain, persecuting, tormenting, a bruising of seeds.
পীড়নীয়, পীড়িতব্য, *a.* sensible, susceptible of pain, deserving to be pained.
পীড়া, *s.* pain, affliction, torture, distress.
পীড়িত, *a.* pained, afflicted, ill, sick.
পীড়্যমান, *a.* suffering pain or distress.
পীত, *a.* yellow; drunk up; *s.* safflower, a topaz, yellow orpiment, turmeric.
পীতচন্দন, পীতসার, *s.* yellow sanders.
পীতরস, *s.* turmeric. [bell-metal.
পীতলোহ, *s.* yellow brass, queen's metal,
পীতাম্বর, *a.* clothed in yellow: *s.* a name of [Krishna.
পীতাশ্ম, পীতসার, *s.* a topaz.
পীন, *a.* fat, plump, sleek, smooth: *s.* a pin. [a peg.
পীনস, *s.* a disease of the nose.
পীনোঘ্নী, *a.* having large breasts or udder,
পীবন্, *a.* fat, plump, large, sleek, fleshy.
পীবর, *a.* plump, fat, large, lusty. [ness.
পীবরতা, -ত্ব, *s.* plumpness, largeness, ful-
পীযূষ, *s.* nectar, water of immortality, [cow's first milk.
পীল, *s.* a young bird.
পীলা, *s.* the spleen: *a.* yellow.
পীষ্, *v. a.* to grind, rub, bruise. [fritters.
পুআ, *s.* a fourth part, a quarter; a kind of
পুআল, *s.* straw, rice straw. [manhood.
পুং, man, male, masculine; -শক্তি, virility,
পুংবৎ, *ad.* manlike, manly, masculine.
পুংবৎস্ত্রী, *s.* a virago, a masculine woman.
পুংলিঙ্গ, *s.* in *gram.* the masculine gender.
পুংশ্চলী, *a.* going to men, loose, whorish.
পুঁএসাপ, *s.* a snake like earthworm.
পুঁচ্, *v. a.* to wipe, to rub off, to wipe off.
পুঁচন, *s.* a wiping, a wiping or rubbing off.
পুঁচা, *v. a.* to cause to wipe, or rub off.
পচান, *s.* the causing to wipe or rub off.
পুঁজ, *s.* purulent matter, pus.
পুঁজময়, *a.* full of purulent matter.
পুঁজী, *s.* a heap, a hoard, wealth, cash, a stock or capital in trade. [goods.
পুঁজীপাটা, *s.* wealth, substance, capital,
পুঁজীবালা, *a.* possessing wealth, rich.
পুঁটলী, *s.* a bundle, a packet, a parcel.
পুঁটলীয়া, *s.* round hand (in writing).
পুটকী, *s.* the anus.

পুঁটা, *a.* low, mean, despicable : *s.* a but-
পুটাঘরা, *s.* a button-hole, a loop. [ton.
পুঁটাতেলী, *a.* greedy, niggardly, avaricious.
পুঁঠী, *s.* the name of a species of fish.[1]
পুঁড়া, *s.* a store-house ; seller of vegetables.
পুক্, *v. n.* to be infected with maggots (as
পুকুর, *s.* a pond, pool, tank. [an ulcer).
পুকুরীয়া, *a.* belonging to a pond.
পুঙ্খ, *s.* the feather of an arrow.
পুঙ্গব, *s.* a bull : *a.* eminent, chief.
পুচ্ছ, *s.* the tail of an animal.
পুছ্, *v. a.* to ask, enquire, to interrogate.
পুছা, *v. a.* to cause to ask or interrogate : *s.* a question, enquiry ; পুছার করণ, to question a person, enquire of a person.
পুঞ্জা, s. a rotten rag, a rag, a fragment.
পুঞ্জ, *s.* a heap, a heap of grain or the like.
পুঞ্জমান, *a.* increasing to heap, plenty.
পুট, *s.* a joining of the hands, a pair, a
পুড়্, *v. a.* to burn, to burn away. [cover.
পুড়ন, *s.* a burning, a kindling.
পুড়ী, *a.* burnt up by the sun : *s.* the teeth of a saw or sickle ; a sort of sugarcane.
পুণ্য, *s.* purity, holiness, virtue, religious merit, a good action : *a.* pure, holy, virtuous, righteous, beautiful, pleasing.
পুণ্যকর্ত্তা, *s.* one who performs holy actions.
পুণ্যকর্ম্ম, *s.* a meritorious or holy action.
পুণ্যকর্ম্মা, *a.* performing holy actions.
পুণ্যফল, *s.* the fruits of purity or holiness.
পুণ্যবন্ত, *a.* pure, holy, virtuous, religious.
পুণ্যবান, পুণ্যশালী, পুণ্যশীল, *a.* righteous,
পুণ্যভূমি, *s.* a holy place. [meritorious.
পুণ্যস্বরূপ, *a.* identified with purity, holiness, or religious merits. [or holiness.
পুণ্যাঙ্কুর, *s.* the first appearance of purity
পুণ্যাচরণ, *s.* a virtuous or holy life.
পুণ্যাচারী, *a.* leading a pure or holy life.
পুণ্যাত্মক, *a.* consisting of or identified with purity, holiness or religious merit.
পুণ্যাত্মা, *a.* holy, pure, religious, virtuous.
পুণ্যাপুণ্য, *s.* holiness and the want of it.
পুণ্যার্থী, *a.* desirous of religious merits.
পুণ্যার্থে, *ad.* for the sake of religious merits.
পুণ্যাহ, *s.* the day on which the tenants make the first payment of their rents.
পুণ্যী, *a.* holy, meritorious, sacred.

পুং, *v. a.* to plant, to set a stake or post in the ground, to bury. [(an abuse).
পুত, *s.* a son ; -খাগী, *fem.* son-devouring
পুতন, *s.* a burying, planting, setting up.
পুতুল, পুত্তলিকা, *s.* an image, a doll, a pup-
পুত্তলী, *s. idem ;* image on the eye. [pet.
পুত্তলীপূজক, an idolater, idol-worshipper.
পুত্তলীপূজা, *s.* idolatry, image worship.
পুত্র, *s.* a son ; -গণ, a number of sons.
পুত্রতা, পুত্রত্ব, পুত্রভাব, *s.* sonship. [son.
পুত্রতুল্য, পুত্রবৎ, *a.* like a son, equal to a
পুত্রপৌত্রাদি, *s.* posterity. [ness for a son.
পুত্র-বৎসল, *a.* fond of a son ; -বাৎসল্য, fond-
পুত্রবতী, *a. fem.* having a son.
পুত্রবধূ, *s.* a son's wife, a daughter-in-law.
পুত্রবান্, *a.* having a son or male children.
পুত্রবিহীন, পুত্রহীন, *a.* sonless, childless.
পুত্রসন্তান, or পুত্রসন্ততি, *s.* male posterity, a
পুত্রার্থী, *a.* desirous of a son. [male child.
পুত্রার্থে, *ad.* for the purpose of a son.
পুত্রিকা, *s* a daughter ; a doll, a puppet.
পুত্রিকাপুত্র, *s.* a daughter's son.
পুত্রী, *s.* a daughter : *a.* having a son.
পুত্রীয়, *a.* filial, relating to a son.
পুত্রেষ্টি, *s.* a sacrifice made for obtaining
পুথী, *s.* a book, a volume. [a son.
পুদিনা, *s.* the herb mint (Mentha sativa).
পুন, *conj.* but. পুনঃ, *ad.* again, once more.
পুনঃপুনঃ, *ad.* repeatedly, again and again.
পুনঃসঙ্কোচন, *s.* a collapsing. [also.
পুনরপি, *conj.* once more, again and again,
পুনরাগমন, *s.* a returning, a recurrence.
পুনরাবৃত্তি, *s.* a return, turning back again.
পুনরায়, *ad.* again, over again.
পুনরাশা, *s.* revived hope.
পুনরুক্ত, *a.* repeated, spoken again.
পুনরুক্তি, *s.* a repetition, a tautology.
পুনরুত্থান, *s.* the resurrection.
পুনরুত্থাপিত, *a.* raised again. [lenting.
পুনরুত্থিত, *a.* risen again. পুনর্দয়া, *s.* a re-
পুনর্জন্ম, *s.* regeneration, second birth, recovery from dangerous illness.
পুনর্জাত, *a.* regenerated, born again.
পুনর্দৃষ্টি, *s.* a revisal, a revision, a review.
পুনর্নবা, *s.* a plant (Boerhaavia diffusa).
পুনর্নিযুক্ত, *a.* re-appointed.
পুনর্নিয়োগ, *s.* a re-appointment.

পুনর্ব্বসু, *s.* the seventh mansion in the zodiac.
পুনর্ব্বার, *ad.* again, another time.
পুনর্ব্বিচার, *s.* a re-investigation.
পুনর্ব্বিচারপ্রার্থনা, *s.* an appeal to another tribunal.
পুনর্ব্বিবাহ, *s.* a second marriage, or first appearance of menses in a married girl.
পুনর্ভব, *s.* a finger or toe nail; regeneration.
পুনর্ভূ, *s.* a twice-married virgin widow.
পুনশ্চ, *ad.* again, yet again, once more.
পুমান্, *s.* a male, a man.
পুর, *s.* a city, a town, a habitation, a place.
পুরঃ, *ad.* in front, formerly.
পুরঃসর, *a.* preceding, going before, going forward.
পুরদ্বার, *s.* a city gate.
পুরন্দর, *s.* Indra, the king of the gods.
পুরন্ধ্রী, *s.* a matron, a housewife.
পুরব, পূর্ব্ব, *a.* east, eastern.
পুরস্করণীয়, পুরস্কার্য্য, *a.* fit to be promoted or rewarded.
পুরস্কর্ত্তা, *s.* he who honours or promotes.
পুরস্কার, *s.* a royal gift, a reward, remuneration, present, promotion, honour.
পুরস্কারবস্ত্র *s.* an honorary dress.
পুরস্কারী, *a.* honouring, promoting.
পুরস্কৃত, *a.* honoured, advanced, promoted, remunerated, rewarded.
পুরস্তাৎ, *ad.* in front, from the forepart: *a.* eastward.
পুরস্ত্রী, *s.* mistress of a family, a housewife.
পুরস্থ, *a.* standing before, staying at home.
পুরস্থিত, *a.* situated before.
পুরা, *ad.* before: *a.* complete, full: *s.* a dose.
পুরাণ, *a.* old, ancient: *s.* the ancient history or mythology of the Hindus.
পুরাণমত, *a.* approved by the puránas.
পুরাণশাস্ত্র, *s.* the writings called puránas.
পুরাতন, *a.* old, ancient, antique.
পুরাতনকথা, *s.* ancient story, legend, tradition.
পুরাধ্যক্ষ, *s.* the governor of a city, or of a house.
পুরি, *s.* a sort of fried pancake.
*পুরিয়া, *s.* a dose; a small packet.
পুরী, *s.* a city, a town, a palace, residence.
পুরীষ, *s.* dung, ordure, excrement.
পুরু, *a.* thick, coarse. পুরুত, *s.* a priest.
পুরুম, *s.* a plumbline, a mason's plumbline.
পুরুষ, *a.* male: *s.* a male, man, a generation, the soul, God, the supreme Being, the sensitive soul, life.
পুরুষকার, *s.* human action or conduct, human exertion.

পুরুষক্রমে, *ad.* in successive generations.
পুরুষত্ব, *s.* manliness, manhood, virility.
পুরুষত্বপ্রকাশ, *s.* a display of manliness.
পুরুষপরম্পরা, *s.* a succession of generations.
পুরুষমাত্র, *s.* merely a man.
পুরুষসিংহ, *s.* an eminent man, a lion of a man.
পুরুষাকার, *a.* human-formed.
পুরুষাঙ্গ, *s.* the male organ of generation.
পুরুষাধম, *s.* a vile or base man.
পুরুষানুক্রম, *s.* a succession of generations.
পুরুষানুক্রমে, *ad.* successively, from generation to generation.
পুরুষার্থ, *s.* manliness, courage, an object of human life.
পুরুষোত্তম, *s.* Vishnu, an eminent man.
পুরোগমন, *s.* a going before or in front.
পুরোবর্ত্তী, পুরোগ, preceding, going before.
পুরোহিত, পুরোধাঃ, *s.* a family priest.
পুর্খা, *a.* shrewd, acute: *s.* an ancestor.
পুল্, *s.* a bank, a dam, a dike, a bridge.
পুল্বন্দি, *s.* an embankment.
পুলক, *s.* erection of the hair of the body through delight or pleasure.
পুলকিত, *a.* overjoyed, glad, delighted, airy, gay.
পুলা, *s.* a sheaf, a bundle, a wisp (of hay).
পুলি, -পিটা, *s.* a sort of cake or sweetmeat.
পুলিন, *s.* a shoal, an island, a strand.
পুলিন্দা, *s.* a bundle, a parcel, a package.
*পুশীদা, *a.* secret, hidden, concealed.
পুষ্, *v. a.* to nourish, to feed.
পুষিত, *a.* nourished, fed, fattened.
পুষ্কর, *s.* water, the sky, the atmosphere, a waterlily, tip of an elephant's trunk, the art of dancing, war, intoxication, union, a cage, a port, a pond, a lake.
পুষ্করদ্বীপ, *s.* name of one of the seven continents in the Hindu geography.
পুষ্করিণী, *s.* a pond, a pool, a tank.
পুষ্কল, *a.* much, many: *s.* feather of an arrow.
পুষ্ট, *a.* nourished, maintained, fed.
পুষ্টতা, *s.* a thriving condition of the body.
পুষ্টি, *s.* nourishment, maintenance, support, increase, prosperity, a good condition of body, a prop, a shore, a bank.
পুষ্টি-কর, -জনক, *a.* nutritious, nourishing.
পুষ্প, *s.* a flower, blossom; the menses.
পুষ্পক, *s.* a flower, calx of brass, copperas, speck on the eye, Kuvera's chariot.

পুষ্পকাসীশ, *s.* the green sulphate of iron.
পুষ্পবৃষ্টি, *s.* a shower of flowers.
পুষ্পময়, *a.* full of flowers, flowery.
পুষ্পরস, *s.* honey, the honey of flowers.
পুষ্পরেণু, *s.* the pollen of a flower.
পুষ্পশয্যা, *s.* a bed of flowers. [an author.
পুষ্পিকা, *s.* a chapter, division of a book ;
পুষ্পিত, *a.* in flower, covered with flowers.
পুষ্পোদ্যান, *s.* a flower garden, a parterre.
পুষ্যা, *s.* the eighth mansion in the zodiac.
পুস্তক, *s.* a book, volume ;-কীট, bookworm.
পুস্তকাগার, or পুস্তকালয়, *s.* a library.
পুস্তা, *s.* an embankment, a shore, a prop.
পুঁই, *s.* an edible plant (Basella alba).
পুঁজ, *s.* pus, matter, the purulent matter.
পূগ, *s.* a multitude, a heap, a quantity, nature, disposition, betel-nut. [shipper.
পূজক, *a.* honouring, worshipping : *s.* a wor-
পূজন, *s.* a showing respect to or honouring of a superior, a worshipping.
পূজনীয়, পূজ্য, *a.* worthy of worship or honour, honourable, worshipful, venerable.
পূজয়িতা, *s.* a worshipper, adorer. [tion.
পূজা, *s.* worship, honour, homage, adora-
পূজারী, *s.* a worshipper, a priest. [ted.
পূজিত, *a.* worshipped, honoured, venera-
পূজ্যতা, *s.* worshipfulness, venerableness.
পূট, *s.* a flux for metals, a menstruum.
পূত, *a.* pure, clean, holy, sincere, honest, speaking truth ; threshed, winnowed.
পূততা, -ত্ব, *s* purity, holiness, sanctity.
পূতাত্মা, *a.* pure, holy : *s.* the Holy Spirit.
পূতি, putrid, musty, corrupted : *s.* purity, sanctity, purification, holiness, truth.
পূতিকা, *s.* a civet-cat ; a potherb ; *vide* পুঁই.
পূতাণ্ড, *s.* the musk-deer ; the flying-bug.
পূপ, *s.* bread, loaf, cake ; -কার, a baker.
পূবীয়, *a.* eastern ; -বাতাস, east wind.
পূবে, *ad.* easterly, eastward, in the east.
পূয়, *s.* putridity ; pus, matter. [an ulcer).
পূর্, *v. n.* to fill or become full, to heal (as
পূর, high, full (as water,) thick : *s.* a city, town, habitation, lake, healing of ulcer.
পূরক, *s.* a multiplier ; inspiration ; a citron : *a.* filling, fulfilling, completing.
পূরট, *a.* filled up, choked up, full.
পূরণ, *s.* the act of filling up, the charging of a gun, the multiplying of numbers, the completing of a work. [pleted.
পূরণীয়, *a.* capable of being filled or com-
পূরা, *s.* a filling up, a completing : *a.* full, complete, perfect, plenary, copious : *v. a.* to fill, to complete, to accomplish.
পূরাণ, *s.* the filling up of a cavity, the making a thing complete : *a.* filled.
পূরিত, *a.* full, filled, completed, accom-
পূরী, *s.* a sort of pancake. [plished.
পূরু, *a.* thick, gross, coarse, full.
পূরুষ, *s.* a man, a male, mankind.
পূর্ব্বা, *a.* shrewd, active, old : *s.* an ancestor.
পূর্ণ, *a.* full, filled, complete, whole, entire,
পূর্ণকাল, *s.* complete or full time. [perfect.
পূর্ণপাত্র, *s.* a full vessel, present to a priest.
পূর্ণমা, or পূর্ণমাসী, *s.* day of full moon.
পূর্ণিত, পূর্ণমাত্রা, *a.* full, complete, entire.
পূর্ণিমা, or পূর্ণচন্দ্র, *s.* the full moon.
পূর্ত্তি, *s.* fulness, repletion, completion.
পূর্ব্ব, *a.* first, preceding, foregoing, former, ancient, prior, preliminary, east, eastern, fronting, before : *s.* the ancestors.
পূর্ব্বজ, *a.* previously produced, first-born,
পূর্ব্বদিক, *s.* the east quarter. [eldest.
পূর্ব্বদিকস্থ, *a.* situated in the east.
পূর্ব্বদিন, *s.* yesterday, the preceding day.
পূর্ব্বদৃষ্টি, *s.* foresight, a former view of an
পূর্ব্বদেশ, *s.* the east country. [object.
পূর্ব্বদেশী, পূর্ব্বদেশীয়, *a.* oriental, eastern.
পূর্ব্বনিয়ম, *s.* a preliminary. [destiny, luck.
পূর্ব্বনির্ব্বন্ধ, *s.* preliminary agreement, fate,
পূর্ব্বপক্ষ, *s.* a thesis, a proposition, the major proposition in a sylogism. [nitor.
পূর্ব্বপুরুষ, *s.* ancestor, forefather, a proge-
পূর্ব্বফল্গুনী, *s.* the eleventh mansion in the
পূর্ব্ববৎ, *ad.* as before, as formerly. [zodiac.
পূর্ব্ববর্ত্তিতা, *s.* precedence. [previouslp.
পূর্ব্ববর্ত্তী, *a.* previous, preceding, existing
পূর্ব্ববাদ, *s.* a former assertion or plea.
পূর্ব্ববাদী, speaking in the first instance. *s.* in *law*, the plaintiff, the first speaker.
পূর্ব্বভাদ্রপদ, *s.* 25th mansion in the zodiac.
পূর্ব্বভাব, *s.* the first or prior state or con-
পূর্ব্বমত, *a.* like the foregoing. [dition.
পূর্ব্বরাত্র, *s.* the past night, yesternight, former part of the night.

পূর্ব্বলিখিত, *a.* abovestated, forementioned, forecited.
পূর্ব্বাধিকারী, *s.* a prior owner.
পূর্ব্বাপর, *a.* in regular order; chronic.
পূর্ব্বাবধি, from antiquity, or a former time.
পূর্ব্বাবস্থা, *s.* a former state or condition.
পূর্ব্বাষাঢ়া, *s.* the twentieth mansion in the zodiac.
পূর্ব্বাহ্ন, *s.* the forenoon, morning.
পূর্ব্বীয়, *a.* eastern, easterly.
পূর্ব্বে, *ad.* before, previously; eastward.
পূর্ব্বেদ্যুঃ, *ad.* on a former day; yesterday.
পূর্ব্বোক্ত, *a.* beforespoken, aforesaid, forementioned.
পূর্য্য, capable of being filled.
পৃক্ত, *a.* smeared, mixed, combined with
পৃথক্, *a.* apart, separate, distinct; -করণ, the making a separation, a separating
পৃথক্ত্ব, *s.* separateness, distinctness.
পৃথক্‌পৃথক্, *ad.* separately, distinctly.
পৃথিবী, *s.* the earth; -তল, the surface of the earth; -পতি, a king, a sovereign.
পৃথিবীমণ্ডল, *s.* the orb of the earth.
পৃথুক, চিড়া, *s.* rice soaked and flattened.
পৃথ্বী, *s.* the earth, the base of a triangle.
পৃষৎ, *s.* the porcine deer; a drop of water.
পৃষ্ট, *a.* asked, interrogated, questioned.
পৃষ্ঠ, flat surface, the back, page of a book.
পৃষ্ঠকণ্টক, *s.* the processes of the spine.
পৃষ্ঠতঃ, *ad.* behind the back, behind, in the rear.
পৃষ্ঠা, *s.* a page, the page of a book.
পৃষ্ঠাবর্ত্তক, *s.* the vertebra of the back.
পেঁক, *s.* mire, mud, the voice of a duck.
পেঁকপেঁক, *s.* the quacking of a duck.
পেঁচ, *s.* a screw, a spiral motion, intricacy, perplexity, an intricate scheme.
পেঁচপাঁচ, *s.* a machination, intricacy.
পেঁচা, *v. a.* to screw: *s.* an owl.
পেঁচাও, *s.* a turning; a schemer: *a.* spiral, intricate.
পেঁচান, spiral, twisted: *s.* a twist, turning.
পেঁচানিয়া, *a.* making things intricate.
পেচাপেঁচি, *s.* an intricacy, a difficulty.
পেঁচাল, *a.* artful, intricate, tortuous, spiral.
পেঁচি, *a.* disputatious, litigious.
পেঁচিমাতাল, *s.* a litigious or quarrelsome sot.
পেঁচুআ, *s.* hysterics: *a.* spiral, intricate.
পেঁচুআনল, *s.* a long huká-snake.
পেঁচুটি, *s.* the sordes of the eyes.
পেঁজন, *s.* the carding of wool or cotton.
পেঁজা, *v. a.* to cause cotton to be carded.

পেঁজান, *s.* a causing to card cotton.
পেঁপিয়া, *s.* a tree and its fruit.[1]
পেকনা, *s.* an excuse, a pretension, coquetry, amorous jest, a mocking, a jesting.
পেকম, *s.* feather, a peacock's expanding of it's feathers.
পেচক, or পেচা, *s.* an owl.
পেট, *s.* the belly, the fœtus, the womb, pregnancy; -কামড়া, -খুঁচ, to have a griping; -খস্, to miscarry; -ফেল, to have an abortion; -নাম, or -চল্, to have a dysentery or purging; -জ্বালা, to starve any one; -ভরা, to satisfy the appetite; -ডক্, to rumble in the bowels; -ফাঁপ্, or -ফুল, to be flatulent, to be hoven; -ধৃ, to stop the purging; -হ, to be pregnant.
পেটআঁটন, *s.* a costive state of the bowels.
পেটকামড়ানী, *s.* a griping of the bowels.
পেটক্কা, intemperate, gluttonous, greedy.
পেটখসা, *s.* a miscarriage, an abortion.
পেটচলা, *s.* a dysentery, a diarrhœa.
পেটধরণ, *s.* the stopping of loose bowels.
পেটন, *s.* a beating, a hammering.
পেটনরম, *a.* lax in the bowels.
পেটনামন, *s.* a looseness of the bowels.
পেটপোড়া, *s.* a medicine used to procure abortion, also, to prevent conception.
পেটফাঁপন, *s.* a distention of the bowels.
পেটফেলন, *s.* the producing of abortion.
পেটবন্ধ, *s.* the cure of a dysentery.
পেট-ভরা, *s.* repletion; -শূল, the colic.
পেটভাঙ্গা, *s.* a diarrhœa, a dysentery.
পেটরোগা, *a.* diseased in the bowels.
পেটসর্ব্বস্ব, *a.* making the belly one's all: *s.* a glutton.
পেটহওন, *s.* a being pregnant.
পেটা, *v. a.* to cause to beat or hammer.
পেটারা, *s.* a clothes-basket, portmanteau; a balloon.
পেটারী, *s.* *idem.*
পেটার্থী, voluptuous, gluttonous, greedy.
পেটাল, *a.* large-bellied, pot-bellied.
পেটিয়াপাড়ন, *s.* the dressing of a woman's hair by parting it on the forehead.
পেটী, *s.* a box, a chest, aw icker basket.
পেটুক, *a.* gluttonous, ravenous, greedy.
পেটুকামী, *s.* gluttony, ravenousness.
পেটুয়া, *a.* included, large-bellied.
পেটোয়াল, *s.* one who is included in another's office or account, a mate.

পেড়া, *v. a.* to grind, squeeze : *s.* a portmanteau, a sort of sweetmeat, young buffalo.
পেড়েমারণ, *s.* a throwing down and beating.
পেতনা, *s.* a sloven, a dirty fellow.
পেতনী, *s.* an apparition, a spectre, a slut.
পেতনীব, পেতনীবৎ, *s.* a slut, a slattern.
পেতিয়া, *s.* a basket, a covered basket.
পেতিয়ান, *s.* a stand to support boxes, bales, etc.
পেদোপোকা, *s.* a flying-bug.
পেনেট, *s.* the female part of the Phallus.
পেয়, potable, drinkable, fit for drinking: *s.* a drink.
পেয়াজ, *s.* onion (Allium cepa).
পেয়াদা, *s.* a footman, a messenger, a peon.
পেয়াদাগিরী, *s.* the business of a footman.
*পেয়ার, *s.* affection, love, fondness.
পেয়ারা, affectionate, beloved: *s.* a guava.
পেয়ালা, *s.* a cup, a teacup, a sneaker, a bowl.
পেরু, *s. Port.* a turkey.
পেরেক, *s.* a nail, a spike.
*পেশ, *s.* the front, forepart : *a.* confided in, trusted.
*পেশকবজ্, *s.* a dagger, a stiletto, a dirk.
*পেশকার, *s.* an agent, a deputy, a manager, an assistant ; পেশকারী, his office.
*পেশগী, *s.* an advance (of wages or cash).
পেশল, *a.* clever, eminent, famous, beautiful, heart-ravishing, crafty, knavish.
পেশা, *s.* a profession, trade, custom, practice, habit ; -দার, holding a profession.
পেশী, *s.* egg of a bird, a scabbard, a muscle, a lump of flesh, spikenard, a bud.
পেষক, *a.* grinding, masticating.
পেষকদন্ত, পেষণদন্ত, *s.* large teeth, grinders.
পেষণ, *s.* grinding of corn, etc. ; a muller ; bandage.
পেষণী, *s.* a millstone, muller.
পেষণীয়, *a.* capable of being ground.
পৈঠা, *s.* one step of a staircase ; a flight of steps.
পৈতা, *s.* the Hindu sacred thread.
পৈতামহ, *a.* relating to a grandfather.
পৈতৃক, *a.* ancestral, paternal ; -ধন, a patrimony ; -বৃত্তি, paternal inheritance.
পৈতৃকাধিকার, *s.* ancestral inheritance.
পৈতৃষ্বস্রীয়, *s.* the son of a paternal aunt.
পৈত্তিক, *a.* bilious, of the nature of bile.
পৈত্র্য, *a.* ancestral, paternal, hereditary.
পৈশাচ, *a.* devilish, demoniacal, infernal.
পৈশাচবিবাহ, *s.* a marriage in which the bride is decoyed away by stratagem.

পৈশুন্য, *s.* defamation, backbiting, slander, spite, cruelty.
পো, *s.* a son, a child.
পোআ, *s.* quarter, 4th part, pedal-posts.
পোআতী, *a.* pregnant, mother of child.
পোআন, *s.* a potter's kiln ; a basking.
পোআল, *s.* straw, rice straw.
পোঁচ, *s.* a whitewash, the plaster of a wall, a coating.
পোঁচড়া, *s.* a whitewashing, plastering ; a wiping brush, a whitewashing brush.
পোঁচমাটি, *s.* a potter's glazing earth.
পোঁচা, *v. a.* to cause to wipe : *s.* the wrist.
পোঁটা, *s.* a gut, entrails of a fish or other animal, the mucus of the nose, snot.
পোঁদ, *s.* the anus, the hips, the posteriors.
পোঁদছেঁচড়ি, *s.* a dragging along by the legs while a person sits on the ground.
পোঁদপট্কা, *s.* laxness of the bowels.
পোঁদাপোঁদি, *ad.* rump to rump, closely.
পোকা, *s.* an insect, a worm, a maggot.
পোকাকাটা, পোকাখেকুয়া, *a.* worm-eaten.
পোক্ত, *a.* ripe, cooked, complete, perfect.
পোক্তান, or পোক্তানী, *s.* ripeness, a being complete, the boiling of salt.
পোগণ্ড, *s.* a beardless boy: *a.* deformed.
পোঙ্গা, *s.* the anus, the privities.
পোট, *s.* a foundation, a basis ; back of a book.
পোটা, *s.* a woman with a beard.
পোড়, *a.* baked, burnt, calcined.
পোড়ল্মাটি, *s.* a kind of burnt earth.
পোড়া, *v. a.* to burn, to destroy by fire, to roast, to scald : *a.* burnt, roasted.
পোড়াকপাল, *s.* a misfortune, bad luck.
পোড়াকপালিয়া, *a.* unlucky, unfortunate, wretched ; *lit.* having burnt forehead.
পোড়ান, *s.* a burning, a searing, a roasting.
পোড়ানারাঙ্গা, *s.* a disease of the skin.
পোড়ানি, *s.* a burning or calcining, calcination : *a.* due for burning things.
পোড়ানিয়া, *a.* incendiary, burning.
পোৎ, *v. a.* the same as পুৎ, which see.
পোত, *s.* a boat, ship, young of an animal, glass beads, foundation, the floor, cloth.
পোতন, *s.* the same with পুতন.
পোতবণিক্, *s.* a merchant who trades by sea, a voyaging merchant.
পোতবাহ, *s.* a boatman, steersman, sailor, rower.
পোতবাহক, *s.* a mariner, a ship-captain.

পোতা, *s.* a burying, the floor, a canton, a seaman, a waterman, the testicles.
পোতাধান, *s.* young fry, a shoal of young fish.
পোদ, *s.* a low caste of Hindus.
পোদ্দার, *s.* a money-changer, a banker.
পোদ্দারী, *s.* the business of a banker.
পোনা, *s.* young fry, the young of fish.
পোনের, *a.* fifteen. পোনেরঞি, fifteenth.
পোয়া, *v. a.* to warm one's self, to bask.
পোয়াতি, *s.* a newly confined woman.
পোরা, *v. a.* to load, fill: *s.* a load, freight.
পোলা, *s.* a son, a child; *fem.* পুলী.
পোলাও, *s.* a dish prepared with rice, butter, flesh, and hot spices.
পোলাত, *s.* steel. পোলো, *s.* a harpoon.
*পোশাক, *s.* clothing, dress.
পোশাকী, *a.* belonging to dress, fit for clothing.
পোশ্তু, *s.* the language of Affghan.
পোষ্, *v. a.* to maintain, cherish, nourish.
পোষক, *a.* nourishing, maintaining.
পোষণ, *s.* a nourishing, a maintaining.
পোষণীয়, *a.* proper to be maintained.
পোষা, *a.* tame, domestic: *s.* maintenance: *v. a.* to cause to nourish, to tame.
পোষাণ, *s.* a causing to be maintained, the recompensing of a person.
পোষ্টা, *s.* one who nourishes or maintains.
পোষ্য, *a.* requiring to be maintained.
পোষ্যপুত্র, *s.* an adopted son.
পোস্ত, *s.* a poppy (Papaver somniferum).
পোস্তা, or পোস্তাবন্দী, *s.* a bulwark, an embankment, a buttress.
পোহা, *v. n.* to become light, to dawn, to pass away.
পৌগণ্ড, *s.* a lad under sixteen years of age.
পৌঢ়ি, *s. properly* প্রৌঢ়ি, which see.
পৌত্র, *s.* a grandson, a son's son.
পৌত্রী, *s.* a son's daughter.
পৌনরুক্ত, *s.* a repetition, tautology.
পৌনর্ভব, *s.* the son of a twice-married woman by her latter husband.
পৌর, *a.* relating to a city, civil, civilized.
পৌরাণিক, *a.* well versed in the puránas: *s.* a professor of the puránas.
পৌরুষ, *s.* manhood, manliness, virility.
পৌর্ণমাসী, *a.* belonging to the full moon.
পৌষ, *s.* a Hindu month containing part of December and part of January.

পৌষ্টিক, *a.* nutritious, fattening.
প্যাঁদ, *s.* a diseased mass protruding from vulva.
প্র, a *prep.* in *comp.* it gives the idea of an increased degree or greater excellency of the action or thing.
প্রকট, manifest, evident, plain, notorious, displayed.
প্রকটিত, *a.* displayed, laid open, apparent.
প্রকরণ, *s.* a treatise, a chapter, a section of a book, the subject of a treatise, an affair, an introduction to a book, a prologue or prelude, a poetical fiction.
প্রকরণীয়, belonging to a treatise, belonging to the subject matter of a book.
প্রকর্ষিত, *a.* made to exceed: *s.* a surplus.
প্রকাণ্ড, *a.* tall, stout, strong, robust, stupendous, excellent, best: *s.* trunk of a tree.
প্রকাণ্ডকায়, *a.* gigantic, large-bodied.
প্রকার, *s.* a sort, a kind, a method, a manner.
প্রকারবিশেষ, *s.* a particular sort.
প্রকারান্তর, *s.* another sort: *a.* dissimilar, other.
প্রকারান্তরে, *ad.* otherwise, in another manner.
প্রকাল, *s.* a noted time; a long time.
প্রকাশ, *s.* expansion, diffusion, manifestation, light, illumination, revelation, discovery, an appearance,; -কৃ, to reveal.
প্রকাশক, *a.* shining, illuminating, displaying, publishing, visible: *s.* a publisher.
প্রকাশকতা, -ত্ব, *s.* the property of manifesting or displaying.
প্রকাশকারক, *a.* making manifest, displaying.
প্রকাশন, shining, manifesting, appearing.
প্রকাশনীয়, প্রকাশিতব্য, *vide* প্রকাশ্য.
প্রকাশমান, *a.* shining, manifesting, appearing.
প্রকাশরূপে, *ad.* openly, publicly, visibly.
প্রকাশিত, *a.* manifested, revealed, blown.
প্রকাশী, *a.* appearing, shining, radiant.
প্রকাশ্য, *a.* discoverable, capable of being revealed or made manifest, visible.
প্রকাশ্যতা, *s.* visibility, manifestness.
প্রকীর্ণ, *a.* scattered about, interspersed, bespread, published, miscellaneous.
প্রকীর্ণক, *s.* a fan made of the tail of Tartar ox; a section or chapter in a book.
প্রকীর্তন, *s.* a mentioning, a declaring.
প্রকীর্তিত, *a.* spoken, declared, explained, mentioned, revealed.
প্রকৃত, *a.* right, genuine, proper, veritable, real, true.

প্রকৃততা, -ত্ব, *s.* rectitude, veracity, genuineness, reality, propriety, accuracy.
প্রকৃতরূপে, *ad.* rightly, properly, veritably,
প্রকৃতার্থ, *a.* the same as প্রকৃত. [truly.
প্রকৃতি, *s.* original and unformed matter, nature, disposition, a subject.
প্রকৃতিপ্রাপক, *a.* elastic, springing back.
প্রকৃতিসিদ্ধ, *a.* natural, effected by nature.
প্রকৃষ্ট, good, excellent, eminent, superior
প্রকৃষ্টতা, goodness, excellency, superiority
প্রকোষ্ঠ, *s.* the forearm; door-frame. [ment.
প্রক্রম, *s.* attempt, beginning, commence-
প্রক্রান্ত, *a.* attempted, begun, commenced.
প্রক্রান্ততা, *s.* a being attempted or begun
প্রক্রিয়া, *a.* bearing royal insignia; adminis-
প্রক্ষারক, *a.* exhalent. [tering remedies.
প্রক্ষালন, *s.* cleansing, the washing or rinsing of a thing, the expiation of a crime.
প্রক্ষালনীয়, প্রক্ষাল্য, *a.* requiring to be, or capable of being, washed or rinsed.
প্রক্ষালিত, *a.* washed, rinsed. [propelled.
প্রক্ষিপ্ত, projected, thrown, cast, injected,
প্রক্ষেপ, *s.* projection, a throwing off, injection, propulsion; share in a joint stock.
প্রক্ষেপক, *a.* propelling, throwing off.
প্রক্ষেপণীয়, *a.* capable of being projected, propelled, thrown, or driven forward.
প্রখর, keen, sharp, acute, acrid, smart, emi-
প্রখরজ্যোতিঃ, *s.* glare, keen lustre. [nent.
প্রখরবুদ্ধি, *s.* acuteness, penetration.
প্রগণ্ড, *s.* the upper arm above the elbow.
প্রগল্ভ, *a.* overpowering, bold, confident, intrepid, audacious, shameless, impudent, strong, insolent, able, firm, ready.
প্রগল্ভতা, *s.* boldness, insolence, audacity, impudence, intrepidity, perverseness.
প্রগল্ভা, *s.* a wanton or lustful woman.
প্রগাঢ়, *a.* steady, serious, firm, much, excessive, hard, difficult, profound.
প্রগাঢ়তা, -ত্ব, *s.* steadiness, seriousness, firmness, abundance, difficulty.
প্রচণ্ড, *a.* passionate, angry, furious, violent, headstrong, intolerable, insupportable, acrid, bold, confident, fierce, presuming.
প্রচররূপে, *ad.* currently, commonly, popularly, publicly. [currency.
প্রচলন, *s.* activity, alacrity, briskness, a
প্রচলিত, *a.* moved, stimulated, current.
প্রচার, *s.* commonness, notoriety, publicity; the tending of cattle. [ing cattle.
প্রচারক, *a.* publishing, manifesting; tend-
প্রচারিত, *a.* made known, published.
প্রচুর, *a.* abundant, sufficient, ample, much.
প্রচুরতা, *s.* abundance, sufficiency, plenty.
প্রচ্ছন্ন, *a.* concealed, covered, disguised.
প্রচ্ছন্নরূপে, *ad.* incog, in disguise, clandes-
প্রচ্ছন্ন হারক, a concealed thief. [tinely.
প্রজা, *s.* an individual, the subject of a king, a tenant, a dependant, an offspring.
প্রজাগণ, প্রজাবর্গ, প্রজাসমূহ, *s.* the body of subjects or dependants, the peasantry.
প্রজাপতি, *s.* Brahmá the sire of all, a king, a prince, a sovereign, a daughter's husband, Vishwakarma, a butterfly.
প্রজ্বলন, *s.* a blazing, a taking fire.
প্রজ্বলনীয়, *a.* combustible, inflammable.
প্রজ্বলিত, *a.* enkindled, made to blaze.
প্রজ্ঞ, *a.* learned, wise, intelligent. [ing.
প্রজ্ঞা, *s.* an intelligent woman, understand-
প্রজ্ঞাবান্, *a.* intelligent, knowing, wise.
প্রণত, *a.* prostrate, humbled, bowed.
প্রণতি, *s.* obeisance, prostration, salutation.
প্রণতিপূর্ব্বক, *ad.* humbly, submissively.
প্রণব, *s.* the mystical syllable ওঁ.
প্রণয়, *s.* intimacy, affection, love, familiarity, concord, friendship, acquaintance.
প্রণয়ী, *a.* intimate, friendly, affectionate.
প্রণষ্ট, *a.* spoiled, lost, ruined. [-কৃ, to bow.
প্রণাম, *s.* prostration, bowing, salutation;
প্রণামী, *a.* bowing, saluting, prostrating: *s.* the present given after bowing to an idol.
প্রণালিকা, *s.* a tube, pipe, vein, a tubular vessel of the body, a conduit. [custom.
প্রণালী, *s.* a water-course, a series, a habit,
প্রণালীপূর্ব্বক, *ad.* customarily, habitually.
প্রণাশ, *s.* destruction, ruin, loss, perdition.
প্রণিধান, *s.* an object of desire, attention, regard, a great effort, stress, energy, profound meditation, access, entrance.
প্রণিধি, *s.* a request, solicitation, a secret agent, an emissary, spy, a place, situation, an agreement, an engagement.
প্রণিপাত, *s.* prostration, a bowing with respect, reverence, obeisance; -কৃ, to bow.

প্রণিহিত, *a.* consigned to, obtained, acquired, received, acknowledged, decided, determined, placed, deposited, fixed.

প্রণীত, *s.* consecrated fire : *a.* cooked, made, done, constructed, compared, thrown, sent, approached, entered.

প্রণেয়, *a.* amiable, docile, tractable, agreeable.

প্রতপ্ত, *a.* ardent, dignified, high-spirited.

প্রতাপ, *s.* splendour, ardour, zeal, power, glory, majesty, dignity, high spirit.

প্রতাপান্বিত, *a.* ardent, zealous courageous, powerful, majestic, dignified, glorious.

প্রতারক, *a.* deceiving, insidious, perfidious: *s.* a deceiver, a cheat, a knave, a rogue.

প্রতারণা, *s.* deceit, imposture, fraud, perfidy, knavery, a trick, an imposition.

প্রতারণাপূর্ব্বক, *a.* deceitfully, fraudulently.

প্রতারণীয়, *a.* deceivable.

প্রতারিত, *a.* deceived, cheated, imposed upon, cajoled.

প্রতি, a *prep.* joined to a word it gives the sense of a reflected or reiterated action : *ad.* every, each, to, back, again.

প্রতিকর্ম্ম, *s.* every work, every action.

প্রতিকার, *s.* an action in return for something done, revenge, retaliation, a reflected action, a remedy, a preventative.

প্রতিকারক, *a.* revenging, retaliating, returning an action, remedying.

প্রতিকার্য্য, *a.* remediable, capable of being retaliated or revenged.

প্রতিকূল, adverse, opposite, contrary, hostile, inverted.

প্রতিকূলতা, -ত্ব, *s.* opposition, contrariety.

প্রতিকৃতি, *s.* retaliation, revenge, a reflected image, a picture, worship, reverence.

প্রতিক্ষণ, *ad.* always, at every moment.

প্রতিক্ষিপ্ত, *a.* dismissed, rejected, opposed, repelled, resisted, calumniated, sent.

প্রতিগমন, *s.* a going back, a returning.

প্রতিগামী, *a.* going back, returning.

প্রতিগৃহীত, *a.* received, accepted, assented to.

প্রতিগ্রহ, *s.* a spitting-pot; a receiving.

প্রতিগ্রহণীয়, or **প্রতিগ্রাহ্য**, *a.* acceptable, fit to be accepted or received.

প্রতিগ্রাহক, *a.* obtaining, receiving : *s.* a person who receives gifts or presents.

প্রতিঘাত, *s.* a blow in return, resistance.

প্রতিচী, *a.* western, west : *s.* the west.

প্রতিচ্ছায়া, *s.* a reflected image, an image, a picture, a bass-relief, a facsimile.

প্রতিচ্ছেদ, *s.* opposition, contrariety.

প্রতিজন, *s.* every man, every one.

প্রতিজ্ঞা, *s.* a promise, engagement, a declaration, a plaint in a lawsuit.

প্রতিজ্ঞাত, *a.* promised, engaged to, declared, affirmed, deposed.

প্রতিজ্ঞাপত্র, *s.* a promissory note, a written declaration.

প্রতিজ্ঞাপালক, one who keeps his promise.

প্রতিজ্ঞাপালন, *s.* the keeping of a promise.

প্রতিজ্ঞাপূর্ব্বক, *ad.* by or through a promise.

প্রতিদত্ত, *a.* given back, returned.

প্রতিদর্শন, *s.* the looking at a person in return.

প্রতিদান, *s.* a recompense, retribution, a remuneration, the returning of a gift.

প্রতিদাপন, *s.* causing a person to return or give back a thing received.

প্রতিদাপিত, *a.* decreed by a court to be returned.

প্রতিদাপ্য, *a.* liable to be returned in consequence of the decree of a court.

প্রতিদিন, *ad.* every day, daily.

প্রতিদেয়, *a.* returnable, subject to be returned.

প্রতিধ্বনি, *s.* an echo, reverberation.

প্রতিনিধি, *s.* a deputy, substitute, representative.

প্রতিন্যাস, *s.* a mutual deposit.

প্রতিপক্ষ, *s.* an enemy, an adversary, a contrary thesis or proposition.

প্রতিপৎ, *s.* the first day of the moon's increase.

প্রতিপত্তি, *s.* obtaining of a thing, accomplishment of an object, acquirement, advancement, promotion, success, acquisition, knowledge, ascertainment, the acknowledgement of a charge, fame, reputation, renown, a demonstration.

প্রতিপত্তিকর, or **প্রতিপাদক**, *a.* ascertaining, working conviction, accomplishing, giving success, demonstrating.

প্রতিপদ, *s.* every step, every place or situation.

প্রতিপন্ন, *a.* effected, accomplished, advanced, demonstrated.

প্রতিপন্নতা, *s.* success, demonstration, promotion.

প্রতিপাদন, *s.* an ascertaining, a demonstrating, a causing to acknowledge, the giving of success, a promoting.

প্রতিপাদনীয়, or **প্রতিপাদ্য**, *a.* ascertainable, demonstrable, obtainable, probable.

প্রতিপাদিত, *a.* ascertained, demonstrated, obtained, promoted, acknowledged.

প্রতিপালক, *a.* providing for, nourishing, supporting, protecting, preserving: *s.* a protector, a provider, a benefactor.

প্রতিপালকতা, -ত্ব, *s.* the circumstance of being a nourisher or protector.

প্রতিপালন, *s.* the nourishing, maintaining, or succouring of a person, the preserving or providing of a person.

প্রতিপালনীয়, প্রতিপাল্য, *a.* proper or requiring to be maintained or nourished.

প্রতিপালিত, *a.* provided for, maintained, nourished, protected, preserved.

প্রতিপালিকা, *s.* a protectress, benefactress.

প্রতিফল, *s.* a retribution, a reward, recompense, a remuneration, a retaliation.

প্রতিবচঃ, প্রতিবচন, *s.* a reply, an echo.

প্রতিবৎসর, *ad.* every year, yearly.

প্রতিবন্ধ, *s.* an impediment, an obstacle.

প্রতিবন্ধক, *a.* obstructing, hindering, impeding, opposing, resisting.

প্রতিবন্ধকতা, -ত্ব, *s.* an obstruction, an impediment, opposition, resistance.

প্রতিবাক্য, প্রতিভাষ, *s.* an answer, a reply.

প্রতিবাদ, *s.* a reply, an answer, litigation, a pleading in reply, a rejoinder.

প্রতিবাদিতা, -ত্ব, *s.* the office of a respondent, litigation, a pleading in reply.

প্রতিবাদী, *a.* replying, rejoining, pleading in reply: *s.* a respondent, pleader. [ing.

প্রতিবাধক, *a.* resisting, opposing, prevent-

প্রতিবাধকতা, -ত্ব, *s.* opposition, resistance.

প্রতিবাধী, *a.* opposing: *s.* an opponent.

প্রতিবাসী, *a.* neighbouring: *s.* neighbour.

প্রতিবিম্ব, *s.* a reflected image, a picture, an image, a shadow, a resemblance. [out.

প্রতিবিম্বিত, *a.* typified, reflected, shadowed

প্রতিবোধ, *s.* a reflected or opposite idea.

প্রতিবোধক, *a.* opposing an idea.

প্রতিভা, *s.* a conception, understanding, intellect, an idea, light, splendour, reflected light, boldness, confidence. [wise.

প্রতিভান্বিত, *a.* bold, confident, intelligent,

প্রতিভূ, *s.* a bondsman, a security, a surety.

প্রতিমা, প্রতিমান, *s.* an image, a likeness, an idol, a picture, a reflected image.

প্রতিমাস, *ad.* every month, monthly.

প্রতিমূর্ত্তি, *s.* a resemblance, image, likeness.

প্রতিযত্ন, *s.* retaliation, revenge, resistance, a strenuous endeavour, a desire, wish, comprehension: *a.* acting aright, retaliating, resisting, making efforts. [ance.

প্রতিযোগ, a counterpart, opposition, resist-

প্রতিযোগিতা, *s.* partnership, mutual union, co-operation, coadjutorship.

প্রতিযোগিতাচরণ, *s.* co-operation.

প্রতিযোগী, *a.* co-operating, counteracting: *s.* a coadjutor, a partner, a second self, one who counteracts. [image.

প্রতিরূপ, *s.* a representation, a likeness, an

প্রতিরূপক, *a.* resembling, substituted.

প্রতিরোধ, *s.* a blocking up, a besieging.

প্রতিরোধক, *a.* blocking up, besieging.

প্রতিলোম, *a.* contrary to the natural course or order, against the hair or grain, reverse, inverted, low, base, depraved.

প্রতিলোমজ, *a.* born of a woman of a superior tribe by a man of an inferior one.

প্রতিশ্যায়, *s.* a catarrh, cold, phlegm.

প্রতিশ্রব, *s.* a promise, engagement, assent.

প্রতিশ্রুত, *a.* engaged by promise, promised, assented to, agreed to, accepted

প্রতিষিদ্ধ, *a.* forbidden, prohibited, denied.

প্রতিষেধ, *a.* prohibition, a denial.

প্রতিষেধক, *s.* denying, prohibiting.

প্রতিষ্ঠা, *s.* fame, renown, celebrity, approbation, reputation, consecration. [ous.

প্রতিষ্ঠান্বিত, *a.* renowned, famous, illustri-

প্রতিষ্ঠিত, *a.* celebrated, famed, renowned, applauded, consecrated.

প্রতিষ্ঠিতা, *a.* possessing wealth, wealthy.

প্রতিহত, *a.* smitten in return, resisted.

প্রতিহন্তা, *s.* one who returns a blow, a re-

প্রতিহিংসা, *s.* revenge, retaliation. [sister.

প্রতিহিংসিত, *a.* injured in return.

প্রতীক, *s.* a member, a limb, a part.

প্রতীকার, *s.* a thing done in return for some other act, a retaliation, remedy, relief.

প্রতীকার্য্য, retaliable, remediable, curable.

প্রতীক্ষণ, *s.* the waiting for or expecting of

প্রতীক্ষা, *s.* expectation, waiting. [a thing.

প্রতীক্ষিত, *a.* expected, waited for. [ern.

প্রতীচী, *s.* the west quarter: *a.* west, west-

প্রতীত, *a.* known, famed, renowned, celebrated, venerated, delighted, past, gone.
প্রতীতি, *s.* fame, notoriety, knowledge.
প্রতুল, *s.* abundance, sufficiency, adequacy.
প্রত্ত, *a.* given, presented: *fem.* betrothed.
প্রত্যক্, *a.* western, subsequent, following.
প্রত্যক্ষ, *a.* evident, visible, plain, obvious, clear to the senses, before the eyes.
প্রত্যক্ষতঃ, *ad.* evidently, clearly, sensibly.
প্রত্যক্ষদর্শন, *s.* an eye-witness.
প্রত্যক্ষপ্রমাণ, *s.* the evidence of the senses.
প্রত্যক্ষফল, *s.* evident consequences.
প্রত্যক্ষর, *ad.* literally, every letter. [ly.
প্রত্যক্ষরূপে, *ad.* clearly, evidently, obvious-
প্রত্যঙ্গ, *s.* an organ of perception, every part, or the extremities, of the body.
প্রত্যবস্কন্দন, *s.* an excuse, a special plea.
প্রত্যবস্থান, *s.* returning to reside at a former residence, return to the late house.
প্রত্যবস্থিত, *a.* inhabited or resided in again.
প্রত্যভিজ্ঞা, *s.* knowledge, idea arising from reflection, recognition, recollection.
প্রত্যভিযুক্ত, *a.* accused in return.
প্রত্যভিযোগ, *s.* a counter accusation.
প্রত্যয়, *s.* faith, belief, trust, confidence, satisfaction, knowledge, apprehension, a custom, usage, practice, fame, celebrity.
প্রত্যয়পূর্ব্বক, *ad.* through faith or trust.
প্রত্যয়যোগ্য, *a.* worthy of belief, credible.
প্রত্যয়িত, *a.* believed, confided in, trusted.
প্রত্যয়ী, *a.* believing: *s.* a believer.
প্রত্যর্থী, *a.* making a counter request: *s.* a defendant in a lawsuit, a respondent.
প্রত্যর্পণ, *s.* the restoring of a thing back.
প্রত্যর্পণীয়, *a.* liable to be restored.
প্রত্যর্পিত, *a.* restored, re-delivered, return-
প্রত্যহ, *ad.* daily, every day. [ed.
প্রত্যাকৃষ্ট, *a.* drawn back. [annulled.
প্রত্যাখ্যাত, *a.* set aside, denied, refused, dis-
প্রত্যাখ্যান, *s.* a refutation, a disannulling, disregard, rejection, a denial, a refusal.
প্রত্যাগমন, *s.* a returning back, a return.
প্রত্যাদান, *s.* retaliation, resumption.
প্রত্যাদানার্হ, *a.* resumable. [published.
প্রত্যাদিষ্ট, *a.* warned, spoken as an oracle,
প্রত্যাদেশ, *s.* an oracular saying, a warning from heaven, an impulse, a revelation.

প্রত্যারম্ভ, *s.* a second commencement.
প্রত্যাশা, *s.* hope, expectation, confidence.
প্রত্যাশাপন্ন, **প্রত্যাশী**, *a.* possessed of hope, hoping, hopeful, expecting, waiting for.
প্রত্যাসন্ন, *a.* near, proximate, contiguous.
প্রত্যাহার, *s.* resumption, the collecting or bringing back of wandering thoughts, an abridgment, a compendium.
প্রত্যাহারী, *a.* resuming, recollecting.
প্রত্যুক্ত, *a.* replied, answered.
প্রত্যুত্তর, or **প্রত্যুক্তি**, *s.* an answer, a reply.
প্রত্যুৎপন্ন, *a.* prompt, ready, reproduced, produced by multiplication: *s.* multiplication, the product in multiplication.
প্রত্যুৎপন্নবুদ্ধি, **প্রত্যুৎপন্নমতি**, *a.* possessed of prompt or ready understanding.
প্রত্যুপকরণীয়, *a.* proper to be done as the grateful acknowledgment of a favour.
প্রত্যুপকর্ত্তা, one who returns assistance or benefits, a grateful person. [kindness.
প্রত্যুপকার, *s.* a grateful return, a return of
প্রত্যুপকারক, **প্রত্যুপকারী**, *a.* helping, helping in return for a kind action, grateful.
প্রত্যুপকৃত, *a.* done as a grateful return.
প্রত্যুপদিষ্ট, *a.* advised or instructed in re-
প্রত্যুপদেশ, *s.* advice in return. [turn.
প্রত্যুপদেশক, *a.* giving advice in return.
প্রত্যূষ, *s.* the morning twilight, the dawn.
প্রত্যেক, *ad.* every one, each, each one.
প্রত্যেতব্য, *a.* credible, worthy of credit.
প্রথম, *a.* the first, first, chief, principal, prior, previous; in *arith.* first product.
প্রথমতঃ, *ad.* in the first place, firstly, pre-
প্রথমসাহস, *s.* a capital crime. [viously.
প্রথমাবয়ব, *a.* embryo: *s.* a fœtus, embryo.
প্রথমে, *ad.* in the first place, firstly.
প্রথমোৎপন্ন, *a.* first-born, first-produced.
প্রথমোৎপন্নাংশ, *s.* an embryo, a fœtus.
প্রথা, *s.* fame, celebrity, custom, usage.
প্রথিত, *a.* famous, renowned, illustrious.
প্রদ, *a.* giving, bestowing, conferring.
প্রদক্ষিণ, circumambulation, going round.
প্রদত্ত, *a.* given, bestowed, conferred.
প্রদপ্ত, *a.* clear, evident, obvious, manifest.
প্রদর, *s.* disease of women (menorrhagia).
প্রদর্শক, *a.* showing, seeing, viewing: *s.* a seer, a person who sees or shows.

প্রদর্শকতা, *s.* the circumstance of being a seer, or a person who shows things.
প্রদর্শন, *s.* a seeing, showing, pointing out.
প্রদর্শিত, *a.* shown, declared, made manifest.
প্রদান, *s.* a gift, a giving, a presenting.
প্রদানীয়, প্রদেয়, *a.* bestowable, conferable.
প্রদীপ, *s.* a lamp. প্রদীপ্ত, *a.* lighted up.
প্রদৃপ্ত, *a.* proud, haughty, elated.
প্রদেশ, *s.* a district, a province, a country, [a place.
প্রদেশিনী, *s.* the forefinger.
প্রদোষ, *s.* evening, forepart of the night.
প্রধন, *s.* war, battle; tearing, rending.
প্রধান, *a.* noble, chief, principal, prime.
প্রধানতা, -ত্ব, *s.* the same as প্রাধান্য.
প্রপঞ্চ, *s.* extension, expanse, expansion, copiousness in style or composition, prolixity, abundance, reverse, opposition, inversion; ideal existence, delusion.
প্রপঞ্চিত, *a.* expanded, extended, dilated.
প্রপন্ন, *a.* obtained, poor, needy, afflicted.
প্রপা, *s.* a watering-place for travellers.
প্রপিতামহ, *s.* paternal great-grandfather.
প্রপিতামহী, *s.* a father's grandmother.
প্রপৌত্র, *s.* a grandson's son, *fem.* প্রপৌত্রী.
প্রফুল্ল, expanded, sparkling, smiling, gay.
প্রফুল্লচিত্ত, *a.* gay-hearted, glad-hearted.
প্রফুল্লতা, or প্রাফুল্ল্য, *s.* expansion, gaiety, cheerfulness, gladness. [with joy.
প্রফুল্লনয়ন, *a.* having the eyes sparkling
প্রফুল্লবদন, *a.* having a sprightly counte- [nance.
প্রফুল্লান্তঃকরণ, *a.* glad-hearted.
প্রফুল্লিত, *a.* expanded, spread open, patent.
প্রবক্তা, *s.* a speaker, orator, an eloquent [man.
প্রবচন, *s.* a treatise, a discourse.
প্রবঞ্চক, *a.* deceiving, insidious, deceitful: *s.* a deceiver, a knave, a cheat.
প্রবঞ্চকতা, -ত্ব, *s.* knavery, deceitfulness.
প্রবঞ্চনা, *s.* deceit, fraud, deception, circumvention, imposition, an imposture.
প্রবঞ্চনাপূর্ব্বক, *ad.* deceitfully, fraudulent- [ly.
প্রবঞ্চনীয়, *a.* deceivable, imposable.
প্রবন্ধ, *s.* a connected narrative, a set discourse, a treatise, composition.
প্রবন্ধকল্পনা, *s.* a feigned story.
প্রবর্ত্ত, *s.* a commencement, excitation.
প্রবর্ত্তক, exciting, stimulating: *s.* a stimu- [lus.
প্রবর্ত্তকশক্তি, *s.* a stimulating power.

প্রবর্ত্তন, *s.* the beginning of an action.
প্রবর্ত্তনা, *s.* a stimulus, an excitement.
প্রবর্ত্তনীয়, *a.* excitable, fit to be stimulated.
প্রবর্দ্ধক, *a.* causing to grow or increase: *s.* that which causeth growth or increase.
প্রবর্দ্ধন, *s.* a growing in size, increasing in riches, growing fat; in *ana.* a process.
প্রবল, *a.* strong, powerful, mighty, cogent, [valid.
প্রবলতা, -ত্ব, *s.* the same as প্রাবল্য.
প্রবলপ্রতাপ, *a.* highly energetic. [tory.
প্রবাচক, *a.* technical, expository, explana-
প্রবাদ, rumour, report, current story; strife.
প্রবাল, *s.* coral, a young shoot, a sprout.
প্রবাস, *s.* temporary residence, a lodging.
প্রবাসী, *a.* residing temporarily in a place: *s.* a sojourner, a lodger.
প্রবাহ, *s.* a stream, a current, a train of circumstances depending on one another.
প্রবাহক, *a.* carrying or flowing off.
প্রবাহকপ্রণালী, *s.* an artery, a vein.
প্রবিষ্ট, *a.* entered, engaged in a thing.
প্রবীণ, clever, learned, eminent, well-vers- [ed.
প্রবীণতা, eminence, cleverness, talent.
প্রবুদ্ধ, *a.* convinced, convicted, stimulated.
প্রবৃত্ত, setting about, engaged, commenced.
প্রবৃত্তি, *s.* an effort, the commencement of an action, excitation, a stimulus, an inclination, a tendency, a predilection; -জন্মা, to incite, to induce, to instigate.
প্রবৃত্তিকর, or প্রবৃত্তিজনক, *a.* stimulating.
প্রবেশ, *s.* entrance into a place, introduction; -কৃ, to enter; -করা, to introduce.
প্রবেশক, *a.* entering: *s.* one who enters.
প্রবেশ -দ্বার, -পথ, *s.* an entrance to a place.
প্রবেশন, *s.* an entering, penetrating. [ble.
প্রবেশনীয়, প্রবেশ্য, introducible, penetra-
প্রবেশিত, *a.* introduced, brought in.
প্রবোধ, *s.* conviction, attention, vigilance, knowledge, understanding, intellect, demonstration, consolation; -জন্মা, to force conviction; -দা, to convince, to console.
প্রবোধক, *a.* convincing, awakening, exciting to vigilance, promoting knowledge.
প্রবোধন, *s.* the convincing of a person.
প্রবোধী, *a.* convincing, awakening. [tion.
প্রভব, *s.* a generative cause, birth, produc-
প্রভা, *s.* splendour, radiance, glory, lustre.

প্রভাকর, radiant, shedding a lustre : *s.* the sun.
প্রভাগ, *s.* the fraction of a fraction.
প্রভাত, *s.* the morning, the dawn of day.
প্রভাব, *s.* majesty, dignity, magnanimity, a high sense of honour, power, influence.
প্রভাবযুক্ত, *a.* energetic, high-spirited.
প্রভু, *s.* a lord, a supreme governor, a master, a sovereign, an owner, a governor.
প্রভুতা, -ত্ব, *s.* lordship, dominion, supremacy, sovereignty, government, superiority, mastery, ownership.
প্রভুভক্ত, *a.* devoted to, obsequious, loyal, faithful.
প্রভুভক্তি, devotedness to a lord or master.
প্রভূত, *a.* much, many, great, sufficient.
প্রভৃতি, *s.* a sort, kind, and the like, etcetera.
প্রভেদ, *s.* a difference, a distinction, a disparity, an inequality, a nick name.
প্রভেদক, *a.* distinguishing, discriminating, separating, severing.
প্রমত্ত, *a.* elated, intoxicated, rash, precipitate, inadvertent.
প্রমদা, *s.* a beautiful woman.
প্রমা, *s.* true knowledge, consciousness, perception.
প্রমাণ, *s.* evidence, proof, a testimony, authority or warrant for an opinion, an attestation, a demonstration, an example, an instance ; -কৃ, or -দা, to attest, prove.
প্রমাণপত্র, *s.* a voucher, an affidavit.
প্রমাতা, *s.* one who gives evidence or proof.
প্রমাতামহ, *s.* maternal great-grandfather.
প্রমাতামহী, *s.* a mother's grandmother.
প্রমাদ, *s.* ruin, confusion, inadvertence, inaccuracy, error, carelessness.
প্রমাদাভিধান, *s.* a plea of error or inadvertence.
প্রমাদী, *a.* inadvertent, inattentive, careless, infatuated, erroneous, ruinous.
প্রমাপক, *a.* giving proof or evidence, testifying.
প্রমিত, *a.* proved, authentic, settled.
প্রমীত, *a.* dead, deceased, defunct.
প্রমুখ, *s.* the face, the mouth.
প্রমুখাৎ, *ad.* from the mouth of, orally.
প্রমুদিত, *a.* overjoyed, elated, delighted.
প্রমেয়, *a.* capable of proof, probable.
প্রমেয়তা, -ত্ব, *s.* a probability.
প্রমেহ, -বিকার, *s.* a gonorrhea, a gleet.
প্রমোচক, *a.* liberating, freeing from.
প্রমোচন, *s.* a liberating, delivering, making free.
প্রমোচনীয়, *a.* capable of being liberated.

প্রমোদ, *s.* excessive joy, delight, rapture.
প্রমোদক, প্রমোদী, *a.* causing excessive joy.
প্রমোদিত, *a.* gladdened, cheered, elated.
প্রয়ত, *ad.* purified, holy, pious, sanctified.
প্রযত্ন, *s.* an endeavour, effort, labour, care.
প্রয়াণ, *s.* a going, an exit, a departure.
প্রয়াত, *a.* gone, departed, deceased.
প্রয়াস, *s.* an endeavour, a desire, a bias of the mind towards an object, a taste for any pursuit, love to an object.
প্রয়াসী, *a.* diligent, ardent, persevering.
প্রযুক্ত, *a.* endowed with, arising from, occasioned by : *ad.* from or because of.
প্রযুজ্য, *a.* capable of being stimulated, susceptible.
প্রযুত, *a.* a million, ten lakhs.
প্রযোক্তা, *s.* a moving, exciting or stimulating cause, one who stirs up or excites.
প্রয়োগ্, *v. a.* to excite, to stimulate.
প্রয়োগ, *s.* an affair, matter, consequence, a result, an effort, an exertion, an act, an action, a text, an authority.
প্রয়োজক, *a.* exciting, causing, instigating : *s.* an exciting, or stimulating cause.
প্রয়োজন, *s.* an affair, necessity, occasion, need, a cause, a motive, an incentive.
প্রয়োজনার্হ, প্রয়োজনীয়, necessary, needed.
প্রয়োজ্য, *idem* : *s.* a capital ; a messenger.
প্রলাপিত, *a.* spoken, mentioned, declared.
প্রলয়, *s.* universal dissolution, the dissolution of nature, destruction, decomposition, death, dissolution, annihilation, fainting, syncope : *a.* vast, excessive.
প্রলয়কাল, *s.* time of universal dissolution.
প্রলাপ, *s.* talk, conversation, delirious talk, ravings of a maniac or delirious person.
প্রলাপদর্শী, *a.* delirious, raving.
প্রলাপী, speaking, conversing, raving, delirious.
প্রলেপ, *s.* a plaster, a salve, an ointment.
প্রলেপন, *s.* the applying of plaster, smearing.
প্রশংস্, *v. a.* to praise, to applaud.
প্রশংসক, or প্রশংসী, *a.* applauding, praising : *s.* one who applauds or praises.
প্রশংসন, *s.* act of applauding or praising.
প্রশংসনীয়, *a.* praiseworthy, laudable.
প্রশংসা, applause, praise, commendation, an encomium, a plaudit, a panegyric.
প্রশংসিত, *a.* applauded, praised.

প্রশংস্য, প্রশস্য, *a.* laudable, praiseworthy.
প্রশমন, *s.* forgiveness, a tranquillizing.
প্রশস্ত, *a.* praised, applauded, happy, excellent; spacious, wide, capacious, roomy.
প্রশস্ততা, *s.* goodness, excellence; width.
প্রশুদ্ধ, *a.* clear, evident, authentic.
প্রশ্ন, *s.* a question, a query, an enquiry.
প্রশ্নকর্ত্তা, *s.* a person who asks a question.
প্রশ্রয়, *s.* love, affection, esteem, fondness.
প্রশ্বাস, *s.* a breathing, respiration.
প্রষ্টব্য, *a.* questionable, fit to be asked.
প্রষ্টা, *s.* an enquirer, one who asks. [chief.
প্রষ্ঠ, *s.* a leader, a conducter: *a.* principal,
প্রসক্ত, *a.* fond; treated of, zealous, eternal, everlasting: *ad.* eternally, ever.
প্রসক্তি, *s.* a topic, a theme; fondness.
প্রসঙ্গ, *s.* the introduction of a topic of conversation, a topic, a subject, a treatise, a sentiment, a passage in a book, introduction, insertion, association, connection.
প্রসন্ন, *a.* gracious, propitious, kind, complacent, favourable, clear, frequented, bright, pellucid, pleased, delighted.
প্রসন্নতা, -ত্ব, *s.* propitiousness, graciousness, kindness, favourableness, complacency, clearness, brightness. [nance.
প্রসন্নবদন, *a.* having a pleasing counte-
প্রসব্, *v. a.* to produce, to bring forth.
প্রসব, *s.* bringing forth, production, birth.
প্রসববেদনা, *s.* pains of labour. [velocity.
প্রসর, *s.* dimension, extent, width; speed,
প্রসহ্য, *ad.* suddenly, forcibly, violently.
প্রসাদ, *s.* grace, favour, kindness, the food which is offered to a god, orts, leavings.
প্রসাদপ্রাপ্ত, favoured, received into favour.
প্রসাদভোগী, *s.* a pensioner.
প্রসাদিত, *a.* graciously bestowed, favoured.
প্রসাদিবস্ত্র, *s.* an honorary dress.
প্রসাদী, *a.* showing favour or kindness.
প্রসাধন, *s.* dress, embellishment, decora-
প্রসাধিত, *a.* finished, decorated. [tion.
প্রসার্, *v. a.* to extend, to spread out.
প্রসার, *s.* width, extent, expansion. [ing.
প্রসারণ, *s.* the act of expanding or unfold-
প্রসারিত, *a.* extended, expanded.
প্রসিদ্ধ, *a.* clear, current, plain, evident, noted, renowned, famous, celebrated.
প্রসিদ্ধি, *s.* fame, celebrity, notoriety.
প্রসূ, *s.* a mother; a spreading creeper.
প্রসূতা, *a.* recently delivered of a child: *s.* a woman in child-bed. [tion, offspring.
প্রসূতি, *s.* a bringing forth, birth, produc-
প্রসূতিকা, *a.* newly delivered of a child.
প্রসৃতি, *s.* the palm of the hand, a palm.
প্রস্তর, *s.* a stone, a gem, bunch of flowers.
প্রস্তরবিশিষ্ট, প্রস্তরময়, *a.* stony, rocky.
প্রস্তাব, *s.* a mentioning, a relation, a story, a topic, the introduction of a topic.
প্রস্তাবনা, *s.* an introduction, a commencement, a prologue, a prelude. [of topics.
প্রস্তাবক্রমে, *ad.* by successive introduction
প্রস্তাবিত, *a.* related, mentioned, told.
প্রস্তার, *s.* width, breadth.
প্রস্তুত, *a.* prepared, ready, prompt, said, revealed, declared, praised, panegyrized.
প্রস্তুততা, -ত্ব, *s.* preparedness, readiness.
প্রস্থ, *s.* a set of utensils, a suit of clothes, width, table-land, a particular measure.
প্রস্থান, *s.* a departure, a going, a marching or setting off; -কৃ, to depart, to go.
প্রস্থাপন, *s.* a sending, a dispatching.
প্রস্থাপনীয়, প্রস্থাপ্য, *a.* fit to be sent or dis-
প্রস্থাপিত, *a.* dispatched, sent. [patched.
প্রস্থিত, *a.* departed, gone, set off.
প্রস্রবণ, *s.* a spring, fountain, the discharging of urine, an oozing, a perspiring.
প্রস্রাব, *s.* the expelling of urine, urine.
প্রহত, smitten, killed, defeated, repelled.
প্রহর, *s.* fourth part of the day or night.
প্রহরিতা, *s.* the office of a watchman.
প্রহরী, *s.* a watchman, sentinel, a sentry.
প্রহর্ত্তা, *s.* he who strikes or beats, a slayer.
প্রহর্ষ, *s.* gladness, joy, hilarity.
প্রহার্, *v. a.* to strike, to smite, to beat.
প্রহার, *s.* a blow, a stroke, punishment.
প্রহারক, *a.* striking: *s.* one who strikes.
প্রহারণ, *s.* the beating of a person.
প্রহারী, *a.* beating, flogging, smiting, kil-
প্রহার্য্য, *a.* deserving a beating. [ling.
প্রহিত, *s.* sauce, gravy, condiment: *a.* discharged, sent, dispatched, suitable.
প্রহৃত, *a.* beaten, struck, smitten. [ed.
প্রহৃষ্ট, *a.* glad, rejoiced; -চিত্ত, glad-heart-
প্রহেলিকা, *s.* a riddle, an enigma, a puzzle.

প্রাংশু, *a.* high, tall, lofty : *s.* the height.
প্রাক্, প্রাক্কালীন, *a.* prior, former; eastern.
প্রাকৃত, *a.* common, vulgar, plebeian.
প্রাক্কাল, *s.* former time, a crisis.
প্রাক্তন, *s.* fate, destiny, luck.
প্রাখর্য্য, *s.* acuteness, ardour, zeal.
প্রাগভাব, *s.* prior non-existence.
প্রাগল্ভ্য, *s.* pomp, parade, bustle.
প্রাগ্‌ভাব, *s.* a prior state or condition.
প্রাঙ্গণ, *s.* a court-yard. প্রাগ্বৎ, *ad.* as before.
প্রাচী, *a.* eastern, east : *s.* the east.
প্রাচীন, *a.* old, ancient, antique, aged.
প্রাচীনগাথা, *s.* tradition. [quity.
প্রাচীনতা, -ত্ব, *s.* oldness, agedness, anti-
প্রাচীনমত, *s.* ancient method : *a.* approved
প্রাচীনা, *s.* antiquity. [by the ancients.
প্রাচীর, *s.* a wall, a fence wall, enclosure.
প্রাচুর্য্য, *s.* sufficiency, plenty, abundance.
প্রাজাপত্য, *s.* a sort of religious penance; a particular sacrifice; a kind of marriage.
প্রাজ্ঞ, *a.* learned, wise, skilful, clever.
প্রাজ্ঞতা, -ত্ব, *s.* erudition, skill, wisdom.
প্রাঞ্জলি, *s.* the open hands joined. [death.
প্রাণ, *s.* breath, life, the spirit, soul; -ত্যাগ,
প্রাণঘাতক, murderous, mortal, fatal, dead-
প্রাণতুল্য, or প্রাণসদৃশ, *a.* equal to life. [ly.
প্রাণদণ্ড, *s.* the punishment of death.
প্রাণদান, *s.* the bestowment of life.
প্রাণধারণ, *s.* the possessing of life.
প্রাণনাথ, *s.* the lord or sovereign of life.
প্রাণপণ, *s.* a staking of life, great exertion.
প্রাণপণে, at the hazard of life, with great
প্রাণপ্রতিম, *a.* equally dear as life. [care.
প্রাণপ্রতিষ্ঠা, *s.* the consecration of an image.
প্রাণপ্রিয়, *a.* beloved of the soul or life.
প্রণবস্তু, *s.* animated matter.
প্রাণবিয়োগ, *s.* the departure of life, death.
প্রাণহিংসা, *s.* injury to life, murder.
প্রাণাধিক, *a.* more than life; -প্রিয়, beloved
প্রাণান্ত, *s.* end of life, death. [above life.
প্রাণী, *a.* animal, animated, vital, living : *s.* a living creature; the soul.
প্রাণেশ্বর, *s.* the lord of life (a submissive
প্রাতঃ, *ad.* the morning, the dawn. [term.)
প্রাতঃ-কর্ম্ম, -কৃত্য, *s.* morning duties of reli-
প্রাতঃকাল, *s.* the morning, dawn, [gion.
প্রাতঃস্নান, *s.* the morning ablution.

প্রাতিকূল্য, প্রাতিলোম্য, *s.* contrariety, oppo-
প্রাতিভাব্য, *s.* suretiship, security. [sition.
প্রাতে, *ad.* in the morni ng, by dawn.
প্রাত্যয়িক, *a.* faithful, trusty, confidential.
প্রাথমিক, *a.* having a right of priority, relating to the first, first, prior, initial.
প্রাথমিকতা, -ত্ব, *s.* priority, precedence.
প্রাদুর্ভাব, *s.* the circumstance of coming to light, manifestation, eliciting. [dent.
প্রাদুর্ভূত, *a.* elicited, manifest, clear, evi-
প্রাদেশ, *s.* thumb and forefinger span.
প্রাধান্য, *s.* pre-eminence, superiority.
প্রাধান্যরূপে, *ad.* pre-eminently. [border.
প্রান্ত, *s.* limit, extremity, outskirts, margin,
প্রান্তর, *s.* an open plain, a prairie, a desert.
প্রাপক, *a.* obtaining, attaining, procuring.
প্রাপণ, *s.* a reaching, obtaining. [able.
প্রাপণীয়, প্রাপয়িতব্য, *a.* obtainable, attain-
প্রাপ্ত, *a.* obtained, found, gained, acquired.
প্রাপ্তব্য, প্রাপ্য, *a.* obtainable, acquirable.
প্রাপ্তব্যবহার, *a.* adult, arived at the legal age, or the age of responsibility.
প্রাপ্তযৌবন, *a.* arrived at age of puberty : *s.* a youth above sixteen. [advantage.
প্রাপ্তি, *s.* gain, profit, acquisition, benefit,
প্রাবর্ত্তক, exciting, stimulating, stirring up.
প্রাবল্য, *s.* strength, power, might, superiority, cogency, validity. [affairs.
প্রাবিড়্ প্রাবীড়্, *s.* a pressure of business or
প্রাবৃট্, *a.* rainy, wet; -কাল, rainy season.
প্রামাণিক, *a.* approved, credible, authentic : *s.* a chairman, a president, a barber.
প্রামাণিকদাঁড়া, *s.* an approved custom.
প্রামাণ্য, probability, credibility, authenti-
প্রায়, *ad.* about, almost, nearly, like. [city.
প্রায়শ্চিত্ত, *s.* an expiation, an atonement.
প্রায়িক, or প্রায়শঃ, *a.* almost, nearly. [ed.
প্রারব্ধ, *a.* begun; caused by fate, predestin-
প্রারম্ভ, *s.* a beginning, a commencement.
প্রার্থক, supplicating, supplicatory : *s.* one who requests, a candidate, a suitor.
প্রার্থনা, *s.* a request, a prayer, a petition, a supplication, a desire; -কৃ, to pray, to request, to solicit, to beseech.
প্রার্থনাপত্র, *s.* a written request, a petition.
প্রার্থনীয়, *a.* proper to be requested, fit to be the subject of a petition.

প্রার্থয়িতা, *s.* one who prays, a petitioner.
প্রার্থিত, *a.* requested, asked, prayed for, solicited, besought.
প্রালব্ধ, *s.* predestination, fate.
প্রাশন, *s.* an eating, a meal, food.
প্রাশস্ত্য, *s.* largeness, extent, capaciousness.
প্রাশী, *a.* eating, feeding.
প্রাসঙ্গিক, *a.* connected with an introduced topic.
প্রাসাদ, *s.* a palace, a house, edifice, temple.
প্রাহ্ন, or পূর্ব্বাহ্ন, *s.* the forenoon.
প্রিয়, *a.* amiable, beloved, grateful, dear, agreeable, esteemed, pleasing.
প্রিয়তম, *a.* most amiable, dearly beloved.
প্রিয়তা, -ত্ব, *s.* amiableness, agreeableness.
প্রিয়দর্শন, *s.* an agreeable sight.
প্রিয়বাক্য, *s.* agreeable words.
প্রিয়ভাষী, প্রিয়ম্বদ, *a.* speaking agreeable things.
প্রিয়াপ্রিয়, *a.* agreeable or disagreeable.
প্রিয়ালাপ, *s.* agreeable conversation.
প্রীণন, *s.* satisfaction, satiety, gratification.
প্রীত, *a.* beloved, esteemed; pleased, glad.
প্রীতি, *s.* love, affection, fondness, regard, intimacy; gratification, enjoyment.
প্রীতিকর, *a.* gratifying, loving, affectionate.
প্রেক, *s.* a nail, spike, peg, pin.
প্রেক্ষক, viewing, seeing: *s.* one who views or surveys.
প্রেক্ষণ, *s.* a viewing, a surveying, a seeing.
প্রেক্ষণীয়, visible, surveyable, discernible.
প্রেক্ষিত, viewed, seen, discerned.
প্রেত, departed, deceased: *s.* a ghost, apparition.
প্রেত-কর্ম্ম, -কার্য্য, -ক্রিয়া, funeral obsequies.
প্রেতপতি, *s.* Yama, the regent of death.
প্রেম, *s.* love, affection, attachment, tenderness, intimacy, enjoyment, pleasure.
প্রেমসাগর, *s.* ocean of love; name of a book.
প্রেমী, *a.* loving, affectionate.
প্রেয়সী, or প্রেয়ান, *a.* dear, most loved, best beloved.
প্রেরক, প্রেষক, *a.* sending, ordering, causing: *s.* a person who sends or orders.
প্রেরণ, *s.* the act of sending, or of giving orders; in *gram.* the causal verb.
প্রেরয়িতা, *s.* one who sends, a commander.
প্রেরিত, *a.* sent: *s.* an apostle, a messenger.
প্রেরিতত্ব, *s.* apostleship, ambassadorship.
প্রেষণ, *s.* a sending, directing, ordering.
প্রেষণীয়, *a.* fit or proper to be sent.
প্রেষিত, *a.* sent, directed, ordered.
প্রেষ্ঠ, *a.* dear, greatly beloved; outstripped.
প্রেষ্য, *a.* fit to be sent: *s.* a messenger.
প্রোক্ত, *a.* spoken, said, uttered, declared.
প্রোক্ষণ, *s.* a sprinkling; the slaughter or immolation of animals for sacrifice.
প্রোক্ষণীয়, *a.* fit to be sprinkled; sacrificial.
প্রোক্ষিত, *a.* sprinkled; immolated.
প্রোথিত, *a.* buried, interred; planted.
প্রোষিত, *a.* abroad, absent from home.
প্রৌঢ়, *a.* controverted, disputed, confident, arrogant; married, full grown, old.
প্রৌঢ়া, *a. f.* married: *s.* a woman from the age of 30 to 55; an amorous woman.
প্রৌঢ়ি, *s.* an investigation, affirmation, controversy, a controverted point, enterprize, zeal, confident or rash exertion.
প্রৌঢ়িবাদ, *s.* a controversy.
প্রোস, *s.* prussiate. প্রোসিক, *s.* the prussic acid.
প্লক্ষদ্বীপ, *s.* one of the seven fabled continents in Hindu geography.
প্লব, *s.* a raft, a float, a frog, a monkey, a sheep, a jumping, leaping, a plunging, diving, a floating, swimming; a declivity, a piece of water, an enemy.
প্লবন, *s.* plunging; a going by leaps or jumps.
প্লাটীনা, *s. Eng.* platina.
প্লাবক, *a.* overflowing, inundating.
প্লাবন, *s.* a deluge, a flood, inundation.
প্লাবিত, *a.* overflown, immersed, flooded.
প্লীহা, *s.* the spleen, the spleen disease.
প্লুত, *a.* overflowed; jumped, leaped: *s.* a gallop, a leap; a grave accent.
প্লুতগতি, *s.* a gallop, a going by leaps.

ফ, the 22nd consonant: *intj.* puh, tush.
ফক, *v. n.* to fail, to miscarry, to mock the expectation, to disappoint.
*ফকৎ, *ad.* only, merely, simply.
ফকা, *v. a.* to cause to fail, to disappoint.
ফকান, *s.* a causing an undertaking to fail, the disappointing of a person.
ফকীর, *a.* poor, needy: *s.* a beggar, a mendicant.
ফকীরী, *s.* beggary, mendicity, poverty.
ফক্কক, *a.* pretending, imposing, delusive.
ফক্কিকা, *s.* a sophism, a deception, a delusion, a trick, circumvention, fraud.
ফক্কু, *ad.* only, alone, merely, simply.

ফকু্া, *a.* penniless, poor, empty-purse.
ফক্ক, *a.* disappointing, failing. [shift.
ফক্কমানি, *a.* unsubstantial, weak, make-
ফচ্কিয়া, *a.* laughing at trifles, playful.
*ফজ্‌র্ *s.* the morning, the dawn. [ness.
*ফজ্‌ল, *s.* mercy, grace, blessing, good-
*ফজ্জিহৎ, *s.* disgrace, ignominy, infamy.
*ফটক, *s.* a gate, an outer, door, a gaol.
ফটকচাঁদা, *s.* a fop, a man of dress.
ফটকবন্দী, *s.* imprisonment, custody.
ফট্কা, *v. a.* to winnow (rice, etc.): *s.* a straggler; a dilemma: *a.* speckled.
ফটিক, *s.* crystal, quartz; -স্তম্ভ, a crystal
ফট্কিরি, or ফট্কারী *s.* alum. [pillar.
ফট্ফট্, *s.* a popping sound. [parade.
ফট্ফটানি, *s.* a crackling sound; pomp,
ফড়, *s.* a gambling, a gambling-house.
ফড়কি, *s.* a twig, a small branch. [stall.
ফড়্খানা, *s.* a gambling-house, gambling-
ফড়িঙ্গ, or *ফন্‌গা, *s.* a grasshopper, a lo-
ফড়িয়া, *s.* a pedlar, a retail dealer. [cust.
ফড়িয়ামী, *s.* retail business, peddling.
ফড়্ফড়্, *s.* tingling sensation, impatience, talkativeness; -কৃ, to talk at random.
ফড়্ফড়ানী, *s.* garrulousness; a fluttering.
ফড়্ফড়িয়া, *a.* loquacious, garrulous: *s.* a
ফণা, *s.* the hood of a serpent. [tattler.
ফণিমনসা, *s.* a shrub (Cactus Indicus).
ফণী, hooded: *s.* the cobra, hooded snake.
ফতুআ, *s.* a waistcoat: *a.* penniless, poor.
ফতুআগিরি, *s.* poverty, pennilessness.
ফতুর, *a.* weak, infirm, poor, wretched.
ফন্দী, *s.* artifice, stratagem, a snare, a trick.
*ফপোলা, *s.* a blister.
*ফয়দা, *s.* gain, profit. [a settlement.
*ফয়শালা, *s.* a doer, the decree of a court,
*ফরৎই; *s.* a Frank, a native of France.
ফরৎইস্তান, *s.* the country of the Franks.
*ফরক, *a.* distant, separate, apart.
*ফরশ্, *s.* a carpet, a floor-cloth. [blank.
ফরসা, *a.* clean, clear, limpid, transparent;
*ফরাশ, *s.* a person whose office it is to spread carpets or to prepare lamps.
ফরিদী, *s.* a small species of paroquet.
*ফরিয়াদ, *s.* a cry for help, a complaint.
ফরিয়াদী, *s.* a plaintiff, a complainant.
*ফরেব, *s.* a trick, fraud, deceit, roguery.
ফরেবী, *a.* lying, crafty, deceitful, roguish.
*ফরোদী, *s.* the backstays of a ship.
*ফর্কাণ, *a.* spread open: *s.* the Qurán.
*ফর্জি, *s.* the queen at chess.
*ফর্জন্দ, *s.* offspring, descendant, progeny.
ফর্দ, ফরদ্, *s.* a vail, a piece, sheet of paper. a list, inventory: *a.* one, single; apart.
ফর্মা, *s. Eng.* a mould, a form.
*ফর্মাইস, *s.* an order, a command.
ফর্মাইসী, *a.* made as per order.
*ফর্মাবর্দার্, *s.* an attendant, a servant.
ফল্, *v. n.* to produce fruit; to grow.
ফল, *s.* fruit, result of an action, an effect, reward, punishment, utility, profit, benefit, success, result, consequence; the blade or head of an instrument.
ফলই, *s.* the same as চিতলমাছ.
ফলক, *s.* a shield, a board, a plough-share.
ফলকী, *a.* carrying or bearing a shield.
ফলগ্রহণ, *s.* the receiving of fruit, or the consequences of an action.
ফলজনক, *a.* advantageous, yielding fruit.
ফলতঃ, *ad.* in reality, virtually, indeed.
ফলদ, *a.* yielding fruit, beneficial, fruitful,
ফলন, *s.* the bringing forth fruit. [fertile.
ফলন্ত, ফলবন্ত, *a.* fruitful, advantageous.
ফলবান, *a.* fruitful, productive, fertile.
ফলমাত্র, *s.* mere fruit or consequence.
ফলমুখ, *s.* harvest, time of harvest.
ফলযুক্ত, *a.* fruitful, advantageous.
ফলা, *v. a.* to bring forth fruit: *a.* abounding with fruit: *s.* a compound letter.
ফলাঙ্গ, *s.* a going by leaps or jumps.
ফলাট, *s.* a stone used to grind paint on; the female organ of a cow. [of paint.
ফলান, *s.* the bringing forth fruit; mixing
*ফলানা, *s.* such a one (or, a person).
ফলাপলাপ, *s.* deceit, a concealment (applied to money or an argument).
ফলাফল, *s.* success or the want of it.
ফলাভিসন্ধি, *s.* interestedness.
ফলাভিসন্ধিরহিত, *a.* disinterestednesss.
ফলার, *s.* a banquet, a feast, a repast.
ফলাহার, *s.* a feeding on fruits.
ফলিত, *a.* filled with fruit, fruit-bearing.
ফলিতার্থ, *ad.* on the whole, in fine.
ফলিন, *a.* fruitful, fertile, advantageous.

ফলী, fruit-bearing : *s.* the head of a spear or arrow, the blade of a knife or other instrument, a plough-share.

ফলোদয়, *s.* advantage, recompense, benefit.

ফলোপভোগ, *s.* the enjoyment of the usufruct of an estate, or of an advantage.

ফলোপভোগী, *a.* enjoying the usufruct of an estate, enjoying advantage.

ফল্গু, *s.* a river in Prayág ; also, *vide* ফাগ্‌.

ফষ্টি, *s.* jest, raillery, mockery, banter.

ফষ্টিযোগ্য, *a.* ridiculous, worthy of a jest.

ফষ্টা, ফষ্টিয়া, *s.* a jester, a wag, banterer.

*ফসল, *s.* a time, a harvest, a crop ; a section, an article, a chapter.

*ফসাদ, *s.* depravity, iniquity, violence, sedition, mutiny, horror, war, an affray.

ফসাদী, *a.* wicked, depraved, violent.

ফস্কা, *a.* loose, flaccid, insecure, slack, lax.

*ফস্ত *s.* phlebotomy ; -খুল, to bleed.

*ফাএদা, *s.* perquisite, profit, gain.

ফাও, *s.* an allowance, a makeweight, overplus.

ফাওড়া, *s.* a spade, a digging-hoe.

ফাঁক, *s.* an aperture ; a slice, a piece.

ফাঁকামারণ, *s.* a chucking in the mouth by handful (a manner of eating).

ফাঁকী, *s.* trick, deceit, evasion ; a powder.

ফাঁড়, *s.* the belly, the impregnated belly.

ফাঁড়া, danger, risk ;-কাট্‌, to avert danger.

ফাঁড়ী, *s.* a post, a guard, district or police station ; an inlet or creek.

ফাঁড়িদার, *s.* the officer of a police station or district.

ফাড়িদারী, *s.* the office of a phánridár.

ফাঁদ্‌, *v. n.* to leap, prance, to commence.

ফাঁদ, *s.* a snare, trap, noose ; -পাত্‌, to set a snare. ফাঁদে পড়ন, to be entrapped.

ফাঁদনী, *s.* a machination, a beginning.

ফাঁপ্‌, *v. n.* to ferment, swell, blister, to be puffed, to be hollow, to become tumid.

ফাঁপ, *s.* a blister, a hollow, a bubble, a puffy or spungy swelling.

ফাঁপন, *s.* a tumifying, a swelling or being puffed up.

ফাঁপনি, *s.* tumidity, spungy texture, puffiness.

ফাঁপর, *s.* a braggadocio ; difficulty.

ফাঁপা, *v. a.* to puff up, inflate, distend : *s.* a spungy swelling : *a.* hollow, tumid.

ফাঁপান, *s.* act of puffing up or inflating : *a.* made hollow, puffed up, inflated.

ফাঁস, *s.* a noose, a loop, a slip-knot.

ফাঁসী, *s. idem ;* strangulation ; -দা, to hang, to strangle ; -কাট, a gallows.

ফাক, *s.* chasm, a chink, open space, a rupture, fracture, an aperture, a vacancy.

ফাকড়া, *s.* an imposition, a cheat, evasion.

ফাকা, *s.* a fasting for want of food.

ফাকাফাকি, *s.* deceit, an imposture, evasion.

ফাকী, *s.* deceit, imposture, an imposition, a fraud, a trick, a stratagem ; powder.

ফাকীজুকী, ফাকীফুকী, *s.* deceit, imposture, imposition, an evasion, a subterfuge.

ফাগ্‌, or ফাগু, *s.* red powder to play with.

ফাজিল, *a.* excellent, learned, virtuous : *s.* abundance, an overplus, a remainder.

ফাট্‌, *v. n.* to break, to crack, to burst.

ফাট, *s.* a cracking, a bursting, a crack.

ফাটল, *s.* a crack, a chink, a peep-hole.

ফাটা, *v. a.* to split, cleave, break : *s.* a fissure : *a.* cracked, burst, rent, torn.

ফাটান, *s.* a causing to crack or split.

ফাটানী, *s. fem.* one who cracks, a crack.

ফাটাফাটি, *s.* cracks in every direction ; (*met.*) great trouble or distress.

ফাটাফুটা, *a.* cracked, chopped, broken.

ফাটাল, *s.* a fissure, a rent, a crack.

ফাটলা, *s.* a crack, a crevice, a peep-hole.

ফাড়্‌, *v. a.* to cleave, to divide, to tear, rive.

ফাড়ন, *s.* a cleaving, tearing, splitting.

ফাড়া, *v. a.* to cause to cleave or tear : *a.* cleft, torn, rent, riven.

ফাড়ান, *a.* torn, cleft, rent : *s.* a causing to tear or cleave.

ফাড়ানি, *s.* a cleaving : *a.* due for cleaving.

ফাণিত, *s.* raw sugar, molasses, the inspissated juice of the sugarcane.

ফাতনা, ফাতা, *s.* a buoy for a fisherman's net, the float of a fishing line.

*ফানস, *s.* a lantern, globe, a table-shade.

*ফারখৎ, *s.* a bill of divorcement, a discharge.

ফারখতী, *s. idem.*

*ফারসী, or পারসী, *a.* Persian.

ফাল, *s.* a plough-share, the head of an arrow or spear, the blade of a knife ; a leap, a jump ; -পাড়্‌, to leap, to jump.

ফালসা, *s.* a tree and its fruit.[1]

ফালা, *s.* a board, a chip, a plough-share, the head of a spear or arrow.

ফালাফালা, *a.* tattered, rent, torn.
ফালী, *s.* a slice, slip, a chip, a small board.
ফাল্গুণ, *s.* an Indian month containing part of February and part of March.
ফাঁক, or **ফাঁকা**, *s.* a chink, a crack, fissure.
*__ফাশ্__, *a.* apparent, manifest, known.
ফিক, *s.* a prop, a shore, a lever, a bambu lever, a sharp pain or stitch in the side.
ফিকব্যথা, *s.* sudden pain in the side.
ফিকনা, *s.* a stanchion, a prop, a lever.
ফিকা, *a.* pale, faded, light-coloured, insipid, saltless, weak (as tobacco, etc.).
ফিকির, *s.* a contrivance, a thought, anxie-
ফিকিরফাকির, *s.* a delusive pretence. [ty.
ফিকিরবন্দ, **ফিকিরী**, cunning, artful, contriving, scheming, thoughtful, anxious.
ফিক্‌ফিকা, *s.* a giggling sound in laughter.
ফিঙ্কি, *s.* a spark, an atom, a particle.
ফিঙ্গা, *s.* a sling; a species of bird.[1]
ফিচ্, *s. Eng.* fees, rewards.
ফিচাল, *a.* cunning, ingenious, artful.
ফিতা, *s. Port.* tape, a ribband.
ফিন্‌কি, *s.* a spark, a small drop.
ফিয়ালি, *s.* an action, a work, an operation.
ফির্, *v. n.* to turn, revolve, veer, walk. **ফিরিয়া দেওন**, to restore, to give back.
ফির, *s.* a revolution, a circle, a roundabout way, an adverse circumstance.
ফিরণ, *s.* a walking, a turning, a changing of the wind, turning round, returning.
ফিরণীয়া, *a.* wandering, roving about, turning about : *s.* a traveller, a rover.
ফিরৎ, *a.* returned, brought back. [ticle.
ফিরতী, *s.* a revolution, turning, return ar-
ফিরা, *v. n.* to cause to turn, to wind, turn, to apply. **ফিরাইয়া লওন**, to take back.
ফিরাণ, *s.* the act of winding or turning, the making of a thing to circulate.
ফিরাণঘুরাণ, **ফিরাফিরি**, *s.* a going in a circuit, a turning to and fro, a shifting.
ফিরালি, *s.* a turning; a plastering.
ফিরালিয়া, *a.* plastering : *s.* a plasterer.
ফিরিঙ্গি, *s.* a *corruption* of **ফরাসী**, which
*__ফিরিস্তা__, **ফেরেস্তা**, *s.* an angel. [see.
*__ফিরিস্তি__, *s.* a list, an inventory, a table of contents, an index, a catalogue.
ফিরে, *ad.* again, back again, once more.

ফিরকি, or **ফিড়কি**, *s.* a wooden latch for a
ফিস্, *intj.* fie! tush! pish! ah! [window.
ফিস্‌ফিস্, *s.* a whispering; -**কৃ**, to whisper.
ফিস্‌ফিসা, *v. a.* to whisper, speak low.
ফিস্‌ফিসানি, *s.* a whispering; drizzling rain.
*__ফিল্__, *s.* elephant, -**খানা**, elephant-stall.
*__ফীল্লি__, *s.* the ankle, the ankle-bone.
ফু *s.* a blast from the mouth : *intj.* pugh!
ফুঃ, *intj.* poh! pugh! oh! foolish! [tush!
ফুঁ, *s.* a blast with the mouth, a blowing.
ফুঁক্, *v. a.* to blow with the mouth.
ফুঁকন, *s.* act of blowing with the mouth.
ফুঁড়্, *v. a.* to pierce, to penetrate.
ফুঁড়ন, *s.* a piercing, a penetrating.
ফুঁপ্, *v. n.* to sob, to breathe short. **ফুঁপিয়া উঠন**, to break out into sobs, to hiss.
ফুঁপা, *v. n.* to sob, to breathe short.
ফুঁপানি, *s.* a sobbing, a breathing short.
ফুঁপি, *s.* the fringe of a piece of cloth.
ফুকর্, *v. n.* to shout, to call aloud, to hoot.
ফুকর, *s.* a vacant space, vent-hole, fissure.
ফুকরণ, *s.* a hooting, a calling aloud.
ফুকরা, *v. a.* to cause a person to call aloud : *v. n.* to hoot, to call aloud.
ফুকরাণ, *s.* the raising of a shout. [space.
ফুকার, *s.* a fissure, a vent-hole, a vacant
ফুট্, *v. n.* to burst, to burst open, expand, to bubble in boiling, to be pierced.
ফুট, single, odd, not a pair : *s.* a menstruum, a drop, a kind of cake; *vide* **ফুটী**.
ফুটন, *s.* a bursting or breaking of a thing, the sudden expansion of a flower, the agitation of liquids when boiling.
ফুটা, *v. a.* to cause to burst, cause liquid to boil so as to be agitated : *a.* burst, expanded, burst open : *s.* a rupture.
ফুটান, *s.* the causing of a thing to burst, the causing of any liquid to boil.
ফুটাফাট্কা, *a.* broken, burst; straggling.
ফুটী, *s.* a cucurbitaceous plant and fruit.[2]
ফুট্‌ফাট্, *a.* manifest, clear, revealed; rum-
ফুৎকার, *s.* the action of blowing. [bling.
ফুয়া, *v. a.* to blow, to exorcise, to kindle.
ফুয়ান, *s.* a blowing, exorcism. [exhausted.
ফুর্, *v. n.* to be wholly spent, finished or
ফুরণ, *s.* a being wholly expended or finished, a being spent or exhausted.

*ফুরসদ, *s.* leisure, opportunity, time.
ফুরা, *v. a.* to exhaust, to finish entirely.
ফুরাণ, *s.* an expending, a finishing : *a.* exhausted, spent; settled (as a bargain,) contract (not daily work). [turgid.
ফুল্, *v. n.* to swell, to become inflated or
ফুল, *s.* a flower, blossom, the chemical preparation called flowers, the placenta, secundines, menstrual flux, the leprosy.
ফুলকা, *s.* the heart, the bronchiæ or gills
ফুলখড়ী, *s.* fine pure chalk. [of a fish.
ফুলগন্ধক, *s.* flower of brimstone, sulphur.
ফুলছড়ী, *s.* bunches of artificial flowers.
ফুলঝরী, *s.* a shower bath; *vide* তুবড়ী.
ফুলড়ী, ফুলরী, *s.* pulse-fritters fried in oil.
ফুলফুলিয়া, *a.* gaudy, foppish, priggish.
ফুলবড়ি, *s.* little balls made of pulse.
ফুলবাগান, ফুলবারী, *s.* a flower garden.
ফুলবাতাসা, *s.* a kind of light sweetmeat.
ফুলবাবু, *s.* a fop, a beau, a man of dress.
ফুলশয্যা, *s.* the bed on which a new married couple sleeps, a bed of flowers.
ফুলশোলা, *s.* the very best lightwood.
ফুলা, *s.* the secundines; a swelling : *v. a.* to bloom, blossom; to inflate, swell.
ফুলান, *s.* the causing of a thing to swell.
ফুলী, *s.* a film or cataract in the eye.
ফুল্ক, ফুল্কা, *s.* the bronchiæ or gills of a
ফুল্ল, *a.* expanded, blown, opened. [fish.
ফুল্লারবিন্দ, *s.* an expanded lotus; a beau, a
ফুষ্কী, *s.* wind expelled backwards. [fop.
ফুস্, term of contempt, pish! tush! pugh!
ফুসী, penniless, poor : *s.* dirt of the teeth.
ফুস্কুড়ী, *s.* a carbuncle, a boil, a pimple.
ফুসফুস, *s.* a whispering; the lungs.
ফসফুসনি, *s.* a whispering, low speaking.
ফুস্লা, *v. n.* to cajole, to wheedle, to inveigle, to coax, to flatter, to seduce.
ফুস্লান, *s.* a wheedling, a cajoling, a coaxing, the seducing of a person.
ফুস্লানিয়া, *a.* wheedling, cajoling : *s.* a ca-
ফে, *s.* the howl of a shakal. [joler.
ফেউ, *s.* a shakal, a jackal.
ফেঁচ, *s.* a flourish in writing. [light, puffy.
ফেঁপড়া, *s.* the lungs : *a.* spungy, hollow,
ফেঁস, *v. n.* to tear, to become lint, to be ineffectual, to disappo int : *s.* a jerking.

ফেঁসাটীয়া, or ফেঁসিয়া, *a.* pale, wan, sallow.
ফেঁসামাছ, *s.* a species of fish, very bony.
ফেঁসুআ, or ফেঁসফেঁসিয়া, *a.* knappy, tomentose, stringy, pale, sallow, wan.
ফেকুআ, *a.* sputtering : *s.* foam, froth.
ফেকুড়া, ফেকুড়ী, *s.* a switch, a twig, a sprig.
ফেটী, *s.* a skein of thread or silk.
ফেণ, ফেণা, *s.* foam, froth, scum, spume.
ফেণআমাণী, *s.* froth and gruel. [ses.
ফেণি, *s.* raw sugar, a cake made of molas-
ফেণিল, *a.* foamy, frothy, foaming.
*ফেতরাজ, *s.* wisdom, sagacity, craftiness.
ফেতরাজী, *a.* wise, sagacious, crafty.
ফেপাতুড়া, *s.* a being non-plussed.
ফের, *ad.* again, back again : *s.* a peril, a disappointment, a reverse; -কর, to repeat, recapitulate; -দেখ, to look again, to review; -পড়, to meet with obstacles.
ফেরৎ, ফেরতা, returned in trade, returned.
ফেরফার, *s.* variation, vicissitude, disorder, confusion, a transposition, a perversion.
ফেরা, *s.* a circuit, a revolution, a turn, a walk, a return, a reverse; a wooden vessel used to measure sand, dry lime, etc.
ফেরেফারে, *ad.* variably, changeably, con-
*ফেরেস্তা, ফিরিস্তা, *s.* an angel. [fusedly.
*ফেরোদী, *s.* the backstays of a boat.
ফেল্, *v. a.* to throw, to throw away. ফেলিয়া, দেওন, to cast or throw away. [away.
ফেলন, *s.* the act of throwing, a throwing
ফেলা, *s.* a refuse, a throwing away : *a.* cast away : *v. a.* to throw, to cast.
ফেলাছড়া, *a.* scattered or thrown about : *s.* a waste or squandering of things.
ফেলান, ফেলানি, *s.* a throwing, a casting.
ফেলানিয়া, *a.* lavish, squandering.
ফেলাফেলি, *s.* a squandering, a throwing
*ফেল্‌ফৌর, *ad.* quickly, speedily. [about.
ফৈজৎ, *s.* disgrace, ignominy, infamy.
ফৈল্, or ফৈলা, *v. n.* to spread about.
ফৈলন, ফৈলান, *s.* the spreading of a thing.
*ফৈসালা, *s.* a decree, a settlement.
ফোঁআ, *v. n.* to drizzle, to mizzle.
ফোঁআন, *s.* a drizzling, mizzling. [hollow.
ফোঁক, *s.* hollow space, a hole, a cavity : *a.*
ফোঁড়ন, *s.* the piercing or transfixing of a thing, the adding of spices to a sauce.

ফোঁড়া, *v. a.* to transfix, pierce, undermine, to stab, to card, to season food : *s.* a boil
ফোঁড়ান, *s.* a causing to pierce, the carding of cotton : *a.* pierced, bored, carded.
ফোঁড়াফোঁড়ি, *s.* a promiscuous piercing or stabbing.
ফোঁপর্, *a.* hollow, spungy.
ফোঁপরদালাল, *a.* officious, extravagant.
ফোঁপরদালালী, *s.* officiousness.
ফোঁপরা, *a.* hollow, spongy, light : *s.* the lungs.
ফোঁপল, *s.* a seed-vessel, a follicle, vegetating kernel of a cocoanut or fan-palm.
ফোঁপা, *v. n.* to sob, heave, breathe short.
ফোঁপান, ফোঁপানি, *s.* a sobbing, a heaving.
ফোঁপাল, *a.* sobbing, heaving, or labouring to breathe, breathing short.
ফোঁস্, *s.* a hissing, the hissing sound.
ফোঁস্ফোঁস্, *s.* a repeated hissing or breathing.
*ফোক্ত, *ad.* only, merely, simply.
ফোট, *v. a.* to pierce, to burst.
ফোটন, *s.* the piercing or bursting of a thing.
ফোটা, *s.* a spot, a drop, a tally, stain.
ফোড়, *s.* a spatula, a weeding-knife, an awl.
ফোড়া, *s.* a tumour, a boil, imposthume.
ফোড়াকৃতি, *a.* in *bot.* spatulate, like a spatula.
ফোপসা, *s.* the lungs, the bladder.
ফোরা, *s.* a pipe, a jet d'eau : *a.* hollow.
ফোলন, *s.* a swelling, a being enlarged.
ফোলা, *v. a.* to provoke to anger, to aggravate, to cause to swell : *s.* a blister.
ফোলান, *s.* the exciting of anger, the causing to swell.
ফোস্কা, *s.* a blister.
*ফোজ, *s.* an army ; -দার, a police-officer.
ফোজদারী, *a.* belonging to the police ; criminal, opposed to দিবানী, civil.
ফোতিক, *s.* perquisites, avails, gain.

ব, the twenty-third consonant ; when it has a dot in the centre it is pronounced like *wa* : *s.* the string which fastens the treddles of a weaver's loom.
বই, *s.* a book : *ad.* without, beside.
বইন, *s.* a sister ; -ঝি, a sister's daughter.
বইনপো, *s.* a sister's son, a nephew.
বউ, *s.* a wife, a son's wife ; also, used in addressing any respectable female.
বউনি, *s.* the first sale of a tradesman in the morning, a handsel ; porterage.

বউৰা, *a.* guilty of incestuous connection with a son's wife (a term of low abuse).
বউৰামী, *s.* incest with a son's wife.
বউভাত, *s.* a meal given the day after a new wife arrives at her husband's house, when she deals out rice to the guests.
বওআ, *s.* a carrying, the bearing of a burden, a flowing, passing away.
বংক্ষণ, *s.* the groin, hips, pubic and iliac region.
বংক্ষণখণ্ড, *s.* in *anatomy*, the ischium.
বংশ, *s.* a family, a race, a stock, a pedigree ; a bambu ; the backbone ; a flute.
বংশকর, *a.* establishing or continuing a family : *s.* the founder of a family.
বংশচরিত্র, *s.* a genealogical table.
বংশজ, *a.* produced in a race or family, born of a noble or kulín bráhman.
বংশধর, *a.* having a race or family.
বংশবৃদ্ধি, *s.* the increase of a race or family.
বংশলোচন, *s.* the manna of the bambu.
বংশানুক্রমে, *ad.* in the order of the family.
বংশাবলি, *s.* a pedigree, a genealogy, a table of lineage, a genealogical table.
বংশী, *s.* a flute, a pipe, a fife, a whistle ; -ধর, -ধারী, holding a flute : one who plays on the flute ; epithet of Krishna.
বংশীয়, or বংশ্য, *a.* lineal, relating to a family.
বঁইচ, *s.* a shrub and its fruit.[1]
বঁধু, বন্ধু, *s.* a relation, a friend, a crony.
বক্, *v. a.* to speak, talk, chatter, prate.
বক, *s.* a heron, a paddy-bird, a crane.
বকন, *s.* a talking, prating, a useless talking.
বকনা, *s.* a heifer, a young cow.
বকনি, *s.* talkativeness, useless prating.
বকম, *s.* a shrub much used in dyeing.[2]
*বকলম, *ad.* with the pen, by the pen of.
বকা, *v. a.* to speak, talk, prattle, perplex one to talk : *a.* talkative, garrulous.
বকাটি, *s.* the rod which lies across the warp in a weaver's loom.
বকাণ্ডপ্রত্যাশা, *s.* vain hope, fruitless expectation ; *lit.* a heron's expecting a meal by the fall of a bull's testicles.
বকান, *s.* the provoking a person to speak.
বকানিয়া, *a.* talkative, garrulous.
বকাবকি, *s.* a mutual prating, a talking in rage.
বকুয়া, *a.* talkative, garrulous, prating.

বকুল, *s.* the name of a tree (Mimusops
বকুলফুল, *s.* flower of M. elengi. [elengi).
বকেয়া, *s.* a remainder, arrears of rent.
বক্ত, *s.* fortune, luck, fate. [mentioned.
বক্তব্য, *a.* fit or necessary to be spoken or
বক্তা, *s.* a fluent person, a speaker, orator.
বক্তৃতা, *s.* a speech, eloquence. [sion.
বক্ত্র, *s.* the mouth; first term in progres-
বক্‌বক্, বক্‌বকানি, বক্‌বকি, *s.* talkativeness,
garrulity, prattle, gabble, a grumbling.
বক্‌বকা, *v. a.* to murmur, to talk much.
বক্‌বকান, *s.* a talking, a murmuring.
বক্‌বকিয়া, *a.* talkative, garrulous, prating.
বক্র, *a.* curved, crooked, awry, distorted,
sinuous, tortuous, askew, churlish.
বক্রগামী, *a.* tortuous, zigzag, flexuous.
বক্রতা, *s.* crookedness, distortedness, churl-
বক্রদৃষ্টি, *a.* squint-eyed. [ishness.
বক্রপাদ, *a.* crook-footed, bandy-legged.
বক্‌রা, *s.* a he-goat. বক্‌রী, *s.* a she-goat.
*বক্‌রিদ্, *s.* a Musalmán festival. [plus.
বক্রী, *s.* a remainder, residue, arrears, sur-
বক্রীকৃত, *a.* bent, made crooked; adverse.
বক্রীভবনীয়, *a.* refrangible, bendable.
বক্রীভাব, *s.* crookedness, refractedness, re-
বক্রীভূত, *a.* become crooked. [fraction.
বক্‌শী, *s.* a paymaster; -খানা, a pay-office.
বক্‌শীস্, *s.* a reward, a gift, a present.
বক্ষ, *s.* the breast, the chest, the bosom.
বক্ষউদর, *s.* the cavity of the stomach.
বক্ষউদরবেষ্ট, *s.* in *anatomy*, the pleura.
বক্ষঃস্থ, *a.* situated on the breast.
বক্ষঃস্থল, *s.* the bosom, the breast.
বক্ষোস্থি, *s.* the breast-bone (sternum).
বক্ষ্যমাণ, *a.* hereafter to be mentioned or
*বখরা, *s.* a share, a portion. [described.
বখরাদার, *s.* a partner, an accomplice.
*বখীল, *a.* greedy, niggardly: *s.* a miser.
বখীলী, *s.* niggardliness, stinginess.
*বখেয়া, *s.* a peculiar stitch in sewing.
বগল, *s.* the armpit; the flank, the side.
বগলী, *s.* a small bag, a purse.
বগী, *s.* a dagger, a hanger: *Eng.* a buggy.
বঙ্ক, *s.* a crook or turn in a river, a reach.
বঙ্কিম, *a.* crooked, bending, tortuous.
বঙ্গ, *s.* lead, tin; the country of Bengal;
cotton; the egg-plant; the calx of tin.

বঙ্গদেশ, *s.* the country of Bengal. [gig.
বঙ্গিলাঠিম, *s.* a top, a teetotum, a whirli-
বঙ্ক্ষণ, or কুচকি, *s.* the hips, the groin.
বচ, *s.* a parrot; the orris root. [tence.
বচন, *s.* a saying, a speech, a word, a sen-
বচনীয়, *a.* utterable, proper to be spoken.
বচসা, *s.* discord, wrangling, quarrelling.
বচস্কর, or বচস্থ, *a.* obedient, subordinate.
বচা, *s.* a word; -বচ, altercation, a dispute.
বজরা, *s.* a large kind of travelling boat; a
species of grain (Panicum spicatum).
*বজা, *a.* right, proper, true, accurate.
*বজাজ্র, *s.* a mercer, a linen-draper.
বজ্জাত, *a.* base-born, vile, of bad caste.
বজ্জাতী, *s.* a being base-born, baseness.
বজ্র, *s.* thunderbolt, diamond: *a.* adaman-
tine, hard, impenetrable, cross, forked.
বজ্রনিস্বন, *s.* a clap of thunder.
বজ্রপাণি, *s.* an appellation of Indra.
বজ্রপাত, *s.* the fall of a thunderbolt.
বজ্রবাঁটুল, *a.* short, hardy, and resolute.
বজ্রাঘাত, *s.* a thunder-stroke, unforeseen
বজ্রাভ, *s.* the precious opal. [calamity.
বজ্রাভ্যাস, *a.* crosswise, zigzag: *s.* recipro-
cal multiplication. [lude.
বঞ্চ্, *v. a.* to deceive, to impose on, to de-
বঞ্চক, *a.* fraudulent, swindling, deceiving,
crafty: *s.* a knave, a deceiver, an im-
postor, a cheat, a rogue, a jackal.
বঞ্চন, *s.* the deceiving of a person.
বঞ্চনা, *s.* deceit, swindling, an imposition,
fraud, a cheat, roguery, knavery.
বঞ্চনাকর্ত্তা, *s.* a swindler, rogue, deceiver,
an impostor, a cheat, a knave.
বঞ্চনাপূর্ব্বক, *ad.* fraudulently, deceitfully.
বঞ্চনীয়, *a.* capable of being deceived.
বঞ্চিত, *a.* deceived, imposed on, deluded,
cheated, defrauded. [of an animal.
বট্, *s.* the Indian fig-tree,[1] a cauri, the gut
বটিকা, or বড়ী, *s.* a pill, a bolus, a ball.
বটিয়া, *s.* a small oar, a paddle. [impost.
বটী, *s.* a fish-knife, a rope, a bead; excise,
বটু, *s.* a priest, a bráhman. [right.
বটে, *ad.* indeed, truly, actually, yes, true,
বটের, *s.* a species of quail.[2]
বট্‌কারা, *s.* a banter, mockery, raillery.
বট্‌কারিয়া, *s.* a wag, one who banters.

বড়, *s.* a tree :[1] *a.* great, large, capacious, spacious, important, chief, supreme: *ad.* very ; -বাড়ী, a large house ; *fig.* a gaol.
বড়বা, *s.* a mare, nymph Ashwiní, a slave-
বড়বাগ্নি, বড়বানল, *s.* submarine fire. [girl.
বড়ভাই, *s.* eldest brother ; a wife's brother
বড়মটর, *s.* the large garden pea. [(in jest).
বড়মা, *s.* (*met.*) misfortune, calamity.
বড়মেথী, *s.* a plant and its seed.[2]
বড়র্বড়র্, *s.* a murmur, a prattle, prating.
বড়ল, *s.* a species of bread-fruit tree.[3]
বড়শা, *s.* a spear, a javelin, a lance, harpoon.
বড়শাধারী, *a.* using a spear : *s.* a spears-
বড়শী, or **বড়িশ**, *s.* a fish-hook. [man.
বড়া, *s.* a kind of cake fried in oil. [deur.
বড়াই, *s.* pride, vaunting, boasting, gran-
বড়িয়া, *s.* a pawn, a man at chess. [bolus.
বড়ী, *s.* little balls made of pulse ; a pill,
বড়ু, *s.* a bráhman who officiates for a shu-
বড়্বড়্, *s.* a murmuring, a prating. [dra.
বড়বড়া, *v. n.* to mutter, grumble, murmur.
বড়বড়ান, *s.* a grumbling, a murmuring.
চড়বড়ানী, *s.* garrulity, murmuring. [ling.
বড়্বড়িয়া, *a.* garrulous, loquacious, grumb-
বড়ৃ, *a.* capacious, great, large, severe.
বঢ়ই, *s.* a carpenter, a joiner.
বণিক, *s.* a merchant, a trader, a banker.
বণ্ট, *s.* a share, a portion. [shares out.
বণ্টক, *a.* dividing, sharing out : *s.* one who
বণ্টন, *s.* sharing out, dividing into shares.
বণ্ড, *s.* one who is circumcised, a tailless animal: *a.* maimed, defective, crippled, castrated, emasculated, impotent, docked.
বৎ, *ad.* like, resembling ; *e. g.* পশুবৎ, like a beast, etc.: *s.* a glutinous substance.
***বতক**, *s.* a duck, a goose, (generic name).
***বতারিখ**, *ad.* on that day of the month.
***বতিশা**, *s.* a kind of sweet electuary.
বত্রিশ, *a.* thirty-two. বত্রিশা, thirty-second.
বৎস, *s.* a calf, a young animal ; also, an affectienate address to any one, O child.
বৎসনাভ, *s.* a very poisonous plant.[4]
বৎসমাংস, *s.* veal, the flesh of a calf.
বৎসর. *s.* a year ;-বৎসর, yearly, every year.
বৎসরান্তরে, *ad.* in another year, yearly.
বৎসল, *a.* fond, affectionate, kind.
‡**বদ্**, *a.* bad, evil : *v. a.* to speak, to say.

বদন, *s.* the face, the countenance, the visage ; the speaking of a thing.
বদরী, *s.* the jujube and its tree.[5]
***বদল্**, *v. a.* to barter, to exchange.
বদল, *s.* exchange, barter, a recompense, a reward, a substitution, a vicissitude.
বদলন, বদলান, *s.* the changing of a thing.
বদলা, *v. a.* to change, to alter, to barter.
বদলাই, বদলী, *s.* thing given in exchange.
বদলাবদলি, *s.* a barter, an exchange. [of.
বদলে, *ad.* in exchange, in lieu of, instead
বদান্য, *a.* bountiful, munificent, liberal.
***বদী**, *s.* a badge of Husain ; evil, wicked-
***বদ্খৎ**, *a.* writing a bad hand. [ness.
***বদ্খেয়াল**, *s.* evil machination or contri-
বদ্খেয়ালী, *a.* contriving evil. [vance.
***বদ্খো**, *a.* malevolent : *s.* a bad conduct.
***বদ্জুবান**, *a.* abusive : *s.* scurrility, abuse.
***বদ্জাত**, *a.* base-born, vile, wicked.
বদ্জাতী, *s.* baseness of birth, vileness.
***বদ্ডৌল**, *a.* ill-formed, ugly, ungraceful.
***বদ্দোয়া**, *s.* a curse, an imprecation.
বদ্ধ, *a.* bound, closed, confined, shut, locked, restrained, stanched, tied, fastened.
বদ্ধক, *a.* styptic, binding : *s.* a styptic.
বদ্ধগোঁআর, *s.* a confirmed idiot, or rustic.
বদ্ধপাগল, *s.* a confirmed fool.
বদ্ধবৈর, *a.* retaining a confirmed enmity.
বদ্ধমূল, *a.* firmly rooted. [evil desire.
***বদ্নজর**, *a.* envious : *s.* envy, evil sight,
***বদ্না**, *s.* an earthen pot with a tube.
বদ্নাম, বদ্নামী, *s.* a bad name, bad cha-
***বদ্নিয়ত**, *a.* inclined to evil. [racter.
***বদ্বখীল**, *a.* parsimonious : *s.* a miser.
***বদ্বো**, *s.* a fetor, an ill scent : *a.* fetid.
***বদ্মজলিশ**, *s.* a bad society or company.
বদ্মজলিশী, *a.* belonging to bad company.
***বদ্মস্লৎ**, *s.* bad counsel, evil advice.
বদ্মস্লতী, *a.* giving evil counsel.
***বদ্মিজাজ**, *a.* ill-disposed : *s.* bad temper.
***বদ্রকম**, *a.* of bad sort, inferior, bad, evil.
***বদ্রঙ্গ**, *a.* bad-coloured : *s.* a tree.[6]
***বদ্রাহা**, *s.* a bad way, a bad road.
বধ্, *v. a.* to kill, to murder. [to kill.
বধ, *s.* slaughter, murder ; -কৃ, to murder,
বধকর্ত্তা, *s.* a murderer, a slayer. [death.
বধদণ্ড, *s.* capital punishment, sentence of

বধনীয়, deserving death, worthy of death.
বধভাগী, *s.* a partaker in the guilt of mur-
বধযোগ্য, *a.* the same with বধনীয়. [der.
বধির, কালা, বহেরা, *a.* deaf.
বধী, or বধিক, *a.* murderous, killing: *s.* a
বধূ, *s.* a wife, a son's wife. [murderer.
বধ্য, *a.* deserving death, vulnerable.
বধ্যতা, -ত্ব, *s.* a being worthy of death.
বন, *s.* a forest, a desert, a thicket, a place overrun with weeds, uncultivated place.
বনআদা, *s.* a plant (Zinziber casumunar).
বনকাটা, *s.* one who cuts wood in a forest.
বনগরু, *s.* a species of ox (Bos grunniens).
বনগাছ, *s.* brushwood, wild plants. [ests.
বনচর, বনেচর, sylvan, traversing the for-
বনচাঁড়াল, *s.* a plant (Hedysarum gyrans).
বনচারক, or বনচারী, *a.* traversing the for-
বনছাগল, *s.* a wild goat. [ests, sylvan.
বনজ, *a.* produced in a forest, sylvan, wild.
বনজাত, *a.* produced in a forest, wild.
বনপূঁই, *s.* a climbing plant.[1] [ascetic.
বনপ্রবেশ, *s.* the entering in a forest as an
বনপ্রস্থায়ী, *a.* going to a forest: *s.* a hermit.
বনবরাহ, or বনশূকর, *s.* a wild hog.
বনবাস, *s.* a residence in a forest.
বনবাসী, *a.* residing in a forest: *s.* a hermit.
বনবিড়াল, *s.* a species of wild cat.[2]
বনভোজন, *s.* the eating a social meal in a forest or garden for recreation.
বনমানুষ, *s.* a wild man, the orang-utang.
বনরাজ, *s.* the lion, king of the forests.
বনস্থ, *a.* situated in a forest: *s.* an ascetic.
বনহলদি, *s.* wild turmeric.[3] [build.
বনা, *v. a.* to make, fabricate, manufacture,
বনাই, or বনুই, *s.* a sister's husband.
*বনাত, or বন্তি, *s.* broad cloth; intimacy.
বনাতী, *a.* made of broad cloth.
বনান, *s.* a making, fabricating, building.
বনায়, *s.* intimacy, friendship, love.
বনিতা, *s.* a wife, a woman.
বনুষ্য, sylvan, wild, belonging to a forest.
বন্দ্, *v. a.* to salute, to pay respects.
বন্দ, *s.* custody, a parcel of land, a girdle, a fastening, a knot, a bandage, a belt, a roller, a string, a knuckle, a mound or fence, an embankment, regularity.
বন্দকরণ, *s.* a confining, a shutting up.
বন্দক, *a.* complimenting, revering: *s.* one who pays respects, a worshipper.
বন্দছন্দ, *a.* orderly, shut up, confined.
বন্দন, বন্দনা, *s.* a salutation, an obeisance, a bow; invocation. [a harbour.
বন্দর, *s.* a market, mart, emporium, a port,
বন্দি, বন্দী, *s.* a captive, prisoner, a parasite; -খানা, -শালা, a prison; -পাল, a jailor.
বন্দীয়ান, বন্দুয়ান, *s.* a captive, a prisoner.
বন্দুক, *s.* a gun, a musket, a fowling-piece.
*বন্দেজ, *a.* inventing, contriving; orderly, fixed: *s.* a binding, elegancy of style.
*বন্দেনেবাজ্, *s.* Sir, Your worship.
বন্দোবস্ত, *s.* a settlement, an arrangement, a covenant, an agreement, regularity.
বন্দ্য, *a.* laudable, praiseworthy, venerable.
বন্ধ, *s.* bonds, intimate union, a tying or fastening: *a.* shut, tied, bound, confined; -কৃ, to tie, shut, shut up, adjourn.
বন্ধক, *s.* a pledge, a pawn, a mortgage.
বন্ধকগ্রহণ, *s.* the taking of a pledge.
বন্ধক-গ্রাহক, -গ্রাহী, *a.* receiving pledges: *s.* a pawn-broker, a mortgagee.
বন্ধন, *s.* a shutting up, fastening, confining, the tying of a knot, a binding, tying; a tie, a bond; -ঘুচা, to liberate.
বন্ধনখোদা, *s.* a dungeon.
বন্ধনশালা, বন্ধনাগার, *s.* a prison. [ment.
বন্ধনী, *s.* a bandage, roller, garter, a liga-
বন্ধনীয়, *a.* capable of being bound or tied, requiring to be confined. [wages.
বন্ধান, *s.* a stipend, a settled pay, a salary,
বন্ধী, *s.* a captive, a prisoner, a felon.
বন্ধু, *s.* a friend, an associate, a kinsman.
বন্ধুগণ, or বন্ধুবর্গ, *s.* relations, friends.
বন্ধুতা, -ত্ব, *s.* friendship, intimacy.
বন্ধুর, *a.* undulated, waved, rough, uneven.
বন্ধ্যা, barren, sterile, unfruitful: *s.* barren
বন্ধ্যাত্ব, *s.* barrenness, sterility. [woman.
বন্য, *a.* of a forest, sylvan, rural, wild; -পশু, a wild beast; -শূকর, a wild boar.
বন্যা, *s.* a deluge, a flood, an inundation.
বপন, *s.* sowing of seed; -কাল, seed-time.
বপা, *s.* fat, synovia. বপুঃ, *s.* the body.
বপ্তা, *s.* a sower, a planter; a father.
বব্বলিয়া, *s.* a shuffler, a liar, false or hired witness, a rogue, a cheat, a swindler.

বভ্রু, *s* a large ichneumon, a weasel.
বমথী, *s.* a vomiting, a spouting out.
বমন, *s.* an emetic; vomit, a vomiting.
বমাল, with the property: *s.* stolen goods.
বমী, *s.* an emetic; any substance vomited.
বম্বেটিয়া, *s.* a pirate; -গিরী, piracy.
বয়, *s.* a scent, a smell, stench.
বয়ঃ, *s.* the period of life, age (attained).
বয়ঃক্রম, *s.* the allotted period of life, age.
বয়ড়া, *s.* a nut used in medicine.
বয়দা, আণ্ডা, ডীম, *s.* an egg. [face.
বয়ঃস্ফোড়া, *s.* pimples which appear on the
বয়স্থা, *s.* prime of life, youth, manhood.
বয়স্য, of the same age, coeval, associate.
বয়া, *a.* fetid, stinking: *s.* a buoy; *vide* বাবুই.
*বয়ান, *s.* a narration, an explanation; the
বয়ার, *s.* the wind, air; a buffalo. [face.
বয়োজ্যেষ্ঠ, *a.* eldest, chief in point of age.
বর্, *v. a.* to betroth, to promise marriage.
বর, *s.* a bridegroom, a gift, boon, blessing, a promise: in *comp.* means chief, great.
বরং, *ad.* rather, in preference.
*বরকৎ, *s.* a blessing, a benediction.
*বরকন্দাজ, *s.* a kind of soldier, an armed footman, a petty police officer.
*বরখাস্ত, *s.* a retiring, cessation of office.
বরগা, *s.* a rafter, battens laid on beams.
বরঞ্চ, *ad.* rather, preferably, in preference.
বরজ, *s.* a betel-plantation. [*fem.* বরটা.
বরট, *s.* a gander; a barbarian; a wasp;
বরণ, *s.* the betrothing of a girl; a giving of earnest money; a freckle, a pustule.
বরণবস্ত্র, *s.* clothes given at a marriage con-
বরণীয়, *a.* eligible, fit to be chosen. [tract.
*বরতরফ্, dismissed from office, put aside.
বরদ, *a.* blessing, giving boons or blessings.
*বরদার, *a.* holding, bearing: *s.* a bearer.
*বরদাস্ত, *s.* patience, a bearing or endur-
বরন্দল, *s.* a defective singer. [ing.
বরপ্রার্থনা, *s.* the requesting a boon.
*বরফ, *s.* snow, ice. [ed to a damsel.
বরপাত্র, *s.* a bridegroom, a person betroth-
বরযাত্রী, *s.* friends or followers of a bride-
বরলা, *s.* a hornet, wasp; a goose. [groom.
বরশা, *s.* a harpoon, fish-hook, spear, lance.
বরষ্, *v. n.* to rain, to fall like a shower.
*বরাঅর্দ্দ, *s.* an estimating, a calculation.

বরাট, *s.* a cauṛi; pericarpium of the lotus.
বরাটক, বরাটিকা, *s* a cauṛi, a cowry-shell.
*বরাৎ, *s.* a commission, a warrant, an assignment, a reference, a letter, a draft, a maintenance; a marriage procession.
বরাতী, *a.* arising from an assignment.
বরাবর, *a.* abreast, even, level, like, plain, uniform, smooth, straight, equal, exact, accurate, alike: *ad.* straight on, up to.
বরামদ, *s.* a backbiting, a tale-bearing, an accusation, an impeachment.
বরার্থী, *a.* desirous of a boon or favour.
বরার্থে, *ad.* for a boon or favour.
বরাহ, *s.* a boar, a hog. বরাহী, *s.* a sow.
বরাহাবতার, *s.* an incarnation of Vishnu.
বরিষ্, *v. a.* to rain down, to shower down.
বরিষণ, *s.* a showering down, the falling of rain, dust, weapons, flowers, or the like.
বরিষা, *v. a.* to shower down, to cause to fall like a shower: *s.* the rainy season.
বরুণ, *s.* the name of the Indian Neptune.
বরেণ্য, *a.* chief, pre-eminent, excellent.
বরেয়া, *s.* the split piece of bambu which runs lengthwise in thatch work.
বর্গ, *s.* a class, a number of synonyms, a section, a square number. [to squares.
বর্গকর্ম্ম, *s.* in *mathe.* an operation relative
বর্গকৃতি, *s.* a square number.
বর্গঘন, *s.* the square of a cube.
বর্গঘনঘাত, *s.* the fifth power or sursolid.
বর্গপদ, or বর্গমূল, *s.* the square foot.
বর্গপ্রকৃতি, *s.* the affected square.
বর্গবর্গ, *s.* the square of a square.
বর্গবর্গঘনঘাত, *s.* the seventh power.
বর্গবর্গবর্গ, *s.* square of a squared square.
বর্গীকৃত, *a.* classified, arranged.
বর্গীভূত, *a.* become a class or genus.
বর্গীয়, *a.* belonging to a class.
বর্চ্ছা, বর্চ্ছি, *s.* a spear, lance; -ধারী, a lancer.
বর্জ্জ্, *v. a.* to except, to relinquish, to abandon, to expel the fæces. [leaving out.
বর্জ্জন, *s.* the making of an exception, a
বর্জ্জনীয়, বর্জ্জ্য *a.* rejectible, exceptionable, fit to be abandoned, censurable.
বর্জ্জিত, *a.* excepted, left out, rejected, abandoned, censured.
বর্ণ্, *v. a.* to narrate, to describe, to detail.

বর্ণ, *s.* a tribe, a class, an order, a colour, a hue, a tint, a syllable, a letter, a quality, a property, fame, celebrity, praise, beauty, lustre, the fineness of gold; in *arith.* a quantity, a co-efficient.
বর্ণক, *s.* a perfume for the body, a paint or pigment, a panegyrist, a bard, one who describes things, the standard of gold: *a.* belonging to a tribe or class.
বর্ণকব্রাহ্মণ, *s.* a bráhman who officiates in religious matters for an inferior class.
বর্ণক্রম, *s.* alphabetical order.
বর্ণগত, *a.* algebraic, pertaining to algebra.
বর্ণন, *s.* the act of describing or narrating.
বর্ণনা, *s.* eulogium, a description, narration, the relation of a thing. [or narrated.
বর্ণনীয়, *a.* describable, fit to be delineated
বর্ণবিপর্য্যয়, *s.* substitution of one letter
বর্ণমালা, *s.* the alphabet. [for another.
বর্ণসঙ্কর, *a.* of mixed blood, mongrel: *s.* a
বর্ণান্তর, *s.* a change of colour. [mixed tribe.
বর্ণাশ্রম, the classes and states of society.
বর্ণিত, *a.* described, narrated, eulogized.
বর্ণী, *a.* of a tribe: *s.* a painter, a describer.
বর্ত্তন, *s.* the existing or subsisting of any thing, a maintenance; a dish, a plate: *a.* fixed, stationed, stable, staying, abiding.
বর্ত্তনীয়, বর্ত্তিতব্য, *a.* possible, probable.
বর্ত্তমান, *a.* being, existing, present, extant.
বর্ত্তমানকাল, *s.* in *gram.* the present tense.
বর্ত্তমানতা, -ত্ব, *s.* present existence, a being.
বর্ত্তি, *s.* a candle, a lamp, a wick, a tent, a
বর্ত্তিকর্ত্তনী, *s.* a pair of snuffers. [bougie.
বর্ত্তিত, *a.* been, become, existed.
বর্ত্তী, *a.* being, existing, standing.
বর্ত্তুল, *s.* a circle, a globe, a ball, a sphere, a pea, a ball or bullet of earth, a marble for play, a pellet, a bullet. [cal, round.
বর্ত্তুলাকার, বর্ত্তুলাকৃতি, *a.* globular, spheri-
বর্ত্তুলাকৃতিসংমিলন, *s.* conglomeration.
বর্ত্ত্যাধার, *s.* a candlestick, a lamp-stand.
বর্ত্মন, *s.* a road, a path; the eyelash.
বর্দ্ধ, *v. a.* to increase, to grow, to enlarge.
বর্দ্ধক, বর্দ্ধমান, *a.* increasing, growing, pros-
বর্দ্ধন, *s.* an increase, a growth. [pering
বর্দ্ধনশীল, *a.* increasing, improving, growing, having a tendency to grow.

বর্দ্ধনীয়, *a.* capable of increase. [ven.
বর্দ্ধিত, *a.* increased, grown, expanded, thri-
বর্দ্ধিষ্ণু *a.* growing, having a tendency to become large, improving. [increase.
বর্দ্ধিষ্ণুতা, -ত্ব, *s.* the having a tendency to
*বর্ফি, *s.* a kind of sweetmeat.
বর্ব্বটী, *s.* a kidney bean.[1] [blockhead.
বর্ব্বর, *s.* one of a low class, a barbarian, a
বর্ম্ম, *s.* armour, coat of mail. বর্ম্মী, mailed,
বর্শি *s.* a fish hook. [accoutred.
বর্ষ, *v. n.* to rain, to shower down.
বর্ষ, a year; -জীবি, annual (as vegetables).
বর্ষণ, *s.* the falling of rain or hail.
বর্ষবৃদ্ধি, *s.* a birthday, an anniversary.
বর্ষা, *s.* rain, a shower, the rainy season: *v. a.* to shower down, to cause to rain.
বর্ষাকাল, বর্ষাৎ, *s.* the rainy season. [son.
বর্ষাকালীন, *a.* belonging to the rainy sea-
বর্ষাতি, *idem*: *s.* a disease in horses; a boat-
বর্ষাবৎ, *a.* rainy. বর্ষোপল, *s.* hail. [cloak.
বর্ষীয়স্, *a.* very old, full of years, eldest.
বর্ষ্মন্, *s.* the body, height, tallness, eleva-
বর্হ, *s.* a peacock's tail, also its crest. [tion.
বর্হী, *s.* a peacock. বর্হিণী, *s.* a peahen.
বল্, *v. a.* to say, to speak, to tell.
বল, *s.* strength, might, force, power, vigour, energy, an army, a chessman.
বলকা, *a.* lukewarm, moderately boiled.
বলদ, *s.* an ox, a bullock; a blockhead.
বলন, *s.* a speaking, a saying. [lent.
বলবৎ, *a.* strong, firm, solid, valid, preva-
বলবত্তা, *s.* strength, power, firmness, solidity, validity, prevalency. [powerful.
বলবান্, বলবন্ত, *a.* strong, vigorous, stout,
বল্লম, *s.* a spear, lance; -বরদার, a lancer.
বলম্ব, *s.* a perpendicular line.
বলয়, *s.* a ring for the wrist; in *ana.* a part
বলয়াকৃতি, *a.* annular. [of the ear (helix).
বলয়িত, *a.* encircled, surrounded. [feeble.
বলযুক্ত, *a.* strong, powerful. বলহীন, weak,
বলরাম, Balarám, the brother of Krishna.
বলা, *s.* a speaking, the saying of a thing: *v. a.* to cause to teach or speak.
বলাট, *s.* the bovine organ of generation.
বলাৎকার, *s.* a rape, violence; -কৃ, to ravish.
বলাৎকারক, বলাৎকারী, *s.* a ravisher.
বলাধান, *s.* a strengthening, invigoration.

বলান, *s.* a teaching or causing to speak.
বলাবলি, *s.* conversation, discourse.
বলি. *s.* a sacrifice, victim; a wrinkle; a tax; -দান, -দেওন, the offering of a sacrifice.
বলিভুক, *a.* feeding on sacrificial food: *s.* a crow.
বলী, *a.* strong, vigorous, powerful.
বলীবর্দ্দ, *s.* an ox, a bullock.
বলক, *v. a.* to wallop, to bubble, to boil, to simmer.
বলকন, *s.* a simmering, bubbling, boiling.
বল্কল, *s.* the bark of a tree; fish-scale.
বলকা, *v. a.* to make a liquid wallop in boiling: *a.* heated, boiling, warm, tepid.
বলকান, *s.* a boiling, making a liquid bubble.
বল্গ বল্গু, *a.* pretty, beautiful, captivating.
বল্গা, *s.* the bit of a bridle, a rein.
বল্মীক, *s.* a whiteant; an ant-hill.
বল্ল, *s.* a weight equal to two rattis.
বল্লব, *s.* a cowherd, a milkman; a cook.
বল্লভ, *a.* beloved, amiable, dear, desired.
বল্লালী, *a.* pertaining to rájá Ballál Sena.
বল্লী, *s.* a climbing plant.
বশ, বশতা, *s.* obedience, submission, subjection, control.
বশতঃ, *ad.* under subjection or control.
বশতাপন্ন, *a.* subject, obedient, under control.
বশিষ্ঠ, *s.* the name of a sage.
বশীকরণ, *s.* a bringing into subjection.
বশীকৃত, বশীভূত, *a.* brought under control, controlled, subjected, subdued.
বশীভূততা, -ত্ব, *s.* subjection, subjugation.
বশ্য, controllable, obedient, docile, tame.
বস, *v. a.* to dwell, to sit, to settle (as any liquid,) to candy, to coagulate, to sink.
*বস, *a.* sufficient, enough: *ad.* no more.
বসৎ, *s.* a dwelling, habitation, residence.
বসৎবাটী, or বসবাটী, *s.* a dwelling house.
বসতি, *s.* a habitation, a dwelling, a residence, an abode; -কৃ, to reside, to dwell.
বসন, *s.* the dwelling in a place, a sitting or settling; clothing, dress, a garment.
বসনিয়া, *a.* dwelling: *s.* an inhabitant.
বসন্ত, *s.* the spring; the small-pox.
বসন্তকাল, *s.* the spring season.
বসন্তকালীন, *a.* vernal, belonging to the spring.
বসন্তবুড়ী, বসন্তবৈরী, *s.* the name of a bird.[1]
বসন্তবাহন, inoculation for the small-pox.
বসন্তী, orange-colored; -রঙ্গ, orange color.
বসা, *v. a.* to cause to sit down, or settle, to compress, to set stones, to drive a nail, to coagulate, to beat down earth, to people a place: *s.* a sitting; fat.
বসাকোষ, *s.* in *anatomy*, a follicle.
বসান, *s.* causing to sit, precipitating, coagulating, settling of liquids: *a.* seated, precipitated, coagulated, candied.
বসু, *s.* a class of eight demigods; tie of a yoke, wealth, substance, matter, a gem, a jewel, water; -দেব, Krishna's father.
বসুমতী, বসুধা, বসুন্ধরা, *s.* the earth.
বস্তব্য, *a.* habitable, fit to live in.
বস্তা, *s.* a bale, a package, bundle, parcel.
বস্তাবন্দী, *s.* making of goods into bales.
বস্তি, *s.* a town, a village, a habitation; the bladder, the abdomen, the pelvis.
বস্তু, *s.* a thing, a substance, stuff, matter.
বস্তুতঃ, *ad.* in reality, in fact, that is.
বস্তুতা, -ত্ব, *s.* substantiality.
বস্তুবিদ্যা, *s.* physiology, doctrine of nature.
বস্তুবিনিময়, *s.* barter, exchange of articles.
বস্তুবিনিময়গণিত, *s.* the rule of barter.
বস্ত্র, *s.* a garment, cloth, clothing, an article of dress; -পর, to dress.
বস্ত্রপরিধান, *s.* the putting on of clothes.
বস্ত্রবিলাস, *s.* foppery, pride of dress.
বস্ত্রবিলাসী, *a.* foppish, proud of dress.
বস্ত্রাগার, *s.* a tent, a clothier's warehouse.
বস্ত্বন্তর, *s.* another thing, not the same.
বহ্, *v. a.* to carry a burden, to bear a load, to flow (as a stream), to blow (as the wind), to pass away (as time), to draw (a plough, etc.), to convey.
বহন, *s.* a carrying of a burden, a flowing, a blowing (of wind), a passing away (of time), circulation or motion of blood.
বহনি, *s.* a carrying of burden; porterage.
বহনীয়, *a.* portable, light; flowing.
বহর, *s.* a fleet, a fleet of boats; width.
বহরী, *s.* a kind of falcon (Falco calidus).
বহা, *v. a.* to impel, to row, to steer a ship.
বহান, *s.* an impelling forward.
বহি, *s.* a book, an account book.
বহিঃ, বহিস্, *ad.* without, viz. on the outside.
বহিঃস্থ, *a.* external, outer, outward.
বহিত্র, *s.* a raft, a float, a raft of any thing.
বহিনী, ভগিনী, বইন, *s.* a sister.

বহিরঙ্গ, *s.* a stranger, a foe; minor rites.
বহিরিন্দ্রিয়, *s.* organs of action, external organs.
বহির্গত, *a.* gone forth, gone out.
বহির্গমন, *s.* a going forth, a going out.
বহির্গামী, *a.* going forth or out.
বহির্দেশ, *s.* a foreign country; outskirts; a privy.
বহির্দ্বার, *s.* a gate, outer door; in *ana.* entrance into the vagina (os externum).
বহির্বাসঃ, *s.* external or outer garment.
বহির্ভূত, *a.* external, excluded, expelled.
বহির্মুখ, turned away; scurrilous, impious.
বহির্লম্ব, *s.* a perpendicular falling on the outside of a triangle.
বহিষ্করণ, *s.* an expelling, expulsion, seclusion.
বহিষ্কৃত, *a.* excluded, expelled.
বহী, *s.* a book, a register; -কার, a book-binder.
বহীবাঁধন, *s.* the binding of a book.
বহু, *a.* much, many: *ad.* very, exceedingly.
বহুকালিক, or বহুকালীন, *a.* of long standing, chronic, old, ancient.
বহুচেষ্টা, *s.* activity, diligence, perseverance.
বহুত, much, many, abundant, numerous.
বহুতা, -ত্ব, *s.* abundance, plenty.
বহুদর্শক, বহুদর্শী, *a.* observant, wise, prudent.
বহুদর্শিতা, prudence, observant condition.
বহু- দলক, polypetalous; -পুরুষক, polyandrous; -পুষ্পক, many-flowered; -ভ্রাতৃক, polyadelphous; -স্ত্রীক, polygynous.
বহুধা, *a.* manifold: *ad.* in various ways.
বহুপত্রক, *a.* having compound leaf.
বহু-পথ, a labyrinth; -পান, drinking to excess.
বহুপ্রকার, বহুবিধ, *a.* many sorts, various.
বহু-প্রজ, populous, prolific; -প্রসূতা, prolific.
বহুফলা, *a.* fruitful, prolific.
বহুবক্রাস্থি, *s.* the ilium; -যাতনা, the iliac passion.
বহুবচন, *s.* in *gram.* the plural number.
বহু- বর্ষক, *a.* perennial; -যতি, polysyllabic.
বহুভার্য্য, *a.* having many wives; -তা, polygamy.
বহুভাষী, *a* talkative, garrulous.
বহুমূত্র, *s.* the diabetes.
বহুমূল্য, *a.* valuable, high-priced, costly, precious.
বহুরঙ্গ, *a.* partycoloured, gaudy, showy.
বহুরূপা, *s.* a chameleon, a polypus.
বহুরূপী, *a.* assuming many forms, multiform.
বহুল, *a.* many, much, abundant, prolix.
বহুস্বামিক, *a.* having many proprietors, common.
বহেরা, বধির, কালা, *a.* deaf.

বহ্নি, *s.* fire, god of fire. বহ্নিমুখ, *s.* a god.
বহ্বপত্য, *a.* having many children.
বহ্বাশা, *s.* large hopes or expectations.
বহ্বাশী, *a.* insatiable, greedy, voracious.
বা, *conj.* or, and, either: *intj.* surprizing!
বাই, *s.* an expression of respect, Lady, Madam; the air of the body, wind, flatulency, enthusiasm; a dancing girl.
বাইচ, *s.* a rowing about in boats for pleasure, a gala.
বাইচা, *s.* a rower.
বাইন, *s.* player on a tambour; a kiln, sugar-boiling furnace; joining in planks, a crevice; an eel; -চাইল, a leak, crack.
বাইমারা, *s.* idleness, laziness, levity.
বাইয়া, *a.* windy, flatulent, hypochondriac.
বাইল, *s.* the leaf of a folding door or table, the turning of a boat; *vide* বালদি.
বাইশ, *s.* an adze, an axe: *a.* twenty-two! *intj.* astonishing! amazing! wonderful:
বাইশা, *a.* the twenty-second.
বাইশী, *s.* a willow tree, the weeping willow.
বাউটি, *s.* ornament for a woman's wrist.
বাউনিয়া, *a.* dwarf, pigmy, short.
বাউরা, বাউড়া, or বাউল, *a.* mad, insane, foolish.
বাউলি, *s.* a pair of tongs used in cookery.
বাউলী, *s.* a large well, a reservoir.
বাও, *s.* the venereal disease; the wind.
বাওআবর, seventy-two. বাওআন্ন, fifty-two.
বাওটাহরিণ, *s.* a swift antelope.
বাওড়, *s.* a lake, a sheet of water.
বাওড়ী, *s.* a circuit, a whirlwind.
বাওরা, *a.* wind-born; -ডিম্ব, a wind-egg.
বাওয়ালী, *s.* small chaff, a wood-cutter, a plant.
বাওরাসার, *s.* the piles, emeroids.
বাওল, *v. a.* to winnow, to toss.
বাঁ, *a.* left (in opposition to right).
বাঁইত, *s.* vomit, the act of vomiting.
বাঁউ, or বাম, *s.* a fathom.
বাঁক, *v. a.* to be crooked, to bow down, to bend, turn.
বাক, *s.* a yoke to carry burden, a turning in a river, a crook or bending, an ornament for the legs; crowing of a cock; a trumpet; -ভাঙ্গ, to straighten.
বাঁকড়া, *a.* impudent, bold, audacious: *s.* a fop.
বাঁকন, *s.* bending, being crooked or awry.
বাঁকা, *v. a.* to bend: *a.* bent, crooked, awry, askew, sinuous, winding: *s.* a fop.

বাঁকাটেড়া, *a.* crooked, tortuous, awry.
বাঁকাপা, *a.* bandy-legged, crook-legged.
বাঁকালোক, *a.* obstinate, foolhardy, rank.
বাঁকী, *s.* a trumpeter, a yoke-porter; remnant, a remainder, residue, a balance.
বাঁচ, *v. n.* to live, to survive, to escape, to remain, to be left, to continue.
বাঁচন, *s.* a living, surviving, an escaping.
বাঁচা, *v. a.* to preserve, protect, shelter, spare, extricate, save: *s.* preservation, an escape: *a.* escaped, saved, preserved.
বাঁচান, *s.* the preserving, defending, sheltering or protecting of a person.
বাঁঝা, বাঁঝী, *a.* barren, sterile. [tion, allot.
বাঁট্, *v. a.* to distribute, to share out, por-
বাঁট, *s.* a share, a portion, a lot, an allowance; the dug of an animal, a teat; the handle of a hatchet or other edge tool.
বাঁটন, *s.* a dealing or sharing out.
বাঁটা, *s.* partition, an allotment, a stigma, discount: *v. a.* to cause to share out.
বাঁটিয়া, বাঁঠিয়া, *a.* dwarfish, short, dwarf.
বাঁটুল, *s.* a ball, a bullet of earth, a pellet.
বাঁট্টা, *s.* a discount, discount on money.
বাঁড়া, *s.* the male organ of generation.
বাঁড়িয়া, *a.* docked, tailless; fine, best, ex-
বাঁদর, *s.* a monkey, an ape. [cellent.
বাঁদী, *s.* a female slave; a kind of garment.
বাঁধ্, *v. a.* to bind, fasten, shut up, confine, tie, stop, block up, to set in a socket, to mount with a metal, to build, to pave.
বাঁধ, *s.* an embankment, a dam, a binding.
বাঁধন, *s.* the act of binding, fastening, or shutting, the stopping of any liquid.
বাঁধনী *s.* a fastening, a tie, a pavement.
বাঁধা, *s.* a pawn, a pledge, a mortgage, a shutting up, a binding or confining: *a.* stopped, stagnant, confined, bound, paved: *v. a.* to confine, to enclose, to repair a dam or bank, to mount with metal.
বাঁধান, *s.* a causing to confine, causing to repair a dam or bank, a causing to set stones, or mount any thing with metal.
বাঁধাবাঁধি, *s.* a mutual tying or confining.
বাঁধাল, *s.* an embankment, bambu partition made in a river to confine fishes.
বাঁধুনি, *s.* a binding, a stitch, a tie.

বাঁয়, *ad.* on the left side; to the left.
বাঁশ, *s.* a bambu; -গাড়ী, the erecting of a bambu as a signal. বাঁশই, a harrow.
বাঁশপাতা, *s.* a bambu leaf; a species of bird,[1] a kind of fish.[2] [a bambu.
বাঁশবাজী, *s.* a sort of sport performed on
বাঁশিনিবাঁশ, *s.* a variety of the bambu.
বাঁশী, *s.* a flute, a pipe, a whistle, a fife.
বাঁশীবালা, *s.* a piper, a fifer. [guage.
বাক্, *s.* a word, speech, utterance, a lan-
বাকল, *s.* bark of a tree, an integument.
বাকস, *s.* the name of a flowering shrub.[2]
বাকার, *s.* *vide* বাখার. [rear, a balance.
বাকী, *s.* remnant, a remainder, residue, ar-
বাক্কৌশল, *s.* eloquence, volubility.
বাক্ছল, *s.* a pretence, an excuse, evasion, prevarication. [of words.
বাক্জাল, *s.* an ensnaring speech, a maze
বাক্তাড়না, *s.* a reprimand, repulse.
বাক্পটু, *a.* eloquent, fluent, voluble, skil-
বাক্পটুতা, *s.* eloquence. [led in words.
বাক্পারুষ্য, *s.* scurrility, abusive language.
বাক্প্রবন্ধ, *s.* a literary composition; pro-
বাক্ব্যয়, *s.* talkativeness. [lixity.
বাক্‌লা, *s.* the bark of a tree or plant, the peel or rind of a fruit, an integument.
বাক্য, *s.* a word, a sentence, an expression, a language, speech.
বাক্যজ্বালা, *s.* provoking language.
বাক্যতাড়না, *s.* a reproof, a reproach.
বাক্যপ্রয়োগ, *s.* a communication, an in-
বাক্যবহির্ভূত, *a.* disobedient. [junction.
বাক্যবিন্যাস, *s.* in *gram.* the syntax.
বাক্যব্যয়, *s.* loquacity, a tautology.
বাক্যার্থ, *s.* the meaning of an expression.
বাক্যালাপ, *s.* conversation, intercourse.
বাখান, *s.* exposition, comment; abusive language, scurrility.
বাখার, *s.* a storehouse, a granary. [lath.
বাখারি, *s.* quicklime; a split bambu, a
বাখারিচূণ, *s.* quicklime, unslaked lime.
বাখ্না, *v. a.* to praise, to laud. [thing.
বাখনান, *s.* the praising of a person or
বাগ, *s.* the rein of a bridle; a garden; a side; *e. g.* এবাগ, this side, etc. [much.
বাগাড়ম্বর, *s.* beginning to talk, a talking
বাগাৎ, *s.* a grove, a garden, gardens.

বাগান, বাগিচা, *s.* a parterre, a garden.
বাগী, *s.* a bubo; a basket to measure grain.
বাগীশ, or বাচস্পতি, *a.* eloquent, fluent:
s. a master of languages; Vrihaspati.
বাগুণ, বার্ত্তাকু, *s.* brinjal, the egg-fruit.
বাগুণীয়া, *a.* purple; -রঙ্গ, purple colour.
বাগুরা, *s.* a net for catching deer. [hunter.
বাগুরিক, *s.* one who catches deer in nets, a
বাগে, *ad.* on the side, in the direction of,
বাগেবাগে, *ad.* on this and that side. [near.
বাগেশ্বরী, বাগ্দেবী, *s.* names of Saraswatí,
the goddess of speech. [locution.
বাগ্জাল, *s.* an ensnaring speech, a circum-
বাগড়া, *s.* an intricacy, a perplexity, a scru-
বাগড়াটিয়া, *a.* intricate, perplexed. [ple.
বাগ্ডোর, *s.* the reins of a bridle.
বাগ্দণ্ড, *s.* a reproof, an admonition.
বাগ্দত্ত, *a.* betrothed, affianced, engaged.
বাগ্দান, *s.* the betrothing of a damsel.
বাগ্দুষ্ট, *a.* evil spoken of, abusive, speak-
ing ill, using ungrammatical speech.
বাগ্বিদগ্ধা, *a. f.* bland, enticing or ensnar-
ing by language or conversation. [ous.
বাগ্মী, *a.* eloquent, talkative, fluent, loquaci-
বাগ্যুদ্ধ, *s.* a disputation, a wrangle, a ver-
bal contest, a strife of words.
বাঘ, *s.* a tiger; -ভেরেণ্ডা, a shrub.[1]
বাঘিনী, বাঘী, *s.* a female tiger; a virago.
বাঙ্গলা, *a.* belonging to Bengal, Bengali:
s. a bungalow, a thatched house.
বাঙ্গালা, *a.* belonging to Bengal, Bengali.
বাঙ্গালী, *a.* *idem*: *s.* a native of Bengal.
বাঙ্নিষ্ঠা, *s.* punctuality, an affirmation.
বাঙ্ময়, *a.* wordy, loquacious, talkative.
বাচক, *a.* expressing, speaking, declaring,
expressive, plain: *s.* a speaker.
বাচকতা, -ত্ব, *s.* expressiveness.
বাচকপদ, *s.* a word expressing a given idea.
বাচড়া, *s.* uncultivated land; a colt, a foal.
বাচনিক, *a.* scriptural; verbal, enjoined,
expressed, mentioned, expressible.
বাচা, *v. a.* to explain. বাচাও, *s.* an expla-
বাচাল, *a.* talkative, garrulous. [nation.
বাচালতা, -ত্ব, *s.* talkativeness, garrulity.
বাচিক, *a.* expressing, expressive, verbal,
vocal, oral, expressible in words.
বাচিত, *a.* mentioned, expressed, said.

বাচ্চা, *s.* the young of an animal.
বাচ্য, *a.* expressible, attributable, predica-
ble, declinable (as an adjective,) vile,
contemptible: *s.* the word or idea to
be expressed, a predicate.
বাছ্ *v. a.* to assort, select, to pick out, to
separate from, to choose out. [things.
বাছন, *s.* the picking out or selecting of
বাছনী, *s.* a sorting, selecting, choosing.
বাছা, *a.* selected: *s.* a little one, a child.
বাছাবাছা, *a.* select, chosen out: *intj.* Oh
বাছুর, *s.* a calf. [child! Oh child!
বাজ্, *v.* to sound as a musical instrument,
to strike, feel pain, to strike as a clock.
বাজ, *s.* a thunderbolt, a wing, speed, ghi
or clarified butter; a species of hawk.[2]
বাজন, *s.* the striking of a clock, the play-
ing of chimes, the uttering of sounds.
বাজনঘড়ী, a clock which strikes the hour.
বাজনা, *s.* a musical instrument, music.
বাজন্দার, বাজনীয়া, *s.* one who plays on a
musical instrument, a musician.
বাজবহরী, বাজবৈরী, *s.* a kind of hawk.[3]
*বাজয়াফ্ত, *s.* dismission, deduction. [ket.
বাজরা, *s.* a kind of grain[4], a market bas-
বাজা, *v. a.* to play on a musical instrument,
to strike a bell: *s.* musical instrument.
*বাজাজ, *s.* a linen-draper, a mercer.
বাজান, *s.* the playing on an instrument.
বাজাবালা, or বাজানীয়া, *s.* a musician.
*বাজার, *s.* a market, a perpetual market.
বাজারু, *a* current, common, belonging to
বাজিন্, *s.* a bird, a horse. [the market.
বাজী, *s.* a horse, a stake, a wager, a game,
tumbling, legerdemain, an exhibition;
a time, *i. e.* twice, three times, etc.
বাজীকর, *s.* a tumbler, one who exhibits
legerdemain tricks or feats of activity.
বাজীভোর, *s* a disappointment.
বাজু, *s.* the arm, ornament for the arm, a
part, side, side posts of a furniture.
বাজুবন্দ, *s.* an ornament for the arm.
*বাজে, *a.* common, incidental, not regu-
lar, job like, some, certain, sundry.
বাজেখরচ, *s.* sundry or incidental expense.
বাজেজমা, *s.* the rents or revenues aris-
ing from charities or incidental profits.

বাজেজমী, *s.* land not subject to taxation.
বাজেদফা, *s.* a certain time, certain times.
বাঞ্ছ, *v. a.* to desire, to wish.
বাঞ্ছক, *a.* desirous, wishing.
বাঞ্ছন, *s.* desiring or wishing for a thing.
বাঞ্ছনীয়, or বাঞ্ছিতব্য, *a.* desirable.
বাঞ্ছা, *s.* a wish, a desire, a propensity.
বাঞ্ছিত, *a.* desired, wished for.
বাট্, *v. a.* to rub in a mortar or on a grinding stone, to grind paint or spices.
বাট, *s.* a road, a way, path.
বাটন, *s.* a grinding, pounding, trituration.
বাটনা, *s.* ground spices for cookery.
বাটনী, *s.* a woman who grinds spices.
বাটপাড়, *s.* a highwayman, a robber.
বাটপাড়ী. *s.* a highway robbery.
বাটপাড়ীয়া, *a.* robbing on the highway.
বাটা, *s.* a grinding; a betel-box; name of a fish.[1]
বাটাখোল, *s.* plate for a betel-box.
বাটালি. *s.* a chisel, a carpenter's chisel.
বাটিবা, *s.* a sort of twine, thin cord.
বাটী, *s.* a house, a habitation, a residence, a cup, a glass, a rod, a mace. a garden.
বাটুয়া, *a.* travelling, infesting the road: *s.* a small bag.
বাটুলা, *s.* a species of pulse.[2]
বাটলাই, *s.* a pot, a caldron.
বাটখারা, *s.* a weight used in weighing.
বাট্টা, *s.* a betel-box, a discount on money; a stigma on a person's family or caste.
বাড়্, *v. n.* to grow, to increase, to thrive, to swell, to jut out, to spread, to abound, to share out boiled rice from a vessel.
বাড়, *s.* a frame, a margin, a column or half a page, a selvage, an edge, a partition to prevent fishes going out with the current, a weir, a volley.
বাড়ই, *s.* a carpenter; a head sugar-boiler.
বাড়ন, *s.* a growing, increasing, jutting out, thriving, a sharing out food; a besom.
বাড়ন্ত. *a.* overgrown, extended; expended.
বাড়ব, বাড়বাগ্নি, বাড়বানল, submarine fire.
বাড়া, *v. a.* to augment, enlarge, extend, multiply, magnify, promote, increase, exalt, raise, excite: *s.* growth, enlargement, excess, abundance, a doling out: *a.* more increasing, exorbitant.
বাড়ান, *s.* a causing to increase, raising of price.
বাড়াবাড়ি, *ad.* prolixly, at large.
বাড়ি, *s.* increase, improvement, interest on grain.
বাড়ী, *s.* home, a house, a residence, a family residence, a staff, a rod, a plot of cultivated vegetable ground.
বাড়ীবালা, *s.* the owner of a house.
বাড়ুন, *s.* a besom, a broom.
বাড়্তী, *s.* increase, an increase or surplus, an excess.
বাড়্তীকথা, *s.* excessive talk, boasting.
বাঢ়াবাঢ়ি, *ad.* excessively, to the utmost.
বাণ, *s.* a dart, an arrow, the versed sine of an arc: *a.* five (figuratively).
বাণা, *s.* the male organ of a child.
বাণি, *s.* the price of making any thing.
বাণিজ, বাণ্য, *s.* a trader, merchant, a banker.
বাণিজ্য, *s.* trade, traffic, commerce.
বাণিজ্যব্যবসায়, *s.* *idem;* also, the profession or employment of commerce.
বাণিজ্যব্যবসায়ী, *a.* following a merchant's business.
বাণিজ্যার্থী, *a.* desirous of trade.
বাণিজ্যার্থে, *ad.* for the purpose of trade.
বাণিয়া, *s.* a tradesman, merchant, a banker.
বাণিয়ানী, *s.* the wife of a banker.
বাণিয়াবহু, *s.* the name of a bird.[3]
বাণী, *s.* a voice, saying, sentence, speech, a word, language; Saraswatí, the goddess of eloquence; price of making.
বাত, *s.* the wind, air, the rheumatism, the gout, the hypochondria, flatulency.
বাতকর্ম্ম, *s.* wind expelled backwards.
বাতগ্রস্ত, বাতকী, *a.* rheumatic, gouty.
বাতজ্বর, *s.* fever from rheumatism.
বাতপৈত্তিক, *a.* attended with excess of bile and wind.
বাতরোগ, *s.* the rheumatism.
বাতশূল, *s.* colic from flatulency.
বাতাবিনেবু, *s.* the pumalose or shadock.[4]
বাতাস, *s.* the wind, the air, an apparition.
বাতাসমুখী, *a.* facing the wind.
বাতাসা, *s.* a kind of light sugar-cake.
বাতাসী, *a.* windy, tempestuous, boisterous.
বাতিক, *a.* flatulent, windy, rheumatic.
বাতিল, *a.* false, vain, absurd, futile; abolished, rejected, null, void.
বাতী, *s.* a candle, wick, bambu rod, stick of wax.
বাতীবালা, *s.* a chandler, a candle-seller.
বাতুয়া, *a.* flatulent, rheumatic, gouty.
বাতুল, foolish, crazy, insane, mad, deranged.

বাতুলতা, *s.* foolishness, insanity, madness.
বাতুআশাক, *s.* edible species of goosefoot.
বাতোল্বণ, *s.* hysterics, convulsion, spasm.
বাত্যা, *s.* strong wind, a gale, a storm, a tempest; a boaster, a braggadocio.
বাৎসল্য, *s.* fondness, affection, love.
বাথান, *s.* cow-pasture, cow-pen, cow-shed.
বাদ্, *ad.* after: *s.* deduction; -দা, to deduct, to subtract; -পড়্. to be deficient.
বাদ, *s.* a word, a sentence; a contradiction, a dispute, discord; resentment.
বাদক, *a.* speaking: *s.* a speaker, a musician.
বাদন, *s.* the playing on an instrument.
বাদবিতণ্ডা, *s.* a reasoning, discussion, disputation.
বাদল, *s.* a cloud, continued rain.
বাদলা, *s.* gold thread, lace, cloudy weather.
বাদলীয় *a.* rainy, connected with rain.
বাদলীয়াপোকা, *s.* an ephemera.
বাদা, *s.* a forest, a desert, a marsh, a fen.
বাদানুবাদ, *s.* a dispute, a controversy.
বাদাম, *s.* an almond; a sail.
বাদামতক্তি, *s.* a sort of flat sweetmeat.
বাদামী, বাদামীয়া, *a.* oval, almond-shaped.
বাদিত, *a.* extorted, made to be uttered.
বাদিয়া, *s.* a snake-catcher, a hunter.
বাদী, *a.* speaking, pleading: *s.* a plaintiff, a suitor.
বাদুড়, *s.* a large bat,[1] flying fox.
বাদ্য, *s.* musical instrument, instrumental music.
বাদ্যকর, *s.* a musician.
বাদ্যভাণ্ড, *s.* a concert of music, harmony.
বাদ্যোদ্যম, *s.* a confused sound of music; a concert, symphony.
বাদ্শা-জাদা, a prince; -জাদী, a princess: -বেগম, a queen.
*বাদ্শাহা, *s.* a king, a sovereign.
বাদ্শাহী, *s.* a kingdom, a government.
বাধ, *v. a.* to hinder, to frustrate.
বাধক, *a.* hindering, preventing, obstructing: *s.* impediment; hinderer, preventer; a disease preventing conception.
বাধকতা, -ত্ব, *s.* opposition, hindrance, prevention, obstruction, detention.
বাধা, *s.* pain, an obstruction, an impediment, a hindrance, an opposition, a detention, stop, a clog to an undertaking.
বাধাই, *s.* Krishna's birth-day songs.
বাধাড়ি, *s.* a shoemaker's scraping tool.
বাধাবাধি, *s.* reciprocal obstacles.
বাধিত, *a.* obstructed, hindered, impeded.
বাধ্য, *a.* obedient, docile, restrainable, capable of being obstructed.
বাধ্যতা, *s.* a capacity of being obstructed.
বাধ্যমান, *a.* suffering obstruction.
বান, *a.* dry (applied to fruit): *s.* flood, heavy sea, the spring tide, the bore.
বানক, *s.* a silk factory, a silk filature.
বানপ্রস্থ, *s.* a hermitage, a hermit's cell.
বানপ্রস্থী, *s.* a hermit, an ascetic.
বানর, *s.* a monkey, an ape; -বৎ, apish.
বানরলাঠি, *s.* long pods of Cassia fistula.
বানা, *v. a.* to build, to make, to fabricate.
বানান, *s.* a making, fabricating; spelling, orthography, combining of vowels with consonants: *a.* made, fabricated.
বান্কী, *s.* a model, pattern, plan, sample, specimen.
বান্তি, *s.* vomiting, disgorging.
*বান্দা, *s.* a slave, a servant, a man.
বান্ধ, *v. a.* to bind, to tie, to confine.
বান্ধব, *s.* a friend, kinsman, relation, ally.
বাপ, *s.* a father: *voc.* বাপরে, Oh father! বাপরেবাপ, Oh father! father! (exclamations of pain, suffering, or surprise).
বাপক, *a.* sowing: *s.* a sower, seedsman.
বাপবাপ, *s.* an exclamation, father! father!
বাপমা, *s.* parents, father and mother.
বাপা, বাপু, *s.* a father; বাপুরে, Oh father!
বাপী, *s.* a large oblong pond, a lake.
*বাফ্তা, *s.* a coarse kind of cloth.
*বাব, *s.* a section, a chapter, a subject, a head, an affair, business, a scope.
বাবই, বাবইতুলশী, *s.* a species of basil.[2]
*বাবৎ, *s.* an item, article, account, business, an affair: *ad.* on account of.
বাবতী, *a.* belonging to an article.
বাবদুক, *a.* loquacious, talkative.
বাবদুকতা, -ত্ব, *s.* loquacity, garrulity.
বাবরচী, *s.* a cook; -খানা, a kitchen, cook-room.
বাবরীচুল, *s.* frizzled or curled hair.
বাবলা, *s.* name of a tree (Mimosa arabica).
বাবা, *s.* a father; a child (erroneously).
বাবাজী, *s.* an affectionate term for a father, a son, a son-in-law, or a nephew.
বাবাডিম, *s.* a wind-egg, an addled egg.
বাবিরঙ্গ, *s.* a shrub and its seed.[3]
বাবু, *s.* Sire, Sir, Master, a Hindu gentleman.

বাবুই, s. the Indian taylor-bird.[1]
বাম, a. left (not right,) contrary, inverted, reverse; beautiful, pleasing: s. a fathom.
বামক, a. emetic, causing vomiting: s. emetic.
বামণ, s. a bráhman; -হাটী, a plant.[2]
বামণী, s. bráhmaness; a species of lizard.
বামন, a. short, dwarfish: s. dwarf, pigmy.
বামবাদ, s. vain or useless expence; an accusation.
বামলোচনা, s. a woman.
বামা, s. a woman; left hand side of drum.
বামাচার, s. heterodoxy, the practice of the Tántrikas.
বামাচারী, a. heterodox.
বায়খা, s. an open airy place, an aperture.
বায়না, s. earnest money.
বায়নাক্কা, s. a relation of things, recital of particulars.
বায়স, s. a crow. বায়সী, s. a female crow.
বায়ু, s. the wind, air, air of the body, hypochondria, flatulency; the god of wind.
বায়ুকোণ, s. the north-west point.
বায়ুগতি, s. motion of the wind: a. swift, fleet.
বায়ুগ্রস্ত, a. inflated; hypochondriac, flatulent.
বায়ুতুল্য, a. like wind, unsubstantial.
বায়ুপ্রক্ষেপককল, s. an air-pump.
বায়ুবৃদ্ধি, s. the increase of flatulence, or wind.
বায়ুবেগে, with the swiftness of the wind.
বায়ুব্যজন, s. the act of fanning, a fan.
বায়ুভক্ষক, a. feeding on air: s. a serpent.
বায়ুভক্ষণ, s. the feeding upon air.
বায়ুভাব, s. gas, a gaseous state.
বায়ুবেচন, s. the act of belching.
বায়ুস্ফীতি, s. a swelling filled with air.
বায্য, a. hypochondriac, insane, deranged.
বায়ুংশ, s. hypochondria, mania, insanity.
বার, s. a time; repetition; water.
বার, s. a day of the week, an occasion, a time or vicissitude, a turn: a. twelve.
বারউড়ানী, বাড়উড়ানী, s. a volley.
বারক, a. hindering, preventing: s. a hinderer.
বারকোল, বারিকোল, s. a turtle, a tortoise.
বারকোষ, s. a wooden tray, a salver.
বারণ, s. a hindering, preventing, forbidding.
বারণীয়, a. preventible, prohibitable.
বারদ্বয়, a. twice. বারদিগর, ad. again.
বারবার, ad. same as বারম্বার.
বারবেলা, s. the close or unlucky part of the day.
বারমাসীয়, a. perennial, perpetual.
বারম্বার, ad. repeatedly, again and again, often.
বারয়িতব্য, a. prohibitable, preventible.
বারস্ত্রী, বারাঙ্গনা, s. a harlot, a prostitute.
বারাণসী, s. the sacred city Benares.
বারাণ্ডা, s. a portico, a porch, a verandah.
বারান্তর, ad. again, once more.
বারি, s. water, tears; -দ, giving water: a cloud.
বারিক, s. Eng. barracks; also, a. thin, fine.
বারিচর, a. aquatic: s. a fish.
বারিজ, a. born in water: s. a lotus, snail, conch-shell.
বারিত, a. hindered, prevented, forbidden.
বারিধি, বারাংনিধি, s. the sea, the ocean.
বারী s. a milk-pail; an elephant's rope.
বারুণি, a. the twelfth.
বারুণী, s. the west; 24th mansion in the zodiac; the bathing festival.
বারুদ, s. gunpowder; -খানা, a powder-magazine.
বারেক, a. once, one time; -দিগর, again.
বারেবারে, ad. the same as বারম্বার.
বারো, a. twelve; -য়ারী, a pleasure-house;
বারোয়ারী, a common, general.
বার্তা, s. a word, talk, conversation, news, tidings, information, a rumour, report.
বার্তাকু, বার্তাকী, s. brinjal, the egg-fruit.[3]
বার্তিক, s. an envoy, one who brings news; a beggar, a gloss, a commentary, a criticism.
বার্দ্ধক্য, s. old age, senility.
বার্দ্ধুষিক, a. living on usury: s. an usurer.
বার্য্য, a. resistible, preventible, prohibitable.
বার্য্যমাণ, a. suffering resistance.
বার্ষিক, a. yearly, annual.
বাল, s. a child, a boy, infant; hair, hair of the privities; a tail: a. infantine.
বালক, s. a child, an infant, a boy; one who represents Krishna at dramatic exhibitions; the great cross-beam.
বালককাল, s. childhood, infancy.
বালককালীন, a. belonging to childhood.
বালকতা, -ত্ব, s. childishness, puerility.
বালকীয়, a. childish, infantine.
বালন, s. a frying pan.
বালসা, s. a fever when it attacks a child.
বালা, s. a female child, a girl, a young woman; a ring or ornament for the wrist.
বালাই, s. a misfortune, calamity, an evil.
*বালাখানা, s. an upper-roomed house.
বালাধিকার, s. pupilage, minority.
বালাম, s. a common variety of rice.

বালি, *s.* a monkey king; sand; a leaf of a folding door; a branch; an earring.
বালিকা, *s.* a female child, a girl under 16;
বালিঘড়ী, *s.* an hour-glass. [sand.
বালিয়া, *a.* sandy, full of sand, made of
বালিয়ামাছ, *s.* a species of fish.[1] [sand.
বালিয়ামাটি, *s.* sandy soil, sandy earth.
বালিশ, *s.* a pillow, a cushion, a bolster: *a.*
বালিহাঁস, *s.* a teal.[2] [childish, ignorant.
বালী, *s.* sand; -দা, to wear down with sand.
বালীময়, *a.* sandy, full of sand.
বালুকা, *s.* sand; -ময়, sandy, full of sand.
বালেন্দু, *s.* new moon (two or three days' old,) a crescent, a lunule or maniscus.
বাল্তি, *a.* destitute, forlorn, bereft: *s.* a wooden water-vessel, a bucket.
বাল্দি, *s.* the spathe or branch of a plantain, cocoanut, and the like trees.
বাল্য,-কাল, *s.* boyhood, childhood, infancy.
বাল্যদশা, বাল্যাবস্থা, *s.* childhood, infancy.
বাল্যভোগ, বাল্যভোজন, *s.* a breakfast.
বাল্মীকি, *s.* the author of the Rámáyana.
বাষট্টি, *a.* sixty-two.
বাষ্টা, *a.* stale, old, stinking, fetid, rotten.
বাস, *s.* a residence, a dwelling, abode, house; a garment, clothing, wearing apparel; a scent, a smell, odour, a perfume; -কৃ, to dwell; -লও, to smell.
বাসক, *a.* dwelling, residing: *s.* a dweller.
বাসকসজ্জা, *s.* one dressed in all her finery.
বাসন, *s.* a plate, a vessel, a dish; liking,
বাসনকুশন, *s.* plates and dishes. [choice.
বাসনা, *s.* a passion, propensity, intention, inclination, a desire, wish, choice.
বাসন্তী, *a.* vernal, belonging to the spring.
বাসযোগ্য, *a.* worthy of a residence.
বাসর, *s.* a day; -ঘর, the house where the married couple sleep the first night.
বাসরাইগোলাব, *s.* a species of rose.[4]
বাসস্, *s.* cloth, clothing, garment.
বাসা, *s.* a temporary residence, an abode, lodging, a bird's nest, lair of an animal.
বাসাঘর, *s.* a temporary dwelling house.
বাসাড়ীয়া, *a.* living in lodgings: *s.* a person who lives in a temporary lodging.
বাসি, *a.* stale, old; well-washed: *s.* an axe: *intj.* Oh! surprizing! astonishing!

বাসিক, *a.* sebacic. [soned, clothed.
বাসিত, *a.* perfumed, scented, spiced, sea-
বাসিধোপকাপড়, *s.* well-washed cloth.
বাসিরে, *intj.* Oh! surprizing! astonishing!
বাসী, বাসিন্, *a.* dwelling, residing: *s.* a re-
বাসুকি, *s.* the king of serpents. [sident.
বাসেন্দা, বাসিন্দা, *a.* dwelling: *s.* a dweller.
বাস্তব, *a.* real, true, genuine, substantiated, material, substantial. [reality.
বাস্তবিক, *a. idem: ad.* really, in truth, in
বাস্তব্য, *s.* habitation, dwelling: *a. vide* বাস্য.
বাস্তু, *s.* the site of a dwelling-house.
বাস্না, *s.* rind of plantain tree; a flower.
বাষ্প, *s.* steam, vapour; allusion; any, the least; -কল, -যন্ত্র, a steam engine; -নৌকা, a steam vessel; -যান, a steam carriage.
বাষ্পধর্ম্মক, *a.* volatile, flying off in steam.
বাষ্পীভাব, *s.* the state or condition of
বাষ্পীভূত, *a.* become steam. [steam.
বাষ্পোদ্গতি, *s.* the ascension of steam.
বাস্য, বাসতেয়, *a.* habitable, inhabitable.
বাহ্, *v. a.* to row a boat; to clamber.
বাহ, *s.* a horse, a bull, air, wind, the arm, a vehicle, conveyance, a porter, cooly.
বাহক, *a.* carrying, bearing: *s.* a porter, a bearer of burden, a rower, a horse.
বাহন, *s.* a carriage, a vehicle, conveyance.
বাহত্তর, *vide* বাহত্তর, বাহাত্তর, seventy-two.
*বাহাদুর, *a.* brave, valiant, courageous: *s.* a hero, a champion, a knight. [ism.
বাহাদুরী, *s.* bravery, courage, valour, hero-
বাহাদুরীকাঠ, *s.* a timber. [a pretext.
*বাহানা, *s.* an excuse, a pretence, evasion,
*বাহার, *s.* beauty, elegance, the spring: *a.*
*বাহাল, *a.* reinstated; prosperous. [out.
বাহিনী, *s.* an army, legion, a cohort, a battalion: *a. fem.* facing, flowing. [officer.
বাহিনীপতি, *s.* a general, a commanding
বাহির, *a.* without, external, out, outside; -কৃ, to exclude, to expel, turn out; -হ, to come forth, to proceed from.
বাহিরনাম, *s.* the direction of a letter.
বাহিরে, *ad.* out of doors, without, outside.
বাহির্ফট্কা, *s.* a straggler, a rambler.
বাহু, *s.* the arm, a fathom.
বাহুড়্, *v. a.* to turn back, to return.
বাহুড়ন, *s.* a returning, a turning back.

বাহুবল, *s.* the strength of the arm.
বাহুমূল, *s.* the shoulder-blade, the armpit.
বাহুযুদ্ধ, *s.* a scuffling, wrestling, pugilism.
বাহুল্য, *s.* abundance, plenty, superfluous.
বাহুল্যাংশ, *s.* a majority, greater portion.
বাহুস্থ, *a.* situated on the arm, brachial.
বাহ্য, *a.* external, outward; portable; -যা, to go forth, to ease nature, to go to stool.
বাহ্যক্রিয়া, *s.* the expulsion of the fæces.
বাহ্যজ্ঞান, *s.* the knowledge of external objects.
বাহ্যস্থান, *s.* a privy, a jakes.
বি, a *prep.* conveying the idea of excellence, though sometimes of privation.
বিআজ, *s.* delay; the interest of money.
বিউনি, *s.* a tail of hair, a plait of hair.
বিংশতি, *a.* twenty; -তম, the twentieth.
বিঁদ, বিঁধ, *s.* a perforation, a hole, a bore.
বিঁধ্, *v. a.* to pierce, to perforate, to bore.
বিঁধন, *s.* a piercing, a perforating, boring.
বিঁধনিয়া, *a.* piercing, perforating.
বিকচ, *a.* blown, expanded, opened, spread open.
বিকট, *a.* formidable, horrible, hideous, distorted: *s.* jeopardy, danger, fear, awe.
বিকটবদন, *a.* having a distorted face.
বিকটাকার, বিকটমূর্ত্তি, *a.* distorted, deformed.
বিকল, *a.* confused, confounded, agitated, defective, imperfect, impaired, out of order, withered, waned, decayed.
বিকলাঙ্গ, *a.* deformed, crippled, maimed.
বিকল্প, *a.* optional, admitting two forms: *s.* an alternative, an option; a doubt.
বিকল্পিত, *a.* admitted as optional
বিকশিত, *a.* expanded, opened (as a flower).
বিকা, বিক্, *v. a.* to sell, to vend, to be sold.
বিকাও, *a.* saleable, vendible: *-ad.* for sale.
বিকার, *s.* a change of form or nature, a transmutation, transformation, change, alteration, deterioration, disease, sickness, passion, feeling, emotion, dangerous symptoms of a disease.
বিকারপ্রাপ্ত, *a.* changed, deteriorated, depraved.
বিকারী, বিকারজনক, *a.* producing or undergoing a change.
বিকার্য্য, *a.* changeable, capable of being deteriorated.
বিকাল, বিকালবেলা, *s.* the evening.
বিকাশ, *s.* expansion, the opening of a flower.
বিকাশিত, *a.* expanded, blown, spread open.

বিকিরণ, *s.* a scattering about, sprinkling.
বিকী, *s.* sale, sale of any thing.
বিকীকিনি, *s.* trade, sale, barter, selling and buying.
বিকীর্ণ, *a.* dispersed, scattered, sprinkled.
বিকীর্য্য, *a.* capable of being scattered.
বিকৃত, *a.* changed, impaired, transformed, transmuted, distorted, estranged, alienated, diseased, imperfect, incomplete.
বিকৃতবদন, *a.* having a distorted face.
বিকৃতাকার, *a.* deformed, distorted, ugly.
বিকৃতি, *s.* a change from the natural state, transformation, transmutation, deviation, distortion, depravity.
বিক্রম, *s.* power, valour, prowess, energy, authority.
বিক্রমী, বিক্রমশালী, *a.* powerful, valorous, daring, courageous, valiant, energetic.
বিক্রয়, *s.* a sale, selling, sale of any thing.
বিক্রয়ণীয়, or বিক্রয়যোগ্য, *a.* saleable, merchantable.
বিক্রয়ার্থে, *ad.* for sale.
বিক্রয়ী, *a.* selling, disposing of.
বিক্রান্ত, *a.* valiant, powerful, heroic, bold, courageous.
বিক্রী, *s.* a sale, a selling.
বিক্রীকর, *a.* selling: *s.* a seller, a vendor.
বিক্রীকরা, *s.* the selling of things: *a.* sold.
বিক্রীত, *a.* sold, disposed off.
বিক্রীৱালা, *s.* one who goes about buying bottles, etc.
বিক্রেতা, *s.* a seller, a vendor, a salesman.
বিক্রেয়, বিক্রেতব্য, *a.* saleable, marketable.
বিক্লব, *a.* panic-struck, overcome by fear, confused, confounded, bewildered.
বিক্লান্ত, *a.* fatigued, exhausted, faint.
বিক্লিন্ন, *a.* shrivelled, decayed, withered, worn out, old, wet, moist.
বিক্ষিপ্ত, *a.* scattered, dispersed, thrown.
বিক্ষেপ, বিক্ষেপণ, *s.* a throwing, a scattering, dispersion; distress of mind.
বিখ্যাত, *a.* famous, renowned, denominated, spoken of, celebrated, praised.
বিখ্যাতি, *s.* renown, fame, praise, celebrity, notoriety.
বিখ্যারা, *s.* a discord in music.
বিগড়্, *v. n.* to alter, change, to be corrupted or deteriorated, to fade.
বিগড়, *s.* deterioration, depravity, discord, a change.
বিগড়ন, *s.* a deteriorating, a changing.
বিগড়া, *v. a.* to spoil, impair, deteriorate.
বিগড়ান, *s.* an impairing, a deteriorating.
বিগড়ানী, *a.* spoiling, vitiating, impairing.

বিগড়াবিগড়ি, *s.* discord, a mutual discord.

বিগত, *a.* departed, gone, separated, severed, parted, obscured, dark : *s.* a span.

বিগন্তব্য, বিগমনীয়, *a.* separable, relinquishable.

বিগম, *s.* separation, departure.

বিগর্হক, *a.* censuring, abusing, hating.

বিগর্হণ, *s.* a censuring, vilifying, hating.

বিগর্হণীয়, *a.* censurable, abominable.

বিগর্হিত, বিগীত, *a.* censured, vilified, abused.

বিগলিত, *a.* fallen, dropped, oozed, removed, made loose, dishevelled.

বিগাড়, *s.* ruin, deterioration, apostacy, discord.

বিগাড়ন, *s.* spoiling of a thing.

বিগুণ, *a.* worthless, pernicious : *s.* an evil quality.

বিগ্রহ, *s.* war, combat ; image, idol ; body.

বিঘটন, *s.* an occurrence, a misfortune.

বিঘটিত, *a* happened, occurred, befallen.

বিঘত, or বিতস্তি, *s.* a span, nine inches.

বিঘা, *s.* a measure of land varying from eighty to eighty-seven cubits square.

বিঘাত, *s.* an injury, destruction, a murder.

বিঘাতী, *a.* killing, murdering, injuring.

বিঘ্ন, *s.* obstacle, danger, obstruction, hindrance, an impediment, a misfortune.

বিচক্ষণ, *a.* learned, clever, skilful, eminent, superior.

বিচক্ষুঃ, *a.* blind, perplexed.

বিচল, *s.* deviation, irregularity, perversity, disobedience ; -বাক্য, slip of tongue.

বিচলা, *s.* a slip, a false step.

বিচলিত, *a.* slipped, bent, unsteady, fickle ; dislocated.

বিচলিতান্তঃকরণ, *a.* fickle-minded, unsteady.

বিচাড়, *s.* a seed-plot.

বিচার্, *v. a.* to judge, investigate, examine, deliberate, discuss.

বিচার, *s.* investigation, examination, an opinion, a determination, judgment, a consultation, discussion, deliberation.

বিচারক, বিচারকারক, *a.* investigating : *s.* he who investigates, a judge.

বিচারকতা, বিচারণা, *s.* judgment, investigation.

বিচারকর্ত্তা, *s.* a judge, one who examines.

বিচারক্ষম, *a.* able to judge or investigate.

বিচারণ, *s.* a judging, an investigating.

বিচারণীয়, or বিচারয়িতব্য, *a.* investigable.

বিচারপ্রার্থনা, *s.* a request to have an affair investigated or judged.

বিচারসূত্র, *s.* a rule for judging, a logical aphorism.

বিচারা, *a.* helpless, destitute of means.

বিচারানুসারে, *ad.* according to judgment.

বিচারান্তরগ্রাহক, *s.* an appellant.

বিচারিত, *a.* judged, investigated, examined, discussed, deliberated on.

বিচার্য্য, *a.* investigable, deserving examination.

বিচার্য্যমাণ, *a.* under investigation.

বিচালী, *s.* straw, rice-straw.

বিচি, বীচী, *s.* a seed, fruit-stone.

বিচিকিৎসা, *s.* a doubt, difficulty, error : *a.* uncouth.

বিচিত্র, variegated, speckled, party-coloured ; surprising, gaudy, handsome, beautiful : *s.* surprise ; a variegated colour.

বিচিত্রিত, *a.* variegated, party-coloured.

বিচ্ছিত্তি, *s.* a cutting off, excision, cutting, a dividing, a fracture, loss, destruction, a limit, the cæsura or pause in a verse.

বিচ্ছিন্ন, *a.* divided, interrupted, shared out, cut, separate, cleft, severed, scattered.

বিচ্ছিন্নাগ্র, *a.* truncated, lopped, shorn.

বিস্কু, *s.* a juvenile sport, hop-scotch.

বিচ্ছেত্তব্য, *a.* divisible, frangible, separable.

বিচ্ছেদ, *s.* a separation, a division, a space between, an interruption of friendship or love, disjunction, removal, disunion, discord, a chapter or division of a book.

বিচ্ছেদক, *a.* separating, dividing, disjoining, interrupting, disuniting.

বিচ্ছেদযন্ত্রণা, *s.* the agony of separation.

বিচ্ছেদানল, *s. fig.* the fire of separation.

বিচ্ছেদ্য, বিচ্ছেদনীয়, *a.* separable, divisible, frangible.

বিচ্‌তাড়ক, *s.* a climbing plant.[1]

বিছটী, বিছুটী, *s.* a sort of stinging plant.[2]

বিছড়া, *v. a.* to scatter, strew ; to fall out : *a.* strewed, scattered ; fallen out.

বিছা, *v. a.* to spread out, to lay in beds : *s.* a scorpion, a centipede, sign Scorpio.

বিছান, *s.* a spreading out, the spreading of a mat or carpet, a laying of things in beds, a bed, a carpet : *a.* spread out.

বিছানা, *s.* a bed, a carpet, a floor mat.

বিজকুচ্ছ, *a.* abominably ugly.

বিজটা, *s.* an ornament for the small of the arm.

বিজন্মা, *a.* illegitimate, bastard, base-born, of spurious birth : *s.* a bastard.

বিজয়, *s.* a conquest, a triumph, a victory.

বিজয়া, *s.* Durgá, one of her attendants, the day her image is cast into the river.

বিজয়ী, *a.* conquering, triumphant, victori-
বিজল, *a.* gummy, viscous. [ous: *s.* a victor.
বিজলী, *s.* lightning, thunderbolt. [brid.
বিজাত, বিজাতক, *a.* base-born, bastard, hy-
বিজাতি, *s.* a different species or kind.
বিজাতীয়, *a.* mongrel, hybrid, base-born, bastard, unnatural, hateful, hostile, unparalleled, unprecedented, dissimilar.
বিজিগীষা, *s.* a desire to conquer, rivalry.
বিজিগীষু, *a.* desirous of victory, emulating.
বিজিত, *a.* subdued, conquered, overcome;
বিজেতব্য, *a.* conquerable. [fanned, wafted.
বিজেতা, *s.* a conqueror, a victor.
বিজ্ঞ, *a.* wise, learned, clever, skilful, intelligent, experienced. [skilfulness.
বিজ্ঞতা, *s.* wisdom, experience, cleverness,
বিজ্ঞপ্তি, *s.* information, a declared opinion, a representation of circumstances.
বিজ্ঞাত, *a.* known, understood, famous, no-
বিজ্ঞাতা, *s.* one who knows. [torious.
বিজ্ঞান, *s.* science, knowledge, learning.
বিজ্ঞাপক, giving information, publishing, conveying knowledge: *s.* an advertiser.
বিজ্ঞাপন, *s.* a making known, a demonstrating, a publishing, advertisement.
বিজ্ঞাপনপত্র, *s.* a petition, an application.
বিজ্ঞাপনীয়, *a.* declarable, publishable.
বিজ্ঞাপয়িতব্য, বিজ্ঞাপ্য, *a. idem.* [vertiser.
বিজ্ঞাপয়িতা, *s.* he who makes known, an ad-
বিজ্ঞাপিত, *a.* published, made known.
বিজ্ঞেয়, *a.* knowable, comprehensible.
বিজ্‌বিজ্‌, *s.* a muttering: full (of maggots).
বিট্‌, *s.* excrement, ordure, a varlet, a catamite, a rogue, a cheat, a scoundrel.
বিটল, বিটলিয়া, বিট্‌ল, vile, vicious, unprincipled, hateful, villainous, abominable.
বিটলামী, *s.* villainy, vice, hatefulness.
বিটাল, *s.* a varlet, villain; -তা, villainy, vice.
বিট্‌খদির, *s.* a fetid species of Mimosa.
বিট্‌লবণ, *s.* a kind of black rock-salt.
বিড়ঙ্গ, *s.* a plant used as a vermifuge.
বিড়ম্ব, *v. a.* to afflict, to vex, to tantalize.
বিড়ম্বনা, *s.* affliction, distress, a tantalizing.
বিড়ম্বনীয়, *a.* capable of being afflicted.
বিড়ম্বিত, *a.* afflicted, distressed, tantalized.
বিড়া, *s.* circular roll of cloth or straw put on the head of a porter or carrier of burden, also, that put under a pot to keep it steady, a packet of betel, a cautery.
বিড়াল, *s.* a tom-cat. বিড়ালী, *s.* a she-cat.
বিড়ালচক্ষুয়া, cat-eyed, wall-eyed. [bling.
বিড়্‌বিড়্‌, বিড়্‌বিড়ান, *s.* a muttering, mum-
বিড়্‌বিড়া, *v. n* to mutter, to mumble.
বিড়্‌বিড়িয়া, *a.* muttering, mumbling.
বিঢপ, বিঢোল, *a.* deformed, distorted, ugly.
বিৎ, or বিদ, *a.* knowing, wise, versed in,
বিতং, *s.* a detail. [acquainted with.
বিতণ্ডা, *s.* criticism, discussion, refutation, a dispute, a debate, a contention, controversy, wrangling, an argument.
বিতত, *a.* stretched, extended, expanded: *s.* a stringed instrument.
বিতরণ, *s.* a giving, distributing, the giving of alms, alms, a largess, a donation.
বিতরণা, *a.* giving alms, distributing.
বিতর্ক, *s.* an inference, a reasoning, discussion, deliberation, consideration, a conjecture, an apprehension, a doubt.
বিতর্কণ, *s.* act of discussing or reasoning,
বিতস্তি, or বিঘত, *s.* a span. [an inferring.
বিতান, *s.* the warp of cloth, an awning, a canopy, an expansion, a spreading out, a verse of 4 lines of 8 syllables each.
*বিতারিখ, *s.* under date.
বিতুষ্ট, *a.* displeased, dissatisfied, averse.
বিতুষ্টি, *s.* dissatisfaction, displeasure.
বিতৃষ্ণা, *s.* satiety, disgust, indifference.
বিত্ত, *a.* acquired, investigated, known, famous: *s.* wealth, property, substance.
বিত্তবান্‌, *a.* wealthy, possessing property.
বিত্তা, or বিত্ত্ব, *s.* wisdom, knowledge.
বিদগ্ধ, *a.* lecherous, amorous, lustful; clever, learned, sagacious, shrewd, witty, intriguing; -রূপে, cleverly, shrewdly.
বিদগ্ধতা, -ত্ব, *s.* shrewdness, learning, skill,
বিদগ্ধনায়ক, *s.* an amorous man. [wisdom.
বিদগ্ধা, *s.* a clever or insinuating woman.
বিদর্‌, *v. n.* to be torn, to be lacerated.
বিদরণ, *s.* a splitting, a rending, tearing.
বিদা, *s.* a harrow, a garden-rake.
বিদাঁড়া, *a.* contrary to custom, irregular.
বিদায়, *s.* a parting with good wishes, leave of absence, leave to depart, dismissal; -কৃ, or -দা, to dismiss, permit to depart.

বিদায়ী, *s.* a leave of absence, a dismissal, a present given at the dismissal.
বিদার্, *v. a.* to tear, to lacerate. [tion.
বিদার, *s.* a crack, a rent, a chink, a lacera-
বিদারক, rending, tearing, cleaving, splitting: *s.* that which rends, tears, etc.
বিদারণ, *s.* the splitting, cleaving, rending, or tearing of a thing, a lacerating.
বিদারণীয়, *a.* that may be torn, lacerable.
বিদারিত, *a.* cleft, split, torn, lacerated.
বিদিক্, *s.* intermediate point of the com-
বিদিত, *a.* known, acquainted with. [pass.
বিদীর্ণ, *a.* torn, rent, split, cleft, lacerated.
বিদুর, *a.* wise, intelligent, learned, clever.
বিদূরজ, *s.* lapis lazuli, a precious gem.
বিদেশ, *s.* a foreign country. [stranger.
বিদেশী, *a.* foreign, strange: *s.* a foreigner,
বিদ্ধ, *a.* pierced, perforated, penetrated.
বিদ্ধকর্ণ, *a.* having the ears bored. [tant.
বিদ্যমান, *a.* existent, existing, present, ex-
বিদ্যমানতা, -ত্ব, *s.* existence, presence.
বিদ্যা, *s.* science, art, literature, knowledge, learning, philosophy; -বান্, *vide* বিদ্বান.
বিদ্যাদাতা, *s.* a tutor, teacher, instructor.
বিদ্যাদান, *s.* the giving of instruction.
বিদ্যাধর, *s.* an order of demi-gods. [ence.
বিদ্যানুশীলন, বিদ্যাভ্যাস, the study of sci-
বিদ্যাবাগীশ, *s.* one eminent in science, a philosopher, a doctor in philosophy.
বিদ্যাব্যবসায়, *s.* the profession of science.
বিদ্যাব্যবসায়ী, professing or following the profession of science or philosophy.
বিদ্যার্জক, *a.* acquiring science: *s.* a stu-
বিদ্যার্জিত, *a.* acquired by science. [dent.
বিদ্যার্থী, *a.* studious, desirous of science: *s.* a tyro, a scholar, a student.
বিদ্যার্থে, for science or philosophy. [tle).
বিদ্যালঙ্কার *a.* adorned with science (a ti-
বিদ্যালয়, বিদ্যাগার, *s.* a college, a school.
বিদ্যালাভ, *s.* the acquisition of learning.
বিদ্যুৎ, *s.* lightning, thundering flash.
বিদ্যুদ্গতি, *a.* quick as lightning, nimble.
বিদ্যুল্লতা, *s.* forked lightning, zigzag flash-
বিদ্যোত, *s.* splendour, glare, light. [ing.
বিদ্যোপার্জন, *s.* the acquisition of science.
বিদ্রব, *s.* flight, escape, retreat; intellect; censure, reproach; liquefaction.

বিদ্রাবক, *a.* pursuing a flying enemy; causing to melt or liquify, jesting, mimicking, jeering: *s.* a jester, mimic, buffoon.
বিদ্রুত, *a.* liquid, fluid, melted, flown, fled.
বিদ্রুম, *s.* coral; the young shoot of a tree.
বিদ্রূপ, *s.* ridicule, mockery, raillery, jesting, a jeer, drollery, mimickry.
বিদ্রূপী, *a.* mimicking, jeering, ridiculing, mocking, railing: *s.* a jester, a mocker.
বিদ্বান্, wise, learned, erudite, intelligent, scientific, knowing, proficient, clever.
বিদ্বিষ্ট, hated, treated with malice. [tion.
বিদ্বেষ, *s.* enmity, hatred, malice, persecu-
বিধ, বিধা, *s.* a manner, sort, kind, a form,
বিধবা, *s.* a widow. [a formula, a rule.
বিধর্ম্ম, apostacy, heterodoxy, irregularity.
বিধর্ম্মী, *a.* heterodox, apostate. [vidence.
বিধাতা, *s.* God, the God of providence, Pro-
বিধান, *s.* a statute, a law, a decree, a rule, an injunction, a precept, an action.
বিধানতা, -ত্ব, *s.* lawfulness, legality.
বিধারা, *s.* an evil habit, an evil custom.
বিধি, *s.* a statute, law, precept, decree, an order, injunction, rule, a form, formula, a text, fate, destiny, luck, an action.
বিধিবিরুদ্ধ, *a.* contrary to law or precept.
বিধিমতে, *ad.* according to law or rule.
বিধু, *s* moon; camphor; -মুখী, moon-faced.
বিধুবদন, *a.* moon-faced: *s.* moon-like face.
বিধেয়, *a.* fit to be enacted as a law.
বিধ্বংস, *s.* destruction, disrespect, enmity.
বিনত, *a.* bowed down, prostrate, humble.
বিনতা, *a. idem*: *s.* the mother of Gaṛura.
বিনতি, বিনয়, *s.* humility, submission, supplication, entreaty, mildness, affability, modesty, decorum, reverence, obedience.
বিনয়পূর্ব্বক, with humility, submissively.
বিনয়বাক্য, *s.* supplicatory speech, humiliating language. [submissive, yielding.
বিনয়ী, humble, modest, affable, suppliant,
বিনশ্বর, *a.* perishable, destructible.
বিনষ্ট, *a.* destroyed, ruined, spoiled, cor-
বিনষ্টতা, *s.* ruin, destruction. [rupted.
বিনা, *ad.* except, without, beside.
বিনাম, *s.* a false name, an assumed name.
বিনামী, *a.* bearing a false name. [Gaṛura.
বিনায়ক, *a.* humble, yielding: *s.* Ganesha,

বিনাশ, *s.* destruction, ruin, loss.
বিনাশক, *a.* ruinous, destructive : *s.* a de-
বিনাশকতা, *s.* destructiveness. [stroyer.
বিনাশকর্ত্তা, *s.* a destroyer, a spoiler.
বিনাশন, *s.* the bringing of a thing to ruin.
বিনাশনীয়, *a.* perishable, destructible.
বিনাশপ্রাপ্ত, *a.* come to ruin or destruction.
বিনাশার্থে, *ad.* for ruin or destruction.
বিনাশিত, *a.* destroyed, spoiled. [to ruin.
বিনাশী, *a.* perishable, destructible, going
বিনাশ্য, *a.* perishable, destructible. [forth.
বিনিঃসরণ, *s.* a going forth : বিনিঃসৃত gone
বিনিগমনা, *s.* the reason of determining to this or that side of an argument.
বিনিময়, *s.* an exchange, a barter, a retaliation, a return, a requital, a reprisal.
বিনির্গম, *s.* a going forth : বিনির্গত, *a.* gone
বিনির্ণয়, *s.* certainty, assurance. [forth.
বিনির্ণীত, *a.* ascertained, settled.
বিনীত, *a.* humble, modest, unassuming, placid, meek, gentle, restrained, decent, compliant, tractable, disciplined, taken, led, conveyed, chastised, humbled.
বিনীতবেশ, *a.* modestly clothed, habited so as to express humility. [disciplined.
বিনীতাত্মা, *a.* lowly, modest, submissive,
বিনেতা, *s.* a leader, guide, an instructor, a
বিনেদন, *s.* divergence. [ruler, a king.
বিনেয়, *a.* fit to be humbled, governable, docile, tractable, humble.
বিনোদ, *s.* eagerness, vehemence, joy, happiness, sport, pastime, play, dismission.
বিন্দু, *s.* a spot, dot, point, drop, the space between the eyebrows ; nasal sign (ঁ).
বিন্দুময়, *a.* dotted, pointed, perforated.
বিন্ধ্, *v. a.* to perforate, to pierce, to bore a hole, to penetrate. [ing of a thing.
বিন্ধন, *s.* the perforating, boring, or pierc-
বিন্ধনী, *a.* piercing, boring, perforating : *s.*
বিন্ধ্য, *s.* a range of mountains. [the colic.
বিন্যাস, *s.* array, arrangement, a dressing of the hair, orderly arranging of things, or putting on of clothes, a deposit, collection, assemblage, a site. [obliqua).
বিপক্ক, *a* ripened, matured ; oblique (folia
বিপক্ষ, *s.* an enemy, an opponent : *a.* hostile, of the enemy's party.

বিপক্ষতা, *s.* enmity, hostility, opposition.
বিপক্ষতাচরণ, *s.* hostile conduct.
বিপণ, *s.* a sale, a contract of sale.
বিপণি, *s.* a shop, market, a market-stall.
বিপৎকাল, *s.* a time of adversity.
বিপৎকালে, *ad.* in a season of misfortune.
বিপত্তি, *s.* misfortune, adversity, calamity.
বিপথ, a byeroad, wrong way, evil course.
বিপথগামিতা, -ত্ব, *s.* perverseness. [way.
বিপথগামী, *a.* perverse, going in an evil
বিপদ্, *s.* a calamity, misfortune, adversity.
বিপদগ্রস্ত, বিপন্ন, *a.* involved in misfortune, sunk in calamity, distressed, afflicted.
বিপরীত, *a.* adverse, reverse, opposed, hostile, repugnant, contrary to. [gitation.
বিপরীতগতি, *s.* retrograde motion, regur-
বিপর্য্যয়, *a.* uncommon, unusual : *s.* contrariety, hostility, repugnance. [tion.
বিপর্য্যাস, *s.* an attributing, false assump-
বিপাক, *s.* a ripening, maturity ; an unexpected result, an occurrence, distress.
বিপিন, *s.* a forest, thicket, wood ; -বিহারী,
বিপ্র, *s.* a bráhman. [roaming in a forest.
বিপ্রকৃত, *a.* reviled, abused, revenged.
বিপ্রকৃতি, *s.* abuse, contumely, censure, an insult, a retaliation.
বিপ্রকৃষ্ট, *a.* deteriorated, inferior, bad.
বিপ্রতিপত্তি, *s.* a dispute, an opposition.
বিপ্রলাপ, *s.* disputation, wrangling.
বিপ্রিয়, *a.* disliked, hated : *s.* sin, a crime.
বিফল, *a.* fruitless, useless, abortive.
বিফলীকৃত, *a.* made useless or ineffectual.
বিফলে, *ad.* uselessly, ineffectually.
বিবক্ষা, *s.* a wish to speak, a desire.
বিবদন, or বিবদমান, *a.* disputing, contradicting, quarrelsome, litigious.
বিবর্, *v. a.* to tell in detail, to narrate.
বিবর, a burrow, hole, cave, animal's hole.
বিবরণ, *s.* a circumstance, a narrative, detail, description, specification. [able.
বিবরণীয়, specifiable, describable, detail-
বিবর্জ্জন, *s.* a relinquishing, a quitting, a leaving, an excepting, a rejecting.
বিবর্জ্জনীয়, *a.* relinquishable, rejectible.
বিবর্জ্জিত, *a.* relinquished, rejected, quitted.
বিবর্ণ, *a.* discoloured, blushing, pale : *s.* one of a low class ; -তা, blush, paleness.

বিবর্ত্ত, *s.* a multitude, collection, heap; a dancing, going round; error, mistake.
বিবশ, *a.* helpless, weak, not under control.
বিবসন, or বিবস্ত্র, *a.* naked, unclothed.
বিবাদ, *s.* a dispute, controversy, wrangle, a lawsuit, an objection.
বিবাদক, *a.* disputing, litigating, controverting.
বিবাদকর্ত্তা, *s.* a disputant, a party in a lawsuit, a controvertist, wrangler.
বিবাদপদ, *s.* a subject of litigation or dispute.
বিবাদান্তর, *s.* another dispute or controversy.
বিবাদার্থী, *a.* desirous of disputes.
বিবাদার্থে, for disputes or controversies.
বিবাদী, *a.* disputing, contentious, disputatious, captious, controversial, quarrelsome, litigious: *s.* a disputant.
বিবাহ, *s.* a marriage, wedding; -দা, to give in marriage; -কৃ, to marry, to wed.
বিবাহিত, *a.* married, wedded: *f.* বিবাহিতা.
বিবাহ্য, or বিবাহযোগ্য, *a.* marriageable.
বিবি, *s.* lady, mistress; -আনা, fit for a lady.
বিবিক্ত, lonely, solitary, disjoined, deserted, judged, pure.
বিবিধ, *a.* various, diverse.
বিবীত, *a.* enclosed: *s.* an enclosed spot.
বিবুধ, *s.* learned man, philosopher, a god.
বিবৃত, *a.* detailed, particularized, narrated, expanded, amplified, displayed.
বিবৃতি, *s.* narration, explanation, commentary, gloss, exposition, interpretation.
বিবৃত্ত, *a.* revolving, whirling, rolling.
বিবেক, *s.* discrimination, discernment, conscience; asceticism.
বিবেকজ্ঞান, *s.* discrimination, consciousness.
বিবেকশাস্ত্র, *s.* that science which teaches to discriminate, or to form distinct and clear ideas, a book on discrimination.
বিবেকী, *a.* discriminating, distinguishing one thing from another: *s.* an ascetic.
বিবেচ্, *v. a.* to discriminate, to judge.
বিবেচক, *a.* judicious, discriminating, examining, reasoning: *s. vide* বিবেচনাকর্ত্তা.
বিবেচনা, *s.* consideration, discrimination. examination, investigation, a trial.
বিবেচনাকর্ত্তা, *s.* one who discriminates.
বিবেচনাদ্বারা, *ad.* by discrimination.
বিবেচনাপূর্ব্বক, *ad.* discriminatingly.
বিবেচনীয়, *a.* worthy of consideration.
বিবেচিত, *a.* discriminated, examined, deliberated.
বিবেচ্য, *a.* same as বিবেচনীয়.
বিব্রত, *a.* distressed, involved in trouble.
বিব্রুবন্, *a.* speaking wrong or improperly.
বিভক্ত, *a.* divided, shared out, allotted.
বিভক্তি, *s.* a division; terminations used to decline nouns and conjugate verbs.
বিভজন, *s.* a dividing into shares or lots.
বিভজনীয়, *a.* divisible into shares or lots.
বিভব, *s.* substance, thing, matter, wealth, property, grandeur, eminence, magnanimity, elevated sentiment, emancipation from matter, superhuman power.
বিভবকর, producing wealth or grandeur.
বিভা, brilliancy, lustre, beauty; marriage.
বিভাগ, *s.* a share, a division, a portion, lot, fraction.
বিভাগী, *a* sharing out, allotting.
বিভাজক, *a.* dividing: *s.* one who divides.
বিভাজ্য, *s.* divisible into shares or lots.
বিভাজ্যতা, divisibility into shares or lots.
বিভাত, *a.* married: *s.* the dawn, daybreak.
বিভাবনা, *s.* discrimination, examination, discussion, a distinguishing, perception of facts, a seeing or discovering.
বিভাবনীয়, বিভাব্য, *a.* discriminable, distinguishable, liable to conviction.
বিভাবরী, *s.* night, turmeric, a bawd, a harlot.
বিভাষা, *s.* an alternative, an option, a different proposal.
বিভাস, *s.* repeating of a note; light, lustre, splendour.
বিভিন্ন, *a.* separated, different, contrary, dispersed, divided, discordant.
বিভিন্নতা, *s.* distinctness, separation, contrariety.
বিভিন্নভাব, *s. idem.*
বিভীষণ, *a.* frightful, terrific, exciting fear, alarming: *s.* a brother of Rávana.
বিভু, *s.* a lord, a sovereign, supreme governor, God: *a.* omnipresent, all-pervading, eternal; strong, firm, solid, hard.
বিভূতি, *s.* supernatural power, affluence, property, glory; -বিশিষ্ট, rich, affluent, wealthy, grand, pompous, glorious.
বিভূতিমান্, *a.* glorious, splendid.
বিভূষ্, *v. a.* to put on ornaments, adorn, dress.
বিভূষণ, *s.* a decorating, adorning, decoration, an ornament, a trinket, jewels.
বিভূষণীয়, *a.* capable of being adorned.

বিভূষিত, ornamented, adorned, decorated.
বিভৃত, *a.* held, retained, upheld, supported, sustained, maintained.
বিভেদ, *s.* separation, a division, a distinction, dispersion, a contradiction.
বিভেদক, *a.* separating, dividing.
বিভেদনীয়, বিভেদ্য, *a.* separable, divisible.
বিভ্রম, *s.* wantonness, caprice, whim, an error, mistake, blunder, a doubt, an apprehension, beauty, a whirling round.
বিভ্রাট্, *s.* an emergency, embarrassment: *a.* elegant, splendid, decorated. [ed.
বিভ্রান্ত, *a.* erring, hurried, alarmed, flurri-
বিভ্রান্তি, *s.* confusion, error, hurry, a flurry.
বিভ্রামক, *a.* erring, mistaking, blundering.
বিমত, *a.* indifferent, averse, opposed to, otherwise-minded, contrary, hostile.
বিমতি, *s.* a different opinion, disapproval, disinclination, disapprobation, dislike.
বিমনস্ক, বিমনাঃ, *a.* inattentive, disordered in intellect, absent in mind, perplexed, averse, sad, dejected, bewildered.
বিমর্দ্দন, *s.* trituration, trituration of perfumes; a compressing, rubbing, grinding, friction; a killing, destruction.
বিমর্ষ, *s.* regret, repentance, displeasure, dislike, dissatisfaction: *a. vide* বিমর্ষী.
বিমর্ষী, *a.* regretting, penitent, dissatisfied, displeased, distressed, downcast, sad.
বিমল, *a.* clear, transparent, immaculate, pure, beautiful, clean, white. [goods.
বিমা, *s* insurance against loss; -কৃ, to insure
বিমাতা, *s.* a stepmother. [mother's son.
বিমাতৃজ, *a.* born of a stepmother: *s.* step-
বিমান, *s.* a chariot a carriage, a car of
*বিমার, বেমার, *a.* sick, ill. [the gods.
বিমারী, sickness, disease. [a brush, broom.
বিমার্গ, a byeroad, wrong road, evil course;
বিমার্গগামী, *a* going astray, perverse.
বিমুক্ত, *a.* liberated, emancipated, pardoned, released, redeemed. [redemption.
বিমুক্তি, liberation, emancipation, release,
বিমুখ, *a.* unfavorable to an object, averse.
বিমোচন, *s.* a releasing, a liberating, the redeeming of a person, pardon.
বিম্কী, *s.* a spouting forth, gushing out.
বিম্ব, *s.* the disc of the sun or moon, a picture, an image, a shadow, reflected image, a bubble, the prismatic spectrum.
বিম্বাকার, *a.* convex, discoid.
বিম্বিত, *a.* reflected, shadowed out.
বিম্বোষ্ঠ, *a.* having red lips, red-lipped.
বিয়৲, *s.* the sky, the firmament.
বিয়ন, বিয়ান, the bringing forth of young.
বিয়নি, *s. idem:* also, plaited hair, a queue.
বিয়াল্লিশ, দ্বিচত্বারিংশৎ, *a.* forty-two.
বিযুক্ত, *a.* separated, disunited, not joined.
বিয়ে, *s.* marriage, wedding; -কৃ, to marry.
বিয়োগ, *s.* a separation, disunion, absence.
বিযোড়, *a.* ill-matched, unsuitable, disagreeable, odd or uneven in number.
বিরক্ত, *a.* displeased, disgusted, dissatisfied, annoyed, averse to.
বিরক্তি, *s.* aversion, displeasure, dislike, disgust, dissatisfaction. [make, fabricate.
বিরচ্, *v. a.* to compose, compile, construct,
বিরচক, *a.* composing, compiling, etc.
বিরচন, *s.* a composing, compiling, a constructing, making, fabricating. [ed.
বিরচনীয়, *a.* fit to be composed or compil-
বিরচিত, *a.* composed, compiled, constructed, made, fabricated. [stopped.
বিরত, *a.* ceased, desisted, relinquished,
বিরতি, *s.* cessation, a stopping, desisting.
বিরল, *a.* fine, delicate, thin; retired, alone, apart, private, loose, relaxed, previous.
বিরস, *a.* insipid, ill-flavoured, nauseous.
বিরহ, *s.* painful absence (especially of lovers,) separation, parting, cessation, forbearance, bereavement, loneliness, a song bemoaning the absence of a lover.
বিরহ-যন্ত্রণা, -যাতনা, *s.* the pain or torment of separation or absence. [absence.
বিরহানল, *s. fig.* the fire or torment of
বিরহিণী, *a. fem.* deserted, forsaken (by a husband or lover). [titute, lonely.
বিরহিত, *a.* absent, separated, bereft, des-
বিরহী, *a.* absent, separate, lonely, bereft.
বিরাগ, *s.* disgust, dislike, disrelish, disapprobation, disregard, the absence of desire or passion, indifference.
বিরাগান্বিত, *a.* filled with disgust. [ing.
বিরাগী, *a.* entertaining disgust, disrelish-
বিরাজ্, *v. n.* to appear, to be conspicuous.

বিরাজ, s. an appearing, splendour, lustre, beauty; -মান, brilliant, conspicuous.
বিরাজনীয়, a. visible in a beautiful form.
বিরাজিত, a. manifested, displayed.
বিরাট, a gigantic, enormous: s. an ancient king; a country in central India.
বিরানই, or বিরানব্বই, a. ninety-two.
বিরাম, s. cessation, rest, repose, a desisting from, a vacation, recess, a proroguing.
বিরামকাল, s. a vacation, a recess.
বিরাল, s. a tom-cat: বিরালী, s. a she-cat.
বিরালচক্ষুয়া, cat-eyed, wall-eyed. [crite.
বিরালতপস্বী, s a feigned devotee, a hypo-
বিরাশী, or দ্ব্যশীতি, a. eighty-two.
বিরিঞ্চি, s. Brahmá, Vishnu, Shiva. [tile to.
বিরুদ্ধ, absurd, contrary, opposed to, hos-
বিরুদ্ধতা, opposition, contrariety, enmity.
বিরুদ্ধভাব, s. opposition, a state of enmity.
বিরুদ্ধাচরণ, or বিরুদ্ধাচার, s. contrary conduct, hostile conduct.
বিরূপ, a. ill-shaped, deformed, uncomely: s. opposition, dislike.
বিরেক, s. a diarrhœa, a purging by stool.
বিরেচক, a. purgative, cathartic, purging.
বিরেচন, s. an operating by stool, purging.
বিরোচন, s. the sun, the moon, fire.
বিরোধ্, v. to quarrel, contradict, oppose.
বিরোধ, s. dissension, quarrel, strife, dispute, discord, opposition, litigation.
বিরোধিতা, s. opposition, a quarrelling.
বিরোধী, বিরোধক, a. quarrelsome, disputatious, litigious, opposing. [parate.
বিল্, v. a. to allot, arrange, dispose, to se-
বিল, a hole, marsh, shallow lake, a valley.
বিলক্ষণ, a. very good, excellent, differing in character: s. a distinction.
বিলগ, a. not in contact. [connected with.
বিলগ্ন, a. unconnected, irrelative; joined to,
বিলঘুঁটিয়া, s. dried cowdung picked up in
বিলঙ্ঘক, a. transgressing. [fields.
বিলঙ্ঘন, s. a transgressing, an overstep-
বিলঙ্ঘনীয়, a. transgressible. [ping.
বিলঙ্ঘিত, a. transgressed, overstepped.
বিলজ্জ, shameless, impudent, immodest.
বিলঞ্চুমাছ, s. fishes of a shallow lake.
বিলন, s. allotting or assigning of shares.
বিলপিত, a. lamented, bewailed, mourned.

বিলম্ব, s. delay, procrastination; -কৃ, to delay, to procrastinate; -করা, to retard.
বিলম্বন, s. the act of delaying. [layed.
বিলম্বনীয়, a. proper to be retarded or de-
বিলম্বিত, a. delayed, procrastinated.
বিলয়, s. dissolution of the world, destruc-
বিলসিত, a. enjoyed, sported. [tion.
বিলা, v. a. to allot, to arrange, to dispose, to give away, to distribute.
বিলাৎ. or বিলাৎ, s. a country; Europe.
বিলাতী, a. of Europe, or, of a country, European, English; -আলু, the common potato;[1] -মেন্দ, the common myrtle.[2]
বিলান, বিলানি, s. alloting, a giving away.
বিলাপ্, v. n. to lament, to bewail.
বিলাপ, s. lamentation, a loud mourning, a complaint, cry of distress. [mourning.
বিলাপক, বিলাপী, a. lamenting, bewailing,
বিলাপকর্তা, s. one who bewails or laments.
বিলাস, s. enjoyment, felicity, sport, pastime, amorous dalliance, wantonness.
বিলাসক, a. sporting, dallying. [sual.
বিলাসী, a. enjoying, happy, dallying, sen-
বিলি, বিলী, বিলিবন্দ, s. division, allotment, arranging or allotting, an assignment.
বিলিমাফিক, a. according to arrangement.
বিলীকরা, the arranging of different parts of any business: a. arranged, allotted.
বিলীন, a. dissolved, melted, extinct.
বিলোক, a. private, uninhabited; defunct.
বিলোকন, s. viewing, seeing. [ceived.
বিলোকিত, a. seen, viewed, surveyed, per-
বিলোম, a. against the hair or grain, reversed, contrary: s. the reverse. [sion.
বিলোমক্রিয়া, an inverse operation, inver-
বিলোমজ, or বিলোমজাত, a. base-born.
বিলোমত্রৈরাশিক, s. the rule of three inverse, an inverse operation, inversion.
বিলোমবিধি, s. an inverse rule, inversion.
বিলোল্, v. n. to swing, to wag, undulate.
বিল্ব, s. the wood-apple, also, the tree.[3]
বিল্লি, s. a cat; a latch, wooden door-bolt.
বিল্‌বিল্, s. a swarm (of bees, flies, fishes).
বিশ, a. twenty. বিশা, the twentieth.
বিশঙ্ক, a. fearless, bold, safe, secure.
বিশল্য, a. free from pain or regret, at ease.
বিশাখা, s. the sixteenth lunar mansion.

বিশারদ, *a.* wise, learned, eminent, large, prevalent, increasing, bold, famous.

বিশাল, *a.* great, large, wide, extensive, enlarged.

বিশালতা, -ত্ব, *s.* width, extent.

বিশিষ্ট, *a.* excellent, genteel, elegant, select, noble, possessed of, having.

বিশিষ্টজ্ঞানী, *a.* rational.

বিশিষ্টতা, *s.* excellence, gentility, superiority, goodness.

বিশিষ্টবুদ্ধি, *s.* conscience, a correct idea.

বিশিষ্টমন্ত্রণা, *s.* thought, a special consultation.

বিশিষ্টাধার, *s.* a cabinet.

বিশিষ্য, *a.* requiring to be discriminated : *s.* in *gram.* a noun, a substantive.

বিংশতি, *a.* the twentieth.

বিশুদ্ধ, *a.* purified, cleansed, rectified, corrected as a writing, pure, clean, virtuous, sanctified, modest.

বিশুদ্ধি, *s.* sanctification, purity, holiness, the correction of a writing or mistake.

বিশূচক, *a.* cathartic, purgative.

বিশৃঙ্খল, *a.* unconnected, irregularly connected, ungrammatical, disorderly.

বিশেষ্, *v. a.* to distinguish, particularize.

বিশেষ, *a.* peculiar, special, different : *s.* a particular, a difference, a peculiarity, a dissimilarity, a variety, a detail, a change for the better in a disease.

বিশেষক, *a.* particularizing, characterizing, attributive, distinguishing.

বিশেষণ, *s.* in *gram.* an adjective, an adverb; a discriminating quality, an attribute, a characteristic mark.

বিশেষণীয়, discriminable, distinguishable.

বিশেষতঃ, *ad.* videlicet, particularly, especially.

বিশেষতাপ, *s.* specific caloric.

বিশেষধর্ম্ম, a particular duty, use or office.

বিশেষফল, *s.* a particular advantage.

বিশেষিত, *a.* distinguished.

বিশেষ্য, *a.* distinguishable : *s.* a noun, substantive.

বিশেষ্যতা, -ত্ব, *s.* discriminableness.

বিশোধনীয়, or বিশোধ্য, *a.* purifiable, corrigible, sanctifiable.

বিশোধিত, *a.* purified, sanctified, cleansed, corrected.

বিশ্রান্ত, *a.* rested, reposed, refreshed.

বিশ্রাম, বিশ্রান্তি, *s.* refreshment, ease, relaxation, rest, repose, rest after fatigue.

বিশ্রামকাল, *s.* a time of rest, a recess.

বিশ্রী, *a.* bereft of splendour or glory, degraded, reduced, denuded.

বিশ্লেষ, *s.* separation, disunion, disjunction.

বিশ্ব, *a.* all, universal : *s.* universe.

বিশ্বকদ্রু, wicked, vile : *s.* a hound; sound, noise.

বিশ্বকর্ম্মা, *s.* the sun; architect of the gods.

বিশ্বখণ্ডক, *a.* difficult to please.

বিশ্বনাথ, *s.* the lord of the universe, a name of Shiva.

বিশ্ব-নিন্দুক, *a.* all-censuring; -বঞ্চক, all-deceptive; -ব্যাপক, -ব্যাপী, all-pervading.

বিশ্বম্ভর, *a.* all-supporting : *s.* the preserver of the world, a name of Vishnu.

বিশ্বম্ভরা, *s.* the earth; a name of Vishnu.

বিশ্বরূপ, *a.* assuming all forms, pantomorphous, polymorphous.

বিশ্বসনীয়, *a.* trustworthy, trusty, credible.

বিশ্বসিত, *a.* trusted, confided in.

বিশ্বস্ত, *a.* believed, confided in, trusty, honest, faithful.

বিশ্বস্তা, *s.* a widow.

বিশ্বস্রষ্টা, বিশ্বসৃক্, *s.* the creator of all, God.

বিশ্বামিত্র, *s.* a sage, who was a king, but by long penance became a bráhman.

বিশ্বাস্, *v. a.* to trust, to believe, to confide.

বিশ্বাস, *s.* trust, trusting, believing, confidence, faith, credence; -জন্মা, to create confidence; -কর্ত্তা, -কারক, a believer.

বিশ্বাসক, *a.* trusting, confiding, believing, faithful.

বিশ্বাসকৃৎ, *a.* believing, trusting.

বিশ্বাসঘাতক, *a.* treacherous : *s.* a traitor.

বিশ্বাসঘাতকতা, -ত্ব, *s.* treachery, perfidy.

বিশ্বাসঘাতী, *a.* treacherous.

বিশ্বাসপাত্র, *s.* a confidant, a trustworthy person.

বিশ্বাসভূমি, *s.* a ground of trust or confidence, a proper object of faith or trust.

বিশ্বাসী, *a.* trusting, believing, trusty, honest, trustworthy, faithful.

বিশ্বাস্য, *a.* worthy of confidence, honest, trustworthy.

বিশ্বেদেবূ *s.* the clitoris.

বিশ্বেশ্বর, *s.* the Lord of all, Shiva's name.

বিষ, *s.* poison, virus, venom, water, the fibres of the stalk of the lotus, myrrh.

বিষঘটিত, *a.* poisonous, mixed with poison.

বিষঘ্ন, or বিষহর, *a.* destroying the effects of poison, acting as an antidote.

বিষণি, *s.* poison, venom, virus.

বিষণ্ণ, *a.* dejected, sad, pensive, cast down.

বিষণ্ণতা, -ত্ব, *s.* dejection, sadness.

বিষণ্ণবদন, বিষণ্ণমুখ, or **বিষণ্ণানন,** *a.* having a dejected countenance, dejected.

বিষ-তুল্য, -বৎ, mortal, deadly; **-ধর,** venemous: a snake; **-দাঁত,** the fang of a serpent; **-দাতা, -দায়ক,** a poisoner; **-পান,** a drinking of poison; **-প্রয়োগ,** the administering of poison; **-বিদ্যা,** the science of poison; **-বিশিষ্ট,** poisonous, venomous; **-বৈদ্য,** a charmer of snake-bites.

বিষম, *a.* unparalleled, irregular, unmanageable, difficult, unequal, alternate.

বিষমকর্ম্ম, *s.* an unparalleled action. [sides

বিষমখাত, *s.* an excavation with unequal

বিষমচতুরস্র, বিষমচতুর্ভুজ, *a.* having all the four angles unequal: *s.* a trapezium.

বিষমজ্বর, *s.* a violent intermittent fever.

বিষমত্রিভুজ, *s.* a scalene triangle. [thy.

বিষমধাতু, *s.* absence of health: *a.* unheal-

বিষমভারী, *a.* very heavy, ponderous.

বিষমসাহস, *s.* temerity, rashness.

বিষমসাহসী, *a.* excessively bold or rash.

বিষমিশ্রিত, *a.* mixed with poison.

বিষয়, *s.* a thing perceivable by the senses, a topic, an object, a thing, a matter, an object of pursuit, wealth, business, trade, any worldly undertaking, a law-suit, a sphere of action, a province, a country, a house, a refuge, an asylum, a department; a lover, a husband.

বিষয়কর্ম্ম, *s.* worldly business; **-কর্ত্তা,** a secular person; **-চ্যুত,** fallen from business.

বিষয়গর্ব্ব, *a.* purse-proud. [ability.

বিষয়চ্যুত, *a.* fallen from office, or respect-

বিষয়জ্ঞান, বিষয়বোধ, *s.* secular knowledge, skill in worldly affairs. [statement.

বিষয়বিবরণ, *s.* a detail of circumstances, a

বিষয়ব্যবস্থা, *s.* the law of nature.

বিষয়ভেদ, *s.* a difference of subject.

বিষয়মদ, *s.* the wine of worldly things.

বিষয়ান্তর, *s.* another object, or topic.

বিষয়াশ্বিত, *a.* busy, engaged in an affair.

বিষয়ী, *a.* secular, engaged in business, having worldly possessions or pursuits.

বিষয়ীভূত, *a.* become an object.

বিষযুক্ত, *a.* poisonous, venomous.

বিষয়ে, *ad.* about, respecting, with regard to, concerning, regarding, relative to.

বিষহর, or **বিষঘ্ন,** *a.* destroying the effects of poison: *s.* an antidote to poison.

বিষহরী, *s.* the serpent goddess Manasá.

বিষাক্ত, *a.* poisoned, mixed with poison.

বিষাণ, *s.* elephant's tusk, a tusk, a horn.

বিষাদ, *s.* dejection, lowness of spirits, lassitude, regret, anxiety, want of energy.

বিষাদিত, *a.* dejected, made low in mind.

বিষাদী, বিষাদক, *a.* dejected, low-spirited.

বিষাপণ, *s.* the poisoning of a thing.

বিষালু, বিষী, poisonous, venomous. [line.

বিষুব, *s.* the equinox; **-রেখা,** equinoctial

বিষুবসংক্রান্তি, *s.* the passage of the sun to the next sign at the equinoxes.

বিষ্ঠা, *s.* excrement, ordure, dung.

বিষ্ণু, *s.* Vishnu, preserver of the world.

বিষ্ণুপদী, *s.* the sun's entering into a new sign just after the equinox.

বিষ্ণুপদীসংক্রান্তি, *s.* the name of the passage of the sun to the next sign.

বিসম্বাদ, *s.* a dispute, a murmuring, a contention, a contradiction, a deceiving.

বিসম্বাদী, *a.* disputatious, contentious.

বিসর্গ, *s.* relinquishment, a gift, a donation, evacuation by stool; the mark (ঃ)

বিসর্জ্জক, *a.* relinquishing, rejecting.

বিসর্জ্জন, *s.* a relinquishing, a casting off; the making of an oblation. [tion.

বিসর্জ্জনীয়, *a.* relinquishable; fit for obla-

বিসূচিকা, *s.* the symptom of a disease.

বিসৃষ্ট, *a.* relinquished, cast off; offered.

বিসৃষ্টি, *s.* relinquishment, a gift, donation.

বিস্তর, *s.* extension, prolixity, abundance, plenty, a sufficiency, amplitude: *a.* extensive, much, many, abundant, plentiful, sufficient, copious, numerous.

বিস্তরণ, *s.* a spreading out, an expanding.

বিস্তার, *s.* prolixity, description at length, extension, diffusion, an amplification, the diameter of a circle, a divergence.

বিস্তারক, *a.* enlarging, amplifying, describing at length, extending: *s.* in *ana.* the musculus extensor; a climbing plant.[1]

বিস্তারকারক, *s.* one who amplifies or enlarges, one who describes at length.

বিস্তারণ. *s.* the extending of a thing, the drawing of a thing out in detail.

বিস্তারিত, *a.* extended,expanded,enlarged, drawn out in detail. [ing out, lax.
বিস্তারী, *a.* amplifying, enlarging, spread-
বিস্তার্য্য, *a.* extensible, dilatable.
বিস্তীর্ণ, *a.* extended, spread out, enlarged, wide, ample, patent, expanded, large.
বিস্তীর্ণতা, *s.* extension,largeness,wideness.
বিস্তৃত, *s.* diameter of a circle ; *vide* বিস্তীর্ণ.
বিস্ফোটক, or বিস্ফোড়া, *s.* a boil, a pustule.
বিস্মৎ, *s. Eng.* bismuth. [agement.
বিস্ময়, *s.* surprize, astonishment, discour-
বিস্ময়াপন্ন, *a.* filled with astonishment.
বিস্ময়াপন্নচিত্ত, *a.* surprized in heart.
বিস্মরণ, *s.* a forgetting, oblivion. [gotten.
বিস্মরণীয়,বিস্মার্য্য, *s.* worthy of being for-
বিস্মিত, *a.* surprized,astonished, confound-
বিস্মৃত, *a.* forgotten, forgetful. [ed.
বিস্মৃতি, *s.* oblivion, forgetfulness. [vour.
বিস্বাদ, *s.* insipidity, tastelessness, ill fla-
বিস্বাদু, *a.* insipid, tasteless. [the sun.
বিহগ, or বিহঙ্গম, *s.* a bird, a fowl ; cloud ;
বিহরণ, *s.* a going for walk or airing, going
বিহা, *s.* a marriage, a wedding. [about.
বিহান, *s.* the morning, the dawn, daybreak.
বিহানে, *ad.* in the morning, by daybreak.
বিহার্, *v. a.* to walk or ride for an airing or for pleasure, to walk for exercise.
বিহার, *s.* motion, exercise, a tour, a walking or riding for exercise, play, pastime
বিহারক, বিহারী, *a.* walking or riding for pleasure or exercise, taking pastime.
বিহারস্থল, or বিহারস্থান, *s.* a play-ground, a place for promenade. [site.
বিহিত, *a.* fit, proper, right, orderly, requi-
বিহীন, *a.* bereft, destitute of, without.
বিহ্বল, *a.* infatuated, delirious, agitated.
বিহ্বলতা, -ত্ব, *s.* infatuation, agitation.
বীক্ষণ, *s* a seeing, a beholding, a viewing.
বীক্ষিত, *a.* seen, beheld, viewed, kened.
বীচ, বীচী, *s.* seed, kernel, a source, origin.
বীচতলা, বীচাড়ি, *s.* a seed-plot, a seed-bed.
বীচধান, *s.* rice for seed, seed-rice. [plot.
বীচপাতন, *s.* the sowing of seed in a seed-
বীচভাঙ্গন, *s.* the transplanting of rice or other plants from the seed-plot.
বীচালি, *s.* straw, rice-straw.
বীচি, *s.* a billow, a wave, a surge, a ripple.

বীজ, *s.* **seed, kernel, the stone of a fruit, a source, principle, origin, semen virile.**
বীজকোষ, *s.* the pericarpium, seed-vessel.
বীজক্রিয়া, *s.* an operation of analysis, an elemental or algebraical resolution.
বীজগণিত, *s.* algebra, the science of, or a treatise upon, arithmetic.
বীজডাঙ্গা, *s.* a seed-bed, a seed-plot.
বীজপুরুষ, or বীজী, *s.* ancestor, progenitor, the progenitor of a tribe or family.
বীজবপন, *s.* the sowing of seed.
বীজমতি, *s.* causal sagacity. [seed-lobe.
বীজাঙ্কুর, *s.* a seed-sprout, a cotyledon or
বীজিত, *a.* fanned. বীজ্যমান, *a.* fanning.
বীজ্য, *a.* produced from seed, produced in a
বীড়া, *s.* a cautery, a searing iron. [family.
বীণা, *s.* a lute, guitar ; -বাদক, a lutanist.
বীণাকার, *a.* lyrate : *s.* in *bot.* folium lyra-
বীণাদণ্ড, *s.* the neck of a lute. [tum.
বীত, *a.* gone, past ; quiet, tranquil.
বীতরাগ, *a.* of subdued passions. [shop.
বীথি, *s.* a road, a row, a line, terrace, stall,
বীপ্সা, *s.* successive order, a being double.
বীর, *s.* a champion, a hero, a combatant, a warrior, a valiant man ; an actor.
বীরখণ্ডি, *s.* a sort of confectionary.
বীরতা, -ত্ব, *s.* prowess, valour, heroism.
বীরত্বপ্রকাশ, *s.* a display of heroism.
বীরপট্ট, *s.* a belt, a girth, a zone.
বীরবল, *s.* name of a celebrated chief and jester who was in the service of Akbar.
বীরবাহু, *a.* chief among heroes.
বীরবৌলি, *s.* a peculiar sort of ear-ring.
বীরভদ্র, *s.* a distinguished hero ; a sacri-
বীরভাব, *s.* heterodoxy. [ficial horse.
বীরহা, *s.* a bráhman without sacred fire.
বীরা, *s.* a matron, a wife and mother.
বীরাসন, *s.* a kneeling posture.
বীর্য্য, *s.* seed, semen virile, heroism, energy, valour, spirit, power, courage, activity.
বীর্য্যবান্, বীর্য্যশালী, *a.* heroic, energetic, courageous, spirited, powerful, active.
বুঁইচ, *s.* the name of a shrub and its fruit.
বুঁদিয়া, *s.* a kind of sweetmeat, a comfit.
বুক, *s.* the breast, the stomach, chest, bosom ; a convexity, a gibbosity ; courage.
বুকজামা, *s.* a jacket, a waistcoat.

বুকড়া, *s.* breast, stomach : *a.* coarse (rice).
বুকনী, *s.* powder of any thing. [breast.
বুকবাছাড়, *s.* wrapping of a cloth over the
বুকশূল, or বুকজ্বালা, *s.* the colic.
বুকাবুকি, *ad.* breast to breast. [ed.
বুকাল, বুকড়, *a.* bold, courageous, undaunt-
বুচর, *s.* a butcher; -খানা, a butcher's shop.
বুজ্, *v. n.* to close (as the eyes), to be filled up (as a pit, well), to be extinguished.
বুজগুড়ি, or বুজবুজ্, *s.* a bubble, a vesicle.
বুজন, *s.* a closing up, (of the eyes,) a being filled up, a being extinguished.
*বুজুরগ, *a.* wise, great, honourable, noble.
বুজুরগী, *s.* greatness, wisdom, skill.
বুজা, *v. a.* to shut, to fill up (a pit), to extinguish (a candle or fire). [guishing.
বুজান, *s.* a shutting or filling up, an extin-
বুঝ, *v. a.* to understand, to perceive, to know, to imagine, to suppose, to think.
বুঝ, *s.* an idea, a guess, an apprehension, thought, understanding. [perceiving.
বুঝন, imagining, understanding, guessing,
বুঝা, *v. a.* to demonstrate, to describe, to make one understand, to convince, to persuade : *a.* supposed, thought.
বুঝান, *s.* the demonstrating of a thing, the causing of a person to understand.
বুঝানি, *s.* persuasion, demonstration.
বুঝানিয়া, *s.* one who demonstrates.
বুঝাপড়া, *s.* a redress ; an understanding.
বুট, *s.* gram, a pulse (Cicer arietinum).
বুটা, বুটী, *s.* flowers wrought in a cloth.
বুটাদার, or বুটীদার, *a.* flowered (cloth).
বুড়্, *v. a.* to dip, to sink, to drown : *s.* immersion ; also, pudendum muliebre.
বুড়, *a.* old, aged ; drowned : *s.* an old man.
বুড়ন, *s.* a dipping, diving, sinking in water.
বুড়নিয়া, *s.* a person who dips or immerses.
বুড়া, *v. a.* to immerse, to baptize, to dip, to squander: *s.* an old man ; immersion, a swamp : *a.* dipped, immersed ; old.
বুড়াঅঙ্গুলা, *s.* the thumb, the great toe.
বুড়াথপ্থপিয়া, *a.* very old, superannuated.
বুড়ান, *s.* the immersing of a thing in water.
বুড়ানি, *s.* an immersion, a dipping.
বুড়ানিয়া, *s.* a baptist, one who immerses.
বুড়াপা, বড়াপনা, বড়ামী, *s.* senility old age.

বুড়ি, *s.* an inundation, a sinking, drowning ; five gandás or 20 cauris. [woman.
বুড়ী, *a.* overflowing ; *fem.* old : *s.* an old
বুড়ীগোপাল, *s.* the name of a small plant.[1]
বুদ্ধ, *a.* known, understood, perceived, felt: *s.* one of the Hindu philosophers.
বুদ্ধি, *s.* understanding, perception, an idea, judgment, sense, intelligence, sagacity.
বুদ্ধিনাশ, *s.* the loss of understanding.
বুদ্ধিমত্তা, -ত্ত্ব, *s.* wisdom, knowledge, sagacity, intelligence. [sagacious.
বুদ্ধিমান্, sensible, intelligent, sage, wise,
বুদ্ধিশুদ্ধি, *s.* knowledge and understanding.
বুদ্ধিহারা, *a.* senseless, infatuated.
বুদ্বুদ, *s.* a vesicle, a bubble. [the gods.
বুধ, *s.* the planet Mercury, the tutor of
বুধবার, *s.* Wednesday. [a sister.
বুন্, *v. a.* to sow seed, to weave, to knit : *s.*
বুনট, বুননি, *s.* the texture of cloth or stuff.
বুনন, *s.* a weaving ; the sowing of seed.
বুনা, *v. a.* to cause to sow, to cause to weave : *a.* sown, cultivated, woven.
বুনাট, *s.* the texture of cloth or stuff.
বুনান, *s.* a causing to sow seed, or weave :
বুনাপ, *s.* a web, film. [*a.* sowed, woven.
*বুনিয়াদ, *s.* a foundation, an origin.
বুনিয়াদী, *a.* fundamental, original.
বুনো, *a.* wild, sylvan, produced in desert.
বুভুক্ষা, *s.* an appetite for food, hunger.
বুভুক্ষিত, *a.* hungry, eager for food.
বুভুক্ষু, *a.* hungry, desirous of eating.
বুভুৎসা, *s.* a desire to know or comprehend.
*বুরুজ, *s.* a battery, a bastion, a cable.
বুরুল, *s.* an inch, 12th part of a foot.
বুর্মা, *s.* a gimlet, a drill, an auger.
বুল্, *v. a.* to stroke, to touch lightly.
বুলন, *s.* a stroking, a touching lightly.
বুলা, *v. n.* to cause to rub or stroke.
বুলান, *s.* the causing to rub or stroke.
বুলী, *s.* voice, word, language ; a chisel.
বুলবুল্, or বুলবুলী, *s.* a species of bird.[2]
বৃক, *s.* a wolf, a hyena ; turpentine.
বৃক্কক, *s.* the pancreas, sweetbread. [park.
বৃক্ষ, *s.* a tree, a plant ; -বাটিকা, a grove, a
বৃক্ষময়, *a.* woody, abounding with trees.
বৃত, *a.* appointed, chosen, selected, approved covered, skreened, enclosed.

বৃতি, *s.* a selection, choice, an approbation, an appointment, a request, solicitation, enclosure, a hedge, a fence, a screen.
বৃত্ত, *a.* been, existed; deceased; round: *s.* a disposition, nature; metre, verse; common practice, custom; a circle.
বৃত্তখণ্ড, *s.* the sector of a circle.
বৃত্তান্ত, *s.* a circumstance, a detail of particulars, a report, tidings, intelligence, a topic, a subject, history, a tale, a story.
বৃত্তান্তলিখন, *s.* a written detail, a report.
বৃত্তি, *s.* a maintenance, wealth, an estate, a pension, a grant, goods, a livelihood, a profession, a gloss, a comment, an explanation, an exposition, existence.
বৃত্তিভোগ, *s.* the living upon a stipend.
বৃত্তিভোগী, *a.* living upon pension. [pose.
বৃথা, useless, futile: *ad.* in vain, to no pur-
বৃথাকথা, *s.* nonsense, useless talk.
বৃথাবাসনা, *s.* a vain wish. [creased.
বৃদ্ধ, *a.* old, aged, enlarged, grown, in-
বৃদ্ধকাল, *s.* old age, the time of old age.
বৃদ্ধতা, -**ত্ব**, *s.* old age, increase, greatness.
বৃদ্ধদশা, *s.* the condition of old age.
বৃদ্ধপ্রপিতামহ, —**মহী**, *s.* a paternal great grandfather's father, and mother.
বৃদ্ধপ্রমাতামহ, —**মহী**, *s.* a maternal great grandfather's father, and mother.
বৃদ্ধা, *s.* increase, old age, senility.
বৃদ্ধাঙ্গুষ্ঠ, *s.* the thumb, the great toe.
বৃদ্ধাবস্থা, *s.* a state of senility or old age.
বৃদ্ধি, *s.* increase, growth, preferment, prosperity, success, consequence, promotion, extension, enlargement, interest on money or goods; -**চা**, to aspire; -**কৃ**, to promote, to enlarge; -**পা**, to flourish, to succeed, to improve, to increase.
বৃদ্ধিকর, *a.* growing, promoting growth, yielding interest or increase. [lender.
বৃদ্ধিজীবী, **বৃদ্ধ্যাজীব**, *s.* an usurer, money-
বৃদ্ধিপ্রমাণ, *s.* the rate of interest. [usury.
বৃদ্ধ্যুপজীবী, *a.* living on interest, or by
বৃন্ত, *s.* a stalk, a footstalk or petiole, a peduncle; a nipple. [flower.
বৃন্তাগ্রী, *s.* a pedicel or partial footstalk to a
বৃন্দ, *s.* a multitude, an assemblage, a congregation, a heap, a quantity, a batch.

বৃন্দাবন, *s.* the name of a famous city.
বৃন্দারক, *s.* a god, an immortal, a chief, the leader of a herd or multitude: *a.* handsome, agreeable, pleasing, reputable, respectable, eminent, best, excellent, chief.
বৃন্দ, *a.* a thousand millions. [Scorpio.
বৃশ্চিক, *s.* a centipede, a scorpion; the sign
বৃষ, *s.* a bull, an ox; the sign Taurus; virtue, moral merit, a strong man. [dha.
বৃষকাষ্ঠ, *s.* a carved post set up at a shrád-
বৃষভ, *s.* a bull; in *comp.* excellent, preemi-
বৃষল, a shudra; lowest caste. [nent, best.
বৃষলী, *s.* a female shudra, a menstruous unmarried girl of 12 years old, the mother of stillborn child, a barren woman.
বৃষ্টি, *s.* rain, a shower; -**হ**, or -**পড়্**, to rain.
বৃষ্টিকাল, *s.* the rainy season. [cent.
বৃহৎ, *a.* large, great, immense, magnifi-
বৃহৎকায়, *a.* gigantic, large-bodied.
বৃহৎকুক্ষি, *a.* corpulent, pot-bellied.
বৃহতী, *s.* a particular measure of verse.
বৃহমস্তিষ্ক, *s.* in *anatomy*, the cerebrum.
বৃহস্পতি, *s.* the planet Jupiter, the tutor
বৃহস্পতিবার, *s.* Thursday. [of the gods.
***বেঅকুফ**, *a.* ignorant, foolish, stupid.
বেঅকুফী, *s.* foolishness, stupidity.
***বেআইন**, *a.* without law, unjust, lawless.
***বেআন্জাম**, *a.* interminable, endless.
বেআড়া, *a.* unproportioned, out of order.
***বেআদব**, *a.* rude, presumptuous.
***বেআন্দাজ**, *a.* immoderate, profuse.
***বেআবরু**, *a.* dishonourable, mean, base.
***বেআবাদ**, *a.* uncultivated, not inhabited.
***বেআরাম**, *a.* unhealthy, sick, ill, uneasy.
বেআরামী, *s.* sickness, illness, a disease.
***বেইখ্তিয়ার**, *a.* incautious, imprudent.
বেইখ্তিয়ারী, *s.* imprudence, inattention.
***বেইন্সাফ**, *a.* unjust, not equitable.
***বেইমান**, *a.* irreligious, unconscionable.
বেউড়বাঁশ, *s.* a thorny species of bambu.
***বেওআ**, *a.* poor, forlorn: *s.* a widow.
***বেওক্ত**, *a.* untimely, premature.
***বেওজুর**, *a.* without excuse, inexcusable.
বেওরা, *s.* a detail of particulars, a circumstance, a report, a recital, a narration.
বেঁউচ্, *v. n.* to be wrenched or sprained.
বেঁউচন, *s.* a being sprained or twisted.

বেঁউচা, *s.* a wrench, sprain: *v. a.* to sprain.
বেঁওৎ, *v. a.* to shape, to cut out cloth.
বেঁওত, *s.* a shape, the cut of a garment, a manner, a method, a kind, a sort.
বেঁওতী, *a.* large, extensive; -জাল, largest net for fishing in the river. [crooked.
বেঁক্, *v. n.* to bow, to wrap, to be awry or
বেঁক, *s.* a crook, a curvature, a bend.
বেঁকন, *s.* a becoming crooked or awry.
বেঁকা, *v. a.* to bend: *a.* crooked, awry.
বেঁকাতেড়া, *a.* crooked, bent, askew.
বেঁকান, *s.* the bending of a thing: *a.* curved.
বেঁকানী, *s.* a bending, a curvature.
বেঁকাপা, *a.* bandy-legged, crook-legged.
বেঁজী, *s.* a shoot, a sprout, a small pustule near larger one; an ichneumon, weasel.
বেঁটে, বেঁটিয়া, *a.* dwarfish, short, diminutive.
বেঁড়ে, বেঁড়া, *a.* the same as বাঁড়িয়া.
*বেকরার, *a.* variable, without promise.
*বেকল, *ad.* out of order: *a.* restless.
*বেকাএদা, *a.* irregular, disorderly.
*বেকাবু, *ad.* out of one's power.
*বেকার, *a.* destitute of employment.
*বেকিম্মত, *a.* worthless, of no value.
*বেখবর, বেখবরদার, careless, incautious, imprudent, inattentive, inadvertent.
*বেখমীর, or বেখমীরী, *a.* unleavened.
*বেখাতির্জমা, *a.* not contented or satisfied.
*বেখাবিন্দ, *a.* want of a master or owner.
বেখাবিন্দী, *s.* the being without an owner.
বেগ, *s.* haste, celerity, swiftness, rapidity, force, speed, impetuosity, an impetus.
বেগড়া, *a.* spoiled, damaged, faulty.
বেগত্ব, *s.* haste, celerity, impetuosity.
বেগবান্, *a.* swift, speedy, violent, impetu-
বেগবিশিষ্ট, or বেগযুক্ত, *a. idem.* [ous.
*বেগম, *a.* free from sorrow: *s.* a queen.
*বেগর, *ad.* without, except, beside.
*বেগানা, *a.* unrelated, foreign, another's.
বেগার, *a.* impressed into service, compelled to work gratis; -ধর, to impress.
বেগারী, *s.* the impressing or forcing a person to labour, work without hire.
বেগী, *a.* swift, impetuous, hasty.
বেগুন, বার্তাকু, *s.* brinjal, the egg fruit.[1]
*বেগুনা, *a.* faultless, sinless, void of fault.
বেগুনীয়া, *a.* purple; -রঙ্গ, purple colour.
বেঙ্গ, *s.* a frog, a toad: বেঙ্গাচী, a tadpole.
বেঙ্গা, *a.* left-handed; -পিত্তল, white brass.
বেচ্, *v. a.* to sell, vend: বেচন, a selling.
বেচা, *v.* to cause to sell: *s.* a sale: *a.* sold.
বেচান, *s.* the causing to be sold: *a.* sold.
*বেচারা, *ad.* without remedy: *a.* helpless.
*বেচাল, বেচালী, *s.* not being customary or common, a bad habit or custom.
*বেজুখম, *a.* free from pain or distress: *ad.* without danger or obstruction.
*বেজুরিব, *a.* not measured, unmeasured.
*বেজানিব, *a.* unacquainted, unknown.
*বেজায়, *a.* useless, unjust, extortionate.
*বেজার, *a.* angry, displeased, out of hu-
বেজী, *s.* an ichneumon, weasel. [mour.
বেটন, *s.* a wrapper, wrapper of a bale.
বেটা, *s.* a son; a fellow (in contempt).
বেটী, *s.* a daughter. [a poor horse.
বেটুয়া, *s.* a purse; a widower, a vagrant;
বেটা, *s.* thin string of jute, cord, rope.
*বেঠৌর, *a.* unsteady, uncertain, not sure.
বেড়্, *v. a.* to encircle, to enclose a field, to surround, to invest a town or fortress.
বেড়, *s.* a fence wall, a hedge, enclosure, the circumference of a circle, a circuit.
বেড়ন, বেড়নি, *s.* a fencing, enclosing.
বেড়া, *v.* to walk about, traverse, ramble: *s.* a fence, a hedge, an enclosure. [lar.
বেড়াঁড়া, *a.* not customary, irregular, singu-
বেড়ান, *s.* a walking or rambling about.
বেড়ানিয়া, rambling, roving: *s.* a rambler.
বেড়ী, *s.* fetters, shackles; a pair of tongs to take off a pot from the hearth, short hair left round the tuft of the crown.
বেডৌল, *a.* contrary to the fashion, ill-
বেঢব, *a.* deformed, ugly. [formed.
বেণা, *s.* a kind of grass,[2] its root is called
বেণিয়া, *s.* the same as বেণ্যা. [*khaskhas.*
বেণী, *s.* tail of hair, braid of hair, a queue; the branch of a river.
বেণু, *s.* a pipe, a flute, a fife, a bambu.
বেণুবাদক, *s.* one who plays on the flute.
বেণ্যা, *s.* a merchant, dealer, trader, banker, dealer in species, a grocer, druggist.
বেত, *s.* a cane, ratan; -বাবী, ratan screen.
*বেতজবীজ, without examination. [pend.
বেতন, wages, salary, hire, reward, fee, sti-

বেতনগ্রাহক, বেতনগ্রাহী, receiving wages : *s.* a hired servant or labourer.
বেতনজীবী, *a.* living upon pension : *s.* a pensioner.
বেতনাধ্যক্ষ, *s.* a paymaster.
বেতর, *a.* uncommon, unusual, strange.
বেতার, *a.* tasteless, insipid, without relish.
বেতাল, *s.* name of a demon, a fiend, goblin.
বেত্তা, *a.* knowing, versed in a science.
বেত্র, *s.* a ratan, a cane, (Calamus rotang).
বেত্রাঘাত, *s.* a blow or stroke with a cane.
বেদ, *s.* knowledge, philosophy, science ; the sacred books of the Hindus.
*বেদখল, *a.* not possessing, not subject to.
বেদখলী, *s.* the not holding possession of a thing : *ad.* without authority over.
বেদজ্ঞ, *a.* well versed in the veda.
বেদজ্ঞান, *s.* the knowledge of the veda.
বেদনা, *s.* a feeling, sensation, pain, ache, an agony, smart, torment, distress.
বেদনীয়, *a.* knowable, perceptible, perceivable, capable of being felt.
বেদবাক্য, *s.* the text of the veda.
বেদবদবা, *ad.* without dignity or pomp.
বেদব্যাস, *s.* a name of the sage Vyása.
*বেদম্, *a.* breathless : *ad.* out of breath.
বেদমাতা, *s.* mystical prayer, secret charm.
*বেদরকার, *a.* unnecessary, useless.
*বেদস্তখৎ, *ad.* without a signature.
বেদস্তখতী, *s.* the want of a signature.
*বেদস্তুর, *a.* not customary, unusual.
বেদাঁড়া, irregular, not customary.
*বেদাগ, বেদাগী, *a.* immaculate, free from stain.
বেদাঙ্গ, *s.* a science appendant on the veda, of these six are reckoned, viz. the formation and arrangement of ideas, logic, grammar, a knowledge of technical terms, astronomy, and prosody.
বেদাঙ্গী, *a.* studying or professing the knowledge of the aforesaid sciences.
*বেদানা, *s.* a pomegranate ; a cooling seed.
বেদান্ত, *s.* one of the six schools of philosophy usually called the darshanas, the vedánta philosophy.
বেদান্তী, *a.* professing the vedánta philosophy.
*বেদাবা, *ad.* without a plaint or claim.
বেদাভ্যাস, *s.* the study of the veda.
বেদার, *s.* a chameleon, a lizard.

বেদি, *s.* an altar, a pillar, mound, elevated terrace, a platform, a stool, bench, seat.
বেদী, *idem* : *a.* versed in, familiar with.
বেদোক্ত, *a.* vedic, related in the vedas.
বেদ্য, *a.* knowable, proper to be known.
বেদ্যা, or বেদিয়া, *s.* a fowler, a hunter.
বেধ্, *v. a.* to pierce, perforate, bore.
বেধ, *s.* a perforation, a hole, an excavation.
বেধন, *s.* a perforating, piercing, boring.
বেধনীয়, *a.* penetrable, vulnerable.
বেধা, *s.* a hole, excavation, wound, scratch.
*বেনাম, *a.* nameless : *s.* assumed name.
বেনামী, *s.* the want of a name : *a.* anonymous, having false or assumed name.
*বেনিশান, *a.* destitute of a sign or mark.
বেপথু, বেপন, *s.* a trembling, a tremor, a quaking.
বেপমান, *a.* trembling, quaking.
বেপরবা, *a.* not in danger or apprehension.
বেপরবানা, *ad.* without a warrant or order.
*বেপর্দা, *a.* without a curtain or screen, open, exposed, shameless.
*বেপসন্দ, *a.* unapproved, choiceless.
বেপার, *s.* a trade, calling, commerce, traffic.
বেপারী, *a.* dealing, trading : *s.* a trader.
*বেফায়দা, *s.* useless, disadvantageous.
*বেফাস্, unfit to be revealed, scurrilous.
*বেফিকির, *a.* thoughtless, careless.
*বেবক্ত, *a.* premature : *ad.* out of season.
*বেবশ, *ad.* not under control or subjection.
বেবা, *a.* poor, forlorn : *s.* a widow.
*বেবাক, *ad.* wholly, without remainder.
*বেবারিস্, *a.* want of a master or owner, not claimable by an heir, heirless.
*বেমজলিসী, *a.* unfit for society, unsocial.
*বেমজা, *a.* insipid, tasteless, untasty.
*বেমরসুম, *a.* untimely, unseasonable.
*বেমর্জী, *a.* not agreeable, not acceptable.
*বেমালিক, *a.* destitute of an owner.
বেমালিকী, *s.* the being destitute of owner.
*বেমাসুল, *a.* free from tribute or customhouse duties, free from postage.
বেমাসুলী, *s.* freedom from tribute or customhouse duties, freedom from postage.
বেমিল, *a.* disunion : *s.* a want of union.
*বেমুরব্বি, *a.* want of patron or protector.
*বেমেরামৎ, *a.* not mended, unrepaired.
বেমেরামতী, *s.* a not being repaired.

*বেরসুম, *ad.* without fees or duties.
বেরসুমী, *s.* the absence of fees or duties.
*বেরুজু, *a.* not agreeing or squaring with.
*বেরোজগার, *a.* want of daily support.
বেরোজগারী, *s.* a want of daily support.
বেল, *s.* the wood apple (Ægle marmelos).
বেলকার, *s.* a lancet, a surgeon's lancet.
বেলন, *s.* a rolling-pin, a pastry-pin.
বেলফুল, *s.* the Tuscan jasmine.[1]
বেলমোক্তা, *s.* an average, gross bargain.
বেলা, *s.* time, the time of the day or night.
বেল্যা, *a.* sandy: *s.* the name of a fish.
বেশ, *a.* good, superior, well. [disguise.
বেশ, *s.* dress, garb, habit, guise, pretext,
বেশ-কারক,-ধারক,-ধারী, assuming a dress or habit: *s.* one who assumes a habit.
বেশধারণ, *s.* the assuming of a habit.
বেশফের, *a.* incognito, disguised.
বেশভূষা, *s.* embellishment, dress, garb.
বেশমাল্য, *s.* a garland, a chaplet.
বেশমুলা, *ad.* high-priced, costly, valuable.
বেশমুলী, or বেশমূল্য, *a. idem.*
বেশর, *s.* a nostril; a nose-ring; a mule.
*বেশরম, *a.* shameless, immodest.
*বেশামিল, *a.* separate, not included.
বেশী, an augment, an increase, overplus.
*বেশুমার, *a.* innumerable, unlimited.
বেশ্মন্, *s.* a house, a dwelling, an abode.
বেশ্যা, *s.* a courtezan, prostitute, harlot.
বেশ্যালয়, *s.* a bawdy-house, a brothel.
বেষ্ট, *s.* bird-lime, size, gum. [round.
বেষ্টক, surrounding, enclosing, wrapping
বেষ্টন, *s.* a girdle, any thing which surrounds or twines round a thing.
বেষ্টনীয়, বেষ্ট্য, *a.* capable of or requiring to be enclosed or surrounded. [passed.
বেষ্টিত, *a.* enclosed, surrounded, encom-
*বেসাত, *s.* a stock, a capital, worth.
বেসাতী, *s.* culinary edible articles.
*বেসালিসী, *s.* the want of an arbitrator.
*বেসুপারিশ, without a recommendation.
*বেসূদ, *ad.* without interest (of money).
বেসূদী, *s.* a running without interest.
*বেসেরেস্তা, *a.* irregular, not customary.
বেস্যাড়া, *a.* stale, old, rancid, stinking.
বেহজমী, *s.* indigestion, want of digestion.
*বেহদ্দ, *a.* boundless, endless, unlimited.
বেহা, *s.* a wedding, a marriage.
বেহাই, *s.* the father of a son-in-law, the father of a daughter-in-law.
*বেহায়া, *a.* shameless, impudent.
বেহারা, *s.* a bearer, a pálki bearer.
*বেহাল, *a.* wretched, miserable: *ad.* in a bad condition: *s.* a state of misfortune.
বেহালা, *s. Port.* a violin, a fiddle.
*বেহুকুম, *a.* contrary to or without orders.
*বেহুরমৎ, *a.* void of honour or respect.
বেহুরমতী, *s.* dishonour, disrespect.
*বেহুশিয়ার, *a.* inattentive, careless, silly.
বেহুশিয়ারী, *s.* inattention, carelessness.
*বেহোশ, *a.* insensible, senseless, insane.
বেহোশী, *s.* want of intellect, insensibility.
বৈ, *ad.* except, besides, else, unless.
বৈকল্য, *s.* confusion, amazement, agitation, defectiveness, imperfection.
বৈকাল, *s.* the evening, afternoon. [ing.
বৈকালিক, বৈকালীন, evening, of the even-
বৈকালী, *s.* evening offering to an idol.
বৈকুণ্ঠ, *s.* Vishnu; paradise of the Hindus.
বৈকৃত্য, *s.* aversion, disgust, deformity.
বৈক্লব্য, *s.* agitation, confusion, disorder.
বৈজয়ন্তী, *s.* a flag, banner, ensign, a kind
বৈটা, বৈঠা, *s.* an oar, paddle. [of garland.
বৈঠক, *s.* a sitting, an assembly; a huká-stand; -খানা, a saloon, sitting or pleasure room, a house for airing or ease.
বৈণবিক, *s.* a player on the flute. [hell.
বৈতরণী, *s.* the Hindu styx or river of
বৈতালিক, a bard, a poet laureate; a singer out of tune; conjurer, a magician.
বৈতালিকী, *s.* magic, the black art.
বৈদগ্ধ্য, *s.* cunning, craft, subtilty, sharpness, skill, wit, dexterity, cleverness.
বৈদিক, *a.* pertaining to the veda, versed or skilled in the veda. [ed in the veda.
বৈদিককর্ম্ম, *s.* an action or work propound-
বৈদূর্য্য, or বৈদূর্য্যমণি; *s.* the lapis lazuli.
বৈদেশিক, বৈদেশী, foreign: *s.* a foreigner.
বৈদ্য, *s.* a physician, a doctor, a surgeon.
বৈদ্যক, *a.* medical: *s.* a doctor; -শাস্ত্র, the science of, or a treatise on, medicine.
বৈধ, *a.* lawful, rational, according to law.
বৈধব্য, *s.* widowhood. [system of religion.
বৈধর্ম্ম্য, *s.* apostacy, heterodoxy, a false

বৈধেয়, *a.* foolish, ignorant : *s.* an idiot, a
বৈনতেয়, *s.* a name of Garura. [fool.
বৈপরীত্য, *s.* opposition, contrariety.
বৈপিত্র, *a.* (a brother) by a stepfather.
বৈবর্ণ্য, *s.* discoloration, tarnish. [বেহাই.
বৈবাহিক, *a.* of a marriage, nuptial : *s. vide*
বৈভব, *s.* riches, wealth, grandeur. [ther.
বৈমাত্র, *a.* (brother or sister) by a stepmo-
বৈমাত্রেয়, *a.* (a brother) by a stepmother.
বৈমাত্রেয়া, *a.* (a sister) by a stepmother.
বৈমুখ্য, *s.* aversion, a turning from.
বৈয়র্থ্য, *s.* inutility, uselessness, vanity.
বৈয়র্থ্যাপত্তি, *s.* uselessness, inutility.
বৈয়াকরণ, a grammarian ; *fem.* **বৈয়াকরণী**.
বৈর, *s.* enmity, revenge, hostility, courage.
বৈরক্ত্য, *s.* aversion, disgust, displeasure.
বৈরক্ত্যজনক, disgusting, causing dislike.
বৈরঙ্গ, *a.* not related to : *s.* one who is not
বৈরভাব, *s.* enmity, hostility. [a relative.
বৈরাগী, *s.* one who is free from passion, a religious devotee, a mendicant, ascetic.
বৈরাগ্য, *s.* freedom from passion, stoicism,
বৈরিতা, *s.* enmity, hostility. [unsecularity.
বৈরী, *s.* an enemy, a foe, an adversary.
বৈলক্ষণ্য, variation, disparity, contrariety.
বৈশ্, *v. n.* to sit, to settle (as water, etc.).
বৈশাখ, *s.* the first Indian month, consisting of part of March and part of April.
বৈশিষ্ট্য, *s.* urbanity, civility, politeness, peculiarity, excellence, validity.
বৈশেষিক, *s.* one of the 6 vedántic schools usually called the darshanas. [phy.
বৈশেষিকশাস্ত্র, *s.* the vaisheshika philoso-
বৈশ্য, *s.* the third tribe of the Hindus.
বৈশ্বানর, *s.* fire, or rather the god of fire.
বৈশ্বামিত্রিক, *a.* copied, imitated, inferior.
বৈষম্য, inequality, unevenness ; severity,
বৈষ্ণব, *s.* a votary of Vishnu. [rigour.
বৈস্, *v. n.* to sit down, take a seat ; to settle to the bottom, to sink as the earth.
বৈস্য, *a.* fit to be sat upon, fit to be seated.
বোআল, or **বোআলী**, *s.* a sheat-fish.[1]
বোঁচা, *a.* deceiving, impudent, rude ; nose-cleft, noseless : *s.* a scoundrel. [nipple.
বোঁট, **বোঁটা**, *s.* a footstalk, petiole, stem ; a
বোকা, *a.* stupid, simple : *s.* a blockhead, a numskull, idiot, simpleton ; a he-goat.

বোকাম, **বোকামী**, *s.* ignorance, stupidity.
***বোক্‌চা**, *s.* a bundle, package, parcel.
বোক্‌চাবোক্‌চি, *s.* packages and bundles.
বোক্‌চি, *s.* a parcel, a bundle, a package.
বোজা, *s.* a burden, a load, a bale.
বোঝা, *s.* the understanding of a thing ; a charge, trust, a burden, a load, a truss.
বোঝাই, *s.* a cargo, lading, a load, burden, the loading of a ship or boat. [load.
বোঝারী or **বোঢ়া**, *s.* a porter, one with a
বোড়াসাপ, *s.* a large species of snake.[2]
বোতাম, *s.* a button, a stud. [damp.
বোদ, *s.* black loam dug up in a pond, etc.;
বোদা, *a.* tasteless, ill-tasted, acrid.
বোদ্ধব্য, *a.* comprehensible, knowable.
বোদ্ধা, intelligent : *s.* intelligent person, a wise man ; bondsman, bail ; caution.
বোধ, *s.* knowledge, intellect, the understanding, an idea, an opinion.
বোধক, *a.* knowing, comprehending, making known, indicating. [mind.
বোধন, *s.* a knowing, a perceiving by the
বোধনীয়, or **বোধগম্য**, *a.* comprehensible.
বোধয়িতা, *s.* one who publishes or makes
বোধাগম্য, *a.* incomprehensible. [known.
বোধান, *a.* intelligent, wise. [vigilant.
বোধিত, *a.* made known, declared ; wary,
বোধ্য, *a.* knowable, perceivable, percepti-
বোনা, *s.* the sowing of seed. [ble.
বোনাই, *s.* a brother-in-law, sister's hus-
বোনাল, *a.* woody, forest, bushy. [band.
বোবা, *v. n.* to lisp : *a.* dumb, speechless.
বোর, *s.* sawdust ; ornament for the waist.
বোরলা, **বোলা**, *s.* a wasp, hornet. [sacks.
বোরা, *s.* a sack, bag ;-বন্দি, packing up in
বোরো, *s.* a bean ; a variety of rice.
বোল্, *v. a.* to speak, say, tell, mention.
বোল, *s.* a speech, a saying, a word ; potter's glazing earth ; liquor for dyeing.
বোলচাল, *s.* discourse, conversation.
বোলতা, *s.* a wasp, hornet ; (*met.*) life, inward agent : *a.* speaking.
বোলা, *s.* a speech, a saying, an expression, a sentence, a recital : *v. a.* to call.
বোলী, *s.* a language, a word, a dialect.
বৌগুণা, *s.* a brass basin or bowl. [ism.
বৌদ্ধ, *s.* a Jaina, a Buddhist ;-মত, Buddh-

ব্যক্ত, *a.* distinct, apparent, clear, evident, manifest, expressed, individual, specific.
ব্যক্তগণিত, *s.* arithmetic.
ব্যক্তরূপে, *ad.* distinctly, clearly, evidently, manifestly, apparently. [of a noun.
ব্যক্তি, *s.* a man, person, individual; case
ব্যক্তিতা, *s.* individuality, personality. [al.
ব্যক্তি-বিশেষ, **-ভেদ**, a particular individu-
ব্যক্তীকরণ, *s.* a making clear or distinct.
ব্যক্তীকৃত, *a.* made evident or apparent.
ব্যক্তীভূত, *a.* become evident or apparent.
ব্যগ্র, *a* eager, zealous, ardent, agitated, bewildered, perplexed, alarmed. [dent.
ব্যগ্রচিত্ত, **ব্যগ্রমনাঃ**, *a.* zealous, eager, ar-
ব্যগ্রতা, *s.* eagerness, zeal, effort, activity, ardency, agitation, alarm, perplexity.
ব্যঙ্গ, distorted, sarcastic: *s.* a sneer, pun, sarcasm, distortion, a frog, a cripple.
ব্যঙ্গক্রমে, *ad.* by or in the way of joke or
ব্যঙ্গবাক্য, *s.* a sarcasm, a sneer. [sarcasm.
ব্যঙ্গযুক্ত, *a.* distorted, garbled, ridiculous.
ব্যঙ্গোক্তি, *s.* a play on words, a witty saying, a jeer, a pun, a sarcasm, a joke.
ব্যঙ্গ্য, *s.* a sarcasm, a jest, a pun, a joke.
ব্যজন, *s.* a fan, a winnowing van.
ব্যঞ্জক, *a.* expressing passion or feeling, indicative, making clear or plain.
ব্যঞ্জন, *s.* a mark, a sign, a token, a spot, a consonant, a condiment, the beard.
ব্যঞ্জনা, **ব্যঞ্জনাবৃত্তি**, *s.* a rhetorical figure, a sarcasm, irony. [verse, reciprocity.
ব্যতিকর, *s.* a misfortune, a calamity, a re-
ব্যতিক্রম, *s.* inversion, opposition, contrariety, repugnance, a reverse. [gressing.
ব্যতিক্রমী, *a.* inverting, reversing, trans-
ব্যতিক্রান্ত, *a.* inverted, reversed, opposed.
ব্যতি-প্রস্ত, **-ব্যস্ত**, *a.* annoyed, vexed, agitated, troubled, distressed, alarmed. [held.
ব্যতিরিক্ত, *a.* excepted, withdrawn, with-
ব্যতিরেক, *s.* an exception, a withholding, separation, a difference. [guishing.
ব্যতিরেকী, *a.* excepting, separating, distin-
ব্যতিরেকে, **ব্যতীতে**, *ad.* without, except, besides, with the exception of. [withheld.
ব্যতীত, *a.* past, gone, excepted, withdrawn,
ব্যতীপাত, *s.* a great and portentous calamity, disrespect, contempt.

ব্যতীহার, *s.* barter, exchange, an exchange of blows or scurrility.
ব্যত্যয়, **ব্যত্যাস**, *s.* variation, deviation, contrariety, opposition, a reverse.
ব্যথা, *s.* pain, ache, smart, distress, agony; -দা, to give pain; -লাগ্, to feel pain.
ব্যথিত, pained, hurt, distressed. [pain.
ব্যথিতব্য, **ব্যথনীয়**, *a.* sensible, able to feel
ব্যপদিষ্ট, *a.* named, imposed on, deceived.
ব্যপদেশ, *s.* a pretence, craft, fraud, dishonesty, a name, an appellation.
ব্যপেত, *a.* opposed, contrary, hostile.
ব্যবকলন, *s.* subtraction; curtailing.
ব্যবকলিত, *a.* subtracted: *s.* a subtraction.
ব্যবচ্ছিন্ন, *a.* divided, cut into pieces.
ব্যবচ্ছেদ, *s.* anatomy, a cutting into pieces.
ব্যবচ্ছেদক, *a.* dividing: *s.* an anatomist.
ব্যবচ্ছেদবিদ্যা, *s.* the science of anatomy.
ব্যবধা, *s.* intervention, interposition.
ব্যবধাতা, *s.* a person or thing which separates, the septum of the nose, a septum.
ব্যবধান, *s.* a partition, a fence, a screen, a covering, a disappearance. [tervene.
ব্যবধানীয়, **ব্যবধেয়**, *a.* fit or suited to in-
ব্যবধায়ক, **ব্যবধায়ী**, *a.* interposing, intervening, concealing, screening.
ব্যবসা, *s.* a trade, a profession, an occupation, an employment. [man.
ব্যবসাদার, *a.* following a trade: *s.* a trades-
ব্যবসায়, *s.* a trade, business, calling, profession, occupation, effort, exertion.
ব্যবসায়দ্রব্য, *s.* merchandize, goods.
ব্যবসায়দ্বারা, *ad.* by trade or profession.
ব্যবসায়ী, *a.* professing a trade or calling.
ব্যবস্থা, *s.* a statute, a law, an established custom, a separation, a placing in order.
ব্যবস্থাকর্ত্তা, *s.* a legislator, a law officer.
ব্যবস্থাদাতা, **ব্যবস্থাদায়ক**, *s.* a lawgiver.
ব্যবস্থাদ্বারা, *ad.* by a law or statute. [ment.
ব্যবস্থান, *s.* a court of law, a place of judg-
ব্যবস্থানুসারে, *ad.* according to a law.
ব্যবস্থাপক, *a.* legislating: *s.* a legislator.
ব্যবস্থাপত্র, *s.* a written law, a document stating the opinion of a law officer.
ব্যবস্থাপন, *s.* a legislating, an enacting.
ব্যবস্থাপনীয়, *a.* capable of being legislated on, requiring to be legislated on.

ব্যবস্থাপয়িতব্য, ব্যবস্থাপ্য, *vide* ব্যবস্থাপনীয়.
ব্যবস্থাপয়িতা, *s.* a lawgiver, a legislator.
ব্যবস্থাপিত, *a.* legislated, enacted.
ব্যবস্থিত, *a.* ordered, arranged, settled, enacted, decreed, regulated. [law or rule.
ব্যবস্থিতবিকল্প, *s.* an option regulated by a
ব্যবস্থেয়, *a.* fit to be an object of legislation.
ব্যবহরণীয়, ব্যবহর্ত্তব্য, customary, usable.
ব্যবহর্ত্তা, *s.* introducer of custom or usage.
ব্যবহার, *s.* a custom, a common usage or practice, the behaviour or conduct of a person, a ceremony, an idiom, a lawsuit.
ব্যবহারক, ব্যবহারী, *a.* acting customarily, bringing into common practice. [usage.
ব্যবহারতঃ, *ad.* customarily, by common
ব্যবহারবিরুদ্ধ, *a.* contrary to custom.
ব্যবহারসিদ্ধ, *a.* established by custom.
ব্যবহারানুসারে, *ad.* according to custom.
ব্যবহারিক, *a.* designed or calculated for practical use. [blished as a custom.
ব্যবহারিত, *a.* brought into practice, esta-
ব্যবহার্য্য, *a.* usable, customary, fit for practice, practicable, defensible by law.
ব্যবহিত, *a.* interposed, intervened.
ব্যবহৃত, *a.* usual, done customarily, used.
ব্যবহ্রিয়মাণ, in use, under customary use.
ব্যভিচরিত, *a.* changed from, corrupted.
ব্যভিচার, *s.* a change of state, fornication,
ব্যভিচারিণী, *s.* an adulteress. [adultery.
ব্যভিচারী, adulterous, whorish. [wasting.
ব্যয়, *s.* outlay, expenditure, expenses, a
ব্যয়কর্ত্তা, *s.* one who spends, a spendthrift.
ব্যয়কুণ্ঠ, ব্যয়কাতর, penurious, stingy, nig-
ব্যয়কুণ্ঠতা, -ত্ব, *s.* penuriousness. [gardly.
ব্যয়পূর্ব্বক, *ad.* by or through expenditure.
ব্যয়ব্যসন, *s.* an expensive habit.
ব্যয়শীল, *a.* extravagant, lavish, expensive.
ব্যয়াভিলাষ, prodigality, profusion. [tion.
ব্যয়ার্থে, *ad.* for expenditure, for consump-
ব্যয়িত, *a.* expended, spent, consumed.
ব্যয়ী, *a.* expensive, extravagant, lavish.
ব্যর্থ, *a.* useless, ineffectual, vain, unmean-
ব্যর্থতা, -ত্ব, *s.* uselessness, vanity. [ing.
ব্যলীক, *a.* displeasing, improper, strange, addicted to an unnatural crime.
ব্যলীকতা, or ব্যলীকাম, *s.* displeasure, dissatisfaction, impropriety, offence.

ব্যসন, *s.* a vice, an affliction, a misfortune.
ব্যসনী, *a.* vicious, unfortunate, distressed.
ব্যস্ত, *a.* distressed, agitated, annoyed, perplexed, separated, decomposed, inverse.
ব্যস্ততা, *s.* agitation, perplexity, separation.
ব্যস্তত্রৈরাশিক, *s.* the rule of three inverse.
ব্যস্তপদ, *s.* an uncompounded word.
ব্যস্তবিধি, *s.* a rule for inversion, inversion.
ব্যাঁত, *s.* mouth; -মেল্, to open the mouth.
ব্যাকরণ, *s.* a grammar; -সিদ্ধ, grammatical; -ব্যুৎপত্তি, a proficiency in grammar; -ব্যুৎপন্ন, proficient in grammar. [mity.
ব্যাকার, a change of form, mimicry, defor-
ব্যাকুড়, *s.* the name of a medicinal plant.[1]
ব্যাকুল, *idem*: *a.* perturbed, troubled, disjoined, disturbed, distracted. [mind.
ব্যাকুলচিত্ত, *a.* distressed or agitated in
ব্যাকুলতা, *s.* agitation, perturbation. [ed.
ব্যাকুলিত, *a.* distressed, confused, dispers-
ব্যাকৃত, *a.* distorted, disfigured, deformed.
ব্যাকৃতি, distortion, disfigurement, change of form, mimicry, deformity.
ব্যাখ্যা, *s.* a statement, commendation, representation, explanation, exposition, a gloss, a comment, an expatiation.
ব্যাখ্যাকর্ত্তা, ব্যাখ্যাতা, *s.* a commentator, a person who states or explains a subject.
ব্যাখ্যাত, *a.* declared, stated, represented, commended, expatiated.
ব্যাখ্যাতব্য, ব্যাখ্যেয়, *a.* capable of being stated or explained, commendable.
ব্যাখ্যান, *s.* a commending, a representing, a commenting, expatiating, explaining.
ব্যাঘাত, *s.* an impediment, an obstacle.
ব্যাঘাতক, *a.* impeding, obstructing. [tion.
ব্যাঘাতকতা, *s.* an impediment, an obstruc-
ব্যাঘাতী, *a.* obstructing, opposing, hinder-
ব্যাঘ্র, *s.* a tiger: *fem.* ব্যাঘ্রী. [ing.
ব্যাঘ্রাদন্তক, *a.* runcinate.
ব্যাজ, *s.* a discount, a deduction, an overplus, a delay, stay, interest on money; -কৃ to delay, loiter; -খেকুরা, an usurer.
ব্যাজে, *ad.* with delay, tardily. [ing.
ব্যাদান, *s.* the opening of the mouth, gap-
ব্যাধ, *s.* a fowler, a hunter, a huntsman.
ব্যাধি, *s.* a disease, malady, sickness.
ব্যাধিগ্রস্ত, *a.* diseased, seized by disease.

ব্যাধিত, or পীড়িত, *a.* ill, sick, diseased.

ব্যান, *s.* one of the five vital airs.

ব্যাপ্, *v. a.* to diffuse, to overspread, to pervade, to occupy space.

ব্যাপক, *a.* spreading, diffusing, pervading *s.* that which pervades or adheres.

ব্যপকতা, influence, prevalence, diffusion.

ব্যাপন, ব্যাপা, *s.* the occupying of space, the being diffused abroad, a pervading.

ব্যাপনীয়, *a.* pervadable, diffusible.

ব্যাপন্ন, *a.* killed, dead, injured, hurt.

ব্যাপার, *s.* an action, transaction, profession, business, affair, occupation, trade.

ব্যাপারবাণিজ্য, *s.* occupation and trade.

ব্যাপারী, *a.* acting, transacting: *s.* a trader.

ব্যাপিকা, *a.* oveerspreading, prevailing: *s.* a termagant, an officiously busy woman.

ব্যাপ্ত, *a.* overspread, overrun, pervaded, penetrated, encircled, encompassed, filled, full, celebrated, formed, fixed.

ব্যাপ্তি, *s.* an overspreading, a pervasion, penetration, a surrounding, a fulness, an adjunct or attribute.

ব্যাপ্য, *a.* capable of being pervaded.

ব্যাপ্যতা, *s.* a capacity of being pervaded.

ব্যাপ্যবৃত্তি, *s.* the being pervadable.

ব্যাবর্ত, or ব্যাবর্তকতা, *s.* a surrounding, an encompassing, a going round.

ব্যাবর্তক, *a.* surrounding, going round.

ব্যাবর্তনা, *s.* an appointing, a setting aside.

ব্যাবর্তনীয়. *a.* capable of being surrounded.

ব্যাবহারিক, *a.* calculated for common practice, designed for practical use.

ব্যাবৃত, *a.* well-screened, well-fenced, well-covered, excluded, excepted.

ব্যাবৃত্ত, *a.* appointed, chosen, surrounded, revolute, excluded, excepted, praised.

ব্যাবৃত্তি, *s.* an appointment, choice, a selection, an encompassing, exemption, rejection, praise, an eulogium.

ব্যাম, বাম, *s.* a fathom, two yards. [ed.

ব্যামুগ্ধ, *a.* afflicted, sick, distressed, molest-

ব্যামোহ, *s.* distress, illness, affliction, trouble, embarrassment, pain, suffering.

ব্যামোহকর, ব্যামোহজনক, *a.* causing distress, afflictive, troublesome, vexatious.

ব্যায়াম, *s.* fatigue, labour ; a fathom.

ব্যালা, *s. Port.* a fiddle, a violin, a lute.

ব্যালাকৃতি, *s.* ponduriform, fiddle-shaped.

ব্যাস, *s.* name of a celebrated sage, author of the purànas, and the founder of the vedánta philosophy ; extension, diffusion, diameter, distribution of parts.

ব্যাসক্ত, *a.* bewildered, confused.

ব্যাসঙ্গ, *s.* loneliness, confusion.

ব্যাসদেব, *s.* an appellation of Vyása.

ব্যাসপীঁড়ি, ব্যাসাসন, *s.* seat on which the reader of the puránas sits. [fused.

ব্যাহত, *a.* smitten, repelled, alarmed, con-

ব্যাহার, *s.* voice, speech, articulate sound ; *bon mot*, a piece of wit.

ব্যাহৃত, *a.* spoken, uttered, announced.

ব্যুৎক্রম, *s.* confusion, an inverted order.

ব্যুত্থান, *s.* opposition, resistance, contradiction, independence, prohibition.

ব্যুৎপত্তি, *s.* proficiency, critical knowledge of science, etymology, derivation, the formation of words, science, learning.

ব্যুৎপত্তিজনক, *a.* producing science or critical knowledge, etymological.

ব্যুৎপন্ন, *a.* proficient, well-versed, learned, studied, derived, generated, begotten.

ব্যুৎপন্নকেশরী, *s.* a man eminently learned.

ব্যুৎপাদক, improving in knowledge, making proficient, forming words.

ব্যুৎপাদ্য, *a.* improvable in science, derivable, capable of being formed.

ব্যূহ, *s.* military array, a phalanx, a flock, a multitude, logic, reasoning, the body.

ব্যোম, *s.* sky, atmosphere, firmament, hea-

ব্রজন, *s.* a going, a moving. [ven, water.

ব্রণ, *s.* a pimple, pustule, boil, carbuncle.

ব্রত, *s.* a vow, voluntary religious observance, an act of devotion. [ceremony.

ব্রতপ্রতিষ্ঠা, *s.* the finishing of a religious

ব্রতভঙ্গ, an interruption of a vow.

ব্রতী, *a.* making or performing vows.

ব্রহ্ম, or ব্রহ্মন্, *s.* God, the all-pervading ; Brahmá the first of the Hindu triad ; a bráhman, an officiating priest ; the veda, sacred knowledge ; one of the yogas.

ব্রহ্মচর্য্য, *s.* the state of a religious student.

ব্রহ্মচারী, *s.* a religious student, a pandit or a student in the veda, an ascetic.

ব্রহ্মজ্ঞান, *s.* the true knowledge of God,
vedántism, a knowledge of the veda.
ব্রহ্মজ্ঞানী, *a.* having the knowledge of God:
ব্রহ্মণ্য, *a.* relating to God. [*s.* a vedántist.
ব্রহ্মতত্ত্ব, *s.* the true doctrine concerning
ব্রহ্মতা, -ত্ব, *s.* the godhead, deity. [God.
ব্রহ্মতালু, *s.* the crown of the head.
ব্রহ্মদৈত্য, *s.* the ghost of a bráhman.
ব্রহ্মবিন্দু, *s.* saliva sputtered in reading the
ব্রহ্মরন্ধ্র, *s.* the suture of the crown. [veda.
ব্রহ্মর্ষি, *s.* a sacred sage.
ব্রহ্মলোক, *s.* the heaven of Brahmá.
ব্রহ্মস্বরূপ, *a.* identified with Brahmá.
ব্রহ্মহত্যা, *s.* the murder of a bráhman.
ব্রহ্মা, *s.* the first of the Hindu triad.
ব্রহ্মাণী, *s.* the wife of Brahmá.
ব্রহ্মাণ্ড, *s.* the mundane egg, the universe.
ব্রহ্মাস্ত্র, *s.* a fabled infallible weapon.
ব্রহ্মাস্ত্রবৎ, *ad.* infallibly, like brahmástra.
ব্রহ্মোপাসক, *a.* diligently serving God.
ব্রহ্মোপাসনা, *s.* the diligent service of God.
ব্রাহ্মণ, *s.* a bráhman; *fem.* ব্রাহ্মণী. [mans.
ব্রাহ্মণ্য, *s.* bráhmanism, multitude of bráh-
ব্রাত্য, *s.* a bráhman who has not been in-
vested with the sacred thread. [rise.
ব্রাহ্মমুহূর্ত, *s.* the hour preceding sun-
ব্রীড়া, *s.* modesty, bashfulness, shame.
ব্রীড়িত, modest, bashful, ashamed, abashed.
ব্রীহি, *s.* rice ripening after the rains.
ব্রৈহেয়, *a.* fit to be sown with rice.

ভ, the 24th consonant of the Bengáli
ভঁইষ, or মহিষ, *s.* a buffalo. [alphabet.
ভইড়, the foot, leg, a lighter-boat. [etc).
ভক, failing, not taking fire (as firearms,
ভক্ত, *a.* devoted to, pious; laid out or-
derly, divided: *s.* boiled rice. [his food.
ভক্তদাস, *s.* servant or slave who serves for
ভক্তবৎসল, *a.* affectionate to the devoted.
ভক্তবিটল, *a.* hypocritical: *s.* a hypocrite.
ভক্তি, *s.* faith, devotedness, homage, at-
tachment, persuasion, a part, portion,
a division, fracture, a metonymy.
ভক্তিকর, *a.* devoted, acting faith.
ভক্তিজনক, *a.* producing faith or piety.
ভক্তিপূর্ব্বক, *ad.* by or through faith.
ভক্তিভাবে, *ad.* under the idea of faith.
ভক্তিমান্, *a.* devoted to, pious, zealous.
ভক্তুয়া, *s.* a dancing boy, a male dancer.
ভক্ষ্, *v. a.* to eat, to feed, to swallow.
ভক্ষক, *a.* voracious, eating: *s.* an eater.
ভক্ষণ, *s.* act of eating, a meal; -কৃ, to eat.
ভক্ষণযোগ্য, *a.* fit for food, eatable, edible.
ভক্ষণীয়, ভক্ষিতব্য, or ভক্ষ্য, *a.* *idem.*
ভক্ষিত, *a.* eaten, swallowed, devoured.
ভগ, glory, fame, praise, excellence, vigour,
knowledge, prosperity, fortune, great-
ness, strength, beauty, splendor, virtue,
love, desire, effort, exertion; the vulva.
ভগন্দর, *s.* a fistula in *ano.*
ভগবৎ, *a.* divine, glorious, omnipotent, il-
lustrious, splendid, beautiful, vigorous.
ভগবদ্গীতা, *s.* the name of a famous work.
ভগবান্, *s.* God: *a.* the same with ভগবৎ.
ভগাঙ্কুর, যোনিলিঙ্গ, *s.* the clitoris. [band.
ভগিনী, *s.* a sister; -পতি, a sister's hus-
ভগীরথ, *s.* a king said to be born by the
copulation of two women. [overcome.
ভগ্ন, *a.* broken, torn, fractured, defeated,
ভগ্নচেষ্ট, *a.* disappointed, discouraged.
ভগ্নপদ, *a.* broken-legged. [ed.
ভগ্নপাখিকা, *a.* broken-winged, incapacitat-
ভগ্নপ্রত্যাশ, ভগ্নাশ, *a.* disappointed, discou-
ভগ্নী, ভগ্নীপতি, *vide* ভগিনী, &c. [raged.
ভঙ্গ, broken: *s.* a breaking, splitting, a fis-
sure, chasm, division, defeat, discomfi-
ture, interruption, disappointment, a
breach, rout of an army, dishonesty,
fraud, circumvention, cheating, hemp.
ভঙ্গভাব, *s.* circumstance of being a frac-
ture or breach, defeat, disappointment.
ভঙ্গরঙ্গ, *s.* sports and dalliance.
ভঙ্গিমা, *s.* a breach, a fracture, a division,
a separation, a trick, dalliance, wit, a
repartee, a deception, disguise, irony.
ভঙ্গিরঙ্গী, *s.* tricks and play, dalliance.
ভঙ্গী, *s.* a wave, a billow; a hint; gesture,
attitude; also, the same with ভঙ্গিমা.
ভঙ্গুর, *a.* crooked, bent, distorted, fraudu-
lent, dishonest, swindling, crafty: *s.*
the elbow or bend of a river. [upon.
ভজ্, *v. a.* to serve, to worship, to attend
ভজন, *s.* the act of serving, adoration,
worshipping; a hymn, a divine song.

ভজনা, *s.* worship, attendance, service.
ভজনানন্দ, *s.* the joy arising from worship.
ভজনীয়, *a.* proper to be served, worshipful, honourable, respectable, venerable.
ভজমান, *a.* right, fit, proper, honourable.
ভজা, *v. a.* to cause to serve or worship, to cause to pay respect. [made to serve.
ভজান, *s.* a causing to serve or worship : *a.*
ভজানিয়া, *a.* causing to serve or worship.
ভজ্যমান, *a.* receiving worship or service.
ভঞ্জ, *v. n.* to break, fracture; to change.
ভঞ্জক, ভঞ্জী, *a.* breaking, changing money.
ভঞ্জন, *s.* a breaking, settling, a changing.
ভঞ্জিত, *a.* broken, changed (money).
ভট, *s.* a warrior; an outcast; a goblin.
ভট্ট, best, excellent: *s.* a learned man, a philosopher; an encomiast; an enemy.
ভট্টাচার্য্য, *s.* a philosopher, a learned man.
ভটভট্, *s.* gibberish, nonsensical talk, an echoing, putrefaction, rottenness.
ভড়, *s.* a large boat of burden. [tation.
ভড়ক, deception, imposition, show, osten-
ভড়কা, *v. a.* to fear, to fret, to be alarmed.
ভড়কাল, *a.* ostentatious, vain-glorious.
ভড়ঙ্গ, *s.* the third or last order of the pilgrims of Jagannáth's temple in Orissá.
ভড়্ভড়্, *im. sd.* expressive of a snoring, or of a rapid discharge of the fæces.
ভণি, *s.* ascribing an author's name.
ভণিত, *a.* spoken, uttered, ascribed.
ভণিতা, *s.* an author, a composer.
ভণ্ড, deceit, imposition, swindling, a wile; a hypocrite, jester, buffoon, an actor.
ভণ্ডতপস্বী, *s.* a hypocritical ascetic.
ভণ্ডতা, *s.* hypocrisy, deceit, buffoonery.
ভণ্ডন, *s.* deceiving, imposing upon. [lity.
ভণ্ডপচাল, *s.* open abuse, shameless scurri-
ভণ্ডামী, *s.* hypocrisy, deceit, imposition.
ভণ্ডুর, ভণ্ডুল, *s.* interruption, imposition.
ভণ্ডুলীয়া, *a.* deceitful, imposing. [flies.
ভণভণ, *s.* the hum of a swarm of bees or
ভণ্ভণা, *v. a.* to buzz, to hum. [ming.
ভণ্ভণান, ভণ্ভণানি, *s.* a buzzing or hum-
ভণ্ভণিয়া, *a.* buzzing, humming.
ভণ্ভণিয়ামাছি, *s.* a large kind of blue fly.
ভদ্র, good, excellent, respectable, prosperous, lucky, propitious, pure, pious, virtuous: *s.* welfare, prosperity, happiness; -গণিত, the making of magical squares.
ভদ্রকর, *a.* beneficent, doing good. [bility.
ভদ্রতা, *s.* goodness, excellency, respecta-
ভদ্রা, *s.* the 2nd, 7th, and 12th days of the lunar fortnight: *a.* good, happy, lucky.
ভদ্রাভদ্র, *s.* good and evil. [stead.
ভদ্রাসন, *s.* a throne, a house and its home-
ভদ্রাসনবাটী, *s.* a dwelling-house.
ভন্দড়, *s.* an animal of the weasel kind.
ভব, *s.* a being, an existing, birth, a state of being; the world; goods, possessions; welfare, prosperity; a name of Shiva.
ভবদীয়, *a.* thine, yours. [being.
ভবন, *s.* a house, an edifice; production,
ভবনীয়, ভবিতব্য, *a.* probable, future, likely
ভবান্, *a.* thou, your honour, [to occur.
ভবানী, *s.* a name of Durgá.
ভবার্ণব, ভবসমুদ্র, *s.* the ocean of the world.
ভবিকা, *s.* prosperity, welfare, happiness: *a.* prosperous, happy, well. [diction.
ভবিষ্যৎ, *a.* future, about to be; -কথা, pre-
ভবিষ্যদ্দর্শক, or ভবিষ্যদ্দর্শী, *a.* foreseeing.
ভবিষ্যদ্বক্তা, *s.* a prophet, one who predicts.
ভবিষ্যদ্বাক্য, *s.* a prophecy, a prediction.
ভবিষ্যদ্বাদী, *a.* predicting, prophesying.
ভব্য, *a.* probable, certain of taking place, polite, well-behaved, fit, proper, right, true, auspicious, prosperous, happy: *s.* a result, being, existence: *ad.* well.
ভব্যতা, *s.* politeness, urbanity, condescen-
ভমরী, *s.* a gimlet, drill, auger. [sion.
ভয়, danger, fear, peril, alarm, dread, awe, terror; -কৃ, to fear; -দেখা, to frighten.
ভয়খেকুআ, *s.* panic-struck, timid, fearful.
ভয়ঙ্কর, *a.* terrific, alarming, terrible.
ভয়জনক, *a.* alarming, causing dread or
ভয়তরাস্যা, *a.* timid, fearful. [fear.
ভয়দর্শক, ভয়দর্শী, *a.* alarming, frightful.
ভয়দেখান, *s.* the act of terrifying a person.
ভয়পূর্ব্বক, *ad.* by or through fear or alarm.
ভয়প্রযুক্ত, *ad.* from or because of danger or
ভয়প্রাপ্ত, *a.* timid, fearful, alarmed. [fear.
ভয়ভাঙ্গা, having overcome fear or terror.
ভয়যুক্ত, *a.* fearful, timorous, dangerous.
ভয়ানক, *a.* alarming, terrific, terrible, awful, fearful, dangerous, frightful.

ভয়ানকতা, *s.* dangerousness, frightfulness.
ভয়ান্বিত, *a.* timid, fearful, alarmed, terrified.
ভয়ার্ত, *a.* fearful, timid, afraid.
ভর্, *v. a.* to fill, to fill up, to load a gun, to make up a deficit: *a.* much, excessive. *s.* a filling, fulfilling: *a.* full, complete.
ভরণ, *s.* a filling up, the making up of a deficiency, the loading of a gun, a maintaining, a supporting, wages, hire.
ভরণপোষণ, *s.* the maintaining of a person.
ভরণী, -নক্ষত্র, *s.* the 2nd zodiacal mansion containing the constellation Musca.
ভরণীয়, *a.* proper or fit to be filled.
ভরণ্য, *s.* wages, hire, maintenance, support.
ভরণ্যভুক্, *a.* living on wages: *s.* a hireling.
ভরত, *s.* brother of Ráma; son of Dushmanta by Sakhuntala; a lark; a weaver.
ভরদ্বাজ, *s.* the name of a celebrated sage; the skylark.
ভরপূর, *a.* full, brimful.
ভরসা, *s.* dependence, hope, expectation; -কৃ, to hope; -দা, to encourage; -রাখ্, to confide, trust; -বাঁধ্, to presume, dare.
ভরসাতী, ভরসান্বিত, *a.* full of expectation.
ভরা, *v. a.* to cause to maintain or fill: *s.* a cargo, a load, fulness: *a.* full.
ভরাট, *s.* filling, the filling up of a hole.
ভরাণ, *s.* a causing to maintain, or make up a deficiency, a causing to fill up.
ভরাণী, *s.* wages, hire, maintenance.
ভরাপূরা, *a.* full, replete, complete.
ভরাবুড়ি, ভরাডুবি, *s.* wreck of a boat, etc. with full cargo (a term of malediction).
ভরাভর, *a.* completely full, thronged.
ভর্জ্জন, *s.* the act of parching, baking, or frying.
ভর্জ্জনকপাল, *s.* a frying-pan.
ভর্ত্তব্য, *a.* proper to be supported.
ভর্ত্তা, *s.* a husband, protector, master of a house; a smashed sauce or condiment.
ভর্ত্তি, *s.* a fulness, a load; any thing given in lieu of, or to make up a deficiency.
ভর্ৎসক, *a.* scolding, vilifying, abusing: *s.* one who reproaches another.
ভর্ৎসন, *s.* a reproaching, scolding, reviling.
ভর্ৎসনা, *s.* reproach, abusive language, reviling, censure, scolding, reprehension.
ভর্ৎসিত, *a.* reproached, reprehended.
ভরমগদুর, *a.* to the extent of one's power.
ভল্ল, *s.* an arrow, a lance; the marking nut and its tree.[1]
ভল্লুক, or ঋক্ষ, *s.* a bear.
ভস্কা, ভস্কান, *a.* insipid, vapid, diluted.
ভস্ত্রা, *s.* a pair of smith's bellows.
ভস্‌ভসীয়া, *a.* boggy, marshy, splashy, soft.
ভস্ম, ashes; -সাৎ, burnt to ashes.
ভা, *s.* light, splendour, beauty, the sun, a shadow.
ভাই, *s.* a brother, cousin, friend.
ভাইখাগী, *a.* eating her brother (abusive term).
ভাইদ্বিতীয়া, *s.* a feast observed in Kártik.
ভাইপো, *s.* a brother's son; *fem.* ভাইঝী.
ভাইফোঁটা, *s.* ceremony of marking foreheads of brethren with liquid sandal.
ভাইবৌ, or ভাউই, *s.* a brother's wife.
ভাইভাতারী, *a.* taking brother for a husband.
ভাউজ, *s.* an elder brother's wife.
ভাও, *s.* price, value of an article; -কৃ, or ঠাহর্, to value an article, to fix a price.
ভাঁইত, *s.* a jest, jibe, jeer.
ভাঁউর, *a.* awry, crooked: ভাঁওতা, an eddy, a whirlpool.
ভাঁজ্, *v. a.* to fold: ভাঁজা, a fold, a roll.
ভাঁজ, *s.* mixture, base mixture, alloy, a sophistication, an adulteration; a fold, a plait; -দা, to adulterate, to alloy.
ভাঁজাল, *a.* adulterated, sophisticated, mixed; folded.
ভাঁটা, *s.* a ball, weir; ebb.
ভাঁটুই, *s.* a snail; a species of grass.[2]
ভাঁড়, *s.* a pitcher, an earthen pot; an impostor, an antic, a buffoon, a juggler.
ভাঁড়া, *v. a.* to deny, to deceive, to impose on a person, to procrastinate.
ভাঁড়ান, or ভাঁড়ানি, *s.* the act of denying, deceiving, or imposing.
ভাঁড়ানিয়া, *a.* deceiving: *s.* a deceiver, an impostor.
ভাঁড়াভাঁড়ি, *s.* procrastination, a repeated putting off, a deceiving repeatedly.
ভাঁড়াম, or ভাঁড়ামী, *s.* a denial, imposition; buffoonery, mimicry, antic tricks.
ভাঁড়ার, *s.* a storehouse, a treasury.
ভাঁড়ি, *s.* a razor-case, a case, a cover.
ভাঁতি, *s.* a sport, a jeering, derision, fun.
ভাকুস, *a.* stupid, maintained but of no use.
ভাক্ত, *s.* one to whom food is constantly given, a dependant.
ভাক্তজ্ঞানী, *s.* a pretender to the knowledge of truth.
ভাক্তদিন, *s.* an hour and half before sunrise and after sun-set.

ভাগ, *s.* a part, share, lot, portion, fraction of the numerator, fortune, luck, degree of a circle; -যা, to run away, to escape.
ভাগকরণ, *s.* a sharing, dividing, partition.
ভাগবত, *a.* pious, devout, holy, devoted to [Vishnu.
ভাগমাতৃ, *s.* a rule of reduction.
ভাগহার, *s.* the rule of division. [thrown.
ভাগাড়, *s.* a place where dead cows are
ভাগাভাগি, *s.* a partition, partnership: *a.* being in partnership: *ad.* in shares.
ভাগিনী, ভাগিনেয়ী, *s.* a sister's daughter.
ভাগিনেয়, ভাগিনা, *s.* a sister's son.
ভাগী, *a.* sharing, partaking with; lucky: *s.* a partner, a sharer, an accomplice.
ভাগীদার, *s.* a sharer, a co-partner. [ges.
ভাগীরথী, *s.* a name of Gangá or the Gan-
ভাগোড়া, *s.* a fugitive, deserter. [destiny.
ভাগ্য, *s.* prosperity, luck, chance, fortune,
ভাগ্যক্রমে, *ad.* by or through good fortune.
ভাগ্যবন্ত, *a.* fortunate, lucky, prosperous.
ভাগ্যবান, *a.* *idem.* [fortune.
ভাগ্যোদয়, *s.* the commencement of good
ভাঙ্, *v. n.* to burst, break: *v. a.* to break, demolish, change money: *s.* a breach.
ভাঙ, *s.* hemp, an intoxicating drug.
ভাঙচি, *s.* obstacle, impediment, suggestions tending to frustrate one's object.
ভাঙড়, *s.* the same with ভাঙী.
ভাঙন, *s.* a breaking; the name of a fish.[1]
ভাঙনবাটা, *s.* a species of fish.[2]
ভাঙনি, *s.* a break, a breaking. [broken.
ভাঙা, *s.* a rupture, a breach, a fracture: *a.*
ভাঙান, *s.* the causing of a thing to break, changing of money or note: *a.* broken.
ভাঙানি, *s.* change, small coin; secret whispering or insinuation. [insinuating.
ভাঙানিয়া, *a.* breaking, causing to break,
ভাঙাভাঙি, *s.* dispute, variance, a falling out, a mutual breaking or bursting.
ভাঙী, ভাঙিজুঙি, *s.* a toper, one addicted to the use of the leaves of hemp.
ভাজ্, *v. a.* to fry, to bake, to parch, to
ভাজক, *s.* in *arith.* a divisor. [scorch.
ভাজন, *s.* a vessel; a confidant, a trustworthy person; division. [fidant.
ভাজনতা, *s.* circumstance of being a con-
ভাজনাখোলা, *s.* a parching or frying pan.

ভাজা, *v. a.* to cause to fry or parch: *a.* fried, parched: *s.* a thing fried or parched.
ভাজান, *s.* the causing of a thing to be fried or parched: *a.* fried, baked, parched.
ভাজি, *s.* any thing fried in oil or ghí.
ভাজু, *s.* an elder brother's wife.
ভাজ্য, *a.* divisible; in *arith.* the dividend.
ভাট, *s.* a panegyrist, a king's messenger.
ভাটা, *s.* the ebb tide: -পড়্, to ebb as tide.
ভাটিয়ারা, *s.* a sutler, an inn-keeper.
ভাটিয়াল, *a.* going down with the ebb.
ভাটী, *s.* a lime-kiln, a distiller's furnace, a still, the way the tide ebbs.
ভাটীবেলা, *s.* the afternoon, evening.
ভাড়ুয়াঘোড়া, *s.* a hack-horse. [to hire.
ভাড়া, *s.* rent, hire of any thing; -দে, to let
ভাড়াটিয়া, *a.* tenanted, hired, let out for hire: *s.* a tenant, a renter. [its husk.
ভাড়ানী, *s. fem.* one who cleanses rice from
ভাণ, *s.* pretence, sham, feigning.
ভাণমতি, *s.* legerdemain, juggling.
ভাণ্ড, *s.* a vessel, a pitcher, a pot, a cup, a razor-case, a case; capital, stock; mimicry, buffoonery; a jester, a buffoon.
ভাণ্ডপ্রতিভাণ্ডক, *s.* barter, the rule of barter.
ভাণ্ডার, *s.* a storehouse, granary, treasury.
ভাণ্ডারী, *s.* a caterer, a storekeeper, a treasurer, a barber, a cook. [ther's interest.
ভাত, *s.* boiled rice; -মারা, injuring ano-
ভাতার, *s.* a husband, provider: -খাগী, devourer of her husband (abusive term).
ভাতারমারী, *s.* one who beats her husband.
ভাতি, *s.* splendour, brightness. [rice.
ভাতী, *a.* living upon rice, pertaining to
ভাতুআ, serving for mere food: rice-eater.
ভাদ্র, *s.* an Indian month containing part of August and part of September.
ভাদ্র-বধূ, -বৌ, *s.* a younger brother's wife.
ভান্, *v. a.* to cleanse rice from its husk.
ভান, *s.* the trumping up of a story; error,
ভাননিয়া, *s.* one who husks rice. [mistake.
ভানা, *v. a.* to cause to husk, to pound.
ভানান, *s.* the causing to cleanse rice, etc.: *a.* pounded, husked. [for husking.
ভানানি, *s.* husking of grain; wages paid
ভানু, *s.* the sun: ভানূদয়, the sunrise.
ভাপ্, *v. n.* to reek, to throw up steam.

ভাপ, *s.* vapour, steam, gas; -উঠ, to reek.
ভাপসাগন্ধ, *a.* mouldy, fusty, musty.
ভাপাপলি, *s.* a kind of boiled cake.
ভাব্, *v. a.* to be anxious, to ponder, contemplate, reflect on, consider, think.
ভাব, *s.* a state, condition, a circumstance, a predicament, entity, an innate property, a disposition, nature, a meaning, drift, a purpose, an intention, a scope, a reality, a probability, familiarity, female infidelity, the state of the mind, emotion, passion, amatory sentiment, an act, an action, birth, a movement, a gesture, wanton sport, pastime, the world.
ভাবক, *s.* external expression of amatory
ভাবচোর, *s.* a plagiarist. [sentiments.
ভাবনা, *s.* thought, reflection, anxiety, care, cogitation, a contemplation, concern, apprehension, uneasiness; -কৃ, to think.
ভাবনীয়, **ভাবয়িতব্য**, *a.* fit to be thought on.
ভাবপদার্থ, a thing which has a real existence, of which 7 kinds are reckoned, viz. things, qualities, actions, genus, species, specific character, and non-existence.
ভাবমাত্র, *s.* mere passion or emotion.
ভাবমূলক, *a.* originating from a state.
ভাবর্, *v. n.* to faulter with fear, to stagger.
ভাবরণ, *s.* a faultering through fear.
ভাবরহিত, *a.* destitute of a scope or object.
ভাবরা, *v. a.* to confuse, to discompose: *s.* the sitting over or breathing in steam.
ভাবরাণী, *s.* amazement, confusion, dismay.
ভাবা, *v. a.* to convict, to prove a charge.
ভাবান, *s.* the convicting of a person.
ভাবান্তর, *s.* another condition or state.
ভাবার্থ, *s.* a scope, an object, purport.
ভাবার্থে, *ad.* for a state or condition, for ex-
ভাবিকল্প, almost future, likely. [istence.
ভাবিত, *a.* thoughtful, anxious, careful, apprehensive, solicitous, convicted. [sees.
ভাবি-দর্শক, **-দর্শী**, foreseeing: *s.* he who fore-
ভাবিবক্তা, *s.* a prognosticator, a prophet.
ভাবিবাক্য, *s.* a prognostication, prophecy,
ভাবী, *a.* future, about to be. [prediction.
ভাবুক, *a.* happy, excellent, right, being, disposed to be, tending to be: *s.* happiness, excellence, advantage, welfare.

ভাবুকী, *s.* a comedian, actor, wag. [stance.
ভাবোদয়, appearing of a scope or circum-
ভাবোন্মাদ, *s.* a kind of madness. [ing.
ভাব্য, *a.* probable, future, necessarily exist-
ভাম, *s.* anger, passion, wrath, a sister's husband; name of an animal. [a vixen.
ভামিনী, *s.* wrathful or passionate woman,
ভায়রাভাই, *s.* relationship between husbands of two sisters, a brother-in-law.
ভায়াদ, or **ভায়াদী**, *s.* consanguinity.
ভার, *s.* a yoke for bearing burdens, a load, a burden, a weight, burden or weight of a charge or trust, responsibility; -ঘচা, to free from a burden or responsibility.
ভারগ্রস্ত, *a.* loaded, responsible. [ther.
ভারণ, *s.* the referring of an affair to ano-
ভারত, *s.* India proper; a great poem usually called the mahábhárata; an actor.
ভারতবর্ষ, *s.* India proper or Hindustán.
ভারতী, *s.* goddess of eloquence, speech, dramatic recitation or the art; quail.[1]
ভারদ্বাজ, *s.* name of a sage; a skylark.
ভারপ্রাপ্ত, *a.* loaded, burdened. [a porter.
ভারবাহ, **ভারবাহক**, *s.* a bearer of burden,
ভারমারণ, *s.* an injuring by incantation.
ভারযষ্টি, *s.* a staff used for carrying a load.
ভারা, *s.* a stage or scaffold for building.
ভারাক্রান্ত, *a.* loaded, laid under a weight of obligation, responsible. [scaffold.
ভারাবাঁধন, *s.* the erecting of a stage or
ভারী, *a.* heavy, weighty, important, big. momentous, sedate, sad, serious: *s.* one who carries a burden, a water-bearer.
ভারুই, *s.* a quail (Perdix chinensis).
ভার্য্যা, **জায়া**, **পত্নী**, **মাগু**, **স্ত্রী**, *s.* a wife.
ভাল্, *s.* a bear; fortune; the forehead.
ভাল, *a.* good, excellent, respectful, honest, healthy, fair (as weather): *ad.* well; -কৃ, to heal, to cure; to do good; -বাস্, to love, esteem, to like, to approve of.
ভালমন্দ, or **ভালবুরা**, *s.* good and evil.
ভালাই, *s.* welfare, goodness, honesty.
ভালুক, **ঋক্ষ**, *s.* a bear (Ursus labiosus).
ভাল্কোবাঁশ, *s.* a species of bambu.
ভাশুর, *s.* a husband's elder brother.
ভাষ, *s.* a word, a sentence, speech.
ভাষণ, *s.* a speaking, talking of a subject.

ভাষপত্র, *s.* a written plaint in the vulgar language delivered to a pandit that he may state the law upon the subject.
ভাষা, *s.* a language, a word, speech, a dialect, the style of a language, a plaint.
ভাষাকথা, *s.* the vernacular dialect, the current language of a country.
ভাষাপাদ, *s.* the first stage of a law-suit.
ভাষাভাষি, *s.* an argument, a disputation.
ভাষিত, *a.* spoken, uttered, said.
ভাষী, or ভাষক, *a.* speaking, conversing.
ভাষ্য, *s.* a commentary, an exposition.
ভাষ্যকার, *s.* a commentator, an expositor.
ভাস্, *v.* to float, swim, overflow: *s.* desire; light, ray, lustre, splendour; a vulture.
ভাসন, *s.* a floating, a swimming on the top.
ভাসমান, *a.* appearing, shining, floating.
ভাসা, *v. a.* to cause to float, to launch a ship or boat: *a.* floating, swimming.
ভাসান, *s.* a setting afloat, launching of a ship or boat: *a.* floated, made to float.
ভাসানি, *s.* a floating, floating of a thing.
ভাস্কর, *s.* the sun; a sculptor, stonecutter.
ভিক, *s.* alms, begging; -দা, to give alms.
ভিক্ষা, *a.* begging: *s.* alms, request, petition; -জীবী, living on alms; -যাচ্ঞ, to beg.
ভিক্ষুক, ভিক্ষক, *a.* begging, poor, needy: *s.* a beggar, a petitioner, a mendicant.
ভিখারী, *s.* a beggar, a mendicant.
ভিজ্, *v. n.* to be wet, moist, or soaked.
ভিজন, ভিজনি, *s.* a being wet or moist.
ভিজা, *v. a.* to wet, steep, soak, moisten: *a.* wet, soaked, moist, damp, clammy.
ভিজাভিজা, *a.* wet, soaked, damp. [soaked.
ভিজান, *s.* a wetting, a soaking: *a.* wet,
ভিটা, ভিটামাটি, *s.* a homestead, ground.
ভিড়্, *v. a.* to approach, come in contact.
ভিড়, *s.* a crowd, concourse, multitude, mob; an encircling, a fence. [arriving.
ভিড়ন, ভিড়নি, coming near, approaching,
ভিড়ভাড়, *s.* crowds and multitudes.
ভিড়া, *v. a.* to bring near, to close with.
ভিড়ান, *s.* bringing of a thing in contact with: *a.* made to approach. [tion.
ভিত, *s.* a wall, thickness of a wall, founda-
ভিতর, *s.* inside, middle, centre, midst, interior, interval: *a.* in, within, between.
ভিতরী, *a.* inner, inward, comprized. [into.
ভিতরে, *ad.* within, between, betwixt: *pr.*
ভিতে, *ad.* towards, in a direction to.
ভিত্তি, *s.* foundation, a wall, breadth of a wall, a thing divided, a breaking, tearing, dividing, a rent, fissure, fragment.
ভিদ্, *v. n.* to enter, to penetrate: *v. a.* to perforate, pierce, penetrate, separate.
ভিন, *a.* separated, distinct, separate.
ভিন্ন, *a.* separate, distinct, divided, distinguished, different, other, split, broken, torn, rent, blown, budded, opened: *s.* a fraction: *ad.* besides; -কৃ, to separate.
ভিন্নগণনা, *s.* multiplication of fractions.
ভিন্নঘন, *s.* the cube of a fraction.
ভিন্নতা, -ত্ব, *s.* a distinction, a difference.
ভিন্নবর্গ, *s.* the square of a fraction.
ভিন্নব্যবকলিত, *s.* subtraction of fractions.
ভিন্নভাগহর, *s.* a division of fractions.
ভিন্নভিন্ন, *ad.* distinctly, separately.
ভিন্নসঙ্কলিত, *s.* addition of fractions.
ভিন্নাধিকার, *s.* a foreign government.
ভিন্নাভিন্ন, *a.* distinct and not distinct.
ভিষক্, *s.* a physician, a doctor. [bag.
*ভিস্তি, *s.* a carrier of water in a leather
ভী, *s.* fear, dread, a panic, terror.
ভীত, *a.* afraid, terrified, alarmed. [bling.
ভীতি, *s.* fear, dread, terror, alarm, a trem-
ভীম, *a.* dreadful, fear-inspiring, awful, tremendous: *s.* horror, fear, terror; name of one of the five Pándava princes.
ভীমরাজ, *s.* name of a bird; also a plant.[1]
ভীমরুল, or ভেমরুল, *s.* a hornet. [timid.
ভীরু, ভীলুক, *a.* timorous, fearful, cowardly,
ভীষণ, *s.* an inspiring of fear, sentiment of fear or horror: *a.* horrible, terrific.
ভীষণতা, -ত্ব, *s.* frightfulness, horribleness.
ভীষ্ম, *s.* that which excites fear or horror, terror, horror, Shiva's name, a goblin.
ভুঁড়ি, *s.* the belly, the intestines. [lent.
ভুঁড়িয়া, *a.* pot-bellied, abdominous, corpu-
ভুক্, *s.* hunger, appetite: *a.* eating.
ভুকা, *a.* hungry; -মরণা, to starve.
ভুক্ত, *v. n.* to be received into a stock, to be added to a stock, to be foisted in.
ভুক্ত, *a.* eaten, devoured, swallowed, included, comprized, comprehended.

ভুক্তাক্ত, left after eating : *s.* orts, refuse.
ভুক্তন, *s.* the adding of new sums to stock or to what is paid off, an interpolating.
ভুক্তভোগ, *s.* a past enjoyment.
ভুক্তি, *s.* food, a meal, an occupation, the enjoyment of property, possession.
ভুখ, *s.* hunger, appetite : **ভুখা**, hungry.
ভুগ্, *v. a.* to suffer, to enjoy, feel. [ing.
ভুগ্ন, bowed down, curved, crooked, stoop-
ভুক্ত্, *v. a.* to interpolate, to foist in.
ভুজ, *s.* the arm, the side of a plane figure.
ভুজগ, ভুজঙ্গ, ভুজঙ্গম, *s.* a serpent, a snake.
ভুজঙ্গভুক্, *s.* a peacock, an ichneumon.
ভুক্তন, *s.* a foisting in of any thing. [corn.
ভুজা, *s.* food, a meal, a refection, parched
ভুঞ্জ, *v. n.* to enjoy, to experience pleasure.
ভুঞ্জন, *s.* the enjoying of a thing, eating.
ভুঞ্জা, *v. a.* to entertain another, to treat.
ভুঞ্জান, *a.* enjoying, possessing, having.
ভুট্, *s.* extirpation, excision, ruin, wasting.
ভুট্ভাট, *s.* a rumbling in the bowels.
ভুড়্ভুড়া, *v. n.* to whisper ; to bubble up.
ভুড়ভুড়ি, *s.* a bubbling up ; a whispering.
ভুণ্, *v. a.* to broil, to bake, to roast, to fry.
ভুণা, *s.* parched grain : *a.* fried, parched.
ভুণি, *s.* a widow's garment. [mankind.
ভুবন, *s.* a world, a sphere, water, heaven,
ভুবনমোহন, *a.* fascinating the world.
ভুবনেশ্বর, *s.* the Lord of the world.
ভুবলোক, ভুবস্, *s.* the atmosphere, the sky, heaven, the æthereal region. [hollow.
ভুয়া, *s.* mildew, smut of corn : *a.* internal,
ভুয়ালাগা, *a.* smutty, mildewed, blighted.
ভুর, ভুরভার, *s.* a boasting, a brag, ostentation, pride, trim, swaggering. [tious.
ভুরভারী, *a.* boasting, swaggering, ostenta-
ভুরা, *s.* a particular sort of sugar.
ভুল্, *v. a.* to mistake, err, forget, omit.
ভুল, *s.* an error, a mistake, a blunder, an oversight, forgetfulness.
ভুল্কা, *s.* a spring of water ; an incantation.
ভুলন, *s.* the making of a mistake or error, the forgetting of a thing.
ভুলা, *v. a.* to mislead, deceive, circumvent, tempt, fascinate, dupe, delude, inveigle.
ভুলান, *s.* the misleading or deluding of a person, a deceiving, a circumventing.

2 P 2

ভুলানি, *s.* a deceiving, a misguiding.
ভুসড়ি, *s.* the seed-pillar of the jak-fruit.
ভুসা, *s.* soot, lampblack ; corn. [a bribe.
ভুসী, *s.* chaff, bran, husk ; -যোগা, to give
ভূ, *v. n.* to be, to exist : *s.* the earth, land, ground, the base of a triangle, a place, a site, a place of abiding, a Hindu hell.
ভুঁই, *a.* ground : *s.* land, ground, planta-
ভুঁইকম্প, *s.* an earthquake. [tion.
ভুঁইকামড়ি, ভুঁইচাঁপা, *s.* name of plants.[1]
ভুঁইচাল, or **ভূকম্প**, *s.* an earthquake.
ভূগোল, *s.* the globe of the earth, geogra-
ভূগোলবিদ্যা, *s.* geography. [phy.
ভূচর, terrestrial, moving on land. [water.
ভূজলচর, amphibious, living on land and
ভূত, *a.* been, gone, past : *s.* a goblin, phantom, ghost, evil spirit, a devil, a demigod, an apparition, a being, an existence ; -ছাড়া, -ঝাড়া, to cast out a devil.
ভূতকাল, *s.* in *gram.* the preter tense.
ভূতগ্রস্ত, *a.* possessed by an evil spirit.
ভূতচতুর্দ্দশী, *s.* 14th lunar day in Kártik.
ভূতড়ীয়া, *a.* expelling evil spirits ; -রোজা, one who expels demons, an exorcist.
ভূতনাথ, ভূতেশ, *s.* Shiva, lord of demons.
ভূতাত্মা, *s.* a name of Shiva; the human body, the elementary or vital principle.
ভূতাবিষ্ট, *a.* possessed by an evil spirit.
ভূতাবেশ, *s.* possession by an evil spirit.
ভূতি, *s.* affluence, grandeur, superhuman power ; ashes ; production, birth.
ভূদেব, *s.* a bráhman, viz. a terrestrial god.
ভূধর, *s.* a king, a mountain, a sandbath.
ভূপ, ভূপতি, ভূপাল, *s.* a king, a sovereign.
ভূপালক, nourishing the world : *s.* a king.
ভূপালন, *s.* the nourishing of the world.
ভূপুত্রী, *s.* a name of Sitá, wife of Ráma.
ভূময়, *a.* earthen. **ভূমন**, *a.* much, many.
ভূমি, *s.* the earth, land, ground, the base of a triangle or other plane figure, the ground of a drawing ; -লাভ, death.
ভূমিকম্প, *s.* an earthquake. [course.
ভূমিকা, *s.* a preface, the ground of a dis-
ভূমিজ, *a.* produced in the earth, earthborn : *s.* a vegetable, the planet Mars.
ভূয়ঃ, *ad.* much, many, repeatedly, again.
ভূর, *s.* pride, a boast, a brag, boasting.

ভরভার, *s.* boasts and brags, vainglory.
ভূরি, *a.* much, many, excessive, exceeding, important: *ad.* plentifully, abundantly.
ভূর্জপত্র, *s.* the bark of a kind of birch used for huká snakes, and in lieu of paper.[1]
ভূলোক, *s.* the earth, habitation of men.
ভূল্কা, *s.* a fountain, a spring; incantation.
ভূষণ, *s.* the putting on of jewels, a dressing, ornamenting, a jewel, dress, ornament, embellishment, decoration.
ভূষণীয়, *a.* capable of embellishment.
ভূষা, *s.* an ornament, a trinket, a jewel, dress; -**কৃ**, to adorn, to dress.
ভূষিত, *a.* adorned, ornamented, decked.
ভূষী, *s.* chaff, bran, husk, tegument.
ভূস্বামী, *s.* a king, a sovereign, a landlord.
ভ্রূকুটি, *s.* a frown, contraction of the eyebrows; hypocrisy, deceit.
ভৃগু, *s.* son of Brahmá, Shukra, regent of planet Venus, a precipice, table-land.
ভৃঙ্গ, *s.* large black bee; a lecher; a golden vase.
ভৃঙ্গরাজ, *a.* the plant **কেশরাজ**.
ভৃঙ্গার, *s.* *idem*; a cricket; golden vase, gold; cloves.
ভৃঙ্গারিকা, *s.* a cricket.
ভৃঙ্গি, *s.* one of Shiva's chamberlains.
ভৃঙ্গী, *s.* the female black bee.
ভৃতি, *s.* nourishment, maintenance; pay, wages, pension; a capital, principal.
ভৃত্য, *s.* a servant, a dependent, a slave.
ভ্রমি, *s.* a whirlwind, an eddy, a whirlpool; swoon, fainting, vertigo, giddiness.
ভৃশ, *ad.* much, exceedingly, eminently.
ভৃষ্ট, *a.* baked, parched, fried, grilled.
ভেউভেউ, *s.* the barking of a dog.
ভেঁউচা, *v. a.* to make faces, to grin, to ridicule.
ভেঁপু, *s.* toy trumpet made of tála leaves.
ভেক, *s.* a frog; a cloud; a disguise, false appearance; -**বদল,** a disguise.
ভেকটী, or **ভেটকী,** *s.* the name of a fish.[2]
ভেকী, *s.* a comedian, an actor, a player.
ভেকুয়া, *a.* simple, foolish, doltish, ignoble.
ভেঙ্গ, *s.* a making faces, mimicry, ridicule.
ভেঙ্গচ, *v. a.* to mouth, ridicule, to mimic.
ভেঙ্গচন, *s.* a ridiculing, a mimicking.
ভেঙ্গা, *v. a.* to make faces, to mimic, mock.
ভেঙ্গান, ভেঙ্গানি, *s.* a making faces at a person, a mocking, mimicking, ridiculing.

ভেজ, *v. a.* to send; to shut: *s.* a sending.
ভেজা, *v. a.* to send; to shut: *s.* the brains.
ভেজান, *s.* the shutting of a door: *a.* shut.
ভেট, *v. a.* to meet, to visit: *s.* a meeting.
ভেট, ভেটী, *s.* a present, gift at a meeting.
ভেটন, ভেটা, *s.* a meeting, a visit.
ভেটীয়ারখানা, *s.* an inn, tavern.
ভেটীয়ারা, *s.* a victualer, a sutler, an inn-keeper.
ভেটীয়াল, *a.* going down with the tide.
ভেড়, *v. n.* to approach, meet: *s.* a sheep.
ভেড়া, *s.* a sheep, a ram, a stupid fellow.
ভেড়াবৎ, *a.* sheepish, stupid, doltish.
ভেড়ামী, *s.* sheepishness, stupidity.
ভেড়ী, *s.* a sheep, an ewe; a mound, a dike.
ভেড়ীবন্ধী, *s.* an embankment.
ভেড়ীয়া, *s.* a wolf, a hyena.
ভেড়ুয়া, *s.* a pander, a pimp, a cuckold.
ভেতো, *a.* serving for food; raw, flabby.
ভেত্তা, *s.* a factious or contentious man, one who sows sedition, a schismatic.
ভেদ, *v. a.* to pierce, perforate, penetrate, to cause separation, to divide, disunite.
ভেদ, *s.* a perforation, an incision, a separation, division, disunion, dissimilarity, a distinction, difference, disagreement, dissent, dissension, penetration, a mystery; a purging by stool; -**কৃ**, to separate, to pierce, to perforate; -**কহ**, to divulge a secret; -**হ**, to purge by stool.
ভেদক, *a.* piercing; sowing dissension; cathartic.
ভেদকৌষধ, *s.* a cathartic.
ভেদন, *s.* a piercing, boring, rending.
ভেদনদন্ত, *s.* a cutting tooth, a foretooth.
ভেদনীয়, *a.* penetrable, distinguishable, separable.
ভেদা, *s.* the name of a fish.[3]
ভেদাভেদ, *s.* distinctions and agreements.
ভেদিত, *a.* divided, separated.
ভেদী, *a.* penetrating, piercing, separating: *s.* a spy.
ভেদ্য, *a.* penetrable, separable, divisible.
ভেবর্, *v. a.* to be alarmed or confounded.
ভেবাচেকা, *s.* confusion of mind, a being confounded.
ভেরী, *s.* a long trumpet.
ভেরেণ্ডা, *s.* the castor oil plant;[4] -**তৈল,** castor oil.[5]
ভেলক, *s.* a raft, a float.
ভেলা, *s.* a dart, a lance; a float, a raft; the marking-nut; the livid colour on the nipples of a pregnant woman.

ভেল্কী, *s.* legerdemain, sleight of hand, sorcery, magic; a conjurer, a magician.
ভেষজ, *s.* a drug, a medicine, physic, medicament.
ভেষজবটিকা, *s.* a pill, a bolus.
ভৈক্ষ্য, *s.* a collection of alms.
ভৈরব, *a.* terrible, dreadful, dangerous, fear-inspiring, frightful: *s.* a name of Shiva.
ভৈরবতা, -ত্ব, *s.* terribleness, dreadfulness.
ভৈরবী, *s.* a name of Durgá; one of the personified musical modes of the Hindus.
ভৈরবীচক্র, *s.* a society formed for lewd purposes.
ভৈষজ্য, *s.* a drug, a medicine.
ভোঁতা, *a.* obtuse, dull, not sharp, blunt: *s.* the unedible parts of the jak-fruit.
ভোঁদড়, *s.* an animal of the weasel kind.
ভোঁস, *a.* satisfied, full, hoven: *s.* an abyss.
ভো, a *voc. part.* O ho, soho.
ভোকছানি, *s.* faintness from hunger or fasting.
ভোক্তব্য, *a.* edible, eatable, fit to be eaten; sufferable.
ভোক্তা, *s.* an eater, a glutton.
ভোগ, *s.* eating, enjoyment or suffering; -কৃ, to enjoy, to suffer, to undergo.
ভোগকর্তা, *s.* one who enjoys or suffers.
ভোগবান্, *a.* enjoying, suffering; playing, dancing, acting, singing.
ভোগরাগ, *s.* possession; a meet-offering.
ভোগা, *v. a.* to cause to enjoy or suffer: *s.* deceit, imposition, a lie, a cheat, deception; -দা, to delude, cheat, dupe.
ভোগান, *s.* the causing to enjoy or suffer.
ভোগান্ত, *s.* end of enjoyment or suffering.
ভোগাভোগ, *s.* enjoyment or non-enjoyment, suffering or not suffering.
ভোগার্থী, *a.* desirous of enjoyment.
ভোগার্থে, *ad.* for enjoyment or suffering.
ভোগিনী, *s.* a king's concubine.
ভোগী, enjoying, possessing, suffering: *s.* a snake.
ভোগ্য, *a.* eatable, sufferable, enjoyable.
ভোজ, *s.* a feast, a meal, a banquet; the name of an ancient king; legerdemain.
ভোজন, *s.* a meal, eating, taking a meal.
ভোজনাগার, *s.* a dining-room.
ভোজনীয়, *a.* eatable, edible, fit for food.
ভোজবাজী, ভোজবিদ্যা, magic, legerdemain, juggling, sleight of hand.
ভোজয়িতব্য, *a.* proper for the feeding of others.
ভোজয়িতা, *s.* one who feeds others, a host.
ভোজরাজ, *s.* an ancient king of Ujjayani.
ভোজ্য, *a.* eatable, edible, fit for food: *s.* an offering, a meat-offering.
ভোজ্যান্ন, *s.* eatable food; a messmate, table-companion.
ভোট, *s.* a red blanket made in Bhoṭán.
ভোড়ঙ্গ, *s.* a trumpet; a kind of boat.
ভোড়ঙ্গিয়, *s.* a trumpeter.
ভোতা, the same as ভোঁতা.
ভোমর, *s.* humble bee; an auger, a drill; a watering-pot.
ভোমা, *s.* the eyebrows: *a.* stupid, foolish.
ভোর, *a.* early: *s.* the morning, the dawn.
ভোরে, *ad.* in the morning, at dawn.
ভোলা, *a.* forgetful, simple: *s.* a fish.
ভৌতিক, *a.* material, belonging to apparitions or evil spirits: *s.* a name of Shiva.
ভৌম, *s.* the planet Mars; ambergris: *a.* earthly, terrestrial.
ভৌমিক, *a.* belonging to land, produced from the earth.
ভৌমী, *s.* a name of Sitá, wife of Ráma.
ভ্যাকা, *v. a.* to con, to commit to memory.
ভ্যাসভ্যাস, *a.* ignorant, stupid, doltish.
ভ্রংশ, *s.* a fall, depravity, fall from virtue, ruin.
ভ্রম্, *v. n.* to err, to mistake.
ভ্রম, *s.* error, mistake, blunder, delusion, a whirling, going round, a whirlpool, whirlwind, a roaming, wandering.
ভ্রমক্রমে, *ad.* through error or mistake.
ভ্রমণ, *s.* a roaming or wandering about, the traversing of a place, a mistaking, an erring, a turning or whirling.
ভ্রমণী, *a.* travelling, wandering, roaming.
ভ্রমপূর্ব্বক, *ad.* erroneously, by mistake.
ভ্রমমাত্র, *s.* a mere mistake, a simple error.
ভ্রমর, *s.* the humble bee; *fem.* ভ্রমরী.
ভ্রমাত্মক, identified with error or mistake.
ভ্রমি, *s.* dizziness, giddiness, vertigo, stupor, fainting, a sceptic, a whirling, an error, mistake, a whirlwind, an eddy.
ভ্রমিলাগন, *s.* a being affected with giddiness, stupor, fainting, forgetfulness.
ভ্রমে, *ad.* through mistake, inadvertently.
ভ্রষ্ট, *a.* fallen from virtue, fallen from an office, depraved, degraded, corrupted; parched, baked, fried, grilled.
ভ্রষ্টতা, *s.* corruption, depravity, degradation.
ভ্রষ্টা, *s.* an adulteress, a bad woman.
ভ্রষ্টাচার, *s.* a depraved line of conduct.

ভ্রষ্টাচারী, *a.* heterodox, acting depravedly.
ভ্রষ্টামী, ভ্রষ্টপনা, *s.* depravity, pollution.
ভ্রষ্টাশঙ্কা, *s.* jealousy of a wife.
ভ্রাজক, *s.* the bile, the bilious humour.
ভ্রাতা, *s.* a brother; -গণ, brethren. [phew.
ভ্রাতুষ্পুত্র, ভ্রাতৃপুত্র, *s.* a brother's son, ne-
ভ্রাতুষ্পুত্রী, ভ্রাতৃপুত্রী, *do.'s* daughter, niece.
ভ্রাতৃ, *s.* a brother, a uterine brother.
ভ্রাতৃকন্যা, *s.* a brother's daughter.
ভ্রাতৃজ, *a.* produced from a brother: *s.* a brother's son; a nephew; *fem.* ভ্রাতৃজা.
ভ্রাতৃ-জায়া, -পত্নী, -বধূ, *s.* a brother's wife.
ভ্রাতৃদ্বিতীয়া, *s.* the same with ভাইদ্বিতীয়া.
ভ্রাতৃব্য, brother's son, nephew; an enemy.
ভ্রাতৃশ্বশুর, *s.* a husband's elder brother.
ভ্রাত্রীয়, *a.* fraternal, brotherly: *s.* a nephew, a brother's son. [error.
ভ্রান্ত, *a.* wandering, mistaken, fallen into
ভ্রান্তি, *s.* a mistake, an error, a delusion, a blunder; -ক্রমে, by means of error.
ভ্রান্তিপূর্ব্বক, *ad.* erroneously, by mistake.
ভ্রামক, *a.* misleading, causing error or mistake: *s.* a magnet, loadstone; a cheat, a swindler; a shakal, a jackal.
ভ্রূ, *s.* the eye-brow. [bidding aspect.
ভ্রূকুটি, ভ্রূক্ষেপ, a frown, angry look, a for-
ভ্রূণ, *s.* a fœtus, embryo, an unborn child.
ভ্রূণঘ্ন, *a.* procuring abortion. [brow.
ভ্রূভঙ্গ, ভ্রূভঙ্গি, *s.* a frown, distortion of the

ম, the twenty-fifth consonant in the alphabet: *v. a.* to churn, to agitate.
মই, *s.* a ladder, the Indian harrow.
মইল, *s.* dirt, filth: মইলা, dirty, filthy.
মউ, *s.* honey; -আলু, a species of yam.[1]
মউআ, মউল, *s.* a tree from the flowers of which a spirituous liquor is made.[2]
মউচাক, *s.* a honeycomb, a bee-hive.
মউচুঙ্গ, *s.* the name of two birds.[3]
মউড়, *s.* a crown, diadem, marriage crown.
মউমাছি, *s.* the common honey-bee.
মউরলা, *s.* the name of a species of fish.[4]
মউরী, *s.* anis-seed and its plant.[5]
মউলা, মৌলা, *s.* a kind of coarse mat.
মওন, মওনী, *s.* churning, act of churning.
মওয়া, *v. a.* to cause to churn: *a.* churned.
*মকদ্দমা, মোকদ্দমা, *s.* the same as মুকদ্দমা.
মকর, *s.* a marine monster probably a seal, a whale? the sign Capricorn; deceit.
মকরকেতন, *s.* the Hindu Cupid. [cine.
মকরধ্বজ, *s.* *idem;* also, a valuable medi-
মকরন্দ, *s.* honey, nectary of a flower, filament of a lotus; a bee; Indian cuckoo.
*মকরর, established, settled, appointed.
মকররাশি, *s.* the sign Capricorn.
মকররী, *s.* appointment. [into Capricorn.
মকরসংক্রান্তি, *s.* the entrance of the sun
মকুট, *s.* a crown, a diadem, a tiara, a crest.
মকুল, or মুকুল, *s.* an opening bud.
মক্কা, *s.* the city of Mecca; also, a plant.[6]
*মক্‌দুর, or মগ্‌দুর, *s.* power, strength, ability.
মক্ষিকা, মাছি, *s.* a fly; মধু-, a bee. [lity.
মখ, *s.* a sacrifice, an oblation. [bean.[7]
মখন, or মখম, *s.* butter; -শিম, a kidney
*মখ্‌মল, *s.* velvet, velveteen; a plant.[8]
*মগজ, *s.* the brain, marrow, pith, a kernel.
*মগজী, *s.* a border, an edging, a hem.
মগরা, *a.* obstinate, headstrong.
মগ্ন, *a.* immersed, sunk, overwhelmed.
মঘা, *s.* the tenth mansion of the Hindu
মঘানক্ষত্র, *idem.* [zodiac.
মঙ্গল, welfare, prosperity, happiness; the planet Mars: *a.* lucky, prosperous; -গা, to congratulate, to sing one's praise.
মঙ্গলকর, *a.* doing good, beneficent.
মঙ্গলঘট, a water-vessel set before an idol.
মঙ্গলবাদ, *s.* congratulation, thanksgiving,
মঙ্গলবার, *s.* Tuesday. [benediction.
মঙ্গলবার্ত্তা, or মঙ্গলাখ্যান, *s.* good news.
মঙ্গলসমাচার, *s.* good news, the Gospel.
মঙ্গলাচরণ, *s.* festivity, a religious action.
মঙ্গলৈষী, *a.* benevolent: *s.* a well-wisher.
মঙ্গল্য, *a.* auspicious, propitious, beautiful, pleasing, agreeable, pure, pious.
মচান, *s.* a shelf, a stage, a platform.
মচক্, *v. n.* to be wrenched or sprained.
মচকন, *s.* a wrenching, spraining, twisting.
মচকা, *v. n.* to sprain, to twist, to wrench.
মচকান, *s.* a wrenching, a spraining: *a.* wrenched, sprained, twisted, torn.
মচকানি, *s.* a wrench, a sprain. [tle.
মচমচীয়া, *a.* crisp, crumping, dried, brit-
মচ্ছড়, *s.* a musquito. মচ্ছলি, *s.* a fish.
মজ্, *v. n.* to be immersed, to be involved.

*মজকুর, *a.* beforementioned, aforesaid.
মজবুত, *a.* strong, firm : মজবুতী, firmness.
*মজলিস, *s.* a society, an assembly, a company.
মজলিসী, *a.* social, fit for a society.
‡মজা, *s.* a flavour, a savour, a taste : *v. a.* to immerse, to plunge, to dip.
মজাক, *s.* the palate, a taste ; a pun, a jibe.
*মজাদার, *a.* well-tasted, savoury, tasty.
*মজিদ, মস্‌জিদ্‌, *s.* a mosque, a temple.
*মজুদ, *a.* present, standing before, ready.
*মজুমদার, *s.* a keeper of the records.
*মজুর, *s.* a labourer, a porter, a cooly.
মজুরী, *s.* labour, wages for labour, hire.
মজ্জ্‌, *v. n.* to sink, plunge, be immersed.
মজ্জন, *s.* a sinking in water or distress, a plunging, immersion, diving.
মজ্জনা, *s.* immersion, dipping, a sinking.
মজ্জা, *v. a.* to immerse, overwhelm : *s.* the brains, marrow, pith, sap.
মজ্জাগত, *a.* affecting the marrow, inward, latent.
মজ্জাগতজ্বর, *s.* the brain-fever.
মজ্জাভেদ, *s.* a touching to the quick.
মজ্জাভেদী, *a.* touching the quick.
মজ্জারস, *s.* in *ana.* the medullary juice.
মঞ্চ, *s.* a shelf, stage, a platform, scaffold, a pulpit, a table, a bed, a bedstead.
মঞ্চোপরি, *ad.* upon a stage or scaffold.
মঞ্ছাল, *s.* red arsenic.
মঞ্জন, *s.* a cleaning, scouring, a dentifrice, tooth-powder.
মঞ্জর্‌, *v. n.* to bud, sprout, germinate, to put forth new leaves.
মঞ্জরী, *s.* a bud, shoot, ear of corn, a spike of flowers.
মঞ্জা, *s.* a species of grass.
মঞ্জিষ্ট, or মঞ্জিষ্ঠা, *s.* the Indian madder.[1]
মঞ্জির, *s.* a ring with bells for the ankle.
*মঞ্জিল, *s.* a journey, day's march, an inn.
মঞ্জুল, *a.* beautiful, agreeable, pleasing.
*মঞ্জুর, *a.* approved, chosen, acquiesced in, admitted ; -কৃ, to acquiesce in, to admit.
মঞ্জুরী, *s.* approbation, consent, choice.
মটর, *s.* peas ; -মালা, a kind of necklace.
মটরাসাড়ী, *s.* a woman's silken garment.
মটী, *s.* a small earthen oil bottle.
মটুক, মকুট, *s.* a crown, a diadem, a tiara.
মট্‌কা, *v. a.* to snap or crack the joints : *s.* ridge of a thatched roof ; a jar ; -মার্‌, to close up the ridge : চক্ষুমট্‌কা, to wink.

মট্‌কান, মট্‌কানি, *s.* a snapping or cracking of the joints : চক্ষুমট্‌কান, a winking.
মট্‌কী, *s.* a jar, large earthen jar.
মঠ, *s.* a monastery, an abbey, a convent, a temple.
মঠাধ্যক্ষ, *s.* an abbot, the chief of a monastery.
মড়ক, *s.* a pestilence, mortality.
মড়ল, *s.* the headman of a village.
মড়া, mortal, dead : *s.* a dead body, corpse.
মড়াকামড়, *s.* a mortal bite ; *fig.* a teazing, dunning, a persevering at all hazards.
মড়াঞ্চিয়া, *a.* all (her) children dying : *s.* a woman whose children are all dead.
মড়ুকচা, *s.* the ridge of a thatched roof.
মড়ুকা, মড়্‌মড়ীয়া, *a.* brittle, fragile, dry.
মড়্‌মড়্‌, *im. sd.* of the fall of a house.
মণি, *s.* a gem, a precious stone, a pearl, the glans penis, semen virile, clitoris.
মণিকর্ণিকা, *s.* name of a pool at Benares.
মণিকার, a jeweller, lapidary, gem-cutter.
মণিপূর, *a.* studded : *s.* the navel, a boddice ; the name of a country.
মণিপ্রভাব, *s.* the power or virtue of a gem.
মণিবন্ধ, *s.* the wrist.
মণিময়, *a.* made of gems, set with gems.
মণিয়া, *s.* name of a kind of little bird.[2]
মণিহারী, *s.* a jeweller ; a seller of toys.
মণ্ড, *s.* rice-gruel, starch, paste, gruel.
মণ্ডন, *s.* an overlaying, a gilding, plating, covering of an article with leather, etc.
মণ্ডপ, *s.* a temple, a house, a booth.
মণ্ডল, *s.* a circle, a halo, a sphere or globe, an orb, the disk of the sun or moon, a ball or globe, headman of a village.
মণ্ডলাকার, *a.* circular, orbiculate, round.
মণ্ডলী, *s* a society, congregation, church.
মণ্ডা, মণ্ডী, *s.* a kind of sweetmeat.
মণ্ডিত, *a.* overlaid, covered, adorned, gilt, plated.
মণ্ডুক, *s.* a frog ; -কূপ, (*met.*) a secret place.
মণ্ডুর, *s.* the rust of iron, dross, scoriæ.
মৎ, a *prohib. part.* used in composition.
মত, *s.* a method, mode, manner, sect, sentiment : *a.* alike, similar, resembling.
মতন, *s.* method, way ; a text, text of a book.
মতবালা, *a.* drunk, intoxicated : *s.* a drunkard.
মতভেদ, *s.* a distinct sect, schism.
মতমত, *ad.* of one mind, of one sect.
*মতর্জিম, *s.* a translator, an interpreter.

মতানুযায়ী, মতানুসারে, *ad.* according with a particular manner or method.
মতান্তর, *s.* another manner, opinion, sect, or party, an alteration : *a.* altered.
মতান্তরীকৃত, *a.* altered, changed, modified.
মতান্তরে, *ad.* otherwise, in another method.
মতাবলম্বন, *s.* the receiving or professing of the sentiments of a particular sect.
মতাবলম্বী, *a.* professing the principles of a particular sect, sectarian.
মতামত, *s.* that which is customary or not : *a.* approved and disapproved.
মতামতি, *s.* approbation or disapprobation.
মতি, *s.* opinion, the mind, will, inclination, imagination ; a pearl. [ranged.
মতিচ্ছন্ন, মতিচ্ছিন্ন, *a.* delirious, crazy, de-
মতিবিশিষ্ট, *a.* intelligent, reflecting, judi-
মতিভ্রম, *s.* a mistake, an error. [cious.
মতিমান্, *a.* wise, reflecting, judicious.
মতিহীন, *a.* injudicious, unintelligent.
মতী, *s.* opinion, mind ; a sect, a party.
মতে, *ad.* according to, agreeably to.
মত্ত, *a.* inebriated, intoxicated, drunk, overcome with joy, eager. [enthusiasm.
মত্ততা, -ত্ব, *s.* intoxication, folly, eagerness,
মত্তমানকলা, *s.* a variety of plantain.[1]
মৎকুণ, *s.* a bug, a flea, a louse. [meaning.
*মৎলব, *s.* a scope, a desire, an opinion, a
মৎলবী, having a scope or wish, desirous.
মৎসর, envious, grudging, covetous, niggardly : *s.* envy, malice ; a musquito.
মৎস্য, *s.* a fish ; one of the puránas ; the fish-formed Vishnu. [ther of Vyása.
মৎস্যগন্ধা, *a.* having fishy scent : *s.* the mo-
মৎস্যণ্ডিকা, *s.* coarse sugar, sugarcandy.
মৎস্যাবতার, *s.* an incarnation of Vishnu.
মথ্, *v. a.* to churn, to agitate violently.
মথন, *s.* a churning, agitating, stirring.
মথিত, *a.* churned : *s.* buttermilk.
মথুরা, *s.* the name of a famous town.
মদ, wine, spirituous liquor, inebriety, intoxication, pride, arrogance, insanity, passion, desire, pleasure, enthusiasm.
মদক, *s.* an opiate, a narcotic medicine, an inebrious prating, a confectioner.
মদকল, *s.* an elephant in rut. [tobacco.
মদৎ, *s.* an intoxicating drug smoked as
মদতী, *s.* one addicted to the use of madat.
মদন, *s.* exhilarating ; Indian Cupid ; the
মদননির্ব্বিবি, *s.* a plant,[2] its root. [spring.
মদনশলাকা, *s.* a provocative medicine ; the female of the Indian cuckoo. [liquor.
মদনা, *s.* a species of parrot ; spirituous
মদবিহ্বল, staggering with liquor, reeling,
মদসার, *s.* alcohol, spirits. [drunk.
*মদার, *s.* a circumference, centre, seat, station, a minister : *s.* the coral tree.[3]
মদিরা, *s.* wine, spirituous liquor.
মদিরাগৃহ, মদ্যগৃহ, *s.* a tavern, an alehouse.
মদিরাজলবণ, *s.* salt of Tartar.
মদীয়, *pron.* my, mine.
মদ্য, *s.* wine, spirituous liquors.
মদ্যজীবী, *s.* a vintner, a tavern-keeper.
মদ্যপ, *s.* a sot, a tippler, a drunkard.
মদ্যপ্রিয়, *a.* fond of liquors, addicted to
মদ্যমণ্ড, *s.* yeast, barm, froth. [wine.
মদ্যশালা, *s.* a tavern, a dram-shop.
মধু, *s.* honey, nectarious juice of flowers, wine, spirit made of grapes. [of lime.
মধুকর, *s.* the humble bee, a lover ; a sort
মধুকোষ, *s.* a honeycomb, hive, testicles of
মধুনাপিত, *s.* a confectioner. [a goat.
মধুমক্ষিকা, or মধুপ, *s.* the honey bee.
মধুময়, *a.* sweet, honeyed, mellifluous.
মধুমালতী, *s.* a climbing plant.[4]
মধুযষ্টিকা, or যষ্টিমধু, *s.* liquorice.
মধুর, *a.* sweet, agreeable, melodious, mellifluous : *s.* sweetness, syrup, treacle.
মধুরতা, -ত্ব, *s.* suavity, sweetness.
মধুরিকা, *s.* the same as মউরী, aniseed.
মধুরিম, *s.* sweetness, the taste of sweet-
মধুশিলা, *s.* the honey-stone. [ness.
মধুসূদন, *s.* a name of Krishna.
মধ্য, *s.* the midst, the middle or inside of a thing, a centre, the waist, an interval, a kind of metre ; ten thousand billions.
মধ্যদেশ, *s.* the waist ; the middle part, the centre of a circle ; India, Bengal.
মধ্যবর্ত্তী, *a.* between, included, situated or standing between, inward, internal : *s.* a mediator, an arbitrator, an umpire.
মধ্যম, মধ্যবিৎ, *a.* middling, intermediate, included, central, temperate. [equation.
মধ্যমখণ্ড, *s.* middle term in an algebraic

মধ্যমসাহস, outrages of the middle class.
মধ্যমা, or **মধ্যা**, *s.* the middle finger; a girl arrived at the age of puberty.
মধ্য -রাত্র, *s.* midnight; -**লোক**, the earth.
মধ্যস্থ, *a.* central, situated between, within, inward: *s.* a mediator, an umpire.
মধ্যস্থতা, *s.* a middle state, mediatorship.
মধ্যস্থল, **মধ্যস্থলী**, *s.* the centre, internal or inward part, the midst. [betwixt.
মধ্যস্থলে, *ad.* inwardly, within, between,
মধ্যস্থালী, *s.* mediatorship, arbitration.
মধ্যস্থিত, *a.* central, inward, standing between, interposing, intervening.
মধ্যান্ত্রত্বক, *s.* the mesentery.
মধ্যাপসরণশক্তি, *s.* the centrifugal force.
মধ্যাপসারী, *a.* centrifugal.
মধ্যাভিসরণশক্তি, *s.* the centripetal force.
মধ্যাভিসারী, *a.* centripetal.
মধ্যাহ্ন, *s.* mid-day, noon: *a.* mid-day; -**ক্রিয়া**, the mid-day religious duties.
মধ্যাহ্নকাল, *s.* the time of mid-day. [midst.
মধ্যে, *ad.* within, between, betwixt, in the
মধ্যেমধ্যে, *ad.* now and then, sometimes.
মন, *s.* the mind, heart, conscience, inclination; forty seras or 78 lbs. [quietude.
মনঃপীড়া, *s.* mental distress, anguish, in-
মনঃপূত, conscientious: *s.* purity of heart.
মনঃপ্রবোধ, *s.* a conviction, consolation.
মনঃশিলা, *s.* red arsenic. [of the mind.
মনঃসংযোগ, *s.* attention, the application
মনন, *s.* a thinking, reflecting, a thought.
মননীয়, *a.* deserving regard. [mind.
মনশ্চাঞ্চল্য, *s.* fickleness, unsteadiness of
মনসা, *s.* the goddess of the serpent race.
মনসাসিজ, *s.* a species of euphorbia.[1]
মনসিজ, *s.* a name of the Indian Cupid.
মনস্কাম, *s.* the desire of the mind, a wish.
মনস্কামনা, *s.* desire or wish of the heart.
মনস্কার, *s.* reflection, perception. [tress.
মনস্তাপ, remorse, mental pain, inward dis-
মনস্তাপী, *a.* afflicting, giving pain to the
মনস্তুষ্টি, *s.* satisfaction of the mind. [mind.
মনস্থ, *a.* situated in the mind or heart: *s.* determination, purpose.
মনস্থৈর্য্য, *s.* steadfastness of mind.
মনস্বী, **মনীষী**, *a.* intelligent, wise, learned; open-hearted, pure-minded.

***মনা**, **মানা**, *s.* a prohibition, prevention.
মনাক, *ad.* minutely, a little, slowly, tardi-
মনীষা, *s.* understanding, intellect. [ly.
মনীষিন্, *s.* a learned man, a wise man.
মনু, *s.* the famous Indian legislator; creator of the world, the progenitor of mankind; a mystical verse or incantation.
মনুজ, *s.* a man, a human being, a mortal.
মনুষ্য, *s.* a man, human being,; -**গণ**, mankind, a multitude of men. [cies.
মনুষ্যজাতি, *s.* mankind, the human spe-
মনুষ্যতা, -**ত্ব**, *s.* humanity, manliness, man-
মনুষ্যআপন্ন, *a.* human, manly. [hood.
মনুষ্যধর্ম্ম, *s.* human duty. [of men.
মনুষ্যবর্গ, *s.* human species, mankind, body
মনুষ্যভক্ষক, **মনুষ্যভোজী**, *s.* a cannibal.
মনুষ্যময়, *a.* populous, full of people.
মনুষ্যমারণ, *s.* murder, manslaughter.
মনুষ্যাভাস, *s.* semblance of a man.
মনে, *ad.* in the mind or memory; -**কৃ**, to think, to recollect, to reflect, to remember; -**হ**, or -**পড়্**, to recal to memory, to recollect; -**রাখ্**, to keep in mind.
মনোগত, *a.* situated or found in the mind.
মনোগ্নি, *s.* jealousy, dissatisfaction.
মনোজ্ঞ, *a.* delectable, beautiful, engaging, tempting, pleasing, agreeable.
মনোজ্ঞতা, *s.* agreeableness, delectableness.
মনোদুঃখ, *s.* grief, pain or distress of mind.
মনোদুঃখী, *a.* pained or distressed in mind.
মনোনিবেশ, *s.* devotedness of the mind, close attention, close study. [object.
মনোনিবেশী, *a.* devoting the mind to an
মনোনীত, or **মনোমত**, *a.* chosen, approved.
মনোবাঞ্ছা, *s.* the desire of the heart.
মনোবৃত্তি, *s.* the operations of the mind, the conception of ideas, a volition.
মনোব্যথা, *s.* pain of mind, grief, jealousy.
মনোভঙ্গ, *s.* an interruption of thought.
মনোভিনিবেশ, *s.* devotedness of the mind to an object, engagedness of mind.
মনোভিলাষ, *s.* the desire of the heart.
মনোভিলাষী, *a.* desirous, zealous.
মনোময়, *a.* intelligent, prudent, wise.
মনোযুক্ত, *a.* engaged in, attentive.
মনোযোগ, *s.* attention, application.
মনোযোগী, *a.* attentive, earnest, zealous.

মনোরঞ্জক, *a.* pleasing, gratifying, agreeable, lovely, pleasant. [of sweetmeat.
মনোরঞ্জন, *s.* pleasure, gratification; a sort
মনোরথ, *s.* a wish, a desire. [pleasant.
মনোরম, *a.* charming, lovely, agreeable,
মনোরম্য, *a.* inviting, pleasant, agreeable.
মনোহর, *a.* captivating, heart-ravishing, winning, enticing, beautiful, amiable.
মনোহরতা, -ত্ব, *s.* a captivating or heart-ravishing property, enticingness.
***মন্‌জীল**, a baiting place, a day's journey.
***মন্‌জুর**, *s.* approval: *a.* seen, approved, acceptable, agreeable; -কৃ, to accept.
মন্তব্য, *a.* requiring to be regarded, ascertained, or fixed in the mind.
মন্তা, মন্ত্রণাকর্ত্তা, *s.* a counsellor, an adviser.
মন্ত্র, *s.* a text of the veda, a charm, an incantation, a form of prayer, a formula, private advice, secret consultation.
মন্ত্রণা, *s.* counsel, advice, persuasion, instigation; -কারক, counselling, advising.
মন্ত্রণাদাতা, *s.* an adviser, a counsellor.
মন্ত্রণাদায়ক, *a.* giving counsel or advice.
মন্ত্রণীয়, *a.* advisable, that may be effected by incantation or formulas. [mentor.
মন্ত্রদাতা, *s.* a guru, spiritual preceptor, a
মন্ত্রসিদ্ধ, *a.* accomplished by a charm.
মন্ত্রসিদ্ধি, *s.* effecting of a purpose by the repetition of a religious formula. [las.
মন্ত্রিত, *a.* consecrated by religious formu-
মন্ত্রী, *s.* a counsellor, adviser, minister of state, a monitor; the queen at chess.
মন্থক, *a.* churning: *s.* a churner.
মন্থন, *s.* a churning, stirring; a churn.
মন্থনদড়ি, *s.* a churning rope.
মন্থনদণ্ড, or **মন্থান**, *s.* a churning staff.
মন্থনীয়, *a.* capable of being churned. [dull.
মন্থর, *a.* slow, heavy, tardy, lazy, stupid,
মন্দ, *a.* evil, bad, vile, vicious, mischievous, low (as a tune), sick, ill, slow, gentle.
মন্দকপাল, *a.* ill-fated: *s.* an evil destiny.
মন্দগতি, *a.* slow, sluggish: *s.* slow motion.
মন্দচাল, *s.* misconduct, evil conduct.
মন্দজুয়ার, *s.* neap tide. [obscurity.
মন্দজ্যোতিঃ, *a.* dim, obscure: *s.* dimness,
মন্দটান, *s.* slack water, a slow stream.
মন্দমন্দ, *ad.* slowly, in a bad manner.
মন্দর, *s.* a fabulous mountain; the space between the breast and the navel.
মন্দরস্থান, *s.* the pit of the stomach.
মন্দা, *s.* low-water, neap-tide: *a.* slow, low, cheap, gentle, little.
মন্দাকিনী, *s.* the celestial Ganges, galaxy.
মন্দাক্ষ, *s.* modesty, bashfulness.
মন্দাগ্নি, *s.* dyspepsia, indigestion. [ful.
মন্দাদর, negligent, inattentive, disrespect-
মন্দার, *s.* coral tree (Erythrina fulgens).
মন্দির, *s.* a temple, a mansion, a house; the
মন্দিরা, *s.* a kind of small cymbal. [ham.
মন্দিরাকার, *a.* conical, tapering.
মন্দিরাচপ, *a.* convex.
মন্দুরা, *s.* a stable for horses.
মন্দেমন্দে, *ad.* slowly, feebly, sluggishly.
মন্দোদরী, *s.* a kind of fine mat; Rávana's
মন্মথ, *s.* a name of Hindu Cupid. [wife.
মন্যত, *s.* approbation, concurrence.
মন্যমান, *a.* under cognizance, under observation or regard, regarding.
মন্যু, *s.* sorrow, regret, dislike; a curse, a malediction, resentment, wrath.
মন্বন্তর, *s.* a period of time consisting of 71 yugas of the gods or 306,770,000 years of mortals; a famine. [nistry.
***মন্‌সব, মন্‌সবী**, *s.* dignity, an office, mi-
মন্‌সুব, *a.* constituted, appointed. [ficer.
মন্‌সুবদার, *s.* a magistrate, a military of-
মন্‌সুবা, *s.* contrivance, scope, intention; -বাজ, prudent, sagacious, ingenious.
***মফ্‌লিস্**, *s.* a bachelor, an unmarried man.
মফঃসল, *s.* the same with **মুফঃসল**.
***মবলগ**, *a.* much, many: *s.* ready money.
মবলগে, *ad.* in the whole. [welcome.
***মবারক**, *a.* blessed, happy, auspicious,
মম, *pron.* my, mine; -কার, appropriation.
মমতা, -ত্ব, *s.* ownership, appropriation; affection, love, attachment, pity.
ময়দা, *s.* meal, flour. [an esplanade.
ময়দান, *s.* a prairee, a plain, an open field,
ময়না, *s.* the name of a bird;[1] also, of a
ময়রা, *s.* a confectioner. [thorny bush.[2]
ময়লা, ময়লাটিয়া, *a.* filthy, dirty, foul.
ময়ান, *s.* leaven, barm. [of a sun-dial.
ময়ূখ, *s.* ray, light, lustre, beauty; gnomon
ময়ূর, *s.* a peacock: **ময়ূরী**, *s.* a peahen.

ময়ূরারি, s. a chameleon, a lizard.
মর্, v. n. to die, dry up, decrease, fail.
মরক, s. mortality, a plague, a pestilence, a contagion, an infectious disease.
মরকত, s. an emerald. [time of death.
মরণ, s. a dying, demise, death; -কাল, the
মরণকালীন, a. of the time of death.
মরণোদ্যত, a. about to die, going to die.
*মর্মর্, সংমর্মর্, marble, marble stone.
*মরসুম্, s. a season, a time. [metal).
মরা, dead: s. a corpse, carcass, base (as
মরাই, s. a granary, barn, storehouse.
মরাটিয়া, a. dying, worn out, impoverished.
মরাধার, a. blunt, dull, obtuse.
মরামাস, s. scurf, dandriff.
মরাল, s. lampblack used as a collyrium, a goose, a duck, a horse, a cloud, a rogue, a scoundrel: a. soft, mild, bland.
মরিচ, s. chilly, pepper, black-pepper.
মরীচি, s. a son of Brahmá; a ray; a miser.
মরীচিকা, মৃগতৃষ্ণা, s. a mirage in a desert.
মরীচিমালা, s. a circle of rays.
মরু, a. unfruitful, sterile, barren, desert, impoverished (as land). [west.
মরুৎ, s. the air, wind, god of wind; north-
মরুৎকোণ, s. the north-west quarter.
মরুৎক্রিয়া, expulsion of wind backwards.
মরুভূমি, s. desert land, barren land.
মর্কট, s. a species of monkey;[1] a spider.
মর্কটজাল, s. a cobweb, a spider's web.
মর্কটী, s. a female monkey.
মর্চ্যা, s. rust, oxide of iron, dross, slag; -ধরা, or -পড়া, rusty, drossy.
*মর্জি, s. will, wish, inclination, pleasure.
মর্ত্ত্য, a. earthly, mortal: s. a man, mankind; the earth; -পুর, or -লোক, the earth, the habitation of mortals.
মর্দ্দ, v. a. to rub, bruise, pound, trample, to thrash corn, to subdue: s. a man.
মর্দ্দক, a. pounding, bruising, subduing: s. one who pounds or grinds any thing.
মর্দ্দন, s. a pounding, grinding, a bruising, a thrashing, trampling, or subduing.
মর্দ্দনীয়, a. capable of being bruised or rub-
মর্দ্দা, a. male: s. a man, a male. [bed.
*মর্দ্দানা, a. man, male: ad. manly, bravely.
মর্দ্দানি, মর্দ্দামি, s. manliness, bravery.

মর্দ্দিত, a. bruised, rubbed, pounded, trampled, thrashed, subdued.
মর্ম্ম, s. a joint; the vital part, core, quick; a secret, a purport, a circumstance; -কথা, secrets; -জান্, to know the secrets.
মর্ম্মজ্ঞ, a. learned, knowing vital or essential doctrines, knowing secrets: s. a spy.
মর্ম্মজ্ঞান, s. a knowledge of the soul or vital circumstances of an affair.
মর্ম্মপীড়া, s. the pain of the inmost soul.
মর্ম্মভেদ, s. a penetrating to the quick.
মর্ম্মভেদক, a. penetrating secrets, piercing
*মর্ম্মর, সংমর্ম্মর, s. marble. [to the quick.
মর্ম্মস্থান, s. the core, quick, vital part.
মর্ম্মস্পৃক্, a. touching to the quick, sharp,
মর্ম্মান্তর, s. another secret. [corrosive.
মর্ম্মান্তিক, a. wounding or destroying the vital parts, mortal, deadly. [polite.
মর্য্যাদক, a. showing honour or respect,
মর্য্যাদা, respect, honour, reputation, rank, esteem; a boundary, limit; rectitude.
মর্য্যাদান্বিত, a. honourable, respectable.
মর্য্যাদাবন্ত, or মর্য্যাদাবান, a. *idem.* [ed.
মর্য্যাদিত, a. respected, esteemed, honour-
মর্ষণ, s. endurance, resignation.
*মর্সিদ, s. an instructor, a guide, a teacher.
*মর্সিয়া, s. an elegy, a funeral eulogium.
মল্, v. a. to rub, squeeze, furbish, thrash.
মল, s. excrement, sediment, dregs, rust, filth, dirt, a soil; ring for the ankles.
মলকক্কা, s. refuse of rice; raisins. [filth.
মলঘ্ন, a. detergent, cleansing, destroying
মলঙ্গা, s. several species of aquatic grass.
মলঙ্গী, s. labourer employed in salt works.
মলজ, a. produced from filth: s. pus.
মলন, s. a rubbing, pressing, squeezing,
মলনিষ্ক্রামক, a. expelling filth. [thrashing.
মলবদ্ধ, a. costive: s. constipation. [ment.
*মলহম, মর্হম, s. a salve, a plaster, oint-
মলমাস, s. an intercalary month.
মলম্বা, a. gilt: s. the gilding of any thing.
মলয়, s. a range of hills, the western ghát, Malabar, a garden, Indra's paradise.
মলয়জ, s. sandal-wood; *vide* চন্দন.
মলয়ানিল, s. south wind of central India, odoriferous wind of Malaya hills.
*মলসারী, s. a tree (Mimusops elengi).

মলা, *a.* dirty, squalid, polluted, sordid, unclean : *s.* filth, sediment, the slag of metals, the dregs of liquids, scum, rust.
মলাধরা, *a.* rusty : *s.* a becoming rusty.
মলাপকর্ষণ, *s.* purification, a cleansing.
*__মলিক__, *s.* a king, a proprietor. [sallow.
মলিন, *a.* filthy, dirty, sullied, faded, sad,
মলিনতা, *s.* filthiness, sordidness, sadness.
মলিনমুখ, *a.* cruel, savage, fierce, wicked : *s.* Agni, fire, a goblin, sad countenance.
মলিম্লুচ, *s.* an intercalary month.
মলুক, *s.* a species of worm. [rice.
মলুকা, **মল্কা**, *s.* broken grains or refuse of
মলমল্ *s.* muslin, book-muslin. [boxer.
মল্ল, *s.* a wrestle, a scuffle ; a wrestler, a
মল্লক্রীড়া, *s.* a wrestling, a scuffling.
মল্লবিদ্যা, *s.* the art of wrestling. [ler.
মল্লবেশ, *s.* the habit or dress of a wrest-
মল্লভূমি, *s.* an arena, an area for wrestlers.
মল্লযুদ্ধ, *s.* a wrestling, a scuffling, boxing.
মল্লযোদ্ধা, *s.* a wrestler, a boxer, a pugilist.
*__মল্লা__, *s.* a teacher, a master, a boatman.
মল্লার, **মল্লারী**, *s.* a note in Hindu music.
মল্লিকা, *s.* the Arabian jasmine.[1] [bag.
মশক, *s.* a musquito, gnat ; a skin water-
*__মশক্কৎ__, *s.* trouble, labour, pain, toil.
মশা, *s.* a musquito, a gnat. [the dead.
মশান, *s.* a cemetery, a place for burning
মশারি, *s.* musquito curtains ; the wind.
*__মশাল__, *s.* a torch ; -চী, a linkboy, a torch-
*__মস্‌লন্দ__, *s.* royal seat, a carpet. [bearer.
*__মসাফির__, *s.* a stranger, a traveller.
*__মসালা__, *s.* spice, pungent ingredient, hot spices, currystuffs ; materials for work.
*__মসাহরা__, *s.* a monthly salary, pay, wages.
মসী, *s.* ink ; -পাত্র, -প্রসূ, an inkstand.
মসীজীবী, *a.* gaining a living by writing : *s.* one who gains a livelihood by writing, a copyist, scribe, writer, amanuensis.
মসীনা, *s.* linseed, flax (Linum usitatissi-
মসুর, *s.* name of a sort of pulse.[2] [mum).
মসূরিকা, *s.* the smallpox ; a small cushion.
মসৃণ, *a.* smooth, unctuous, bland.
*__মস্ক__, *s.* musk ; *vide* মৃগনাভি. [andrew.
মস্করা, *s.* a low jester, a buffoon, merry-
মস্করামী, **মস্করাপনা**, *s.* buffoonery, jesting.
*__মস্‌জেদ__, *s.* a mosque, a Moslem temple.

*__মস্ত__, *a.* drunk, lustful, wanton, proud.
মস্তক, *s.* the head, the top of any thing.
মস্তকোপরি, *ad.* vertically, over the head.
*__মস্তানা__, *a.* wanton, lewd, lustful, drunk.
মস্তানী, *a. fem.* wanton : *s.* drunkenness.
মস্তি, *s.* wantonness, lust, drunkenness.
মস্তিষ্ক, *s.* the brain ; also, মজ্জা.
মস্তিষ্কত্বক্, *s.* in *ana.* the Dura mater.
মস্তু, *s.* whey, the watery part of curds.
*__মস্‌লহৎ__, *s.* an action, counsel, advice.
মস্যাধার, *s.* an inkstand, an inkhorn.
মহৎ, *a.* great, important, noble, chief, good, excellent, illustrious.
মহতী, *s.* the egg-plant ; Nárada's lute.
মহত্ত্ব, *s.* greatness, dignity, importance.
মহত্রাণ, *s.* a sort of free charity land.
মহৎবরীবচ, *s.* orris root (good for cough).
*__মহরম__, *s.* the 1st Hijirí month ; a bodice ; a festival in honour of Imám Husain.
মহরীর, *s.* a writer, a scribe, a secretary.
মহরীরী, *s.* the office of a scribe, etc.
মহর্ষি, *s.* a great sage.
*__মহল__, *s.* a place, a building, a mansion, a house, a seraglio, a district, a quarter.
মহলদার, *s.* a person holding a district.
মহলদারী, *s.* the office of a mahaldár.
*__মহলা__, *s.* the story of a building. [trict.
*__মহল্লা__, *s.* a quarter or part of a town, a dis-
মহা, *a.* great, large, important, noble, excellent ; in *comp.* a substitute for মহৎ.
মহাকবি, *s.* a great poet.
মহাকাব্য, *s.* a regular and classical poem.
মহাকায়, *a.* gigantic, large-bodied. [nity.
মহাকাল, *s.* a name of Shiva, Yama, eter-
মহাকুল, *s.* a great or noble family.
মহাকুলীন, *a.* most noble.
মহাঘোর, excessively dreadful or horrid : *s.* great gloom or darkness ; Hindu hell.
মহাজন, *s.* a powerful or upright man, a merchant, a money-lender, a creditor.
মহাজনী, *s.* business of a merchant, commerce, trade ; interest on money lent.
মহাত্মা, *a.* magnanimous, great-minded, generous, noble-spirited. [consort.
মহাদেব, Shiva : **মহাদেবী**, Durgá, Shiva's
মহাধন, *s.* great riches, any thing costly,
মহাধনী, *a.* very rich, most opulent. [gold.

মহান্, *a.* great, vast, important, eminent,
মহানস, *s.* a kitchen, a cookroom. [grand.
মহানাদ, *s.* a loud sound, an elephant, a
মহানিদ্রা, *s.* death, the great sleep. [lion.
মহানিশা, মহারাত্র, *s.* midnight.
মহানুভব, *a.* magnanimous, generous.
মহাপথ, *s.* a high road ; death.
মহাপদ্ম, ten hundred thousand millions, a gem of Kuvera, the large white lotus.[1]
*মহাপা, *s.* a litter, a kind of pálki.
মহাপাতক, মহাপাপ, *s.* a mortal sin. [sins.
মহাপাতকী, মহাপাপী, *a.* guilty of mortal
মহাপুরুষ, *s.* a great personage, a saint.
মহাপ্রভু, *s.* a king, lord, holy man, also applied to Shiva, Vishnu, Jagannáth, etc.
মহাপ্রলয়, *s.* the destruction of the world.
মহাবংশ, *s.* a noble family, noble descent.
মহাবংশজ, *a.* born of a noble family. [ler.
মহাবল, *a.* very strong, powerful : *s.* a wrest-
মহাবাক্য, *s.* the mystic syllable ওঁ, or Om.
মহাবারুণী, *s.* a Hindu festival in Chaitra.
মহাবিদ্যা, *s.* nature, great science.
মহাবিষুব,-সংক্রান্তি, *s.* the vernal equinox.
মহাবীজ্য, *s.* the septum of the scrotum with part of the perinæum.
মহাবীর, *s.* a great hero, a lion, Garuṛa.
মহাব্রাহ্মণ, *s.* eminent bráhman, a funeral
মহাভূত, *s.* five primary elements. [priest.
মহামতি, *a.* magnanimous, noble.
মহামদ, *s.* an elephant in rut. [ficent.
মহামনস্ক, *a.* magnanimous, liberal, muni-
মহামহিম, *a.* majestic, noble, most exalted,
মহামহোপাধ্যায়, *a.* most learned. [great.
মহামাত্র, *s.* a king's prime minister, a chief counsellor, a person of consequence.
মহামায়া, *s.* Durgá ; worldly illusion, the vanity of the world, vanity and illusion.
মহামায়ী, *s.* Durgá, Sitalá, the small-pox.
মহামারী, *s.* plague, pestilence, mortality.
মহামূল্য, *a.* costly, precious : *s.* a ruby.
মহাযজ্ঞ, *s.* the five essential sacrifices.
মহারজত, *s.* gold.
মহারণ্য, *s.* a large forest.
মহারথ, *s.* a large car ; a wish, a desire.
মহারথী, *s.* a great or eminent charioteer.
মহারাজ, *s.* a great king ; Sir, your honour, your majesty (a respectful address).

মহারাজাধিরাজ, *s.* an emperor, a king by his own right, a great king.
মহারাত্র, *s.* midnight. মহারূপ, *s.* resin.
মহারৌরব, *s.* one of the Hindu hells.
মহার্ঘ্য, dear, costly, high-priced, precious.
মহাল, *s.* the same with মহল.
মহালক্ষ্মী, *s.* Saraswatí, wife of Brahmá.
মহালয়, *s.* God, the supreme refuge, a place of pilgrimage, a place of refuge, an asylum, a sanctuary.
মহালয়া, *s.* the moon's change in Bhádra.
মহাশঙ্খ, *s.* the forehead, a human bone, a necklace of bones ; one thousand billions ; one of Kuvera's treasures.
মহাশয়, *s.* a gentleman, Sir, Sire, your honour (used in respectful address).
মহাসাহস, *s.* excessive violence, brutal assault, an outrage of the highest class.
মহাসাহসিক, *a.* excessively outrageous.
মহাসুখ, *s.* sexual commerce, copulation.
মহাহ্লাদ, *a.* great joy, excessive mirth.
মহিম, *s.* greatness, war, battle. [glory.
মহিমসাগর, *s.* an ocean of greatness or
মহিমা, *s.* greatness, majesty, glory, dig-
মহিষ, *s.* a buffalo. [nity, grandeur.
মহিষা, *a.* belonging to a buffalo.
মহিষী, *s.* a female buffalo ; a queen.
মহী, *s.* the earth, the base of a triangle.
মহীতল, *s.* the earth, the earth itself.
মহীপতি, মহীপাল, *s.* a king, a sovereign.
মহীরুহ, *s.* a tree, a vegetable.
মহীলতা, *s.* an earthworm, a worm.
মহীলা, মহিলা, *s.* a woman, a female, a wife.
মহু, *s.* mell, honey ; -মাছী, the honey bee.
মহুরী, *s. vide* মউরী, anise-seed.
মহেচ্ছ, *a.* magnanimous, liberal, generous.
মহেন্দ্র, *s.* Indra, the ruler of swarga and the gods ; the northern ghâts.
মহেশ, মহেশ্বর, *s.* titles of Shiva.
মহোক্ষ, *s.* a great or fierce bull.
মহোৎপল, *s.* an aquatic plant.*
মহোৎপাত, *s.* a great outrage or violence.
মহোৎসব, *s.* a feast, a great festival.
মহোৎসাহ, *s.* great perseverance or ener-
মহোদধি, *s.* the great ocean. [gy of mind.
মহোদয়, *a.* prosperous, dignified : *s.* final liberation, a lord, pride.

মহোদ্যম, *s.* great effort, energy, exertion, zeal: *a.* diligent, persevering, zealous.
মহৌষধ, *s.* a sovereign remedy; garlic.
মা, *s.* a mother; it is often used as an affectionate or respectful address.
মাই, *s.* the breast, the paps, a dug, teat, udder; -খাওয়া, or -দা, to suckle. [a tree.
মাইজ, *s.* pith of a plant, marrow, heart of
মাইজকাঠ, a timber, timber of rotten pith.
মাইটগাড়া, *s.* a cellar, place under ground.
মাইয়া, *s.* a woman, a girl, a daughter.
মাইয়ামর্দ্দা, *s.* a virago, masculine woman.
মাইয়ামুখ, *a.* shame-faced, woman-faced.
মাংস, *s.* flesh, meat; -খাদক, -ভক্ষক, -ভোজী, carnivorous: one who eats flesh.
মাংসগ্রন্থী, *s.* a gland; -বিদ্যা, adenology.
মাংসপেশী, *s.* a muscle; -বিদ্যা, myology.
মাংসবিক্রয়, *s.* the sale of flesh.
মাংসবিক্রয়ী, *a.* selling flesh, or a daughter; a nickname of persons betrothing their daughters for a sum of money.
মাংসবিদ্যা, *s.* sarcology. [of flesh.
মাংসবৃদ্ধি, *s.* increase or fungous growth
মাংসল, *a.* fleshy, plump, fat, corpulent.
মাংসাদ, or মাংসাশী, *a.* carnivorous.
মাঁজ্, *v. a.* to scour, rub, cleanse, polish.
মাঁজন, *s.* a scouring, rubbing, polishing.
মাঁজা, *a.* scoured, cleansed, polished: *v.* to cause to scour, rub, cleanse, or polish.
মাঁদা, *s.* a seedplot, a ridge round a tree; -বাঁধা, -মারা, a ridge round a tree-root.
মাকড়, or মাকড়সা, *s.* a spider.
মাকড়জাল, *s.* a cobweb, a spider's web.
মাকড়জালী, *s.* a species of grass.[1] [ter.
মাকড়া, *s.* a spider; (*fig.*) a person, mas-
মাকন্দ, *s.* a mango; a beardless man.
মাকাটিয়া, মাকাট্যা, *a.* unkind, greedy, mi-
মাকাটী, *s.* the seed of cotton. [serly.
মাকাল, *s.* a climbing plant and its fruit.[2]
মাকু, *s.* a weaver's shuttle.
মাকুন্দ, *s.* a beardless man.
*মাকুল, *a.* well-versed, just, proper. [gross.
মাকা, *a.* mixed, average, general, in the
মাক্ষিক, *s.* cubic pyrites of various kinds.
মাখ, or মাখা, *v. a.* to smear, to spread over, to plaster, to knead, to mix.
মাখন, *s.* butter; a smearing or mixing.
মাখনওয়ালা, *s.* a butterman.
মাখনি, *s.* a smearing, a plastering over.
মাখনিয়া, *s.* a butterman; one who smears.
মাখান, *a.* mixed, plastered: *s.* a smearing or plastering over, a mixing. [tering.
মাখামাখি, *s.* a mutual smearing or plas-
মাগ্, *v. a.* to ask, to pray for, to beg.
মাগী, *s.* a woman, an old woman, a crone.
মাগু, ভার্য্যা, পত্নী, জায়া, স্ত্রী, *s.* a wife.
মাগুর, মদগুর, *s.* the name of a fish.[3]
মাগ্রাম, *s.* self-applause, a boast, vaunt, a puff; -কৃ, to boast, to puff. [vaunting.
মাগ্রামবাক্য, *s.* a rhodomontade, a boasting,
মাগ্রামীয়া, *a.* boasting, vaunting, puffing.
মাঘ, *s.* an Indian month containing part of January and part of February.
মাঘী, *s.* the full moon in Mágha.
মাঙ্, *v. a.* to ask, to request, demand, to solicit, beg: *s.* the vagina; *vide* শিঁথী.
মাঙন, *s.* asking for, requesting, begging.
মাঙনা, *a.* gratuitous, for nothing. [ging.
মাঙনিয়া, মাঙন্তেড়িয়া, *a.* habitually beg-
মাঙ্গতা, *s.* one who begs for a thing. [cial.
মাঙ্গলিক, *a.* propitious, auspicious, benefi-
মাঙ্গা, *v. a.* to cause to request, to send for: *s.* a request: *a.* dear, opposed to cheap.
মাঙ্গান, *s.* a sending for, a causing to beg.
মাচা, or মাচান, *s.* a platform, a pulpit, a stage, a scaffold, a shelf, a shed.
মাচিয়া, *s.* a chair, a stool, a bench.
মাছ, *s.* a fish; -রাঙ্গা, a kingfisher.
মাছী, *s.* a fly; (*met.*) a man; -টেপা, parsimonious, niggardly, penurious, stingy.
মাছুয়া, *s.* a fisherman, a fishmonger.
মাছুয়ানী, *s.* a woman who sells fish.
মাছেতা, *s.* blackish shade on the cheeks.
মাজ্, *v. a.* to wipe, clean, scour, rub.
মাজ, *s.* the pith, middle of a thing, internal crack or rottenness in timber.
মাজন, *s.* a scouring, a rubbing; dentifrice.
মাজমরা, *a.* inwardly or internally dead.
মাজা, *v. a.* to cause to scour: *s.* the waist, loins: *a.* internally cracked, scoured.
মাজান, *s.* a causing to scour, rub, or clean: *a.* scoured, rubbed, cleansed.
মাজী, মাঝী, *s.* a steersman, a helmsman.
মাজীকাঠ, *s.* inwardly unsound timber.

মাজুফল, *s.* gall-nut, a medicinal dry fruit.
মাজুরী, মাদুরী, *s.* a kind of sleeping-mat.
মাজুম, *s.* an intoxicating electuary.
মাঝ, *s.* the midst, the middle, the centre.
মাঝখান, *s.* the centre or middle part.
মাঝদাদা, *s.* the second brother.
মাঝামাঝি, *ad.* in the midst, centrally, mid-
মাঝার, *s.* the middle, the centre. [way.
মাঝারী, *a.* middling, central.
মাঝে, *ad.* in the midst, within, in.
মাঞ্জন, *s.* a dentifrice, tooth-powder.
মাঞ্জা, *s.* glue and bottle powder applied as a starch to the silk of a paper-kite.
মাট, *a.* slow, sluggish, bad, inert.
মাটী, earth, soil; -কাটা, an earth-digger.
মাটীয়া, *a.* earth-coloured, brown, earthen.
মাটীয়াতৈল, *s.* naphtha, earth-oil.
মাঠ, *s.* a field, plain, meadow, common, pasture: *v. a.* to smooth a plank. [ed.
মাঠা, *s.* buttermilk, sourmilk: *a.* smooth-
মাঠান, *s.* a smoothing: *a.* smoothed.
মাঠানজমী, *s.* land belonging to a plain.
মাঠুয়া, belonging to or situate in a plain.
মাঠে, *ad.* in the field; -যা, to ease nature.
মাঠো, stiff, slow, inert, scarcely movable.
মাড়্, *v. a.* to thrash corn, tread out corn; to rub or grind (medicine). [paste.
মাড়, *s.* a raft, a float; rice-gruel, starch,
মাড়ন, *s.* the thrashing of corn, a rubbing.
মাড়নি, *s.* a thrashing, rubbing, grinding.
মাড়নিয়া, *s.* a thrasher of corn, a grinder.
মাড়া, *v. a.* to stamp or tread down, to thrash, to cause to be thrashed.
মাড়ান, *a.* trampled, stamped, thrashed: *s.* a stamping, a trampling, a thrashing.
মাড়ানি, *s.* trampling, treading, stamping.
মাড়ুআ, or **মারুআ**, *s.* a kind of grain.[1]
মাঢ়ি, মাড়ি, *s.* a double tooth, grinder, the
মাঢ়িলগ্রন্থী, *s.* a maxillary gland. [gums.
মাণবক, *s.* a youth, a hobbledehoy.
মাণিক, or **মাণিক্য**, *s.* a ruby, a carbuncle.
মাণিকযোড়, *s.* the name of a large bird.[2]
মাৎ, *v. n.* to be drunk, to be intoxicated: *s.* whey, the whey of curds.
মাৎলামী, *s.* drunkenness, intoxication.
মাৎসর্য্য, *s.* envy, avarice, malice. [mate.
মাত, whey; thin sort of treacle; a check-

মাতঙ্গ, *s.* an elephant, a man of a degraded caste, a mountaineer. [or Durgá.
মাতঙ্গী, *s.* mountain-born goddess Párvati
মাতন, মাতনি, *s.* a being intoxicated. [ard.
মাতবালা, *a.* sottish, drunken: *s.* a drunk-
মাতলা, *s.* an arch, the capital of a pillar or arch, a cornice; a bedding, a mattress.
মাতা, *s.* a mother, a goddess, the smallpox.
মাতান, *s.* a making drunk, exciting.
মাতামহ, *s.* a maternal grandfather.
মাতামহী, *s.* a maternal grandmother.
মাতাল, *a.* drunk, drunken; great, important: *s.* a toper, a tippler, a drunkard.
মাতাল্যা, *s.* a drunkard, a toper, a sot.
মাতি, *s.* measure, weight; the head or internal tender part of a palm tree.
মাতুল, *s.* a maternal uncle.
মাতুলানী, *s.* a maternal uncle's wife.
মাতৃ, *s.* a mother; -তুল্য, motherly, like a mother; -হীন, motherless.
মাতৃকা, *s.* a foster-mother; a class of sixteen goddesses, an alphabet, a body of preliminary rules.
মাতৃঘাতক, *a.* matricide: *s.* a matricide.
মাতৃবন্ধু, মাতৃবান্ধব, *s.* a maternal relation.
মাতৃভ্রাতা, *s.* an uncle, a mother's brother.
মাতৃষ্বসা, *s.* an aunt, a mother's sister.
মাতৃষ্বস্রীয়, *s.* the child of a maternal aunt.
মাতৃহত্যা, *s.* the murder of a mother.
মাত্র, *s.* an unit, a single individual, a mere circumstance: *a.* only: *ad.* merely.
মাত্রা, *s.* a quantity, an instant, half a short syllable; the head-stroke of a letter.
মাথ্, *v. a.* to mount upon, to put forth or protrude the head in birth.
মাথট, *s.* a collection, a subscription.
মাথা, *v. a.* to climb upon any thing: *s.* the head, a pinnacle, top or upper part; -ঘুর, to be giddy; -ভাঙ্গা, headstrong.
মাথাঘুরা, *s.* a vertigo, giddiness. [born.
মাথাটানা, *a.* obstinate, headstrong, stub-
মাথান, *s.* interfering with another's business, a going foremost in an affair.
মাথাপাগলা, *a.* crack-brained, obstinate,
মাথাব্যথা, *s.* the head-ache. [stubborn.
মাথাভারী, *a.* top-heavy: *s.* a blockhead.
মাথামাথি, *s.* head to head, up to the head.

মাথাল, *s.* a sort of wicker hat ; capital of a
মাথালাড়া, insolent, pragmatical. [pillar.
মাথ্লা, *s.* abacus, capital of a pillar, a cor-
মাদক, *a.* intoxicating, inebriating. [nice.
মাদকতা, *s.* intoxicating quality or power.
মাদল, *s.* a tamborine, a drum, a tabor.
*মাদা, মাদী, *a.* female : *s.* a female animal.
মাদার, *s.* coral tree (Erithrina fulgens).
মাদুর, মাদুরি, *s.* a particular kind of mat.
মাদুলী, *s.* a charm, an amulet, a brooch.
*মাদোআন, *s.* a mare : বাছেড়ী, a filly.
মাধব, *s.* a name of Krishna.
মাধবী, মাধবীলতা, *s.* a climbing tree.[1]
মাধুর্য্য, sweetness, agreeableness, suavity,
মাধুশিল, *s.* in *chem.* mellite. [mildness.
মাধুশিলিক, *a.* in *chem.* mellitic. [day.
মাধ্যাহ্নিক, *a.* midday, belonging to mid-
মান্, *v. a.* to esteem, to regard, venerate, observe, to mind, to obey, to submit.
মান, *s.* honour, respectability, reputation, rank, value, weighing, measuring, measure, weight, particular measure ; hauteur, pride ; -ভাঙ্, to expose a person's faults, put one to shame ; -রাখ, to preserve one's reputation ; a kind of arum.
মানকচু, মানক, *s.* a kind of arum.[2]
মানচিত্র, *s.* a map, a chart, a sketch.
মানত, মাননা, মাননী, *s.* a vow, a voluntary
মানন্তা, *s.* one who vows. [obligation.
মানন, *s.* the regarding of a person, the observing or obeying of one's dictates.
মাননি, *s.* a honouring, a showing respect.
মাননীয়, *a.* obligatory, honourable, estimable, venerable. [multitude of men.
মানব, *s.* a man, human creature, a mortal,
মানভঙ্গ, or মানভঞ্জন, *s.* a dishonouring.
মানস, *a.* mental, ideal : *s.* a volition, intention, design, thought, a wish, a desire.
মানসসরোবর, *s.* a lake on the Himálaya
মানসিক, mental, ideal, imaginary. [hills.
মানহানি, *s.* the wounding of one's honour, or lessening his respectability.
মানহীন, *a.* disreputable, destitute of honour or respect, humble, free from pride.
মানা, *s.* the regarding of a person ; a prohibition, warning : *v. a.* to prevail on, to persuade, to cause to fit, to adjust.

মানানি, *s.* persuasion, a prevailing on.
মানিত, *a.* honoured, made respectable.
মানী, *a.* minding ; honoured ; proud, sulky.
মানুষ, *s.* a man, a human being.
*মানে, *s.* the meaning of a word, a mean-
মান্দাস, *s.* a raft, a float. [ing, a scope.
মান্দ্য, *s.* badness, vileness, slowness, infe-
মান্দ্যগতি, *s.* slowness, tardiness. [riority.
মাস্থিক্ষণ, *s.* an auspicious moment.
মান্য, মানীতব্য, *s.* honourable, venerable, deserving of regard, respectable.
মান্যতা, -ত্ব, *s.* respectability, honour.
মান্যমান, *a.* receiving honours, in the act of receiving honours.
মাপ্, *v. a.* to measure, to gauge.
মাপ, *s.* a measuring, measure, weight.
মাপক, *a.* measuring : *s.* a measurer.
মাপন, *s.* a measuring, weighing.
মাপনি, or মাপযোঁক, *s.* a measurement.
মাপনীয়, *a.* measurable. [sured.
মাপা, *v. a.* to cause to measure : *a.* mea-
মাপান, measured : *s.* causing to measure.
*মাফ, *a.* absolved, forgiven : *s.* pardon, forgiveness, exemption. [with, suiting.
*মাফিক, *a.* conformable, like to, agreeing
মামক, *pron.* my, mine.
মামড়ী, *s.* scurf, scab, scale.
*মামলতী, *a.* fit for business, active.
মামলা, মামলৎ, *s.* an affair, a business, ne-
মামা, *s.* a maternal uncle. [gotiation.
মামাতুয়া, *a.* of an uncle ; -ভগিনী, or -ভাই, an uncle's daughter or son.
মামাশশুর, *s.* husband's or wife's mother's
মামাশাশুড়ী, *s.* their wives. [brother.
মামী, মামানী, *s.* a maternal uncle's wife.
মায়া, *s.* fraud, fascination, magic, illusion, a trick, deceit, wickedness, villainy, a deception, idealism, want of reality or substance, vanity ; affection, tenderness, love, attachment, sensibility, a woman.
মায়াজাল, *s.* the net of illusion or magic.
মায়াপূর্ব্বক, *ad.* illusively, deceptively.
মায়াবদ্ধ, *a.* bound by magic or illusion.
মায়াবী, *a.* magical, using magic, illusive, fascinating : *s.* a magician, a juggler.
মায়াশূন্য, *a.* unfeeling ; free from illusion.
মায়াস্বরূপ, *a.* identified with illusion.

মায়িক, *a.* magical; affectionate, clement, [fascinating.
মায়ী, *a.* illusive, deceptive.
মায়ু, *s.* the bilious humour, gall, bile.
মার্, *v. a.* to smite, strike, beat, to kill; মারিয়া ফেল্, to kill, to slay.
মারক, *a.* destructive, smiting, killing: *s.* a plague; he who smites. [pugnacious.
মারকুটিয়া, *a.* quarrelsome, ready to beat,
মারণ, *s.* a smiting, a striking, a killing.
মারণীয়, *a.* punishable, to be beaten or [killed.
মারত্মক, *a.* fatal, mortal, deadly.
মারপেঁচ, *s.* a catch in conversation, a difficulty, a dilemma, a quibble. [cause.
*মারফত, *ad.* by means of, through, by: *s.*
মারা, *v. a.* to beat, kill: *s.* a beating, killing; -পড়্, to be killed, to be ruined.
মারাণ, *s.* a causing to be beat or killed; *fem.* the admitting of coition. [beats.
মারাণিয়া, *a.* smiting, beating: *s.* one who
মারাণী, *a. fem.* admitting coition. [tal.
মারাত্মক, *a.* murderous, mortal, deadly, fa-
মারাধরা, *s.* a beating, a striking. [scuffle.
মারামারি, *s.* reciprocal smiting, a battle,
মারী, *s.* a pestilence, a contagion.
মারীভয়, *s.* fear of a pestilential disease.
মারুত, বায়ু, বাতাস, *s.* the wind, air.
মারুরাগ, *s.* a mixed rága or air in music.
মার্কণ্ডেয়, *s.* name of a sage; পুরাণ, one of the puránas or ancient histories.
মার্গ, *s.* a road, path, way, passage, a section.
মার্গণ, *s.* a seeking, search, enquiring for.
মার্গণীয়, or মার্গয়িতব্য, *a.* searchable.
মার্গশীর্ষ, *s.* the Hindu month Agraháyan.
মার্গি, *a.* sought, enquired, searched.
মার্ঘা, *a.* dear, high-priced, expensive.
মার্জক, *a.* scouring, cleansing, forgiving: *s.* one who cleanses, he who forgives.
মার্জন, *s.* a scouring, cleansing, rubbing, polishing, the forgiving of a crime.
মার্জনা, *s.* polish, scouring, cleansing, purification, forgiveness, pardon, remission.
মার্জনার্হ, মার্জনীয়, venial, pardonable, puri-
মার্জনী, *s.* a towel, rubber, duster. [fiable.
মার্জা, *s.* barter, exchange, permutation.
মার্জার, বিড়াল, *s.* a cat; *fem.* মার্জারী.
মার্জিত, *a.* purified, cleansed, scoured, pol-
মার্তণ্ড, *s.* the sun. [ished, pardoned.

*মার্তেল, *s. Port.* a hammer. [mridanga.
মার্দঙ্গিক, *s.* a player on the drum called
মার্দব, *s.* softness, mildness, politeness.
*মাল, merchandise, wares, goods, property; a hero, a wrestler, a snake-catcher; the whirling cord of a spinning wheel.
মালখানা, *s.* a storehouse. [holder.
মালগুজার, *s.* one who pays tribute, a land-
মালগুজারী, *s.* the rent of land. [perty.
মালজামিন, *s.* a security or surety for pro-
মালজামিনী, *s.* suretiship for property.
মালঞ্চ, *s.* a parterre, a flower-garden.
মালতী, name of Lakshmí; three shrubs.[1]
মালসাট, *s.* boasting, a throwing down the gauntlet; -মার্ to boast, to challenge.
মালা, *s.* a wreath, a necklace, a garland, a rosary, neck-beads; a cocoanut shell.
মালাইচাকি, *s.* the rotula, the kneepan.
মালাকর, মালাকার, *s.* a florist, a gardener, one who sells necklaces or garlands.
মালাকাক্সামরুল, *s.* a tree and its fruit.[*]
মালাকাবেত, *s.* the Malacca ratan.
*মালামাল, *s.* things, goods, merchandise.
মালামী, wrestling, heroism, wrestlership.
মালিক, *s.* a florist, a gardener, a flower-seller; a king, a governor, an owner.
*মালিকানা, *s.* allowance paid to a land-holder: *ad.* like an owner. [supremacy.
মালিকী, royalty, governorship, ownership,
মালিন্য, *s.* filthiness, sordidness, squalidness, dirtiness, gloominess.
মালিম, *s.* a ship-officer next to a captain.
মালী, *s.* a gardener, a florist; *fem.* মালিনী.
*মালুম, *a.* known, acquainted with.
মালো, *s.* a fisherman: *intj.* O mother!
মাল্য, *s.* a necklace, a garland, a chaplet.
মাল্যগ্রহণ, *s.* the wearing of a necklace.
মাল্যচন্দন, *s.* a necklace and sandalwood (an offering of respect and honour).
মাল্যবান্, *a.* wearing a necklace of flowers.
মাল্সা, *s.* a kind of earthen pot. [pulse.[2]
মাষ, *s.* a skin-disease; -কলায়, a kind of
মাষা, or মাষক, *s.* a goldsmith's weight.
মাস, *s.* a month; flesh, meat.
মাসকাবার, *s. Port.* the end of the month
মাসকাবারী, *a.* of the month, monthly.
মাসতুতভাই, *s.* a mother's sister's son.

মাসবৃদ্ধি, *s.* an intercalary month. [ed.
মাসাল, fleshy, fat, plump, well-condition-
মাসাস, *s.* a husband's or wife's mother's
মাসিক, or মাসুড়া. *a.* monthly. [sister.
মাসী, *s.* a mother's sister, a maternal aunt.
মাসুড়া, *s.* a film on the eye, a cicatrix.
*মাসুল, *s.* tax, duty, excise, custom.
*মাসুর, *a.* celebrated, published, divulged, conspicuous, famous, well-known.
মাসুহা, মহোআরী, monthly, per mensem.
মাস্তুর, মাস্তুল, *s.* the mast of a ship or boat.
মাহাত্ম্য, *s.* magnanimity, greatness, glory, praise, celebrity. [monthly pay.
*মাহিনা, *s.* monthly pay; -দার, receiving
মাহিয়ানা, *a.* monthly: *s.* monthly pay.
মাহিষ, *a.* produced by or from a buffalo.
মাহুত, *s.* an elephant-driver.
মাহেশ্বরী, *s.* a name of Durgá.
মিচক্, *v. n.* to simper, to smile.
মিছরী, or মিসরী, *s.* sugarcandy.
মিছা, *a.* false: *s.* falsehood, vanity; -ঠমক, -ঠাট, -ভুর, false pride, vain boasting.
মিছামিছি, *ad.* falsely, pretendedly.
*মিজাজ, *s.* temperament, complexion, constitution, temper, disposition. [extinct.
মিট্, *v. n.* to subside, wear out, fail, to be
মিট, *s.* absolving of a person, expiation.
মিটন, *s.* a subsiding, a wearing out.
মিটা, *v. a.* to dispel, efface, suppress, settle, to expiate a crime, to extinguish.
মিটান, *s.* a dispelling of danger or gloom, the effacing of a thing, terminating of a dispute, the expiating of a crime: *a.* dispelled, effaced, suppressed, expiated.
মিট্মাট, decision of an affair, settlement.
মিট্মিট্, *s.* the twinkling of a lamp.
মিটমিটিয়া, *a.* dying, expiring, twinkling.
মিঠ, মিঠা, *a.* sweet: মিঠানি, sweetness.
মিঠা, *v. a.* to sweeten: *s.* sweetness, suavity.
মিঠাই, *s.* sweetmeat, confectionary.
মিঠান, *a.* seasonable, opportune, slow.
মিত, *a.* measured, moderate, regular.
মিতব্যয়, *s.* measured expenditure, economy, frugality. [in expenses.
মিতব্যয়ী, *a.* economical, frugal, prudent
মিতা, *s.* a friend, a namesake. [Hindu law.
মিতাক্ষরা, *s.* a celebrated commentary on
মিতাচার, *s.* properly regulated conduct.
মিতাচারী, *a.* acting in a moderate manner.
মিতাশন, or মিতাহার, *s.* abstemiousness.
মিতাশী, or মিতাহারী, *a.* abstemious.
মিতি, *s.* a measure, weight; interest. [ny.
মিত্র, a friend, companion, confidant, cro-
মিত্রঘ্ন, treacherous to, or killing a friend.
মিত্রতা, মিতালি, *s.* friendship, intimacy.
মিত্রদ্রোহী, *a.* injuring or killing a friend.
মিত্রনাম, *s.* a namesake, one of same name.
মিত্রলাভ, *s.* the acquisition of a friend.
মিত্রহত্যা, *s.* the murder of a friend.
মিত্রাক্ষর, *s.* rhyme in poetry. [ly, in secret.
মিথস্, *ad.* mutually, reciprocally, private-
মিথুন, *s.* a couple, twins; sign Gemini.
মিথুনরাশি, *s.* the sign Gemini.
মিথ্যা, *a.* false, counterfeit, delusory, apparent: *s.* a denial; falsehood, vanity.
মিথ্যাঠাটঠমক, *s.* glare, false grandeur.
মিথ্যাপত্তি, *s.* an imaginary misfortune or distress, a false pretension.
মিথ্যাবাদী, *a.* lying: *s.* a liar. [picion.
মিথ্যাশঙ্কা, *s.* imaginary fear, a false sus-
মিথ্যা -শপথ -দিব্য, *s.* false oath, perjury.
মিনতি, মিন্নৎ, *s.* prayer, supplication, en-
মিয়ানা, *s.* a litter, pálki. [treaty, request.
মির্গি, *s.* the epilepsy: রোগী, epileptic.
মির্চাই, *s.* pepper, chilly; a cathartic seed.
মির্জাই, or মের্জাই, *s.* a kind of jacket.
*মির্দাহ, *s.* the chief man of a village.
মিল্, *v. n* to coalesce, agree, rhyme, associate, to correspond, match, tally with, unite, incorporate, suit, to be reconciled, to be obtained, to meet (a person).
মিল, *s.* concord, union, consent, society.
মিলন, *s.* a coalescing, a coming in contact, agreeing, joining, according with, a being reconciled, obtaining of a thing.
মিলনসার, *a.* affable, social, friendly.
মিলনস্থান, *s.* a place of rendezvous.
মিলা, *v. a.* to unite, reconcile, to revise, compare, to check accounts, to collate, adjust, join, to mingle, mix, to procure.
মিলান, *s.* the making of things agree with one another, a reconciling, a uniting.
মিলাপ, *s.* social intercourse, sociality.
মিলাপী, *a.* social, affable, friendly.

মিলিত, *a.* mixed, united, met with, coalesced, compounded, found, obtained.
মিলিতযন্ত্র, *s.* a set of chimes.
মিল্‌মিলা, হাম, *s.* the measles. [with.
মিশ্‌, *v.* to mix together, to unite, mingle
মিশা, *v. a.* to incorporate, to mix, mingle, to compound, to jumble together.
মিশাল, *s.* the composition of a medicine, a mixture: *a.* mixed, compounded.
মিশালঘোশাল, *s.* a jumble, a mixture.
মিশ্র, *s.* a proper name; mixture. [mixing.
মিশ্রণ, *s.* in *arith.* addition; mixture, a
মিশ্রিত, *a.* mixed, compounded.
মিশ্রিতভাষা, *s.* a mixed language, a jargon.
মিষ্ট, *a.* sweet, pleasant, agreeable. [ness.
মিষ্টতা, *s.* sweetness, suavity, agreeable-
মিষ্টবক্তা, *s.* an agreeable or kind speaker.
মিষ্টবাক্য, মিষ্টকথা, *s.* agreeable language.
মিষ্টভাষী, *a.* speaking agreeably: *s.* kind
মিষ্টান্ন, *s.* sweetmeat, frumenty. [speaker.
মিসরী, মিছরী, *s.* sugarcandy. [teeth.
মিসি, *s.* a kind of powder to blacken the
*মিসিল, *s.* a session in a court of justice.
*মিহী, মিহীন, *a.* fine, not coarse, slender,
মীন, *s.* a fish; the sign Pisces. [delicate.
মীনরাশি, *s.* the sign Pisces.
*মীনা, enamel; -কার্‌, an enameller; -কারী, act of enamelling. [an arbitrator.
মীমাংসক, acting as umpire: *s.* an umpire,
মীমাংসনীয়, *a.* discriminable, decidable.
মীমাংসা, *s.* one of the Hindu philosophical systems founded by Jaimini; a logical decision, a settling of differences, the reconciling of different opinions.
মীমাংসাকর্ত্তা, *s.* the author of the mímánsá system, viz. Jaimini; an umpire.
মীমাংসার্হ, *a.* worthy of a logical decision.
মীমাংসিত, *a* decided, adjudged, settled.
মীমাংস্য, *a.* discriminable, decidable.
*মীয়াদ, *s.* a time allotted or agreed upon.
মিয়াদী, *a.* of agreed or allotted time.
*মীর, *s.* a chief, a title of sayad tribe of
মীরসিকার, *s.* a hawk, a falcon. [Moslems.
মীরসিকারী, *s.* a hunter, a falconer. [birth.
*মীর্জা, মের্জা, a title of Mogals: chief by
মুই, *pron.* I; used in a humiliating sense.
*মুকদ্দমা, a preamble, a law suit, an affair.

*মুকাবিলা, *s.* a meeting, a confronting.
মুকুট, *s.* a crest, a crown, a diadem, tiara.
মুকুন্দ, *s.* a liberator; a name of Vishnu.
মুকুর, *s.* a looking glass, mirror. [a bud.
মুকুল্‌, *v. n.* to blossom, to bud, to open as
মুকুল, *s.* a blossom, a bud. [rous.
মুকুলজ, *a.* produced from a bud, gemmipa-
মুকুলিত, *a.* set with blossom buds.
মুক্ত, *a.* free, liberated, acquitted, delivered, emancipated, rescued, open, loose.
মুক্তকেশী, *s.* a name of the goddess Kálí.
মুক্তহস্ত, open-handed, liberal, munificent.
মুক্তা, মুক্তাফল, *s.* a pearl; -দাম, -মালা, or -হার, a necklace of pearls.
মুক্তাগার, *s.* the pearl-oyster.
মুক্তি, *s.* freedom, liberation, emancipation, salvation, an acquittal, a discharge, a deliverance, beatitude.
মুক্তিদ, *a.* liberating, giving salvation.
মুক্তিদাতা, *s.* a saviour, a deliverer.
মুখ, *s.* a commencement, the mouth, face, aperture, opening: *a.* foremost, first, initial, chief, principal, pre-eminent; -ঢাক্‌, to veil, cover the face; -ধর্‌, or -লাগ্‌, to salivate, itch the mouth; -বাঁধ্‌, or -মার্‌, to bribe, to stop the mouth.
মুখচোরা, *a.* sheepish, shame-faced, bash-
মুখচোরামী, *s.* sheepishness. [ful, shy.
মুখছোব, *s.* a shrinking, a being bashful.
মুখজোবানী, মুজবানী, *s.* a deposition, a verbal report: *a.* verbal: *ad.* verbally.
মুখড়, or মুখফটু, *a.* scurrilous, abusive.
*মুখ্‌তার, *s.* an agent, an attorney, a substi-
মুখ্‌তারনামা, *s.* a power of attorney. [tute.
মুখ্‌তারী, *s.* attorneyship, agency.
মুখনল, *s.* a huká mouth-piece.
মুখনিরীক্ষক, *a.* looking in the face, partial.
মুখপাত, *s.* the front, outer fold (of cloth).
মুখপ্রক্ষালন, *s.* the washing of the mouth.
মুখবন্ধ, *s.* a gag, a bribe, a gift for secrecy; a preface, an introduction to a writing.
মুখবন্ধন, *s.* the giving of a bribe. [mouth.
মুখব্যাদান, *s.* gaping, the opening of the
মুখমণ্ডল, *s.* the orb of the face, the face.
মুখযন্ত্রণ, *s.* the bit of a bridle.
মুখর, *a.* impudent, insolent, scurrilous, foul-mouthed: *s.* a conch-shell, a crow.

মুখরতা, -ত্ব, *s.* a scurrility, abusiveness.
মুখরোগ, *s.* a cancer in the mouth.
মুখশুদ্ধি, or মুখশোধন, *s.* cleanness of the mouth, sharpness, pungency, flattery.
মুখশোষ, *s.* dryness of the face. [fle.
মুখস, *s.* a mask; the bit of a bridle, a snaf-
মুখস্থ, *a.* in the mouth, verbal, oral, by rote.
মুখা, *v. n.* to face, approach: *s.* split pieces of bambu used to edge a mat door.
মুখাগ্নি, *s.* a kind of goblin; the putting of fire into the mouth of a corpse.
মুখাচ্ছাদন, or মুখাচ্ছাদনী, *s.* a veil.
মুখাপেক্ষক, or মুখাপেক্ষী, *a.* partial.
মুখাপেক্ষা, *s.* partiality, partial regard.
মুখামুখি, *ad.* face to face, front to front, vis a vis: *s.* a dispute, a wrangling.
মুখামৃত, *s.* a propitious or favorable look (a term of flattery); saliva, spittle.
মুখাল, মুখাস, *s.* a muzzle, a mask, a gag.
মুখাসব, *s.* saliva, spittle, drivel.
মুখী, *s.* a sprout, a shoot, a germ. [nent.
মুখ্য, *a.* primary, chief, principal, pre-emi-
মুগ, *s.* the bean of Phaseolus mungo.
মুগডালি *s.* husked bean of P. mungo.
মুগসামলী, *s.* a sort of cake.
মুগুর, *s.* a mallet, a club, a bludgeon.
মুগ্ধ, *a.* bereft of sensation or reflection, infatuated, stupified, stupid, ignorant.
মুগ্ধা, *a. fem.* arrived at the age of puberty.
মুগরা, *s.* the large variety of Jasminum
মুগরিফুল, the same as বেলফুল. [zambac.
মুক্তা, *s.* coral; a sort of Ásám silk.
মুজি, or মুজিবালাম, *s.* a variety of rice.
মুচ্ *v. a.* to release, liberate, emancipate, resign, to vacate, to desert, to wipe.
মুচ্‌ক, মুচ্‌কা, *v. n.* to smile, to simper.
মুচ্‌কি, *s.* a smile, simper; a kind look: *ad.*
মুচজ, *s.* a Jew's harp. [smilingly.
মুচি, মুচী, *s.* a shoemaker, a currier, a cobbler; a small cocoanut; a crucible; —খোলা, a kind of earthen dish and cover to make rice-flour cakes in.
মুচড়্, *v. n.* to twist, to squeeze, to sprain.
মুচড়া, মুচড়ান, মুচড়ানি, *vide* মোচড়া, &c.
মুচনী, *s.* a female shoemaker or currier.
*মুচলকা, *s.* recognizance. [distress, fear.
*মুজাকা, *s.* compression, straitness, penury,

মুঞ্জী, *s.* a mean person; the name of a fish.
মুঞ্চন, *s.* act of setting free, emancipation, a releasing, the expelling of the fæces.
মুঞ্জ, *s.* a species of grass;[1] an arrow.
মুঞ্জর্, *v. n.* to shoot, shoot up into flower.
মুঞ্জরা, *s.* a shooting up to flower.
মুঞ্জরী, *s.* a spike of flowers, an ear of corn.
মুটরী, *s.* a small bundle, a parcel, a pack.
মুটী, *s.* a cork, a stopper, the bung of a cask, a plug, a hilt or handle, the fist.
মুটিয়া, *s.* a porter, a bearer of burden.
মুটুমহাত, *s.* a cubit with closed fingers.
মুট্‌কী, *s.* cracking the finger joints; a fat
মুটমুটিয়া, *a.* crumbling, brittle. [woman.
মুঠ, *s.* the fist; hilt of a sword, a handle; a handful; -বাঁধ্, to clench the fist.
মুঠা, *s.* a handful, fist; -মুঠা, by handfuls.
মুঠি, মুঠী, a handful, the clenched fist, the handle of a weapon, a plug, a cover.
মুড়্, *v. a.* to crop, shave; to overlay, cover with leather, cloth, etc., to gild; to turn, twist, tack, shut (a clasp-knife).
মুড়, cropped, lopped, headed (as a pollard tree): *s.* the head, a border, a boundary.
মুড়কী, *s.* parched rice mixed with sugar.
মুড়ন, *s.* a cutting of the hair, a shaving, a covering, an overlaying, a gilding.
মুড়নি, *s.* a shaving, the cutting of hair.
মুড়নিয়া, মুড়ানিয়া, cutting hair: *s.* a barber.
মুড়া, *v. a.* to shave, lop off the head of a tree: to cover, overlay, gild: *s.* the head; end, extremity; a stump, pollard.
মুড়ান, মুড়ানি, *s.* a shaving, a lopping off.
মুড়ামুড়ি, *ad.* from end to end. [head.
মুড়ী, *s.* parched rice; the head, severed
মুড়মুড়িয়া, *a.* crumbling, brittle.
মুণ্ড্, *v. a.* to shave the head, to cut off the hair, to lop off a tree.
মুণ্ড, *s.* the head, the forehead, a pollard; Ráhu: *a.* shaven, shorn, bald, cropped.
মুণ্ডক, *s.* a barber, a shaver, one who shaves.
মুণ্ডন, *s.* a shaving, pruning, overlaying.
মুণ্ডা, *v. a.* to be shaved; to cause to lop off: *s.* a kind of shoes. [covered, gilt.
মুণ্ডিত, *a.* shaven, shorn, lopped, overlaid
মুণ্ডী, *s.* a kind of sweetmeat; a barber.
মুত, *s.* urine; a bulbous-rooted grass.

*মুতসদ্দি, *s.* an accountant, a scribe, writer.
মুতিআবেল, *s.* a variety of jessamine.
মুথা, *s.* a bulbous-rooted grass.[1]
মুদ্, *v. a.* to fill up, to cover; to close the eyes; to move on hinges, to shut.
মুদন, *s.* a filling or covering up, the closing of the eyes, the shutting of a door.
মুদা, *s.* a button, a plug, a covering; the strangury; a gift to a fortune-teller.
মুদাঘরা, *s.* a button-hole, a loop.
মুদিত, *a.* shut, closed, filled up; gratified.
মুদিতা, *a. fem.* pleased, gratified.
মুদী, *s.* a retail shop-keeper, a grocer.
মুদীখানা, *s.* a storehouse, a grocer's shop.
মুদ্গ, মুগ, *s.* the bean of Phaseolus mungo.
মুদ্গর, *s.* a mallet, hammer, a mace, a club, a bludgeon, a staff, dumb-bells.
*মুদ্দই, *s.* a plaintiff, a suitor, an enemy, a foe.
*মুদ্দত, *s.* a space of time, a long time, antiquity.
মুদ্দতী, *a.* ancient, of old standing.
*মুদ্দা, *s.* a scope, an object, a meaning, a view, a wish, a desire.
মুদ্রা, *s.* a coin, a seal, a medal, a die, a stamp, cash.
মুদ্রাকর, মুদ্রাকার, *s.* an engraver, a coiner.
মুদ্রাঘটিত, pecuniary, monetary.
মুদ্রাঙ্কিত, *a.* sealed, stamped with a mark, printed.
মুদ্রান্বিত, *a.* impress, sealed, stamped.
মুদ্রাযন্ত্র, *s.* a machine to print or stamp impression, a printing press.
মুদ্রাসংখ, *s.* litharge, (Plumbi oxyde).
মুদ্রিত, sealed, imprest, printed, cut, closed (as flower).
*মুনাফা, *s.* profit, perquisite.
মুনাল, *s.* a huká mouth-piece.
মুনি, *s.* a Hindu sage, a philosopher, a law-giver.
*মুনিব, *s.* a master, a patron, a lord.
মুনিবাক্য, *s.* the sayings of philosophers.
*মুনসী, *s.* a scribe, a tutor, a teacher, a writer, a secretary.
*মুন্সীফ, *a.* equitable, just: *s.* a judge, an arbitrator.
*মুফঃসল, *s.* the inside, the interior, the country in opposition to the city.
*মুফ্ত, *a.* gratuitously, freely, gratis.
*মুফ্তী, *s.* a law-giver, a judge.
মুমুক্ষা, *s.* a desire for freedom or liberty.
মুমুক্ষু, *a.* desirous of emancipation.
মুমূর্ষা, *s.* the approach of death, a desire to die.
মুমূর্ষু, *a.* about to die, at the point of death.

*মুরগ, *s.* a cock, fowl, bird; *fem.* মুরগী.
*মুরচা, -বন্দি, *s.* a bastion, a rampart, a battery.
*মুরব্বা, *s.* a preserve, a confection.
*মুরব্বী, *s.* a patron, a guardian, a protector; -আনা, like a patron or guardian
মুরলী, *s.* a flute, a fife, a pipe, a whistle.
*মুরাতিবা, মুর্তবা, *s.* dignity, rank, honour.
*মুরাদ, *s.* a desire, a wish, an inclination, a design.
*মুরিদ, *s.* a disciple, a pupil.
মুরজ, *s.* a small drum, a tabour.
*মুর্গা, *s.* coxcomb flower;[2] a cock; *fem.* মুর্গী.
*মুর্দা, *a.* dead: *s.* a corpse; -ফরাস্, a plebeian, an undertaker; -সং, litharge.[3]
মর্দার, *s.* corpse, dead body; -সং, litharge.[3]
*মুলাকাৎ, *s.* a meeting, an interview.
*মুলুক, *s.* a kingdom, a country.
মুলুকগিরী, *a.* territorial, provincial: *s.* government, supremacy, political affairs.
*মুল্তবী, *a.* delayed, postponed, spun out.
মুলতান, *s.* a tune; হিং, best asa fœtida.
*মুশককৎ, *s.* trouble, labour, pain, toil.
*মুশ্কিল, *a* difficult, intricate, hard.
*মুশ্কী, *s.* dark bay colour; the trussing of a fowl; -বাঁধ্, to pinion, to truss.
মুষল, *s.* a pestle, pestle of a rice-mortar.
মুষলধারে, *ad.* in torrents, heavy (as rain).
মুষ্ক, *s.* the scrotum, a testicle.
মুষ্কগ্রন্থি, *s.* in *ana.* the testes.
মুষ্কগ্রন্থিলুণ্ঠকবন্ধনী, *s.* the ligament of the testicles.
মুষ্কব্যবধায়ক, *s.* in *ana.* the septum scroti.
মুষ্কমুক্ত, *a.* gelt, gelded, castrated.
মুষ্কমোচন, *s.* a castrating, gelding, castration.
মুষ্কশূন্য, *a.* gelt, castrated: *s.* a eunuch.
মুষ্কান্তঃত্বক্, *s.* the tunica vaginalis.
মুষ্টামুষ্টি, *ad.* fist to fist, fisticuffs.
মুষ্টি, *s.* the clenched fist, a handful, a grasp, the hilt, handle.
মুষ্টিযোগ, *s.* quack medicine; a striking with the fist.
মুষ্টিবন্ধন, *s.* the act of clenching the fist.
*মুসব্বর, *s.* aloes, a medicinal gum.
*মুসলমান, *s.* a Moslem, a Musalmán.
মুসলমানী, *s.* Moslemism, circumcision.
*মুসাফের, *s.* a traveller, alien, stranger.
*মুসাবিদা, *s.* rough draught of a writing.
*মুসাহেব, *s.* a companion, an aid-de-camp.
*মুসাহেরা, *s.* monthly wages, salary, pay.
মুস্তক, *s.* the same with মুথা.

মুহনা, *s.* the conflux of two rivers, the outlet or mouth of a river. [tary.
*মুহরির, *s.* a writer, book-keeper, a secre-
মুহরিরগিরী, *s.* the office of a muharir.
মুহরী, *s.* a drain, a gutter, a trench, a sink, a sewer; a scribe, writer, an accountant, a book-keeper, a secretary. [harí.
মুহরীআনা, *s.* the office and pay of a mu-
*মুহসিল, *s.* a tax-gatherer, a bailiff, a dun.
*মুহিম, *a.* important, urgent, great: *s.* war.
মুহুঃ, *ad.* repeatedly, again and again.
মুহুর্মুহুঃ, *ad.* again and again, frequently.
মুহূর্ত, *s.* a division of time, an hour of forty-five minutes, a short time, a moment.
মুক, *a.* dumb: *s.* a fish, a demon, a pauper.
মুচী, *s.* a crucible, a pan for melting metals.
মুঢ়, *a.* stupid, rustic, ignorant, clownish, rude, cold, apathetic, phlegmatic. [thy.
মুঢ়তা, *s.* stupidity, gross ignorance, apa-
মুৎ, *v. n.* to discharge urine, make water.
মুত্র, মুত, প্রস্রাব, লঘী, *s.* urine. [urine.
মুত্রকৃচ্ছ্র, *s.* strangury, a suppression of
মুত্রনিঃক্ষেপাত্র, *s.* a catheter, surgical tool.
মুত্রপথ, মুত্রপ্রণালী *s.* the urinary passage.
মুত্রপ্রবাহকপ্রণালী, মুত্ররন্ধ্র, *s.* the urethra.
মুত্রবর্দ্ধক, মুত্রোপকারক, *a.* diuretic.
মুর্খ, *a.* ignorant, stupid, silly, clownish, awkward: *s.* a dunce, a fool, an idiot.
মুর্খতা, ignorance, stupidity, silliness, awkwardness; -পূর্ব্বক, stupidly, ignorantly.
মুর্চ্ছনা, *s.* purification of oil; *vide* মুর্চ্ছা.
মুর্চ্ছা, *s.* syncope, loss of sensation, swoon, a stupor, a state of torpor, a fainting fit.
মুর্চ্ছাগত, *a.* swooned, fainted. [swooning.
মুর্চ্ছাপন্ন, *a.* bereft of sensation, senseless,
মুর্চ্ছাবায়ু, *s.* the epilepsy, falling sickness.
মুর্চ্ছারোগ, *s.* syncope, a fainting fit.
মুর্চ্ছিত, *a.* senseless, in a swoon, fainted.
মুর্ত্ত, *a.* solid, material, having a shape.
মুর্ত্তি, *s.* a form, a shape, a resemblance, likeness, an image, a picture, a statue.
মুর্ত্তিমান্, *a.* having a visible form, embodied, possessing a shape; clever.
মুর্ত্যন্তর, a different form, another shape; transformation, metamorphosis.
মুর্দ্ধন্য, cerebral, lingual; -বর্ণ, the class of lingual letters, viz. ঋ ৠ ট ঠ ড ঢ ণ র ষ.

মুর্দ্ধসন্ধি, *s.* the coronal suture. [head.
মুর্দ্ধা, *s.* the head, the upper part of the
মুর্দ্ধাভিষিক্ত, *s.* a kshetriya, a king, prince.
মুল, *s.* a radix, root, bulbous root; the first cause, origin, source, a foundation, a cause; root of a number, as the square or cube root; a capital or stock in trade, a principal lying at interest; a radish: *a.* radical, original, near, proximate.
মুলক, *a.* originating from, founded upon, springing from a root: *s.* a radish.
মুলকারণ, *s.* the radical cause, a source.
মুলগণ, *s.* the co-efficient of a root.
মুলগাইন, *s.* the chief of a set of singers.
মুলজ, *a.* radical, primitive, produced from
মুলধন, *s.* capital, stock in trade. [the root.
মুলা, *s.* a radish, an edible root.
মুলী, *a.* fundamental, original: *s.* a radish.
মুলীভূত, *a.* become a source or origin.
মুলোৎপাটন, *s.* subversion, a rooting out.
মুল্য, *a.* purchasable, valuable: *s.* a price, value, worth, wages, hire; -কৃ, to bargain; -ঠাহর্, -ধর্, to value, appraise.
মুল্যবান, *a.* valuable, precious. [pan.
মুষা, *s.* a rat, a mouse; a crucible, melting
মুষিক, ইন্দুর, উন্দুর, উন্দুর, *s.* a rat, a mouse.
মুষী, মুচী, *s.* a crucible, a melting pan.
মৃগ, *s.* deer, stag, antelope, a beast, game.
মৃগতৃষ্ণা, মরীচিকা, *s.* mirage, illusive scene.
মৃগধূর্ত্তক, *s.* a shakal, a jackal. [eyed.
মৃগনয়নী, মৃগলোচনী, মৃগাক্ষী, *a. fem.* fawn-
মৃগনাভি, মৃগমদ, *s.* musk, a bag of musk.
মৃগব্য, *s.* game, hunting; a butt in archery.
মৃগয়া, *s.* the chase, diversion of hunting.
মৃগয়ু, *s.* Brahmá; a jackal, a hunter.
মৃগরাজ, মৃগেন্দ্র, *s.* the lion, king of beasts.
মৃগশাবক, *s.* a fawn, the young of a deer.
মৃগশালা, *s.* a stable for deer, a deer park.
মৃগশিরা, *s.* the fifth mansion of the zodiac.
মৃগশৃঙ্গ, *s.* a buck's horn, hartshorn.
মৃগাঙ্ক, চন্দ্র, চন্দ্রমা, শশধর, শশী, *s.* the moon.
মৃগাল, *s.* the name of a species of fish.
মৃগালয়, *s.* a park, a forest, hunting place.
মৃগিত, *a.* hunted, chased, pursued, sought.
মৃগী, *s.* a doe, female deer; the epilepsy.
মৃড়, *s.* one of the names of Shiva. [lily.
মৃণাল, *s.* the stalk of the lotus or water-

মৃণালী, *s.* waterlily, an assemblage of lotus.
মৃণ্ময়, *a.* earthen, made of clay.
মৃৎ, *s.* earth, clay, mould, soil.
মৃত, *a.* dead, deceased, defunct.
মৃতকল্প, *a.* dying, nearly dead, almost dead.
মৃততুল্য, *a.* like a dead person. [legacy.
মৃতদত্ত, *a.* bequeathed, given at death: *s.* a
মৃতদার, *a.* bereft of his wife: *s.* a widower.
মৃতপ্রায়, *a.* almost dead, like one dead.
মৃতান্তর, *a.* after death, after the demise of.
মৃতি, *s.* death, decease, demise, dying.
মৃত্তিকা, *s.* earth, soil, clay, mould, ground.
মৃৎপিণ্ড, *s.* a lump of earth, a clod.
মৃত্যু, *s.* death, decease, demise, dying; regent of death, Yama. [causing death.
মৃত্যু-কর, -জনক, *a.* deadly, mortal, baneful,
মৃত্যুঞ্জয়, *s.* Shiva, the conqueror of death.
মৃৎসা, *s.* rich soil, good or fertile ground.
মৃদঙ্গ, *s.* a kind of egg-shaped drum.
মৃদু, *a.* mild, gentle, meek, peaceable, quiet, tender, affable, kind, placable, soft, pacific, tame, supple, blunt, not sharp.
মৃদুতা, *s.* mildness, gentleness, meekness, quietness, affability, tenderness, kindness, suppleness, softness, tameness.
মৃদুল, *a.* gentle, mild, tender, pliable.
মৃদুস্বভাব, *a.* naturally mild or tame, gentle, kind, peaceable, quiet, supple.
মৃদু-স্বর, *s.* a mild voice; -হাস্য, a smile.
মৃদ্বীকা, *s.* a grape, a raisin.
মৃন্ময়, *a.* earthen, made of clay.
মৃষা, *ad.* falsely, uselessly, in vain.
মেঁ, *s.* the bleating of a sheep or goat.
মেই, *s.* a nipple: also, *vide* মেইখুঁটি, মেধী.
মেইখুঁটি, *s.* centre post of a threshing-floor.
মেইয়া, মাইয়া, *s.* a girl, a female, a woman, a daughter; -মানুষ, a woman, female.
মেইয়ামর্দ্দা, *s.* a virago, a masculine woman.
মেইয়ামী, *s.* effeminacy, womanishness.
মেইয়ামুখ, shamefaced, womanish, bashful.
মেক, *s.* a nail, an iron pin, a spike, a plug of base metal, a tent pin, a hook, tenter.
মেকদার, *s.* quantity, measure, space, num-
মেকদারশির, *s.* a balance, a surplus. [ber.
মেকরাজ, *s.* a pair of scissors or shears.
মেকলী, *s.* a fine sort of sackcloth.
মেকী, *a.* counterfeit, plugged (as a coin).

মেখলা, *s.* a thin cord worn by women round the waist, a swordbelt, a swordknot, the sea, a fine sort of sackcloth.
মেঘ, -ডম্বুর, *s.* a cloud; -গর্জ্জন, thunder.
মেঘজ্যোতিঃ, *s.* a flash of lightning.
মেঘনাদ, মেঘনির্ঘোষ, *s.* a clap of thunder,
মেঘমালা, a collection of clouds. [thunder.
মেঘলা, *a.* cloudy, lowering, overcast.
মেঘাচ্ছন্ন, overcast, covered with clouds.
মেঘাড়ম্বর, *s.* a clap of thunder, thunder.
মেঘান্ধকার, *s.* the darkness of clouds.
মেঘারম্ভ, *s.* the gathering of clouds.
মেচ্যা, *s.* a stool, a chair, a bench. [wife.
মেছুনী, *s.* a fisherwoman, a fisherman's
মেছুয়া, *s.* a fisherman, a fishmonger. [egg.
মেছোতা, *s.* spots on the cheeks; a fly's
মেজ, *s.* *Port.* a table; -লাগা, -সাজা, to prepare a table, to lay a table for a meal.
*মেজাজ, *s.* the habit of body or mind.
মেজিয়া, মেজ্যা, *s.* the floor of a house.
মেঝ, *s.* the middle, the floor of a house.
মেঝিয়া, *a.* middlemost: *s.* floor of a house.
মেঝেম, *s.* flooring, the flooring of a house.
মেটমাট, *s.* the settling of an affair.
মেটা, *v. a.* to adjust, obviate, remove, confute: *a.* confuted, obviated, adjusted.
মেটান, *s.* the settling or adjusting of an affair, removing of a doubt. [clayey.
মেটিয়া, মেট্যা, *s.* a jar; kidneys: *a.* earthy,
মেট্যাচিল, *s.* the common Bengál kite.
মেট্যাতেল, *s.* naphtha, earth-oil.
মেড়, *s.* a frame, framework of an image.
মেড়া, মেঢ়া, *s.* a ram, sheep: মেড়ী, an ewe.
মেড়ুয়া, *a.* starched, blunt, dull, rusty: *s.* a small hammer; also, *vide* মাড়ুআ.
মেঢ্র, *s.* the penis; a ram; -অক, the pre-
মেঢ্ররোগ, *s.* the venereal disease. [puce.
*মেতর, *s.* a sweeper, a nightman. [wind.
মেতরাণী, *s.* a female sweeper; (*fig.*) the
মেথী, মেথিকা, *s.* the name of a plant.[1]
মেদ, *s.* lymph, serum, fat, marrow; corpulence; -ধুৎ, lymphatic.
মেদা, *a.* stupid, dull, sluggish, slow.
মেদিনী, ধরণী, ভূমি, মহীতল, *s.* the earth.
মেধ, *s.* a sacrifice; apprehension.
মেধা, *s.* aptness to learn, intellect, apprehension, conception, understanding.

মেধাবী, *a.* apt, intelligent, retentive, of good abilities, of quick parts, docile.
মেধী, *s.* the stake or post placed in the centre of a threshing floor.
মেধ্য, *a.* pure, fit for sacrifice or offering.
মেনকা, *s.* the mother of Durgá.
মেনা, *s.* a woman's breast, the udder of a beast.
মেনী, *s.* a female; -বিড়াল, a female cat.
মেনীমুখা, shunning company, reserved, retired, bashful, shamefaced, sly.
মেনীমুখামী, bashfulness, shamefacedness, slyness.
মেন্দি, মেঁদি, *s.* an ornamental shrub.[1]
মেবা, *s.* a fruit, a particular fruit:[2] *a.* delicious, sweet-tasted, good-tasted.
*মেয়ানা, *a.* middling: *s.* a sort of pálki.
*মেয়ানী, *s.* the flap of a pair of breeches.
মেয়ে, *a.* female: *s.* a woman, a female, a daughter; -মানুষ, a woman.
*মেরাপ, *s.* a round building; a picture frame.
*মেরামৎ, *s.* repairs; -কৃ, to mend, repair.
মেরামতী, *s.* repairs, a mending: *a.* repaired, mended, due for repairing.
মেরু, *s.* a fabulous mountain, the axis, the backbone of the earth; the north pole.
মেরুগ্রন্থি, *s.* the kidneys.
মেরুদণ্ড, *s.* the spine, the backbone.
মেল্, *v. a.* to extend, to unfold, to open.
মেল, *s.* peace, reconciliation, intimacy, society, union, a conjunction, concord, accord, agreement, consent, comparison.
মেলক, *a.* social, meeting: *s.* a reconciler.
মেলন, *s.* a meeting, a coming together, a reconciling, laying open, unfolding.
মেলা, *s.* a fair, an assembly, a crowd: *a.* spacious, open, free, unrestrained.
মেলান, *s.* a spreading out, a causing to be opened: *a.* open, extended, expanded.
মেলানি, *s.* an assembly, an association, a multitude, union, a friendly dismissal.
মেলাপ, *s.* union, peace, amicability, agreement, an accommodation.
মেষ, *s.* a ram, a sheep; the sign Aries.
মেষঘোষ, *s.* a confused crowd, a mixture.
মেষপাল, *s.* a flock of sheep; a shepherd.
মেষপালক, *s.* a shepherd, keeper of sheep.
মেষরাশি, *s.* the sign Aries.
মেসুয়া, মেসো, *s.* a mother's sister's husband.

মেস্যাড়া, *s.* a film, skin over a wound.
মেহ, *s.* a gleet, a gonorrhea, an inflammatory disease of the urethra, urine.
মেহকর, মেহজনক, মেহবৰ্দ্ধক, *a.* diuretic.
*মেহনৎ, *s.* labour, toil, exertion, activity.
মেহনতী, *a.* laborious, toilsome, active.
মেহবিকার, *s.* a gleet, a gonorrhea.
মেহরবানী, *s.* favour, mercy, compassion.
মৈত্র, *a.* friendly, amicable: *s.* friendship, amity, intimacy, friendliness.
মৈত্রী, *s.* friendship, intimacy, amity.
মৈথিলী, *s.* a name of Sitá.
মৈথুন, *s.* marriage, union, association; copulation.
মো, or মোআ, *s.* a kind of sweetmeat.
মোই, *s.* a ladder, the Indian harrow.
মোক্তব্য, *a.* capable of being liberated.
মোক্তা, *s.* a liberator, deliverer, saviour: *a.* all at once, including every item.
মোক্তাফুরান, *s.* an agreement for any work including materials and workmanship.
মোক্ষ, *s.* liberation, freedom, beatitude, final emancipation.
মোক্ষজ্ঞান, *s.* the knowledge or idea of the liberation of spirit from matter.
মোক্ষণ, *s.* liberation, final beatitude, emancipation, death; a letting out (as blood).
মোক্ষপ্রাপ্ত, *a.* possessed of final beatitude.
মোক্ষপ্রাপ্তি, *s.* the acquisition of beatitude.
মোঘ, *a.* vain, useless, ineffectual, abandoned, left: *s.* a fence, a hedge; tuberose.
মোচ, *s.* a blossom; moustache, whiskers; a nib, point.
মোচক, *a.* freeing, liberating.
মোচড়্, *v. a.* to twist, twist round, wring.
মোচড়, *s.* a sprain, a twist, a wrench; -দা, to twist; -লাগ্, to sprain, to wrench.
মোচড়া, *v. a.* to twist, to wrench: *s.* a twist, a sprain, a wrench; -দা, to twist, sprain.
মোচড়ান, *s.* the twisting or wrenching of a limb: *a.* twisted, wrenched.
মোচড়ামি, *s.* a sprain, a twist, a wrench.
মোচন, *s.* a liberating, a forgiving, a delivering from, a wiping or cleansing.
মোচনা, *s.* pair of pincers, tweezers, tongs.
মোচনীয়, *a.* capable of being liberated.
মোচরস, *s.* the gum of the silk-cotton tree.
মোচা, *s.* the blossoms of a plantain tree; -ফেল্, to blossom (as a plantain tree).

মোচাফল, কবলী, রম্ভা, কলা, *s.* a plantain.
মোচিত, *a.* caused to be set free or released.
মোছ্, *v. a.* to wipe, to cleanse, to shave.
মোছা, *v. a.* to cause to wipe. [hosier.
*মোজা, *s.* a stocking, a boot; -বালা, a
মোট, *s.* gross, total; a burden, load, bundle, package.
মোটরী, *s.* a small bundle.
মোটা, *a.* thick, coarse, fat, corpulent, bulky; -বুদ্ধি, dull, thick-headed, stupid.
মোটামোটি, *ad.* in the gross, cursorily.
মোটাসোটা, *a.* thick, coarse, fat, corpulent.
মোটিয়া, *s.* a porter, bearer of load, coolie.
মোড়, *s.* a twist, crook, bend, a turning, a strain, an udder, ornament for a pillar.
মোড়ক, *s.* a dose, a paper-packet, a squib.
মোড়ন, *s.* a turning, the bending of a thing.
মোড়মাড়, *s.* a turning and bending.
মোড়ল, *s.* the chief man of a village.
মোড়া, *v. a.* to turn a boat or plough, to make crooked, to turn, bend, warp, to twist, to overlay, to plate, to cover with paper, leather or cloth: *s.* a rubbing or twisting round, a screw, a crook, a foot-stool, a roll, a packet wrapped in paper.
মোড়ান, *s.* the causing a boat, etc. to turn, a covering, overlaying, bending: *a.* bent, turned, covered, overlaid.
মোড়ানি, *s.* a turning, a bending, a twist.
মোদক, *a.* exhilarating, gladdening: *s.* a confectioner; a sweetmeat, electuary.
মোদন, *s.* an enlivening, delighting, giving pleasure.
মোদা, shut, close: *s.* a closing.
মোনা, *s.* the pestle-like part of the pedal.
মোন, *s.* 40 sers or 82 lbs. মোনী, tonnage.
মোম, *s.* wax, bees' wax; -বাতী, wax-candle.
মোমজামা, মোমচাল, *s.* waxcloth, cerecloth.
মোরচঙ্গ, মুচঙ্গ, *s.* a jew's-harp. [in a fort.
মোরচাল, *s.* lines of entrenchment, lines
মোরব্বা, *s.* preserved fruit, confectionary.
মোল, *s.* price, value; a blossom. [ler.
মোষক, *s.* a robber, a freebooter, a swind-
মোষণ, *s.* swindling, withholding the due.
মোহ্, *v. n.* to lose sensation or reflection, to be fascinated, stupified, or fainted.
মোহ, *s.* loss of sensation or reflection, stupefaction, infatuation, fascination, delusion, fainting, ignorance, folly, stupidity.

মোহক, *a.* fascinating, stupifying, delusive.
মোহজনক, *a.* causing stupefaction or loss of sensation: *s.* a sorcerer.
মোহন, *s.* a becoming fascinated, a fascinating.
মোহনভোগ, *s.* a kind of meat-offering.
মোহনী, *s.* incantation; churning. [cant.
মোহন্ত, *s.* a devotee, ascetic, hermit, mendi-
মোহর, *s.* a coin, a gold coin, a seal, stamp.
মোহরকন্দ, *s.* an engraver of seals.
*মোহাফেজ, *s.* a record-keeper. [dered.
মোহিত, *a.* infatuated, fascinated, bewil-
মোহিনী, fascinating: *s.* a fascinating woman.
মোহী, *a.* fascinating, infatuating.
মৌ, *s.* honey, nectar of flowers; -চাক, a honeycomb, hive; -মাছি, the honey bee.
*মৌকুফ, *a.* deferred, postponed, left off.
মৌক্কল, *s.* (*corruption* মক্কেল) a client.
মৌক্তিক, মুক্তা, *s.* a pearl. [ness.
মৌখর্য্য, *s.* insolence, scurrility, abusive-
মৌখিক, *a.* immediate, speaking to the face; verbal, oral; pretended, outward.
*মৌজা, *s.* a village, a district; a wave.
*মৌজুদ, present, existing, standing near,
*মৌত, *s.* death, decease, demise. [found.
মৌতাদ, *a.* usual, of daily use: *s.* a custom, usage.
মৌত্রিক, *a.* uric, relating to urine.
মৌন, *a.* silent, tacit: *s.* silence, sadness, gloominess; -ব্রত, a vow of silence.
মৌনসম্মতি, *s.* a silent consent.
মৌনী, *a.* silent, reserved, taciturn.
মৌনে, *ad.* in silence, taciturnly. [thers.
মৌরছোল, *s.* a fan made of peacock's fea-
মৌরলা, *s.* the name of a fine fish.
মৌরি, the same with মউরী.
*মৌরস, or মৌরসী, *a.* hereditary.
মৌরসীপাট্টা, *s.* a hereditary lease of land.
মৌর্ব্বী, *s.* a bowstring, the cord of an arc.
মৌল্, *v. n.* to blossom, to bud; to winnow.
মৌল, radical, of pure extraction: *s.* pure extraction; a sort of mat; a blossom.
*মৌলবী, *s.* a learned or erudite man.
‡মৌলা, *s.* God; a kind of coarse mat.
মৌলী, *s.* the head; a diadem, a topknot.
*মৌসুম, *s.* a season, a time.
*মৌসিল, *s.* a bailiff, a dun.
মৌহূর্ত্তিক, *s.* an astrologer. [a tom-cat.
ম্যাও, *s.* the mewing of a cat, the voice of

ম্যাড়ম্যাড়, *s.* disgust, viscidity, dirtiness.
ম্রুক্ষ, *v. a.* to smear, to anoint. [ing.
ম্রুক্ষণ, *s.* a sprinkling, smearing, anoint-
ম্রিয়মাণ, *a.* dying, expiring, about to die.
ম্লান, *a.* faded, pale, grieved, dejected, sad.
ম্লানবদন, *a.* downcast, dejected, sad.
ম্লানি, *s.* sadness, languor, dejection, a fad-
ম্লেচ্ছ, *a.* barbarian : *s.* a barbarian. [ing.

য, the twenty-sixth consonant; when it has a dot thus (য়,) it is pronounced ya.
যক, *s.* Kuvera's treasurer, a fairy, a demon who superintends wealth.
যকৃৎ, *s.* the liver; the liver-complaint; -কোষ, the hepatic cyst. [same as যক.
যক্ষ, *s.* a kind of fabled beings; also, the
যক্ষধূপ, *s.* incense, turpentine.
যক্ষ্মা, *s.* pulmonary consumption.
যক্ষ্মী, *a.* consumptive, afflicted with con-
যখন, *ad.* when, whenever. [sumption.
যখনতখন, *ad.* now and then, occasionally.
যগঝম্প, *s.* a particular sort of music.
যগাতালয়, *s.* a custom-house; *vide* জগাৎ.
যজন, *s.* act of sacrificing or worshipping.
যজমান, *a.* sacrificing: *s.* the person for whom the sacrifice is made. [vedas.
যজুর্বেদ, যজুঃ, যজুস্, *s.* one of the four
যজুর্বেদী *a.* pertaining to the Yajur-veda.
যজ্ঞ, *s.* a sacrifice, a religious worship.
যজ্ঞকুণ্ড, *s.* an altar, a sacrificial pit.
যজ্ঞডুম্বুর, *s.* a species of fig-tree.[1]
যজ্ঞবেদি, যজ্ঞবেদী, *s.* an altar for sacrifice.
যজ্ঞাঙ্গ, *s.* an essential part of a sacrifice.
যজ্ঞার্থ, *a.* having sacrifice for its object.
যজ্ঞার্থী, *a.* desirous of worship or sacrifice.
যজ্ঞীয়, *a.* sacrificial, fit for sacrifice. [up.
যড়, *a.* collected, amassed, united, closed
যড়ক, *a.* in gross, in a lump, heaped.
যড়া, *v. a.* to collect, bind, hoard, amass, to fold, wrap, to roll up, to furl a sail.
যড়াও, *a.* enamelled: *s.* an enamelling.
যড়ান, *s.* a collecting, amassing, a folding, wrapping, rolling, the furling of a sail: *a.* folded, wrapped, rolled, furled.
যড়ানসড়ান, *a.* folded and wrapped.
যড়িত, *a.* collected, folded, squeezed together, rolled, furled, amassed.

যৎ, *pron.* which, what.
যত, *pron.* as many as, as much as.
যতঃ, *ad.* wherefore, hence, because.
যতকাল, যতক্ষণ, যতদিন, *ad.* as long as.
যতন, *s.* the same with যত্ন.
যতনীয়, *a.* proper to be taken care of.
যতবার, *ad.* how often, as often.
যতি, *s.* cessation, rest, restraint, a check, pause, stop or rest, space in writing, a syllable; -রাখ্, to observe the pauses.
যতী, *a.* temperate: *s.* an ascetic, a sage.
যতুক, *s.* a portion, a marriage portion; a
যতেক, *ad.* so many, as many as. [freckle.
যৎকাল, *s.* which time, the time which.
যৎকালীন, *a.* belonging to which time.
যৎকিঞ্চিৎ, *ad.* a little, a few, ever so little.
যত্ন, *s.* active endeavour, effort, exertion, zeal, care, labour, application, toil, energy, perseverance; -কৃ, to apply closely, to exert, to toil, to endeavour; -পূর্ব্বক, with care or endeavour. [active.
যত্নবান্, *a.* strenuous, laborious, zealous,
যৎপরোনাস্তি, *ph.* ne plus ultra, utmost.
যতাচার, *s.* act of an ascetic, abstemious
যতাচারী, *a.* acting as an ascetic. [habit.
যত্র, where, in which; -কুত্রাপি, anywhere.
যত্রা, *ad.* wherever, in whatever place.
যৎসংখ্যক, *a.* of which number. [mean.
যৎসামান্য, *a.* vulgar, common, inferior,
যথতত্র, *ad.* as, like as, for instance; where.
যথাকাম, *ad.* as you please, at will.
যথাকাল, according to the time. [ledge.
যথা-জ্ঞান, -বুদ্ধি, *ad.* to the extent of know-
যথাতথা, *ad.* the same, so as, as much of; any how, as you like.
যথান্যায়, *ad.* according to right or justice.
যথায়, *ad.* where, in which place. [ties.
যথাযথা, *ad.* as much as, of equal quanti-
যথাযোগ্য, *ad.* as deserved, as is suitable.
যথারুচি, *ad.* as you like, as you please.
যথার্থ, *a.* real, genuine, correct, just, right,
যথার্থতা, *s. vide* যাথার্থ্য. [proper, true.
যথার্থবক্তা, *s.* one who speaks the truth.
যথার্থব্যয়, *s.* frugality, economy.
যথার্থব্যয়ী, *a.* frugal, economical.
যথার্হ, *a.* as is fit or proper, as is right.
যথাশক্তি, *ad.* to the utmost of one's power.

যথাশাস্ত্র, *ad.* according to law or science.
যথাসম্ভব, *ad.* as circumstances require.
যথাসাধ্য, *a.* as is possible, to the utmost, to the extent of a person's power.
যথাস্থান, *ad.* according to the place.
যথেচ্ছ, *ad.* as you please, as you like.
যথেষ্ট, *a.* as much as you please, enough, plenty, abundant, copious, ample.
যথেষ্টাচরণ, *s.* unrestrained conduct.
যথেষ্টাচারী, *a.* acting without restraint.
যথোক্ত, *ad.* as it was said, as related.
যথোচিত, *a.* merited, condign: *ad.* as is fit, to the extent of what is proper.
যথোদিত, *ad.* as it turns up. [proper.
যথোপযুক্ত, *ad.* properly, as much as is
যদবধি, *ad.* since, whilst, while, till, until.
*যদা, *ad.* when, at the time when.
যদি, *ad.* if, though, since.
যদিস্যাৎ, *phrase.* if it may be, if.
যদু, *s.* a king who is the eldest son of Yajáti and the ancestor of Krishna.
যদুআর, *s.* zedoary (Curcuma zedoaria).
যদুবংশ, *s.* the family or race of Yadu.
যদৃচ্ছা, *s.* independence, wilfulness: *ad.* voluntarily, spontaneously.
যদ্যপি, *ad.* although, if, if also, even if.
যদ্যপিস্যাৎ, *phrase.* if it may be, if, in case.
যন্ত্র, *s.* an engine, a machine, a mechanical instrument, a diagram, a sort of vessel.
যন্ত্রক, *s.* pain, anguish, a binding, a confining, a checking, a controlling.
যন্ত্রণা, *s.* anguish, agony, pain, torture, torment, suffering; -দাতা, a tormentor.
যন্ত্রণাপূর্ব্বক, *ad.* by or thro' pain or agony.
যন্ত্রতন্ত্র, *s.* instruments and machines, diagrams and cabbalistical figures. [ed.
যন্ত্রিত, fettered, restrained, bound, check-
যন্ত্রী, *a.* ingenious, mechanical, projecting.
যব, *s.* barley, a barleycorn or 3rd part of
যবক্ষার, *s.* nitre, saltpetre. [an inch.
যবক্ষারজ, *a.* nitrous, nitric.
যবক্ষারজাম্ল, *s.* nitric-acid, aquafortis.
যবক্ষারজাম্লবায়ুভাব, *s.* nitrous oxide gas.
যবক্ষারবায়ুভাব, *s.* nitrous gas, nitric gas.
যবথব, যবস্থব, *ad.* neither moving one way nor the other, as it was. [a Moslem.
যবন, *s.* a western foreigner, a Musalmán,
যবনিকা, *s.* a curtain, the screen of a tent.
যবান, *a.* young, youthful. [plant.[1]
যবানী, যমানী, *s.* an aromatic seed and its
যবান্ন, *s.* barley, boiled barley, barley food.
যবার, *ad.* as often as, as many times.
যবে, when, at which time. [barley crop.
যব্য, *a.* barley, sown with barley, ready for
যব্‌যব্, *s.* wetness, complete wetness.
যবযবীয়া, *a.* wet, clammy, splashy, watery.
যম, *s.* death, Yama, the regent of death, the Hindu Pluto; a pair.
যমক, *s.* twins; alliteration, rhyme.
যমজ, *s.* twins, one of a pair.
যমদূত, যমকিঙ্কর, *s.* a messenger of death.
যমদ্বার, *s.* Yama's door, gates of death.
যমধার, *s.* a dagger, a stiletto, a poniard.
যমপুরী, *s.* the abode or city of Yama.
যমভয়, *s.* the fear of death.
যমরাজ, *s.* Yama, the regent of death.
যমালয়, *s.* the residence of death.
যশঃ, *s.* fame, renown, celebrity.
যশন, or যশম, *s.* enjoyment, pleasure.
যশস্, *s.* glory, fame, celebrity, renown, praise, eulogium, panegyric.
যশস্বী, *a.* renowned, famous, glorious.
যশো -গাথক, -গায়ক, *a.* panegyrizing: *s.* a panegyrist, a flatterer, a sycophant.
যশোভাগ্য, *s.* fame and good fortune.
যষ্টা, *s.* a worshipper, a priest, a sacrificer.
যষ্টি, *s.* a stick, a wand, a mace, a staff, a
যষ্টিমধু, মধুযষ্টিকা, *s.* liquorice. [club.
যা, *v. a.* to go, to depart, to move: *s.* a husband's brother's wife. [rice.
যাউ, *s.* ricegruel, gruel made of broken
যাওন, যাওয়া, *s.* act of going, a departing.
যাওয়াআসা, *s.* intercourse, going and com-
যাঁতা, *s.* millstone; pair of bellows. [ing.
যাঁতি, *s.* a betelnut-cutter, a nut-cracker.
যাগ, *s.* a sacrifice, an act of religious worship; any thing used to ripen fruits.
যাগান, ripe by force: *s.* causing to ripen.
যাচ্, *v. a.* to ask, petition, request, pray.
যাচক্, *a.* asking, begging: *s.* one who asks, a petitioner, beggar, candidate, suitor.
যাচন, *s.* a praying, requesting, petitioning;
যাচনদার, *s.* an appraiser. [appraising.
যাচনা, যাচ্ঞা, *s.* a request, petition, prayer.

যাচনীয়, or যাচ্য, *a.* fit to be requested.
যাচাযাচি, *s.* a requesting and praying.
যাচিত, *a.* asked, requested, petitioned.
যাচ্যমান, *a.* being the subject of a petition.
যাজক, *s.* a priest, a sacrificing priest.
যাজকতা, *s.* priesthood, office of a priest.
যাজন, *s.* the performing of a sacrifice.
যাজ্য, *a.* proper to be offered in sacrifice.
যাজ্ঞিক, *a.* of a sacrifice, sacrificial.
যাত, *a.* past, gone, departed, escaped.
যাতনা, *s.* torment, anguish, pain, agony.
যাতনাকর, *a.* painful, causing torment or agony.
যাতনাদাতা, *s.* a tormentor.
যাতযাম, *a.* old, spent, worn out, impaired, used, rejected, abandoned, faded.
যাতা, *s.* a husband's brother's wife.
যাতায়াত, *s.* intercourse, a going and coming.
যাতু, *s.* one who goes; also, *vide* যাত্রা.
যাত্রা, *s.* a journey, a march, a going, the setting off on a journey, a travelling, a pilgrimage; theatrical representation.
যাত্রাকাল, *s* time of a march or journey.
যাত্রাবালা, *s.* a person who acts a part on the stage, the performer of yátrá.
যাত্রী, যাত্রিক, *a.* marching, journeying, travelling: *s.* a traveller, a pilgrim.
যাথার্থিক, *a.* real, genuine, true, righteous, just.
যাথার্থ্য, যাথার্থিকতা, genuineness, reality, truth, righteousness, justice, propriety.
যাদ্, a recollection, remembrance.
যাদব, *a.* of the race of Yadu: *s.* Krishna's name.
যাদৃক্, or যাদৃশ, *ad.* as, like as, such as.
যাদৃচ্ছিক, *a.* wilful, self-willed, obstinate.
যান, *s.* a vehicle, a carriage, a pálki, a conveyance.
*যানবর, animal: *s.* an animal.
যানবাহ, যানবাহক, *s.* an animal or person by which a vehicle is drawn or carried.
যানবাহী, *a.* carrying or drawing a vehicle.
যাপ্, *v. a.* to cause to go or pass away, to pass or spend (time).
যাপক, *a.* causing to go or pass away, spending.
যাপন, *s.* a causing to pass or go, the spending or passing (of time).
যাপনীয়, যাপ্য, *a.* concealable, dormant, latent; requiring to be spent, passable.
যাপিত, made to go, caused to pass away, spent, past; concealed, secret.

যাবক, *s.* half ripe barley; lac.
যাবক্ষার, *a.* nitrous. যাবক্ষারিক, *a.* nitric.
যাবক্ষারিকাম্ল, *s.* nitric acid, aquafortis.
যাবজ্জীবন, *ad.* while life continues, as long as life, as long as one lives.
যাবৎ, *ad.* while, whilst, until, as long as, as much as: *a.* all, entire, the whole.
যাবত্তাবৎ, *ad.* as much as, as long as.
যাবদীয়, যাবতীয়, *a.* all, entire, the whole.
যাবদ্দেশে, *ad.* throughout, everywhere.
যাবনিক, *a.* belonging to a foreigner.
যাম, *s.* a watch, the 4th part of the day or night.
যামাতা, *s.* a daughter's husband.
যামিক, *a.* relating to the watches of the day or night; -ভট, a watchman.
যামিনী, *s.* a night; -পতি, the moon.
যাম্য, *s.* the south quarter.
*য়ার, a friend; -কী, friendship; -বাস, fond of friends; -বাসী, attached to friends.
যিনি, *hon. pr.* who, he who, the person who.
যুক্, or যুক্ত্, *v. a.* to measure, to weigh, to take dimensions.
যুক, *s.* a pair of scales for weighing, a steelyard.
যুকৎ, *s.* art, skill, habit, knack, dexterity.
যুক্ত, *a.* connected with, yoked, joined to, united with, being in contact with, fit, right, proper, proved, possessed of, endowed with, intent on, attached to.
যুক্তাক্ষর, *s.* a compound letter.
যুক্তি, *s.* a logical conclusion, advice, counsel, policy, a contrivance, propriety, fitness, usage, custom, reason, an inference, a specification, union, connection.
যুক্তিকর্তা, *s.* a person who draws a conclusion or inference, a reasoner.
যুক্তিদাতা, *s.* a counsellor, one who gives advice.
যুক্তিপূর্ব্বক, *ad.* by or through reason.
যুক্তিবিরুদ্ধ, *a.* contrary to reason.
যুক্তিবিশিষ্ট, *a.* reasonable, proper, right, fit.
যুক্তিসিদ্ধ, *a.* concluded by reason, logical.
যুগ, *s.* an age of the world, a dispensation; the Hindus reckon four yugas, viz. the Satya, Tretá, Dwápara, and Kali; a yoke, a pair, a couple, measure of four cubits, a period of twelve years.
যুগধর্ম্ম, *s.* religion or duties peculiar to an age.
যুগপদ্, যুগপৎ, *ad.* at once, at one time.

যুগল, যুগ্ম, *s.* a pair, couple, brace, a yoke, two animals of the same kind, an animal which matches with another; a mate.
যুগান্ত, *s.* the end of an age.
যুজ্যমান, *a.* under process of being joined or united.
যুঝ্, *v. a.* to fight, to resist.
যুট্, *v. n.* to assemble, to come to a person or place, to be provided, to be supplied.
যুড়্, *v. a.* to join, to cement, to unite, to commence: *v. n.* to be overspread.
যুড়ন, *s.* the joining or uniting of things, a cementing, a commencing.
যুড়া, *v. n.* to become cool, to be comforted, to be glad, to be gratified: *s.* cool.
যুড়ান, *a.* cooled, comforted, gratified: *s.* a becoming cool, a being gratified.
যুড়ি, *s.* a pair, a match.
যুত, *a.* connected, united, endowed or in contact with, joined to: *s.* connexion.
যুথ, *s.* a herd, a drove, a flock, multitude.
যুদ্ধ, *s.* a battle, war, a combat, a conflict.
যুদ্ধকর্ত্তা, *s.* one who makes war, a warrior.
যুদ্ধকুশল, যুদ্ধনিপুণ, *a.* eminent in war.
যুদ্ধকৌশল, *s.* skill in war.
যুদ্ধবিরতি, যুদ্ধবিরাম, *s.* a cessation of war, a truce.
যুদ্ধভঙ্গ, *s.* a defeat, a desisting from war.
যুদ্ধসজ্জা, সাঁজআ, *s.* armour, war dress.
যুদ্ধসামগ্রী, *s.* ammunition, warlike stores.
যুদ্ধস্থল, *s.* the field of battle, battle-field.
যুদ্ধোপক্রম, *s.* the commencement of war.
যুধিষ্ঠির, *a.* firm in battle: *s.* the name of the eldest of the five Pándavas.
যুব, যুবক, young, youthful, adult: *s.* a young man.
যুবতী, *a.* youthful: *s.* a young woman.
যুবত্ব, or যুবতা, *s.* youth, youthfulness.
যুবন্, *a.* young, good, excellent, arrived at the age of puberty.
যুবরাজ, *s.* a prince, the heir-apparent.
যুবা, *a.* young, youthful: *s.* a young man.
যুষ্মদ্, *pron.* you, thee, thou.
যুষ্মদীয়, *a.* thy, thine, yours, belonging to you.
যূই, যূথী, যূথিকা, *s.* a species of jasmine.[1]
যূঁইপাণা, *s.* a shrub (Justicia nasuta).
যূক, *s.* a louse; a pair of scales.
যুতি, *s.* a mixture, a junction, an additive number, addition.
যূথ, *s.* a flock, herd, drove, swarm, covey, a multitude.
যূপ, *s.* a sacrificial post, post, pillar, stake.
যূষ, *s.* soup, broth, gravy, pease porridge.
যে, *pron.* he who, that which: *conj.* that.
যেঅবধি, *ad.* from which time.
যেকালে, *ad.* when, at what time.
যেকিছু, *pron.* whatever, whichever.
যেকেহ, *pron.* whosoever, whoever.
যেকোন, *pron.* whoever, whatever.
যেক্ষণে, *ad.* when, at what time.
যেখনতেখন, *ad.* now and then, occasionally.
যেথা, or যেখানে, *ad.* where, whither.
যেন, *ad.* in order that, therefore; as if.
যেপর্য্যন্ত, *ad.* till, until, whilst.
যেপ্রকার, *ad.* what sort, what kind.
যেমত, যেমন, *ad.* as, like, like as.
যেমনতেমন, *ad.* the same, just as it was, any way.
যেযে, *pron.* whoever, whatever.
যেরূপ, *s.* what manner: *ad.* as, such as, like as.
যেরূপে, *ad.* as, like as, in what manner.
যেস্থানে, *ad.* where, wherever.
যেহেতুক, *conj.* because, for, forasmuch as.
যো, *s.* a stock, a capital; *vide* যোকাঠি.
যোঁকা, *v. a.* to measure, take dimensions: *s.* measure, dimensions; also, a plant.
যোঁকান, *s.* a taking the measure of a thing.
যোঁকানি, *s.* the dimensions of a thing.
যোঁয়ালি, *s.* a yoke, a yoke for cattle.
যোকাঠি, *s.* the rods which run across the warp of a piece of cloth in the loom.
যোক্তা, *s.* he who joins or unites; a purveyor, provider.
যোক্ত্র, *s.* the tie of a yoke.
যোগ, *s.* contact, a conjunction, a union, a mixture, a junction, addition, a consequence, result, a juncture, contemplation, the abstraction of the mind from all foreign objects and fixing it on one alone, an expedient, lucky conjuncture, propriety, fitness, the connection of one thing with another as the cause with the effect, the predicate with the subject, the quality with the substance, etc.
যোগক্ষেম, *s.* the transport of goods, preservation of acquired articles, articles of property not divisible to co-heirs.
যোগধর্ম্ম, *s.* religious merit of meditation.
যোগনিদ্রা, *s.* sleep which admits of the full exercise of the mental powers.

যোগপাদুকা, *s* magical shoes having the property of conveying one anywhere.

যোগপাদুকারোহণ, *s.* the putting on of the shoes having the aforesaid property.

যোগপূর্ব্বক, *ad.* by or through junction or union, or fixed contemplation on God.

যোগবল, *s.* virtue of meditation, the power arising from contemplation on God.

যোগভঙ্গ, *s.* a breaking off the mind from contemplation on God.

যোগরূঢ়, *a.* used only in a particular sense, having a particular meaning.

যোগা, *v. a.* to supply, furnish, provide.

যোগাড়, *s.* assistance, a supply, assisting of a workman, a workman's assistant.

যোগাড়িয়া, *s.* an assistant, an auxiliary, a bricklayer's assistant or labourer.

যোগান, *s.* supplying of necessaries for an occasion, or of materials for a work.

যোগানিয়া, যোগান্যা, *a.* supplying necessaries, providing: *s.* one who supplies.

যোগারূঢ়, *a.* continuing in a state of abstraction, or contemplation upon God.

যোগাসন, *s.* a posture assisting the mind in close contemplation upon God.

যোগিনিদ্রা, *s.* light slumber, a doze: *vide* [যোগনিদ্রা,

যোগিনী, *s.* a female devotee.

যোগী, *s.* an ascetic, a devotee; a weaver.

যোগীশ্বর, *s.* Shiva, a name of Yájnávalká.

যোগে, *ad.* conjointly, through, by means [of.

যোগেযাগে, *ad.* somehow or other.

যোগ্য, *a.* worthy, capable, suitable, fit, adequate, proper, liable to, able.

যোগ্যতা, *s.* worthiness, fitness, a capacity, ability, a qualification. [thiness.

যোগ্যতাপন্ন, *a.* possessed of fitness or wor-

যোঙড়া, *s.* a bivalve shell, cockle-shell.

যোজক, *a.* uniting, joining, causing union: *s.* a negotiator, marriage, matchmaker.

যোজন, *s.* a uniting; a measure of distance containing 4 krosha or about 8 miles.

যোজনা, *s.* the supplying of materials or necessaries; union, conjuncture.

যোজনীয়, or যোজ্য, *a.* capable of being brought into union or contact.

যোট্, *v. a.* to connect, to pair, to yoke animals, to mix, to incorporate.

যোট, *s.* one of a pair, a match.

যোটক, *s.* a broker, factor, an agent, manager, a matchmaker, a negotiator.

যোটন, যোটনা, *s.* the yoking of animals to a carriage or plough, a cementing.

যোটপাট, *s.* the supplying of any thing.

যোটা, *v. n.* to match, to pair, to yoke animals, to incorporate: *a.* matched, paired, yoked: *s.* the same as যোটান.

যোটান, *s.* a joining, matching, pairing, yoking, negotiating: *a.* yoked, paired.

যোটাযোটি, *s.* a reciprocal matching or [pairing.

যোটী *s.* one of a pair, a match.

যোড়, *a.* joined: *s.* a pair, couple, junction, union, one of a pair, a match: a patch, seam, joining, suture; -লাগ্, to match, pair, unite, cohabit; -দা, to patch, join.

যোড়ন, *s.* a joining, cementing, uniting, a commencing; rennet to curdle milk.

যোড়া, *a.* joined: *s.* a couple, pair, suit (of clothes,) union, connection: *v. a.* to connect, unite, affix, add, cement together.

যোড়ান, *s.* a connecting or uniting, a joining or adding, the grafting of a tree: *a.* united, joined, added, affixed, grafted.

যোড়িত, *a.* embroidered, united, connected, cemented, grafted. [rhyme.

যোড়েতাড়ে, *ad.* in a rhyming manner, in

যোত, *s.* a farm; the string which fastens the plough to the yoke of the cattle.

যোতদার, *a.* holding a farm: *s.* a farmer.

যোতা, *s.* a farm, ploughed land.

যোত্র, *s.* a capital, a stock, wealth, a person's capital or ability to expend.

যোত্রাপন্ন, *a.* possessed of stock or capital, rich, wealthy, opulent. [combatant.

যোদ্ধা, *s.* a warrior, a soldier, a wrestler, a

যোনি, *s.* a cause, origin, the original of things, the vulva, womb, site of birth.

যোনিকীট, *s.* a lecher, a lascivious person.

যোনিজ, *a.* viviparous, producing young.

যোনিপার্শ্ব, *s.* in *ana.* labiæ pudendæ.

যোনিভাঁজ, *s.* the nymphæ.

যোনিলিঙ্গ, *s.* the clitoris. [youthfulness.

যোবান, *a.* young, youthful. যোবানি, *s.*

যোষিৎ, *s.* a woman, a female.

যোষিদ্বর্গ, *s.* womankind, class of females.

যৌ, *s.* lac, gum lac, wax; -বাতী stick-lac.
যৌক্তিক, *a.* founded on reasoning, logical, inferrible, proper. [from the root.
যৌগিক, *a.* derivative, formed regularly
যৌগিকশব্দ, *s.* a word formed from the root, a derivative word.
যৌতুক, *s.* a dower, a marriage portion.
যৌবন, *s.* the age of puberty, youth, youthfulness; -বিশিষ্ট, young, youthful.
যৌবনাবস্থা, *s.* state of youth, youthfulness.
যৌবরাজ্য, *s.* office of a prince associated with his father in the government.

র, the twenty-seventh consonant in the Bengáli alphabet: *v. n.* to stay, to stop.
রইকাঠ, *s.* a post placed erect in a pond to measure its depth.
রওআনা, *s.* a pass for goods; a going.
রকম, *s.* a sort, kind, species, a manner.
রক্ত, *a.* red, blood-red: *s.* blood; -ক্ষর, -পড়্, to bleed; -স্রু; -ভাঙ্গ, to discharge blood, to have the lochia or issue of blood.
রক্তক, রক্তকম্বল, *s.* a species of waterlily.[1]
রক্তক্ষরণ, *s.* the oozing of blood, bleeding.
রক্তখেকুয়া, *a.* sanguinary; drinking the blood of the menses (a term of abuse).
রক্তগঙ্গা, *s.* a Ganges of blood; (*met.*) copious streams of blood.
রক্তচন্দন, *s.* red sanders,[2] red sandalwood.
রক্তজনক, hæmapoietic, blood-producing.
রক্তজ্বরা, *s.* slight fever attending a convalescent person recovered from fever.
রক্তদুষ্ট, *s.* a diseased state of the blood.
রক্তধমনাড়ী, *s.* a vein, artery, a blood-vessel.
রক্তপঙ্কল, *s.* the lochia, the issue of blood.
রক্তপদ্ম, *s.* the large red waterlily.[3]
রক্তপা, *s.* a leech, a blood-sucker. [ing.
রক্তপাত, *s.* the shedding of blood, a bleed-
রক্তপিত্ত, *s.* a vitiated state of blood and bile causing the spontaneous discharge of blood from the nose or mouth.
রক্তপ্রবাহক, রক্তবাহক, -নাড়ী, *s.* a vein, an
রক্তবন্ধ, *s.* a stopping of blood. [artery.
রক্তবর্ণ, *a.* red, blood-colour. [the blood.
রক্তবিকার, *s.* a change or diseased state of
রক্তভাঙ্গন, *s.* a morbid discharge of blood from the uterus, lochia, issue of blood.
রক্তময়, *a.* bloody, full of blood. [blood.
রক্তমোক্ষক, *s.* a phlebotomist, one who lets
রক্তমোক্ষণ, *s.* phlebotomy, the act of letting blood; -কৃ, to phlebotomise.
রক্তযুক্ত, রক্তযুত, *a.* bloody, full of blood.
রক্তলিপ্ত, রক্তাক্ত, *a.* smeared with blood,
রক্তস্রাব, *s.* an hemorrhage. [bloody.
রক্তারক্তি, *s.* a mutual shedding of blood.
রক্তিকা, *s.* the seeds of Abrus precatorius.
রক্তিমা, *s.* redness; -বর্ণ, red colour.
রক্তোৎপল, *s.* a kind of lotus; *vide* রক্তক.
রক্তোপল, *s.* red-ochre; red-stone, a ruby.
রক্ষক, *s.* a keeper, one who preserves or guards, a watchman, a protector.
রক্ষণ, *s.* the preserving or taking care of a thing, the protecting of a person.
রক্ষণীয়, রক্ষিতব্য, *a.* capable of being preserved, salvable, defensible, preservable.
রক্ষা, *s.* preservation, salvation, protection, defence, escape, security; -কৃ, to save.
রক্ষাকর্তা, রক্ষিতা, *s.* a preserver, keeper, saviour, defender, protector, guardian.
রক্ষিত, kept, preserved, defended, guarded, protected, saved. [tion or defence.
রক্ষ্যমাণ, *a.* under the process of preserva-
রগ, or রগ্গা, *s.* a sinew, a nerve, a vein.
রগচটানা, convulsed, distorted, headstrong.
রগড়্, or রগড়া, *v. a.* to rub as clothes, to rub the body, to rub out corn or seed.
রগড়, *s.* the quick beating of a drum.
রগড়ন, রগড়ান, *s.* a rubbing, scrubbing,
রগসন্ধি, *s.* a tendon, ganglion. [treading.
রঘু, *s.* proper name, Ráma's grandfather.
রঘুনন্দন, রঘুনাথ, *s.* names of Ráma.
রঘুবংশ, *s.* the race of Raghu; the poem which treats of the ancestors of Ráma.
রঙ্, *v. a.* to colour, to dye, to paint.
রঙ্গ, *s.* paint, colour, dye; dancing, acting, singing, sport, fun, merriment; field of battle; -দা, or -কৃ, to paint, dye, colour.
রঙ্গকর, রঙ্গানিয়া, *a.* dying: *s.* a dyer.
রঙ্গচঙ্গ, *s.* gaudiness, glaring or fine colour.
রঙ্গচঙ্গিয়া, *a.* glaring, fine, gaudy, showy.
রঙ্গজীবিক, *s.* an actor, a dancer, a painter.
রঙ্গণ, *s.* a dying, colouring; a red flower.
রঙ্গভঙ্গ, *s.* dramatic antics, lascivious gestures, wantonness, sport, merriment.

রঙ্গভূমি, *s.* field of battle, a theatre, stage, [arena.
রঙ্গমাতৃকা, *s.* lac, the lac insect.
রঙ্গরস, *s.* merriment, sport, fun, pleasure.
রঙ্গরেজ, *s.* a dyer, a dyer of native clothes.
রঙ্গা, *v. a.* to colour, to paint, to dye.
রঙ্গাণ, *s.* the communicating of a colour, the making of a person blush. [showy.
রঙ্গিল, রঙ্গিলা, *a.* gay, gaudy, splendid,
রঙ্গী, *a.* colouring, painting, dying; exhibiting shows or sports; impassioned.
রঙ্গীন, *a.* coloured, gaudy; impassioned.
রচ্, *v. a.* to compose (a work), to invent, make, fabricate, to string flowers, etc.
রচক, *a.* making, composing, fabricating: *s.* an author, a compiler, a maker.
রচন, *s.* a making, forming, composing.
রচনা, *s.* an orderly arrangement of parts, the decoration of the hair, the stringing of flowers, fabrication, composition, a making, a contriving, an inventing.
রচনীয়, রচয়িতব্য, *a.* fabricable, formable, capable of being made or composed.
রচয়িতা, *s.* an author, a maker, fabricator.
রচা, *s.* a making, composition: *a.* made, composed, fabricated. [cated.
রচিত, *a.* made, composed, written, fabri-
রজঃ, or রজস্, *s.* dust, powder, farina or pollen of a flower, the menses; secularity, the quality of activity or passion.
রজক, *s.* a washerman; *fem.* রজকী.
রজত, *s.* a necklace, silver, ivory: *a.* white.
রজনী, *s.* night; turmeric; -কর, the moon.
রজনীগন্ধ, *s.* the tuberose (Polianthes tuberosa).
রজস্বলা, *a.* menstruous.
রজোগুণ, *s.* the second quality inherent in matter, *viz.* the motive or active power (applied to inanimate matter), passion or activity (applied to animate matter).
রজ্জু, *s.* a halter, rope, cord, line, string.
রঞ্জক, *a.* jovial, merry, pleasing, cheering, exciting: *s.* priming powder; a painter; a stimulant; -দিয়া, to prime a gun.
রঞ্জকঘরা, *s.* the touch-hole of a gun.
রঞ্জন, *s.* an exciting, pleasing; painting.
রট, রটা, *v. a.* to speak, to proclaim, to report, to announce. [licity, fame.
রটনা, রটন, *s.* a talk, report, rumour, pub-
রটা, *s.* a speech, a declaration, a report.
রটান, *s.* a speaking, proclaiming, publish- [ing.
রটিত, *a.* spoken, uttered, rumoured.
রড়্, রড়া, *v.* to run, fly; to cause to run.
রণ, *s.* war, battle, a fight, a conflict.
রণকর্তা, *s.* one who makes war, a warrior.
রণকুআসা, *s.* a thick fog or mist.
রণজয়, *s.* victory. রণজয়ী, *a.* victorious.
রণজেতা, *s.* a conqueror in battle, a victor.
রণপণ্ডিত, *a.* skilled in the art of war.
রণ-বিরতি, -বিরাম, *s.* the cessation of war.
রণভঙ্গ, *s.* a defeat, the breaking of ranks, [a rout.
রণ-ভূমি, -স্থল, *s.* a field of battle.
রণসজ্জা, *s.* the accoutrements of war.
রণসিঙ্গা, *s.* a war-conch, a war-trumpet.
রণ্ড, *a.* forlorn, dying without male issue, irreligious: *s.* a widower; barren tree.
রণ্ডা, barren, sterile, childless; *s.* a widow.
রণ্ডী, *s.* a widow, woman; -বাজ, a lecher.
রত, *a.* delighted with, devoted to: *s.* copu- [lation.
রতার্থী, lewd, lascivious, lustful.
রতি, *s.* sensual enjoyment, pleasure, coition; -ক্রিয়া, coition; -দান, the act of coition; -পতি, the Indian Cupid; -শক্তি, virile power; also, *vide* রত্তি.
রতিরঙ্গ, *s.* sport and pleasure, coition.
রত্তি, রত্তিকা, *s.* the seed of Abrus precatorius; a little, a small quantity, a grain.
রত্ন, *s.* a gem, jewel, precious stone, any [thing valuable.
রত্নকন্দল, *s.* coral.
রত্নখচিত, *a.* set with jewels or gems.
রত্নগর্ভা, *s.* the earth; a woman whose children are blessings to her.
রত্নজীবী, *a.* living by gems: *s.* a jeweller.
রত্নময়, *a.* gemmy, abounding with gems.
রত্নসিংহাসন, *s.* a jewelled throne.
রত্নাকর, রত্নগর্ভ, *s.* a mine of gems; the [sea.
রত্নাবলী, *s.* a string of jewels.
রত্নি, *s.* a cubit with closed fingers.
রত্যাসক্ত, *a.* lascivious, lecherous, fond of [pleasure.
রথ, *s.* a car, chariot, carriage.
রথকার, *s.* a wheelwright, a coachmaker.
রথযাত্রা, *s.* the car festival of Jagannáth.
রথযাত্রী, *a.* attending the car festival.
রথী, *s.* a charioteer, coachman. [highway.
রথ্যা, *s.* a public street, a carriage road, a
রদ, *s.* a tooth, a tusk; rejection, rescind-

ing of a law, prevention; -কৃ, to prevent, stop work, to hinder, rescind, disprove.
রদন, s. a tooth, a tusk.
রদী, a. toothed; rejected: s. an elephant.
*রদ্দজবাব, s. a rejoinder.
*রদ্‌বদল, s. argument, discussion, altercation.
রন্ধ্, v. a. to cook food, to dress, to boil.
রন্ধন, s. the cooking or dressing of food.
রন্ধনশালা, s. a kitchen, a cookroom.
রন্ধনার্হ, a. fit or proper for cooking.
রন্ধ্র, s. a cavity, a hole, the eye of a needle, a vent, a fissure, a chasm, a fault.
*রপ্টু, রপ্টা, v. a. to toil, to wander about.
রপ্টানি, s. toil, endeavour, labour.
*রপ্তানি, s. the exporting of goods.
*রফা, s. the settlement of a dispute.
রফাদার, s. the settler of disputes.
রফানামা, s. a deed of settlement.
*রফু, s. the mending or darning of clothes.
রফুকর, s. a tailor, one who darns cloth.
*রফ্তু, s. a going; practice, habit, use.
রফ্তানি, s. a going, the exporting of goods.
রব, s. a sound, a voice, a noise, rumour.
*রবানা, s. a going, a pass for goods.
রবাহূত, a. led by report, called, invited.
রবি, s. the sun; -বার, Sunday.
রবিশস্য, a. ripened by the sun: s. cold season crop.
রমণ, s. sensual enjoyment, coition, sport, play, amorous dalliance, a lover, a gallant, Indian Cupid, a husband, memory.
রমণা, s. a park, pleasure ground; *vide* রমণী.
রমণার্থী, a. lascivious, lecherous.
রমণী, s. woman, agreeable woman, a wife, mistress; -গণ, body of amorous women.
রমণীয়, a. beautiful, pleasing, pleasant, delightful, charming, lovely.
রমা, s. a name of Lakshmí, wife of Vishnu.
রম্ভা, s. plantain;[1] a celestial dancing girl.
রম্য, a. lovely, beautiful, charming, pleasing, pleasant, pleasurable, agreeable.
রলা, s. a shoot, sprout, scion, twig, a small branch; a rod, a thin post or timber.
রল্লক, s. a blanket, a rug; an eyelash.
রশনা, s. a bridle, a rein, a halter.
রশুন, s. a garlic (Allium sativum).
রশুনা, s. a species of cive or shalot.[2]
রশুনীয়া, s. the cat's eye gem.

রশ্মি, s. a sunbeam, a ray of light.
রষাণ, s. a touch-stone.
রস্, v. n. to swell, to become œdomatous, to become puffy, to fester, to be damp.
রস, s. savour of a thing, taste, flavour, relish, carnal enjoyment, sensuality, the pith or marrow of a discourse, taste or sentiment in a literary sense, wit; an affection of the mind, passion, juice, sap, exudation, a fluid, liquid, semen virile, metal, quicksilver, water, primary fluid of the body, chyle, serum and other fluids, gum, myrrh, mineral salt.
রসক, a. rosacic: s. stewed meat.
রসকরা, made savoury: s. a kind of sweetmeat.
রসকর্পূর, রসকাপূর, s. a white muriate of mercury, quicksilver.
রসকস, s. sentiment and feeling, pith and juice.
রসগর্ভ, s. vermillion; a kind of stibium.
রসজ, a. produced in liquids: s. an animalcule produced in liquids; blood.
রসজ্বর, s. fever arising from indigestion.
*রসদ, s. grain or provision for an army.
রসন, s. a tasting, taste; a festering, rotting; dampness; sound, noise.
রসনা, জিহ্বা, s. the tongue, organ of taste.
রসনেত্রিকা, s. red arsenic.
রসনেন্দ্রিয়, s. the organ of tasting, the tongue.
রসবৎ, or রসবান্, a. tasteful, juicy, well-flavored.
রসবাত, s. rheumatism, gout.
রসময়, a. sentimental, juicy, savoury.
রসযুক্ত, রসযুত, a. sapid, savoury, juicy.
রসরাজ, s. quicksilver, mercury.
রসশোধন, s. borax; *vide* সোহাগা.
রসসিদ্ধ, s. an alchymist, a chymist.
রসসিদ্ধি, s. the knowledge of alchymy.
রসা, v. a. to wet, make tumid: s. the earth; a rope, a halter, a line: a. wet, juicy.
রসাঞ্জন, s. a kind of stibium.
রসাতল, s. lowest division of the infernal regions.
রসাদান, s. suction, drying up, absorption.
রসান, s. a causing to swell.
রসানি, s. purulent matter, sanies, serum.
রসাভাস, a. hiding the feelings: s. strife.
রসায়ন, s. poison, a medicine to prolong life (elixir vitæ), alchymy, chymistry.
রসায়নবিদ্যা, s. chymistry, alchymy.

রসায়নাকর্ষণশক্তি, s. elective attraction.
রসাল, savoury, juicy, delicious: a mango.
রসাসিন্দুর, s. a medicinal cinnabar made of zinc, mercury, blue vitriol and nitre.
রসাস্বাদ, s. realizing the taste.
রসাঢ্য, s. turpentine, resin. [morous.
রসিক, a. jocose, droll, merry, witty, hu-
রসিক-চূড়ামণি, -শিরোমণি, s. one eminent for wit or jocularity, an eminent wit.
রসিকতা, -ত্ব, s. jocularity, wittiness, drollery, merriment, humour.
রসিকরাজ s. an eminently witty or jocose person, an eminent wit; quicksilver.
রসিকা, a. jocose, witty: s. a coquette.
রসিদ, s. *Eng.* a receipt, an acknowledge-
রসী, s. a cord, a line, a halter. [ment.
রসুই, s. the cooking of food, cookery.
রসুন, s. garlic: *vide* রশুন. [quisite.
*রসুম, s. postage, duty, toll, tax, a fee, per-
রসুয়া, a. cooking: s. a cook. [stone.
রসেন্দ্র, s. quicksilver, the philosopher's
রহ্, v. n. to stop, to desist, to cease, to continue, to stay, to endure, to subsist.
রহণ, s. a staying, remaining, continuing
রহনিয়া, a. residing: s. an inhabitant.
রহস্, ad. alone, in solitude, privately.
রহস্য, s. a common saying, a proverb; a sight, a show, diversion; a retirement, solitude; -স্থান, a place of retirement.
রহা, s. a remaining, staying, a desisting.
রহিত, a. destitute, bereft, free from.
রা, s. a word, sound. [monger, a lecher.
রাঁড়, s. a widow, woman; -বাজ, a whore-
রাঁড়বাজী, s. whoremongery, licentiousness.
রাঁড়া, রাঁড়াল, a. barren, sterile, fruitless.
রাঁড়াগাছ, s. a barren or fruitless tree.
রাঁধ্, v. a. to cook, to cook or dress food.
রাঁধন, s. the cooking or dressing of food.
রাঁধনি, a. cooking: s. a cook, cookery.
রাঁধনিয়া, a. cooking: a cook. [cook.
রাঁধনী, s. the Bengal parsley;[1] a female
রাই, s. mustard, a species of mustard.[2]
*রাইয়ৎ, s. a tenant, a subject, tenantry.
রাইয়তী, a. tenantable, tenanted.
রাঈ, s. a species of mustard;[2] a name of Rádhá the mistress of Krishna.
রাউটী, s. a small tent, a travelling tent.

রাং, রাংতা, s. *vide* রাঙ্গ, &c. [moon.
রাকা, s. the full moon, the day of the full
রাকাড়্, v. n. to reply to a call, to answer.
রাক্ষস, s. a monster, a demon, a giant, a cannibal, a fiend, a titan, goblin, ogre.
রাক্ষসী, s. a female Rákshasa, a giantess, a female cannibal, a virago, a vixen.
রাক্ষসীবেলা, s. the evening twilight.
রাক্ষসেন্দ্র, s. Rávana, king of giants.
রাখ্, v. a. to keep, preserve, lay down, to place or put by, to defend, to protect.
রাখন, s. keeping, preserving, or placing of a thing, a defending or protecting; the keeping of cattle. [keeper.
রাখলামী, s. guardianship, the office of a
রাখা, a. kept, preserved: s. a keeping or preserving: v. a. to cause to keep, preserve, or lay by, to cause to tend cattle.
রাখাঢাকা, a. laid down, kept secret.
রাখাণ, s. a causing to lay a thing down: a. laid down, guarded, preserved.
রাখাল, s. a keeper, a cowherd, shepherd.
রাখালি, s. business of a keeper or shepherd, the pay of a guardian or keeper.
রাখিপূর্ণিমা, s. the day of the full moon of Shrávana observed as a festival.
রাগ্, v. n. to madden with anger or passion, to be angry, to be irritated.
রাগ, s. passion, love, anger, envy, the passion in general, distress, lust, a tune: -কৃ, to be angry, to be irritated.
রাগকর, a. exasperating, provoking.
রাগতঃ, a. angry, passionate, irascible.
রাগপূর্ব্বক, ad. passionately, angrily.
রাগসম্বরণ, s. the restraining of passion.
রাগান্ধ, a. blind with anger. [irritable.
রাগান্বিত, রাগাসক্ত, a. passionate, irascible,
রাগারাগী, s. anger, exhibition of passion.
রাগাল, the same as রাগী. [tion of tunes.
রাগিণী, s. in *music*, a female personifica-
রাগী, a. passionate, irascible, irritable.
রাগীভূত, a. become passionate or irascible.
রাঘব, s. Ráma, the descendant of Raghu; uninvited guest; a fortune-teller.
রাঘববোআল, a fish (Silurus pelorius?)
রাঙ্গ, s. tin; paint, colour; -ঝালি, solder, a
রাঙ্গতা, s. leaf tin, tinfoil. [soldering.

রাঙ্গা, *s.* tin : *a.* red, scarlet : *v. a.* to colour, to dye ; -নটীয়া, a common potherb.[1]
রাঙ্গাচোঙ্গা, *a.* red. রাঙ্গাণিয়া, *s.* a dyer.
রাঙ্গাটিয়া, রাঙ্গড়াটিয়া, reddish, rather red.
রাঙ্গাণ, *s.* a dying, colouring of any thing.
রাঙ্গামুখ, *a.* red-faced ; (*fig.*) a master.
রাঙ্গামুলা, *s.* a red radish ; (*fig.*) handsome but ignorant. রাঙ্গাশাক, *s.* a potherb.[2]
রাজ, *s.* a bricklayer, a mason ; in *comp.* it means royal ; also, a king, a prince.
রাজকর, *s.* a tax, tribute, royal revenue.
রাজকর্ম্ম, রাজকার্য্য, *s.* royal duty, the duty of a king, a government affair, politics.
রাজকীয়, *a.* royal, kingly, belonging to a
রাজকুমার, *s.* a prince, king's son. [king.
রাজকুমারী, or রাজকন্যা, *s.* a princess.
রাজকুল, *s.* a royal family, royal race.
রাজগাঁড়, *s.* a boil on the belly. [regicide.
রাজঘাতক, *a.* king-killing, treasonous : *s.* a
রাজজ্ঞান, politics, science of government.
রাজটীকা, রাজতিলক, *s.* the coronation of a king, the installation of a sovereign.
রাজতা, *s.* kingship, royalty, government.
রাজতী, *s.* empire, government. [sway.
রাজত্ব, *s.* royalty, government, empire,
রাজদণ্ড, *s.* a sceptre, a fine paid to a king.
রাজ-দ্রোহ, *s.* treason, rebellion ; -দ্রোহী,
রাজদ্বার, royal gate ; a levee. [treasonous.
রাজধর্ম্ম, *s.* the royal duties or virtues.
রাজধর্ম্মানুষ্ঠান, *s.* practice of royal duties.
রাজধানী, *s.* the royal residence, a king's palace, the capital city of a kingdom.
রাজন্, *s.* a king, a sovereign. [al ethics.
রাজনীতি, *s.* political science, politics, roy-
রাজন্য, *a.* of royal birth : *s.* a kshyetriya, a royal descendant, a prince.
রাজপথ, রাজমার্গ, *s.* king's highway, pub-
রাজপাট, *s.* a royal throne. [lic road.
রাজপুত, রাজপুত্র, *s.* a king's son, a kshyetriya, a person of the military tribe.
রাজপুর, রাজপুরী, *s.* royal city, a capital.
রাজবংশীয়, রাজবংশ্য, connected with or relating to a royal family. [residence.
রাজবাটী, রাজবাড়ী, *s.* a king's palace or
রাজবুদ্ধি, *s.* the science of government, po-
রাজব্যবহার, *s.* a royal custom. [litics.
রাজমন্ত্রী, *s.* a king's minister or adviser.

রাজমল্ল, *s.* a king's wrestler. [chief wife.
রাজমহিষী, রাজরাণী, *s.* a queen, a king's
রাজযক্ষ্মা, *s.* a pulmonary consumption, an
রাজর্ষি, *s.* a royal sage. [atrophy.
রাজলক্ষণ, *s.* sign of royalty, royal mark.
রাজলক্ষ্মী, রাজশ্রী, *s.* the fortune of a king.
রাজশাসন, *s.* the discipline or government exercised by a king. [royal assembly.
রাজসভা, *s.* a king's court, privy council,
রাজসম্পর্কীয়, belonging to a king, royal.
রাজস্ব, *s.* revenue, tribute, the king's tax.
রাজহংস, রাজহাঁস, *s.* a gander, a goose.
রাজহংসী, *s.* a goose. [at chess.
রাজা, *s.* a king, sovereign prince ; a king
রাজাজ্ঞা, *s.* royal edict, command or decree.
রাজাজ্ঞাবর্ত্তী, *a.* loyal, obedient to the laws.
রাজাধিরাজ, *s.* a sovereign king, emperor.
রাজাবলি, *s.* a list or genealogy of kings.
*রাজ়ী, *s.* pleasure, consent, acquiescence, agreement, satisfaction ; -কৃ, to satisfy.
রাজ়ীনামা, *s.* a written consent or agree-
রাজী, *s.* a row, rank, series, line. [ment.
রাজীব, *s.* a waterlily, lotus ; -লোচন, lotus-
রাজ্ঞী or রাজপত্নী, *s.* a queen. [eyed.
রাজ্য, *s.* a kingdom, empire, realm, region, a nation, government ; -কৃ, to reign.
রাজ্যচ্যুত, *a.* deposed from the kingdom.
রাজ্যছাড়া, *a.* outlandish, foreign.
রাজ্যনীতি, *s.* the laws of a kingdom.
রাজ্যভার, *s.* the weight of the affairs of a
রাজ্যভ্রষ্ট, *a.* *vide* রাজ্যচ্যুত. [kingdom.
রাজ্যাঙ্গ, *s.* the constituent part or requisite member of regal administration, viz. the sovereign, the prime minister, an ally, wealth, territory, strongholds, an army, subjects, and a priest.
রাজ্যাধিকার, *s.* a right to a kingdom.
রাজ্যাধিকারী, *a.* having a right to a kingdom, possessing a kingdom. [dom.
রাজ্যাধিপতি, *s.* the sovereign of a king-
রাজ্যাধিপত্য, *s.* sovereignty. [ment.
রাজ্যাভিষিক্ত, *a.* installed into a govern-
রাজ্যাভিষেক, *s.* the installation of a king.
রাজ্যেশ্বর, *s.* the lord of a kingdom, a king.
রাঢ়, *a.* clownish, rude, uncivilized, barbarous : *s.* country west of the Hugli river.
রাঢ়ামী, *s.* unmannerliness, clownishness.

রাঢ়ি, or রাঢ়ীয়, *s.* a class of bráhmans.
রাণা, *s.* a flight of steps at the landing-place of a river.
রাণী, *s.* a queen.
রাতারাতি, *ad.* in the night, by night.
রাতি, *s.* night; -কাণা, blind at night.
রাতিচরা, *s.* a bat, an imp, a goblin.
রাত্রি, রাত্রী, *s.* a night, night; -কাল, night time.
রাত্রিচর, *a.* prowling by night: *s.* a bat, an imp, a goblin, ghost, a night-prowler.
রাত্রিযোগ, night, the setting in of night; a thief, a robber, a watchman, a guard.
রাত্র্যন্ধ, *a.* blind at night.
রাত্র্যন্ধতা, *s.* the disease of night blindness.
রাদ্ধান্ত, *s.* a logical conclusion.
রাধা, *s.* the 16th mansion in the zodiac; the favourite mistress of Krishna.
রাধিকা, *s.* the mistress of Krishna.
রান্না, *s.* the cooking of food, cookery.
রান্নাঘর, *s.* a kitchen, a cookroom.
রাব, *s.* a sound, a noise, a shout, a yell.
রাবণ, *s.* the giant-sovereign of Lanká.
রাবণি, *s.* a name of Rávana's son Indrajit.
রাম, *s.* Ráma, a king of Ajodhyá and the hero of the Rámáyana, an incarnation of Vishnu; pleasure, enjoyment.
রামকুঁড়্যা, *s.* a cottage, a hut, a cabin.
রামখড়ী, *s.* chalk of a superior quality.
রামঘুঘু, *s.* a beautiful species of dove.[1]
রামচন্দ্র, *s.* one of the names of Ráma.
রামচাকী, *s.* a whirligig, a teetotum.
রামছাগল, *s.* the large beardless goat.[2]
রামতুলসী, *s.* a large species of basil.[3]
রামধনুক, *s.* Ráma's bow, the rainbow.
রামরম্ভা, রামকলা, *s.* a sort of plantain.[4]
রামশালি, *s.* a variety of rice.
রামা, *s.* a woman, a beautiful woman.
রামাৎ, *s.* a votary or follower of Ráma.
রামায়ণ, *s.* a celebrated Hindu epic poem.
রায়, *s.* a prince, a title of honour.
রায়বাঁশ, *s.* a spear, a bambu spear.
রায়বাঁশিয়া, *s.* a spearman, lancer.
রায়বাঘিনী, *s.* a termagant, a virago, a vixen.
রায়রায়ান্, *s.* prince of princes (a title).
রাশি, *s.* a heap of corn, sand, or any loose article, a congeries, a heap, a quantity, a constellation, a sign of the zodiac.
রাশিগত, *a.* arithmetical, algebraic.
রাশিচক্র, *s.* the zodiac.
রাশিনাম, *s.* the name by which any person is called.
রাশিভাগ, *s.* a fraction of an unit.
রাশিভোগ, *s.* passage of the sun, moon, or planets through a sign of the zodiac.
রাশীকৃত, *a.* made into heaps, heaped up, in heaps, accumulated, abundant.
রাশীভূত, become heaps, heaped, abundant.
রাষ্ট্র, *s.* a country, a kingdom, a realm, a province, a public plague, a display.
রাষ্ট্রভঙ্গ, *s.* insurrection, revolution.
রাস, *s.* play, sport, toying, gambol, dalliance; a festival in honour of Krishna.
রাসযাত্রা, *s.* a festival in honour of the gambols of Krishna and the milkmaids.
রাসন, *a.* relating to the organ of tasting.
রাস্তা, *s.* a road, a street, a path, a way.
রাস্না, *s.* the name of a species of Acacia; also, another plant;[5] a sort of perfume.
রাহা, *s.* a road, a path, a way; -খরচ, travelling expenses; -গির্, a traveller.
রাহাজানী, *s.* highway robbery or murder.
রাহাদারী, *s.* a travelling, a pass for goods.
রাহু, *s.* the ascending node or dragon's head; an Asura; -পীড়া, an eclipse.
রাহুগ্রস্ত, *a.* seized by Ráhu, eclipsed (applied to sun and moon).
রাহুগ্রাস, *s.* immersion of a luminary at an eclipse.
রিক্ত, empty, void, destitute, poor, purged by stool: *s.* a forest, emptiness, space.
রিক্তহস্ত, *a.* empty-handed.
রিক্থ, *s.* hereditary property, patrimony, wealth.
রিক্থী, *a.* possessing patrimony: *s.* an heir, successor.
রিজ্, *v. a.* to be glad, to rejoice.
রিঠা, *s.* soapberry, its tree;[6] a sort of fish.[7]
রিপু, *s.* a foe, enemy, adversary.
রিপুগণ, *s.* a body of enemies, a hostile band.
রিষ্ট, *s.* misfortune, loss, injury, privation, destruction, sin; the soapberry tree.[6]
রিষ্টি, *s.* a sword; misfortune, loss, injury.
রিষ্য, *s.* a species of deer; -মুখ, the name of a mountain.
রীঢ়ক, *s.* the backbone.
রীত, *s.* a custom, an usage, a fashion.
রীতি, *s.* a local observance, a custom, a manner, usage, habit, rite, method, natural property or disposition.
রীতিজ্ঞ, *a.* acquainted with usages or customs.

রীতিজ্ঞতা, *s.* an acquaintance with customs
রু, *v. a.* to plant, to set up. [or usages.
রুই, *s.* white-ant; a sort of fish;[1] cotton.
রুক্মন্, *s.* gold; the name of a prince.
রুক্মিণী, *s.* Lakshmí, the goddess of for-
রুক্মিণীকান্ত, *s.* a name of Vishnu. [tune.
রুক্ষ, or রুক্ষী, *a.* morose, rough, scabrous.
রুক্ষিতা, *s.* roughness, scabrosity, morose-
রুধ্, *v. n.* to be angry, be irritated. [ness.
রুশ, *a.* lean, thin, ugly, spare, empty, dry.
রুগ্ন, *a.* diseased, sick, ill, emaciated.
রুগ্নতা, *s.* a diseased condition, sickness.
রুচ্, *v. n.* to be agreeable to the mind or palate, to be approved, to be relished.
রুচি, *s.* a ray, light, lustre, beauty, passion, inclination, wish, desire, appetite, hunger, agreeableness to the senses, taste of food, relish, taste, approbation.
রুচিকর, *a.* provoking appetite or desire.
রুচির, *a.* agreeable, beautiful, charming, amiable, pleasant, sweet, stomachic, restorative, cordial. [ence, comparison.
*রুজু, *s.* appearing, confronting, a refer-
রুটী, *s.* bread, a loaf; -বালা, a baker.
রুদিত, *a.* wept, deplored, lamented. [ed.
রুদ্ধ, *a.* shut, closed, blocked up, obstruct-
রুদ্র, *a.* wrathful, furious, vengeful: *s.* the sun; a demigod; a name of Shiva.
রুদ্রাক্ষ, *s.* a tree,[2] of its seeds rosaries are
রুদ্রাণী, *s.* Durgá, Shiva's wife. [made.
রুদ্রাবতার, *s.* a name of Hanumán.
রুধির, or শোণিত, *s.* blood. [ceedings.
*রুবকারী, *s.* a deposition, a report of pro-
*রুবরু, *ad.* face to face, in the presence
*রুমাল, *s.* a handkerchief. [of, before.
রুয়া, *s.* cotton, hair, wool; thatched-roof rafters, the seeds of a pomegranate.
রুরু, *s.* a species of deer; a giant or evil
রুষ্, *v. n.* to be angry, to fret. [spirit.
রুষ্ট, *a.* vexed, angry, displeased, enraged, furious, passionate, severe.
রুষ্টি, *s.* anger, rage, fury. [raging.
রুষ্টিকর, *a.* provoking to anger, wrathful,
রূঢ়, *a.* produced, born, sprung from seed, sprouted, budded, blown, famous, notorious, certain, ascertained, current.
রূঢ়বচন, or রূঢ়বাক্য, *s.* a word used in a peculiar but well known acceptation, abusive, harsh, or forbidding language.
রূঢ়ি, or রূঢ়িশব্দ, *s.* a word used in a peculiar but well known sense.
রূপ্, *v. a.* to plant, to seminate.
রূপ, *s.* a form, shape, manner, mode, species, kind, nature, beauty, an appearance, a semblance, declension of a noun, conjunction of a verb, the inflection of nouns or verbs, a discrete quality, an unit, an integer, a figure, image, a play, a dramatic poem; in *comp.* like, resembling, identically the same. [rical.
রূপক, *a.* figurative, metaphorical, allego-
রূপকবাক্য, রূপকশব্দ, *s.* a figurative word, a metaphorical expression. [qualities.
রূপগুণবিশিষ্ট, *a.* having beauty and good
রূপচাঁদ, *s.* a prig, a coxcomb, fop, dandy; the name of a bird,[3] also, of a fish.[4]
রূপবন্ত, রূপবান্, *a.* beautiful, symmetrical,
রূপভাগ, *s.* a fraction of an unit. [elegant.
রূপসী, *a.* elegant, beautiful, comely, hand-
রূপস্থান, *s.* a multiple. [some.
রূপা, *s.* silver; -লী, silver, made of silver.
রূপালাপ, *s.* the striking of the key note before singing or playing a tune.
রূপী, *s.* a silver coin, a rupee; a monkey.
রূপ্য, *s.* silver; -ময়, silver, made of silver.
রূপ্যাধ্যক্ষ, *s.* the master of the mint.
রে, রেরে, *voc. par.* employed in addressing a person in contempt, hear, you.
*রেআৎ, *s.* pardon, favour, abatement.
রেউআ, *s.* a class of impostors pretending to know the secrets of providence.
রেউচিনী, *s.* rhubarb, China rhubarb.
রেউড়ি, *s.* a sort of nut-like sweetmeat.
রেঁদা, *s.* a carpenter's plane. [ness.
রেক, *s.* a basket to measure grain; a loose-
*রেকাব, *s.* a stirrup. রেকাবী, *s.* a plate.
রেখা, *s.* a streak, stripe, line, slit; -পড়া, streaked, striped; -ভূমি, the equator.
রেখাকার, রেখাকৃতি, *a.* striped, striated.
*রেখতা, *a.* mixed: *s.* a mortar; a mixed Persian language; a kind of song.
রেচ্, *v. n.* to breathe; to purge by stool.
রেচক, *s.* an expiration of the breath; a cathartic, a purge: *a.* purgative, aperient.

রেচন, *s.* a purging by stool, a looseness;

রেজকি, *s.* a quarter rupee. [respiration.

রেজলা, *a.* impassionate, obstinate, headstrong, vile, base, wicked.

রেজা, *v. a.* to please, to gratify: *s.* a boy who serves a mason, a remnant.

রেজাই, *s.* a quilt, a bed quilt.

রেজান, *s.* a gratifying: *a.* gratified.

রেণু, or রেণুক, *s.* dust, sand, an atom, the pollen of a flower. [charge of semen.

রেতঃ, *s.* semen; sand; -পতন, -স্খলন, dis-

রেতস্, *s.* semen, the seminal fluid.

রেতী, *a.* sandy: *s.* sandy land, a sandbank.

রেপ, *s.* the wards of a lock.

রেফ, *s.* the letter র, or the symbol (ʼ).

রেবত, *s.* the name of an ancient king.

রেবতী, *s.* the wife of Balarám; the last mansion of the Hindu zodiac.

রেবা, *s.* a name of the Narmadá river.

*রেবাজ, *s.* a usage, custom, fashion; fat.

রেভন, *s.* the lowing of kine. [bráhmans.

রেয়ো, *a.* uninvited, uncalled: *s.* a class of

রেল, রেলা, *s.* plenty, a multitude, resort.

*রেশা, *s.* fibres in ripe mangoes or other

রেশাদার, *a.* fibrous, stringy. [fruits.

*রেসবৎ, *s.* a bribe; -খোর, he who takes

রেসবতী, *s.* one who takes bribes. [bribes.

*রেসম, *s.* silk. রেসমী, *a.* silken, of silk.

*রেসালা, *s.* a mission; a troop of horse.

রেসালাদার, *s.* the commander of a resálá.

রৈ, *s.* wealth, riches, a post erected in the midst of a pond when it is consecrated.

রো, *v. a.* to sow, to plant; to cry. [rice).

রোআ, রোআলি, *a.* planted (applied to

রোঁদ, *s. Eng.* a patrol, a round.

রোঁয়া, *s.* hair of the body, or of a beast.

রোঁয়াফোড়া, *s.* a kind of boil of the body.

রোক্, *v. a.* to stop, hinder, prevent, to obstruct, withstand, ward off, to bore.

রোক, *s.* ready cash; an incision, a blemish.

রোকড়, *s.* a cash-book. [banker.

রোকড়িয়া, *s.* a cash-keeper, a treasurer, a

রোকা, *s.* prevention; a letter, short note: *v. a.* to provoke to anger; *vide* রোক্.

রোকাণ, *s.* the provoking one to anger, hindering or obstructing of a thing.

রোক্থোক্, *s.* ready money, cash.

রোক্বিক্রী, *s.* a sale for ready money.

*রোখশোদ, *s.* a dismissal, a discharge.

রোখাল, *a.* passionate, peevish, cross.

রোগ, disease, illness, distemper, sickness.

রোগগ্রস্ত, *a.* taken ill, diseased. [nish.

রোগণ, *s.* varnish, colour, paint; -কৃ, to var-

রোগশান্তি, *s.* the alleviation of disease.

রোগসঞ্চার, *s.* communication of a disease.

রোগান্তক, *a.* curing disease. [sickly.

রোগা, রোগান্বিত, রোগার্ত্ত, *a.* diseased, ill,

রোগিতা, *s.* diseased state, illness, sickness.

রোগী, sick, ill, diseased, sickly: a patient.

রোচক, *a.* gratifying, pleasant, agreeable, exciting appetite, savoury.

রোচনা, *s.* an approval, persuasion; the exciting of appetite; a pigment.

রোচিস্, *s.* light, splendour, brightness.

*রোজ, *s.* a day; -গার, service, earning; -গারী, he who earns; -নামা, a daybook, a journal; -রোজ, daily, every day.

*রোজা, *s.* a voluntary fast. [baker.

রোটী, রোটিকা, *s.* bread, a loaf; -বালা, a

রোদন, *s.* a weeping, a wailing, a lamenting, a crying; -কৃ, to weep, cry, lament.

রোদনীয়, *a.* proper to be wept over or be-

রোদিত, *a.* weeping, wept, cried. [wailed.

রোদ্ধব্য, রোধনীয়, *a.* that may be hindered, obstructed, blockaded or besieged.

রোদ্ধা, *s.* a besieger, one who blockades a place, one who hinders or obstructs.

রোধ্, *v. a.* to obstruct, block up, besiege.

রোধ, *s.* a hindrance, obstruction, obstacle, blockade of a port or city, an embargo, a prohibition, stoppage. [ing.

রোধক, prohibitory, obstructing, blockad-

রোধন, *s.* the fencing round a place, a besieging, a blockading, an obstructing.

রোধিত, *a.* blockaded, obstructed, stopped, shut up, hindered, besieged. [seedsman.

রোপক, *a.* planting: *s.* a planter, sower,

রোপণ, *s.* the planting of trees, the fixing of a stake or pole in the ground.

রোপণকারক, *s.* a person who plants.

রোপণীয়, *a.* fit to be planted or sown.

রোপিত, *a.* sown, planted, inserted, fixed.

রোম, *s.* the hair of the body, or of a beast; down, pubes, the nap of cloth, wool.

রোমকূপ, *s.* the pores of the skin.
রোমন্থায়মান, *a.* chewing the cud; -জন্তু, a ruminating animal. [pilation.
রোমহর্ষ, রোমাঞ্চ, *s.* a bristling up, horri-
রোমাঞ্চিত, *a.* affected with horripilation.
রোমাবলী, *s.* a line or row of hair on the
রোয়ালী, *s.* a seedplot; seedling. [body.
*রোশনচৌকী, *s.* an orchestral music containing Indian hautboy, drum, etc.
রোশনাই, রোশনী, light, splendour, lustre.
রোষ, *s.* anger, passion, wrath, fury.
রোষা, *v. a.* to exasperate, to provoke.
রোষান্বিত, রোষাল, রোষী, angry, choleric, wrathful, passionate, peevish, fretful.
*রোসুম, *s.* a fee, postage, duty, toll, tax.
রোহিণী, *s.* the 4th mansion in the Hindu zodiac; a girl nine years' old. [diac.
রোহিণীনক্ষত্র, *s.* the 4th mansion of the zo-
রোহিত, *s.* a fish much used for the table.[1]
রৌচনিক, *s.* the tartar of the teeth.
রৌদ, *s.* solar heat, sunshine, glare.
রৌদ্র, *s.* solar heat, sunshine, warmth, heat: *a.* acute, sharp, fearful, terrible, dreadful, violent, wrathful, irascible.
রৌপ্য, *a.* silver, made of silver. [hell.
রৌরব, *a.* terrible: *s.* a division of the Hindu
*রৌশন, *a.* conspicuous, light, manifest.
রৌহিণেয়, *s.* Balarám, Mercury; emerald.

ল, the 28th consonant: *v. a.* to take, to receive, to obtain. লইয়া আইসন, to fetch, to bring. লইয়া যাওন, to take away.
লওন, *s.* the taking, receiving, or obtaining of a thing, the accepting of a gift.
লওয়া, *s. idem;* also, *v. a.* to persuade, to convince, to prevail on, to bias a person.
লওয়াজিমা, *s.* necessary things, requisites, furniture, property, effects, baggage.
লওয়ান, *s.* persuasion, the act of biasing.
লক, or লখ, *s.* silk thread for kite-string.
লক্কা, *s.* a species of fan-tailed pigeon.
লকুচ, *s.* lac, lac-dye. [vibrating.
লক্‌লকিয়া, *a.* slender, moving by the wind,
লক্ষ্, *v. a.* to perceive, to mark, to discriminate, to see or notice, to observe.
লক্ষ, *s.* aim, a mark, a sign, a butt, a mark to shoot at: *a.* a hundred thousand.

লক্ষণ, *s.* a discriminating sign or mark, a badge, a token, a mark, an indication.
লক্ষণা, *s.* a metaphor, ellipsis in writing.
লক্ষণাক্রান্ত, *a.* distinguished by a sign.
লক্ষ্মণ, *s.* the brother of Ráma.
লক্ষ্মী, *s.* Vishnu's wife, goddess of fortune, fortune, prosperity; -কান্ত, Vishnu.
লক্ষ্মীছাড়া, abandoned by fortune or prosperity, unfortunate, luckless. [ous.
লক্ষ্মীবন্ত, লক্ষ্মীবান, *a.* fortunate, prosper-
লক্ষ্য, *a.* observable, perceptible, noticeable; a hundred thousand: *s.* aim, mark, a butt, a sign; fraud, disguise.
লগা, *s.* a rod or staff to beat down fruits.
লগী, *s. idem;* a boat-pole, a boat-hook.
লগুড়, *s.* a staff, stick, a club, a bludgeon.
লগ্ন, *a.* adhering to, touching, connected: *s.* junction, a particular portion of time.
লগ্নক, *s.* a bondsman, a surety, a bail.
লগ্নকতা, *s.* suretiship, security for another.
লগ্নকথা, *s.* a speech to the purpose.
লগ্নপত্র, a writing specifying a particular portion of time reckoned propitious.
লগ্নবগ্ন, *ad.* abreast, side by side.
লগ্নিকা, *s.* a girl ten years' old. [tory.
লগ্‌বগীয়া, লগ্‌লগীয়া, *a.* vibrating, vibra-
লঘু, *a.* small, unimportant, light, trifling, trivial; in *algebra,* a lesser surd, the lesser quantity connected with it.
লঘুচ্ছন্দ, *s.* a cadence. [insignificance.
লঘুতা, -ত্ব, *s.* levity, lightness, trivialness,
লঘুত্বপরিমাপক, *s.* a micrometer.
লঘুদোষ, *s.* a small fault, a venial sin.
লঘুপাক, *a.* easy of digestion.
লঘুব্যয়, *s.* thriftiness, frugality, economy.
লঘুব্যয়ী, *a.* frugal, economical. [light.
লঘুভার, *s.* a light burden: *a.* portable,
লঘুভোজন, লঘ্বাহার, *s.* a light meal.
লঘুমূল, *s.* in *algebra,* the least root with reference to the additive qualities.
লঘুমূল্য. *s.* a low price: *a.* low-priced.
লঘুরাশী, a set consisting of fewer terms.
লঘুসমর, *s.* a skirmish, slight war. [urine.
লঘ্বী, *s.* a lesser surd; urine; -কৃ, to expel
লঘ্বীক্রিয়া, *s.* the act of making water.
লঙ্কা, *s.* in *mytho.* a famous city, capital of Rávana, Ceylon island; capsicum.

লঙ্কামরিচ, *s.* capsicum of several species.
লঙ্কাশিজ, a shrub (Euphorbia terecaulis).
লঙ্গ, লং, *s.* clove, clove-tree; *vide* লবঙ্গ.
লঙ্গর, *s.* anchor; -কৃ, to anchor; -তোল, to weigh anchor, (*fig.*) to depart, to die.
লঙ্ঘ, *v. a.* to transgress, to go beyond, to step over, to pass the bounds.
লঙ্ঘক, *a.* transgressing: *s.* a transgressor.
লঙ্ঘন, *s.* the transgressing of a law, a stepping over, or going beyond a limit.
লঙ্ঘনীয়, লঙ্ঘ্য, *a.* transgressible, fit to be transgressed or exceeded. [ed beyond.
লঙ্ঘিত, *a.* transgressed, overstepped, pass-
লজ্জা, *s.* shame, modesty, bashfulness.
লজ্জাকর, *a.* shameful, ignominious. [ful.
লজ্জান্বিত, *a.* modest, shamefaced, bash-
লজ্জাপূর্ব্বক, *ad.* by or through shame.
লজ্জাপ্রযুক্ত, *ad.* from or because of shame.
লজ্জাবান্, লজ্জাবিশিষ্ট, *a.* ashamed, modest, bashful, shamefaced, sheepish.
লজ্জালু, *idem; s.* sensitive plant.[1] [coy.
লজ্জাশীল, *a.* shamefaced, modest, bashful,
লজ্জাহীন, নির্লজ্জ, *a.* shameless, immodest.
লজ্জিত, *a.* ashamed, abashed, coy.
লজ্জুক, *a.* bashful, shamefaced, sheepish.
লট্‌ক্, *v. n.* to hang, swing, be suspended.
লট্‌কন, *s.* a hanging, a being suspended; a species of parrot;[2] the Anotta tree.[3]
লট্‌কা, *v. a.* to hang up, suspend a thing: *s.* magic spell, a charm. [suspending.
লটকান, hanged, suspended: *s.* a hanging,
লট্‌খট্, লট্‌খটিয়া, *a.* intricate, perplexing, troublesome, vexatious, litigious. [cy.
লট্‌খটী, *s.* a labyrinth, perplexity, intrica-
লট্‌পট, *s.* unsteady motion thro' weak-
লটুয়া, *a.* lewd, lascivious, profligate.[ness.
লড়্, *v. n.* to stir, to move, to vibrate, to quiver, to shake, to wag, to fight.
লড়চড়, *a.* unsteady, movable: *s.* motion.
লড়চড়িয়া, wavering, inconstant, moving.
লড়ন, *s.* a shaking, moving, a vibrating, a wagging, stirring; fighting. [and fro.
লড়নচড়ন, *s.* a moving about, a moving to
লড়নী, *s.* agitation, motion, a shaking.
লড়া, *v. a.* to fight, shake, jolt, agitate: *v. n.* to cause to stir, or fight: *s.* motion, a stirring, moving, a shaking; the arm.
লড়াই, *s.* a battle, fight, war; -কৃ, to fight.
লড়াক, *a.* fighting: *s.* a warrior, fighter.
লড়াচড়া, *s.* a moving to and fro, a shaking.
লড়ান, *a.* shaken, agitated, moved about: *s.* a causing to shake, vibrate, or fight.
লড়ালড়ি, *s.* a mutual fighting or scuffling.
লড়িয়াভোলা, *a.* dull, stupid, decrepit.
লড়ী, *s.* a staff, a wand, a cane, a mace, a stick, a switch; a class of Hindus who make lac rings for the wrist of women.
লড়ুকা, *v. n.* to bait a hook, to lay a bait: *s.* a child, a son; *fem.* লড়ুকী.
লডডুকা, *s.* a sweetmeat ball. [dangling.
লড়্‌বড়্, *s.* a shaking about, a staggering,
লড়্‌বড়া, *v. a.* to move about, reel, stagger.
লড়্‌বড়িয়া, *a.* dangling, shaking, unsteady.
লণ্ড, tossing, agitation, staggering; penis.
লণ্ডভণ্ড, *a.* dishevelled, disordered, confused: *s.* ruin, confusion, disorder.
লতা, *s.* a climbing plant, a vine, creeper; -কৃ, to cling to another, creep as a vine.
লতাকদম, *s.* a climbing species of nettle.[4]
লতিকা, *s.* a vine, a creeper.
লনী, লবনী, *s.* butter; (*properly* ননী).
লপন, *s.* a speaking; the mouth.
লপেট, *s.* a wrapping round, wrapping up.
লপেটা, *s.* a kind of ornamented shoes.
লপ্‌ট্, *v. n.* to cling, to adhere, to stick to.
লপ্‌টা, *v. a.* to twine, fold, stick, to wrap.
লপ্‌টান, *s.* a twining together.
লব, *a.* small, little, minute: *s.* a cutting; a son of Ráma; littleness, minuteness.
লবঙ্গ, *s.* clove, the clove tree.[5]
লবঙ্গলতা, *s.* a beautiful scandent shrub.[6]
লবণ, salt, factitious salt; saltness; -সমুদ্র,
লবণাকর, *s.* a salt mine. [the salt sea
লবণাক্ত, *a.* salted, smeared with or steeped
লবণাম্বু, *s.* brine, salt water. [in salt.
*লবাদা, *s.* a cloak, a great-coat.
*লবান, *s.* frankincense, its tree,[7] gum ben-
লবি, *s.* a sickle, a reaping hook. [zoin.
*লব্জ, *s.* a word, a saying. [a son.
লব্ধ, *a.* obtained, gained, got; -পুত্র having
লব্ধক, *s.* the star Sirius, the dogstar.
লব্ধকার্কযোগদিন, *s.* the dog-days.
লব্ধধন, *a.* having acquired wealth.
লব্ধপ্রতিষ্ঠ, *a.* possessed of acquired fame.

লব্ধবিদ্য, *a.* possessed of acquired science.
লব্ধসুখ, possessed of acquired happiness.
লব্ধি, *s.* profit, gain, acquisition, an obtaining, the quotient in division.
লভ্য, *a.* obtainable: *s.* an object of gain, probable gain, profit, the interest of money, a prospect of gain or success.
লভ্যভুক্, *s.* a rapacious person, an usurer.
লভ্যার্থী, *a.* desirous of gain.
লভ্যার্থে, *ad.* for gain. [lewd, libertine.
লম্পট, *a.* immoral, lascivious, dissolute,
লম্পটতা, *s.* lasciviousness, lewdness, lechery, libertinism, fornication.
লম্ফ, *s.* a jump, a leap; -দা, to jump, leap.
লম্ফঝম্ফ, *s.* a jumping or frisking about.
লম্ফন, *s.* the act of jumping or leaping.
লম্ব, *a.* long, tall, pendulous: *s.* a perpen-
লম্বকর্ণ, *a.* long-eared. [dicular.
লম্বজাঙ্ঘী, long-legged, spindle-shanked.
লম্বন, *s.* a being suspended, a hanging, a depending from. [stretching.
লম্বমান, *a.* hanging, dangling, suspending,
লম্বা, *a.* long, tall, high: *s.* a perpendicular.
লম্বাই, *s.* length, tallness: *a.* lengthwise.
লম্বাইচৌড়াই, *s.* the length and breadth of a thing, profuse expenditure, prodigality: *ad.* in all its length and breadth.
লম্বালম্বি, *s.* the whole extent in length.
লম্বিকা, *s.* the uvula or soft palate.
লম্বিত, *a.* pendant, hanging down.
লম্বোদর, *a.* lank, long-bellied: *s.* Ganesha.
লয়, *s.* an adhering, a clinging to, an em. bracing, loss, destruction, dissolution, an absorption, dispersion, concealment or disappearance, a melted state. [tion.
লয়কাল, *s.* time of absorption or dissolu-
ললাট, *s.* the forehead, fate, destiny, luck.
ললিত, *a.* hanging in collops, desired, coveted, beautiful, lovely, wanton, dallying: *s.* female amorous dalliance, or signs and gestures indicative of passion.
লশুন, *s.* garlic (Allium sativum).
লশুনীয়া, *s.* the cat's eye gem.
***লস্কর**, *s.* an army, a soldier, a ship's crew
লস্করী, *a.* belonging or relating to an army.
লহর, *s.* an aqueduct, a drain for water.
লহরী, *s.* a wave, billow, surge; a whim.

লা, *s.* lac, sealing-wax; -বাতী, stick-lac.
লাউ, *s.* a pumpkin, gourd (Cucurbita la-
লাক, *a.* a hundred thousand. [genaria).
লাক্ষা, **লাক**, *s.* lac, the lac insect.
লাক্ষিক, *a.* laccic, impregnated with or relating to lac; in *chy.* the laccic acid.
লাখেরাজ, rentfree land, a freehold; -দার, a
লাখেরাজী, *a.* free from taxes. [freeholder.
লাগ, *v. n.* to touch, to come in contact, to stick, to adhere, to strike: লাগিয়া থাক্, or রহ্, to stick, to adhere.
লাগন, *s.* the coming in contact with a thing, the adhering to a thing.
লাগা, *v. a.* to cause to touch, to bring into contact, to apply, smear, plaster, attribute, ascribe, impute, spread (a table); to land (a boat): *s.* a being in contact, adherence: *a.* joined, put in contact.
লাগাইদ, *prep.* unto, until: *a.* continual.
লাগাইল, *s.* a vestige, reach, the place of a person or thing which is sought after.
লাগান, *s.* bringing into contact, a smearing, applying, the landing of a boat.
লাগানঘাট, *s.* a port, a landing place.
***লাগাম**, *s.* a bridle, rein, halter, the bit of a bridle; -কামড়া, to champ the bit.
লাগালাগি, *ad.* in contact, close to, adjoin-
লাগি, *s.* contact, junction. [ing, abreast.
লাঘব, *s.* lightness, levity, smallness, insignificance, alleviation, minuteness.
লাঘবী, *a.* sparing, frugal, faring hard.
লাঙ্গল, *s.* a plough; -দণ্ড, a plough-beam.
লাঙ্গলফাল, *s.* plough-share. [plough-ox.
লাঙ্গলা, *s.* a cultivator, ploughman, tiller, a
লাঙ্গলাগরু, *s.* a plough bullock.
লাঙ্গলিক, of a plough: *s.* a kind of poison, probably the root of Gloriosa superba.
লাঙ্গলিয়া, *a.* ploughing: *s.* a ploughman.
লাঙ্গলী, *s.* the name of various plants.[1]
লাঙ্গুল, *s.* the tail of an animal. [ness.
লাচার, *a.* helpless, forlorn: লাচারী, helpless-
লাজ, *s.* parched grain; shame, bashfulness, modesty; -খেকুরা, shameless, immodest.
লাজমণ্ড, *s.* a kind of sweetmeat.
লাজুক, *a.* modest, bashful, shame-faced: *s.* the sensitive plant (Mimosa pudica).
লাজুলমা, *a.* modest, bashful, shamefaced.

লাঞ্ছন, *s.* a stain, a spot, a mark. [abuse.
লাঞ্ছনা, *s.* reprehension, reproof, reproach,
লাঞ্ছিত, *a.* marked, notorious, reproved, reprehended : *s.* reprehension. [per kite.
লাট, *s.* entanglement ; the whirling of a pa-
লাটাঘাটা, *s.* confusion, disorder.
লাটিম, *s.* a top to play with, a plaything.
লাঠামাছ, *s.* the name of a species of fish.[1]
লাঠালাঠি, reciprocal striking with clubs.
লাঠী, *s.* a staff, a stick, a walking stick, a mace, a club, a bludgeon, a cudgel.
লাড়্, *v. a.* to shake, to displace, to remove.
লাড়ন, *s.* a shaking, the removing a thing.
লাড়া, *v. a.* to move, shake, remove, displace : *s.* a shaking motion, agitation ; stubble : *a.* shaken, agitated, moved.
লাড়ান, *s.* the causing of a thing to shake or move : *a.* shaken, moved, displaced.
লাড়ালাড়ি, *s.* a mutual moving or shaking.
লাড়ু, *s.* a kind of sweetmeat-ball. [fancy.
লাড়ুগোপাল, *s* Krishna's image of his in-
লাৎ, or লাথ, *s.* a kick ; -মার্, to kick.
লাথালাথি, *s.* a reciprocal kicking.
লাথী, *s* a kick ; -মার্, or -ছাড়্, to kick.
লাফ্, *v. a.* to jump, spring, leap, flounce.
লাফ, *s.* a jump, leap, bound ; -ছাড়্, -মার্, to jump, leap, flounce. [insolent, daring.
লাফডিঙ্গরা, overleaping all bounds, bold,
লাফা, *v. a.* to jump, spring, bound : *s.* a hare ; a jump or leap. [flouncing.
লাফান, লাফানি, *s.* a jumping, a leaping, a
লাফালাফি, *s.* a leaping or jumping about.
লাবণিক, *a.* salted, relating to salt : *s.* a vender of salt, a salt-seller.
লাবণ্য, *s.* saltness ; charm, beauty, loveliness, amiableness, agreeableness.
লাবণ্যকারক, *a.* adorning, beautifying.
লাবণ্যবান্, লাবণ্যবিশিষ্ট, *a.* beautiful, elegant, handsome, graceful, agreeable.
লাভ, *s.* gain, profit, advantage, income, benefit, an acquisition. [geous.
লাভকর, লাভজনক, *a.* profitable, advanta-
লাভাকাঙ্ক্ষা, *s.* a desire for gain or profit, a mercenary spirit. [mercenary.
লাভাকাঙ্ক্ষী, *a.* desirous of gain or profit,
লাভালাভ, *s.* profit and loss. [ousness.
লাম্পট্য, *s.* immorality, lewdness, lascivi-

লাল, *a.* red : *s.* slaver, saliva ; also a small
লালকরবী, *s.* the red oleander.* [bird.*
লালচ, *s.* covetousness, inordinate desire.
লালচিয়া, লালচী, *a.* desirous, covetous.
লালন, *s.* a caressing, a fondling, a petting ; -পালন, a caressing and nourishing.
লালশাক, *s.* a species of red amaranthus.
লালসর্বজয়া, *s.* a flower plant.* [lust.
লালসা, *s.* excessive desire, covetousness,
লালসিক, *a.* covetous, inordinately desir-
লালা, *s.* slaver, saliva ; sir, master. [ous.
লালাটিক, *a.* referring every thing to fate.
লালিত্য, *s.* sweetness, flavour, agreeableness, beauty, loveliness, pleasure.
লালী, *s.* redness ; -ঘা, a fistula, a cancer.
লালুক, লালুয়া, *a.* sputtering : *s.* a driveller,
*লাশ, *s.* a corpse, dead body. [sputterer.
লাস, লাস্য, *s.* singing and dancing, dalliance, wantonness, unseemly gesture.
লাসক, dancing, dallying, using unseemly
লাস্ফোটনী, *s.* a gimlet, auger. [gestures.
লাহা, *s.* lac, sealing-wax ; -বাতী, stick-lac.
লিখ্, *v. a.* to write, to draw, to paint.
লিখন, *s.* a writing, a letter, a record, a written document, the act of writing.
লিখনপ্রণালী, *s.* style of a writing.
লিখনীয়, লিখিতব্য, *a.* fit or proper to be written, requiring to be written.
লিখিত, *a.* written : *s.* a literary composi-
লিগা, *s.* an axletree. [tion.
লিঙ্গ, *s.* pudendum virile, the penis ; mark, sign, token ; in *gram.* gender ; the Phallus, representation of Shiva ; an inference, matter, crude matter, nature.
লিঙ্গী, *a.* having a mark : *s.* a betokening.
লিচি, *s.* a China fruit (Scytalia litchi).
লিপি, *s.* a writing, a record, a letter, epistle, a drawing, a written document.
লিপিকর, *s.* a writer, a painting artist.
লিপিধারা, *s.* the method of writing.
লিপ্ত, *a.* smeared, tainted, infected with ;
লিপ্তপা, *a.* palmipede, webfooted. [joined.
লিপ্সা, *s.* a desire to gain or acquire, covetousness, cupidity, a hope of gain.
লিপ্সিত, *a.* coveted, greedily sought after.
লিপ্সু, *a.* covetous, desirous of gain.
লীন, *a.* taken, dissolved, mixed, absorbed

লীলা, *s.* play, sport, pastime, diversion, lasciviousness, amorous sport. [tacle.
লীলাপ্রকাশ, *s.* a display of sport, a spec-
লীলাবতি, *s.* a Sanskrit arithmetical work.
লীলাসম্বরণ, *s.* a restraining of sport.
লুআড়ি, *s.* an edible fruit and its tree.[1]
লুই, *s.* a kind of flannel, woollen cloth.
লুক্, *v. n.* to be concealed, to be unperceived: *s.* meteor, a fiery meteor.
লুকা, *v. n.* to hide, to conceal, suppress.
লুকাচুরি, *s.* the sport of hide and seek.
লুকান, *s.* a concealing: *a.* concealed.
লুকিবিদ্যা, *s.* the science by which a person is able to render himself invisible.
লুক্কায়িত, *a.* concealed, hid, hidden.
লুঙ্গী, *s.* a kind of coloured dress.
লুচি, *s.* a kind of pancake. [লুচ্চী.
*লুচ্চা, *a.* lewd, lascivious, wanton; *fem.*
লুচ্চাপনা, লুচ্চাম, লুচ্চামী, *s.* lewdness.
লুট্, *v. a.* to plunder, rob, pillage, ransack, to toss or tumble: লুটিয়া যাওন, to tumble or toss about: লুটিয়া পড়ন, to lie prostrate: লুটিয়া লওন, to pillage.
লুট, *s.* plunder, a booty, prey, plundering.
লুটন, *s.* act of plundering or pillaging.
লুটনিয়া, *a.* plundering: *s.* a plunderer.
লুটা, *s.* plunder, a booty, a prey: *v. a.* to plunder, to ransack, ravage, to cause to rob or plunder; to waste or squander.
লুটান, *s.* a squandering, a causing to be plundered: *a.* plundered, ransacked.
লটী, *s.* a clew, skein, a ball of thread, a wadding, a cricket ball, a ball of cloth.
লুটীসুটী, *a.* tousled, disordered, confused.
লুটেরা, লুটিয়ারা, *s.* a plunderer, an open robber, a pindárá, a rapacious person.
লট্পাট্, or লুট্পুট, *s.* plunder, robbery; a prey, rapine, spoil; a rolling about.
লুট্পুটা, *v. a.* to throw into disorder, to drag, to roll or tumble over and over.
লুঠ্, *v. n.* to roll, to wallow, to tumble about, to plunder, to ravage.
লুঠন, *s.* a wallowing about; a plundering.
লুঠিত, *a.* plundered, ravaged. [ry ticket.
লুড়ী, *s.* a ball, fragments of bricks, a lotte-
লুণ, *s.* salt; -দা, -ছড়া, to salt.
লুণিয়া, *s.* a dealer in salt; also, purslain.[2]

লুণ্ঠ্, *v. a.* to plunder, to ravage, to tumble or toss about, to tousle, to roll about.
লুণ্ঠক, *a.* plundering, rolling, wallowing: *s.* a plunderer; one who rolls about.
লুণ্ঠন, *s.* a plundering; a tossing about, a wallowing or rolling about. [vanished.
লুপ্ত, obsolete, concealed, effaced, extinct
লুফ্, *v. a.* to catch a flying ball, etc.
লুব্ধ, *a.* coveted, desired. [hunter.
লুব্ধক, *a.* greedy, avaricious: *s.* a fowler, a
লুভ্, *v. n.* to be desired, to be coveted.
লুভী, *a.* desirous, covetous, avaricious.
লুরী, *s.* a species of red parrot.[3]
লুলা, *a.* lame of hand, maimed. [lops.
লুলিত, *a.* flabby, wrinkled, hanging in col-
লূতা, *s.* a spider; -তন্তু, or -জাল, a cobweb.
লূতাতন্তুবিতান, *s.* a spider's web, a cobweb.
লে, *voc. part.* take; the calling or setting
লেই, *s.* paste, starch. [of a dog.
লেংট, লেংটা, *a.* naked, unclothed, bare.
লেংটি, *s.* the same as নেংটি, which see.
লেংটাইন্দুর, *s.* a mouse.
লেকড়া, *s.* a rag.
লেকড়্যাবাঘ, or নেকড়্যা, *s.* a hyena.
লেখক, *s.* a writer, a scribe, a painter.
লেখন, *s.* the act of writing or drawing; a letter, a writing. [and reading.
লেখনপড়ন, *s.* written documents; writing
লেখনিক, *s.* a letter-carrier, a postman, one who signs a writing for another.
লেখনী, *s.* a pen, a pencil, a style, a graver.
লেখা, written: *s.* a writing, handwriting, act of writing: *v. a.* to cause to write.
লেখাজোকা, *s.* accounts, reckonings.
লেখান, *s.* a causing to write: *a.* written.
লেখাপড়া, *s.* a studying, records or writings, writing and reading. [writing.
লেখালেখি, *s* a correspondence, a mutual
লেখিত, *a.* written, engrossed, recorded.
লেখিতব্য, লেখনীয়, *a.* fit or proper to be written, requiring to be written.
লেখ্য, *a. idem*: *s.* a writing, a document.
লেঙ্গড়া, *a.* lame, limping, crippled, halt.
লেঙ্গা, *a.* left-handed: *s.* left-handed man.
লেঙ্গুচা, *s.* a sausage, a hog's pudding.
লেজুড়, or লেজ, *s.* the tail of an animal.
লেজাড়, or দুমচী, *s.* a crupper.

লেঠা, *s.* a difficulty, obstruction, embarrassment, obstacle; a left-handed man.
লেঠাবধান, *s.* impeachment, legal censure.
লেড়া, *a.* bald: *s.* a man who shaves off all his hair, a sect of mendicants.
লেপ, *v. a.* to smear over, plaster, anoint.
লেপ, *s.* a smearing, an unguent, plaster, salve, ointment, mortar or lime; a rug.
লেপক, *a.* smearing, plastering: *s.* a plas-
লেপন, *s.* a smearing, plastering. [terer.
লেপনীয়, *a.* requiring to be plastered.
লেপা, *s.* a plastering, smearing: *a.* plastered, smeared: *v. a.* to cause to plaster.
লেপান, *a.* plastered: *s.* a causing to plas-
লেপাপা, *a.* palmipede, webfooted. [ter.
লেপাপোঁচা, *a.* plastered, whitewashed: *s.* a plastering and whitewashing.
লেপিখুঁচি, *s.* the repairing of a thatch.
লেপিত, *a.* smeared, plastered. [per.
*লেফাফা, *s.* a cover, an envelope, a wrap-
লেবু, *s.* a lime, orange; it is a generic name to all the species of Citrus.
লেম, *s.* agreement, unity, peace.
লেলান, *s.* the setting a dog on to attack.
লেলে, *voc. part.* used to set a dog.
লেশ, *s.* a tinge, a trace, a small portion, minuteness; the least connection.
লেশদৃষ্টি, *a.* seeing very small objects.
লেহন, *s.* a licking, lapping, tasting.
লেহাই, *s.* paste, starch, hasty pudding.
লেহ্য, *a.* proper to be licked. [women.
লো, *voc. part.* used in addressing inferior
লোক, *s.* a person, a man, folk, people, the world; the three worlds, viz. heaven, earth, and infernal regions. [popularly.
লোকতঃ, *ad.* according to common usage,
লোকন, *s.* a looking, a viewing, a survey-
লোকনাথ, *s.* name of Shiva, Brahmá. [ing.
লোকনিন্দা, *s.* reproach or censure of the
লোকনীয়, *a.* visible, surveyable. [world.
লোকন্দরা, *a.* dissolute, lewd, lascivious.
লোকবাদ, *s.* a common report, a rumour.
লোকভয়, *s.* a fear of public opinion.
লোকসমূহ, *s.* a mob, crowd, concourse.
লোকান্তর, *s.* another world; death. [dead.
লোকান্তরগত, *a.* gone to another world,
লোকান্তরপ্রাপ্ত, *a.* arrived in another world.
লোকাপবাদ, *s.* the censure or accusations of the world, or that of public opinion.
লোকারণ্য, *s.* a crowd, a multitude of people, a mob, a large population. [veyed.
লোকিত, *a.* seen, perceived, viewed, sur-
লোঙ্গর, *s.* anchor; -ফেল্, to cast anchor.
লোচন, *s.* the eye; act of looking. [low.
লোট্, *v. n.* to tumble about, to roll, wal-
লোটন, *s.* a tumbling about, wallowing; a tumbler pigeon; a braid of hair.
লোটনবাঁধন, *s.* the curling of hair.
লোটা, *v. a.* to hang loosely, to wallow, to roll or toss about: *s.* a brass pot, a pot.
লোটান, *s.* a hanging loosely, wallowing, rolling or tossing: *a.* rolled, dangling.
লোড়া, *s.* the muller of a grinding stone.
লোণ, লবণ, *s.* salt; -দা, or -ছড়া, to salt.
লোণা, salt, saltish, brackish: *s.* a kind of custard-apple;[1] -আতা, bullock's heart.[2]
লোণামাছ, *s.* a salt-water fish, salted fish.
লোণামাটী, *s.* salt land; a burial place.
লোৎ, or লোত, *s.* a booty, a prey, plunder, stolen article, a tear; a note or mark.
লোধ, or লোধ্র, *s.* a tree and its bark.[3]
লোপ, *s.* a wiping out, extinction, disappearance, discontinuance, abrogation, obsoleteness, the erasing of a writing, a disannulling, rescinding, obliteration.
লোপক, or লোপী, *a.* causing to disappear, discontinuing, disannulling, erasing.
লোপনীয়, লোপ্য, *a.* expungible, capable of being obliterated or made obsolete.
লোপ্ত্র, *s.* stolen article, booty. [ball).
লোফ্, *v. a.* to throw up and catch (as a
লোফা, *s.* the throwing and catching of a
লোবা, *a.* covetous, avaricious. [ball, etc.
লোবিয়া, *s.* a species of kidney bean.[4]
লোভ, *s.* covetousness, desire, avarice; -কৃ, to covet; -দেখা, to allure, to persuade, to tempt, to entice, excite. [alluring.
লোভজনক, *a.* exciting desire, tempting,
লোভনীয়, *a.* covetable, exciting desire.
লোভপূর্ব্বক, *ad.* covetously, greedily.
লোভা, *a.* covetous, avaricious, greedy.
লোভান্বিত, *a.* covetous, desirous.
লোভামী, *s.* a grasping, covetousness.
লোভিত, *a.* coveted, desired, grasped at.

লোভী, *a.* greedy, covetous, desirous.
লোম, *s.* hair of the body, hair of beasts, [wool.
লোমকূপ, *s.* a pore of the skin.
লোমকূপবৎ, *a.* porous, cellular.
লোমড়ী, *s.* a fox: also, খিখি, খেঁকশিয়ালী.
লোমশ, *a.* hairy, shaggy, woolly.
লোমশ্রেণী, *s.* a row of hairs extending from the breast to the navel.
লোমহর্ষ, লোমহর্ষণ, *s.* hairs standing erect through fear or surprise, horripilation.
লোমাঞ্চ, *s.* *idem.*
লোমাঞ্চিত, *a.* having the hair standing erect through fear or surprise, horrific.
লোমাঞ্চিতকলেবর, লোমাঞ্চিততনু, *a.* *idem.*
লোমাবলি, *s.* the same with লোমশ্রেণী.
লোল, *a.* tremulous, hanging loosely, shaking, slackening; desirous, eager, cupidinous, fickle; -দা, to let loose, to slacken.
লোলক, *a.* pendant, swinging: *s.* a pendulum; a jewel for the nose of women.
লোলা, *s.* a name of Lakshmí; desire, cupidity, eagerness: *a.* fickle.
লোলিত, *a.* pendant, tremulous, hanging in collops or wrinkles, flabby. [sirous.
লোলুপ, *a.* covetous, greedy, eagerly de-
লোষ্ট, লোষ্ট্র, *s.* a clod, a lump of earth.
লোহ, *s.* iron, metal in general; blood.
লোহকান্ত, অয়স্কান্ত, *s.* magnet, loadstone.
লোহকার, *s.* a blacksmith, an iron founder.
লোহচূর্ণ, লোহাচুর, *s.* iron filings. [anvil.
লোহপ্রতিমা, *s.* an iron image, a smith's
লোহময়, *a.* iron, made of iron. [iron.
লোহা, *s.* iron; -ঘু, the scoriæ or rust of
লোহাঘটিত, *a.* chalybeate. [smith's shop.
লোহার, *s.* a blacksmith; -খানা, a black-
লোহিত, *a.* red, sanguine: *s.* blood.
লোহিতনয়ন, *a.* red-eyed, angry, wrathful,
লোহিতনাড়ী, *s.* a red vein. [furious.
লোহিতমুখ, *a.* blushing, red-faced, angry.
লৌ, or লৌহু, *s.* blood. [parting gift.
লৌকতা, *s.* civility, urbanity, a present, a
লৌকিক, *a.* popular, current, vulgar, commonly practised; worldly, mundane.
লৌকিকতা, *s.* popularity, usage, civility.
লৌজারি, *s.* an appearance of blood.
লৌহ, *s.* iron; preparation of iron.
লৌহময়, *a.* iron, made of iron.

ব, the twenty-ninth consonant. The natives of Bengal make no distinction between ব *wa* and ব *ba.* *See* ব. A few Hinduí words are here introduced.
বক্ত, *s.* time, season.
বাকিফ্, *a.* acquainted with, knowing; -হাল, having knowledge of an affair.
বাজিব, or বাজিবী, *a.* right, just, proper, necessary: *s.* justice. [*fem.* বালী.
বালা, *s.* in *comp.* seller, owner, inhabitant;
বারিশ্, *s.* an heir. বারিশান্, *s.* *pl.* heirs.
বাসিল, *a.* received, credited, arrived, met.
বাসিলবাকি, *s.* the state of an account, bal- [ance.
বাস্তা, *s.* a cause, sake, a reason.
বাস্তি, *s.* a writing reed, a reed pen.
বাস্তে, *ad.* on account of, for, because.
বাহবা, or বাহবাবাহবা, *interj.* bravo! admirable! wonderful! surprising!

শ, is the thirtieth consonant in the Bengáli alphabet: *a.* a hundred.
*শওক, *s.* pleasure, a wish, eager desire.
শওকীন, *a.* fond of pleasure, eagerly desirous: *s.* a person fond of pleasure.
শং, *ad.* happily, fortunately, auspiciously.
শংযু, *a.* happy, fortunate, auspicious.
শক, *s.* a king who gives his name to an era, an era, epoch; a wish, a desire.
শকট, *s.* a cart, a waggon, hackery, chariot; the constellation Rohiní or the fourth mansion of the Hindu zodiac.
শকড়া, *s.* a cat, a waggon, hackery; -বালা, a carter, a carman, a hackeryman.
শকরকন্দ, *s.* the sweet-potato; *vide* শর্কর-
শকল, *s.* a shell, a part, share. [কন্দ.
শকাব্দা, *s.* a year of any era, but chiefly confined to that of Shálivàhana.
শকুন, শকুনী, *s.* a carrion-bird, a vulture.
শক্ত, *a.* firm, strong, tight, tough, valid, hard, compact, fast, difficult, austere.
শক্ততা, -ত্ব, *s.* the same with শক্তাই.
শক্তদর, *a.* dear, high-priced. [rigour.
শক্তাই, *s.* strength, toughness, hardness,
শক্তি, *s.* strength, power, ability, energy, validity, authority; a spear. [man.
শক্তিধর, *a.* holding virile power: *s.* a wo-
শক্তিপূর্ব্বক, *ad.* with power or energy.

শক্তিমান, *a.* strong, powerful, mighty, energetic.
শক্তু, *s.* the same with ছাতু.
শক্তোত্তর, *s.* a sharp or hard reply.
শক্য, *a.* possible, practicable; -তা, possibility.
শক্র, *s.* name of Indra; -ধনু, the rainbow.
শগুন, *s.* a vulture; an oath.
শঙ্ক্, *v. n.* to be afraid, to be in awe, to suspect.
শঙ্কনীয়, *a.* worthy of fear or suspicion.
শঙ্কর, *a.* auspicious: *s.* a name of Shiva; -মাছ, the scate fish.
শঙ্করচিল, *s.* the Bráhmani kite, the Coromandel eagle.[1]
শঙ্করজটা, *s.* a plant (Hedysarum pictum).
শঙ্কা, *s.* fear, dread, danger, peril, terror, awe, a panic, a suspicion.
শঙ্কাকর, *a.* fearing, causing fear or awe, suspecting.
শঙ্কাকুল, *a.* distressed with fear or dread.
শঙ্কাক্রমে, *ad.* by or through fear.
শঙ্কাজনক, *a.* causing fear or awe, terrifying, alarming, causing suspicion.
শঙ্কান্বিত, fearful, filled with awe, suspicious.
শঙ্কাভূমি, *s.* a ground or object of fear.
শঙ্কাসূচক, *a.* indicating fear or danger.
শঙ্কাস্পদ, *s.* an object of fear or suspicion.
শঙ্কিত, *a.* afraid, involved in doubt, hesitated, doubted, suspected.
শঙ্কু, *s.* a gnomon, a staff used to measure heights by the shadow, a scate fish, a pin, a stake, a pole, a javelin, a fibre.
শঙ্খ, *s.* conch shell; temporal and frontal bone; a military drum; a shell-bracelet.
শঙ্খক, *a.* a hundred billions.
শঙ্খকার, *s.* a shell-worker.
শঙ্খজ, *s.* a large pearl shaped like a pigeon's egg.
শঙ্খধ্বনি, *s.* the sound of a conch.
শঙ্খাসুর, *s.* a giant killed by Krishna.
শঙ্খাস্থি, *s.* the temporal and frontal bone.
শঙ্খিনী, *s.* a highly irascible woman, a vixen, a virago, an apparition, a fairy.
শচী, *s.* the wife of Indra; -পতি, Indra.
শজারু, *s.* a porcupine, hedgehog.
শজিনা, *s.* a tree[2], its root is used as horseradish.
শটরবটর, *s.* an intrigue, an artifice.
শটা, *s.* the matted hair of an ascetic.
শটিত, *a.* stale, mouldy, musty.
শটী, *s.* wild turmeric;[3] also, *vide* শঠী.
শঠ, *a.* artful, crafty, knavish, over-reaching, deceitful, swindling, wicked.
শঠতা, craftiness, artifice, knavery, deceit.
শঠতাচরণ, *s.* deceitful or knavish conduct.
শঠী, *s.* mango-scented ginger.[4]
শড়, *s.* collusion; *a.* the same as শড়া.
শড়ঙ্গা, *a.* tall, slender: *s.* a canoe.
শড়া, *a.* small, little, minute, slender, thin.
শড়াৎ, *im. sd.* expressive of a quick motion.
শড়িঙ্গা, *a.* thin, slender, tall, long.
শড়্শড়ি, *s.* a kind of sauce or gravy.
শণ, *s.* hemp plant,[5] hemp; -খদড়, tow.
শণসূত্র, **শণসুতলি**, *s.* twine, thin hemp cord.
শণ্ড, *s.* a eunuch; a clown; a bull at liberty.
শণ্ডতা, *s.* emasculation, castration.
শণ্ডা, *s.* a clown, a bumpkin, a boor.
শত, *a.* a hundred; -গুণ, hundred-fold; -তম, the hundredth; -ধা, -প্রকার, -বিধ, a hundred kinds; -বার, hundred times.
শতক, *s.* a hundred, a collection of a hundred.
শতক্রতু, *s.* a name of Indra.
শতঘ্ন, *s.* a destructive engine, a cannon.
শতপথিক, *a.* following many doctrines.
শতপদী, *s.* a centipede, a julus.
শতভিষা, *s.* 25th mansion of the Hindu zodiac.
শতমুখী, *a.* hundred-faced: *s.* a broom.
শতমূলী, *s.* Indian climbing asparagus.[6]
শতরঞ্চ, *s.* a carpet, a chess board or cloth; the game of chess; -খেলা, the play at chess; -বাজ, a chess-player.
শতরঞ্চি, *s.* a carpet, a floor-cloth.
শতানিক, *s.* an old man; a pupil of Vyása.
শতাব্দী, *s.* a century, 100 years.
শত্রু, *s.* an enemy, a foe, adversary, an opponent.
শত্রুক্ষয়, *s.* the decay of enemy.
শত্রুগ্রস্ত, *a.* surrounded by enemies, taken captive.
শত্রুঘ্ন, *a.* killing the enemy: *s.* the name of one of the brothers of Ráma.
শত্রুতা, -ত্ব, *s.* enmity, hostility.
শত্রুতাচরণ, *s.* a course of hostility or enmity.
শত্রুতাপূর্ব্বক, *ad.* by or through enmity.
শত্রুপ্রার্থিত, *a.* ill-designed, malevolent.
শনি, *s.* the planet Saturn; young fruits.
শনিবার, **শনিচর**, *s.* Saturday.
শন্নি, *s.* a cypher, a dot, a point, an odd.
শনৈঃ, *ad.* slowly, gently, softly.
শনৈঃশনৈঃ, *ad.* slowly, deliberately.
শনৈশ্চর, *s.* the planet Saturn.
শপথ, *s.* oath, imprecation; -কৃ, to swear, take oath.

শপথপত্র, *s.* an affidavit of an oath.
শপ্ত, *a.* cursed, execrated, anathematised.
শফ, *s.* hoof; the root of a tree; floor-mat.
শফরী, *s.* a species of carp;[1] -আম, the guava.[2]
শব, *s.* a corpse, a dead body.
শবদাহ, *s.* the burning of a dead body.
শবদাহক, *s.* one who burns a dead body.
শবদাহী, *a.* burning a dead body.
শবল, *a.* variegated, brindled, gray, ashy.
শবসাধন, *s.* a ceremony or incantation performed by sitting on a dead body.
শবাচ্ছাদনী, *s.* a shroud.
শব্দ, *s.* a sound, noise, a voice, a word; in *gram.* a noun.
শব্দকর, *a.* sounding, sonorous.
শব্দকোষ, শব্দসংগ্রহ, *s.* a dictionary, vocabulary.
শব্দচোর, *s.* a plagiary, a plagiarist.
শব্দপ্রমাণ, *s.* oral testimony.
শব্দবোধ, *s.* the knowledge of sounds or words.
শব্দভেদিবাণ, *s.* a fabled arrow.
শব্দশাস্ত্র, *s.* philology.
শব্দযোনি, শব্দাকর, *s.* a dhátu or radix of a word, verbal root.
শব্দহরণ, or শব্দচুরি, *s.* plagiarism.
শব্দাতীত, *s.* the supreme God, *viz.* he who is beyond the reach of sound.
শব্দার্থ, *s.* the meaning of a sound or word.
শম, *s.* restraint of the senses, tranquillity, placidity, quietness, calmness, rest, stoicism, indifference. alleviation.
শমতা, *s.* a state of tranquillity or quietude,
শমন, *s.* mental tranquillity, placidity, immolation of beasts for sacrifice; Yama.
শমী, *s.* a bean, a pod, a legume.
শমীধান্য, *s.* leguminous grain.
শমীর, *s.* the name of a tree (Acacia suma).
শম্ব, *s.* the iron head of a pestle.
শম্বল, *s.* money or provision for a journey.
শম্বূক, শামুক, *s.* a snail, a bivalve shell.
শয়চান, *s.* a hawk. শয়তান, *s.* Satan, devil.
শয়তানাংশ, *s.* in *anatomy*, morsus diaboli.
শয়তানী, *a.* satanic, devilish: *s.* wickedness.
শয়ন, *s.* a lying down, a reclining, a reposing, repose, a sleeping; -কুটীর, -কুঠরী, -ঘর, -মন্দির, a bed-room, a dormitory.
শয়নভঙ্গ, *s.* the interrupting of repose.
শয়নাগার, *s.* a dormitory, a bed-room.
শয়নীয়, শয়িতব্য, *a.* fit for repose.
শয়নৈকাদশী, a fast in honour of Vishnu's repose.
শয়ান, *a.* reclining, taking repose, procumbent.
শয়িত, *a.* reclined, reposed, asleep.
শয্যা, *s.* a bed; -গত, gone to bed, confined to bed, bedridden.
শয্যাচ্ছাদন, *s.* a bed sheet, a coverlet or counterpane.
শয্যাপতিত, শয্যাপ্রাপ্ত, *a.* fallen on the bed, gone to bed, confined to bed, bedridden.
শর, *s.* a reed, a species of grass;[3] an arrow, cream, the versed sine of an arc.
শরট, *s.* a chameleon, a lizard.
শরণ, শরণং, *s.* a shelter, a protection, a refuge; a protector; -পুঠী, a fish.[4]
শরণাগত, শরণাপন্ন, *a.* refuged, taken refuge: *s.* a protégé, a refugee.
শরণ্য, *a.* fit to be taken refuge in, trusty: *s.* a protector, defence, protection.
শরৎ, -কাল, *s.* autumn; -কালীন, autumnal.
শরপুঙ্খ, *s.* feather of an arrow.
শরফল, *s.* the head of an arrow.
*শরবৎ, *s.* lemonade, sherbet, a beverage.
শরবর্ষণ, *s.* the showering down of arrows.
শরবৃষ্টি, *s.* a shower of arrows.
শরব্য, *s.* a mark or butt to shoot at.
*শরম, *s.* shame, bashfulness, modesty.
শরমঙ্গলা, *s.* a musical instrument made of the dry stalks of Saccharum sara.
*শরমিন্দা, *a.* ashamed, modest, bashful.
শরমিন্দাবিল্লি, *s.* the name of an animal.
শরল, শরলতা, *vide* সরল, সারল্য.
শরস্, শরেস্, *a.* good, excellent, better, best.
শরা, *s.* an earthen basin, cover for a pot.
*শরা, শরাই, *s.* an inn, a baiting-place.
*শরাকৎ, শরাকতী, *s.* partnership.
শরাকৎনামা, *s.* an indenture of copartnership.
শরাঘাত, *s.* a stroke with an arrow.
শরাব, *s.* a cover, a lid, the cover of a pot.
*শরাব, wine, spirits, liquor; -খানা, grog-shop, liquor-shop; -খোর, *vide* শরাবী.
শরাবী, *a.* drinking spirits or wine; *s.* one addicted to wine or spirits, a drunkard.
শরাসন, *s.* a bow to shoot arrows.
শরাহত, *a.* smitten with an arrow.
*শরীক, *s.* a copartner, a colleague.
*শরীর, *a.* wicked, vicious; -পনা, wickedness, vice.
শরীর, *s.* the body, matter.
শরীরগ, moving as a reptile: *s.* a reptile.
শরীরজ, *a.* produced from the body.

শরীরপণ, *s.* the staking of the body, maceration of the body. [body, death.
শরীরপতন, or শরীরপাত, *s.* the fall of the
শরীরপাক, *s.* a wasting of the body, ema-
শরীরবন্ধক, *s.* a hostage. [ciation.
শরীরসংস্কার, *s.* bodily purification.
শরীরী, *a.* bodily, corporeal, material: *s.* an
*শরীরী, *s.* wickedness, vice. [animal.
শরু, *a.* thin, slender, fine: *s.* an arrow.
শরুমোটা, *a.* uneven, thick and thin.
শর্করকন্দ, *s.* sweet-potato, (Convolvulus
শর্করা, *s.* sugar, sugarcandy. [batatus).
শর্করিল, *a.* gravelly, full of gravel.
শর্করোদক, *s.* lemonade, sherbet.
*শর্ত, *s.* a condition, a stipulation, wager.
শর্টী, *s.* *Port.* a lottery, a raffle.
শর্ব্বরী, *s.* night, a night.
শর্ব্বলা, *s.* an iron crow-bar.
শর্ম্মা, *a.* happy, prosperous, glad: *s.* happiness, pleasure; a Bráhmanical epithet.
শল, *s.* a porcupine's quill.
শলভ, *s.* a locust, a grasshopper.
শলা, or শলাকা, *s.* a thin rod or peg, a skewer, rod of metal or wood, javelin, a dart, an arrow, a brimstone match, a thin slip of bambu; a tent or probe.
শলাটু, *a.* unripe, moist. [of rice.
শলি, *s.* a measure of 20 seras or pasuris
শলিতা, *s.* the wick of a lamp or candle.
শলিল, *s.* water: শলিলজ, *a.* aquatic.
শলুফা, or শুলফা, *s.* the Indian fennel.[1]
শনৈশনে, *ad.* by slow degrees, slowly.
শল্ক, *s.* the scales of a fish; bark, rind.
শল্কময়, *a.* full of scales, scaly, flaky.
শল্য, *s.* iron crow or club, a dart, arrow, a javelin, a spear, a blade, a peg, a pin, a spit, a bambu rod or stake; difficulty, embarrassment, distress; a porcupine.
শল্যাকার, শল্যাকৃতি, *a.* cuspidate. [arrow.
শল্যোদ্ধার, *s.* the extracting of a dart or
শল্লকী, *s.* a porcupine; frankincense.
শশ, *s.* a hare, the dark part of the moon supposed to resemble a hare.
শশক, or শশারু, *s.* a hare, a rabbit.
শশবিষাণ, *s.* (*lit.*) a hare's horns; (*met.*) that which has no existence in nature.
শশিলেখা, *s.* a digit of the moon.

শশিশেখর, *s.* one of the names of Shiva.
শশী, শশধর, শশাঙ্ক, *s.* the moon.
শশোর্ণ, *s.* the fur of hares or rabbits.
শশ্বৎ, *ad.* repeatedly, frequently, perpetu-
শশা, *s.* a cucumber. [ally, eternally.
শষ্কুলি, *s.* the ear-hole, opening of the ear.
শস্ত, *a.* happy, comfortable, praised, good, best, excellent: *s.* happiness, excellence.
শস্তা, *a.* low-priced, cheap: *s.* cheapness.
শস্ত্র, *s.* a weapon, armour, defensive armour, a sword, a cimetar, iron, steel.
শস্ত্রগ্রহণ, *s.* the taking of arms.
শস্ত্রজীবী, *a.* living by arms: *s.* a soldier.
শস্ত্রধারী, *a.* bearing arms, armed.
শস্ত্রনির্ম্মাতা, *s.* an armourer, a cutler.
শস্ত্রপাণি, wielding weapons, bearing arms.
শস্ত্রাজীব, *a.* living by arms: *s.* a soldier.
শস্ত্রাভ্যাস, *s.* military exercise, fencing.
শস্ত্রী, *a.* armed, accoutred, having arms.
শস্ত্রোপজীবী, *a.* living by arms: *s.* a soldier.
শস্প, *s.* young tender grass.
শস্য, *s.* grain, corn, a harvest, kernel of a
শস্যক্ষেত্র, *s.* a corn-field. [nut or drupe.
শস্যখাদক, শস্যভক্ষক, *a.* granivorous.
শস্যশালী, *a.* abounding in corn.
শস্যসংগ্রহ, *s.* the collecting of corn.
শস্যসংস্থান, *s.* a stack of corn.
শহর, *s.* a city; -কোতবাল, a bailiff, the chief officer of a city-police.
শহরকোতবালী, *s.* the office of a bailiff.
শহরতলী, *a.* near a city: *s.* a suburb.
শহরপনা, *s.* a wall or ditch round a city.
শহরপাশাড়ী, *a.* bordering on a city.
শহরবদল, or শহরবদলী, *s.* transportation.
শহরী, or শহরীয়, *a.* city, urban.
শাঁই, শাঁইজী, *s.* a Musalmán mendicant.
শাঁখ, *s.* a conch, univalve shell. [parition.
শাঁখচিন্নী, *s.* a hag, a female goblin, an ap-
শাঁখপোকা, শাঁকপোকা, *s.* a ladybird, a coc-
শাঁখা, *s.* a bracelet made of shell. [cinella.
শাঁখারি, *s.* a shell-cutter; -করাত, his saw.
শাঁখিনী, *s.* a goblin, spectre; an amphis-
শাঁখী, *a.* testaceous, shelly. [bena.
শাঁড়ক, *s.* a bambu lath used in thatching.
শাঁস, *s.* fruit, kernel, the nutricious part.
শাক, *s.* a potherb, an esculent vegetable.
*শাকী, *s.* a cup-bearer.

শাকুনিক, *s.* the occult sciences.
শাক্ত, *s.* a worshipper of the goddess Káli.
শাক্তিক, *a.* fighting with javelins.
শাখা, *s.* a branch, a bough ; philosophy of the veda.
শাখানগর, *s.* a suburb, village.
শাখামৃগ, *s.* a monkey, an ape.
শাখী, *s.* a tree ; a veda.
শাক্ষিশাক, *s.* a potherb (Achyranthes triandra).
শাটী, *s.* a garment worn by Hindu women.
শাটেন, *s.* *Eng.* satin, shining silk.
শাট্‌বাট্‌, শটর্‌বটর্‌, *s.* an artifice.
শাঠ্য, *s.* deceit, a trick, collusion, craftiness.
শাঠ্যব্যবহার, *s.* the practice of deceit.
শাঠ্যাচরণ, *s.* a course of deceit.
শাড়া, *s.* sound, word, speech ; -দা, to answer.
শাড়ী, *s.* a garment worn by Hindu women.
শাণ, *s.* a whetstone ; coarse kind of cloth.
শাণ্ডিল্য, *a.* relating to the sage Shaṇḍila.
শাত্রব, *s.* enmity, hatred, strife, opposition
শাদা, *a.* white ; (*fig.*) betel-lime.
*শাদী, *s.* a marriage ; a famous Persian poet.
শান্‌, *v. a.* to sharpen, to whet, to grind.
শান, *a.* small : *s.* a whetstone, a hone ; a whetting or grinding ; a paved floor ; -দা, to whet or grind, to sharpen, to polish.
শানক, শানকী, *s.* an earthen dish, a platter.
শানকরমজ্জা, *s.* a tree (Carisca diffusa).
শানবাঁধা, or শানবাঁধান, *a.* paved : *s.* the paving of a floor, pavement.
শানবাঁধাঘাট, শানবাঁধানঘাট, paved wharf or landing-place on a river or pond.
শানশিল, *s.* a whetstone, a hone.
শানা, *s.* a weaver's sley or reed.
শানিত, *a.* whetted, ground, sharpened.
শান্ত, *a.* tranquil, at rest, peaceable, allayed, appeased, calm, quiet.
শান্তি, *s.* tranquillity, calmness, quietness, rest, peace.
শান্তিকর, *a.* tranquillizing, calming, appeasing.
শান্তিজল, *s.* holy-water.
শাপ্‌, *v. a.* to curse, to imprecate.
শাপ, *s.* an imprecation, a curse ; -দা, to curse.
শাপগ্রস্ত, *a.* lying under a curse.
শাপবাণী, *s.* a curse, maledictory sentence.
শাপবিমুক্ত, *a.* liberated from a curse.
শাপভ্রষ্ট, *a.* fallen or ruined by a curse.
শাপান্ত, *s.* end or termination of a curse.
শাবক, *s.* the young of an animal.

2 x

শাবল, or শর্ব্বলা, *s.* an iron crow-bar.
শাবান, *s.* *Port.* soap ; -জল, soap suds.
*শাবুদ, *s.* testimony, a proof, evidence.
শাব্দ, *a.* sonorous, sounding, belonging to a noun, nominal : *s.* Saraswatí.
শাব্দবোধ, *s.* a knowledge of words.
শাব্দিক, *a.* of sounds or words, of nouns.
শামলা, *a.* tawny, yellowish black.
শামা, *s.* mouldiness ; a kind of bird ;[1] two species of grass ;[2] -দান, a candlestick.
*শামিআনা, *s.* an awning, a canopy.
*শামিল, *a.* connected with, included in, belonging to, joined with, adjoining.
শামুক, *s.* a snail, large snail,[3] a shellfish.
শারঙ্গ, *s.* a cuckoo ; a deer ; the black bee.
শারদা, *s.* Saraswatí, goddess of learning.
শারদীয়, *a.* autumnal ; also used as the adjective of the worship of Durgá.
শারী, *s.* the name of two birds.[4]
শারীরিক, *a.* bodily, corporeal, material.
শার্ঙ্গ, *a.* horny, corneous ; -ত্বক্‌, a cornea.
শার্দ্দূল, *a.* eminent, dignified : *s.* a tiger.
শাল, *s.* a shawl ; an edifice ; a gallows, a gibbet, stake on which criminals are impaled ; a timber tree ;[5] a kind of fish.[6]
শালকাঁটা, *s.* the remains of the footstalks of the leaves of Phœnix sylvestris.
শালপর্ণী, শালপাণী, *s.* name of a plant.[7]
শালা, *s.* a house, a hall, a room ; a wife's brother, (also used as an abusive term).
শালাই, *s.* a skewer, a brimstone match.
শালাজ, *s.* a wife's brother's wife.
শালাপো, *s.* a wife's brother's son ; *fem.* শালাঝি.
শালি, *s.* a kind of winter rice.
শালিআনা, *a.* annual, yearly.
শালিক, *s.* the name of a common bird.[8]
*শালিস, *s.* a mediator, arbitrator, umpire.
শালিসী, *s.* arbitration.
শালী, *a.* inclined to, tending towards : *s.* a wife's sister.
শালুক, *s.* the tuberous root of the lotus.[9]
শালতী, *s.* a canoe made of a shála tree.
শাল্মলী, *s.* the silk-cotton tree ; -দ্বীপ, one of the fabled continents of the Hindus.
শাশুড়ী, *s.* a mother-in-law.
শাশুড়ীয়া, criminally intimate with wife's mother (a vulgar term of reproach).
শাশ্বত, *a.* eternal, perpetual, always.

শাস্, *v. a.* to discipline, to reprove, to correct, to punish : *s.* a mother-in-law.
শাসক, or শাস্তা, *s.* the same as শাসনকর্তা.
শাসন, *s.* the exercising of discipline, discipline, governing, government, command, reproof, correction, punishment; -কৃ, to discipline, to correct.
শাসনকর্তা, *s.* a governor, one who maintains discipline, a corrector, reprover.
শাসনার্হ, *a.* fit for or deserving discipline.
শাসনীয়, *a.* the same as শাস্য.
শাসা, *v. a.* to discipline, reprove, correct, punish.
শাসান, *s.* a disciplining, a reproving, correcting.
শাসানি, *s.* correction, discipline.
শাসিত, *a.* disciplined, controlled, corrected, reproved, punished, chastised.
শাস্তি, discipline, correction, award, chastisement, punishment; -দাতা, chastiser.
শাস্ত্যর্হ, *a.* worthy of punishment.
শাস্ত্র, *s.* a sacred book, a law, a treatise on laws or maxims, a science, religion.
শাস্ত্রতত্ত্ব, *s.* the truths of the shástras.
শাস্ত্রবহির্মুখ, *a.* lawless, unrestrained.
শাস্ত্রবেত্তা, *s.* one acquainted with the shástras or sacred books, a philosopher.
শাস্ত্র-মত, -সম্মত, *a.* approved by the shástras.
শাস্ত্রসিদ্ধ, *a.* proved by the shástras.
শাস্ত্রার্থ, *s.* the true intent of the shástras.
শাস্ত্রীয়, *a.* according to the shástras.
শাস্ত্রোক্ত, *a.* declared in the shástras.
শাস্য *a.* disciplinable, corrigible, punishable.
*শাহ, *s.* a king, a sovereign.
শিউলি, *s.* the name of a flower tree.[1]
শিংশপা, *s.* the name of a timber tree.[2]
শিঁথী, *s.* a parting of hair on the forehead.
শিঁথী, শিঁথিমুকুট, a wreath, chaplet, tiara.
শিকড়, *s.* a root, a fibrous root, an origin.
*শিকদার, *s.* a revenue officer of a division.
শিকদারী, *s.* the office of a Shikdár.
শিকপা, *s.* a horse's rearing up; -কৃ, to rear up.
*শিকরা, *s.* a hawk, a bird of prey.
শিকল, *s.* chain, fetters, shackles; a cleaning, polish; -কর, a furbisher, polisher.
শিকস্ত, *a.* broken, disjointed, nonplused.
শিকা, শিক্য, *s.* the rope-shelves of a water-bearer, a hanging-shelf of rope, a sling.
*শিকার, *s.* a hunting, chase, game.
শিকারী, relating to hunting : *s.* a hunter.
শিক্ষ্, *v. n.* to learn, to study, to acquire knowledge, to be trained up.
শিক্ষক, *s.* a learner; a teacher, a tutor.
শিক্ষা, *v. a.* to instruct, educate, teach : *s.* doctrine, instruction, teaching; -কৃ, to learn; -করা, to teach, to instruct; -কর্তা, a learner, student; -দাতা, a teacher.
শিক্ষাকারক, *s.* a teacher; a student.
শিক্ষাগুরু, *s.* a tutor, instructor, preceptor.
শিক্ষার্থে, *ad.* for doctrine, for instruction.
শিক্ষিত, *a.* taught, instructed, studied.
শিক্ষিতব্য, শিক্ষ্য, *a.* fit to be taught, teachable.
শিখ্, *v. n.* the same with শিক্ষ্.
শিখণ্ড, *s.* a peacock; locks of hair left on the head at the tonsure.
শিখণ্ডী, *s.* a cock, a peacock, a peacock's tail; a tuft.
শিখন, *s.* a learning, a receiving instruction.
শিখনী, *s.* snot, mucus of the nose.
শিখর, *s.* a summit, a mountain peak, the top of a tree, a point or forepart.
শিখরিণী, *s.* an acid liquor, vinegar.
শিখরী, *s.* a craggy mountain; vegetable.
শিখা, *v. a.* to teach, instruct, train in, to break in an animal : *s.* flame, a crest, a tuft of hair or feathers, a spike of corn, a mountain peak, a pinnacle, a pyramid.
শিখাকার, or শিখাকৃতি, *a.* pyramidal.
শিখান, *s.* a teaching, the breaking in of an animal : *a.* taught, broken in.
শিখানি, *s.* punishment, vengeance, teaching.
শিখাবান্, *a.* flaming; crested, tufted : *s.* Agni or fire.
শিখাবৃক্ষ, *s.* a chandelier.
শিখামূল, *s.* a carrot, a top root, a fusiform root.
শিখিনী, বর্হিণী, ময়ূরী, *s.* a peahen.
শিখিপুচ্ছ, *s.* a peacock's tail.
শিখী, *a.* crested, tufted : *s.* a peacock; fire.
শিঙ্গ, *s.* a horn; a mountain peak.
শিঙ্গড়া, *s.* oak tree. শিগ্রু, the horseradish.
শিঙ্গা, *s.* a cupping glass, a horn used for cupping, or for blowing; -বসা, to cup.
শিঙ্গাড়া, *s.* an aquatic plant and its fruit.[3]
শিঙ্গার, *s.* a woman's adorning and beautifying herself; also, *vide* শৃঙ্গার.
শিঙ্গী, *s.* the name of a species of fish.[4]
শিঙ্গেল, *a.* having horns, horned.
শিঙ্ঘাণ, *s.* snot, mucus of the nose.

শিচ্কা, *s.* an iron rod to clean huká-tube.
শিঞ্জ, *v.* to jingle: শিঞ্জন, jingle, jingling.
শিঞ্জিত, *a.* jingling, sounding, sonorous.
শিটা, *s.* dregs, refuse, sediment, dross.
শিড়শিড়া, *v. n.* to tingle, to feel chilly, to feel cold as on the access of a fever.
শিড়শিড়ানি, শিড়শিড়, *s.* a tingling, the hair standing on end, horripilation.
শিড়ী, *s.* a ladder, a step, a flight of steps.
শিত, *a.* whetted; reduced, made thin.
শিতান, *s.* a pillow, cushion, bolster, that side of the bed where the head lies.
শিথিল, *a.* slack, dilatory, inactive, relaxed, remiss; -তা, -ত্ব, *vide* শৈথিল্য. [ty.
শিব, *s.* Shiva; an apple; welfare, prosperi-
শিবচতুর্দ্দশী, or শিবরাত্রি, *s.* a religious fast observed in Mágha in honour of Shiva.
শিবধাতু, *s.* the milkwhite opal.
শিবপুরী, *s.* the city of Benares. [Durgá.
শিবা, *s.* a shakal, a jackal; Shiva's wife,
শিবানী, শিবদূতী, *s.* Shiva's wife, Durgá.
শিবালয়, *s.* Shiva's temple; a cemetery.
শিবিকা, *s.* a palankeen, a pálki, a litter.
শিবির, *s.* a tent, a camp; -কৃ, to encamp.
শিবোত্তর, *s.* an estate devoted to Shiva.
শিম, *s.* a kidney-bean, a legume.
শিমুল, *s.* the silk-cotton tree.[1] [bean.
শিম্বা, শিম্বী, *s.* a legume, a pod, a kidney-
শিয়র, *s.* the head of the bed, place where a person's head lies when he sleeps.
শিয়াল, *s.* a jackal, shakal; -কাঁটা, a plant.[2]
শির, *s.* the head, the top part; a nerve, sinew, vein, artery, a blood-vessel, any tubular vessel of the body; a furrow.
শিরঃ, *s.* the head; -কম্প, the vertigo.
শিরঃপীড়া, শিরোরোগ, *s.* the head-ache.
শিরকা, শিখরিণী, *s.* vinegar. [of a book.
শিরনামা, *s.* superscription, address, title
শিরপা, *s.* honorary dress; restiveness in a horse; -কৃ, to be restive, to rear up.
শিরশ্ছেদন, *s.* a beheading, decapitation.
শিরস্ত্র, *s.* a helmet, a hat, a turban.
শিরস্থ, *a.* situated on the head or top.
শিরা, *s.* a vein, a nerve, a tendon, a blood-vessel, any tubular vessel of the body.
শরাচ্ছাদন, *s.* a covering for the head.
শিরাবিদ্যা, *s.* in *anatomy*, Neurology.

শিরাময়, *a.* sinewy, abounding with nerves.
শিরীস, *s.* glue, a viscous cement.
শিরোধার্য্য, *a.* fit to be respected. [head.
শিরোনমন, *s.* a bowing or nodding of the
শিরোমণি, *s.* a jewel in the crest.
শিরোরুহ, *s.* the hair of the head.
শিরোলুণ্ঠন, *s.* a hanging down of the head.
শিল, *s.* a mountain, a stone, a hone, a curry-stone, a hailstone, arsenic.
শিলনোড়া, *s.* the flat stone and muller with which condiments are ground.
শিলা, *s.* a rock, a stone, a hailstone, a muller, a threshold, a transverse beam.
শিলাজ, *s.* benzoin, gum benjamin.
শিলাজতু, *s.* bitumen, a fat unctuous resin.
শিলাধাতু, *s.* chalk, red chalk.
শিলাপুত্র, *s.* a rolling stone, a muller.
শিলাবল্কা, *s.* a species of lichen, moss.
শিলাবৃষ্টি, *s.* hail, a shower of hailstones.
শিলীপদ, *s.* the elephantiasis. [business.
শিল্প, *s.* the mechanical arts, handicraft,
শিল্পকর, শিল্পকার, *s.* a mechanic, an artificer, a tradesman, a handicraftsman.
শিল্পকর্ম্ম, manual labour, handicraft work.
শিল্পকর্ম্মকারক, or শিল্পকারক, *a.* working at handicraft work: *s.* a mechanic.
শিল্পবিদ্যা, *s.* the science of mechanics.
শিল্পবিশিষ্ট, *a.* mechanical, manual.
শিল্পী, *a.* working at a trade or manual art: *s.* a workman at any manual art.
*শিশ, *s.* glass; a hiss, whistle; -মহল, a crystal palace, a house made of glass.
শিশি, *s.* a glass, a phial, glass, crystal.
শিশির, *s.* dew, frost, hoar, dewy season.
শিশু, *s.* a child, an infant, a babe, a young
শিশুক, শিশুমার, শুশুক, *s.* a porpoise. [one.
শিশুকাল, *s.* infancy, childhood, nonage.
শিশুগণ, *s.* a number or class of children.
শিশুতা, -ত্ব, *s.* infancy, childhood. [na.
শিশুপাল, *s.* a king who was slain by Krish-
শিশ্ন, *s.* the male organ, penis. [sensual.
শিশ্নোদরপরায়ণ, *a.* devoted to sensuality,
শিষ, *s.* ear of corn; flower spike; a flame.
শিষ্ট, disciplined, trained, polished, civil, polite, gentle, tractable, docile, genteel.
শিষ্টতা, *s.* politeness, gentleness, tractableness, civility, urbanity, docility.

শিষ্টাচার, s. politeness, civility, urbanity, gentleness, gentlemanly conduct.
শিষ্টাচারী, a. behaving in a polite or urbane manner, acting like a gentleman.
শিষ্য, s. a disciple, a pupil, a scholar.
শিষ্যতা, -ত্ব, s. discipleship, pupilage.
শিস, s. flame, an ear of corn, a whistle, a hiss; -দা, to whistle, to hiss.
শিহর, v. n. to feel, to feel the sensation of cold: s. horripilation.
শিহর্, v. n. to feel, feel a gratifying or disagreeable sensation: s. horripilation.
শিহরাণ, s. the feeling of a gratifying or disagreeable sensation. [the wind.
শীকর, s. rain, thin rain, rain driven by
শীঘ্র, ad. quickly, speedily, immediately, hastily: a. soon, speedy, quick, rapid.
শীঘ্রগ, শীঘ্রগামী, a. swift, fleet, rapid, pas-
শীঘ্রগমন, a. *idem*: s. a quick pace. [sing.
শীত, a. cold, frigid: s. cold, cold weather, cold season, coldness, the moon; -কাল, the cold season, winter; -শিব, rock salt.
শীতকালীন, a. wintery, of the cold season.
শীতড়ী, s. a garment for the cold season.
শীত -ভীত, -ভীরু, a. afraid of cold, chilly.
শীতল, a. cool, cold, refreshing: s. green vitriol or sulphate of iron, coldness, frigidity, chilliness, the moon, turpentine.
শীতলতা, s. coolness, frigidity, coldness.
শীতলপাটী, s. a fine sort of Sylhet mat.
শীতলষষ্ঠী, s. a cold collation; a goddess.
শীতলা, s. smallpox; goddess of smallpox.
শীতলী, s. a swelling in the axils or on the
শীতার্ত, a. cold, affected by the cold. [arm.
শীতাশ্ম, s. crystal, the moon gem.
শীৎকার, s. a quailing, a thrilling.
শীধু, s. rum made from molasses.
শীর্ণ, a. fallen off (as leaves,) shrivelled, withered, emaciated, lean, thin, slender.
শীর্ণতা, s. emaciated or withered state.
*শীর্ণি, s. an offering, a meat-offering.
শীর্ষ, s. the head: শীর্ষণ্য, s. a helmet.
শীর্ষক, s. a helmet; a skull; judgment.
শীল, s. the bias or inclination of the mind, a tendency, an inclination, a bias: a. endowed with, possessed of, tending to.
শীলক, a. tending towards, inclined to.

শীলতা, -ত্ব, s. a tendency or bias of the mind, a good tendency or inclination.
শীলিত, a. learned, acquired by study.
শীশ, s. a hiss, a whistle; -দা, to whistle
শুঁটী, s. a legume, a pulse; -কলাই, peas.
শুঁঠ, s. dry ginger; -পিষ্টক, a gingerbread.
শুঁড়, s. a proboscis, elephant's trunk. [ler.
শুঁড়ী, শুণ্ডিক, s. a dramseller, vintner, distil-
শুক্, v. n. to become dry, to be exsiccated, to wither, to fade, to heal, to shrivel.
শুক, s. parrot; -দেব, the son of Vyása.
শুকচীনা, s. China root (Smilax China).
শুকতারা, s. the planet Venus.
শুকন, s. a becoming dry, a withering, a fading, the healing of a wound or ulcer.
শুকনা, a. dry, sapless, withered, lean.
*শুকর, s. thanks; -গুজারী, thanksgiving.
শুকা, v. a. to dry, to dry up, evaporate, to cause to shrivel or waste: a. dry, dried up, emaciated, lean: s. drought, dryness.
শুকাটা, or শুকানি, s. dryness, withering.
শুকান, s. a drying up, withering, the causing of a thing to dry up or waste.
শুকানিয়া, a. drying: s. one who drys.
শুক্টী, dry, dried, lean; -মাছ, dried fish.
শুক্ড়িয়া, a. shrivelling; -যা, to shrivel up.
শুক্ত, sour gruel, vinegar; a bitter potherb.
শুক্তনী, s. bitter condiment or sauce.
শুক্তি, s. dryness, a shrivelling up, a consumption; pearl-oyster, cockle, shell.
শুক্তিকা, s. sorrel; a pearl-oyster (Ostrea
শুক্তিজ, মুক্তা, s. a pearl. [ephippium).
শুক্র, a. white: s. the planet Venus; semen; -কোষ, vesiculæ seminales; -বার, Friday.
শুক্ল, a. bright, white, pure: s. whiteness.
শুক্লতা, -ত্ব, s. whiteness, brightness, purity.
শুক্লপক্ষ, s. the light or lunar fortnight.
শুক্লপক্ষীয়, of the light or lunar fortnight.
শুক্লিমা, s. whiteness, brightness, purity.
শুঙ্গ, v. a. to smell: s. beard of corn or grass.
শুঙ্গা, v. a. to cause to smell: s. a smelling.
শুচনা, s. correction, a table of errata.
শুচি, a. pure, clean, cleansed, purified, correct: s. Agni, fire; a tried friend, purification by ablution, moral purity, holiness, virtue, goodness, accuracy, correctness.
শুচিকর, sanctifying, purifying, cleansing.

শুচিতা, *s.* sanctity, purity, holiness, virtue.

শুজি, *s.* flour, rolam, grits, coarse flour.

শুড়ী, *a.* straight and narrow, narrow.

শুড়্শুড়্, শুড়্শুড়ী, *s.* the sensation of ting-

শুড়্শুড়ান, শুড়্শুড়ানী, *s.* a tingling. [ling.

শুণ্ঠী, dried ginger; -পিষ্টক, gingerbread

শুণ্ড, *s.* a proboscis, an elephant's trunk.

শুণ্ডিক, *s.* a vintner, a distiller, dram-seller.

শুদ্ধ, *a.* pure, clean, unmixed, unadulterated, right, correct, purged from faults.

শুদ্ধতা, -ত্ব, *s.* the same as শুদ্ধসত্ত্বতা.

শুদ্ধমতি, *a.* pure-minded, upright. [holy.

শুদ্ধসত্ত্ব, *a.* perfect, right, righteous, pure,

শুদ্ধসত্ত্বতা, correctness, perfection, righteousness, uprightness, purity, rectitude.

শুদ্ধি, *s.* purity, sanctity, simplicity, rectitude, correctness, unadulteratedness.

শুদ্ধিকর, *a.* purifying, sanctifying, cleansing, purging from errors or impurities.

শুধ্, শুধরা, *v.* to be cleansed or purified; to cleanse, purify, correct or improve, to purge from impurity, error or fault, to expiate, to forgive, to mend, modify.

শুধরাণ, *s.* a cleansing, purifying, the correcting of a writing, the purging away of faults, errors, or impurities, the amending or modifying of a law. [ly.

শুধু, *a.* bare, empty: *ad.* only, merely, bare-

শুন্, *v. a.* to hear, to regard, to attend to.

শুনন, or শুননি, *s.* the hearing of a thing.

শুনা, *v. a.* to cause to hear, to mention in one's hearing: *a.* heard: *s.* a hearing.

শুনান, শুনানি, *s.* a causing to hear, rehearsing in one's hearing: *a.* sounded out.

শুনী, *s.* the female of a dog, a bitch.

শুভ, good, right, pleasant, agreeable, propitious, favourable, auspicious, beautiful, handsome, splendid, shining, illustrious, eminent, distinguished, learned: *s.* good, good fortune, happiness, auspiciousness, goodness, welfare.

শুভংযু, *a.* happy, prosperous, fortunate.

শুভকর, *a.* auspicious, doing good.

শুভকর্ম, or শুভকার্য্য, *s.* a good or auspicious act, a religious action. [moment.

শুভক্ষণ, *s.* propitious time, an auspicious

শুভগ্রহ, *s.* an auspicious planet.

শুভঙ্কর, *a.* auspicious, propitious: *s.* an arithmetician, an accountant.

শুভদৃষ্টি, *s.* an auspicious or favourable glance, mutual interview of the bride and bridegroom on the wedding day.

শুভদ্বেষ, *s.* envy, malice, ill-will.

শুভদ্বেষ্টা, *s.* an envious person. [of time.

শুভলগ্ন, *s.* an auspicious hour or portion

শুভসংবাদ, or শুভসমাচার, *s.* an auspicious report, good news, the gospel.

শুভাদৃষ্ট, *s.* good fortune, good luck.

শুভানুধ্যায়ী, শুভধ্যায়ী, *a.* benevolent, seeking the good of others: *s.* a well-wisher.

শুভান্বিত, *a.* fortunate, lucky.

শুভাশীর্ব্বাদ, *s.* a benediction, a blessing.

শুভিতা, *s.* ease, convenience, favourableness of circumstances, seasonableness.

শুভোদয়, *s.* the rise of one's good fortune.

শুভ্র, *a.* white, fair, bright; -তা, whiteness.

শুভ্রদন্তী, *a.* having white teeth: *s.* she who has fine teeth; the guardian elephant

শুভ্রাংশু, *s.* the moon. [of N. W. quarter.

*শুমার, *s.* calculation, number; attention.

শুম্ভ, *s.* the Asura or giant slain by Durgá.

শুল্ক, *s.* custom, a toll, fee, duties on imports and exports, port duties, a present made to the bride by the bridegroom, money given to the bride's parents.

শুল্কগ্রহণ, *s.* the taking of toll or duty.

শুল্কগ্রাহক, *a.* taking toll or duty: *s.* a toll-gatherer, a collector of port duties.

শুল্কগ্রাহী, *a.* taking toll or duty.

শুল্‌ফা, *s.* the common way of filling tobacco for smoking; also, *vide* শল্‌ফা.

শুশুক, শিশুক, শিশুমার, *s.* a porpoise. [vant.

শুশ্রূষক, *a.* serving obsequiously: *s.* a ser-

শুশ্রূষা, *s.* service, attention, care, obedi-

শুষণ, *s.* the drying of things. [ence.

শুষির, *s.* a hole, vacuity, a chasm, a tube, the vacuity within a tube. [up.

শুষ্ক, *a.* dry, sapless, withered, shrivelled

শুষ্কতা, -ত্ব, *s.* dryness, saplessness.

শূআ, *s.* an awn, a spiculæ, the hairs on a caterpillar, a bristle; name of a bird.

শূআপোকা, *s.* a hairy caterpillar.

শূআর, *s.* a hog, a boar; *fem.* শূআরনী.

শূঁআ, *s.* an awn, a spiculæ, a bristle.

শূক, *s. vide* শঙ্গা ; -কীট, a hairy caterpillar.
শূকধান্য, *s.* bearded rice or corn.
শূকময়, শূকী, *a.* awned, bristly, setaceous.
শূকর, *s.* a pig, a hog, a boar ; *fem.* শূকরী.
শূক্ষ্ম, *a.* small, fine ; (*properly* সূক্ষ্ম).
শূঙ্গা, *s.* an awn, spiculæ, a bristle. [class.
শূদ্র, শূদ্রা, *s* a shúdra, or man of the 4th
শূদ্রধর্ম্ম, *s.* the duties of the shúdra tribe.
শূদ্রাণী, শূদ্রী, *s.* a female of shúdra caste.
শূনা, *s.* shambles, slaughter-house. [lems.
শূন্নৎ, *s.* circumcision : শূন্নি, a class of mos-
শূন্য, *a.* lonely, desert, empty, void, blank, vacant, hollow : *s.* the atmosphere, a vacuum, a dot, cypher, an odd ; -গৃহ, empty house ; -তা, -ত্ব, emptiness, vacuity ; -বাদ, atheism ; -বাদী, an atheist : -স্থান, an empty place ; -হস্ত, empty-handed.
শূম, *s.* a niggard, a miser. [caterpillar.
শূয়, *s.* an awn, a spike, a bristle, a hairy
শূয়াপোকা, *s.* a hairy caterpillar.
শূয়ার, *s.* a pig, a hog, a boar ; *fem.* শূয়ারী.
শূর, *a.* bold, brave, heroic, courageous, intrepid : *s.* a hero, a champion, warrior.
শূরতা, *s.* heroism, courage, bravery, intre-
শূরত্ব, *s. idem.* [pidity.
শূরত্বপ্রকাশ, *s.* a display of bravery.
শূল, *s.* a stake on which criminals are impaled, a spear, dart, a spit, sharp pain, a pang, the colic, rheumatic pains, death.
শূলঘ্ন, *s.* removing pain, anodyne.
শূলন, *s.* excruciating pain, the colic.
শূলফী, *s.* a javelin, a dart, a pike, a spear.
শূল -বেদনা, -ব্যথা, -রোগ, *s.* the colic.
শূলী, armed with a spear : *s.* an impaling, a stake on which convicts are impaled.
শৃগাল, *s.* a shakal, a jackal ; *fem.* শৃগালী.
শৃঙ্খল, শিকল, *s.* a chain, fetters, shackles.
শৃঙ্খলতা, *s.* a series, arrangement, connection (of things), concatenation, order.
শৃঙ্খলা, *s. idem ;* also, a chain, fetters.
শৃঙ্খলী, *s.* a chain for an elephant's feet.
শৃঙ্গ, *s.* a horn, a mountain-peak, a sign, a mark, sovereignty, mastership, elevation, an artificial fountain or jet-d'eau.
শৃঙ্গাটক, *s.* the same with শিঙ্গাড়া.
শৃঙ্গার, *s.* passion, love, copulation ; in *poetry*, the sentiment of love.
শৃঙ্গাররস, *s.* the sentiment of love, amatory sentiment in poetry. [ing gaily.
শৃঙ্গারী, *a.* impassioned, lascivious, dress-
শৃঙ্গী, *a.* horned, armed with horns, peak-
শৃত, *a.* boiled, dressed. [ed, crested.
শেওড়া, *s.* a small tree (Trophis aspera).
শেওরা, *s.* pudendum muliebre.
*শেখ, *s.* title of a class of Musalmáns.
শেখর, *s.* a crest, a garland of flowers for
শেফালিকা, *s.* same as শিউলি. [the head.
শেয়ান, *a.* cunning, subtle, sly, artful.
শেয়াল, *s.* a jackal ; -কাঁটা, a thorny shrub.
শেয়ালা, *s.* conferva, moss, aquatic weed.
শেয়ালাপড়া, *a.* overrun with moss, mossy.
শের, শেট, *s.* a sera, seer, 2lbs avoirdupoise.
শেল, *s.* a javelin, spear, pike, dart, a spit.
শেলেষ্মা, *s.* the same with শাক্ষিশাক.
শেষ, *s.* end, limit, termination of a thing, an ultimatum, a result, a remainder.
শেষকাল, *s.* the last time, the latest time, the time of death. [part of a book.
শেষখণ্ড, শেষগ্রন্থ, *s.* a supplement, the last
শেষদশা, শেষাবস্থা, *s.* the last state or condition, final state of a person, old age.
শেষবেলা, *s.* the afternoon, end of the day.
শেষভাগ. *s.* the last or remaining part.
শেষভুক্, *a.* eating remnants of food.
শেষভোজ্য, *s.* dessert, what is eaten after a
শেষমন্দ, *s.* catastrophe, ill result. [meal.
শেষরাত্রি, *s.* the last watch or close of the
শেষে, *ad.* finally, lastly, in fine. [night.
শৈখরিণ, *s.* a lactate : শৈখরিণিক, *a.* lactic.
শৈত্য, *s.* coldness, chilliness, frigidity.
শৈথিল্য, *s.* slackness, dilatoriness, delay.
শৈব, *a.* devoted to Shiva : *s.* a devotee of Shiva ; a malate : শৈবিক, *a.* malic.
শৈবাল, *s.* conferva, moss, aquatic weed.
শৈল, *s.* a rock, a mountain.
শৈলজ, a produced on a rock, rock-born : *s.* bitumen, or storax, benzoin.
শৈলভিত্তি, *s.* a stone-cutter's chisel.
শৈলি, contrivance, stratagem, art, knack ; a queen's maid or female attendant.
শৈলী-ভবন, *s.* petrifaction ; -ভূত, petrified.
শৈলেয়, *a.* benzoate : *s.* benzoin or storax.
শৈলেয়িক, *a.* benzoic, benzoate. [niness.
শৈল্য, *s.* a stony substance, hardness, sto-

শৈশব, *a.* infantile, juvenile: *s.* childhood, infancy, minority. [*vide* শলুফা.
শোআ, *v. a.* to lay one down to sleep: *s.*
শোআন, *a.* sleeping, lying: *s.* a causing one to sleep, the putting a child to bed.
শোঁক, শোঁকা, *v. a.* to smell. [*s.* a smelling.
শোঁকা, *v. a.* to cause to smell: *a.* smelled:
শোঁটা, *s.* a mace, a club, a bludgeon; -বর্দার, a mace-bearer; -বর্দারী, his business.
শোক, *s.* grief, mourning, sorrow, woe.
শোকজনক, *a.* distressing, mournful.
শোকসাগর, *s.* an ocean of grief. [sorrow.
শোকাকুল, *a.* grieved, overwhelmed with
শোকানল, *s.* the fire or torment of grief.
শোকান্বিত, *a.* sad, sorrowful, grieving.
শোকাবিষ্ট, শোকার্ত, *a.* grieved, sorrowful.
শোকী, *a.* grieving, lamenting, mourning.
শোচ, *s.* grief, sorrow, sadness, distress.
শোচক, *a.* occasioning grief, distressing.
শোচনা, *s.* grief, anxiety, regret, sorrow.
শোচী, *a.* grieving, mourning, regretting.
শোণ, *s.* hemp;[1] the name of a river.
শোণা, শোণামুখী, *s.* senna (Cassia senna).
শোণিত, রুধির, রক্ত, *s.* blood. [limbs.
শোথ, *s.* a swelling or intumescense of the
*শোদা, *s.* a fop, a vagabond, a libertine.
শোধ, *s.* the clearing off of a debt, payment, retaliation, purifying; -কৃ, to pay, to liquidate a debt, to retaliate.
শোধক, *a.* cleansing, purifying, correcting, paying off a debt, retaliating: *s.* he who purifies, one who corrects writings.
শোধন, *s.* a liquidating or clearing off, retaliation, the correcting of a writing, a calcining of poison, subtraction. [paid.
শোধনীয়, *a.* payable, due, requiring to be
শোধবোধ, *a.* liquidated, cleared off, paid.
শোধা, *v. a.* to cause to purify, correct or cleanse: *s.* a cleansing, the correction of a writing, purification, a paying off.
শোধিত, *a.* paid off, cleared, corrected.
শোধ্য, *a.* payable, due requiring to be paid, corrected, cleansed, or purified
*শোবে, *s.* a doubt, suspicion.
শোভন, *s.* a being comely or pleasing to the sight: *a.* shining, splendid, beautiful, handsome, propitious, auspicious.
শোভনীয়, *a.* requiring to be beautified, worthy of being made illustrious.
শোভা, *s.* light, lustre, radiance, splendour, beauty, elegance, glory, comeliness.
শোভাকর, *a.* shining, radiant, resplendent, comely, beautiful, ornamental.
শোভাঞ্জন, *s.* same as শজিনা. [illustrious.
শোভান্বিত, *a.* beautiful, comely, splendid,
শোভিত, *a.* splendid, adorned, beautified.
*শোর, *s.* a noise, a clamour, a sound.
শোরসার, *s.* a clamour, a noise, a voice.
শোরা, *s.* nitre, saltpetre.
শোলা, *s.* lightwood, Indian cork-plant.[2]
শোলাবৎ, *a.* suberous, like lightwood.
শোষ, *s.* pulmonary consumption, dryness, wasting, drying up, imbibition, suction.
শোষক, *a.* drying, absorbent. [dry.
শোষটান, *s.* a drawing off or drinking till
শোষণ, *s.* a drying or imbibing, a becoming dry, an absorbent vessel. [ed.
শোষণীয়, *a.* capable of being dried or wast-
শোষা, *s.* dryness, a drying up.
শোহাগ, *s.* a caress, indulgence, dalliance.
শোহাগিনী, *a. fem.* caressing, dallying.
*শৌক, *s.* desire, inclination, love, curiosity, gaiety, cheerfulness, pleasure.
শৌকিন, *a.* loving, desirous, intent upon, fond of pleasure or curiosity, gay.
শৌক্ত, *a.* acetous: শৌক্তিক, *a.* acetic.
শৌচ, *s.* stool, the evacuation of the excrements; purification by ablution.
শৌচপ্রস্রাব, *s.* stool and urine.
শৌণ্ডিক, *s.* a vintner, a distiller. [flesh.
শৌনিক, *s.* a butcher, a seller of birds'
শৌর্য্য, *s.* heroism, bravery, prowess, cour-
শৌর্য্যদ্বারা, *ad.* by bravery. [age, valour.
শৌর্য্যধন, *s.* wealth acquired by bravery.
শৌর্য্যান্বিত, *a.* brave, courageous, heroic.
শ্মশান, *s.* a place to burn the dead, a cemetery, a sepulchre, a burying ground.
শ্মশ্রু, *s.* a beard; -মুখী, a bearded woman.
শ্যাকুল, *s.* a shrub (Ziziphus scandens).
শ্যাব, brown; -দন্ত, brown or black toothed: *s.* a tooth produced between the two front teeth of the upper jaw.
শ্যাম, *a.* black, the colour of a peacock's neck, dark-blue; -তা, -ত্ব, blackness.

শ্যামল, *a.* black, dark-blue, yellowish blue.
শ্যামা, *s.* the black goddess Káli, a name of Durgá ; the name of a song bird.[1]
শ্যাল, শ্যালক, শালা, *s.* a wife's brother.
শ্যালকী, শালী, *s.* a wife's sister.
শ্যেন, or শ্যেনপক্ষী, *s.* a hawk, a falcon.
শ্রদ্ধা, *s.* faith, credence, devotedness, fidelity, respect, reverence, a desire, purity.
শ্রদ্ধাকর, *a.* exercising faith or veneration.
শ্রদ্ধান্বিত, *a.* believing, showing veneration.
শ্রদ্ধালু, *a.* believing, trusting, venerating.
শ্রবণ, *s.* a hearing, attending ; the ear ; the hypothenuse of a triangle, a diagonal.
শ্রবণকর্ত্তা, *s.* a hearer, an auditor.
শ্রবণসহ্য, *a.* tolerable to the hearing.
শ্রবণা, -নক্ষত্র, *s.* the 23rd mansion of the zodiac.
শ্রবণানার্হ, *a.* unfit to be heard.
শ্রবণার্হ, *a.* fit to be heard.
শ্রবণীয়, *a.* audible, fit or proper to be heard.
শ্রবণেন্দ্রিয়, *s.* the organ of hearing, the ear.
শ্রবণোপযুক্ত, *a.* proper or fit to be heard.
শ্রম, *s.* fatigue, weariness, labour, toil, exertion, diligence, military exercise.
শ্রমকাতর, *a.* distressed with toil or fatigue.
শ্রমপূর্ব্বক, *ad.* with toil or fatigue.
শ্রমসহ, *a.* supporting fatigue, unwearied.
শ্রমসাধ্য, *a.* accomplished by toil.
শ্রমাকাতর, *a.* unwearied, very laborious.
শ্রমান্বিত, *a.* connected with toil or fatigue.
শ্রমাসক্ত, *a.* sedulous, assiduous, laborious.
শ্রমী, *a.* laborious, sedulous, assiduous, diligent, industrious, painstaking.
শ্রাদ্ধ, *s.* an offering made to deceased ancestors at appointed times.
শ্রাদ্ধীয়, *a.* belonging to the shráddha.
শ্রান্ত, fatigued, wearied, tired, exhausted.
শ্রান্তি, *s.* fatigue, weariness, languor, lassitude.
শ্রান্তিকর, *a.* fatiguing, wearisome.
শ্রাবণ, *a.* connected with hearing : *s.* the sense of hearing ; an Indian month containing part of July and part of August.
শ্রাবণপ্রত্যক্ষ, *a.* known by the hearing.
শ্রাবণীয়, শ্রাবয়িতব্য, *a.* audible, proper to be spoken in the hearing of another.
শ্রাবিত, *a.* caused to be heard, spoken in another's hearing.
শ্রাব্য, *a.* audible, proper to be made audible.

শ্রী, *s.* fortune, prosperity, success ; a name of Lakshmí the goddess of prosperity ; glory, beauty, elevation, consequence, splendour. When prefixed to a person's name it means glorious, illustrious.
শ্রীকণ্ঠ, *s.* one of the names of Shiva.
শ্রীকাতর, *a.* envious, invidious, malicious.
শ্রীখণ্ড, *s.* the sandal-wood.
শ্রীদ, giving beauty or splendour, conferring glory.
শ্রীপতি, *s.* a name of Vishnu.
শ্রীপঞ্চমী, *s.* a festival in honour of Saraswatí.
শ্রীফল, *s.* wood-apple, the Bel-fruit.[2]
শ্রীবৎস, *s.* a mark on Vishnu's breast.
শ্রীভ্রষ্ট, *a.* fallen from glory or splendour, ill-fated, poor, degraded.
শ্রীমান্, *a.* glorious, prosperous, beautiful, illustrious, fortunate.
শ্রীমুখ, *s.* the word শ্রী, written on the back of a letter.
শ্রীযুক্ত, শ্রীযুৎ, *a.* glorious, prosperous, illustrious, splendid, beautiful, fortunate.
শ্রীযুত, শ্রীল, শ্রীবিশিষ্ট, *a. idem.*
শ্রুত, *a.* heard, reported : *s.* a hearing.
শ্রুতমশ্রুত, *a.* despised, disregarded.
শ্রুতাধ্যয়নসম্পন্ন, *a.* learned, possessed of a knowledge of the veda and shástras.
শ্রুতি, *s.* the vedas ; audience, hearing, a rumour, the ear ; the hypothenuse of a triangle, a diagonal.
শ্রুতিকটু, *s.* a cacophony, unpleasant sound.
শ্রুতিমূলক, *a* originating from the vedas.
শ্রুতিসিদ্ধ, *a.* proved or established by the vedas.
শ্রুত্যধীন, *a.* subject to the vedas.
শ্রুব, *s.* a sacrificial spoon ; a sacrifice.
শ্রেণী, *s.* a row, a range, a rank, a tier, a row of trees, an avenue.
শ্রেণীপূর্ব্বক, *ad.* orderly, in a line or row.
শ্রেণীবদ্ধ, *a.* in a row, arranged in lines.
শ্রেণীভূত, *a.* disposed in ranks or rows.
শ্রেঢ়ি, a set of distinct substances placed in order, consequence, progression.
শ্রেঢ়িগণিত, or শ্রেঢ়িফল, *s.* the sum of all the terms in progression.
শ্রেয়ঃ, *s.* prosperity, beatitude.
শ্রেষ্ঠ, *a.* best, chief, prime, superior.
শ্রেষ্ঠতা, -ত্ব, *s.* superiority, excellence.
শ্রেষ্ঠাসন, *s.* a principal seat, a chief seat.
শ্রোণি, *s.* the hip, the loins, the rump.

শ্রোণিফলক, *s.* the hip and loins, hip-bone.
শ্রোতব্য, *a.* audible, proper to be heard.
শ্রোতা, *s.* a hearer, an auditor.
শ্রোত্র, *s.* the organ of hearing, the ear.
শ্রোত্রীয়, *a.* modest, docile, well-behaved: *s.* a bráhman versed in the vedas.
শ্রৌত, *a.* prescribed by the vedas.
শ্লথ, *a.* slack, loose, flaccid, remiss: *s.* slackness, indifference, carelessness.
শ্লাঘনীয়, শ্লাঘ্য, *a.* praiseworthy, laudable, deserving of applause. [one's self.
শ্লাঘা, *s.* praise, applause, an eulogy, priding
শ্লাঘী, *a.* praising, applauding, puffing.
শ্লিষ্ট, *a.* embraced, connected, joined.
শ্লীপদ, *s.* the elephantiasis or swelled leg.
শ্লেষ, *s.* an irony, sarcasm, a double entendre, a speech admitting of a double meaning, a jest, a pun; an embrace, union, junction, contact, presence.
শ্লেষকাব্য, *s.* a poem intended to convey a double meaning, a sarcastic poem.
শ্লেষপ্রবন্ধ, *s.* a composition or set speech intended to convey a double meaning.
শ্লেষবচন, শ্লেষবাক্য, *s.* an irony, a sarcasm, a double entendre, a word admitting of double meaning, a jest, a pun.
শ্লেষ্মঘ্ন, *a.* destroying phlegm or cold.
শ্লেষ্মন্, শ্লেষ্মা, *s.* a catarrh, serum, rheum, a cold, phlegm, the phlegmatic humour.
শ্লোক, *s.* a stanza, a verse of poetry.
শ্লোককাটাকাটি, *s.* a mutual spouting of
শ্লোকচুরি, *s.* plagiarism. [verses.
শ্লোকচোর, *s.* a plagiary, a plagiarist.
শ্লোকরচক *s.* a versifier, a poet. [verses.
শ্লোকরচনা, *s.* versification, a composing of
শ্বঃ, *ad.* to-morrow.
শ্বদন্ত, *s.* the canine teeth.
শ্ববৃত্তি, *s.* service, slavery, servitude.
শ্বসন, *s.* a breathing, wind, air, breath.
শ্বশুর, *s.* a father-in-law.
শ্বশ্রূ, *s.* a mother-in-law.
শ্বা, *s.* a cur, a dog.
শ্বাপদ, *a.* having digitated feet, rapacious.
শ্বাস, *s.* breath, respiration, a sigh; asthma.
শ্বাসকাস, শ্বাসরোগ, *s.* an asthma, a wheez-
শ্বাসরোগী, *a.* asthmatic, wheezing. [ing.
শ্বিত্র, *s.* a kind of leprosy.

শ্বিত্রী, *a.* leprous: *s.* a leper.
শ্বেত, *a.* fair, white: *s.* whiteness.
শ্বেতকরবী, *s.* the white oleander.[1]
শ্বেতপার্শ্ব, *s.* the white of the eye.
শ্বেতপুনর্নবা, *s.* a variety of hogweed.[2]
শ্বেতবর্ণ, *a.* white coloured: *s.* white colour.
শ্বেতমুর্গা, *s.* the white cockscomb flower.[3]
শ্বেতরাই, *s.* a species of mustard.[4]

ষ, the 31st consonant in the alphabet.
ষট্, *a.* six; -কর্ণ, a kind of lute.
ষট্ক, *a.* six, six-fold.
ষট্কর্ম্ম, *s.* the six prescribed duties, *viz.* 1. adoration, 2. sacred duty, 3. alms-giving, 4. sacrifice, 5. giving instruction, and 6. receiving lawful gifts.
ষট্কোণ, *a.* hexagonal, six-cornered.
ষট্ক্ষণ, *s.* an hour [the 46th.
ষট্চত্বারিংশৎ, forty-six: ষট্চত্বারিংশত্তম,
ষট্ত্রিংশৎ, thirty-six: ষট্ত্রিংশত্তম, 36th.
ষট্পঞ্চাশৎ, fifty-six: ষট্পঞ্চাশত্তম, 56th.
ষট্পদ, *a.* six-footed: *s.* a bee.
ষট্পুরুষ, *a.* hexandrous: *s.* six lineal an-
ষট্প্রকার, *a.* six sorts or kinds. [cestors.
ষট্ষষ্টি, *a.* sixty-six; -তম, the sixty-sixth.
ষট্সপ্ততি, *a.* seventy-six; -তম, the seventy-
ষট্স্ত্রী, *a.* hexagynous. [sixth.
ষড়্, a *prefix* meaning six.
ষড়ঙ্গ, *s.* six parts of the body collectively, *viz.* the two hands, the two feet, the head and the loins; the six sciences appendant to the vedas, *viz.* 1. grammar, 2. prosody, 3. astronomy, 4. pronunciation, 5. the meaning of unusual terms, and 6. the religious ritual.
ষড়শীতি, *a.* eighty-six: *s.* the passage of the sun from Aquarius to Pisces, from Taurus to Gemini, from Leo to Virgo, and from Cancer to Sagittarius.
ষড়শীতিতম, *a.* the eighty-sixth.
ষড়ানন, *a.* six-faced: *s.* a name of Kártik.
ষড়্গুণ, *a.* six-fold, six times.
ষড়্ধা, ষড়্বিধ, *a.* six sorts or kinds. [sixth.
ষড়্বিংশতি, twenty-six; -তম, the twenty-
ষড়্ভুজ, *a.* six-armed, hexagonal: *s.* a hexagon, a quadrilateral and two triangles.
ষড়্ষড়্, *s.* a rustling noise, titillation.

ষণ্ড, *s.* a eunuch ; a bull at liberty.
ষণ্ণবতি, *a.* ninety-six ; -তম, ninety-sixth.
ষষ্টি, *a.* sixty ; -তম, the sixtieth.
ষষ্টিক, *a.* belonging to or connected with sixty, ripening in sixty days.
ষষ্ঠ, *a.* the sixth ; -ধা, of six sorts, six-fold.
ষষ্ঠী, *a.* the sixth (lunar day) : *s.* Durgá.
ষাইট, *a.* sixty, threescore ;-গুণ, sixtyfold.
ষাঁড়, ষণ্ড, *s.* a bull, an ox, a bull at liberty.
ষাট্‌পৌরুষিক, *a.* belonging to or connected with six generations.
ষিড়্গ, *s.* a whoremonger, a catamite.
ষেটেরাপূজা, *s.* a ceremony observed on the sixth day of the birth of a child.
ষোড়শ, *a.* sixteen. [ingredients.
ষোড়শাঙ্গ, *a.* composed of sixteen parts or
ষোল, *a.* sixteen ; -ক্রি, the sixteenth.
ষোলআনা, *a.* complete, full, entire, the whole : *s.* sixteen annas or a rupee.

স is the thirty-second consonant : when used as a *prefix*, it means *with* : *v. a.* to bear, to endure, to suffer, to support.
***সহিস**, *s.* a groom ; *fem.* সহিসনী.
সই, *s.* a female companion or friend, a female namesake ; also, a signature.
***সওআর**, *s.* a rider : সওআরী, a vehicle.
***সওআল**, *s.* an interrogation, a question.
***সওদাগর**, *s.* a merchant, trader. [chant.
সওদাগরী, *s.* merchandise ; office of a mer-
সওদাপত্র, *s.* written contract. [number.
সওয়া, *s.* a quarter more than the given
সং, a *prefix*, in *comp.* it usually conveys the idea of the action being done compactly, well, in the society of some one, or in connection with some thing.
সংকল্প,সংক্রান্তি,সংক্ষেপ,&c. *vide* সঙ্কল্প, সঙ্ক্রান্তি, &c. Also *see* ADDENDA.
সংজ্ঞা, *s.* a noun, a name, appellation, a term, a denomination, a class, thought, mind, idea, intellect, the Gáyatrí or sacred verse of the veda, one of the wives of the sun ; -সুত, Saturn.
সংবৎসর, *s.* a year, a full year.
সংবৎসরীয়, *a.* annual, yearly.
সংবাদ, *s.* a report, news, an intelligence, notice, information.
সংবাদদ্বারা, *ad.* by or through a report.
সংবিৎ, *s.* intellect, understanding, knowledge, a contract, an engagement, assent, a promise, a sign, signal, a watchword, an appellation, a name, an institute, a preserved ceremony or custom.
সংবিদ্ব্যতিক্রম, *s.* violation of a promise or
সংয, *s.* a human skeleton. [engagement.
সংযত, *a.* restrained, bound, confined, imprisoned, fettered, concrete, frozen.
সংযন্তা, *s.* one who restrains or coerces.
সংযম, *s.* restraint, confinement, forbearance, concretion, ceremonial fast.
সংযম্য, *a.* coagulable, concretive.
সংযম্যমেদ, *s.* coagulable lymph.
সংযুক্ত,*a.*conjoined, united to, joined with, related to, connected with, attached to, mixed with, endued with. [war, battle.
সংযুগ, *s.* the meeting of armies in battle,
সংযোগ, *s.* close contact, intimate union, adhesion, cohesion, union, connection.
সংযোগযুক্ত, *a.* adhesive, cohesive.
সংযোগী, *a.* joining, connecting, uniting, adhering, cohering. [concurrence.
সংযোজন, a joining, uniting, connection,
সংযোজিত, *a.* joined, united, connected.
সংরক্ষক, *a.* preserving, guarding : *s.* a preserver, a keeper, a guardian. [ing.
সংরক্ষণ, *s.* a preserving, guarding, keep-
সংরক্ষণীয়, সংরক্ষ্য, *a.* proper or requiring to be kept or preserved.
সংরক্ষিত, *a.* kept, preserved, guarded.
সংলগ্ন, *a.* brought into contact, joined, stuck together, adhered, connected.
সংশপ্তক, *s.* a chosen soldier, a soldier who is sworn never to retreat from battle, a brother in arms, a military comrade.
সংশয়, *s.* a doubt, hesitation, suspicion.
সংশয়জ্ঞান, *s.* an idea of doubt, doubt, uncertainty, a suspicion.
সংশয়প্রাপ্ত, *a.* doubtful, hesitating. [cion.
সংশয়যোগ্য, *a.* worthy of doubt or suspi-
সংশয়াত্মক, *a.* consisting of or identified with doubt or suspicion. [cious.
সংশয়াপন্ন, *a.* doubting, hesitating, suspi-
সংশয়ী, *a.* *idem.* [ablution.
সংশোধন, *s.* correcting, a cleansing by

সংশ্রব, *s.* a promise, an agreement, assent.
সংশ্রয়, *s.* protection, a refuge, an asylum.
সংশ্রিত, *a.* protected, defended, preserved, [secured.
সংশ্লিষ্ট, *a.* united, embraced.
সংশ্লেষ, *s.* an embrace, union, connection, junction, association, aggregation.
সংসক্ত, *a.* near, adjoining, contiguous, endowed with, effected by, connected, associated, attached to, acquainted with.
সংসক্তি, *s.* acquaintance, intimacy, union, connection, junction, associated connection, proximity, contact.
সংসর্গ, *s.* proximity, contact, union, junction, acquaintance, intimacy, society, intercourse, the junction of the sexes.
সংসর্গদোষ, *s.* the fault or evil of society.
সংসর্গবর্ব্বর, *s.* a stupid or foolish man owing to the society in which he moves.
সংসর্গাধীন, *a.* subject to society.
সংসর্গী, *a.* social, maintaining intercourse.
সংসার, *s.* the world, the mundane state or condition, the state of man in society, a person's family and worldly concerns.
সংসারাশ্রম, *s.* a secular condition.
সংসারাশ্রমী, *a.* secular, worldly. [worldly.
সংসারী, going on as mundane affairs do,
সংসিদ্ধ, *a.* accomplished, perfected.
সংসিদ্ধি, *s.* the accomplishment of a work, perfection, completion, nature, the natural state, quality, or disposition.
সংসৃষ্ট, *a.* connected, united, connected as partners in trade, re-united, connate, congregated, combined, coadunited.
সংসৃষ্টতা, *s.* union, association, fellowship.
সংসৃষ্টি, *s.* a connection, an union, a reunion, coparcenership, copartnership.
সংসৃষ্টী, *s.* a coparcener, a relation reunited with his relations after a separation.
সংস্কার, *s.* a completing, accomplishing, finishing, perfection, purity, apprehension, idea, conception, recollection, memory, a habit, instinct, a faculty, embellishment, decoration, elegance, consecration, purification, the preparation of an article of food or medicine, a chemical process, a purificatory rite.
সংস্কারক, *a.* completing, accomplishing, perfecting, purifying, consecrating, embellishing, decorating : *s.* a purifier.
সংস্কারকর্ত্তা, *s.* a consecrator, a purifier.
সংস্কারবিশিষ্ট, *a.* complete, full, perfect, pure, consecrated, sanctified, recollected as a habit, cooked, concocted.
সংস্কারযোগ্য, *a.* worthy of sanctification or consecration, worthy of recollection.
সংস্কারাপন্ন, *a.* connected with habit or recollection, connected with prescribed religious observance.
সংস্কারী, *a.* completing, accomplishing, effecting, conceiving, consecrating, purifying, sanctifying, recollecting.
সংস্কার্য্য, *a.* perfectible, accomplishable, conceivable, requiring to be consecrated, requiring to be recollected.
সংস্কৃত, *a.* wrought, exquisitely formed, compact, artificially produced, excellent, highly decorated, embellished, purified, cleansed, consecrated, completed, finished, perfected, formed by accurate grammatical rules : *s.* the classical and sacred language of the Hindus.
সংস্তর, *s.* bed or couch, a bed of leaves.
সংস্থ, *s.* a spy, an emissary, a fellow-countryman, neighbour, an inhabitant, correct conduct, a state, a condition of being, the period of life, a stop or stay, a likeness, a resemblance, an assembly, a staying, an association.
সংস্থান, *s.* a form, a figure, a shape, fabrication, construction, a heap, a quantity, a stock, pecuniary state, property, wealth, primary formation.
সংস্থাপক, *a.* establishing, causing to stand, settling, fixing : *s.* he who establishes.
সংস্থাপন, *s.* a fixing, establishing, settling.
সংস্থাপনীয়, সংস্থাপ্য, *a.* fixable, capable of being settled or established.
সংস্থাপিত, *a.* established, fixed, settled.
সংস্থিতি, *s.* a stock, capital, wealth, a residence, an abode, a station, a standing.
সংস্পর্শ, *s.* close contact, a touch, a grasp.
সংস্পৃষ্ট, *a.* brought in contact, grasped, [joined.
সংস্রব, *s.* connection, mixture.
সংহত, *a.* strongly knit, well compacted,

close, welded, joined, approximated to, closed, shut, struck, wounded, killed.

সংহতজানুক, *a.* knock-kneed. [heap

সংহতি, *s.* an assemblage, a collection, a

সংহরণ, *s.* a destroying, ruin, destruction.

সংহর্তা, *s.* a destroyer, a murderer.

সংহার, *s.* destruction, ruin. [stroyer.

সংহারক, *a.* destructive, ruinous : *s.* a de-

সংহারমুদ্রা, *s.* a particular ceremony of Hindu worship consisting of locking the fingers of each hand together back to back and then turning them round.

সংহারী, *a.* destructive, ruinous.

সংহার্য্য, *a.* destructible, requiring to be or worthy of being killed or destroyed.

সংহিত, *a.* attached, joined, collected, assembled, compounded.

সংহিতা, *s.* an arrangement of the sacred text of the veda into short sentences, a compilation, collection. [scattered.

সংহৃত, *a.* killed, destroyed, ruined, seized,

সকণ্টক, *a.* thorny, spiny, prickly, attended with trouble and difficulty. [venue.

সকর, *a.* attended with revenue, paying re-

সকরুণ, *a.* compassionate, pitiful. [verbs).

সকর্ম্মক, *a.* in *gram.* active, transitive (as

সকল, *a.* all, entire, the whole. [of stains.

সকলঙ্ক, *a.* contaminated, defiled, rusty, full

সকল্যাণ, *a.* happy, prosperous. [ful.

সকাম, *a.* desirous, lascivious, sensual, lust-

সকারবকার, *s.* nonsense, obscene talk.

সকাল, *ad.* early, in the morning, betimes.

সকালে, *ad.* early, early in the morning.

সকুল, *a.* belonging to the race or family : *s.* a kinsman, a relation.

সকুল্য, *a.* belonging to the same family and entitled to drink the same water : *s.* a distant relation.

সকৃৎ, *s.* fæces, ordure : *ad.* at once, with, together with, always : *a.* once.

সকোপ, or সক্রোধ, *a.* angry, wrathful.

সখা, *s.* a companion, a friend, associate.

সখিত্ব, *s.* friendship, intimacy.

সখী, *s.* a female friend or companion.

সখীভাব, *s.* friendship, companionship.

সখ্য, *s.* friendship, intimacy. [fumed.

সগন্ধ, *a.* having a fragrance, scented, per-

সগর, *s.* the name of a fabled king of Ajodhyá who had sixty thousand sons.

সগর্ব্ব, *a.* proud, haughty, arrogant.

সগর্ভ্য, *s.* brother of full blood, uterine bro-

সগর্ভা, *a.* with child, pregnant. [ther.

সগুণ, *a.* possessed of good qualities, virtuous, talented : *s.* teak tree, teak wood.

সগোত্র, *a.* together with the race or family : *s.* a kinsman, of the same family name.

সঘন, *a.* thick, impervious, frequent.

সঙ্কট, *a.* narrow, contracted, difficult, impervious : *s.* a strait, defile, difficulty.

সঙ্কটপ্রাপ্ত, *a.* involved in difficulties.

সঙ্কটাপন্ন, *a.* afflicted with difficulties.

সঙ্কর, *a.* mixed, compound, mongrel, of two castes : *s.* a scate ; -মাছ, scate fish.

সঙ্করসম্পর্ক, *s.* in *chym.* compound affinity.

সঙ্কলন, *s.* addition, contact, junction, a blending, an intermixing, a heaping.

সঙ্কলিত, *a.* added, joined, blended, twined, intermixed, folded : *s.* in *arith.* addition, the first addition of arithmetical quantity ; in *bot.* folium conduplicatum.

সঙ্কল্প, *s.* a religious ceremony of consecration, a thought, volition, a contrivance.

সঙ্কল্পজ, *a.* produced from thought or consecrating ceremonies. [tended.

সঙ্কল্পিত, *a.* thought, contrived, willed, in-

সঙ্কারকাকর্ষণ, *s.* attraction of composition.

সঙ্কীর্ণ, clustered, close, aggregated, thickly strewed, crowded, contracted, strait ; in *bot.* an aggregate flower.

সঙ্কীর্ত্তক, *a.* celebrating, praising, extolling.

সঙ্কীর্ত্তন, *s.* the uttering of praises aloud, the celebration of a person's praises.

সঙ্কুচিত, *a.* contracted, shrivelled. [hint.

সঙ্কেত, *s.* a sign, an allusion, an inuendo, a

সঙ্কেতদ্বারা, *ad.* by means of sign or token.

সঙ্কেতবাক্য, *s.* a hint, a suggestion.

সঙ্কেতস্থান, *s.* a place appointed by a hint or sign, the place of an assignment.

সঙ্কেতে, *ad.* indirectly, by sign, by a hint.

সঙ্কোচ, *s.* a contracting, shrivelling up, a withdrawing, a shrinking from.

সঙ্কোচক, *a.* causing to contract, shrivelling, contracting : in *ana.* a sphincter.

সঙ্কোচমৎস্য, *s.* a scate, scate fish.

সঙ্কোচী, *a.* contracting, shrivelling up.

সঙ্ক্রম, *s.* a bridge; a changing of station.

সঙ্ক্রমণ, *s.* the removing from one station to another (chiefly applied to the passing of the sun from one sign to the next); transition, transposition, concurrence.

সঙ্ক্রান্ত, passed from one station to another.

সঙ্ক্রান্তি, *s.* a passing from one station to another; a sun's entering on a new sign, at which time the Hindu months begin.

সংক্ষিপ্ত, *a.* abridged, compressed, condensed into a small compass, brief.

সংক্ষেপ, *s.* an abridgment, a compendium, brevity; -কৃ, to abridge, to shorten.

সংক্ষেপক, *a.* abridging: *s.* he who abridges.

সংক্ষেপনীয়, *a.* comprisable in an abridgment or compendium.

সংক্ষেপবক্তা, *s.* one who expresses much in a few words.

সংখ্যা, *s.* a number, a calculation, a reckoning, an account, a muster, a sum.

সংখ্যাত, *a.* numbered, enumerated, calculated.

সংখ্যাতব্য, *a.* calculable, numerable

সংখ্যান, *s.* an enumerating, a calculating.

সংখ্যাবিদ্যা, *s.* arithmetic, science of number.

সংখ্যাবেত্তা, *s.* an arithmetician.

সংখ্যেয়, *a.* calculable, numerable.

সঙ্গ, *s.* company, society, an association, a meeting, a joining, the junction of rivers; -ছাড়, to secede, quit a society.

সঙ্গছাড়া, *a.* lonely, quit of society.

সঙ্গত, *a.* collected, united, adequate, proper, relevant, probable, likely, consistent, appropriate, applicable, apposite.

সঙ্গতকর্ম্ম, *s.* an appropriate or apposite action.

সঙ্গতব্যয়, *s.* economy, frugality.

সঙ্গতব্যয়ী, *a.* economical, frugal.

সঙ্গতি, *s.* society, an association, a meeting, an agreement with, an accession to a party, a person's income or means.

সঙ্গদোষ, *s.* an evil of, or a fault in, society.

সঙ্গম, *s.* meeting, association, a concourse, a coming together, a junction, union, the meeting of friends or lovers, the connection of the sexes, copulation.

সঙ্গী, *a.* accompanying, attending, going with, uniting with, attached to: *s.* a companion, an associate, an attendant.

সঙ্গীত, *a.* sung in a choir: *s.* choral song, a public entertainment consisting of song, dancing and music, a concert.

সঙ্গীতবিদ্যা, *s.* the science of singing in a choir.

সঙ্গীতশাস্ত্র, *s.* the science of music.

***সঙ্গীন**, *s.* a bayonet, a musket-dagger.

সঙ্গুপ্ত, *a.* concealed, hidden, suppressed, closely concealed, kept secret.

সঙ্গুপ্তি, *s.* concealment, suppression, privacy.

সংগৃহীত, *a.* collected, compiled, gathered.

সঙ্গে, *ad.* with, in company with, in society with.

সঙ্গোপক, *a.* concealing, hiding.

সঙ্গোপন, *s.* concealment, suppression.

সঙ্গোপনীয়, or **সঙ্গোপ্য**, *a.* concealable.

সঙ্গ্যা, *s.* a companion, an associate.

সংগ্রহ, *s.* a collection, a compilation, a selection, a taking, a seizing, assent, a promise, the clenching of the fist.

সংগ্রহণ, *s.* the collecting of things together, the compiling of a book, a catalogue.

সংগ্রহণীয়, **সংগ্রহীতব্য**, **সংগ্রাহ্য**, *a.* capable of being gathered or collected.

সংগ্রাম, *s.* a battle, war, conflict, an attack.

সংগ্রামকুশল, *a.* skilled or eminent in war.

সংগ্রাহক, *s.* a collector, a compiler.

সঙ্ঘ, *s.* an assemblage, a flock, a multitude, a collection, a heap, a quantity.

সঙ্ঘট, *s.* a crowd, a conflux of people, close contact, adhesion; a pimp, a pander.

সঙ্ঘটন, *s.* an accession to a party, a meeting, an occurring, the acceding to a proposal, an adhering, a cohering.

সঙ্ঘটনা, *s.* a meeting, a junction, a union, a concurrence in sentiment, or of circumstances, an occurrence, accession, close contact, adhesion, cohesion.

সঙ্ঘটিকা, *s.* a bawd, a procuress.

সঙ্ঘটিত, *a.* concurred with, occurred, fallen in with, acceded to, met, joined, fallen out together.

সঙ্ঘট্ট, *s.* a concourse, a crowd, a conflux; a pimp.

সঙ্ঘন, *a.* solid, impervious, condensed.

সঙ্ঘাত, an assemblage, a multitude, a heap, a collection, the composition of words, a formation of compound terms.

সচকিত, *a.* startled, vigilant, alert; -কৃ, to spring game, to awaken, to stimulate.

সচর, *a.* connected with moving creatures.
সচরাচর, *a.* universal, current, connected with movable and immovable things.
সচল, *a.* moving, able to move, mobile, active.
সচা, *a.* true, right : সচাই, *s.* truth.
সচিন্ত, *a.* thoughtful, anxious, careful.
সচিব, *s.* a counsellor, friend, companion, an associate.
সচী, *s.* the wife of Indra.
সচেত, *a.* sensible, feeling, vigilant, wary.
সচেতন, *a.* sensible, animate, aroused.
সচেষ্ট, *a.* strenuous, zealous, active.
সচ্চরিত্র, *a.* well-disposed, acting virtuously.
সচ্চিদানন্দ, *s.* the existent, good, wise, and happy, an appellation of the Deity.
সচ্ছ, *a.* clear, pellucid, pure, transparent.
সচ্ছল, beneficent, generous, kind, liberal.
সচ্ছলতা, *s.* beneficence, generosity, benevolence, liberality, kindness.
সচ্ছিদ্র, *a.* faulty, blameworthy, guilty.
সজল, *a.* moist, wet, watery, marshy.
সজাগ, *a.* wakeful, awake, vigilant, wary.
সজাতি, *s.* a similar kind, genus, or class.
সজাতীয়, *a.* similar, belonging to the same kind, genus, species, class, or tribe.
সজাতীয়কণা, *s.* similar particles of matter.
সজারু, *s.* a porcupine, hedgehog.
সজীব, alive, living, extant; -কৃ, to revive, revivify.
সজোর, *a.* hale, strong, able, powerful.
সজ্জ, *a.* springing from virtue or truth.
সজ্জন, *s.* a good man, a virtuous person.
সজ্জা, *s.* outfit, furniture, equipage, ornaments, apparatus, armour, dress, accoutrements, harness; -বিশিষ্ট, harnessed.
সজ্জিত, *a.* armed, accoutred, dressed.
সজ্বর, *a.* sick of a fever, feverish.
সঞ্চ, *s.* a joint, joining.
সঞ্চয়, *s.* a collection, gathering, amassing, a hoard, a heap, accumulation.
সঞ্চয়ন, *s.* the collecting of things.
সঞ্চয়নীয়, সঞ্চেতব্য, *a.* accumulable, colligible.
সঞ্চয়ী, *a.* collecting, hoarding, laying up.
সঞ্চরিত, *a.* moving by a communicated power, communicated, begun.
সঞ্চার, *s.* a communication, a communication by contagion, a commencement, the access of a disease, the communication of motion or power, impulse.
সঞ্চারক, *a.* commencing, spreading by communication, communicating motion.
সঞ্চারণ, *s.* the communicating of motion or disease, communicating of influence.
সঞ্চারিত, *a.* communicated, begun, communicated by contagion or contact, brought near or into contact.
সঞ্চারী, *a.* acting upon, influencing, communicating motion or influence.
সঞ্চার্য্য, *a.* communicable by contact, communicable by contagion, capable of being brought near or into contact.
সঞ্চিত, *a.* collected, hoarded, accumulated.
সঞ্চেয়, *a.* accumulable, colligible.
সঞ্জআ, *s.* armour. সঞ্জাব, facing of a garment.
সটীক, *a.* furnished with a commentary.
সটক, সট্কা, *v. a.* to run away : *s.* a small huká-snake.
সড়, *v. a.* to putrify, to rot.
সড়ক, *s.* a highway, a road, a street, way.
সড়কা, *a.* long and narrow, oblong, perpendicular : *a.* slipknot : *v.* to run away.
সড়কীপথ, *s.* a lane, alley, narrow passage.
সড়গড়, *s.* practice, conning, by rote, a committing to memory.
সড়ঙ্গা, *s.* a canoe.
সড়া, *a.* rotten, putrid, musty, tainted : *v. a.* to cause to rot or putrify, to macerate.
সড়িঙ্গা, *a.* thin and tall : *s.* a canoe.
সড়্সড়্, সড়্সড়ান, *s.* a tingling, itching sensation.
সড়্সড়া, *v. n.* to tingle, to itch.
সড়্মড়ো, *a.* dry, parched, friable, crisp.
সৎ, *a.* existent, being, good, true, virtuous, excellent, best, venerable, respectable, wise, learned, fit, proper, firm, steady : *s.* the omnipresent and all-wise God.
সৎ, or সদ্, *a.* good, real, genuine, true.
সতত, *ad.* continually, always, even, perpetually : *a.* eternal, continual, perpetual.
সততজ্বর, *s.* a perpetual fever.
সতর, *a.* seventeen : সতরুক্রি, seventeenth.
সতরঞ্চী, *s.* a carpet, a carpet or cloth worked as a chessboard to play upon.
সতরঞ্চ, game of chess ; -বাজ, chess-player.
সতর্ক, *a.* investigating, reasoning, acute, vigilant, on the alert, careful.
সতর্কতা, *s.* acuteness, sagacity, vigilance.
সতল, *a.* having a bottom, bottomed.
সতা, or সতিন, *s.* a co-wife, a rival wife.

সতী, *a.* virtuous, chaste, pure : *s.* one who burns on her husband's funeral pile.
সতীতা, -ত্ব, *s.* chastity, female purity.
সতীর্থ, *a.* connected with a sacred place : *s.* fellow student or disciple, a classmate.
সতৃষ, সতৃষ্ণ, *a.* thirsty, greedy, covetous, rapacious, avaricious.
সতেজ, *a.* vigorous, fertile, splendid, luxuriant.
সৎকথক, *a.* eloquent : *s.* a good speaker.
সৎকর্ম্ম, *s.* a good act, piety, charity, virtue, worship, homage, a respectful salutation, a welcome to a guest, courtesy, funeral obsequies, purificatory ceremony.
সৎকার, *a.* good, producing good, performing good : *s.* funeral obsequies, a pious action, respect, a welcome, a reward.
সৎকার্য্য, *s.* religious duties, good works.
সৎকৃত, *a.* worshipped, adored, honoured, respected, revered, welcomed, saluted.
সৎক্রিয়া, *s.* a good action, good works, respectful treatment, funeral rites.
সত্তা, *s.* existence, being, goodness, excellence.
সত্ত্রী, *s.* a liberal or munificent householder, an ambassador, an agent.
সত্ত্ব, *s.* goodness, holiness, entity.
সত্ত্বগুণ, *s.* moral goodness, entity, one of the three qualities attributed by the Hindus to matter, *i. e.*, existence when applied to matter, and moral rectitude when applied to rational creatures.
সৎপথ, *s.* a good way, a good course of conduct.
সৎপুরুষ, *s.* a good man.
সৎপ্রতিপক্ষ, *s.* the opposite or contrary reasons by which two propositions one declaring the existence and the other the non-existence of a thing are defended.
সৎপ্রসঙ্গ, *s.* a good topic.
সৎমা, *s.* a step-mother ; *masc.* সৎবাপ.
সত্য, *a.* true, real, genuine, sincere : *s.* truth, an oath, a demonstrated conclusion : *ad.* yes, verily, truly, indeed ; -কৃ, to aver, to affirm, to promise, to swear ; -জান্, to believe, admit a thing as true.
সত্যঙ্কার, *s.* ratification of a bargain, an earnest given to bind a bargain, pledge.
সত্যতা, -ত্ব, *s.* truth, reality, certainty, the truth of any proposition or assertion.
সত্যপ্রতিজ্ঞা, *s.* an affirmation, firm promise.
সত্যবক্তা, *s.* a speaker of truth.
সত্যবতী, *s.* the mother of the sage Vyása.
সত্যবাদী, *a.* faithful to what is spoken, speaking the truth, truth-speaking.
সত্যবোধ, *s.* conviction.
সত্যব্রত, true, veracious, honest, sincere : *s.* name of a king.
সত্যভামা, *s.* one of Krishna's wives.
সত্যভাষী, *a.* speaking the truth.
সত্যযুগ, *s.* the first of the four Hindu ages.
সত্যসন্ধ, *a.* aiming at truth : *s.* Bharata.
সত্যানাশ, *s.* ruin, perdition, destruction.
সত্যানৃত, *s.* trade, commerce, a mixed system of truth and falsehood.
সত্র, *s.* sacrifice, oblation ; liberality, munificence, fraud, cheating ; a house.
সত্বর, speedy, hasty, quick, swift, active.
সত্বরতা, *s.* celerity, activity, swiftness, quickness.
সৎশঙ্কা, *s.* pregnancy.
সৎসংসর্গ, সৎসঙ্গ, *s.* good society or company.
সথূৎকার, *a.* sputtering in speech.
সদঃ, *s.* an assembly, a meeting.
সদৎ, *ad.* always, continually, perpetually.
সদন, or **সদ্মন্**, *s.* a house, a residence.
সদয়, *a.* compassionate, merciful, kind.
সদয়তা, -ত্ব, *s.* compassion, mercifulness.
***সদর**, *a.* chief, supreme : *s.* government ; the outer or upper side, the right side, the breast, pre-eminence, exaltation.
সদর আদালৎ, *s.* the chief court of justice.
সদর আমীন, *s.* a commissioner, a judge or chief officer at a chief station.
সদরদেবানী, *s.* the chief civil court.
সদর দ্বার, *s.* the chief or public gate.
সদরমালগুজার, *s.* one who is accountable to government for the revenue.
সদরমালগুজারী, *s.* government revenue.
সদর্থ, *a.* the substance of `an argument, scope, meaning, an object of endeavour.
সদর্প, *a.* haughty, boastful, arrogant.
সদসৎ, *s.* good and evil.
সদসদবিবেচক, *a.* not judging between good and evil.
সদসদ্বিবেচক, *a.* investigating, discriminating between right and wrong.
সদসদ্বিবেচনা, *s.* a judging or discriminating between right and wrong.
সদসদ্ভেদ, *s.* distinction beween good and evil.

সদস্য, *s.* assistant at a sacrifice ; a spectator, a by-stander. [petually.
সদা, সদাকাল, *ad.* always, continually, per-
সদাচার, *s.* good conduct, good behaviour.
সদাতন, *a.* constant, eternal, incessant, con-
সদানন্দ, *a.* always joyful, happy. [tinual.
সদানুগত, *a.* constantly attached to a person : *s.* a tame animal.
সদাপীড়িত, *a.* valetudinary, always ill.
সদার, *a.* having a wife, with a wife.
সদালাপ, *s.* good conversation, familiarity.
সদাশয়, magnanimous : Sir, your honour.
সদাশিব, *a.* always prosperous : *s.* Shiva.
সদাসন্দিগ্ধ, *a.* always doubtful or suspici-
সদুত্তর, *s.* a good or proper reply. [ous.
সদৃক্, সদৃক্ষ, *a.* similar, alike, resembling.
সদৃশ, *a.* like, similar, resembling, analo-
সদৃশতা, -ত্ব, *s.* similarity, likeness. [gous.
সদেশ, *a.* of the same country, near, proximate : *s.* the same country. [place.
সদেশী, সদেশীয়, *a.* of the same country or
সদোষ, সদোষী, *a.* faulty, guilty, criminal.
সদোষকর, *s.* an accuser, one who con-
সদ্গতি, *s.* virtue, prosperity, bliss. [demns.
সদ্গুণ, *s.* a good quality, virtuous habit.
সদ্বক্তা, *s.* a very eloquent person.
সদ্বক্তৃতা, *s.* magniloquence.
সদ্বিবেচক, *a.* discriminating properly.
সদ্বিবেচনা, *s.* proper discrimination.
সদ্বৃত্ত, *a.* well-behaved, amiable, acting virtuously ; well-rounded.
সদ্ভাব, *s.* entity, goodness of disposition, kindness, goodness, courtesy.
সদ্ভাবী, *a.* well-conditioned, good-natured.
সদ্যঃ, *ad.* forthwith, immediately, at the moment, instantly, in an instant.
সদ্যোজাত, *a.* new, recent, fresh : *s.* a calf.
সধন, *a.* opulent, wealthy, having wealth.
সধবা, *s.* a married woman, a wife, a woman whose husband is living.
সধর্ম্ম, *a.* like, equal, having the same nature or properties, performing the same duties : *s.* the same uses or duties.
সধর্ম্মাক্রান্ত, *a.* subject to the same rules or duties, possessed of same properties.
সধর্ম্মিণী, *s.* a lawful wife, a wife married according to the law of the veda.
সধর্ম্মী, *a.* having similar nature or properties, performing similar duties.
সন, সাল, অব্দ, সম্বৎ, *s.* a year.
*সনদ, or সনন্দ, *s.* a grant, an order, a signature, the seal of a magistrate ; a prop or support, relation, connection.
সনসনাৎ, *ad.* yearly, year by year. [stant.
সনাতন, eternal, perpetual, incessant, con-
সন্তত, *a.* extended, spread, eternal, perpetual, continual ; -জ্বর, a continual fever.
সন্ততি, *s.* posterity, descendants, progeny.
সন্তপ্ত, *a.* heated, distressed, grieved.
সন্তমস, *s.* great or blinding darkness.
সন্তরণ, *s.* a swimming, a floating.
সন্তর্পণ, *s.* a gratifying ; care, attention.
সন্তান, *s.* lineage, a race, a descendant, offspring, progeny ; spreading, expansion.
সন্তাপ, *s.* heat, burning heat, pain, distress, remorse, woe, anguish, passion.
সন্তাপকর, *a.* giving pain or distress.
সন্তাপন, *s.* one of the arrows of Káma-deva, a scorching, affliction, pain, acute distress, the exciting of passion.
সন্তাপনীয়, *a.* capable of being distressed, liable to distress or woe. [pained.
সন্তাপিত, heated, distressed, hurt in mind,
সন্তুষ্ট, *a.* glad, pleased, gratified, satisfied.
সন্তুষ্টচিত্ত, সন্তুষ্টান্তঃকরণ, *a.* pleased, glad, gratified, satisfied at heart. [tion.
সন্তুষ্টি, *s.* pleasure, satisfaction, gratifica-
সন্তোলন, *s.* a spicing or seasoning of food.
সন্তোষ, *s.* pleasure, gratification, satisfac-
সন্তোষক, *a.* the same as সন্তোষী. [tion.
সন্তোষণীয়, *a.* placable, may be pleased.
সন্তোষী, *a.* pleasing, satisfying, gratifying.
সন্দর্ভ, *s.* a stringing of flowers or beads, a collecting, the arrangement of things.
সন্দিগ্ধ, *a.* doubted, questioned, suspected, doubtful, suspicious, questionable.
সন্দিগ্ধচিত্ত, or সন্দিগ্ধমনাঃ, *a.* suspicious, sceptical, doubtful-minded. [debt.
সন্দিগ্ধার্থ, *s.* a doubtful meaning ; disputed
সন্দেশ, *s.* news, a design, information, a report ; a kind of sweetmeat. [suspicion.
সন্দেহ, *s.* a doubt, uncertainty, scepticism,
সন্দেহকর, exercising doubts, suspicious.
সন্দেহবিশিষ্ট, সন্দেহযুক্ত, *a.* *vide* সন্দেহী.

সন্দেহভঞ্জন, *s.* the resolving of doubts, the clearing up of suspicions. [suspicious.

সন্দেহী, *a.* doubting, uncertain, sceptical,

সন্ধান, *s.* distillation, a mixing, a joining, adhering, combination, intimate union, a sustaining, supporting, a recovering; an aim, a guess, a tracing, seeking, a search, scrutiny; a boundary.

সন্ধানলওন, *s.* a searching, tracing, seeking.

সন্ধানী, *a.* searching, aiming, guessing.

সন্ধানীকৃত, *a.* made an aim or scope.

সন্ধায়ী, *a.* aiming, uniting, combining, investigating, searching, scrutinizing.

সন্ধি, *s.* a junction, a joining, a joint, the place of juncture or union; peace after war, an alliance; the junction of letters or syllables, a connecting limb, intervention, a stop or pause, articulation.

সন্ধিগ্রন্থি, *s.* a synovial gland.

সন্ধিচ্যুত, *a.* dislocated: *s.* a dislocation.

সন্ধেয়, *a.* proper to be aimed at.

সন্ধ্যা, *s.* the evening, the twilight, both of the morning and evening, a period of time, *viz.* the morning, mid-day, or afternoon, religious ceremonies to be performed at the aforesaid times, meditation.

সন্ধ্যাকাল, *s.* the evening, the twilight.

সন্ধ্যাকালীন, *a.* belonging to or connected with the evening or twilight. [amulet.

সন্নদ্ধ, *a.* armed, accoutred, wearing an

সন্নামক, *a.* pressing downwards.

সন্নিকর্ষ, *s.* attraction, a drawing near or together, attraction of cohesion. [ther.

সন্নিকৃষ্ট, *a.* attracted, drawn near or toge-

সন্নিধান, **সন্নিধি**, *s.* vicinity, nearness, prox-

সন্নিধিবর্ত্তী, *a.* near, proximate. [imity.

সন্নিপাত, *s.* morbid state of the humours, an inflammatory affection of the body.

সন্নিপাতবিকার, *s.* a change to a morbid state of the humours.

সন্নিবেশ, *s.* devotedness; a plain near a city, a vicinity, neighbourhood. [hand.

সন্নিহিত, near, proximate, adjacent, close at

সন্নেদন, *s.* a conniving, a converging.

সন্ন্যাস, *s.* religious mendicity, asceticism, monastic life, mendicity. [cant.

সন্ন্যাসধর্ম্ম, *s.* duties of a religious mendi-

সন্ন্যাসী, *s.* a religious mendicant, an ascetic, a devotee.

সপ, *s.* a mat, a floor-mat.

সপক্ষ, *a.* winged; of the same party.

সপক্ষ্ম, *a.* fringed with soft hairs, ciliated.

সপত্নী, *s.* a co-wife; **-পুত্র**, son of a co-wife.

সপরিবার, *a.* connected with a family, attended by a family or attendants.

সপর্ব্ব, *a.* jointed, geniculated.

সপর্য্যা, *s.* reverence, worship.

সপিণ্ড, *s.* a kinsman connected by a right to offer the funeral cake to the manes.

সপিণ্ডীকরণ, *s.* the investing of a person with the right to offer the funeral cake.

সপুত্রক, *a.* attended by a son, having a son.

সপ্ত, **সাত**, *a.* seven: **সপ্তম**, *a.* the seventh.

সপ্তক, *a.* the seventh: *s.* a series or total of seven; a woman's girdle. [the 47th.

সপ্তচত্বারিংশৎ, *a.* 47: **সপ্তচত্বারিংশত্তম**, *a.*

সপ্ততি, **সত্তরি**, seventy, threescore and ten.

সপ্তত্রিংশৎ, *a.* 37: **সপ্তত্রিংশত্তম**, *a.* the 37th.

সপ্তদশ, *a.* seventeen, the seventeenth.

সপ্তধা, *ad.* of seven sorts or kinds.

সপ্তধাতু, *s.* the seven constituent parts of the body, *viz.*, chyle, blood, flesh, fat, marrow, bone, and semen. [seventh.

সপ্তপঞ্চাশ, or **সপ্তপঞ্চাশত্তম**, *a.* the fifty-

সপ্তপঞ্চাশৎ, *a.* fifty-seven. [seventh.

সপ্তবিংশতি, *a.* twenty-seven, **-তম**, twenty-

সপ্তপদীগমন, *s.* a bridal ceremony.

সপ্তমী, *s.* the seventh day of the moon.

সপ্তরাশিকা, *s.* the rule of proportion with seven terms. [lation ursa major.

সপ্তর্ষি, *s.* a class of seven sages, the constel-

সপ্তাস্র, *a.* seven-cornered: *s.* a heptagon.

সপ্তাহ, *s.* seven days, a week. [obstacle.

সপ্রতিবন্ধ, *a.* attended with an intervening

সপ্রতিভ, ready, shrewd, having ready wit, understanding or presence of mind.

সপ্রমাণ, *a.* having proof, authentic, self-

***সফর**, *s.* a journey, a voyage. [evident.

সফল, *a.* efficacious, effectual, successful, fruitful, profitable, advantageous.

সফেণ, *a.* foaming, attended with froth.

***সফেদ**, *a.* white. **সফেদা**, *s.* whitelead.

***সফ্তালু**, *s.* the peach fruit. [a reason.

***সব**, *a.* all, the whole, entire. **সবব্**, a cause,

সবংশ, *a.* attended by a race or family.

সবর্ণ, *a.* of the same class in society, homogeneous, of the same colour, coloured.
সবল, *a.* strong, vigorous, powerful, energe-[tic.
সবস্লোট, *a.* lustful, lascivious, lewd.
সবস্ত্র, or **সবাস**, *a.* clad, clothed, dressed.
সবিদ্য, *a.* scientific, learned, erudite.
সবিনয়, *a.* humble. **সবৃন্ত**, *a.* petiolated.
সবিশেষ, *a.* special, circumstantial.
***সবুর**, **সবুরী**, *s.* patience, forbearance.
***সবুজ**, *a.* green, fresh : *s.* a green colour.
সবৃদ্ধিক, *a.* reckoned with interest.
***সবজী**, *s.* an edible plant, vegetable.
সব্য, *a.* left (not right) : *s.* the left hand.
সব্যসাচী, using the left hand equally well with the right : *s.* a name of Arjuna.
সভয়, *a.* timorous, fearful, timid. [lord.
সভর্তৃকা, **সপ্রভুকা**, *a.* having a husband or
সভা, *s.* a company, assembly, a session, a meeting, a royal court, the sitting of the king in council. [moderator.
সভাপতি, *s.* a president, a chairman, a
সভাসৎ, **সভাসদ্**, *a.* having a right to sit in an assembly, belonging to an assembly.
সভাস্থ, *a.* having a place in an assembly.
সভ্য, social, polite, civilized, fit for society.
সভ্রূভঙ্গ, *a.* frowning, distorting the brows.
সম, *a.* like, similar, same, equal, even, level, smooth ; all, whole, entire, full, complete, good, virtuous, proportional.
সমকটিবন্ধ, *s.* the temperate zone.
সমকর্ণ, *s.* an equi-diagonal tetragon.
সমক্ষ, *ad.* before, in presence of, in sight : *a.* near, evident, visible. [own eyes.
সমক্ষদর্শন, *s.* a seeing of a thing with one's
সমখাত, *s.* an excavation which will contain a solid with regular sides.
সমগন্ধক, *s.* a compounded perfume. [full.
সমগ্র, *a.* all, the whole, entire, complete,
সমচতুরস্র, *s.* an equilateral quadrangle, a
সমচতুর্ভুজ, *s.* a square. [square.
সমচ্ছেদন, *a.* having like denominators.
সমজ, *s.* a set of fools or blockheads, a pack
সমজ্ঞা, *s.* fame, reputation. [of beasts.
সমজ্যা, *s.* a society, an assembly, a meeting, an association, fame, celebrity.
সমঝ, *s.* knowledge, comprehension, sense.
সমঞ্জস, *a.* proper, right, earnest, accurate, virtuous, good, experienced : *s.* propriety, consistency, fitness, truth, accuracy.
সমতা, *s.* equality, similarity, sameness, completeness, evenness, equilibrium.
সমতুল্য, *a.* alike, similar, equal, same.
সমতুল্যতা, *s.* equality, similarity.
সমত্রিভুজ, *s.* an equilateral triangle.
সমদর্শী, *a.* viewing all alike, impartial.
সমদ্বাদশাস্র, *s.* a dodecahedron. [of sides.
সমদ্বিদ্বিভুজ, *s.* a rhomboid with equal pairs
সমদ্বিভুজ, *a.* equilateral : *s.* a rhomboid having two equal sides.
সমধাতু, *s.* health, an equilibrium of the elementary parts of the body.
সমধিক, *a.* excessive, exceeding. [dary.
সমন্ত, *s.* a limit, an end, a frontier, a boun-
সমন্ততঃ, **সমন্তাৎ**, *ad.* all around, all about, on every side, wholly, altogether.
সমন্বয়, *s.* a connection with or following as a consequence, the receiving of a person into his former rank of society after he has made atonement for his fault.
সমন্বিত, *a.* possessed of, endued with, ef-
সমপ্রকার, *a.* homogeneous. [fected by.
সমবয়স্ক, *a.* coeval, being of the same age.
সমবায়, *s.* a multitude, assemblage, a collection, aggregate, a junction, combination, union, concord, the connection or comprehension of species in a genus.
সমবায়সম্বন্ধ, *s.* the connection or relation of qualities with the subject, the connection of the species with the genus.
সমবায়িকারণ, *s.* the material cause, or the material of which a thing is made.
সমবায়ী, *a.* mixing, blending, assembling, collecting under one head, comprising.
সমবেত, *a.* mixed, assembled, collected under one head, comprised in one genus.
সমবেধ, *s.* an equal or mean depth. [ble.
সমব্যথনীয়, *a.* sympathetic, equally sensi-
সমভাব, *s.* the same as **সমতা**. [being with.
সমভিব্যাহার, *s.* a society, association, a
সমভিব্যাহারী, *s.* a companion, associate.
সমভিব্যাহৃত, *a.* attended, accompanied by.
সমভূমি, level ground, flat surface, a plain.
সমমর্য্যাদ, *a.* possessing equal honours ; near, proximate, bounded, limited.

সমমাত্র, *a.* having the same dimension.
সমমিতি, *s.* a mean or equal measure.
সময়, *s.* time, a season, fit time, leisure, an opportunity ; an oath, an affirmation on oath ; an established religious custom.
সময়শিরে, *ad.* in the nick of time.
সময়োচিত, *a.* suited to the time or season.
সমর, *s.* war, battle, conflict ; -**তরঙ্গ**, sharp
সমর্জু, or **সমসরল**, *a.* parallel. [conflict.
সমর্থ, *a.* able, strong, powerful, capable, adequate to, fit, proper, successful, connected in sense or object.
সমর্পক, *a.* committing to another.
সমর্পণ, *s.* a delivering over, the committing of a thing to the care of another.
সমর্পণীয়, *a.* requiring to be delivered over or committed to another.
সমর্পিত, *a.* delivered over, committed to.
সমল, *a.* filthy, sordid, squalid, dirty.
সমলম্ব, *a.* having equal perpendiculars.
সমশিরাঃ, *a.* equal in height : a flower
সমশোধন, *a.* equal subtraction. [spike.
সমসমকাল, *ad.* that very time : *s.* a crisis.
সমসূত্রপাত, *a.* putting in parallel lines.
সমস্ত, *a.* compounded, all, the whole, entire, complete : *s.* a whole, an aggregate.
সমস্যা, *s.* a part of a stanza given to be filled up as a trial of skill. [*s.* a year.
সমাংশী, *s.* an equal sharer, a co-heir. **সমা**,
সমাংসমীনা, *s.* a cow calving every year.
সমাকুল, *a.* distressed, agitated in mind.
সমাখ্যা, *s.* a namesake; reputation, honour.
সমাগত, *a.* come together, assembled.
সমাগম, *s.* a coming together, a meeting or assembling, a concourse. [formation.
সমাচার, *s.* a report, news, intelligence, in-
সমাজ, *s.* an assembly, a meeting, a congregation, a society, association. [our.
সমাদর, *s.* respect, veneration, esteem, hon-
সমাদরণীয়, **সমাদর্য্য**, *a.* honourable, respectable, venerable, reverend.
সমাদরপূর্ব্বক, *ad.* respectfully, honourably.
সমাদৃত, *a.* honoured, respected, venerated.
সমাধা, *s.* a reconciling, settling of differences, adjusting of an affair, decision.
সমাধান, *s. idem ;* also, a meditating or fixing of the mind on God alone.

সমাধি, *s.* deep meditation, silence ; the settling of an affair, the reconciling of differences, perseverance in difficulties, a promise, an engagement ; cremation, a burial, a grave.
সমাধিকর্ত্তা, *s.* a settler of affairs or differences ; one who meditates.
সমান, *a.* equal, alike, similar, same, uniform, level : *s.* one of the vital airs.
সমানতা, -**ত্ব**, *s.* equality, similarity, uniformity, levelness. [to one another.
সমানসম্পর্কতা, *s.* general relation of things
সমানোদক, *s.* a relation connected by right to make offerings of water to the manes.
সমাপক, a finishing, concluding.
সমাপকক্রিয়া, the finishing stroke. [ing.
সমাপন, a completing, terminating, finish-
সমাপনীয়, **সমাপয়িতব্য**, **সমাপ্য**, *a.* requiring to be finished or concluded.
সমাপ্ত, **সমাপিত**, *a.* finished, ended. [tion.
সমাপ্তি, *s.* a finishing, conclusion, comple-
সমাবিষ্ট, *a.* entered, engrossed by, engag-
সমাবেদন, *s.* a representation. [ed by.
সমাবেশ, *s.* entrance, accommodation, absorption in contemplation or business.
সমারোহ, magnificence, grandeur, pomp.
সমারোহী, *a.* magnificent, pompous, grand.
সমাস, *s.* a compound state, term, or word, the formation of words, or compound terms, aggregation, composition. [sis.
সমাসাধ্যাহার, *s.* the supplying of an ellip-
সমাহার, *s.* aggregation, a collection, an assemblage, an artificial arrangement of letters so that any two being expressed the intermediate ones are included.
সমাহিত, *a.* meditating, having the senses restrained, reconciled, settled, cautious.
সমাহ্বয়, *s.* a match, prize-fighting, fighting of animals, a challenge, battle, conflict.
সমিতা, *s.* wheaten flour.
সমীকরণ, **সমীকার**, **সমীক্রিয়া**, *s.* an equalizing, a levelling, a making even.
সমীকৃত, *a.* equalized, made level or even.
সমীক্ষ, Sánkhya system of philosophy, nature, crude matter, understanding, intellect, sight, survey, inspection, supervision, superintendence, investigation.

সমীচীন, *s.* truth, reality : *a.* true, genuine, real, right, correct, accurate, proper.
সমীপ, *a.* near, contiguous, proximate : *s.* vicinity, proximity, neighbourhood.
সমীপবর্ত্তী, or **সমীপস্থ**, *a.* near, neighbouring, contiguous, proximate.
সমীপাগত, *a.* approached, come near.
সমীর, or **সমীরণ**, *s.* wind, air. [fitting.
সমুচিত, *a.* proper, fit, right, suitable, be-
সমুচ্চয়, *a.* whole, entire : *s.* a collection, as-
সমুদয়, **সমুদায়**, all, the whole. [semblage.
সমুদাহৃত, *a.* elucidated by example.
সমুদ্র, *s.* the sea, the ocean ; also, *a.* sealed, stamped, ten million millions.
সমুদ্রফেণ, *s.* cuttle fish bone.
সমুদ্রফেণাখ্যজীবী, *s.* a cuttle fish.
সমুন্নত, *a.* elevated, exalted, prosperous.
সমুন্নতি, *s.* elevation, exaltation, prosperity.
সমূহ, *s.* a multitude, assemblage, totality.
সমৃদ্ধ, increased, grown rich or powerful.
সমৃদ্ধি, *s.* prosperity, increase, greatness.
সমেত, *a.* come together, assembled, collected, associated with : *ad.* with. [perity.
সম্পত্তি, **সম্পদ**, *s.* wealth, substance, pros-
সম্পত্তিকর, *a.* making rich or prosperous.
সম্পন্ন, *a.* accomplished, effected, completed, obtained, enriched, prospered.
সম্পর্ক, *s.* relationship, connection, a mixture, contact, affinity, chemical affinity.
সম্পর্কী, *a.* relating to, connecting, coming in contact with, mixing with.
সম্পর্কীয়, *a.* liable to come in connection. relating to, connected or blended with.
সম্পাদক, *a.* effecting, completing, accomplishing, prospering : *s.* a manager.
সম্পাদন, *s.* the effecting or completing of a thing, the accomplishing of a work.
সম্পাদনীয়, *a.* procurable, accomplishable.
সম্পাদয়িতব্য, **সম্পাদ্য**, *a. idem.* [plished.
সম্পাদিত, *a.* effected, completed, accom-
সম্পূর্ণ, *a.* full, filled, replete, complete, perfect, whole, entire, finished. [tion.
সম্পূর্ণতা, *s.* fulness, completeness, perfec-
সম্পৃক্ত, *a.* related, connected, mixed, joined, united, blended, inlaid. [educated.
সম্পোষ্য, *a.* requiring to be nourished or
সম্প্রতি, *ad.* now, at present, of late.

সম্প্রতিপত্তি, *s.* consent, agreement to what is said, assent, a confession.
সম্প্রদত্ত, given, bestowed, conferred, communicated, delivered (as a tradition).
সম্প্রদাতা, *s.* a person who gives, bestows or communicates traditions.
সম্প্রদান, *s.* a giving or bestowing, a communicating ; in *gram.* the dative case.
সম্প্রদানীয়, *a.* communicable, bestowable.
সম্প্রদায়, *s.* traditional doctrine : *s.* gang, a party, a body, a band of musicians.
সম্বৎ, *s.* a year, an æra.
সম্বৎসর, *s.* a whole year, a year.
সম্বৎসরীয়, *a.* annual, yearly, perennial.
সম্বন্ধ, *s.* connection, relation, natural or essential connection of a property or quality with a substance, fitness, propriety ; in *gram.* the possessive case : *a.* fit, proper, right, connected, adjunct, inherent.
সম্বন্ধী, *a.* related to : *s.* a wife's brother.
সম্বন্ধীয়, *a.* appertaining to, connected with, possessed by, relating to, relative.
সম্বৃ, *v. a.* to conceal, to withdraw.
সম্বরণ, *s.* a withdrawing, a concealing.
সম্বল, *s.* provender, provision for a journey, travelling expenses ; water, spikenard.
সম্বলাক্ষর, *s.* arsenic, white arsenic.
সম্বুল, *s.* spikenard (Valeriana jatamansa).
সম্বোধন, *s.* a call ; in *gram.* vocative case.
সম্ভব, *s.* birth, production : *a.* probable.
সম্ভাবনা, *s.* fitness, suitableness, adequacy, probability, possibility, practicability, worship, honour, potentiality.
সম্ভাবনীয়, **সম্ভাবয়িতব্য**, *a.* producible, possible, adaptable, suitable, adequate, fit.
সম্ভাবিত, *a.* suited to, adequate, made fit, made possible, adapted to.
সম্ভাব্য, *a.* producible, possible, adaptable, suitable, adequate, fit. [sation.
সম্ভাষ, **সম্ভাষণ**, *s.* communication, conver-
সম্ভাষণীয়, *a.* conversable, communicable.
সম্ভুক্ত, *a.* enjoyed, partaken of.
সম্ভূত, *a.* born, produced, sprung from.
সম্ভূয়সমুত্থান, *s.* fellowship in trade.
সম্ভোগ, *s.* enjoyment, possession, copulation, a particular sentiment of love.
সম্ভোগী, *a.* enjoying, sensual, cohabiting.

সম্ভ্রম, *s.* honour, respect, reverence, haste, hurry, flurry, confusion, a whirling or turning round, error, ignorance.

সম্ভ্রমজনক, *a.* producing honour or respect.

সম্ভ্রমবিশিষ্ট, or সম্ভ্রমযুক্ত, *a.* honourable, reverend, venerable, respectable.

সম্ভ্রমযোগ্য, *a.* worthy of honour or respect.

সম্ভ্রমার্থী, *a.* desirous of honour. [respect.

সম্ভ্রমার্থে, *ad.* for the purpose of honour or

সম্ভ্রান্ত, *a.* honoured, respected, reverenced, hurried, flurried. [ed, chosen.

সম্মত, *a.* of the same mind, willing, approv-

সম্মতি, *s.* approbation, assent, consent, acquiescence, permission, a wish, regard, affection, respect, true knowledge. [sion.

সম্মর্দ্দক, *a.* compressing: সম্মর্দ্দন, compres-

সম্মান, *s.* honour, respect, reverence, veneration; -কর, showing honour or respect.

সম্মাননীয়, সম্মান্য, *a.* the same as সম্মানীয়.

সম্মানবিশিষ্ট, *a.* the same as সম্ভ্রমবিশিষ্ট.

সম্মানযোগ্য, *a.* worthy of honour or respect.

সম্মানিত, *a.* honoured, respected, venerated.

সম্মানীয়, *a.* honourable, venerable, respect-

সম্মার্জ্জনী, *s.* a brush, broom, besom. [able.

সম্মীলক, *a.* shutting or closing the eyes.

সম্মুখ, *s.* the front or opposite part, the situation in front of a place, presence. সম্মুখে আইসন, to come in presence.

সম্মুখবর্ত্তী, *a.* opposite to, facing, fronting.

সম্মুগ্ধ, সম্মূঢ়, infatuated, astounded, stupi-

সম্মোহ, *s.* infatuation, stupefaction. [fied.

সম্যক্, *a.* good, perfect; all, whole, entire: *ad.* wholly, entirely, properly, fitly.

সম্রাট্, *s.* a paramount sovereign, an em-

সন্নত, *a.* submissive, humble. [peror.

সযোনি, *s.* Indra; proximity to a wife; a female friend; a nut-cutter.

সর্, *v. n.* to move, to go, to remove.

সর, *s* cream, thick milk; motion, a going, a lake, a pool, a cascade, a water-fall.

সরক, *a.* going, moving, preceding: *s.* spirituous liquor, especially rum.

*সরকশ, *a.* obstinate, disobedient, proud.

*সরকার, *s.* a king's court, government, an estate, property, a district comprising several smaller divisions, a steward, superintendent, a writer, an accountant.

সরকারী, *a.* belonging to the estate, public: *s.* superintendence, stewardship. [ter.

সরজ, made of cream: *s.* butter, fresh but-

সরজস্কা, *a.* menstruous, menstruating.

*সরঞ্জাম, *s.* articles, things, furniture, apparatus, materials, ingredients.

সরট, *s.* a chameleon, a lizard.

সরতা, *s.* a betel-nipper, a nut-cracker.

সরত্নি, *s.* a short cubit.

*সরদাই, *s.* cold, cooling things. [man.

*সরদার, *s.* a chieftain, a captain, a head-

সরদারী, *s.* supremacy, the business of a

*সরদী, *s.* cold, wetness, damp [headman.

*সরপোশ, *s.* a cover or lid. [guished.

*সরফরাজ, *a.* exalted, dignified, distin-

সরফরাজী, *s.* exaltation, distinction.

*সরবরা, *s.* a supply, travelling expenses.

সরবরাকার, *s.* one who supplies necessaries for a work, a steward, purveyor.

সরবরাকার, *a.* supplying necessaries for a work: *s.* the office of a surbarákár.

সরভাগ, *s.* boiled-milk cream, custard.

সরভাজা, *s.* fried cream, baked custard.

সরমা, *s.* the wife of Vibhishana; a bitch.

সরযু, *s.* air, wind; the name of a river.

সরল, *a.* straight, rectilinear, upright, honest, sincere, frank: *s.* a kind of bird.

সরলতা, -ত্ব, *s.* the same as সারল্য.

সরলদ্রব, *s.* turpentine, tar. [hearted.

সরলহৃদয়, সরলান্তঃকরণ, *a.* sincere, open-

সরস, *a.* having flavour, taste or sentiment, juicy, sappy, excellent, good: *s.* the cypress tree (Cypressus sempervirens).

সরসরী, *a.* easy, facile, simple. [water.

সরসী, সরস্, *s.* a pond, a lake, a sheet of

সরসীজ, সরসীরুহ, *s.* a water-lily, a lotus.

সরস্বতী, *s.* the goddess of speech and eloquence, affirmed to be the inventress of Deva-nágari letters and the Sanskrit language, and the patroness of music and the arts; speech, the faculty of speech, eloquence; the name of a river.

সরস্বান্, *s.* the ocean, a male river.

*সরহদ্দ, *s.* a boundary, a limit, a border.

সরা, *v. a.* to remove, to use: *s.* a moving, a removing: *a.* moved, removed, used.

*সরাই, *s.* an inn, a baiting place.

সরাগ, সরোষ, *a.* angry, wrathful, passion-
সরাণ, *s.* the removing of a thing. [ate.
*সরাব, *s.* wine, spirituous liquor. [pler.
সরাবী, সরাবখোর, *s.* a winebibber, a tip-
সরালি, *s.* a species of wild duck.
*সরাসর, *a.* all, the whole : *ad.* entirely.
*সরাসরী, *a.* summary, concise.
সরি, *s.* a water-fall, a cascade. [partner.
*সরিক, সরিকদার, *s.* a partaker, a sharer, a
সরিৎ, *s.* a river, thread, a clue ; -পতি, the
সরিদ্বরা, *s.* the river Ganges. [ocean.
সরিষা, *s.* mustard, mustard plant. [shrill.
সরু, *a.* fine, thin, slender, small, minute,
সরূপ, *a.* having a form or shape, having a similar form or shape, resembling.
সরোগ, *a.* diseased, sick. সরোজ, a lotus.
সরোতা, *s.* a betelnut-cracker. [water.
সরোবর, *s.* a large pond, a lake, a sheet of
সর্গ, *s.* creation, a created thing, nature, effort, perseverance, a chapter, section, abandonment, relinquishment. [ta).
সর্জ্জ, *s.* resin ; the shála tree (Shorea robus-
সর্জ্জক, *s.* the shála tree ; also, the Creator, nation, alkali : *a.* creating. [quishing.
সর্জ্জন, *s.* a forming or creating, a relin-
সর্জ্জরস, *s.* the resin of the shála tree.
সর্জ্জিকা, *s.* the impure carbonate of soda.
সর্প, *s.* a serpent, snake, twining or serpentine motion, a gliding along ; *fm.* সর্পিকা.
সর্পক, *a.* moving or gliding along, creep-
সর্পভ্রম, *s.* error in perception. [ing.
সর্পমণি, *s.* a gem said to be produced in the head of a serpent, a carbuncle?
সর্পরাজ, *s.* Vásuki, the king of serpents.
সর্পিস, *s.* ghí or clarified butter.
সর্ব্ব, *a.* all, the whole, entire, universal.
সর্ব্বকাল, *s.* all times, all seasons: *ad.* always.
সর্ব্বকালীন, *a.* belonging to all times.
সর্ব্বগ, all-pervading, going everywhere : *s.* the soul, spirit, water, Brahmá, Shiva.
সর্ব্বগন্ধা, *s.* four aromatic substances.[1]
সর্ব্বজনীন, *a.* applying to all men, univer-
সর্ব্বজয়া, *s.* a flower plant.[2] [sal.
সর্ব্বজিৎ, *a.* all-conquering, all-subduing.
সর্ব্বজ্ঞ, all-wise, omniscient, all-knowing.
সর্ব্বজ্ঞতা, -ত্ব, *s.* omniscience.
সর্ব্বজ্ঞাতা, *s.* one who knows all things.

সর্ব্বতঃ, *ad.* universally, in every respect, every way, wholly, entirely, on all sides.
সর্ব্বতোভদ্র, *a.* good on all sides : *s.* a square temple or palace ; a kind of charade in which the same word answers to several questions, a sort of verse so contrived as to express the same meanings when read from whatever direction.
সর্ব্বতোভাবে, সর্ব্বথা, *ad.* in every respect, by all means, wholly, fully, completely.
সর্ব্বত্র, *ad.* everywhere, in every place.
সর্ব্বত্রগ, সর্ব্বত্রগামী, *a.* going everywhere, all-pervading, omnipresent.
সর্ব্বদর্শী, *a.* omniscient, all-seeing.
সর্ব্বদা, *ad.* always, at all times, continually.
সর্ব্বদেশী, সর্ব্বদেশীয়, *a.* universal, general.
সর্ব্বধুরীণ, *s.* an ox trained both to draught
সর্ব্বনাম, *s. gram.* a pronoun. [and carriage.
সর্ব্বনাশ, *s.* complete ruin or destruction.
সর্ব্বনাশী, *a.* all-destroying, all-destructive.
সর্ব্বপ্রকার, *s.* all kinds or sorts.
সর্ব্বপ্রিয়, *a.* beloved by all, dear to all.
সর্ব্ববল্লভা, *s.* a common woman. [senting.
সর্ব্ববাদিসম্মত, *a.* approved by all, all-con-
সর্ব্ববিধ, *a.* every way, every sort or kind.
সর্ব্বব্যাপক, সর্ব্বব্যাপী, *a.* all-pervading, extending to all circumstances of a case.
সর্ব্বমঙ্গলা, *s.* one of the names of Durgá.
সর্ব্বময়, universal, general, all-abounding.
সর্ব্বরী, রজনী, নিশা, *s.* the night.
সর্ব্বশক্তিমান, *a.* almighty, omnipotent.
সর্ব্বশাস্ত্র, all sciences, all books of science.
সর্ব্বশাস্ত্রজ্ঞ, *a.* versed in all books of science.
সর্ব্বশ্রেষ্ঠ, *a.* chief of all, pre-eminent.
সর্ব্বসহ, সর্ব্বসহা, bearing all : *s.* the earth.
সর্ব্বসাক্ষী, *s.* the universal witness, God.
সর্ব্বসুদ্ধ, *ad.* altogether, inclusively.
সর্ব্বস্ব, *s.* whole of a person's property.
সর্ব্বস্বান্ত, *s.* an end of one's whole proper-
সর্ব্বাঙ্গ, *s.* the whole body. [ty.
সর্ব্বাঙ্গসুন্দর, *a.* completely beautiful : *s.* a perfect beauty ; *fem.* সর্ব্বাঙ্গসুন্দরী.
সর্ব্বাঙ্গী, *a.* affecting all parts of the body.
সর্ব্বাণী, *s.* a name of Durgá. [things.
সর্ব্বান্তর্যামী, *a.* pervading all hearts, or all
সর্ব্বান্ন, *s.* all sorts of food. [persons.
সর্ব্বান্নীন, *a.* eating the food of all sorts of

সর্ব্বাপেক্ষা, *ad.* than all, beyond all.
সর্ব্বাবস্থা, *s.* all states or conditions.
সর্ব্বার্থ, সর্ব্বীয়, *a.* general, universal. [tion.
সর্ব্বেন্দ্রিয়, *s.* all organs of perception and ac-
সর্ব্বোপরি, সর্ব্বোপরিস্থ, *ad.* supreme, above
সর্ব্বৌষধি, a class of medicinal drugs.[1] [all.
সর্ষপ, সর্ষা, *s.* mustard, seed and plant.[2]
সলজ্জ, *s.* modest, abashed, ashamed.
*সলা, *s.* peace, concord, advice, counsel.
সলাভ, *a.* connected with gain, gainful.
সলিল, উদক, নীর, বারি, জল, *s.* water.
সশঙ্ক, *a.* afraid, timid, doubtful, suspicious.
সশঙ্কিত, *a.* fearful, timid, suspicious.
সশরীর, *a.* with the body, embodied.
সশা, *s.* a cucumber. [harnessed.
সসজ্জ, সশস্ত্র, *a.* dressed, armed, accoutred,
সসত্ত্বা, *a.* with child, pregnant, quick.
সসৈন্য, *a.* attended by an army.
সস্ত্রীক, *a.* attended by a wife or woman.
সস্য, *s.* corn, grain ; -কাট্, to reap.
সহ্, *v. a.* to bear, to suffer, to sustain.
সহ, a *prefix*, meaning *with*, *attending*.
সহকার, *s.* help, assistance, co-operation.
সহকারিতা, -ত্ব, *s.* an acting in concert with, assistance, help, co-operation.
সহকারী, *a.* co-operating, assisting, aiding.
সহকৃত, done in concert with, co-operated.
সহক্রীড়, *s.* a play-fellow, a play-mate.
সহগন্ত্রী, সহগামিনী, *s.* a woman who burns herself with her deceased husband.
সহগমন, *s.* a woman's burning herself with her deceased husband, a going with.
সহগামী, *a.* going with, following.
সহচর, সহচারী, *a.* moving with, attending : *s.* an attendant, a companion.
সহচরিত, *a.* moved with, attending.
সহচরী, *s.* a female follower or attendant, a female companion.
সহজ, *a.* light, easy, without difficulty.
সহদেব, *s.* the name of one of the five Pán-
সহধর্ম্মিণী, *s.* a lawful wife. [davas.
সহন, *s.* a bearing, enduring, suffering.
সহনশীল, *a.* patient, disposed to bear suf-
সহনীয়, *a.* bearable, tolerable. [ferings.
*সহবৎ, *s.* society, assembly, a fair; coition.
সহবতী, *a.* social, fit for society. [ciety.
সহবর্ত্তিতা, *s.* a being with, attendance, so-
সহবর্ত্তী, *a.* with, being with, attending, associating with : *s.* a companion.
সহবাস, *s.* a residence with, society.
সহবাসী, *a.* residing with, living in society.
সহমরণ, *s.* a woman's dying or burning herself with her deceased husband.
সহমৃতা, *a.* dead with her husband : *s.* a woman who dies with her husband. [soft.
*সহল, *a.* easy, not difficult, simple, facile,
সহসা, *ad.* suddenly, hastily, without re-
সহস্র, *a.* a thousand. [flection.
সহস্রাক্ষ, *s.* the thousand-eyed Indra.
সহায়, *s.* an ally, a coadjutor, a co-operator, a helper, an assistant.
সহায়তা, *s.* an alliance, co-operation, assist-
সহার্দ্দ, *a.* tender, affectionate. [ance.
সহিত, *ad.* with, together with.
সহিষ্ণু, *a.* enduring, patient, bearing afflic-
সহিষ্ণুতা, *s.* patience, forbearance. [tion.
সহোদর, *s.* own brother, uterine brother.
সহ্য, *a.* tolerable, bearable, bearing.
সাইঙ্গ, *s.* the pole with which articles are borne or carried on the shoulders.
*সাইদ, *s.* a witness, testimony, proof.
সাইর, *s.* songs sung by Chittagong boatrowers ; also, the same with সারি.
সাংঘাতিক, *a.* deadly, fatal, mortal.
সাংযুগীন, *a.* coming in close engagement with an enemy, closely combating.
সাংবৎসরিক, *a.* annual, yearly. [mundane.
সাংসারিক, *a.* secular, worldly, of the world,
সাঁইত্রিশ, thirty-seven : সাঁইত্রিশা, the 37th.
সাঁকো, সেতু, পুল, *s.* a bridge. [of betel-leaf.
সাঁচি, *a.* new, fresh, recent ; -পাণ, a fine sort
সাঁকো, *a.* recently made, new, fresh, recent.
সাঁজোআ, armed, accoutred : *s.* armour, har-
সাঁজোকাপড়, *s.* fresh washed cloth. [ness.
সাঁজোদই, *s.* fresh curds. [dusk.
সাঁঝ, *s.* the evening twilight, candle-light,
সাঁড়ক, *s.* a bamboo lath used in thatching.
সাঁড়াশী, *s.* a smith's tongs, pair of pincers.
সাঁতর, or সাঁতরা, *v. a.* to swim in water.
সাঁতরাণ, *s.* a swimming, a swimming from place to place : *a.* crossed by swimming.
সাঁতলা, *v. a.* to put the spices and other additions to a condiment. [seasoned.
সাতলান, *s.* the seasoning of condiment : *a.*

সাঁতার, *s.* a swimming; -দা, খেল্, to swim.
সাঁধ্, *v. a.* to enter, to go in, to creep into.
সাঁধান, *s.* a going in, creeping in, entering.
সাঁধি, *s.* a crevice, a chink, a perforation.
সাঁস, *s.* the nutritious substance of corn or seeds, the kernel of a fruit. [totality.
সাকল্য, *s.* wholeness, entireness, amount,
সাকার, *a.* having a form or shape, bodily.
সাক্ষাৎ, *ad.* in the presence: *a.* immediate: *s.* interview, meeting, presence, sight.
সাক্ষাৎকার, *s.* presence, personal presence.
সাক্ষাদ্দর্শন, *s.* an immediate sight or view.
সাক্ষিতা, -ত্ব, *s.* the office of a witness.
সাক্ষী, *a.* bearing testimony: *s.* a witness, an ocular witness, an eye-witness.
সাক্ষ্য, *s.* testimony, evidence.
সাগম, *a.* attended with valid credentials.
সাগর, সমুদ্র, *s.* the ocean, the sea. [dis).
সাগুআনী, *s.* the teak tree, (Tectona gran-
সাঙ্খ্য, *s.* one of the atheistical darshanas or views of the veda. [philosophy.
সাঙ্খ্যতত্ত্ব, *s.* the doctrine of the Sánkhya
সাঙ্খ্যশাস্ত্র, *s.* the Sánkhya philosophy.
সাঙ্গ, *a.* complete, finished, ended: *s.* completion, finis, the end, conclusion.
সাঙ্গাৎ, *s.* a friend, comrade, associate.
সাঙ্গীন, *s.* a bayonet, a musket-dagger.
সাঙ্গোপাঙ্গ, *a.* complete, entire, the whole.
সাঙ্ঘাতিক, *a.* deadly, fatal, mortal.
সাজ্, *v. a.* to accoutre, dress, adorn one's self, to put on dress or ornaments.
সাজ, *s.* accoutrements, armour, harness, outfit, articles of dress or use.
সাজা, *v. a.* to accoutre, dress, harness, to set furniture in order in a house, to set out a table for a meal: *s.* punishment; rennet for curds; cornice of a building.
সাজান, the harnessing of an animal, the accoutering of a person, the putting of things in order, setting out of a table for a meal: *a.* accoutered, harnessed, furnished with articles, set in order.
সাজিমাটি, *s.* fuller's earth, unctuous marl.
সাজী, *s.* a flower-basket; fuller's earth.
সাড়, *s.* a sense of feeling, sensitiveness.
সাড়া, *s.* sound, voice, answer, signal, nod.
সাড়ে, *a.* connected with half, half: *ad.* with one-half over; *e. g.* সাড়ে তিন, three and a half, সাড়ে চার, four and a half, &c.
সাত, *a.* seven: সাতৈ, *a.* the seventh.
সাতচল্লিশ, 47. সাতষট্টি, 67. সাতাইশ, 27. সাতাইশা, the 27th. সাতাত্তর, 77. সাতানব্বই, সতানব্বই, 97. সাতান্ন, 57. সাতাশী, 87.
সাতনলা, *s.* a bird catcher's rod or wand.
সাত্ত্বিক, *a.* true, virtuous, excellent, well-disposed.
সাথ, *a.* attended by, with. [disposed.
সাথী, *s.* a. companion, an attendant, an associate.
সাদর, *a.* respectful, honourable. [sociate.
সাদৃশ্য, *s.* likeness, resemblance, similitude.
সাধ, *v. a.* to effect an object, to accomplish a desired thing, to obtain one's wishes, to prevail upon a person.
সাধ, *s.* a desire, wish, solicitation, prayer, labour to accomplish an object.
সাধক, *a.* effecting, accomplishing: *s.* one who accomplishes an undertaking.
সাধন, *s.* an accomplishing, the effecting of a purpose, an expedient, means, the instrument or means for accomplishing.
সাধনা, *s.* effort, entreaty, worship.
সাধনার্হ, *a.* worthy of being accomplished.
সাধনীয়, *a.* possible, accomplishable.
সাধর্ম্য, *s.* a professing of the same religion, an answering the same purpose.
সাধারণ, *a.* common, general, universal.
সাধারণ্য, *s.* a common right or interest, communion, community.
সাধিত, *a.* effected, accomplished, prevailed on, persuaded, well-versed. [suadable.
সাধিতব্য, *a.* accomplishable, possible, per-
সাধিষ্ঠ, সাধীয়ান্, *a.* very hard or heavy.
সাধু, *a.* righteous, good, pious, holy, pure, pleasing, beautiful, well-born, fit, right, proper; classical (as language): *s.* a creditor, a money-lender. [holiness.
সাধুতা, *s.* righteousness, piety, goodness,
সাধেসাধে, *ad.* spontaneously, voluntarily.
সাধ্য, *a.* possible, able, within one's power: *s.* an object to be effected, power, ability, a kind of demi-god, a god.
সাধ্যক্রমে, সাধ্যানুসারে, *ad.* to the extent of one's power, according to ability.
সাধ্যতা, -ত্ব, *s.* possibility, ability.
সাধ্যপক্ষ, *s.* the plaint in a lawsuit.

সাধ্যমত, *a.* corresponding with power : *ad.* to the utmost of one's ability.
সাধ্যসাধনা, *s.* urgent entreaty.
সাধ্যসিদ্ধি, *s.* success, success in an object.
সাধ্যসিদ্ধিপাদ, *s.* the last stage of a lawsuit or a decree for the plaintiff. [suit.
সাধ্যাসিদ্ধি, *s.* want of success, loss of a law-
সাধ্বস, *s.* fear, terror, alarm.
সাধ্বী, *a. fem.* righteous, holy, just, good, pious, chaste : *s.* a virtuous woman.
সান, *s.* feeling, sensation, sense of feeling, sensibility ; paved or smoothed floor ; a whetstone, a whetting wheel.
সানকর, *s.* a whetter, sharpener. [festive.
সানন্দ, joyful, happy, pleasant, delightful,
সানা, *s.* a weaver's sley ; a fine sort of cloth.
সানায়ী, *s.* a bagpipe, a flute, a pipe, a fife.
সানু, *s.* table-land on a mountain.
সানুকূল, *a.* helping, favourable, propitious.
সান্ত্ব, *a.* consolatory, soothing, agreeable, pacific, sweet, docile, quiet. [person.
সান্ত্বন, *s.* the comforting or consoling of a
সান্ত্বনা, *s.* comfort, consolation, condolence.
সান্ত্বনাকারক, *a.* consoling : *s.* a comforter.
সান্দ্র, *a.* dense, thick, gross, coarse, unctuous, oily, impervious, clustered.
সান্দ্রস্নিগ্ধ, *a.* thick or coarse and unctuous.
সান্নিধ্য, *s.* nearness, vicinity, proximity.
সান্নিপাতিক, attended by morbid humours.
সাপ, *s.* a serpent, snake ; -লেজাড়ে, conical,
সাপকর্ষ, *a.* bad, evil, vile. [pyramidal.
সাপত্ন্য, *s.* the condition or state of the co-
সাপত্য, *a.* together with children. [wives.
সাপরাধ, *a.* guilty, in fault, criminal.
*সাপসন্দ, *s.* choice, wish, desire, volition.
সাপুড়িয়া, *s.* a snake-charmer. [pendant.
সাপেক্ষ, *a.* attended with expectation, de-
*সাফ, *a.* clean, pure, pellucid, transparent,
সাফল্য, *s.* effectualness, success. [clear.
*সাফিনামা, *s.* a writing declaring a dispute to be settled by arbitration.
সাবক, *s.* the young of an animal.
সাবকাশ, *a.* at leisure, disengaged. [dent.
সাবধান, attentive, cautious, careful, pru-
সাবধানতা, *s.* caution, care, attention.
সাবধানপূর্ব্বক, *ad.* attentively, carefully.
সাবয়ব, *a.* having its constituent parts.

সাবর্ত্তক, *a.* vertebral as applied to animals.
*সাবাশ, *interj.* brave ! well done ! bravo !
সাবাশী, *s.* an encouragement, applause.
সাবিত্রী, *s.* the gáyatrí or hymn to the sun.
*সাবুৎ, or সাবুদ, *s.* witness, testimony, a confirmation, proof ; -কৃ, to prove.
সাব্যস্ত, সাভ্যস্ত, *a.* confirmed, established, settled ; -কৃ, to prove, to establish.
সাম, *s.* the third veda ; conciliation.
সামক, *s.* a whetstone, a grinding-stone.
সামগ, *s.* one who chants the Sáma veda.
সামগ্রী, *s.* things, articles, materials, goods.
সামঞ্জস্য, *a.* right, proper, good, virtuous : *s.* reconciliation, agreement, union.
সামন, or সামবেদ, *s.* the Sáma veda.
সামন্ত, *a.* bordering, neighbouring : *s.* a chieftain, a military officer, retinue.
সাময়িক, *a.* temporary, seasonable, adopted to particular times or seasons.
সামর্থ্য, *s.* capability, strength, power.
সামলা, সামাল, *v. a.* to take care, to keep in safety, to recover from sickness, etc., to attend, to be careful, to ward off.
সামলান, *s.* attention, care, a warding off, a recovering : *a.* carefully kept.
সামাজিক, *a.* belonging to a society, community, or fraternity. [or community.
সামাজিকতা, *s.* the belonging to a society
সামানাধিকরণ্য, *s.* a being in the same predicament or condition. [al, vulgar.
সামান্য, *a.* common, general, ordinary, usu-
সামান্যবনিতা, *s.* a common prostitute.
সামান্যরস, *s.* a general fluid of the body.
সামাল, *s.* care, caution, attention, careful
সামিয়ানা, *s.* an awning, canopy. [keeping.
সামিল, *a.* comprised in, appending to, included in : *s.* a connection, a whole.
সামীপ্য, *s.* nearness, vicinity, proximity.
সামুদ্র, *a.* marine, sea, sea-born : *s.* a muriate, muriatic salt, cuttle-fish bone ; lines of the hands. [a palmister.
সামুদ্রক, *s.* a fortune-teller, a chiromancer,
সামুদ্রিক, *s. idem* : *a.* muriatic ; sea, marine, relating to the sea.
সামুদ্রিকবিদ্যা, *s.* the science of fortune-telling, chiromancy, palmistry.
সামুদ্রিকাম্ল, *a.* muriatic acid.

সাম্প্রতং, *ad.* now, at present.
সাম্প্রদায়িক, *a.* fit for society, respectable.
সাম্বৎসরিক, *a.* yearly, annual.
সাম্বর, *a.* clad, clothed, dressed.
সাম্বরী, *s.* a female juggler.
সাম্বলক্ষার, *s.* arsenic, white arsenic.
সাম্বলক্ষারিক, *a.* arsenical.
সাম্য, *s.* an equilibrium, an equality, similarity, equanimity.
সাম্রাজ্য, *s.* a kingdom, an empire, government, the duties of government.
সায়, *s.* assent, acquiescence, acknowledgment.
সায়ং, or সায়ঙ্কালীন, *a.* evening.
সায়ক, *s.* an arrow, a dart.
সায়ঙ্কাল, সায়াহ্ন, *s.* the eventide, the evening.
সাযুজ্য, *s.* final absorption.
*সায়ের, *s.* a going, walking, wandering; the whole.
সার্, *v. n.* to amend, to be reproved, to get well of a disease: *v. a.* to repair, to mend, to accomplish, to overthrow.
সার, *s.* quintessence of a thing, essence, alcohol, the heart of a tree, cream of milk, vigour, strength, firmness, hardness, prowess, heroism, dung, manure.
সারক, *a.* cathartic, purgative.
সারকুণ্ড, *s.* a dunghill, a heap of dung or manure.
সারঙ্গ, *s.* a strong man, the melancholy cuckoo;[1] a species of crane;[2] one of the names of Shiva, a deer, a bow, a bow made of horn, a sort of fiddle, hair colour, a kind of note or tune.
সারণ, *s.* a repairing, a mending, a setting right, an improving, a recovering.
সারথি, *s.* a charioteer, a coachman.
সারথ্য, *s.* the office of a charioteer.
সারভাগ, *s.* the quintessence, cream, the most substantial part of a thing.
সারমাটী, *s.* manure, soil for land.
সারল্য, *s.* straightness, uprightness, honesty, sincerity, frankness, integrity.
সারসংগ্রহ, *s.* compilation, summary collection, abstract, compendium.
সারস, *s.* a species of crane.[3]
সারসী, *s.* a female crane; window-glass.
সারা, *v. a.* to repair, to mend: *a.* repaired, finished, ended; all, whole, entire.
সারাণ, *s.* the repairing of things: *a.* repaired.
সারাণিভাটা, *s.* slack water at ebb tide.
সারাংসার, *s.* quintessence, the best part.
সারি, *s.* a row, a rank, a line, a file.
সারিকা, সারী, *s.* the name of a bird.[4]
সারিসারি, *a.* in rows or ranges, in files.
সারেঙ্গ, *s.* a chief lascar or mariner.
সারূপ্য, *s.* identity, a perfect resemblance.
সারোদ্ধার, *s.* compendium, drift, scope, design.
সার্থ, *a.* having a meaning; wealthy.
সার্থক, *a.* answering its end or purpose.
সার্থক্য, সার্থকতা, *s.* the answering of its scope or purpose, effectiveness.
সার্দ্ধ, *a.* connected with half, half: *ad.* with one-half over.
সার্দ্ধং, *ad.* with, together with.
সার্দ্র, *a.* moist, wet, damp, watery.
সার্ব্বকালিক, suited to all seasons, belonging to all seasons, perenniel.
সার্ব্বত্রিক, *a.* universal, belonging to every place.
সার্ব্বভৌম, *s.* a king, a universal sovereign.
সাল, *s.* a shawl to cover; a timber tree,[5] a species of fish;[6] also, a year.
সালগ্রাম, *s.* a sort of stone worshipped by the Hindus as an emblem of Vishnu.
সালসা, *s.* the sarsaparilla.
সালিয়ানা, *a.* yearly, belonging to a year.
সালিক, *s.* a common species of bird.[7]
সাস্র, *a.* angular, polygonous.
সাস্রস্তম্ভ, *s.* a pillar with several angles.
সাহচর্য্য, *s.* association, companionship.
সাহস, *s.* violence, rapine, aggression, oppression, boldness, courage, cruelty, ravishment, rape, hatred, a daring, rashness, temerity, impudence, a boasting.
সাহসপূর্ব্বক, *ad.* boldly, courageously.
সাহসিক, সাহসী, *a.* bold, courageous, audacious, insolent, rash, boasting, daring.
সাহস্র, *a.* relating to a thousand: *s.* a captain, or army, of a thousand men.
সাহায্য, co-operation, mutual help, assistance, patronage, confederacy, alliance.
সাহিত্য, *s.* society, association with another; literature, rhetoric.
সাহুকার, *a.* rich, wealthy, opulent: *s.* a rich man, a great man, a man of credit.
সাহুকারী, the condition of a rich person.
*সাহেব, *s.* a lord, a master, a gentleman;

-লোক, a gentleman ; -জাদা, son of do. ; -জাদী, daughter of do. *Pl.* সাহেবান্.
*সিআ, *v. a.* to sew, to stitch : *a.* black : *s.* a sect or class of Musalmáns.
সিউনী, *s.* a baling-vessel, a kind of basket for baling out water from a pond, etc.
সিংহ, *s.* a lion, a king ; a title, signifying courageous, eminent, chief ; sign Leo.
সিংহদ্বার, সিংহদরজা, *s.* a portal, a palace gate, the principal gate of a temple.
সিংহনাদ, *s.* the roaring of a lion, the shout of combatants or warriors.
সিংহার, *s.* decoration ; *vide* সিউলি. [ed.
সিংহাসন, *s.* a throne ; -চ্যুত, -ভ্রষ্ট, depos-
সিংহাসনোপবিষ্ট, *a.* seated on a throne.
সিঁআ, *v. a.* to sew, to stitch, to seam.
সিঁআন, *s.* the sewing of cloth : *a. vide* সাানা
সিঁআনি, *s.* a sewing, needlework, a stitch,
সিঁউতী, *s.* the white rose.[1] [a seam.
সিঁড়ী, *s.* a flight of steps, a ladder.
সিঁধ, *s.* a mine, a hole, a hole made through a wall by thieves or burglars.
সিঁধকাটী, *s.* instrument used by burglars.
সিঁধাল, *s.* a burglar, thief, house-breaker.
সিঁধালী, *s.* burglary, house-breaking.
সিকতা, *s.* sand, sandy soil, the gravel (dis-
সিকতাময়, *a.* sandy, gravelly. [ease).
সিকদার, *s.* a petty revenue collector.
সিকদারী, *s.* the business of a Sikdár.
সিকনি, *s.* snot, the mucus of the nose.
সিকি, সুকি, *s.* a quarter, a quarter rupee.
সিক্কা, *a.* sterling, current : *s.* an impression on money, stamped coin, a rupee.
সিঙ্গাড়া, সিঙ্গারা, *s.* the same as শিঙ্গাড়া.
সিজ, *v. n.* to boil, to be boiled.
সিজন, *s.* a boiling, a being boiled.
সিজা, *v. a.* to boil, to cook by boiling.
সিজান, *s.* a boiling : *a.* boiled, sodden.
সিড়সিড়, *s.* a tingling, a tingling sensation.
সিত, *a.* white, light, bright.
সিথিল, *a.* slack : সিথিলতা, *s.* slackness.
সিদা, *s.* a gift of rice, etc. to a guest.
সিদি, *s.* an African, a negro, a Caffre.
সিদ্ধী, *s.* hemp leaves, an intoxicating drug.
সিদ্ধ, *a.* effected, accomplished, concluded, boiled, cooked, prepared, made ready : *s.* a sort of demi-gods ; -পুরুষ, holy man.

সিদ্ধচাউল, *s.* rice which has been cleansed from the husk by previous boiling.
সিদ্ধসাধ্য, সিদ্ধার্থ, successful, prosperous.
সিদ্ধান্ত, *s.* an end accomplished, the final result, a decision, a demonstration, a logical conclusion, the astronomical system of the Hindus. [clusion.
সিদ্ধান্তকোটি, সিদ্ধান্তপক্ষ, *s.* a logical con-
সিদ্ধান্তী, *a.* belonging to a decision, appertaining to a logical conclusion : *s.* one versed in the Mimánsá philosophy.
সিদ্ধান্ন, *s.* prepared food, boiled rice.
সিদ্ধি, *s.* the effecting of a work or purpose, accomplishment of an object, perfection, success, the sentence of a court.
সিদ্ধ্যর্থে, *ad.* for success, for a final result.
সিধা, *a.* straight, honest, upright, sincere.
সিন্দুক, *s.* a chest, a box : সিন্দুকচি, a small
সিন্দূর, *s.* vermillion, redlead. [chest.
সিন্ধু, *s.* the ocean, the river Indus.
*সিপাহী, *s.* a soldier ; -গিরী, business of
সিরকা, শিখরিণী, *s.* vinegar. [a soldier.
*সিরিস্তা, custom, usage, current practice.
সিরিস্তাদার, chief native officer in a court.
সিরিস্তাদারী, the business of a Siristádár.
*সিলা, *s.* a weapon, armour.
সিলাখানা, *s.* an arsenal, an armoury.
সিসৃক্ষা, *s.* a desire to create.
সিসৃক্ষু, *a.* desirous of creating.
সীর, *s.* thin drizzling rain. [of Ráma.
সীতা, *s.* a parting the hair ; a furrow ; wife
সীতাফল, *s.* an apple, a custard-apple.
সীতাময়, *a.* furrowed, sulcate.
*সীনা, *s.* the breast ; -বন্দ, a waistcoat.
সীমন্ত, *s.* a bringing the hair over the temples so as to part it on the forehead.
সীমন্তিনী, *s.* a woman, a female.
সীমন্তোন্নয়ন, *s.* a peculiar ceremony observed by women during pregnancy.
সীমা, *s.* a border, a margin, a limit, an end, a boundary, a frontier.
সীমান্তর, *s.* another border or boundary.
সীসক, or সীসা, *s.* lead. সীর, *s.* a plough.
সু, an *insepar. part.* giving the idea of excellence when prefixed to a noun, and of ease or facility when joined to verbals : *a.* good, excellent, easy.

সুঁচ, সূঁচি, সুচ, or **ছুঁচ,** *s.* a needle.
সুঁড়ী, *s.* a vintner, a distiller, a liquor-man.
সুঁতী, *s.* the space between a river's shoal where the water runs in a slow stream.
সুঁদর, *a.* beautiful, handsome, good.
সুঁদরী, *a. f. idem: s.* name of a tree[1] used as
সুঁধি, *s.* two species of waterlily.[2] [fuel.
সুঁধিনারিকেল, *s.* a cocoanut the woody shell of which is easily separated. [waterlily.
সুঁধিমালুক, *s.* the edible root of a species of
সুকর, *a.* easy, easily done, practicable.
সুকর্ম্মা, *a.* virtuous, good, benevolent, dili-
সুকল, *a.* liberal, benevolent. [gent, active.
সুকুমার, *s.* a fine son, a docile or pleasant
সুকুলীন, *a.* noble, most noble. [child.
সুকৃত, *a.* well done, easily done: *s.* a good deed, virtue, merit. [tuous work.
সুকৃতি, *s.* a good or auspicious act, a vir-
সুকৃতিপত্র, সুকৃতিনামা, *s.* a written affirmation, a written affidavit or oath.
সুকৃতী, *a.* virtuous, happy, good.
সুক্রিয়া, *s.* a good action, a good work.
সুখ, *s.* pleasure, happiness, ease, enjoy-
সুখজনক, *a.* producing pleasure. [ment.
সুখজ্ঞান, *s.* the idea of pleasure. [glad.
সুখড়, *a.* happy, easy, pleasant, delighted,
সুখদ, *a.* giving pleasure, pleasant.
সুখদায়ক, *a.* giving pleasure. [and pain.
সুখদুঃখাত্মক, *a.* identified with pleasure
সুখদোহ্যা, *a.* easily milked. [pleasure.
সুখবোধ, *s.* a knowledge or sensation of
সুখভঙ্গ, *s.* an interruption of pleasure.
সুখভেদ্য, *a.* easily separable or divided.
সুখভোক্তা, *s.* a luxurious person. [luxury.
সুখভোগ, *s.* the enjoyment of pleasure,
সুখভোগী, *a.* enjoying pleasure, luxurious.
সুখময়, *a.* happy, full of happiness.
সুখসংবাদ, *s.* good or pleasing news.
সুখসাগর, *s.* an ocean of pleasure. [sure.
সুখসাধন, *s.* the means of obtaining plea-
সুখসাধ্য, *a.* easily accomplishable.
সুখসেব্য, *a.* easily attended or served.
সুখস্বরূপ, সুখাত্মক, *a.* identified with, or strongly resembling pleasure. [ness.
সুখাবহ, productive of pleasure, or happi-
সুখাভিলাষ, সুখাকাঙ্ক্ষা, *s.* a desire of plea-
সুখিন্, সুখী, *a.* happy, easy, at ease. [sure.
সুখোপবিষ্ট, *a.* seated at ease.
সুখ্যাত, *a.* well-named, of good repute, well spoken of, famed, renowned.
সুখ্যাতি, *s.* fame, renown, celebrity, reputation, a good name or character.
সুখ্যাতিজনক, *a.* producing renown, famous.
সুখ্যাতিবিশিষ্ট, *a.* famous, renowned.
সুখ্যাত্যাপন্ন, *a.* reputed, famous, renowned.
সুগঠন, *a.* well-made, well-formed, well-executed: *s.* good workmanship.
সুগতিক, *s.* a good state, a happy state, ease: *a.* having a good gait.
সুগন্ধ, fragrance, odour; a trader. [spicy.
সুগন্ধি, fragrant, sweet-scented, aromatic,
সুগন্ধিতা, *s.* fragrance, a pleasing scent.
সুগম, *s.* easy, accessible, easily done, easily understood: *s.* ease, convenience.
সুগম্য, *a.* easily practicable or attainable.
সুগহন, *a.* impervious, thick, close.
সুগৃহ, *s.* the tailor-bird (Sylvia sutoria).
সুগৃহীত, *a.* firmly held, fast seized, auspiciously received. [end of a work.
সুগোচ, *s.* an easy accomplishment, a finis,
সুগোচর, *a.* evident, clear, obvious, well-
সুগ্রাহ্য, *a.* easily grasped. [known.
সুগ্রীব, *a.* having a fine neck: *s.* a fabled monkey chief and ally of Ráma.
সুঘটন, *s.* auspicious event, good luck.
সুচতুর, *a.* very clever or active, dexterous.
সুচরিত, *a.* well done, easily done, easily effected, easily practised.
সুচরিত্র, *a.* virtuous, well-behaved: *s.* a clear history or narration.
সুচিত্ত, *s.* a good heart or mind.
সুচিন্তা, *s.* proper care or anxiety.
সুচির, *a.* very long, very late.
সুচেষ্টিত, *a.* heartily or diligently sought.
সুজন, *a.* good, good-natured, honest, civil, polite, kind, benevolent: *s.* a good man.
সুজনতা, kindness, urbanity, benevolence. goodness, politeness, civility, honesty.
সুজন্মা, *a.* lawfully begotten, legitimate.
সুজাতি, *s.* a good or respectable nation, a good class of men. [or class of men.
সুজাতীয়, *a.* respectable, of a good nation
সুজি, *s.* grits, coarse flour, rolam; an in-
সুজীর্ণ, *a.* worn out; well-digested. [dex.

সুজ্ঞাত, *a.* easily known, well known.
সুজ্ঞান, *s.* accurate knowledge, a right idea.
সুজ্ঞেয়, *a.* easily knowable.
সুঞি, or or সুঁই, *s.* a needle, *vide* সুঁচ, সুচ.
সুট্, *s. Eng.* a suit (of clothes, etc.).
সুড়ঙ্গ, *s.* a hole, excavation in the earth, a passage under ground, a mine. [path.
সুড়ী, narrow, strait, confined : *s.* a narrow
সুডৌল, সুচপ, *a.* well-shaped, well-formed, handsome, elegant, beautiful. [to itch.
সুড়সুড়, an itching, tingling sensation ; -কৃ,
সুড়সুড়নি, সুড়সুড়ি, *s.* a tingling sensation.
সুণ্ডিক, *s.* a vintner a distiller, a liquor-man.
সুণ্ডিকালয়, *s.* a grog-shop, a liquor-shop.
সুত, *s.* a son : সুতা, *s.* a daughter. [der.
সুতনু, a beautiful, slender : *ad.* very slen-
সুতপাঃ *s.* a devotee, a doer of austerities.
সুতরা, *a.* fine, good, beautiful. [tainly.
সুতরাং, *ad* of course, consequently, cer-
সুতল, *s.* the foundation of a building, a division of the infernal regions.
সুতার, *a.* nice, savoury, palatable, tasteful.
সতীক্ষ্ণ, *a.* very keen or sharp, very pungent, acutely painful.
সুতুষ্টি, *s.* high pleasure or gratification.
সুতেজস্, *s.* great splendour or energy.
*সুদ, *s.* interest, usury ; -খোর, an usurer.
সুদন্ত, *a.* having fine teeth.
সুদরিদ্র, *a.* very poor, needy.
সুদর্শন, *a.* beautiful, pleasing ; *s.* clear sight, a fine view ; the discus of Vishnu.
সুদর্শনচক্র, *s.* the discus of Vishnu.
সুদাঁড়া, *s.* a good custom, a good rule.
সুদিন, *s.* a fine day, an auspicious day.
সুদৃঢ়, *a.* very firm, very hard. [handsome.
সুদৃশ্য, *a.* easily perceptible, clearly visible ;
সুদৃশ্যতা, *s.* a being clearly visible. [merely.
সুদ্ধ, *ad.* with, along with, inclusive, only,
সুধা, *v. a.* to ask, question, enquire : *s.* ambrosia, nectar ; -দান, a gift of nectar.
সুধাকর, or সুধাংশু, *s.* the moon.
সুধান, *s.* a questioning, asking, enquiring.
সুধাপান, *s.* the drinking of nectar.
সুধাবৃষ্টি, *s.* a shower of ambrosia or nectar.
সুধাময়, *a.* nectarious, ambrosial.
সুধী, *a.* highly learned, sensible, clever.
সধীর, steady, constant, deliberate, grave.

সুধু, *ad.* only, merely, barely, simply.
সনয়ন, *s.* a fine eye : *a.* having fine eyes.
সুনিদ্রা, *s.* a sound sleep. [conduct.
সুনীতি, *s.* good morality, sound ethics, good
সুন্দর, *a.* beautiful, handsome, elegant, excellent, fine, of exquisite beauty.
সুন্দরী, *a. fem. idem : s.* a beautiful woman.
সুন্ধি, or সুঁধি, *s.* two species of waterlily.
সুপক্ক, *a.* well-ripened, well-boiled.
সুপণ্ডিত, *a.* well-learned : *s.* a highly learned man, a good philosopher.
সুপথ, *s.* a good road, a virtuous line of ac-
সুপথ্য, *s.* good or wholesome diet. [tion.
সুপর্ণ, *s.* a name of Garura the regent
সুপাঠক, *s.* a good reader. [of birds.
সুপাঠ্য, *a.* easy to be read. [fied man.
সুপাত্র, *s.* a worthy person, a good or quali-
সুপারী, *s.* the betel-nut (Areca catechu).
*সুপারিস, *s.* a recommendation.
সুপারীসী, *a.* recommendatory.
সুপুত্র, *s.* a fine son, a good or obedient son.
সুপুরুষ, *s.* a good man, a beautiful man.
*সুপুর্দ, *s.* a delivering over in charge.
সুপ্ত, *a.* asleep, sleeping ; -ঘাতক, killing a sleeping person : *s.* one who thus kills.
সুপ্তি, *s.* sleep, slumber, drowsiness.
সুপ্তিজনক, *a.* somniferous, causing sleep.
সুপ্রকৃত, *a.* exceedingly right or proper.
সুপ্রজ্ঞ, *a.* well-learned. [good character.
সুপ্রতিষ্ঠা, *s.* a sort of metre ; great renown,
সুপ্রভ, *a.* splendid, brilliant, glorious.
সুপ্রভাত, *s.* a fine or pleasant morning.
সুপ্রযোগ, *s.* dexterity, expertness, contact.
সুপ্রলাপ, *s.* good or free conversation.
সুপ্রসন্ন, *a.* very gracious, highly favorable.
সুপ্রসাদ, *s.* great grace or favour.
সুপ্রাপ্য, *a.* easily obtainable or procurable.
সুফেণ, *s.* yeast, barm, froth.
সুবচন, *s.* a good or elegant language.
সুবচনী, *s.* a lizard ; also, a goddess.
সুবর, a good boon or gift, a good blessing.
সুবর্ণ, *s.* gold, a gold coin, goldmohur ; a fine colour, a good rank or class in society.
সুবর্ণক, *a.* golden : *s.* a tree (Cassia fistula).
সুবর্ণগণিত, *s.* alligation medial, the calculation of gold, as to its fineness, etc.
সুবর্ণগণিত, *a.* mixed with or made of gold.

সুবর্ণবণিক, *s.* a trader in gold, a class of Hindus.
সুবর্ণময়, *a.* golden, made of gold.
সুবর্ণযূথি, *s.* yellow jasmine.
সুবর্ণাত্মক, *a.* identified with gold.
সুবসন্ত, *s.* a festival kept in honour of Kámdeva.
*সুবা, *s.* a province; a Nawáb, a governor.
সুবাদার, *s.* the governor of a province.
সুবাদারী, office of a Nawáb or governor, the government of a province, a province.
সুবাস, *s.* a good scent, a good residence.
সুবিদ্য, *a.* learned, scientific, philosophic.
সুবিধ, সুবিধা, *a.* easy, of a good kind.
সুবিনীত, *a.* well-humbled, very humble.
সুবুদ্ধি, wise, sensible, well-informed, intelligent: *s.* a good idea or understanding.
সুবেশ, well-dressed, neat: *s.* good clothing.
সুবোধ, *a.* wise, intelligent, well-informed, docile, good-natured: *s.* a correct idea or judgment, accurate knowledge.
সুবোধ্য, *a.* easily comprehensible.
সুভগ, *a.* beloved, fortunate, favoured.
সুভগা, *a. fem. idem: s.* a beloved wife.
সুভদ্রা, *a.* very good: *s.* Jagannáth's sister.
সুভব্য, *a.* very polite, genteel.
সুভিক্ষ, *s.* a time of plenty; successful begging.
সুভোক্তা, *s.* a dainty eater, an epicure.
সুভোজ্য, *a.* wholesome to be eaten.
সুক্ষ, *a.* having beautiful or fine eyes.
*সুম, *s.* a horse's hoof; a miser.
সুমতি, well-disposed, benevolent: *s.* a kind mind.
সুমনাঃ, *a.* well-intentioned, good-minded.
সুমর, *a.* numerable: *s.* a multitude.
সুমর্য্যাদক, *a.* highly respectable.
সুমানুষ, *s.* a respectable man, a gentleman.
সুমার, *a.* numerable, calculable.
সুমিত্রা, *s.* the mother of Ráma.
সুমুখ, *s.* a fine face: *a.* having a fine face, pretty.
সুমেধাঃ, *s.* a good capacity to learn, good parts: *a.* sensible, of good capacity.
সুমেরু, *s.* a fabulous mountain celebrated in Hindu romance, the north pole.
সুযোগ, *s.* an opportunity, convenient time.
সুর, *s.* a god, a demigod; tune; a vowel.
*সুরৎ, *s.* a form, a fashion, a countenance, visage, a portrait, an appearance.
সুরৎহাল, *s.* a coroner's inquest, a judicial investigation of murder or robbery.

সুরত, *a.* greatly enjoyed, well-pleased.
সুরতি, *s.* great pleasure or enjoyment.
সুরপুরী, *s.* Indra's capital, heaven of gods.
সুরভি, *s.* a perfume; spring; a fabulous cow which granted every wish.
সুরমণীয়, সুরম্য, *a.* easily enjoyable, very pleasant.
সুরর্ষি, *s.* a divine sage.
সুরলোক, *s.* the heaven of the gods.
সুরস, *a.* nice, savoury, sweet, well-tasted.
সুরসরিৎ, *s.* Gangá, the river Ganges.
সুরা, *s.* wine, spirits, spirituous liquors.
সুরাচার্য্য, সুরগুরু, *s.* epithets of Vrihaspati the preceptor of the gods.
সুরাপ, *a.* drinking spirits: *s.* a tippler, a sot.
সুরাপান, *s.* a drinking of spirits or wine.
সুরাভাগ, or সুরামণ্ড, *s.* yeast, barm.
সুরারি, *s.* a titan or enemy of the gods.
সুরালয়, *s.* the residence of the gods.
সুরাহা, *s.* a good road, a fine way.
সুরূপ, handsome, well-shaped, well-formed.
সুরেন্দ্র, *s.* Indra, the king of the gods.
*সুর্ম্মা, *s.* collyrium, antimony.
সুলক্ষণ, *s.* a good sign, or distinguishing mark.
সুলভ, সুলভ্য, *a.* cheap, easily obtainable, procurable, acquirable, or attainable.
সুলাভ, *s.* a good gain or acquisition.
সুলুপ, *s. Eng.* a sloop, small vessel.
সুলেখক, *a.* writing a fine hand: *s.* a good writer.
সুলোক, *s.* a good person; a good world.
সুলোচন, *a.* having fine eyes *fem.* সুলোচনা.
সুলতান, *s.* a king, a Sultán; *fem.* সুলতানা.
সুলতানী, *a.* kingly, royal, befitting a king.
সুশাসন, *s.* good government or discipline.
সুশাসিত, *a.* well governed or disciplined.
সুশাস্য, *a.* easily disciplinable or governable.
সুশীতল, *a.* very cool, well cooled.
সুশীল, *s.* a good or kind disposition, good nature: *a.* good-natured, amiable.
সুশীলতা, -ত্ব, *s.* goodness of disposition.
সুশোভন, *s.* a looking handsome, comely or well: *a.* comely, beautiful.
সুশ্রাব্য, *a.* easy to be heard, very audible, melodious, harmonious, agreeable.
সুশ্রাব্যতা, *s.* audibleness, melodiousness.
সুশ্রী, *a.* handsome, beautiful, comely.
সুষণি, *s.* a kind of needle-worked cloth.
সুষণিশাক, *s.* a plant used as a pot-herb.

সুষি, সুষির, s. a tube, apipe, ahole, a cavity, an excavation ; a wind instrument.
সুষিদ্ধ, a. well effected or accomplished, completely proved or established.
সুষুপ্ত, a fast asleep, sleeping soundly.
সুষুপ্তি, s. a sound sleep, a dead sleep.
সুষুপ্তিকর, causing sound sleep, soporific.
সুষুপ্তিজনক, a. somniferous, soporific.
সুষুপ্ত্যবস্থা, s. a state of profound sleep.
সুষ্ঠু. ad. well. excellent, plentifully, abundantly.
সুসংস্কৃত, a. well wrought or done.
সুসজ্জ, a. well armed, dressed or harnessed.
সুসন্তান, s a good son or descendant.
সুসময়, s. a fine time, an auspicious time.
সুসহ, a. easy to he borne, tolerable.
সুসাধ্য, a. easily, practicable.
সুসার, sufficiency, pecuniary means, ease, help.
সুসি, s. a kind of striped cloth made of silk and thread.
সুসেবিত, a. well-served.
সুসেব্য, a. easy to be served.
*সুস্ত, a. dejected, low-spirited, indolent, lazy, slow.
*সুস্তি, a. indolent, lazy, slow, dilatory : s. indolence, laziness.
সুস্তিগিরী, সুস্তিপনা, s. indolence, laziness.
সুস্থ, a. well situated, placed in comfortable circumstances, hale, healthy, easy.
সুস্থতা, -ত্ব, s. health, ease, comfort.
সুস্থির, a. very firm or stable, steady, still.
সুস্পষ্ট, a. clear, distinct, evident, very plain, intelligible, articulate.
সুস্পষ্টরূপে, ad. clearly, distinctly, plainly, evidently, intelligibly, articulately.
সুস্বপ্ন, s. a good or auspicious dream.
সুস্বর, s. an agreeable sound : a. fine-toned.
সুস্বাদু, a. well-tasted : s. a good taste.
সুহিত, a. fast held, satiated, satisfied, fit, right, kind, friendly.
*সুহেল্, s. the dogstar, the star Sirius.
সুহেল্সূর্য্যযোগাদিন, s. the dogdays.
সুহৃদ্, s. a friend, an associate, ally, crony.
সুহৃদয়, a. good-hearted, friendly, kind.
সুহৃচ্ছেদ, s. the separation of friends, the breach of friendship.
সূঁই, সূচ, সূচি, ছুঁচি, s. a needle.
সূক্ষ্ম, a. minute, attenuated, fine, thin, subtile, atomic, delicate, precise, exact, neat, accurate, correct, ingenious.

সূক্ষ্মতা, s. fineness, minuteness, attenuated state, thinness, delicateness, ingenuity.
সূক্ষ্মদর্শী, a. sharp-sighted, intelligent.
সূক্ষ্মবুদ্ধি. or সূক্ষ্মবোধ, s. a keen intellect, penetration : a. ingenious, keen, penetrating, sharp, witty, shrewd.
সূক্ষ্মশরীর, s. a fine or subtile body.
সূক্ষ্মীভূত, a attenuated, become fine, minute, delicate, or ingenious.
সূক্ষ্মীভূতহওন, s. rarefaction, a being attenuated.
সূচক, a. informing, pointing out, indicating, making known : s. an informer.
সূচনা. s. information, an indication.
সূচনীয়, or সূচ্য, a. informable, indicable.
সূচি, s. a needle, a pyramid, a cone.
সূচিখাত, s. an excavation of a conical form.
সূচিত, a. informed, indicated, made known.
সূচিমুখ, s. a particular kind of arrow.
সূচীপত্র, s. a table of contents, an index.
সূচ্যগ্র, s. the point of a needle : a. acuminated.
সূচ্যগ্রাকৃতি, a. conical, muricated.
সূচ্যমান, a. receiving information.
সূঁচ্যাকৃতি, a. needle-shaped, acerose.
সূত্র, সূত্রপত্র, s. an index, table of contents.
সূত, a charioteer ; thread ; -কাট, to spin.
সূতক, a. birth : s. impurity after childbirth.
সূতকাটা, s. the spinning of thread.
সূতকাশৌচ, s. the impurity of childbirth.
সূতলী, s. twine, packthread, string.
সূতা, s. thread, twine, yarn ; -কাট্, to spin.
সূতিকা, a. delivered : s. a lying-in woman.
সূতিকাগৃহ, s. a lying-in woman's room.
সূতিকারোগ, s. the diarrhœa or dysentery when it attacks a lying-in woman.
সূত্র, s. thread, line, twine, a clue, an axiom, aphorism, maxim, general rule.
সূত্রধর, ছুতার, s. a carpenter, a joiner.
সূত্রব্যাখ্যা, the amplification of an axiom.
সূত্রিত, a. composed or delivered in axioms.
সূনু, s. a son ; the penis of a child.
সূপ, s. soup, broth, pease soup, sauce, gravy ; a winnowing fan ; -কার, a cook.
সূরণ, s. the same with ওল, which see.
সূর্প, s. a wicker fan for winnowing corn.
সূর্পনখা, s. a giantess, the sister of Rávana.
সূর্য্য, s. the sun ; -কান্ত, crystal, a gem.
সূর্য্যগ্রহণ, s. an eclipse of the sun.

সূর্য্যমণি, *s.* a beautiful flowering plant.[1]
সূর্য্যমণ্ডল, *s.* the orb of the sun.
সূর্য্যমুখী, *s.* the annual sun-flower.[2]
সূর্য্যসুইহেল্সঙ্গম, *s.* the approach of the star Sirius and the sun to each other.
সূর্য্যসুইহেল্সঙ্গমদিন, *s.* the dogdays.
সূর্য্যেন্দুসঙ্গম, *s.* the approach of the sun and moon to each other at the new moon.
সূর্য্যোদয়, sunrise: সূর্য্যাস্ত, sunset.
সৃক্ক, সৃক্কণী, *s.* the corners of the mouth.
সৃজ্, *v. a.* to create, form, to make, frame.
সৃজন, *s.* a creating, a forming, a making.
সৃণি, *s.* a hook or goad for an elephant.
সৃণিকা, *s.* slaver, spittle, phlegm.
সৃষ্ট, *a.* created, formed, made, fabricated.
সৃষ্টি, *s.* creation, formation, fabrication.
সৃষ্টিকর্ত্তা, *s.* the Creator, a maker; God.
সৃষ্টিকর্ত্তৃত্ব, *s.* creatorship, makership.
সৃষ্টিধর, *s.* sustaining the creation: *s.* God.
সৃষ্টিনাশ, *s.* the destruction of the creation.
সৃষ্টিপ্রক্রিয়া, *s.* the work of creation.
সে, *pron.* it, that, he or she *(inferior)*.
সেঅবধি, *ad.* from that time or place.
সেই, *pron.* that, even that, that same.
সেঁওতী, *s.* the Indian white rose.[3]
সেঁকট্, *v. a.* to turn up the nose.
সেঁকট্বেকট্, *ad.* crookedly, distortedly.
সেঁচ, *v. a.* to water, to throw up water from a pond, to bale water from a boat.
সেঁটক্, or সেঁট্কা, *v. a.* to turn up the nose, to distort the face through disgust.
সেঁট্কান, *s.* a distorting the face or turning up the nose in disgust: *a.* distorted.
সেঁতান, *a.* wet, damp, swampy, marshy.
সেক্, *v. a.* to foment, to toast, bake, heat.
সেক, *s.* heat, a fomenting; -দা, to foment.
সেকন, a toasting, baking, heating, fomenting.
সেকন্দর, *s.* Alexander the Great.
সেকন্দরী, *a.* pertaining to Sekandar.
সেকপাত্র, *s.* a vessel to bale water from a boat.
সেকরা, স্বর্ণকার, *s.* a goldsmith.
সেক্তা, *s.* a fomenter, he who waters a garden or street, one who bales out water.
*সেখ, *s.* a class of Musalmáns.
সেখানে, *ad.* there, thither, in that place.
সেগুণ, *s.* the teak tree (Tectona grandis).
সেঙ্গাত, *s.* a friend, companion, an associate.
সেচক, *a.* watering, baling out water.
সেচন, *s.* a watering, a baling out water.
সেচনী, সেকপাত্র, *s.* a baling-vessel.
সেজ, *s.* a table-shade; the name of a plant.
*সেতখানা, *s.* a necessary, a privy, jakes.
সেতার, *s.* the Indian guitar.
সেতু, *s.* a mole or dam, an embankment, a bridge.
সেতুবন্ধ, *s.* the making of a mole or dam (as Ráma's fabled dam in Ceylon).
সেতুবন্ধরামেশ্বর, *s.* island of Ceylon.
সেথা, *ad.* there, thither, in that place.
সেনা, *s.* a soldier, an army, troops.
সেনাগণ, সেনাসমূহ, *s.* a body of troops.
সেনাঙ্গ, *s.* a constituent part or thing necessary to an army.
সেনানী, *s.* a leader or general of an army; Kártika.
সেনাপতি, *s.* a general, commander of an army.
সেনাবর্গ, *s.* troops, military men.
সেনাভঙ্গ, *s.* a flight of troops in disorder.
সেনামুখ, *s.* a division of an army or battalion, a particular company of troops.
সেনাসঙ্গ্রহ, *s.* the collecting of troops.
সেনাসামন্ত, *s.* retinue, attendants, soldiers and officers.
সেপঞ্জ, *a.* fifteen (at dice).
সেপর্য্যন্ত, *ad.* till then, to that place.
সেপায়া, *s.* a tripod, a teapoy.
সেপ্রকার, *ad.* of that kind, of that sort.
সেপ্রযুক্ত, *a.* the same with সেহেতুক.
সেব্, *v. a.* to serve, to attend upon, to take (medicine).
সেবক, *a.* serving, attending on: *s.* a servant, attendant.
সেবকানুসেবক, *s.* the servant of a servant.
সেবতী, *s.* the white rose; *vide* সেঁওতী.
সেবত্যাকৃতি, *a.* rosaceous, rose-formed.
সেবন, a serving, attending on, taking medicine.
সেবনীয়, *a.* requiring to be served.
সেবা, *s.* service, attendance, a serving.
সেবাতী, *s.* a temple clerk, one who performs the service of a temple for hire.
সেবাধর্ম্ম, *s.* the duty or religion which consists in serving or attendance.
সেবিত, *a.* served, attended upon.
সেবিতব্য, সেব্য, *a.* requiring to be served.
সেব্যমান, *a.* receiving service or attendance.
সেমত, *ad.* that sort, that kind.
সেয়াকোল, *s.* a bushy plant and its fruit.[4]
সেয়াখত, *s.* papers relating to landed estate.

সের, *s.* a seer; *vide* শের. সেরগন্ধ, *s.* a bird.[1]
সেরূপ, *a.* of that form, of that kind.
সেরূপে, *ad.* in that form, in that manner.
সেহেতুক, *a.* caused by or arising from that: *ad.* from or because of that.
সৈকত, *s.* a sandy place.
সৈনিক, *s.* a sentinel, a guard, a picquet: *a.* belonging to an army, military.
সৈন্ধব, *s.* rock-salt, fossil-salt.
সৈন্য, *s.* a soldier, an army. [army.
সৈন্যগণ, সৈন্যসমূহ, *s.* a body of troops, an
সৈন্যবর্গ, *s.* troops, military men.
সৈন্যভঙ্গ, *s.* the flight of troops in disorder.
সৈন্যসংখ্যা, *s.* the number of troops.
সৈন্যসংগ্রহ, *s.* the collecting of troops.
সৈন্যসামন্ত, *s.* the same with সেনাসামন্ত.
সৈন্যাধিপতি, সৈন্যাধ্যক্ষ, *s. vide* সেনাপতি.
সৈরিন্ধ্রী, *s.* an independent female artizan, a female attendant of a seraglio.
*সৈলাব, *s.* an inundation, a deluge.
সোআগা, সৌভাগ্যসম্ভব, রসশোধন, *s.* borax.
সোঁটা, *s.* a mace, a bludgeon, a truncheon, a club; -বরদার, a mace-bearer.
সোঁত, *s.* a stream; dysenteric swellings.
সোঁতা, *s.* a stream, a rivulet, a creek.
সোঁদাগোঁদা, *s.* a cosmetic, perfumed un-
সোঁদালি, *s.* Cassia fistula. [guents.
সোঁপন, *s.* a delivering up, entrusting to one's care, a submitting.
সোজা, *a.* straight, straightforward, easy, light, simple; -কৃ to straighten.
সোঢব্য, *a.* tolerable, bearable.
সোঢ়া, *s.* one who bears or endures. [fish.[2]
সোণা, *s.* gold; -খড়কী, the gold or silver
সোণামুখী, *s.* senna (Cassia senna).
সোণামুগ, *s.* a species of pulse.[3]
সোণালা, *a.* gold, golden, gilt: *s.* gilding.
সোণালী, *a.* gold, golden: *s.* Cassia fistula.
সোণ্না, *s.* a small pair of pliers, a pair of pincers, tweezers, nippers.
সোদয়, *a.* connected with the rise of the heavenly bodies, connected with gain.
সোদর, সোদর্য্য, *s.* a full brother, or one born of the same father and mother.
সোপকার, or সোপকৃতি, *a.* connected with help or assistance. [eclipsed.
সোপপ্লব, *s.* the sun or moon when
সোপাধি, সোপাধিক, *a.* surnamed; connected with qualities or attributes.
সোপান, *s.* a staircase, stairs, steps, ladder, a way, a road. [an acid plant.[4]
সোম, *s.* the moon; nectar; the name of
সোমবার, *s.* Monday. [at a sacrifice.
সোমরস, *s.* the juice of Soma plant drank
সোমরাজী, *s.* a common plant.[5]
সোমলতা, *s.* the Soma or moon-plant.
সোমাস্ক্রি, *s.* a thatching-needle, a bamboo
*সোরা, *s.* nitre, saltpetre. [needle.
সোহাগ, *s.* affection, love, fondness, fond-
সোহাগা, রসশোধন, *s.* borax. [ling.
সোহাগিনী, *s.* a beloved wife or woman.
সৌগন্ধিক, *a.* perfumed, sweet-scented.
সৌগন্ধ্য, *s.* a perfume, fragrance, scent.
*সৌগাৎ, *s.* a present, largess; a rarity.
সৌচিক, *s.* a tailor, one who sews.
সৌজন্য, *s.* kindness, good-naturedness, benevolence, civility, goodness, honesty.
*সৌদা, *s.* trade, commerce, articles.
*সৌদাগর, *s.* a merchant, a trader.
সৌদাগরী, *s.* trade, traffic, commerce.
সৌদাপত্র, *s.* a written agreement to deliver goods to a purchaser. [du heaven.
সৌদামিনী, lightning; a courtezan of Hin-
সৌধ, *s.* a place, a site, a mansion; opal.
সৌন্দর্য্য, *s.* beauty, elegance, neatness.
সৌন্দর্য্যবিশিষ্ট *a.* beautiful, elegant, neat.
সৌবর্ণ, *a.* gold, golden, made of gold.
সৌবিদ, *s.* a eunuch, guard of the seraglio.
সৌভাগিনেয়, *s.* the son of a beloved wife.
সৌভাগ্য, *s.* good fortune, good luck.
সৌভাগ্যচিন্তামণি, *s.* a febrifuge, a kind of
সৌভাগ্যসম্ভব, *s.* borax. [fever pills.
সৌম্য, *a.* handsome, pleasing, gentle, placid, quiet, kind, mild, soft, sacred to the moon, lunar: *s.* Mercury.
সৌর, *a.* solar, belonging to the sun.
সৌরজগৎ, *s.* the solar system.
সৌরভ, *s.* fragrance, perfume, scent, odour, beauty, reputation, fame, character.
সৌরমাস, *s.* a solar month.
সৌরি, *s.* Saturn, or the son of Sun. [ness.
সৌষ্ঠব, *s.* excess, excellence, beauty, fleet-
সৌষ্ঠবান্বিত, *a.* excessive, abundant, excel-
সৌহার্দ্দ, *s.* friendship, intimacy. [lent.

সৌহৃদ্য, *s.* friendship, intimacy, amity.
সৌহৃদ্যভঙ্গ, *s.* a breach of friendship.
স্কন্দ, *s.* Kártika, the general of the gods.
স্কন্ধ, *s.* the shoulder, the head of the humerus, the body, the trunk of a tree, a large branch ; a section, a chapter.
স্কন্ধাস্থি, *s.* the shoulder bone (scapula).
স্খলদ্বাক্য, *s.* slip in speaking, a lapsus lin-
স্খলন্, *a.* slipping, tripping, erring. [guæ).
স্খলন, *s.* a slipping, a falling, erring, skipping of words or letters, a moral slip.
স্খলনীয়, *a.* liable to slip or mistake.
স্খলিত, *a.* slipped, mistaken, fallen. [der.
স্তন, the female breast, the pap, dugs, ud-
স্তনদ্বয়, *s.* the two breasts. [or udder.
স্তনপান, স্তন্যপান, *s.* sucking of the breast
স্তনপায়ী, স্তন্যপায়ী, *a.* sucking the breast.
স্তনবৃন্ত, স্তনাগ্র, *s.* the nipple of the breast.
স্তনভর, *s.* a man who has large breasts.
স্তনমর্দ্দন, *s.* the pressing of a woman's
স্তনিত, *s.* the rattle of thunder. [breasts.
স্তন্য, *s.* milk; -ভুক্, feeding at the breast.
স্তব, *s.* praise, an eulogium, a panegyric, applause, flattery ; কৃ, to eulogize.
স্তবক, *s.* a cluster of blossoms, a bunch, a bouquet, nosegay, thyrsus, a multitude.
স্তবকারক, *s.* the same with স্তাবক.
স্তব্ধ, *a.* hardened, stiffened, paralysed, stopped, become rigid, stupid, benumbed.
স্তব্ধি, *s.* rigidity, hardness, stupidity, the absence of feeling or excitability.
স্তম্ব, *s.* a shrub, a stemless plant, a clump of grass, a sheaf, a bunch, tuft, central column of a seed-vessel, a mountain, a post, a pillar, stupidity, insensibility.
স্তম্ভ, *s.* a post, a pillar, column, stupidity, insensibility, rigidity, unfeelingness.
স্তম্ভাকৃতি, *a.* cylindrical. [sensible, fixed.
স্তম্ভিত, *a.* benumbed, paralysed, become in-
স্তর, *s.* a layer of any substance, a stratum.
স্তাবক, *a.* praising, eulogizing, flattering : *s.* an eulogist, a panegyrist, a flatterer.
স্তাবকতা, *s.* praise, an eulogium, flattery.
স্তুত, *a.* praised, eulogized, panegyrized, applauded, celebrated, flattered.
স্তুতি, *s.* praise, eulogy, panegyric, flattery, entreaty ; -পাঠক, a panegyrist, eulogist.

স্তুতিবাদ, *s.* an expression of eulogy, theme of praise, praising, coaxing.
স্তুতিবাদী, *a.* uttering praises or eulogiums.
স্তুত্যর্থ, *a.* having praise for its object : *s.* the object or subject of praise.
স্তুত্যর্থে, *ad.* for praise, applause, or flattery.
স্তূপ, *s.* a heap, a pile, a mound of earth.
স্তূপাকার, স্তূপাকৃতি, *a.* formed like a heap, much, large, abundant, various.
স্তেন, *s.* a thief ; theft, a stealing, robbery.
*স্তৈমরাত্রি, *a.* continuing, perpetual.
স্তেয়, *a.* liable to be stolen : *s.* theft, robbery, plunder, the thing stolen.
স্তোক, *a.* little, small : *s.* a drop of water.
স্তোতব্য, *a.* laudable, worthy of praise.
স্তোতা, স্তুতিকর্ত্তা, *s.* a person who praises, an eulogist, a panegyrist, a flatterer.
স্তোত্র, *s.* praise, eulogy, panegyric, flattery,
স্তোভ, *s.* consolation, comfort. [entreaty.
স্ত্রংস, *s.* Strontium. [to iron linen.
স্ত্রি, *s.* a washerman's smoothing iron ; -কৃ,
স্ত্রী, *s.* a wife, a woman, a female.
স্ত্রীগ্রহণ, *s.* the taking a wife, a marrying.
স্ত্রীচিহ্ন, *s.* the female organ of generation.
স্ত্রীজিত, *a.* henpecked, governed by a wife.
স্ত্রীতা, or স্ত্রীত্ব, *s.* womanhood.
স্ত্রীধন, *s.* a wife's own property, property given to a woman on her marriage.
স্ত্রীধর্ম্ম, *s.* menstruation ; female duties.
স্ত্রীধর্ম্মিণী, *s.* a menstruous woman.
স্ত্রীপর, *a.* devoted to women, uxorious : *s.* a
স্ত্রীপরতা, -ত্ব, *s.* uxoriousness. [libertine.
স্ত্রীপরায়ণ, *a.* fondly attached to a wife.
স্ত্রীপরিগ্রহ, *s.* the marrying of a woman.
স্ত্রীপুংধর্ম্ম, *s.* duty of man and wife, duties of the sexes towards each other. [wife.
স্ত্রীবিয়োগ, *s.* separation from, or death of a
স্ত্রীলিঙ্গ, *a.* female : *s.* feminine, female ; in *gram.* the feminine gender.
স্ত্রীলোক, *s.* a woman, a female.
স্ত্রীসংসর্গ, স্ত্রীসঙ্গ, *s.* the society of women, sexual intercourse. [ried woman.
স্ত্রীসংগ্রহণ, *s.* seduction, seduction of a mar-
স্ত্রীসম্ভোগ, *s.* carnal commerce, coition.
স্ত্রীস্বভাব, *s.* feminine nature ; a eunuch.
স্ত্রীহত্যা, *s.* the murder of a woman.
স্ত্রীহরণ, *s.* seduction, adultery, rape.

স্ত্রৈণ, *a.* female, feminine, effeminate : *s.* a man who is governed by his wife.

স্ত্র্যংশ, *s.* the female parts of generation ; the anther of a flower.

স্থ, *a.* standing, situated, (used in *comp.* as the last member of a compound word).

স্থকিত, স্থগিত, *a.* stopped, ceased, obsolete.

স্থগ, *a.* concealed, deceitful, swindling.

স্থণ্ডিল, *s.* an altar made of sand, a square piece of sacrificial ground, a boundary.

স্থপতি, an architect, master mason or carpenter, mason, carpenter, stone-cutter.

স্থবির, *a.* old, aged, steady, firm : *s.* an old man.

স্থবিষ্ঠ, *a.* very thick or corpulent.

স্থল, *s* place, situation, dry land, a text in a book ; -কমল, -পদ্ম, a flowering shrub.

স্থলচর, *a.* moving or living on dry land.

স্থলচ্যুত, স্থলভ্রষ্ট, *a.* fallen from a place or situation.

স্থলপথ, *s.* a way by land.

স্থলী, *s.* a place, land, a valley.

স্থলীয়, *a.* of a place, of the land, terrestrial.

স্থাণু, *s.* a lopped or pollard tree ; Shiva ; a pillar, a post, a stake or pin.

স্থাতব্য, স্থানীয়, *a.* proper to be placed or fixed.

স্থাতা, *s.* a person who remains in a place.

স্থান, *s.* a place, spot, site, situation, room, space, a stay, a continuance, a square in a city, leisure, opportunity, a home, a house, a chapter or section of a book.

স্থানচ্যুত, স্থানভ্রষ্ট, *a.* the same with স্থলচ্যুত.

স্থানান্তর, *s.* another place, elsewhere.

স্থানাভাব, *s.* the want of place or room.

স্থানীয়, *a.* local.

স্থাপক, *a.* placing, fixing : *s.* he who sets up.

স্থাপন, *s.* a placing, a fixing, a setting up.

স্থাপনকর্ত্তা, *s.* one who places or fixes.

স্থাপনীয়, *a.* may be placed or fixed.

স্থাপয়িতব্য, *a.* fixable, may be established.

স্থাপয়িতা, *s.* a person who places or fixes.

স্থাপিত, *a.* placed, fixed, established, set up.

স্থাপ্য, *a.* fixable, fit to be placed or established : *s.* property, deposited, a deposit.

স্থাবর, *a.* fixed, stable, stationary, immovable : *s.* landed property, unalienable or immovable property, a mountain.

স্থাবরধন, *s.* immovable property.

স্থাবরাস্থাবর, *s.* fixed and movable property.

স্থাবির, *s.* old age, steadiness, slowness.

স্থায়িতা, -ত্ব, *s.* steadiness, fixedness, permanency.

স্থায়িভাব, *s.* *idem.*

স্থায়ী, *a.* standing, continuing, permanent, enduring, staying, fixed, stationary.

স্থাল, *s.* a charger, a dish, a metalic dish.

স্থালী, *s.* a cooking vessel, a pot, a pan, the socket of the gums or jawbone.

স্থাস্নু, *a.* firm, immovable, durable, eternal.

স্থিত, *a.* situated, being, fixed, placed.

স্থিতি, *s.* a situation, state, condition, continuance, stay, permanency, a staying, durability, a fixed state, a stop, pause.

স্থিতিকর, স্থিতিকারক, স্থিতিকারী, *a.* giving continuance, making permanent.

স্থিতিস্থাপক, *a.* elastic : *s.* a supporter.

স্থিতিস্থাপকতা, -ত্ব, *s.* elasticity.

স্থিতিস্থাপন, *s.* elasticity, a being elastic.

স্থির, *a.* steady, firm, steadfast, stable, settled, fixed, permanent, still, calm.

স্থিরকুট্টক, *s.* a steady pulverizer ; in *algebra,* a general divisor.

স্থিরচিত্ত, steady-hearted, firm of purpose, determined.

স্থিরতর, *a.* very steady, very firm or steadfast, durable, permanent.

স্থিরতা, *s.* steadiness, firmness, steadfastness, durability.

স্থিরত্ব, *s.* *idem.*

স্থিরবুদ্ধি, স্থিরধী, *a.* steady-minded, firmly purposed, determined, convinced.

স্থিরযৌবন, *a.* possessing unfading youth.

স্থিরীকৃত, *a.* confirmed, established, settled.

স্থূণা, *s.* an iron image, an anvil ; the post or pillar of a house.

স্থূল, thick, corpulent, stout, bulky, gross, inactive, blunt, large, great, coarse.

স্থূলকায়, *a.* bulky, corpulent unwieldy.

স্থূলতা, স্থৌল্য, thickness, bulkiness, grossness.

স্থূলফল, *s.* gross measure, or result.

স্থূলবুদ্ধি, স্থূলধী, *a.* dull, stupid, incapable.

স্থূলমধ্যকাঁচ, *s.* a lens, a round convex glass.

স্থূললক্ষ্য, *a.* very liberal, munificent.

স্থূলশরীর, *s.* the gross or material body.

স্থূলান্ত্র, *s.* the large intestines.

স্থূলীভূত, *a.* enlarged, thickened.

স্থেয়, *a.* fixable, requiring to be placed or fixed.

স্থৈর্য্য, steadiness, stability, steadfastness, firmness, certainty, calmness, stillness.

স্নাত, *a.* having bathed, bathed, washed.
স্নাতক, *s.* an initiated householder.
স্নাতব্য, স্নাপনীয়, *a.* requiring to be bathed, proper for bathing. [who bathes.
স্নাতা, *s.* one who practises ablutions, one
স্নান, *s.* a bathing, ablution, a washing.
স্নানযাত্রা, *s.* bathing festival of Jagannáth.
স্নানযাত্রী, *a.* going to see the Snánjátrá.
স্নানীয়, *a.* proper for bathing or ablution.
স্নাপিত, immersed, bathed, washed, rinsed.
স্নায়ী, *a.* bathing, practising ablution.
স্নায়ু, *s.* a tendon, the tail of a muscle.
স্নিগ্ধ, smooth, oily, unctuous, lubricated, soft, refreshing, cool, amiable, beloved, coarse, thick: *s.* a friend, marrow.
স্নিগ্ধকর, *a.* lubricating, refreshing, cool.
স্নিগ্ধতা, *s.* smoothness, unctuosity, oiliness, agreeableness, coolness, lubricity.
স্নুষা, *s.* a daughter-in-law, a sons's wife.
স্নেহ, smoothness, unctuosity, love, agreeableness, tenderness, affection. [ness.
স্নেহকর, *a.* exercising affection or tender-
স্নেহপাত্র, *s.* an object of affection, a favou-
স্নেহযোগ্য, *a.* worthy of affection. [rite.
স্নেহী, *a.* unctuous, agreeable, affectionate, tender-hearted. [a vibration.
স্পন্দ, *s.* a shaking, a trembling, agitation,
স্পন্দকর, *a.* shaking, trembling, agitating.
স্পন্দন, *s.* a trembling, a quaking, a fluttering, agitation, vibration.
স্পন্দনীয়, *a.* agitable, vibratory. [ing.
স্পন্দবিশিষ্ট, *a.* shaking, trembling, vibrat-
স্পন্দিত, *a.* shaken, agitated, vibrated.
স্পর্দ্ধা, *s.* defiance, a daring, a challenging.
স্পর্দ্ধাকারক, স্পর্দ্ধাকারী, treating with defiance, provoking, challenging, daring.
স্পর্দ্ধিত, *a.* defied, dared, challenged.
স্পর্শ, *s.* touch, touching, contact, feeling; -কৃ, to touch, to feel, to come in contact.
স্পর্শক, *a.* touching, coming in contact.
স্পর্শন, *s.* a touching, a feeling. [gible.
স্পর্শনীয়, *a.* fit to be felt or touched, tan-
স্পর্শাক্রামক, *a.* contagious, infectious.
স্পর্শাতীত, *a.* past feeling, intangible.
স্পষ্ট, *a.* clear, evident, manifest, plain.
স্পষ্টবক্তা, *s.* a plain speaker. [plainly.
স্পষ্ট-বাদী, -ভাষী, *a.* speaking clearly or

স্পষ্টবোধ, *s.* clear knowledge or idea.
স্পষ্টরূপে, *ad.* clearly, plainly, evidently.
স্পষ্টার্থ, *s.* having clearness or plainness for an object: *s.* a clear object. [poses.
স্পষ্টার্থতা, *s.* clearness, plainness of pur-
স্পষ্টার্থে, *ad.* for clearness or plainness.
স্পষ্টীকরণ, *s.* a making clear or plain.
স্পষ্টীকৃত, *a.* made clear or plain.
স্পষ্টীভূত, *a.* become clear or plain.
স্পাগুল, *s.* a plant (Plantago ispagoola).
স্পৃশ্য, *a.* tangible; -তা, -ত্ব, tangibility.
স্পৃষ্ট, *a.* touched, brought into contact.
স্পৃহা, *s.* a wish, a desire, longing, hope.
স্পৃহাজনক, *a.* producing wishes or desires.
স্পৃহাবিশিষ্ট, *a.* desirous, longing, eager.
স্ফট, *s.* the hood of a serpent; alum.
স্ফটিক, *s.* crystal, quartz; -স্তম্ভ, crystal pil-
স্ফটিকময়, *a.* crystal, quartzose. [lar.
স্ফটিকারী, ফিটকারী, *s.* alum.
স্ফিচ, *s.* the buttocks, the posteriors.
স্ফীত, *a.* swollen, extended, enlarged; risen in wealth or importance. [perity.
স্ফীতি, *s.* a swelling, enlargement; pros-
স্ফীতিকর, *a.* causing a swelling or enlargement; causing prosperity. [breaking.
স্ফুট, স্ফুটন, *s.* a bursting, a cracking, a
স্ফুটফল, *s.* precise area, superficial con-
স্ফুটিত, *a.* burst opened, manifest. [tent.
স্ফুটী, *s.* a kibe, tumour, swelling; a fruit.[1]
স্ফুলিঙ্গ, *s.* a spark of fire, a drop of water.
স্ফূর্জথু, *s.* thunder, a clap of thunder.
স্ফূর্ত্তি, *s.* a palpitation occasioned by surprise or joy, alacrity, expansion, excitation, stimulation, utterance.
স্ফূর্ত্তিজনক, *a.* exciting, stimulating.
স্ফূর্ত্তিমান্, exciting, stimulating, palpitat-
স্ফোটক, *s.* a boil, a tumour, abscess. [ing.
স্ফোটন, *s.* a rupture, a hernia, a bursting, a rending; a gimlet, an auger.
স্মর্, *v. a.* to recollect, to remember.
স্মর, *a.* recollecting, remembering: *s.* memory; the Indian Cupid. [mory.
স্মরণ, *s.* a recollection, remembrance, me-
স্মরণকর্ত্তা, *s.* one who recollects.
স্মরণীয়, স্মর্ত্তব্য, স্মার্য্য, *a.* memorable, recognisable, fit to be remembered. [Cupid.
স্মররিপু, স্মরারি, *s.* Shiva, the enemy of

স্মারক, *a.* reminding, memorable, retentive: *s.* a remembrancer, a recorder.

স্মার্ত্ত, *a.* embraced by the memory, recollected; skilled in jurisprudence.

স্মার্ত্তকাল, *s.* the time which a person can recollect. (It is stated to be 100 years.)

স্মিত, *a.* smiled, smiling: স্মের, *s.* smile, sim-

স্মৃত, *a.* recollected, remembered. [per.

স্মৃতি, recollection, memory, remembrance, the body of Hindu laws, jurisprudence.

স্মৃতিশাস্ত্র, the science of Hindu law, the books on Hindu jurisprudence.

স্মৃতিসম্মত, *a.* approved by the writings upon Hindu jurisprudence.

স্মৃতিসাধ্য, *a.* capable of being established by the writings upon jurisprudence.

স্মৃতিসিদ্ধ, *a.* proved or established by the writings upon Hindu jurisprudence.

স্যন্দন, *s.* a trickling, oozing, air, wind, water, a going swiftly, a car, war-chariot.

স্যন্দিনী, *a.* oozing, trickling: *s.* saliva.

স্যাগোষ, a fierce animal of feline genus.

স্যানা, *a.* grown up, adult; sensible, wise,

স্যাল, *s.* a wife's brother. [ingenious.

স্যূত, *a.* sewed, stitched: *s.* a sack. [age.

স্যূতি, a sewing, stitching, offspring, line-

স্রব্, *v. n.* to ooze, drop, to flow as a liquid.

স্রব, স্রাব, *s.* a flow, oozing, trickling, flow-

স্রবণ, *idem*; also, perspiration, urine. [ing.

স্রষ্টা, স্রষ্টৃ, *s.* a creator, inventor, maker.

স্রষ্টৃতা, -ত্ব, *s.* creatorship, inventorship.

স্রুক্, *s.* a wooden sacrificial ladle.

স্রুত, *a.* dropped, flowed, dropping, flowing.

স্রোতঃ, *s.* a current, a stream, the flow or course of water, an organ of sense.

স্রোতস্বতী, *a.* having a stream: *s.* a river.

স্রোতোঞ্জন, *s.* antimony.

স্রোতোঞ্জনভস্ম, *s.* the calx of antimony.

স্ব, *s.* self, identity, individuality, wealth, property, the soul: *a.* own. [self.

স্বকর্ম্মকৃৎ, *s.* one who does work for him-

স্বকার্য্য, স্বকর্ম্ম, *s.* the duties peculiar to a person, a person's own work or duty.

স্বকীয়, or স্বক, *a.* own, peculiar, proper.

স্বগণ, *a.* of one's own party: *s.* a partisan.

স্বগত, kept to one's self, exclusive, aside,

স্বঙ্গ, *a.* handsome, well-shaped. [apart.

স্বচ্ছ, *a.* pure, clear, transparent, pellucid, white, sound, healthy, convalescent.

স্বচ্ছতা, -ত্ব, *s.* purity, transparency, clearness, pellucidness, soundness.

স্বচ্ছদ্রব্য, *s.* the crystalline humour.

স্বচ্ছন্দ, *a.* spontaneous, independent, free, unrestrained, uncontrolled, self-willed, voluntary: *s.* a person's own will.

স্বচ্ছন্দপূর্ব্বক, *ad.* spontaneously, volunta-

স্বচ্ছন্দে, *ad. idem.* [rily, freely.

স্বচ্ছপত্র, *s.* talc mineral.

স্বচ্ছল, *a.* generous, liberal, munificent.

স্বজ, *a.* born or produced from a person: *s.* an offspring, a son; perspiration.

স্বজন, *s.* distant relation, a friend, a person of one's own family.

স্বজাতি, *s.* a person's own class or nation.

স্বজাতীয়, *a.* of one's own class or nation.

স্বজ্ঞান, *s.* self-knowledge, one's own know-

স্বতঃ, *ad.* of itself, from itself. [ledge.

স্বতন্ত্র, *a.* independent, unrestrained, not, subject, uncontrolled, separate, apart.

স্বতন্ত্রতা, independence, unrestrainedness.

স্বত্ব, *s.* proprietary right, proprietorship, ownership, self-existence.

স্বত্ববান, *a.* wealthy, possessed of property, having a right of property.

স্বদেশ, *s.* own country, one's own country.

স্বদেশী, *s.* a fellow-countryman. [try.

স্বদেশীয়, *a.* belonging to one's own coun-

স্বধর্ম্ম, *s.* nature, characteristic, one's own religious profession, or peculiar duties.

স্বধর্ম্মচ্যুত, *a.* fallen from one's own religious profession, apostatized.

স্বধর্ম্মত্যাগ, *s.* apostasy; -কৃ, to apostatize.

স্বধর্ম্মত্যাগী, *s.* an apostate, a turncoat.

স্বন, *s.* sound: স্বনিত, *a.* sounded.

স্বনাম, *s.* a namesake, one's own name.

স্বপক্ষ, *a.* of one's own party, adherent.

স্বপথ, *s.* a person's own way or course of

স্বপ্ন, *s.* a dream, vision, a sleep. [conduct.

স্বপ্নদোষ, *s.* nocturnal impurity.

স্বপ্নবৎ, *a.* like a dream, visionary.

স্বপ্নবিচারী, *s.* an interpreter of dreams.

স্বপ্রকাশ, a display of one's self, ostenta-

স্বপ্রকাশক, *a.* displaying one's self. [tion.

স্ববশ, *a.* subject to one's own control.

স্বভাজন, *s.* civility, courtesy, adieu, welcome, one who gives a polite welcome or dismissal to a guest.

স্বভাব, *s.* nature, disposition, natural temper or disposition, a natural tendency.

স্বভাবতঃ, *ad.* naturally, by nature.

স্বভাববিরুদ্ধ, *a.* contrary to nature.

স্বভাবসিদ্ধ, *a.* effected by nature, natural.

স্বভূ, *s.* the self-existent, Vishnu, Brahmá.

স্বয়ং, *pron.* self, himself, of itself.

স্বয়ংসিদ্ধ, *a.* famed for one's own merits.

স্বয়ংকৃত, *a.* self-done, spontaneous, done by a person's own self.

স্বয়ন্দত্ত, *a.* self-given : *s.* a child who has given himself to adoptive parents. [ed.

স্বয়মুপাগত, *a.* come of himself (to be adopt-

স্বয়ম্বর, *s.* the ceremony of a woman choosing her own husband.

স্বয়ম্বরা, *s.* a bride choosing her husband.

স্বয়ম্ভূ, *s.* the self-existent, God.

স্বর্, *s.* heaven, paradise, sky, ether, beauty, splendour; a division of the universe.

স্বর, *s.* a sound, a noise, the voice, a musical note ; the vowels ; -বান্ধ, to tune.

স্বরবত্তা, *s.* vocality, noisiness.

স্বরবান্ *a.* vocal, sounding, noisy, having a pleasant voice. [pleasant voice.

স্বরভঙ্গ, *s.* hoarseness, fluttering or un-

স্বরাংশ, *s.* a half or quarter tone in music.

স্বরাজ, *s.* a measure of verse used in the veda, a verse of three lines, *viz.* two of eight and one of ten syllables.

স্বরিত, *s.* the circumflex accent : *a.* accented, articulated, sounded as a note.

স্বরুচি, *a.* self-willed, wilful, uncontrolled.

স্বরূপ, *a.* identified with, like : *s.* a defini-

স্বরূপতঃ, *ad.* identically, like. [tion.

স্বরূপতা, -ত্ব, *s.* likeness, identity.

স্বর্গ, *s.* heaven, celestial abode, Indra's

স্বর্গগত, *a.* gone to heaven. [paradise.

স্বর্গগমন, *s.* the going to heaven.

স্বর্গগামী, *a.* going to heaven. [way.

স্বর্গঙ্গা, *s.* the celestial Ganges, the milky

স্বর্গবিদ্যাধরী, *s.* a kind of demi-goddesses.

স্বর্গলোক, or **স্বর্গপুর**, *s.* the same with **স্বর্গ**.

স্বর্গস্থ, or **স্বর্গস্থিত**, *a.* situated in heaven.

স্বর্গাগত, *a.* come to or arrived at heaven.

স্বর্গাপগা, *s.* Gangá, the river Ganges.

স্বর্গারোহণ, *s.* the ascending to heaven.

স্বর্গী, **স্বর্গীয়**, **স্বর্গ্য**, *a.* heavenly, celestial.

স্বর্ণ, *s.* gold ; -যূথি, yellow jasmine.

স্বর্ণকার, **স্বর্ণকৃৎ**, *s.* goldsmith, a jeweller.

স্বর্ণজ, *s.* tin. **স্বর্ণবর্ণ**, *a.* gold-coloured.

স্বর্ণজনক, *a.* producing gold, auriferous.

স্বর্ণবণিক্, *s.* a money-changer, money scri-

স্বর্ণময়, *a.* golden, made of gold. [vener.

স্বর্ণমাক্ষিক, *s.* iron or copper pyrites, cubi-

স্বর্ণাঙ্গুরীয়ক, *s.* a gold ring. [cal pyrites.

স্বর্বেশ্যা, *s.* a heavenly courtezan.

স্বর্বৈদ্য, *s.* the physician of the gods, Dhanwantari, the Hindu Esculapius.

স্বর্ভানু, *s.* Rághu, the ascending node.

স্বর্লোক, *s.* heaven, the paradise of Indra.

স্বল্প, *a.* very few, very small, very little.

স্বসা, **স্বসৃ**, *s.* a sister, an own sister.

স্বসৃপতি, *s.* a sister's husband.

স্বস্তি, *intj.* excellent ! well done ! success or good attend you ! be it so, amen.

স্বস্তিক, *s.* a sort of temple or palace, auspicious object ; meeting of four roads.

স্বস্তিবাচন, *s.* a blessing, a preliminary invocation, a religious rite for invoking the blessing of the gods.

স্বস্ত্যয়ন, *s.* prayers and offerings made to bring down a blessing, a thankoffering ; also, a deprecation of evil.

স্বস্থ, *a.* confident, resolute, firm, relying on

স্বস্রীয়, *s.* sister's son, nephew. [one's self.

স্বাকার্, *v. a.* to accept a bill or other notes, to sign or subscribe a person's name.

স্বাকার, or **স্বাকৃতি**, *s.* a fine form, a person's own form : *a.* beautifully formed.

স্বাক্ষর, *s.* a signature, autograph ; -কৃ, to sign, to subscribe.

স্বাগত, *a.* welcome ; a word used as a welcome or salutation. [to one's self.

স্বাতন্ত্র্য, *s.* independence, accountableness

স্বাতী, *s.* one of the wives of the sun, the star Arcturus, the 15th lunar asterism.

স্বাদ, *s.* flavour, taste, relish, tasting.

স্বাদন, *s.* the tasting of food or drink.

স্বাদিত, *a.* tasted, touched with the lips.

স্বাদু, *a.* sweet, tasty, savoury, nice : *s.* the taste or relish of a thing.

স্বাদুল, *a.* well-tasted, relishing, savoury, [tasty.
স্বধর্ম্ম, *s.* a person's own religion.
স্বাধিকার, *s.* one's own right or title to a [thing.
স্বাধীন, *a.* independent, free.
স্বাধীনতা, *s.* independence, freedom.
স্বাধ্যায়, *s.* an inaudible reading of the veda, a reading to one's self.
স্বাধ্যায়ী, *a.* reading to himself: *s.* a person who reads the veda; a tradesman.
স্বান, *s.* sound, noise. **স্বাপ**, *s.* sleep.
স্বান্ত, *s.* the mind, thought, intellect; a cave.
স্বাপরাধ, *s.* a person's own crime.
স্বাভাবিক, *a.* natural, inherent, innate.
স্বাভিপ্রায়, *s.* one's own scope or object.
স্বাভিলাষ, *s* a person's own wish or desire.
স্বামিতা, or **স্বামিত্ব**, *s.* mastery, ownership, lordship, sovereignty, possessorship.
স্বামী, *s.* a husband, master, owner, a lord, sovereign, a spiritual guide, a god.
স্বার্জ্জন, *s.* a person's own acquisitions.
স্বার্জ্জিত, self-acquired. [ject or interest.
স্বার্থ, *a.* self-interested: *s.* one's own ob-
স্বার্থপর, *a.* selfish, self-interested.
স্বার্থপরতা, *s.* self-interestedness, selfish-
স্বার্থে, *ad.* for the sake of self. [ness.
স্বাস্থ্য, *s.* health, ease, comfort, relief, good
স্বিৎ, *ad.* hey, what! is it true? [health.
স্বীকরণ, *s.* an acknowledging, a consenting, an agreeing to, a confessing.
স্বীকর্ত্তা *s.* one who acknowledges or confesses, one who consents to a thing.
স্বীকার, *s.* an acknowledgment, consent, agreement, confession, acquiescence.
স্বীকারী, **স্বীকারক**, *a.* confessing, acknowledging, consenting to, acquiescing.
স্বীকার্য্য, **স্বীকরণীয়**, *a.* requiring to be confessed, acquiesced in, or consented to.
স্বীকৃত, *a.* confessed, acknowledged, acquiesced, consented to, promised, engaged.
স্বীয়, *a.* own, private; -কার্য্য, one's own
স্বীয়া, *a.* own: *s.* a virtuous woman.[work.
স্বীয়াপরাধ, *s.* a person's own crime.
স্বেচ্ছা, *s.* a person's own will, voluntariness.
স্বেচ্ছাক্রমে, or **স্বেচ্ছামতে**, *ad.* according to one's own will, voluntarily.
স্বেচ্ছাচার, *a.* acting according to one's own will, unrestrained, uncontrolled.
স্বেচ্ছাচারী, *a. see* **স্বেচ্ছাচার**, *s.* one following his own inclinations. [steam, warmth.
স্বেদ, *s.* perspiration, sweat, warm vapour,
স্বেদজ, *a.* engendered by heat and moisture (applied to insects and worms).
স্বেদন, *s.* a perspiring, a sweating.
স্বেদনী, *s.* a frying pan, a caldron.
স্বৈর, *a.* unrestrained, self-willed, lazy.
স্বৈরতা, *s.* obstinacy, self-will, laziness.
স্বৈরিণী, *s.* an unchaste woman, adulteress.
স্বৈরী, *a.* self-willed, unrestrained, obsti-
স্বোপার্জ্জিত, *a.* self-acquired. [nate.
স্বোরস, *s.* the sediment of oil.

হ, the 33rd and last consonant of the alphabet: *v n.* to become, to be, to exist.
হইতে, *v.* to be: *ad.* from; than. [coming.
হওন, **হওয়া**, *s.* a being or existing, a be-
হংস, *s.* a drake, a gander, a swan; duck, goose, (the generic name). [flamingo.
হংসক, *s. fem.* ornament for the feet; the
হংসকূট, *s.* the same with **ককুৎ**.
হংসগামিনী, *a. fem.* walking gracefully.
হংসনাদ, *s.* the voice of geese or ducks.
হংসনাদিনী, *a. fem.* having graceful voice.
হংসপদ, *s.* a caret to mark omission.
হংসমণ্ডল, **হংসমালা**, *s.* a flock of geese.
হংসী, *s.* a duck, a goose. [rectitude.
***হক**, *a.* just, true, right: *s.* justice, truth,
***হকিকৎ**, *s.* narration, a detail of particulars, a relation, an explanation.
***হকিম**, *s.* a physician, a doctor. [wrong.
***হক্‌নাহক**, *ad.* for nothing: *a.* right or
***হজম**, digestion; -কৃ, to digest, embezzle.
হজমী, *a.* digestive, promoting digestion.
হট্ট, *s.* a market, a fair; -চোর, a market-
হট্টবিলাসিনী, *s.* a harlot; a whore. [thief.
হট্, *v. a.* to move backwards, to recede.
হঠ, *s.* violence, rapine, outrage.
হটন, *s.* a receding, falling back, retreat.
হটা, *v.a.* to cause to move backwards: *s.* a causing to move backwards.
হঠাৎ, *ad.* on a sudden, accidentally, suddenly, unexpectedly, easily, forthwith.
হড়্, *v. a.* to slip, to falter, to stumble.
হড়্গড়া, *v. n.* to roll on uneven ground.
হড়্গড়ানিয়া, rough, uneven, up and down.

হড়্বড়ান, *s.* a being confused or puzzled.
হড়্বড়ি, *s.* haste, hurry, bustle, confusion.
হড়্বড়িয়া, *a.* speaking in a noisy and hur-
হড়্মড়িয়া, *a.* rustling, brittle. [ried way.
হড়রবড়র, *s.* hurried and inarticulate talk.
হড়্হড়, *im. sd.* of sudden slipping or falling.
হড়্হড়ান, হড়্হড়ী, *im. sds.* expressive of a thundering, rattling of the wheels, etc.
হড়া, *s.* a quantity of pulse in stalks to be parched by setting fire to the sheafs.
হড়াগড়া, *s.* difficulty, intricacy. [হড়া.
হড়াপোড়া, *s.* parched pease or pulse, as in
হড়ি, *s.* a pair of stocks, wooden fetters.
হড্ড, *s.* a bone: *a.* low, mean, vulgar.
হড্ডক, *s.* a sweeper, a man of low caste.
হণ্ডিকা, হণ্ডী, *s.* cooking-vessel, a pot, a pan.
হত, *a.* killed, smitten, struck. [rited.
হতচিত্ত, *a.* bereft of spirit or sense, dispi-
হতজ্ঞান, *a.* bereft of sense or knowledge.
হতপর, *a.* ruined as it respects a future state, reprobate, profligate, perfidious.
হতপ্রতিভ, *a.* bereft of manifestation.
হতপ্রায়, *a.* almost dead, nearly killed.
হতবুদ্ধি, *a.* senseless, bereft of sense or understanding, crazy, demented. [ill-fated.
হতভাগা, হতভাগ্য, *a.* unfortunate, unlucky,
হতাদর, *a.* bereft of respect or honour.
হতাশ, *a.* disappointed, desponding, bereft of hope, hopeless, despairing.
*হতিয়ার, *s.* a weapon, a tool; the penis.
হতিয়ারবন্দ, *a.* armed, bearing arms.
হত্যা, *s.* killing, slaying, murder, slaughter; -কৃ, to murder, to kill, to slay.
হত্যাকর্ত্তা, *s.* a murderer, one who kills.
হত্যাশীল, *a.* bloody-minded, murderous.
*হদ, or হদ্দ, *s.* a boundary, a limit.
হদ্দমদ্দ, *ad.* at farthest, to the extent of.
হন্, *v. a.* to kill, to murder. [plication.
হনন, *s.* a smiting, killing; in *arith.* multi-
হননযোগ্য, *a.* deserving to be killed.
হননশীল, *a.* bloody-minded, revengeful.
হননীয়, *a.* worthy of being smitten or killed, intended for slaughter. [monkey.
হনু, *s.* the jaw, the jaw-bone; the deified
হনূমান, *s.* a baboon, the deified monkey.
হন্ত, *interj.* woe! alas! [murderer.
হন্তা, or হন্তৃ, *s.* one who smites or kills, a

হন্যমান, *s.* in the state of being beaten or
*হফ্তকলম, *s.* forgery: *a.* forged. [killed.
হফ্তকলমি, *s.* a forger; forgery: *a.* forged.
হবন, *s.* a sacrifice, an oblation.
*হবলদার, a native sergeant in the army.
হবিঃ, *s.* *ghi,* clarified butter; an oblation.
হবিষ্য, *s.* clarified butter; a meal taken once in 24 hours during mourning.
হবিষ্যান্ন, *s.* sacred food. [sacrifice.
হব্য, or হবনীয়, *a.* sacrificial, intended for
হব্যপাক, *s.* oblation dressed for the gods.
হম্মা, হম্বা, *im. sds.* of the lowing of kine.
হয়, *a.* occurring, happening: *s.* a horse.
*হয়রাণ, *a.* astonished, confounded, troubled, disturbed, fatigued, wretched.
হৃ, *v. a.* to steal, to take unlawfully.
হর, *s.* a name of Shiva; division. [loss.
*হরকৎ, *s.* action, hinderance, prevention,
*হরকরা, *s.* a footman, a messenger.
হরগৌরী, *s.* Shivá and Durgá in a united
*হরঘড়ি, *ad.* at every hour. [state.
হরণ, *s.* a taking by fraud or force, a stealing, a taking away; in *arith.* division.
হরণীয়, *a.* proper to be taken by force.
হরদর, *ad.* on an average, in the gross.
*হরফ, *s* a letter of the alphabet; printing
*হরবক্ত, *ad.* always, at all times. [types.
*হরবোলা, imitating the voices of all animals, talkative, speaking all languages.
*হরাম, *a.* unlawful, impure, forbidden, sacred: *s.* a seraglio, female apartments.
*হরামজাদা, *s.* a bastard, a baseborn person, a rogue, a rascal; *fem.* হরামজাদী.
হরি, a name of Vishnu; a horse, a monkey, a lion: *a.* green, yellow, tawny.
হরিচন্দন, *s.* a yellow kind of sandal-wood, saffron, the farina of the lotus.
হরিণ, *a.* yellowish white: *s.* a deer, a buck, a stag; -বাটী, -বাড়ী, a deer-park, a jail, a prison, a house of correction.
হরিণকাণা, *a.* infatuated, insensible.
হরিণনয়নী, *a.* deer-eyed, fawn-eyed.
হরিন্মণি *s.* an emerald, a sapphire.
হরিৎ *a.* green, verdant: *s.* vegetation.
হরিৎখন্দ, *s.* a field of greens for food.
হরিতাল, *s.* orpiment, yellow arsenic.
হরিতালভস্ম, *s.* the calx of yellow arsenic.

হরিতালিকা, *s.* the 4th lunar day in Bhádra.
হরিদ্রা, yellow : *s.* turmeric (Curcuma longa).
হরিদ্রাক্ত, *a.* smeared with turmeric.
হরিদ্বার, *s.* a famous place of pilgrimage.
হরিমণি, *s.* an emerald, a sapphire.
হরিপ্রিয়া, *s.* a name of the goddess Lakshmí.
*হরিফ, *a.* clever, cunning, facetious : *s.* a rival, an enemy ; an associate, a friend.
হরিফী, *s.* cleverness, cunning, facetiousness ; rivalry, enmity ; friendship.
হরিবাসর, *s.* the eleventh lunar day.
হরিশ্চন্দ্র, *s.* the name of a noted king.
হরিহরাত্মক, *a.* identified with Vishnu and Shiva in their united state.
হরীতকী, *s.* a kind of myrobalan and its tree.[1]
হরেক, *ad.* every one : *a.* various.
হরেদরে, *ad.* on an average, in the gross.
হর্ত্তা, or হর্ত্তৃ, *s.* one who takes unlawfully, a thief, a robber, a plunderer.
হর্ত্তাকর্ত্তা, *s.* the absolute disposer.
হর্ম্মন্, *a.* gaping, yawning.
হর্ম্ম্য, *s.* a palace, mansion, brick or stone house.
হর্ষ, *s.* joy, pleasure, merriment, delight, happiness, gladness.
হর্ষক, *a.* delighting, giving pleasure, delightful.
হর্ষণ, *s.* a cause of joy or pleasure, a thing which gives pleasure, a rejoicing.
হর্ষবিষাদ, *s.* joy and dejection, sadness in joy.
হর্ষমাণ, *a.* joyful, cheerful, glad, happy.
হর্ষান্বিত, *a.* joyous, happy, glad, merry.
হর্ষিত, *a.* glad, delighted, made happy.
হর্ষিতমনাঃ, *a.* glad-hearted, joyful-minded.
হল, *s.* a plough ; the consonants.
হলকষা, *s.* the name of a common plant.[2]
*হলকা, *a.* light in weight ; mean, silly, soft, cheap : *s.* a boat-hook ; a tendril.
হলদী, or হলুদ, *a.* yellow : *s.* turmeric.
হলধর, *a.* holding a plough : *s.* Balarám.
হলায়ুধ, *a.* wielding a plough : *s.* Balarám.
হলাহল, *s.* a kind of deadly poison.
হলিদা, *s.* turmeric ; the name of a bird.[3]
হলী, *s.* ploughing : *a.* ploughman, a tiller.
হল্য, *a.* ploughed, tilled ; proper or designed for tillage : *s.* a multitude of ploughs.
হল্‌হল্, *a.* lax, loose, shaking, dangling.
‡হল্লক, *s.* the throat ; the red lotus.
হসন, *s.* laughing, smiling, simpering.

হসন্ত, *s.* in *writing*, this mark (্). When affixed to a consonant, it denotes that the inherent vowel is suppressed.
হসিত, *a.* laughed at, smiling, laughing.
হস্ত, the hand, a cubit ; elephant's trunk.
হস্তগত, *a.* come to hand, delivered in hand.
হস্তধারণ, *s.* a holding the hand, handing.
হস্তা, *s.* the thirteenth lunar mansion.
হস্তান্তর, *s.* another hand, another's hand.
হস্তান্তরকরণ, *s.* the transfer of property.
হস্তান্তরকরণপত্র, *s.* a deed of transfer.
হস্তান্তরকৃত, হস্তান্তরগত, *a.* transferred.
হস্তার্পণ, *s.* the laying one's hands on.
হস্তিদন্ত, *s.* ivory ; a peg to hang things on.
হস্তিনাপুর, *s.* the name of Delhi or the ancient capital of Hindustán.
হস্তিপক, *s.* an elephant-driver.
হস্তিপাল, *s.* an elephant-keeper.
হস্তিশালা, *s.* a stable for elephants.
হস্তিশুণ্ড, *s.* an elephant's proboscis.
হস্তী, *s.* an elephant ; *fem.* হস্তিনী.
হা, *intj.* oh ! alas ! well ! excellent ! *ad.* yes.
হাই, *intj.* oh ! alas ! *s.* breath.
হাউড়া, *a.* gluttonous, ravenous, greedy.
*হাওলদিল, *s.* palpitation of the heart.
হাওলাৎ, *s.* a thing given in charge, money or any thing taken on trust or credit.
হাওলাতী, *a.* taken on trust or credit.
হাওলে, *ad.* slowly, coolly, deliberately.
হাওলেহাওলে, *ad. idem.*
হাঁ, *ad.* yes, certainly : *intj.* make haste ! take care ! let it not be ! God forbid !
হাঁই, *s.* breath, breath emitted by drowsiness, gaping, yawning.
হাঁক্, *v. a.* to drive, to call, to shout : *s.* a call, a shout, a bawling, outcry.
হাঁকন, হাঁকনি, *s.* the driving an animal, a calling, a shouting, a bawling.
হাঁকনিয়া, *s.* one who drives, or shouts.
হাঁকা, *v. a.* to drive, to cause to drive : *s.* a driving, a calling : *a.* driven, called.
হাঁকান, *s.* a causing to drive, a driving.
হাঁকার্, *v. a.* to hoist, to pull up, to shout, to call, to assent : *s.* assent.
হাঁকাহাঁকি, *s.* a reciprocal shouting or driving.
হাঁচ্, *v. n.* to sneeze, to emit wind by nose.
হাঁচন, *s.* the act of sneezing, sternutation.

হাঁচা, *v. a.* to provoke sneezing, to cause to
হাঁচি, *s.* a sneezing. [sneeze : *s.* a sneezing.
হাঁট্, *v. a.* to walk, to go afoot.
হাঁটন, *s.* a walking, a going afoot.
হাঁটা, *v. a.* to walk, to cause to walk.
হাঁটান, *s.* the causing a person to walk.
হাটু, *s.* the knee ; -গাড়ন, a kneeling down.
হাঁড়ল, *s.* a hole or cavity at the bottom of a pond to which the fish resort.
হাঁড়া, *s.* a large pot, a boiler, a caldron.
হাঁড়ি, *s.* a pot for cooking food, a pan.
হাঁড়িকুঁড়ি, *s.* pots and pans, cooking uten-
হাঁড়িচাঁচা, *s.* the Indian magpie.[1] [sils.
হাঁপ, *v. n.* to pant, to breathe short : *s.* steam ; panting, breathing short. [ing.
হাঁপান, *s.* breathing short, panting, wheez-
হাঁপা, *v. a.* to pant, to wheeze, to be tired
হাঁপানি, *s.* a panting, a wheezing, asthma.
হাঁপানিকাশ, *s.* a wheezing cough, asthma.
হাঁপাহাঁপি, *s.* a violent panting.
হাঁস্, *v. a.* to laugh, to smile ; to cut.
হাঁস, *s.* the same with হংস. [collar-bone.
হাঁসলী, *s.* an ornament for the neck ; the
হাঁসা, *v. a.* to cause laughter : *a.* white ; cut but not entirely divided (applied to water-melon, etc.) : *s.* a drake, a gander.
হাঁসি, হাঁসী, *s.* laughter ; a duck, a goose.
*হাকিম, *s.* a governor, a ruler, a judge
হাকিমী, *s.* rulership, government.
হাকুচ, *s.* the name of a tree.[2]
হাকুচকাঁটা, *s.* the holly-leaved Acanthus.[3]
হাঙ্গর, *s.* a shark, a voracious sea-fish.
*হাজ়ৎ, *s.* necessity, need, a wish ; prison.
হাজা, *a.* destroyed by rain or floods (applied to crops of corn or other plants).
হাজ়াম, *s.* a barber, a scarifier.
হাজ়ামৎ, *s.* the shaving of a person.
*হাজ়ার, *a.* a thousand. [thousand.
হাজ়ারী, *a.* worth, producing, or having a
হাজ়ির, *a* present, ready, willing, content.
হাজ়িরজামিন, *s.* a bail, a surety for another's appearance. [appearance.
হাজ়িরজামিনী, *s.* suretyship for another's
*হাজ়িরী, *s.* a breakfast, a levee, presence, attendance, an audience.
হাজ়িরীনবীস, *s.* one who takes account of workmen present, a muster-master.
হাজ়িরীনবীসী, *s.* the office of a házirínawís.
হাজ়িরীবহি, *s.* a muster-roll, a register of workmen in attendance. [thief.
হাট, *s.* a market, a fair ; -চোর, a market-
হাটুরিয়া, *a.* going to market : *s.* a market-
হাড়, *s.* a bone ; -কাটা, a bone-cutter. [man.
হাড়গিলা, *s.* an adjutant, a gigantic crane.[4]
হাড়চারা, হাড়যোড়া, *s.* a plant having the property of joining broken bones.[5]
হাড়ঙ্গ, *s.* a manger, earthen pan. [stocks.
হাড়ি, *s.* a sweeper, a scavenger, hogherd ;
হাড়িকাঠ, *s.* wooden stocks or fetters, a small post for sacrificing animals.
হাত, *s.* the hand to the elbow; a cubit ; -কড়ি, handcuffs, manacles.
হাতকরাত, *s.* a hand-saw, a small saw.
হাতচালা, *s.* the moving of a person's hand by the force of incantations.
হাতছাতা, *s.* a parasol, a small umbrella.
হাত-ছেঁচড়, -ছেঁচড়া, *s.* a pilferer, petty thief.
হাতছেঁচড়ামি, *s.* a pilfering, petty theft.
হাতড়া, *v. a.* to feel by the hands in dark, or as a blind person does.
হাতড়ান, *s.* a groping for, a feeling for, a feeling by the hands in the dark.
হাতড়ী, *s.* a hammer, mallet. [abandoned.
হাতব্য, *s.* relinquishable, that should be
হাৎযোড়া, *s.* a joining of hands, a joining of the hands in token of humility.
হাতল, *s.* a handle, a knob, a wrench, hilt.
হাতা, *s.* a spoon, a ladle, a fire shovel, an ash rake, a slice, a tiger's paw, a glove.
হাতাহাতি, *s.* a scuffle, a grappling, fisticuffs, a struggling hand to hand : *ad.* from hand to hand.
হাতিশুঁড়া, *s.* the name of a plant.[6]
হাতী, *s.* an elephant ; *fem.* হাতিনী.
হাতুড়িয়া, *s.* a quack doctor ; a pilferer.
হাতুয়া, *s.* a cow milked without its calf.
হাতোহাত, immediate, instant : *ad.* immediately, instantly, from hand to hand.
হান্, *v. a.* to smite, injure, pierce, transfix.
হান, *s.* a relinquishing, an abandoning.
হানা, *v. a.* to cause to injure : *s.* damage, destruction, a flood, an inundation, swamping, a killing, an injuring, a giving pain : *a.* destructive, injurious.

হানাবাড়ি, *s.* a house or ground which is supposed to be destructive to its owner.
হানি, *s.* loss, detriment, injury, hurt, destruction, a blow, murder, slaughter.
হাপর, *s.* a crucible, a smelting furnace, a goldsmith's hearth.
হাপরমালী, *s.* a climbing shrub.[1] [dered.
হাপিত, caused to be abandoned or surren-
হাব, হাবভাব, *s.* wanton dalliance, amourous gestures, coquetry.
হাবজা, or হাবজাগোবজা, *s.* trash, dregs.
হাবা, *a.* stupid, foolish, dumb. [hall.
*হাবা, *s.* air, wind; -খানা, a saloon, airy
হাবাৎ, *s.* a ruin, loss, misery, indigence.
হাবাতীয়া, *a.* ruinous, profuse, wasteful.
*হাবালে, *a.* in the care or custody of.
হাবী, *s.* a stupid or dumb woman.
হাবুগেলা, *a.* fearful, timid, foolish, idiotic,
হাম, *s.* the measles. [stupid.
হামরাই, *s.* attendants, companions.
হামলা, *v. a.* to low, to bellow.
হামলান, *s.* a lowing, a bellowing.
হামা, হামাগুড়ি, *s.* the creeping or crawling of infants, a creeping on all fours, as little children do; -দা, to creep or crawl.
*হামানদিস্তা, *s.* a mortar and pestle.
*হামাম, *s.* a bath; a kind of fine cloth.
হামামখানা, হামামঘর, *s.* a bath, a bagnio.
হামার, *s.* a cable, a thick rope; a heap.
হামি, *s.* a protector, a defender; affirmation; -দা, to affirm, to agree. [child.
*হামেল, a fœtus, pregnancy, a being with
হামেলা, *a.* pregnant; a pregnant woman.
*হামেস, or হামেসা, *ad.* often, frequently.
হায়, *intj.* ah! alas! হায়হায়, alas! alas!
হায়ন, *s.* the year, a twelvemonth.
*হায়া, *s.* modesty, shame. [in a lawsuit.
হার্, *v. a.* to lose, to be overcome, to lose
হার, *s.* a necklace, a wreath, a vessel to measure oil, a rate, common rate, a loss.
হারক, *a.* taking unlawfully, taking by force or fraud: *s.* one who takes thus; a thief, a robber; a divisor.
হারণ, *s.* a losing, failing, suffering loss.
হারা, *v. a.* to lose, to cause to lose: *a.* lost.
হারাণ, *s.* the losing of a thing: *a.* lost.
হারাণি, *s.* the losing of a thing.

হারাণিয়া, *a.* causing to lose, losing: *s.* a person who loses or causes to lose.
হারি, *s.* the losing of a game, defeat, discomfiture: *a.* handsome, captivating.
হারিত, *a.* lost: *s.* the green dove.[2] [low.
হারিদ্র, *a.* stained with turmeric, dyed yel-
হারিদ্রমেহ, *s.* a yellow gleet or gonorrhea.
হারিমুগ, or হালিমুগ, *s.* a species of pulse.[3]
হারিষ, *s.* the running of blood thro' the nose; the hemorrhoids, piles. [fraud.
হারী, *a.* taking unlawfully or by force or
হার্দ্দ, *s.* affection, kindness, love. [fraud.
হার্য্য, *a.* liable to be taken by force or
হাল, *s.* a plough, the rudder or helm of a boat; a state or condition: *a.* present.
হালকা, *a.* light, mild, vain, empty, weak.
*হালবান, *s.* a kid, a lamb.
*হালাক, *a.* lost, weary, fatigued. [mals.
*হালাল, *a.* right, lawful: *s.* killing of ani-
হালালখোর, *s.* a sweeper, a privy-cleaner.
হালাহল, *s.* poison, venom, virus.
হালি, *a.* present, recent: *s.* a rudder, helm.
*হালিম, *s.* garden cresses.[4]
হালিয়া, *a.* belonging to a plough: *s.* a tiller; a ploughman; -গরু, a plough bullock.
হালিয়াসাপ, *s.* a kind of harmless snake.
*হালুআ, *s.* a kind of sweetmeat.
হালুই, or হালুইকর, *s.* a confectioner.
হাস্, *v. n.* to laugh, to smile, simper.
হাস, *s.* laughing, laughter, smile.
হাসকুটিয়া, *a.* laughing, lively, funny, jovial: *s.* a laugher, a playful person.
হাসা, *v. a.* to cause to laugh: *a.* white.
হাসি, *s.* laughter, smile, simper. [cloth.
*হাসিয়া, *s.* a border, margin, the hem of
*হাসিল, *s.* custom on goods, port duties.
হাসিলদফতর, *s.* board of customs.
হাসিলী, *a.* subject to custom or duties.
হাসুয়া, *s.* a sickle, a scythe.
হাস্য, *s.* laughing, laughter, smile. [face.
হাস্যবদন, *a.* smiling faced: a smiling
হাস্যরস, *s.* the sentiment of jocularity.
হস্যার্ণব, *s.* a sea of laughter.
হাহতোস্মি, *intj.* ah! it is all over with me.
হাহা, *intj.* alas! alas! *s.* a class of demigods.
হাহাকার, *s.* loud lamentation, wailing.
হাহাকারধ্বনি, *s.* a noise of lamentation.

হি, an *imphatic particle,* indeed, truly; also, a sound expressive of laughter.
হিং, or হিঙ্গু, *s.* asafœtida.
হিংস্, *v. a.* to injure, hurt, to do mischief.
হিংসক, *a.* injurious, hurtful, malicious.
হিংসন, *s.* injuring or hurting of a person.
হিংসা, harm, injury, hurt, malice, mischief.
হিংসাকর, *a.* injuring, hurting, molesting.
হিংসাকর্ত্তা, *s.* an injurer, one who hurts.
হিংসিত, *a.* hurt, injured, molested.
হিংস্য, *a.* liable to be hurt or injured.
হিংস্র, হিংস্রক, *a.* injurious, hurtful, malicious, mischievous, noxious, ravenous.
হিঁচকি, *s.* a hiccup; -উঠন, rise of a fit of hiccup.
হিঁচকিপিটন, *s.* a fit of hiccup.
হিঁদু, *s.* a Hindu; *fem.* হিঁদুনী.
হিঁয়ালি, *s.* an enigma, a riddle, a puzzle.
*হিকমৎ, হিকমতী, *vide* হেকমত, &c.
হিক্কা, *s.* a hiccup, a fit of hiccup.
হিঙ্গু, or হিঙ্গুনির্য্যাস, *s.* asafœtida.
হিঙ্গুল, *s.* vermillion.
হিঙ্গুলী, বার্ত্তাকু, *s.* the egg-plant and its fruit.
হিচ্‌কন, *s.* a hiccuping, a sobbing.
*হিজড়া, *s.* a eunuch, a hermaphrodite.
হিজরী, *s.* the æra of the Muhammadans.
হিজল, *s.* a tree;[1] -দাগড়া, an incorrigible villain.
হিজলিবাদাম, *s.* the cashew nut.
হিণ্ডীর, *s.* cuttle-fish bone.
*হিণ্ডোলা, *s.* a swing, a cradle.
হিত, *s.* benefit, advantage, welfare: *a.* held; good.
হিতকর্ত্তা, *s.* a beneficent person.
হিতকারক, হিতকারী, *a.* doing good, beneficent.
হিতবক্তা, *s.* a person who speaks beneficially, a moral instructor, a good adviser.
হিতবাক্য, *s.* good advice, or conversation.
হিতবাঞ্ছক, or হিতাকাঙ্ক্ষী, *a.* benevolent.
হিতবাদী, হিতভাষী, *a.* giving good advice.
হিতাভিলাষ, হিতাকাঙ্ক্ষা, *s.* benevolence.
হিতৈষী, *a.* seeking another's welfare, benevolent: *s.* a well-wisher.
হিতোপদেশ, *s.* salutary instruction.
হিতোপদেষ্টা, *s.* a moral instructor.
হিন্তাল, or হিঁতাল, *s.* a small palm.[2]
হিন্দু, *s.* a Hindu; *fem.* হিন্দুনী.
হিন্দুস্থান, *s.* country of the Hindus, Hindustán.
হিন্দুস্থানী, belonging to Hindustán.
হিন্দোল, *s.* a swing, cradle, swinging festival.
হিবা, *s.* a gift, a grant; -নামা, a deed of gift.
হিম, cold, frigid, frosty: *s.* cold, dew, frost.
হিমকণা, *s.* frigorific particle, snow-particle.
হিমকর, *a.* cooling, chilling, refreshing: *s.* the moon, camphor.
হিমকুট, or হিমাগম, *s.* the cold season, winter.
হিমজনক, *a.* producing cold, frigorific.
হিমৎ, *a.* belonging to the cold season.
হিমধান, *s.* the cold season rice.
হিমবান্, *a.* cold, frigid, frosty, dewy.
হিমসাগর, a succulent plant;[3] -তৈল, a medicinal oil made of Himságar plant.
হিম্‌সিম্, *s.* fatigue, panting with exertion.
হিমাংশু, *s.* the moon.
হিমাঙ্গ, *s.* coldness, a shivering or cold fit, ague.
হিমাদ্রি, *s.* Himálaya ridge of mountains.
হিমানী, হিম্‌মিকা, hoarfrost, snow, ice, frost.
*হিমায়ৎ, *s.* auspice, protection, defence, patronage, guardianship.
হিমায়তী, protecting, having a guardian or protector.
হিমালয়, a range of snowy mountains separating India from Chinese Tartary.
*হিম্মৎ, spirit, courage, boldness, resolution, daringness, hardihood.
হিম্মতী, bold, undaunted, resolute, daring, hardy.
হিয়া, *s.* the heart, the mind.
হিরণ্ময়, *a.* made of gold, golden.
হিরণ্য, *s.* gold, any precious metal, crude bullion, unwrought gold or silver.
হিরণ্যগর্ভ, *s.* prolific nature, mundane egg.
হিরণ্যরেতাঃ, *s.* fire; the sun; Shiva.
হিরণ্ময়, *a.* golden: *s.* one of the geographical divisions of the earth; Brahmá.
*হিরফৎ, হিরফতী, *vide* হেরফৎ, হেরফতী.
*হিরসফ, *s.* an artichoke.
হিলমোচিকা, হিলঞ্চা, the same as হেলেঞ্চা, which see.
*হিল্লা, *s.* care, shelter, a refuge.
হিসাব, *s.* a reckoning, an account, a calculation.
হিসাবী, *a.* belonging to an account: *s.* an accountant, a calculator.
*হিস্সা, *s.* a share, a lot, a part, a portion.
হিস্সাদার, a sharer, a partner, a partaker.
হিস্সাদারী, *s.* partnership.
হিহি, হীহী, an *intj.* indicating laughter or surprise.
হী, *interj.* an exclamation of assent, surprise, sorrow, or despondency.
হীন, *a.* relinquished, destitute, bereft, de-

fective, deficient, bad, low, vile, base, mean, wasted, worn out. [cast, base.
হীনজাতি, s. an outcast : a. degraded, out-
হীনপক্ষ, a. destitute of relations, forlorn.
হীনবাদ, s. a departing from former affirmation and asserting other things.
হীনাঙ্গ, a. maimed, crippled, defective.
হীরক, হীরা, s. a diamond; a thunderbolt.
হীরাকষ, s. copperas, blue vitriol.
হীরামন, s. a beautiful species of parrot.[1]
হু, pron. he, that person.
হুঁ, intj. ha! aye! yes.
হুঁকশাস্ত্র, ad. speedily, quickly, without delay, as if by charm. [smoking tobacco.
হুঁকা, s. the huká, or apparatus used for
হুঁকাবর্দার, s. one whose office it is to pre-
হুঁচট, s. a stumbling. [pare the huká.
হুঁচটীয়া, a. stumbling. [an edict, a law.
*হুকুম, s. a command, an order, a decree,
হুকুমনামা, s. a written command or order.
*হুকূমৎ, s. magisterial authority, sovereignty, dominion. [-বর্দারী, obedience.
হুকুম-বর্দার, a. obedient, obeying orders;
হুঙ্কার, s. a loud and frightening sound.
*হুজুর, s. presence, appearance; sir, Mr.
হুজুরী, s. an attendant : a. attending.
*হুজ্জত, s. an argument, altercation, disputation, pertinacity, obstinacy.
হুজ্জতী, a. disputatious, pertinacious, obstinate : s. an obstinate person.
হুট, an expression of contempt.
হুটপাট, im. sd. expressive of a sudden scuffling noise, or of a speedy motion.
হুটহাট, s. the grumbling of the bowels.
হুড়্, v. n. to crowd together. [bustle.
হুড়, a. rude : s. a crowd, multitude, uproar,
হুড়কা, হুড়ুকা, s. a bolt, a bar, a bar for a door or gate, a fastening.
হুড়কী, s. a woman who flies from her husband to her father's house.
হুড়মুড়, s. a sudden falling with a crash : হুড়মুড় করিয়া, with a crash, suddenly.
হুড়হাড়, s. the grumbling of the bowels.
হুড়হুড়, s. a quick discharge by stool, a gushing : হুড়হুড় করিয়া, gushingly.
হুড়হুড়িয়া, s. name of a common plant.[2]
হুড়া, v. a. to knock, shove, kick, butt.
হুড়ান, s. a knocking, shoving, butting.
হুড়ামুড়ি, হুড়াহুড়ি, s. a scuffling, a tumult.
হুড়ুম, s. thunder, distant thunder.
হুণ্ডী, s. a draft, a bill of exchange.
হুণ্ডীয়ান, s. the fee or price paid for granting a bill of exchange. [an offering.
হুত, offered in sacrifice, called, invited : s.
হুতভুক্, a. eating the offering : s. fire.
হুতাশ, a. eating the offering : s. fire, fear, terror, dread, alarm, horror.
হুতাশন, s. fire, Agni, the god of fire.
হুতাশে, ad. through fright or alarm.
হুদ্দা, s. an office or post, employment.
হুদ্দাদার, a. holding an office or post.* [da.
হুন, s. a coin current on the coast, a pago-
*হুনর, s. skill, ingenuity, art, cleverness.
হুনরী, a. skilful, ingenious : s. an artist.
হুপ্, হুপ্‌হাপ্, হুপ্‌হুপ্, im. sds. expressive of the noise made by baboons.
হুপাল, a. resolute, brave, undaunted.
*হুব, s. spirit, courage, boldness.
*হুবহু, a. identical, exactly like.
হুমবাঘ, s. a large royal tiger.
হুমা, s. bore on a river, strong tide.
*হুর্, s. a nymph of the Moslem paradise.
*হুরমৎ, s. dignity, character, chastity, honour, reputation. [ter or honour.
হুরমতী, হুরমৎবালা, s. a person of charac-
হুরা, interj. huzza, hurra.
হুল, s. a sting, a sharp point; the two ends of a bow; -ফুটা, to sting. [ing.
হুলান, s. the setting on (as a dog,) excit-
হুলাহুলি, s. an inarticulate sound made by women as an expression of pleasure.
হুলি, s. the festival of playing with red powder called huli at the Dola-yáttrá.
হুলু, হুলুধ্বনি, s. the same with হুলাহুলি.
*হুশিয়ার, a. intelligent, attentive, careful, alert, clever, sensible, sober. [ness.
হুশিয়ারি, s. sobriety, carefulness, clever-
হূঙ্কার, s. a loud and frightening sound.
হূম, a particle of assent, yes, well, amen.
হূলস্থূল, s. commotion, fray, tumult.
হূহূ, s. a kind of demi-gods; the roaring of blazing fire or the velocity of water.
হৃ, v. a. to take, to steal, to take unlaw-
হৃৎ, হৃদ, s. the same with হৃদয়. [fully.

হৃত, *a.* seized, stolen, robbed, bereft, swindled.

হৃতজ্বালাভাব, *a.* dephlogisticated.

হৃৎকোষ, *s.* the pericardium.

হৃৎপদ্ম, *s.* the heart.

হৃৎপিণ্ড, *s.* the heart, *viz.* the fleshy mass so called.

হৃৎপিণ্ডবাহকনাড়ী, *s.* the vena cava.

হৃৎপ্রবাহকরক্তনাড়ী, *s.* the aorta.

হৃদয়, *s.* the heart, the mind, the seat of thought and the affections.

হৃদয়ঙ্গম, affecting, touching the heart, impressive.

হৃদয়ালু, *a.* good-hearted, affectionate.

হৃদাবর্ত্ত, *s.* a curl of hair on a horse's chest.

হৃদুদর, *s.* a ventricle of the heart.

হৃদ্য, *a.* dear, beloved, amiable, grateful, agreeable, pleasant, affectionate, kind.

হৃদ্যতা, *s.* agreeableness, gratefulness, pleasantness, intimacy, affection, kindness.

হৃদ্রোগ, *s.* the heart-burning disease.

হৃষীকেশ, *s.* a name of Vishnu.

হৃষ্ট, *a.* glad, joyful, merry, delighted.

হৃষ্টচিত্ত, হৃষ্টমনাঃ, *a.* glad, glad-hearted.

হৃষ্টতা, হৃষ্টত্ব, *s.* joy, gladness, merriment.

হৃষ্টপুষ্ট, *a.* good-looking, plump, fat, sleek.

হৃষ্টপুষ্টতা, *s.* plumpness, fatness.

হৃষ্টি, *s.* joy, gladness, merriment.

হে, a *vocative particle* used among equals; also, in addressing the Deity.

হেঁগল, হেঙ্গল, *s.* a dog, a cur.

হেচ্‌কা, *v.* to pull; -টান্‌, -মার্‌, to pull with a jerk.

হেচ্‌কাটান, *s.* a pulling with a jerk.

হেচ্‌কি, *s.* hiccup; -উঠ, to hiccup.

হেঁট, *a.* low, slanting, inclined, bent.

হেঁঠ, *ad.* low, down, below, beneath.

হেঁঠমুখ, *a.* downcast, dejected, lowspirited.

হেঁড়ে, *a.* very large, like a pot, very deep.

হেঁতাল, *s.* the same with হিন্তাল.

হেঁদলা, *s.* a swing, a cradle, a hammock.

*হেকমত, *s.* wisdom, knowledge, art, skill, cleverness, philosophy.

হেকমতি, *a.* wise, clever, ingenious, skilful.

হেঙ্গলা, *a.* emaciated, lank, meagre, poor.

হেতু, *s.* a cause, the reason of a thing, an occasion, a motive.

হেতুক, *a.* causal, instrumental: *s.* an active cause, an instrument or agent: *ad.* because, on account of, caused by.

হেতুতা, -ত্ব, *s.* causality, motivity.

হেতুবাদ, *s.* an expressed cause or reason, the preamble of a law.

হেতুবাদী, *a.* expressing causes or reasons.

হেতূপন্যাস, *s.* the producing of reasons or causes.

হেথা, here; -আইস, come here.

হেদে, a *voc. part.* oh! heyday!

হেম, *s.* gold; a celestial courtezan.

হেমন্ত, *s.* the cold season, winter.

হেমপুষ্পিকা, *s.* a species of yellow jasmine.

হেমবর্ণ, *a.* gold-coloured.

হেয়, *a.* relinquishable, despicable, untenable, low.

হেয়জ্ঞান, *s.* contempt, disesteem, a low idea or opinion of a thing; -কৃ, to despise, to abhor, to detest, to hate.

হেয়তা, -ত্ব, *s.* lowness, relinquishableness, despicableness, untenableness.

হের্‌, *v. a.* to see, to observe, to attend to.

*হেরফৎ, ingenuity, cleverness, cunning, artifice, skill, contrivance.

হেরফতী, *a.* skilful, ingenious, clever, cunning, artful.

হেরম্ব, *s.* Ganesha; one inflated with an idea of his own prowess; a buffalo.

হেল্‌, *v. a.* to disregard, to treat with levity, to neglect; to swim.

হেলক, disregarding, neglecting, treating with levity.

হেলন, *s.* a disregarding, a treating with levity; a swimming, a swinging.

হেলা, *v. a.* to cause to disregard, to cause to swing or oscillate: *s.* disregard, light and trifling conduct: *a.* aslant, sloping.

হেলাগোছা, *s.* regularity and irregularity.

হেলান, aslant, sloping: *s.* a causing to disregard, or oscillate, a prop, a support.

হেলানীয়া, *a.* aslant, not erect, bent.

হেলায়, *ad.* easily, without difficulty.

হেলিত, *a.* disregarded, neglected, slighted; sloping, slanting, aslant, bent.

হেলিঃমুখতুম্ব্যাকৃতি, *a.* bagpipe-shaped.

হেলেঞ্চা, *s.* an aquatic plant (Hingcha repens).

হৈ, a vocative particle.

হৈম, *a.* cold, frigid; golden.

হৈমন্তিক, *a.* wintry, produced in winter.

হৈয়ঙ্গবীন, *s.* clarified butter prepared the day before it is used.

*হৈরাণ, *a.* astonished, confounded, disturbed, distressed, fatigued.

হৈরাণী, *s.* fatigue, astonishment, perturbation.

হোঁকা, *s.* a person who exerts himself in a work without reflection.

হোঁকাটিয়া, *a.* using excessive or violent exertion without reflection. [sheds.

হোগলা, *s.* a species of sedge used to erect

হোড়, *a.* muddy: *s.* clay, mud, slush, plashiness, miriness; a wager.

হোড়ন, *s.* the causing of a crowd.

হোড়া, *v. a.* to cause a crowd. [of oblations.

হোতা, হোতৃ, *s.* a sacrificial priest, a maker

হোথা, *ad.* there, in that place.

হোম, *s.* an oblation, a burnt-offering.

হোমদ্রব্য, *s.* a sacrificial article.

হোরা, *s.* the rising of a sign of the zodiac, an hour, a mark, a line: *intj.* huzza.

হোল, *s.* the scrotum, the testicles.

হোলা, *s.* a tom-cat; a large boat: *a.* slack.

হোলী, *s.* the festival of হুলি, which see.

হৌজ, *s.* a cistern, a vat, a reservoir, a pond.

হৌজখানা, *s.* a factory containing vats.

হ্রদ, *s.* a lake, a large and deep sheet of water, a cistern, a pond.

হ্রদিনী, *s.* a river, a flowing stream.

হ্রস্ব, *a.* short, dwarf, low in stature; -কৃ, to shorten, to abridge, to abstract.

হ্রস্বইকার, *s.* the letter ই, or the symbol ি.

হ্রস্বউকার, *s.* the letter উ, or the symbol ু.

হ্রাস, *s.* shortness, diminution, a wearing,

হ্রাসক, diminishing, shortening. [decline.

হ্রী, *s.* shame, bashfulness, modesty.

হ্রেষা, *s.* the neighing of a horse.

ক্ষ, is a compound of ক and ষ, and the last letter of the Bengáli alphabet.

ক্ষণ, *s.* a measure of time equal to about four minutes; a moment, a while, an instant; centre. ক্ষণদা, *s.* night, the night.

ক্ষণকাল, *s.* an instant, a momentary time.

ক্ষণধ্বংসী, *a.* perishing in a moment.

ক্ষণপ্রভা, *s.* lightning, a flash, a momentary splendour or brilliance.

ক্ষণভঙ্গুর, *a.* perishing in a moment.

ক্ষণমাত্র, *s.* an instant, a mere moment.

ক্ষণার্দ্ধ, *s.* half a moment.

ক্ষণিক, *a.* momentary, fleeting, transient.

ক্ষণুয়া, *a.* diseased with scars in the feet.

ক্ষণো, *s.* a disease in the soles of the feet.

ক্ষত, *a.* wounded, hurt: *s.* a scar, a sore.

ক্ষতজ, *s.* blood, pus, matter. [a wound.

ক্ষতবিক্ষত, *a.* full of cuts and wounds.

ক্ষতব্রত, *s.* one who breaks a vow.

ক্ষতান্বিত, *a.* wounded, full of wounds.

ক্ষতি, *s.* hurt, detriment, harm, damage, loss, injury, evil.

ক্ষতোদর, *s.* a bloody flux. [Hindus

ক্ষত্র, *s.* the second or military tribe of

ক্ষত্রিয়, *s.* a person of the military tribe.

ক্ষপা, *a.* mad, foolish, raving, passionate: *s.* night; passion, madness, folly.

ক্ষপাকর, *a.* provoking: *s.* the moon.

ক্ষবথু, *s.* a cough, a consumption.

ক্ষম, *a.* patient, calm, enduring, benevolent, friendly, able, capable, adequate: *s.* propriety, capability, fitness. [rity.

ক্ষমতা, *s.* power, capacity, ability, autho-

ক্ষমতাপন্ন, *a.* able, capable, powerful.

ক্ষমা, *s.* forbearance, patience, pardon, forgiveness; the earth; a name of Durgá.

ক্ষমাপন্ন, *a.* forbearing, patient, compassionate, long-suffering, forgiving, gracious.

ক্ষমাবান্, or ক্ষমী, *a. idem.*

ক্ষয়, *s.* decay, waste, loss, destruction, decline, consumption; -কৃ, to wear, to waste; -যা, to be wasted, to wear off.

ক্ষয়কর, causing decay or loss, removing, destroying, causing to wear away.

ক্ষয়কাস, *s.* the consumptive cough.

ক্ষয়জ, *a.* arising from waste or decay, arising from consumption.

ক্ষয়মাস, *s.* an intercalary month.

ক্ষয়রোগ, *s.* an atrophy, a consumption.

ক্ষয়া, ক্ষয়িত, *a.* decayed, tending to ruin.

ক্ষর্, *v. a.* to distil, leak, flow, trickle, ooze

ক্ষরণ, *s.* a leaking, oozing, trickling. [out.

ক্ষরণপ্রস্তর, *s.* a dripping stone.

ক্ষরণশীল, *a.* having an oozing tendency.

ক্ষরণার্হ, *a.* fit or proper to ooze out or to

ক্ষরণীয়, *a. idem.* [leak.

ক্ষরা, *v. a.* to cause to leak, trickle or ooze

ক্ষরিত, *a.* leaked, oozed out. [out, to distil.

ক্ষান্ত, *a.* desisted, forborne, led to stop.

ক্ষান্তি, forbearance, forgiveness, desisting.

ক্ষার, *s.* alkali, potash, salt, ashes, soda.

ক্ষারবিশিষ্ট, *a.* alkaline, salt, brackish.

ক্ষারমাটি, *s.* fuller's earth, earth impregnated with salt, alkali, or nitre.
ক্ষারমেহ, *s.* a gonorrhœa, a saltish gleet.
ক্ষাররস, *s.* alkaline or brackish taste.
ক্ষারিত, *a.* distilled from alkaline matter.
ক্ষালন, *s.* the washing or rinsing of a thing.
ক্ষালনীয়, *a.* requiring or fit to be washed.
ক্ষালিত, *a.* washed, rinsed, cleansed.
ক্ষিণ্ণ, *a.* excited, agitated, stimulated.
ক্ষিতি, *s.* the earth; a house, abode; loss, destruction, waste, wane; -রুহ, a tree.
ক্ষিতিজ, *s.* planet Mars, son of the earth.
ক্ষিতিধর, *s.* a mountain; a king. [reign.
ক্ষিতি -পতি, -পাল, -পালক, *s.* a king, a sove-
ক্ষিতিপালন, *s.* the governing of a country.
ক্ষিপ্ত, *a.* thrown, cast; distracted, mad.
ক্ষিপ্র, *a.* active, quick, soon, rapid.
ক্ষীণ, *a.* lank, thin, slender, weak, feeble, emaciated, decayed, exhausted.
ক্ষীণতা, *s.* slenderness, thinness, feebleness,
ক্ষীণমধ্যা, *a.* slender-waisted. [weakness.
ক্ষীণশরীর, or ক্ষীণাঙ্গ, *a.* weak, emaciated.
ক্ষীর, *s.* milk, inspissated milk, milk thickened by boiling, frumenty; water.
ক্ষীরুই, *s.* most of the species of Spurge or leafy Euphorbia.
ক্ষীরপুলী, *s.* a sort of sweetmeat.
ক্ষীরসা, *s.* inspissated or thickened milk.
ক্ষীরা, *s.* a cucumber; -জালী, a gherkin.
ক্ষীরী, *s.* the udder of a cow. [of milk.
ক্ষীরোদ, *s.* a kind of white silk cloth; sea
ক্ষুঁৎ, *s.* a mark, a bruise, a blemish, a fault.
ক্ষুঁজ, small, little: *s.* a sort of net-like cloth.
ক্ষুঁচুৎ, *im. sd.* of cutting any vegetable.
ক্ষুচুরক্ষুচুর, *ad.* a little and a little; quickly.
ক্ষুদরা, *a.* small, trifling, insignificant, little: *s.* retail, a little at a time.
ক্ষুণ্ণ, *a.* crushed, pounded; perplexed, sad, distressed; marked, blemished.
ক্ষুণ্ণপাদ, *a.* having scars in sole of the feet.
ক্ষুণ্ণমনাঃ, *a.* regretting, contrite, distressed in mind, penitent, grieved.
ক্ষুৎ, *s.* a sneeze; a stain, a flaw, blemish.
ক্ষুদ্, *v.* to dig the earth, to carve, to engrave: *s.* broken fragments of grain.
ক্ষুদন, *s.* a pounding, a digging, carving.
ক্ষুদিয়া, *a.* minute, small, trifling, little.

ক্ষুদ্বোধ, *s.* sensation of hunger, appetite.
ক্ষুদ্র, *a.* small, minute, little, trifling, low, mean; -দৃষ্টি, miserly, penurious.
ক্ষুদ্রতা, *s.* smallness, insignificance, littleness, minuteness, meanness.
ক্ষুধা, *s.* hunger, an appetite for food; -কর, or -কৃৎ, causing hunger. [famished.
ক্ষুধাতুর, *a.* afflicted with hunger, hungry,
ক্ষুধান্বিত, ক্ষুধার্ত্ত, or ক্ষুধিত, *a.* hungry.
ক্ষুন্নিবারণ, *s.* the prevention of hunger.
ক্ষুন্নিবৃত্তি, *s.* the appeasing of the appetite.
ক্ষুপ্, or ক্ষুপ্ক্ষুপ্, *a.* quick, in short steps: ক্ষুপ্ করিয়া, or ক্ষুপ্ক্ষুপ্ করিয়া, speedily, quickly, hastily, suddenly. [cage.
ক্ষুপ, *s.* a shrub, a bush; a fowl or pigeon
ক্ষুবরী, *s.* a pigeon house; a hut. [seed.
ক্ষুবি, *s.* a tuft, a clump, a spot sown with
ক্ষুব্ধ, *a.* affected, agitated, distracted, stimulated, excited, pained, distressed.
ক্ষুব্ধতা, -ত্ব, *s.* alarm, agitation, stimulation, excitation, pain, distress.
ক্ষুমা, *s.* flax, linseed.
ক্ষুর, *s.* a razor; hoof; -ধার, razor-edged.
ক্ষুরপা, ক্ষুরপ্র, *s.* a spud, an instrument to grub up grass for horses. [coughing.
ক্ষুসক্ষুস, *s.* a wheezing sound which attends
ক্ষেত, *s.* a field, a wife, the body.
ক্ষেতপাপড়া, *s.* a small annual plant.[1]
ক্ষেত্র, *s.* a field, a wife, the body; a place of pilgrimage; (রণ-) a field of battle.
ক্ষেত্রজ, *a.* born of a married woman by an adulterous connection: a son thus born is owned by the husband as a legitimate child according to the Hindu law.
ক্ষেদো, *a.* coarse and broken (as rice).
ক্ষেপ্, *v. a.* to be angry, irritated, distracted, or foolish, to fall into a passion.
ক্ষেপ, *s.* a throw, a cast, a load which is carried to a place at one time, a throw (of a casting net), a stroke of an oar.
ক্ষেপণ, *s.* a casting, a throwing, a rowing.
ক্ষেপণী, *s.* an oar, a paddle; a net.
ক্ষেপলা, *a.* proper to be cast or thrown.
ক্ষেপলাজাল, *s.* a casting net.
ক্ষেপা, *v. a.* to provoke to anger, to make a person distracted: *a.* vexed, provoked, angry, passionate, distracted, foolish.

ক্ষেপাণ, *s.* act of provoking, a distracting.
ক্ষেম, *s.* happiness, good fortune, welfare.
ক্ষেমঙ্করী, *s.* same as **শঙ্করচিল**. [basket.
ক্ষেমী, *a.* happy, fortunate: *s.* a trinket-
ক্ষেয়ারী, *s.* a rower, a waterman, a dáṇṛi.
ক্ষো, *s.* the refuse of sugar-cane after the juice has been expressed by the mill.
ক্ষোক্ষস্, *s.* a giant-killer, a cruel person.
ক্ষোণা, *s.* a particular kind of spear.
ক্ষোণি, or **ক্ষোণী**, *s.* the earth.
ক্ষোপ, *s.* a pigeon-house, a dovecot.
ক্ষোপচাল, *s.* side roof of a thatched house.
ক্ষোপা, *s.* a hair-knot tied on the top of or behind the head of a woman.
ক্ষোপাল, *a.* having a hair-knot, having sufficient hair for a hair-knot.
ক্ষোভ, *s.* excitation, stimulation, confusion, perplexity, distress of mind.
ক্ষোভকারক, ক্ষোভকারী, ক্ষোভজনক, *a.* exciting, stimulating, agitating the mind.
ক্ষোভান্বিত, ক্ষোভিত, *s.* agitated, excited, stimulated.
ক্ষৌণি, ক্ষৌণী, *s.* the earth.
ক্ষৌদ্র, *s.* honey, water, liquid.
ক্ষৌম, *s.* an airy room on the top of a house; wove silk or linen, silk cloth.
ক্ষৌর, ক্ষৌরী, *s.* the shaving of the head or beard.
ক্ষ্মা, *s.* the earth.
ক্ষ্বেড়, *s.* venom, poison, virus; sound.

APPENDIX.

অকটাক্ষ, *s.* a full stare at any thing.
অকড়িয়া, *a.* penniless, very poor.
অকল্পন, *a.* genuine, inartificial.
অকল্পনা, *s.* machination, ill design.
অকষ্টবদ্ধ, *s.* the utmost degree of distress.
অকায, *a.* the same with **অকায্**.
অকুশল, *s.* misfortune, ill luck.
অকুপার, *s.* the ocean; a tortoise.
অকৃতকর্ম্মা, অকৃতকার্য্য, *a.* unsuccessful.
অক্রেয়, *a.* not purchaseable, dear.
অক্ষম, *a.* unable, impotent, insufficient.
অক্ষমালা, *s.* myrobalan rosary or necklace.
অক্ষরমালা, *s.* the alphabet.
অক্ষাংশ, *s.* a degree of latitude or longitude.
অক্ষাগ্র, *s.* an axletree, an axis.
অক্ষান্ত, *a.* unforbearing, persevering.
অক্ষান্তি, *a. idem*: *s.* impatience.
অখড়ি, *s.* childish whim, caprice, fancy.
অখণ্ড, *a.* unbroken, whole.
অখিল, *a.* whole, all, entire.
অগ্নিতুল্য, *a.* fire-like, haughty, passionate.
অগ্নিবিসর্প, অগ্নিবীসর্প, *s.* a violent pain.
অগ্নিশিখা, flame of fire; name of a plant.[1]
অগ্ন্যবতার, *a.* violently passionate, furious, mad with rage: *s.* a furious person.
অঙ্কগ, *s.* (a child) in arms.
অঙ্গরাগ, *s.* a cosmetic, colouring for the body.
অঙ্গাঙ্গী, partnership, collusion, chicanery.
অঙ্গুলিত্র, অঙ্গুলিত্রাণ *s.* a guard for the thumb or finger, a thimble.
অচিরক্রিয়, *a.* prompt in action.
অচিরাৎ, অচিরায়, *ad.* promptly, forthwith.
অচৈতন্য, *a.* the same with **অচেতন**.
অচ্ছত্র, *a.* without an umbrella or a king.
অচ্ছন্ন, অচ্ছাদিত, *a.* uncovered.
অচ্ছল, *a.* without fraud, honest, upright, sincere.
অজিন, *s.* a hide, leather.
অজীর্ণ, *a.* not worn out, undigested: *s.* indigestion.
অটন, *s.* the act of moving or walking.
অটবী, *s.* a forest, wood, thicket.
অট্ট, অট্টালক, *s.* a palace, upper-roomed house.
অণিমা, *s.* a species of superhuman power.
অণুবীক্ষণ, *s.* a microscope.
অতন্দ্রতা, *a.* not procrastinating, punctual.
অতিক্রান্ত, *a.* transgressed, surpassed.
অতিপন্থা, *s.* a highway, high road.
অতিপর, *s.* a decided enemy.
অতিপাত, *s.* a deviation from fixed rules.
অতিপ্রসঙ্গ, *s.* verbosity, prolixity.
অতিবাত, *s.* a storm, hurricane, cyclone.
অতিভাব, *s.* great friendship, intimacy.
অতিমাত্র, *a.* the same with **অতিশয়**.
অতিরথী, *s.* a great warrior, a hero.
অতিসর, *a.* exceeded, excessive.

অতিসুগ্রাহ্য, *a.* highly acceptable.
অতিসুহৃদ, *s.* a very great friend.
অতীব, *ad.* exceedingly.
অতুন্দ, অতুন্দিল, *a.* lank, thin, lean.
অতুল, *a.* unequalled, unrivalled, peerless.
অত্যন্তবাসী, *s.* a devotee, an ascetic.
অত্যয়, *s.* a surpassing, excess, outrage.
অত্যয়িত, *a.* exceeded, overstepped, outraged.
অত্যুক্তি, *s.* garrulity, exaggeration.
অত্যুত্তর, *a.* last: *s.* complete reply or refutation; extreme north.
অত্রপ, অত্রপান্বিত, *a.* immodest, shameless.
অধঃপাত, *s.* downfall of a person or thing.
অধঃপ্রস্তর, *s.* the seat of an unclean person.
অধিক্রম, *s.* invasion, infringement.
অধিত্যকা, *s.* table-land on a mountain.
অধিদৈব, *s.* demigods, demons, titans.
অধিপ্রজ, *s.* a continuation of the world.
অধিমাত্র, *s.* a knowledge of the properties of the mysterious syllable ওঁ, namely, অ, উ and ম.
অধিলোক, *s.* the universe.
অধিশ্রয়ণ, *s.* a receptacle, a focus.
অধীর, *a.* not slow, not tardy, hasty.
অধোগত, *a.* descended, gone down.
অধোদেশ, *s.* pudendum muliebre.
অধোভব, *a.* inferior, subordinate.
অধোমুখ, *a.* the same with অধোবদন.
অধ্যগ্নি, *s.* wedding present to a bride.
অধ্যধীন, *a.* wholly subject: *s.* a slave.
অধ্যবসায়, perseverance, devotedness to
অধ্যারূঢ়, *a.* mounted upon, riding on.
অধ্যারোপণ, the imputing of deeds falsely
অধ্যারোহণ, a mounting on, a climbing up.
অধ্যাস, *s.* substituting one thing for another.
অধ্যাসিত, *a.* inhabited, seated on.
অধ্যাসীন, *s.* a being placed or seated on.
অধ্যুষিত, *a.* inhabited, seated on.
অধ্যূঢ়া, *s.* a superseded wife.
অধ্যেষণা, *s.* solicitation, prayer.
অধ্বনীন, অধ্বন্য, *s.* a traveller, messenger.
অধ্বর, *s.* a sacrifice.
অনক্ষর, *s.* illiterate, unlettered, ignorant.
অনডুহী, অনড়াহী, *s.* a cow.
অনড্বান্, *s.* an ox, a bull.
অনন্যপূর্ব্বক, *a.* unprecedented, not preceded.
অনপর, *a.* own: *s.* a name of Brahmá.

অনপরাধী, *a.* guiltless, innocent.
অনবকাশ, *s.* want of leisure or opportunity.
অনবদ্য, *a.* irreproachable, honourable.
অনবসর, *a.* busy: *s.* want of leisure.
অনবসাদ, *a.* unwearied, unexhausted.
অনবস্থা, *s.* want, need, adversity.
অনর্গল, *a.* unrestrained, free, fluent.
অনাকারণ, *a.* preternatural, causeless.
অনাগত, *a.* not yet come, future.
অনাগমন, *s.* a not coming, non-arrival.
অনাজ, *s.* corn, edible vegetables.
অনাটন, *s.* lacking, insufficient.
অনাড়, *a.* secret, not easily discovered.
অনাড়িপনা, অনাড়ী, *vide* আনাড়িপনা.
অনাঢ্য, *a.* not wealthy, not affluent, poor.
অনাতপ, *a.* cool, shady: *s.* shade, coolness.
অনাবিষ্ট, *a.* not fully engaged in.
অনাম, *a.* nameless, anonymous.
অনামক, *a.* anonymous, nameless: *s.* the piles.
অনামুখ, *a.* unsightly, unwelcome.
অনার্য্য, *a.* inferior, mean, base, barbarian.
অনালাপ, *s.* taciturnity: *a.* taciturn, unsocial.
অনালাপী, *a.* unsocial, not affable.
অনালাপ্য, *a.* not affable, cynical.
অনাশ্য, অনাশনীয়, *a.* imperishable.
অনীশ, void of authority, subject, depending.
অনীশ্বর, *s.* that which is not God.
অনিশ্বরত্ব, *s.* atheism, a denial of God.
অনীশ্বরপ্রতিপাদন, *s.* defence of atheism.
অনুদ্বাহ, *s.* celibacy, single life.
অনুবন্ধ, *a.* connected, bound, related to.
অনুবন্ধী, *s.* a hiccough, hiccup.
অনুবর্জ্জন, *s.* relinquishment.
অনুবর্ত্তন, *s.* a following; complaisance.
অনুবাদক, *a.* replying: *s.* one who quotes.
অনুবাদী, *a.* replying, responding, quoting.
অনুমত, *a.* permitted, allowed.
অনুমোদন, *s.* cheerful approbation.
অনুলাপ, *s.* tautology, repetition.
অনুশয়, *s.* repentance; ancient enmity.
অনুশয়ী, penitent, feeling regret.
অনুশাসন, *s.* a giving rules, order, discipline.
অনুশাস্তা, *s.* a teacher, a disciplinarian.
অনুশিষ্ট, docile, teachable, subject to rules.
অনূপ, *a.* wet, overflowed: *s.* a buffalo.
অনৃত, not affected with; untrue: *s.* falsehood.
অনেকশঃ, *ad.* by large numbers.

অনৈকাগ্র্য, *s.* a divided attention.
অনৈক্য, *s.* want of union or unity, discord.
অনৌচিত, *s.* unfitness, inaptitude.
অন্তঃপট, *s.* privacy, secresy.
অন্তঃপ্রজ্ঞ, *a.* acquainted with the heart.
অন্তঃসত্ত্বা, pregnant, with child : *s.* name of a tree (Semicarpus anacardium).
অন্তরাত্মা, *s.* the inward spirit, the soul.
অন্তর্গর্ভ, *a.* included, within.
অন্তর্গৃহ, *s.* the inside of a house. [tion.
অন্তর্দাহ, *s.* inward burning or inflamma-
অন্তর্যজন, or অন্তর্যাগ, *s.* mental worship.
অন্তেবাসী, *s.* an outcast ; a pupil, a disciple.
অন্দু, *s.* a ring or chain for the ankle.
অন্নদাস, *s.* a mercenary, serving for food.
অন্নব্রহ্ম, *s.* Brahmá as identified with food.
অন্নযোগ, *s.* the providing of food.
অন্নাদ, *s.* an eater ; Vishnu.
অন্নাদি, *s.* food and other necessaries.
অন্নাহারী, *a.* eating food : *s.* an eater.
অন্যগামী, *a.* going to others, adulterous.
অন্যৎ, *ad.* another, other, otherwise.
অন্যথাচরণ, *s.* perversity, disobedience.
অন্যথাচারী, *a.* disobedient, perverse.
অন্যপ্রকার, *a.* another sort : *ad.* otherwise.
অন্যভৃৎ, *s.* a crow. অন্যভৃত, *s.* a cuckoo.
অন্যমনাঃ, *a.* otherwise minded. [spect.
অন্যাং, *a.* yet, otherwise, in another re-
অন্যাদৃক্, অন্যাদৃশ, *a.* otherwise, of another
অন্যাধীন, subject, dependent. [kind.
অন্যায্য, *a.* unjust, unlawful, wrong.
অন্বয়, *s.* race, lineage ; in *gram.* the regimen or government of words in a sentence ; in *logic*, a direct consequence.
অন্বয়ী, *a.* agreeing with another word or part of a sentence, following upon.
অন্বহ, *ad.* daily, continually.
অন্বাধি, *s.* a pledge, trust, a deposit made in order to be credited to another.
অন্বায়তন, *a.* latitudinal. [ral feast
অন্বাহার্য্য, *s.* a monthly shraddha or fune-
অন্বাহিত, *a.* deposited for another.
অপকরণ, *s.* an injuring, an obstructing.
অপকীর্ত্তি, *s.* ill fame, disgrace, infamy.
অপকৃষ্টতা, *s.* inferiority, meanness.
অপক্ক, *a.* raw, unripe, imperfect.
অপগম, *s.* a departure, a deviation.

অপঘন, অবয়ব, *s.* a limb, member. [tion.
অপচার, অজীর্ণ, *a.* undigested : *s.* indiges-
অপটু, *a.* unskilled, awkward, incapable.
অপড়, *a.* lasting, durable ; saleable.
অপত্য, সন্তান, *s.* a child, offspring.
অপত্রপ, *s.* bashfulness, modesty.
অপত্রপিষ্ণু, *a.* bashful, modest.
অপথ্য, *a.* unwholesome, not salutary.
অপদ, *a.* out of office ; feetless : *s.* a reptile.
অপদস্থ, *a.* out of employ, cashiered.
অপদান, *s.* an approved occupation.
অপদার্থ, *s.* non-entity, nothing, vanity.
অপদিশ, *s.* intermediate point of the com-
অপদেশ, *s.* a pretence, a pretext. [pass.
অপধ্বংসক, *a.* abominable, accursed.
অপনাম, *s.* a nickname.
অপবর্গ, *s.* emancipation, beatitude.
অপবর্ত্ত, *s.* abridging, a reducing.
অপবাহ, *s.* an inference, a deduction.
অপবিত্রতা, -ত্ব, *s.* impurity, uncleanness.
অপবিদ্ধ, *a.* pulverised, broken into bits.
অপভ্রংশ, *s.* vulgar term, vulgar expres-
অপররাত্র, *s.* the end of the night. [sion.
অপরম্পার, *a.* continual, continued.
অপরাদ্ধ, *a.* guilty, criminal.
অপরিণত, *a.* immature, unripe.
অপরিণামদর্শী, *a.* imprudent, improvident.
অপরিণীতা, *s.* an unmarried woman.
অপরিসর, *a.* distant ; narrow, strait.
অপরুদ্ধ, *a.* vexed, mortified, annoyed.
অপরেদ্যুঃ, *ad.* another day, the morrow.
অপর্য্যাপ্ত, *a.* insufficient, unlimited.
অপসব্য, *s.* the right-hand side.
অপহনন, *s.* murder, slaughter.
অপহন্তা, অপহা, *s.* a murderer.
অপহর্ত্তা, *s.* a robber, thief, plunderer.
অপাত্র, *a.* unworthy : *s.* a mean vessel.
অপান, *s.* the anus ; air inhaled.
অপাবৃত, *a.* unrestrained, self-willed.
অপায়, *s.* destruction, a hindrance.
অপারক, unable, incapable, incompetent.
অপারকতা, *s.* inability, incompetency.
অপিচ, অপিতু, *conj. vide* অপি. [father.
অপিতৃক, *a.* fatherless, not pertaining to a
অপিধান, *s.* a covering, concealing.
অপীনস, *s.* a catarrh, cold.
অপূপ, *s.* bread, a cake of flour.

অপৃষ্ট, *a.* unasked, unsought. [liloquy.
অপৃষ্টাভিধান, unrequired discourse, a so-
অপেয়, *a.* unpotable, unfit for drinking.
অপেশল, *a.* inexpert, not handsome.
অপোগণ্ড, *a.* not deformed, not beardless.
অপৌরুষ, *s.* unmanliness, cowardice.
অপ্পতি, *s.* the sea, the lord of waters.
অপ্রকাণ্ড, *s.* a shrub, a bush.
অপ্রণয়, *s.* want of affection, inaffability.
অপ্রণয়ী, unaffable, unfriendly. [peerless.
অপ্রতিমেয়, অপ্রতিমাতব্য, *a.* incomparable.
অপ্রতিষ্ঠ, *a.* of no renown, infamous.
অপ্রসিদ্ধ, *a.* infamous; -পদ, an obsolete
অপ্রৌঢ়, *a.* unmarried; timid. [word.
অপ্রৌঢ়া, *a. fem.* unmarried: *s.* a spinster.
অবকথন, *s.* fulsome flattery, low talk.
অবকর, *s.* sweepings, refuse, a dunghill.
অবকর্ত্তন, *s.* a spinning-wheel; excision.
অবকলন, *s.* an incorrect calculation.
অবকুঞ্চিত, *a.* dishevelled; contemned.
অবকুট্টন, *s.* needless fear, timidity.
অবকুণ্ঠন, *s.* querulousness, complaining.
অবকূজন, অবক্কূজন, *s.* hideous groaning.
অবকৃষ্ট, *a.* expelled, rejected, removed.
অবক্রন্দন, *s.* clamorous weeping.
অবক্রীড়ন, *s.* improper play. [rage.
অবক্রোধ, *a.* unreasonable anger, fury,
অবক্ষুধা, *s.* a ravenous appetite.
অবক্ষুধিত, ravenous, ravenously hungry.
অবখণ্ডন, *s.* a digging, a piercing.
অবখাত, *s.* a cavern, a pit.
অবগম, *s.* knowledge, acquaintedness.
অবগম্য, অবগমনীয়, *a.* knowable.
অবগুণ্ঠন, অবগুণ্ঠিকা, *s.* a veil.
অবগুণ্ঠিত, *a.* veiled.
অবগোচর, *a.* imperfectly perceived.
অবগোরণ, *s.* the raising of a weapon to
অবগ্রন্থন, *s.* bad construction. [strike.
অবগ্রহ, disrespect; drought; elephant's
অবঘাত, murder, a fatal blow. [forehead.
অবঘূর্ণ, *s.* a whirling, a whirlpool.
অবঘ্রাণ, *s.* a disagreeable smell.
অবচ্ছেদাবচ্ছেদ, *s.* the whole of any thing.
অবজীর্ণ, *a.* superannuated, old, worn out.
অবতংশ, *s.* a crest, an earring, a gem, gold, wealth, a ray of light, a halter or rein, the tie of a yoke for oxen.

অবদান, *s.* an oblation, an offering.
অবদূন, *a.* regretted, lamented.
অবদ্য, *a.* unutterable, unspeakable.
অবদ্যোত, *s.* glimmering.
অবদ্রুত, *s.* precipitate flight.
অবধারণ, *s.* a determining; emphasis.
অবধারণার্হ, *a.* fit to be determined.
অবধীরিত, *a.* disrespected, despised.
অবধূক, *a.* wifeless, unmarried, widowed.
অবধুত, *a.* shaken out, brushed.
অবধেয়, *a.* proper to be ascertained or at-
অবধৌত, *a.* badly washed. [tended to.
অবনায়, *s.* a precipitating; disagreement.
অবন্দনীয়, *a.* not worthy of salutation.
অববাদ, *s.* censure, accusation, reproach.
অববৃত, *s.* ablution after a sacrifice.
অববোধ, *s.* false idea, prejudice.
অবভৃথ, *s.* a bathing after sacrifice.
অবমান, *s.* dishonour, disgrace.
অবমূর্দ্ধময়, *a.* precipitating, headlong.
অবমৃষ্ট, defloured, defiled, forced.
অবর, *a.* younger, junior, inferior, least.
অবরবর্ণ, *a.* of an inferior class or tribe.
অবরস, *a.* ill-tasted, insipid: *s.* insipidity.
অবল, *a.* weak, infirm, feeble, powerless.
অবলাঞ্ছন, *s.* mark of disgrace.
অবলাঞ্ছিত, *a.* marked disgracefully.
অবলিপ্ত, *a.* smeared over; proud, self-im-
অবলীঢ়, *a.* lapped, licked. [portant.
অবলীলা, *s.* merriment, sport, loose mirth.
অবলেহন, *s.* a lapping with the tongue.
অবশ্যম্ভব, *a.* inevitably coming to pass; *s.* urgency. [surrounded.
অবষ্টব্ধ, *a.* near; protected, supported;
অবষ্টম্ভ, *s.* a pillar; a beginning; beauty.
অবসাদ, *s.* weariness, lassitude, flaccidity.
অবসারণ, *s.* a disbanding (of troops,) a dislodging (of an enemy,) a discharging (of a servant,) a dismissing any one.
অবস্কন্দ, *s.* a camp; an assault. [ling.
অবস্কন্দন, *s.* the act of refuting or repel-
অবস্কর, *s.* sweepings, refuse.
অবস্তাৎ, *ad.* posteriorly, lastly, finally.
অবস্বন, *s.* a harsh sound, yell.
অবহা, *a.* permanent, standing, stagnant.
অবহার, *s.* a removing; forgiveness; a
অবহিত্থা, *s.* dissimulation. [shark.

অবাক্শিরঃ, অবাঙ্মুখ, *a.* downcast, hanging down the head, nodding. [nodding.
অবাগ্র, *a.* bowed, hanging down, deflexed,
অবাচ্যদেশ, *s.* pudendum muliebre.
অবাদে, *ad.* without opposition, smoothly.
অবাধে, *ad.* without obstruction, easily.
অবাস্তব, *a.* not genuine, not real, unsubstantial, fictitious. [preservation.
অবি, *s.* a sheep ; a mountain ; the sun ;
অবিকট, *s.* a flock of sheep.
অবিকল, *a.* entire, perfect, regular, unim-
অবিকলতা, *s.* regularity, order. [paired.
অবিকল্প, *a.* not optional, not admitting two forms : *s.* a positive precept.
অবিগীত, *a.* not reproached or censured.
অবিঘ্ন, *a.* free from obstruction or hinder-
অবিদিত, unknown, unacquainted. [ance.
অবিধা, *s.* want of method or distinction.
অবিনীত, *a.* unhumbled, not docile.
অবিবেকী, *a.* rash, undiscriminating, judging in the gross.
অবিভক্ত, *a.* undivided, not shared out.
অবিহর্ষ, *s.* cheerlessness, gloom.
অবী, *s.* a woman in her courses.
অবীক্ষিত, *a.* unsurveyed, not viewed.
অবেদন, *a.* not knowing or perceiving.
অবৈগুণ্য, *a.* consistent : *s.* consistency.
অবৈচক্ষণ্য, *a.* unlearned : *s.* ignorance.
অবৈজয়ন্তী, *a.* destitute of a flag.
অব্জজ, *a.* produced from the moon : *s.*
অব্জযোনি, *s.* a name of Brahmá. [Brahmá.
অব্জিনী, *s.* a bed of lotuses ; -পতি, the sun.
অব্ধি, *s.* the sea, a receptacle for water.
অভিক, or **অভীক**, *a.* wanton, lascivious.
অভিখ্যা, *s.* a name, appellation ; beauty.
অভিঘাত, *s.* destruction, smiting, murder.
অভিচার, *s.* incantation for injuring one.
অভিজন, *s.* a family, the head of a family ; a birth-place, a family residence.
অভিজ্ঞান, *s.* certainty, conviction, a token, a signal, the colour of a fleet
অভিধেয়, *a.* explicable : *s.* an appellation.
অভিধ্যা, *s.* a coveting another's goods.
অভিপন্ন, *a.* guilty, subdued, involved in.
অভিব্যক্ত, *a.* expressed, declared, revealed.
অভিব্যাপ্তি, *s.* co-extension, contact.
অভিভাবক, *s.* a guardian, a protector.

অভিলেখন, *s.* a writing down, inserting.
অভিষব, *s.* distillation ; ablution before a sacrifice ; a sipping the juice of Soma.
অভিসন্ধি, *s.* a joint, juncture ; cheating.
অভিসম্পাত, *s.* a curse, an imprecation ; conflict, war, devastation.
অভিসর, *s.* a follower, an attendant, a companion, a comrade, an ally.
অভিসার, *s.* *idem ;* an assignation, an appointment to meet.
অভিসারিকা, *s.* a woman who attends an assignation with her lover.
অভিহিত, *a.* spoken, disclosed.
অভীক, *a.* lascivious, lustful.
অভীক্ষ্ণ, *ad.* repeatedly, frequently.
অভেদ্য, অভেদনীয়, *a.* indivisible, inseparable, impenetrable, impervious.
অভ্যঙ্গ, অভ্যঞ্জন, *s.* a rubbing the body with oil, unction. [sent.
অভ্যনুজ্ঞা, অভ্যনুজ্ঞান, *s.* a permission, con-
অভ্যনুজ্ঞাত, *a.* permitted, consented to.
অভ্যবহরণ, *s.* act of eating or taking food.
অভ্যর্থনা, *s.* a petition, request ; welcom-
অভ্যাগত, *a.* come : *s.* a guest, visitor. [ing.
অভ্যাপাত, *s.* a misfortune, calamity, ruin, loss, misery, disappointment.
অভ্যুদাহরণ, *s.* illustration by its reverse.
অভ্যুপগত, *a.* acknowledged, consented to.
অভ্যুপগন্তব্য, *a.* recognisable. [sent.
অভ্যুপগম, admission, acquiescence, con-
অভ্যুপায়, *s.* good or applicable expedient.
অভ্রংশ, *s.* not a fall from virtue or dignity.
অভ্রমু, *s.* female of the elephant ঐরাবত.
অম্, *a.* quick, small : *s.* swiftness.
অম, *a.* raw, unbaked, (earthen-ware).
অমত, *s.* disapprobation, dislike.
অমতে, *ad.* disapprovingly.
অমন্তব্য, *a.* not knowable, not assented to.
অমানুষ, *s.* not a man : *a.* not human, unmanly ; uninhabited, desolate.
অমায়িক, *s.* sincere, upright.
অমায়ী, *a.* not practising sorcery.
অমিত্র, *a.* friendless : *s.* an enemy.
অমিশ্রিত, *a.* unmixed, uncompounded, sim-
অমী, *a.* sick, diseased. [ple.
অমুত্র, *ad.* in another world.
অমৃষ্টি, *s.* an oblong drinking vessel.

অমৃত্যু, *s.* immortality : *a.* immortal.
অমেধ্য, *a.* unclean, impure : *s.* impurity.
অম্বক, *s.* an eye, organ of seeing.
অম্বল, *a.* acid, sour, tart ; -বেল, a plant.[1]
অম্বষ্ঠ, *s.* a physician, or the descendant of a Bráhman by a Vaishya woman.
অম্বুজ, *s.* an aquatic plant ; a lotus.
অম্বুদ, অম্বুবাহ, অম্বুভূৎ, *s.* a cloud.
অম্বুধি, অম্ভোনিধি, *s.* the ocean, the sea.
অম্বুর, *s.* the threshold of a door.
অম্বূকৃত, *a.* sputtered, drivelled.
অম্ভোজ, *s.* a lotus, waterlily ; the moon.
অম্ভোদ, অম্ভোধর, অম্ভোধি, *s.* a cloud.
অযথা, *a.* disproportioned, unlike, inconsistent.
অযথাব্যয়, *s.* extravagance.
অরণ্যানী, *s.* a large or extensive forest.
অরত্নি, *s.* a cubit measured from the elbow to the tip of the little finger.
অরিত্র, *s.* the rudder of a ship or boat.
অরিন্দম, *a.* foe-subduing : *s.* a conqueror.
অরুক, অরুগ, অরুগ্ন, *a.* healthy, hale.
অর্চিষ্মান্, *a.* brilliant, illustrious, radiant, bright, clear, striking conviction.
অর্চিস্, *s.* flame, light, splendour, radiance.
অর্ত্তিক, *s.* a sort of cake or gingerbread.
অর্থতঃ, *ad.* according to the sense ; namely.
অর্থপর, *a.* parsimonious, niggardly.
অর্থবত্তা, *s.* the answering of a purpose.
অর্থবাদ, *s.* a petition, a plea ; the exaggerating of advantages.
অর্থবান, *a.* rich, wealthy, opulent ; apposite, answering a purpose, relevant.
অর্দ্দনা, *s.* a begging, a request, a petition, a prayer, solicitation, suffering.
অর্দ্দিত, *a.* requested, asked, petitioned, prayed for, tormented : *s.* convulsions.
অর্দ্ধনীরী, cultivating land for half share.
অর্দ্ধাবভেদক, *s.* a violent head-ache.
অর্দ্ধার্দ্ধি, *ad.* half and half.
অর্দ্ধাশন, *s.* half a meal, a tiffin.
অর্দ্ধেন্দু, *s.* a half moon, a crescent.
অর্ব্বন, *a.* low, inferior, base : *s.* a horse.
অর্ব্বাক, *a.* prior, former, antecedent : *ad.* formerly, antecedently.
অর্ভক, *s.* a child, little one, young of an animal.
অর্ম্ম, *s.* a disease of the eyes.
অর্য্যমা, *s.* the sun ; the ancestors.

অর্য্যা, *s.* a belonging or appertaining to.
অর্হন, *s.* a being right, proper or deserving.
অলবড্ড, *a.* ignorant, awkward, clumsy.
অলর্ক, *s.* a dog excited to pursue a game.
অলাত, *s.* a firebrand, charcoal.
অলাবু, *s.* the bottle gourd (Cucurbita lagenaria).
অলিজিহ্বা, *s.* the uvula or epiglottis.
অলিঞ্জর, *s.* a water-jar, a large pitcher.
অলিন্দ, *s.* a terrace before a house, a balcony.
অলুক, *a.* insuppressible : *s.* a potato.
অলৌকিক, *a.* unpopular ; supernatural.
অলমারা, *s.* *Eng.* a chest of drawers, a cabinet, a bureau, a book-case.
অল্পবয়স্ক, *a.* young, not advanced in age.
অল্পিষ্ঠ, *a.* very few, fewest, very small.
অশনাচ্ছাদন, *s.* food and clothing.
অশনায়া, *s.* hunger, desire for food.
অশনায়িত, *a.* hungry, desirous of food.
অশনি, *s.* a thunderbolt ; lightning.
অশনীয়, *a.* eatable, fit for food.
অশমতা, *s.* want of tranquillity, perturbation.
অশরীরিতা, *s.* incorporeity, immateriality.
অশরীরী, *a.* incorporeal, immaterial.
অশশ্বৎ, *a.* temporary, not eternal.
অশিব, *a.* unpropitious, unhappy, unlucky.
অশ্রোত্র, *a.* earless, deaf.
অশ্মন, or অশ্মা, *s.* a stone.
অশ্মন্ত, *s.* a portable fire-place or hearth.
অশ্মভাল, *s.* a mortar and pestle.
অশ্লীল, *s.* rustic or obscene language.
অশ্বীন, *s.* a day's journey for a horse.
অষ্টময়সিদ্ধি, *s.* a full accomplishment of a person's desires.
অষ্ঠীনিকা, অষ্ঠীলা, *s.* costiveness.
অসতামী, *s.* unchastity, sin, turpitude, unholiness.
অসতীতা, -ত্ব, *s.* unchastity, impurity.
অসন, *s.* a throwing ; the name of a tree.[2]
অসমীর, *a.* airless, still, calm.
অসাঙ্গতা, *s.* poverty, want, indigence, need.
অসান্ত্বনা, *s.* a want of consolation.
অসান্ত্বনীয়, *a.* inconsolable.
অসামাজিক, *a.* unsocial, holding no rank in society : *s.* not a member of society.
*অসামী, a client, a defendant, a convict.
অসাম্প্রতৎ, *ad.* not now.
অসিক্নী, *s.* a lady's maid.
অসু, *s.* life, vital breath : *a.* swift.

অসুধী, *a.* not wise, ignorant.
অসৃক, শোণিত, রক্ত, লহু, *s.* blood.
অসেচনক, *a.* very beautiful, charming.
অস্তিত্ব, *s.* existence, being.
অস্ত্রীক, *a.* destitute of a wife. [of sleep.
অস্বপ্ন, *s.* bad or ominous dream, a want
অস্বভাব, *a.* unnatural, ill-natured.
অস্বর, *a.* having a bad or hoarse voice.
অহংযু, *a.* proud, self-important.
অহঙ্কারপূর্ব্বক, *ad.* by or through pride.
অহঙ্কারপ্রযুক্ত, from or because of pride.
*অহদ্, *s.* a promise, an agreement. [ter.
অহদ্‌নামা, *s.* a will, a deed of gift, a char-
*অহমক, *a.* ignorant, stupid, clownish.
অহর্ম্মণি, *s.* the sun, the luminary of day.
অহর্ম্মুখ, *s.* the morning, the dawn.

আ.

আঁজন, *s.* a salve for the eyelids. [active.
আঁটরাকাট, *a.* stout, robust, young and
আঁড়ুবাঁড়ু, nausea, qualmishness, sickness.
আঁতরসামারণ, *s.* the parboiling, or half dressing of fish or flesh. [a person.
আঁদীকরণ, আঁধীকরণ, *s.* the blindfolding of
আকড়, *a.* difficult, hard to be performed.
আকড়িয়া, *a.* penniless, poor, indigent.
আকণ্ঠা, *a.* reaching up to the throat.
আকর্ণ, *a.* reaching up to the ear.
আকর্ণন, *s.* a listening, a hearing.
আকর্ণিত, *a.* listened to, heard.
আকর্ষণী, *s.* a hooked stick for pulling fruit.
আকল্প, ornament, sale, increase. [ance.
আকারতঃ, *ad.* from the likeness or appear-
আকুণ্ডকুণ্ড, *s.* the increase of a quarrel by the interference of a third person.
আক্রমণকর্ত্তা, *s.* one who seizes, an invader.
আগদোগ, *s.* the forepart of a thing.
আগমকী, *s.* a plant (Bryonia scabrella).
আগস্, *s.* sin, guilt, crime.
আগোড়বাইগির, *a.* sure, firm, unalterable.
আগোবরা, *a.* preceding; (cash) advanced.
আগোনে, beforehand, in advance. [army.
আগদেলিয়া, *a.* leading the vanguard of an
আগ্রহ, *s.* zeal, eagerness, perseverance, tenacity, obstinacy.
আগ্রহায়ণ, *s.* the same as অগ্রহায়ণ. [year.
আগ্রহায়ণিক, preceding or beginning the
আগ্রহায়ণী, day of full moon in অগ্রহায়ণ.

আঘাবিঘা, hindrance, obstruction, oppo-
*আঙ্গিয়া, a bodice, a sort of stays. [sition.
*আঙ্গোঠা, *s.* the thumb, the great toe.
আচারপূত, *a.* of good conduct, polite.
আট্‌কপালিয়া, *a.* ill-fated, unlucky.
আটকাঁটালিয়া, octangular; of eight sorts.
আটপটাঙ্গীয়া, *a.* sumptuous, pompous.
আটেকাঠেদড়, *a.* firm, holding firmly on all
আড়ুচা, *s.* an unreasonable longing. [sides.
আড়পাপড়া, *s.* a cudgel, a bludgeon.
আড়ষ্ট, *a.* cramped, stiffened, benumbed.
আড়িপাতনীয়া, *a.* lying in wait, lurking, insidious: *s.* an assassin.
আড়েগিলনীয়া *a.* ravenous, gluttonous.
*আণ্টা, *s.* a ball to play with;-খেলা, a play at billiards; -ঘর, a billiard-room.
আততায়ী, *a.* ready to murder or injure.
আতর্পণ, *a.* cleansing up for a festival.
আতারিকাতারি, *s.* a groan, agony, a writhing about with pain.
আতালিপাতালি, *ad.* everywhere, high and low, above and below.
আতুআতু, *a.* subject to, dependent on.
আতেলা, *a.* destitute of oil, not oiled.
আদ্যপ্রান্ত, অদ্যোপান্ত, *ad.* from the first, all along, from first to last.
আদ্যশ্রাদ্ধ, first funeral obsequies. [gies.
আদ্যা, goddesses reckoned divine ener-
আদ্যূন, selfishly voracious, greedy, gluttonous, luxurious, not emulous.
আধআধ, *ad.* half and half, by halves.
আধকপালিয়া, *s.* half a head-ache.
আধপাগল, *a.* half a fool, weak, foolish.
আধপাগলাটীয়া, inclined to idiocy, foolish.
আধভোজন, *s.* half a meal, a tiffin.
আধলা, *s.* half of a paisá, half a brick.
আধসের, *s.* half a seer, or about a pound.
আধ্যাত্মিক, *a.* internal, inherent.
আনক, *s.* a kind of trumpet, a drum.
আনদ্ধ, *a.* bound, tied, fastened, shut, imprisoned, confined: *s.* a kind of drum.
আনাহ, epistasis, a suppression of urine, constipation, costiveness.
*আনোঠাজলেবী, *s.* a kind of sweetmeat.
*আন্দর্শা, *s.* a fine kind of sweetmeat.
আপন্নসত্ত্বা, *s.* a pregnant woman.
আপা, আবাপ, *s.* an interlineation.

আপাদমস্তক, cap-a-pie, from head to foot.
আপান, *s.* an assembly of druukards.
আপীড়, *s.* a chaplet for the head.
আব, or আবু, *s.* a wen.
আবপন, *s.* a receptacle, a vessel.
আবাপন, *s.* a thread reel.
আবিল, *a.* muddy, sinful, guilty, foul.
আবিষ্কার, a making apparent ; a reviling.
আভিচারিক, *s.* one who uses incantations.
আভিধানিক, *a.* relating to a dictionary.
আয়ুষ্টোম, a sacrifice to ensure longevity.
আর্জ্জব, straightness, rectitude, honesty.
আর্ত্তধ্বনি, আর্ত্তনাদ, আর্ত্তস্বর, *s.* a groan, a shriek, a cry of distress. [ern sea.
আর্য্যাবর্ত্ত, country from eastern to west-
আলন, *s.* a putrefying ; a going home.
আলাৎপালাৎ, *s.* nonsensical talk, a foolish or ridiculous reply. [safe.
আল্‌গানি, a clothes-horse, a shelf, a meat-
আল্‌তাপাতা, *s.* cotton leaves impregnated
আলীঢ়, licked, lapped, eaten. [with lac.
আলুনা, *a.* fresh, unsalted, insipid.
আশীবিষ, *s.* a serpent, a snake.
আশুগ, *a.* swift, fleet: *s.* an arrow, the
আসাধন, *s.* completion, finis. [wind.
আহ্বায়, *s.* an appellation ; a lawsuit arising from a squabble for gambling.

ই.

ইকড়, *a.* solid, not porous : *s.* a kind of reed.
ইকড়া, *s.* a bandicoot ; a kind of grass.
ইতরেতর, *a.* mutual, reciprocal.
ইভ, *s.* an elephant.
ইমন্‌, *s.* in *music*, the concord of two notes.

ঈ.

ঈশা, *s.* the beam of a plough. [God.
ঈশ্বরসেবা, *s.* the service or worship of
ঈশ্বরাজ্ঞা, *s.* a command of God. [God.
ঈশ্বরারাধনা, or ঈশ্বরপূজা, *s.* the worship of
ঈশ্বরোপাসনা, *s.* attendance or waiting on God, the service of God.

উ.

উক্করী, or উক্কলী, *s.* a sort of drum.
উক্ষা, *s.* a bull, an ox.
উখড়ন, a getting loose, passing off. [low.
উচ্চনীচ, *a.* uneven, up and down, high and
উচ্চমনাঃ, *a.* high-minded, magnanimous.
উজড়ন, *s.* a rooting up ; a vomiting.
উজড়ীয়া, *a.* the same with উজ্জড়ীয়া.
উজুমীয়া, *a.* out of one's element, wandering out of its place (as a fish). [lavish.
উজ্জড়ীয়া, *a.* wasteful, spendthrift, ruinous,
উড়কুড়, *ad.* from first to last.
উতরণ, *s.* a coming, arriving, alighting.
উত্তরসংজ্ঞিত, *s.* a witness from hearsay.
উত্তুঙ্গ, *a.* high, loud, elevated.
উৎসৃজন, *s.* the offering of an oblation.
উৎসৃজ্য, *a.* proper to be offered.
উদকাধার, *s.* a receptacle of water.
উদকার্থী, *a.* desirous of water, thirsty.
উদধি, উদন্বা, *s.* the sea, ocean.
উদন্যা, *s.* thirst, desire for water.
উদপান, *s.* a well, a tank, a pond, a cistern.
উদয়াচল, *s.* the eastern mountain.
উদয়াস্ত, *ad.* from sunrise to sunset.
উদরবেদনা, *s.* a griping, the colic.
উদরভঙ্গ, উদরপীড়া, dysentery, diarrhœa.
উদরম্ভরি, selfishly voracious, gluttonous.
উদর্ক, *s.* a remote consequence, future time, result, profit, advantage.
উদাত্ত, *s.* the acute accent.
উদান, *s.* one of the five vital airs.
উদীরিত, *a.* spoken, uttered, announced.
উদ্‌গুম্ফন, *s.* act of building up ; edification.
উদ্‌গ্রহ, *a.* attainable, possible. [bench.
উদ্‌ঘন, *s.* a chopping block, a carpenter's
উদ্‌ঘাটন, *s.* a leathern bucket, a rope and bucket of a well.
উদ্‌ঘাত, *s.* a beginning ; a weapon.
উদ্দণ্ড, *a.* elevated on a staff. [dance.
উদ্বর্দ্ধন, *s.* an increasing, abounding, abun-
উধস্‌, *s.* the udder of a cow.
উন্মাথ, *s.* a snare, a trap.
উন্মিষিত, *a.* expanded, opened (as the eyes), full-blown (as a flower).
উপগুরু, *s.* an usher, an under-teacher.
উপদ্রোহ, annoyance, oppression, an out-
উপনিক্ষেপ, *s.* a deposit of goods. [rage.
উপযাচনা, *s.* a request, prayer, petition.
উপস্থান, *s.* proximity, nearness, assiduity.
উপস্থাপন, *s.* a keeping or placing near.
উপস্পর্শ, *s.* a touching, washing, bathing.
উপাংশু, *a.* muttering prayers ; solitary.
উপাকৃত, *s.* a victim ; a portent. [ing.
উপাগমন, *s.* an arrival ; a promise ; a bod-

উপালম্ভ, *s.* an abuse, a reproach, reviling.
উপোঢ়, *a.* near; married; arrayed.
উপ্ত, *a.* sown, disseminated, strewed.
উবন, *s.* a departing, a disappearing; উবে যাওন, to depart, disappear, vanish.
উজ্জ, *a.* straight, unconnected. [and land.
উভয়চর, *a.* amphibious, living in water
উম্বর, *s.* a lintel, the upper part of a door-
উরঃসূত্রিকা, *s.* a pearl necklace. [frame.
উরণ, *s.* a ram; a cloud.
উরসিজ, *s.* the female breast.
উরসিল, *a.* broad-chested.
উরস্ত্রাণ, *s.* a coat of mail, a cuirass.
উরস্য, *a.* lawful, legitimate; cordial.
উরুজ, *a.* born from the thigh: *s.* a Vaishya.
উল্লন, *s.* a coming down, a descending.
উল্লাপ, *s.* a groaning, a moaning, a wailing.
উল্লোল, *s.* a surge, a wave, a billow.
উল্লসন, *s.* a being delighted.

এ.

একতান, *a.* closely attentive, intent.
একতাল, *s.* unison, harmony in music.
একতুম্বী, *s.* a kind of lute, snake-catcher's
এতদীয়, *ad.* relating to this, of this. [lute.

ও—ঔ.

ওয়াক, ওয়াকবক, *s. vide* ওআক.
ঔপনিধিক, *a.* relating to a deposit.

ক.

কচারি, *s.* a razor; a barber.
কচ্চর, *a.* foul, vile, ugly.
কছহরি, *s.* a court of justice.
কটকোল, *s.* a spittoon, a pikdán.
কটোল, *s.* a person of a degraded caste.
কট্‌কট্‌, *s.* a twinging, throbbing, a clatter.
কঠশাখা, *s.* a part of the Rig-veda.
কড়িকান, *s.* a drying up, healing (as a sore).
কড়্‌কড়্‌, *s.* a rattling or thundering noise.
কড়্‌মড়্‌, *s.* a crackling or crunching noise.
কণাদ, *s.* a goldsmith; a sage, a Muni.
কণিত, *s.* a shriek, a piercing cry.
কণ্টকাল, *s.* the Indian bread-fruit tree.[1]
কনীনিকা, *s.* the iris of the eye.
কফোণি, কুণী, কুণুই, *s.* the elbow.
করটক, *s.* a crow; *fem.* করটকী.
করপাত্র, *s.* a vessel of joined open hands.
করপাল, *s.* a sword, a scimitar.
কর্ম্মেন্দ্রিয়, *s.* the five organs of action, *viz.* the hand, the foot, the larynx or organ of the voice, the penis, and the anus.
কলঙ্ক, *s.* an animal stricken with a poisoned arrow. [del, a fort.
কলত্র, *s.* a wife; the hip and loins; a cita-
কলহকর্ত্তা, *s.* a brawler, a wrangler.
কলহংস, *s.* aquatic bird, a teal, a drake, a
কলাকন্দ, *s.* a sort of sweetmeat. [gander.
কলানিধি, *s.* the moon.
কল্পদ্রুম, কল্পবৃক্ষ, *s.* the same as কল্পতরু.
কল্পান্ত, *s.* the end of a kalpa, the destruction of the world.
কাঁই, or কাঁইবিচি, *s.* the seeds of tamarind and Bakul fruit (Mimusops elengi).
কাকোল, *s.* a black poison; a drug; a raven.
কাকোলী, *s.* a cooling medicinal drug.
কাজসারা, *s.* the finish of a business.
কাঠগড়, *s.* a large wooden mortar.
কাঠজালী, *s.* a coarse kind of salt.
কাঠরিয়া, *s.* a wood-cutter, a woodman.
কাঠাকীয়া, *s.* a table of land-measure.
কাদড়া, *a.* soft with rain, muddy, miry.
কাদাবাদী, *a.* contentious, quarrelsome.
কানট, *a.* warped, twisted, awry. [fellow.
কানীপোদা, *s.* a tatterdemalion, a ragged
কান্দন, *s.* a howling, weeping, lamenting.
কান্দিশীক, *a.* running away through fear, flying, fleeing, put to flight.
কাপথ, *s.* a bad road, a dangerous road.
কাপটীয়, কাপট্য, *a.* selfish, unfeeling, parsimonious, stingy, sordid, niggardly.
কাপট্যাপনা, or কাপট্যামি, *s.* niggardliness, stinginess, parsimony, sordidness.
কাপ্যকর, *s.* a penitent, confessing.
কারণিক, *a.* investigating, causative.
কারণোত্তর, *s.* a special plea.
কারুণিক, *a.* compassionate, kind.
কারুণ্য, *s.* pity, tenderness, kindness.
কার্ষাপণ, *s.* a káhan or 16 pana of cauri.
কালকীল, *s.* an uproar, a hubbub.
কালবেলা, *s.* an unlucky hour.
কালিঙ্গা, *s.* old or decayed thatch.
কিখি, *s.* a fox, a small jackal.
কীকট, *a.* miserly, avaricious, penurious, poor, needy: *s.* the name of a country.
কীচক, *s.* a hollow bamboo, a bamboo whistling or rustling with the wind.

কুর্দ্দন, *s.* a frisking, gambolling, sport.
কুলজ্ঞ, *s.* a genealogist, a family registrar.
কুলপতি, *s.* the head of a family.
কুলতিলক, *s.* a person who makes an illustrious figure in a family.
কুলপ্রদীপ, *s.* one who is an honour to his family; *(lit.)* the lamp of a family.
কুলীনসভা, *s.* the House of Lords.

ন.

নিরীহ, *s.* tranquil, limpid, harmless.
নিরেট, *a.* solid, not hollow, sound.
নির্দ্দায়, *a.* irresponsible, released.
নির্দ্ধারণ, *s.* a bringing to an issue.
নির্ব্বাত, *a.* calm, tranquil, happy.
নির্ব্বেশ, *s.* enjoyment, marriage.
নির্ব্যূঢ়, *a.* deserted; completed.
নির্ভর্ৎসন, *s.* reproach, abuse, blame.
নির্ভাজন, *s.* a being disinherited.
নির্ভিন্ন, *a.* pierced, wounded; identical.
নির্ভুল, *a.* free from mistake, infallible.
নির্মর্য্যাদ, *a.* disrespectful, irreverent.
নির্মাপণ, *s.* a causing to make.
নির্মোক, *s.* the cast skin of a snake.
নির্যাতন, *s.* requiting, retaliation.
নির্যাণ, *s.* a going forth, departure.
নির্হাদ, *s.* a sound, a noise, a report.
নির্হার, *a.* extracting, evacuating.
নির্হারী, *s.* widely fragrant.
নির্হেতুক, *a.* without reason or motive.
নিলয়, *s.* a house, habitation, abode.
নিলয়ন, *s.* absorption, extinction.
নিলীন, *a.* enwrapt, absorbed.
নিশীথ, *s.* midnight, the midnight.
নিশীথিনী, *s.* night, the night.
নিশ্চার, *s.* the wind; wilfulness.
নিশ্চীয়মান, *a.* under investigation.
নিশ্ছিদ্র, *a.* without a hole or flaw.
নিষঙ্গ, *s.* a quiver, a case for arrows.
নিষেবন, *s.* service; the taking of medicine.
নিষ্ক, *s.* a certain gold-weight.
নিষ্কাশ, *s.* a portico, a verandah.
নিষ্কাশন, *s.* an expelling, ejecting, dismissing.
নিষ্কুল, *a.* out of caste, put out.
নিষ্কৃত্রিম, *a.* genuine, not artificial.
নিষ্ক্রয়, *s.* a ransom, wages, salary, fee.
নিষ্কাথ, *s.* soup, broth, gravy.
নিষ্পেষণ, *s.* the grinding of a thing to powder.
নিষ্প্রতিভ, *a.* dull, stupid, frigid.
নিষ্প্রভ, *a.* gloomy, dark, without light.
নিসূদন, *s.* a killing, slaughter.
নিস্তরণ, *s.* a getting over, deliverance.
নিস্ত্রপ, *a.* shameless, immodest.
নিহনন, *s.* a killing, the smiting of a person.
নিহন্তা, *s.* a murderer, a slayer.
নিহানী, or নিহালী, *s.* an anvil.
নিহিত, *a.* placed, deposited with.
নিহ্নুতি, *s.* concealment, reserve.
নিহ্নাতা, *s.* one who mistrusts.
নীকাশ, *a.* like, resembling, equal.
নীচগ, *a.* tending downwards.
নীড়জ, *a.* born in a nest: *s.* a bird.
নীবর, *s.* a beggar, a vagrant, mendicant.
নীবী, *s.* a woman's zone; a capital.
নীয়ন্তা, *s.* a receiver, a dealer.
নীরজাঃ, *a.* without pollen.
নীহার, *s.* frost, hoar frost, ice.
নুণী, or নুনিয়াশাক, *s.* purslain.
নেত্রাম্বু, *s.* tears, tears of the eye.
নেপথ্য, *s.* a dressing-room.
নেলান, *a.* exciting, stimulating, setting a dog on.
নেহাই, or নেহালী, *s.* an anvil.
নৈধানী, *s.* an imperishable landmark.
নৈষ্ঠিক, *s.* a theological student, a student of religion or theology.
নোয়ান, *s.* a binding down, a lowering.
ন্যাকা, *a.* ignorant, stupid, awkward: *s.* he who pretends to be ignorant.

প.

পক্ষতি, *s.* first day of a lunar fortnight.
পক্ষব্যাপী, *a.* embracing a whole theme.
পঙ্কিল, *a.* clayey, miry, muddy, plashy.
পঙ্গ, *s.* a grasshopper, a locust.
পচাকাল, *s.* dirty or sloppy weather.
পঞ্চরঙ্গী, *a.* variegated, motley.
পঞ্চশাখ, *a.* five-branched: *s.* the hand.
পঞ্চসূনা, *s.* five sources of death.
পঞ্চাঙ্গুল, *a.* digitated, forked out like fingers, having five fingers: *s.* five fingers.
পঞ্চায়িত, *s.* the midst; arbitration.
পটময়, *a.* made of canvass: *s.* a tent.
পটল, *s.* the formulary of worship.
পটহ, *s.* a kettle-drum.
পটীর, *s.* sandal-wood; a field.
পটুয়া, *s.* a limner, a sculptor; *vide* পটুআ.

পট্টিশ, *s.* a two-edged sword.
পট্পটী, *s.* a kind of rush ; a pop-gun.
পড়ন, *s.* a falling, happening ; a reading.
পতদ্গ্রাহ, *s.* spitting-utensil, a spittoon.
পত্তি, *s.* a foot-soldier ; a troop.
পত্রিকা, *s.* a letter, a document.
পত্রোল্লাস, *s.* a flower-bud.
পদ্মাকর, *s.* a pond full of waterlilies.
পদ্যপাড়ন, *s.* a behaving, conducting.
পন্নগাশন, a name of Garuṛa king of birds.
পরচর্চ্চা, *s.* a busybody, a quiz.
পরচ্ছন্দ, *a.* dependent, subservient.
পরচ্ছুতী, *s.* the eaves of a house.
পরব্রহ্ম, *s.* the supreme Deity.
পরভৃত, *s.* the black Indian cuckoo.
পরম্পর, *a.* successive, lineal.
পরম্পরায়, *ad.* by tradition, traditionally.
পরান্ন, *s.* food of another party.
পরারি, *s.* the year before last.
পরার্দ্ধ, *s.* the highest of all numbers.
পরাশ্রয়, *s.* a dependent, a parasite.
পরিকর, *s.* a bed ; retinue ; family.
পরিকল্পনা, *s.* a contrivance, a stratagem.
পরিকীর্ত্তন, *s.* a mentioning, an eulogizing.
পরিক্রম, *s.* a walking for pleasure, play.
পরিগত, *a.* understood, sought, gained.
পরিচার্য্য, *a.* worthy to be served.
পরিণাহ, *s.* width, circumference.
পরিদর্শন, *s.* a comprehensive view.
পরিধাপন, *s.* a clothing, causing to dress.
পরিপণ, *s.* a stock in trade, capital.
পরিপালন, *s.* an observing, a nourishing.
পরিভাষণ, *s.* an address, an agreeing with.
পরিভ্রমণ, *s.* a wandering or roving about.
পরিমণ্ডল, *s.* a circle, a sphere, an orbit.
পরিমল, *s.* perfume, scent, redolence.
পরিশ্লেষ, *s.* embracing, hugging, embrace.
পরিসেবন, *s.* a serving, taking of medicine.
পর্ণশালা, *s.* an arbour, a hermitage.
পর্য্যবস্থান, *s* an opposition, contradiction.
পর্য্যালোচন, *s.* a looking attentively.
পর্য্যুদস্ত, *a.* prohibited ; unsuitable.
পলব, *s.* a wickerwork fish-trap. [ing.
পাইল, *s.* a fulcrum, a prop ; a sail, an awn-
পাওনিয়া, *s.* an heir, a creditor.
পাংক্তেয়, *a.* of equal rank in society.
পাকতঃ, *ad.* reluctantly ; inevitably.

পাকন, *s.* suppurating, ripening, maturity.
পাকিম, *a.* quite ripe, mellow.
পাকে, *ad.* for, on account of.
পাখনা, *s.* a wing, feather, shoulder-joint ; an eddy, a whirlpool.
পাজন, *s.* a perceiving, a forming an idea.
পাঠনা, *s.* a teaching to read, tuition.
পাণিগৃহীত, *a.* married, wedded.
পাণিনি, *s.* name of a celebrated gramma- [rian.
পাণিশঙ্খ, *s.* a species of conch.
পাতঞ্জি, *a.* fit to be spread : *s.* a bedding.
পাতন, *s.* a spreading out, a laying flat.
পাথোধি, *s.* the sea, the ocean. [cringes.
পাদগ্রাহী, *a.* cringing, fawning : *s.* one who
পাদত্রাণ, *s.* a shoe, a sandal, a patten.
পাদবিহরণ, *s.* a stepping, walking, proceed- [ing.
পাদসেবা, *s.* obsequious attendance.
পাদানত, *a.* humbled to the feet.
পাদাবন, *s.* a stamping with the foot.
পানীয়শালিকা, *s.* a watering-place.
পাপরোগ, *s.* the small-pox.
পাম, *s.* an eruption, itch, a ringworm.
পারশ্বধিক, *a.* armed with an axe.
পারিণায্য *s.* marriage presents.
পালাশ, *a.* green, green colour.
পাল্টান, *s.* an overturning, subverting.
পাশকথা, *s.* a trifling or empty talk.
পাসরাণ, *s.* a walking, a moving on.
পিছন, *s.* a falling back, receding, desist- [ing.
পিচ্ছট, *s.* the rheum of the eyes.
পিঞ্জন, *s.* the carding of cotton or wool.
পিঞ্জিকা, *s.* a roll of cotton.
পিণ্ডভাগ, *s.* a partaking of funeral cake.
পিণ্ডীশূর, *a.* lazy, indolent : *s.* a braggart, [a fop.
পিতৃপ্রসূ, *s.* the evening, twilight.
পিতৃবন, *s.* a place for burning the dead.
পিপ্পল, *s.* longpepper ; name of a tree.
পীঠস্থান, *s.* the shrine of a goddess.
পীড়ি, *s.* a stool, a platform, an altar.
পীতমণি, or পীতরক্ত, *s.* a topaz.
পীলক, *s.* the large black ant.
পুংসবন, *s.* a ceremony on conception.
পুংস্ত্ব, *s.* manhood, virility.
পুঙ্খানুপুঙ্খ, *s.* minute consideration.
পুঞ্জ, *s.* a heap, collection, a row.
পুণ্ডরীক, *s.* a white lotus ; a tiger.
পুতনা, *s.* a squadron of horse.

পুরশ্চরণ, *s.* a mode of religious service.
পুরাবৃত্ত, *s.* ancient history, tradition, legend.
পুরীতত্তি, *s.* an entrail, guts.
পুরুষক্রম, *s.* successive generations.
পুরোডাশ, *s.* a sacrificial cake.
পুলাক, *s.* shrivelled grain; celerity.
পুলায়িত, *s.* a horse's gallop.
পুষ্পধম্বা, *a.* having a bow of flowers.
পুষ্পাঞ্জলি, *s.* a handful of flowers.
পূজার্হ, *a.* worthy of veneration.
পূতিগন্ধ, *s.* stench, putrid odour.
পূর্ণমাস, *s.* a sacrifice at full moon.
পূর্ত্ত, *s.* an act performed for merit.
পূর্ব্বক, *ad.* with, by means of.
পৃচ্ছা, *s.* a question, interrogation.
পৃথগ্বিধ, *a.* of various kinds, multiform.
পৃষ্ঠমাংসাদ, *s.* a backbiter, a slanderer.
পোত্র, *s.* a hog's snout; a ploughshare.
পোয়া, *s.* a fourth part; a plant.
পোয়ান, *s.* the warming of one's self.
পোয়াল, *s.* rice-straw, straw for fodder.
পোরাণ, *s.* a causing to fill or load.
পোষ্যবর্গ, *s.* a household, a retinue.
পোহান, *s.* a dawning, becoming light.
পোঁছন, *s.* an arriving, a succeeding to.
পোঁছান, *s.* a causing to arrive, a conveying.
পৌত্তলিক, *s.* an image-worshipper.
পৌরোহিত্য, *s.* the office of a family priest.
প্রকর্ষ, *s.* excellence, superiority.
প্রকৃতার্থিক, *a.* just, righteous, honest.
প্রখ্যাত, *a.* celebrated, notorious.
প্রগত, *a.* diverging, gibbous.
প্রগুণ, *a.* honest, upright, sincere.
প্রগ্রহ, *s.* string suspending a balance.
প্রগ্রীব, *s.* a lattice, window, railing.
প্রঘাত, *s.* combat, battle, conflict.
প্রচরদ্রূপ, *a.* current, common, rife.
প্রতিগ্রহণ, *s.* an acceptance; a consent.
প্রতিজঙ্ঘা, *s.* the forepart of the thigh.
প্রতিজিহ্বা, *s.* the uvula, the epiglottis.
প্রতিজ্ঞাপন, *s.* a causing to declare.
প্রতিতাল, *s.* a key, a picklock.
প্রতিদারণ, *s.* war, battle, conflict.
প্রতিনপ্তা, *s.* a son's grandson.
প্রতিপ্রসব, *s.* cancelling a prohibition.
প্রতিবল, *a.* of equal power, adequate.
প্রতিরব, *s.* an echo, reverberation.
প্রতিলিপি, *s.* a written reply; a transcript, copy.
প্রতিসীরা, *s.* cloth screen, curtain.
প্রতিসূর্য্য, *s.* a chameleon.
প্রতিস্পন্দন, *s.* a throbbing, palpitation.
প্রতিহনন, *s.* the returning of a blow.
প্রতোদ, *s.* a goad, a whip, a cane.
প্রত্যক্ষসিদ্ধ, *a.* known by the senses.
প্রত্যন্ত, *a.* contiguous, bordering.
প্রত্যবায়, *s.* sin, crime; separation.
প্রত্যভিজ্ঞান, *s.* knowledge, a memento.
প্রত্যাসর, *s.* the rear of an army.
প্রত্যুত্থান, *s.* a respectfully rising.
প্রত্যূহ, *s.* an obstacle, an impediment.
প্রপদ, *s.* the tip of the toes.
প্রবর, *s.* a line of ancestors.
প্রবোদ্ধা, *s.* a comforter, a consoler.
প্রব্রজ্যা, *s.* a pilgrim, an ascetic.
প্রভাস, *s.* a place of pilgrimage.
প্রভিন্ন, *a.* totally different, distinct.
প্রভুপণা, *s.* lordship, a domineering.
প্রমদ, *s.* joy, delight, rapture, ecstacy.
প্ররোচনা, *s.* encouragement, excitement.
প্রলোভ, *s.* covetousness; a bribe.
প্রষ্ঠা, *s.* a page, page of a book.
প্রসঙ্গসঙ্গতি, *s.* converse, conversation, discourse.
প্রসরণ, *s.* the outflanking of an enemy.
প্রসূত, *a.* born, brought forth.
প্রসূন, *s.* a blossom, a bud; a fruit.
প্রস্ফোটন, *s.* a winnowing; expansion.
প্রহনন, *s.* a smiting, wounding, killing.
প্রাকার, *s.* enclosure, a wall, a rampart.
প্রাঙ্ন্যায়, *s.* former trial of a cause.
প্রাঙ্মুখ, *a.* facing eastward.
প্রাঞ্জল, *a.* honest, upright, liberal.
প্রাড়্বিবাক্, *s.* a judge, a magistrate.
প্রাণহা, *a.* deadly, fatal: *s.* a murderer.
প্রাণাধার, *s.* a living body, the body.
প্রাণায়াম, *a.* holding the breath.
প্রাণিদ্যূত, *s.* a cock-fighting.
প্রাণেশ, *s.* the lord of life, a husband.
প্রাতরাশ, *s.* a morning meal, breakfast.
প্রাদোষ, *a.* evening, of the evening.
প্রান্তশূন্য, *s.* a long wearisome road.
প্রাপ্তপঞ্চত্ব, *a.* dead, deceased, defunct.
প্রাবরণ, *s.* an outer garment, a screen.
প্রাবৃত, *a.* screened: *s.* an outer garment.
প্রিয়ঙ্কর, *a.* pleasing, amiable, affectionate.

প্রেঙ্খন, *s.* a hanging, swinging, being pendent.
প্রেতাকার, *a.* ghost like, like a goblin.
প্রোৎসাহ, *s.* great zeal, ardour.
প্রোৎসাহক, *s.* an instigator, a stimulator.
প্রোষিতভর্তৃকা, *s.* the wife of an absentee.
প্লক্ষ, *s.* the sacred fig-tree.
প্লবগ, *s.* whatever goes by leaps.

ফ.

ফক্কা, *s.* assertion, thesis; a baulking.
ফরফরাণ, boasting, bragging, swaggering.
ফলশ্রুতি, *s.* special parts of the vedas.
ফল্গূৎসব, *s.* Dol-játrá, the festival of hulí.
ফাঁসা, *s.* a hole, rent, chink, fissure.
ফাকফাক, *a.* apart, separately.
ফুলন, *s.* a blossoming, a swelling out.
ফেরব, ফেরু, crafty, deceitful: *s.* a jackal.

ব.

বক্রোক্তি, *s.* evasion, pun, irony.
বক্ষোজ, *s.* the breast of a female.
বজ্রনির্ঘোষ, *s.* a thunder-stroke.
বড়বাভৃত, *s.* the gallant of a slave-girl.
বণ্ঠর, *s* a palm shoot, bamboo-sheath.
বৎসতরী, *s.* a steer, a heifer.
বনপ্রিয়, *s.* the Indian cuckoo.
বনমালী, *s.* a name of Krishna.
বনস্পতি, *s* a tree yielding fruit without apparent flowers.
বনৌকস, *s.* a hermit, a forester, an ape.
বন্দনীয়, *a.* venerable, worshipful.
বন্ধুল, *s.* a bastard, an adulterine.
বন্ধ্যা, *a.* unproductive, unfruitful.
বয়ঃপ্রাপ্ত, *a.* grown up, of age, adult.
বয়স্ক, *a.* of a certain age.
বরণডালা, *s.* provision for a ceremony.
বরিষ্ঠ, *a.* the best of all, greatest.
বর্ণাট, *s.* a singer, a painter, an actor.
বর্ত্তিক, *s.* a paint-brush; a candle, a wick.
বর্ত্তিকা, *s.* a wick, a candle, a lamp.
বর্ষাভ্বূ, *s.* a frog.
বর্ষিষ্ঠ, *a.* old, aged, very old.
বলভি, *s.* the turret on a house-top.
বলাকা, *s.* a flight of cranes.
বলিপ্রিয়, *a.* predacious: *s.* birds of prey.
বলিষ্ঠ, *a.* powerful, very strong, able.
বল্গিত, *s.* a horse's gallop, a canter.
বশগ, *a.* brought under control.
বশী, *a.* of subdued passions.

বসিন্দা, *s.* an inhabitant, a dweller.
বসুধারা, *s.* the consecrating of a house.
বস্তুতঃ, *ad.* in reality, in a word.
বহুঘণা, *s.* a brass basin or cooking-vessel.
বহুব্রীহি, *s.* a compound adjective.
বাঁচাও, *s.* rescue, escape, deliverance.
বাঁটখারা, *s.* a weight for weighing things.
বাক্চাতুরী, *s.* a joke, sally, witticism.
বাক্চাপল্য, *s.* gossip, chat, idle talk, chitchat.
বাক্যুদ্ধ, dispute, wrangling, war of words.
বাক্সিদ্ধ, *a.* as good as one's word.
বাক্যস্থ, *a.* minding what is said.
বাগ্বজ্র, *s.* imprecation, curse, ill-wish.
বাঙ্নিষ্পত্তি, *s.* a keeping one's word.
বাঙ্মুখ, *s.* an exordium, a preface.
বাজপেয়, *s.* a kind of sacrifice.
বাড়তী, *s.* increase, overplus.
বাতায়ন, *s.* a window, an air-hole.
বাদী, *s.* a speaker, plaintiff; the key-note.
বাধ, *s.* a stop, interruption, hindrance.
বান্ধন, *s.* a binding, fastening, a tie.
বায়ব্য, *a.* relating to the wind: *s.* the north-west quarter.
বায়ুপুত্র, *s.* the black-faced monkey, Hanumán.
বারনারী, বারবধূ, *s.* a harlot, a prostitute.
বার্ত্তায়ন, *s.* a spy, an emissary.
বার্হস্পত্য, *s.* ethics, morality.
বাস্তুদেব, *s.* a household god.
বাহাবাহবি, *a.* grappling, hand to hand.
বিউল, *s.* shelled pulse.
বিকসন, *s.* expansion, opening out.
বিকাররোগ, *s.* collapse before death.
বিকির, *s.* funeral cake for the friend less.
বিক্লৃপ্ত, *a.* variously done, multiform.
বিক্রীড়িত, *a.* played, having played.
বিক্লেদ, *s.* dampness, suppuration.
বিক্ষুব্ধ, *a.* agitated, disturbed, anxious.
বিক্ষোভ, *s.* agitation, anxiety, care.
বিগণ, *s.* an adversary, enemy, foe.
বিগোছ, *s.* a mixture; an ill omen.
বিঘূর্ণন, *s.* a whirlpool, eddy, a whirlwind.
বিঘ্নরাজ, *s.* a name of Ganesha.
বিঘ্রাণ, *a.* smelling: *s.* odour, smell.
বিচয়ন, *s.* a search, investigation.
বিচর্চ্চিকা, *s.* the itch, a ringworm.
বিচাল, *a.* intervening, interval.
বিচেষ্টিত, *a.* carefully sought.

বিজন, *a.* solitary, lonely, private.
বিজিল, *a.* mixed with rice-water.
বিটপ, *s.* a bunch ; a profligate.
বিটপী, *s.* a tree.
বিঠৌর, *a.* confused, disconcerted.
বিতথ, *a.* false, untrue, unsubstantial.
বিতল, *s.* one of the Hindu infernal regions.
বিতৃষ্ণ, *a.* having slaked the thirst.
বিত্রপ, *a.* impudent, audacious.
বিত্রস্ত, *a.* affrighted, terrified.
বিদল, *a.* of an opposite party.
বিদূষক, *a.* censorious : *s.* a detractor.
বিদ্বেষ্টা, *s.* a malignant enemy.
বিদ্যুতি, *s.* light, a sunbeam, energy.
বিদ্রোহ, *s.* malevolence, malice.
বিধায়ক, *s.* an ordinance ; a prescriber.
বিধিবৎ, *a.* according to precept.
বিধূত, *a.* agitated, sifted, ventilated.
বিধুন্তুদ, *s.* Ráhu, the ascending node.
বিধুর, *a.* destitute, distressed, afflicted.
বিধুনন, *s.* agitation, trembling.
বিধৃত, *a.* upheld, sustained, propped.
বিনান, *s.* the plaiting of the hair.
বিনামা, *s.* a shoe, a boot.
বিনায়াস, *a.* without difficulty, easily.
বিনাশোন্মুখ, *a.* almost destroyed.
বিনাসাধ, *a.* involuntary, unwilling.
বিনিগমক, *a.* conclusive, decisive.
বিনিপাত, *s.* a fall, downfall, calamity.
বিনিয়োগ, *s.* an appointment, installation.
বিন্যস্ত, *a.* placed in order, deposited.
বিপাদিকা, *s.* a blister on the foot.
বিপুল, *a.* abundant, much, plentiful.
বিফুল্ল, *a.* expanded, open, blown.
বিবাস, *s.* banishment : *a.* unclothed.
বিবোঢ়া, *s.* a bridegroom, a husband.
বিভক্তজ, *a.* born after division of property.
বিভাকর, *s.* the sun, fire.
বিভাষিত, *a.* spoken, expressed ; doubtful.
বিভীষিকা, *s.* fear, object of terror.
বিভোল, *a.* foolish, demented, crazy.
বিমুগ্ধ, *a.* fascinated, infatuated.
বিমোক্তা, *s.* a liberator, a deliverer.
বিমোহ, *s.* fascination, stupefaction.
বিরজা, *a.* past menstruation.
বিলক্ষণা, *s.* a present at a shráddha.
বিলিখিত, *a.* striped, marked in lines.
বিলোচন, *s.* the eye.
বিলোড়ন, *s.* a stirring up, churning, wallowing.
বিশাখ, *a.* without branches, lopped.
বিশোক, *a* free from grief or sorrow.
বিশোচন, *s.* a consoling, comforting.
বিশোধন, a purifying, cleansing, correcting.
বিশ্রব্ধ, *a.* trusted ; tranquil, rested.
বিশ্রম্ভ, *s.* trust ; hilarity, affection.
বিশ্রুত, *a.* renowned, celebrated.
বিশ্বতঃ, *ad.* everywhere, universally.
বিশ্বভণ্ড, *a.* all-deceptive.
বিশ্বসৃক, *a.* all-creating : *s.* God.
বিষকণ্ঠ, *s.* a name of Shiva.
বিষয়ক, *a.* relating to, about, concerning.
বিষ্কম্ভ, *s.* the diameter of a circle.
বিষ্টম্ভ, *s.* the hardening of cement.
বিষ্টর, *s.* a tree, a seat, kushá grass.
বিষ্টি, *s.* unpaid labour.
বিসঙ্কট, *s.* danger, strait, jeopardy.
বিসর্পণ, *s.* a moving, extending, spreading.
বিসারণ, *s.* expansion, a spinning out.
বিসারিত, *a.* extended : *s.* axis of a sphere.
বিসৃপ্ত, *a.* diffused, extended, spread out.
বিস্পন্দ, *s.* tremulous motion, tremor.
বিস্পষ্ট, *a.* manifest, evident, clear.
বিস্ফার, *s.* the twang of a bowstring.
বিহর্ষ, *s.* gladness, joy, pleasure.
বিহায়স, *s.* the sky, the atmosphere.
বীনাহ, *s.* the top of a well.
বীভৎস, *a.* mischievous : *s.* abhorrence.
বীরেশ্বর, *s.* a chief among heroes
বুকফুলন, *s.* a strutting, a swaggering.
বুকন, *s.* the barking of a dog.
বুদ্ধীন্দ্রিয়, *s.* the organs of sense.
বুননিয়া, *s.* a seedsman, a sower, a weaver.
বৃংহিত, *a.* grown, increased, nourished.
বৃক্ষরুহা, *a.* tree-climbing : *s.* a parasite.
বৃজিন, *s.* hair ; sin, crime, wickedness.
বৃষোৎসর্গ, *s.* the offering of a bull.
বেচনিয়া, *s.* a seller, a vender, a salesman.
বেঠন, *s.* a cloak, overall, mantle, a wrapper.
বেদিতব্য, perceptible, ascertainable.
বেহাই, *s.* same as বৈবাহিক ; *fem.* বেহাইন.
বৈগুণ্য, *s.* hostility, unpropitiousness.
বৈচক্ষণ্য, *s* skill, tact, proficiency.
বৈজনন, *s.* the last month of pregnancy.
বৈড়ালব্রতিক, *a.* hypocritical, deceitful.

বৈতনিক, *s.* a hired labourer, a hireling.
বৈদুষ্য, *s.* learning, science, wisdom.
বৈবাহিক, *s.* relationship between a wife's and husband's father; *fem.* বৈবাহিকা.
বৈরস্য, *s.* disagreeable taste, insipidity.
বৈষয়িক, *a.* relating to the affairs of life.
বৈসন, *s.* a sitting down, taking a seat.
বোধাতীত, *a.* past comprehension.
ব্যপদেষ্টা, *s.* an impostor; a denominator.
ব্যবহারজ্ঞ, *a.* acquainted with usages.
ব্যর্থীকৃত, *a.* rendered useless, nullified.
ব্যাই, *s.* the same as বৈবাহিক; *fem.* ব্যান.
ব্যাপাদন, *s.* a killing, malevolence.
ব্যাপী, *a.* pervading, diffusive.
ব্যামোহক, *a.* afflictive: *s.* a nuisance.
ব্যাল, *s.* a snake, a wild beast.
ব্যালগ্রাহী, *s.* a snake-catcher.
ব্রজ, *s.* the name of a district about Agra.
ব্রহ্মজীবী, *s.* a mercenary bráhman.
ব্রহ্মপুত্র, *s.* the Brahmaputra river.
ব্রহ্মবাদী, *s.* a vedantist.
ব্রহ্মযজ্ঞ, *s* study of the vedas.
ব্রাহ্ম, *s.* a kind of marriage; a vedantist.
ব্রাহ্মণব্রুব, *s.* a secular bráhman.

ভ.

ভইল, *s.* form, shape; a mark.
ভঞ্জন, *s.* a breaking, a defeating.
ভজিষ্ণু, devout, pious, obsequious.
ভড়কান, *s.* a being afraid, a leaving from fear.
ভণন, *s.* act of speaking, a composing.
ভণ্ডকথা, *s.* a low saying, a slang, scurrility.
ভয়শীল, *a.* timid, fearful, cowardly.
ভষণ, *s.* a barking, scolding, railing.
ভাওলিয়া, *s.* a pleasure boat, a large house-boat.
ভাঁজন, *s.* a folding; adulterating.
ভাগ্যভাব, *s.* a course of destiny.
ভাগ্যভাবা, *a.* adventuring, risking.
ভানুমান, *a.* invested with rays: *s.* the sun.
ভাববোদ্ধা, *a.* discerning, sagacious.
ভাবুনিয়া, *s.* a fop, a dandy, a coxcomb.
ভাস্বর, *a.* light, luminous, splendid.
ভিন্নভাব, *s.* separation, change.
ভীমরথী, *s.* extreme age, dotage.
ভুক্তাবশিষ্ট, *s.* leavings after eating, orts.
ভূতল, *s.* the earth, surface of the earth.
ভূমিজীবী, *s.* an agriculturist, a husbandman.
ভূমিপ, *s.* a king, a sovereign.
ভূমিষ্ঠ, *a.* flat on the ground; born.
ভূমিসাৎ, *ad.* on the ground.
ভূয়োভূয়ঃ, *ad.* again and again, repeatedly.
ভোগদেহ, *s.* the body, the seat of enjoyment and suffering.
ভোগবতী, *s.* the Hindu river of hell.
ভোগলালী, *s.* deception, hypocrisy.
ভোগ্যা, *s.* a harlot, a concubine.
ভোগ্যাধি, *s.* a loan to be used.
ভ্রাজিষ্ণু, *a.* elegant, adorned.

ম.

মকরালয়, *s.* the sea, the ocean.
মদোদ্ধত, *a.* tipsy, intoxicated, drunk.
মধুপর্ক, *s.* oblation of curds and honey.
মধ্যবিধ, *a.* of a middling kind.
মরীচিমালী, *a.* radiant: *s.* the sun.
মানসূত্র, *s.* a measuring line.

য.

যজ্ঞসূত্র, *s.* the bráhminical thread.
যতেন্দ্রিয়, *a.* of subdued senses.
যথাকথঞ্চিৎ, *ad.* in whatever way.
যথাক্রম, *ad.* in order, successively.
যবস, *s.* meadow grass, fodder.
যবসুর, *s.* malt liquor, beer.
যবাগূ, *s.* rice gruel, rice frumenty.
যবিষ্ঠ, *a.* youngest, very young.
যাটি, *s.* a stick, a staff, a wand, a club.
যাঠা, *s.* a stick, a staff, a walking-stick.
যিহুহা, *s.* Jehovah, God Almighty.
যীশু, *s.* Jesus, the Redeemer of mankind.
যীশুখ্রীষ্ট, *s.* Jesus Christ, the Saviour.

র.

রক্তবটী, *s.* the small-pox.
রক্ষস, *s.* a cannibal, an ogre, a goblin.
রঙ্গশালা, *s.* a theatre, a ball-room.
রঙ্গানিয়া, *s.* a dyer, a painter.
রঙ্গাবতারী, *s.* an actor, a mimic, a buffoon.
রজনীমুখ, *s.* the evening, nightfall.
রজোরস, *s.* darkness, gloom.
রথাঙ্গ, *s.* a wheel, part of a car.
রসজ্ঞ, *a.* of refined taste: *s.* an alchymist.
রসজ্ঞা, *a.* knowing the flavours: *s.* tongue.
রাজস, *a.* springing from passion.
রাজসদন, *s.* a palace, a royal residence.
রাজসী, *s.* a worshipping with sacrifice.
রাজসূয়, *s.* a sacrifice offered by an emperor.
রাজ্যেশ, *s.* the reigning sovereign.

রামদূত, *s.* the monkey-god Hanumán.
রিঙ্গন, *s.* a slipping, tumbling, falling.
রুণরুণ, *s.* a tingling sound.

ল.

লঘিমা, *s.* lightness, diminution.
লঘীয়স, *a.* light, contemptible.
লত্থা, *s.* a blow, a stroke, a beating.
লত্থালত্থি, *s.* a boxing, fisticuffs.
লড়্‌চড়্‌, *a.* fidgetty, fickle, tottering.
লুলাপ, *s.* a buffalo.
লোকপাল, *s.* a king, sovereign.
লোকযাত্রা, *s.* human affairs ; a fair.
লোকালয়, *s.* an inhabited place, a town.
লোকালোক, *s.* the boundary of the world.

শ.

শপশপ্যা, *a.* wet, sloppy, liquid.
শবযান, *s.* a bier, a hearse.
শবর, *s.* a barbarian, a savage.
শব্দগ্রহ, *s.* knowledge of sounds ; the ear.
শয়ালু, *a.* sleepy, drowsy.
শাড়ুভাই, *s.* the same with ভায়রাভাই.
শালীপতি, *s.* the same with ভায়রাভাই.
শিলোচ্চয়, *s.* a mountain, a rock.
শিলোঞ্ছ, *a.* following several trades.

স.

সংক্রম, *s.* a passage, a pass, a bridge.
সংক্রান্ত, *a.* passed over, transferred to.
সংক্রান্তি, *s.* sun's entrance into a new sign.
সংক্ষিপ্ত, *a.* abridged, condensed, brief.
সংক্ষেপ, *s.* brevity, a compendium.
সংখ্যা, *s.* a number, a reckoning.
সংগুপ্ত, *a.* concealed, suppressed.
সংগৃহীত, *a.* collected, compiled.
সংগোপন, *s.* a concealing, suppressing.
সংগ্রহ, *a.* collecting, compiling.
সংগ্রাম, *s.* conflict, war, battle.
সংগ্রাহক, *s.* a compiler, a collector.
সংঘটনা, *s.* concurrence, embracing.
সংঘটিত, *a.* concurring ; through.
সংঘট্ট, *s.* a concourse, a crowd.
সংরম্ভ, *s.* anger, wrath, fury, rage.
সংরুদ্ধ, *a.* shut up, obstructed.
সংস্মৃতি, *s.* remembrance, memory.
সঙ্কাশ, *a.* like, similar : *s.* splendour.
সঙ্কুল, *a.* agitated, pestered, vexed.
সন্দংশ, *s.* a pair of tongs, pincers, nippers.
সন্দর্শন, *s.* a looking, viewing, visiting.
সন্দেহকল্প, *s.* uncertainty, contingency.
সন্নাহ, *a.* putting on armour, arming.
সন্নিকট, *a.* near, close at hand.
সন্নিবিষ্ট, *a.* intent upon, absorbed in.
সপদি, *ad.* instantly, forthwith, quickly.
*সমধী, *s.* same as বৈবাহিক; *fem.* সমধীনা.
সমাবর্ত্তন, *s.* the finishing of one's educa-
সমিধ, *s.* fuel for a sacrifice. [tion.
সমীহা, *s.* endeavour ; modesty.
সমুখ, *a.* eloquent ; opposite ; obvious.
সমুদিত, *a.* risen into view, manifest.
সম্পাত, *a.* descending, alighting.
সম্বর্ত্ত, *s.* the end of the world.
সম্বর্দ্ধক, *a.* honouring, augmenting.
সম্বর্দ্ধনা, *s.* honour, respectful welcome.
সম্বলিত, *a.* provided with, containing.
সম্বাদ, *s.* intelligence, news, tidings.
সম্ভবন, a corresponding or agreeing with,
সম্ভার, *s.* fulness, multitude. [tallying.
সম্মীলন, *s.* a closing, shutting (as the eyes).
সম্মিশ্লিষ্ট, *a.* mixed with, joined to. [way.
সরণ, *s.* a budging, moving, sliding, giving
সলগ্ন, *a.* appropriate, consistent.
সহমান, *s.* a sustaining, enduring.
সহযোগে, *ad.* in company, at once. [ing.
সাঁজড়ন, *s.* an equipping, harnessing, yok-
সাঁটন, *s.* a writhing, cramming, thriving.
সাচিব্য, *s.* ministry ; friendship, aid.
সাটোপ, *a.* proud, imperious, haughty.
সাবন, *s.* a solar month.
সারার্থ, *s.* the pith, chief meaning.
সারাল, *a.* vital, pithy, vigorous.
সারাসার, *s.* substance and vanity.
সারি, *s.* a line, a row, range, tier.
সারিন্দা, *s.* a lute, guitar, violin, fiddle.
সারিসারি, *ad.* in rows, in files.
সালোক্য, *s.* a dwelling with the gods.
সাশ্রয়, *s.* cheapness, abundance.
সাস্না, *s.* the dewlap of an ox.
সাহঙ্কার, *a.* proud, imperious, haughty,
সীয়ন, সীঙ্গান, *v.* to sew, stitch : *s.* a sew-
সুখায়ন, *s.* heaven, abode of bliss. [ing.
সুতান, *a.* melodious, harmonious.
সুদূর *a.* distant, very far off.
সুনৃত, *s.* an agreeable truth.
সুবদন, *a.* having a fine face.
সুমেল, *s.* symmetry, a good fit.

সুরাজক, *a.* ruled by a good king.
সুরঙ্গা, *s.* an excavation, a mine.
সুশৃঙ্খল, *a.* well-arranged, orderly.
সূত্রপাত, *a.* measuring, planning.
সেক, *s.* a wetting, sprinkling, pouring.
সেথুয়া, *s.* a fellow-traveller, a guide.
সৌঁধান, *s.* a perfuming, making fragrant.
সৌর্য্য, *s.* learning, literature, literary eminence.
স্তম্ভন, *s.* a stupifying; a stupor.
স্তিমিত, *a.* wet, moist; taciturn.
স্থায়ক, *s.* a surety, an overseer, a chief.
স্থিরবাদী, *a.* keeping one's word; exact.
স্নিগ্ধমূর্ত্তি, *a.* clement, placid, mild.
স্নেহদ্রব্য, *s.* any greasy liquid, oil.
স্রক্, *s.* a chaplet of flowers, a necklace.
স্বরস, *s.* attachment, love, fondness.
স্বরূপযোগ্য, *a.* capable, able, qualified.
স্বরূপাখ্যান, *s.* a stating the real facts.
স্বাধিকৃত, *a.* made one's own, subjected.
স্বাপদ, *s.* a wild beast.
স্বিন্ন, *a.* expanded by heat, sodden.

হ.

হন্যা, *a.* snappish, snarling, surly.
হস্তদোহার, *s.* an assistant; a weapon.
হস্তপাদাদি, *s.* the extremities.
হাঁসফাঁস, *s.* a puffing and blowing.
হা, *intj.* alas! *s.* a gaping, yawning.
হাইড়, *s.* stocks, wooden fetters.
হাইর, *s.* loss, failure, defeat.
হাইল, *s.* a rudder, a helm.
হালবাহক, *s.* a ploughman, a tiller.
হালা, *s.* intoxicating liquor; poison.
হাসিখুসি, *s.* laugh and sport, merriment.
হাস্কুড়্যা, *a.* always laughing, merry.
হিলোন, *s.* a cool breeze.
হিল্লোল, *s.* a wave, a billow, a breaker.

NOTES.

Scientific Names of Birds, Beasts, Fishes, Reptiles, Trees, &c., &c.

Page

2.—1 & 3 Aquillaria agallocha. 2 & 4 Amaris agallocha. 5 Plumbago zeylanica.

4.—1 Morinda tinctoria, used in dyeing.

5.—1 Eclipta prostrata. 2 Cytisus cajan.

7.—1 Periploca indica, or Asclepias pseudasarsa. 2 Hedysarum alhaji.

8.—1 Arundo bifaria?

15.—1 Nymphæa lotus.

17.—1 Viz. the fruits of Terminalia chebula, Phylanthus emblica, and Menispermum cordifolium. 2 Tamarindus indicus.

20.—1 Jonesia Asoca. 2 Physalis flexuosa.

25.—1 Helicteres Isora. 2 Calotropis gigantea. 3 Juglans regia.

34.—1 Spondias mangifera. 2 Clupea prinoides of *Gmelin*, and Clupée apalike of *Lacépède*.

35.—1 Tamarindus indicus. 2 Eupatorium Aya Pana.

37—1 Carpopogon pruriens, *Roxb.* 2 Cymbidium tessaloides. 3 Cucurbita lagenaria. 4 Prunus triflora.

Page

40.—1 Nymphæa cœrulea; also, Asparagus racemosus.

41.—1 Coccinella of several species. 2 Wrightea antidysenterica. 3 Vitex negundo. 4 Clupea alosa.

42.—1 Termes bellicosus.

44.—1 Ficus glomerata.

47.—1 Ficus glomerata.

51.—1 Saccharum cylindricum.

52.—1 Andropogon muricatum.

57.—1 Ricinus communis. 2 Alpinia cardamomum, 3 Cyprea caput serpentis.

58.—1 Gallinula nictycorax. 2 Viz. *Xiris* indica, Verbena nodiflora, and Hibiscus esculenta. 3 Hibiscus rosa sinensis.

59.—1 Lutianus scandens, *Lacépède;* Perca vagabunda, *Buch. Mss.*

60.—1 Esox scolopax, *Buch. Mss.* 2 Allangium hexapetalum. 3 Momordica mixta. 4 Bauhinia variegata and purpurea. 5 Lanius excubitus. 6 Cæsalpinia bonducella.

3 F

Page

7 Wrightea antidysenterica, *Brown;* also, Calotropis gigantea, *Brown.* 8 Feronia elephantium.

61.—Artocarpus integrifolia.

62.—1 Musa sapientum. 2 Cucurbita lagenaria 3 Viz. Butea frondosa, Datura metel, Mesua ferrea, and Bauhinia variegata. 4 Pterospermum acerifolium. 5 Datura fastuosa.

64.—1 Nelumbium speciosum. 2 Carrisa Carandas.

65.—1 Nerium odorum. 2 Bucco corula. 3 Momordica carantia. 4 Ardea nivea maxima. 5 Falco halietus. 6 Asclepias dominata?

66.—1 Convolvulus repens.

68.—1 Crinum zeylanicum. 2 Rhyzophora gymnorrhiza. 3 Lacerta scutata? 4 Cucumis utilissimus. 5 Amomum zedoaria.

69.—1 Amaranthus spinosus. 2 Quercus armata. 3 Artocarpus integrifolia. 4 Turdus jocosus, *Buch.;* Lanius jocosus, *Latham.*

70.—1 Psittacus accipitrinus. 2 Commelina bengalensis, and C. salicifolia. 3 Bauhinia variegata. 4 Datura metel. 5 Picus medius, and some other species. 6 Æschynomene paludosa.

71.—1 Plotosis anguillaris, *Lacépède:* Silurus unitus, *Buch. Mss.* 2 Cyprinus niloticus, *Linn.* 3 Scolopus glariola; Tringa glariola of *Latham.*

72.—1 Gossipium of several species. 2 Averrhoa carimbola.

73.—1 Cassia or senna sophora. 2 Sorex cœruleus, the bite of which is supposed to be mortal. 3 Eugenia jambolana. 4 Sesamum indicum. 5 Ocymum sanctum. 6 Datura fastuosa. 7 Sylvia Kala Phutkee, *Buch. Mss.*

74.—1 Perdix olivacea. 2 Cyprinus atratus. 3 Phaseolus max. 4 Saccharum spontaneum. 5 Tantalus denudatus, *Buch. Mss.*

76.—1 Muræna apterygia, *Buch. Mss.;* Synbranche of *Lacépède.* It is said that the bite of this fish is mortal to cows. 2 Strychnos nux vomica. 3 Boswellia thurifera. 4 Acheiris Kookoor Jihwa, *Buch. Mss.* 5 Conyza terebinthina, and some other species. The dogs are fond of smelling this plant before they pass urine. 6 Cuculus castaneus, *Buch. Mss.*

Page

78.—1 Falco halietus. 2 Hedysarum triflorum.

79.—1 Boswellia thurifera. 2 Cucurbita pepo. 3 Aloe perfoliata. 4 Nymphæa esculenta, and Nymphæa rubra. 5 Cyprinus Koorchi, *Buch. Mss.*

80.—1 Zizyphus jujuba. 2 Capparis spinosa. 3 Poa cynosuroides. 4 Carthamus tinctorius.

81.—1 Zizyphus jujuba.

82.—1 Plumbago zeylanica. 2 Mirabilis jalapa, and Poinciana pulcherrima. 3 Ocymum pilosum. 4 Antilopa cervicapra. 5 Pandanus odoratissimus. [trispinosus.

83.—1 Verbesinia calendulacea. 2 Holocentrus.

84.—1 Anas casarca. 2 Paspalum Kora. 3 Hedysarum triflorum.

86.—1 Serratula anthelmintica.

87.—1 Falco halietus. 2 Mimosa catechu.

88.—1 Viverra zibetha.

89.—1 Clupea fornicata. 2 Cucumis melo. 3 Mugil protuberans, *Buch. Mss.* 4 Phœnix sylvestris.

90.—1 Perca setacea, or Trichopodus Kolisha, *Buch. Mss.* 2 Andropogon muricata. 3 Saccharum spontaneum.

95.—1 Lathyrus sativus. 2 Ardea cinnamomea.

97.—1 Pelecanus onocratulus. 2 Pothus officinalis.

98.—1 Premna spinosa.

99.—1 Viverra Gunda, *Buch. Mss.* 2 Andropogon schœnanthus. 3 Artimisia indica. 4 Echites caryophyllata. 5 Gardenia florida.

100.—1 Cucumis momordica. 2 Ficus cordifolia. 3 Rhizophora decandra. 4 Silurus ascitus. 5 Dipterocarpus incana.

102.—1 Pelecanus onocratulus.

103.—1 Silurus ascitus, *Linn.;* Pimelodes barbatus, *Lacépède.* 2 Capsicum annuum.

104.—1 The white and red variety of the Boerhaavia diffusa. 2 Diospyros glutinosa. 3 Arundo bengalensis. 4 Vultur Coromandeliana.

105.—1 Lacerta striata. 2 Anethum Panmorium. 3 Aquillaria agallochum. 4 Alpinia cardamomum. 5 Abrus precatorius.

106.—1 Capparis sepiaria. 2 Perdix Coromandelica.

Page

107.—1 Areca catechu.

108.—1 Chrysanthemum indicum. 2 Narcissus tazetta. 3 Impatiens balsamica. 4 Menispermum glabrum. 5 Ficus Gooloorees. 6 Plumeria acuminata 7 Ocymum caryophyllatum. 8 Mimosa farnesiana. 9 Sturnus Gosalica, *Buch. Mss.*

109.—1 Tagetes patula, and Tagetes erecta. 2 Tribulus lanuginosus.

111.—1 Ajuga disticha.

116.—1 Aloe perfoliata, var. succotrina.

117.—1 Phaseolus lobatus. 2 Deeringia celosioides. 3 Anas casarca. 4 Tetrao rufa, *Linn.*; Perdix rufa, *Lath.*

118.—1 Bauhinia acuminata.

120.—1 Chrysanthemum indicum. 2 Michelia Champaca. 3 Jasminum grandiflorum.

122.—1 Zeus oblongus. 2 Musa sapientum. 3 Amaranthus polygamus. 4 Muscicapa laticauda. 5 Hemionitis cordifolia.

124.—1 Dillenia indica. 2 Perdix rufa.

125.—1 Trichosanthes anguina. 2 Achyranthes lappacea. Mystus Chitula. 4 Plumbago rosea and zeylanica.

126.—Buchanania latifolia. 2 Gentiana Cherayta. 3 Falco ater.

127.—1 Triphasia aurantiola. 2 Rumex vesicarius. 3 Dioscorea globosa.

128.—1 Mangifera indica. 2 Ophiocephalus aurantiacus, *Buch. Mss.* 3 Gobius Boddarti.

129.—1 Cyprinus cultrata, *Buch. Mss.*

136.—1 Euphorbia chamæsyce. 2 Portulaca meridiana. 3 Cicer arietinum.

137.—1 Dalrympelia pomifera. 2 Valeriana Jatamansi.

138.—1 Andropogon bicolor. 2 Hibiscus rosa sinensis.

139.—1 Eugenia jambolana. 2 Andropogon saccharatum.

140.—1 Elæocarpus serrata.

142.—1 Jasminum grandiflorum. 2 Eugenia jambolana. 3 Eugenia alba. 4 Dolichos lignosus.

143.—1 Lagerstrœmia regina.

144.—1 Celtis orientalis. 2 Cuminum cyminum. 3 Jasminum auriculatum. 4 Justicia nasuta.

Page

145.—1 Trochus perspectivus.

149.—1 Luffa acutangula. 2 Ardea Coromandeliana. 3 Passiflora citrifolia.

150.—1 Tabernæmontana coronaria.

151.—1 Melochia corchorifolia.

152.—1 Tetrodon sceleratus. 2 Silurus ascita?

156.—1 Cyprinus barbiger, *Buch. Mss.* 2 Tringa goensis.

157.—1 Tringa goensis. 2 Podiceps Doobaroo, *Buch. Mss.* 3 Artocarpus lacucha. 4 Amaranthus lividus.

159.—1 Ipomea grandiflora.

162.—1 Polynemus paradiseus.

163.—1 According to some, Xanthocymus pictorius; according to others, Diospyros tomentosa. 2 Luffa acutangula. 3 Aloe perfoliata, var. succotrina. 4 Cucurbita citrullus. 5 Falco fasciatus, *Buch. Mss.* 6 Ipomea quamoclit.

165.—1 Corypha taliera.

166.—1 Borassus flabelliformis. 2 Mimosa dulcis.

167.—1 Sinapis patens? 2 Corchorus capsularis, var. viridis. 3 Tamarindus indicus. 4 Sesamum orientale. 5 Cucurbita lagenaria, var. punctata.

168.—1 Loxia rosea, and L. alba. 2 Cucurbita lagenaria.

169.—1 Morus indica and other species 2 Lathyrus sativus. 3 Tamarindus indicus. 4 Euphorbia antiquorum. 5 Laurus cassia.

170.—1 Momordica monadelpha.

172.—1 Viz. Terminalia chebula, T. bellerica, and Phyllanthus emblica.

173.—1 Hibiscus mutabilis.

174.—1 Achyranthes lanata. 2 Turdus saularis, *Carey*; Gracula saularis, *Linn.*

175.—1 Croton polyandrum.

177.—1 Panicum stagninum. 2 Parra indica? [*Lath.*

178.—1 Cassia alata.

181.—1 Ligusticum Ajwaen.

183.—1 Impatiens balsamina. 2 Certhia zeylanica.

184.—1 Hedychium coronarium.

185.—1 Panicum dactylon.

186.—1 Andropogon saccharatus. 2 Pinus longifolius.

189.—1 Vitis vinifera.

Page
192.—1 Coriandrum sativum.
194.—1 Luffa pentandra.
195.—1 Hibiscus esculentus.
197.—1 Amaranthus prostratus, A. lanceolatus, A. oleraceus, A. fasciatus, and A. spinosus. 2 Cedrela Toona. 3 Halicacabum cordiospermum.
198.—1 Arundo tibialis.
199.—1 Nelumbium speciosum. 2 Arundo Karka. 3 Valeriana Jatamansi.
200.—1 Mesua ferrea. 2 Bauhinia anguina. 3 Cyperus pertenuis. 4 Mimosa pudica. 5 Cæsalpinia bonduccella. 6 Euphorbia antiquorum.
201.—1 Perca nebulosa, *Buch. Mss.*; Holocentra, *Lacépède.*
206.—1 Melia Azad-dirachta.
210.—1 Kyllingia monocephala. 2 Strychnos potatorum.
212.—1 Vitex negundo.
213.—1 Indigofera tinctoria 2 Coracias indica. 3 Nymphæa cyanea. 4 Simia ferox. 5 Psittacus Lory.
214.—1 Silurus porosus. *Buch. Mss.* 2 Annona squamosa.
216.—1 Gryllus migratorius. 2 Viz. long-pepper, its root, Piper chuvya, Plumbago zeylanica, and dry ginger. 3 Viz. the twigs of Spondias mangifera, Eugenia jambos, Ægle marmelos, Citron, and Feronia elephantum.
217.—1 Trichosanthes dioica.
218.—1 Nelumbium speciosum.
220.—1 Hibiscus populneoides.
223.—1 Butea frondosa.
224.—1 Ophidium punctatum, *Buch. Mss.*
225.—1 Silurus sagittatus, *Buch. Mss.*
226.—1 Corchorus olitorius and C. capsularis. 2 Polygonum flaccidum.
227.—1 Plectranthus aromaticus. 2 Flacourtia cataphracta. 3 Pelecanus fusicollis.
228.—1 Trapa bicornis. 2 Silurus asotus. 3 Erythrina fulgens.
229.—1 Mugil latus, *Buch. Mss.* 2 Beta bengalensis. 3 Erythrina fulgens.
230.—1 Trigonella corniculata.
231.—1 Buchanania latifolia. 2 Pentaptera tomentosa.

Page
232.—1 Cyprinus chrysoparus.
235.—1 Carica Papaya.
248.—1 Grewia asiatica.
249.—1 Corvus balicassius. 2 Cucumis momordica.
250.—1 Clupea ensiformis.
251.—1 Flacourtia sapida. 2 Cæsalpinia sappan.
252.—1 Ficus indica. 2 Perdix olivacea, *Buch.*
253.—1 Ficus indica. 2 Trigonella fœnum grecum. 3 Artocarpus lacucha. 4 Aconitum ferox. 5 Zizyphus jujuba. 6 Fagara Budrunga.
254.—1 Basella rubra. 2 Felis caracal. 3 Curcuma zedoaria.
255.—1 Terminalia bellerica.
256.—1 Dolichos catjang.
257.—1 Bucco corula and B. philippensis.
259.—1 Merops philippensis, and Merops viridis. 2 Cyprinus radiatus. 3 Justicia adhatoda.
260.—1 Jatropha curcas. 2 Falco nisus. 3 Falco calidus. 4 Panicum spicatum.
261.—1 Cyprinus Bata, *Buch. Mss.* 2 Cicer arietinum. 3 Turdus melanocephalus, *Carey*; Oriolus melanocephalus, *Linn.* 4 Citrus decumana.
262.—1 Vespertillio vampyrus. 2 Ocymum pilosum. 3 Embelia ribes.
263.—1 Loxia philippensis. 2 Siphonanthus indica. 3 Solanum melongena.
264.—1 Cyprinus denticulatus, *Buch. Mss.* 2 Anas creeca. 3 Rosa centifolia.
266.—1 Lettsomia nervosa. 2 Tragia involucrata.
272.—1 Solanum tuberosum. 2 Myrtus communis. 3 Ægle marmelos.
274.—1 Lettsomia nervosa.
275.—1 Flacourtia sapida.
276.—1 Ruellia ringens. 2 Lanius emeria, *Linn.*; Turdus emeria, *Carey.*
277.—1 Bambusa spinosa.
278.—1 Solanum melongena. 2 Andropogon muricatus.
280.—1 Jasminum zambac, flor. plen.
281.—1 Silurus pelorius. 2 Boa constrictor.
283.—1 Solanum indicum.
287.—1 Semicarpus anacardium. 2 Andropogon aciculatus.
288.—1 Mugil cephalotis, also Cyprinus mullus, *Buch. Mss.* 2 Cyprinus ariza, *Buch.'s Mysore.*

Page

289.—1 Perdix chinensis.

290.—1 Verbesinia calendulacea.

291.—1 Convolvulus reniformis and Kempferia rotunda.

292.—1 Betula Bhoorja. 2 Coius Vacti, *Hamilton's Fishes.* 3 Perca nebulosa, *Buch. Mss.*; Holocentra, *Lacépède.* 4 Ricinus communis. 5 Oleum ricini.

294.—1 Dioscorea aculeata. 2 Bassia longifolia. 3 Certhia zeylanica, and C. cruentata. 4 Cyprinus Morala, *Hamilton's Fishes.* 5 Anethum Panmorium. 6 Zea mays. 7 Dolichos gladiatus. 8 Lettsomia nervosa.

295.—1 Rubia Munjistha. 2 Fringilla amandava.

296.—1 Musa sapientum. 2 Kempferia angustifolia. 3 Erythrina fulgens. 4 Asclepias volubilis.

297.—1 Euphorbia ligularia.

298.—1 Gracula religiosa. 2 Vangueria spinosa.

299.—1 Simia erythrina.

300.—1 Jasminum zambac. 2 Ervum hirsutum, also, Cicer lens.

301.—1 Nelumbium speciosum, var. alba. 2 Nelumbium speciosum.

302.—1 Eleusine Ægyptiaca. 2 Trichosanthes palmata, also, Cucumis colocynthus. 3 Silurus batrachus, *Linn.*; Macropteranoton granuillar, *Lacépède.*

303.—1 Eleusine corocana. 2 Ardea leucocephala.

304.—1 Gærtnera racemosa. 2 Arum indicum.

305.—1 Jasminum grandiflorum, Echites caryophyllata, and Gærtnera racemosa. 2 Eugenia Malaccensis. 3 Phaseolus radiatus.

308.—1 Saccharum Munja.

309.—1 Cyperus rotundus. 2 Celosia cristata. 3 Plumbi oxyde.

310.—1 Cyprinus Mrigala, *Hamilton's Fishes.*

311.—1 Trigonella fœnum grecum.

312.—1 Lawsonia inermis. 2 Annona squamosa.

314.—1 Ficus glomerata.

315.—1 Ligusticum Ajowan.

317.—1 Jasminum auriculatum.

319.—1 Nymphæa rubra. 2 Pterocarpus santalinus. 3 Nelumbium speciosum.

321.—1 Musa paradisiaca. 2 Allium ascalonicum.

322.—1 Apium involucratum. 2 Sinapis ramosa.

323.—1 Amaranthus atropurpureus. 2 Amaranthus gangeticus.

Page

324.—1 Columba indica. 2 Capra imberbis, *Buch. Mss.* 3 Ocymum gratissimum. 4 Musa paradisiaca. 5 Much used in Hindu Materia medica. 6 Sapindus of several species. 7 Pimelodus Rita, *Hamilton's Fishes.*

325.—1 Cyprinus Rohita, *Hamilton's Fishes.* 2 Elæocarpus ganitrus. 3 Meleagris satyra. 4 Chætodon argus, *Lacépède.*

327.—1 Cyprinus denticulatus, or C. Rohita, of *Hamilton.*

328.—1 Mimosa pudica. 2 Psittacus minoo. 3 Bixa orellana. 4 Urtica nauclifolia. 5 Eugenia caryophyllata. 6 Limonia scandens. 7 Boswellia thurifera.

329.—1 Viz. Gloriosa superba, Commelina salicifolia, Nama repens, and Jussiena repens.

330.—1 Ophiocephalus Lata, *Hamilton's Fishes*; Ophiocephale Karaivey, *Lacépède.* 2 Fringilla amandava. 3 Nerium odorum. 4 Canna indica, var. rubra.

331.—1 Phyllanthus longifolia. 2 Portulaca oleracea and meridiana. 3 Psittacus Lory.

332.—1 Annona squamosa. 2 Symplocos racemosa. 3 Dolichos sinensis.

334.—1 Falco ponticerianus. 2 Hyperanthera Morunga. 3 Curcuma Zerumbet. 4 Curcuma Amhuldi. 5 Crotolaria juncea. 6 Asparagus racemosus.

335.—1 Cyprinus Sophore, *Hamilton's Fishes.* 2 Psidium pyriforme and maliforme. 3 Saccharum Sara. 4 Cyprinus Sarana, *Hamilton's Fishes.*

336.—1 Anethum Sowa.

337.—1 Turdus macrourus. 2 Panicum frumentaceum and colonum. 3 Helix ampullacea. 4 Viz. Gracula religiosa, and Turdus Salica. 5 Shorea robusta. 6 Ophiocephalus Wrahl, *Hamilton's Fishes.* 7 Hedysarum gangeticum. 8 Turdus Salica. 9 Nymphæa lotus.

338.—1 Nyctanthes tristis. 2 Dalbergia Sissoo. 3 Trapa bispinosa. 4 Silurus Singio, *Hamilton's Fishes.*

339.—1 Bombax heptaphylla. 2 Argemone Mexicana.

343.—1 Crotolaria juncea. 2 Æschynomene paludosa.

344.—1 Turdus macrourus. 2 Ægle marmelos.

345.—1 Nerium odorum. 2 Boerhaavia diffusa. 3 Celosia cristata. 4 Sinapis glauca.

Page
358.—1 Viz. Kakkola, cloves, agallochum, and gum benjamin. 2 Cana indica.

359.—1 Consisting of Moora, Valeriana Jatamansa, Calamus aromaticus, Koorha, a kind of moss called Shileya, turmeric, red sanders, dried ginger, Machelia Champaca, and Cyperus rotundus. 2 Sinapis dichotoma.

362.—1 Cuculus melancholicus. 2 Ardea Sarunga, *Carey*. 3 Ardea Sibirica. 4 Turdus Salica, *Buch. Mss.* The natives of Bengal, however, apply the name to the female parrot. 5 Shorea robusta. 6 Ophiocephalus Wrahl. 7 Turdus Salica, *Buch. Mss.*

363.—1 Rosa glandulifera.

364.—1 Herritiera minor. 2 Nymphæa cyanea, and N. esculenta.

366.—1 Marsilia quadrifolia.

368.—1 Hibiscus phœniceus. 2 Helianthus annuus. 3 Rosa glandulifera. 4 Zizyphus scandens.

369.—1 Corvus venatorius, *Buch. Mss.*, perhaps Gracula cristatella, *Linn.* 2 Cyprinus auratus. 3 Phaseolus aureus. 4 Sarcostema viminalis. 5 Serratula anthelmintica.

Page
371.—1 Hibiscus mutabilis.

372.—1 Cucumis momordica.

377.—1 Terminalia chebula. 2 Phlomis zeylanica. 3 Oriolus melanocephalus, *Linn.*; Turdus melanocephalus, *Carey*.

378.—1 Corvus mendicantium. 2 Croton polyandrum. 3 Acanthus cilicifolius. 4 Ardea Argala. 5 Cissus quadrangularis. 6 Heliotropium indicum.

379.—1 Echites dichotoma. 2 Columba Hariala. 3 Phaseolus mungo. 4 Lepidium sativum.

380.—1 Barringtonia acutangula. 2 Phœnix paludosa. 3 Cotyledon laciniata.

381.—1 Psittacus sinensis. 2 Achyranthes aspera.

383.—1 Typha elephantinum.

384.—1 Oldenlandia biflora, and perhaps one or two more species.

385.—1 Gloriosa superba.

390.—1 Arum bulbiferum. 2 Pentaptera tomentosa.

393.—1 Artocarpus integrifolia.

CALCUTTA, BAPTIST MISSION PRESS.